CW01390802

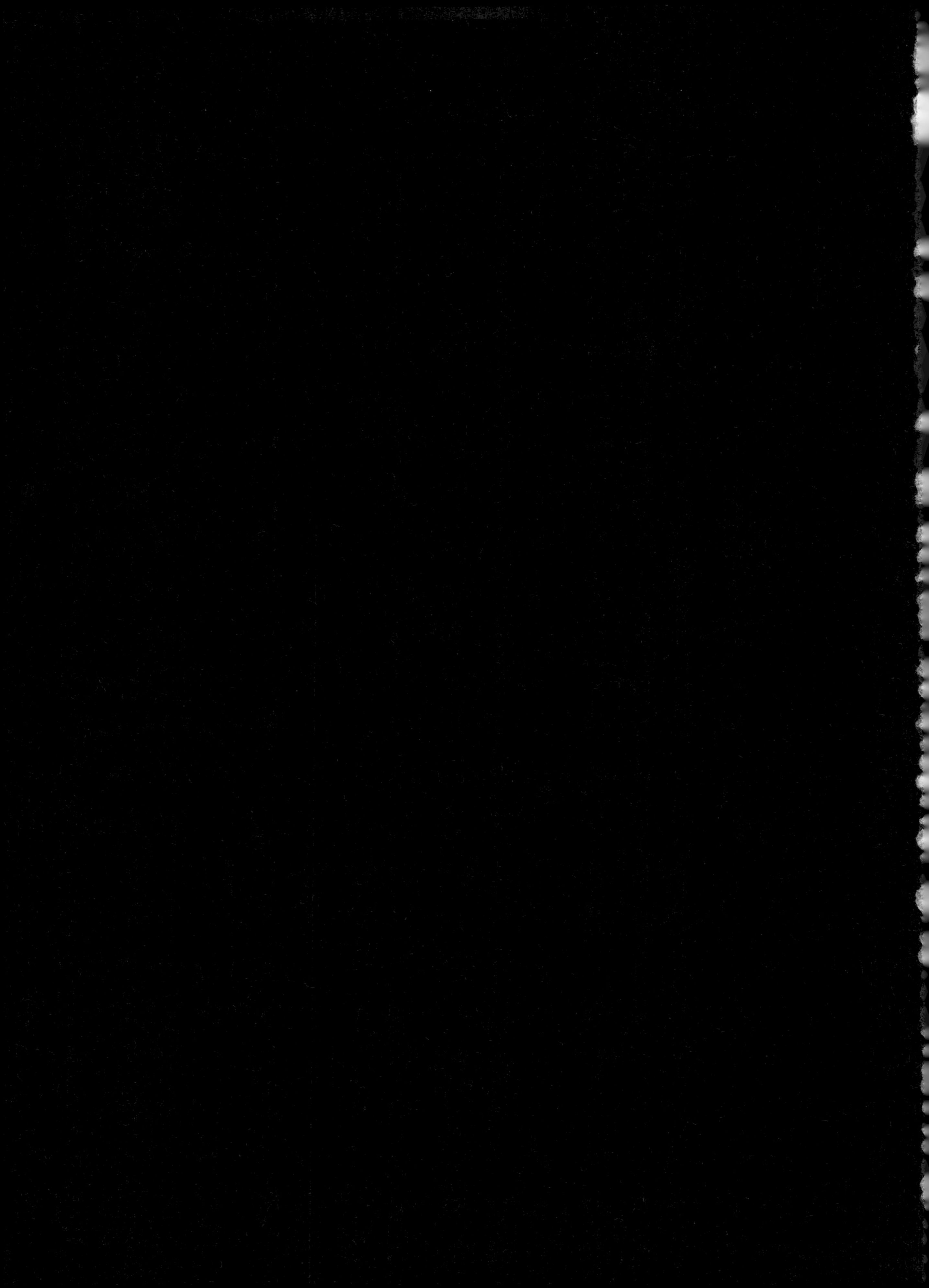

dig it!
Building Bound to the Ground

dig it! Building Bound to the Ground

Bjarne Mastenbroek
Esther Mecredy
SeARCH
Iwan Baan

TASCHEN

Building is one of very few endeavours that are physically connected to the surface of the earth, fixed and enduring. Yet it seems as if we have a simplistic understanding of its true workings. The ground is often used as a passive foundation for going higher, but we can also dig deeper into the rich and endless possibilities of buildings that merge with their surroundings and the earth.

For millennia, people have tried to move away from an environment seen as insecure and hostile. It started as a retreat from natural elements, and now we retreat from each other. We know we need to reconfigure our position in relation to nature, and after a long period of destructive behaviour things have started to shift.

This book acknowledges efforts to reconnect architecture and landscape and merge building and ground.

There has been a pulse throughout history. At times, we considered ourselves separate and above nature – with classical antiquity, Enlightenment and modernism we drifted away and defined our own systems and order. At other times, we sought connection, drawing on nature for ritual and religion, relying on topography for fortified protection and more recently for calculating ecological balance.

Having sifted through the history of building across the millennia, architect Bjarne Mastenbroek of SeARCH and photographer Iwan Baan highlight historically overlooked projects and fascinating examples in the following pages. Six different strategies were identified and analysed:

Bury
Embed
Absorb
Spiral
Carve
Mimic

dig it! is not an exhaustive encyclopaedia, nor a complete atlas, but it does guide you on a global tour to reveal the beauty and diversity of building cultures – clever and utterly relevant as we face challenges in both urban and natural environments.

Nature's Lack of Design

An essay that traces the history of humanity to better understand the relationship between the built environment and the ground on which it sits.

Introduction

The year 1964 was a pivotal moment in history. Our global population growth rate hit its peak and has never been higher. Humans were racing to leave the earth and biologist Rachel Carson had just witnessed a *Silent Spring*, awaking one morning to find the birds had stopped singing.[1] With ever-quickening speed, humankind's relationship to the earth had shifted from symbiosis to commensalism to parasitism. We went from guest to stalker to thief and, in the end, to killer.

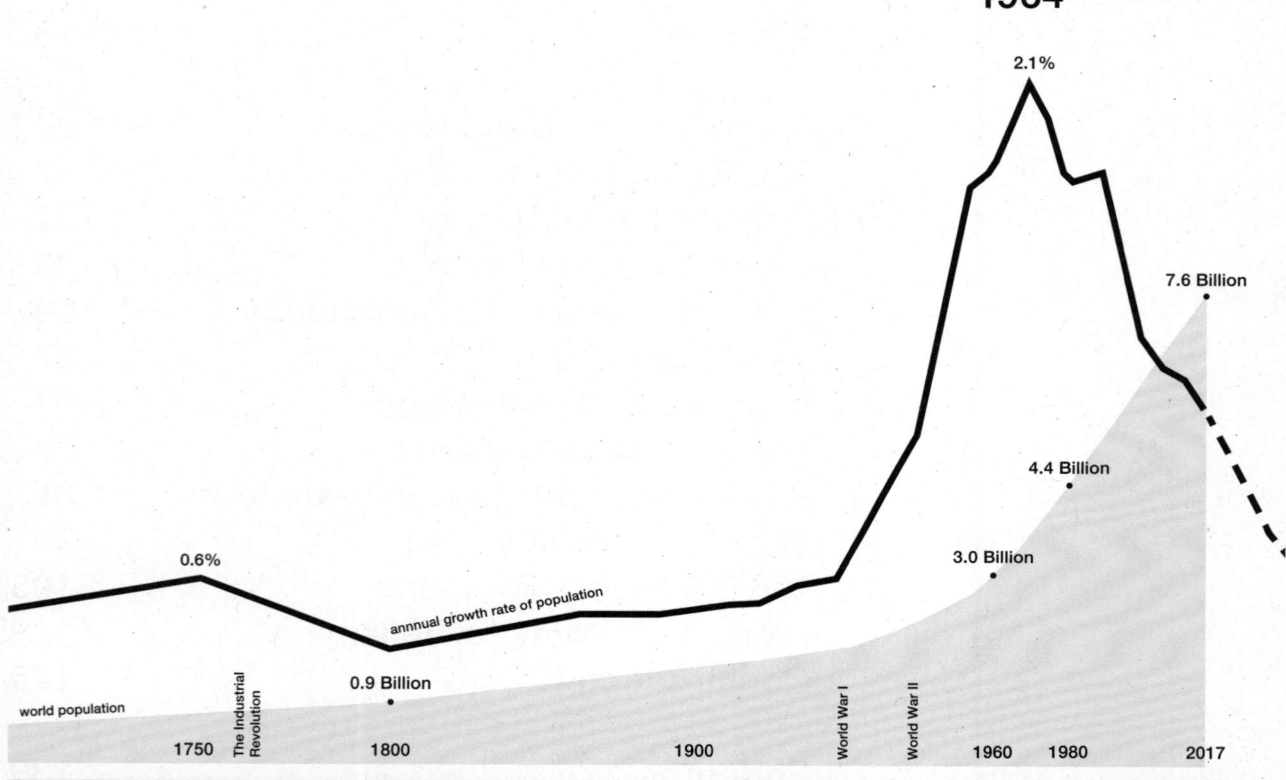

Growth rate of global population, Max Roser, *Our World in Data*, 2015.

Nature's silence represented the fading out of humankind. By poisoning nature, we were poisoning ourselves. Carson's words shook the myth of infinite growth to its core and challenged the doctrine of progress that saw humanity sprinting towards its own extinction.

As Western society confronted nature's frailty and the damaging role humans play at the centre of this narrative, the absurdity of modern urban life came into sharp focus. In his film *Playtime*, Jacques Tati held a mirror up to society and the austere and antiseptic city in which it was aspiring to live.

Playtime, Jacques Tati, 1963–1967.

Playtime was an absurdist take on the homogeneous and ubiquitous character of modern architecture, where only the colour of a bus allows a tourist to differentiate Paris from London. It highlighted a dogmatism that had stripped buildings down to their bare formal elements, rendering them highly efficient, abstract containers.

Vattenfall Haus, Hamburg, Arne Jacobsen, 1963–1969.

The fundamental 'shelter' built into the crust of the earth had become a highly sophisticated building envelope separating us from the elements of our own ecosystem. With nature excluded and reduced to a mere backdrop, it was so much easier to silence. The year 1964 was both the peak and a tipping point.

Until then, buildings had evolved to improve on basic comforts: heating, light and ventilation, equipment and lifts. The focus was on the hardware. But post-1964, the blueprint of the future was no longer self-evident. If modernism had got it right, why was the modern city not comfortable? And why was it so damaging?

With *The Death and Life of Great American Cities*, Jane Jacobs criticized what she labelled the 'Radiant Garden City Beautiful': approaches which dispersed and segregated the urban realm.[2] Jacobs saw the principal planning theories of the time as being utterly at odds with urban realities and human sensibilities.[3] While technological and chemical development attacked nature, suburban sprawl and the automobile attacked the city, like a snake that bites its own tail.

Los Angeles scarred its landscapes, divided communities, and displaced a quarter of a million people in the construction of its freeway system.

With the dissolution of the Congrès Internationaux d'Architecture Moderne (CIAM) in 1959, the first vague contours of an alternative presented themselves. The younger architects of this platform, Team 10, questioned modernism's technocratic approach. There was more to building than hardware, and in order to reconnect nature and the city, software was crucial. Brutalism can be seen as a step backwards, or at least sideways, from a modern conception of progress, hoping to show how a new roughness could be comfortable.

Only now, in the early days of the Anthropocene, are the true origins of human settlement becoming clearer, and recent findings are forcing a reconsideration of long-held assumptions.[4] Agriculture did not make the city: humankind did. A desire to settle together, to exchange transience for comfort and continuity, predates agricultural practice.[5] For over 14 000 years we have been 'urban farmers', more than farmers turned urban, but today we see the city hitting back at fertile lands and becoming its own competitor.

Architecture and landscape are merging, and both the hardware and software of the city are evolving together.[6] We harvest buildings for recycling purposes and reconstruct a natural environment. We are not building buildings any more; we are redesigning our world and the line between nature and culture is completely blurred.

The High Line in New York breathes new life into a disused railway; here the hardware of an industrial past supports a new urban ecology.

This essay traces a tumultuous history to reveal the times in which humanity pulled away from the environment, pivotal moments of almost complete separation and the resounding efforts since to reconnect. This is an uneven, non-linear and entirely personal narrative of how our built culture has evolved. If you look closely you will see how buildings were, and are, inextricably linked to the natural environment, to the surrounding landscape and to the ground.

Paleolithic
3 000 000 – 10 000 BCE

Neolithic
10 000 – 3000 BCE

Homo neanderthalensis
450 000–40 000 BCE

Northern migration to Europe and Siberia
60 000–30 000 BCE

Homo habilis
2 800 000–1 500 000 BCE

Agriculture practices Indus Valle
9000–7500 BCE

Homo heidelbergensis
700 000–300 000 BCE

Migration through the Americas
22 000–12 000 BCE

Eastern migration through Asia and Australia
70 000–25 000 BCE

Agricultu
7700–200

First migration to Fertile Crescent
100 000–75 000 BCE

Homo erectus
1 800 000–350 000 BCE

Agriculture practices Fertile Crescent
10 000–5000 BCE

350 000 BCE: Homo sapiens
200 000 BCE: Homo sapiens develop collective learning
125 000 BCE: Widespread control of fire

64 000 BCE
20 000 BCE
9000 BCE

Context and key moments

Case studies page n°

Louvre extension 282
Phillip Island House 288
Roof Made City 298
Museum aan de Strom (MAS) 860
Scherf 13 1282
Villa Vals 326
Synagogue LJG 1088
Casa No Tempo 1116
Hotel Jakarta 1346
Yourtopia 376
El Paradiso 372
Summertime 1338

Árbol para Vivir 1274
Amdavad Ni Gufa 302
Mercedes Benz Museum 864
Braga Stadium 572
Skewed Stolp 600

Morella School 548
Hexenhaus 508
Therme Vals 558
The High Line 1294
Zeitz MOCAA 1120
Chalet Anzere 594

50
Landscape Urbanism
1995–present
Antinori Winery 308
Forest Tower 1308
Junior College 926
Roy and Diana Vagelos
Education Center 954

Entelechy II 1248
Monument to Tolerance 266
Danish Maritime Museum 358
Mountain Dwellings 1320
54

econstructivism
980–present
Espai Verd 1268
ACROS 1278
Serpentine Gallery Pavilion 750
Favrholm Conference Centre 344

Igualada Cemetery 292
Neue Staatsgalerie 542
Neanderthal Museum 856
Villa KBWW 1072
Isbjerget 1324
House &
Restaurant 278

Parametricism
1990–present
Biosphere 2 1163
Kunsthal 716
Olympic Archery Range 554
Posbank Pavilion 896
Dutch Embassy 722
IJdock 1076
Borneo Housing 566
Seattle Central Library 912
NotOna 270
Monte Rosa Hütte 908
Markthal 1094
Khalifeyah Library 1100
Danish Pavilion 938
The Truffle 274
Fort Vechten 362
Hunting Ranch 368
Friendship Centre 578
Katendrecht 950

Ten, Charles and Ray Eames
1986: Court & Garden, Michael Dennis
1992: Environmental Summit, Rio de Janerio
1997: The Kyoto Protocol
2015: The Anthropocene
epoch proposed
2002: The Rise of the Creative Class, Richard Florida
2007: Apple releases the iPhone

2000

Richard Sennett

Constructing Nature 2000 – present

125

From Cave to Canopy

The popular story of human progress is that of successive revolutions. As society evolves, so too does its building culture. With the 'cognitive revolution' 70 000 years ago, humans began to build shelters. With the 'agricultural revolution' 11 000 years ago, humans built structures to store and protect resources. With the rapid accumulation of knowledge under the scientific revolution 500 years ago, built structures became more sophisticated, articulated and ordered. With inventions such as the lift during the Industrial Revolution some 200 years ago, buildings reached great heights. And with the information revolution last century, distances stretched and society spread out.[7]

This impressive narrative skips lightly over the last 2.6 million years, focusing on how far we have advanced. It misses a strange yet fascinating truth – that for ninety-nine per cent of our existence, all but a measly 11 000 years, humankind enjoyed a symbiotic relationship with nature. The Biotechnological Revolution today is an acknowledgement that a rebalancing of biology and technology, the living and the built, is paramount.

Vindija Cave near Varazdin, Croatia, was occupied by Neanderthals more than 40 000 years ago.

Early hunter-gatherers manipulated the surface of the earth, sheltering in caves and beneath overhanging cliffs, or carving spaces out of the ground. It was an existence devoted to pure subsistence. Humankind was completely dependent on the crust of the earth, surviving by foraging for food and water. They used the raw materials they found to shelter themselves. All activities took place within a space ranging from two metres above to two metres below the ground.

The first 'buildings' were fashioned from materials in their immediate environment: loose stones, trees, branches, leaves. Later, clay or animal faeces provided semi-durable shelter for semi-nomadic hunter-gatherers.[8] Unlike their invasive descendants, the early hunter-gatherers left few traces. The little archaeological evidence we have suggests a transient, non-territorial relationship to the ground, over which small, widely-dispersed communities migrated in search of food.

Typically, it takes two hours for a group of Hadza women to build a new camp, making huts by bending tree branches into round structures and covering them with grass.

Subsistence, transience and living in small numbers afforded a level of egalitarianism.[9] Division of labour according to age or gender existed, but leadership (if any) would change depending on the task. There was no overarching organizational form and no central authority. Anthropologists believe transience negated the need to stockpile assets or territory. Without property, there was no need for protection or protectionism, and thus no competition or theft.

Migrating with wild herds and the seasons, the Hadza are East Africa's last remaining nomadic hunter-gatherers. They settle temporarily around Lake Eyasi in present-day Tanzania in camps of twenty to forty huts. The Hadza exhibit a striking social equality. They are non-territorial and bilocal, they reject group aggression and competition, they share their resources freely and they value personal autonomy.

Lithic materials suggest that the Hadza have continuously occupied the Eyasi Basin since the Middle Stone Age.[10] Like their ancient ancestors, they live in a symbiotic relationship with their environment, utterly dependent, just another element in the natural world. This position is a fraught one. Living at nature's mercy is dangerous and insecure. Where possible, shelter is sought to keep the natural world out. Humankind dug inwards away from the elements and climbed upwards to avoid competition. As humankind has migrated, extending its habitat across the globe, we see a stretching beyond the threshold of two metres above and below the crust of the earth.

Korowai tree house, West Papua.

The Korowai of West Papua build their houses atop living trees. Constructed in a few days and lasting up to five years, these incredible timber structures sit between 8 and 45 metres above the ground. This height affords protection from spirits, mosquitoes and unwelcome neighbours. All materials are sourced from the jungle below; low houses are constructed around sturdy banyan or wanbom trees, branches are used for framing, the bark of the sago palm lines the floor and walls, the roof is woven from leaves and everything is tied together with rattan bindings. The Korowai tree house is an ingenious example of how to extend the boundary between humankind and the natural world, without severing ties for ever.

The Ritualization of Life

Just twenty years ago we thought we understood the rough sequence of the Neolithic Revolution, how hunter-gatherer transience was exchanged for a settled agricultural life, and how small scattered groups became organized, sophisticated societies that exchanged rudimentary structures for more permanent constructions. But recently, with the discovery of Göbekli Tepe, this chronology has been challenged.[11]

Aerial view of Göbekli Tepe, a monumental enclosure for gathering and feasting, 11 500–9000 BCE.

The structures of Göbekli Tepe in south-eastern Anatolia (11 500–9000 BCE) were not driven by pragmatic concerns but by an ancient preoccupation with the rituals of life and death. There are no domestic structures or signs of permanent occupation; it was the ritual centre for a nomadic culture of hunter-gatherers. Predating Stonehenge by 6000 years, this early evidence of prehistoric worship upends the conventional view that only after the advent of farming did humans have the time, organization and resources to construct great temples and towers.

The extensive effort necessary to elaborately carve, erect and arrange seven-ton stone pillars in circles, and the subsequent burying and layering of these rings over centuries to create the gently rounded mound of Göbekli Tepe (belly hill), would have required a large and coordinated community. Archaeologist Klaus Schmidt believes that the collective construction and participation in this ritual practice was a key mechanism in motivating a nomadic culture to take part in a communal lifestyle, thus influencing the emergence of settled communities, like Nevalı Çori and Çayönü (± 9000 BCE) and Çatalhöyük (± 7000 BCE) nearby.[12]

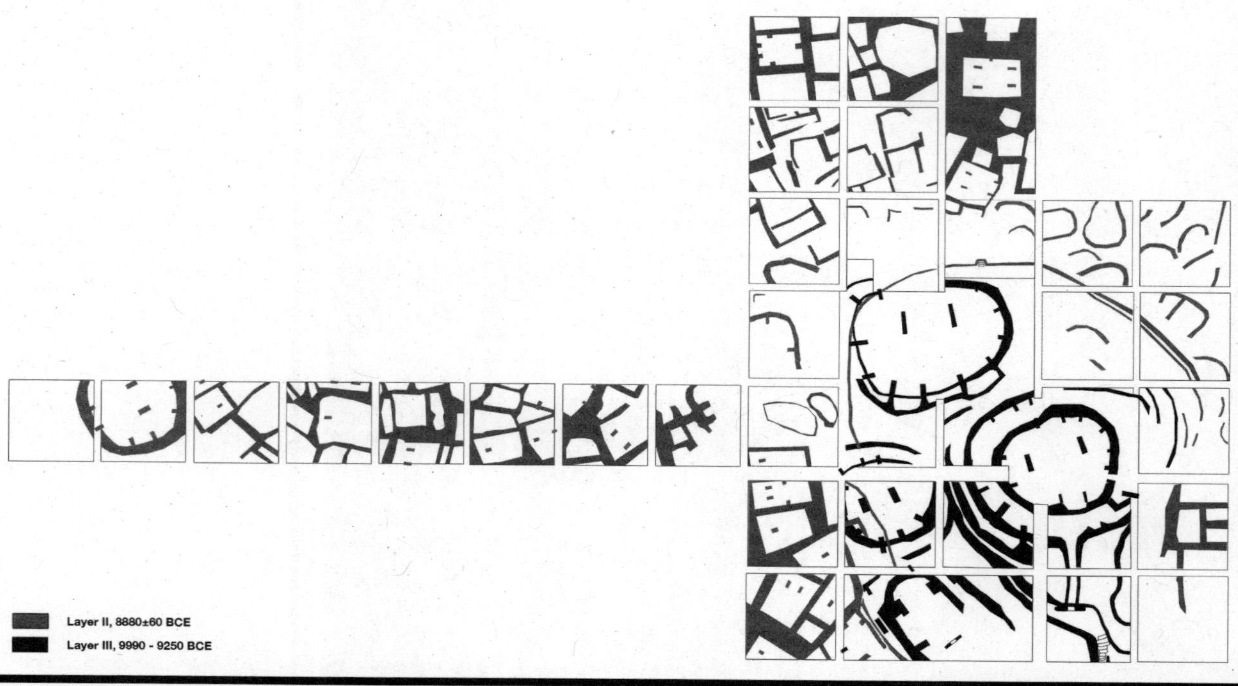

Layers of structures within Göbekli Tepe. German Archaeological Institute.

Ritual offered a way to establish continuity and routine, and building offered a way to cement this existence within the physical world. Pier Vittorio Aureli argues that the daily patterns of behaviour in early nomadic communities shaped the very

Plan and section of part of a Natufian settlement at Ain Mallaha (Eynan), 10000–8200 BCE. Derived from the work of Gil Harklay and Avi Gopher.

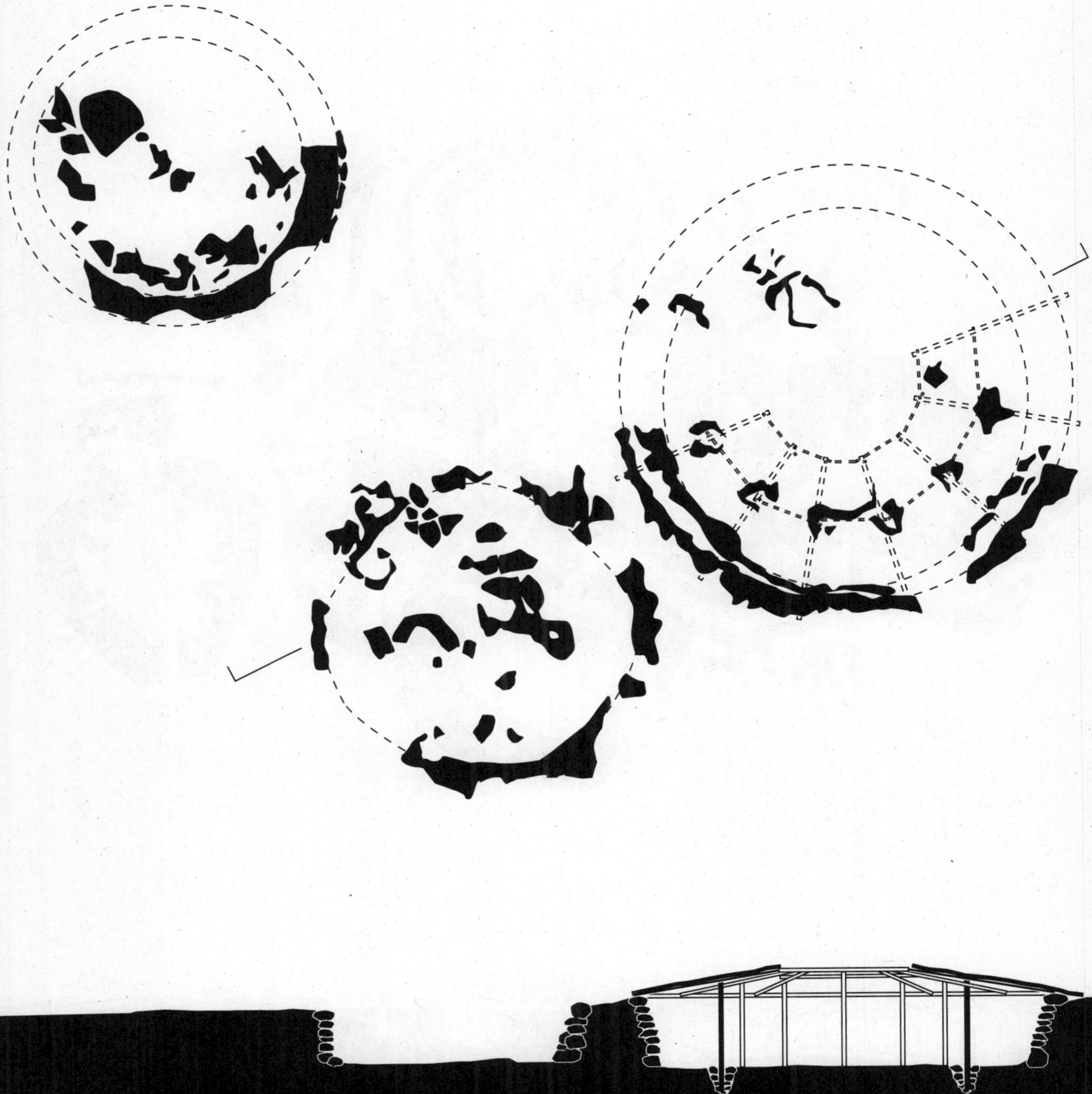

Dwellings separated by sunken passages at Skara Brae, Orkney Island, 3180–2500 BCE. Derived from the work of Vere Gordon Childe.

layout of prehistoric dwellings, that the will to geometrically organize space was a natural reaction to the precariousness of their daily lives.[13]

The Natufians were the first people of the Levant to establish permanent villages, making Ain Mallaha one of the first known sites of the settled hunter-gatherer. Here, very precise circular dwellings were cut into the earth, walls and floor were lined with dry stone and timber posts supported a roof. Five thousand years later and thousands of kilometres away in Scotland, the Neolithic Skara Brae curiously shares the same logic, with circular dwellings clustered together and embedded in the ground. Skara Brae was continuously occupied for 600 years. Semi-subterranean dwellings were literally carved from the waste of prior habitation and this midden served as highly efficient insulation. At this incredibly well-preserved site it is possible to see the gradual shifting from circular to more rectangular space.

The dwellings of Skara Brae are set into the ground with 2.4-metre-high stone walls lining the interior.

Domesticating Nature

According to Greek mythology, we owe our ability to cultivate crops to the goddess Demeter. In a burst of goodwill, Demeter bestowed grain on a trusted priest, who traversed the earth, sowing the dual blessings of agriculture and civilization. Fourteen thousand years ago a more sedentary existence was followed by the cultivation rather than the chasing of our food. This Neolithic Revolution saw the development of ever more sophisticated tools and thousands of small, systematic improvements to the practices of collecting and increasing the food supply.

The adoption of agricultural practices fostered a new typology, and for the first time humankind needed a place to store excess production. Excavations at Dhra', Jordan, provide evidence of sophisticated, purpose-built granaries that represent a critical evolutionary shift in the relationship between people and plant foods. The ancient logic of the granary, of raising food off the ground to protect it from animals and the elements, was adopted by agricultural societies on (almost) every continent.[14]

Excavations at Dhra', Jordan, showing the likely structure that supported a suspended floor.

Systematic domestication fundamentally altered our relationship to the ground. Humans started to groom the natural environment, removing organisms they did not want and controlling and manipulating the reproduction of plants and animals for human consumption. Derrick Jensen and Lierre Keith describe this as 'biotic cleansing', a destructive clearing of all living things, down to bacteria.[15]

Whilst farming increased our species' biological success through a cycle of ever-increasing population and production, intensification brought vulnerability. The hunter-gatherer's life was undoubtedly short, but it was comparatively healthier than the sedentary lifestyle of farming. With agriculture, humans became fifteen centimetres shorter, brain size declined by more than ten per cent, teeth deteriorated, diseases were transmitted between humans and animals, and muscles and bones suffered under heavy work.[16] The birth of agriculture marks a shift from a quality of life to a quantity of life.

A. Dogon tower granaries, Cliff of Bandiagara, Mali, 1000–1700.
B. Fortified Granary of Gasr Al-Hajj, Libya, 700–1300 CE.
C. Berber granaries of Agadir Inoumar, Morocco, 1700.
D. Anasazi granary, Montezuma Canyon, Utah, 1150–1300.
E. A Minangkabau rice barn in Batipu, West-Sumatra.
F. A granary built with the kath khuni method, Chitkul, India, 1000 CE.

The hunter-gatherer once inhabited the same space as their food source but as settlements and agriculture expanded, so too did the distance between them, and the reciprocal relationship between human and habitat was broken. Land was cleared of competition and soil became a resource for growth. From this point on agriculture and the city became intertwined. Global population exploded, communities intensified, and so did our demands on resources. Growing food (rather than chasing it) overwhelmingly reshaped the perceived value of the land. We shifted from seeing the natural environment as a habitat to seeing it as a resource or commodity needed to support the human population. This dependence on agriculture was the beginning of our carbon footprint, the growth of which we continue to witness today.

The migration and dispersion of Homo sapiens, and the first instances of agriculture. National Center for History in the Schools, UCLA.

Possible Landward Routes
Possible Coastal Routes
Migrations in Oceania
Regions of Early Plant and Animal Domestication

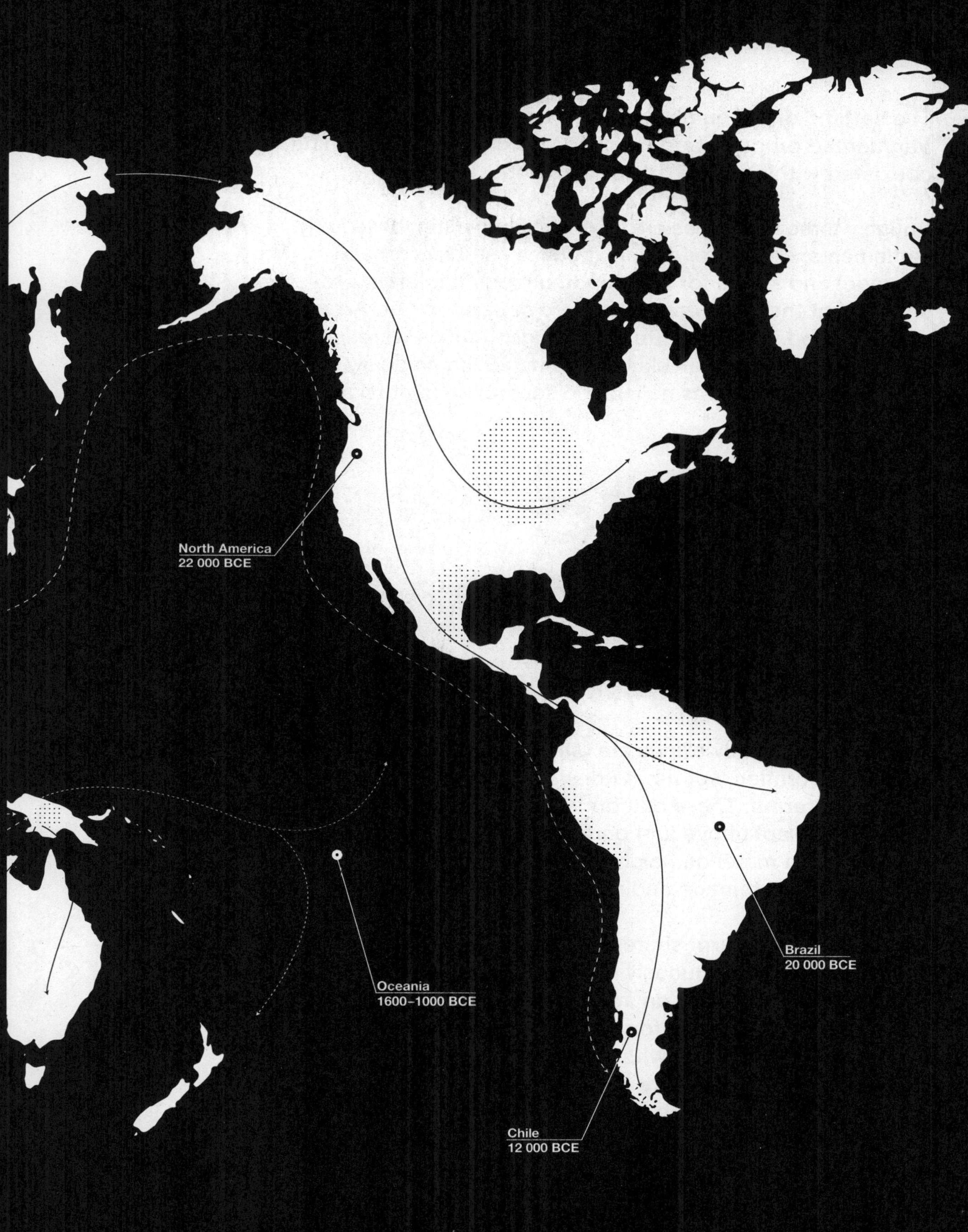
North America
22 000 BCE
Brazil
20 000 BCE
Oceania
1600–1000 BCE
Chile
12 000 BCE

From Shelter to Shed

The settling of the hunter-gatherer was a slow, uneven, fragmented process, and practices of foraging and farming coexisted within many early settlements.

Roughly three typologies are distinguished within these early settlements: shelter for people (houses), shelter for food (storage) and space for worship (temples). It is often presumed that these programmes were separated out. Art was concentrated in special ritual buildings, houses were laid out in zones, and human skulls were buried communally.[17] But in Çatalhöyük there was no marked separation of ritual and domestic functions.[18]

Quadrangular mud-brick houses (left) and storage for cereals (right), Mehrgarh, 5000–4000 BCE.

At Çatalhöyük, all dwellings are different in shape, size and level of decoration, yet most consist of a central room with raised platforms. These platforms had a double function: inhabitants slept above and buried their dead below. Subtle differences in material, height and colour described function, and space was remade and reworked for different purposes.

The larger urban form shared this fine-grained complexity. Dwellings were continuously built, levelled and rebuilt upon previous dwellings with an immediate and abundant material: earth. Çatalhöyük's built form was a topography. Dwellings were clustered together with mutually supporting walls; there were no gaps, passages or 'streets'. Instead, inhabitants traversed the honeycomb-like maze of Çatalhöyük's rooftops, accessing their homes through an opening in the ceiling.

The efficiency of this urban form is evident. Every surface is maximized, while structure and material are kept to a minimum. Roofs are not purely elements of shelter but a space

The plan (top) and axonometry (bottom) shows how dwellings were clustered together, sharing walls and accessed from the roof. Çatalhöyük, 7400–5700 BCE.

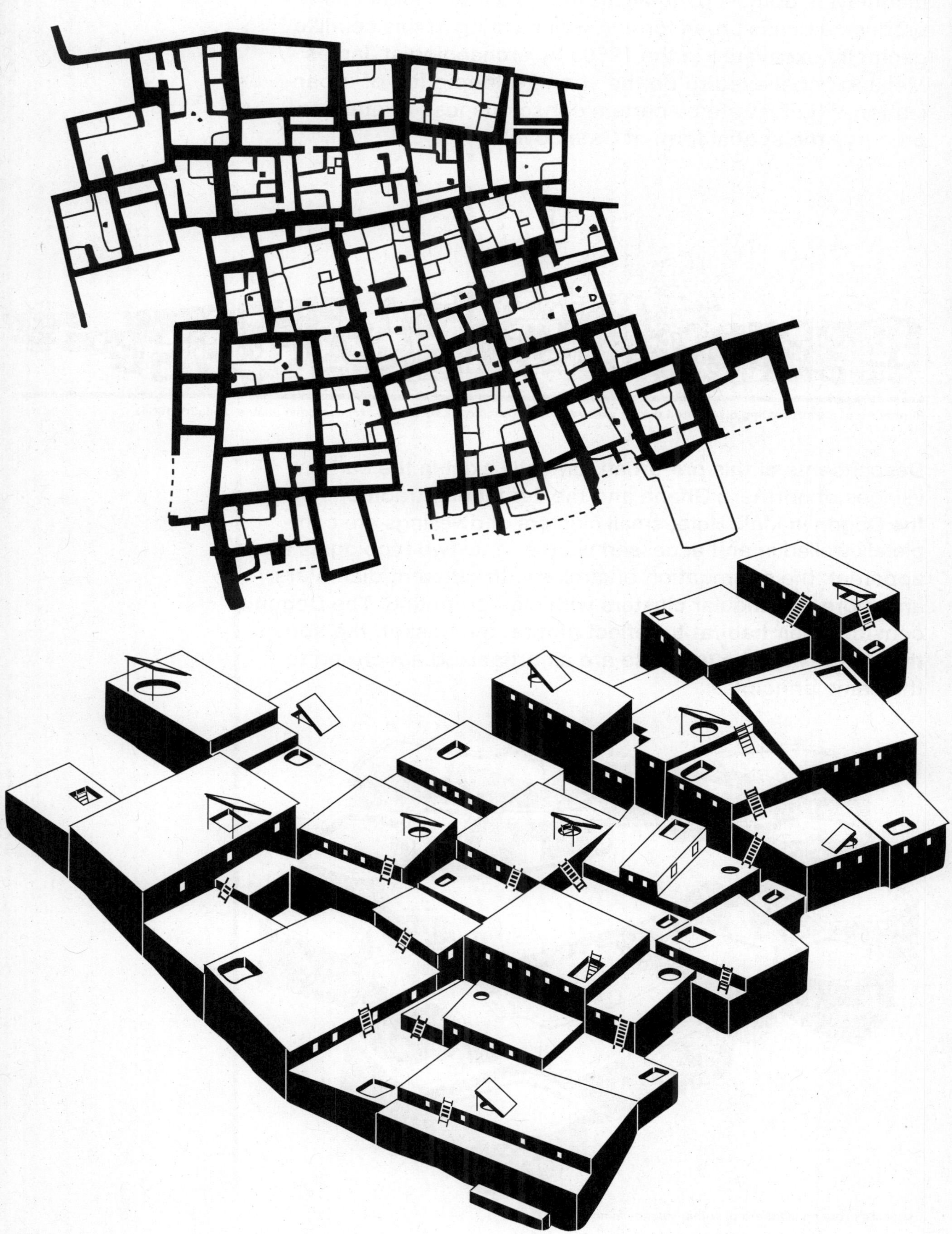

of circulation and exchange as well as a productive surface, widely used for drying food and storage. This ancient settlement layers domestic, ritualistic and pragmatic functions to produce a dense urban form. A wall painting of this cell-like geometry excavated in the 1960s by archaeologist James Mellaart is believed to be the very first depiction of urbanization.[19] It illustrates a certain consciousness or effort to preserve the spatial form of Çatalhöyük.

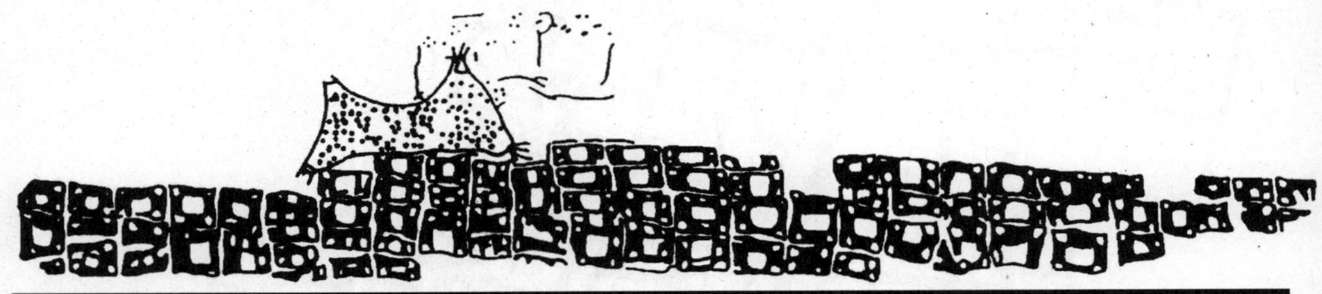

Rendering of a wall painting discovered during excavations of Çatalhöyük by British archaeologist James Mellaart, 1964.

Descendants of this pre-urban form still exist in the earthen villages of northern Ghana and the vernacular traditions of the Dogon in Mali. Here, small clusters of dwellings are completely walled in and accessed via the roof. Two typologies are apparent: the aggregation of circles with different diameters, and more rectangular clusters with clearer routing. The Dogon consider their habitat to reflect nature; the basket, the house, the village and the universe are all organized according to the same principles.

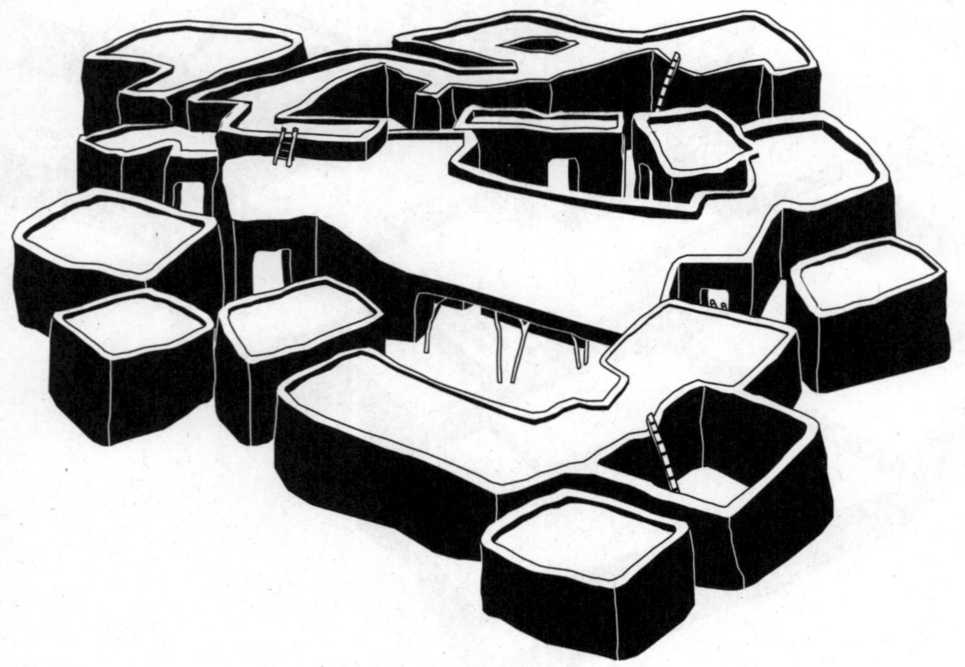

Secondary routing via the roof within villages in northern Ghana.

The Dogon cosmology and approach to ordering space had a profound impact on the thinking of Dutch architect Aldo van Eyck. He interpreted the Dogon relativity as 'twin-phenomena', exploring the exchangeability of large and small space.[20] For Van Eyck, "a city is not a city unless it is also a huge house". He expressed these ideas in his Amsterdam Municipal Orphanage in the aggregation of spaces below a roof of cupolas in three different sizes. To create space for the individual and the collective, Van Eyck argued for architecture to structure the relationships between part and whole.

Amsterdam Municipal Orphanage, Aldo van Eyck, 1960–1961.

The formal and programmatic intelligence embedded in vernacular urban form should not be overlooked. In fact, with the overwhelming erasure of adobe structures globally, there is an urgent need for the value, potential and efficiency of this highly contextual, highly sensitive building culture to be communicated before it disappears.

From Compound to Community

For almost 150 000 years there were neither rulers nor cities. Then something shifted. Six thousand years ago our ancestors crossed a historic divide, swapping small settlements for dense concentrations of resources and people.

Experts trade theories on what sparked this era of conflict, competition, expansion and empire building. Settlement brought a huge acceleration in population growth. Agriculture, by its very nature, invites intensification. Irrigation brought new wealth. Trade constructed new relationships based on surplus stock or scarcity. Religion bound together new, fragile groups, salving tensions and uniting individuals in a common view of the world. Across the Fertile Crescent, villages began to amalgamate, huddling together and hiding behind great walls. What is most intriguing is how and why these ancient settlements developed into concentric or radial forms. What informed Jericho's double circle?

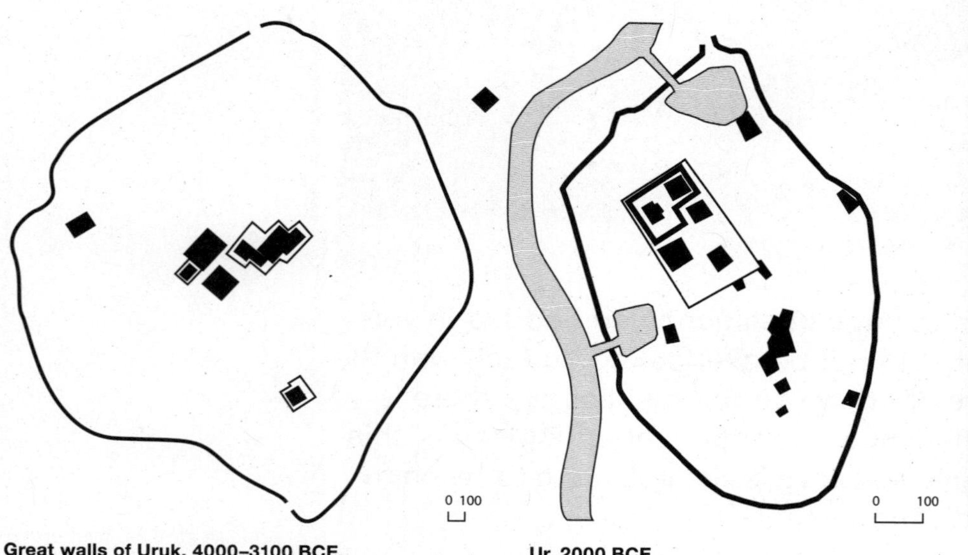

Great walls of Uruk, 4000–3100 BCE.

Ur, 2000 BCE.

Agricultural humans' means of survival, subjugating nature to grow resources, required huge amounts of time and energy. The subsequent division and distribution of this labour drove new hierarchies and stratification within agrarian society. An elite minority of imperial leaders, religious leaders and military leaders began to exercise control over the labour and social behaviour of the majority, creating centralized systems of government, greater specialization in labour, hierarchy in

The fourth city wall of Jericho was a double enclosure, 1800 BCE.

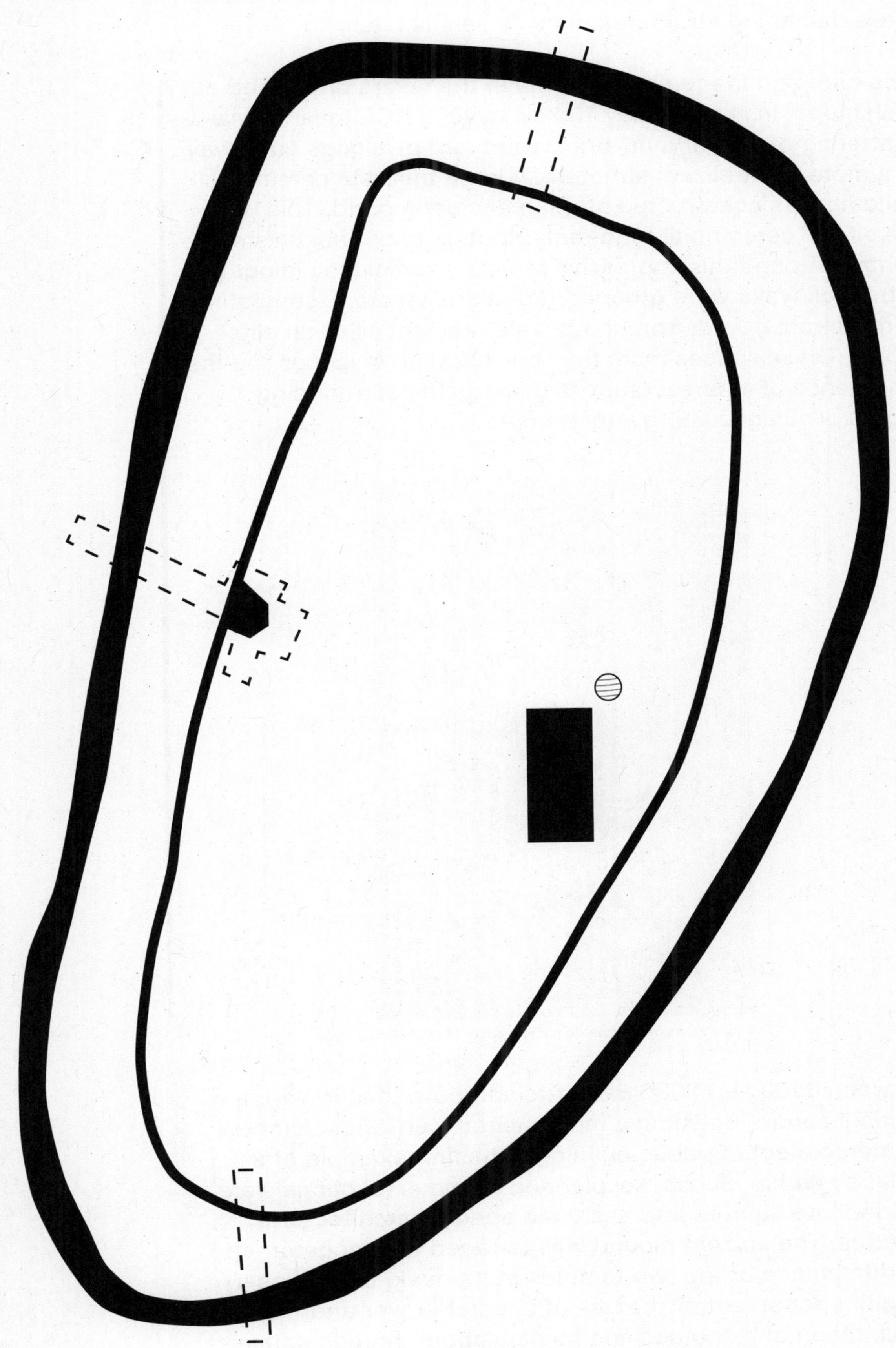

wealth, power and privilege, the emergence of the patriarchy and the enslavement of people. We are still trying to dismantle these damaging structures many millennia later.

This creeping inequality is visible in the layers unearthed at Arslantepe, in modern-day Turkey. In 4000 BCE the informal scattering of similar mud-brick courtyard dwellings gave way to a more 'centralized' structure. A large tripartite ceremonial building was constructed atop an ancient mound. This was the site of ceremonial food redistribution under administrative control. Around this impressive structure, official buildings with thick walls were grouped together in sectors, separating administrative work from the private residences of an elite group. These spaces mark the specialization of labour and the emergence of a bureaucracy to manage the surrounding region of villages and pastoral nomads.

Excavations of Arslantepe palace, 3350–3000 BCE.

Between 3350 and 3000 BCE, Arslantepe was a powerful political centre, boasting a monumental mud-brick complex of interconnected public buildings, the first example of a 'palace'. Within, public, secular and religious functions were divided into sectors and assigned specific architectural features. The ancient mound was terraced to exaggerate the predominance of the two temples at its peak. It remains a tangible document of the rise of secular power and the exploitation of resources and human labour through administration, and later force.[21]

Aptly christened 'the cradle of civilization', the ancient cities of Mesopotamia mimicked the established religious, political and military hierarchies in their urban form. Areas for the elite were highly planned, centrally located and demarcated by their monumental form. Beyond this, urbanization was unplanned, growing organically as population increased.

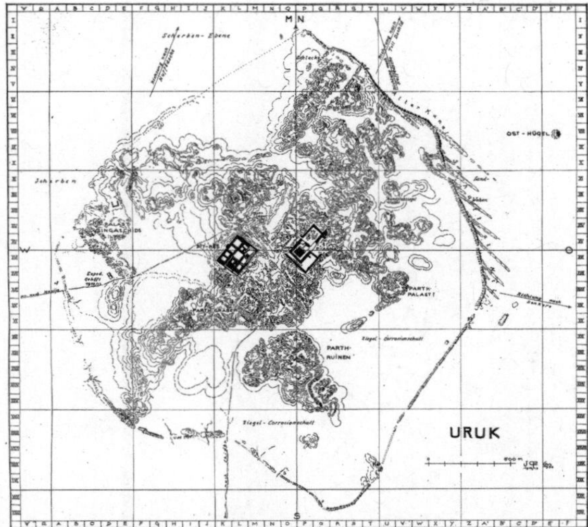

Plan of the ancient city of Uruk showing city walls around a large settled area with two central high points, the Eanna temple complex and Anu temple complex. By 3100 BCE, the population of Uruk may have reached 50,000 people.

Remains of the Eanna temple complex, where a Ziggurat once rose above a complex system of walls and courts that separated this holy district from the rest of the city.

Within the vast plains of Mesopotamia, elevation signalled monumentality. Palaces and administrative buildings of an elite class were raised above those they controlled, supported by terraced earth substructures. Above the elite in Mesopotamian social hierarchy sat the ancient gods. To honour them, humans built artificial mountains.

The enormous stepped structure of the ziggurat was the link between heaven and earth. At its summit is the site of an elaborate temple, honouring the patron of the city. No ziggurat is preserved to its original height, but the most famous is perhaps Etemenanki, the temple of Marduk, in ancient Babylon. Described by Herodotus in 460 BCE as an eight-tiered structure ascended by a spiralling path, Etemenanki is often associated with biblical accounts of the Tower of Babel.

City walls of Babylon surrounding the Hanging Gardens and the Tower of Babel, Athanasius Kircher, 1679. Division of Rare and Manuscript Collections, Cornell University Library.

Hanging Gardens of Babylon, Athanasius Kircher, 1679. Division of Rare and Manuscript Collections, Cornell University Library.

While dense centralized cities were being established in Mesopotamia, radial or oval-shaped Tripol'ye 'mega-sites' extended from modern-day Serbia to Ukraine. Although similar in scale, they bear no other resemblance.

Ziggurat of Etemenanki, Babylon, by Nebuchadnezzar II, 604–562 BCE.

The Tripol'ye 'mega-sites' were not organized around a monumental structure like the ziggurat. There are no palaces, no large temples and no large storage spaces. Although buildings radiate outwards in concentric circuits, most are homogeneous in size, style and decoration. The Tripol'ye 'mega-sites' betray few signs of an imposed hierarchy or deliberate planning.[22] They are like some colossal ancient suburb, with thousands of highly regular 'house-and-garden' typologies loosely connected in strips and clusters.

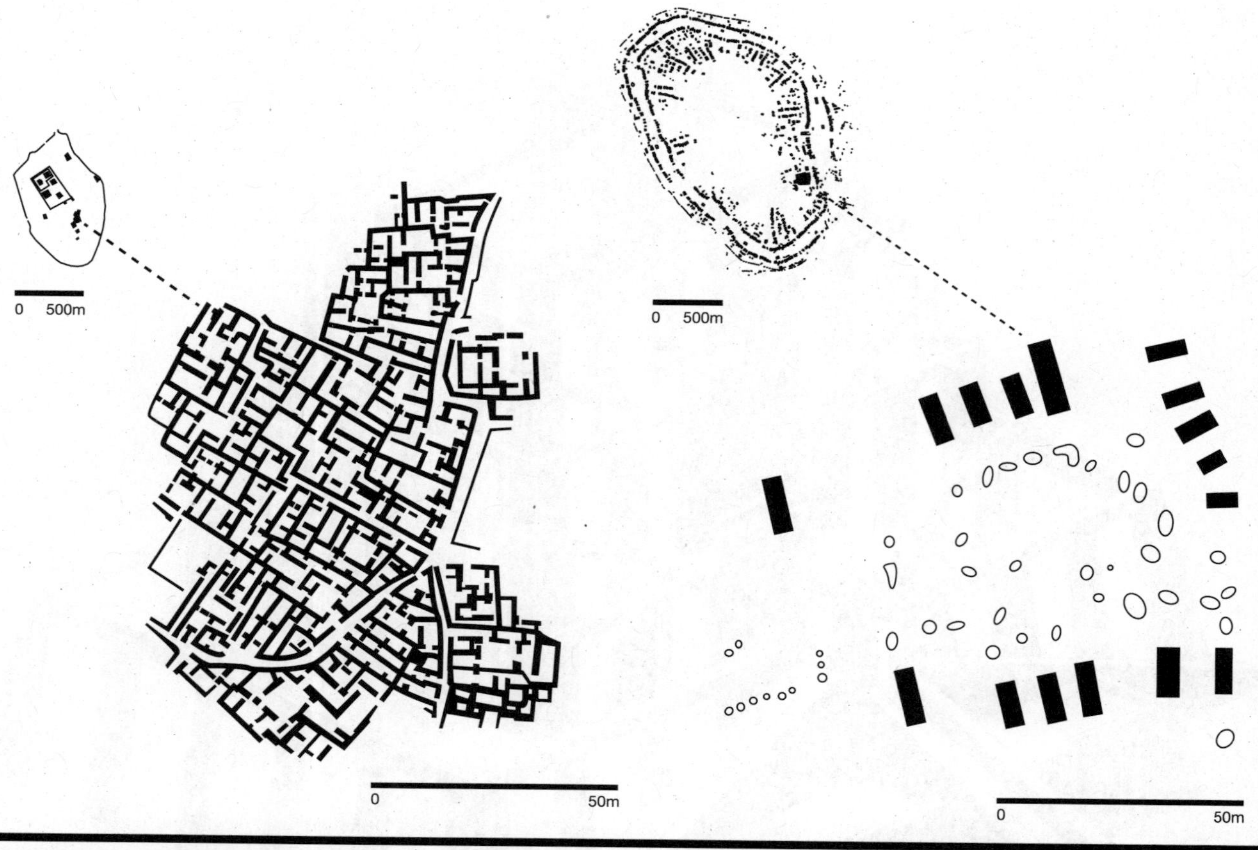

The urban form of the Mesopotamian city of Ur (left) is markedly denser than the Tripol'ye settlement of Nebelivka (right).

Identifying these radial streets or small courtyards has led to speculation about how this sprawling form operated. Was there an intermediary level between household and whole settlement? Could clusters have operated semi-autonomously, without a tight, top-down hierarchy? Tripol'ye sites were visibly rural, peaceful and non-hierarchic societies with a population of up to 10 000 people spread over areas as great as 450 hectares. They constitute the only exception to the global model of settlement limits established by Roland Fletcher.[23] How such massive agglomerations functioned, how resources were managed and communications were effective without inequalities materializing through architecture, craft or burial practice is fascinating.

Maidanets'ke Settlement, Ukraine, 3800–3600 BCE. Derived from the work of Dr Mikhaylo Videiko.

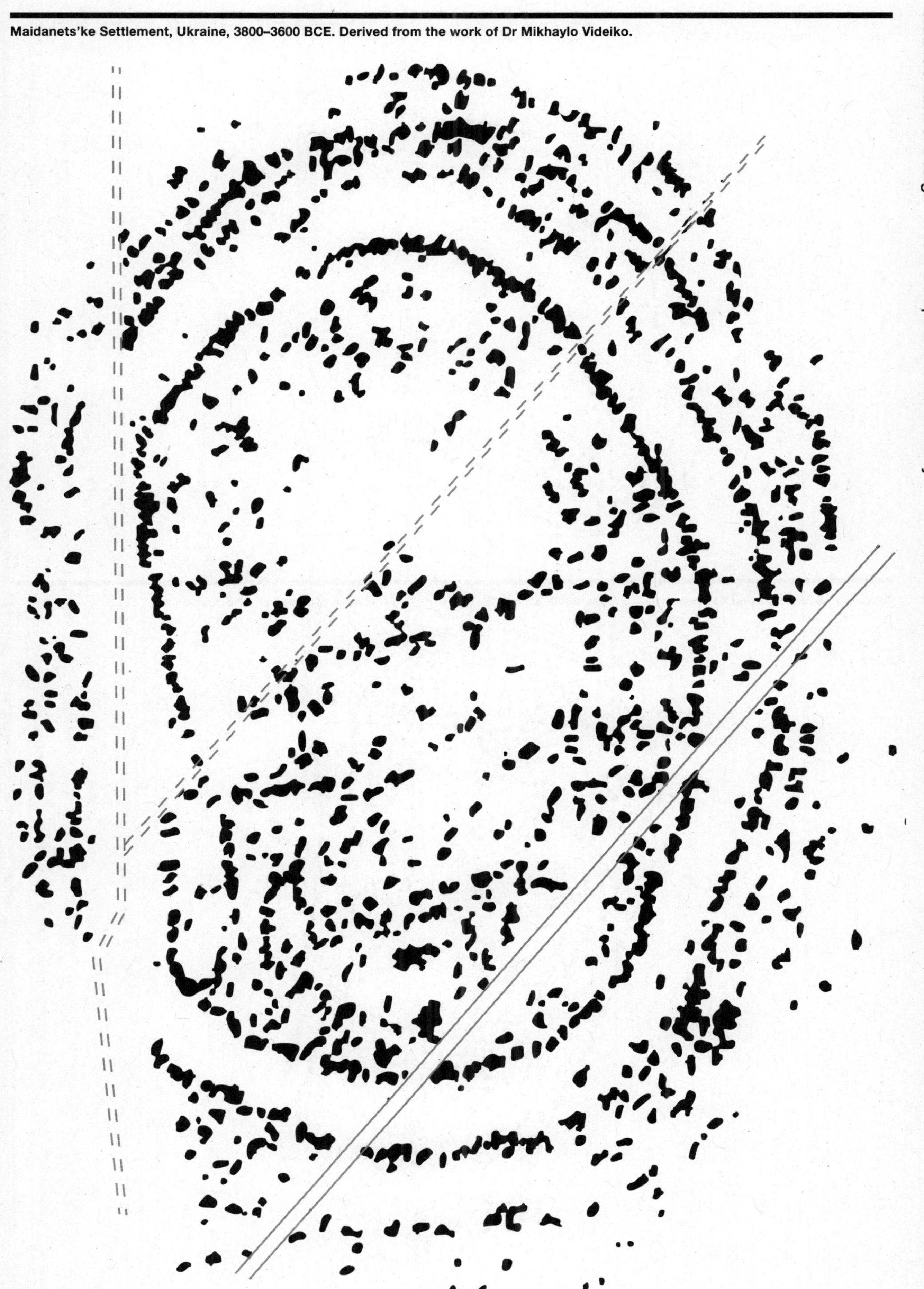

Nebelivka, Ukraine, 4000 BCE. Derived from the work of Dr John Chapman.

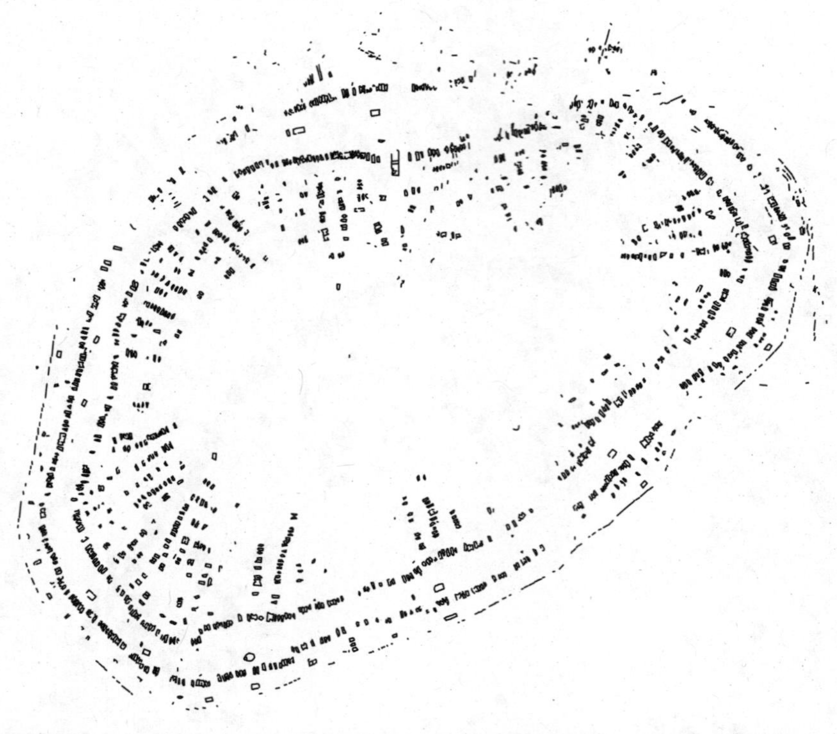

Tallyanky covered around 450 hectares, Ukraine, 3600–3300 BCE. Derived from the work of Dr Korvin-Piotrovskiy.

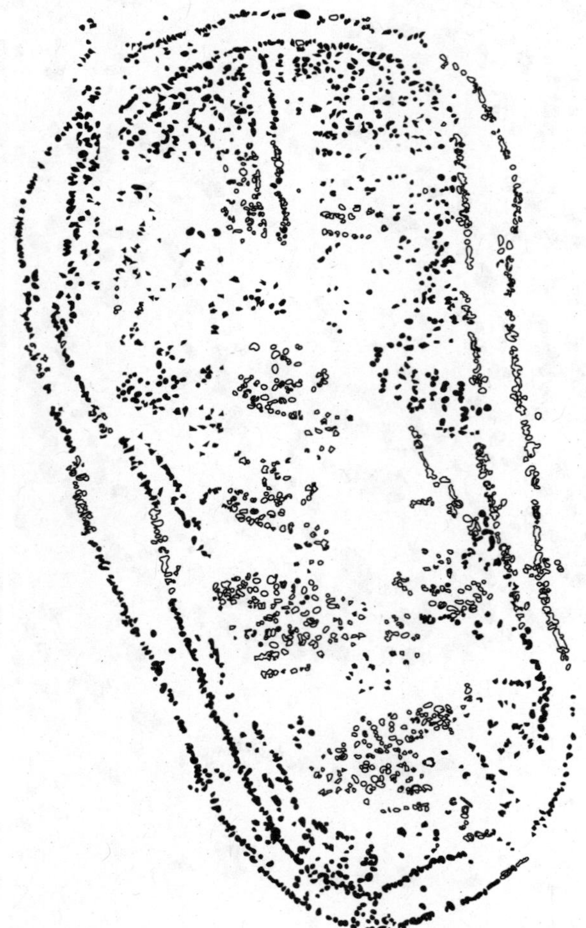

Establishing Order

"Enjoy Nature!... My own experience is that the more we study Art, the less we care for Nature. What Art really reveals to us is Nature's lack of design, her curious crudities, her extraordinary monotony, her absolutely unfinished condition. Nature has good intentions, of course, but as Aristotle once said, she cannot carry them out. When I look at a landscape I cannot help seeing all its defects... If Nature had been comfortable, mankind would never have invented architecture."[24] –Oscar Wilde

Primates craft a primitive hut in *Architecture: Its Natural Model,* Joseph Gandy, 1838.

Over a few thousand years, humankind has redefined the once symbiotic system of our survival, separating 'human' from 'nature'. Architecture's very natural beginnings became shrouded in mythology, and with every ancient civilization humanity's habitat grew in complexity.

One of the biggest, largely unresolved secrets of history is the complex of Giza, built around 2560 BCE. It is almost without doubt a ritualistic burial building and it took 3800 years before it was surpassed in height by Lincoln Cathedral, a religious building.

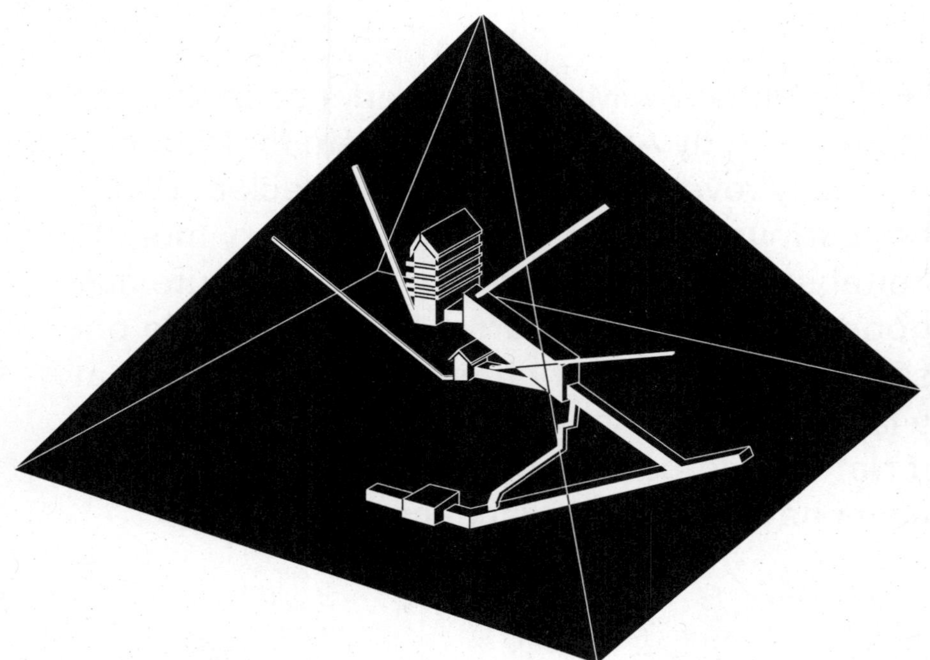

Diagram showing the system of circulation tunnels and chambers inside the Great Pyramid of Giza.

Giza pyramid complex, Khufu, 2580–2560 BCE.

Why and how did ancient Egyptians move stones as heavy as 80 tons over a distance of 800 kilometres, putting possibly 800 tons per day into place in order to finish within twenty years? This could only have been done with a very high level of organization and almost limitless powers over more than 20 000 workers at any time. The section shows an unprecedented and amazingly intricate system of passages, shafts and chambers, extending down into the bedrock on which the great pyramid is built as well as upwards into it. The organizational skills and the infinite motivation to pay tribute to the dead far outweighed the much simpler constructions for everyday life, at least as far as we know. It is totally unclear how they managed and why they felt the urge to do it.

The ancient Greek world untied itself from nature, developing its own rules. We see incredible material and immaterial invention. Space and habitation was organized, not by the laws of nature but by the abstract ideals of humans. Classical orders, systems of proportions and the separation of domestic and political space shaped humankind's new environment.

The dichotomy set up by the ancient Greek notions of *nomos* and *physis* has undoubtedly shaped a troubled relationship with nature over the last millennia. Under this logic, humans and their attempts to order the natural world, through mathematics, music or architecture, resided with the rationalism of *nomos*, while pre-godly nature was generally seen as purely chaotic. This conception of humans (and specifically men) as separate from nature, and in fact a necessary force against nature, is perhaps the greatest misunderstanding of humanity.

We see nature being pushed further and further away, no longer an essential element but an unattainable paradise. With Adam and Eve's expulsion from Eden, humankind fell from grace. No longer residing in paradise, humankind abandoned their existence within nature and reduced it to a utopia. This religiously impelled divide, this symbolic separation of humanity and nature, has shaped Western consciousness until its very recent emancipation. God granting human beings dominion over nature allowed them to consider nature the 'other' – an entity to be admired, owned, controlled, contested and consumed.[25]

A sweeping panorama of hedonistic abandon in *The Garden of Earthly Delights*, Hieronymus Bosch, 1510.

The Roman Empire took a more pragmatic approach to nature. Extending across modern-day Europe and into northern Africa, the land of the empire was a resource to be owned, and building infrastructure was a mechanism to attain or retain dominance. Enormous aqueducts carried clean water vast distances, where it was distributed to the homes and businesses of those who could afford it.[26] The Romans adapted and invented their way out of multiple environmental obstacles or climatic inconveniences. They are credited with inventing floor heating, heating an open space, known as a hypocaust, beneath a private home or bath with a fire or furnace.

Pont du Gard, France, 40–60 CE. © Roberto Ferrari.

In the civilizing of humankind we witness a considerable effort to civilize nature and exclude natural elements from our habitat. It started innocently enough, but exclusion bred contempt and what was once an instinct for shelter became a conscious effort to escape an environment ever more degraded by human actions.

Middle-Age Fortifications

With fortification, humankind drew the ground upwards for a more sinister purpose. Using the material at hand and exaggerating existing topography, it constructed new mountains, impenetrable walled fortresses to command the countryside.

Before towns ballooned into cities and density exploded under the Industrial Revolution, Europe was a smattering of small dense settlements. From the eleventh to the fourteenth century, landlords, great and small, ramped up their building programme. A vast number of new fortified settlements were established across Europe. Together, this scattered urbanization formed a network of nucleated settlements that went on to kill and conquer one another with monotonous regularity.

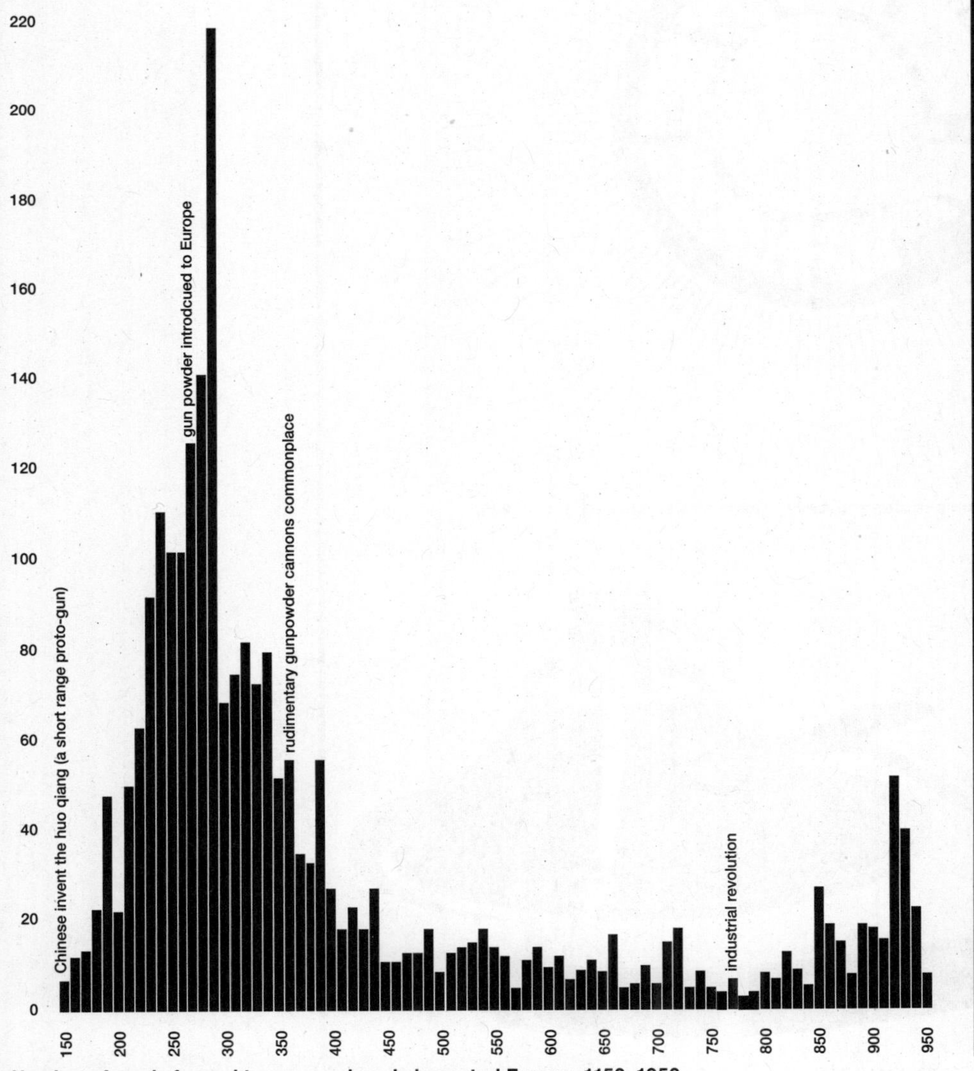

Number of newly formed towns per decade in central Europe, 1150–1950.

The motte-and-bailey was a popular typology for about 200 years. It preceded the real castle as we know it today and was easy to build. Often an existing hill was slightly manipulated to save time and material. A dry ditch was dug, a palisade was built around the lower bailey, and the scarp was smoothed to form a motte, on which was built a wooden keep. At the end of the twelfth century this typology fell into disuse as raiders developed new techniques to set fire to the wooden keep and attack from all sides. Stone gradually replaced wood. First the enclosure and later the internal wooden buildings were remade in stone.

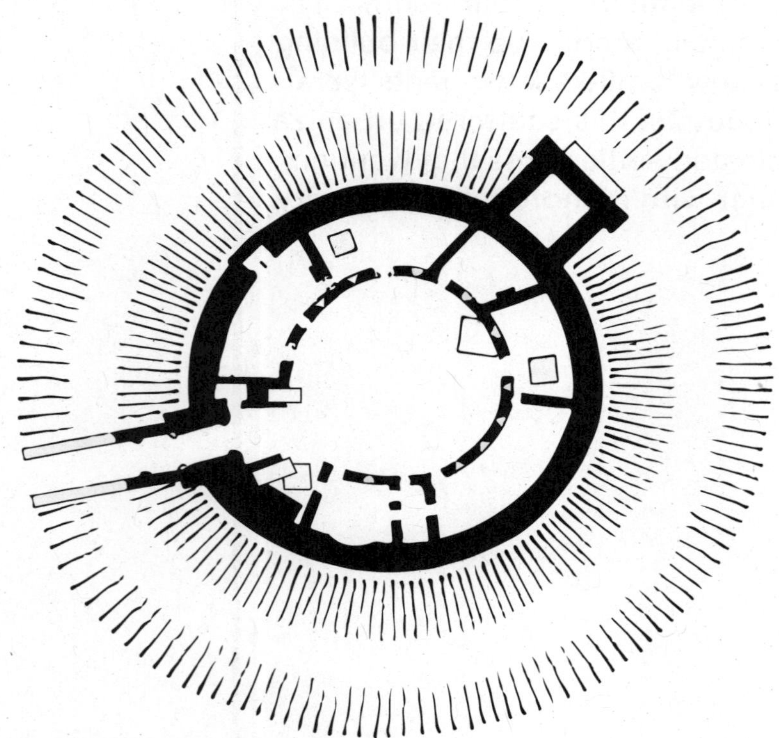

Restormel Castle was converted from a motte-and-bailey castle to a shell keep, 1192–1225.

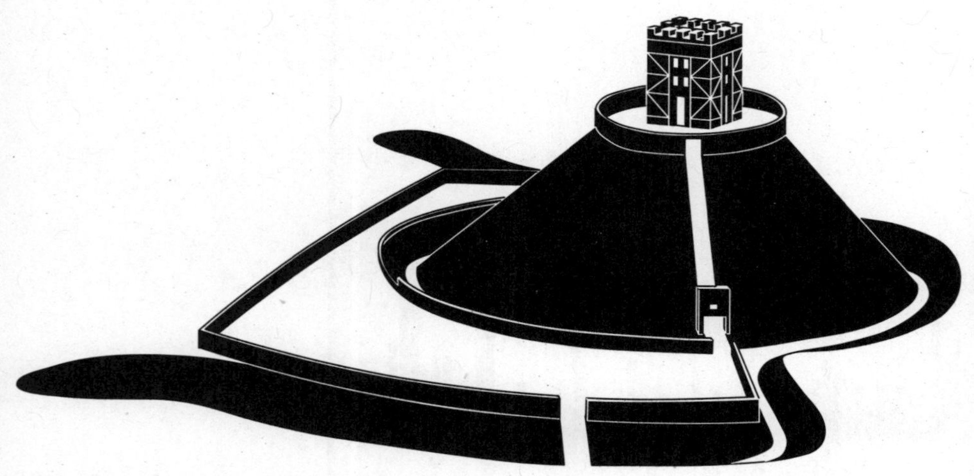

Timber motte-and-bailey Windsor Castle after 1085.

The castle, high on the hill, denying its enemies higher ground, is the image that typifies the Middle Ages. The widely held view that the castle was a defensive structure, built to protect a lord and his subjects within, is erroneous. Rather, the construction of a castle was an overtly hostile action, a marking of territory and an instrument for expansion.[27] Each fortress was a base for the exploitation of the surrounding agricultural land and population. Its sphere of influence was determined by the distance a group of soldiers could safely travel in a day.[28]

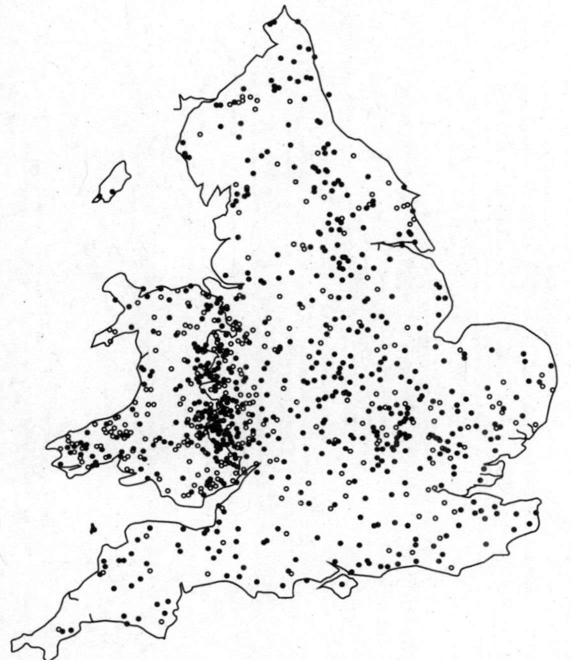

Distribution of motte-and-bailey castles in Britain, 1000–1200.

In the eleventh century Windsor Castle was established as part of William the Conqueror's defensive ring of motte-and-bailey castles to protect an important part of the River Thames and London. Each was a day's march from both the city and each other, allowing for easy reinforcement. While the wooden keep withstood numerous sieges, it was replaced by a stone shell keep by Henry I (1110–1135). During the twelfth century the three wards of Windsor Castle were transformed into impressive stone fortifications and a royal palace was built within the same enclosure.

Wenceslaus Hollar made a splendid etching of Windsor Castle in the mid-seventeenth century. This self-constructed and highly accurate axonometry shows the impressive motte, completely covered by what looks like an edible garden. This detailed drawing does not depict a smoothed scarp, cleared for the line of fire, but a manicured planted mound.

Windsor Castle transformed into a stone fortress by 1272. This etching by Wenceslaus Hollar shows the impressive central motte, 1650.

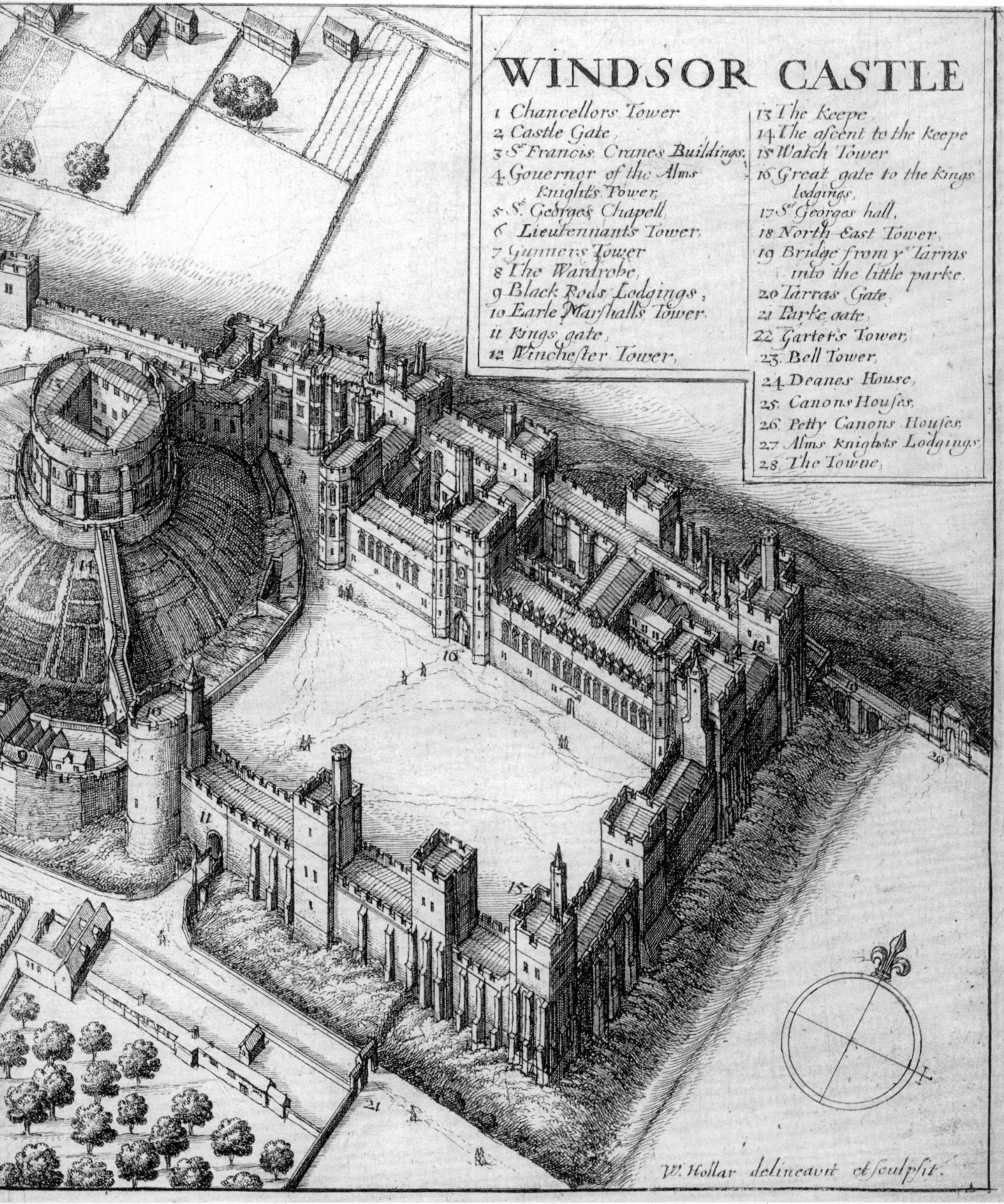
WINDSOR CASTLE
1 Chancellors Tower
2 Castle Gate,
3 Sr Francis Cranes Buildings,
4 Gouernor of the Alms Knights Tower,
5 St Georges Chapell,
6 Lieutennants Tower,
7 Gunners Tower
8 The Wardrobe,
9 Black Rods Lodgings,
10 Earle Marshalls Tower.
11 Kings gate,
12 Winchester Tower,
13 The Keepe,
14 The ascent to the Keepe
15 Watch Tower
16 Great gate to the Kings lodgings,
17 St Georges hall,
18 North East Tower,
19 Bridge from ye Tarras into the little parke.
20 Tarras Gate,
21 Parke gate,
22 Garters Tower,
23 Bell Tower,
24 Deanes House,
25 Canons Houses,
26 Petty Canons Houses,
27 Alms Knights Lodgings
28 The Towne,
W. Hollar delineavit et sculpsit.

Perhaps this was urban agriculture, built within the safety of an enclosure, to feed those trapped when the castle was under siege. Through verticality, this militant architecture asserted its dominance over its surroundings. Standing 500 metres above the Jordan River Valley, the Belvoir Fortress (Kochav HaYarden) is the archetypal concentric castle.[29] Two circuits of three-metre-thick basalt walls are surrounded by a dry moat cut 14 metres deep and 20 metres wide into the bedrock. Here the undulation of wall and ditch is used to amplify height. Material extracted from the moat was amassed within the thick curtain walls, exaggerating its elevated position. The fortification acts like an extension of the ground, fusing with the site to overwhelm those beyond its enclosure.

Measured from the moat, the outer wall of Belvoir would have once been 25 metres high.

Within the castle walls, architecture was an instrument of control. The concentric arrangement of walls, the articulation of openings and the complexity of internal circulation combines to force and coerce the intruder along predetermined routes.

Approaching Belvoir Fortress, intruders are forced along a double bent entrance, ramping up towards a barbican within the external tower and then switching back towards a corner tower. This narrow passage slowed the enemy, trapped them within the walls of the outer fortress and exposed them to fire from the towers and through arrow slits along the walls. Once inside, the outer fortress acts like a large 'zwinger',[30] or killing ground, for the internal fortress, trapping intruders

Plan (top) and axonometry (bottom) of Belvoir Fortress, 1168. The arrow shows the intruder's path through the double bent entrance.

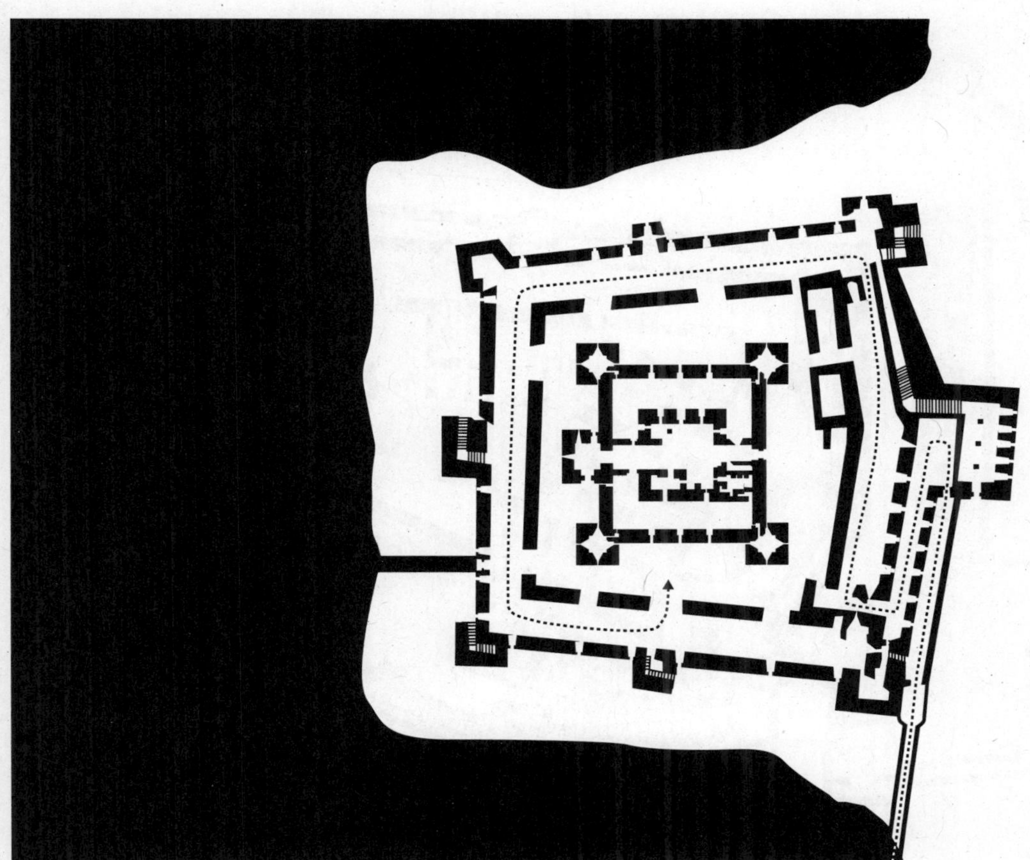

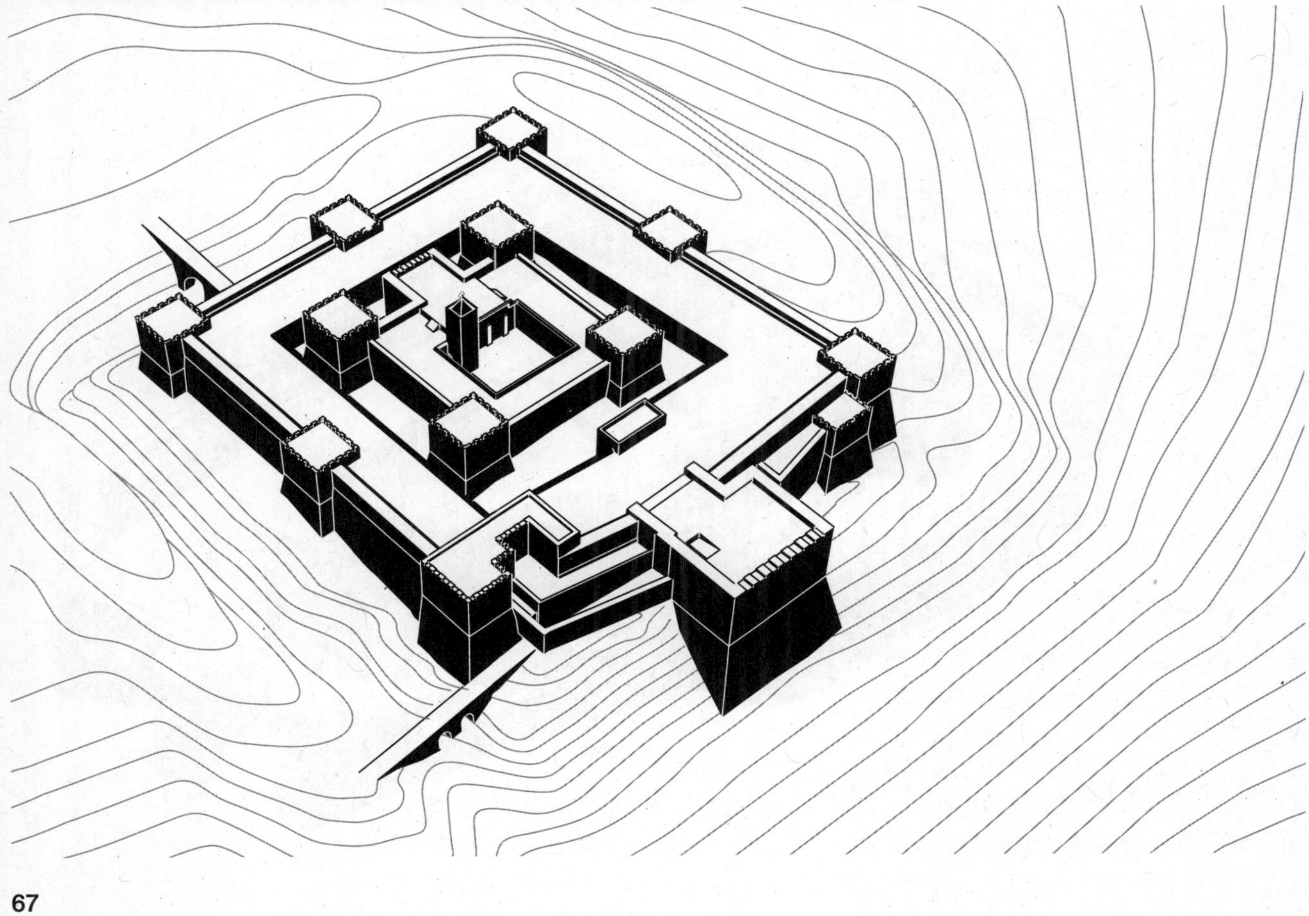

Plan (top) and axonometry (bottom) of Krak de Chevaliers, 1142–1271. Note the bent entrance at the bottom of the plan.

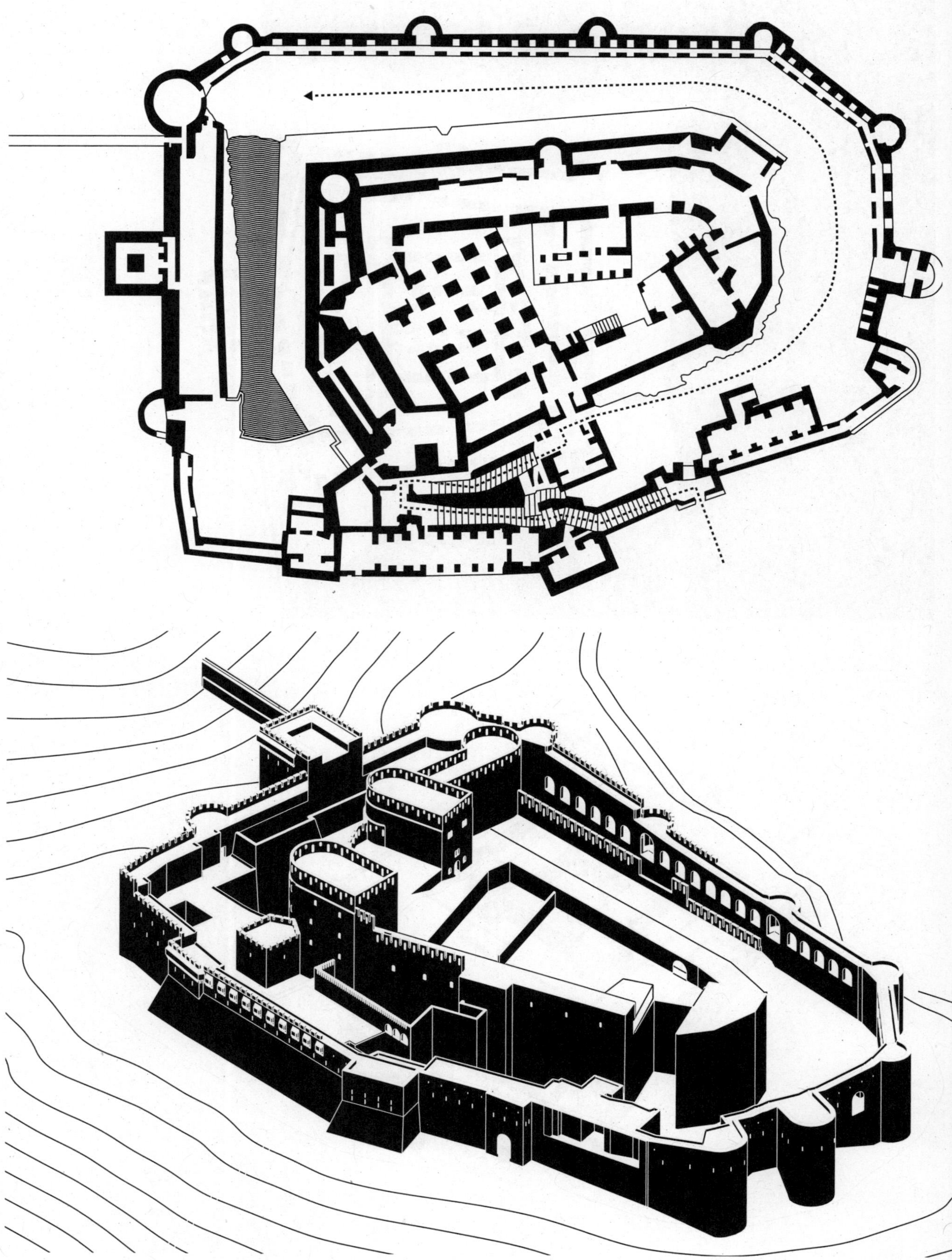

within and forcing them to circumnavigate the castle from the eastern outer gateway to the western inner gateway.[31] One of the most elaborate bent entrances is found in Syria at the Krak de Chevaliers. Housed between the inner and outer walls on the eastern side is a 200-metre-long killing zone. This vaulted ramp leads intruders upwards while making tight elbow turns, slowing and confining intruders into a tight formation. Along this passage, intruders were vulnerable to attack from towers, the machicolations (stone parapets) above and posterns at each turn.

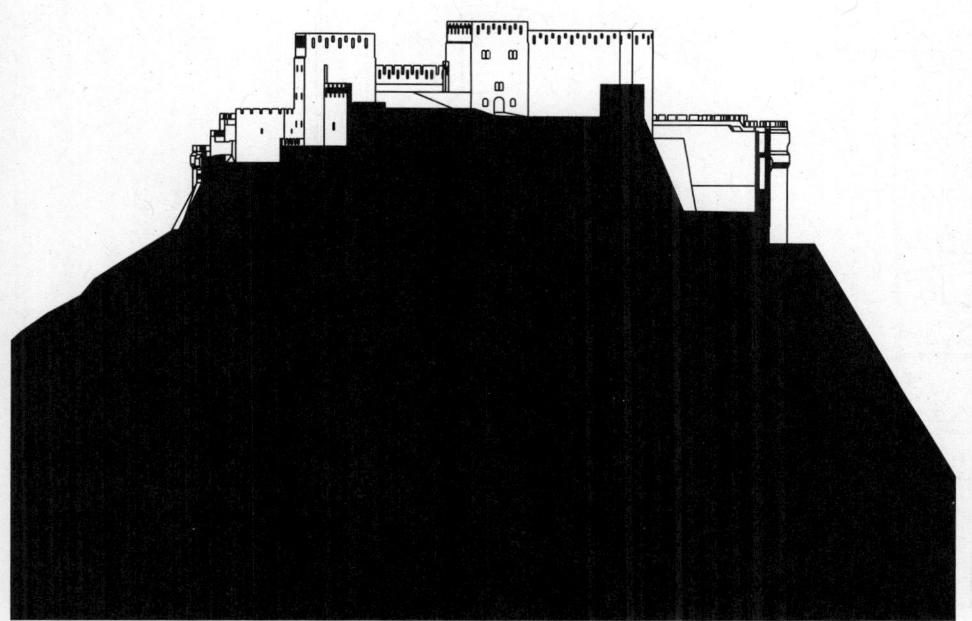

Section of Krak de Chevaliers showing how the castle extended the existing topography.

Originally, mortals laid an articulated, dynamic route to spiritual enlightenment in the temples and the houses of the gods. Within fortifications, defenders constructed elaborate passages to slow, impede, disable and kill intruders. While the Middle Ages can be seen as an apex of this architecture of control or coercion, these techniques have been repetitively translated and transposed. Whether it is Le Corbusier's *promenade architecturale* or the more inward-focused *Raumplan* of Adolf Loos, these concepts can be seen as modern manifestations of a bent entrance, albeit with slightly less menace.

Designing a continuous procession through space was irresistible to the modern architect. Like the medieval castle, Adolf Loos articulated space within exterior load-bearing walls. The Raumplan gave Loos control over the placement of partitions within a set enclosure. Passages snake and branch through Villa Moller. For Loos, unfolding space around a central pathway was a necessity; the architect had to design the relationship and transition between spaces. Le Corbusier took it further. With the free plan, structure and enclosure are separated. Anything was now possible, and so he enlivened space by curating a sequence of images to unfold before the eyes of the observer.

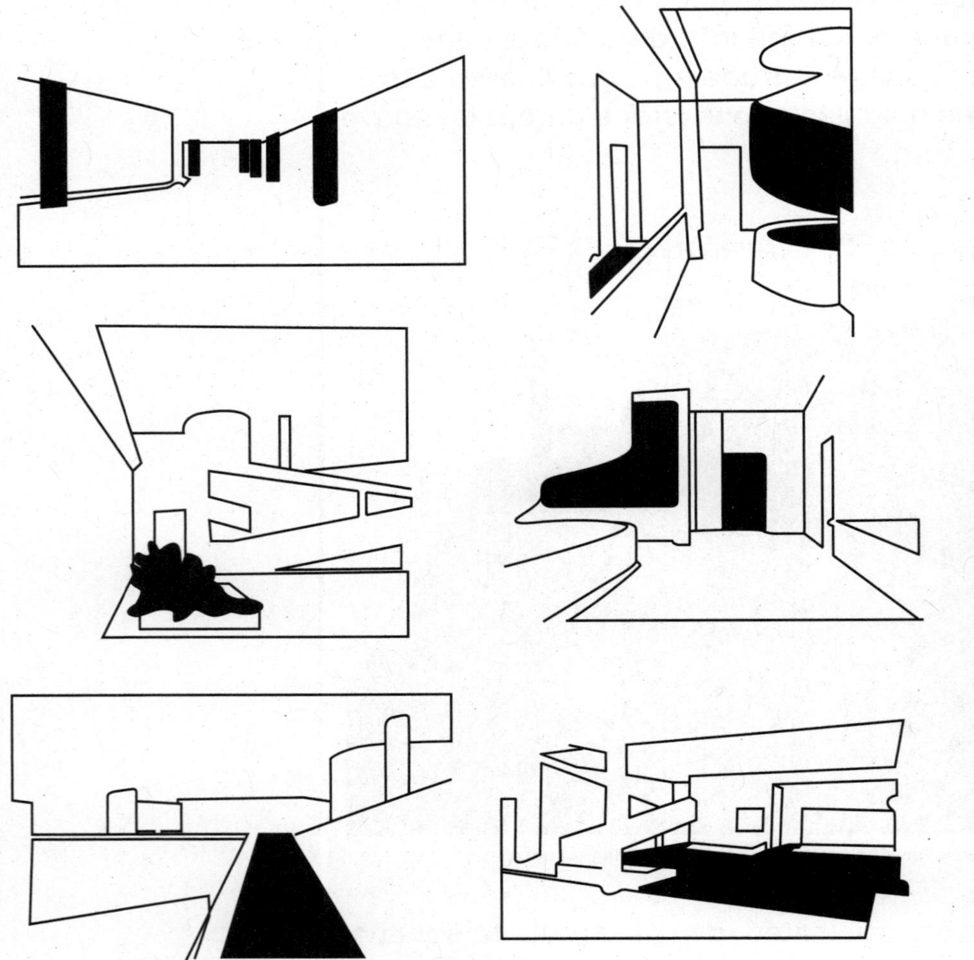

Promenade Architecturale through the Villa Savoye.

While the building itself became less and less articulated under modernism, architecture today remains enamoured with this coercion of movement and controlling of experience. A visitor to a contemporary gallery or museum is led through a series of spaces in a predetermined fashion. Descending the spiral ramp of Frank Lloyd Wright's Guggenheim or losing a sense of direction within Daniel Libeskind's Jewish Museum, the viewer obligingly follows an unavoidable, unalterable experience.

This totalitarian control of the architect is rightly criticized. An architect's desire to elevate or divert the spatial experience of the user denies individual participation and self-direction, and ultimately leads to the standardizing of space.

Axonometry, plans and section of Villa Moller, Vienna, Adolf Loos, 1928.

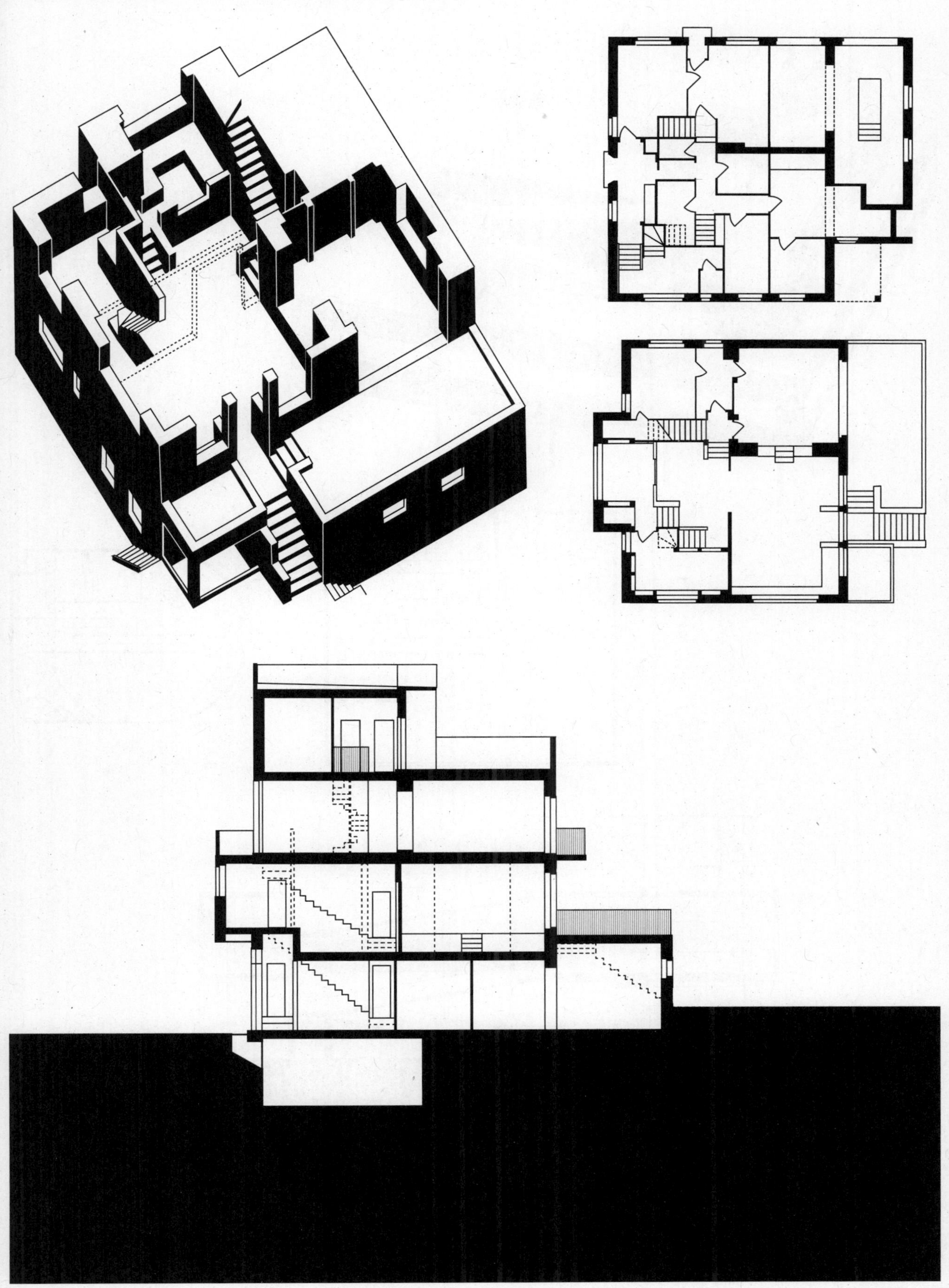

Axonometry, plans and section of Villa Savoye, Poissy, Le Corbusier, 1929.

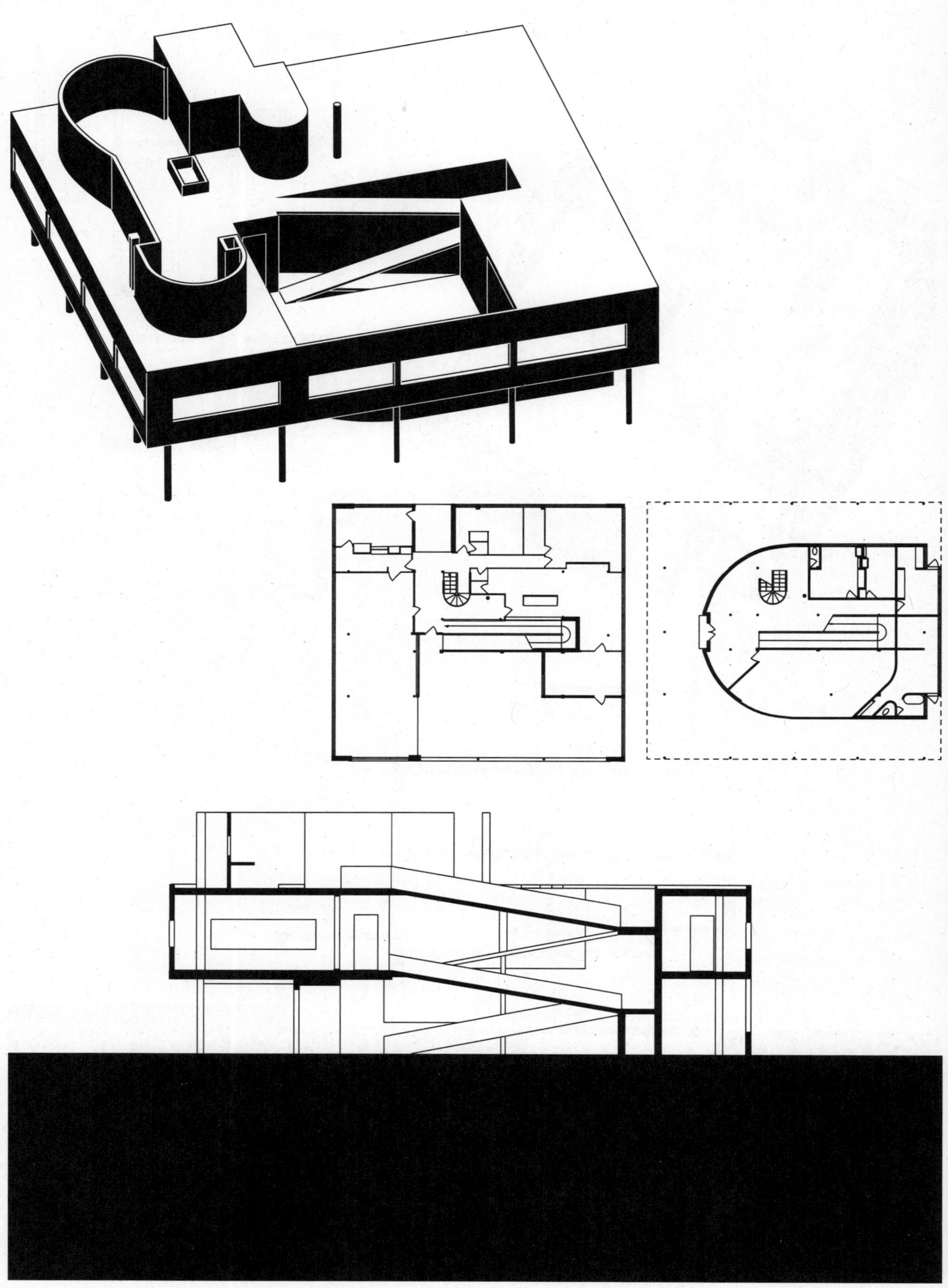

The Age of Gunpowder

With the introduction of gunpowder and the refinement of explosive weaponry, the traditional walled fortification, impregnable for centuries, was now vulnerable.[32] In response, verticality was replaced with depth. Forts became both lower and larger in area with tiers of defences radiating outwards. Walls were lowered, towers levelled, fortifications embedded in ditches and fronted by earthen slopes. The ground dissipated the explosive power of the manoeuvrable siege cannon.

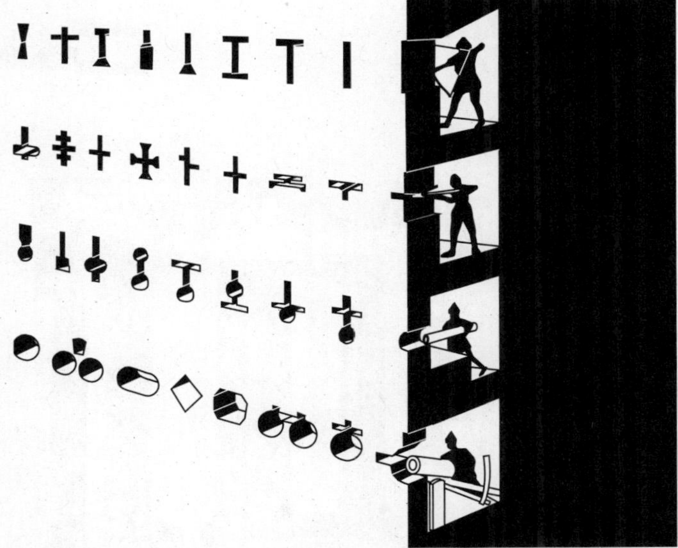

The articulation of openings within the curtain wall shifted with the sophistication of weaponry.

Throughout history, elevation and height have been associated with concepts of superiority, divinity and supreme power. The tower as a medieval edifice was utilized as both reinforcement of outer fortifications and the central, last defence within the concentric castle, the king's keep.

The inert square keep or great tower of Dover Castle sits at the summit of the hill. Its walls are almost six metres thick, with small openings splayed inward for the occupant. The mass of the walls is further exaggerated by a series of auxiliary spaces, winding passages and staircases contained within. The depth and complexity of this vertical circulation draws on the logic of the bent entrance, slowing and controlling the intruder, protecting its patron on the top level. Even the spiral stairs twist to the right to give a right-handed defender the advantage.

The inhabited wall of Dover Castle's keep, 1180.

First Unitarian Church, Louis Kahn, 1962.

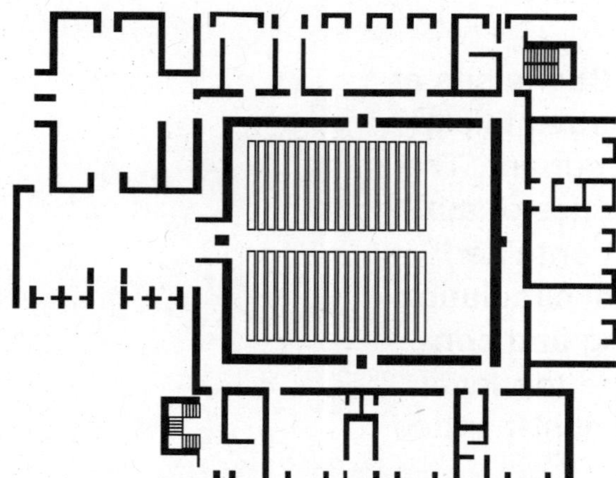

Housing mural chambers, stores and galleries within the ex terior wall serves a double purpose: strengthening the keep and buffering the central space. The potential of this inhabited wall was explored centuries later by Louis Kahn in his design of the First Unitarian Church. Here classrooms are strung along a corridor and wrapped around the central church space to create a sanctuary.[33]

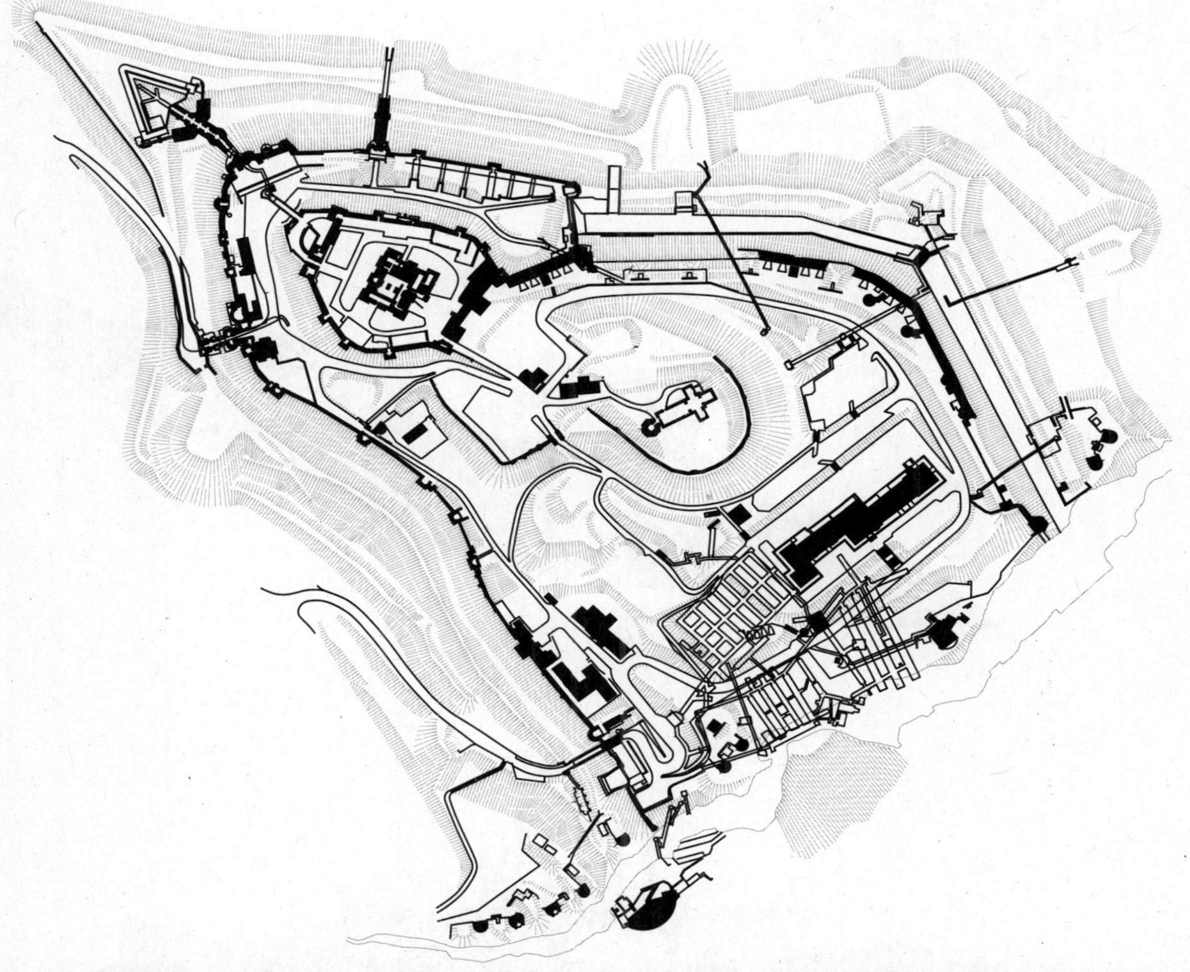

Initially constructed in 1180, Dover Castle's defences were adapted to meet the changing demands of weapons and warfare from 1217 to 1815.

Fortified for 2000 years, the chalk of Castle Hill in Dover has been shaped and reshaped over the centuries into immense earthworks, ditches and mounds. Anticipating a cannon-wielding Napoleonic France, Dover Castle's outer walls were lowered and backed by an earth rampart. Towers were levelled to form gun platforms and clear the line of fire from the keep. To increase depth of field, a large ditch was cut around the front of the outer curtain. A raised gun platform faced inland and a network of tunnels were dug into the cliff-face to provide cover towards the sea. Gunpowder forced Dover Castle to duck down and ground itself within its site.

Dover Castle's outworks, erected 1217–1260, and defences, reshaped for artillery 1740–1815.

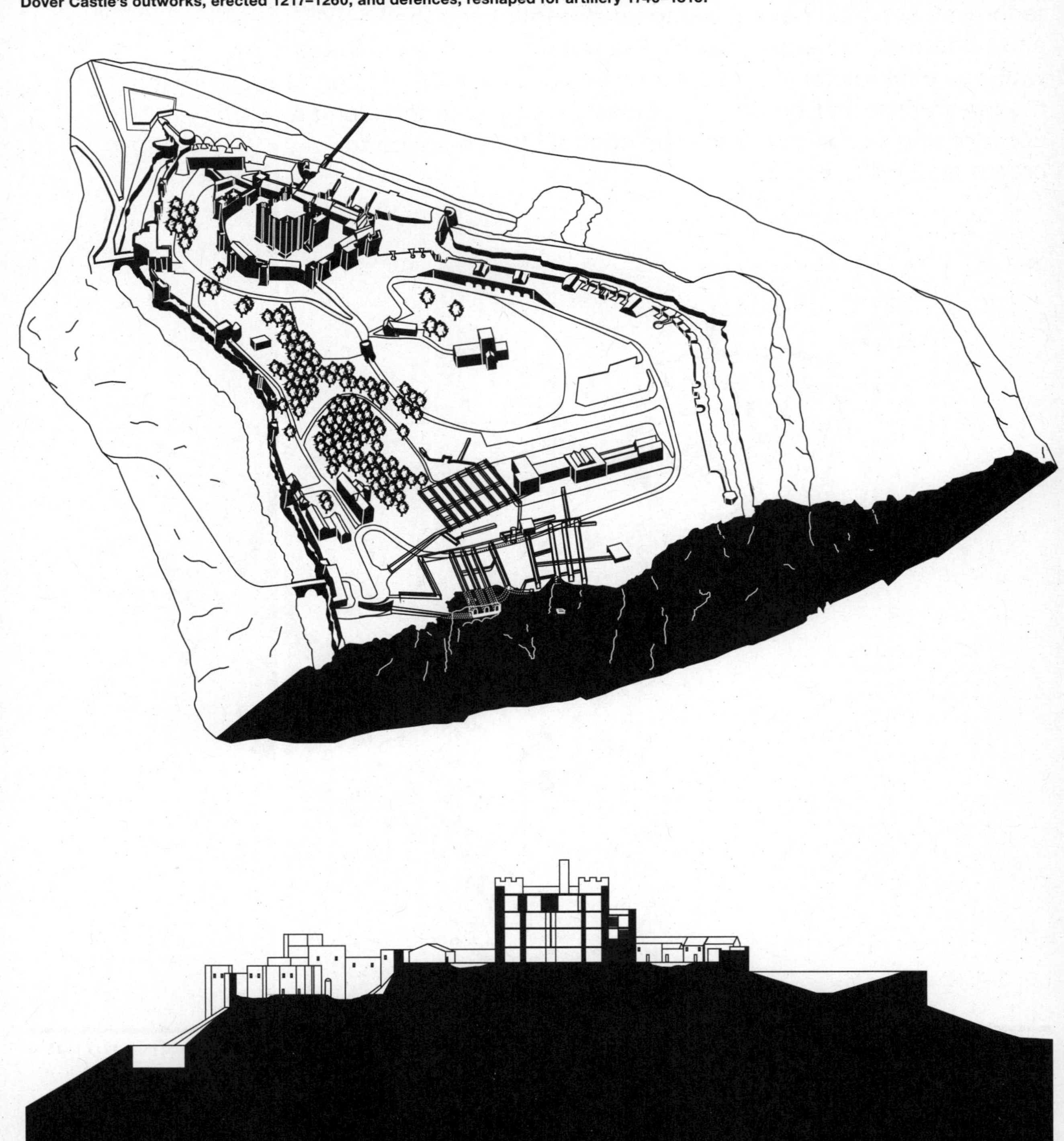

A ten-metre-high entrance gate (A) blocks the only approach from the mainland, and a postern gate (B) is built above the only part of the cliff approachable by boat. Dunnotar Castle, 1396–1600.

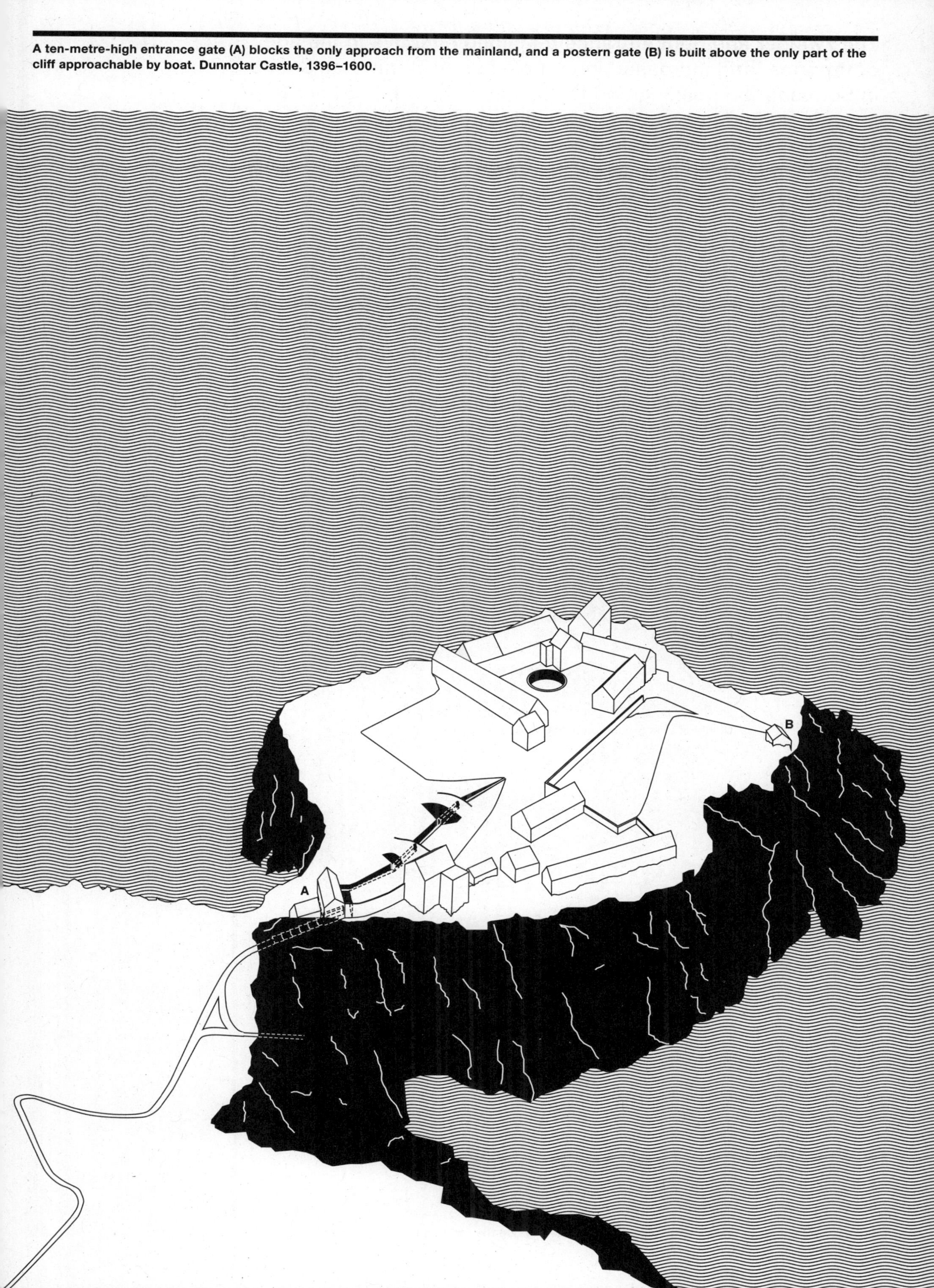

The zwinger and bent entrance remained effective in the age of firearms, and increased in complexity. At Dunnottar Castle in Scotland the building and the landscape work together to impede, confine and ultimately kill intruders. A carefully choreographed entry system is concentrated along a narrow strip of land, which connects Dunnottar to the mainland, exploiting its naturally fortified position.

The new fortifications of the fifteenth century were focused on increasing depth of field and depth of mass. Vauban's Citadel of Lille was an acknowledgement that no fort is totally impenetrable. Instead, a sequence of obstacles slowed the enemy's progress. Beyond the enclosure of the citadel the earth was cut and folded into a layered defence. Ravelins, hornworks, crownworks and wide ditches and moats radiated outwards in uneven lines, like the teeth of a saw.[34]

Citadel of Lille ground plan, 1667–1670.

Soay sheep keep vegetation low above the fortifications.

In the remarkable starlike fortress of Nossa Senhora da Graça in Portugal, an entire hill was moulded into interlocking fields of fire. Three defensive lines – the central stronghold, the masterful compound and the exterior works – radiated outwards to cover the distance of a cannon shot. Each layer was interdependent and separated by deep pits. Beyond this, massive gently sloping banks of earth (glacis) fronted ditches so that the fortress walls were almost totally hidden.

Aerial view of Forte de Nossa Senhora da Graça, 1763–1792. © Starforts.com.

The evolution of European society, from feudalism to the beginnings of the modern nation-state, can be tracked through the construction and evolution of its fortifications.[35] Constant conflict and competition reshaped Europe. The resources needed to build, arm and besiege ever more sophisticated fortifications drove a consolidation of power.[36] Those unable to compete were simply swallowed up by their more powerful neighbours. Gunpowder produced a new remoteness between ever-larger armies and ever-expansive fortifications.

The geometric rigour of the star-shaped fortification had a formative influence on the patterning of the ideal Renaissance city. Fortifications encased cities within a regular geometry. Points, lines and grids enabled city designers to create a series of nodes, axes and networks as the defining elements of urban space.[37] Rejecting the irregularity and informality of the medieval city, Renaissance urbanism emphasized regularity, harmony and order.[38] Symmetry, perspective, the positioning of monuments along an axis, the convergence of axes and the closed vista: all combined to shape a highly centralized urban form.

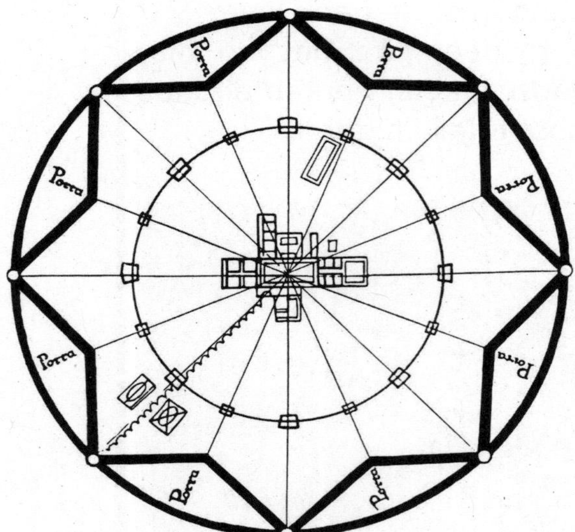

Ideal city of Sforzinda, Antonio di Pietro Averlino, 1457.

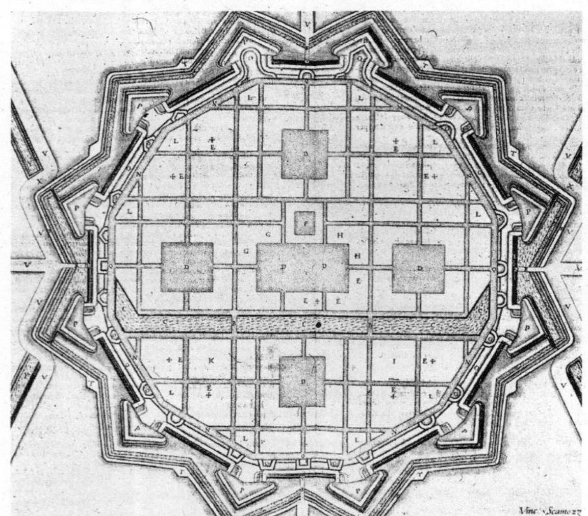

Plan of an ideal city by Vincenzo Scamozzi, 1615.

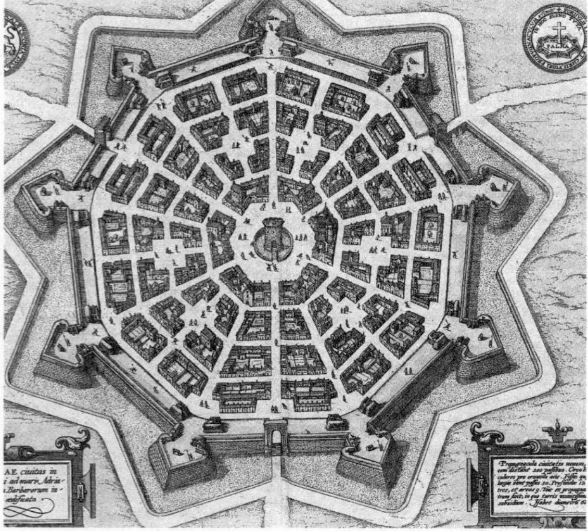

Seventeenth-century map of the city of Palmanova, c.1597.

From Public Space to Private Icon

For centuries the city was the setting for a highly active public life. With the social and intellectual revolution of the mid-eighteenth century, a belief in the right of the individual to liberty, privacy, security and property led to the conception of a private realm. According to Richard Sennett, the erosion of public space and public life that followed represents 'the fall of public man'.[39] Retreating into the private realm, Western society has become paralysed by an almost pathological obsession with personal matters.

Completed during the reign of Septimius Severus, the Forma Urbis Romae was a ground-floor plan of the city of Rome carved into marble slabs. This served as a cadastral survey, a public register of property in which to settle spatial disputes.[40] Here, private space is separated from the public realm, or rather the city was partitioned into spaces deemed not tradable (res publica and res sacra) and the remainder deemed private and exchangeable (res privata).

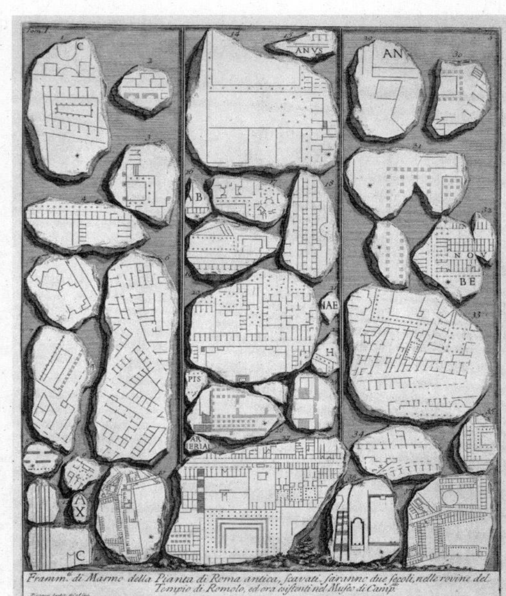

Depiction by Giovanni Battista Piranesi, Antichità Romane, 1756.

Fragment of the Forma Urbis Romae, 200–300 CE.

The attention given to representing the architectural form of the public or sacred sphere demonstrates its dominance. In the Forma Urbis Romae, monumental or public structures are described in detail. The thickness of walls and the arrangement of columns suggest both form and programme, while private space is denoted as a single line, like the modern site boundary. The parcelling of land into public and 'other' was a ritual practice in Ancient Rome. In each survey of a new city, space was set aside for the empire. Pier Vittorio Aureli argues that public and private space were once mutual conditions, and that without a clearly demarcated public space, private space could not exist. [41]

Over a thousand years later, Giovanni Battista Nolli mapped the Eternal City.[42] The graphic figure-ground nature of the Nolli plan has become a modern benchmark for urban representation. The built fabric of the city is rendered solid and public space, both outdoor and indoor, is carved out. Alongside the street and the square, the interiors of church, theatre and palace courtyard combine to represent a continuum of accessible urban space. Again, particular care is given to representing this public realm. The dynamic interplay between interior and exterior, solid and void, figure and ground, underscores a dialectical relationship between buildings and their context. The context conditions the building and the building in turn exerts an outward pressure on the city fabric.[43]

A section of La Nuova Topografia di Roma, Giovanni Battista Nolli, 1748.

From the seventeenth century onward, we see a gradual inversion of the European city fabric. As society sought liberation and autonomy, enclosed urban space and an active public life was eroded in favour of privacy and personal life. In his book *Court & Garden*, Michael Dennis beautifully describes the physical manifestations of this growing individualization of society, tracing the physical tug of war between public and private space within the French hôtel.[44]

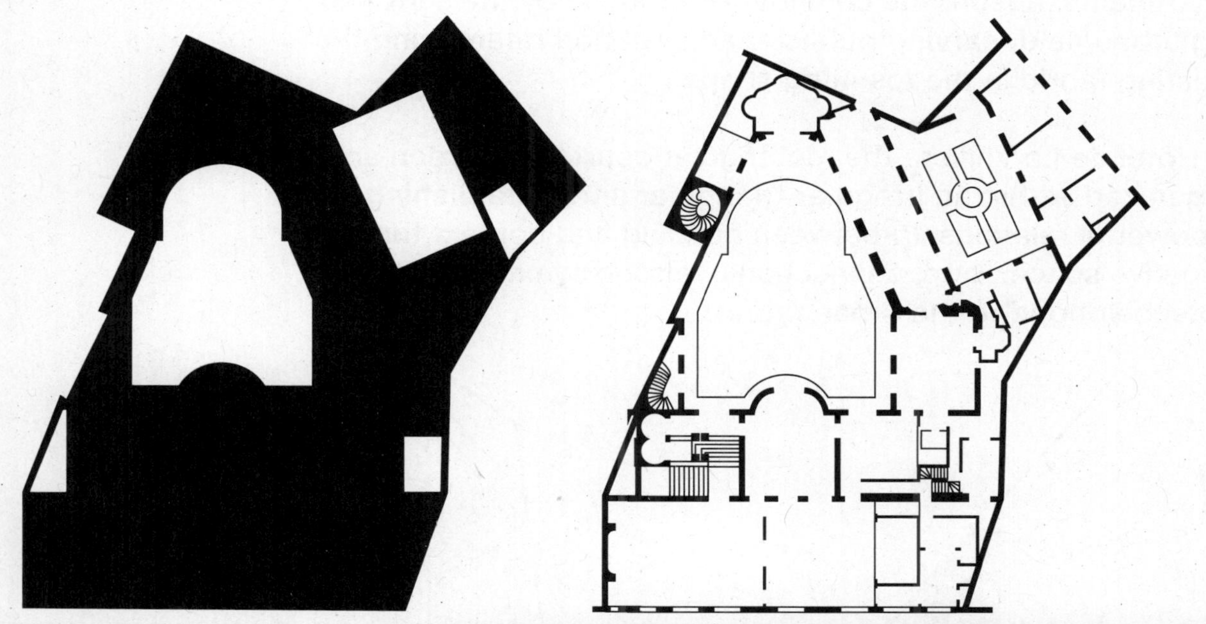

Hôtel de Beauvais by Antoine Le Pautre, 1652–1655.

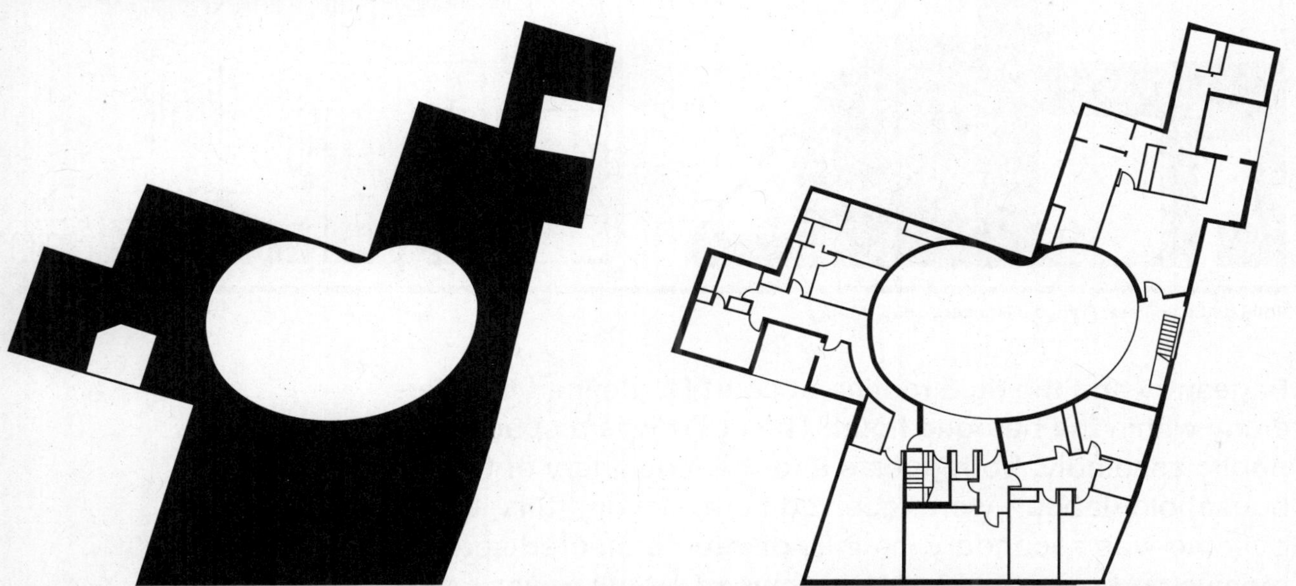

Doña Maria Apartments, Seville, by Cruz y Ortiz Arquitectos, 1974–1976.

Instead of adhering to a rigid axial composition, the French hôtel was organized around a court and a garden. These two interconnected open spaces were arranged within the hôtel to allow a contiguous urban fabric. Locked between party walls, the hôtel exploited asymmetry and site irregularity. To describe the court and the garden as 'voids' is to diminish their position. These central open spaces were outdoor rooms, embodying a material, pliable fullness.[45] They acted as the figure within the ground, conscious products which both respond to the urban fabric in which they were placed and define the buildings that bound them. Both Hôtel de Beauvais and its twentieth-century counterpart, Doña Maria Apartments, absorb the constraints imposed by the surrounding urban field, carving public space out and referencing the existing fabric in the resulting shape.

In Hôtel de La Vrillière the rectangular court and garden are organized within an irregular triangular site, establishing a powerful relationship between building and context through negative space. Here, connection overrode symmetry. The hôtel belonged to the urban fabric.

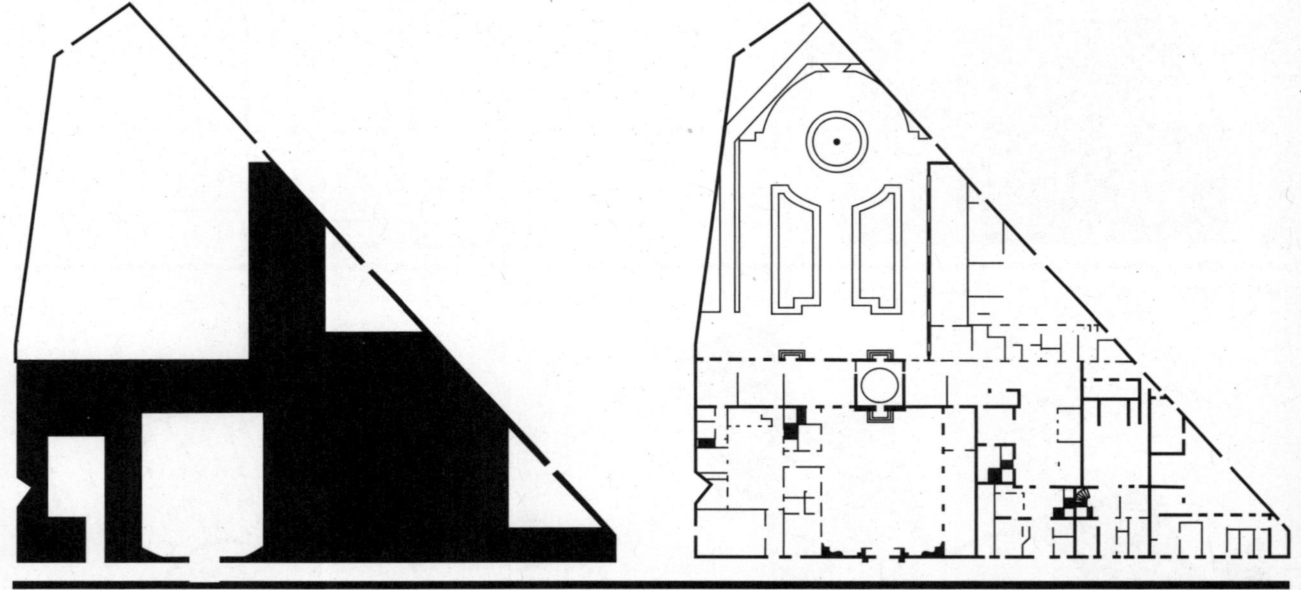

Hôtel de La Vrillière, François Mansart, 1635–1640.

Pageantry and the rigid routine of court life defined the hierarchy within the baroque hôtel. The court was a space of public assembly; both guests and the machinery of the household (labour) were received here. Beyond this, the building was secondary, an infill of interconnected spaces to receive and entertain. In many ways personal privacy did not exist. Reception took precedence over comfort, and display was more important than intimacy. As society became enamoured with ideas around personal privacy, intimacy and the individual, an architecture of intrigue replaced an architecture of pageantry.[46] The rococo hôtel can be seen as a negotiation between display and retreat.

Internal space became articulated and specialized, and rooms were assigned programmes. Guests transitioned across ever more thresholds: from the vestibule to the *antichambre*, the *salle à manager* to dine, the *grande salle* for a party, the library, the chapel, various galleries, and finally the *chambre* – the principle reception room. As the hôtel grew, so too did the service spaces. The *garderobe*, cabinet and finally *privé* became extensions of the *chambre*. An internal hierarchy of *pochés* managed the transition from the most public to the most private.

Hôtel Lambert is organized around a highly public life. The ground floor manages flows through the household. Guests enter the main court and progress up a grand stair to the first floor, where a series of rooms connected in enfilade form the primary spatial sequence.

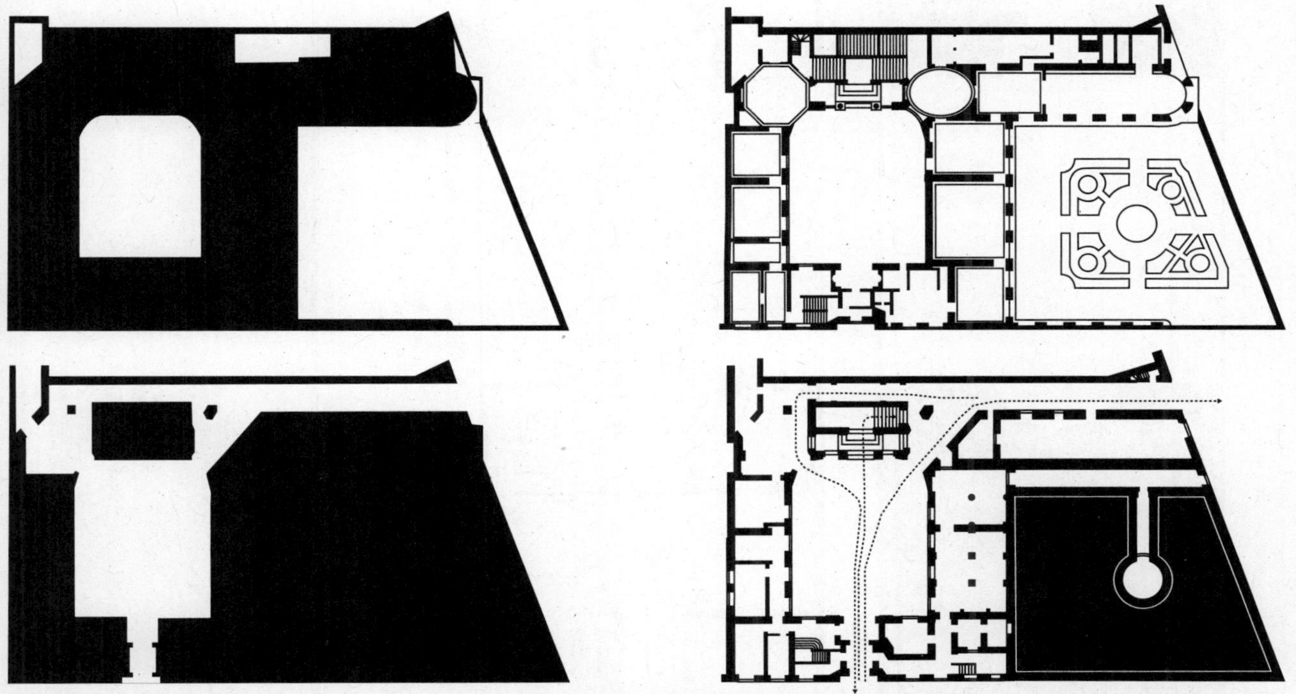

Ground floor (bottom) and first floor (top), Hotel Lambert, Louis Le Vau, 1642–1644.

As we loaded buildings with technology, programmatic complexity grew and architecture sought order. Internal space became compartmentalized, increasingly articulated as public or private, living or service. Rooms were grouped in rows (*enfilade*) or clustered (*massée*). Gradually, both were arranged as a double zone of rooms (*corps-de-logis*) for greater flexibility, and the corridor was born. The interior became ever more intricate, and the building became ever more rationalized and precise. This signalled the rise of modern functional planning. Architecture could now demonstrate its virtuosity and its value through form and programme.

The court was pushed forward to become a forecourt and the garden was pushed backwards. The building ripped one side away from the boundary, and then another, retreating within the site and defining its own extremities. In Hôtel Guimard the building divides the site, centring itself and organizing the open space. With Hôtel de Thélusson the building has fully detached itself from the city fabric to become a free-standing pavilion in a garden.

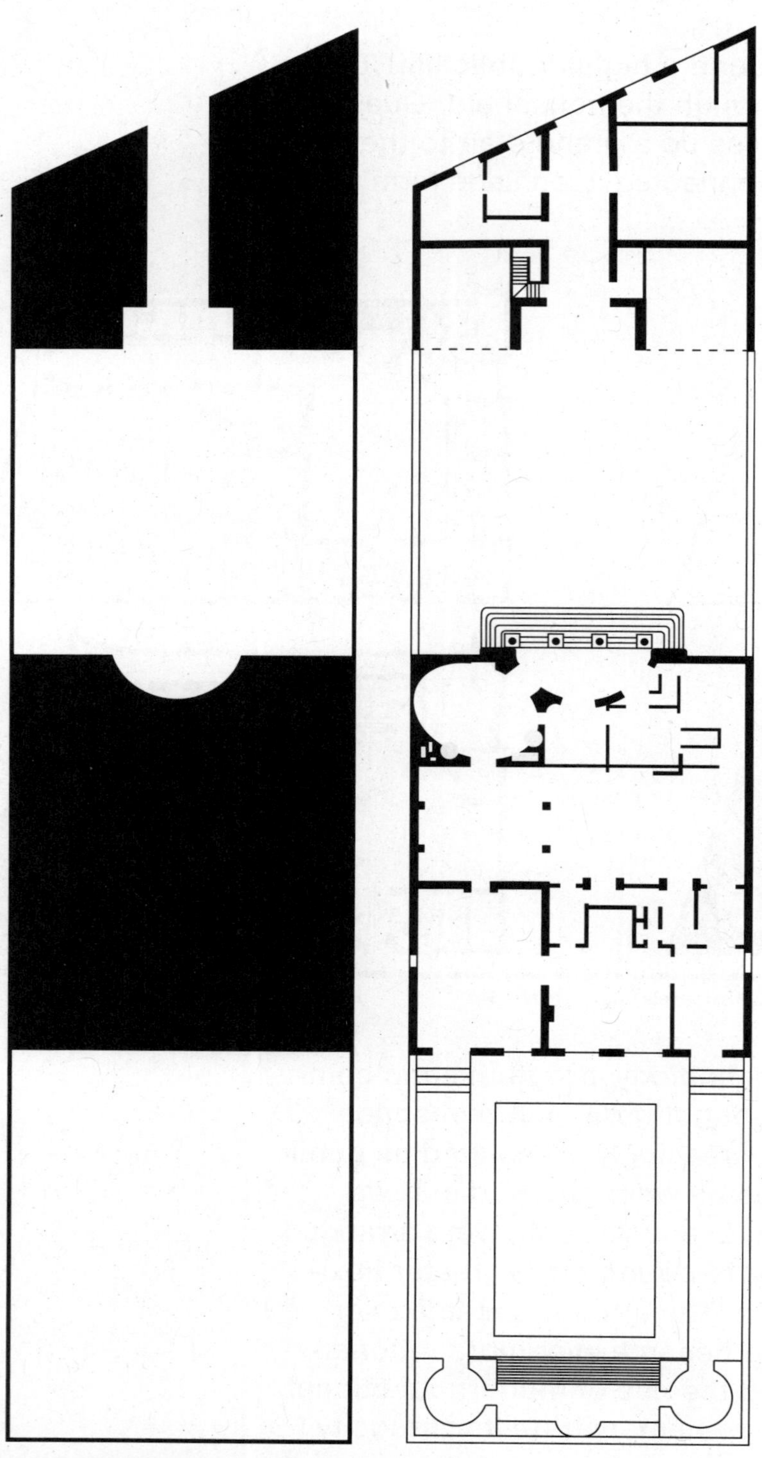

Hôtel Guimard, Claude-Nicolas Ledoux, 1770–1772.

Hôtel de Thélusson, Claude-Nicolas Ledoux, 1778–1783.

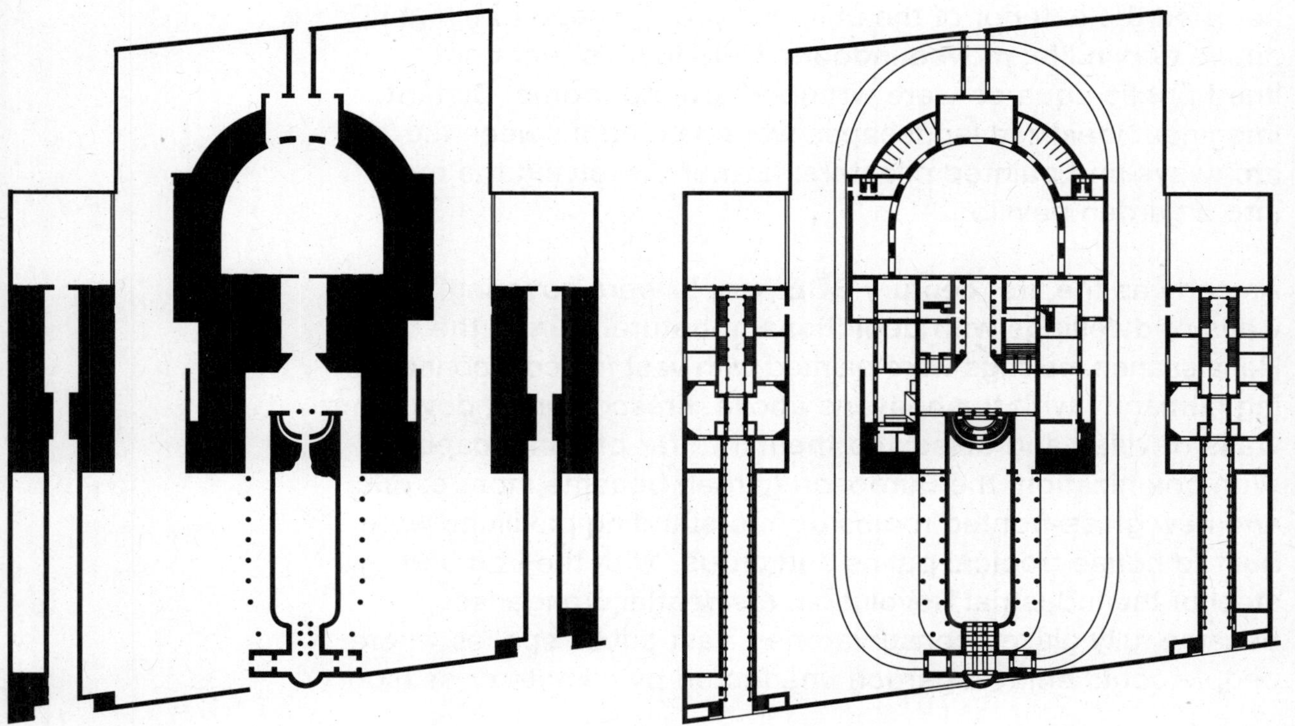

The neoclassical hôtel liberated itself from the city. In reversing the established figure-ground relationship, the building became an object and the city became the background. The enclosed public space was inverted, and the private icon was born. Rationalized solids set within continuous open space became the ideal urban system.[47] Palladio's Villa Rotonda is perhaps the most extreme product of this – a temple to the ideal architectural volume, a highly abstract form floating in open space.

Villa Almerico Capra, commonly known as La Rotonda by Andrea Palladio, 1567–1592.

An obsession with the private realm is also legible in the surface of the architectural object. Ornamentation that once adorned the exterior of the building, giving shape to a highly active public life, moved indoors. Colonnades that once lined public squares were wrapped around rooms. Distant, imagined, idealized landscapes were painted between the archways and painted pilasters, further dissolving the room into a garden pavilion.

As early as the first century BCE people were covering the walls of dwellings with depictions of nature. During the Renaissance, ceilings were painted with vast frescos, connecting humanity with the heavens above. Frescos crept down the walls of villas and dissolved them into far-off landscapes. With colonization, the European garden became more exotic and new glass-fronted rooms or free-standing pavilions were built to house tropical palms and citrus. With the iron and steel of the Industrial Revolution, residential orangeries became fully glazed conservatories, vast public spaces where people could enjoy a garden unaffected by climate or season.

A.

B.

C.

D.

E.

F.

A. Painted garden, Villa of Livia in Rome, 39 BCE.
B. The walls of Palladio's Villa Barbaro painted by Paolo Veronese, 1560–1561.
C. Painted wallcoverings of the Bartolotti House by Isaac de Moucheron, eighteenth century.
D. The Crystal Palace, Joseph Paxton, 1851.
E. Farnsworth House, Mies van der Rohe, 1945–1951.
F. *The Paintings (with Us in the Nature)*, Gilbert & George, 1972.

Nature became scenographic, a romanticized backdrop to our private lives. The building detached itself from its surroundings, reduced it to a picturesque view and then looked back at it from a distance. Nature became landscape and landscape became scenery, reduced to a toothless built or painted folly. Landscape painting from the fifteenth to the sixteenth century depicted the land as a vast terrain with deeply receding space and a distant horizon, stretching the distance between viewer and environment, and the technological progress of the Enlightenment confirmed humanity's sense of superiority. We were masters of nature and the laws of nature, so why shouldn't we hang our conquest on the wall?

Painted garden, Villa of Livia in Rome, 39 BCE.

The walls of Palladio's Villa Barbaro, painted by Paolo Veronese, 1560–1561.

Wallcoverings of the Bartolotti House, painted by Isaac de Moucheron, eighteenth century.

The Crystal Palace, Joseph Paxton, erected for the Great Exhibition of 1851.

Farnsworth House, Mies van der Rohe, 1945–1951.

The Paintings (with Us in the Nature), Gilbert & George, 1972.

The City in the Garden

The twentieth century fundamentally altered the DNA of Western urban form. Summed up remarkably simply by Cedric Price, the compact ancient city encircled by defensive walls ballooned concentrically under the Industrial Revolution, only to finally choke and collapse in the twentieth century. The modern city abandoned a dense urban core in favour of a networked, mobile, decentralized urban realm.

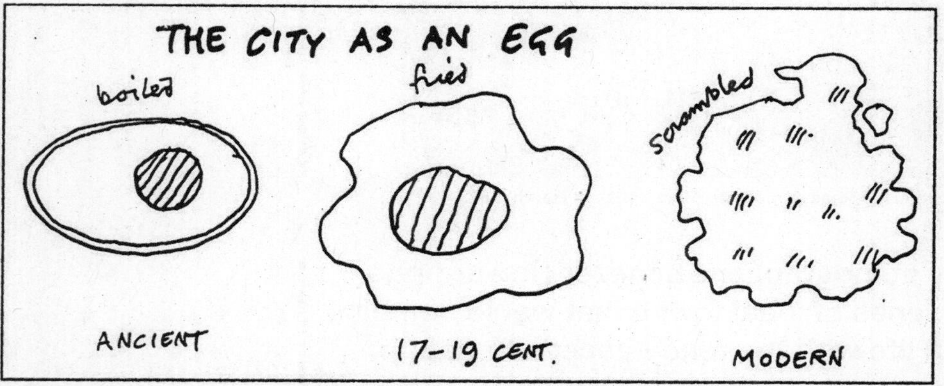

The City as an Egg, Cedric Price, 1982.

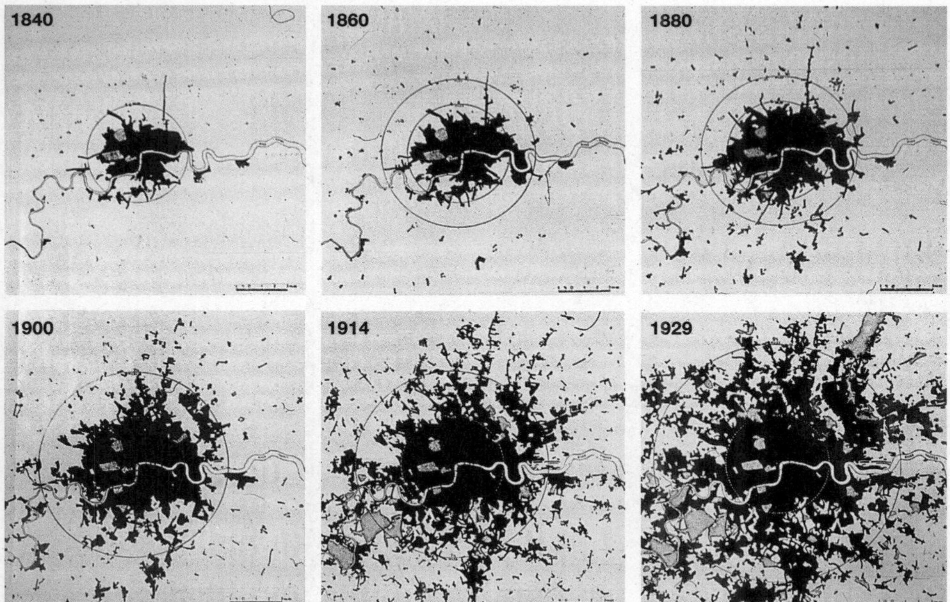

Urban sprawl of Greater London, Patrick Abercrombie, 1944.

In the eighteenth century, only three per cent of the world's population lived in cities. Spurred by industrialization, Europe and America rapidly urbanized. In this revolution's birthplace, Britain, the population virtually doubled every fifty years and the enormous wave of migration into cities resulted in overcrowding, poor sanitation, disease, contaminated air and water, and structural unemployment. The urban ideas of the twentieth century can be seen as a collection of attempts to reform, cleanse, erase or abandon this dystopian urbanization.

The Thames in London was referred to as a 'monster soup', William Heath, 1828.

In 1898, parliamentary stenographer Ebenezer Howard published his vision for a series of ideal towns that would combine the amenities of urban life with the ready access to nature typical of rural environments.

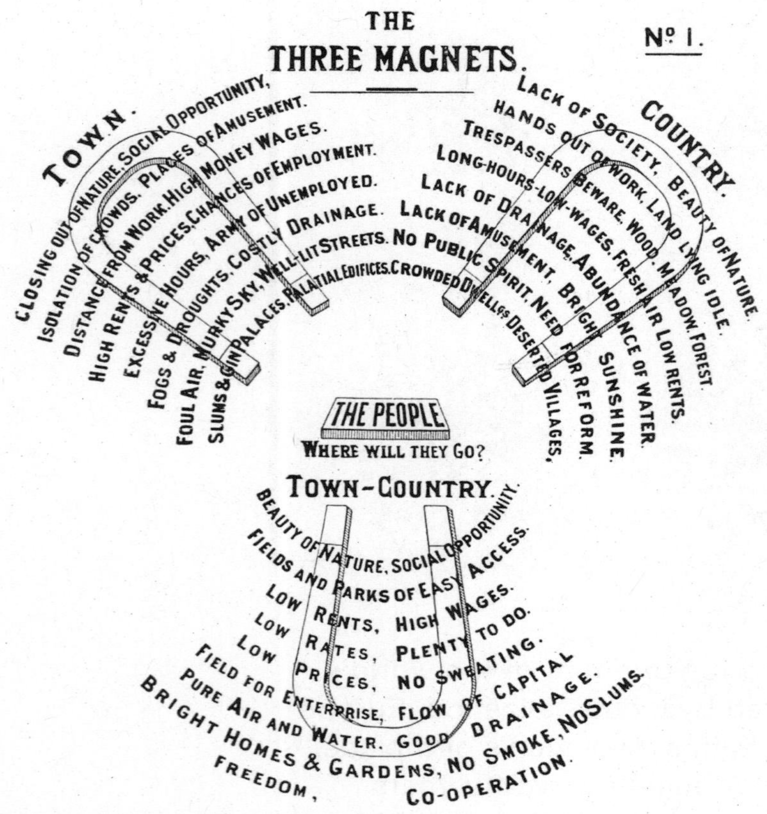

The three magnets of Ebenezer Howard's *Garden Cities of Tomorrow*, 1902.

Garden Cities were intended to be planned and integrated new communities, distancing themselves from the haphazard and unpredictable development within the contemporary city. Separating housing from industry and contained by a large green belt of agriculture, these small cities were arranged concentrically. Civic functions were housed within a central park, ringed by a large shopping arcade. Beyond this, housing and schools radiated outwards, encircled by peripheral factories and services.[48]

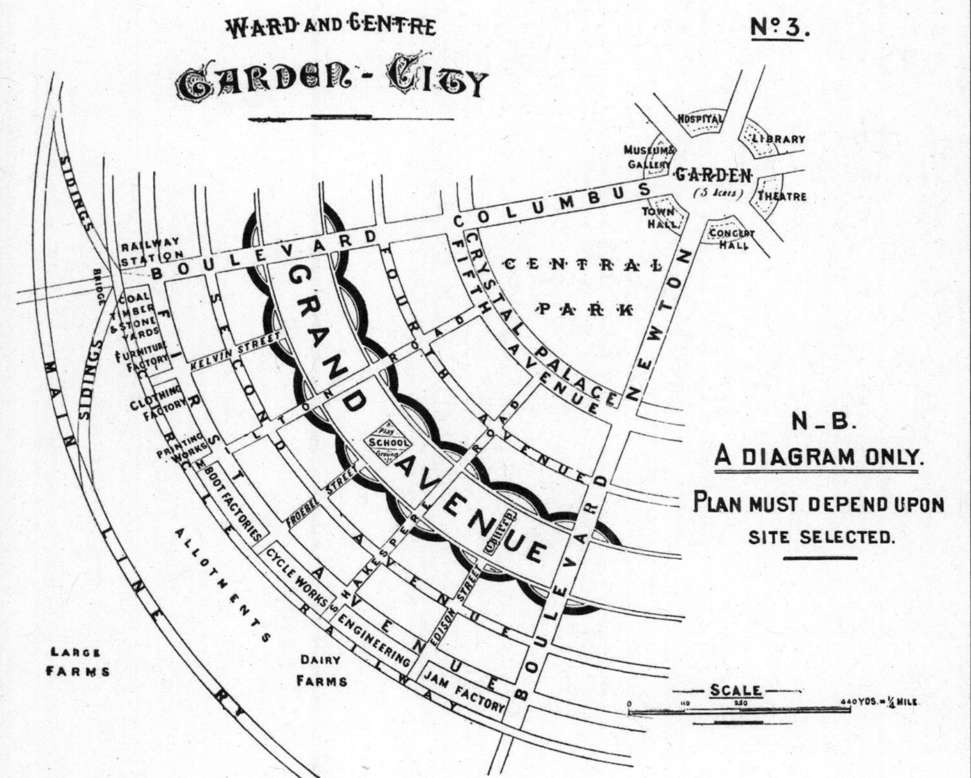

Model for a ward and centre of a Garden City, Ebenezer Howard, 1902.

“There are in reality not only, as is so constantly assumed, two alternatives – town life and country life – but a third alternative, in which all the advantages of the most energetic and active town life, with all the beauty and delight of the country, may be secured in perfect combination; and the certainty of being able to live this life will be the magnet which will produce the effect for which we are all striving – the spontaneous movement of the people from our crowded cities to the bosom of our kindly mother earth, at once the source of life, of happiness, of wealth, and of power.”[49] – Ebenezer Howard

These small urbanities were intended to be self-sufficient, capitalizing on the abundance of cheap land for development within the countryside. Land and resources were to be co-operatively owned and every citizen was to be a shareholder, retaining and reinvesting value rather than encouraging speculation. However, the realized cities of Letchworth and Welwyn struggled to remain affordable, resembling ex-urban dormitory towns or affluent garden suburbs.

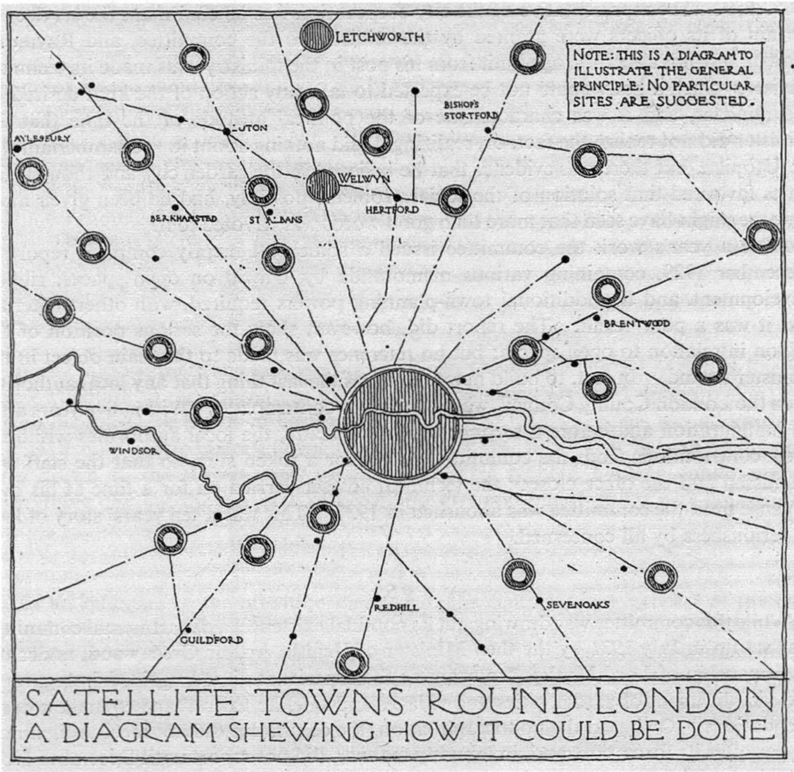

Satellite towns around London, C. B. Purdom, 1921.

At its core, the Garden City argues for a more balanced growth, an integrated approach that goes beyond urban-rural, architecture-nature dichotomies. But the closer the Garden City came to large-scale application, both at home through the New Towns programme or outside Britain, the further it was removed from its original ideals and designs.[50] With the centralization of civic and commercial functions and the pushing of the industrial periphery further and further away, the Garden City was reduced to a space for dwelling.

Attempts to connect the Garden City, or rather a Garden Town, with the urbanism it wished to escape from further diluted the connections it sought to create. Although formally influential, the Garden City was watered down to an unobtrusive pastoral ideal, more of a leafy suburb than a radical alternative to the contemporary city.

Aerial view of Letchworth Garden City.

The New Town of Milton Keynes is an odd mix of Garden City ideals and car-based planning.

Modernism recognized the similar symptoms of the Industrial Revolution but sought a very different antidote to this 'urban disease'.[51] Highly idealistic, early modernists argued it was architecture's responsibility to revolutionize the city, clearing away the oppressively filthy and congested traditional city and creating a new space of order, light and freedom.

Modernist space was defined by air, light and freedom, Le Corbusier, 1935.

Le Corbusier sought to 'free the ground plane', raising towers on stilt-like columns, so that citizens might stroll through a park-like city without having to encounter anything as vulgar as the common street.[52] Standing on pilotis, the ideal modernist building would hover above the landscape, dominating the surroundings and literally detaching the living functions from the ground. Le Corbusier saw the ocean liner as a symbol of this new era, a feat of design and engineering that allowed humans to float in a self-contained city.

> "A city! It is the grip of man upon nature. It is a human operation directed against nature, a human organism both for protection and for work. It is a creation."[53] —Le Corbusier

For Le Corbusier, the formula for the modern city involved the marriage of humankind, nature and technology. Building upwards maximized density and open space. His Ville Contemporaine was envisioned as a new city of repetitive monolithic skyscrapers to house three million people, spread evenly across a vast green area. Here nature transforms the unhealthy chaotic and dense city into a place of peace and pure air.

In the twentieth century, nature became so clinical that the park was referred to as the 'lungs' of the city.[54] Urban nature was considered infrastructure, a green carpet to be built with the same intensity as water and sewage systems, highway networks and housing developments. Perhaps the modern movement sought a vertical garden city, but the strict order, symmetry and standardization of modern form offered little space for negotiation with its surroundings. Lewis Mumford notes that by mating the utilitarian and financial image of the skyscraper to a romantic image of the environment, Le Corbusier had in fact produced a sterile hybrid.[55]

Ville Contemporaine, Le Corbusier, 1922.

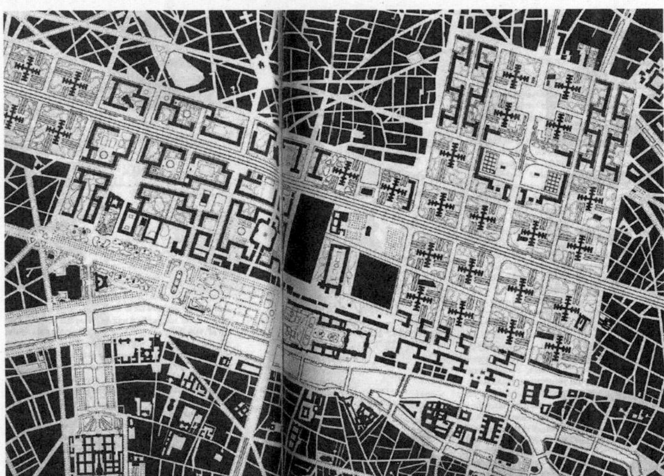

Le Corbusier's Plan Voisin proposed the erasure of the traditional urban fabric of Paris in favour of a grid of twentieth-century towers, 1925.

Both Le Corbusier and Jane Jacobs visited New York for the first time in 1935 and were equally excited. However, their reasons for this excitement could not be more different. Le Corbusier was thrilled about the wild brutality, the *sauvagerie*, and looked at it as an experiment of a new order, probably his order.[56] Le Corbusier studied the 'hardware' of New York, seeing potential to improve the efficiency of its gridded high-rise form.

For Le Corbusier the 'software' of the nineteenth-century urban street represented wasted ground. It would be much more logical to scrap it and build the twentieth-century skyscraper within a twentieth-century master plan.

In contrast, Jane Jacobs wrote four articles for *Vogue* between 1935 and 1937 on the inextricable relation between rural and city economies and the tremendous physical and social infrastructure that brought raw materials to market as city products. "Where the Fur Flies", "Leather Shocking Tales", "Diamonds in the Tough" and "Flowers Come to Town" communicated the essence of New York through its vibrant street life.[57] Instead of focusing on the powerful image of New York skyscrapers, Jacobs saw value in the activity the traditional urban space supported.

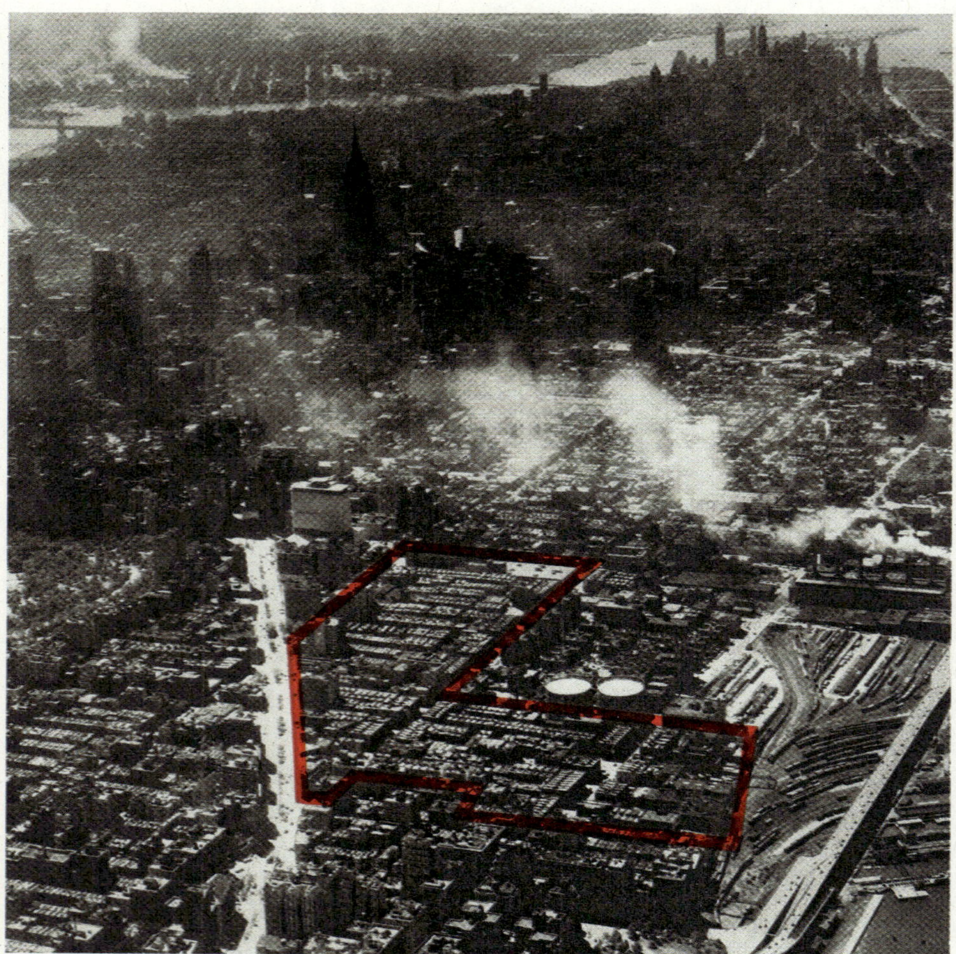

During the 1950s large areas of central New York City, like the site above (now the Lincoln Center), were demolished. This slum clearance displaced thousands and for ever altered the urban fabric.

However, hardware won out and modernist ideals drove urban development and planning theory in the early twentieth century. With unprecedented post-war growth and intensive building programmes on both sides of the Atlantic, the

Western city shifted attention away from the urban core and towards the urban periphery. A central premise of the Congrès Internationaux d'Architecture Moderne (CIAM) doctrine was the organization of the city into different zones of activity. The separation of residential from commercial and industrial space created a physical and mental split between work and home, urban and domestic space.

As automobiles became available to every middle-class family, and government policies favoured their ubiquity, the city splintered further to create a decentralized urban realm. Sky bridges and expressways replaced mixed-use, walkable neighbourhoods. Despite Jane Jacobs's eloquent attack on the dispersed and segregated anti-city of Ebenezer Howard and Le Corbusier in *The Death and Life of Great American Cities*, by the time it was published in 1961 much of the damage had already been done.

Los Angeles's Four Level Interchange was a connector within the modern decentralized metropolis.

Over the next century, the modern icon, standing alone and defined by a fluidity of space around it, was disseminated across all scales, from the urban tower to the detached house. Ideals of autonomy, privacy and individualism ignited in the Enlightenment had found a physical form under modernism. Aligning with the ideological positions of the era, modernism was associated with progress, democracy and, as it infiltrated the United States, capitalism.[58]

The 1939 and 1964 World's Fairs held in New York City illustrate the incredible corporatization of modernist principles. Instead of CIAM's egalitarian city segregated according to function, Edward Bernays presented Democracity, a future city of capitalism.[59] At the centre of the 1939 fair was a perisphere, which housed an enormous rotating model of this future city. The Centerton (the social and cultural centre), Pleasantvilles (middle-class residential towns), Milvilles (industrial towns), and Farms were arranged concentrically, with the most luxurious at the centre, like a corporate pyramid. Just twenty years later capitalism had turned the World's Fair into a grand consumer show. The 1964 World's Fair was a parade of American corporations, where architecture was a billboard for products.[60] But just as the World's Fair celebrated the arrival of a corporate utopia, cracks were starting to appear.

Democracity designed by Henry Dreyfuss, 1939.

New York World's Fair organized by Robert Moses, 1964.

1964: A Pivotal Moment

In 1964, a highly efficient mutation of modernism hit its peak just as the global population saw its greatest increase in known history. Before and after 1964, this growth rate was never equalled. This was no coincidence. The year 1964 represents a pivotal moment in which humankind confronted the reciprocal relationship between our actions and our habitat, calling into question the doctrine of progress that saw humanity sprinting towards its own extinction.

> "The history of life on earth is a history of the interaction of living things and their surroundings. To an overwhelming extent, the physical form and the habits of the earth's vegetation and its animal life have been moulded and directed by the environment. Over the whole span of earthly time, the opposite effect, in which life modifies its surroundings, has been relatively slight. It is only within the moment of time represented by the twentieth century that one species – man – has acquired significant power to alter the nature of his world, and it is only within the past twenty-five years that this power has achieved such magnitude that it endangers the whole earth and its life."[61] –Rachel Carson

Nuclear weapons testing at Bikini Atoll, mid-1946, less than a year after the destruction of Nagasaki.

After World War II, humankind manipulated nature to feed a growing population. The Green Revolution brought chemical technology (pesticides, herbicides, fertilizers) and new breeds of high-yield crops to greatly increase global food production.[62] Technology allowed crops to be cultivated in places they otherwise wouldn't grow. Humankind developed a false sense of security and progress, ever more reliant on chemicals and irrigation to prop up overpopulation.

Aerial spraying of DDT to control the tussock moth, Latah County, Idaho, 1947.

With the revelatory work *Silent Spring*, biologist Rachel Carson detailed the devastating effects of DDT and pesticides and condemned this utterly unsustainable practice. Carson calmly and eloquently explained how, in a rush to feed an ever-growing population, humankind was foolishly poisoning its own habitat, and thus itself. This awakening coincided with humankind's first attempts to leave the planet. The release of the first satellite image of Earth from Apollo 8 brought the fields of science and ecology to the fore. Seeing our environment from this new vantage point reinforced a growing comprehension of the earth as delicate and finite.

Apollo 8's view of Earth rising over the moon has proved to be the most enduring image we have of our fragile world. NASA, 1968.

Deep ploughing of virgin topsoil caused severe dust storms from 1934 to 1940 in Texas and Oklahoma.

This affected 400 000 square kilometres of land, earning the area the name Dust Bowl.

The Great Leap Forward was an effort to rapidly transform the People's Republic of China from an agrarian to an industrial society, 1958–1962.

The modern world was a space of nuclear, extraterrestrial, chemical and antibiotic activity.[63] Through plain naivety and vain domination, humankind had constructed a potentially deadly habitat. As humankind confronted its frailty, the nature of modern life and the direction of the modern city no longer seemed like a viable blueprint for the future.

Modernity was a gradual process, but the modernization and mechanization of the Western household came with a heavy thud. Machines intruded on a relatively insular, parochial society accustomed to doing things by hand, and the speed, absurdity and confusion of this new world was perfectly captured by popular culture. Lining up the films of Jacques Tati illustrates the rush to keep up with global progress (*Jour de Fête*, 1949), the struggle with a technologically advanced suburban life-style (*Mon Oncle*, 1957), and the austere and antiseptic nature of a highly efficient modern city (*Playtime*, 1964–67).

François, a local postman, becomes obsessed with keeping up with the speed and efficiency of the US postal service air delivery by retrofitting his bicycle. *Jour de Fête*, Jacques Tati, 1949.

Frustrated with automated, ultra-modern surburbia, Monsieur Hulot pines for his muddled urban apartment. *Mon Oncle*, Jacques Tati, 1957.

The homogenous architecture of the modern city in *Playtime*, Jacques Tati, 1967.

Although Tativille's architecture was actually composed of enormous fake facades glued to scaffolding, it was a scarily accurate depiction of the modern city. Colin Rowe notes that as European modernism infiltrated the United States, it was largely purged of its ideological or socialist rhetoric.[64]

The five Hötorget buildings (1952–1966) of Stockholm were designed by various architects but their similarity highlights a certain dogmatism. They would be completely at home in Tati's *Playtime*.

The substitution of socially driven ideas of functionality for Fordist or capitalist notions of efficiency fundamentally shifted the building from being in service of a user to being in service of a client. This sharpening stripped the modernist agenda down to its barest formal elements (open plan, column, grid, and free facade), oversimplifying, abstracting and standardizing modern architecture. The site-specific, spatially complex early modernism of Le Corbusier and Jean Prouvé seems practically romantic when compared to the ruthless regularity and replication of this economic hyper-modernism.

CENTRE SOCIAL D'UNE USINE, BADEN, SUISSE

ARMIN MEILI, ARCHITECTE

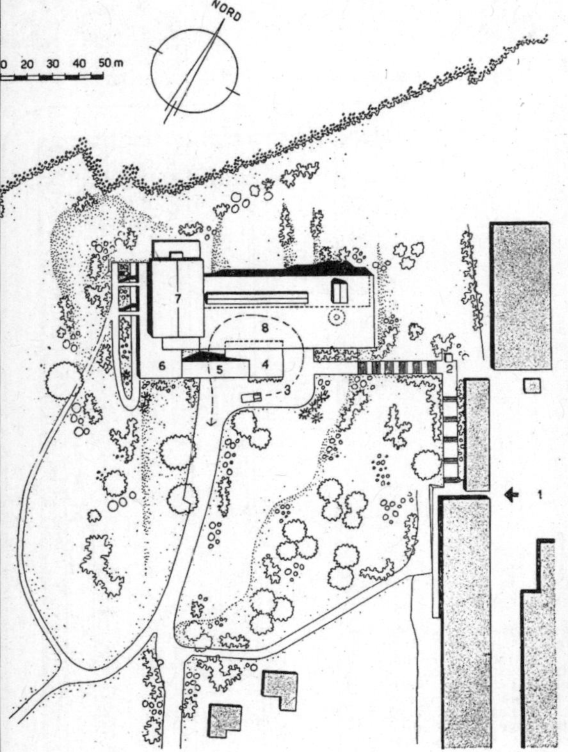

Social centre for a factory in Baden, Switzerland.

IMMEUBLE DE LA J. HANCOOK C° A KANSAS CITY

SKIDMORE OWINGS ET MERRILL ARCHITECTES

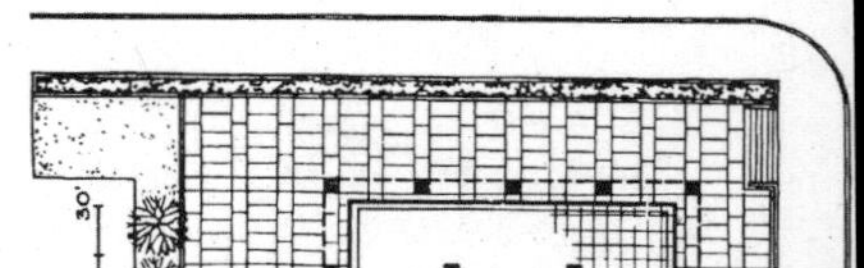

Vue d'ensemble et de détail du bâtiment dont la structure extérieure aux façades vitrées, est réalisée au moyen d'éléments préfabriqués formant brise-soleil (voir texte page précédente). Ci-contre : Plan du rez-de-chaussée.

GARAGE

The J. Hancock Company, Kansas (this page) and Commerzbank, Düsseldorf (opposite page).

NOUVEAU BATIMENT DE LA BANQUE DU COMMERCE A DUSSELDORF

P. SCHNEIDER ESLEBEN ARCHITECTE

D. HOOR ET J. RINGEL INGÉNIEURS

Ci-dessous : Vue d'ensemble du nouveau bâtiment lié à la tour des circulations verticales et, par une passerelle, à l'ancienne construction. Le béton a été particulièrement soigné : pour les coffrages, il a été utilisé un bois d'Epicéa nordique non raboté (planches variant de 7 à 10 cm). Le mur-rideau, étudié spécialement par l'architecte pour ce bâtiment est réalisé selon des méthodes propres à la fabrication des wagons et des carrosseries automobiles (cadres en aluminium hauts de deux étages avec panneaux sandwich faits de deux feuillets d'aluminium de 2 mm d'épaisseur séparés par une matière isolante).

A. Coupe transversale sur l'immeuble et les parkings qui le dégagent de l'environnement.

B. Plan au niveau de la passerelle.

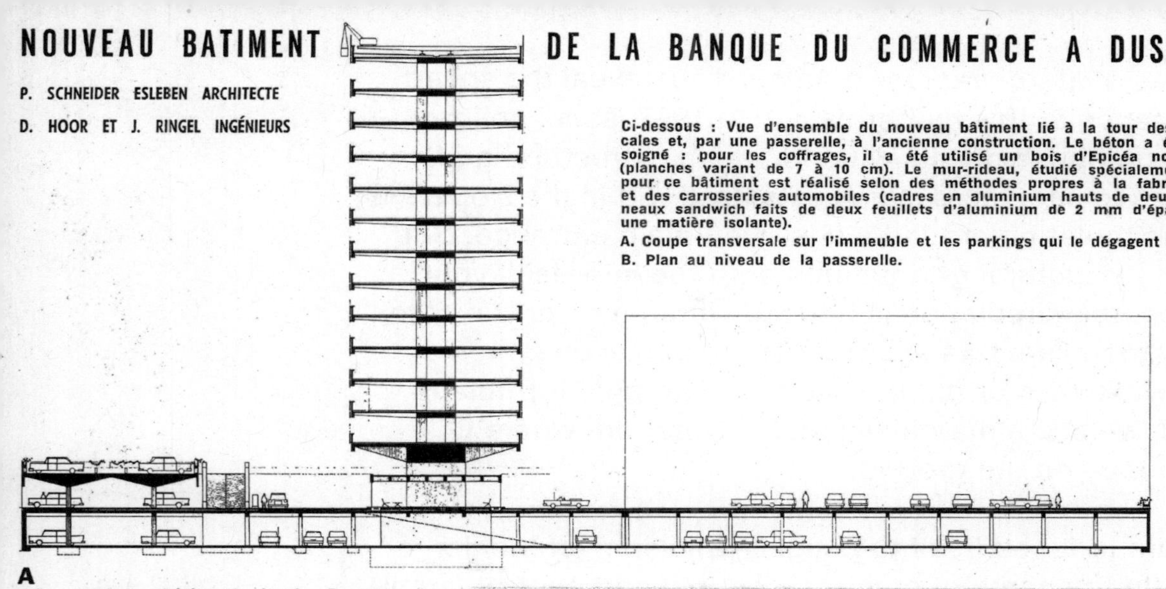

A

Le nouveau bâtiment de la Banque du Commerce représente l'extension du siège social situé en vis-à-vis de l'autre côté de la rue Kasernen, à la liaison du noyau ancien et du quartier des affaires de Dusseldorf.

Deux problèmes ont été particulièrement difficiles à résoudre en raison de réglements d'urbanisme en vigueur. Le premier portait sur la liaison entre l'ancienne et la nouvelle construction, l'autre, sur les circulations, accès et parkings.

Il avait été envisagé tout d'abord de relier les deux bâtiments par un tunnel sous la rue, solution qui n'apparut pas réalisable en raison du tracé du métro. Il a donc été décidé de créer pour les piétons une passerelle suspendue (27 tonnes) enjambant la rue Kasernen. Cette passerelle part de la tour des circulations verticales du nouvel immeuble.

Le second problème : circulation et accès, a été étudié pour que le trafic d'arrivée et de départ des voitures puisse se dérouler selon un flot continu à sens unique. C'est pourquoi l'ossature repose sur trois supports en béton armé, libérant un espace accessible aux voitures (drive in Bank). Deux des supports sont situés en façade principale ; le troisième, en façade postérieure, qui comprend les sanitaires et l'escalier de secours, s'enfonce jusqu'aux fondations servant de chevalet coupe-vent.

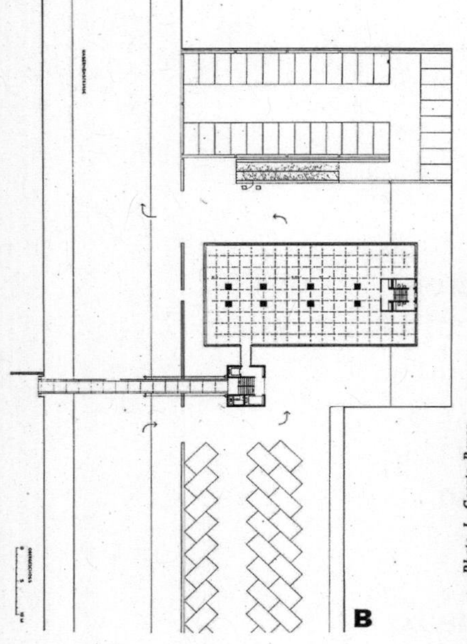

B

Photo I. Goertz Bauer.

Back issues of *L'Architecture d'Aujourd'hui* reveal the speed and dominance of this modernism. In a 1957 issue, an irregular spatial composition sits within a regular structural grid. Responding to site, the building sets itself within the slope, wrapping circulation around a sheltered main entrance. But by 1964 the structural grid defines both the internal layout and facade, the circulation is housed within the central core, and pedestrians are raised above ground level on either elevated walkways or plinths. As the building's formula is optimized, we see a marginalization of freedom where it matters most – on the ground.

Architecture reduced itself to a highly efficient, yet sterile, container. In the name of comfort, security and control, architecture had detached and isolated itself from its surroundings. Never was the distance between humankind and nature further.

Dreischeibenhaus, Düsseldorf, Germany, Helmut Hentrich & Hubert Petschnigg, 1957–1960.

But this peak was also a tipping point. Against the backdrop of nuclear threat, protest, economic instability and political disillusionment, a deep suspicion of the status quo developed in all facets of cultural production. This paradigm shift in political reality and philosophical thought fundamentally challenged the doctrine of modernism. Architecture began searching to reconnect.

Emerging from, and in response to the Congrès Internationaux d'Architecture Moderne (CIAM), Team 10 was a loose group of autonomous practitioners who questioned the technocratic approach and universal design ethos of modernism. Team 10 was not a singular movement to supplant modernism, but an important space of investigation and discussion, which propelled the new ideas of New Brutalism and Structuralism.

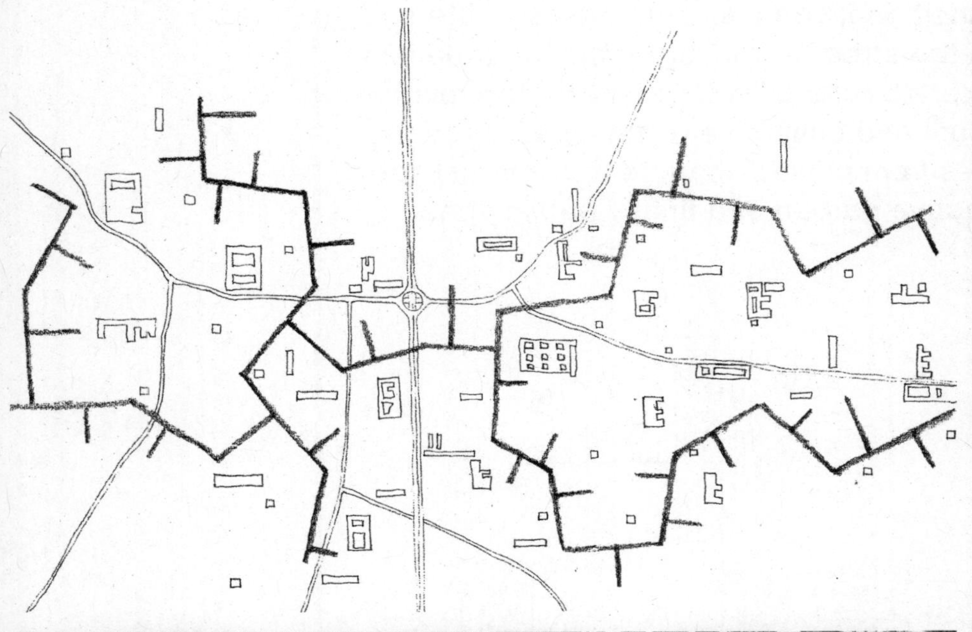

Golden Lane project, Alison & Peter Smithson, 1952.

The Brutalism of Alison and Peter Smithson sought to anchor early modernism to site, exploiting its proficiencies (structure, production, prefabrication) but focusing on the experience of the user. Rejecting the imposition of the high modernist grid, the Smithsons' Golden Lane project proposed a networked, flexible architecture. This continuous branch-like structure was seen as another layer of urbanism, responding to existing urban fabric and topography. The architectural object stepped back to consider its surroundings.

In the Netherlands, Structuralism concerned itself with designing relationships or frameworks that could respond or adapt to change. Jaap Bakema called for 'total space', 'total life' and 'total urbanization', articulated architecturally as an interrelated system of transitional spaces, elements and filters from the doorstep to the street to the larger city and the landscape.[65] In Herman Hertzberger's De Drie Hoven, the relationship between individual and collective is managed through the transition of spaces from private apartment to internal street, internal square, collective garden and finally public space.

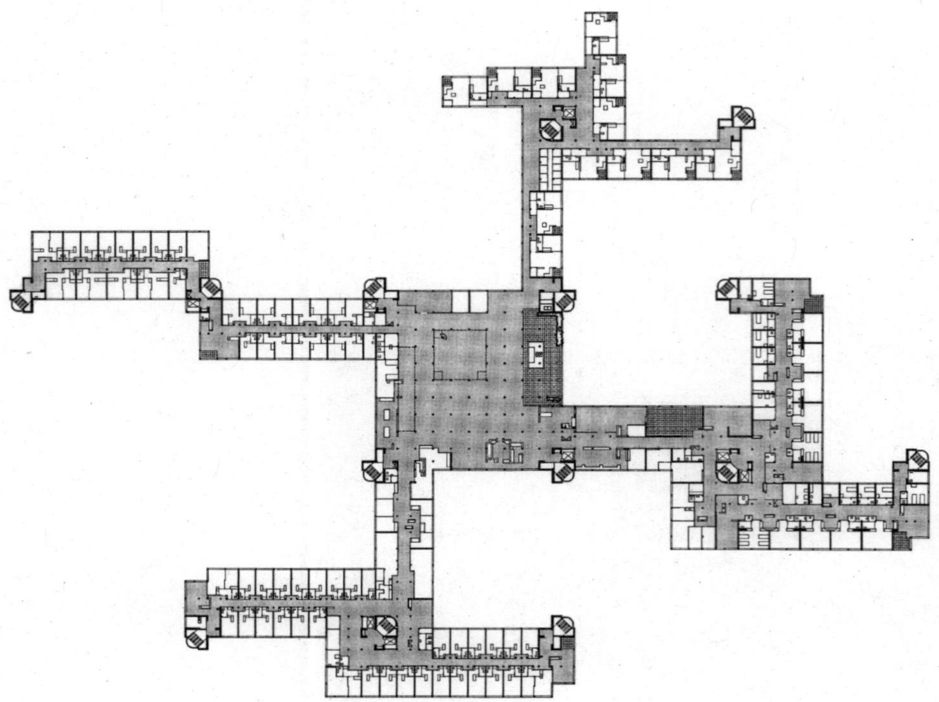

Housing for the elderly. De Drie Hoven, Amsterdam (Demolished). Herman Hertzberger.

Internal street of De Drie Hoven, 1975. © Willem Diepraam.

Both New Brutalism and Structuralism shared modernism's claim that architecture was a social project but rejected "... the universalizing, homogenizing, dehumanizing qualities of Modern architecture."[66]

It was an era of questioning and free speculation. While some architects attempted to remake or expand the modern project, others sought to tear it down, citing the failures of social housing, the impact of gentrification and urban renewal, and the corporate rationalization of modernism. On both sides of this much-laboured schism between modernism and post-modernism, there was an overwhelming optimism in humankind's ability to liberate itself through architecture and technology.[67]

In 1966, Sigfried Giedion wrote a new and extended introduction for the fifth edition of his milestone book *Space, Time and Architecture*, 1941, which he entitled "Architecture of the 1960s: Hopes and Fears". In this he declared the 1960s a new and third era of architectural development since ancient history, while at the same time he recorded a certain fatigue or confusion. Particularly astute was his reading of the spatial implications of the era where he highlights movement as an inseparable element of architecture. This might be the reason why it all feels increasingly unstable, to this day.[68]

From Dichotomy to Holism

Architecture had begun its turn towards integration and connection. Strategies observed in the microscope were replicated in utopian buildings and cities. A new breed of architects proposed that architecture was more than the creation of isolated structures, and that it also required social and environmental considerations. The recognition that architecture has a relationship with its surroundings resulted in a new trend of melding structure with environment and ecology.

As early as the 1950s, architects and critics such as Reyner Banham, Yona Friedman and the Archigram group proposed the dawn of a second machine age, questioning the relationship between technology, society and architecture. Through speculation, Archigram developed an experimental architecture that animated and automated the city. Architecture could be nomadic, temporal and adaptive to its ecology and inhabitants. Pushing this further, Buckminster Fuller saw the earth as a planetary system, which we could optimize through design. For Fuller, architecture should play a critical role in balancing the stewardship of the environment with the advancement of humanity.[69]

Yona Friedman envisioned a Spatial City of adaptable habitats suspended over Paris, 1960.

Cushicle, Michael Webb, 1964.

Buckminster Fuller's geodesic dome, US pavilion, Expo '67, Montreal.

Inspired by Fuller's *Operating Manual for Spaceship Earth*, the *Whole Earth Catalog* focused on self-sufficiency, ecology, alternative education and holism. The brainchild of renegade biologist Stewart Brand, it documented the adaptive strategies and radical ideas of a cohort committed to thoroughly renovating America's industrial society along ecological and social lines. Published between 1968 and 1972, it is an artefact of an incredible era in which 'ecology' was all-encompassing, where architecture, nature and the human habitat were one and the same.

"We are as gods and might as well get used to it. So far, remotely done power and glory – as via government, big business, formal education, church – has succeeded to the point where gross defects obscure actual gains. In response to this dilemma and to these gains a realm of intimate, personal power is developing – power of the individual to conduct his own education, find his own inspiration, shape his own environment, and share his adventure with whoever is interested. Tools that aid this process are sought and promoted by the Whole Earth Catalog."[70] —Stewart Brand

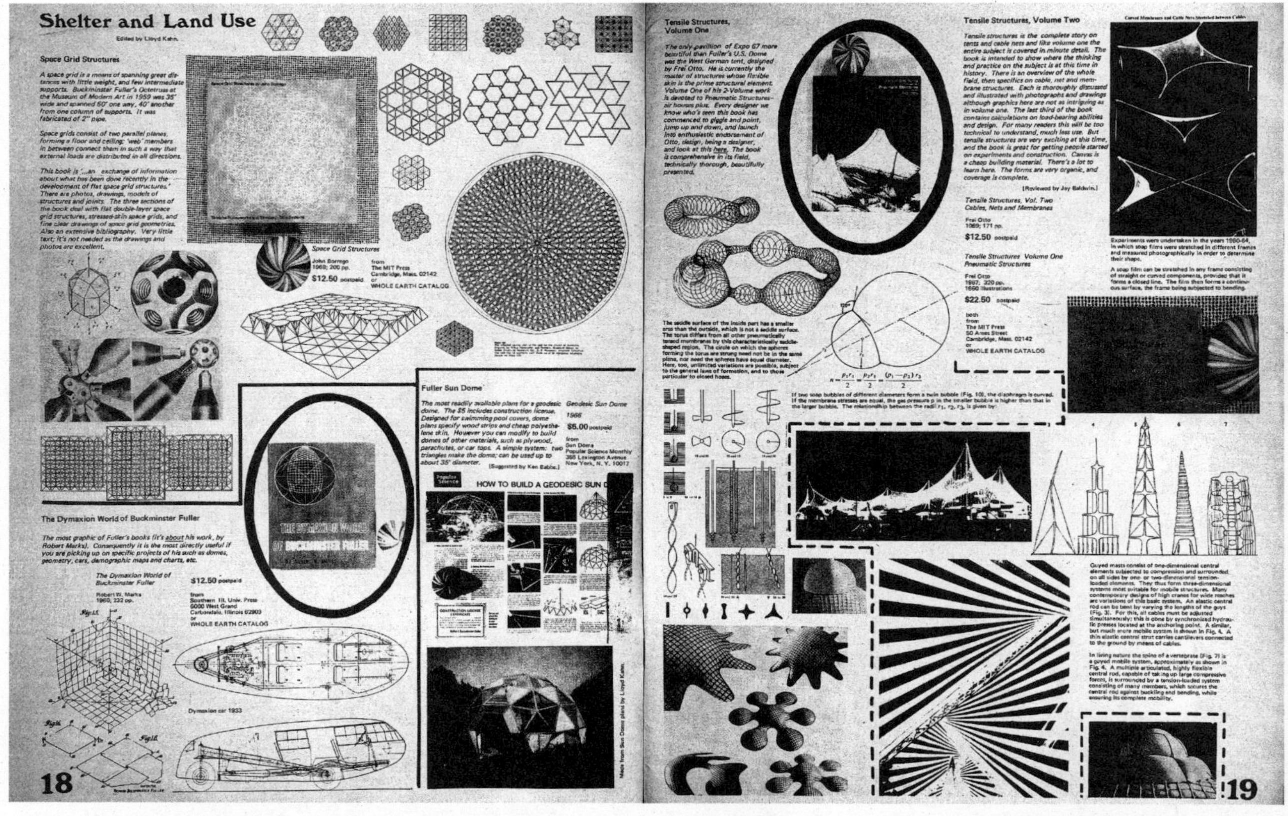
Shelter and Land Use

Edited by Lloyd Kahn.

Space Grid Structures

A space grid is a means of spanning great distances with little weight, and few intermediate supports. Buckminster Fuller's Octetruss at the Museum of Modern Art in 1959 was 35' wide and spanned 60' one way, 40' another from one column of supports. It was fabricated of 2" pipe.

Space grids consist of two parallel planes, forming a floor and ceiling; 'web' members in between connect them in such a way that external loads are distributed in all directions.

This book is '...an exchange of information about what has been done recently in the development of flat space grid structures.' There are photos, drawings, models of structures and joints. The three sections of the book deal with flat double-layer space grid structures, stressed-skin space grids, and fine clear drawings of space grid geometries. Also an extensive bibliography. Very little text; it's not needed as the drawings and photos are excellent.

Space Grid Structures

John Borrego
1968; 200 pp.

$12.50 postpaid

from
The MIT Press
Cambridge, Mass. 02142
or
WHOLE EARTH CATALOG

The Dymaxion World of Buckminster Fuller

The most graphic of Fuller's books (it's about his work, by Robert Marks). Consequently it is the most directly useful if you are picking up on specific projects of his such as domes, geometry, cars, demographic maps and charts, etc.

The Dymaxion World of Buckminster Fuller

Robert W. Marks
1960; 232 pp.

$12.50 postpaid

from
Southern Ill. Univ. Press
6000 West Grand
Carbondale, Illinois 62903
or
WHOLE EARTH CATALOG

Dymaxion car 1933

Fuller Sun Dome

The most readily available plans for a geodesic dome. The $5 includes construction license. Designed for swimming pool covers, dome plans specify wood strips and cheap polyethelene skin. However you can modify to build domes of other materials, such as plywood, parachutes, or car tops. A simple system: two triangles make the dome; can be used up to about 35' diameter.

[Suggested by Ken Babbs.]

Geodesic Sun Dome

1966

$5.00 postpaid

from
Sun Dome
Popular Science Monthly
355 Lexington Avenue
New York, N. Y. 10017

HOW TO BUILD A GEODESIC SUN D

18

Tensile Structures, Volume One

The only pavilion of Expo 67 more beautiful than Fuller's U.S. Dome was the West German tent, designed by Frei Otto. He is currently the master of structures whose flexible skin is the prime structural element. Volume One of his 2-Volume work is devoted to Pneumatic Structures-air houses plus. Every designer we know who's seen this book has commenced to giggle and point, jump up and down, and launch into enthusiastic endorsement of Otto, design, being a designer, and look at this here. The book is comprehensive in its field, technically thorough, beautifully presented.

Tensile Structures, Volume Two

Tensile structures is the complete story on tents and cable nets and like volume one the entire subject is covered in minute detail. The book is intended to show where the thinking and practice on the subject is at this time in history. There is an overview of the whole field, then specifics on cable, net and membrane structures. Each is thoroughly discussed and illustrated with photographs and drawings although graphics here are not as intriguing as in volume one. The last third of the book contains calculations on load-bearing abilities and design. For many readers this will be too technical to understand, much less use. But tensile structures are very exciting at this time, and the book is great for getting people started on experiments and construction. Canvas is a cheap building material. There's a lot to learn here. The forms are very organic, and coverage is complete.

[Reviewed by Jay Baldwin.]

Tensile Structures, Vol. Two Cables, Nets and Membranes

Frei Otto
1969; 171 pp.

$12.50 postpaid

Tensile Structures Volume One Pneumatic Structures

Frei Otto
1967; 320 pp.
1650 Illustrations

$22.50 postpaid

both
from
The MIT Press
50 Ames Street
Cambridge, Mass. 02142
or
WHOLE EARTH CATALOG

Experiments were undertaken in the years 1960-64, in which soap films were stretched in different frames and measured photographically in order to determine their shape.

A soap film can be stretched in any frame consisting of straight or curved components, provided that it forms a closed line. The film then forms a continuous surface, the frame being subjected to bending.

The saddle surface of the inside part has a smaller area than the outside, which is not a saddle surface. The torus differs from all other pneumatically tensed membranes by this characteristically saddle-shaped region. The circle on which the spheres forming the torus are strung need not be in the same plane, nor need the spheres have equal diameter. Here, too, unlimited variations are possible, subject to the general laws of formation, and to those particular to closed hoses.

$$n = \frac{p_1 r_1}{2} = \frac{p_2 r_2}{2} = \frac{(p_1 - p_2) r_3}{2}$$

If two soap bubbles of different diameters form a twin bubble (Fig. 10), the diaphragm is curved. If the membrane stresses are equal, the gas pressure p in the smaller bubble is higher than that in the larger bubble. The relationship between the radii r_1, r_2, r_3 is given by:

Guyed masts consist of one-dimensional central elements subjected to compression and surrounded on all sides by one- or two-dimensional tension-loaded elements. They thus form three-dimensional systems most suitable for mobile structures. Many contemporary designs of high cranes for wide reaches are variations of this basic system. An elastic central rod can be bent by varying the lengths of the guys (Fig. 3). For this, all cables must be adjusted simultaneously; this is done by synchronized hydraulic presses located at the anchoring point. A similar, but much more mobile system is shown in Fig. 4. A thin elastic central strut carries cantilevers connected to the ground by means of cables.

In living nature the spine of a vertebrate (Fig. 7) is a guyed mobile system, approximately as shown in Fig. 4. A multiple articulated, highly flexible central rod, capable of taking up large compressive forces, is surrounded by a tension-loaded system consisting of many members, which secures the central rod against buckling and bending, while ensuring its complete mobility.

19

The *Whole Earth Catalog* assembled an encyclopaedia of pragmatic, vernacular and radical tools for an imminent future, 1968.

Architectural thought gradually shifted from a space of 'knowing' and an architecture that provides a solution to an architecture that acknowledges complexity and aims to communicate meaning through ambiguity. Robert Venturi introduced 'inflection', the consideration of the building in the context of its surroundings.[71] Kenneth Frampton's critical regionalism sought to do the same but geographically, connecting architecture to the immediate topography, climate, material and light.[72]

While postmodernism called for a revival of ornament, or references to place and past, deconstructivism sought to break architecture down to its elements, fragmenting the geometries of the building.

At its best, there was a playfulness, whimsy and wit. Architecture loosened up, drawing on historical decoration, symbolism, colour and pattern to create a 'messy vitality'.[73] Sculptural forms, ornaments, anthropomorphism and trompe l'oeils became common physical characteristics. The discipline splintered in all directions to accommodate self-expression.

Fontainebleau Hotel's trompe l'oeil, Miami Beach, Richard Haas, 1986.

Sea Ranch Condominium, California, MLTW, 1964–1966.

Residence and poolhouse, Llewellyn Park, Robert A. M. Stern, 1982.

At its worst, postmodern architecture became inward-looking and regressive. Appropriated by the commercial mainstream, bloated houses were hidden behind a thin veneer of vernacular styles and car-orientated neighbourhoods were rendered less alienating with watercolours. As eclecticism became fashionable, Manfredo Tafuri noted that the search for constant newness resulted in architectural languages and types that were outdated before even being built.[74]

Alongside proliferation and stylistic chaos, an understanding of the city as a complex, contradictory, dynamic condition prevailed. As cities experienced extreme fluctuations in growth and deindustrialization, the relationship between infrastructure, water management, biodiversity and human activity became a space of investigation. A restructuring of public policy and development practices further supported this shift towards integration. The soiled spaces and brownfield sites on urban fringes and waterfronts became testing sites, and architects, planners, urban designers and landscape architects were busy with procedures of rehabilitation, renewal, remediation and restoration. Landscape became a lens through which to examine our cities, and approaches that sought to realign architecture with the dictates of the environment gained momentum.

The collective behavior of flocks, herds, and schools was modelled and simulated in the mid-1980s.

An expansion of knowledge within mathematics and computation allowed for the behaviour of natural systems to be described and modelled. The fields of architecture and landscape architecture latched onto this, translating immaterial forces, flows and systems into the physical realm. Stan Allen's essay 'Field Conditions' marked a shift in both language and practice. The city changed from an accumulation of objects within zones to a field of shifting patterns, networks and territories.[75]

Diagrams of Field Conditions, Stan Allen, 1996.

Emerging theories of landscape urbanism, infrastructural urbanism, mat urbanism and phylogenesis worked with, not against, a site's existing conditions. Foreign Office Architects believed architecture could integrate multiple systems through a relational taxonomy, Mohsen Mostafavi extracted data from site and then fed this back in to shape architectural form, and James Corner took a softer approach, realizing landscape's hidden potential, an act located between people and nature.[76] Finally, the built environment was listening to natural systems, embedding their needs within the design process to repair prior neglect.

The High Line in New York has become a much-celebrated example of how to design urban nature, Diller Scofidio + Renfro, James Corner Field Operations & Piet Oudolf, 2003–2014.

The built landscape of the Yokohama International Passenger Terminal, FOA, 2002.

At the turn of the twenty-first century, buildings were twisting and contorting themselves to manage flows, forces and complexity. A fascination with new tools, or perhaps toys, led Moshe Safdie to proclaim that architects have been designing drunk for the last twenty years.[77] The very real and urgent project of connecting nature and culture got lost among the sculptural free-for-all of parametricism and the bloated mechanisms of sustainability.

Constructing Nature

Alongside the industrial, chemical, medical and digital revolution, all exceptionally invention-driven, the environmental revolution was treated as reactionary and anti-progressive. A killjoy, for three generations, picking away at the objects and practices of comfort and indulgence we hold dear. In the fifty years since our awakening, a holistic attitude to ecology has been replaced by sustainability, which is noticeably narrower and quantifiable. Technological utopianism has been swapped for market fundamentalism, and the belief that the economy will provide the solution still largely drives development.

Renault advertisement, 1961. Subaru advertisement, 1985. Lexus advertisement, 2007.

Nathaniel Rich pronounced the decade between 1979 and 1989 as 'The Decade We Almost Stopped Climate Change'. An effort worthy of celebrating, but for the alarming reality of the title that precedes it: 'Losing Earth'.[78] Rich details how for a brief moment the world's major powers came close to a binding, global framework to reduce carbon emissions. The data collected since 1957 confirmed what scientists predicted, and the US government seemed set to regulate its way out.

Then, politics faltered. The existential problem facing the climate was passed over for the hole in the ozone, an issue with an obvious political solution: the banning of CFCs.[79] At least you could witness the *fixing* of an ozone hole, whereas you cannot witness a sea level that does not rise thanks to tireless climate-saving efforts. It is really that cynical.

Back on land, things were even worse. The malicious exploitation of the crust of the earth in the name of oil kicked into overdrive. During the 1960s, the United States invested in the development of techniques to use nuclear explosives for peaceful purposes, one instance of which was for the recovery of oil from the Athabascan tar sands in Canada. While this technique was abandoned due to political controversy, the largest mine in the world opened in 1978 and has grown to mind-blowing proportions.[80] The Athabascan tar sands have been dubbed the largest and most destructive industrial project in human history.

All of this digging is literally the fuel (the oil) that supports the growth of the concrete skin of the contemporary city above ground. What is frightening is that we are scarring the skin of the earth in two directions at once and with increasing speed. This current generation will dig out the same volume of earth that has been built on its surface.

The Athabasca mine in Alberta, Canada, goes 60 metres into the ground. It is currently only at a fifth of its capacity and could potentially cover 140 000 square kilometres. © 2018 Google Earth.

Architecture and the construction industry do not exist in a vacuum. While the climate debate got bogged down for three decades in technicalities, a holistic approach to architecture, ecology and society has been watered down and replaced by shallow practices of efficiency. Sustainability has become an accepted financial instrument; nations buy and sell carbon credits and cities chase liveability metrics. The architectural manifestation of this exists as a series of certifications, green stars and building performance calculations. The optimized building is a container for rudimentary technologies to harness energy and reduce waste.

Syncrude Mildred Lake North Mine, Athabasca Oil Sands Region, Alberta, Canada. Hereward Longley, 2014.

Chuquicamata copper mine, Antofagasta, Chile. Simone Cardullo, 2019.

Burj Khalifa, the tallest structure in the world, in Dubai, a city that has grown out of the desert with the discovery of oil in the late 1960s.

Despite emission regulations since 1967, Los Angeles has the worst ozone pollution in the USA, with 145 days of unhealthy air per year.

As of 2010, more than four million of the six million inhabitants of Caracas, Venezuela, live in a self-built informal city.

In the aftermath of Hurricane Sandy, 818 000 inhabitants lost power for ten days, New York City, 2012.

We live in a strange time in which we have to financially incentivize the survival of our own habitat. George Monbiot recently noted that we discuss our habitat as though it is tradable and exchangeable. Natural processes are 'ecosystem services', and hills, forests and river catchments are now 'green infrastructure' within an 'ecosystem market'.[81] Nature is a commodity and the value ascribed to the land is so ingrained within our culture that the thought of leaving it alone when its value is evident is described as a waste.

Longyangxia Dam Solar Park. Jesse Allen, NASA Earth Observatory, 2017.

Within this context, a rather arbitrary line has been drawn between rural and urban space. While we shape, debate and redefine urban space, rural space continues to be considered separately, a periphery (often agricultural) beyond the suburbs. But this delineation does not exist. For the last 11 000 years the periphery has been harvested to fuel urbanization. Grain is cultivated, oil extracted, and more recently solar energy absorbed. Rural space is economically and ecologically bound to the city, and the mental and physical distance we impose between centre and periphery, urban and rural, is perverse and damaging.

While the countryside is ignored or romanticized, humans have destroyed a tenth of the earth's remaining wilderness, and much of this peripheral space is more synthetic and unnatural than the cities in which we live.[82] Since the 1980s a small coastal plain near Almería, Spain, has developed into the largest concentration of greenhouses in the world. Seen from space, this plastic field looks like a geographical feature.

These 320 million square metres of greenhouses feed urban Europe. This patch of plastic is an environmental nightmare and economic miracle at the same time.

Although our cities are getting smarter, they did not densify. *The Atlas of Urban Expansion* has charted cities like Addis Ababa in an effort to understand this growth.[83] In the next forty years, global population is set to double while the total area covered by the world's cities is set to triple.[84] The 'urban' share within global land use seems relatively slight, but when we consider all the land subjugated in supporting this ever-growing urban realm, there is not much habitable space left over. As Richard Florida and cronies rush back downtown with fervent enthusiasm, touting density and cultural capital and echoing Jane Jacobs's 'ballet of the city sidewalk', the unevenness of development and the reality of the periphery are obscured.[85]

At least 50% of all habitable land on Earth is needed to support the 1–2% taken up by the urban realm. Global Land Use, 2016.

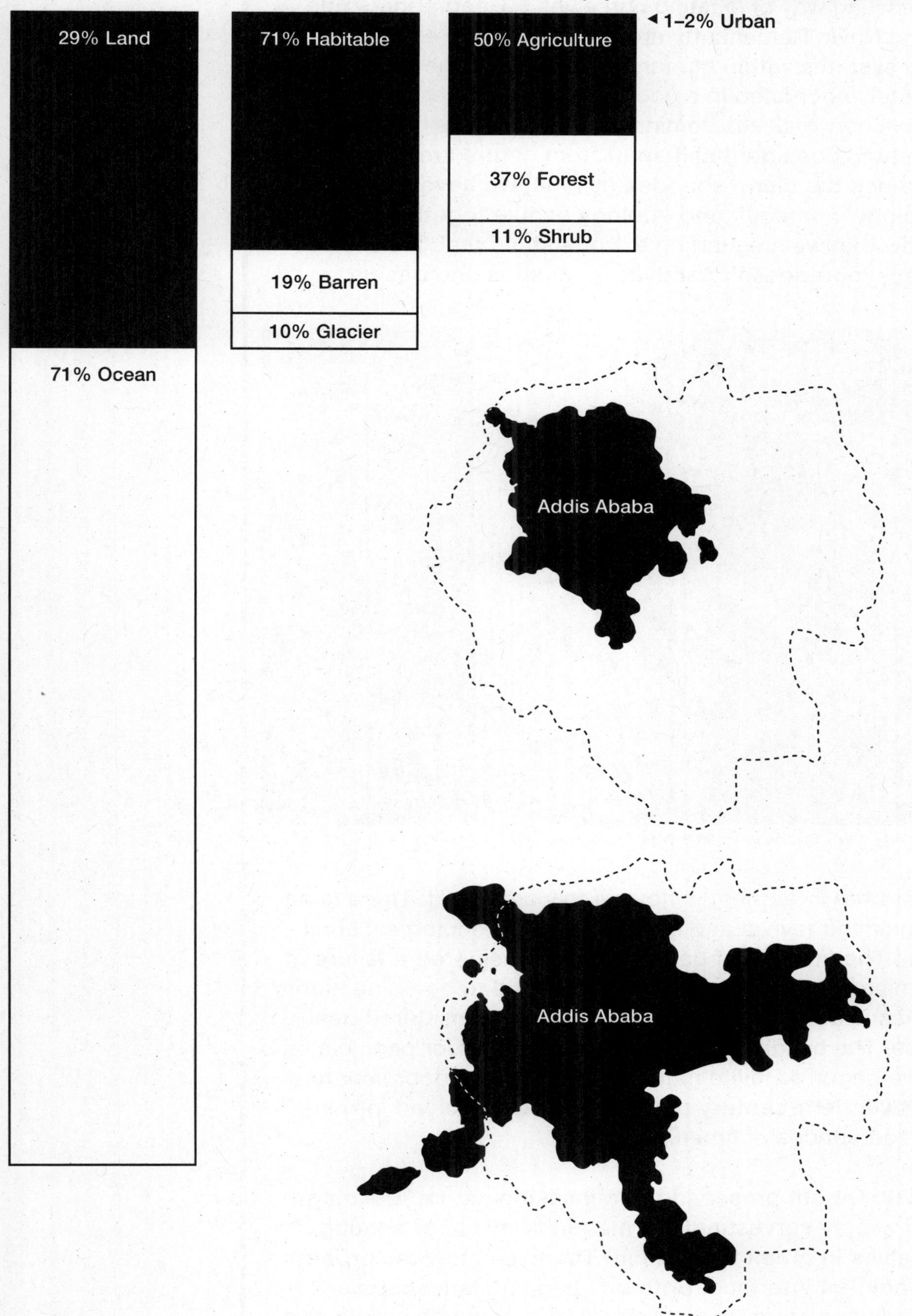

Addis Ababa 1987 (top) to 2010 (bottom). Derived from *The Atlas of Urban Expansion*.

The Anthropocene, a problem of our own creation, does offer an interesting way of locating ourselves.[86] Geographers Erle Ellis and Navin Ramankutty argue that we have embedded natural systems within human ones and that the planet is completely encrusted in a geological layer of design.[87] Due to our previously reckless dominance, dichotomies that allowed humanity to consider itself apart from nature are being reconciled. Since the alarm sounded in 1964, we have known that technology, humanity and ecology evolve together. But it is only now that we are starting to understand that this endless feedback loop doesn't paralyse innovation and design.[88]

Bosco Verticale, Milan, Stefano Boeri, 2009–2014.

What started in earnest is now widely accepted. There is an overwhelming revival and investment in an ecological architecture. The urban roof garden, once considered a failure of modernism, is now coveted, and the need to combine higher densities with humanized public space is considered best practice. The building is no longer a container for people alone; we have begun to invite nature inside. The outdoor sanatoria of the twentieth-century public park have evolved into internalized spaces of amenity.[89]

This is not about preserving or mimicking nature. Buildings are not simply harvesting information from site or coating themselves in green to blend in. There is a new reciprocity at the point of interface. Both building and landscape are being designed in concert, and the line between nature and culture has begun to blur.

A provocation for architecture and ecology inscribed on the steel door of Yourtopia, Rotterdam, SeARCH, 2014.

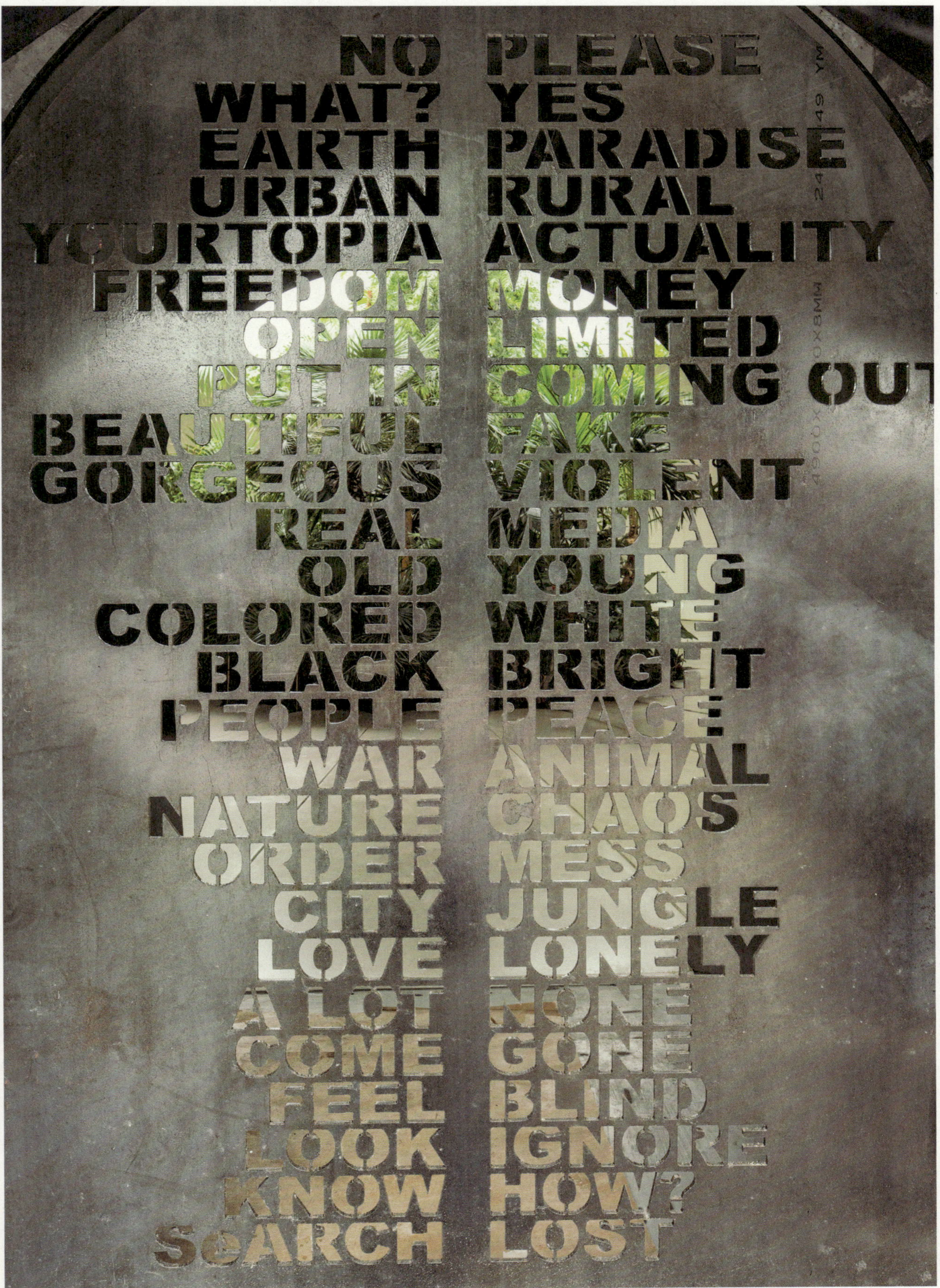

Endnotes:

1 [p. 14] Carson detailed the devastating environmental effects of DDT and pesticides, explaining how in the rush to grow more and feed an ever-growing population we were poisoning nature and ourselves. Rachel Carson, *Silent Spring* (Boston: Houghton Mifflin, 1962).

2 [p. 16] While the book broadly criticized the modernist approach to urban planning, Jacobs took Le Corbusier's Radiant City and Ebenezer Howard's Garden City to task for visions that informed the physical destruction of inner city suburbs and the segregation of the city into different zones of activity. Jane Jacobs, *The Death and Life of Great American Cities* (New York: Random House, 1964).

3 [p. 16] Stephen Ward. "Jane Jacobs: Critic of the Modernist Approach to Urban Planning Who Believed That Cities Were Places for People". Obituary in *The Independent* (3 June 2006). Accessed 20 August 2018.

4 [p. 17] Experts have been debating whether or not humanity's impact on the earth is so profound that we have permanently marked the geological record, warranting the declaration of a new geological epoch: the Anthropocene. In July 2018 the International Commission on Stratigraphy (ICS) subdivided the Holocene into Greenlandian, Northgrippian and Meghalayan Age (beginning roughly 2200 BCE with a 200-year drought). This is based entirely on climatic evidence, whereas the Anthropocene would be based on evidence of human impact. Other scientists criticize this, arguing that the division between natural and human activity is incorrect as humans are an inseparable part of nature. Jonathan Amos, "Welcome to the Meghalayan Age: A New Phase in History", *BBC*, 18 July 2018. Accessed 16 August 2018.

5 [p. 17] Bread-like products were prepared by Natufian hunter-gatherers 4000 years before the emergence of the Neolithic agricultural way of life. Amaia Arranz-Otaegui, Lara Gonzalez Carretero, Monica N. Ramsey, Dorian Q. Fuller, and Tobias Richter, "Archaeobotanical Evidence Reveals the Origins of Bread 14,400 Years Ago in North-eastern Jordan", *Proceedings of the National Academy of Sciences* (16 July 2018). Accessed 23 July 2018.

6 [p. 17] See Beatriz Colomina and Mark Wigley, *Are We Human? Notes on an Archeology of Design* (Zürich: Lars Müller Publishers, 2016); Bruno Latour, *Facing Gaia: Eight Lectures on the New Climatic Regime* (New York: Wiley, 2017); and Koert van Mensvoort, *Next Nature* (Amsterdam: Next Nature Network, 2015).

7 [p. 24] An architectural adjustment of Yuval Noah Harari, *Sapiens: A Brief History of Humankind* (London: Vintage Books, 2015).

8 [p. 25] This 'raw material' could be called the first semi-manufactured product, even though humans were not the 'producer'.

9 [p. 25] Woodburn makes a distinction between 'immediate-return' hunter collectors (egalitarian) and 'delayed-return' hunter collectors (non-egalitarian). James Woodburn, "Egalitarian Societies", *Man, New Series* 17, no. 3 (September 1982), 431–451.

10 [p. 26] There is a consistent pattern of mobility and use of rock shelters right through to present-day Hadza campsites. A. Z. P. Mabulla. "Tanzania's Endangered Heritage: A Call for a Protection Program", *African Archaeological Review* 13 (1996), 197.

11 [p. 27] Charles C. Mann. "The Birth of Religion", *National Geographic* (June 2011).

12 [p. 28] Andrew Curry. "Gobekli Tepe: The World's First Temple?", *Smithsonian Magazine* (2008). Accessed 5 November 2017.

13 [p. 31] Pier Vittorio Aureli. "Life, Abstracted: Notes on the Floor Plan", Architecture and Representation Lecture Series, Het Nieuwe Instituut (19 October 2017). Accessed 8 March 2018.

14 [p. 32] Ian Kuijt and Bill Finlayson, "Evidence for Food Storage and Predomestication Granaries 11 000 Years Ago in the Jordan Valley", *Proceedings of the National Academy of Sciences* 106, no. 27 (July 2009).

15 [p. 32] Derrick Jensen and Lierre Keith, *Earth at Risk: Building a Resistance Movement to Save the Planet* (PM Press, 2012), 145.

16 [p. 33] "The change from hunting-gathering to farming was a change from high mortality, low morbidity and low numbers to low mortality, high morbidity and high numbers". Hillary J. Shaw, *The Consuming Geographies of Food: Diet, Food Deserts and Obesity* (London: Routledge, 2017). 14.

17 [p. 36] Ian Hodder, "This Old House", *Natural History Magazine* (June 2006). Accessed 2 November 2017.

18 [p. 36] B. S. Düring, "The Articulation of Houses at Neolithic Çatalhöyük, Turkey", in R. Beck (ed.), *The Durable House: House Society Models in Archaeology* (Carbondale: Center for Archaeological Investigations, 2017), 146.

19 [p. 38] A. K. Schmitt et al, "Identifying the Volcanic Eruption Depicted in a Neolithic Painting at Çatalhöyük, Central Anatolia, Turkey", *PLOS ONE* (8 January 2014). Accessed 10 September 2017.

20 [p. 47] Aldo van Eyck, "Dogon: Mand-Huis-Dorp-Wereld", *Forum* 17, no. 4 (1963).

21 [p. 50] Permanent Delegation of Turkey, "Archaeological Site of Arslantepe". Tentative Lists of States Parties, UNESCO World Heritage Centre, (15 April 2014).

22 [p. 54] John Chapman, "Houses, Households, Villages and Proto-cities in Southeastern Europe", in David W. Anthony and Jennifer Y. Chi (eds.), *The Lost World of Old Europe: The Danube Valley, 5000 –3500 BC* (New York: Institute for the Study of the Ancient World, 2010), 82.

23 [p. 54] Roland Fletcher argues that the built environment becomes a constraint on the long-term development of a settlement, and that the initial layout of buildings, and forms of communication that result from it, may come to shackle further development, and also to place constraints on social and political change. Tripol'ye sites have a residential density higher than 300–600 per hectare and area greater than 100 hectare – above limits set by Fletcher and thus challenging his hypothesis regarding the transformation of human settlement from mobile to sedentary, sedentary to urban, and urban to industrial.

Roland Fletcher, *The Limits of Settlement Growth* (Cambridge: University of Sydney, 1995).

24 [p. 57] Oscar Wilde, "The Decay of Lying: An Observation", *The Complete Writings of Oscar Wilde*, vol. 7 (New York: Nottingham Society, 1909).

25 [p. 59] Then God said "Let us make man in our image, after our likeness. And let them have dominion over the fish of the sea and over the birds of the heavens and over the livestock and over all the earth and over every creeping thing that creeps on the earth". Genesis 1:26.

26 [p. 60] M. Gargarin and E. Fantham, *The Oxford Encyclopedia of Ancient Greece and Rome*, vol. 1 (Oxford: Oxford University Press, 2010), 145.

27 [p. 63] R. Allen Brown, *Castles: A History and Guide* (Dorset: Blanford Press, 1980), 16.

28 [p. 63] Ibid. 14.

29 [p. 66] The principle of concentric design used at Belvoir "was to influence castle design for the next several centuries", H. J. A. Sire, *The Knights of Malta* (New Haven: Yale University Press, 1994).

30 [p. 66] The 'zwinger' was an open area between two defensive walls believed to come from the German word *zwingen*, meaning 'to force'. Otto Piper, *Burgenkunde: Bauwesen und Geschichte der Burgen* (Würzburg, 1995), 684.

31 [p. 66] Georg Ulrich Großmann, *Burgen in Europa* (Regensburg: Schnell & Steiner, 2005).

32 [p. 73] Gunpowder travelled the Silk Road to Europe in the 13th century but it wasn't until the 16th century that manoeuvrable cannons capable of reducing the fortifications to rubble were developed.

33 [p. 75] Louis Kahn's fascination with the nestling of auxiliary spaces into the thick walls of Scottish castles is discussed in David B. Brownlee and David G. De Long, *Louis I. Kahn: In the Realm of Architecture* (Museum of Contemporary Art & Rizzoli, 1991), 68.

34 [p. 78] Leon Battista Alberti, *De re aedificatoria* (Florence, 1485).

35 [p. 79] See M. Roberts, *The Military Revolution, 1560–1660: An Inaugural Lecture Delivered before the Queen's University of Belfast*, (Belfast: Boyd, 1956); and Geoffery Parker, 'Military Revolution 1560–1660 a Myth?', *The Journal of Modern History* 48, no. 2 (June 1976), 203.

36 [p. 79] Geoffrey Parker, *The Military Revolution: Military Innovations and the Rise of the West 1500–1800* (Cambridge: Ohio State University, 1996).

37 [p. 79] Ali Madanipour, *Designing the City of Reason: Foundations and Frameworks* (London: Routledge, 2007), 45.

38 [p. 80] Ibid. 43.

39 [p. 81] Richard Sennett, *The Fall of Public Man* (New York: Knopf, 1977).

40 [p. 81] Liba Taub, "The Historical Function of the 'Forma Urbis Romae'", *Imago Mundi* 45 (1993), 9–19.

41 [p. 82] Aureli, "Life, Abstracted: Notes on the Floor Plan". (above, note 13).

42 [p. 82] A few centuries earlier and unaware of the Forma Urbis Romae, Leonardo Bufalini provided an unparalleled measured, unified portrayal of Rome (1551).

43 [p. 82] James Tice, "The Nolli Map and Urban Theory", *Nolli Map* website. Accessed 13 January 2018.

44 [p. 83] Michael Dennis, *Court and Garden: From the French Hotel to the City of Modern Architecture* (Cambridge: MIT Press, 1986), 126.

45 [p. 84] Norman T. Newton, *Design on the Land: The Development of Landscape Architecture* (Cambridge, Mass: Belknap Press of Harvard University Press, 1971).

46 [p. 84] Michael Dennis discusses the work of Talbot Hamlin in *Court and Garden*, 91.

47 [p. 87] Dennis, *Court and Garden*, 126.

48 [p. 97] Merijn Oudenampsen, "Re-tracing the Garden City", *MO* (3 April 2013). Accessed October 2017.

49 [p. 97] Ebenezer Howard, *Garden Cities of Tomorrow* (London: Swan Sonnenschein & Co, 1902).

50 [p. 98] Peter Hall and Colin Ward, *Sociable Cities: The Legacy of Ebenezer Howard* (Chichester: Wiley, 1998).

51 [p. 100] Frederic James Osborn, *New Towns after the War* (London: J. M. Dent and Sons Ltd, 1918).

52 [p. 100] Five Points of Architecture manifesto in Le Corbusier, *Towards an Architecture* (Paris: Cres & Cie, 1923).

53 [p. 100] Le Corbusier, *The City of To-morrow and Its Planning* (London: Rodker, 1925).

54 [p. 101] Lev Bratishenko, "No Parks?", article 14 of 17, Nature Reorganized, *CCA* (May 2017). Accessed 20 November 2017.

55 [p. 101] Lewis Mumford, "Yesterday's City of Tomorrow", *The Lewis Mumford Reader* (New York: Pantheon Books, 1986), 139–144.

56 [p. 101] Peter L. Laurence, *Becoming Jane Jacobs* (Philadelphia: University of Pennsylvania Press, 2016), 24–28.

57 [p. 102] Ibid.

58 [p. 103] Colin Rowe notes that as European modernism was adopted in the United States, it was largely purged of its ideological or socialist rhetoric. Colin Rowe, *Five Architects: Eisenman, Graves, Gwathmey, Hejduk, Meiser* (New York: Oxford University Press, 1975).

59 [p. 103] Bernays considered capitalism inherently democratic. Jonas Staal, "Art. Democratism. Propaganda.", *E-flux Journal* no. 52, (February 2014). Accessed 18 September 2017.

60 [p. 104] Both the 1939 and 1964 World Fairs were not endorsed by the Bureau of International Expositions (BIE), who citied issues of private financing of fairs and the collecting of rent from the pavilions.

61 [p. 105] Carson, *Silent Spring* (above, note 1).

62 [p. 106] Research by agronomists Nazareno Strampelli (Italy) and Norman Borlaug (US) on high yield wheat varieties increased agricultural production worldwide, particularly in the developing world.

63 [p. 109] From the ancient Greek αντιβιοτικά (antibiotiká), meaning opposing life.

64 [p. 109] Colin Rowe, *Five Architects*.

65 [p. 116] Dirk van den Heuvel, "Total Space: Considering Dutch Structuralism Today", *Archis* 50 (2017).

66 [p. 117] Mary McLeod, "Architecture and Politics in the Reagan Era: From Postmodernism to Deconstructivism", *Assemblage* 8 (February 1989), 38.

67 [p. 117] "While Charles Jencks will pinpoint the break between modernism and postmodernism to 3.32 p.m. on 15 July 1972, the moment the Pruitt-Igoe housing project was demolished, others acknowledge the emergence of postmodernity as a changing sensibility through a range of diverse fields". David Harvey, *The Condition of Postmodernity: An Enquiry into the Origins of Cultural Change* (Oxford: Blackwell, 1989), 39–41.

68 [p. 117] Sigfried Giedeon, *Space Time and Architecture; The Growth of a New Tradition*, 5th ed. (Cambridge: Harvard University Press, 1966), XXXII, IV and IVI. See also "Introduction", Carve, 965–993.

69 [p. 118] David Langdon, "AD Classics: Montreal Biosphere / Buckminster Fuller", *ArchDaily* 25 (November 2014). Accessed 19 December 2017.

70 [p. 120] Stewart Brand, *Whole Earth Catalog* (Fall 1968).

71 [p. 120] Robert Venturi, *Complexity and Contradiction in Architecture* (New York: Museum of Modern Art, 1966).

72 [p. 121] Kenneth Frampton, "Towards a Critical Regionalism: Six Points for an Architecture of Resistance", in Hal Foster, *The Anti-Aesthetic: Essays on Postmodern Culture* (New York: New Press, 1998).

73 [p. 121] Robert Venturi, *Complexity and Contradiction in Architecture*.

74 [p. 122] Fernando Donis, "Evolution in the Age of Crisis", *Conditions* 1 (2009), 24–27.

75 [p. 123] Stan Allen's "Field Conditions" (1999), reflects on the expansion of knowledge within mathematics and computation and translates this into the physical realm of architecture, in *Points + Lines: Diagrams and Projects for the City* (New York: Princeton Architectural Press, 1999).

76 [p. 124] Foreign Office Architects, *Phylogenesis: FOA's Ark* (London: Actar Publisher, 2004), 11; Mohsen Mostafavi and Gareth Doherty, *Ecological Urbanism* (Zürich: Lars Müller, 2010); and James Corner, *Recovering Landscape: Essays in Contemporary Landscape Architecture* (New York: Princeton Architectural Press, 1999).

77 [p. 124] Moshe Safdie, "Moshe Safdie Tells the Tale of Habitat 67 and Predicts Housing's Future", *Metropolis* (16 June 2017). Accessed 23 April 2018.

78 [p. 125] Nathaniel Rich, "Losing Earth: The Decade We Almost Stopped Climate Change", *New York Times Magazine* (1 August 2018). Accessed 21 August 2018.

79 [p. 125] This article details how Rafe Pomerance and Al Gore, among others, have worked since the late 1970s to convince the US Congress and the media to put climate change on the international agenda. They made progress until 1983, somewhat surprisingly with the help of Republicans, who demanded action. But under Ronald Reagan the environmental achievements of previous administrations were reversed. By the end of his second term, in 1989, very few regulations and measures to curb atmospheric carbon dioxide were left. Nathaniel Rich, "Losing Earth".

80 [p. 126] The cumulative production of the Syncrude Canada Ltd mine exceeds 2.8 billion barrels. The total extent of bitumen deposits throughout Alberta is 1.7 trillion barrels across 140,000 square kilometres. However, the amount that can be extracted with current technology and prices is 10% of this, 165 billion barrels. Hereward Longley, "Conflicting Interests: Development Politics and the Environmental Regulation of the Alberta Oil Sands Industry, 1970-1980." *Environment and History* (Cambridge: White Horse Press, Forthcoming 2020).

81 [p. 133] George Monbiot discusses the 2013 report of the Ecosystem Market Task Force. George Monbiot, "Putting a Price on the Rivers and Rain Diminishes Us All", *Guardian* (6 August 2012). Accessed 28 November 2017.

82 [p. 134] Adam Vaughan, "Humans Have Destroyed a Tenth of Earth's Wilderness in 25 years – Study", *Guardian* (8 September 2016). Accessed 14 February 2018.

83 [p. 134] Data of Addis Ababa, *The Atlas for Urban Expansion*, NYU Urban Expansion Program, Marron Institute of Urban Management, Stern School of Business of New York University, UN-Habitat and Lincoln Institute of Land Policy (2016). Accessed 19 January 2018.

84 [p. 134] Mark Swilling, "The Curse of Urban Sprawl: How Cities Grow, and Why This Has to Change", *Guardian* (12 July 2016). Accessed 2 February 2018.

85 [p. 134] Jane Jacobs, *The Death and Life of Great American Cities* (above, note 2).

86 [p. 136] Humanity's impact on the earth is so profound (a permanent mark in the geological record) that experts are calling for the declaration of a new geological epoch – the Anthropocene.

87 [p. 136] Erle C. Ellis, Kees Klein Goldewijk, Stefan Siebert, Deborah Lightman and Navin Ramankutty, "Anthropogenic Transformation of the Biomes, 1700 to 2000", *Global Ecology and Biogeography* 19 (September 2010), 589–606.

88 [p. 136] According to Van Mensvoort, the transformation of our natural environment offers an opportunity to co-evolve. Koert van Mensvoort, *Next Nature* (Amsterdam: Next Nature Network, 2015).

89 [p. 136] Lev Bratishenko, "No Parks?". (above, note 54).

Building Bound to the Ground

Six strategies for reconnecting architecture and landscape, merging building and ground.

344 Favrholm Conference Centre, Hillerød
358 Danish Maritime Museum, Helsingør
800 Rundetårn, Copenhagen
830 Silkeborg Museum, Silkeborg
1320 Mountain Dwellings, Copenhagen
1324 Isbjerget, Aarhus
860 Museum aan de Stroom, Antwerp
864 Mercedes Benz Museum, Stuttgart
856 Neanderthal Museum, Mettmann
508 Hexenhaus, Bad Karlshafen
542 Neue Staatsgalerie, Stuttgart
256 Temppeliaukio Church, Helsinki
1202 Centraal Beheer, Apeldoorn
1308 Forest Tower, Putten
926 Junior College, Julianadorp
896 Posbank Pavilion, Rheden
1346 Hotel Jakarta, Amsterdam
1338 Summertime, Amsterdam
1088 Synagogue, Amsterdam
1076 IJdock, Amsterdam
600 Skewed Stolp, Jisp
566 Borneo Housing, Amsterdam
298 Roof Made City, Utrecht
1072 Villa KBWW, Utrecht
1282 Scherf 13, Leidsche Rijn
362 Fort Vechten, Bunnik
1094 Markthal, Rotterdam
716 Kunsthal, Rotterdam
376 Yourtopia, Rotterdam
950 Katendrecht, Rotterdam
750 Serpentine Gallery Pavilion, London
282 Louvre Extension, Paris
996 Piscine des Amiraux, Paris
1210 Jeanne Hachette, Paris
644 Sainte-Marie de La Tourette, Eveux
836 Musée Gallo-Romain, Lyon
494 Prouvé House & Studio, Nantes
1036 Holy Cross Church, Chur
326 Villa Vals, Vals
372 El Paradiso, St.Moritz
514 Siedlung Halen, Bern
558 Therme Vals, Vals
594 Chalet Anzere, Anzère
908 Monte Rosa Hütte, Gorner Glacier
368 Hunting Ranch, Bratislava
Antinori Winery, Bargino 308
Il Magistero, Urbino 536
Villa Malaparte, Capri 632
Lingotto factory, Turin 814
292 Igualada Cemetery, Barcelona
470 Park Güell, Barcelona
554 Olympic Archery Range, Barcelona
1042 Walden 7, Barcelona
274 The Truffle, Costa de Morte
548 Morella School, Morella
1268 Espai Verd, Valencia
1116 Casa No tempo, Montemor-o-Novo
810 Quinta de Regaleira, Sintra
572 Braga Stadium, Braga
1050 Doña Maria Coronel, Seville
266 Monument to Tolerance, Fuerteventura
1242 Hotel Las Salinas, Lanzarote
404 Ancient Theatre, Epidaurus
1234 Ramot Polin, Jerusalem
784 Dur Sharrukin, Khorsabad
794 Minaret al-Malwiya, Samarra
788 Etemenanki Ziggurat, Babylon
782 Nanna Ziggurat, Uruk
222 Biete Ghiorgis, Lalibela
722 Dutch Embassy , Addis Ababa
1100 Khalifeyah Library, Muharraq
458 Sar Agha Seyed, Chaharmahal-Va-Bakhtiyari
1120 Zeitz MOCAA, Cape Town
502 Die Es, Cape Town
450 Surya Kund, Modhera
442 Rani Ki Vav, Patan
302 Amdavad Ni Gufa, Ahmedabad
438 Adalaj ni Vav, Ahmedabad
1012 Indian Institute of Management, Ahmedabad
204 Kailasa Temple, Ellora
446 Panna Mia Baori, Jaipur
454 Nahargarh Fort Baori, Jaipur
434 Agrasen ki Baoli, New Delhi
578 Friendship Centre, Gaibandha

912 Seattle Central Library, Seattle
1054 Westin Bonaventure, Los Angeles
488 The Eames House, Los Angeles
648 Frey House II, Palm Springs
Beinecke Library, New Haven 664
Habitat 67, Montreal 1188
The Whitney Museum, New York 1032
The High Line, New York 1294
Solomon R. Guggenheim, New York 824
Education Center, New York 954
The Ford Foundation, New York 1018
Fallingwater, Mill Run 482
Entelechy II, Sea Island 1248
House & Restaurant, Ube 278
ACROS, Fukuoka 1278
Danish Pavilion, Shanghai 938
The Yaodong, Loess Plateau 178
The Sydney Opera House, Sydney 1174
Seidler House, Sydney 704
Phillip Island House, Phillip Island 288
Athfield House & Studio, Wellington 522
NotOna, Patagonia 270
Árbol para Vivir, Lechería 1290
El Helicoide, Caracas 870
Casa Gerber, Angra dos Reis 708
Costa Brava Clube, Rio de Janeiro 680
MASP, São Paulo 1004
Casa de Vidro, São Paulo 638

AFRICA

Biete Ghiorgis
Lalibela, Ethiopia
1100–1200
222

Monument to Tolerance
Moñtana Tindaya, Canary Islands
Eduardo Chillida
1995–present
266

Die Es
Cape Town, South Africa
Gawie & Gwen Fagan
1964–1965
502

Dutch Embassy
Addis Ababa, Ethiopia
SeARCH & Dick van Gameren
1998–2005
722

Zeitz MOCAA
Cape Town, South Africa
Heatherwick Studio
2014–2017
1120

Hotel Las Salinas
Lanzarote, Canary Islands
Fernando Higueras
1973–1977
1242

NORTH AMERICA

Fallingwater
Mill Run, USA
Frank Lloyd Wright
1936–1939
482

The Eames House
Los Angeles, USA
Charles & Ray Eames
1945–1949
488

Frey House II
Palm Springs, USA
Albert Frey
1959–1964
648

Beinecke Rare Book &
Manuscript Library
New Haven, USA
Gordon Bunshaft (SOM)
1960–1963
664

Solomon R. Guggenheim
Museum
New York City, USA
Frank Lloyd Wright
1943–1959
824

Seattle Central Library
Seattle, USA
OMA
1999–2004
912

Roy and Diana Vagelos
Education Center
New York City, USA
Diller Scofidio + Renfro
2013–2016
954

The Ford Foundation
New York City, USA
Kevin Roche John Dinkeloo and
Associates
1963–1968
1018

The Whitney Museum
New York City, USA
Marcel Breuer with
Hamilton P. Smith
1964–1966
1032

The Westin Bonaventure
Los Angeles, USA
John C. Portman
1974–1976
1054

Habitat 67
Montreal, Canada
Moshe Safdie
1967
1188

EUROPE

OCEANIA

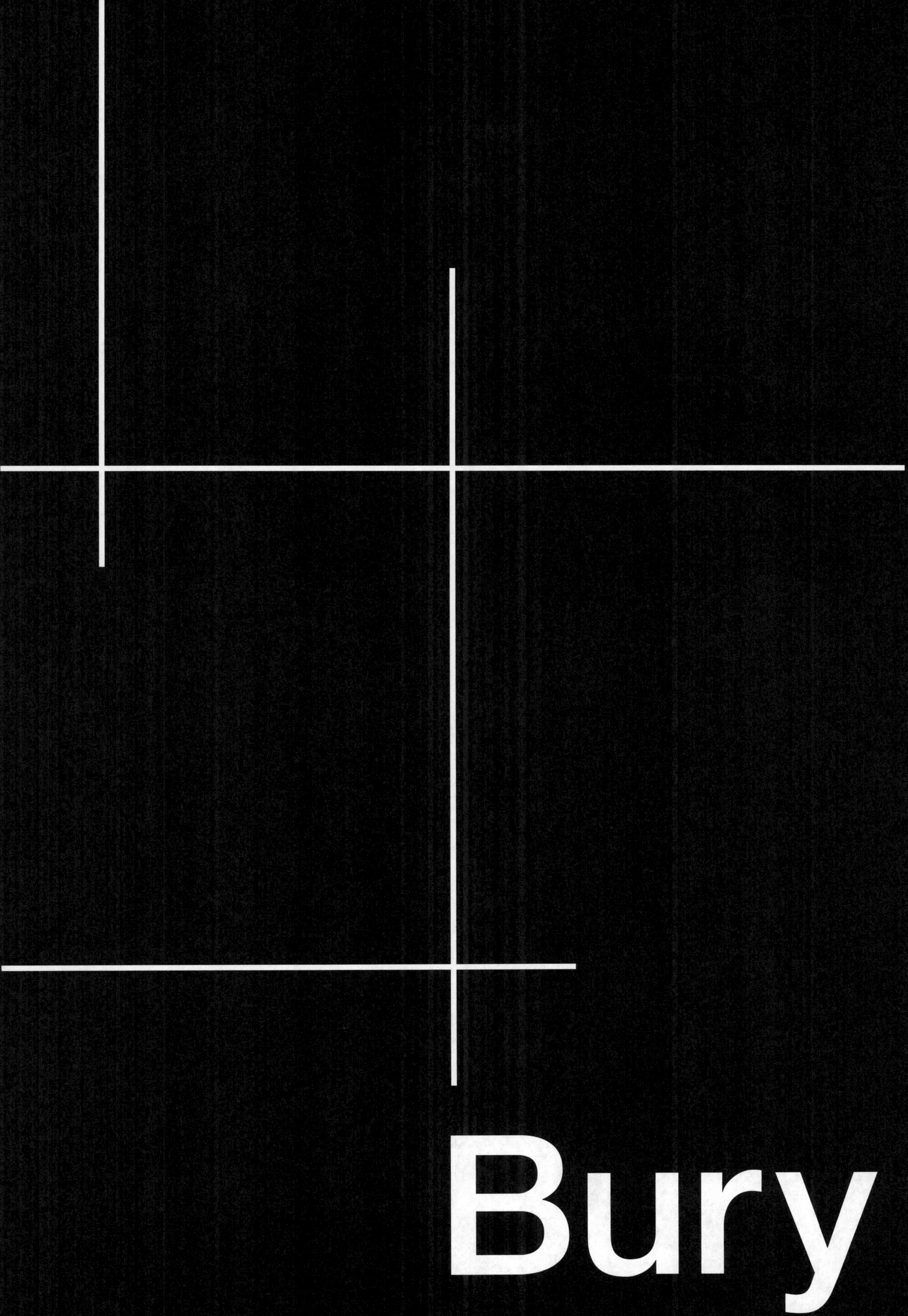
Bury

The building sits below the earth's crust, allowing for an uninterrupted landscape above.

"Design is a funny word. Some people think design means how it looks. But of course, if you dig deeper, it's really how it works."[1] —Steve Jobs

There is something paradoxical about an underground architecture. In a field where icons compete for attention, the underground building hides, forcing the architecture to be judged not on its image but on how it functions, how it manages the vital lifelines of structure, temperature, air and light.

For millennia humankind has dug downwards for shelter, security and comfort. Born out of pure necessity, using nothing but the ever-present earth, humankind created architecture by subtraction.[2] In Ethiopia, monolithic churches were hewn out of rich volcanic rock. In India, elaborate temples were carved from cliffs. And in China's Loess Valley, underground dwellings were constructed within the porous ground.

The Yaodong, China, 300 BCE–present.

Within much of this earthen vernacular, habitation is described by what is removed. The ground is sculpted into *poché* and manipulated to define interior space.[3] Taking away, often by hand, only what is essential, humankind exists within niches of the earth's crust. The structural limit of the material, the nature of the tools and the intended purpose of the space define this subtractive construction.

Troglodyte dwellings, Matmata, Tunisia.

A sparse landscape and scarcity of resources for construction often drove this innovative sculpting of the ground. After all, necessity is the mother of all invention. The economy and efficiency of this subtractive building practice is remarkable. Nothing is wasted, and nothing is superfluous. The material excavated is a resource for constructing above ground. Depth and mass offer insulation and protection, and openings provide light and ventilation. There is an inherent sustainability and natural circularity embedded in this form of construction.

Plan of Troglodyte dwellings, Matmata, showing dwellings around open courtyard.

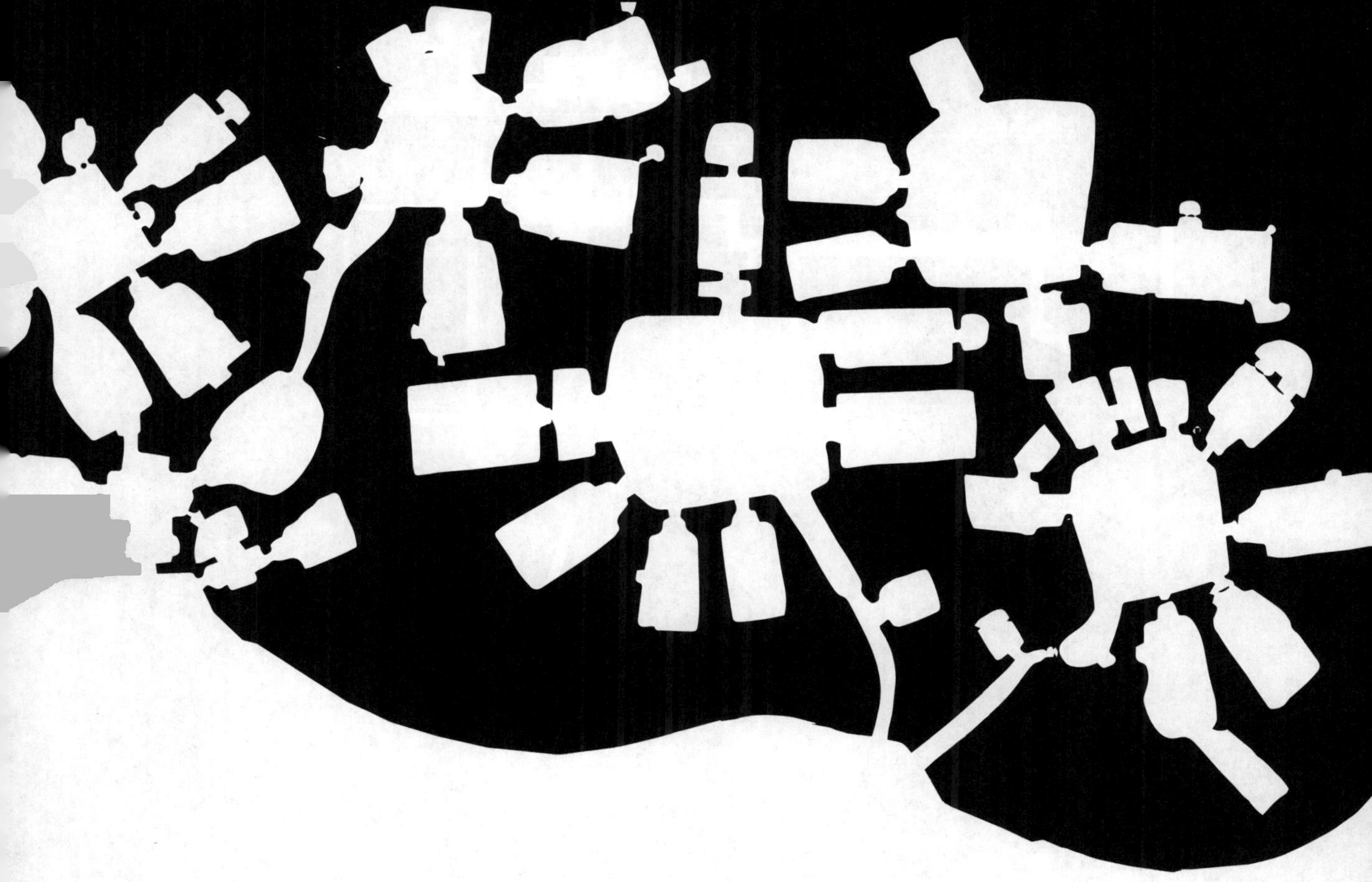

Plan of Toronto's PATH, an underground network of walkways which connect to the buildings above ground, 1900–present.

On close inspection, we see that the same instinct or logic that shaped ancient cave dwelling has been adopted beneath the contemporary city. The Yaodong in China and the troglodyte dwellings of Tunisia and Libya use the high thermal performance of the earth to buffer large fluctuations in temperature, from day to night or summer to winter. In Montreal and Toronto, citizens traverse the city below ground, avoiding the sub-zero temperatures above. Aptly named PATH, a 30-kilometre-long pedestrian shopping complex runs under Toronto, connecting the skyscrapers above.

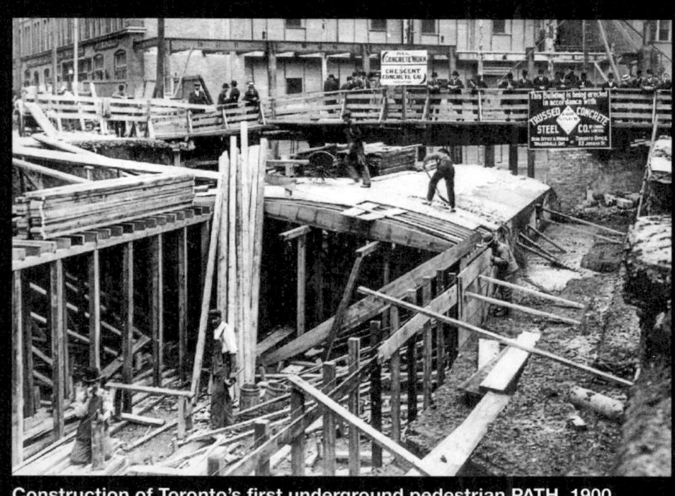

Construction of Toronto's first underground pedestrian PATH, 1900.

Centuries apart and separated by enormous distances are examples of humankind tunnelling downwards away from a harsh environment above, seeking control. The underground cities of Cappadocia were designed to keep thousands of people hidden for months at a time. The sanctuary of Derinkuyu, dug deep within the belly of the earth, involved a complex system of tunnels that managed waste and food storage, and shafts that allowed light and air to penetrate.

The stone wheel doors of Derinkuyu in Cappadocia were rolled across tunnel entrances to cut the city off from dangers above.

Plan of Derinkuyu tunnels below ground, inhabited from 800 BCE–1923.

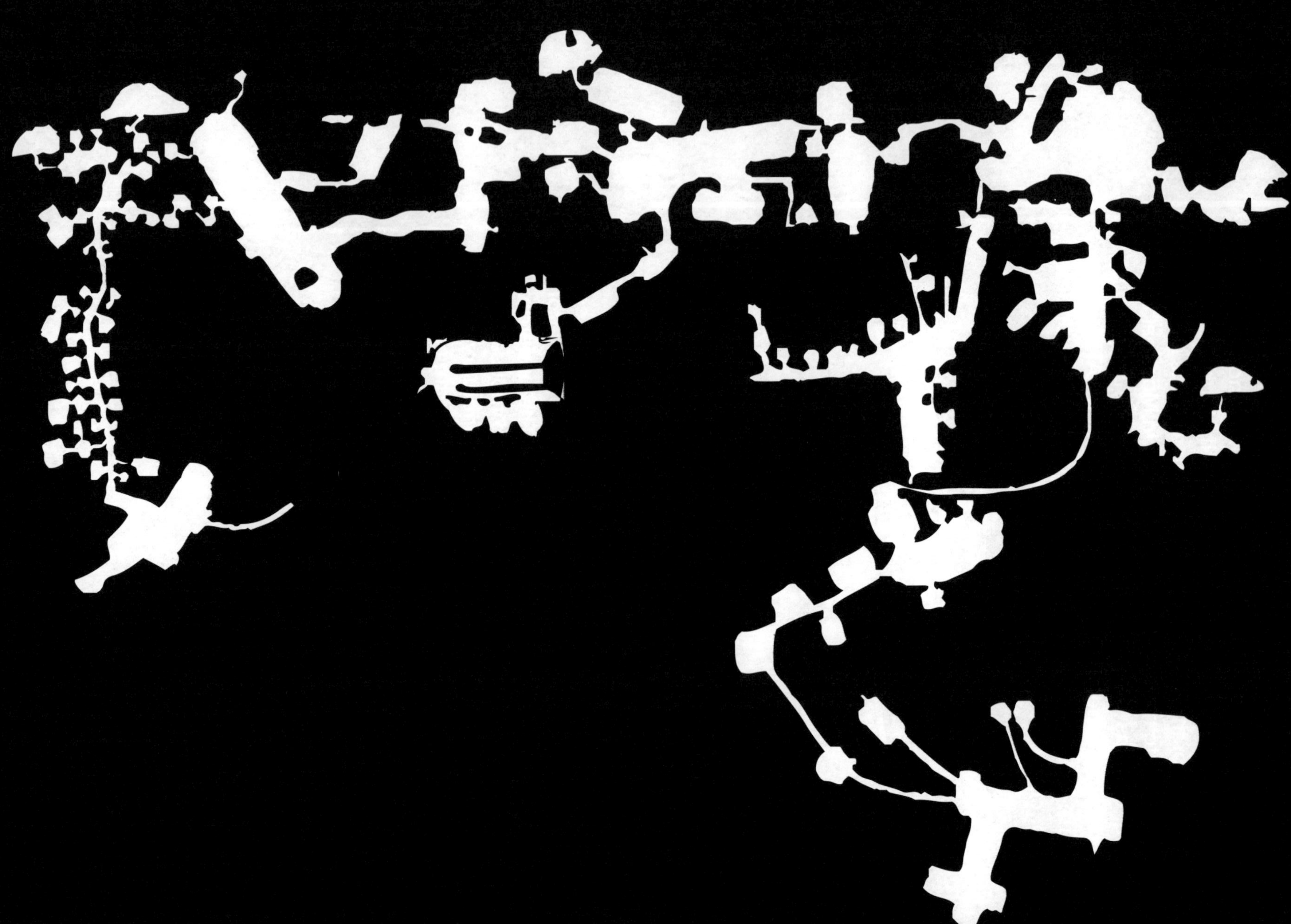

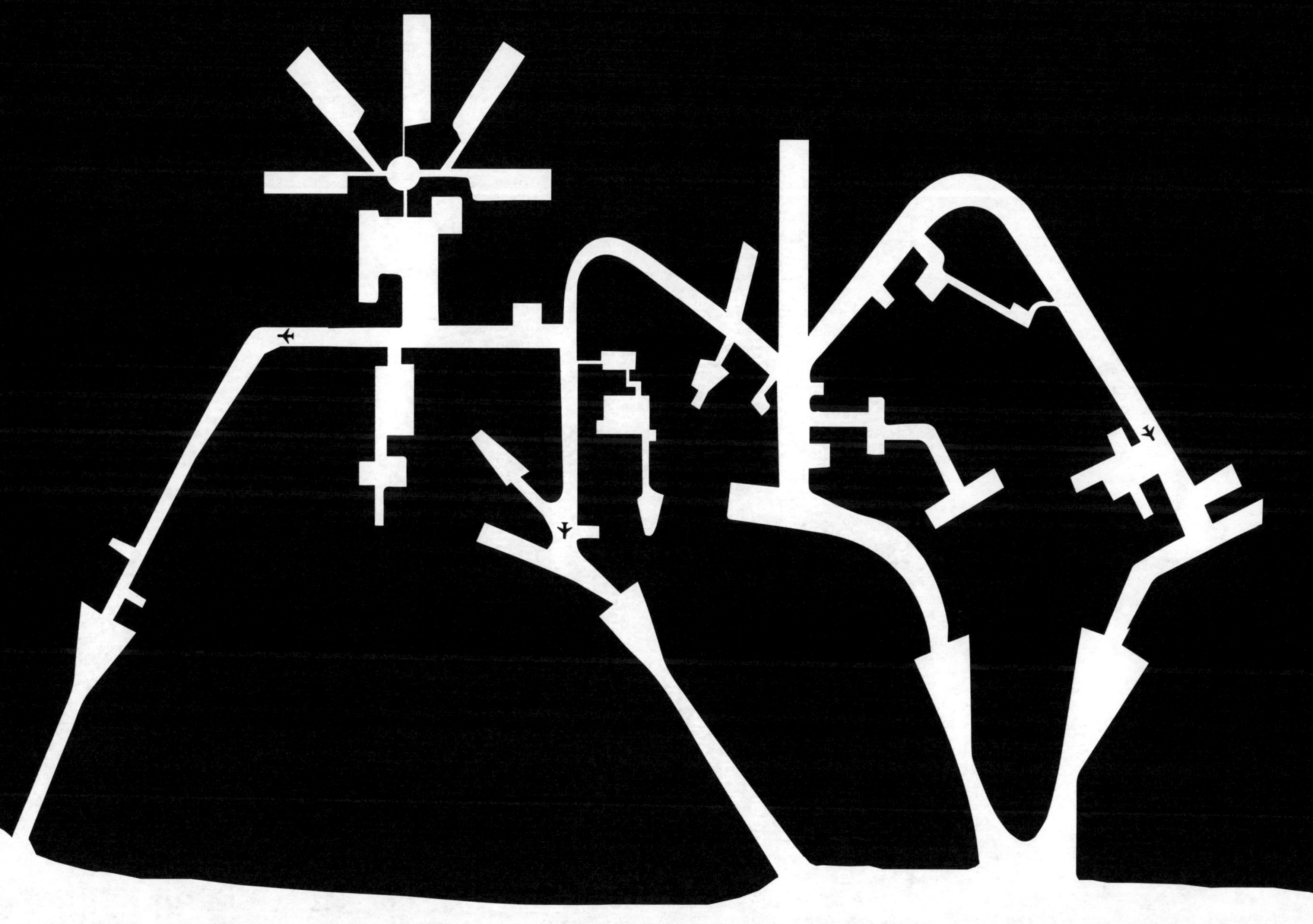

Plan of Željava Air Base, 1948–1968.

New York City imagined as a nuclear metropolis, Oscar Newman, 1969.

The underground city of Dixia Cheng Beijing, was reportedly able to house 300 000 people, 1968–1972.

Subterranean spaces are easily isolated and insulated from the fickleness and volatility above, making them the preferred spot in an apocalypse. Both China and Russia constructed vast underground cities during the Cold War in anticipation of nuclear fallout. Likewise, the subterranean Željava Air Base in former Yugoslavia was designed to withstand a nuclear bomb equivalent to the one that devastated Nagasaki.

On a lighter note, depth and isolation also make subterranean space an opportune place for observation. One thousand metres below ground, the Super-Kamiokande detector has been built in anticipation of the next supernova. Here, deep within the earth, we investigate the creation of matter in the universe above.[4]

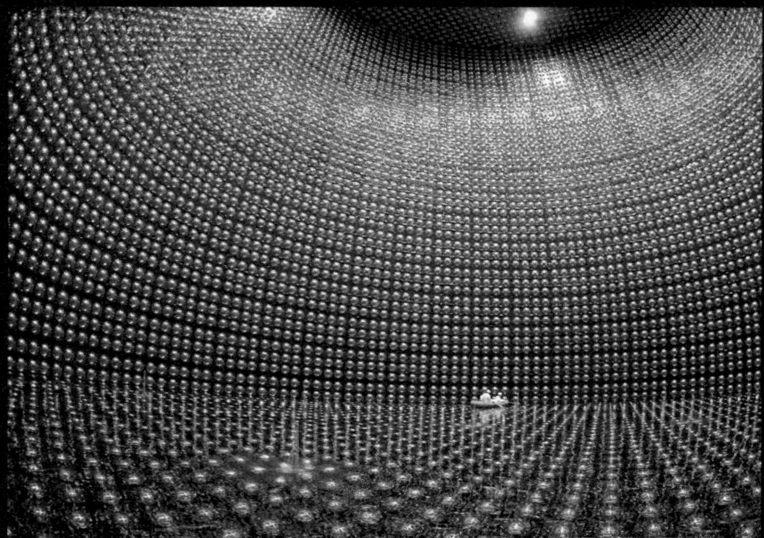

Physicists floating within the Super-Kamiokande detector, a space the size of a 15-storey building, buried 1000 metres under Mount Ikeno in Japan. Kamioka Observatory, ICRR (Institute for Cosmic Ray Research), The University of Tokyo.

The earth has always been a resource and a source of fuel for our cities. The 'matter' of the buildings around us has been mined from beneath our feet. Apparently, sixty per cent of Naples rests on nothing. Enormous cathedral-like caves were quarried out to build the original city. These artificial caves, ancient tunnels, aqueducts, cisterns and catacombs weave together to form an underground city beneath the city. Surviving centuries of changing use, these incredible spaces were used as a shelter from war and an underground aeroplane factory in World War II. Today, however, they are largely used as car parks.

Citizens of Naples living in the caves, 1945.

Subterranean Morelli car park beneath Naples, 1992.

Caves and tunnels below Naples, 400 BCE–present.

Stockholm's T-Centralen, an enormous metro hub below ground, first opened 1957, extended in 1975 and again in 2009.

An immense demand for space has pushed the mechanics of our lives underground. Over the last 200 years, virtually every urban lifeline, ninety per cent of our transport infrastructure and a colossal amount of cables, pipes, wires and tunnels have been buried. In their midst, buildings have grown downward, digging out more and more space to support structure, services and the pesky car. This space beneath our feet has become essential. A subterranean city grows beneath the city above, an ingenious space-saving solution for our ever-expanding cities. In Kansas City, ten per cent of the total commercial real estate is underground. Since 1964, space has been carved from a 270-million-year-old limestone deposit to create SubTropolis, the world's largest underground business complex.

SubTropolis is serviced by 13 kilometres of road and 3 kilometres of rail.

The constant internal temperature makes it the perfect place for data centres and archives.

Plan of SubTropolis, Kansas City, USA. The total excavated mine covers over five million square metres.

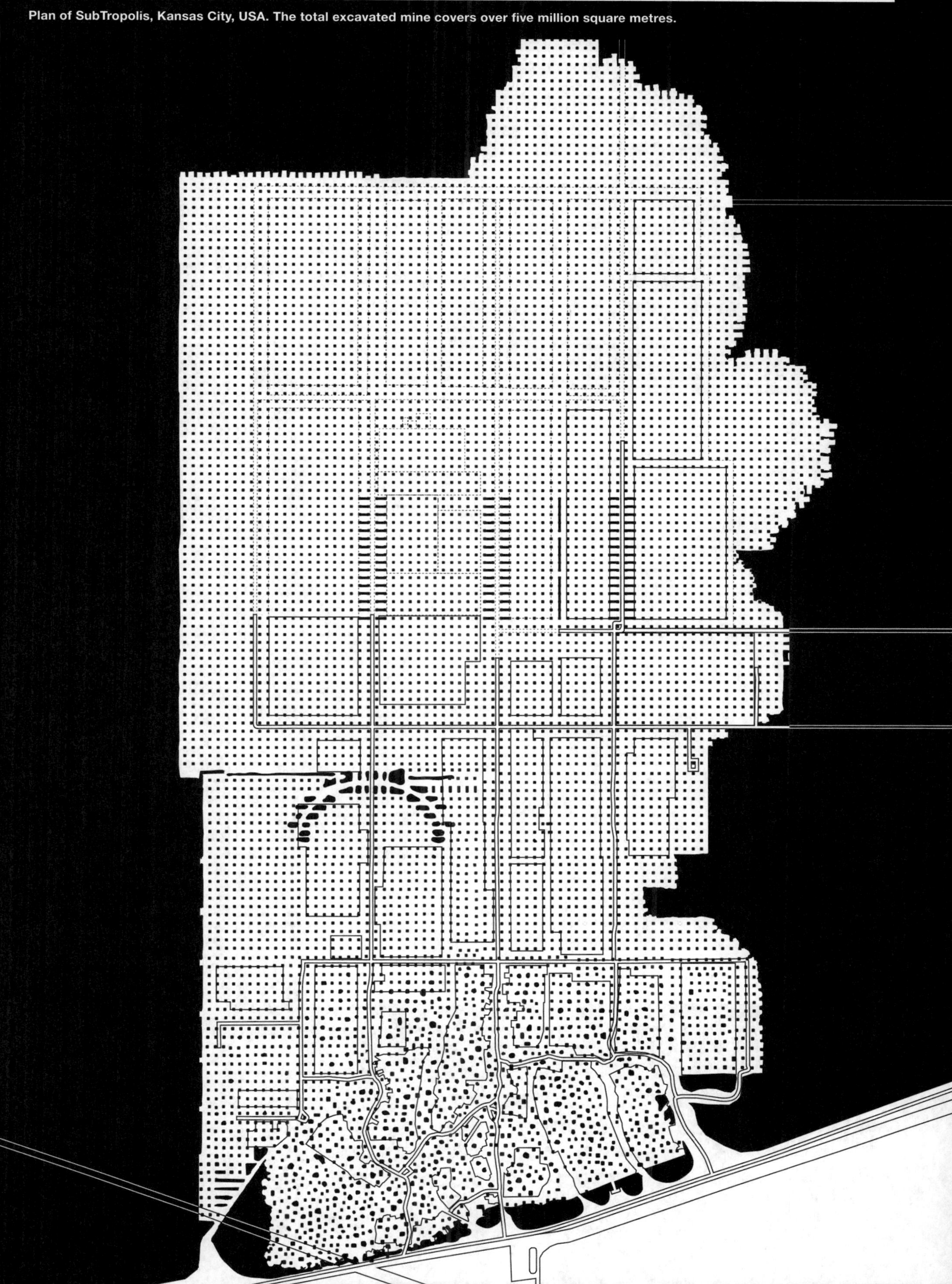

Further densification has begged for several other programmes to follow suit. The new is tucked below so as not to interfere with the image of a crystallized, memorialized past. In museums all over the world, the underground extension strategy is by far the most preferred option. In this scenario, UNESCO heritage arguments seem to be decisive, but if you ask the organization, it's a bit like discussions between the EU and national governments. The city administrations and UNESCO blame each other for the misconception that going underground is the only option. Regardless, extending the collections of historic museums underground has become the status quo. The Grand Louvre in Paris and the Rijksmuseum in Amsterdam are tiny in comparison to the extensions built beneath them.

Looking up through the foundations, sewers and wires of the city in David Macaulay's fascinating children's book *Underground*, 1976.

How strange that we put so much of our history, our most beloved artefacts, underground and out of sight. Why do we relegate them to the same space as the infrastructure of modern life? Unsightly power lines, wires, pipes, transport tunnels and drains banished from our streetscapes are woven around the objects we pay to see.

A. Silkeborg Museum, Silkeborg, Denmark, Jørn Utzon, 1963 (unbuilt).
B. Musée Gallo-Romain, Lyon, France, Bernard Zehrfuss, 1966–1975.
C. Louvre extension, Paris, France, I. M. Pei, 1983–1989.
D. Rijksmuseum, Amsterdam, Netherlands, Cruz y Ortiz Architects, 2001–2013.
E. Museum Judenplatz, Vienna, Austria, Jabornegg & Palffy, 2000.
F. Andalucia's Museum of Memory, Granada, Spain, Alberto Campo Baeza, 2005–2010.
G. Städel Museum, Frankfurt, Germany, Schneider+Schumacher, 2007.
H. Chichu Art Museum, Naoshima, Japan, Tadao Ando, 2008.
I. Earthquake Museum, Wenchuan, China, Cai Yongjie and Cao Ye, 2008.
J. New Acropolis Museum, Athens, Greece, Bernard Tschumi, 2009.
K. Museo del Bicentenario, Buenos Aires, Argentina, B4FS Arquitectos, 2009.
L. Joanneum Museum extension, Graz, Austria, Nieto Sobejano, 2006–2011.
M. Open Air Exhibition Grounds of the Estonian Road Museum, Varbuse, Estonia, Salto AB, 2010.
N. Drents Museum, Assen, Netherlands, Erick van Egeraat, 2011.
O. Museum of Sacred Art, Adeje, Spain, Menis Arquitectos, 2006–2011.
P. Department of Islamic Arts, Louvre Museum, Paris, France, Mario Bellini Architects, Rudy Ricciotti, 2012.
Q. Danish Maritime Museum, Copenhagen, Denmark, BIG, 2013.
R. Amos Rex, Helsinki, Finland, JKMM, 2013.
S. Archeopark Pavlov, Pavlov, Czech Republic, Architektonicka kancelar Radko Kvet, 2016.
T. TIRPITZ, Blåvand, Denmark, BIG, 2017.
U. Lascaux IV, Lascaux, France, Snøhetta + Duncan Lewis Scape Architecture, 2017.

Plan of the wine cellars of Cricova, built within the tunnels of a fifteenth-century limestone mine.

The regulating temperature of the earth also makes it an opportune place in which to bury our (liquid) treasures. In recent times, the subterranean wine cellar has become the subterranean winery. The surge in this underground typology is noticeable, culminating in the extraordinary Antinori Winery by Archea Associati, near Florence. Here the client, the twenty-seventh generation of the Marquis family, made the difference. Their profound commitment to this typology meant that any delay or extra costs associated with what seemed at first a simple project was absorbed and accepted.

A. Bodegas Ysios, Laguardia, Spain, Santiago Calatrava, 1998–2001.
B. Quintessa, California, USA, Walker Warner Architects, 2000–2006.
C. Niepoort Vinhos, Vila Nova de Gaia, Portugal, Andreas Burghardt, 2000–2008.
D. Tenuta Manincor, Caldaro, Italy, Rainer Köberl, Walter Angonese, 2001.
E. Distilleria Nardini, Bassano del Grappa, Italy, Massimiliano and Doriana Fuksas, 2002–2004.
F. Peregrine Winery, Queenstown, New Zealand, Architecture Workshop, 2003–2004.
G. Faustino Winery, Gumiel de Izán, Spain, Foster + Partners, 2004–2010.
H. Leo Hillinger Winery, Jois, Austria, Gerner Gerner Plus, 2004.
I. Bodega Clos Apalta, Colchagua, Chile, Roberto Benavente & Amercanda, 2004–2012.
J. Cascina Adelaide, Barolo, Italy, Archicura, 2004.
K. Antinori Winery, Bargino, Italy, Archea Associati, 2004–2013.
L. Winery Cheval Blanc, Saint-Emilion, France, Christian de Portzamparc, 2006–2011.

The meditative power and pleasure of the underground structure is experiencing a renaissance in the West. At one end of the scale sits the eco-home or earth shelter, a response to our precarious environmental situation. At the other are opulent mansions, which bury their cars, pools, cellars, gyms, cinemas and galleries below ground. In London, Roger Burrows has uncovered a 'luxified troglodytism' where one, two and three-storey luxury basements (larger than the average UK home) are being excavated below ground.[5]

n London, luxury basement extensions are almost the same size as the homes above. Drawing by Sophie Baldwin and Elizabeth Holroyd.

Sadly, this fascination for subterranean space is not evenly spread. Until recently, an estimated forty million Chinese people lived in the Yaodong. But much of this is being swept away by modernization.[6] Adobe structures in the Dadès Valley in Morocco are meeting a similar fate. Globally, this earthen vernacular is being eroded at an incredible pace, only to be replaced by ubiquitous concrete units.

Corte San Pietro Hotel, Matera, Daniela Amoroso, 2012.

The tourism industry is doing its bit to resuscitate these habitats. The Yaodongs in China and the Sassi di Matera in Italy are being transformed into hotels for those who wish to get 'back to basics' with a smattering of luxury. The jury is still out on whether this represents a preservation or perversion of these underground structures, but the tourist looks like a necessary evil in combating the shrinking biodiversity of our habitats.

The underground building inverts a modern fascination with size, height and facade. To bury architecture alive is to force it to engage with the interior, to communicate its value not through visual expression or image but through its use and its users' experiences. Although rooted in pragmatism, the power and poetry of this architecture is undeniable. This architecture by subtraction successfully blurs the line between architecture and ground.

Ancient cave dwellings below the city of Matera, Italy.

Not all underground developments are successful. In our research we have seen that digging down carries the same risk as stretching upwards. A desire for greater control often breeds isolation, alienation and disconnection.

The success (or failure) of these underground structures can be found in the degree of enclosure and how they manage often-competing interests of enclosure, light, depth and orientation. Those that are successful blur the line between building and ground. They shift their expression from plan to section to confront and design the connection between the context above and space below. This moment of exchange within the crust of the earth is where their intelligence lies.

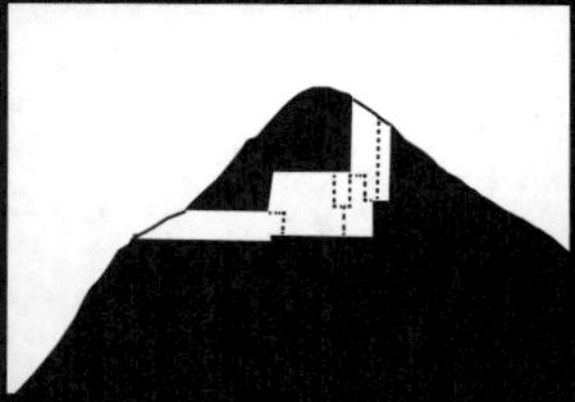

The Yaodong
Loess Plateau, China
300 BCE–present

Both Mao Zedong and Xi Jinping lived in a cave dwelling for several years. Mao used the time he spent here for reading, writing and gardening right after the Long March in 1935, when his ascent to power started. Xi was sent to the Shaanxi province for educational purposes in 1968. He immediately escaped, but his mother allowed him to be sent back, and he lived another seven years in a cave. He only cried twice: when he was sent down to this region and when he moved away in 1975, both in sorrow. It shaped their lives and is in some way proof of the classless qualities of the Yaodong.

Mao Zedong, Yan'an cave dwelling, 1938.

"The cave the Chinese president called home". Xi Jinping visits former cave dwelling in Liangjiahe, 2015.

Subterranean dwellings arranged around a sunken courtyard.

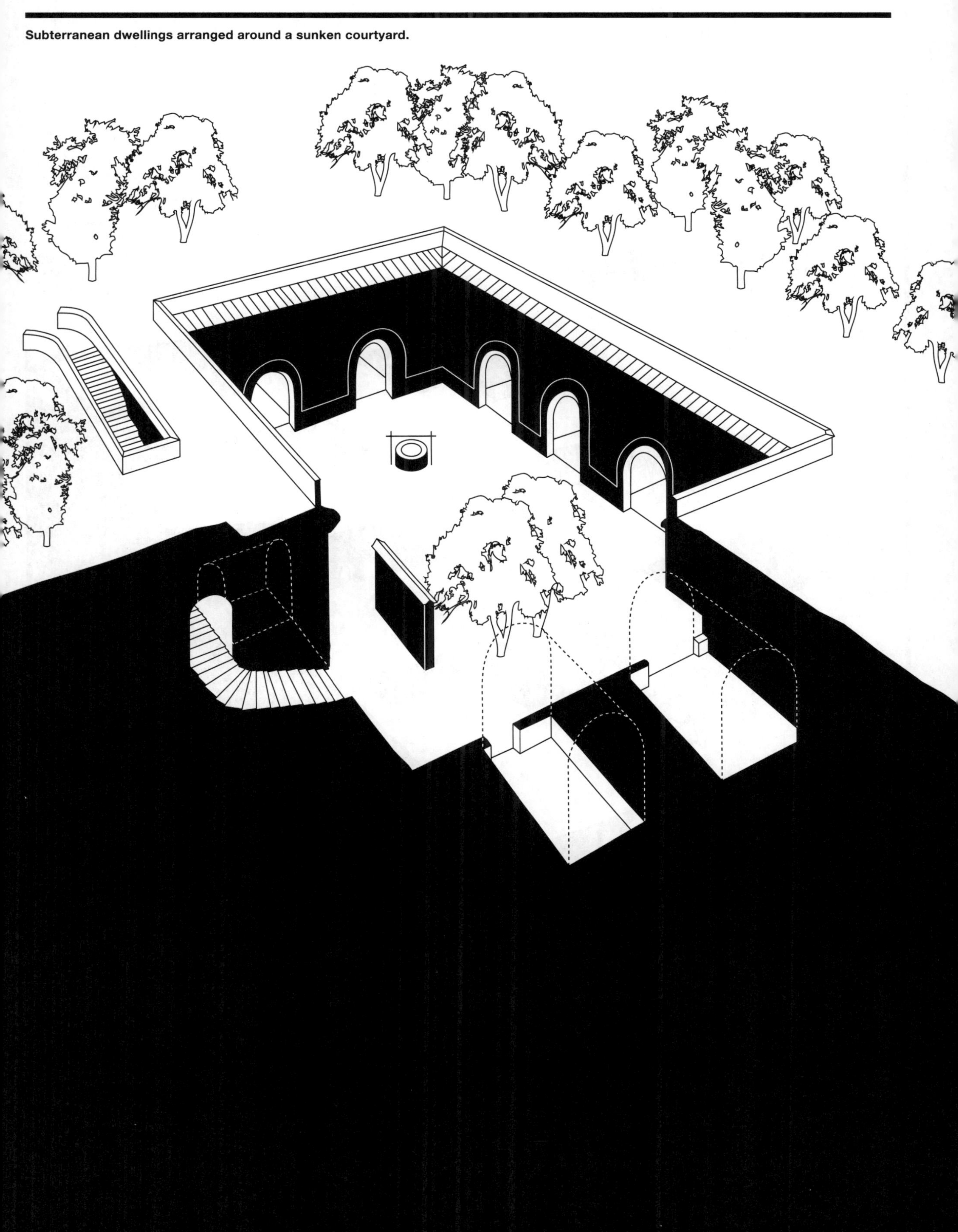

Sectional axonometry of Xi Village, Gong County, Henan.

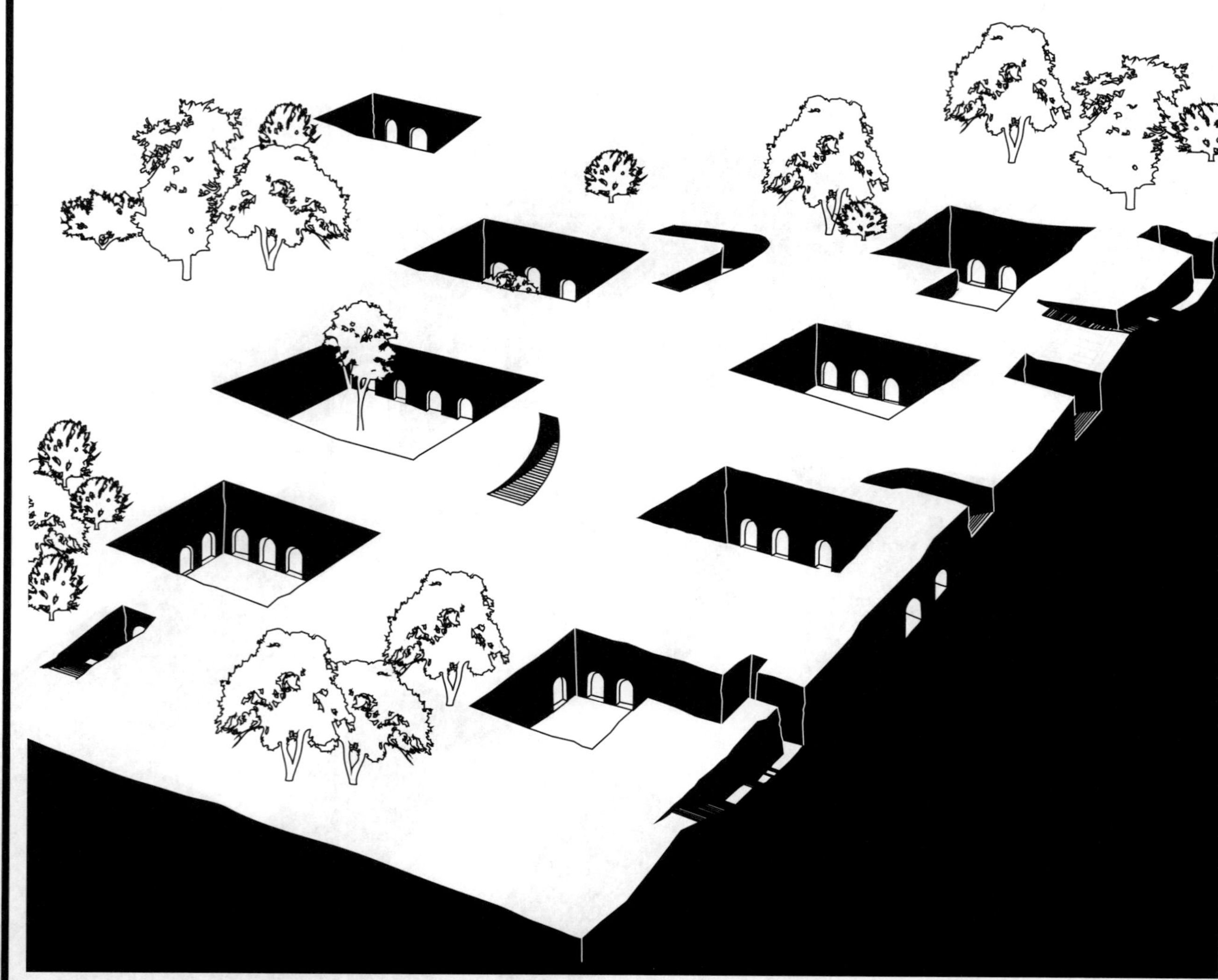

Constructed within the incredibly porous ground of China's Loess Plateau, the Yaodong epitomizes an architecture of subtraction. Here, villages are carved out of the flat plain or the sides of valleys. It is an excavation born out of necessity. The vast landscape offers very little to construct with, is highly exposed to weather and experiences sharp fluctuations in temperature, from hot days to cold nights. The Loess Plateau is a landscape sculpted by wind. Layers upon layers of dust blown in from the Mu Us Desert have accumulated to form a highly erodible, yet fertile condition. Exploiting this, the Yaodong digs down, arranging a series of underground dwellings around a sunken courtyard, open to the sky and leaving much of the productive surface above available for farming.

温馨家园
天天向上鋪就錦綉前
步步登高创造宏基伟業

福

奇强

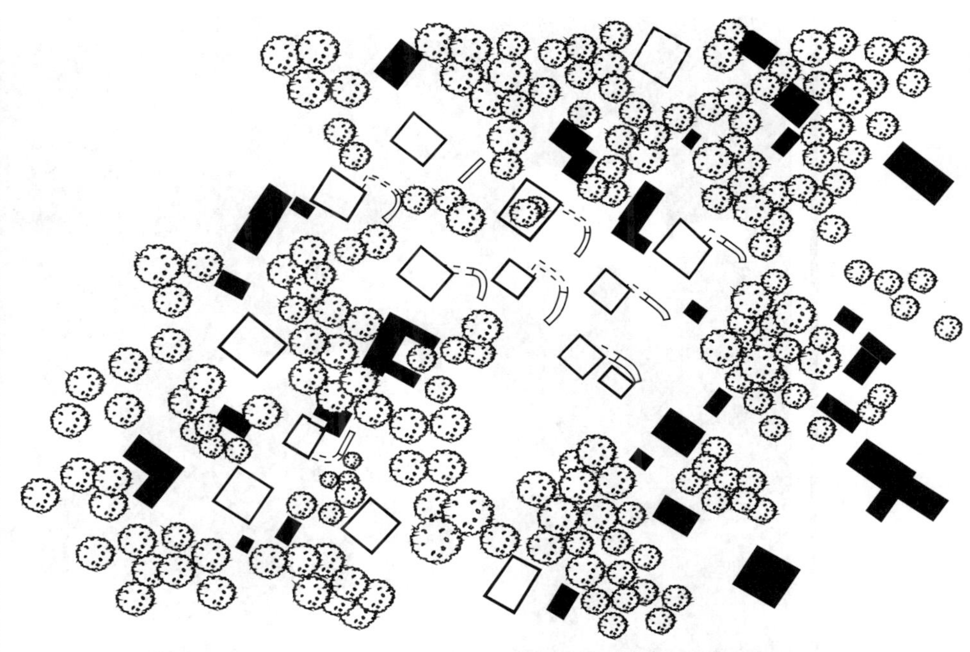

Section and site plan of Yaodong dwellings.

The Yaodong emulates traditional Chinese neighbourhoods above ground. It is as if the walled courtyard dwellings of the *Siheyuan* are lowered five metres into the ground and narrow *Hutong* are excavated between them. The Yaodong represents an architecture responsive to its context, a way of building derived from physical, economic and social considerations.

What makes this typology distinctive is the presence of a community, literally looking down on each family living around a sunken courtyard. This is clearly a community protecting its members instead of looking for privacy or retreating from society.

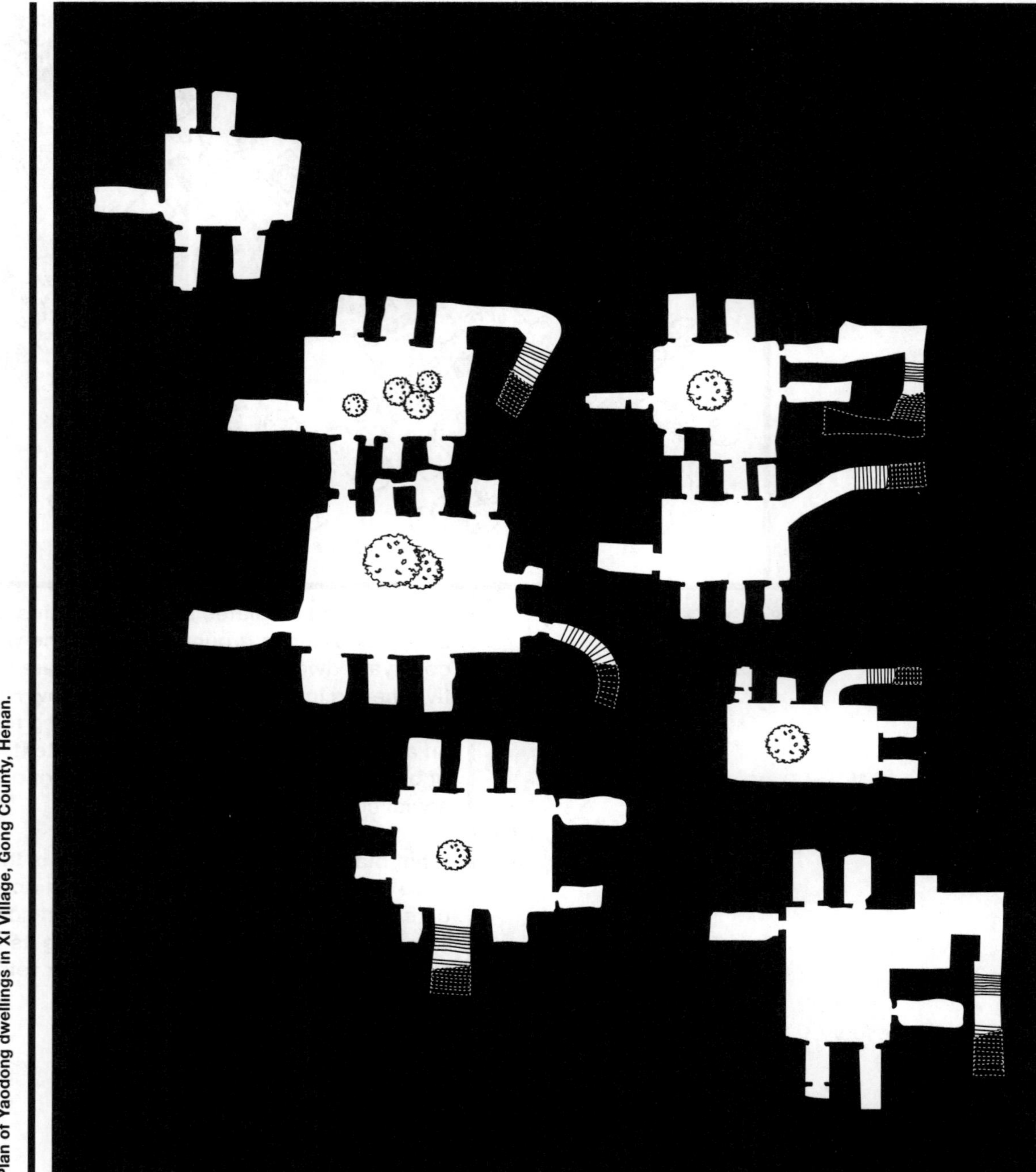

Plan of Yaodong dwellings in Xi Village, Gong County, Henan.

But this way of life and these ingenious structures are being eroded by China's rapid urbanization. An estimated ninety per cent of the forty million inhabitants on the vast Loess Plateau still lived in cave dwellings in 2005. But in analysing satellite images, you can see the amazing checkerboard pattern of sunken patios being replaced by corrugated sheet sheds, leaving the adjacent Yaodongs to implode and be used as a farmer's waste bin. We may bear witness to their disappearance in our lifetime.

Is this alarming? The younger generation no longer wishes to live in a cave; they long for a 'modern' concrete house. The same could be said of Ethiopia, Kenya or Nigeria, where straw and adobe housing is being replaced by standardized four- to six-storey concrete structures, built by the Chinese in return for agricultural and mining leases.[7]

The radical erasure of two Yaodong villages, 2005–2016.
© 2005 & 2016 Digital Globe, Google Earth.

Paradoxically, renewed scientific interest shows that Yaodong cave dwellings perform far better than a standard brick house in the same conditions, and a modernized cave dwelling could reduce energy consumption by eighty-three per cent. The potential of this typology should be obvious; but unfortunately, the real benefits will probably only be clear when most of the dwellings are history.[8]

Kailasa Temple
Ellora, India
756–773 CE

More than any other region in the world, India possesses the most intricate art in rock sculpture. Although the ancient civilization of the Indus Valley was thoroughly capable of building extensive cities with sophisticated infrastructure by 2500 BCE, carving spaces from rock continued up until the sixteenth century.[9]

Interior of Lomas Rishi cave.

Lomas Rishi cave entrance, 260 BCE.

Early rock caves exhibit interesting details. At Barabar Hills in Bihar, the Lomas Rishi cave is an exact copy of a wooden structure cut into the living rock, including the planking and even straw ceilings on the inside of the room. The cave entrance is a perfect imitation of the gable end of a wooden structure, including wood details completely chiselled in stone.

Building knowledge develops incredibly slowly. Techniques and tools are added and structure is tested and calibrated, almost like a biological evolution. The Shore Temple of Mahabalipuram was built as a free-standing temple completely cut from whale-backed rock. Despite having a new and novel form, this temple employed known techniques. Stone was shaped into beam-heads, rafters and purlins, meticulously replicating a timber structure. What was the objective and intention of recording so faithfully and with such infinite toil each architectural type, as if it were a full-sized model?[10]

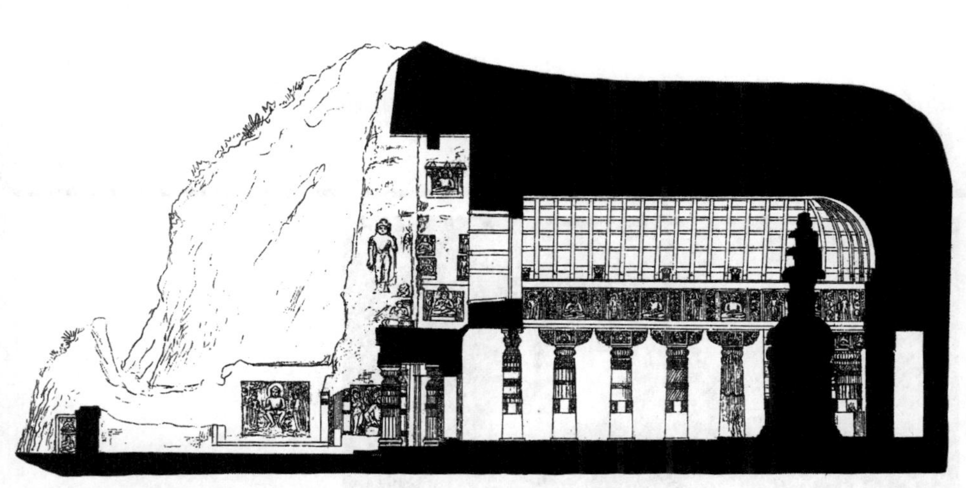

Section through Chaitya hall, 200–100 BCE.

Looking at early masonry temples in comparison to rock-cut structures built a century earlier, we see a considerable regression in conception and technique. It turns out that putting one stone on top of another so as to form a strong and shapely structure had a clumsy beginning. But masonry construction did advance architectural thought. Its free-standing nature revealed the exterior elevation, an aspect and dimension previously not considered by the rock architect, who dealt almost exclusively with the interior. Once perfected, masonry buildings were more pliant, more ductile, and in certain respects more durable.

It is like the transition from hunter-gatherer to farmer. There it took millennia to overcome the decline in health, strength and size, but in the end, it turned out to be an inevitable transition, born out of necessity and fuelled by growth. Building masonry temples was in part also a necessary solution to prevent scarcity. Buildings carved in stone were only to be found where the conditions were right, in cliff sides and exposed rock formations, while structures constructed in stone or other material could stand almost anywhere.

Still, we must not forget the highly efficient and economical way in which these carved-out structures were fashioned. For example, above the Chaitya hall porches is a large round opening.[11] It is from here that the temple was carved in situ from solid rock. Debris excavated from the interior was used to construct the forecourt in front of the facade. Beginning from above was practice, taking advantage of the rough rock below for footholds, thus dispensing with the need for scaffolding. In the interior the same procedure was followed; the ceiling or roof was first cut and completely finished, and the work gradually continued downwards.[12]

Built during this transitory period from rock sculpture towards masonry work, the Kailasa Temple at Ellora draws from both.

Section of the Kailasa Temple.

Kailasa Temple, section of central spine and three-storey columned arcades.

Kailasa Temple, lower floor plan.

Kailasa Temple, upper floor plan.

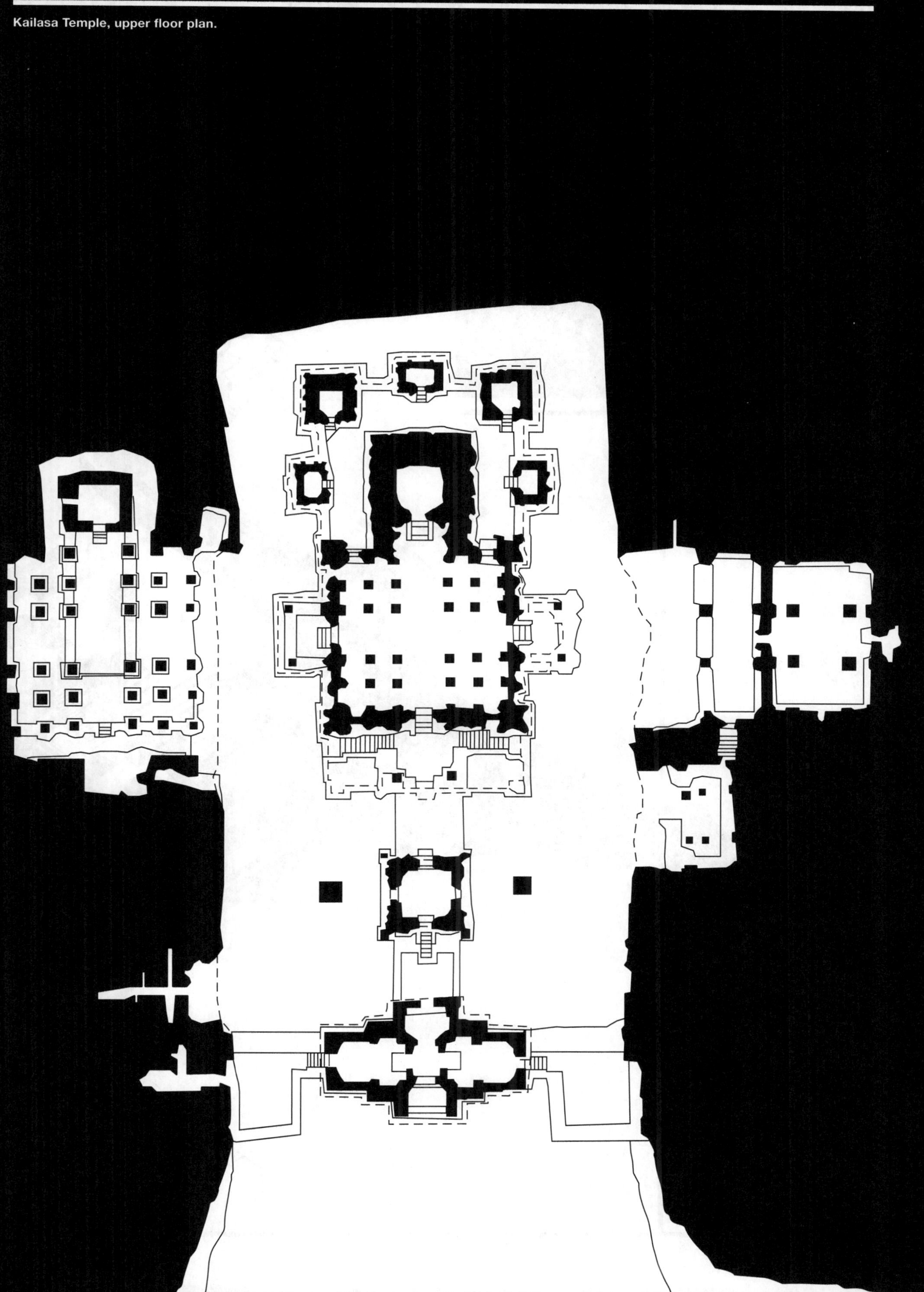

It is not purely an interior, for it reveals its facades as well. Here they chiselled from the top of the cliff down to build the largest and most intriguing temple out of one piece of solid rock.

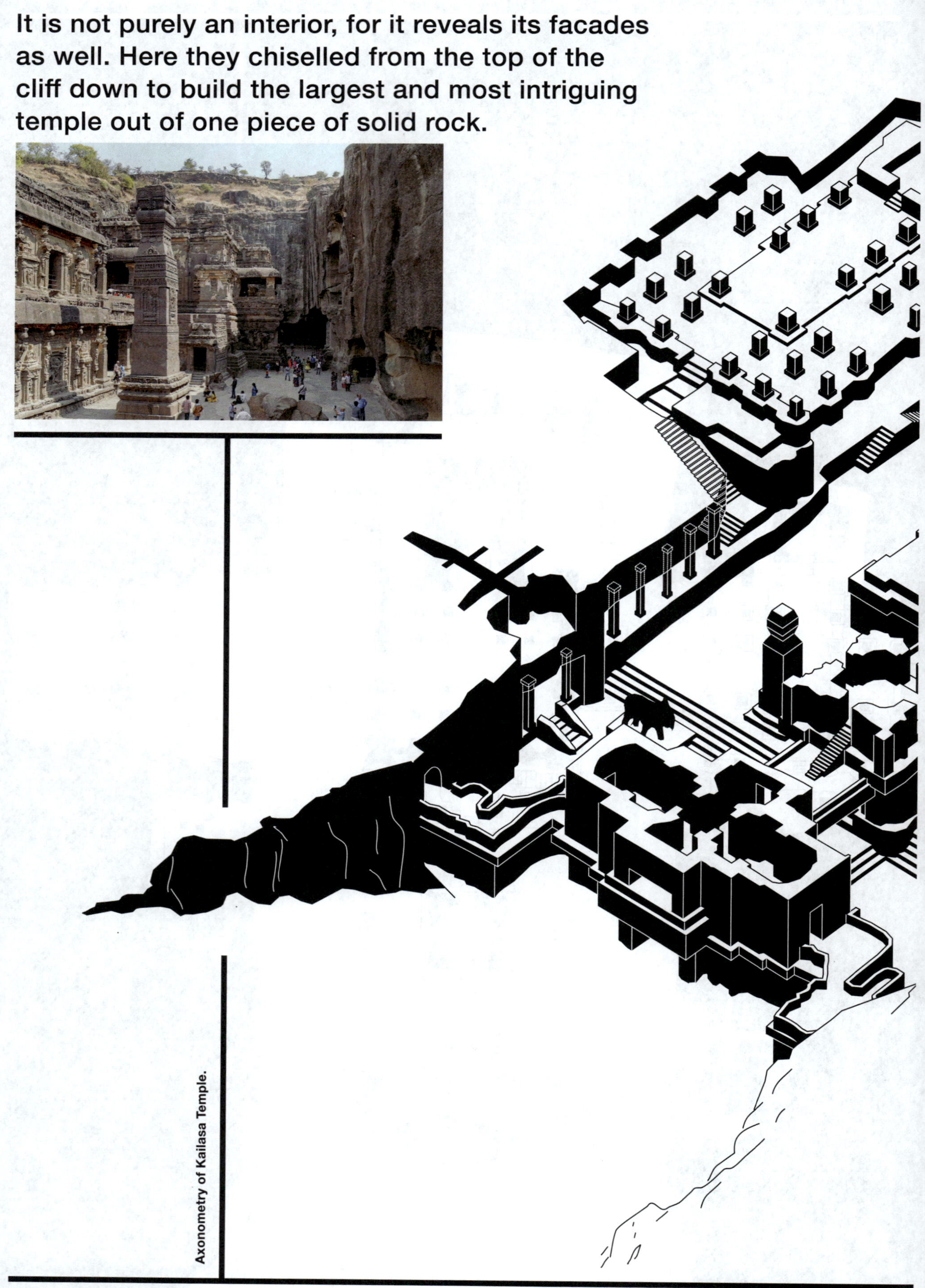

Axonometry of Kailasa Temple.

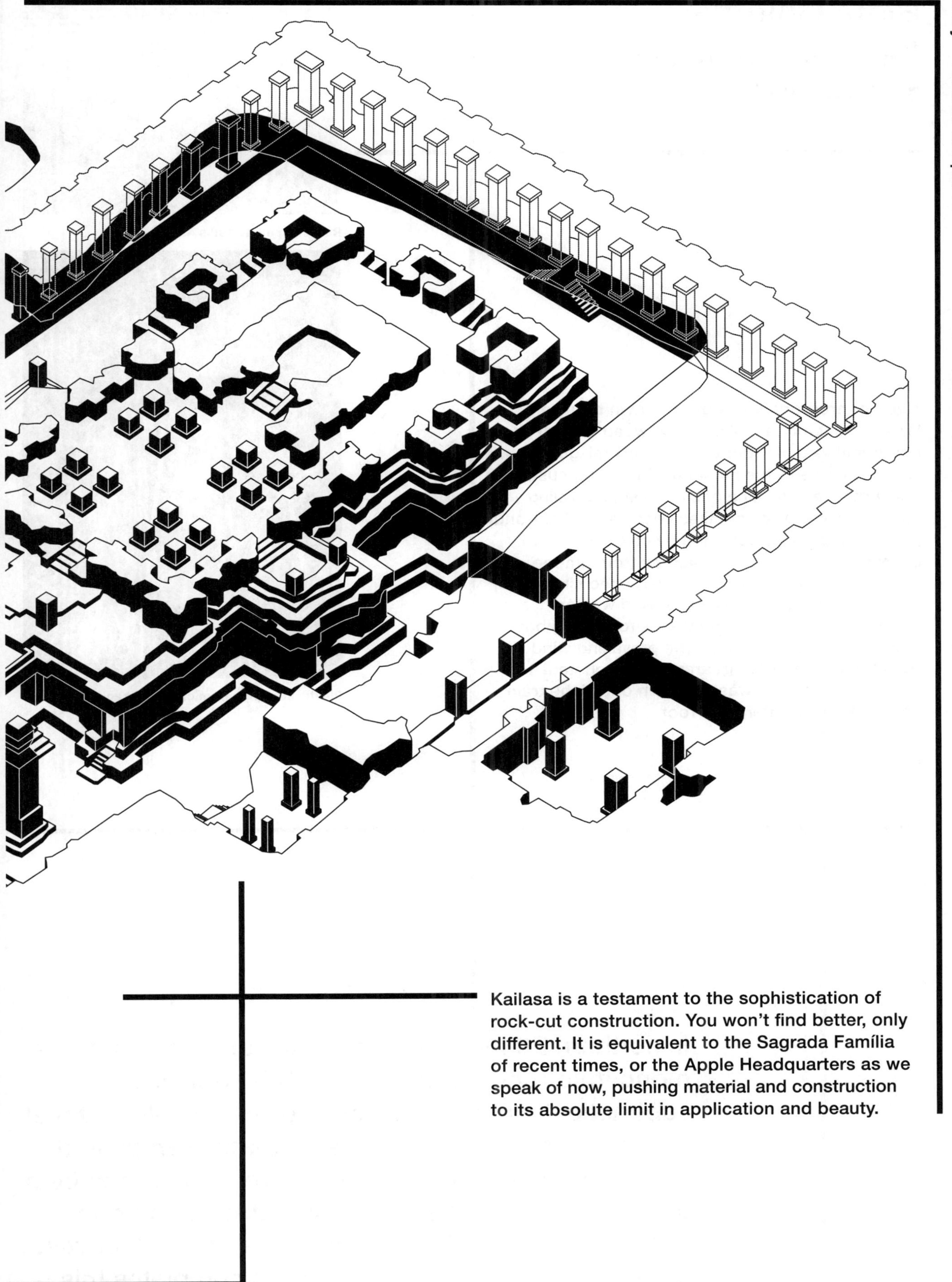

Kailasa is a testament to the sophistication of rock-cut construction. You won't find better, only different. It is equivalent to the Sagrada Família of recent times, or the Apple Headquarters as we speak of now, pushing material and construction to its absolute limit in application and beauty.

Biete Ghiorgis
Lalibela, Ethiopia
1100–1200

Recycling nails, Addis Ababa.

Plastic strapping from cargo packaging.

A rather arbitrary line is often drawn between Western society and Africa, between a modern and primitive state. But this is utterly misguided. Africa is home to the most intelligent and sustainable practices, the king of smart use, upcycling and efficiency. Worn-out tires become flip-flops and plastic strapping is collected by colour and sold on. Nails are endlessly reclaimed from timber structures, straightened and sharpened since it is cheaper than buying new ones. And why are all straw and mud huts along the railroad to Djibouti built on the Western side? The prevailing wind from the Gulf of Aden guarantees a constant accretion of plastic waste thrown out of the train and ideal for a waterproof roof.

In northern Ethiopia sits a complex of twelfth-century monolithic rock-cut churches. This ‘building by subtraction’ embodies a similar efficiency. No material is needed, only the ever-present earth. Ramps and staircases lead to an *enfilade* of covered antechambers and open courtyards. The monolithic *poché* conceals a complex of sacred rooms and monk caves. Smart drainage of all these cavities completes this.

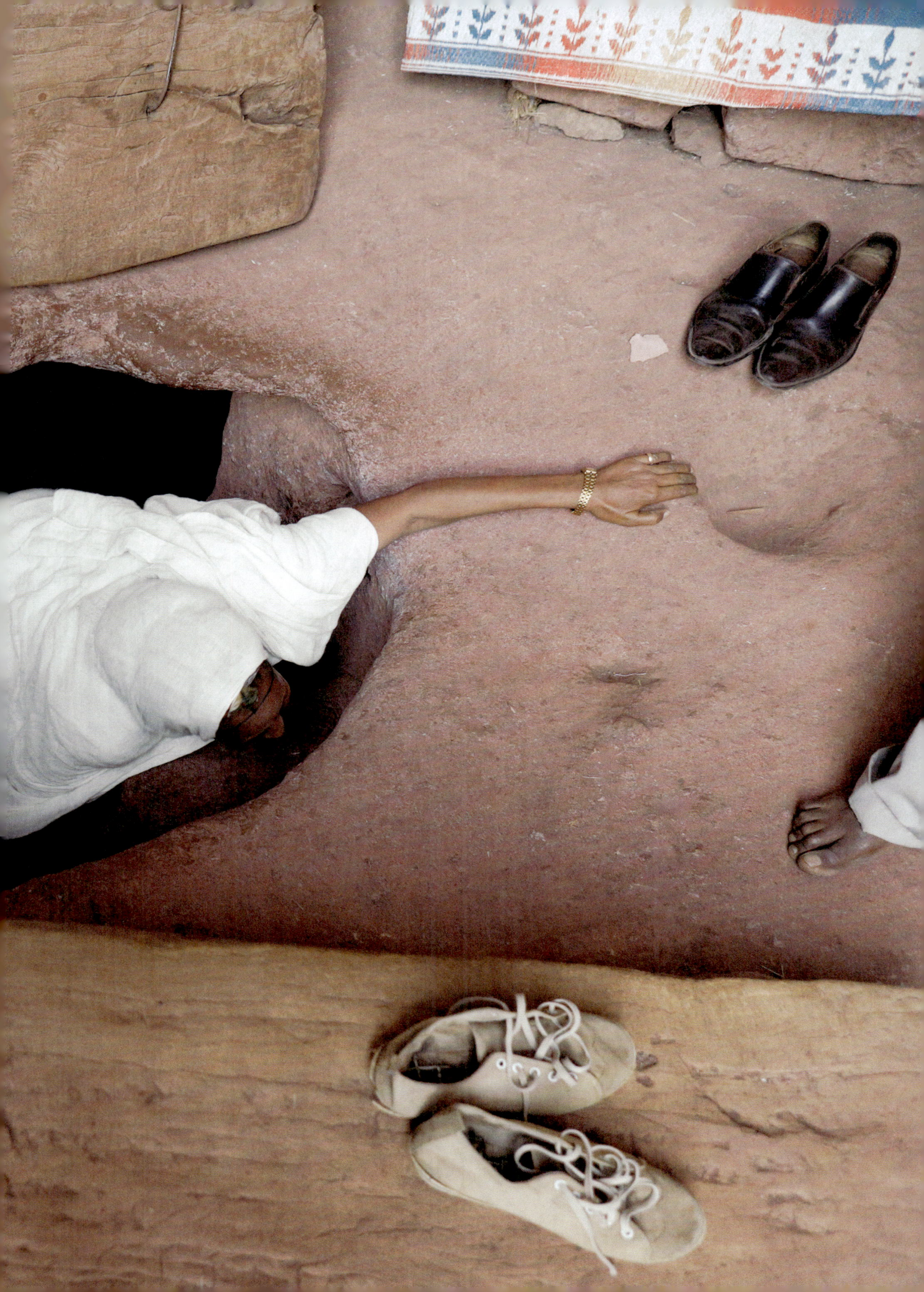

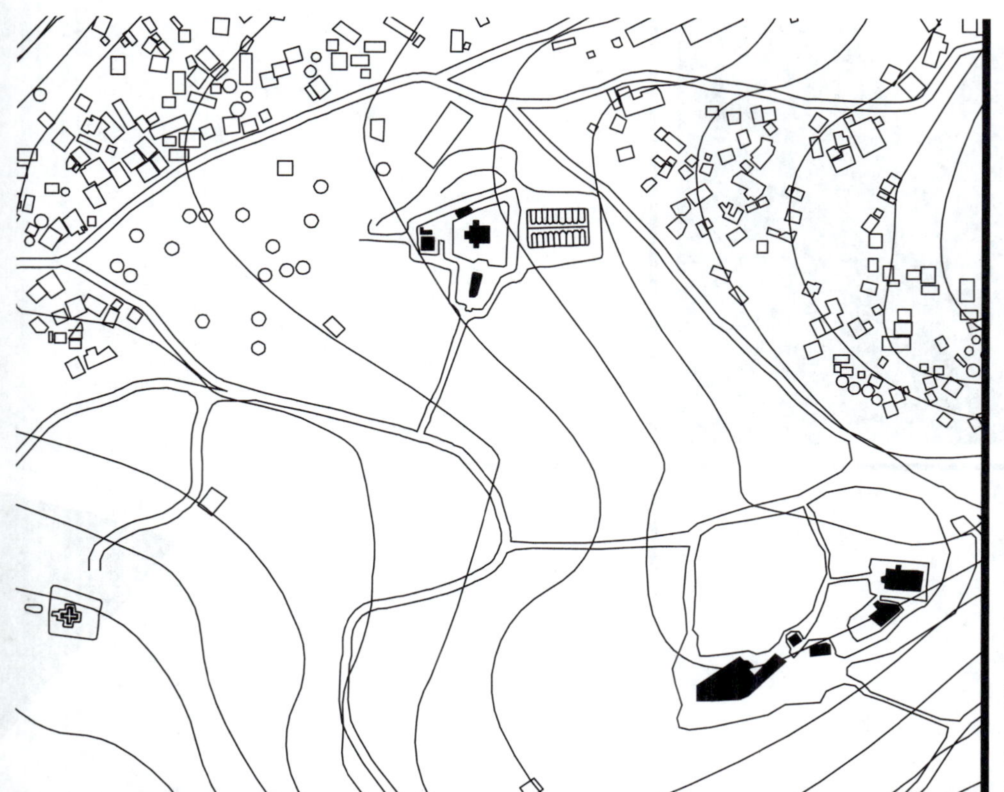

Site plan of Biete Ghiorgis in the mountain.

Lalibela was said to be the 'New Jerusalem', carved out of the rock landscape to symbolize spirituality and humility. When taking part in pilgrimage, people literally disappear into the ground and come up as if they were born again, thus undergoing a strong landscape experience.

At Biete Ghiorgis, the entry is via a slit in the earth, pictured here on the lower right.

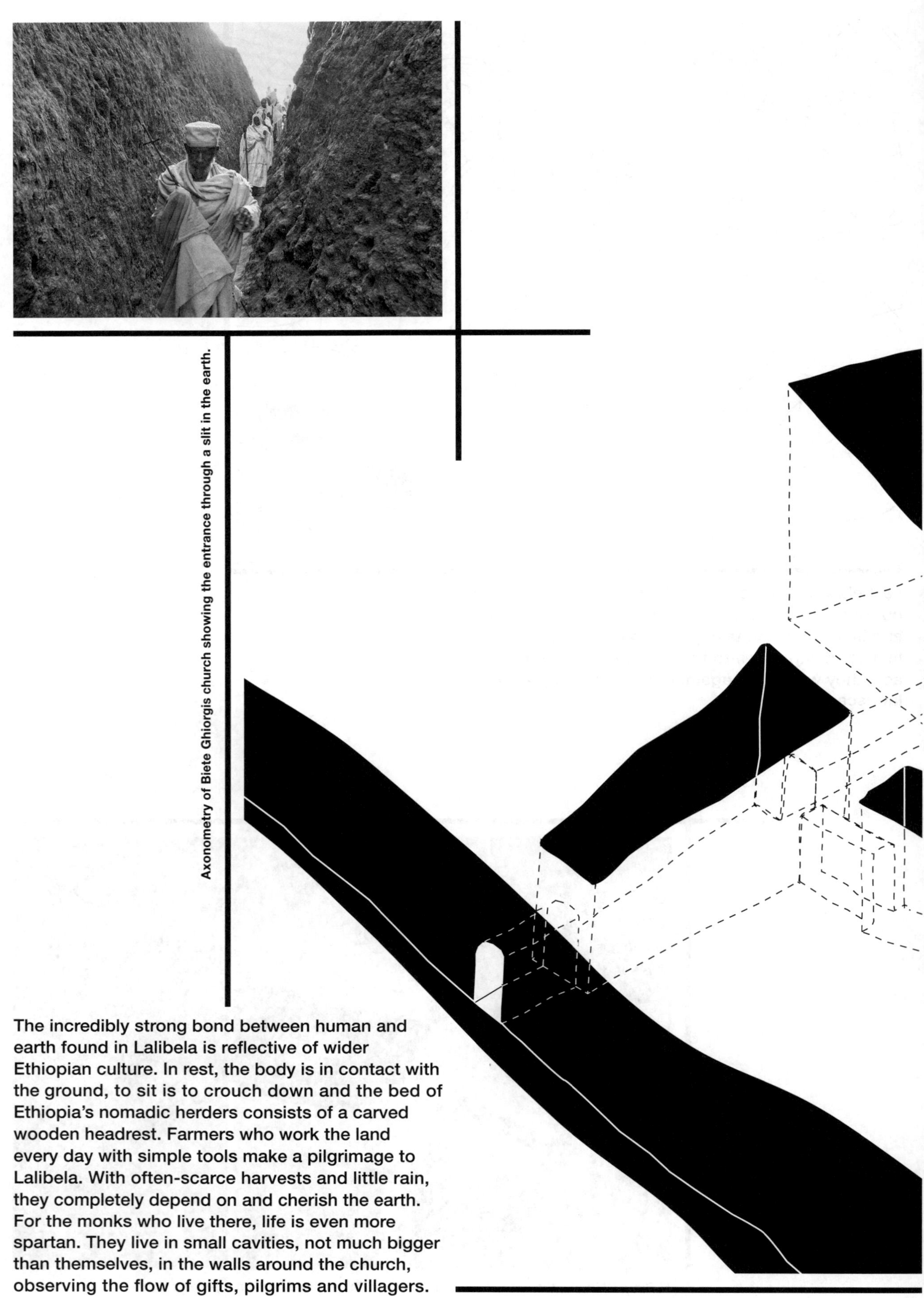

Axonometry of Biete Ghiorgis church showing the entrance through a slit in the earth.

The incredibly strong bond between human and earth found in Lalibela is reflective of wider Ethiopian culture. In rest, the body is in contact with the ground, to sit is to crouch down and the bed of Ethiopia's nomadic herders consists of a carved wooden headrest. Farmers who work the land every day with simple tools make a pilgrimage to Lalibela. With often-scarce harvests and little rain, they completely depend on and cherish the earth. For the monks who live there, life is even more spartan. They live in small cavities, not much bigger than themselves, in the walls around the church, observing the flow of gifts, pilgrims and villagers.

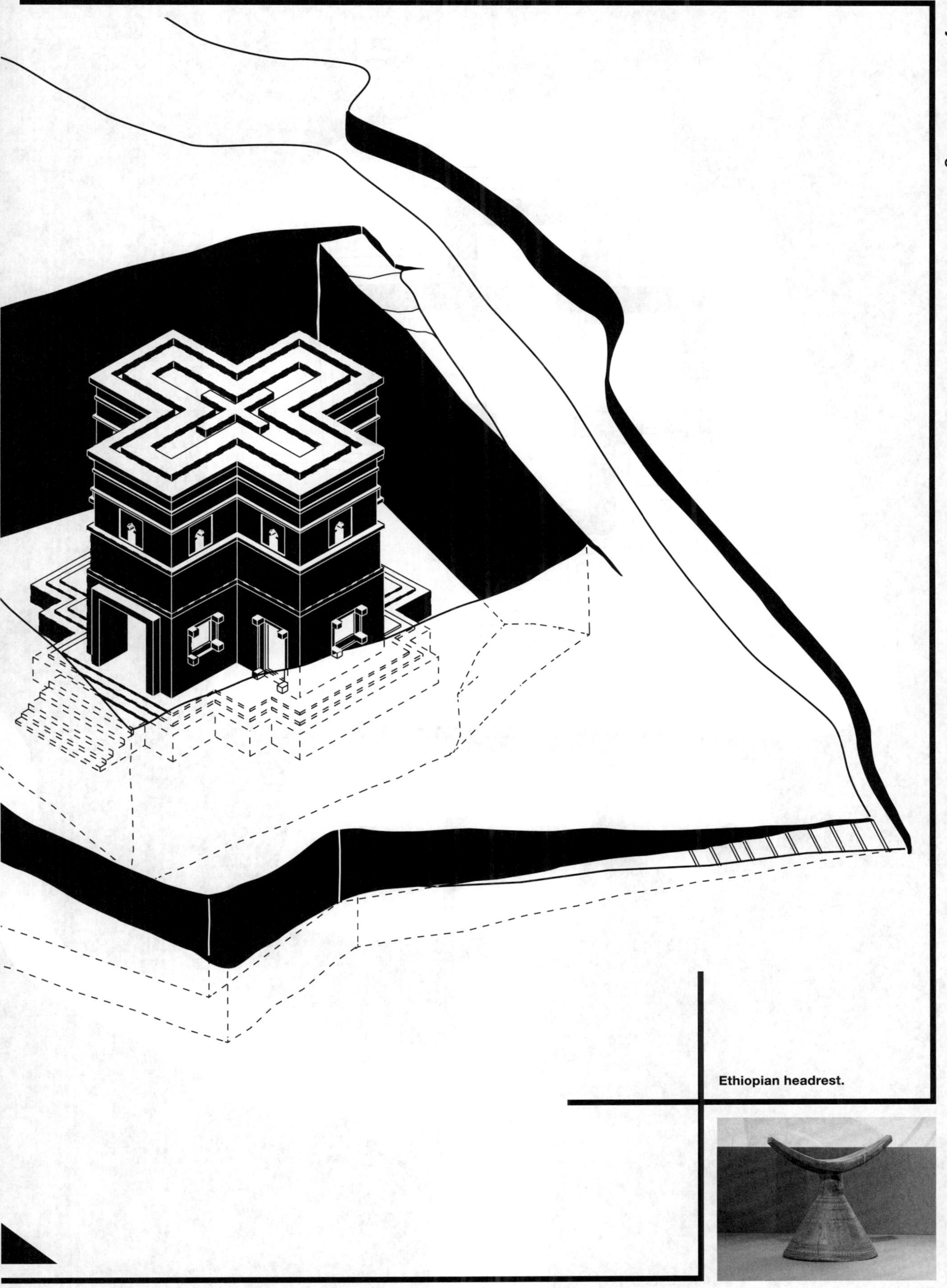

Ethiopian headrest.

Plan of Biete Ghiorgis.

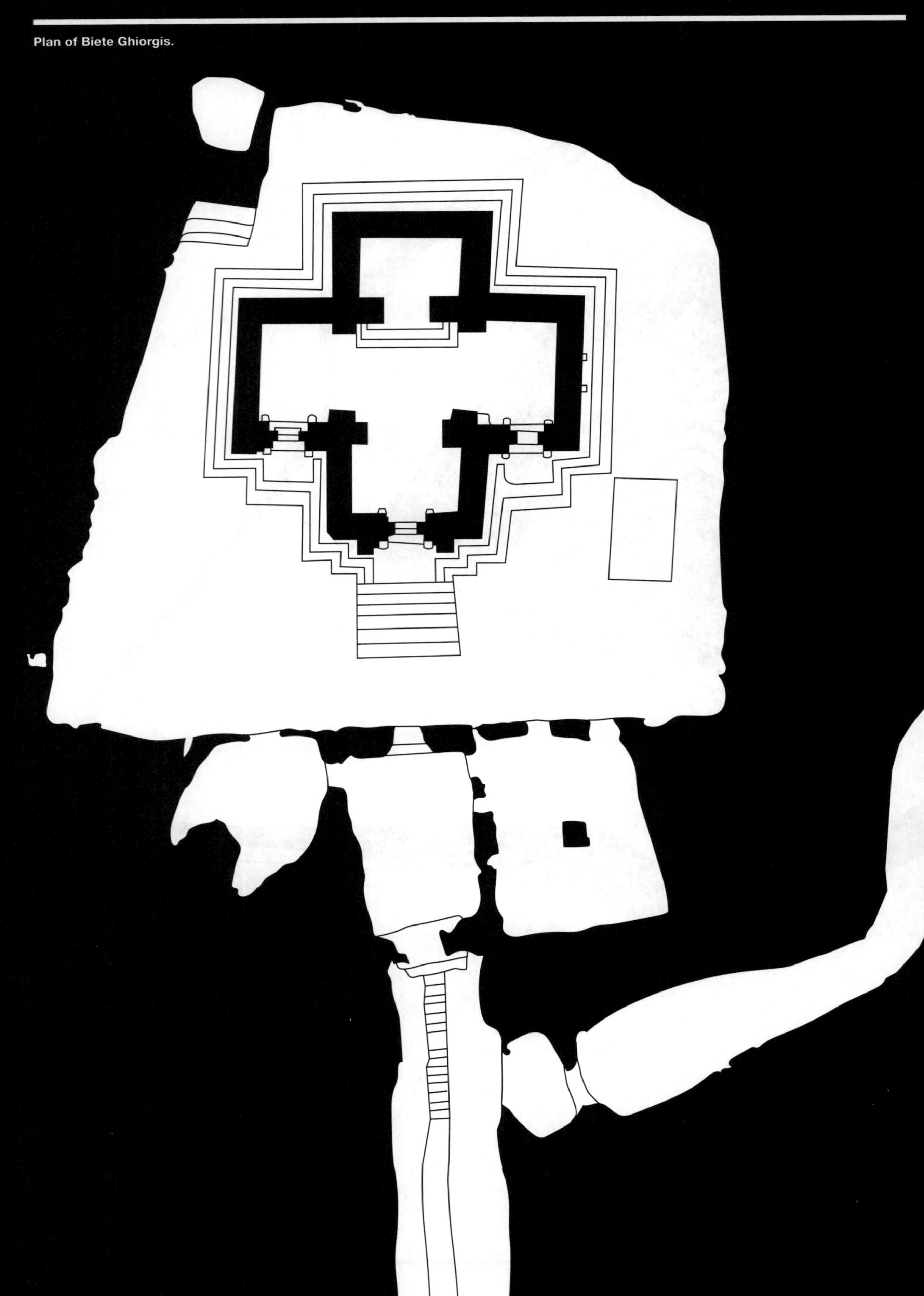

Despite the considerable difference in height between the landscape, the sunken courtyard around the church and the high platforms around the other churches, there is no fencing or security. Previous attempts to apply them have failed because people want to sit on the edge and witness the spectacle.

Section of Biete Ghiorgis through to the dry riverbed on the far left.

Although cut from the landscape, these spaces obey the rules of nature. They are still part of a continuous landscape with artificial ponds, riverbeds, grottoes and abysses, bringing with them the inconveniences and dangers.

Temppeliaukio Church
Helsinki, Finland
Timo & Tuomo Suomalainen
1961–1969

Newgrange burial mound, Ireland 3200 BCE.

Clava Clairn burial mound, Scotland, 2500 BCE.

Barclodiad y Gawres burial mound, Wales, 3000 BCE.

On a slightly elevated rock plate in central Helsinki a highly anachronistic scene unfolds. It is caught between a lava-like eruption, a Bronze Age burial mound and a UFO landing station. Temppeliaukio Church lies in the middle of this rocky city square, one city block in size. While the true volume of this domed church is hidden within the rock, the Brutalist concrete walls that line the base of the rock and the stonework that encircles the skylight atop signal its hiding place.

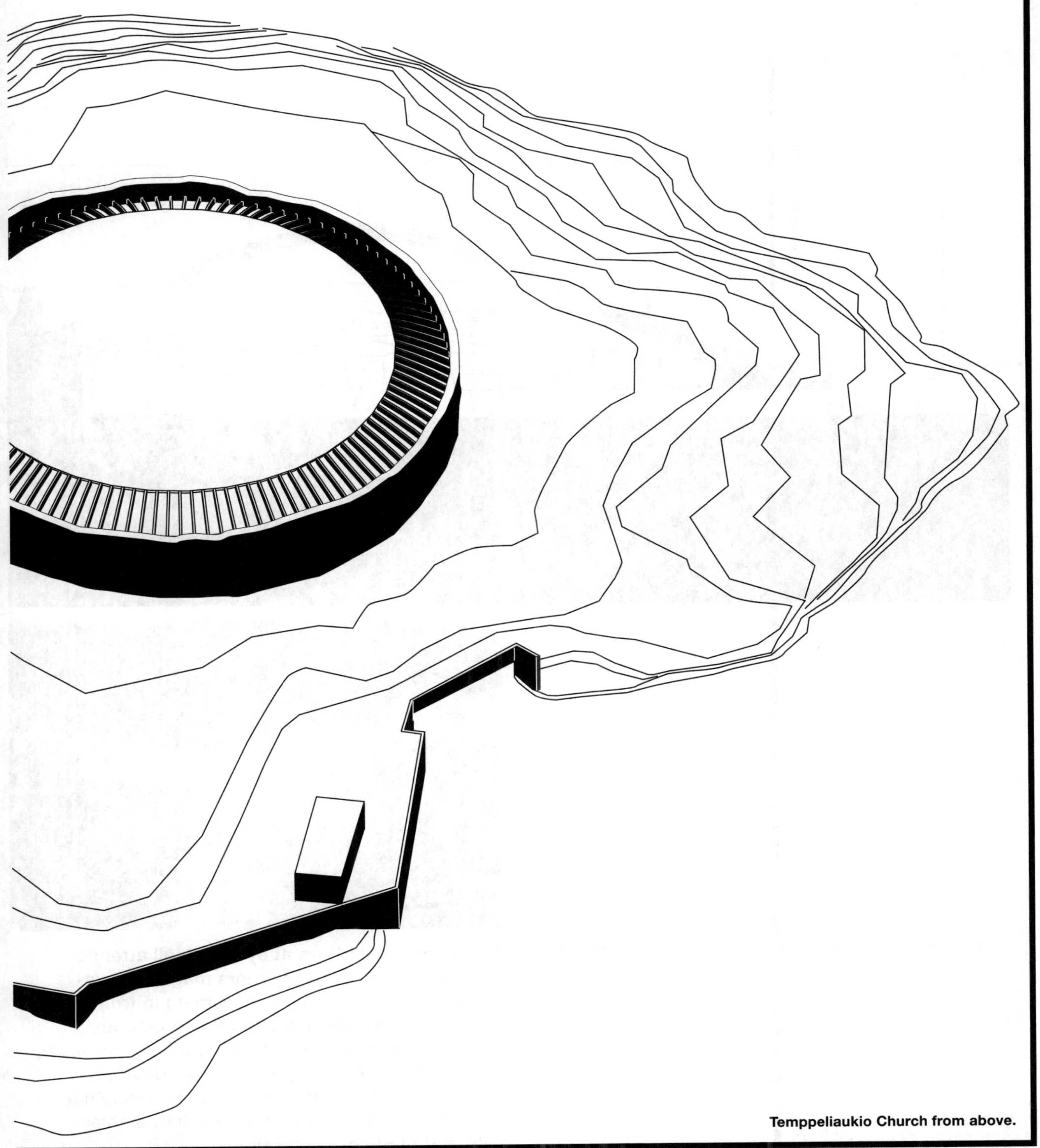

Temppeliaukio Church from above.

Excavating right into the rock and using the stone to build upwards creates a tall central hall. Thanks to the uneven walls of masonry and absorbent slits in the blocks, the space boasts excellent acoustics.

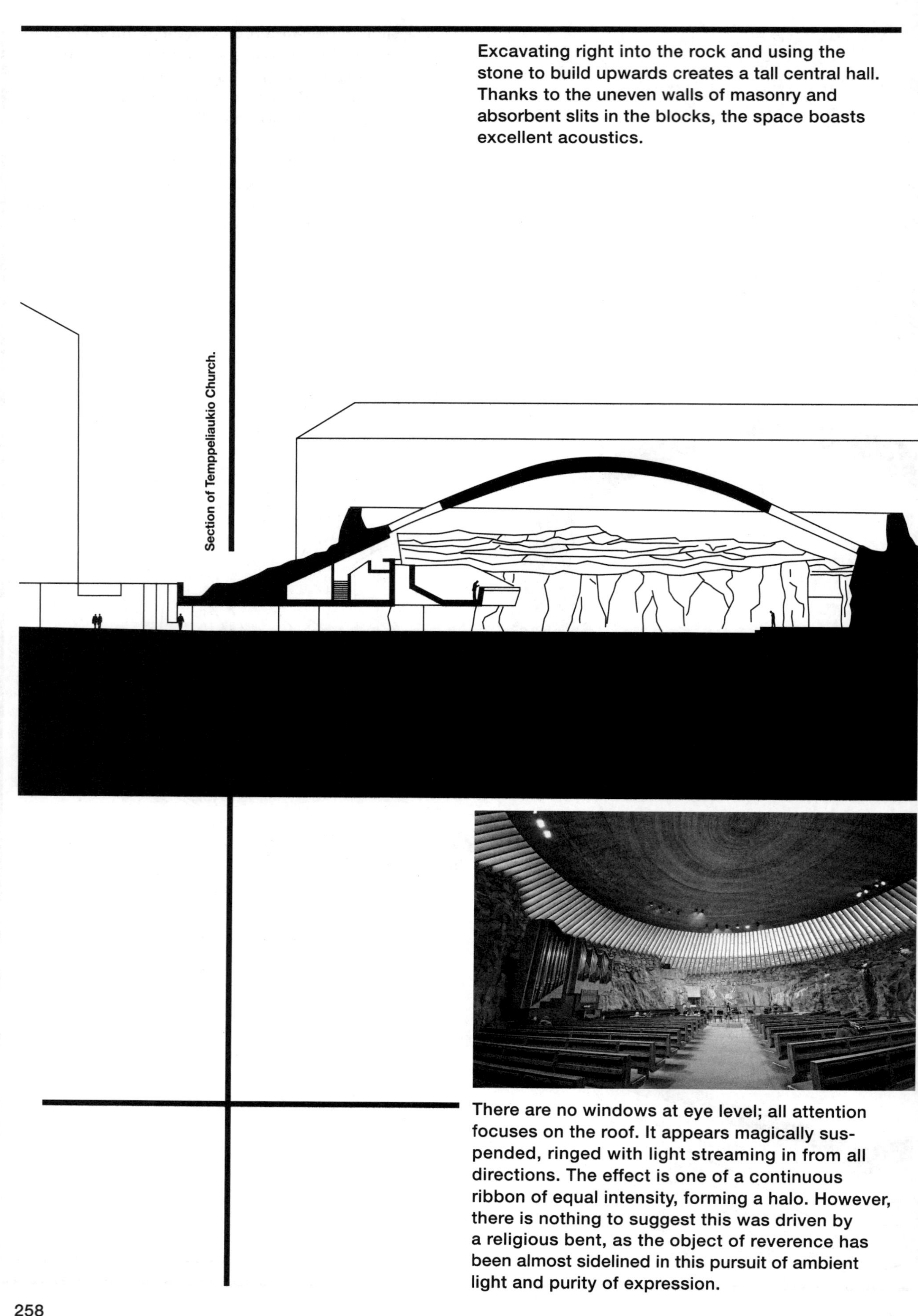

Section of Temppeliaukio Church.

There are no windows at eye level; all attention focuses on the roof. It appears magically suspended, ringed with light streaming in from all directions. The effect is one of a continuous ribbon of equal intensity, forming a halo. However, there is nothing to suggest this was driven by a religious bent, as the object of reverence has been almost sidelined in this pursuit of ambient light and purity of expression.

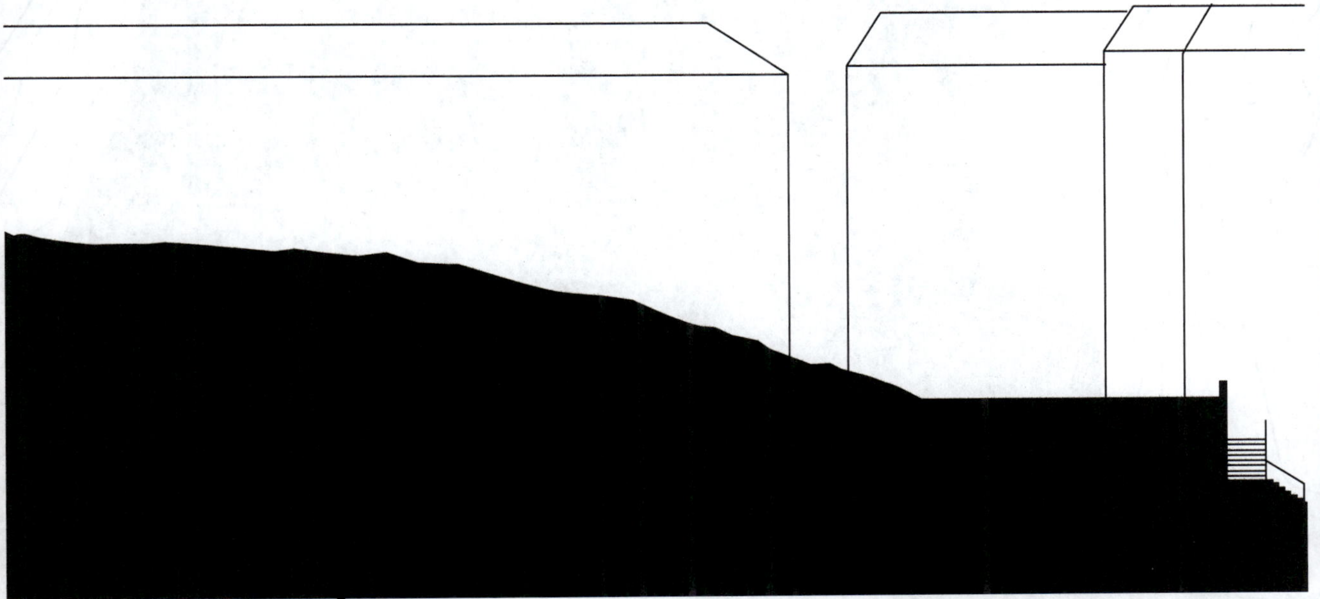

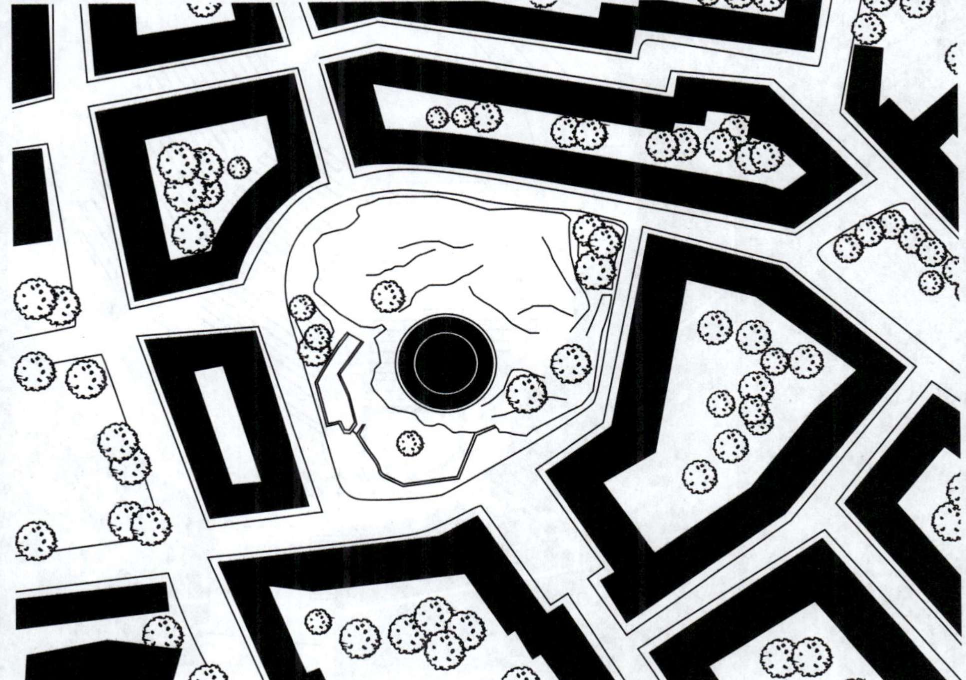

Site plan of Temppeliaukio Church.

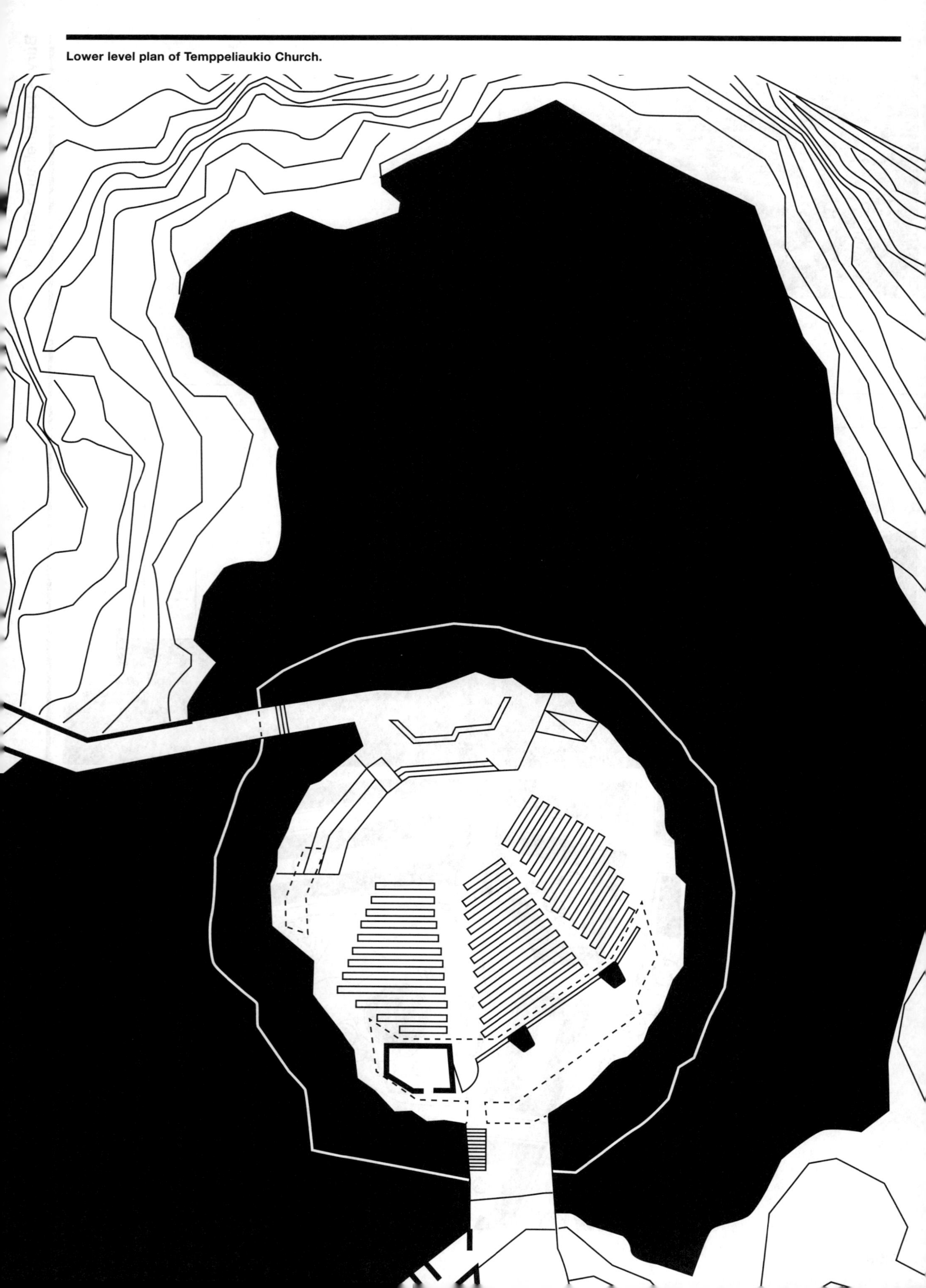

Lower level plan of Temppeliaukio Church.

The most spectacular architectural act is the conscious retreat from the everyday world to the revered space inside, with a complete absence of stimuli or cacophony from outside.[13] The design combines a park and a church in a compassionate way without any religious dominance. The level of the church floor and the height of the domed roof are perfectly calibrated. The church sits low, obstructing the park as little as possible, and the crown of the dome is raised by a two-metre-tall tomb-like base that prevents easy access to the delicate skylight and roof. Everybody shares, preserving the double function of this public space.

This minimalist approach is perhaps the biggest achievement of all, especially since it is achieved whilst referencing widely divergent moments of humanity. With such ease, this building links the Bronze Age to Brutalism.

Land Art

The 1960s were pivotal in history.[14] Against the backdrop of nuclear threat, economic instability and political disillusionment, a deep suspicion of the status quo developed in all facets of modern society. Citizens, mainly students, realized their potential to shape the world around them and began to mobilize.[15] A more participatory democracy, where government was more active yet held less authority, was demanded. An environmental movement grew rapidly, and society began not only to question unbridled land use, but also to actively legislate against it.[16]

This bold challenging of the establishment was echoed in both architectural discourse and the art world. As early as 1945, French painter Jean Dubuffet rebelled against a perceived elitism in art, launching art brut.[17] Dubuffet embraced the spontaneous and inventive character of art that originated from obscure people foreign to the professional artistic milieu. For Dubuffet, established art, or *art culturel*, was dominated by the 'clan of career intellectuals' and thus could never be honest.[18]

Wilderness Act of the United States, 1964.

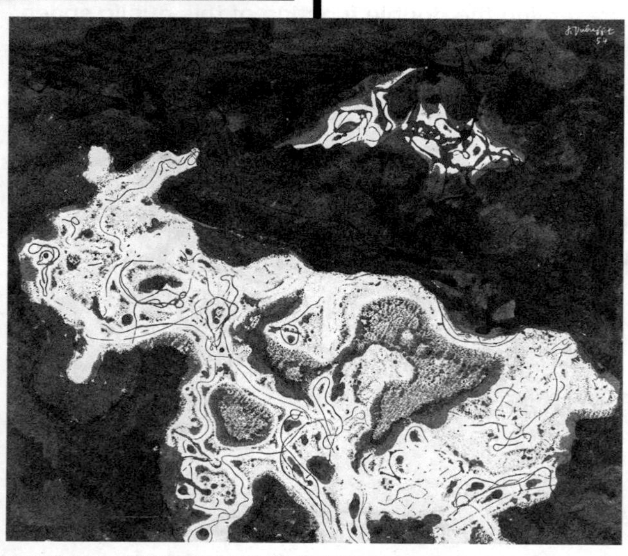

Goat with a Bird by Jean Dubuffet, 1954.

Running parallel to this, within architectural discourse, Team 10 had abandoned the Congrès Internationaux d'Architecture Moderne (CIAM) and rejected modernism's technocratic approach to improving living standards. They began to foster an attitude that was less strict and controlled. Brutalism was a return to basics, a celebration of ruggedness and imperfection more in sync with the world they observed around them.

Parallel to this the Land Art movement emerged. A growing disillusionment with the commercialization of art, particularly in the United States, led artists to experiment beyond the galleries and the museums, and the crust of the earth became their new canvas.[19]

Although not known for making Land Art himself, artist Donald Judd saw this medium as an antidote to the art world of the 1960s.[20] According to Judd, "most of the art of the past that could be moved was taken by conquerors. Almost all recent art is conquered as soon as it's made".[21] Contemporary artists did not have a say in how the work was presented; it was passed from one museum to another every month or so. Judd argued that "art should be where the artist wanted it to be and the best is that which remains where it was painted, placed or built... There is no constructive effort; there is no cooperative effort. This situation is primitive in relation to a few earlier and better times."[22]

Donald Judd and Virginia Dwan, heiress of the 3M conglomerate, were early patrons of the Land Art movement. Both the Dia Art Foundation and the Chinati Foundation financed artists' perseverance, as a particularity of working with the earth was that it often took decades of costly work.

City, Michael Heizer, 1972–2020. © 2019 Google Maps.

In 1970, Michael Heizer moved 244 000 tons of stone for *Double Negative* in Nevada. Since acquiring land in 1979, James Turrell has been constructing the enormous Roden Crater, which celebrates the sharp contrast in light conditions of the Arizona desert. Not surprisingly, the Land Art movement was firmly established in the south-west of the United States. Vast uninhabited landscapes were the perfect setting for large-scale art projects. The earth was not just a canvas; it was also mined as the main material to sculpt the projects. As a result, most projects dig in and earthly material is repositioned, to create the work of art.

“I think earth is the material with the most potential because it is the original source material.”[23] –Michael Heizer

“At Roden Crater, I was interested in taking the cultural artifice of art out into the natural surround. I wanted the work to be enfolded in nature in such a way that light from the sun, moon and stars empowered the spaces. I wanted to bring culture to the natural surround as if one was designing a garden.”[24] –James Turrell

***Roden Crater*, James Turrell, 1979–present. © 2019 Google Earth.**

In Mildam, Friesland, self-proclaimed ‘ecotect’ Louis Guillaume le Roy constructed a beautiful Ecokathedraal by reusing concrete paving. Central to Le Roy’s idea is that humans should not control nature but should work together with nature’s vigour to achieve the highest degree of complexity. This act requires long-term interaction between human and nature. The Ecokathedraal will take a thousand years to build, supposedly standing 300 metres tall.[25]

Ecokathedraal, Louis Guillaume le Roy, 1970.

The essence and the challenge of Land Art is scale. As they take on architectural dimensions and qualities, the works become inseparable from the earth's crust and thus impossible to display in a museum. This immovability kept Land Art relatively safe from the traditional trading and commercialization artists had hoped to untie themselves from. However, in securing funding for larger, more ambitious, and more costly projects, artists produced photos, videos and plans for the very institutions they had chosen to break ties with.

Although Michael Heizer originally refused both the conservation and sale of his work *Double Negative*, believing it should be reclaimed by nature, he did permit Virginia Dwan to donate it to the Museum of Contemporary Art in Los Angeles in 1984, and now expresses a wish for it to be restored.[26]

A recurring theme within Land Art is digging. Just as Homo sapiens did many millennia ago, this excavation is not purely out of necessity.[27] There is a contemplative aspect. Undergoing the resonance of the earth is something between desire and religious subjugation. Working with the ground is a recurring driver in the history of humankind and the all-encompassing nature of the work blurs the boundary between art and architecture.

Land Art

—

Monument to Tolerance
Montaña de Tindaya, Canary Islands
Eduardo Chillida
1995–present

"My sculpture wants this mountain, it is now time to see whether the mountain wants my sculpture."[28] –Eduardo Chillida

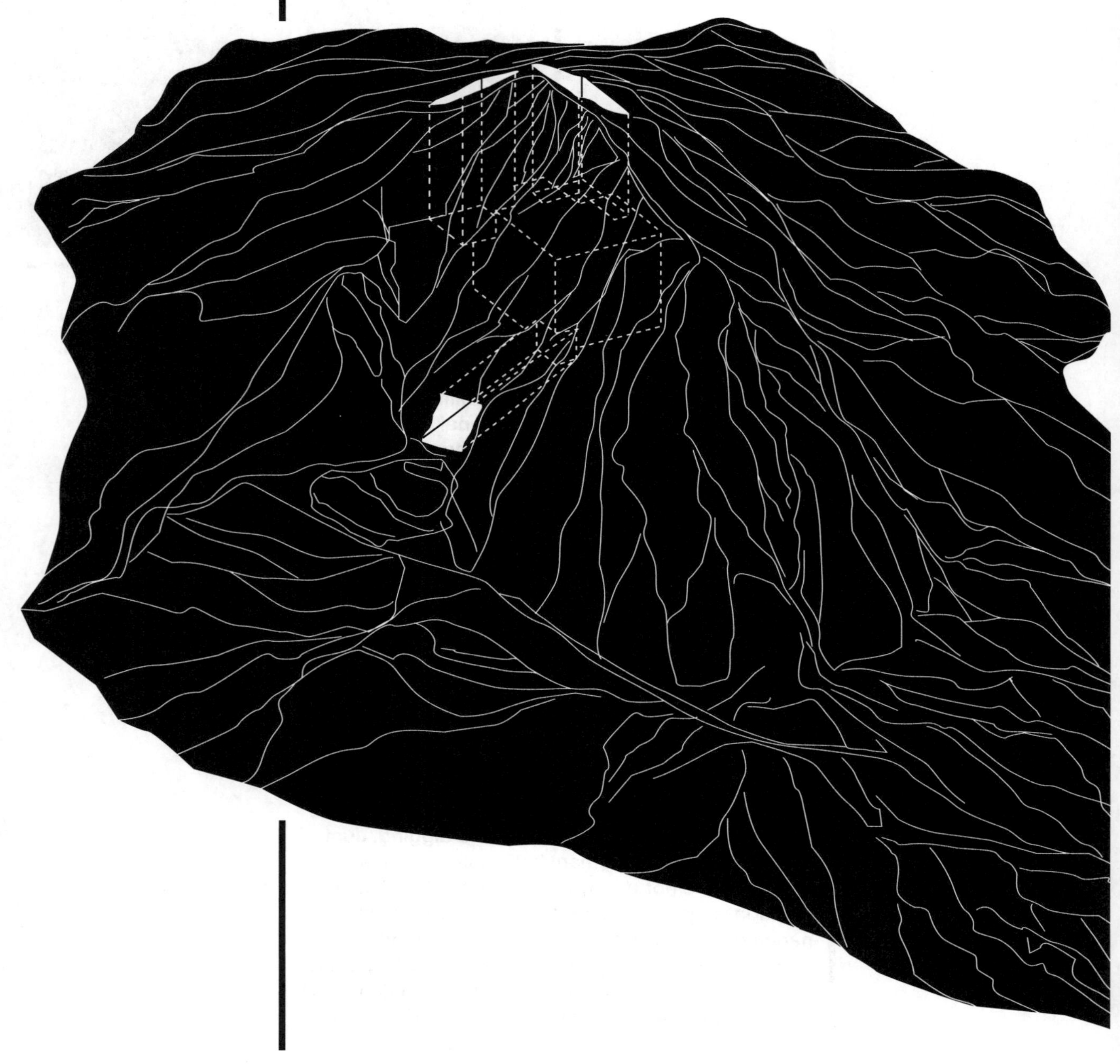

Eduardo Chillida's sentiment exemplifies the inherent challenge of Land Art. He chose a mountain guarded by environmental groups and sacred to others. His vision was to carve almost 150 000 cubic metres out of the mountain, which would make it one of the largest underground caverns ever constructed. The Fuerteventura government, to whom Chillida's widow Pilar Belzunce transferred the rights, is still seeking funding, but they haven't given up yet. The mountain has yet to make its final decision.

Montaña de Tindaya.

Axonometry of Montaña de Tindaya showing the Monument to Tolerance.

A physical, tactile experience is an important component of the work of Chillida. His steel sculptures, often deformed through bending, show a thickening and stretching in the corners, creating intriguing details in form. His sculptures are as much about solid as void, shaping space, and embracing the body of the viewer. Instead of just standing and observing, you are invited to both touch the physical form and enter the interior of the void.

Consejo al Espacio (*Advice to Space VIII*), Eduardo Chillida, 2000.

Plan of Plaza de los Fueros, Vitoria-Gasteiz & Eduardo Chillida, 1987.

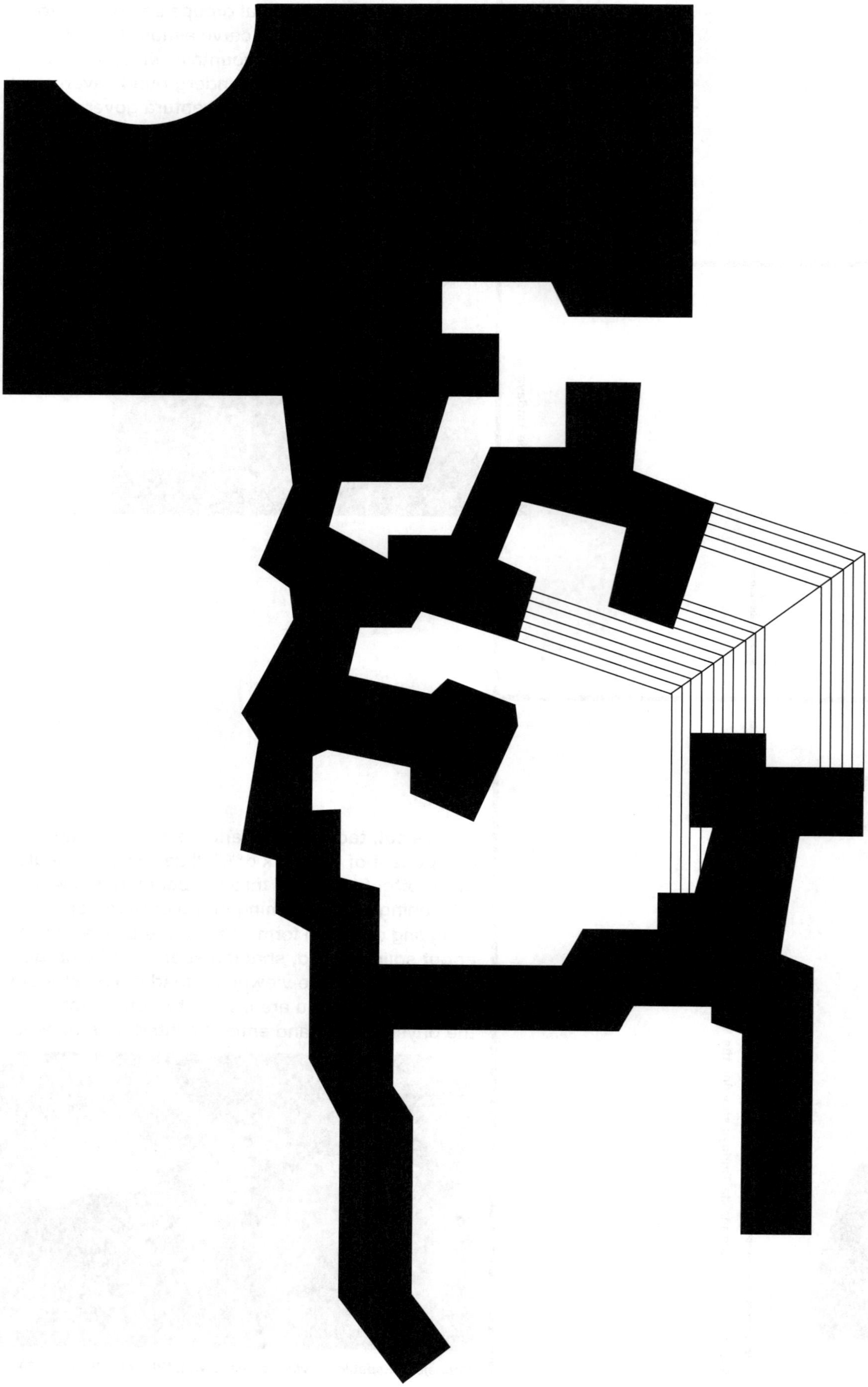

Although presented as a work of art, Chillida's Monument to Tolerance undeniably reads as a piece of cathedral-like architecture.

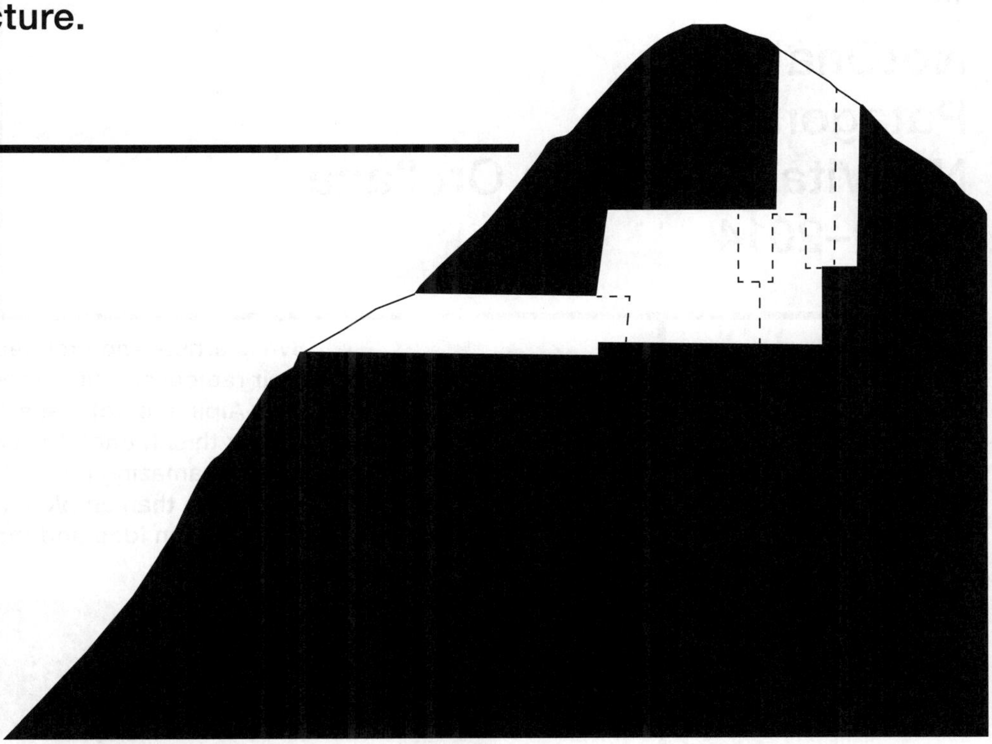

While Chillida had tolerance in mind, the government of Fuerteventura wants to see it built for touristic reasons. Perhaps both can be satisfied. Whoever takes on the incredible challenge of realization could have a return of investment by charging an admission fee. Chillida never intended this work to be a cause for division or a pawn in political point scoring; he simply wanted visitors to experience the immensity of the space.[29]

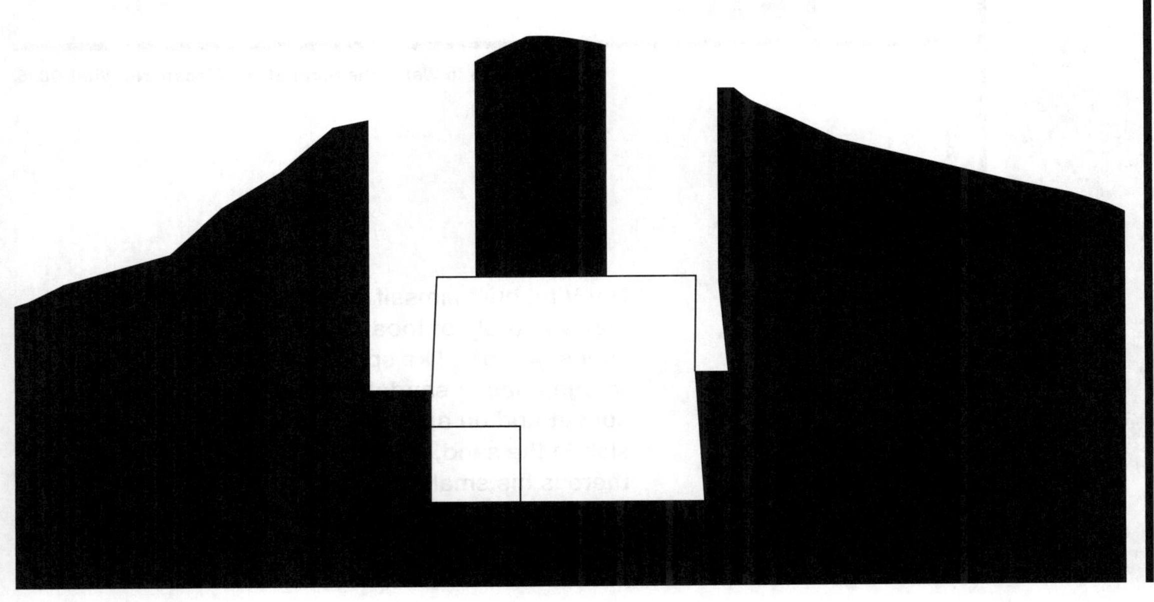

Sections of the Monument to Tolerance.

Land Art

—

NotOna
Patagonia, Chile
Not Vital & Cristián Orellana
2009–2014

Swiss artists and architects are renowned for their radical and uncompromising ideas. Perhaps their Alpine remoteness and an extreme climate trigger this. It can't be a coincidence. The artist with the amazing name, Not Vital, is no exception. With more than ample means, he creates works that push an idea and the subsequent space to the extreme.

House to Watch the Night Skies, Aladab, Not Vital, 2006.

JOSUJO (Disappearing house), Sent, Not Vital, 2007.

Not Vital built himself a home in Agadez, Niger, made entirely of local materials. He also built a series of monk-like spaces of contemplation: a refuge against sandstorms, a tower to watch the sunset and an abstract adobe volume, a huge slab in the sand, in which to watch the moon. Then there is his small house in Sent, Switzerland, which is topped with grass and disappears into the earth at the push of a button. His work is provocative: why see a house if it is not in use?

Plan of NotOna cut through an island.

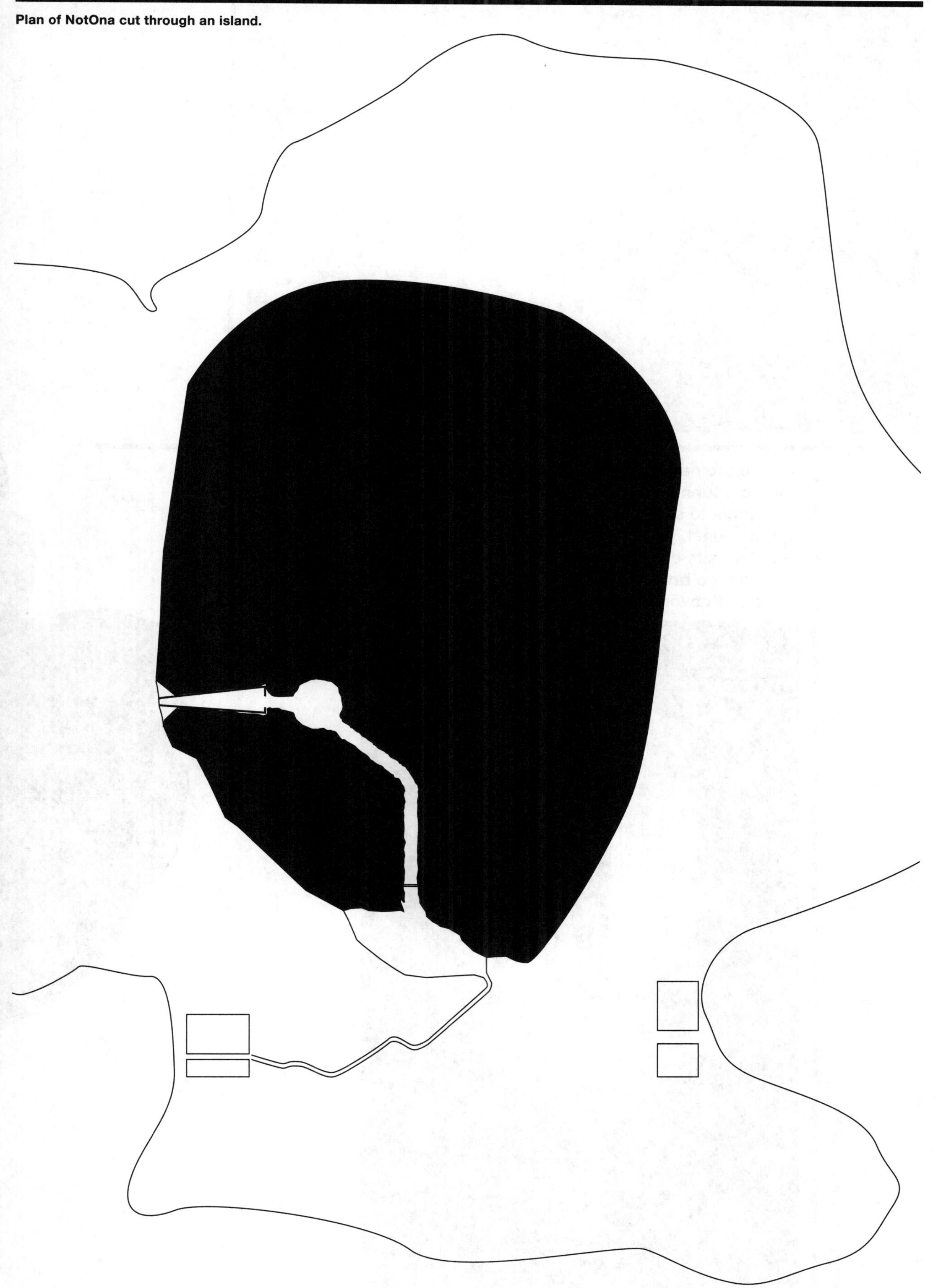

True to the nature of these projects, Not Vital carved a tunnel through a rocky marble island in Patagonia to see the sunset. In the middle of a quirky tunnel, you will find a dome-shaped room. The deposits of the carving are used to make an entrance box on the other side of the island and a path over the whale-shaped rock.

NotOna, Patagonia by Not Vital.

"No sound, no noise, no smell, no phone. The womb of the earth. Since childhood I wanted to enter the world, the stone, to be inside, to be protected and see the world from within. The surface was not enough for me it seems."[30] —Not Vital

Axonometry of NotOna.

Not Vital talks about a white fox, the only creature on the island to accompany him while he sleeps on a bare mattress in a sleeping bag. Again, this project is all about approaching the essence of earthly life and its natural beauty as closely as possible without any distractions. It is a lesson in modesty as a counterpart to the overwhelming and harmful lifestyle of today.

Land Art

—

The Truffle
Costa da Morte, Spain
Ensamble Studio
2010

Ensamble Studio straddles the space between the disciplines of art and architecture. They describe their practice as thinking with their hands. In 2010, they cast a holiday retreat within the earth. The Truffle was formed by pouring concrete on top of a square-ish volume of hay bales set within a hole they had dug.[31] Then the comic part started with Pauline, a young cow, brought to the site to empty the volume by eating the hay away.

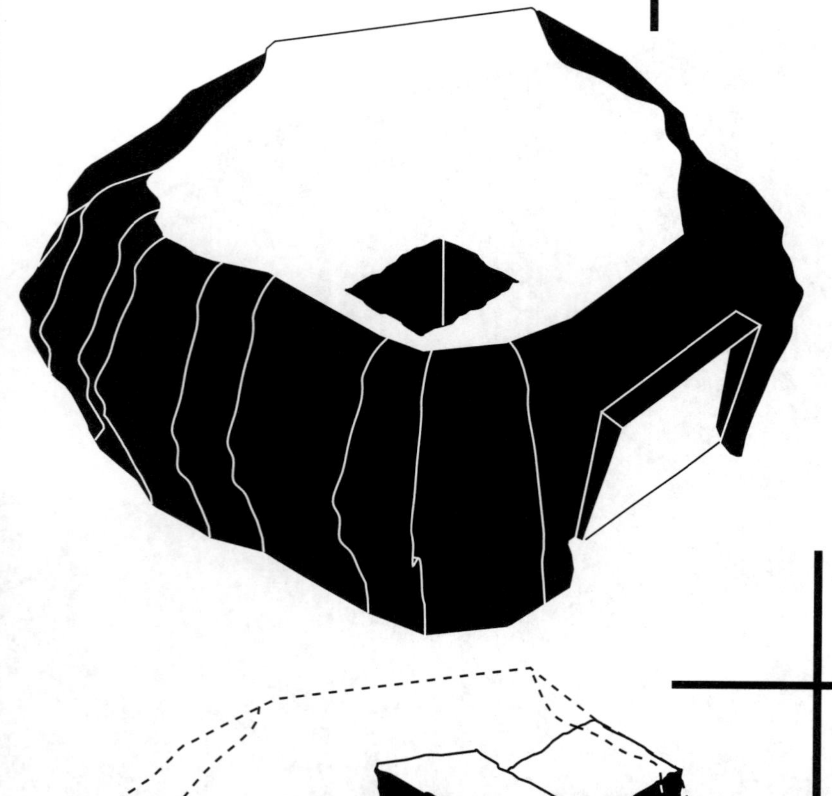

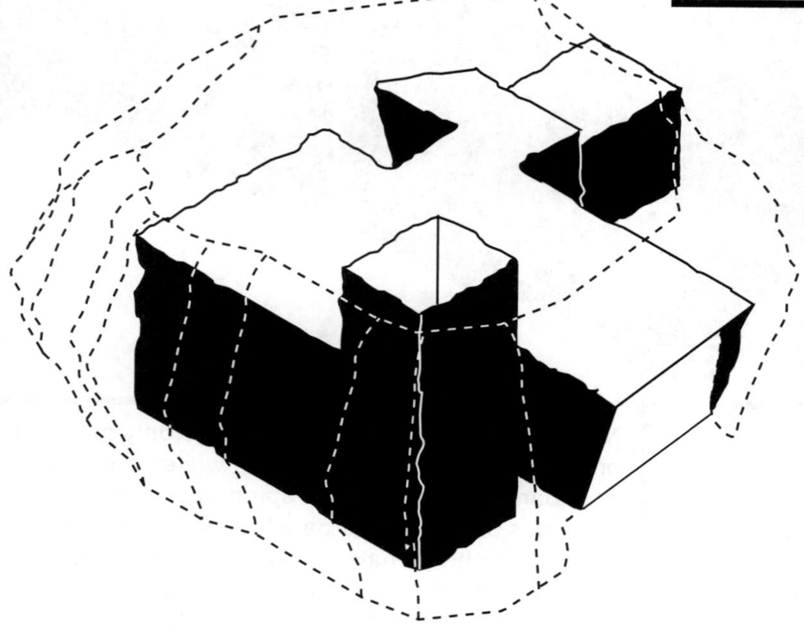

Axonometry of the Truffle (top) and the void within (bottom).

Once both the exterior and interior had been exhumed, two elevations were sliced off the irregular volume: one facing the sea view in which they fixed a steel-framed window, and one in which they placed the entrance.

Section of the Truffle.

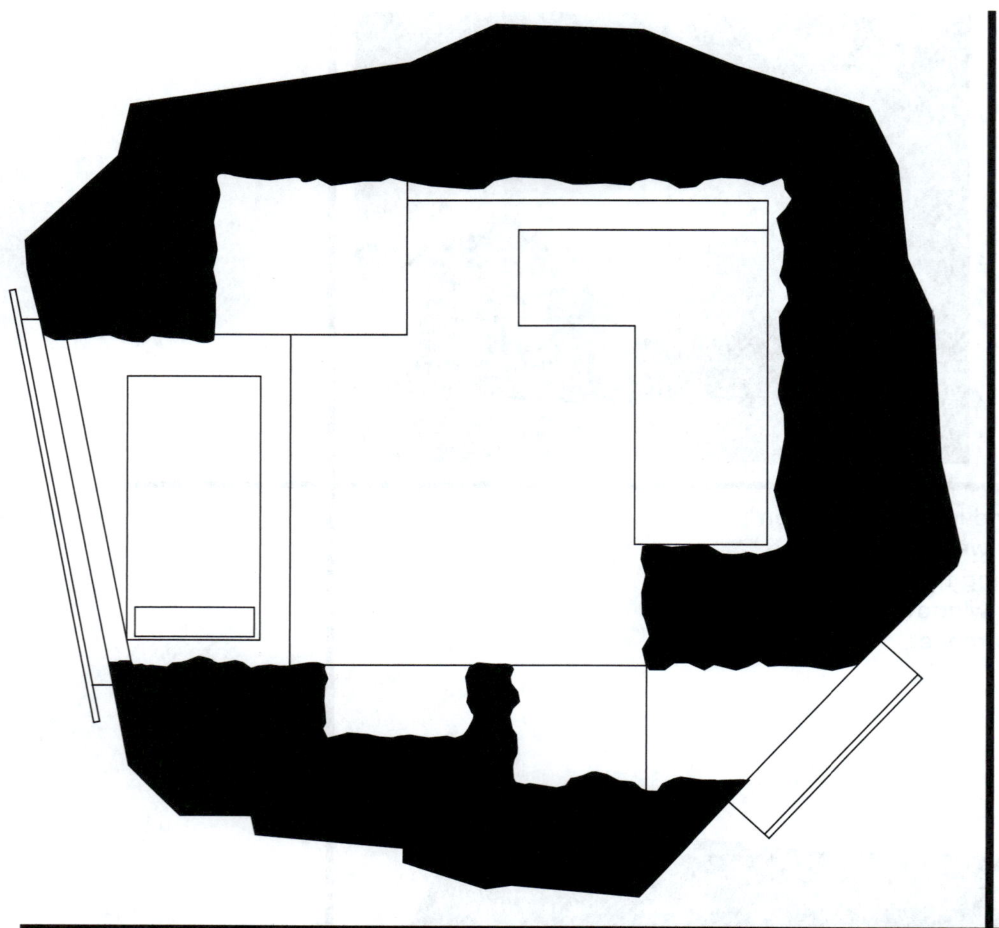

Plan of the Truffle.

Domo (top) and *Beartooth Portal* (bottom), Structures of Landscape, Tippet Rise Art Center, 2016.

Extending on the Truffle, Ensamble created two immense artworks, *Beartooth Portal* and *Domo* for the Tippet Rise Art Center in Fishtail, Montana. Both works consist of discus-shaped concrete forms, cast in a sand mass. The *Domo* is excavated and left in place, while the *Beartooth Portal* is erected using a tilt-slab method, standing tall against the vast backdrop.

With the current Ca'n Terra project in Menorca, Ensamble are unlocking an old subterranean quarry, making it into a room to contemplate nature. Dubbed by the studio as the house of the earth, the project is a perfect example of the architects' inextricable relationship with nature.

Iwan Baan using his drone to film the cutting of the first skylight at Ca'n Terra. The olive tree had just dropped down.

"We don't like pastoral representations of nature or domesticated beauty. We understand that nature is brutal and can kill you."[32] —Antón García-Abril

Through a smart reworking of the earth, architectural intervention is minimized. Processes of digging and casting are employed to maximum effect, making these projects impressively site-specific. Their almost obsessive approach to stone and concrete construction methods avoids the need for excessive structural support like formwork and scaffolding. Low-tech is the new high-tech.

Land Art
—
House & Restaurant Ube, Japan Junya Ishigami 2018

"I imagine a world where buildings don't exist. A place with no rustic cottages nor gleaming skyscrapers, no classicism nor modernism, no preconceived idea of what a house or an office block should be. How would we make spaces from scratch if anything was possible? Freed from the conventions of architecture and construction, what would this world look like?"[33] —Junya Ishigami

For a proposal in Dali, south-west China, Ishigami used the big boulders on site as structural pillars, forming a megalithic indoor landscape. He meticulously arranged the rooms and furniture of the homes around the great rocks and topped it with a 300-metre-long wafer-thin roof. He says you should approach designing a house "as if you were putting together a garden, a little at a time... If we forget everything we know, just imagine how many more kinds of architecture there could be."

Eight villas in Dali, China, Junya Ishigami, 2017. © Giovanni Emilio Galanello.

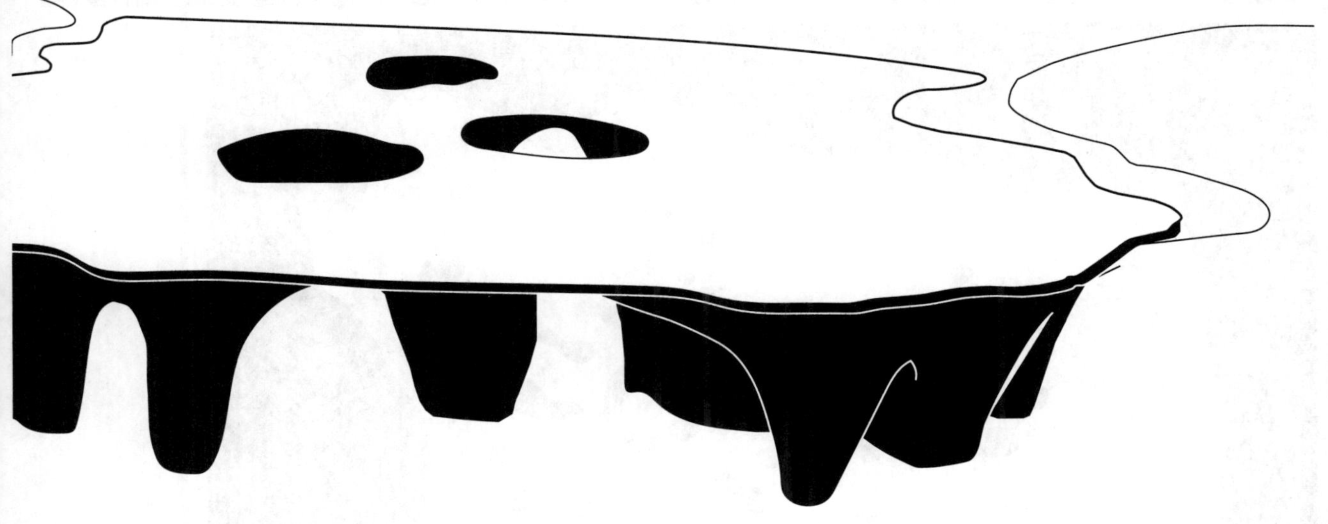

Axonometry of the poured concrete 'slab'.

With the House & Restaurant project, Ishigami comes close to what he calls 'a building that does not exist'. Ishigami tweaked the original request from the client to make a house with a restaurant like a rustic wine cellar into something that looks like an ant nest. He dug holes into the earth, keeping earth volumes in between. A concrete slab was poured on top, and then the earth removed, inverting solid and void. The earth became space and the holes in return pop out as fat columns, almost like an obese viaduct of Gaudí's Park Güell.

Construction of House & Restaurant.

Plan of House & Restaurant built below ground level.

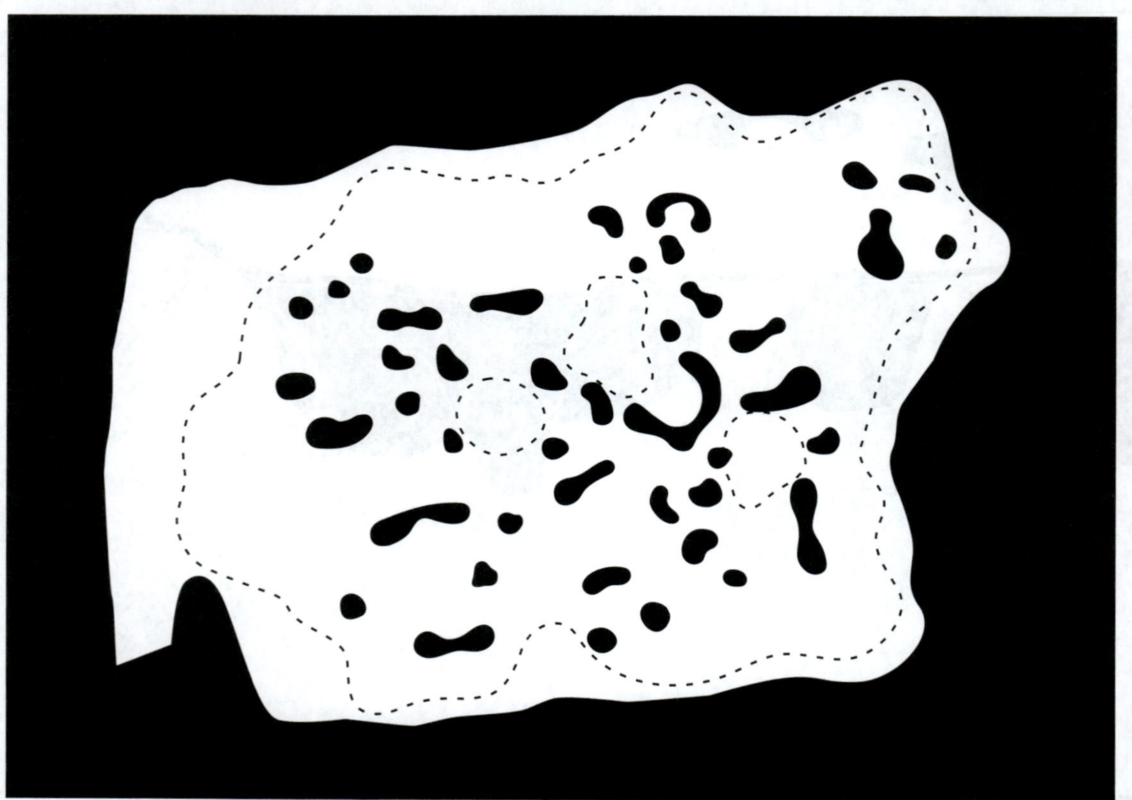

The plan shows no reference whatsoever to any preexisting typology. It is a sequence of amorphous spaces and courtyards, subservient to the continuity of the cave-like structure. It wants to be a rock, not a house or restaurant; more of a landscape. This feeling is strengthened by the fact that at certain points you must stoop down in order to go from one space to another.

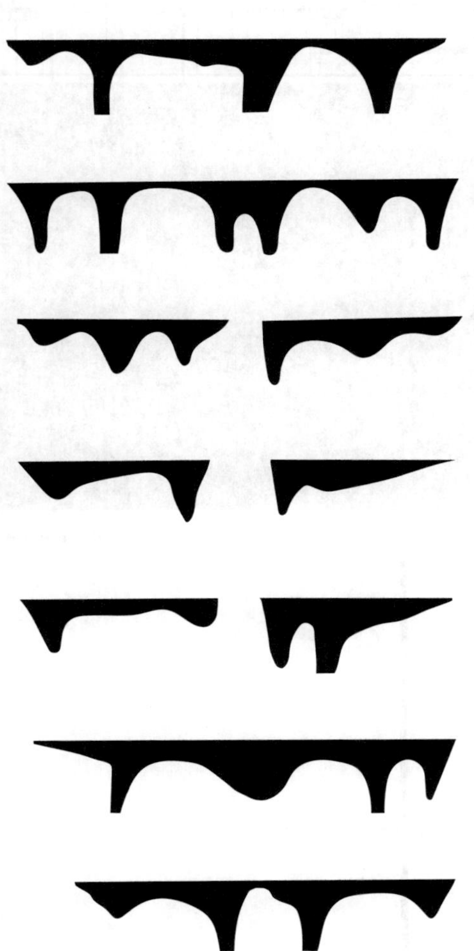

Successive sections of the project.

Louvre Extension
Paris, France
I. M. Pei
1983–1989

Architecture holds a key position between nature and culture, between our history and the way we live now. How it functions, however, remains surprisingly vague, especially if you look at the first 10 000 years of humankind as a settled species. We debate the whys and whats, but everything that has not been 'carved in stone' has perished or been digested, leaving almost no traces. Ironically it is often the spaces shrouded in mystery that are the most enduring.

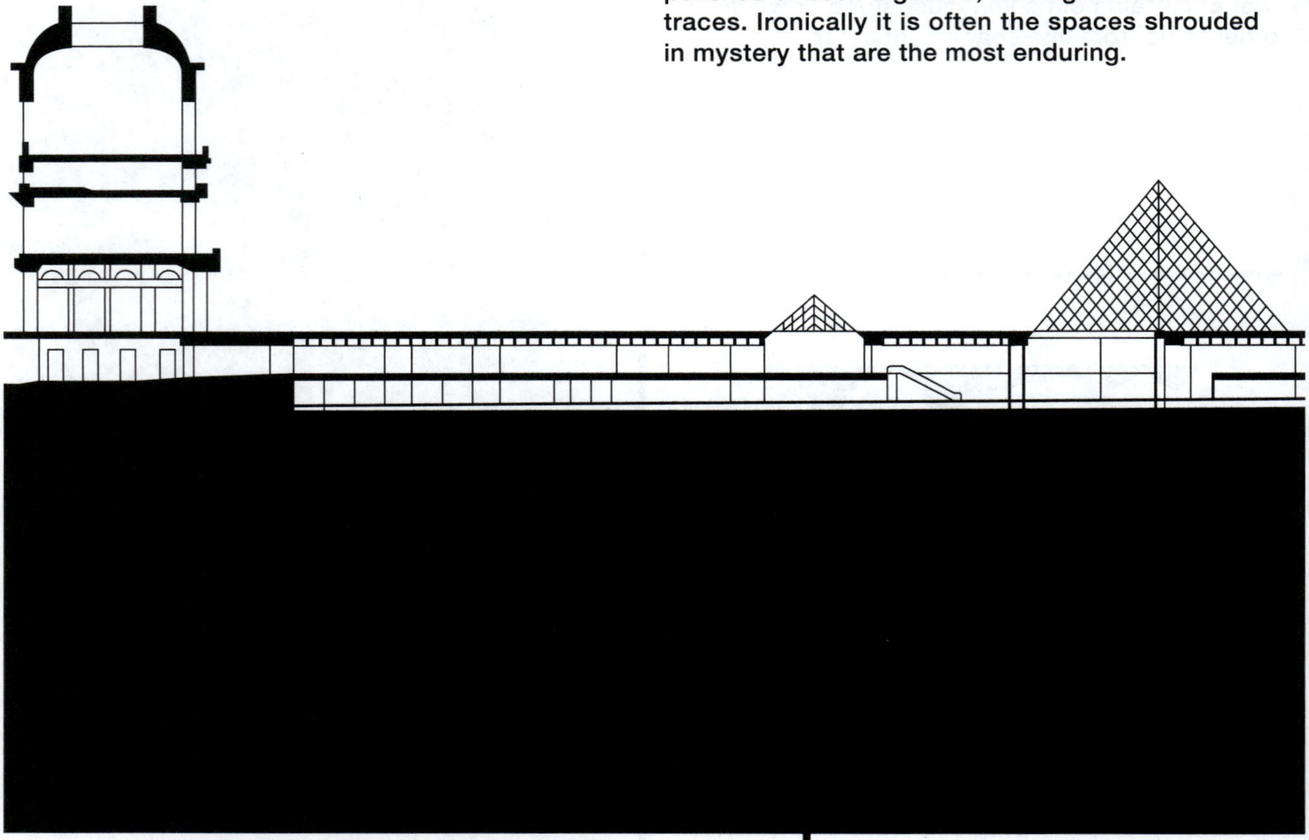

Section of the Louvre extension.

© Gordon Calder.

I. M. Pei's extension to the Louvre figures prominently in the bestselling book *The Da Vinci Code.* Assuming that Pei's archival registrations and documentations of the building are far less prolific than the eighty million copies of Dan Brown's book, it is interesting to consider what might be remembered in a thousand years' time. Will it be seen as a gripping solution to a lack of space in the centre of Paris, or a ritualistic act within a grand scheme? In light of the Seine's recent flooding, the chosen solution is far from obvious.

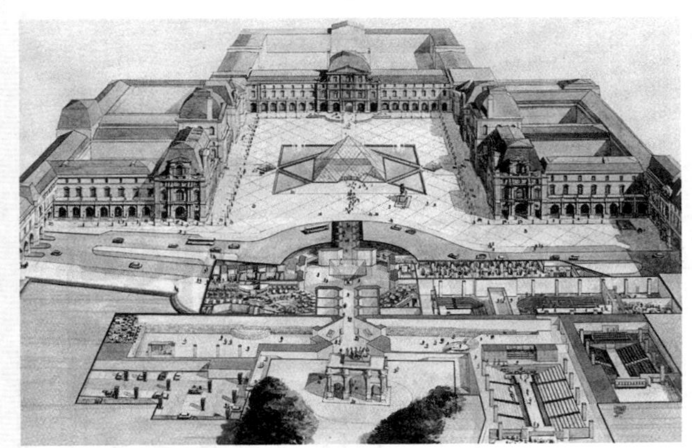

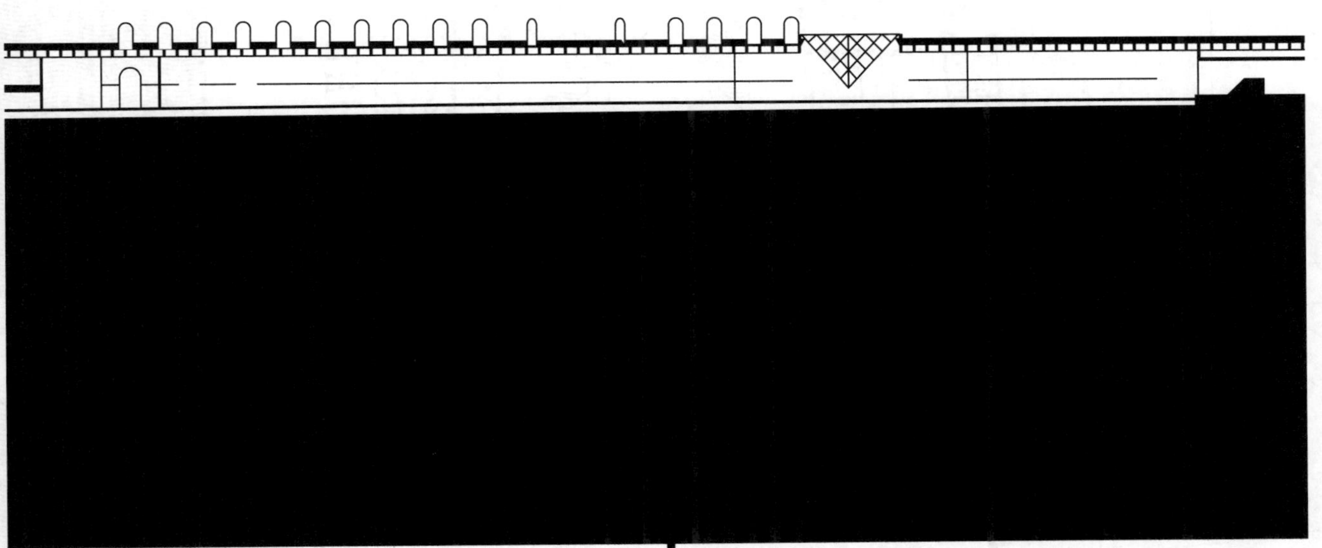

Although I. M. Pei's 21-metre-high pyramid of glass originally raised eyebrows, in context it is an impressively modest addition to the historic square. If you scratch away the surface of the square, you see that the delicate U-shaped Louvre sits on an immense plateau, a 'placenta' of subterranean infrastructure that connects and feeds everything. François Mitterrand knew that without this new motherboard, the Louvre was about to die. This colossal space holds and organizes parking for cars and buses, a conference centre, a mall, technical and mechanical space, access to the city's metro system and the other ninety-two per cent of the collection not on display.[34]

Louvre extension above ground.

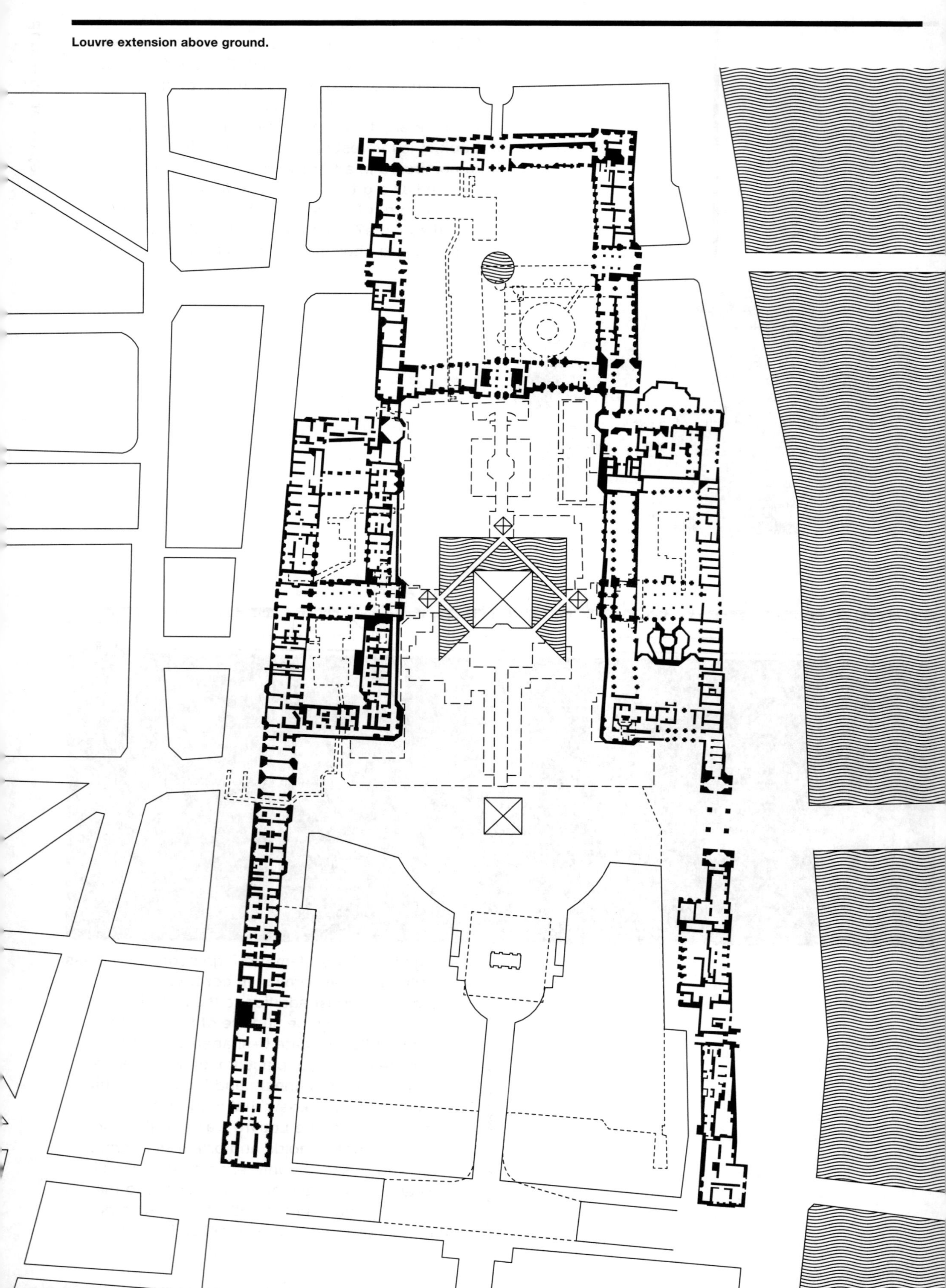

Louvre extension below ground.

In the past, people approached the Louvre through the Tuileries Garden. Now most visitors filter up. It is as if the world has been inverted, and even the pyramid here points down. There are countless precedents, but the Louvre has set the standard for underground, inner-city museum extensions. What makes it so convincing is its equal treatment of territory above and below ground.

Section of the extension showing its connection to the existing museum.

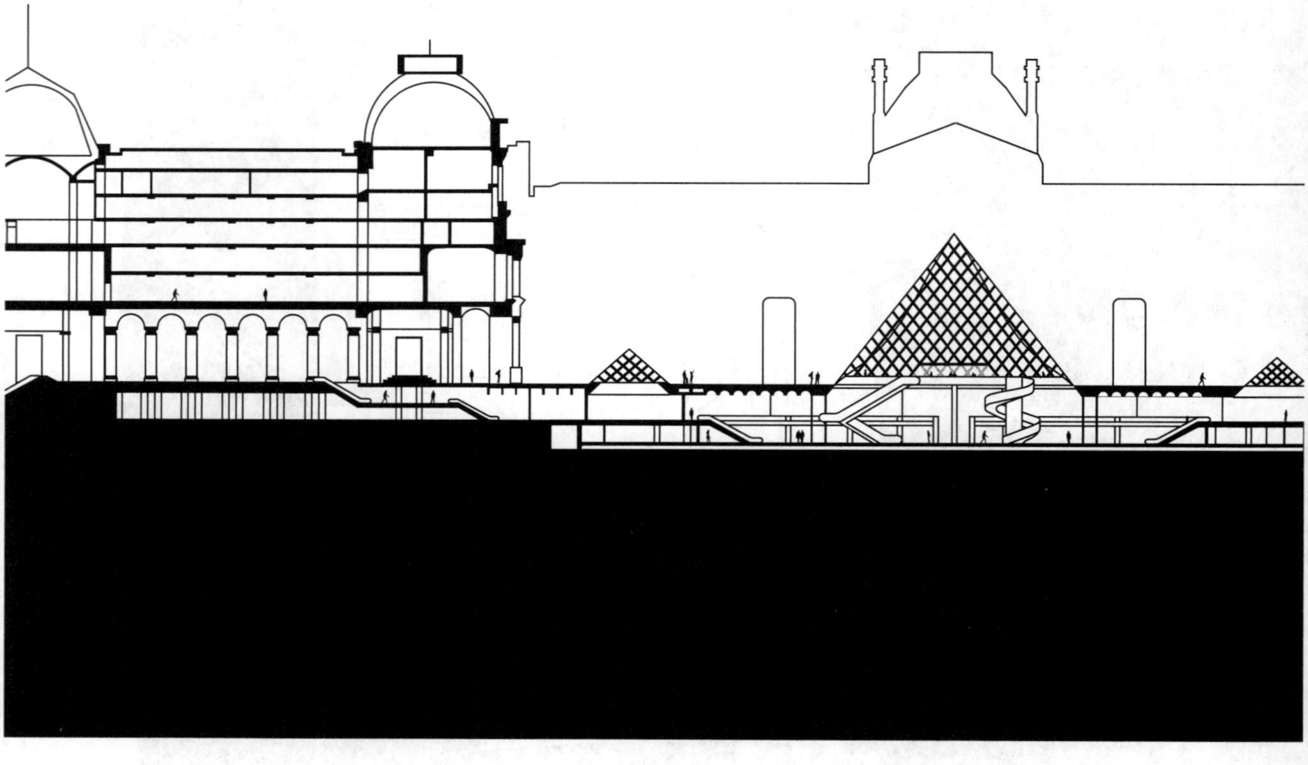

The pomp and circumstance around the central pyramid masks the fact that you spiral down, slide sideways under the old foundations and resurface in the original museum. That begs the question: is it simply adding modern services and auxiliary spaces or does it also rewrite history?

It is amazing to see such an archaic form spice up the debate. Love or despise them, contemporary storytelling and social media work; an immersive experience and a selfie with a pyramid reaches the crowds more easily than the inconclusive story of the *Mona Lisa*. This is because the design never touches the historical buildings. It landed in Paris and parked itself in the forecourt, with reference to the stars and the centre of the earth, as if transcending worldly importance.

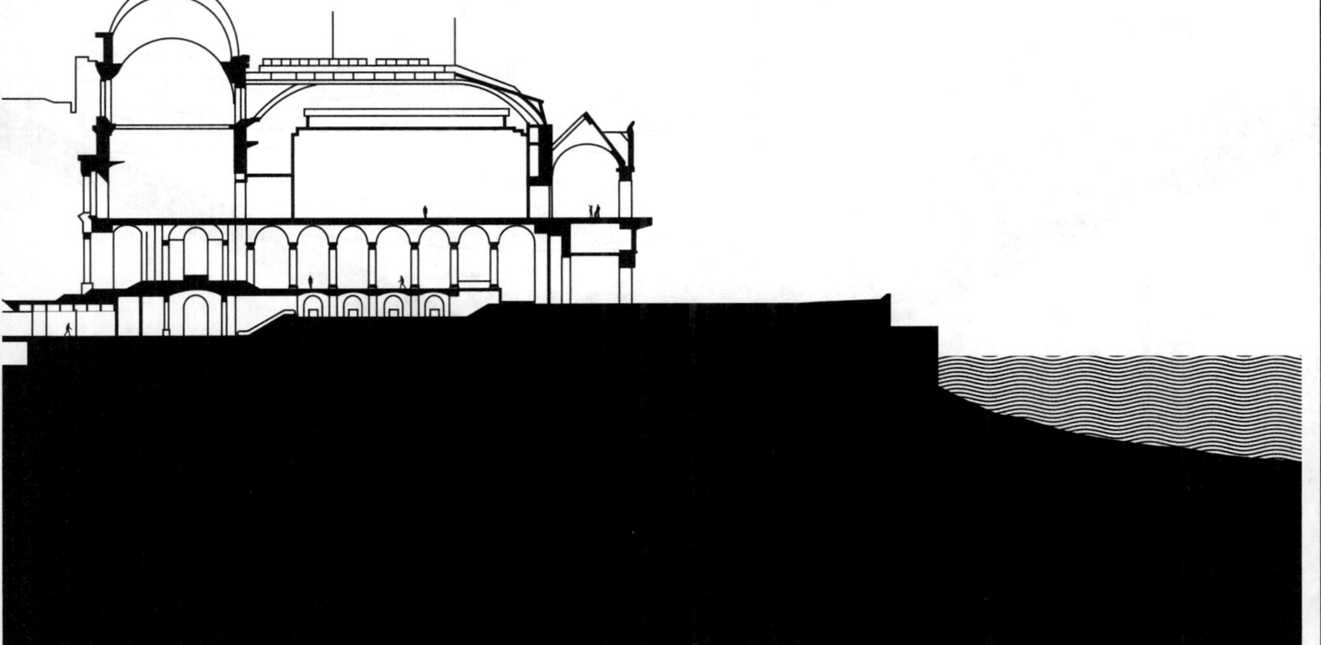

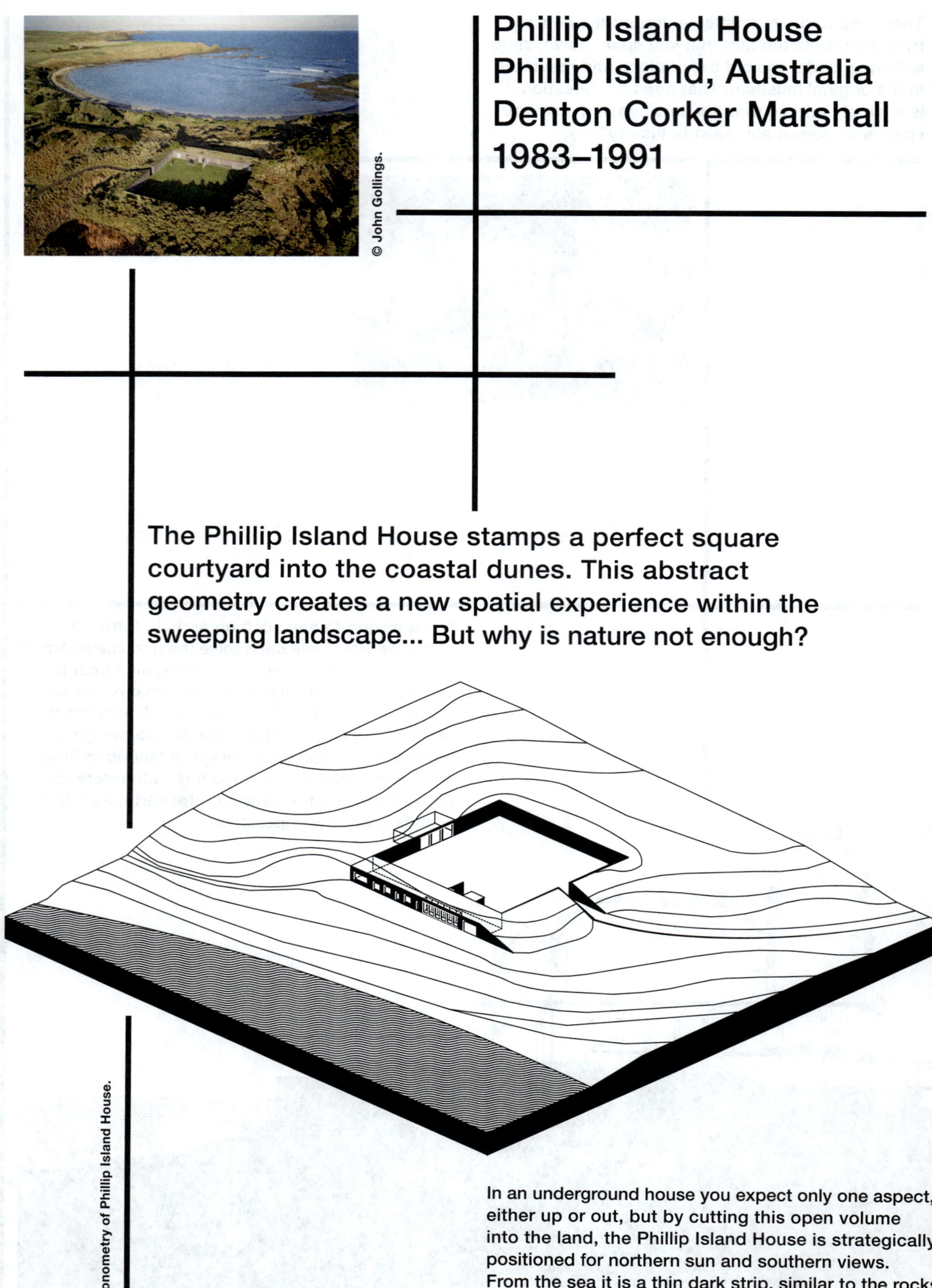

© John Gollings.

Phillip Island House
Phillip Island, Australia
Denton Corker Marshall
1983–1991

The Phillip Island House stamps a perfect square courtyard into the coastal dunes. This abstract geometry creates a new spatial experience within the sweeping landscape... But why is nature not enough?

Axonometry of Phillip Island House.

In an underground house you expect only one aspect, either up or out, but by cutting this open volume into the land, the Phillip Island House is strategically positioned for northern sun and southern views. From the sea it is a thin dark strip, similar to the rocks below; from the land it is buried within the dunes.

Plan of the Phillip Island House cut into hillside.

Section of Phillip Island House.

The courtyard acts like a sort of bailey. Upon approach, you are confronted by a number of strong architectural features that are reminiscent of the reinforcement of a medieval castle. Navigating the road, past a strait, you arrive within a walled enclosure.

Small windows along the bottom of the dark concrete walls give the appearance of an upside-down battlement wall. A galvanized screen perpendicular to the house accentuates the front door. Each element is in service of a dramatic architectural experience, with, as icing on the cake, a dramatic view from the interior over the beaches and cliffs of the Australian coast.

The courtyard is hidden from view by a dike that blends into the rolling dunes. The landscape extends over the roof and slopes down to meet the ground, obscuring the house's position. Is it built up or excavated down? The slanted chimney stands like a shovel in the ground, waiting to be picked up again to finish the work. This house shows in a profound way the dichotomy of seclusion and unification with the landscape and its vistas.

Igualada Cemetery
Barcelona, Spain
Enric Miralles
1984–1996 (unfinished)

"A cemetery is not a tomb. It is, rather, a relationship with the landscape, and with forgetting."[35] –Enric Miralles

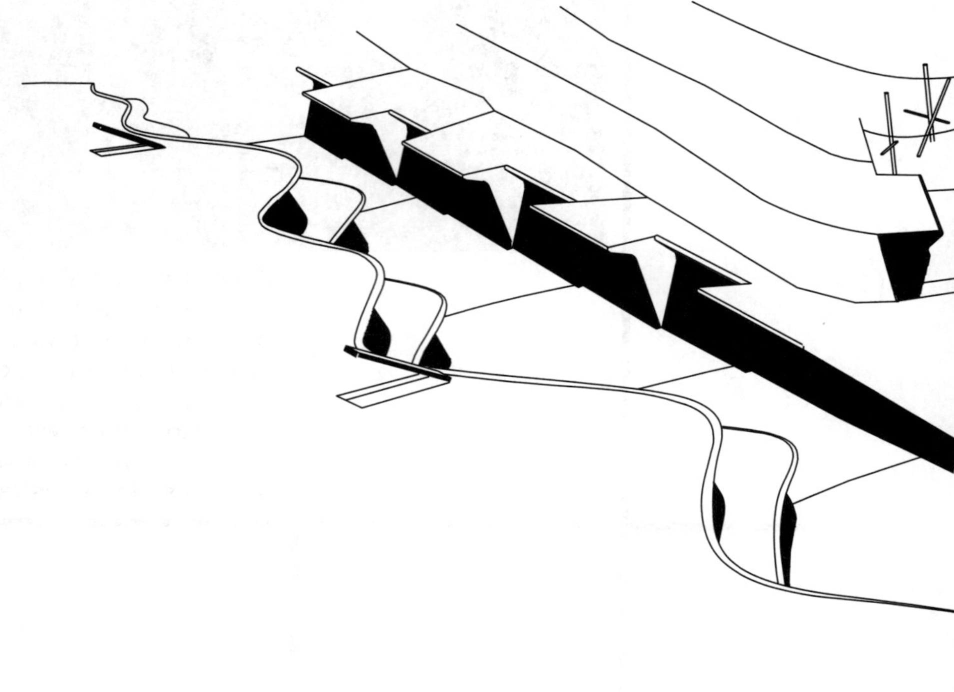

Igualada Cemetery does not ask one to forget death. It is about how landscape can soothe loss. It invites the mourner to forget the brutal industrial zone in which the cemetery is located and enter the ground. One descends down the path and, as Enric Miralles stated, "the tombs will be in its interior and trees will make the space dense, like characters inhabiting shadows of the walls produced by the cut in the earth."[36]

Axonometry of Igualada Cemetery.

It is impossible to look at the meandering walls and turning points without bearing in mind the surprisingly poetic drawings of an assassinated multi-talent some fifty years ago. You will witness the exact same transparency and overlay of forms. If this is not a three-dimensional tribute to Federico García Lorca, who never had a grave of his own, what else could it be?[37]

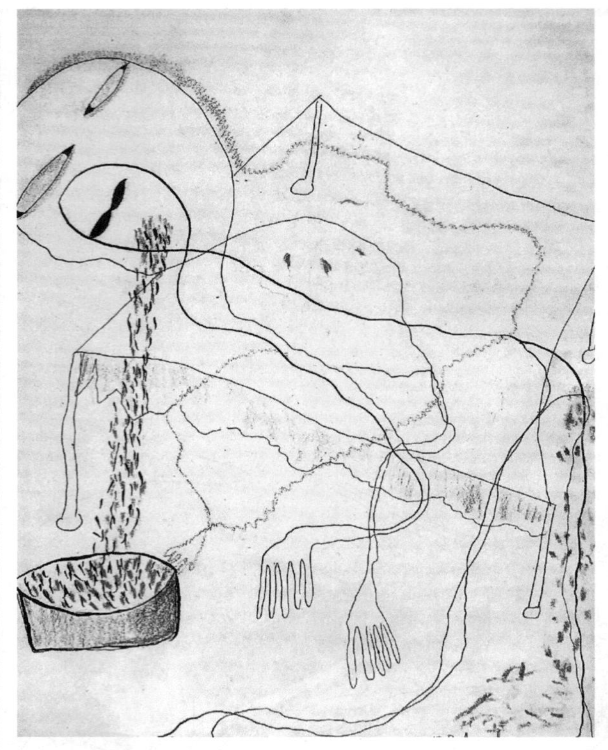

***The Death of Santa Rodegunda*, Federico García Lorca, 1929.**

Drawing up this project while simultaneously including the change and movement of lines that continued through construction was almost more important than the final 'static' forms, cast in concrete. If you look at Federico García Lorca's doodling drawings like *Muerte de Santa Rodegunda* or *Two Figures over a Grave*, you will see all the ingredients of the Igualada Cemetery laid out. Death and dream, the cross and the scattering of tombs and trees are all mentioned by García Lorca, and it is amazing how Miralles used this to create a project that, as he mentioned, 'already existed'.

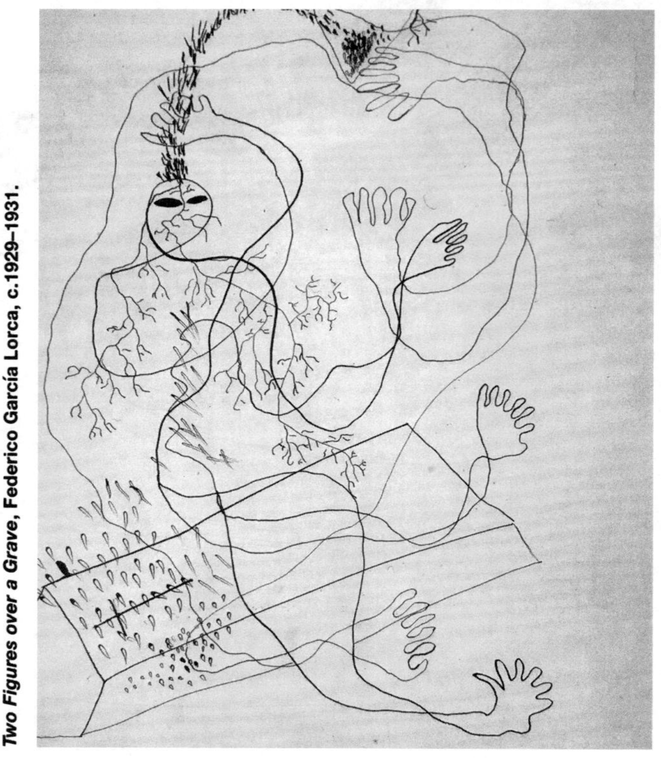

***Two Figures over a Grave*, Federico García Lorca, c.1929–1931.**

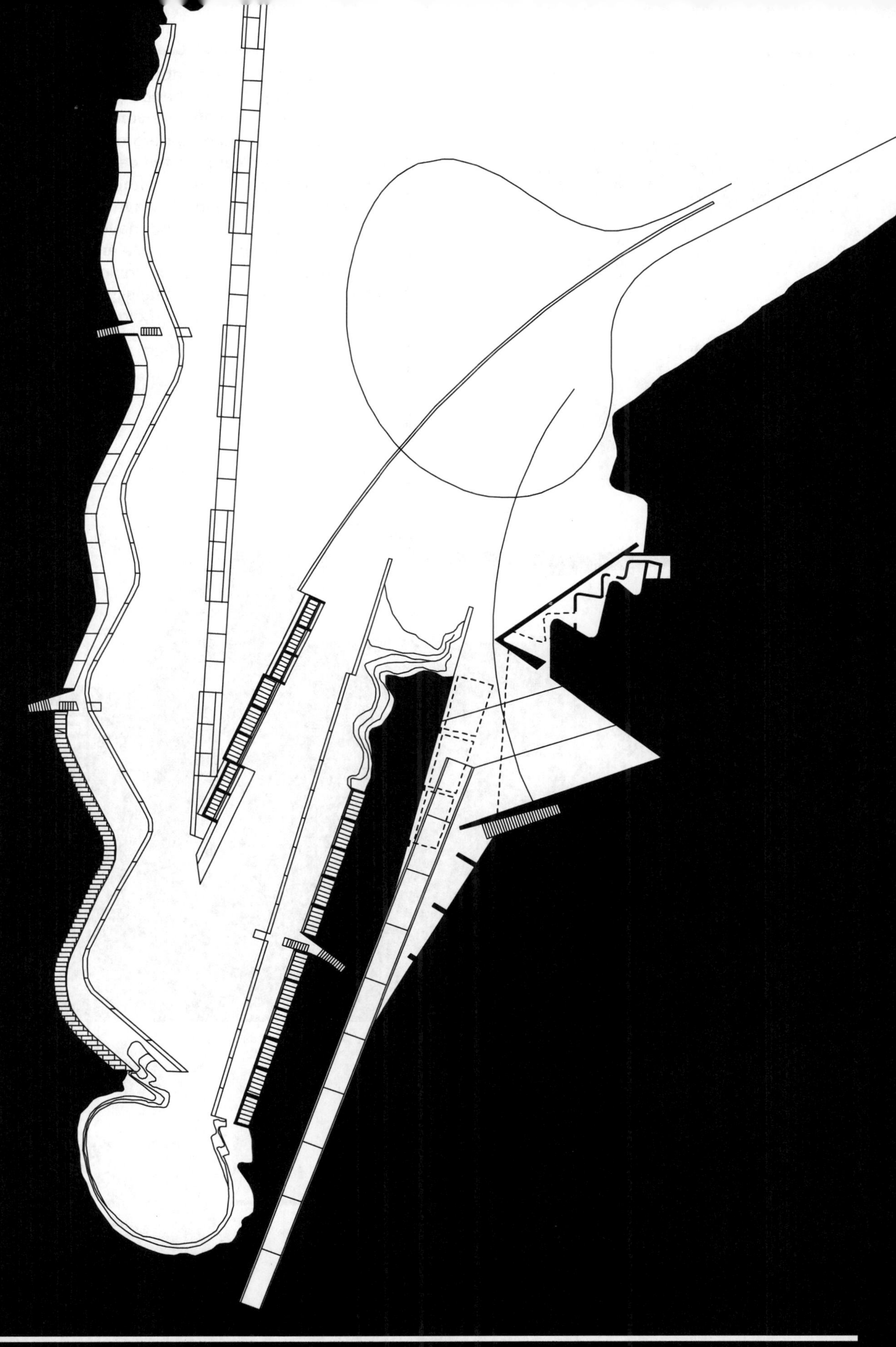

Plan of Igualada Cemetery.

Igualada Cemetery is all about trying to stay 'flexible', being able to change and adapt like the growing of trees, the flux of rivers and the changing of seasons. It is neither underground nor above ground. The fence around the cemetery exemplifies this. Reinforced steel mesh without the concrete allows its thin steel ends to wave in the wind. This project enriches fissures and movement in the natural terrain. Most remarkable are the similarities between Miralles's way of designing and the different techniques artist Wassily Kandinsky uses to 'penetrate' the paper, as if digging into the earth.

Section of Igualada Cemetery.

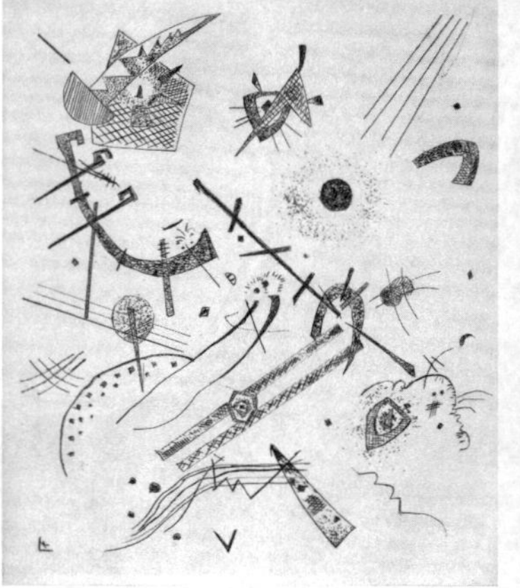

Kleine Welten XI, Wassily Kandinsky, 1922.

© Dieter Janssen.

Igualada Cemetery is the ground itself, manipulated and converted into a place, even spaces. It draws on humankind's first building efforts, stepping back as far as the Neolithic period when humankind was utterly preoccupied with building both ritual and ritualistic space.

Roof Made City
Utrecht, Netherlands
SeARCH
1993 (unbuilt)

The 'pied-de-poule', originally called the hound-stooth check, was not Christian Dior's invention. First woven around 360–100 BCE, it is a simple, highly efficient technique, creating a moisture-resistant and durable fabric. This interlocking of two identical forms also inspired graphic artist Maurits Cornelis Escher. An interesting element in his drawings is that these mathematical tessellations were made as negatives, since he mainly did woodcuttings and lithographs. His etchings start from a black 'page', gouging out the white. But ultimately, as with his etching *Day and Night*, woodblock and print are the same through their line-symmetry. In the end you see both day and night, black and white, mass and void, land and water, town and countryside.

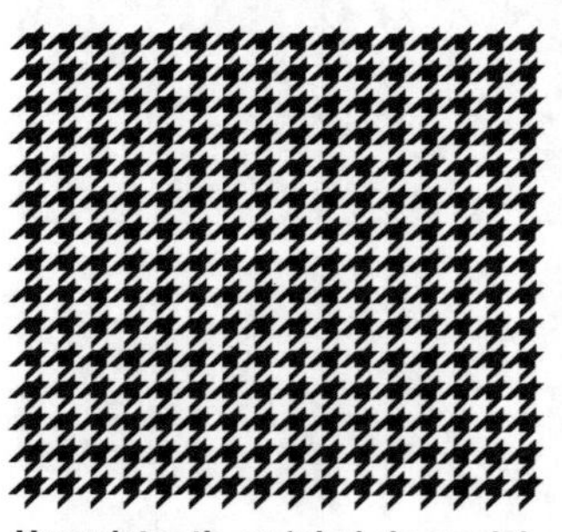

Houndstooth, or 'pied-de-poule'.

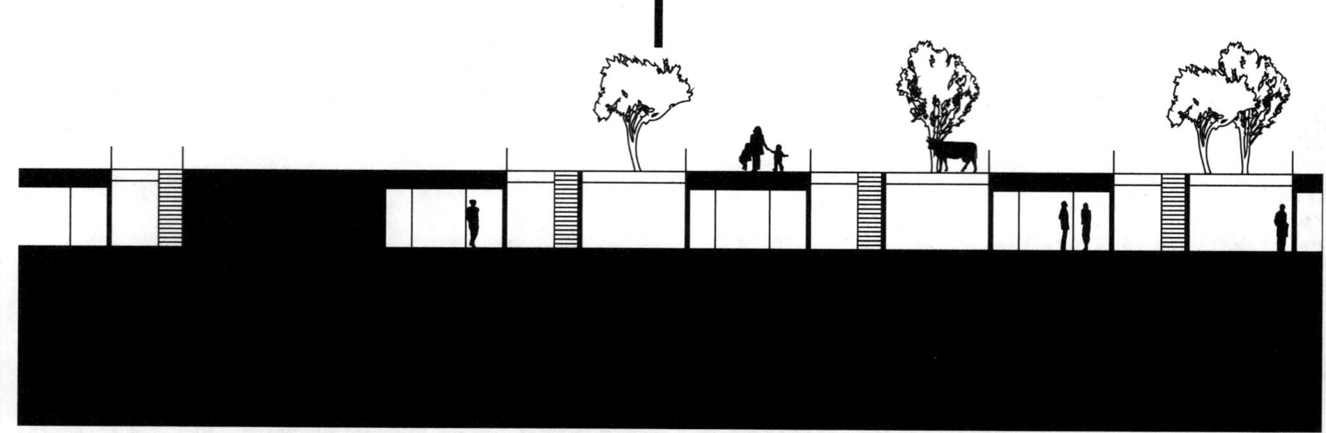

***Day and Night*, M. C. Escher, 1938.**

Roof Made City interlocks in a similar way, inter-weaving nature and buildings, shifting every row of houses by three metres to allow for a tree hole.

This neighbourhood of identical houses nestles between train tracks, a highway and a provincial road with a high level of sound pollution. All living quarters are protected by the endless mass of houses. The roofscape has an orchard-like set-up with trees planted in a grid measuring 13 x 19 metres. Two patios per unit allow for daylight and are interconnected with neighbouring houses, complying with the rule that there must be two escape routes per unit. By giving up the idea of a traditional house with facades and windows, one can roll out this typology in places considered unsuitable for housing.

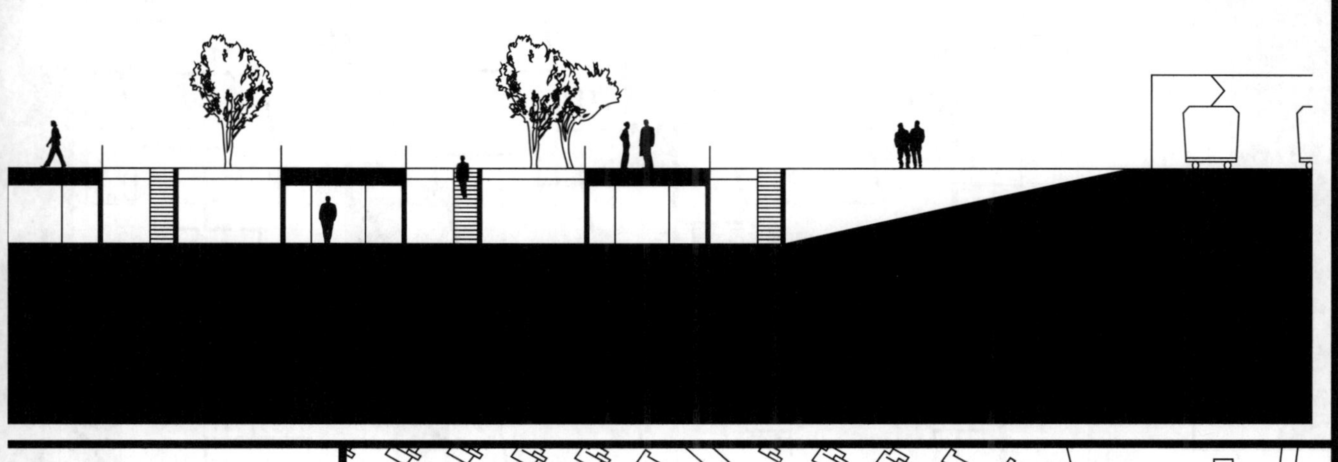

Section of Roof Made City.

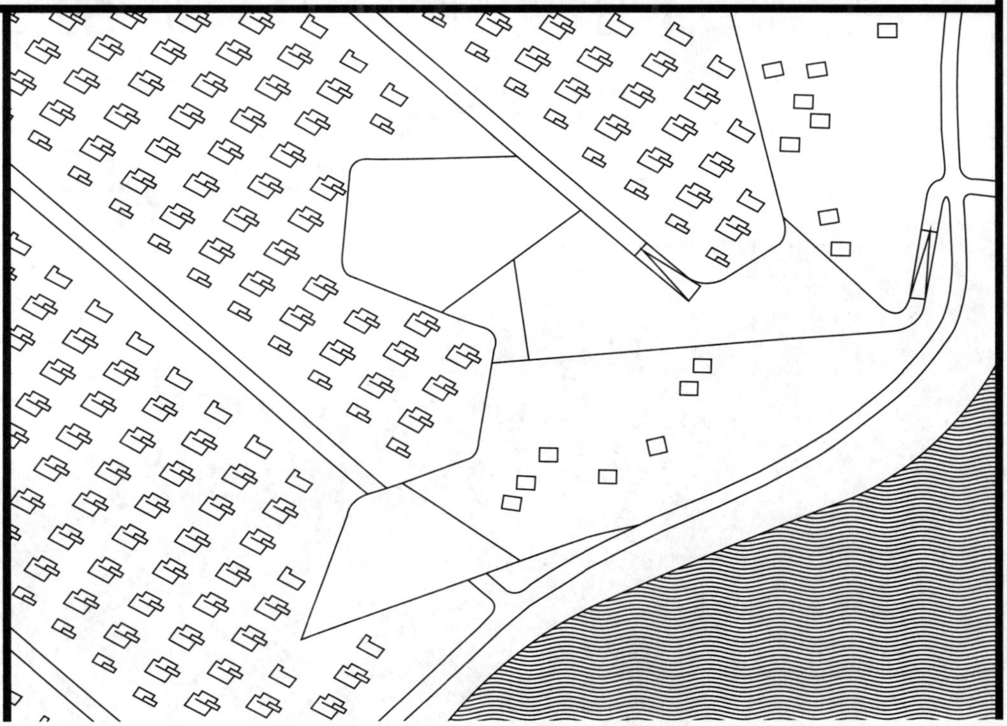

Roof Made City seen from above.

Plan of Roof Made City.

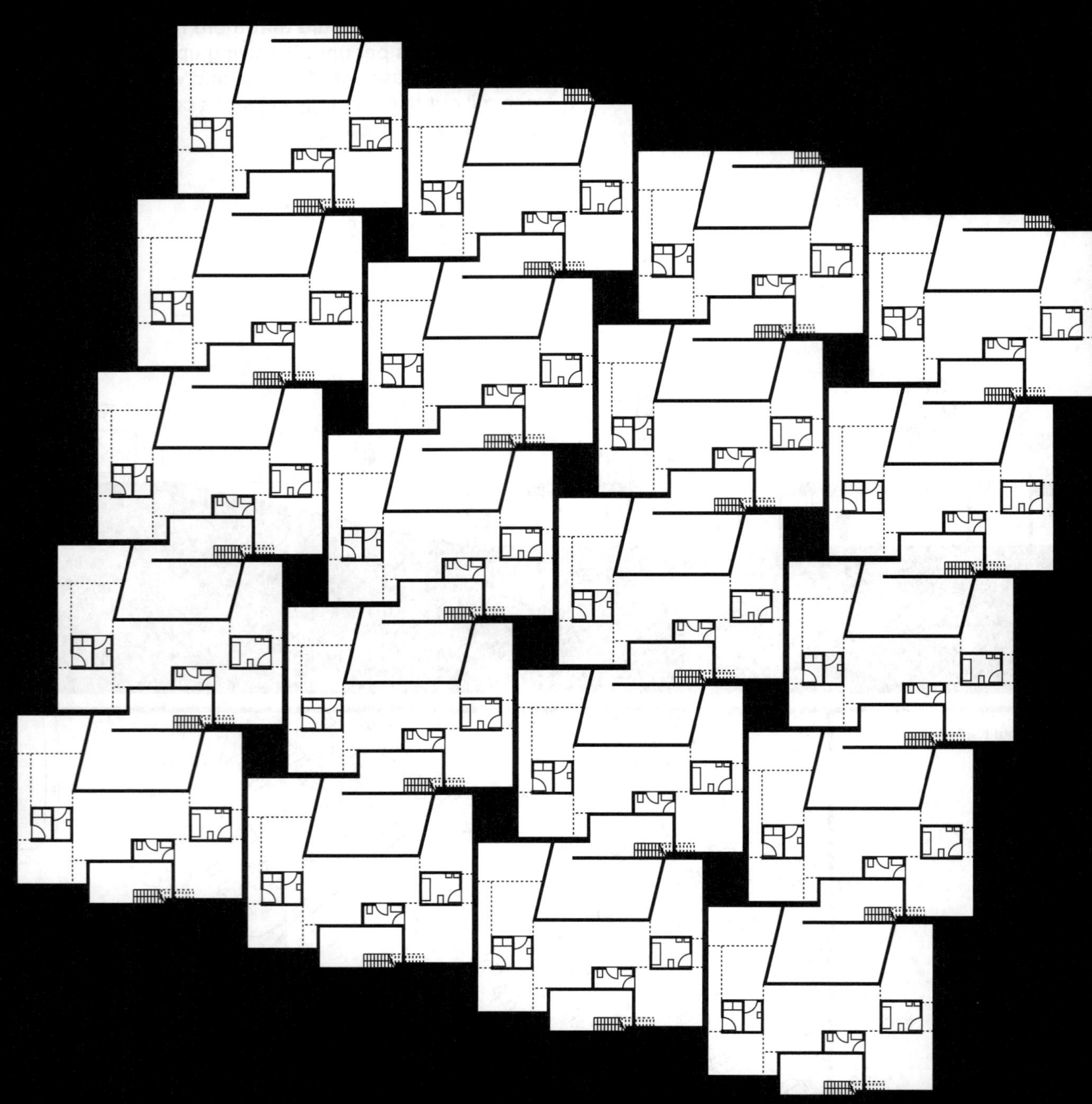

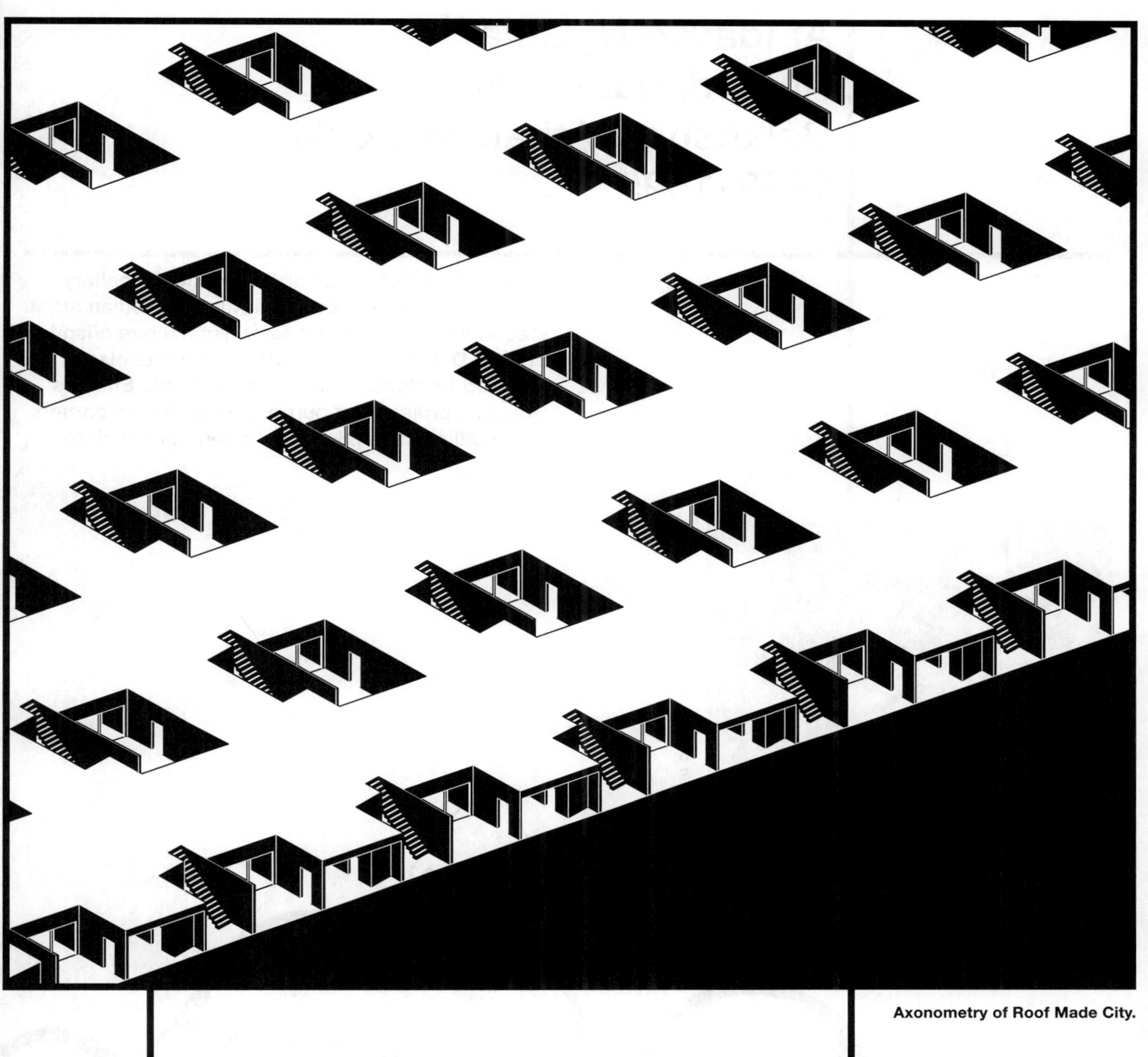

Axonometry of Roof Made City.

The landscape above can be supplemented with small allotment-like buildings, an orchard or the odd grazing cow or sheep, creating beautiful views over this polder-like landscape. Small structures and allotment garden facilities don't have to comply with strict Dutch housing regulations. Moreover, any infrastructure added does not need to be sealed off from its surroundings with sound barriers, therefore exaggerating a very characteristic virtue of the Dutch landscape: its spectacular flatness.

Amdavad Ni Gufa
Ahmedabad, India
Balkrishna Vithaldas Doshi
1993–1995

Amdavad Ni Gufa is an underground art gallery exhibiting paintings and sculptures by Indian artist Maqbool Fida Husain. It seems like the rare offspring of Jean Dubuffet's *Jardin d'émail* with its playful roof and Frederick Kiesler's biomorphic Endless House, a project that purposely erased the corners and rectilinear simplicity of modern architecture.

Jardin d'émail, Jean Dubuffet, 1974.

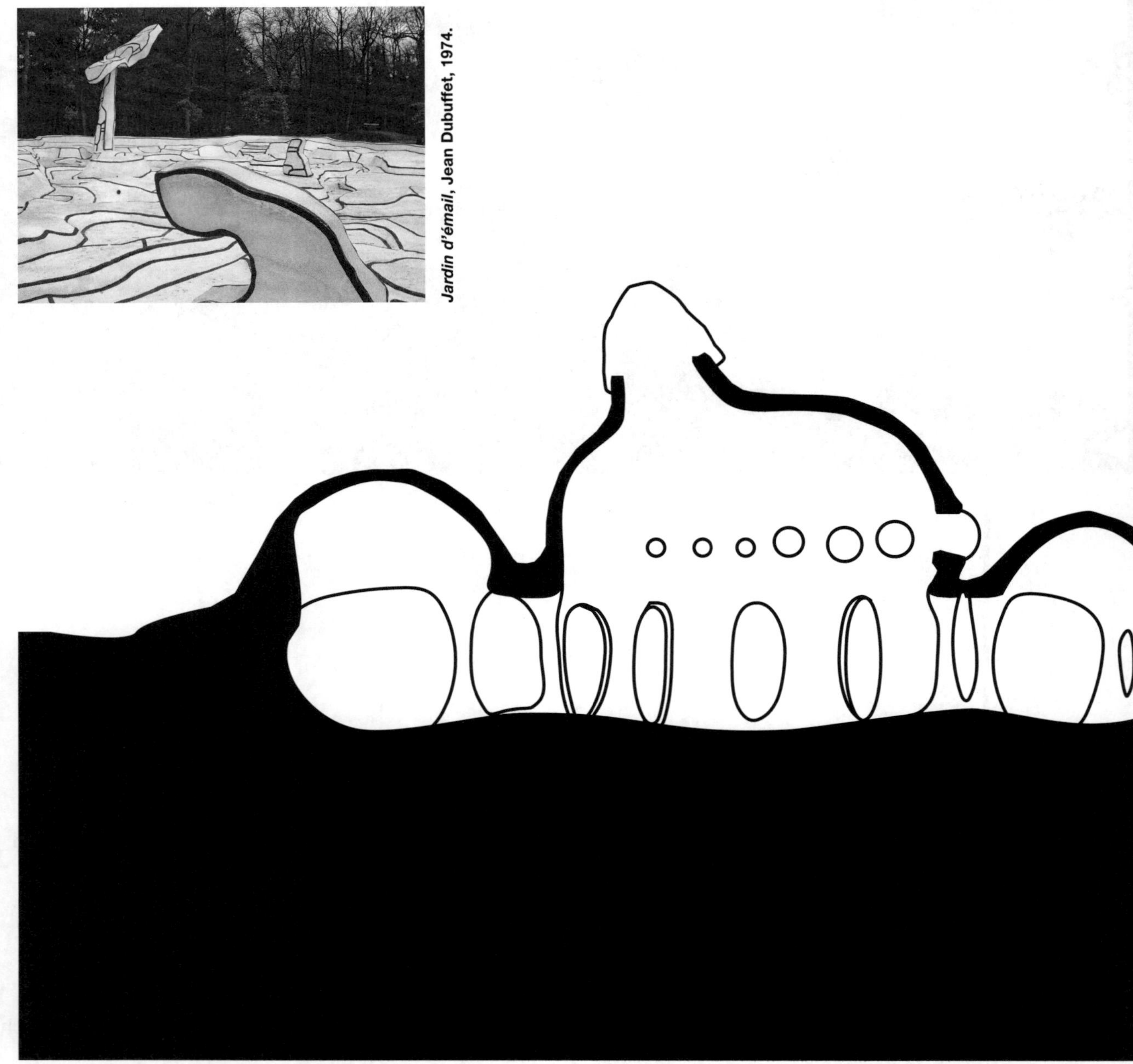

Frederick Kiesler presented his plans for the Endless House as early as 1924 in Vienna. This blunt criticism of the functionality of modernism and the International Style was dismissed by both the architecture and the art community, and it took until 1960 before the work was presented in the exhibition *Visionary Architecture* at the Museum of Modern Art. And even then, Kiesler's ideas were considered too visionary to be built.[38]

The Endless House, Frederick Kiesler, 1950–1960.

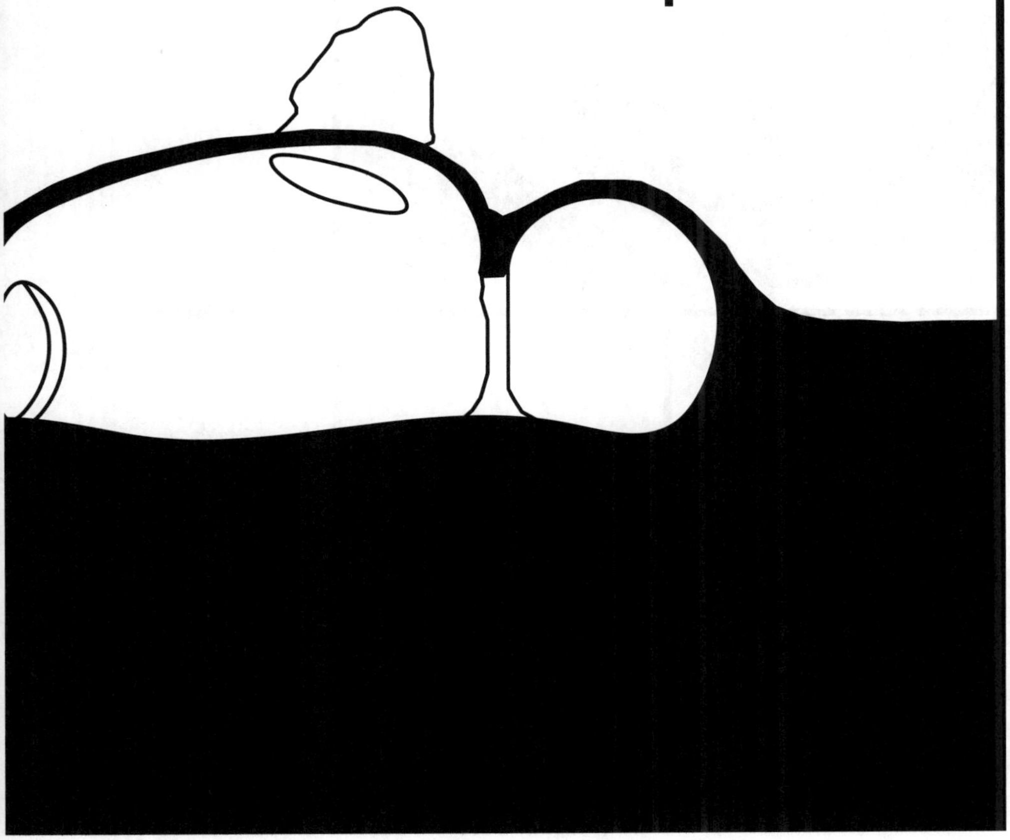

Section of Amdavad Ni Gufa.

Balkrishna Vithaldas Doshi had more luck with timing, using the humble computer to resolve Amdavad Ni Gufa's unorthodox design. Inspired by soap bubble structures and the shells of tortoises, there is not a single straight wall. The design is comprised of intersecting circles and ellipses, and although the geometries are complex, all was built by labourers with nothing but hand tools.

View of Amdavad Ni Gufa from above.

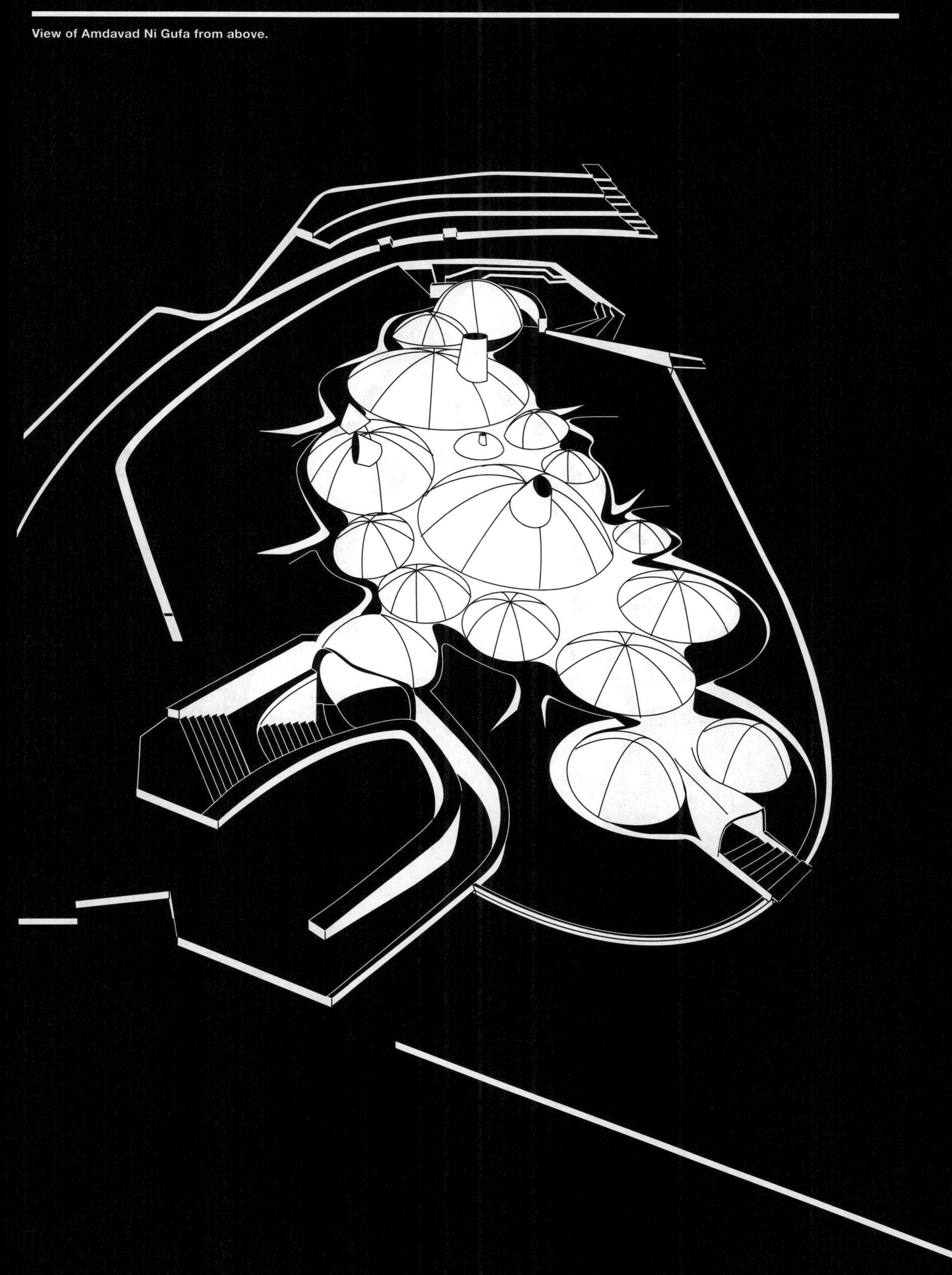

Plan of Amdavad Ni Gufa.

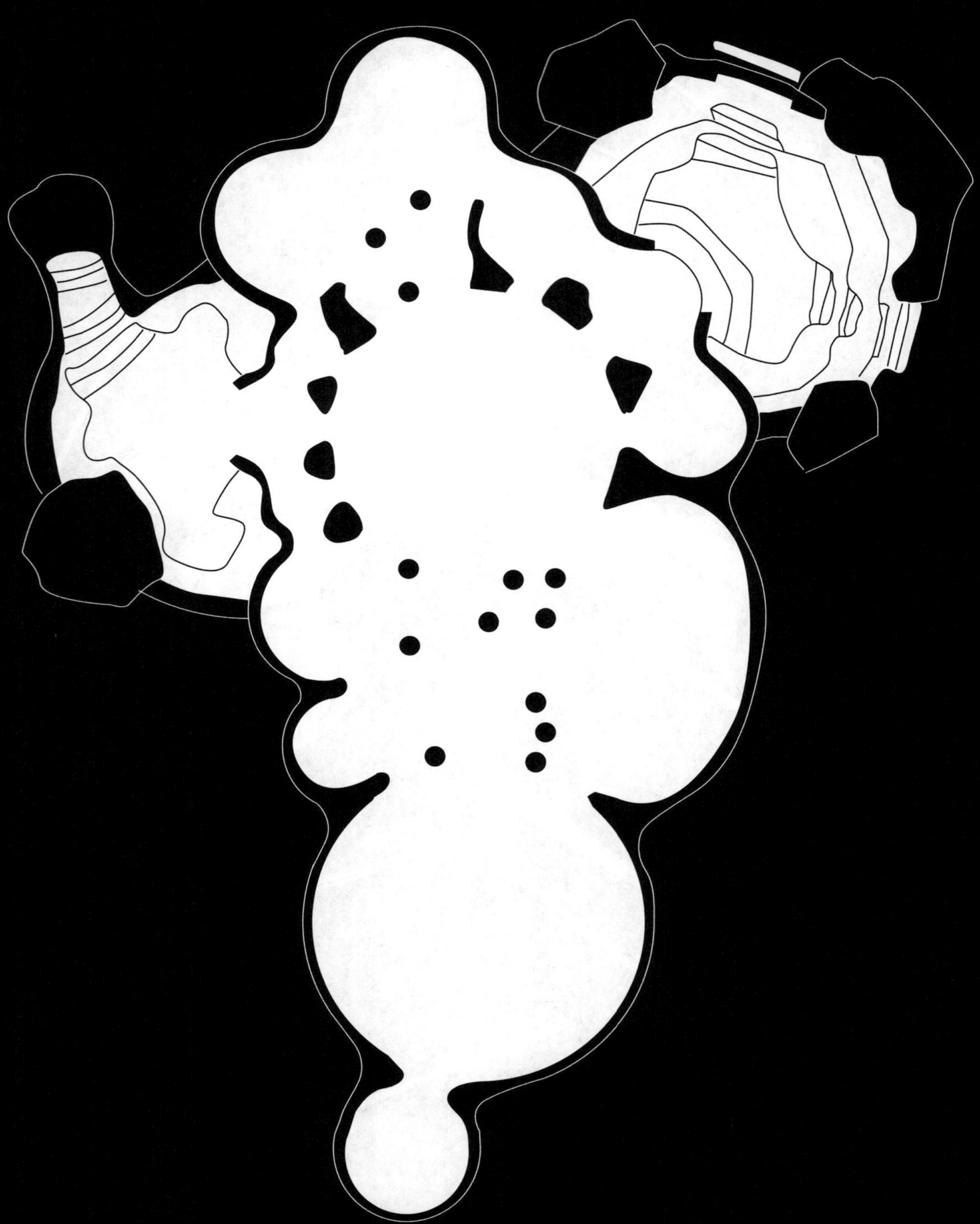

"Its fluid space, which has now become a natural garbhagriha, or 'golden womb', is where one is able to discover previous births and reincarnations. Such unexpected experiences make one ask: Who am I? Where do I come from? What time is it? How much and whose time do we have? Yet these questions become irrelevant as one delves deeper, as in a yogic trance. In the gufa, the past, present, and future are fused into a seamless continuum. There is no beginning and no end: in that space, time stands still."—Balkrishna Vithaldas Doshi

Antinori Winery
Bargino, Italy
Archea Associati
2004–2013

Since 1385, twenty-seven generations of Marchesi Antinori have lived off the vineyards around Florence, and they particularly cherish this land. When the present generation decided to move back to the vineyards from the patriarchal head-quarters of Palazzo Antinori in the centre of Florence, their passion and deep understanding of the place made all the difference.[39] What at first sight was a simple project became highly complex when the 11-metre-deep excavation altered the water management of this vast hillside. Without water, there are no grapes and no wine, but luckily the family knew how to rebalance this equation.

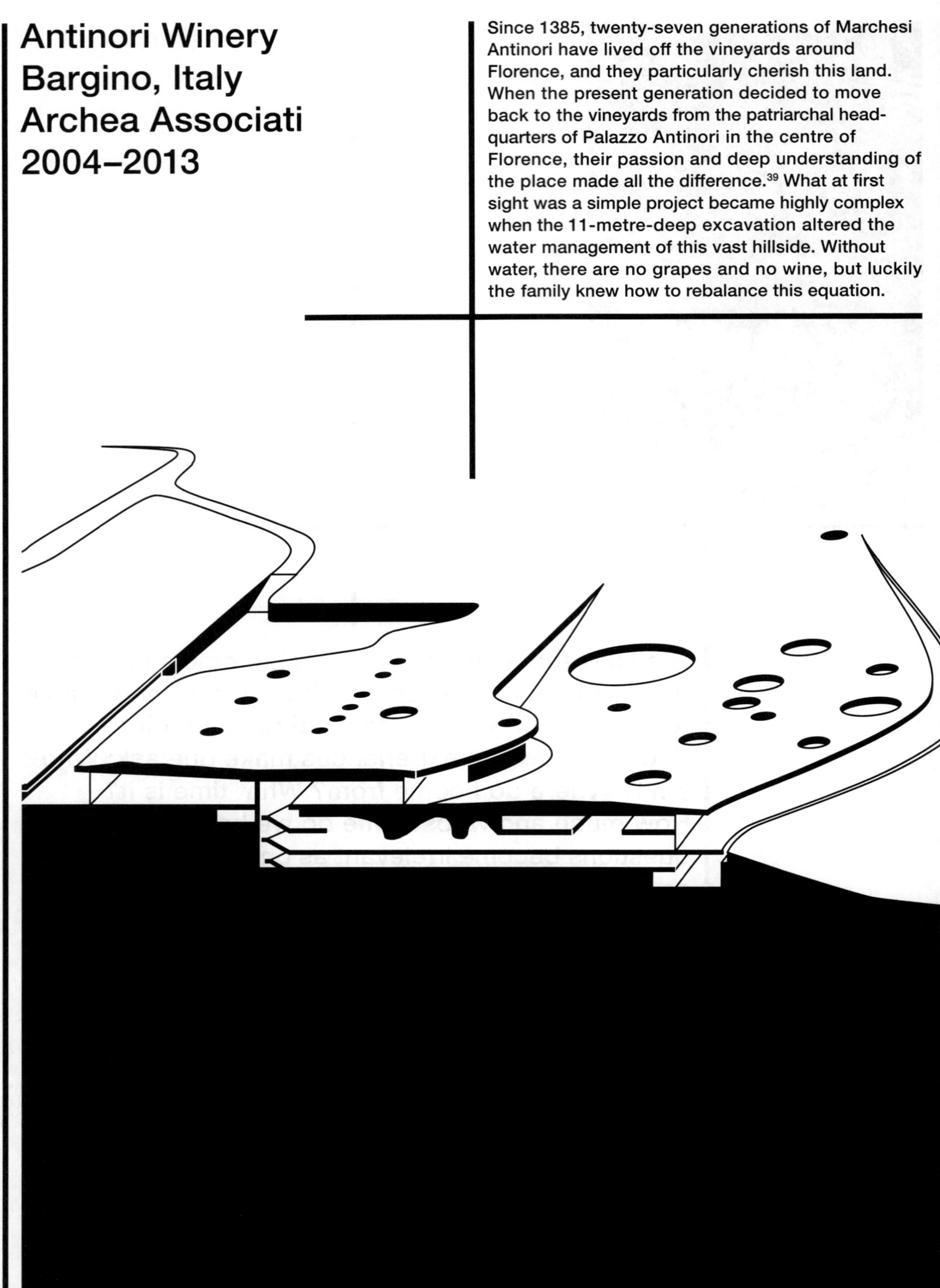

© Leonardo Finotti.

Sectional axonometry of Antinori Winery.

The new headquarters is a combination of offices, visitor centre, restaurant, shop, wine production and cellars. Trucks as well as visitors move in and out. The building convincingly pairs an iconic idiom with a subservient position under the vineyard. The delineation of architecture and landscape within this project is appropriately blurred. Both building and landscape have been designed; nature manipulated and cultivated.

Horizontal fissures in the landscape give access to the building and open up wide views over the rolling Tuscan landscape. Vertical skylights admit light and air. A winding 'corkscrew' staircase connects the lower parking level with a front plaza under a very spacious double-height canopy. Here you enter the visitor centre and offices, and inside you find an undulating ceramic-tiled ceiling covering the caves.

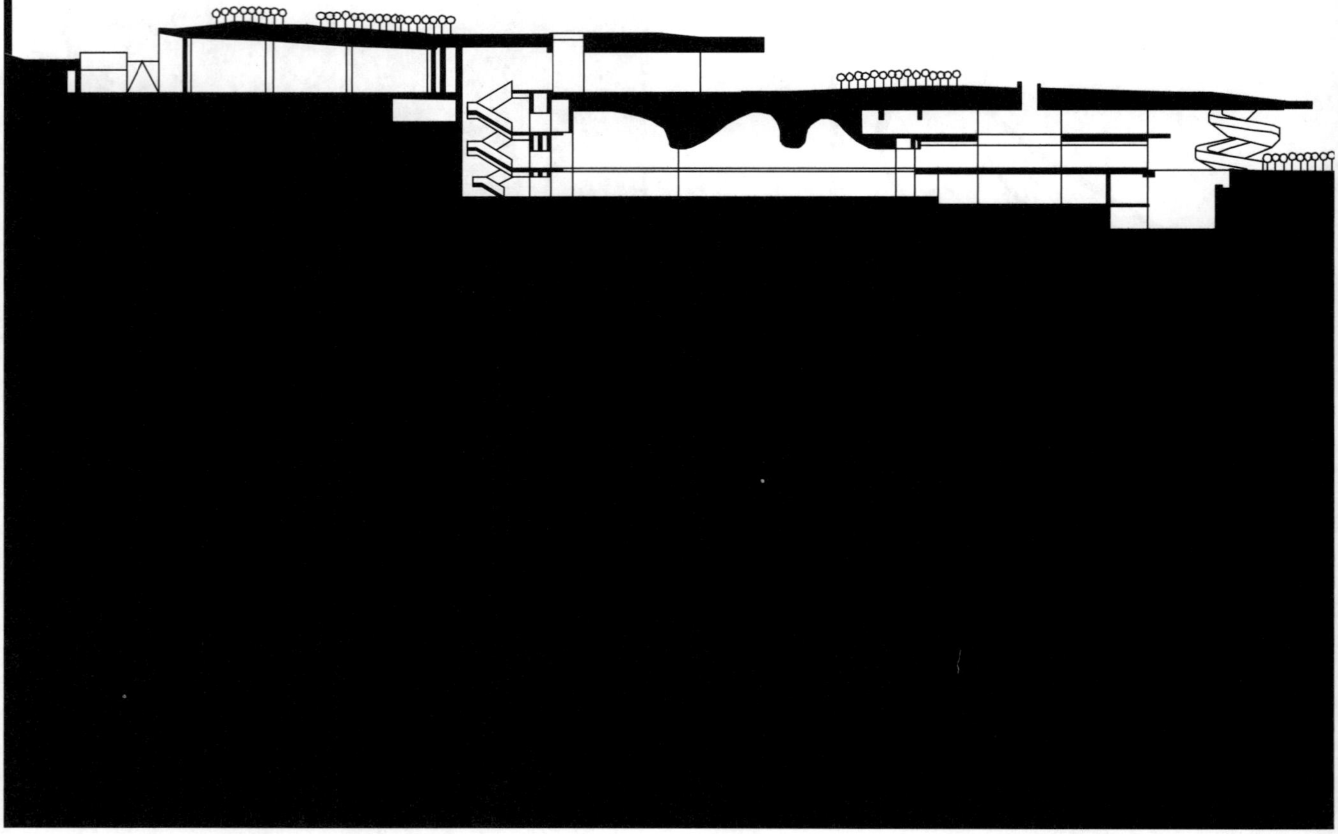

Cross sections of the building rise and fall with the landscape. What makes this building so convincing, so impressive, yet humble and discreet? It's not the section as such. It is the way in which, at both ends, the building blends into the landscape, allowing enough space for building and nature to come together. The two turns in the road to access the lower and upper level have an important role in this transition.

In the end, appearances are deceiving. This looks and feels like an underground building. In fact, it is only perched on the hill. It lies against a retaining wall at the back, where you will find a practical service street and loading bay. Antinori Winery goes back to the roots and an age-old understanding of what winemaking is about. It's a timeless building, without compromises, just like winemaking.

Section of Antinori Winery.

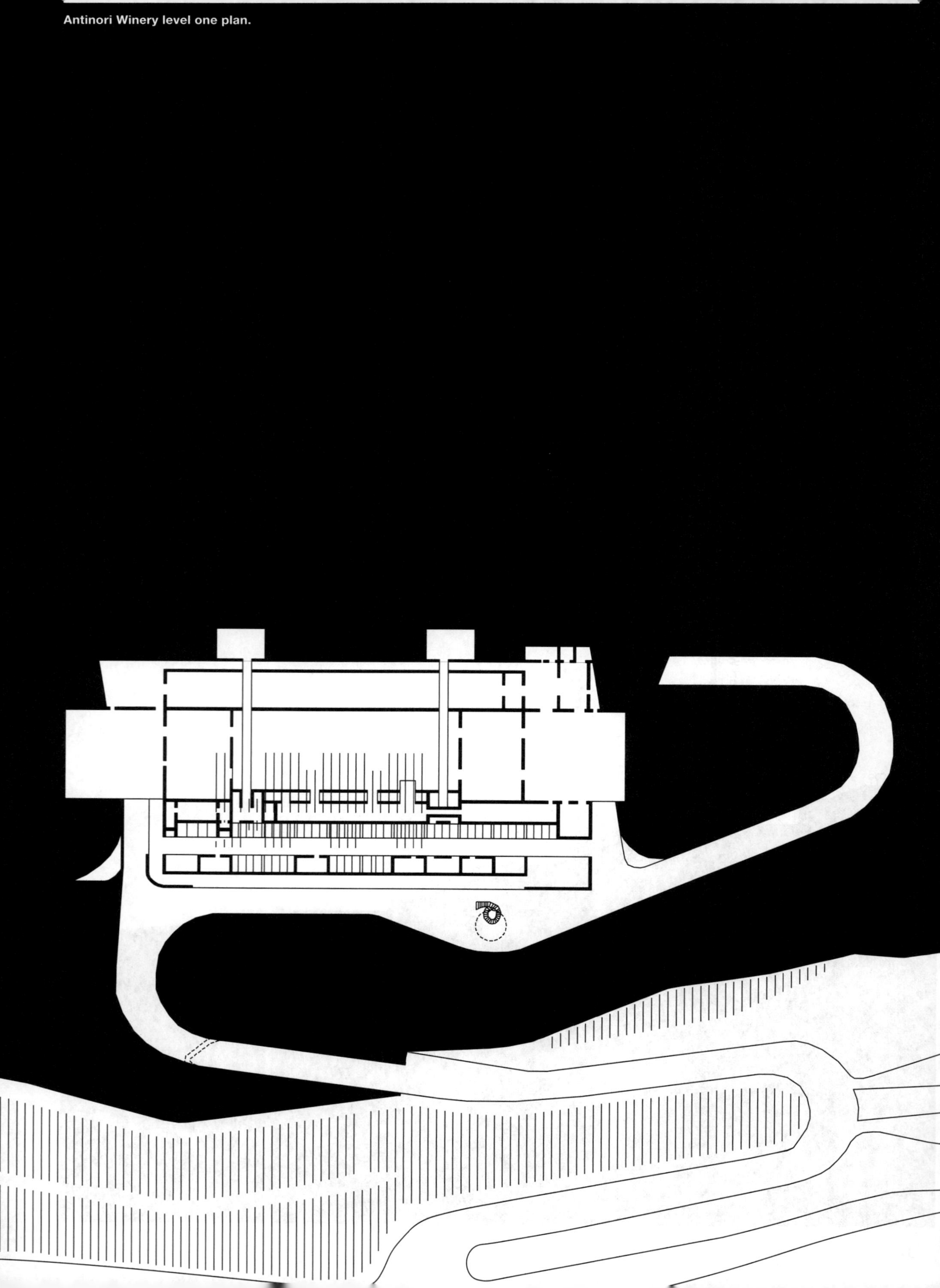

Antinori Winery level one plan.

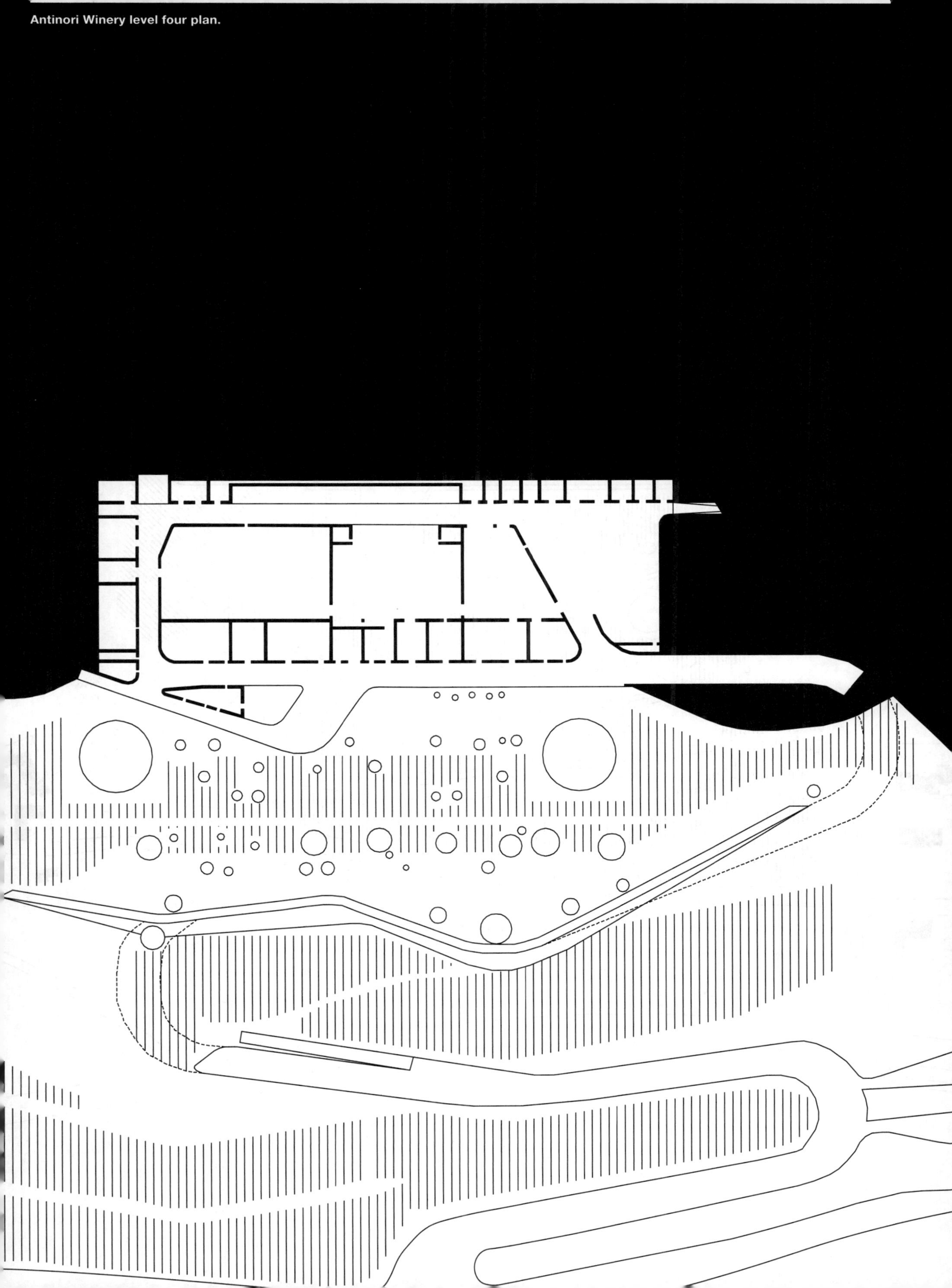

Antinori Winery level four plan.

Antinori Winery site plan.

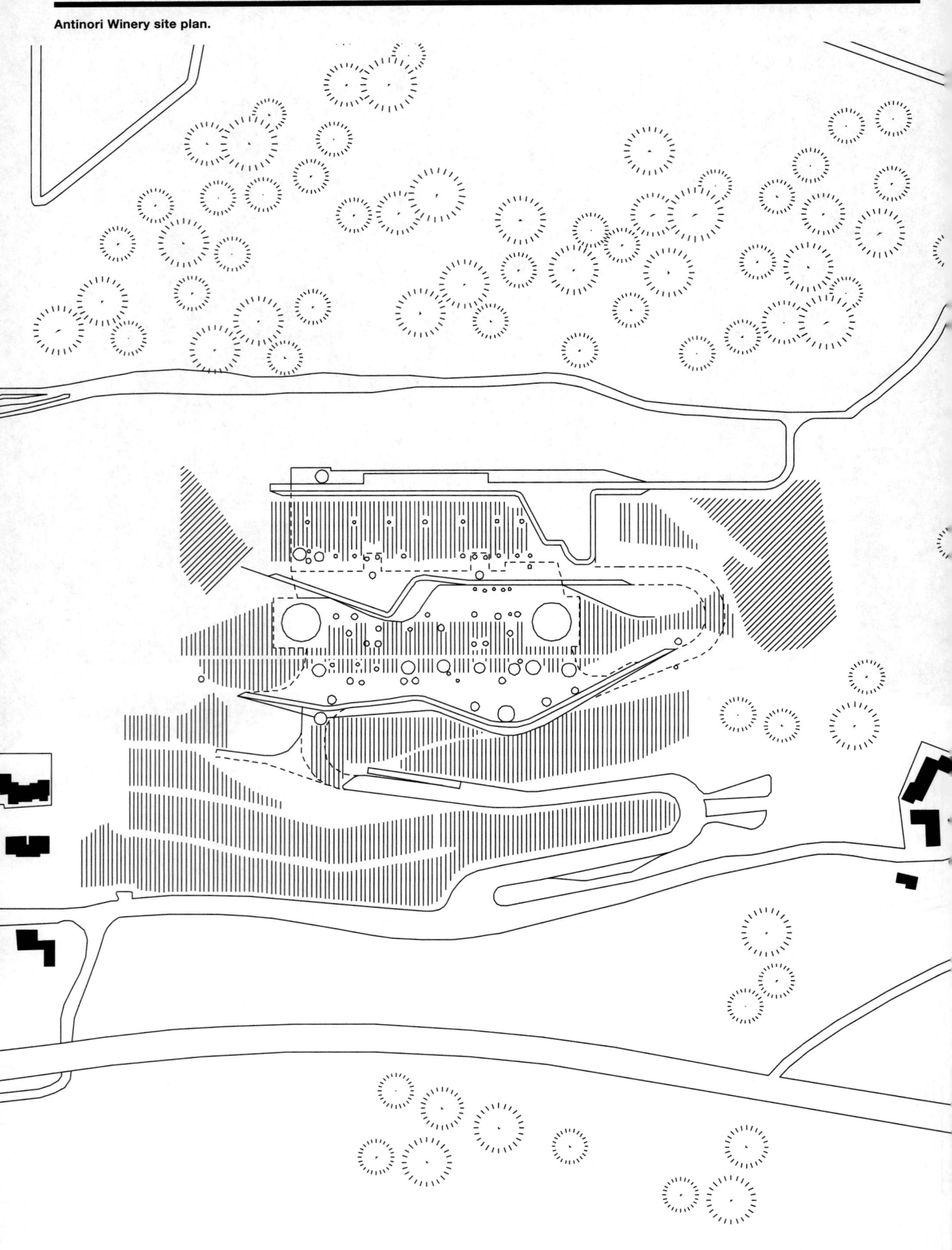

In Conversation

In 2014 Bjarne Mastenbroek interviewed founding partner of Archea Associati Marco Casamonti about the Antinori Winery, and his practice's wider position on sustainability, cultivating landscape and burying architecture.

Allegorical engraving of the Vitruvian primitive hut in the frontispiece of Marc-Antoine Laugier, *Essai sur l'architecture*, 2nd ed. 1755.

[Bjarne Mastenbroek] In your project Antinori Winery, there is a particular attention to the contextual specifics of the site, as if it sprung from them. Is this an underlying theme of your work? And was your decision to go underground a conscious effort to preserve the landscape or something more?

[Marco Casamonti] We believe it is impossible to design without a deep understanding of the context, and such an approach can lead to very interesting results. Intermingling concepts of beauty and nature were particularly influential in the eighteenth century, when Marc-Antione Laugier compared the primitive hut to the Greek temple. In the primitive hut, the horizontal beam was supported by tree trunks planted upright in the ground and the roof was sloped to shed rainwater. Laugier believed this was the inspiration behind the basic Doric order, that it was the standard form, which all architecture embodied. In the twentieth century we see the opposite, Le Corbusier's Villa Savoye started to detach architecture from nature, with a suspended and light object overlooking and dominating its context. But contemporary architecture is free from preconceived models. After classicism and modernism it is time to reconsider architecture as a whole. We need to look back to nature where we can find inspiration for both a different aesthetic and advanced technology.

[BM] I agree, architecture seems to be trying to connect, drawing inspiration or meaning from nature and landscape. I have my theories for why, but what do you think is driving this?

[MC] Firstly, I think that this reconsideration is linked to the acknowledgement that everything is artificial. Technology and virtual reality has taken us very far from

Gerard Noodtstraat, Nijmegen, Netherlands, SeARCH, 1993–1996.

nature. Nature is a basic necessity, so we need to reintroduce it in our cities. Secondly, we have to save energy and money. The world population is growing fast and therefore we should manage the space we inhabit carefully. It is essential to understand that each time we build, we lose natural ground, and it is impossible to reproduce it. This is the main reason why Archea works extensively underground. A variety of activities can be moved underground with the aim to keep the existing landscape intact for a different and complementary use, like in the case of Antinori where we safeguarded the cultivation of Chianti grapes.

[BM] A winery is a very interesting typology to study how architecture relates to its context and to landscape in general. The winery has enjoyed a bit of a renaissance of late, transforming from purely a production space to a destination. Hiding a winery below ground is a rather brave or risky move, no?

[MC] Ten years ago I interviewed Mr Antinori for a book about wineries. He knew everything about traditional wine production but asked for my help to develop a new representative building for his company. We made a winery that is at the same time a church, a farm and an industry. A church, for its symbolic and monumental value; a farm, because it is immersed in nature and right in the production site; an industry, for the complexity of programmes and its dimensions. The aim was to merge the building and the rural landscape. This was achieved through creating a new ground, a roof cultivated with vines.

[BM] So the complex roofscape shifts the ground to a new level, like its fighting to stay visible while still supporting the vines above?

[MC] Yes, the farmland is interrupted, along the contour lines, by two horizontal cuts allowing an exchange between the inside and the outside. By enhancing the landscape we express the cultural and social value of the place where wine is produced.

[BM] We think this strategy can be applied to a dense urban context. In one of our first projects, a housing block in Nijmegen, we displaced the car park from the backyard to the roof of the building, freeing the ground for more interesting activities. Is the future of the city the hybridization between urban and rural?

[MC] Yes, car parking, community centres and housing projects can all carry nature within them, not only metaphorically in their shapes and technologies, but also physically with green terraces or rooftops. In this way we can save public ground which would otherwise be occupied by buildings. We can compare this strategy to the tradition of terracing in agriculture.

[BM] Not to play devil's advocate, but agriculture is highly artificial. Surely the integration of nature in the city must go beyond urban farming or a generic green roof?

[MC] Green space should be conceived as a communal element not only at ground level but also at different heights, with a diffuse system of terraces and green roofs covering the lower buildings that form the primary fabric of the city. A second layer of high-rise towers overlays the green city, increasing density. The result is similar to Le Corbusier's Ville Radieuse, although it presents a greater integration between nature and architecture, not just towers standing on an empty green field but merging with a complex and hybrid system.

[BM] These ideas are not new, I think the challenge lies in how to make projects like these more resilient to commercial impact. How do we show that connecting architecture, landscape and nature can improve people's lives while being profitable?

[MC] We need to communicate the value of transferring the ground that the building occupies to the roof. Roofs are usually convenient spots to place installations, but that is old technology. We can easily and conveniently use geothermal energy. One metre of planted ground is an efficient and cheap thermal insulator and filter for rainwater. The natural place for installations is under the building, leaving the roof available for new uses. We need to harness natural processes and ancient construction methods. In the Antinori Winery we cool down the double space where wine ages in barrels naturally. Taking inspiration from Brunelleschi's dome of Florence's Cathedral of Santa Maria del Fiore, we produced a special brick that can be suspended on a steel structure. This created a hollow space between vault and concrete structure keeping the temperature at a constant 17°C. A city that is able to truly hybridize with nature means advanced technology, sustainability and even profit!

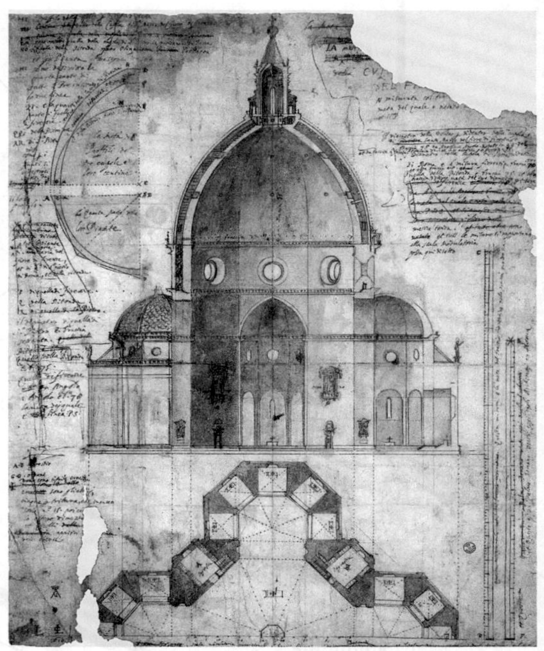

Section of the dome of Santa Maria del Fiore, 1613.

Villa Vals
Vals, Switzerland
SeARCH & CMA
2005–2009

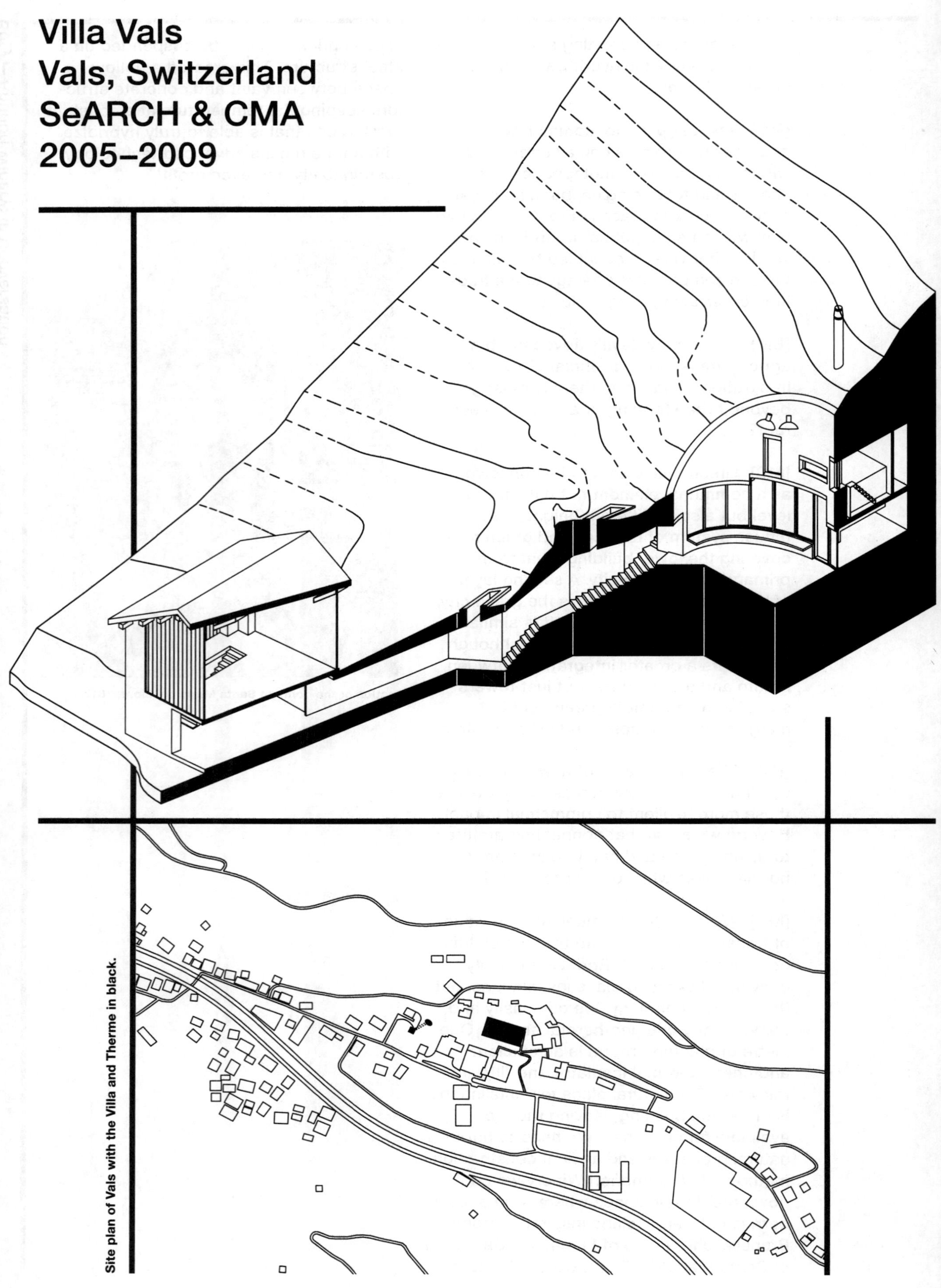

Site plan of Vals with the Villa and Therme in black.

Surprised it was permissible to construct so close to the world-famous thermal baths and in the line of sight of the historic village of Vals, the client seized the opportunity. Not to petulantly obstruct the view but to realize a childhood dream of making an underground house, like the huts he used to build with friends. Some memories stay sharp and easy to conjure up, like a familiar scent.

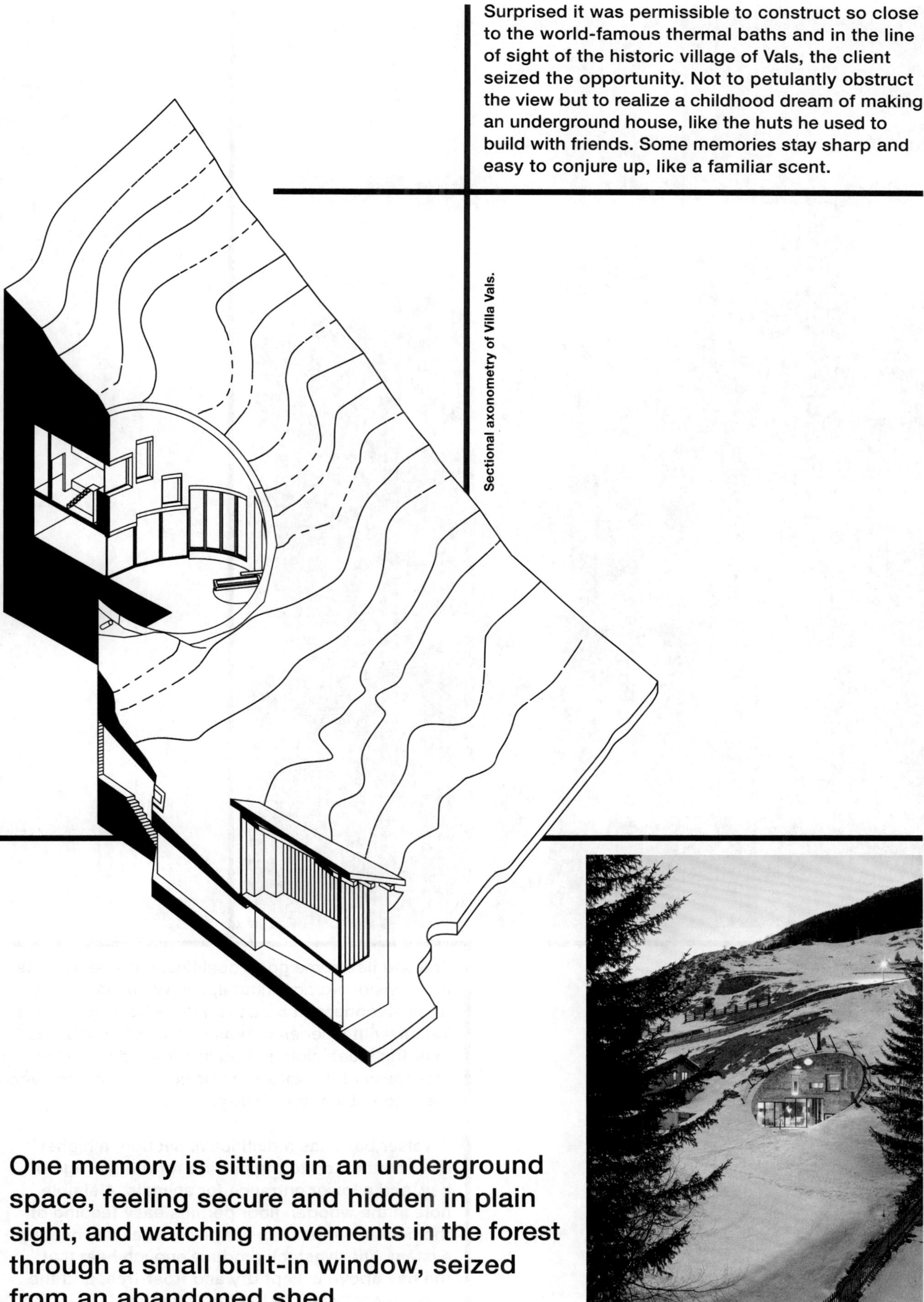

Sectional axonometry of Villa Vals.

One memory is sitting in an underground space, feeling secure and hidden in plain sight, and watching movements in the forest through a small built-in window, seized from an abandoned shed.

Typical Valser barns.

The site has some good qualities. It is cheap since it is considered agricultural, and unbuildable due to its steepness. It boasts an incredible view of Piz Tomül, with a series of typical Valser barns spread over the steep slopes. And in winter, despite the steepness of the valley, the rising sun appears over the ridge as early as half-past nine.

A Valser barn has a distinctive section, a higher level connected to the hillside for the storage of hay, and a lower entrance for animals. A simple hole in the wooden floor permits easy feeding of the herd in winter. It is the perfect passive heating system. The livestock produce enough heat that the hay above is kept dry and frost-free, and the dung is easily ejected at the lower level.

New European rules on animal welfare prohibit the future use of these barns, so a new function has to be found. Most barns are abandoned or demolished, but in the case of Villa Vals, the lower level of the existing barn is used as an entrance hall and the upper level as a garage. This sensitivity to the Valser barn's value made this project possible. The old farmer had, until then, prevented every sale without telling why. It turned out that he, too, wanted to preserve his shed.

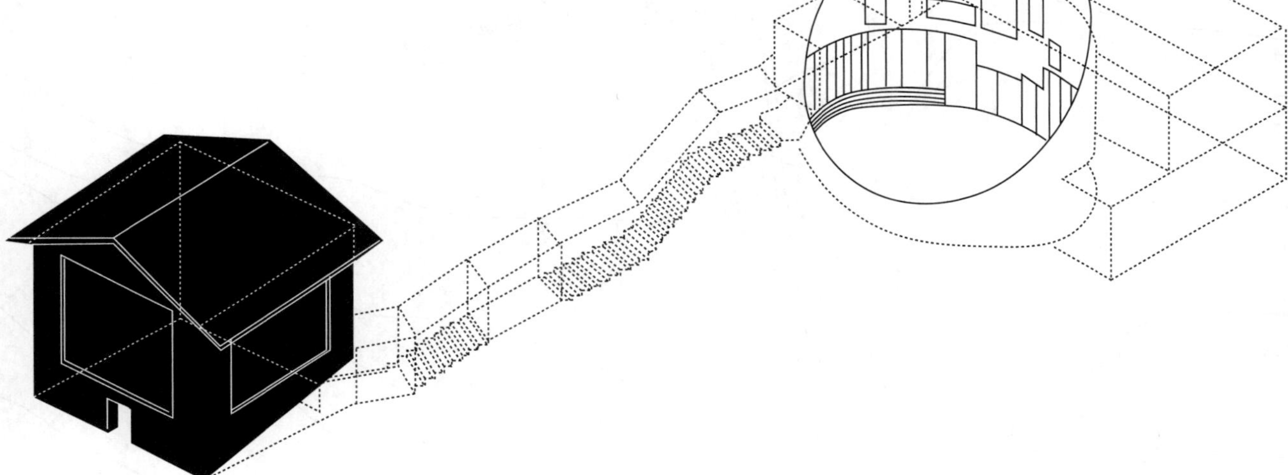

Axonometry of Villa Vals showing the entrance through the barn.

The use of the section affords an architecture that is simultaneously underground, yet open to the landscape. A spherical incision into the steep incline denotes a central patio. With this new ground slightly lowered, the viewing angle is inclined. Standing within the patio, you can tilt your head up towards a dramatic view of the mountains on the opposite side of the narrow valley. The incision into the landscape frames the view beyond.

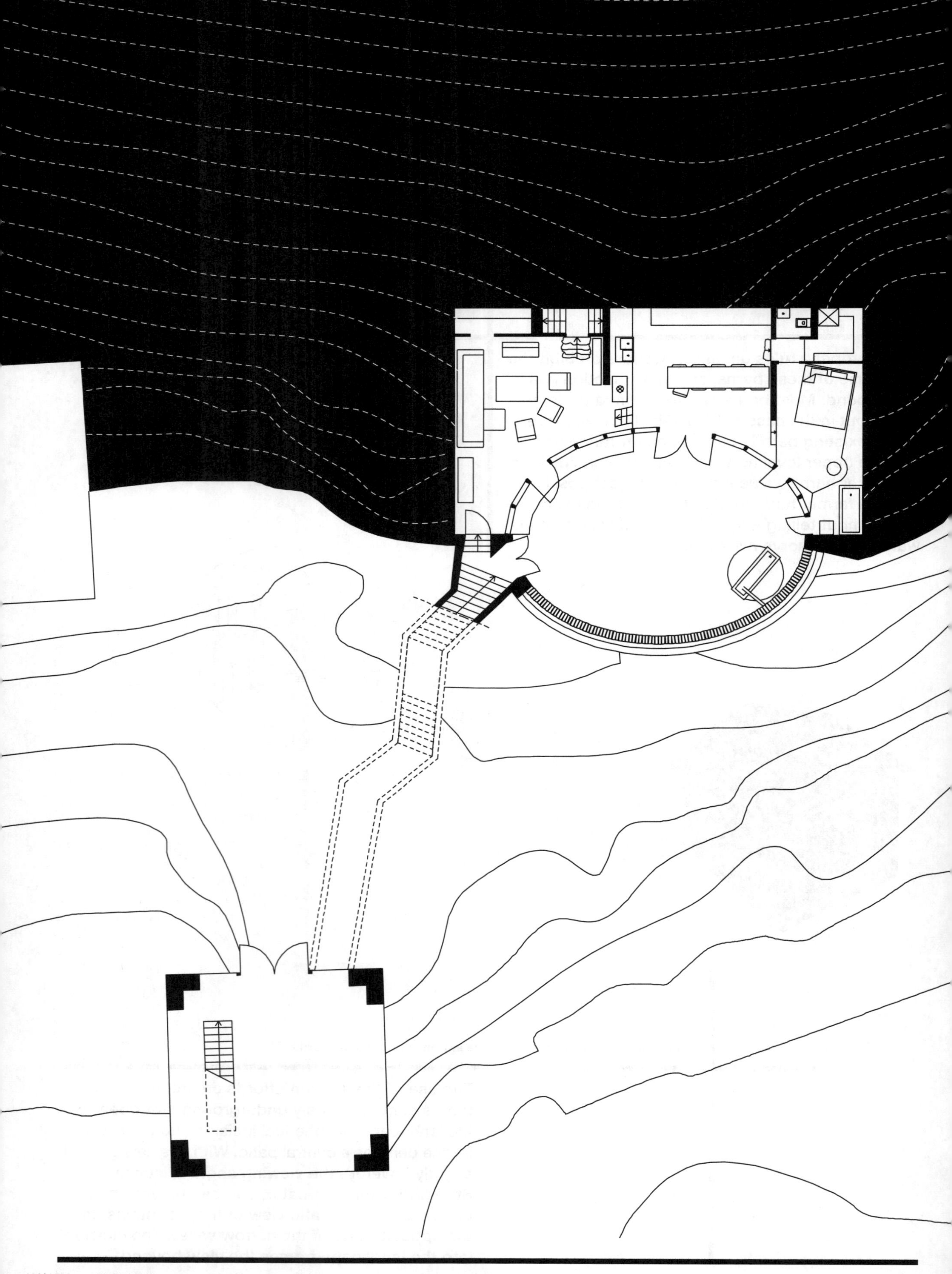

Plan of Villa Vals.

dutchtub

656

dutchtub
114

Section of Villa Vals.

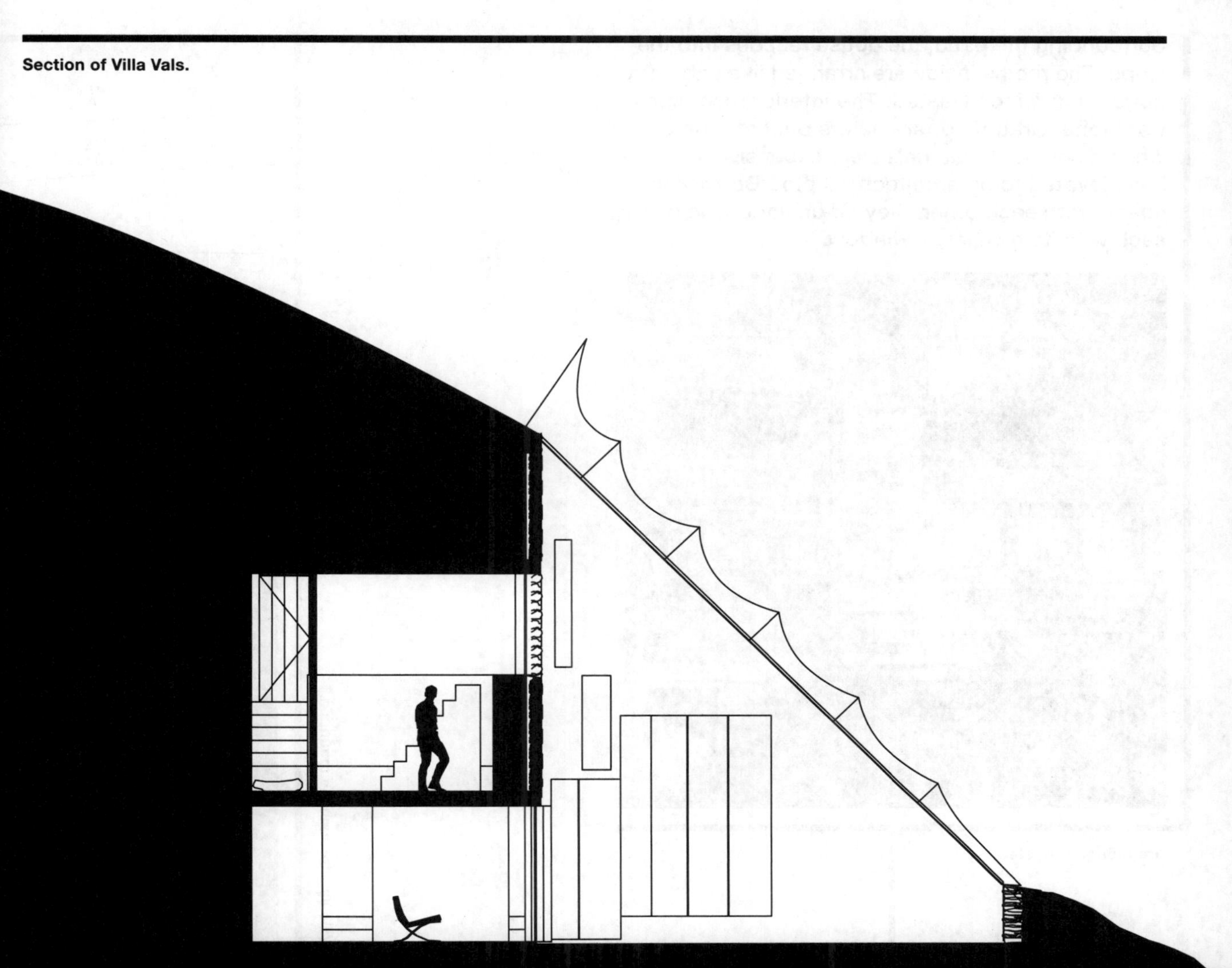

Surrounding the patio, the house recedes into the slope. The rooms inside are arranged like cabinetry, not a square inch wasted. The interior resembles traditional Graubündner chalets built at a time when labour and materials were expensive, but here it is elevated to an architectural plot. Borrowing space from each other, they sit on various levels, each with its own large window.

Graubündner chalet.

Section of Villa Vals through the mountain.

The earth, which surrounds these internal spaces, insulates the building, reducing energy consumption and increasing internal comfort. Villa Vals exploits both the pragmatic and the exceptional nature of this site to create a unique embedded architecture.

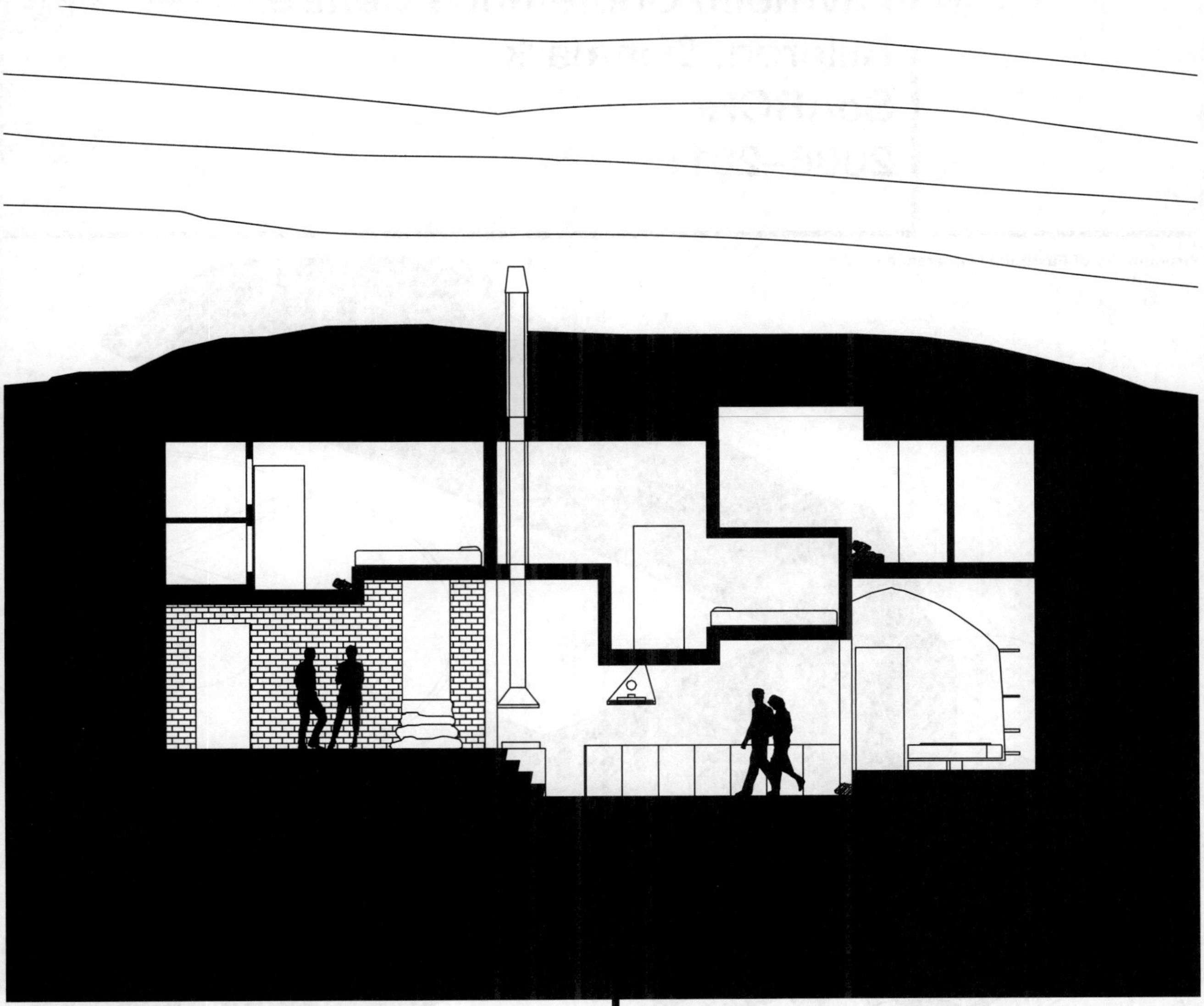

The best things in life are free. While digging the hole to create a building site we found an old water source. This is now a wellspring on the main terrace.

Favrholm Conference Centre
Hillerød, Denmark
SeARCH
2006–2011

Axonometry of Favrholm Conference Centre.

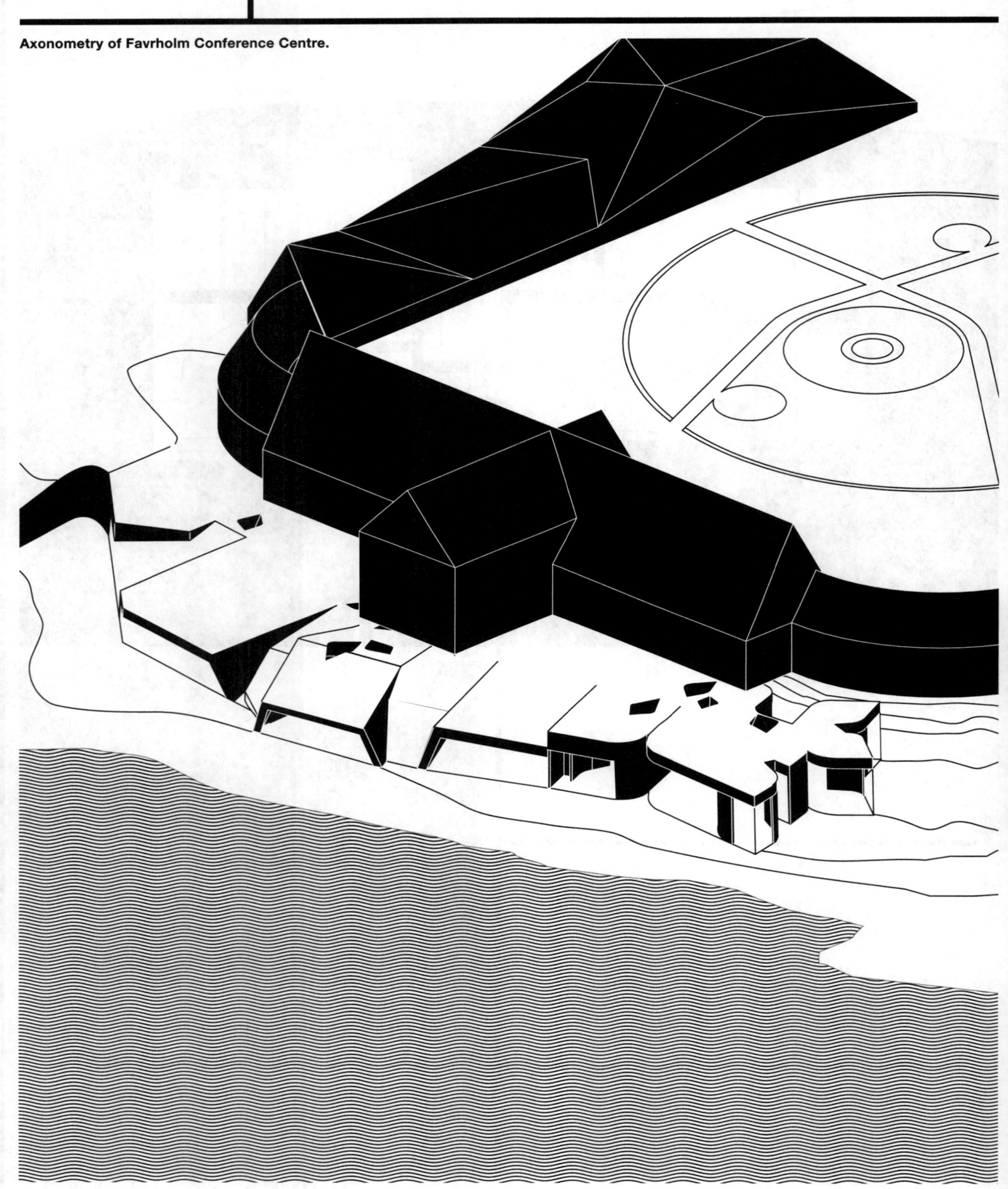

GEZONDHEIDSDIENST VOOR DIEREN
GLD
212 1008252
516 245 744
01-09-89
VRI
2B
W F Bunt
Schoolstraat 2
6674-AK Herveld
02-11-89
V.V.B. KESTEREN

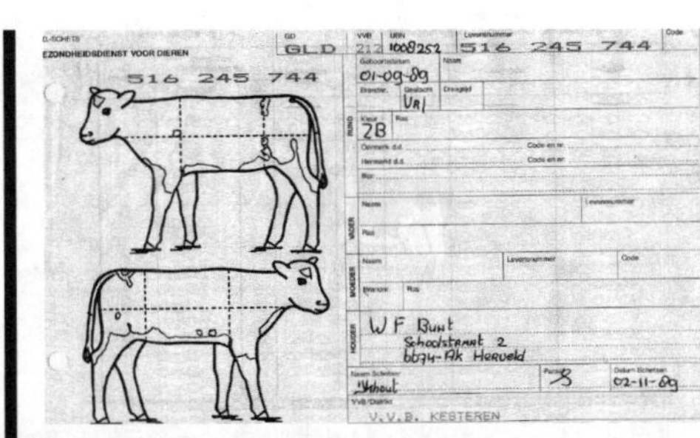

Cow identifier.

Before the gaudy yellow ear tags became the obligatory standard in farming, a cow sketcher came to the farm when a calf was born. A black and white pattern (or brown-white) was drawn like a unique fingerprint, allowing the cow to be identified throughout his life. It is amazing how they were able to precisely identify every cow by this simple and relatively fast technique.

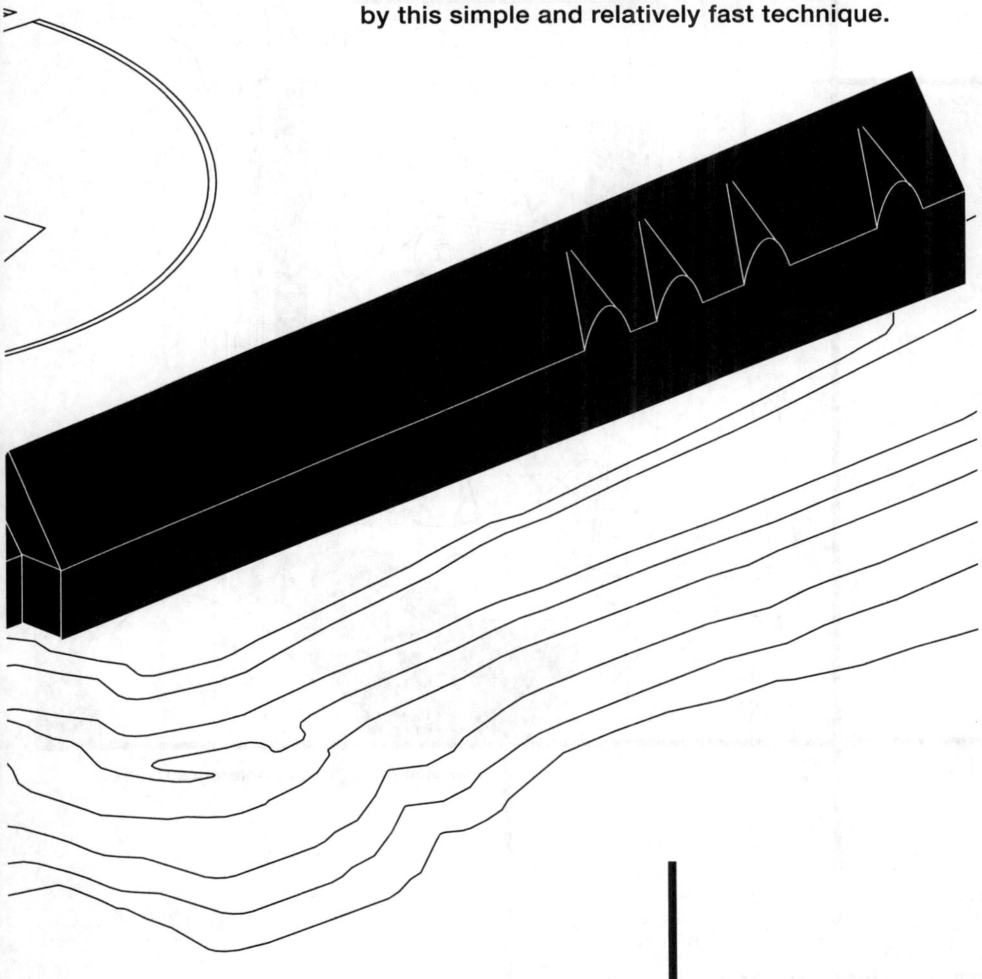

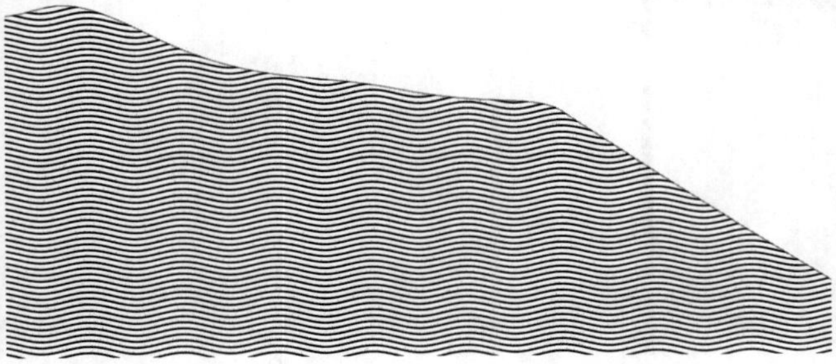

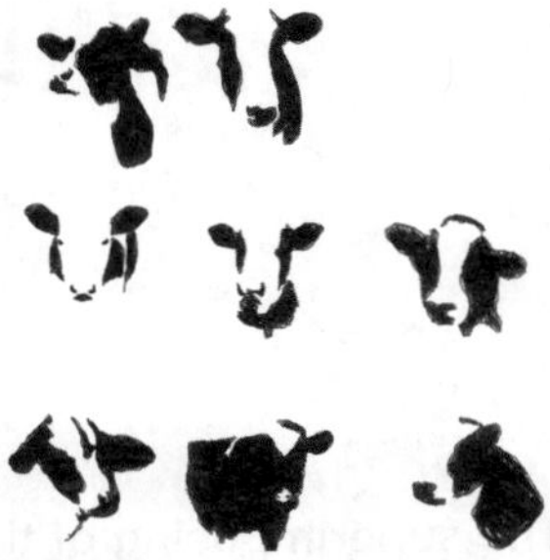

Cow sketches.

As a tribute to the late Enric Miralles, SeARCH re-enacted the cow sketches he once made in response to a very Dutch postcard sent to him by Bjarne Mastenbroek. The sketches provide proof that from a very rudimentary black and white pattern, a full image with depth can be rendered relatively quickly.

The Favrholm site has been a stud, dairy and research farm over history, and cows have played a crucial role in its development. In designing a substantial extension of the farm to house Novo Nordisk's global conference centre, we made an abstract collage from these cow silhouettes.

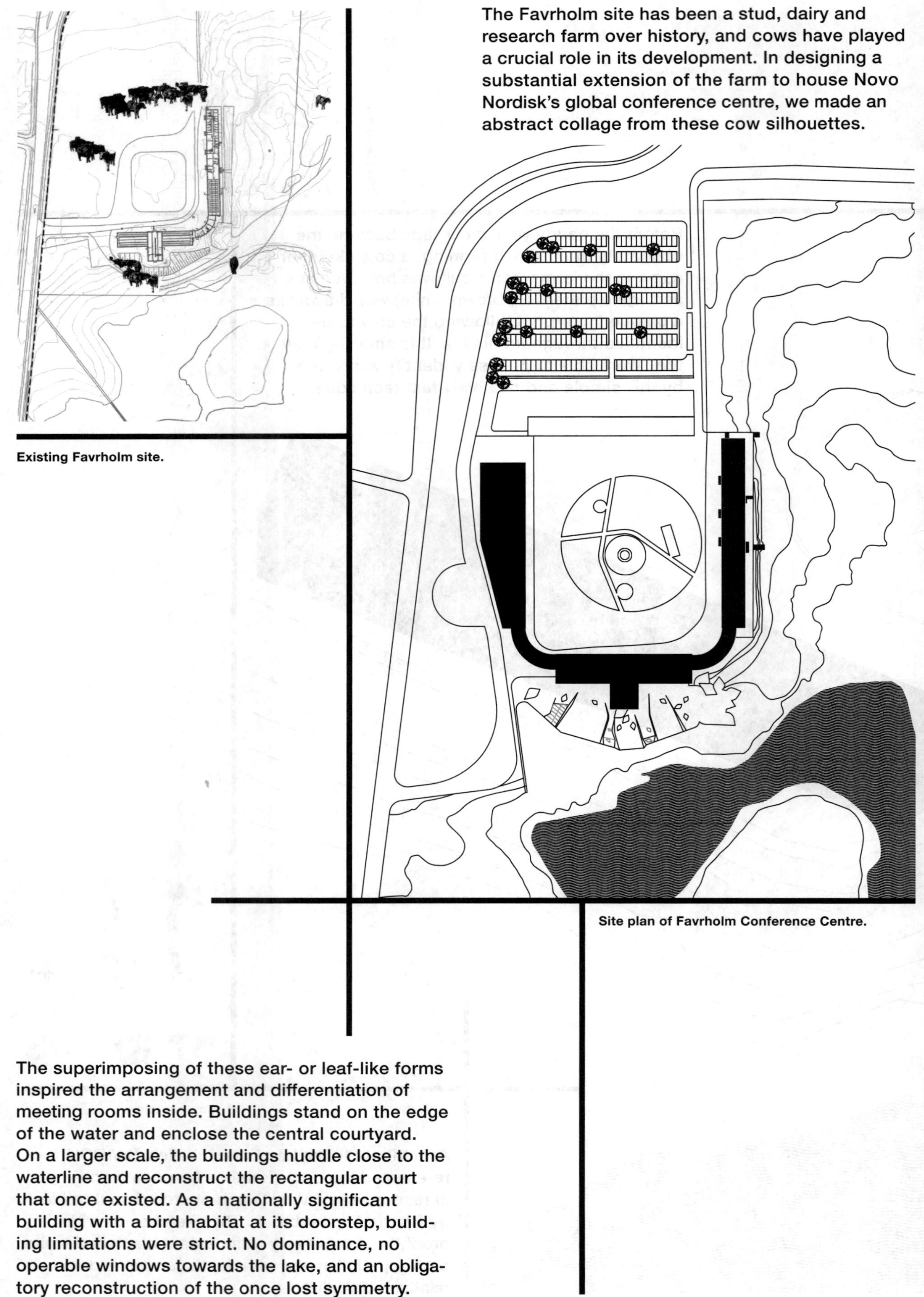

Existing Favrholm site.

Site plan of Favrholm Conference Centre.

The superimposing of these ear- or leaf-like forms inspired the arrangement and differentiation of meeting rooms inside. Buildings stand on the edge of the water and enclose the central courtyard. On a larger scale, the buildings huddle close to the waterline and reconstruct the rectangular court that once existed. As a nationally significant building with a bird habitat at its doorstep, building limitations were strict. No dominance, no operable windows towards the lake, and an obligatory reconstruction of the once lost symmetry.

NOVO

On the north side, the conference rooms and meeting areas are 'laid down' in the grass, with the sun in the back and away from the noise, overlooking the bird-foraging lake and rural setting. The difference in level between the court and lakeside is exploited and a significant amount of programme is dug into the bank. At the western tip the cow-ear-shaped small meeting rooms slowly detach from the hill-shaped volumes. Some are found scattered in the surrounding landscape as tree houses or terraces.

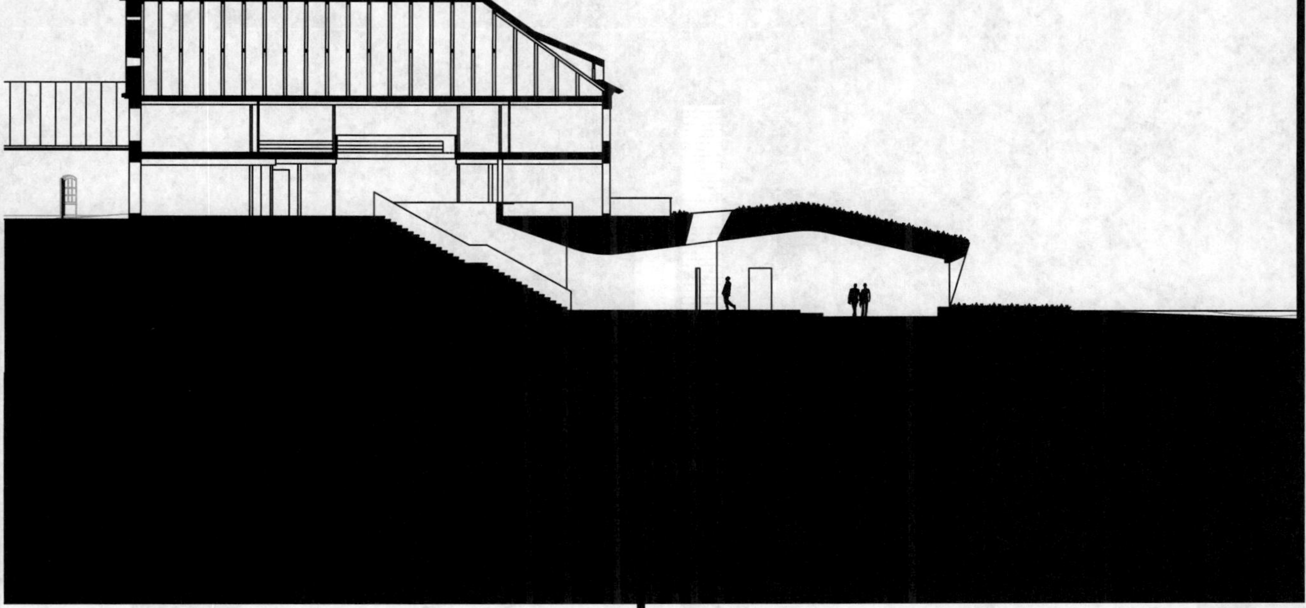

Section of Favrholm Conference Centre.

By connecting the central farmhouse with the 'underground' conference rooms and both ends of this linear building, we made a loop between old and new. This permits people to bypass the narrow wing of the main building and keep views free on both sides.

When it comes to an underground building, the loss of orientation is an issue. Especially in a conference facility where people from all around the world will come maybe once or twice in their lives. Big skylights in the roof and small meeting rooms alternating with small patios ensure that people can always orientate themselves towards the central farmhouse above. The feeling of being underground is gone.

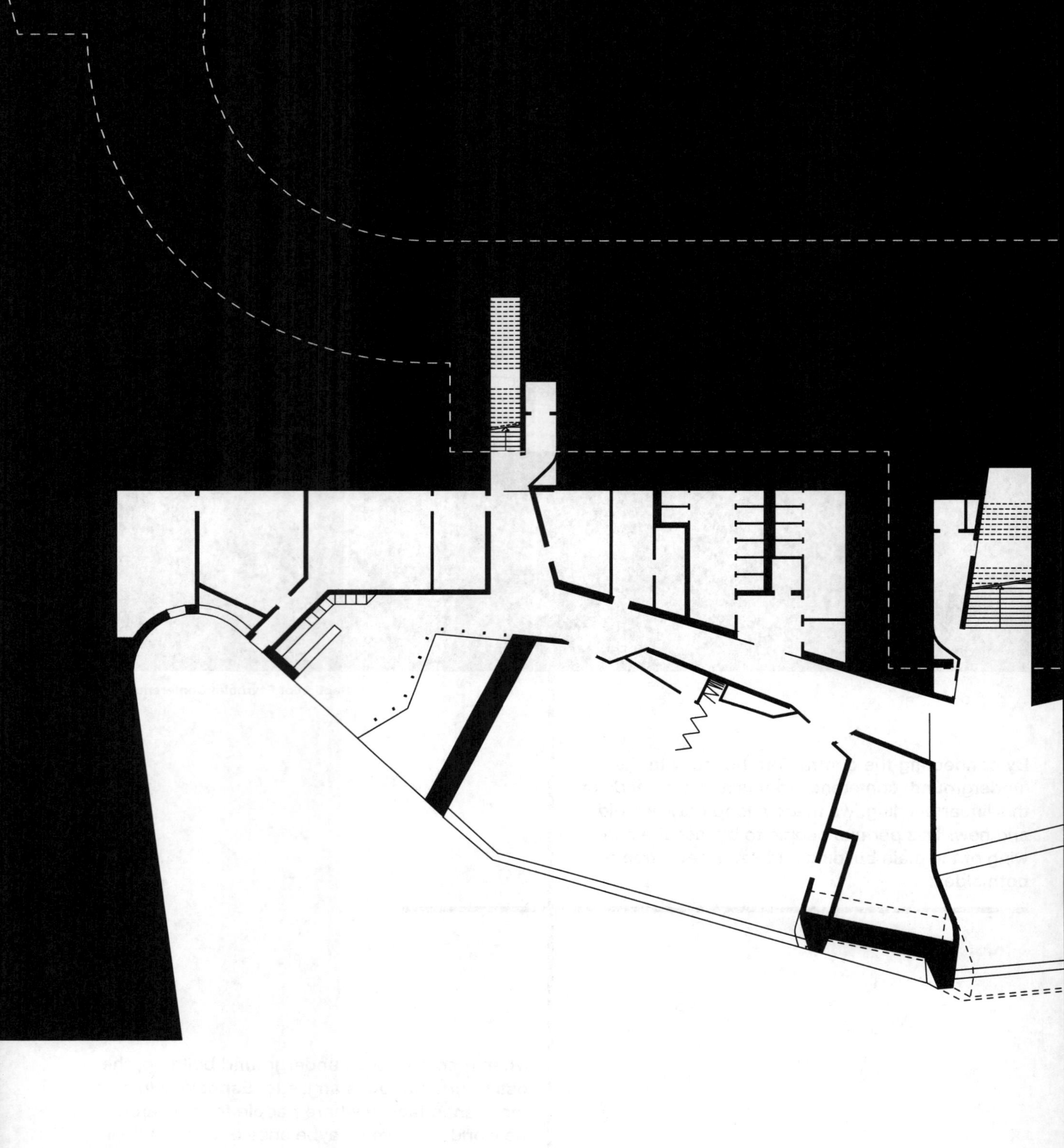

Plan of Favrholm Conference Centre.

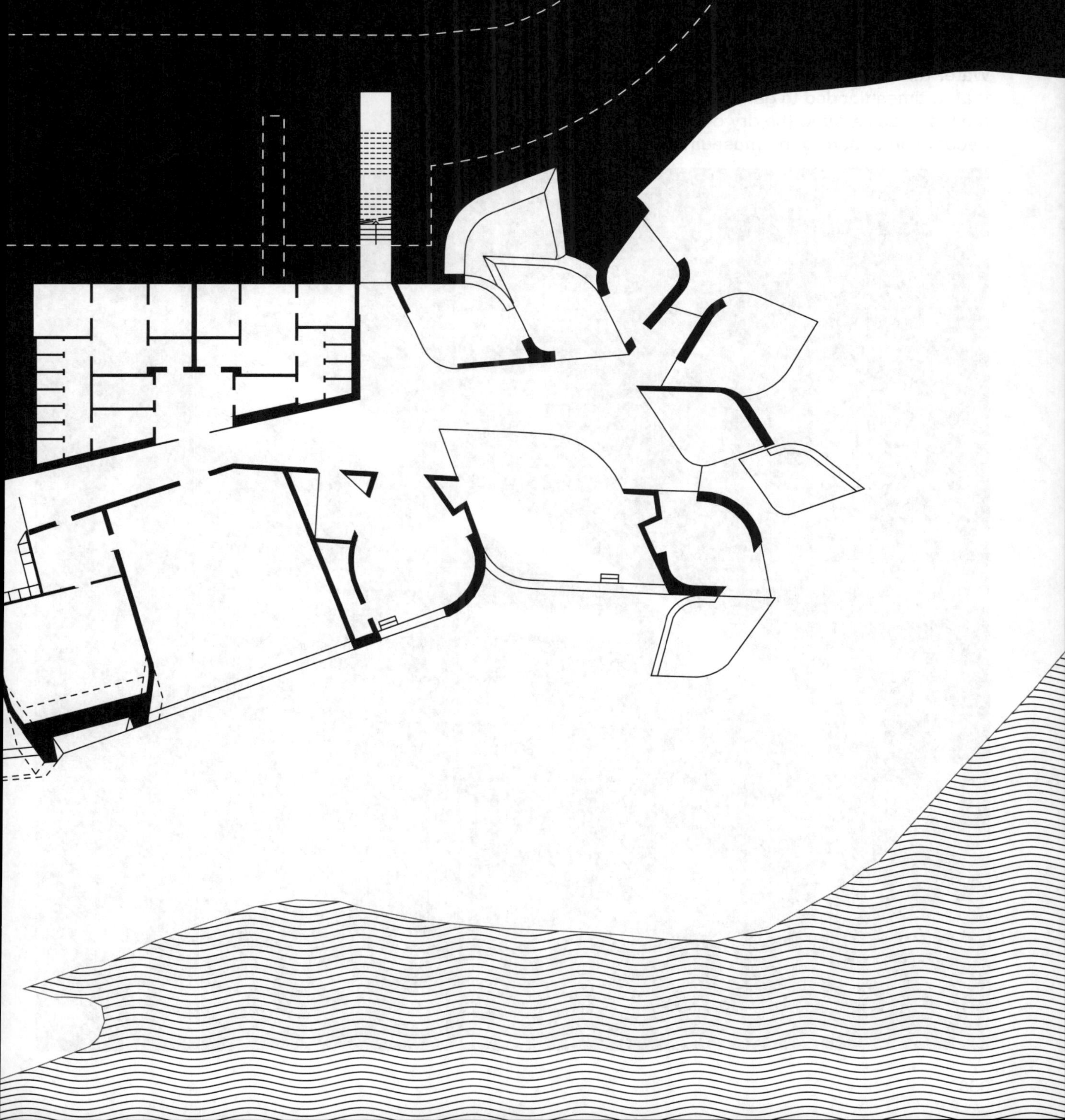

Danish Maritime Museum
Helsingør, Denmark
BIG
2008–2013

Throughout history, this site has been a double play between land and water, void and mass. Water turned into land turned into void: a dry dock that at times flooded to get a ship in or out. Now the landmass around the dry dock is excavated to become an underground museum.

Axonometry of the Danish Maritime Museum.

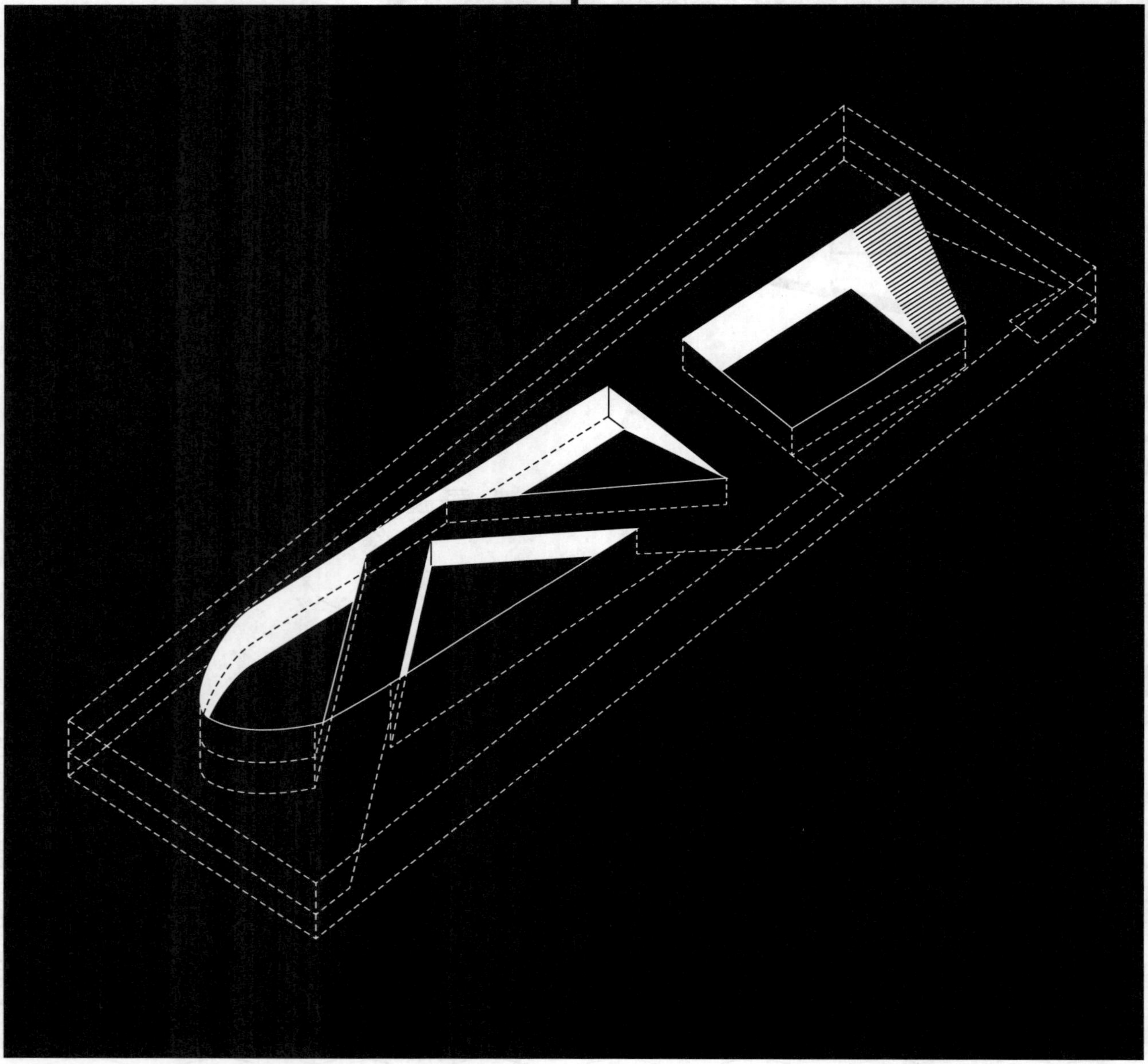

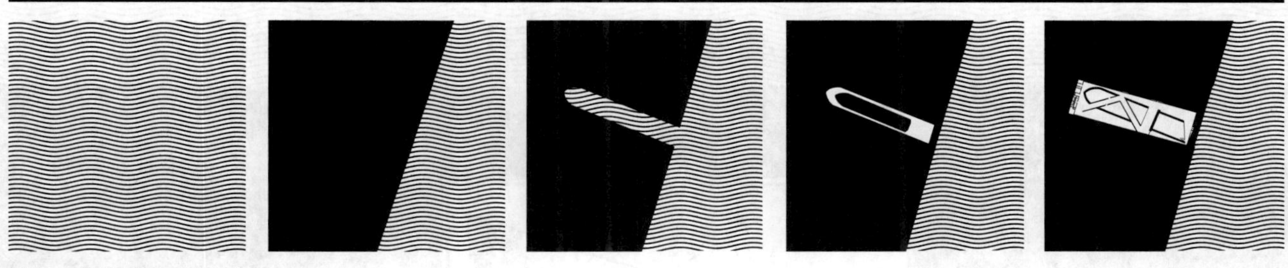

Site evolution from dike to museum.

The map of the city of Helsingør reads like a palimpsest. Nothing is erased. Instead, each layer of history is superimposed on another, from military fortress to industrial port to cultural waterfront.

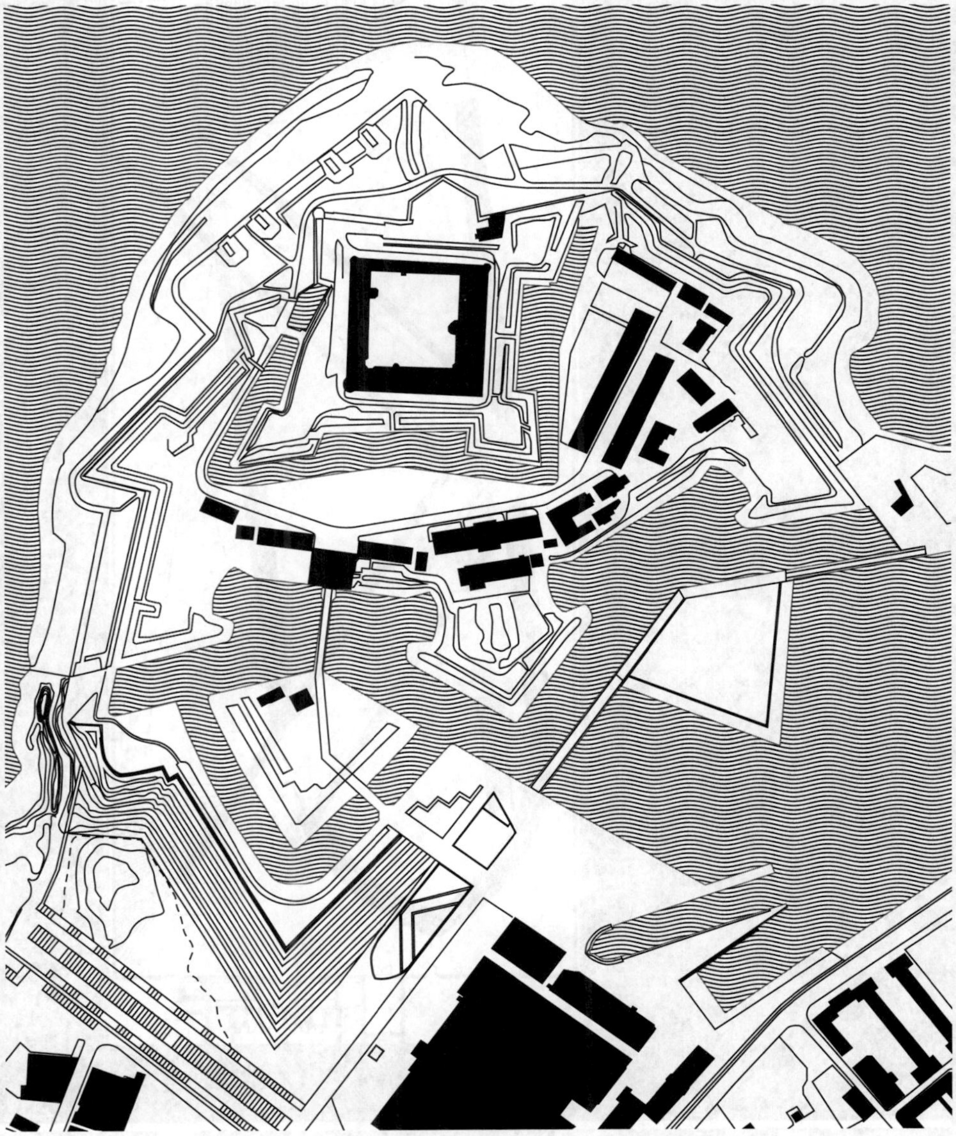

Map of Helsingør's waterfront, with the Danish Maritime Museum in the centre.

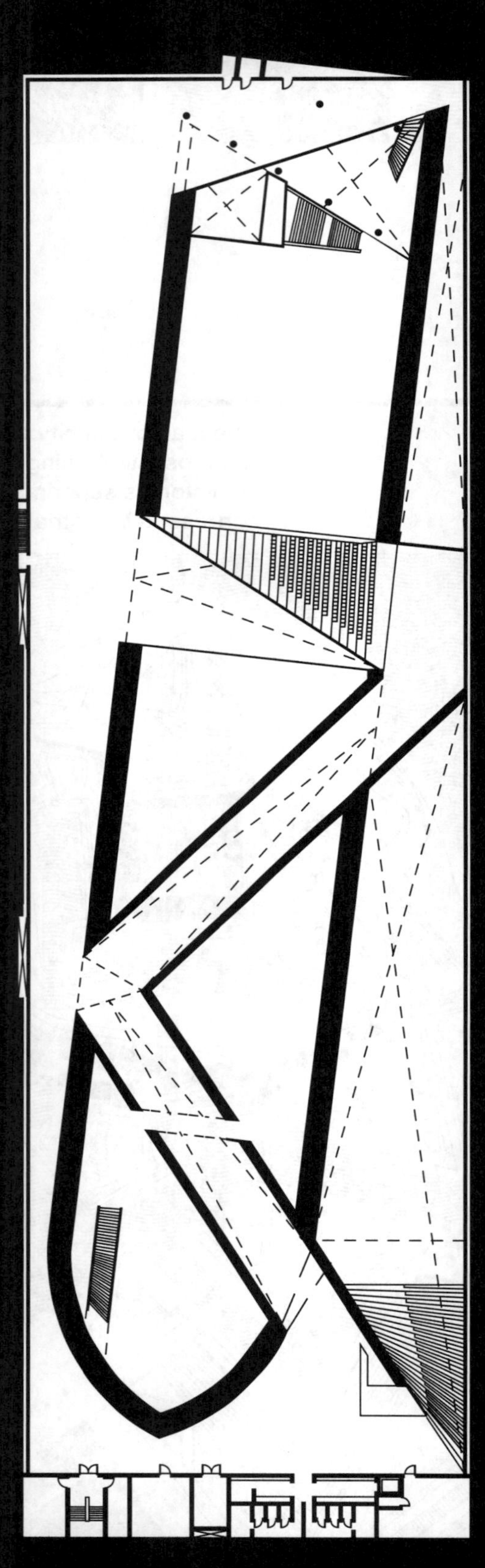

Plan of Danish Maritime Museum.

The museum successfully hides in plain sight, tucked behind the walls of a sixty-year-old dry dock. The geometry of this sunken space commands a strong public presence, yet only a single glass balustrade peeks above ground level.

Jonah and the Whale, Pieter Lastman, 1621.

Once you get to the edge of the untreated dry dock, the only visible, iconic elements are slanted, glazed bridges, serving both as an urban connection and a shortcut for visitors within the bowels of the museum.

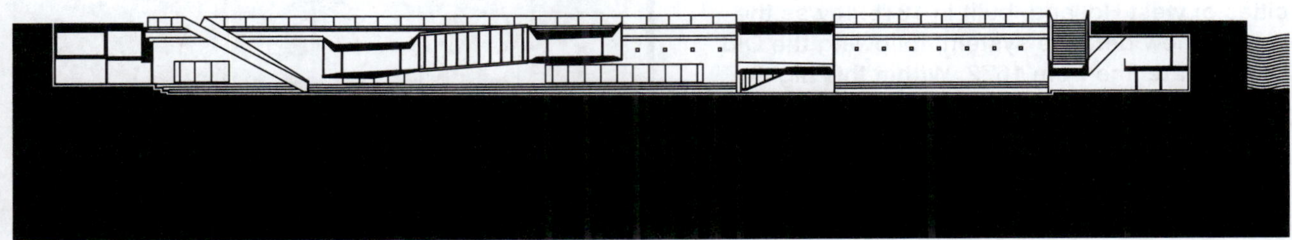

Short section (top) and long section (bottom) of the Danish Maritime Museum.

Fort Vechten
Bunnik, Netherlands
Anne Holtrop
2011–2015

Axonometry of Fort Vechten integrated in the landscape.

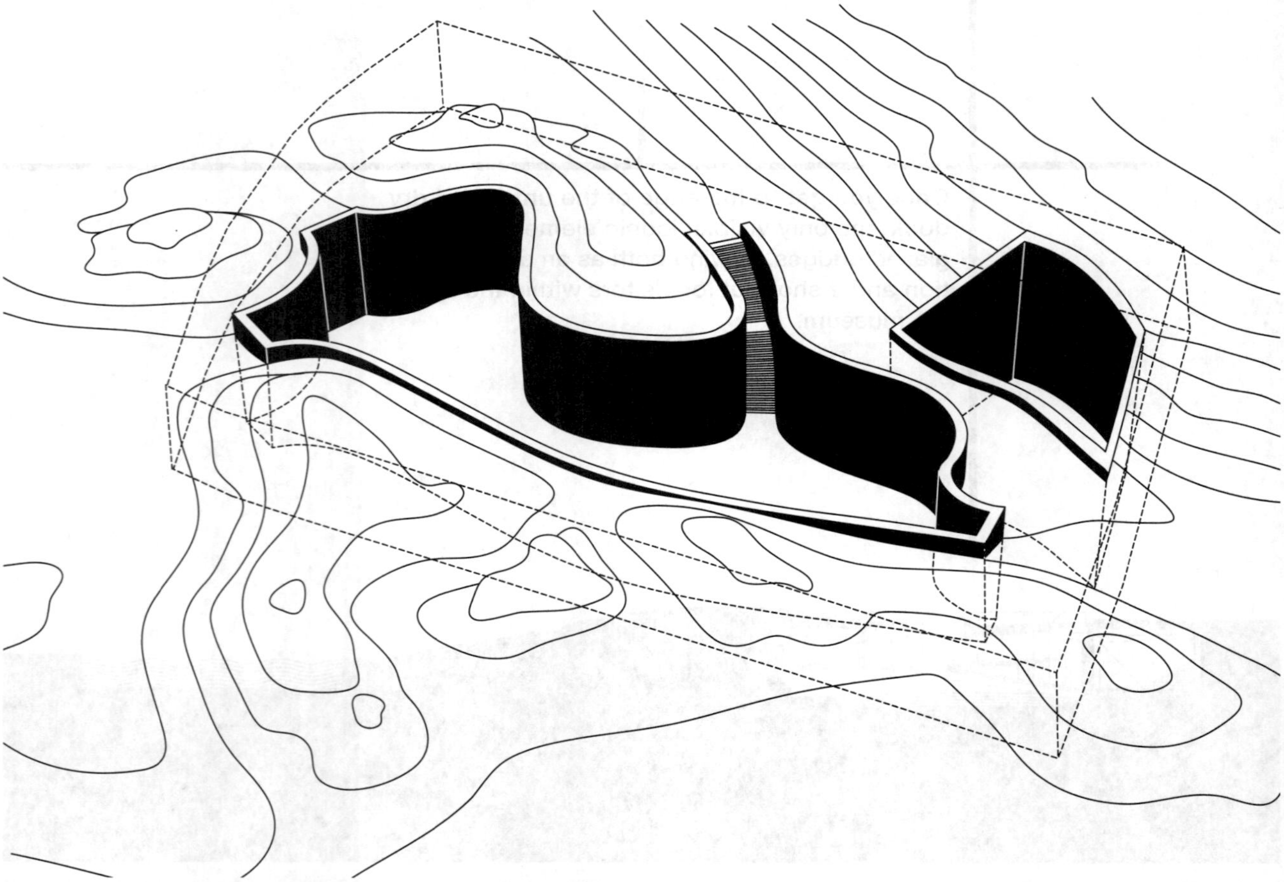

Map of the New Dutch Waterline, 1815.

Fort Vechten is a minuscule piece of an 85-kilometre-long and three-to-five-kilometre-wide defence line, the New Dutch Waterline, for the cities of west Holland, built in 1815. It was the second new defence system, following the Old Dutch Waterline from 1672. Within this highly intricate system of walls, locks and fortresses, the locks play a key role. When opened, water inundated this vast strip of the Dutch landscape, making it too deep for infantry and too shallow for boats to cross. It only became obsolete when German planes flew over it in 1940.

Fort Vechten, 1925. Netherlands Institute of Military History.

© Ossip van Duivenbode.

The museum design at Fort Vechten shows little mercy for these precise adjustments of water level. It digs a five-metre-deep hole in the central bastion and obscures most of the museum. The 50-metre-long concrete walls follow the landscape contours like an intuitive line drawing. By doing so they become subordinate to the relief of this abandoned star fort and emphasize defence and natural conditions.

A scale model of the New Dutch Waterline in the courtyard, together with the 'site sensitive' curvy walls, make the building a museum piece in itself. The whole fort is a celebration of sculpted ground – bastion and gun lines (past) and New Dutch Waterline (present). Somewhat hermetic, but that was what the Waterline was all about in the first place.

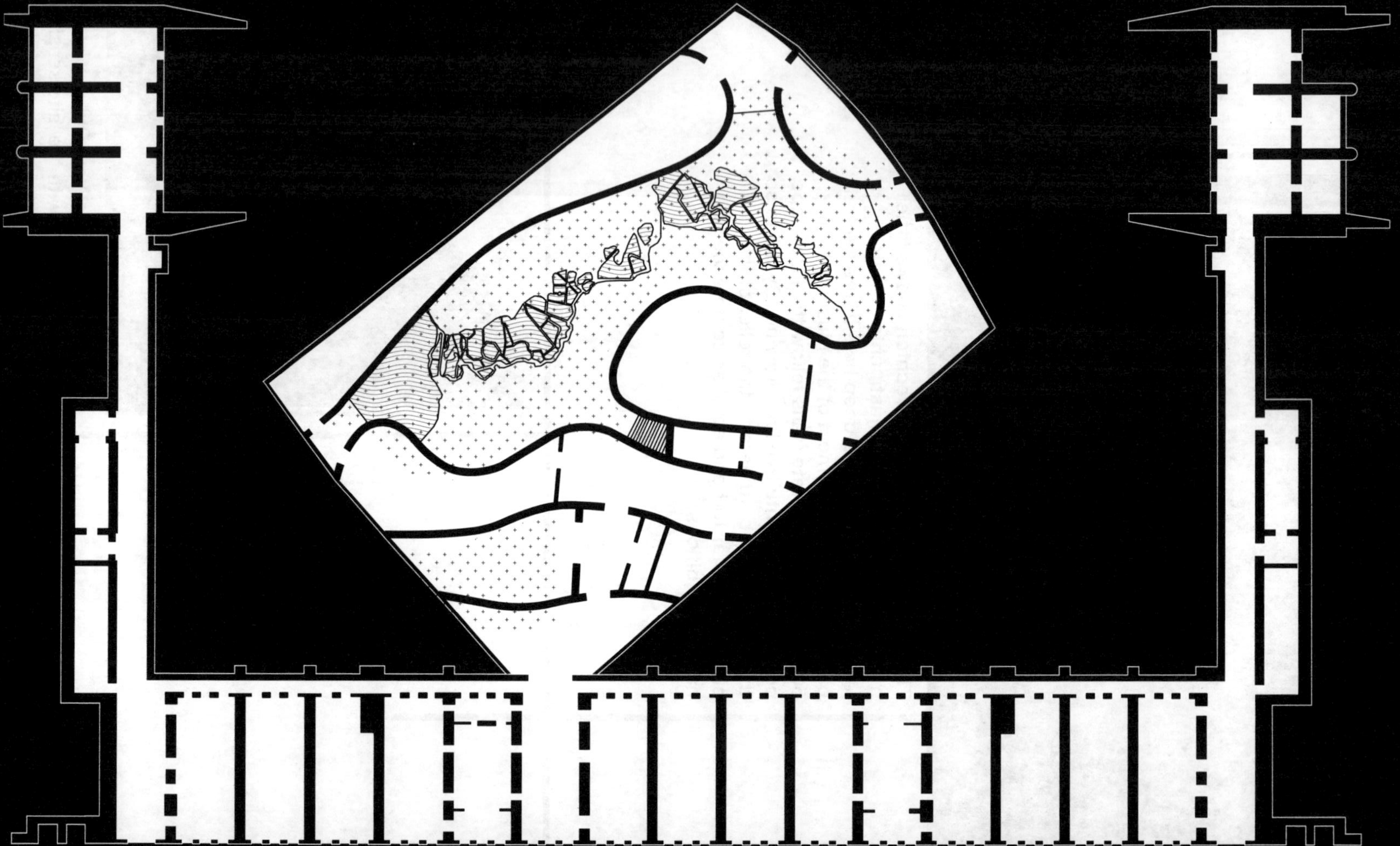

Plan of Fort Vechten below ground.

Plan of Fort Vechten above ground.

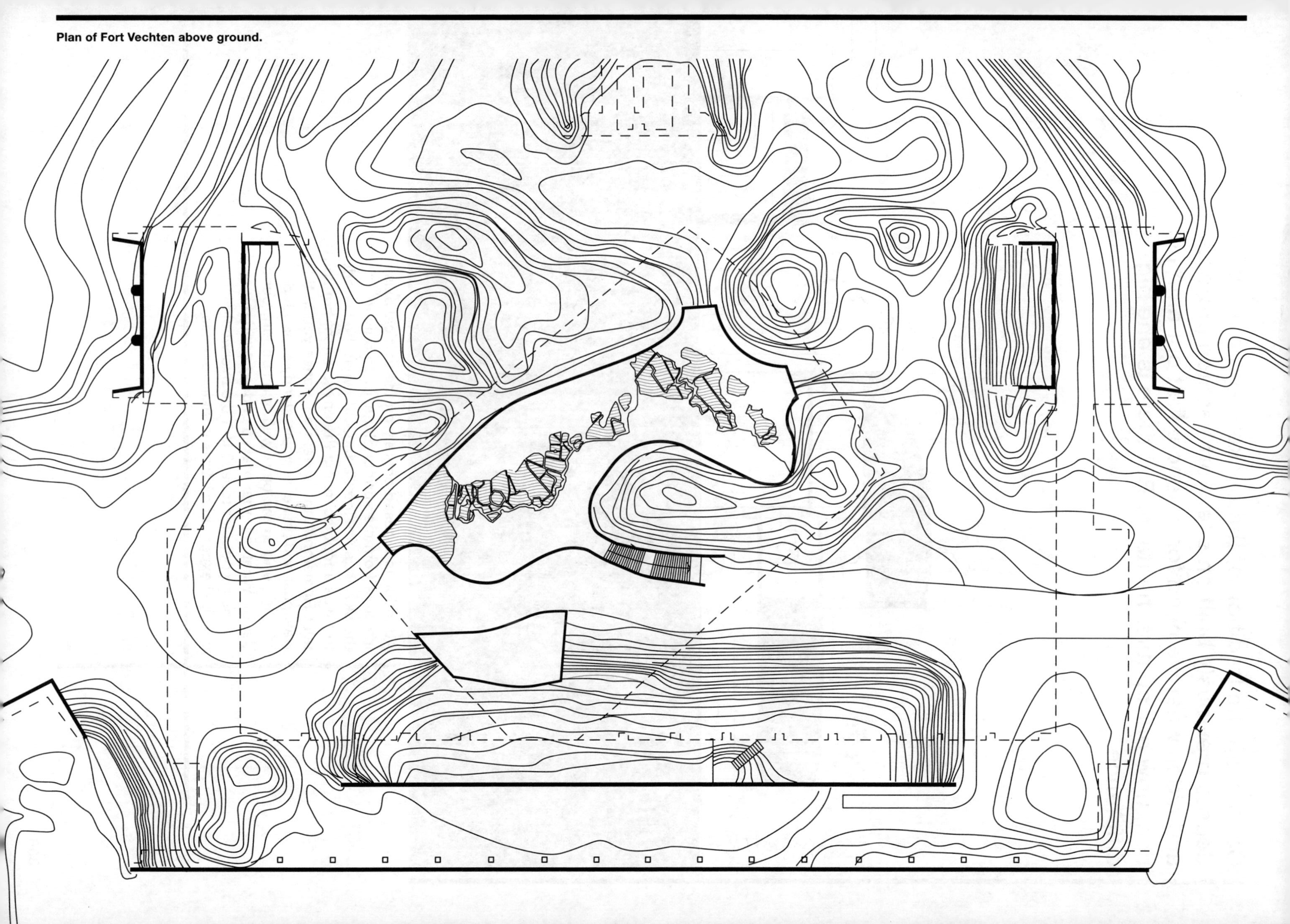

Continuing the tradition of the bunkers and ammunition depots previously built on site, Fort Vechten protects and hides what we need for defence: first our ammunition, now our cultural heritage. But there is one big difference.

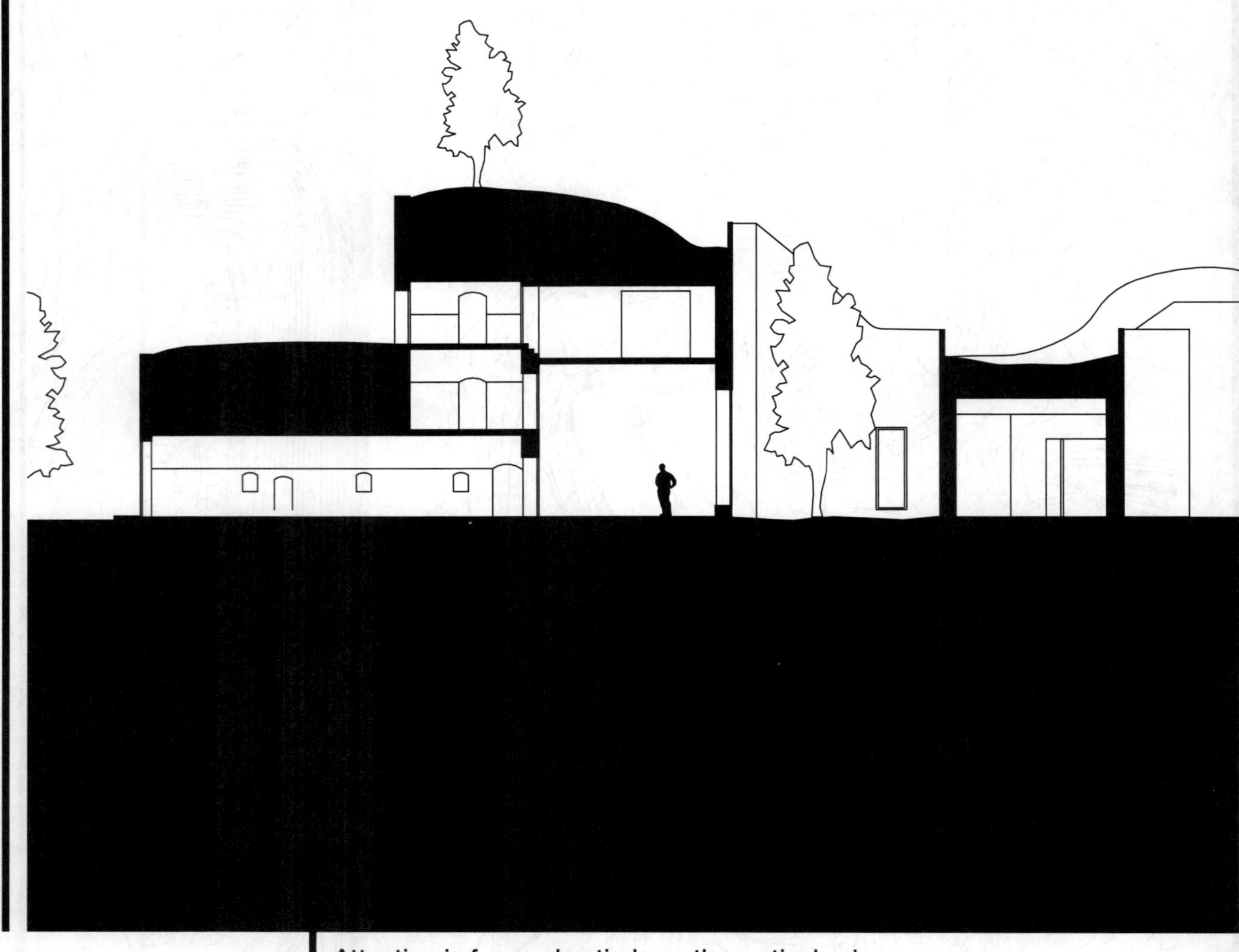

Attention is focused entirely on the vertical axis. Invisible from the surroundings, open only to the sky, thus not interfering with what the historic fort was about: scanning the environment horizontally. Remember, there were no planes yet! In this way, past and present remain clearly separated, meeting only at the back wall of an underground depot. What is it that makes underground museums so popular today? Is it the overwhelming physical experience? Or is it their absence?

It seems like the art of *polderen* (poldering), reclaiming land from the whimsical waters, has become a proverbial way of negotiating, seeking compromises instead of changing nature by toil. The deal struck to be able to build on a historically listed site is not to do it well, but to build it out of sight. This has become so prevalent that we increasingly hide our cultural institutions underground. It is a funny contradiction: exhibiting our past by hiding the future.

Section of Fort Vechten.

Hunting Ranch
Bratislava, Slovakia
SeARCH
2011–2018

The design of the Hunting Ranch draws on OMA's Maison à Bordeaux by pairing guiding principles and contradictory wishes.

Axonometry of Hunting Ranch.

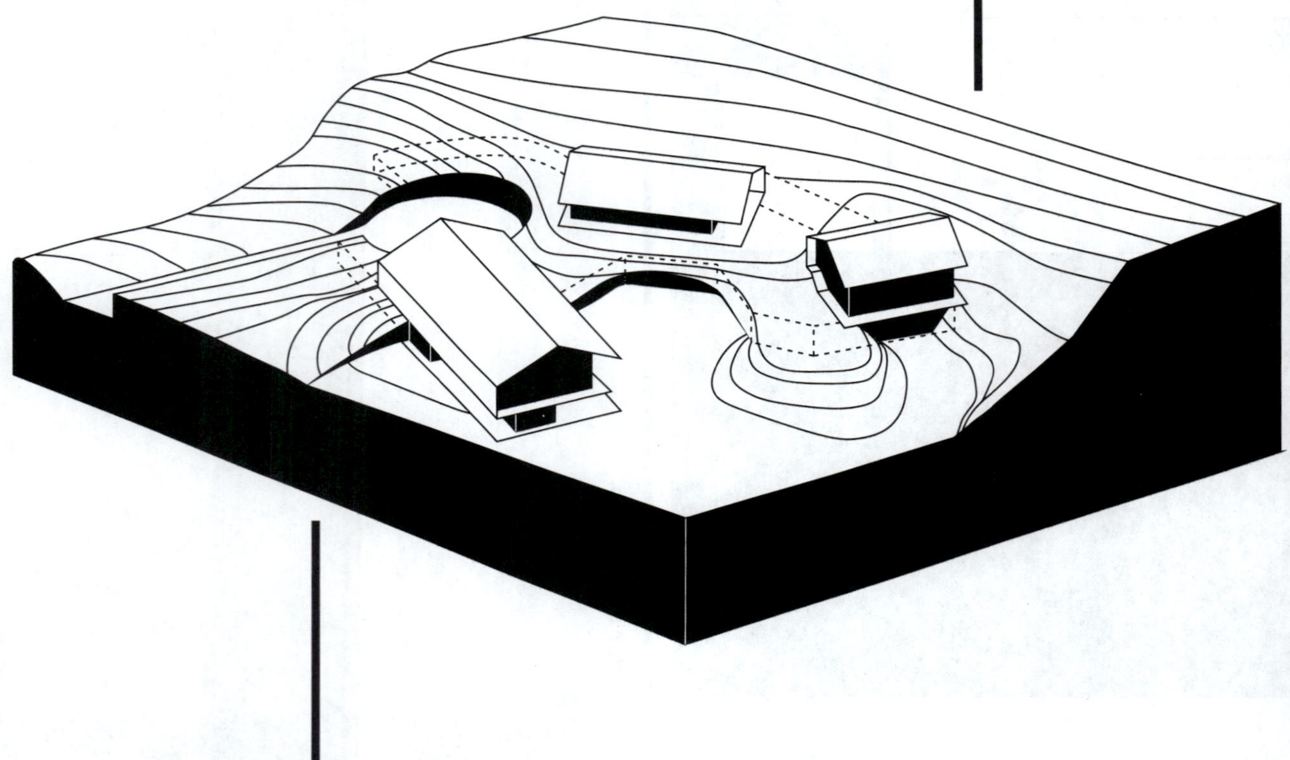

Partly sunken car park.

The Maison à Bordeaux by OMA breaks a single house into a series of disparate spaces – in, on, hovering and submerged. The structure adds to this feeling with a high degree of ballet-like balance. Does it want to hide, is it even there, or is it floating away?

Maison à Bordeaux, OMA, 1998.

Houselife, an intriguing documentary made by Ila Bêka and Louise Lemoine, shows Maison à Bordeaux through the eyes of the exasperated cleaning lady. Confronted with these (rather hilarious) scenes, architect Rem Koolhaas replies, “You can observe the collision here between two systems: the system of the platonic conception of house cleaning and the system of the platonic conception of architecture.” Collision seems inevitable, but it feels like each level wants to be autonomous. A lift that could easily fit a car is used as a library. Moving over the three floors, it allows its wheelchair-bound owner to reach every shelf. However, other parts of the house are inaccessible. A spiral stair in the basement is enclosed by a snaking retaining wall and the bedroom feels aloof, separated from the rest of the house.

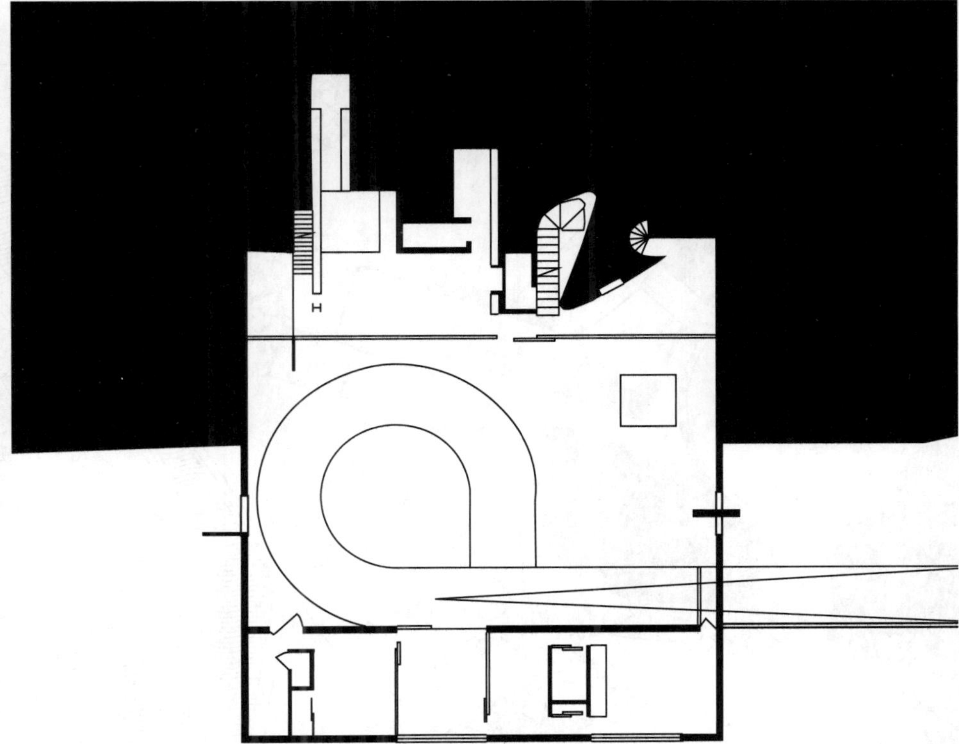

Plan of OMA's Maison à Bordeaux.

Lower level plan of the Hunting Ranch.

Like Maison à Bordeaux, the Hunting Ranch is a bit of a Frankenstein, a haphazard stitching together of autonomous programmes. Above ground, it creates a small village. Three volumes – one for the owner, one for the family, and one for guests – are orientated around a sunken courtyard, looking to the landscape to soften its edges. Luckily, a considerable amount of auxiliary and amenity space doesn't need daylight, so this serves as a foundation, organizing the domestic programme. A 'back of house', including technical rooms, ten-car garage, wine cellar and security is concealed along with a cinema, wellness space, fitness area and large reception room.

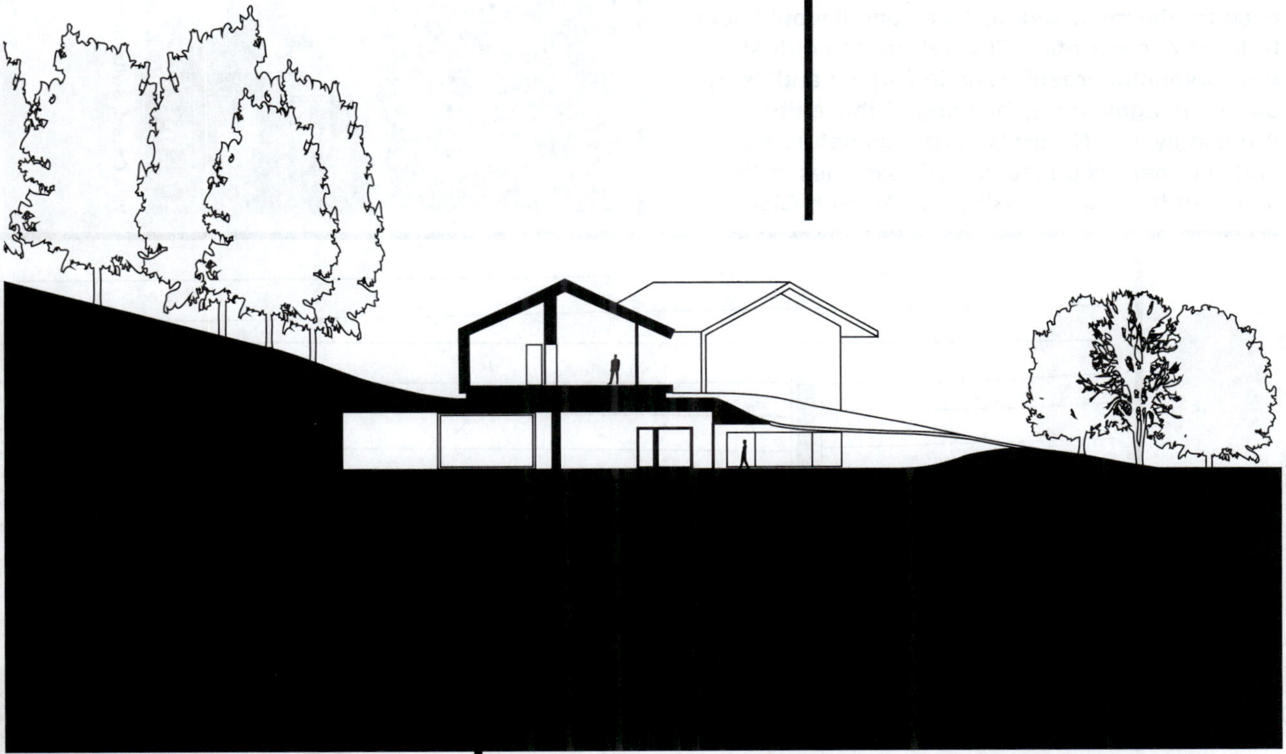

Section of Hunting Ranch.

The house withdraws from the meadow. The lower part of the house mediates between a hillside of dark woods and the low-lying open meadow and lake. All programmatic elements too big for the site are embedded in the hillside, snaking around existing trees.

The Hunting Ranch draws on hunting traditions without taking any animal lives. It is a space for gathering, festivities and the telling of tall tales. The only space reserved for trophies is one small room, a man's cave with a window facing a massive pine tree. In the end it is for a client with a great love of the woods.

El Paradiso
St Moritz, Switzerland
SeARCH & CMA
2014 (unbuilt)

The most efficient house type is probably the igloo. Water is frozen into a building material in winter and returned to the ground in summer, leaving no traces whatsoever. It's the ultimate dream of sustainable and circular design.

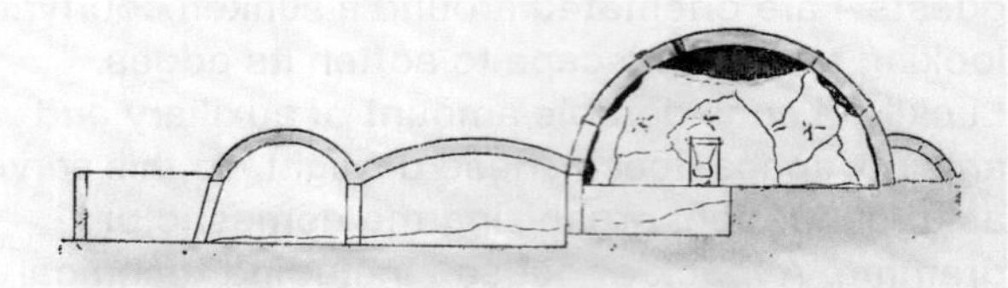

Cross section of an Iglulik Snowhouse (igloo), Franz Boas, 1888.

Designing a remote hotel as an extension to the renowned El Paradiso restaurant at an altitude of 2200 metres is the architectural equivalent of walking on thin ice. Any visual gem would disappear completely under a thick pack of snow for almost eight months of the year, timed perfectly with the busy season. During the few snowless months, 2200 metres is an ambitious position, even for the most serious hiker, and it would need to keep a low profile. Pro Natura, the oldest environmental organization in Switzerland, is by definition against any building at this altitude. Amusingly, Pro Natura's gorgeous nature centre and summer residence, Villa Cassel, lies at the same altitude, overlooking the Aletsch Glacier.

Villa Cassel, Switzerland.

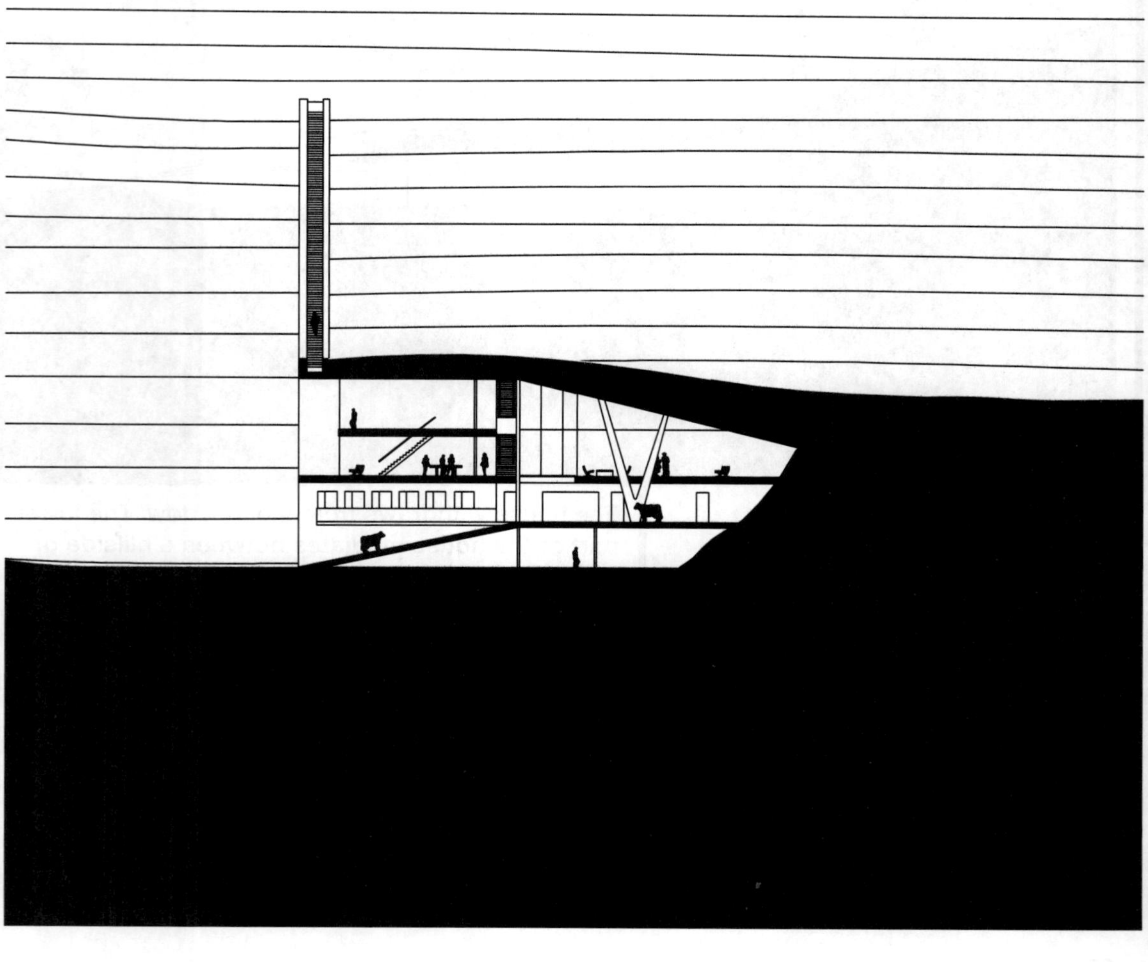

Section of El Paradiso in the mountain.

So embracing the challenge, this project builds an igloo for the super-rich within the thick pack of snow. Completely autarkic, with no access by car or helicopter and no services besides what it builds for itself, this building submits to the whims of the alpine winter.

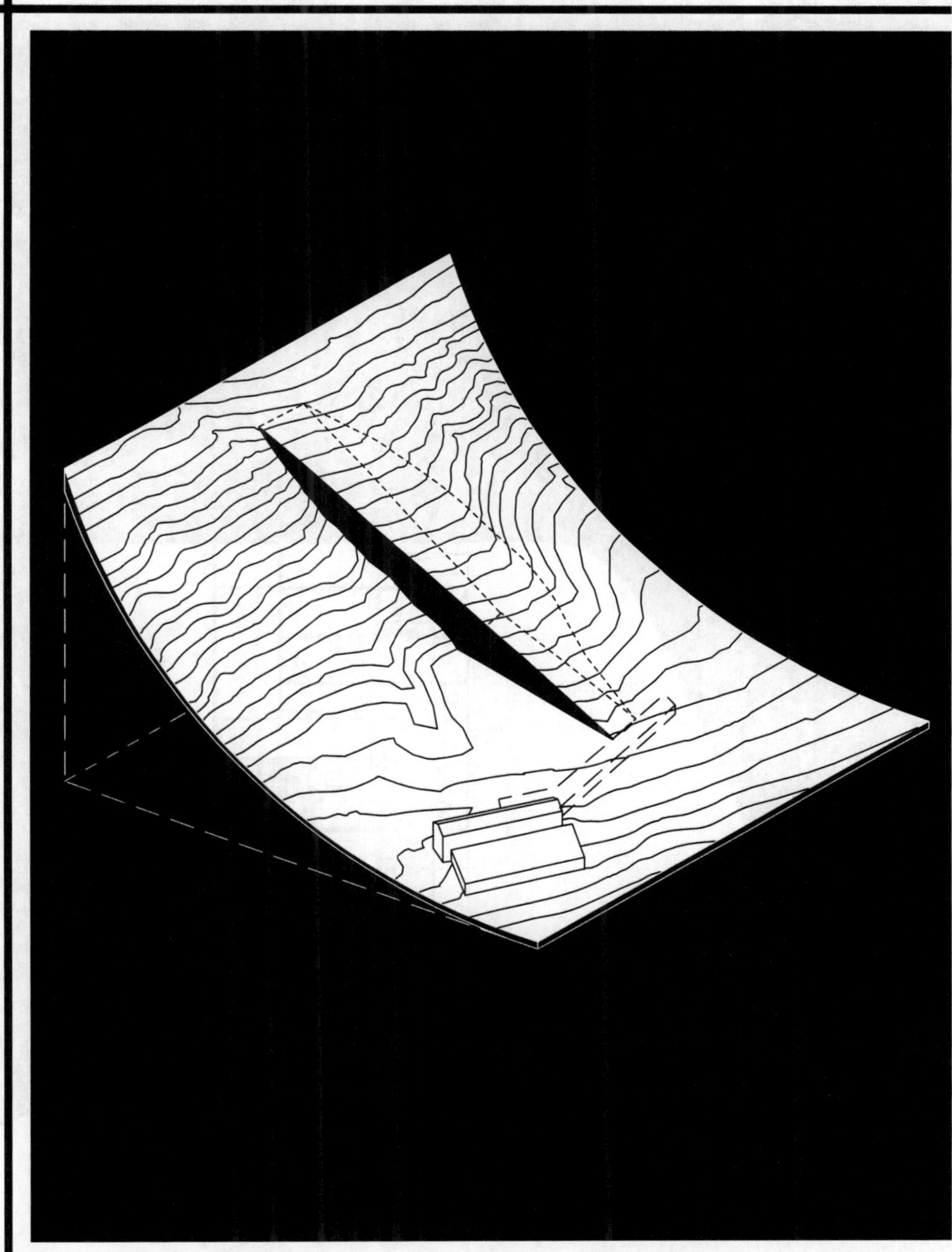

Axonometry of El Paradiso in the mountain.

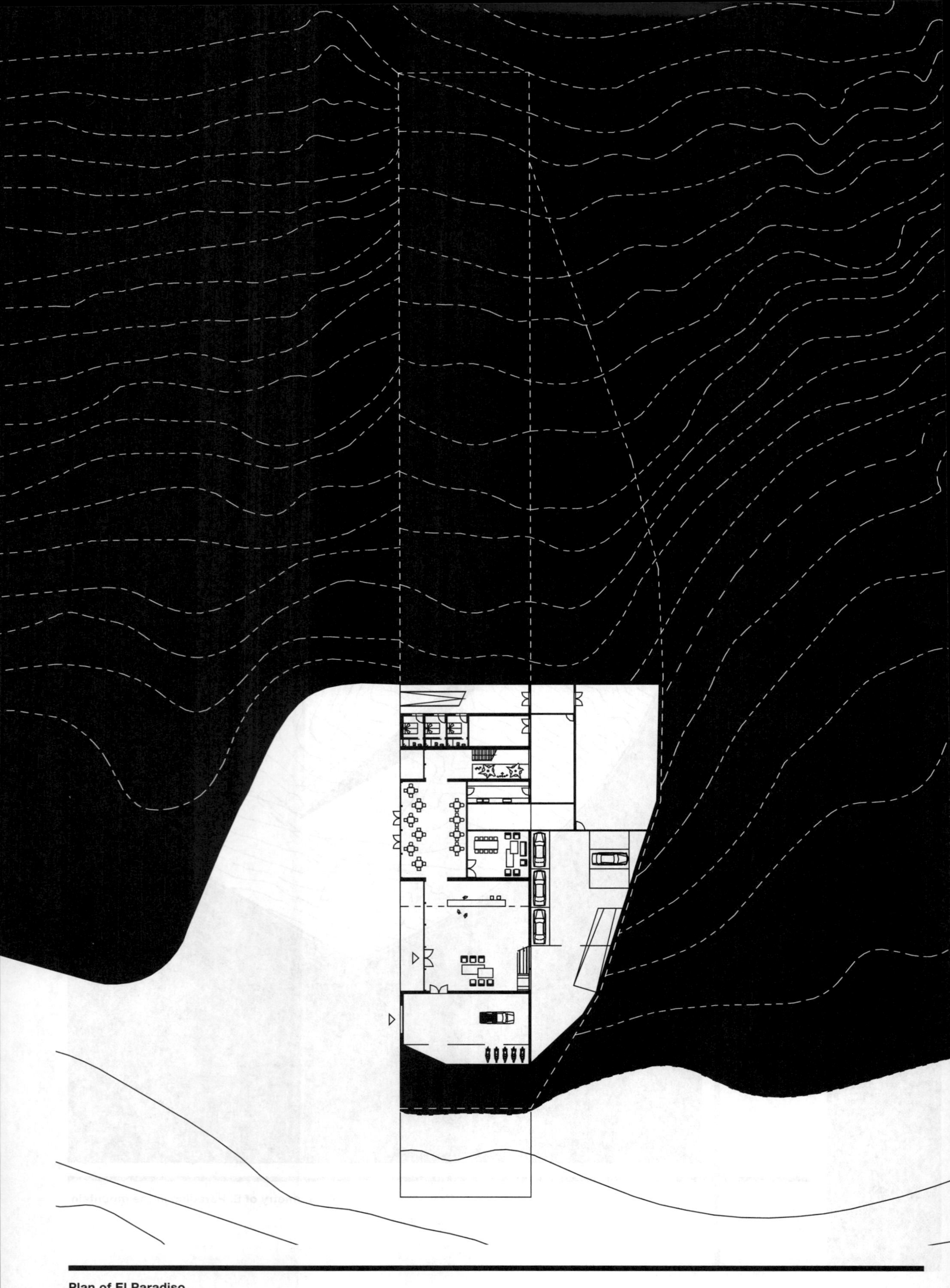

Plan of El Paradiso.

El Paradiso borrows the wise logic of a nearby cowshed. The cow is an inefficient way of feeding people, but a highly efficient heat producer. Stick your head in an old barn in winter and you'll experience their warmth. Since each animal produces over one kilowatt-hour, you need just over fifty cows to power and heat a luxury hotel. What could be more romantic than being dog-sledded from the valley to the hotel and all the milk, cheese and yoghurt is homemade on-site by your warm neighbours?

El Paradiso is tucked into a natural dent in the steep slope and orientated towards the sun for additional heat intake.

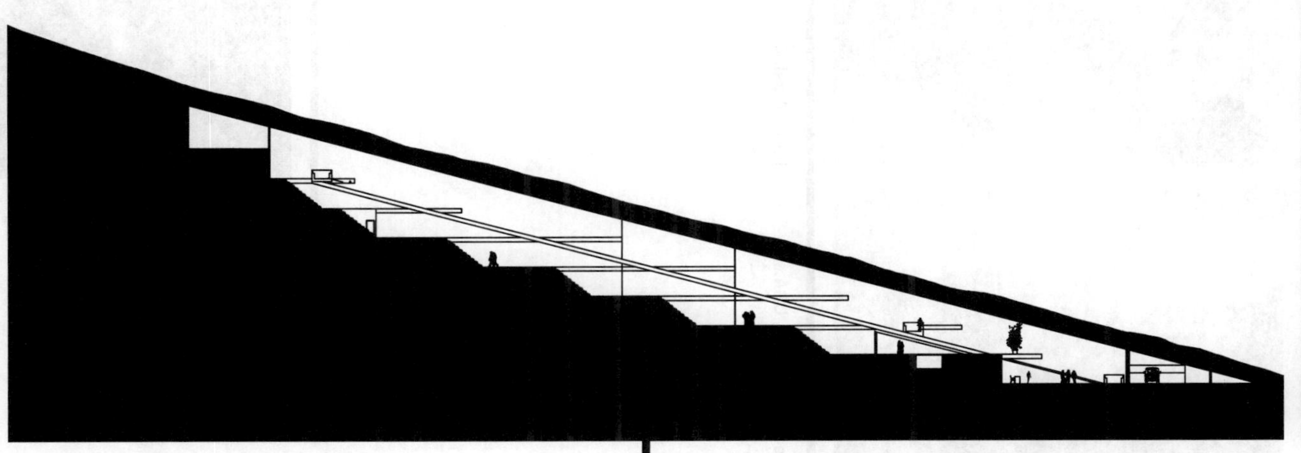

Successive sections through El Paradiso.

Twenty suites, a lobby, indoor pool and a cow entrance line the facade, while the barn, vehicles and technical services sit in a large half-dome behind, all below a two-to-five-metre-thick layer of snow. Igloos often featured an inner layer of animal skins to protect against water and further insulate the interior by ten degrees. El Paradiso's 'inner skin' is the hotel itself.

The most important elements in this project are a complete 'absence' of architecture, an intensified perception of nature and the basic necessities of life: pure air and water, food, complete silence and an extremely clear, starry sky.

Yourtopia
Rotterdam, Netherlands
SeARCH
2014

Clochán (beehive hut), Ireland.

Igloo, Alaska.

Ocmulgee earth lodge, USA.

Maasai hut, Tanzania.

Archaic forms of vernacular shelters around the world are largely circular. The South African rondela, the Ethiopian tukul, the Native American tipi, the Inuit igloo, the Brazilian maloca, the North American pit house, the Mongolian yurt and many more. Humankind has also tried countless times to invent or design the ideal city, even an ideal society, based on a rigid, circular pattern.[40] There is something about the circle, the only singular form without beginning or end, without corners, a geometry implying unity and focus. But why should a round space create more unity than a square or rectangular one? Is it a myth, or did our ancestors know something we do not?

As the most practical, efficient form, the circle has been used and abused for all kinds of conspiracies and religious babble. That begs the question: do we really understand the round thing? It is both an emblem of equality and for the very same reasons a closed circuit, excluding everyone beyond its enclosure. Like Plato's Allegory of the Cave, Yourtopia is about the "the effect of education and the lack of it on our nature".[41] In Plato's Cave, prisoners watch shadows projected on the wall from objects passing in front of a fire behind them and give names to these shadows.

Section of Yourtopia.

The shadows are the prisoners' reality. Yourtopia, instead, puts a tiny piece of nature, call it paradise, in the centre, probably the most precious element we have on this globe.

In nature, circular structures are abundant and apparent. But in building, the circle has become almost extinct, the exception, the odd one. By definition, a circular domed structure is the most stable. It relies on nothing extra and uses the least amount of material. It is this efficiency that shaped a penchant for the circle in our past, and it will only be a matter of time, and a little advancement in our building techniques, before we see a huge revival.

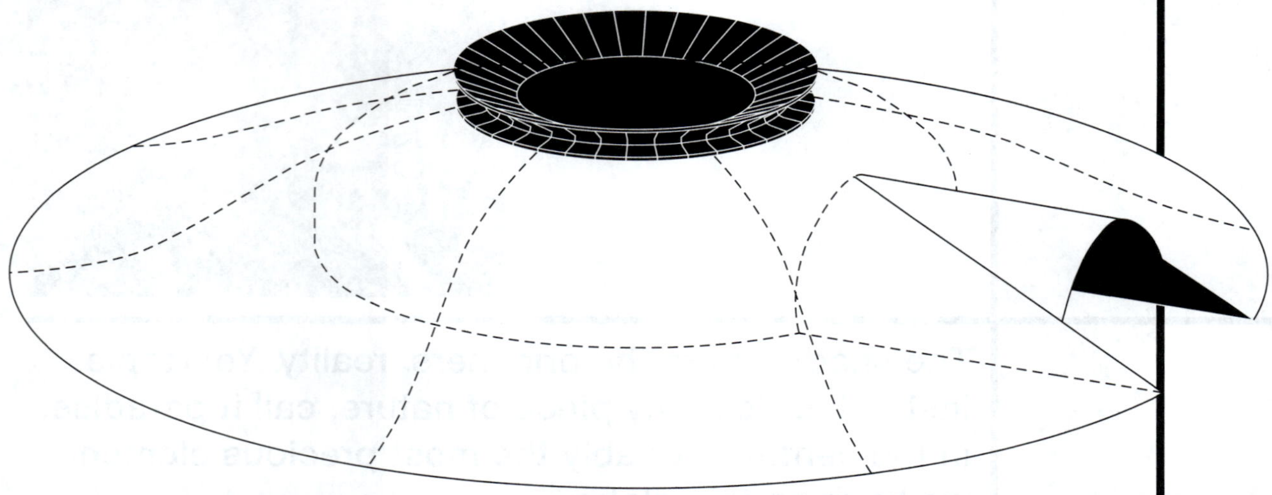

Axonometry of Yourtopia.

Exploded axonometry showing components.

Connecting round shapes is complicated to say the least, but as society tends towards individualism and 'real connections' become digital, we may need a rethink. For robots, the artisans of the future, circular movement is a natural one. Looking at the rotating and kowtowing limbs of a robot as it mills building elements makes a person quite Zen.

Carel Weeber once said he always designed symmetrical buildings because it would save him half the time. With a circle you could state that an infinitely small portion of time suffices.

But let's face it, the majority of vernacular shelters weren't about design trickery but about basic protection from the elements, a place to sleep and maybe cook. Dwelling is more luxurious today. Mukesh Ambani built a fifty-storey skyscraper in Mumbai as a private home, with a garage for 168 cars and nearly 600 staff at a time when a staggering sixty million people live in emergency shelters. Things are clearly off-kilter and the time seems ripe for a fundamental reset.

In this globalized world, Yourtopia asks: why not unite all these vernacular species? Perhaps this form can match the consequences of population increase, finite resources, globalization, a longing for privacy and other pressing issues with a back-to-basics attitude.

Assuming that we intelligent creatures acknowledge the alarming numbers, what is essential? What do we really need to enjoy a maximum quality of life?

Feels Blind by Matthew Stadler

An essay on Yourtopia, a temporary pavilion commissioned by Het Nieuwe Instituut, Rotterdam, 2014

The sweet young barista at my local cafe told me he'd seen a 'spaceship grotto' at the Museumpark. He's an art student; he goes to the Museumpark a lot. The spaceship grotto was the New Pavilion, and I asked him what he thought of it. He said it looked "kind of scary" and he didn't go inside. Yes, this is anecdotal; but I start here because I was also scared by the pavilion's green scrim of innocence. It frightened me too, many times, in many different ways. But I went inside.

His remark reminded me of endless encounters I had in the 1980s when friends would tell me that punk rock was interesting, but the shows were too frightening, so they never went. Had they bothered to walk through the door, they would have found the sweetest, most timid people, bedecked comically in safety pins and chains, trying to hold convincing sneers despite laughing and smiling all of the time. In the assaultive musical environment we endure today, punk's basic sweetness and humanity is crystal clear, but back then it seemed scary to exactly those for whom it *could have been liberatory*.

Not everyone is scared of the New Pavilion. I asked a man emerging from its doorway in a cloud of marijuana smoke what this building was. "This is a temple", he told me, nodding sagely. Every morning, scores of empty bottles remain from the parties Rotterdammers improvise on the pavilion's verdant exterior. During the day teens slouch on its shoulders, remote and sullen on 'smoker's hill', while fashion photographers circle models posed by the pavilion's steel door before swooping inside, where the models stretch and swing their hair across the tropical greenery.

Skaters have tried skating the interior walls; impromptu concerts are held; tourists pose; children squeal with excitement and speak of Teletubbies. In time it has become active. Oddly, this is largely through neglect. An ambitious programme of deliberate 'activation' proved impossible and the pavilion spent most of the summer alone in the rain. Then the creatures of the night came out and began to leave their traces, the residue of their pleasure. It reminded me of the American city where I once lived, where skaters roamed the streets a few steps ahead of the police, looking for neglected places to colonize. In Portland, the underside of a bridge proved foul and hidden enough that the skaters managed to build an entire park out of poured concrete, the Burnside Skatepark, without anyone stopping them. Eventually the city bought the land and granted it back to the skaters, rather than chase them further, or destroy what they'd built. Maybe neglect can be a deliberate part of city development.

The New Pavilion looks both futuristic *and* prehistoric, as much like Fred Flintstone's cave/house as like George Jetson's saucer-shaped home in the sky. Its relation to time – to other buildings, past or future, to the grass which enfolds it, to the city it is part of, to this greater world that connects to it in infinite, precise, nearly invisible ways – is scrambled and vast. The love I feel for this confounding, unresolved building nests inside this confusion of time and effects. Robert Smithson described something like it in his 1966 essay "Entropy and the New Monuments". (Bjarne Mastenbroek pointed me to this.) "Instead of causing us to remember the past, like the old monuments, the new monuments seem to cause us to forget the future. Instead of being made of natural materials, such as marble, granite, or other kinds of rock, the new monuments are made of artificial materials... they are not built for the ages but rather against the ages. They are involved in a systematic reduction of time down to fractions of seconds, rather than in representing the long spaces of centuries. Both past and future are placed in an objective present. This kind of time has little or no space; it is stationary and without movement, it is going nowhere."

This systematic reduction of time – which, as it approaches zero, becomes also a boundless exploding of time – this confounding of time's measure – fits well the New Pavilion's blunt affect. It bears no mark of time because nothing is remote or discontinuous from it. In this it also resembles the sixteenth-century monad of John Dee, a densely overloaded symbol that purports to collect all human knowledge in the modest labyrinth of a mark on a page.

I've grown to love the New Pavilion, despite strong negative first impressions that deepened with repeated viewing. This building does not seduce you. It actively repels some, and I only grew to love it because I love poetry. I kept coming back and listening. I paid attention. I accepted its contradictions and broadened my view. I heard the music it takes part in. The New Pavilion is one of the most challenging and honest contributions to Dutch architecture in the last few years, and it rewards serious engagement – it even demands it. I'm not surprised a building like this is rare. Architects are rarely asked for honesty or conflict. Bjarne Mastenbroek had the advantage of an ambitious client, Het Nieuwe Instituut, who really needed something smart, and of a brief that expressly called for a challenge. (The brief specifically asked the architect to "design a 1:1 model of a process to be", not "a house of the future with the usual emphasis on technology". So, this is not Rotterdam's 'Tomorrow Land'.)

You've no doubt noticed it is impossible to sit in the shadow of the New Pavilion, which cannot be said of the client's HQ, Het Nieuwe Instituut by Jo Coenen. This modesty is just one of the myriad, poetic and contradictory assertions made by Mastenbroek's design. Among the others is boastfulness, beauty, harsh ugliness, innocence, blindness, vision, tranquility, imprisonment, vitality, death and, underlying them all, I believe, a barely repressed rage.

They're all part of what the brief called for – an example of process; the way the architect thinks – not a futurist's prognostication of how we'll live. The New Pavilion is a tool for thinking – thinking by building – not the house we'll live in in 2050. It's interesting to see the Sonneveld House sitting confidently across the street, a house we visit by imagining the pleasures of living in it. Mastenbroek concedes that pleasure to the Sonneveld and its neighbouring villas. His New Pavilion has little or no dialogue across the street, despite sharing a home address. The pavilion is too strange, too indifferent to middle-class notions of comfort. It is completely alien, babbling alone in a foreign language, like a refugee family that's been plunked down on the block who, in their incoherent way, have no thoughts about comfort because they are simply hoping not to die.

The pavilion is more obviously tied to the bulky headquarters it sits beside, like a broken water main fountaining in the yard. But nothing has burst, yet. The swelling in the grass betrays some sort of pressure deep in the bowels of Dutch architecture. But is the New Pavilion a disaster about to explode upon us or the reassuring performance of a reliable back-up system, that admirably resilient bladder called 'the architect' – a miraculous organ into which rivers of poison can be poured that the architect will smilingly swallow so the system can bring forth its great, golden stream of buildings; how much abuse can be heaped into this holding tank without breaking it?

About this question, the New Pavilion is poker-faced, or no-faced. There is no facade, only this pressured swelling of the earth. Architecture, here, is completely interior. It makes no sculptural claims. True, the architect's process distorts the earth, pushing against the surface, but it barely breaks the skin. The breaks are in two places – on top, to open a kind of defenseless eye that can only see the sky, and nothing else; and on the front, to open the throat that lets us pass and be swallowed. The pavilion's interplay with the external, material context is as close to zero as Mastenbroek could dial it, so that all that's left is this set of buried pressures shaping whatever the architect can give us to help relieve the pressure; which, given the brief, must be 'architecture', or all that's left of it. So, how does that feel?

All the doves that fly past my eyes
Have a stickiness to their wings
In the doorway of my demise I stand
Encased in the whisper you taught me

How does it feel?
It feels blind

How does it feel?
Well, it feels fucking blind
What have you taught me? Nothing
Look at what you have taught me
Your world has taught me nothing

If you were blind and there was no Braille
There are no boundaries on what I can feel
If you could see but we're always taught
What you saw wasn't fucking real yeah
How does that feel?
It feels blind
How does that feel?
Well it feels fucking blind
What have you taught me? Nothing
Look at what you've taught me
Your world has taught me nothing

As a woman I was taught to always be hungry
Yeah women are well acquainted with thirst
Yeah, I could eat just about anything
I could even eat your hate up like love

I eat your hate like love
I'd eat your fucking hate up like love

The poem on the pavilion's door, composed by Mastenbroek's design team, led me to this. Near the bottom, the door says "FEEL BLIND". The song is "Feels Blind", by Bikini Kill. I saw the band in Olympia, Washington: Kathleen Hanna, Billy Karren, Kathi Wilcox, and Tobi Vail, circa 1992. Another band there, then, (Tobi's boyfriend Kurt's band) was recording "Smells Like Teen Spirit". But 'Feels Blind' is the song that history will remember. Such majesty. That beautiful pale flower that blossoms open at the end, Tobi Vail's desultory cymbal crash, is exactly where Bjarne Mastenbroek's angry pavilion begins. He has swallowed the considerable rage that precedes it, knowing that rage was not part of the brief, even if it is part of his process. But he has barely swallowed it, and it keeps pushing up, like a gut full of bile. If the New Pavilion is "kind of scary", that's maybe because the swollen pregnancy it houses begins in these deeply negative emotions of refusal, a refusal that feels so urgent it threatens to annihilate hope.

The pavilion does not offer us any easy way out. We can only exit through the same narrow passage that led us in. Mastenbroek has rigorously stripped the interior of decoration or distractions, except, notably, the plants. Which is not to say the building is indifferent to context. The New Pavilion is a more deeply contextual and engaged building than, for example, the larger one it sits beside. Context is not only visual or material; it also lies hidden in massive accumulations of pressure, adjacency, and connections from which visual pleasures and play often distract us. The New Pavilion foregrounds this web of connectedness by stripping away the distractions we normally fix upon.

Mastenbroek has subtracted all of the pleasantries, the aesthetic and intellectual puzzles of style and context that normally take up the attention of architecture's consumers. He's robbed us of the chance to consume, giving us, anyway, hammocks, so we can sway while we wait, but for what? The green is nice, but the plants are also prisoners, refugees. And they look beaten. Huddled together, their tips burned by the sun, their tops broken, they might be victims of a hate crime.

They've come from across the globe. Not one of them belongs here. They have been pulled from their beds and put on life support. Now, in the lean-to refugee shelter, the provision of even that is in question. But isn't this the case for architecture now? That the lives it must house, those who need shelter, are as displaced and complex as these plants? Their faces are just as pleasant to look at as the relaxing green of the prisoner-plants, but their lives are as intractably difficult.

Hosting these alien, imported plants, the New Pavilion gives us green ecology, the nonhumans with whom we must share our destiny, while refusing to give us 'Nature'. The same can be said for the industrial lawn that's been rolled over the pavilion's steel shell outside. It looks like 'nature' but it was trucked here from an indoor grass factory that produces the stuff by the metre using (one imagines) the most hideous of chemical processes. In the New Pavilion we are undeniably enfolded in a green world, the realm of the ecology-minded architect, literally so; but we are equally enfolded in the brutal politics and economics that frame that puzzle. Writer and literary critic Timothy Morton calls this entanglement the 'dark ecology'. The 'dark ecology' is a universe of things – including the 'things' that are writing and reading this text, you and I – as well as the things it is printed on and that move through the world in concert with it. Persons, animals, objects, concepts, have an equivalent complexity and shroudedness in this densely interconnected world. All are shaped mutually in a 'mesh' – to use another of Morton's terms – that was well described by Darwin. Morton extends Darwin's deep, agnostic appreciation for the incredible surprise and specificity of living things to a world, our world, riven too with the virtual, the remembered, the forgotten, and the merely imagined. To inhabit this world, Morton says, is to fall into the shadow of 'the ecological thought'.

"The ecological thought", Morton wrote in his 2010 book of the same name, "is a virus that infects all other areas of thinking. Ecology isn't just about global warming, recycling and solar power – it is not just to do with everyday relationships between humans and nonhumans. It has to do with love, loss, despair and compassion. It has to do with depression and psychosis. It has to do with capitalism and what might exist after capitalism. It has to do with amazement, open-mindedness, and wonder. It has to do with doubt, confusion, and skepticism... Like the shadow of an idea not yet fully thought, a shadow from the future (that wonderful phrase of the poet Shelley), the ecological thought creeps over other ideas until nowhere is left untouched by its dark presence."

The New Pavilion is Morton's 'ecological thought' expressed as architecture. It is the spot where this shadow from the future touches ground. But Morton's time-sense is rather like Robert Smithson's. Things run backwards, so that causality is inverted. The future arrives to tell us what happened, not what will be happening next. There is no element of prediction in Morton's work, nor in the New Pavilion, just this radical overloading of the present moment so that our view broadens, bringing time to a standstill by crowding as much as possible into a singular present, what Morton has also called 'ecology without nature'.

"One of the things that modern society has damaged", Morton says, "along with ecosystems and species and the global climate, is thinking". The ecological thought is a way of thinking, a quality of attention, a breadth and generosity of regard – it is very specifically *not* a laundry list of correct positions but the complete absence of such a list. The ecological thought is the demand that we, at each moment, remain thoughtful, that we be intelligent in public. Morton sees specific barriers to our public intelligence in the long Romantic discourse of Nature. "Like a dam, Nature contained thinking for a while", he writes, "but in the current historical situation, thinking is about to spill over the edge... the concept 'nature' has had its day and no longer serves us well. The main reason is that nature is a kind of backdrop – and we are living in a world where there is no backdrop: it's all foreground now. When we replace nature with the ecological thought, we discover a much stranger, more intimate, more jaw-dropping world."

The New Pavilion is a portal to this intimate, stranger world. There is no getting out of it. The pavilion presents a kind of Klein bottle (that Möbius 3D space) melding inside and outside, plant and human, shelter and threat so completely they become legible only as a totality, a permanent temporariness that holds us in our constant flight. Structurally, the pavilion is built, as a Klein bottle, around the outside's clever interpenetration of the putative 'interior'. The green environment circles back in through the ground to erupt inside the sterile white room, in the form of the hostage plants, bathed in the world's natural light that enters, also Möbius-like, through the dome's open eye, above.

There is no clear inside or outside to the pavilion, just as there is no separation of human and nonhuman, temporary or permanent, refuge or prison. For all of its solid clarity, the structure simply shapes a permanent entanglement in flux, a vast yet precise dynamism that is the world we live in, the world we're part of – 'the ecological thought'. This is a setting without shelter because there is no separation of parts, no *other* to be threatened by or take shelter from. Old dichotomies have collapsed. What is 'home' when there is no place apart? With no *domus* there can be no domesticity.

The New Pavilion keeps our attention fixed on this condition, the pleasures and perils of the permanent refugee; rather than indulging the usual distractions of virtuoso engineering or visual fondling that most architecture invites us to consume. Mastenbroek gives us the bare minimum that architecture can do – and it doesn't look like much – only a distortion in the course of things, the accommodation an inherently violent system makes to house us. Which again reminds me of punk rock, which turned out to be such a utopian movement, so full of vegans and macrobiotic saints, neo-hippies, really, wearing their scuffed fake leather, refusing all the crap.

At the heart of Mastenbroek's refusal is his disgust with all of the glittery extras that threaten to crowd out architecture's core mission, its gift – the intelligent provision of shelter to those who need it. He stages our encounter with 'the ecological thought' as honestly and efficiently as possible. Architects are typically asked to make villas for rich people, a degrading task Mastenbroek convincingly describes (in the case of Zaha Hadid's villa for Naomi Campbell) as providing a starlet with a cross between a rocket and a shoe.

Architecture has become such an incredibly huge accumulation of stuff, of ambitions and purposes, of capabilities – the architect's eager and constant offer to help – anything the architect can horde or claim as his own, wanting an identity, a reassurance, like a layer of fat, as bulwark against his disappearance. There are many things more virtuous than making rocket-shoes for starlets and which architecture has also become – visual entertainment, branding apparatus, social control, a substitute for democracy or an advanced cultural weapon – but I'll let Mastenbroek's 'designing rocket-shoes for starlets' stand in for them all. If the architect is not providing intelligent shelter for those who need it, what is he doing? The bloating of architecture is precisely corollary to the incredibly swift internal shrinkage of the profession's native purposes and identity. The architect is willing to take on, to *be anything*, so desperate is he to survive, and so uncertain is he of architecture's survival.

The New Pavilion is, first and foremost, a refusal to continue with all of the nonsense that architecture has become. It is a zero reset for the profession. Henceforth we get the bare minimum, a distortion in the system that swells to shelter us, and that will shrink again or disappear in time. And yet, miraculously, the New Pavilion also refuses to look like poverty. Exploring the minimum, the pavilion nevertheless insists on industrial materials and a machine-tooled finish. Structurally, it is nothing more than a lean-to with a tarp roof – about as distant from designing rocket-shoes for starlets as you can get. This is architecture's equivalent of the 1-4-5 blues chord structure off of which ninety per cent of punk rock built its culture ("Feels Blind" cleverly inverts this formula into a 5-4-1) – but its materials and the precision of its engineering invite a wholly other discourse than the one invited by, say, the work of Samuel Mockbee/Rural Studio or, in art, Oscar Tuazon. The New Pavilion does not trade in any coin except architecture, not even the paradoxical glamour of *arte povera*. It is architecture minus everything that architecture is not.

Formally, the New Pavilion is a poem constructed with a purely architectural vocabulary. Poetry – with all of its complexity, its internal contradictions, its unresolvability, its compact concision and resistance to either mastery or complete surrender – a form that I understand to be relational, demanding a fully-engaged reader, yielding its meanings only via the vibrant agency of both writer and reader committed to a shared text – is the design process evident in the New Pavilion.

Poems oblige all of us – author and audience – to live cheek-by-jowl with unresolved paradox, fear, hope and failure. We are, after all both ethical and rational creatures. We can't help but want to do right, to be virtuous, even while knowing we'll fall short. We will try and fail, and try and, as Beckett said, fail better.

Of the many 'right responses' to the poem of Bjarne Mastenbroek, I include the herb smokers, those who lay back in the hammocks and deepen their entanglement by smoking the dried leaves of the plant world that died to become their sacrament. I also include the daily ministrations of Het Nieuwe Instituut's staff who figured out which plants needed how much water and endeavoured to give it to them, to lengthen their lives, even amidst such suffering, to save some, even if they could not save them all. And I include the initial act, the architect's response to a challenging brief in the form of serious, deeper challenge. He followed his instincts to undefended assertions, the unresolved beauty of this peculiar structure. He took risks in public.

Robert Smithson, in his last, most productive years, focused on the exhausted sites of old strip mines, using art to turn the dead residue of that industry into new life. His most completely realized project was in the Netherlands, near Emmen, where he built Broken Circle and Spiral Hill in 1971. Smithson had no interest in disguising the industrial past that defined his sites. He did not do as, say, James Turrell and find rich art patrons and troll for unencumbered real estate on which to impose his artistic vision. Smithson worked directly with mining companies and municipalities. His interventions are a kind of last phase of mining, after the industry arrives at its deepest contradictions – strip mining destroys the earth it profits from – his work finessed a future out of it.

In 1972, a year before his death, Smithson wrote, "a dialectic between mining and land reclamation must be developed. The artist and the miner must become conscious of themselves as natural agents. In effect, this extends to all kinds of mining and building. When the miner or builder loses sight of what he is doing through the abstractions of technology he cannot practically cope with necessity. The world needs coal and highways, but we do not need the results of strip-mining or highway trusts. Economics, when abstracted from the world, is blind to natural processes. Art can become a physical resource that mediates between the ecologist and the industrialist. Ecology and industry are not one-way streets; rather they should be crossroads. Art can help to provide the needed dialectic between them."

It's possible that the industry of architecture has reached the same deep contradictions as mining. The work is exhausted. It's renewal depends on a kind of intellectual jiu-jitsu, like Smithson's, to redirect the considerable force that expended itself making rocket-shoes for starlets. I see Mastenbroek's pavilion as similar to Smithson's strip-mine recoveries. This is architecture, pure and simple. Mastenbroek does not mask its contradictions or brutalities; he finesses them into something possible, something with a future. And it doesn't look like much.

In keeping with Smithson's radically collapsed time sense, the New Pavilion has already become a ruin. The tarp ceiling caved in and the pole that once held it taut now protrudes from the hole like the broken mast of a shipwreck. The captive plants look alternately liberated, as if this pole were the lead thrust of their breakout, and in agony; they are neglected, broken, turning brown, and dying. As a ruin, the New Pavilion is the site of radical upheaval and change. But the door is locked. Legal requirements make closure the only possible institutional response to the pavilion's structural failure. The next step will be removal, expulsion. It's only a pavilion, after all, and all pavilions are built to be temporary. So it is with any refugee. The end of the story is always the same. Asylum ends, the refugee centre is closed, and everyone must move along. But to where?

Endnotes:

1 [p. 157] Gary Wolf, "Steve Jobs: The Next Insanely Great Thing", *Wired* (1 February 1996). From the same interview: "To design something really well, you have to get it... It takes a passionate commitment to really thoroughly understand something, chew it up, not just quickly swallow it. Most people don't take the time to do that". Accessed March 2017.

2 [p. 157] Bernard Rudofsky, *Architecture without Architects: A Short Introduction to Non-pedigreed Architecture* (New York: Museum of Modern Art, 1964), 25.

3 [p. 158] *Poché* refers to areas of an architectural plan or section that are filled in, often by cross hatching or solid black, to show wall thicknesses, floor thicknesses and all other solid areas that intersect the plane of the section.

4 [p. 164] "About Super-Kamiokande", *Super Kamiokande* website. Accessed March 2018.

5 [p. 173] Sophie Baldwin, Elizabeth Holroyd and Roger Burrows, "Luxified Troglodytism? Mapping the Subterranean Geographies of Plutocratic London", *ResearchGate* (May 2018). Accessed May 2018.

6 [p. 174] Fang Wang, Fengyao Yu, Xiaohua Zhu, Xiaoli Pan, Ruimin Sun and Hongru Cai, "Disappearing Gradually and Unconsciously in Rural China: Research on the Sunken Courtyard and the Reasons for Change in Shanxian County, Henan Province", *Journal of Rural Studies* 47, part B (October 2016), 630–649.

7 [p. 203] Specifically G-plus-3, 4 or 5 (ground floor and 3 to 5 storeys) are built in return for land. Michiel Hulshof and Daan Roggeveen, A Go West Project, "Facing East; Chinese Urbanism in Africa", *Storefront for Art and Architecture* (2015). Accessed June 2018.

8 [p. 203] Xinrong Zhu, Jiaping Liu, Liu Yang and Rongrong Hu, "Energy Performance of a New Yaodong Dwelling, in the Loess Plateau of China", *Energy and Buildings* 70 (February 2014), 159–166.

9 [p. 204] The most widespread civilization of the Old World during the Bronze Age, the Indus Valley Civilization (IVC) or Harrapan Civilization. Rita P. Wright, *The Ancient Indus: Urbanism, Economy, and Society* (Cambridge: Cambridge University Press, 2009), or 2010 in an interview connected to this book.

10 [p. 204] Percy Brown, "Buddhist Rock-cut Architecture: The Early or Hinayana Phase, 2nd Century B.C. to 2nd Century A.D.", ch. V and "The Dravidian Style, Its Genesis under the Pallavas (6th–9th Century A.D.)", ch. XVI, in *Indian Architecture: Buddhist and Hindu Periods,* vol. 1 (Bombay: Taraporevala Sons, 1940), 308ff.

11 [p. 205] See the round opening of Chaitya Hall at Ajanta built in the sixth century CE.

12 [p. 205] Percy Brown, "Buddhist Rock-cut Architecture" (above, note 10).

13 [p. 261] Amit Khanna Design Associates, "The Profanity of Solace by Amit Khanna", *WAN, World Architecure News* (17 December 2012).

14 [p. 262] Michael Hauben, "Participatory Democracy from the 1960s and SDS into the Future On-line" Columbia University, 1995; and James Miller, *Democracy Is in the Streets* (New York: Simon and Schuster, 1987).

15 [p. 262] Michel Crozier, Samuel P. Huntington and Joji Watanuki, *The Crisis of Democracy: On the Governability of Democracies to the Trilateral Commission* (New York: New York University Press, 1975).

16 [p. 262] Growing conservation advocacy from the 1950s led to the signing of the Wilderness Act of the United States in 1964. This legally defined wilderness and established a mechanism for protecting it.

17 [p. 262] In 1948 Dubuffet founded Compagnie de L'Art Brut with the spiritual father of surrealism André Breton.

18 [p. 262] *Jean Dubuffet: Soul of the Underground* exhibition, 18 October 2014–5 April 2015, Museum of Modern Art, New York.

19 [p. 263] Also referred to as Earth Art or Environmental Art.

20 [p. 263] Courtney Jordan and Samantha Sanders, "Seriously, Why Marfa?", *Art Opening(s)* podcast, episode 5, Artists Network.

21 [p. 263] Donald Judd, "Statement for the Chinati Foundation/La Fundación Chinati", VAGA New York (1987).

22 [p. 263] Ibid.

23 [p. 264] Nick Tarasen, "About Michael Heizer", *Double negative* website. Accessed 15 May 2019.

24 [p. 264] Mark Holborn, "Under the Volcano", *Independent* (11 April 1993). Accessed 15 May 2019.

25 [p. 264] Louis Guillame le Roy, Piet Vollaard and Rob Hendriks, "Leven en Werken in Ruimte en Tijd", *Stichting Tijd* (2006).

26 [p. 265] Dana Goodyear, "A Monument to Outlast Humanity", *New Yorker* (29 August 2016). Accessed 4 August 2018.

27 [p. 265] See "The Ritualization of Life", Nature's Lack of Design, 27–31.

28 [p. 266] Raj Patel, "One of the Largest Underground Caverns Ever Constructed", *Arup* website. Accessed 15 May 2019.

29 [p. 269] Giles Tremlett, "Spanish Island Allows Massive Cave to Be Bored into 'Magic' Mountain", *Guardian* (20 January 2011). Accessed 18 August 2018.

30 [p. 273] Not Vital in conversation with Andrew O'Haganot, "Inside the Many Houses of Not Vital, Maker of Dreamscapes for Adults", *New York Times Style Magazine* (18 October 2013). Accessed September 2018.

31 [p. 274] Kieron Marchese, "Millions of Lasers Project 3D Scan Allowing Ensamble Studio's Contemporary Intervention of Abandoned Quarry", *Designboom* (29 May 2018). Accessed 5 August 2018.

32 [p. 277] Antón García-Abril in conversation with Vladimir Belogolovsky, "The New Generation Will Not Accept Standard Solutions. We Need an Entirely Different City", *Arch Daily* (8 October 2015). Accessed 4 August 2018.

33 [p. 278] Junya Ishigami in conversation with Oliver Wainwright, "I Want to Make the Sky", *Guardian* (3 April 2018). Accessed 1 August 2018.

34 [p. 283] Kimberly Bradley, "Why Museums Hide Masterpieces Away", *BBC* (23 January 2015). Accessed 15 May 2019.

35 [p. 292] Enric Miralles, "Mixed Talks", *Architectural Monographs* no. 40 (London: Academy Editions, 1995).

36 [p. 292] *Enric Miralles, Works and Projects 1975–1995* (New York: Monacelli Press, 1996), 52.

37 [p. 294] See also Mario Hernandez and Christopher Maurer, *Line of Light and Shadow: The Drawings of Federico García Lorca* (Durham: Duke University Press in association with Duke University Museum of Art, 1991).

38 [p. 303] Press release for the exhibition *Visionary Architecture!* MoMA, New York, 29 September 1960.

39 [p. 308] Palazzo Antinori in the center of Florence had been the headquarters since 1506.

40 [p. 376] See "From Compound to Community", Nature's Lack of Design, 48–56.

41 [p. 377] Plato, "The Allegory of the Cave", book 7, *The Republic*, 380 BCE.

Embed

Embed — Sitting within slope

Building and landscape share an equal position within the earth's crust. The building is embedded in the landscape, and the landscape is manipulated to accommodate the building.

"Everything that does not have a roof is landscape; and the moment I have a roof above me, I'm passing into another realm and into another, totally different scale."[1] —Diana Balmori

Drawing the imaginary line between architecture and landscape is a joyful tug of war. The jury is still out but we would argue that walls have a deciding vote when it comes to unravelling the two disciplines' domains. We'd like to claim back walls without a roof: the stepwells of Northern India are surely in the realm of building. But what is a single floor with furniture atop a mountain? Is this the pinnacle to which the architect should aspire, the 'beinahe nichts', or almost nothing, of Mies van der Rohe?[2]

Null Stern Hotel, Teufen, Switzerland, Atelier für Sonderaufgaben, 2009.

Stepwell Agrasen ki Baoli, New Delhi, India, c.1400.

Rotated Glass House study, Japan, Bjarne Mastenbroek, 2001.

If the roof can be boiled down to the master of shelter, then the wall masters enclosure. It sits perpendicular to the earth, bound to it by gravity yet reaching to the sky. Analysing how we handle walls over the centuries offers fascinating insight into the tumultuous relationship between mass (earth) and void (sky).

In the eighteenth century, public space was defined by its boundaries, the solid mass of built fabric around it, whereas within modern society isolated buildings are defined by the fluidity of space around them. The built fabric of our cities has been inverted; the private realm has overtaken the public realm, focus has shifted inside, and buildings have become a more abstract matter.

Lever House, New York, US, Gordon Bunshaft and Natalie de Blois, 1952.

The twentieth century took architecture to lofty new heights. But supported by densification and technological progress, buildings became minimalist containers. Full-figured dames in richly attired costumes with crinolines shrunk to scrawny supermodels. The enclosed spaces of the medieval centre were repressed and ridiculed. Why look backwards to the humble room when presented with the *free* plan and *free* facade made possible by the steel column?

Modernists took our walls and dissolved the room into open, universal spaces defined by columns. Today we live and work within these spaces, exhilarated but exposed. In the end, what's more prison-like, a dungeon with a splinter of light or a glass house without curtains amidst the urban buzz? Not being able to hide is tantamount to being held captive, which is not something we generally like to admit. Luckily, buildings need shafts, storage, toilets and other facilities, but these spaces are a poor substitute for what used to be our hiding places.

Zonnestraal Sanatorium, Hilversum, Netherlands, Jan Duiker, 1931.

The skyscraper, once celebrated as a symbol of progress, expressing the city's commercial and cultural dominance, is now associated with global homogeneity, Through its affordable and efficient construction system, the curtain wall became an increasingly invincible, standardizing force.[3] Architect Annabel Koeck argues that the curtain wall is making buildings and even entire cities invisible thanks to its sheer ubiquity – at the expense of architectural expression.[4] The reflective glass facades of the contemporary city abuse the term 'transparency'. You only have to look at the Zonnestraal Sanatorium of 1931 to see the high natural light transmittance that is possible.

The projects on the following pages do not reflect the rigour or efficiency of modernism. There are too many walls, too many rooms, too many flourishes. They boldly look backwards to satisfy something more elemental – a desire to dwell with our backs covered and an open view.

A. Olympic Archery Range, Barcelona, Spain, Enric Miralles & Carme Pinos, 1989–1991.
B. Siedlung Halen, Bern, Switzerland, Atelier 5, 1955–1961.
C. Buddhist Academy, Larung Gar, Tibet, 1980.
D. Settlement of Oia, Greece.
E. Rockland Ranch, Moab, Utah, 1980–present.
F. Sar Agha Seyed, Chaharmahal and Bakhtiari Province, Iran.
G. Athfield House & Studio, Wellington, New Zealand, Ian Athfield, 1965–present.
H. Guadix, Spain.
I. Il Magistero, Urbino, Italy, Giancarlo De Carlo, 1968–1976.
J. Nawarla Gabarnmang, Australia.
K. Hanging Temple, Datong, China, 490 CE.
L. Kumbum chorten, Tibet, 1427–1437.
M. The Great Wall of WA, Western Australia, Australia, Luigi Rosselli Architects, 2015.
N. Alemdoune, Morocco.
O. Vardzia Monastery, Georgia, twelfth century.
P. Positano, Italy.
Q. Acusa Seca, Canary Islands.
R. Mühlehalde Housing, Umiken, Hans Scherer, Strickler & Weber, Switzerland, 1962–1971.
S. Tolo House, Ribeira de Pena, Álvaro Siza, Portugal, 2005.
T. Wadi Qelt, Israel, second century BCE.
U. Pok Fu Lam cemetery, Hong Kong, China, 1882.

Looking at the village of Sar Agha Seyed dug out of the hillside, the sprawling village of Athfield or the strict logic of Siedlung Halen, we see how building within the slope or mediating a slope with a building can satisfy a modern desire for panorama and an ancient desire for enclosure. The interior of the building becomes a transitory element between the back wall and the exterior, ignoring the building as a separate element by comforting its occupants. The roof becomes the ground and the ground becomes the roof, further complicating any attempts to neatly separate building and landscape.

Constructed centuries apart and on different continents, buildings twist the surface of the earth upwards, downwards, or both simultaneously, like some kind of deranged Escher painting. The Ancient Theatre of Epidaurus, the stepwells of India or the more recent Friendship Centre in Bangladesh all create a new topography without truly leaving the ground. Stone is piled upwards to support or give shape to human activity. Surface is manipulated to amplify sound, channel water or provide shade.

Relativity, M. C. Escher, 1953.

Surya Kund temple, Modhera, India, 1026 CE.

Friendship Centre, URBANA, Bangladesh, 2011.

A building embedded into its environment is more than a position. The projects included in this chapter know this. They are not bound together aesthetically, geographically, historically or culturally, but connected by deep concern with site.

There is a beautiful tension between natural formation and human construction in the city of Petra, Jordan.

They share a strong material consideration, as if each was vernacular to the place, scratching around upon the surface for the immediate material to work with. Each project unlocks the qualities of its site in different ways. For Charles and Ray Eames, what mattered was an incredible control of scale, not just designing for the human scale but understanding the relativity of humankind and their surroundings. For Enric Miralles, it was about sensitivity to every delicate curve in the landscape. His buildings creep along the slope and ease themselves into position.

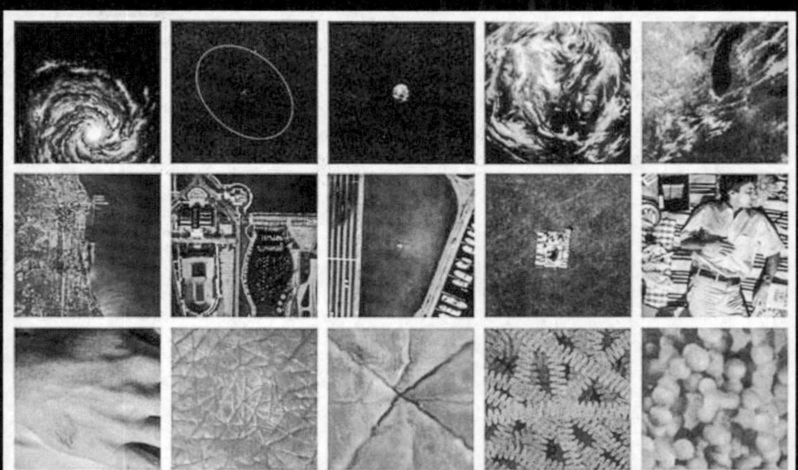

From the galaxy to the microscopic, *Powers of Ten*, Charles & Ray Eames, 1977.

"For too long, buildings in the West have been conceived as isolated objects that float in naturalistic landscapes. Inverting the relationship – considering building and landscape as reciprocal entities – reconciles this division."[5] – Diane Balmori, Hans Ibelings and Bjarne Mastenbroek

This chapter celebrates buildings unimaginable without their natural setting, and they in return create a site unthinkable without its built form.

Buildings are not imposed but embedded in the landscape. Conversely, landscape is not the dominant entity. Buildings do not disguise themselves – each competes for equal attention. It is as if their architecture was a comfortable, enfolding lounge chair within an infinite landscape. They bring a natural friction to the fore: the dichotomies between building and landscape, mass and void, object and space, earth and sky, are interrogated on the following pages.

Let the battle begin.

Ancient Theatre Epidaurus, Greece Polykleitos the Younger 330–200 BCE

Ancient Greece is the celebrated birthplace of Western civilization, a pivotal era in which humankind untied itself from nature, developing its own rules. Society was conceived, democracy was installed, and a political, religious, cultural and educational system was refined. Space and habitation were organized, not by the laws of nature but by the abstract ideals of humans, and an architecture of classical orders, mathematical systems of proportions and ornamentation was invented.

Axonometry of the Ancient Theatre of Epidaurus.

The architectural forms of the earliest temples (600–500 BCE) were made from timber.[6] But gradually, solidified and polished stone replaced timber, as if the structure had undergone petrification.[7]

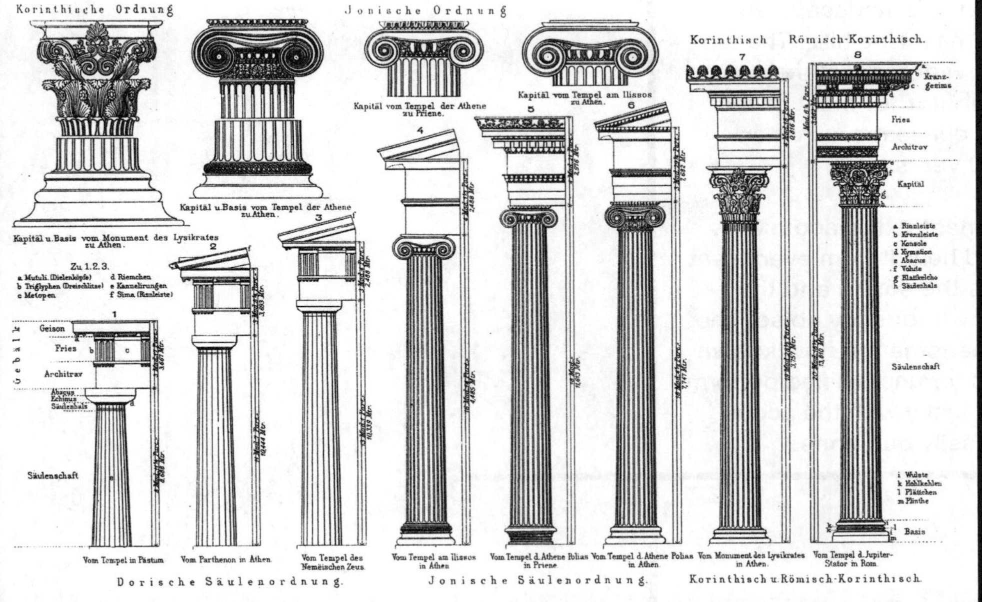

The orders of Ancient Greece: Doric, Ionic and Corinthian.

Whilst the Ionic and Corinthian order still referenced nature with their cochlea and acanthus shape, the simpler Doric order did not. Stronger and cheaper to build, the Doric order emerged as the predominant element and classical architecture no longer referenced natural elements.

There were some constructions, like the Ancient Theatre of Epidaurus, that couldn't do without. And why should they? The backdrop behind the *skênê* is perfect for dramatic performances, and the semicircular site made it a perfect fit for an otherwise huge building to be erected.

Section of the theatre.

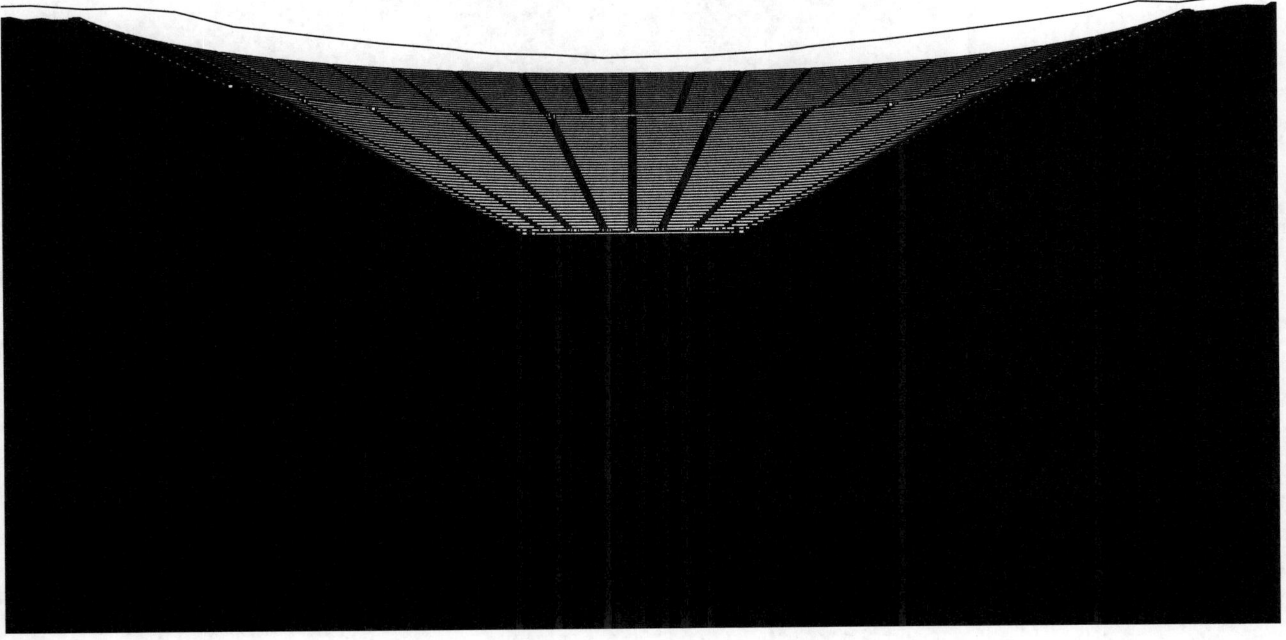

The Ancient theatre, sits 'in' the landscape and has an open view towards the rolling hills. The top row of this original theatre, wider in dimension and functioning as a distributor for most of the seats, separates it from the epitheatre, an extension atop built roughly 150 years later.

The most astonishing element is the acoustics. You can strike a match and hear it from every seat because its shape reflects the sound and the limestone seats absorb low frequency noise. The high clarity of sound, a phenomenon now known as virtual pitch, is priceless for unamplified performances. Maybe humans got lucky with the acoustics, but nature is not so easily outshone.

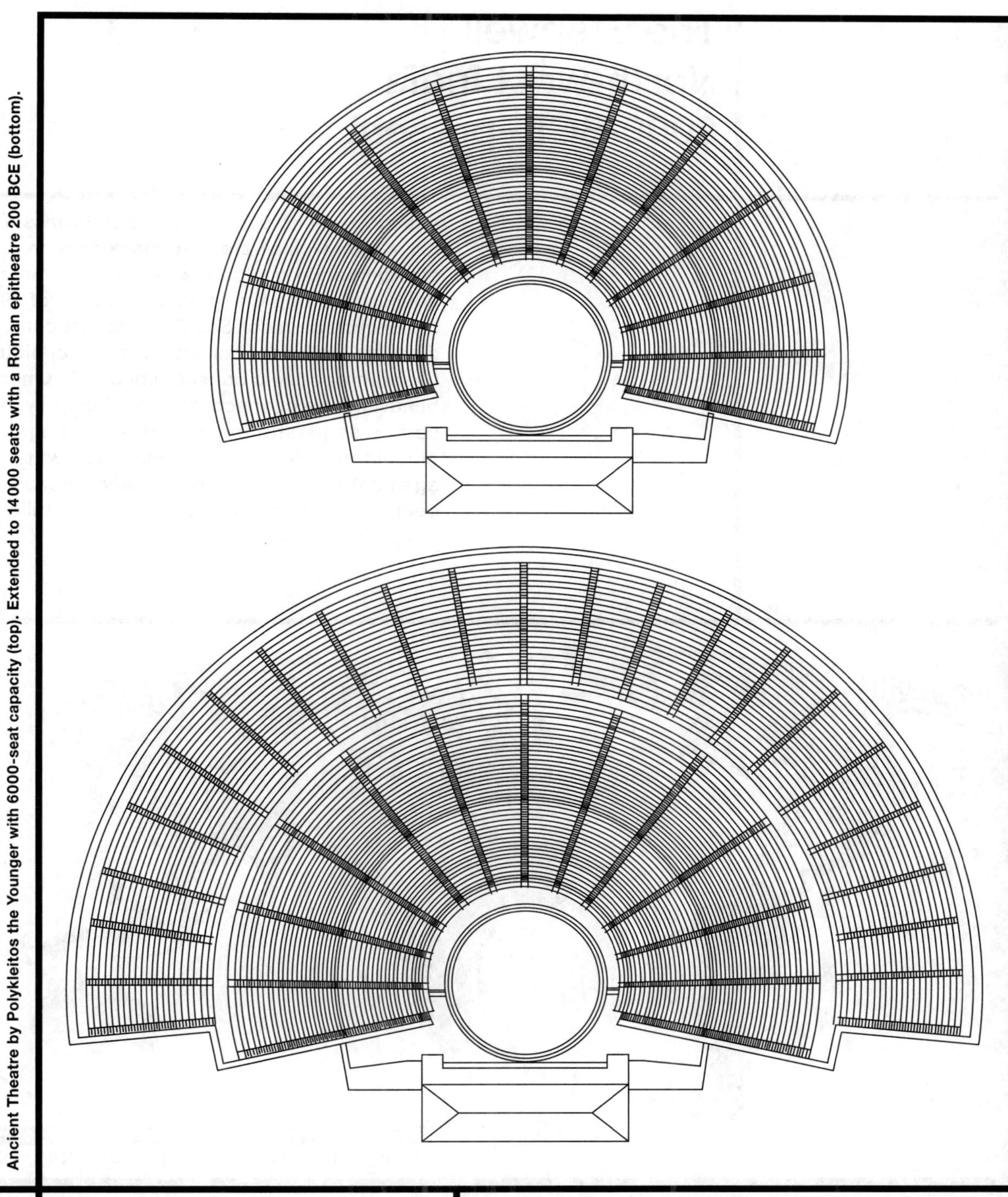

Ancient Theatre by Polykleitos the Younger with 6000-seat capacity (top). Extended to 14 000 seats with a Roman epitheatre 200 BCE (bottom).

If it wasn't for the determination of Panagíotis Kavvadías and the Greek Archaeologist Society, the Ancient Theatre of Epidaurus might still be buried under a six-metre-deep layer of soil and covered with olive trees. Following a hunch that ancient geographer Pausanias had indeed seen "the most remarkable theatre of the ancient world at Epidaurus", Kavvadías started digging. And in 1881 he discovered what nature had preserved for over a millennium.[8]

The Stepwell
North-west India
2000 BCE–present

It is probably no coincidence that Professor Rattan Lal, a man well aware of humankind's precarious environmental position, was born in India and educated during the 'pivotal moment' of 1964. In his *Encyclopedia of Soil Science*, Lal compiled dizzying statistics, building a very real picture of the anthropogenic consequences of humankind's behaviour. He connects climate change with soil carbon sequestration, climate-smart agriculture, global food security, soil health, soil-water management and erosion control, and forecasts a decrease in renewable freshwater for billions of people by 2025.[9]

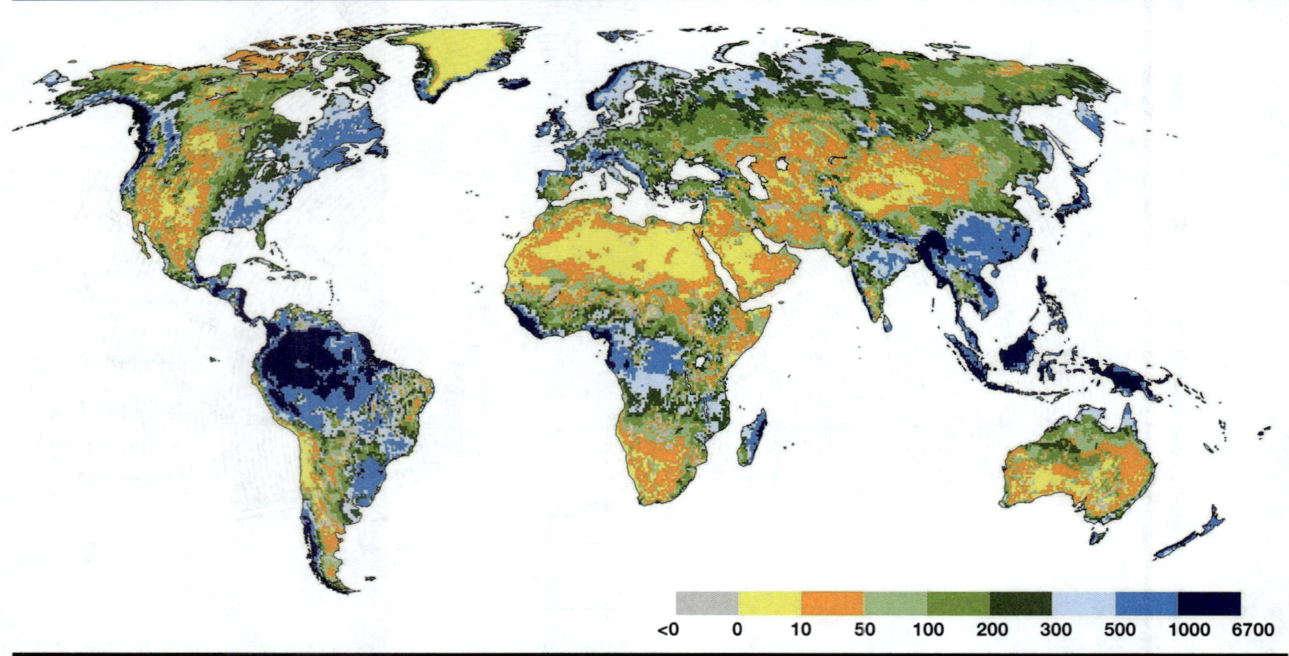

Total renewable freshwater resources in millimetres per year.

The encyclopaedia focuses on the most basic of all natural resources: the soil. This thin upper surface of the earth's crust supports most living organisms, including us. It is precisely summed up by an old Chinese proverb, "despite his artistic pretentions, his sophistication and many accomplishments, [man] owes his existence to a six-inch layer of topsoil and the fact that it rains." This fragile position is felt more acutely in western India, where rainfall is low for much of the year until the monsoon sweeps by.

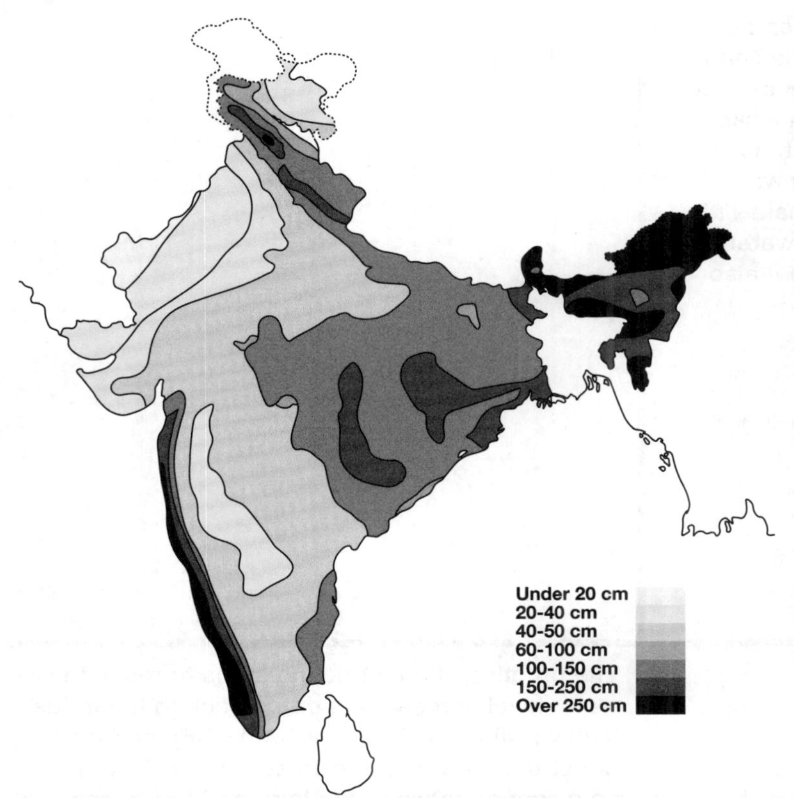

Average annual rainfall, India.

Position and concentration of stepwells.

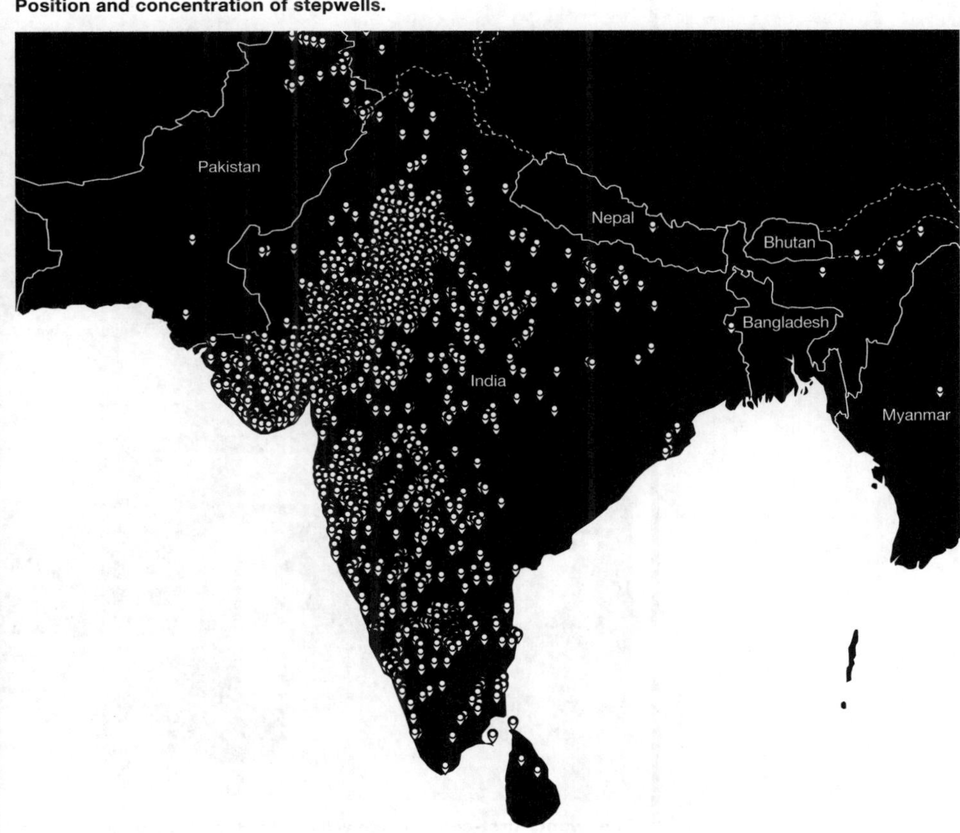

A dazzling number of stepwells have been built in the arid and semi-arid climates of Rajasthan and Gujarat to balance seasonal fluctuations in water availability. The wells function as irrigation tanks, their wide surface collecting water in intensive downpours and their deep form holding water in the months of no rainfall. The terracing makes it easier for people to reach the changing water level in the tank. Maintenance and management also play a role.

The practice of constructing steps to reach the water level in reservoirs dates back to the Indus Valley civilization (roughly 2000 BCE), and the construction of rock-hewn stepwells started somewhere between the third and fourth century.[10] Despite considerable damage and neglect under British rule, stepwell construction continues today. We have observed roughly three typologies: strict and linear, open and geometric, and free-form and geologic.

The twenty-first-century stepwell Birkha Bawari, Jodhpur, Anu Mridul, 2009.

EOS DIGITAL

DO NOT TOUCH SCULPTURES

Seen here in the Adi Kadi Vav in Junagadh, a thin pathway to the well is cut 41 metres into solid rock.

120 rock-hewn steps of Adi Kadi Vav, Junagadh.

The linear or sometimes crucifix typology is roughly characterized as a narrow slit in the earth. A tank is positioned at one end, and steps descend from the other, towards a fluctuating water level. The most significant element of this stepwell is the architecture of soil retention. In areas where the ground is stable, two opposite, arched walls suffice. But in less stable conditions, impressive constructions with flying buttresses, absorbing lateral forces, appear. Meticulously chiselled ornamentation between does the rest.

Rudimentary buttresses were employed in Europe in late antiquity (200–300 CE) but it took until the Gothic period (1100–1500) before they came anywhere close to the sophistication India had achieved hundreds of years earlier.

Rotunda of Galerius, Thessaloniki, 305–311 CE.

Notre-Dame d'Amiens, 1200–1300.

The Stepwell
—
Agrasen ki Baoli New Delhi, India c.1400

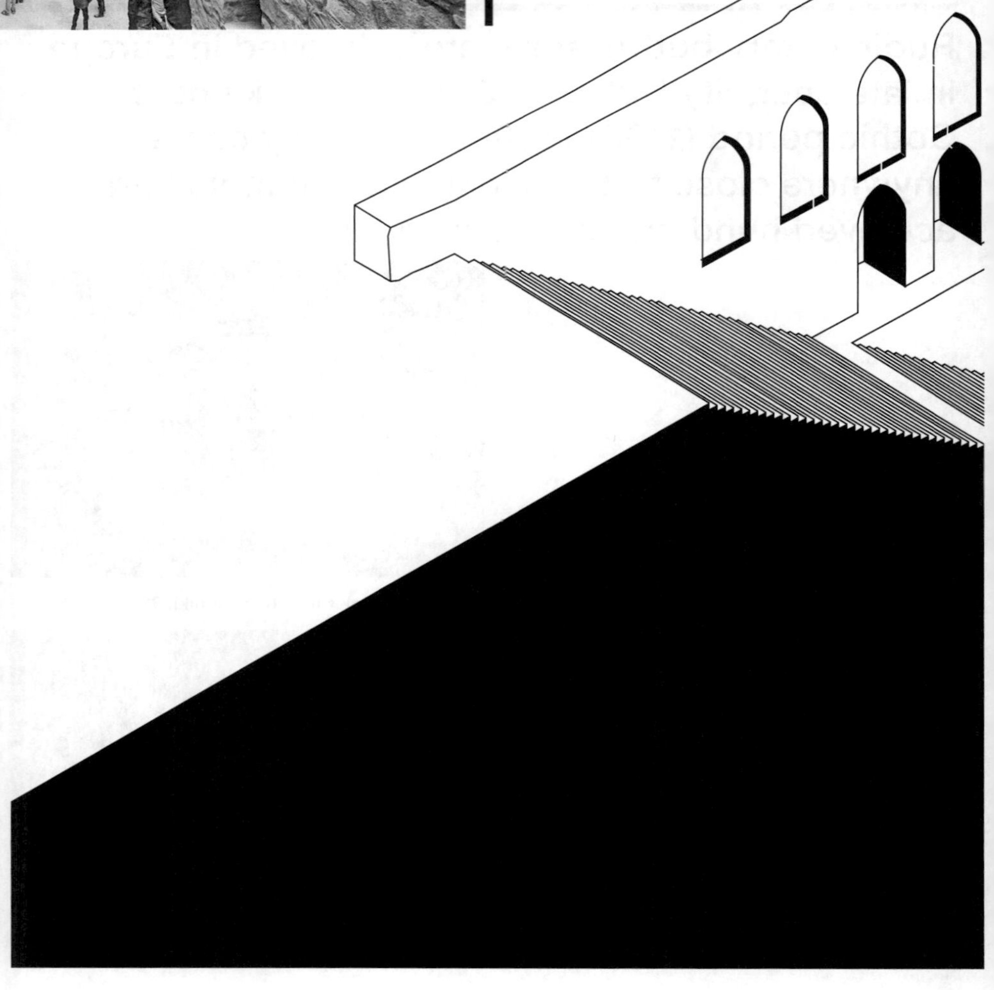

Sectional axonometry of Agrasen ki Baoli.

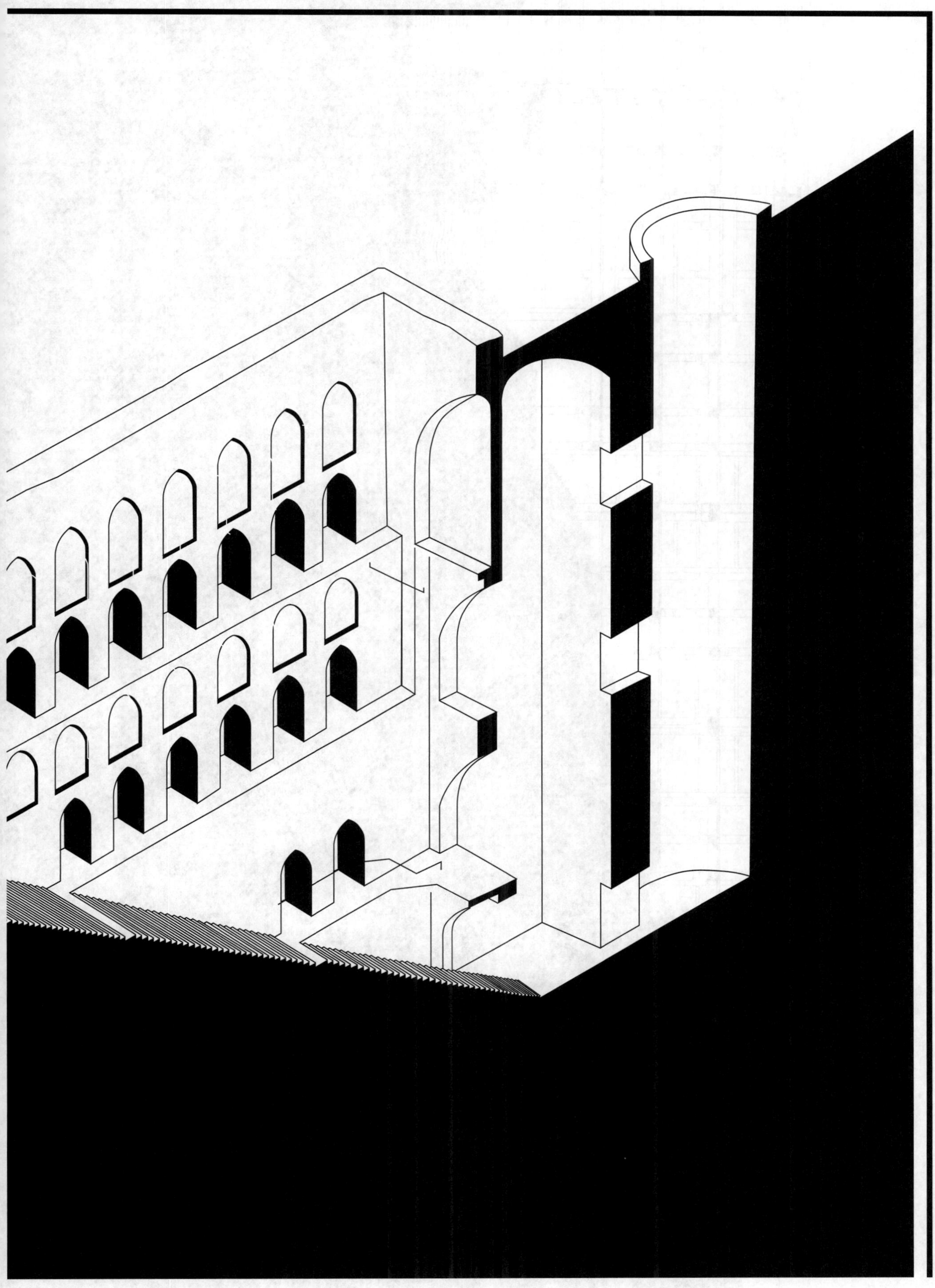

Section of Agrasen ki Baoli.

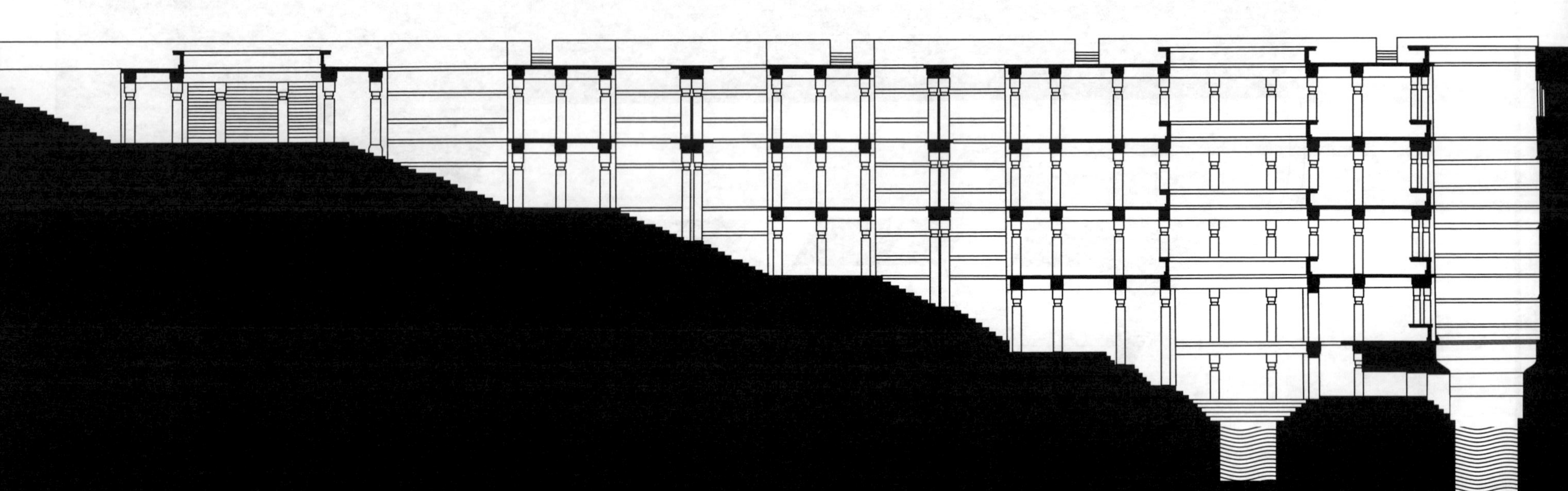

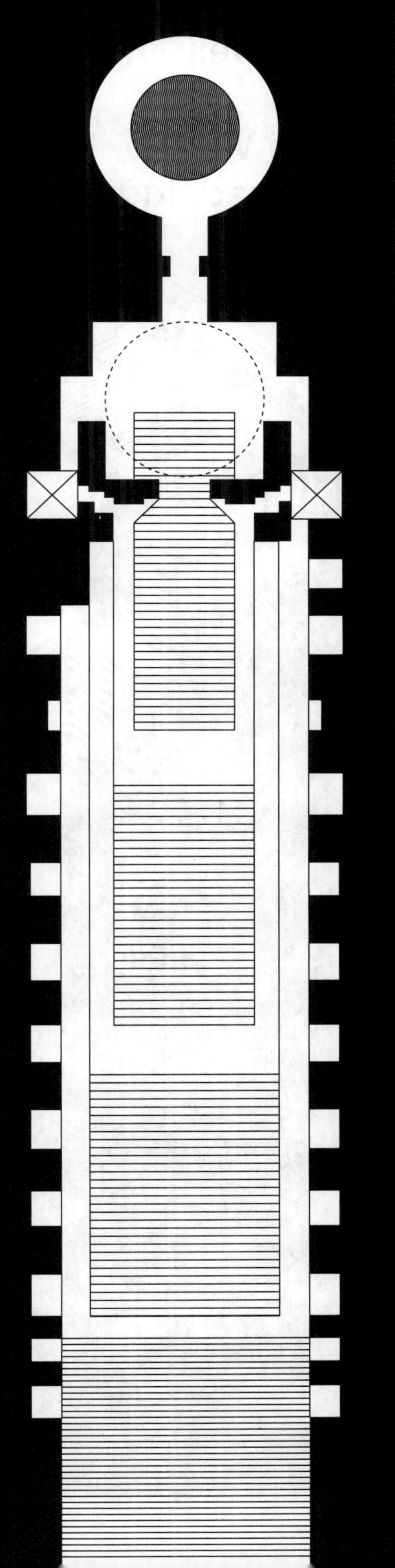

Plan of Agrasen ki Baoli.

The Stepwell
—
Adalaj ni Vav
Ahmedabad, India
1495–1505

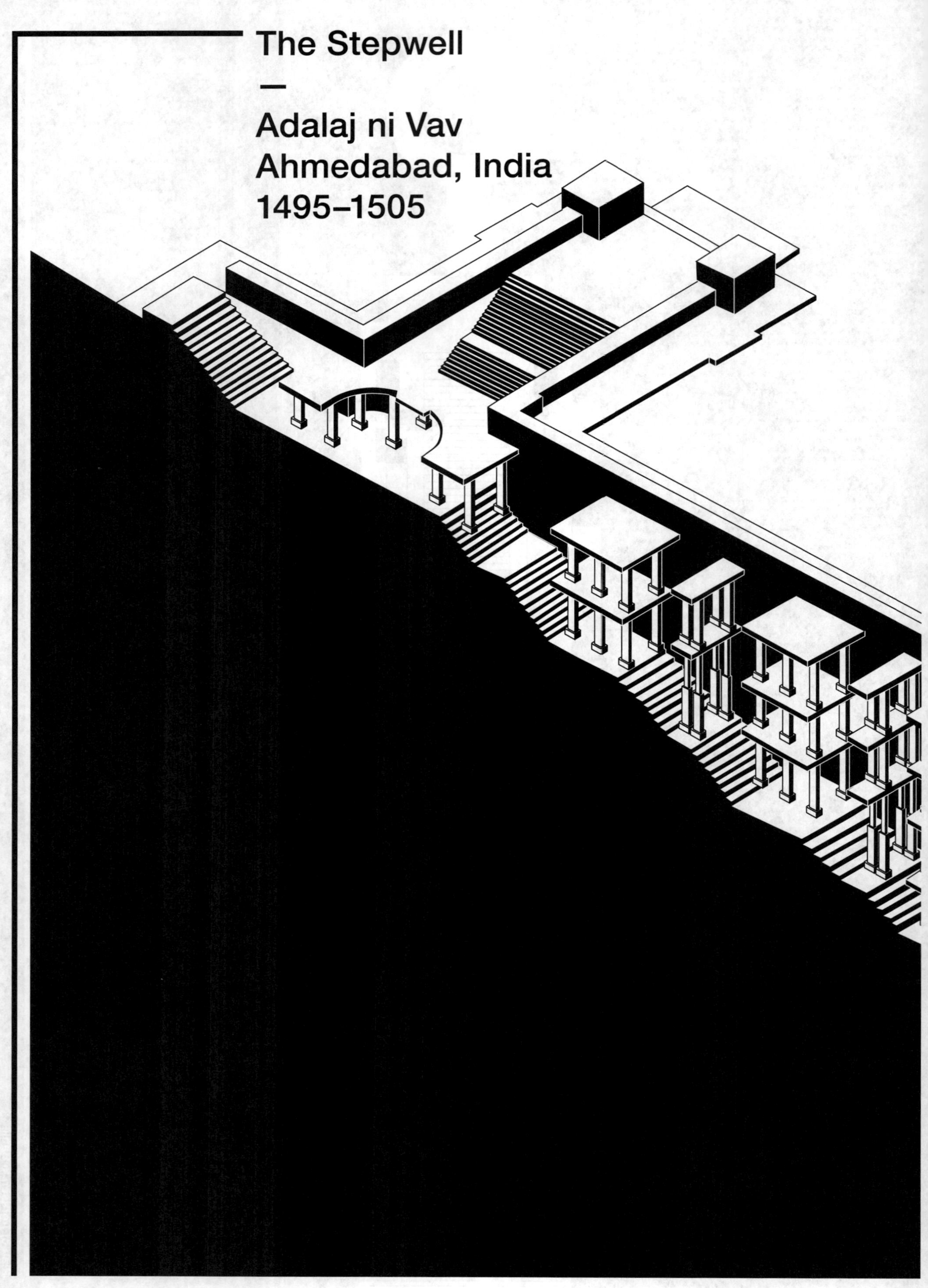

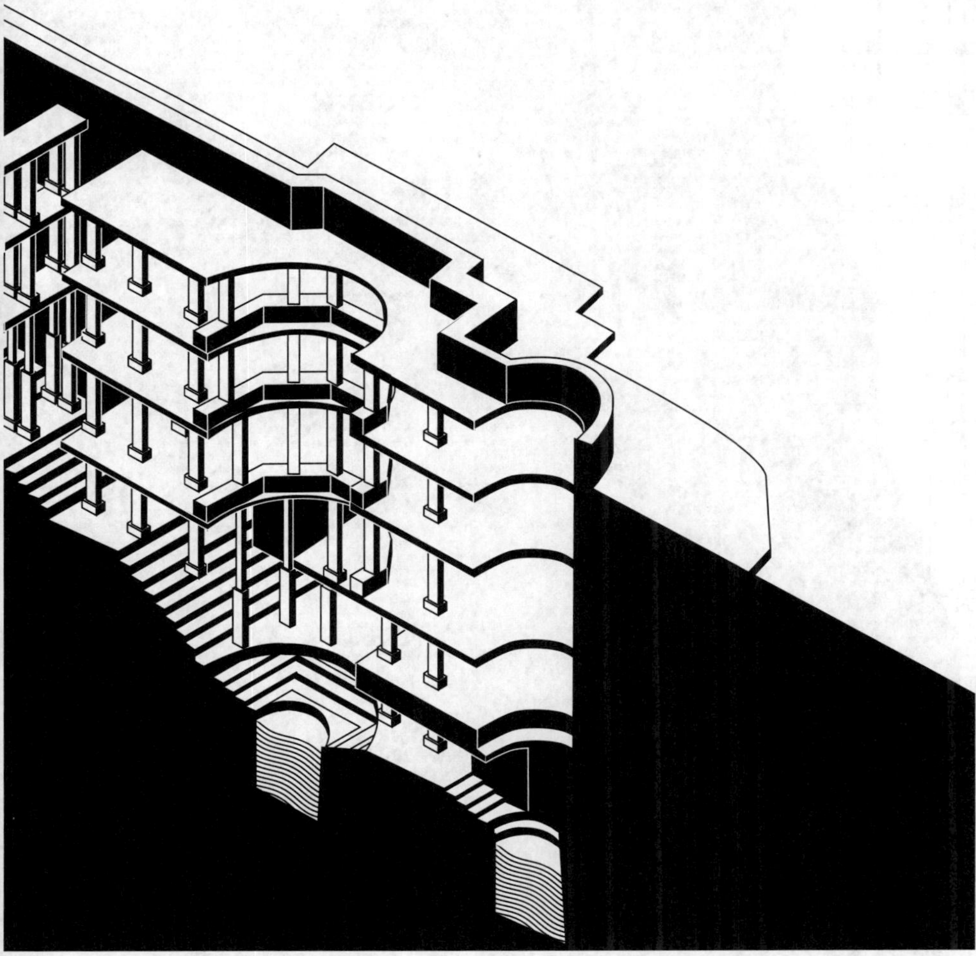

Sectional axonometry of Adalaj ni Vav.

Section of Adalaj ni Vav.

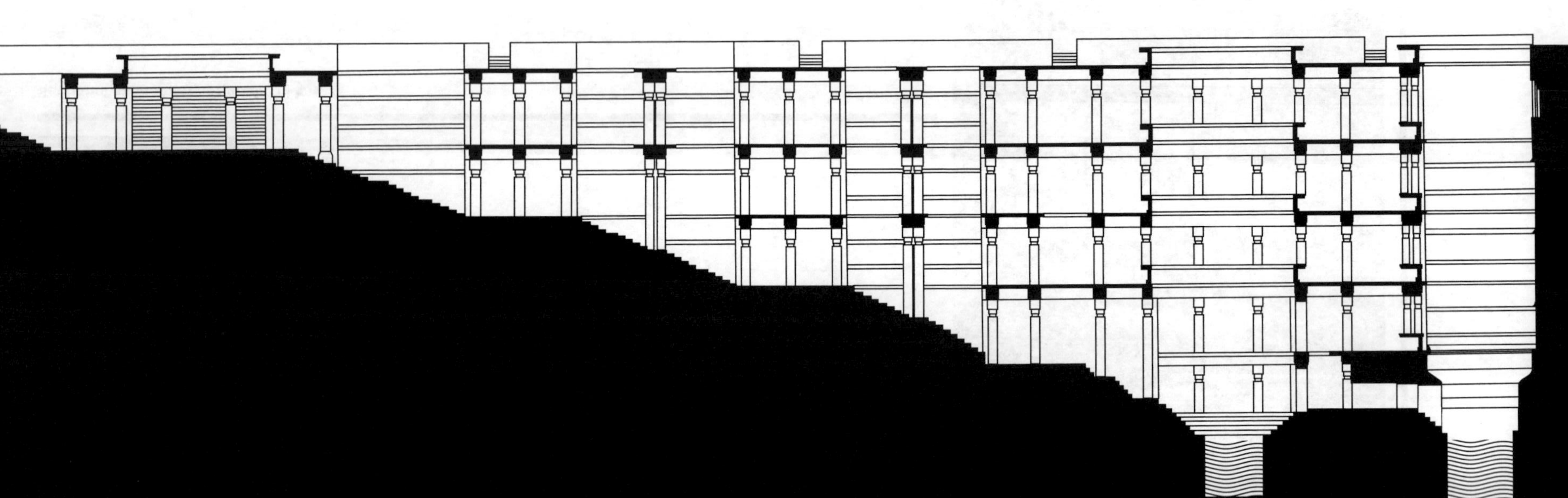

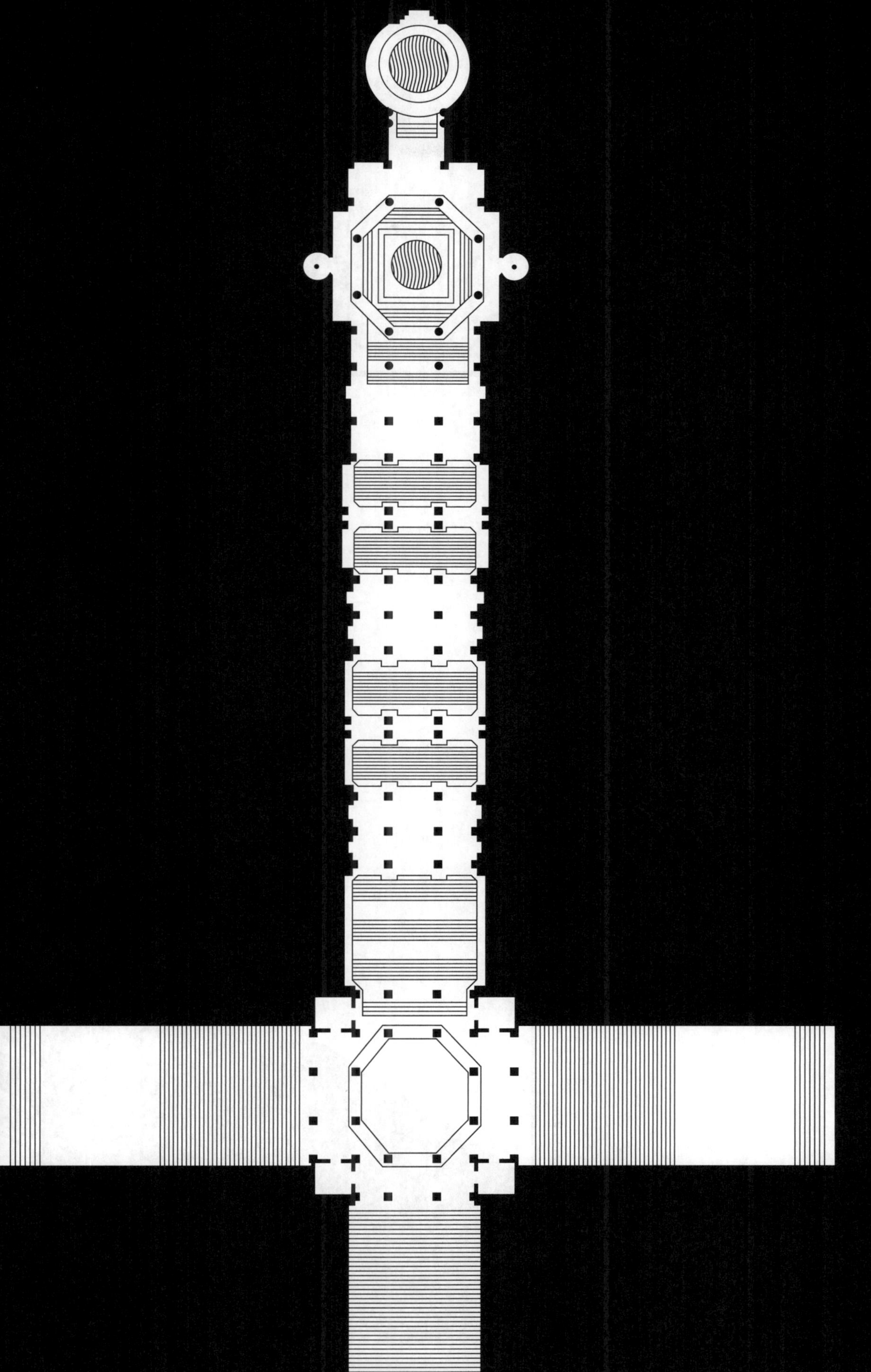

The Stepwell
—
Rani ki Vav
Patan, India
1063 CE

Sectional axonometry of Rani ki Vav.

Section of Rani ki Vav.

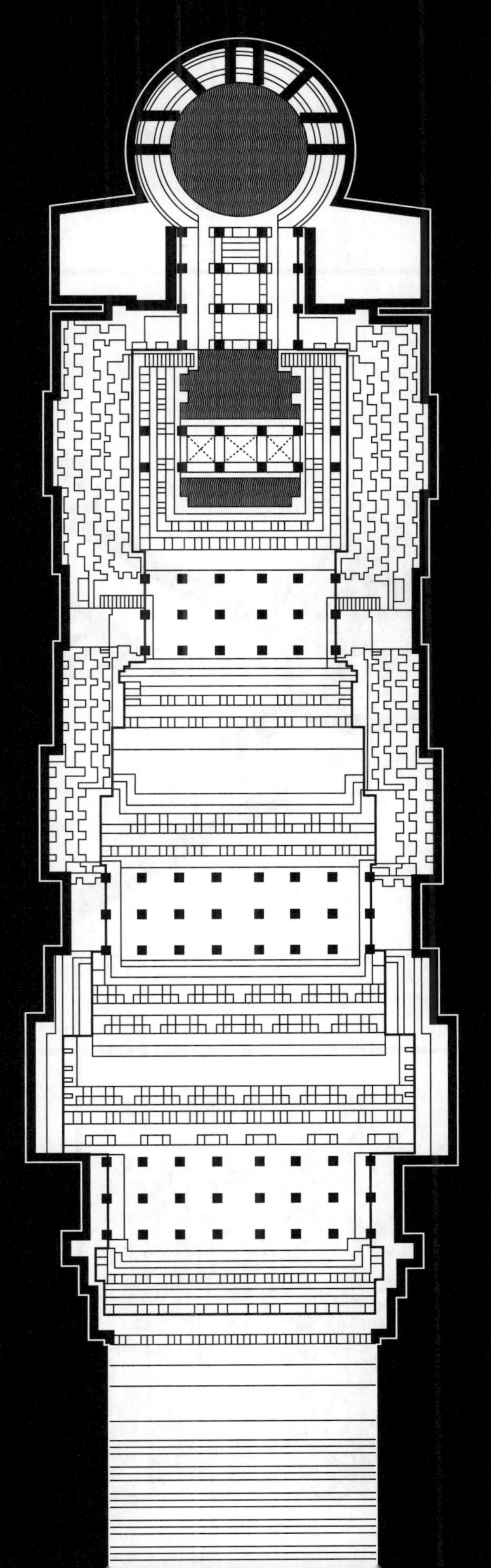

Plan of Rani ki Vav.

The Stepwell

—

Panna Mia Baori
Jaipur, India
c.1500

The square or rectangular typology terraces down around an open well, commonly referred to as a stepped pond. It has a hallucinating layout reminiscent of an Escher drawing. Maze-like stairs descend in a seemingly endless pattern, either on all four sides or often on just three sides, facing a temple frontispiece. Inclination varies from shallow to extremely steep. One stepwell, Nagar Sagar Kund, descends to a stunning 40-metre depth along an almost vertical stone retaining wall until you reach the water tank. Walking up with heavy canisters of water must have been an arduous and potentially deadly trip.

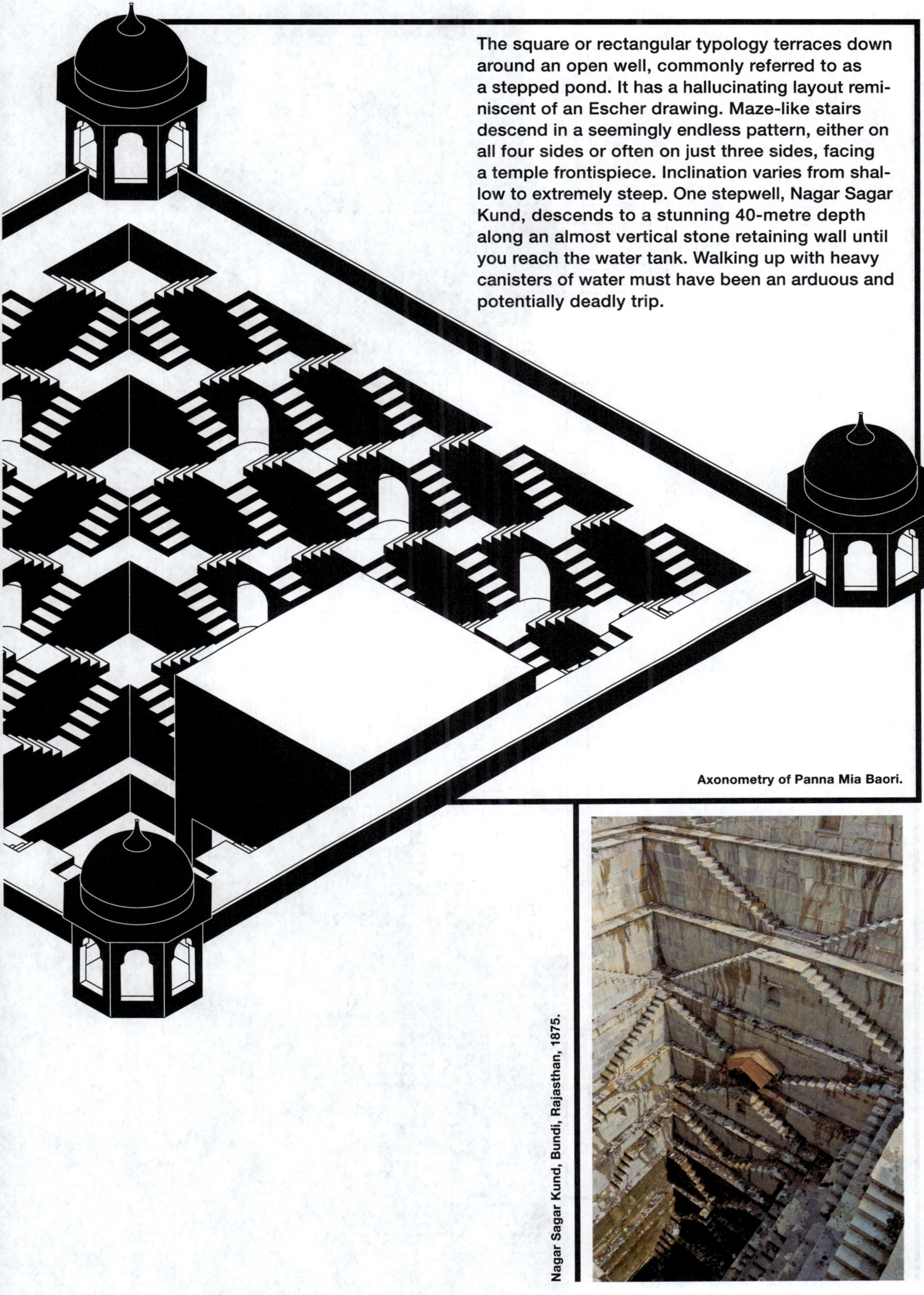

Axonometry of Panna Mia Baori.

Nagar Sagar Kund, Bundi, Rajasthan, 1875.

Section of Panna Mia Baori.

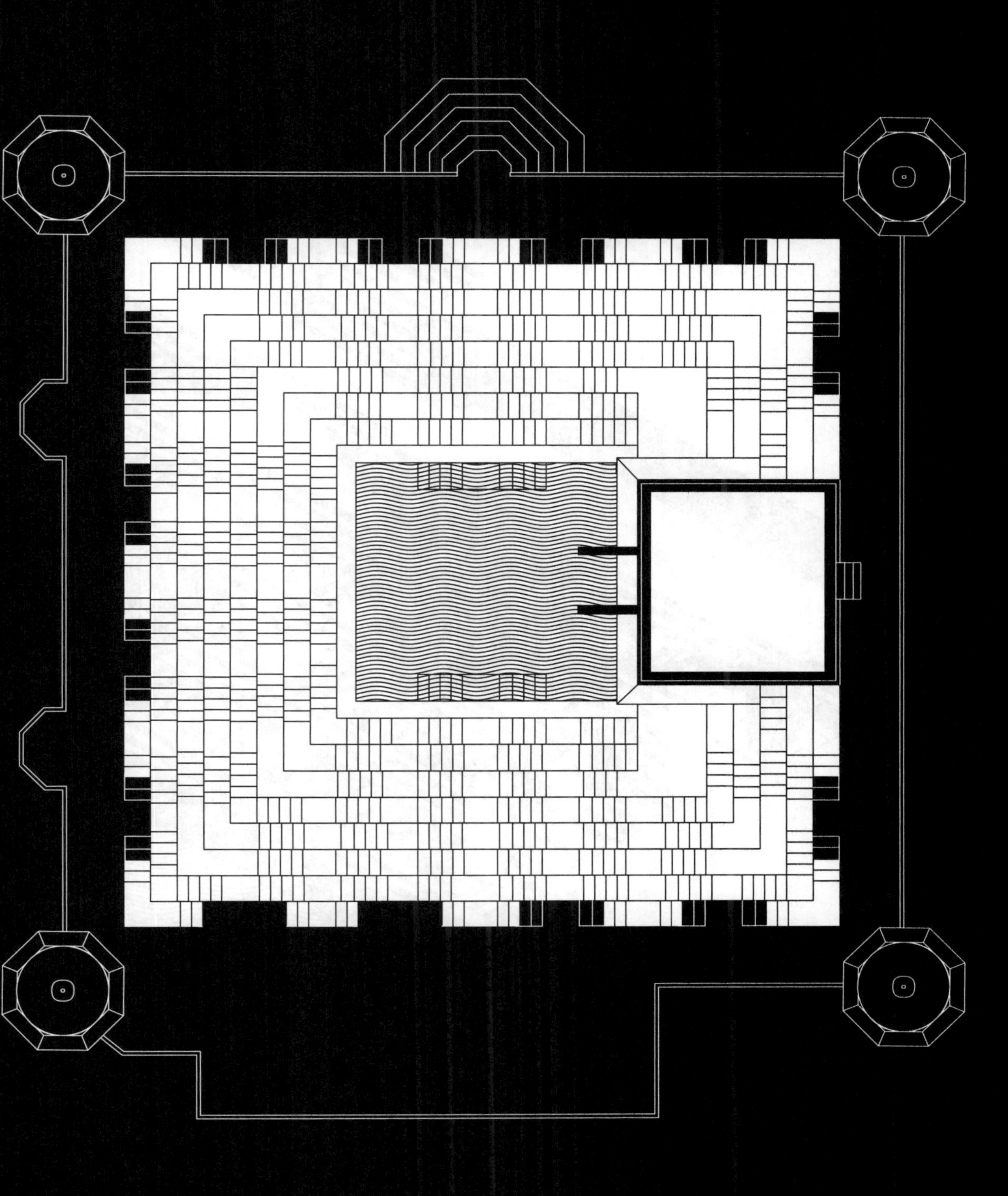

The Stepwell

—

Surya Kund
Modhera, India
1026 CE

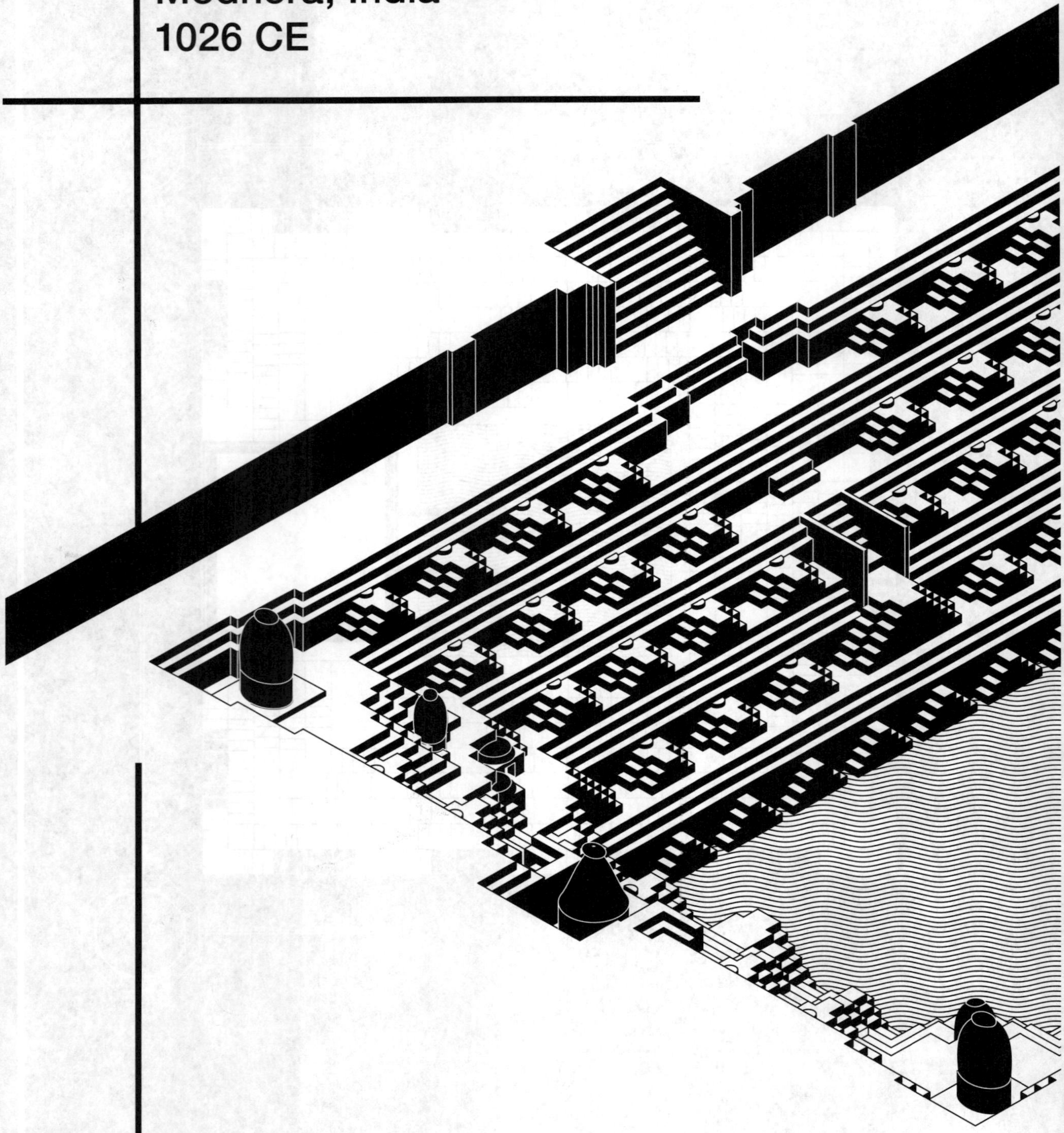

Axonometry of Surya Kund.

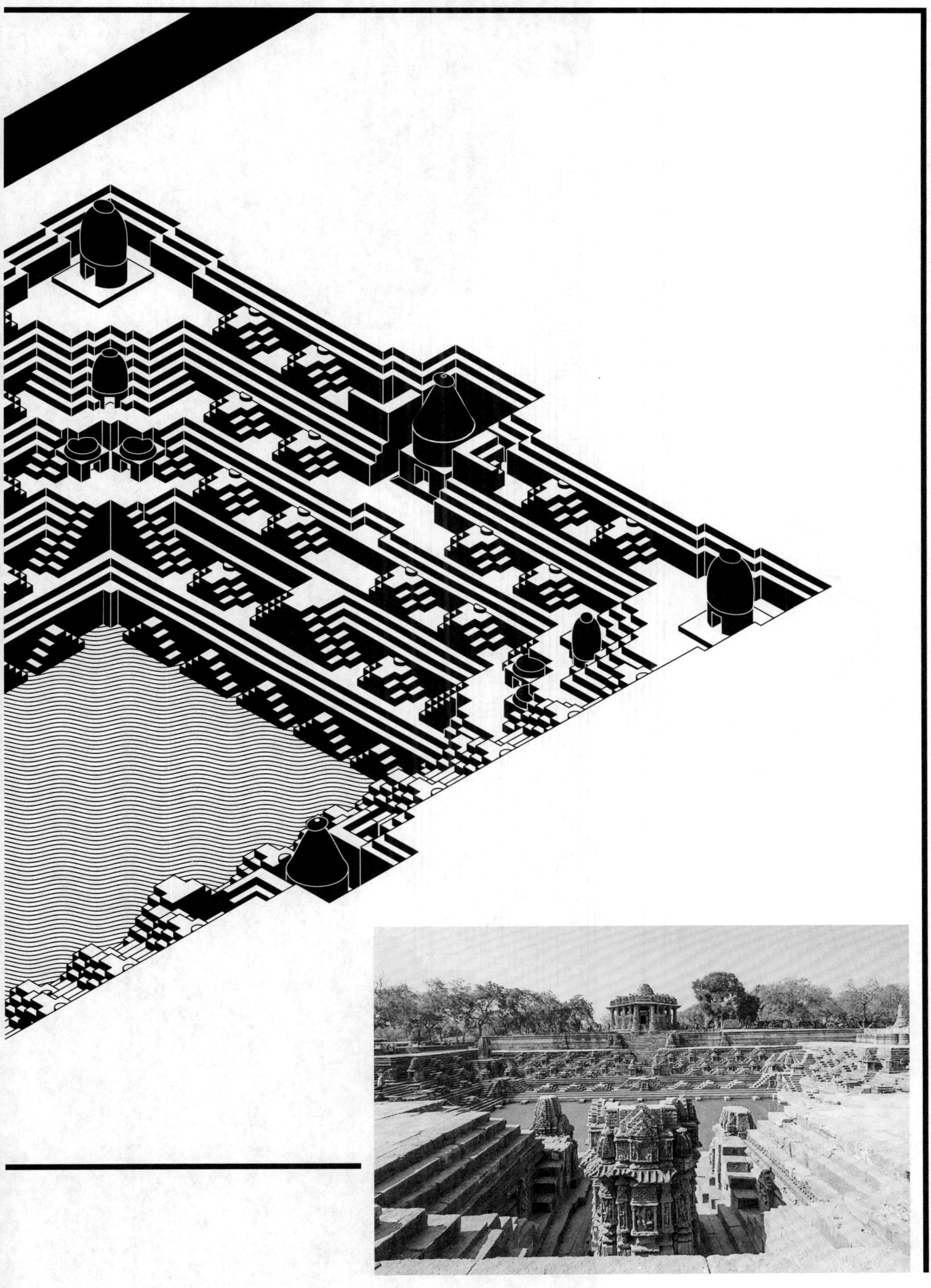

Section of Surya Kund.

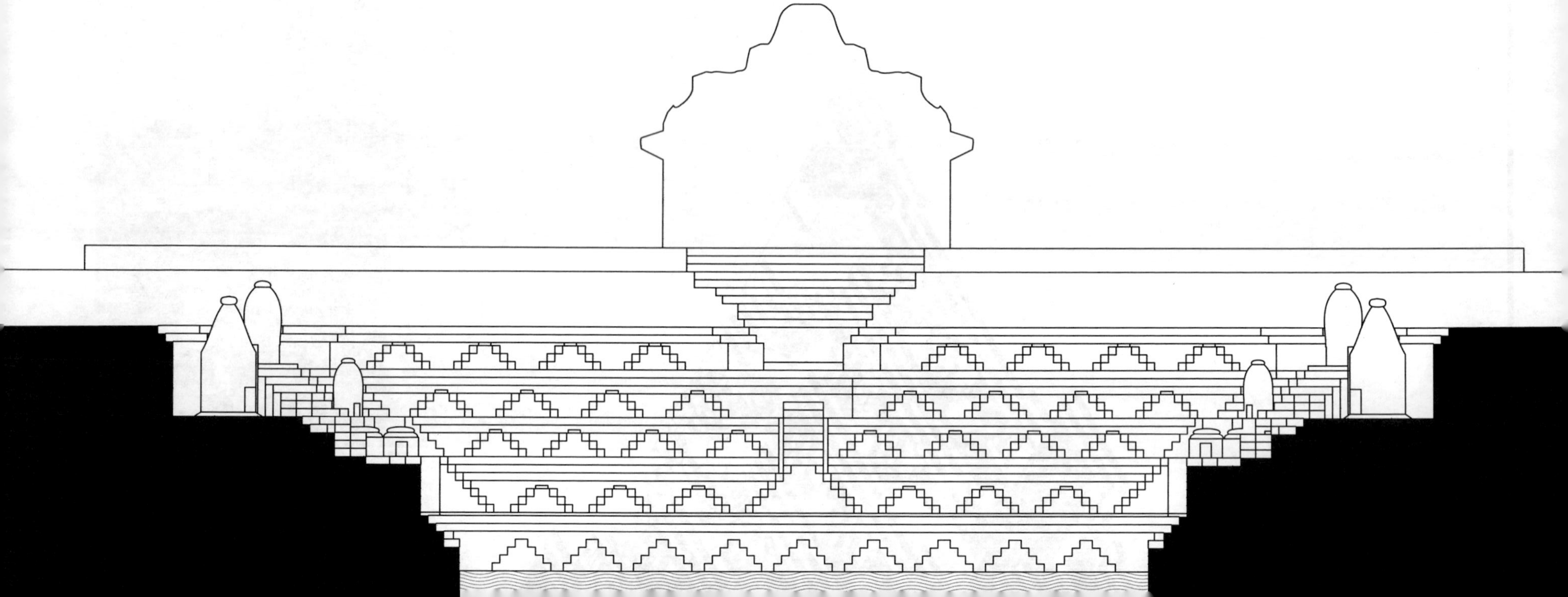

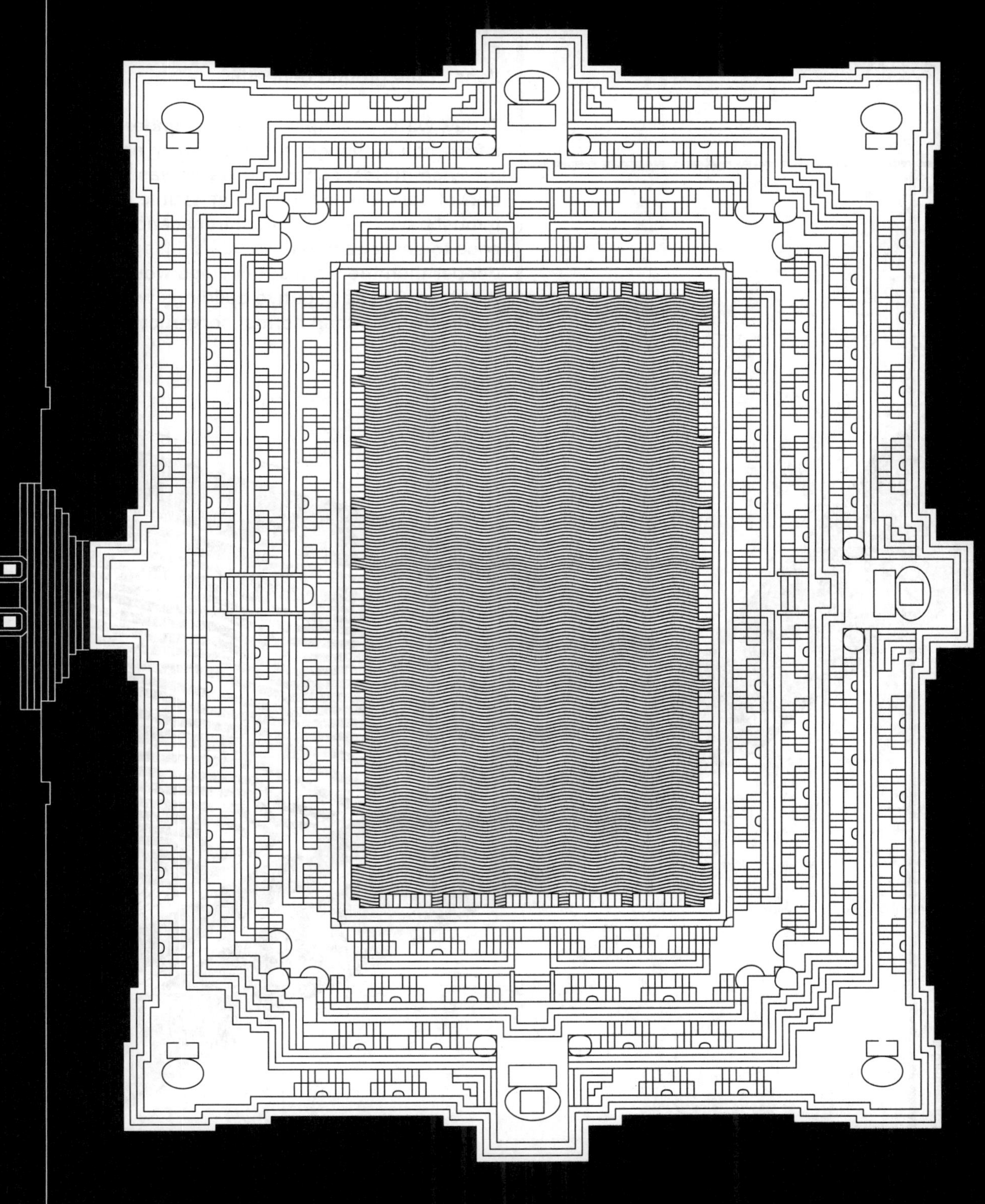

The Stepwell
—
Nahargarh Fort Baori Jaipur, India 1732

There are uncountable free-form stepwells that follow the topography. Some are natural pits of sandy soil in low-lying ground or inside caves. Others boast an intricate system of water inlets and outlets that prevent dirt from entering the basin. The two built next to the Nahargarh Fort in Rajasthan look like giant contour models, abstractions of the ground beneath.

Today, water is supplied invisibly underground. An infrastructure thoughtlessly turned on and off. For many centuries, accessing water was an essential part of daily life. In India it was visible and valued. It must have been an almost transcendental experience to descend into this cool, calm space, going deeper than the highest buildings would rise up at that time. These negative buildings were in fact more essential than normal constructions.

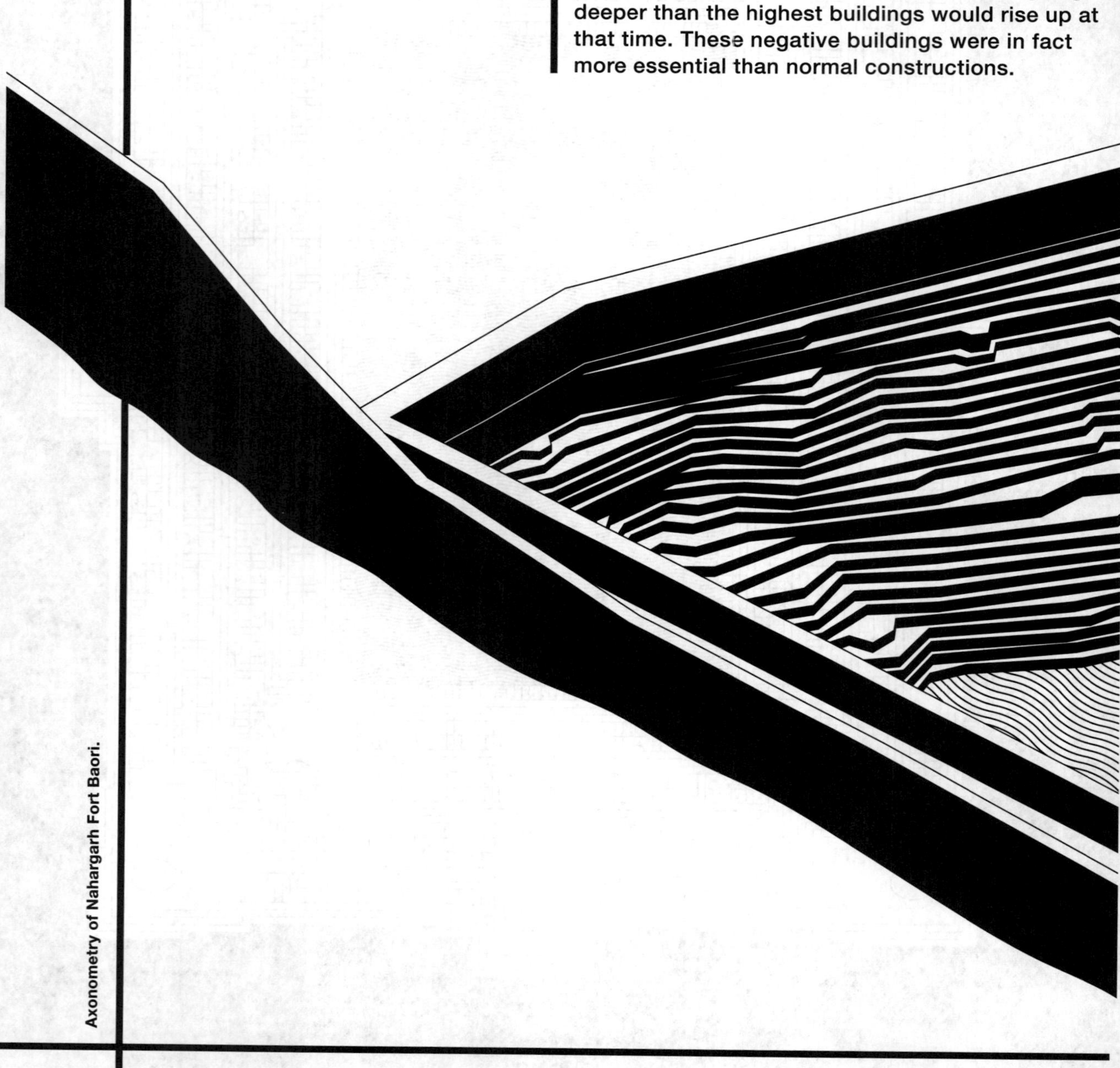

Axonometry of Nahargarh Fort Baori.

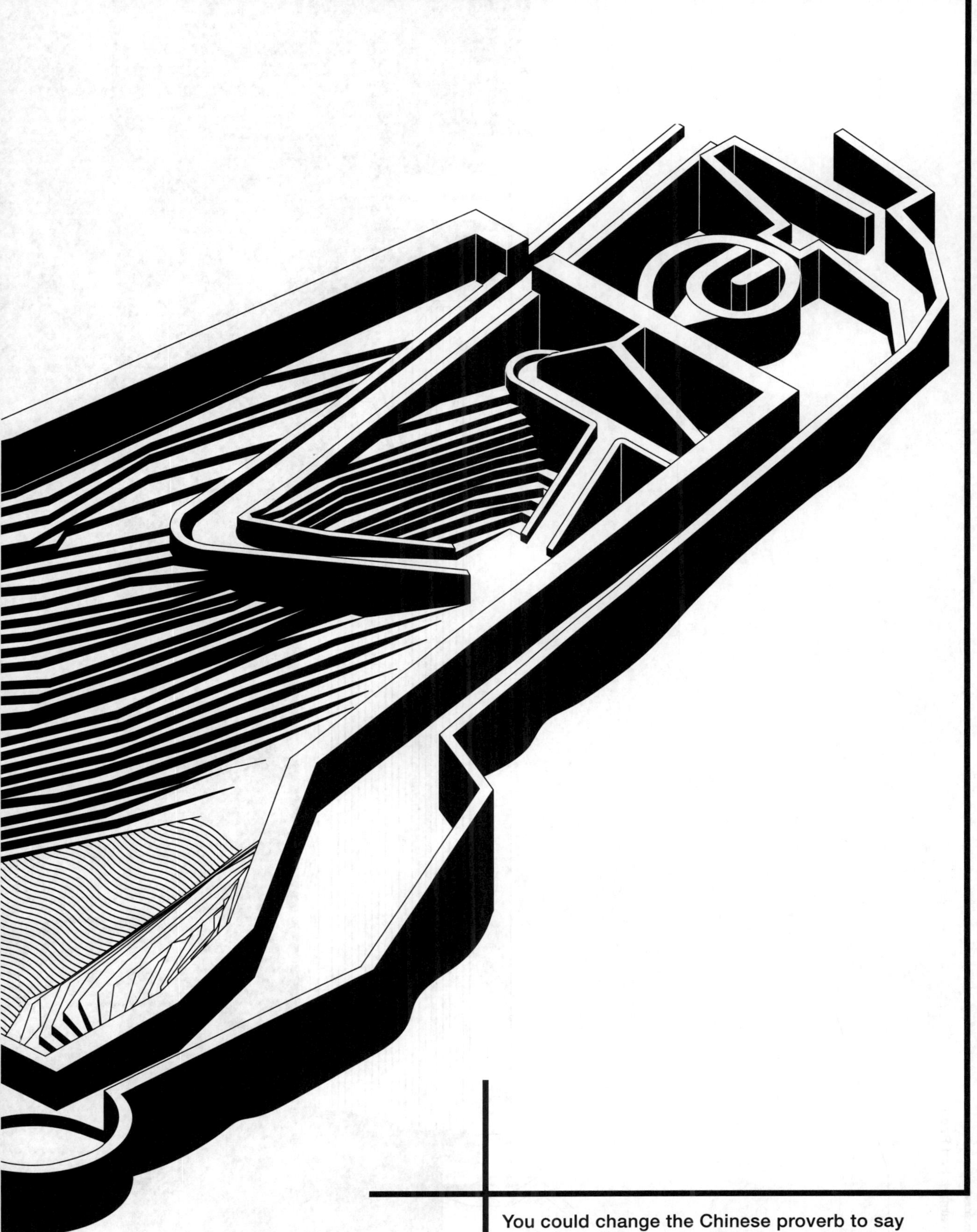

You could change the Chinese proverb to say that the stepwell owes its existence to the simple fact that humankind, with all their artistic pretentions, sophistication and many accomplishments, need water, also during periods when it hardly rains.

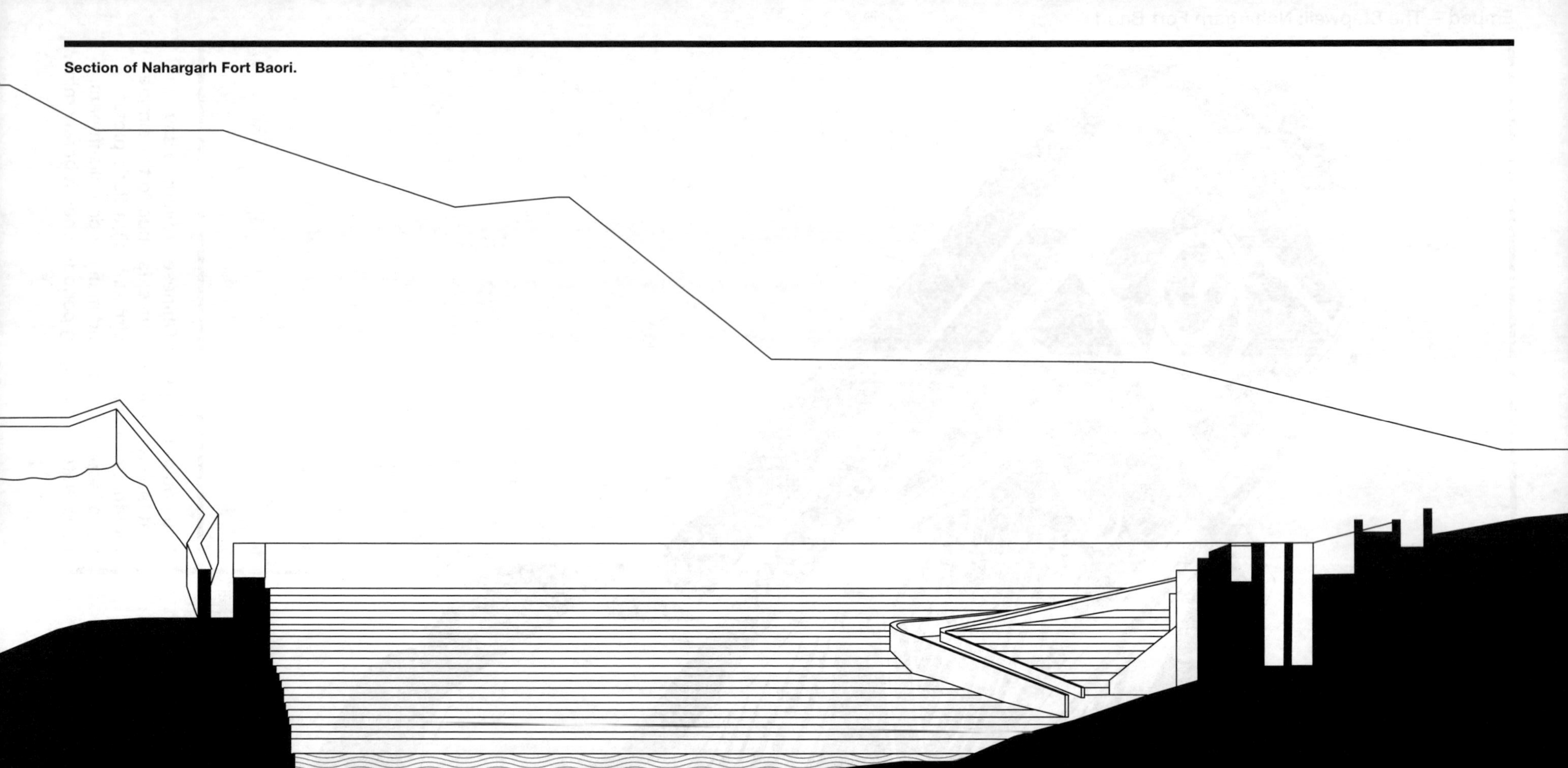

Section of Nahargarh Fort Baori.

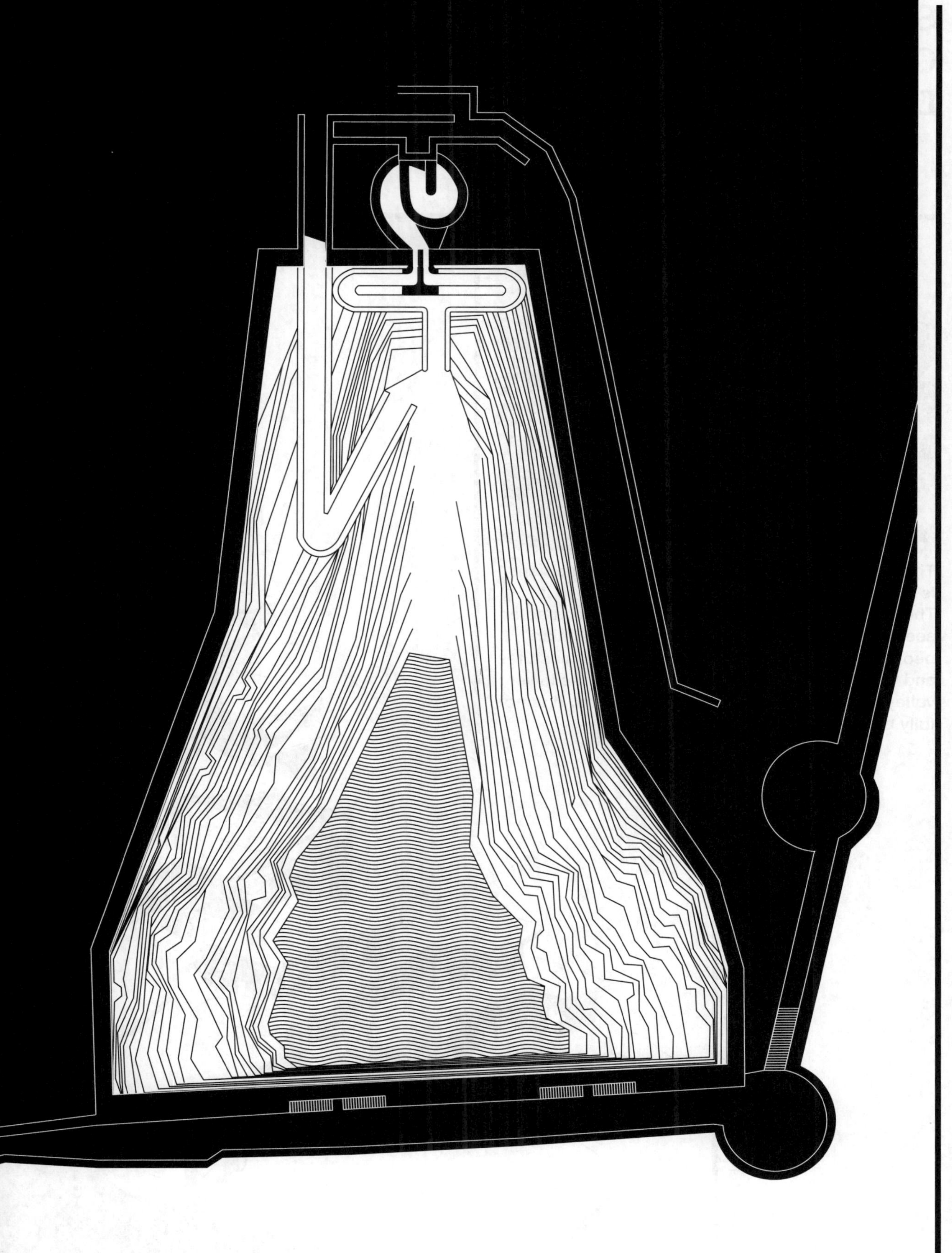

Plan of Nahargarh Fort Baori.

Sar Agha Seyed
Chaharmahal and Bakhtiari Province, Iran
Date unknown

The story behind the Sar Agha Seyed settlement is just as mysterious as the path leading to it. There is actually no road, and its remote character seems deliberate. The once nomadic Bakhtiari people used to migrate between summer pastures and winter *garmsīr*, or seasonal tents, in the lower valleys of the mountain ranges of Zagros. It is not fully clear when and why they settled.

Axonometry of Sar Agha Seyed.

The urban layout of Sar Agha Seyed consists of a haphazard stitching together of houses and barns. Unlike the stepped villages of Palangan or Masuleh, Sar Agha Seyed is embedded in the hill. Exploiting the slope, Sar Agha Seyed simply adds a level to the hillside, blending in with the landscape. Roofs are not rectilinear squares but a smooth sweeping landscape that dips down to ground level occasionally to allow villagers to navigate the steep slope.

The roof edges are reminiscent of tent cloth. Villagers use the flat roofs just as the Bakhtiari nomads dried crops in front of their tents, except for the fact that here they use the roof of neighbours living one or two levels below them. Paths leading to all houses are a combination of narrow back alleys, stairways in between and roof paths, flat, stepped or slightly inclined to reach the next level. The absence of clear boundaries, routing and the communal use of roofs has great similarities with the first-known urban settlement in Çatalhöyük and the existing small villages of northern Ghana and Mali.[11]

Çatalhöyük, 7500–5700 BCE.

Village in northern Ghana, 2006.

Axonometry showing the flat roofs of the settlement.

Site plan of Sar Agha Seyed.

The informal organization and compactness of dwellings seem intrinsic or innate. As if their nomadic lifestyle ended and communal form was created before they developed any rules. It is said that the construction of new houses led to irritation, since there was no demarcation of ownership and houses were often built in between. These insertions, where possible and close to relatives, left no place for drying crops in summer and no space to sweep the snowfall off roofs in winter.[12]

Park Güell
Barcelona, Spain
Antoni Gaudí
1900–1914

Site plan of Park Güell.

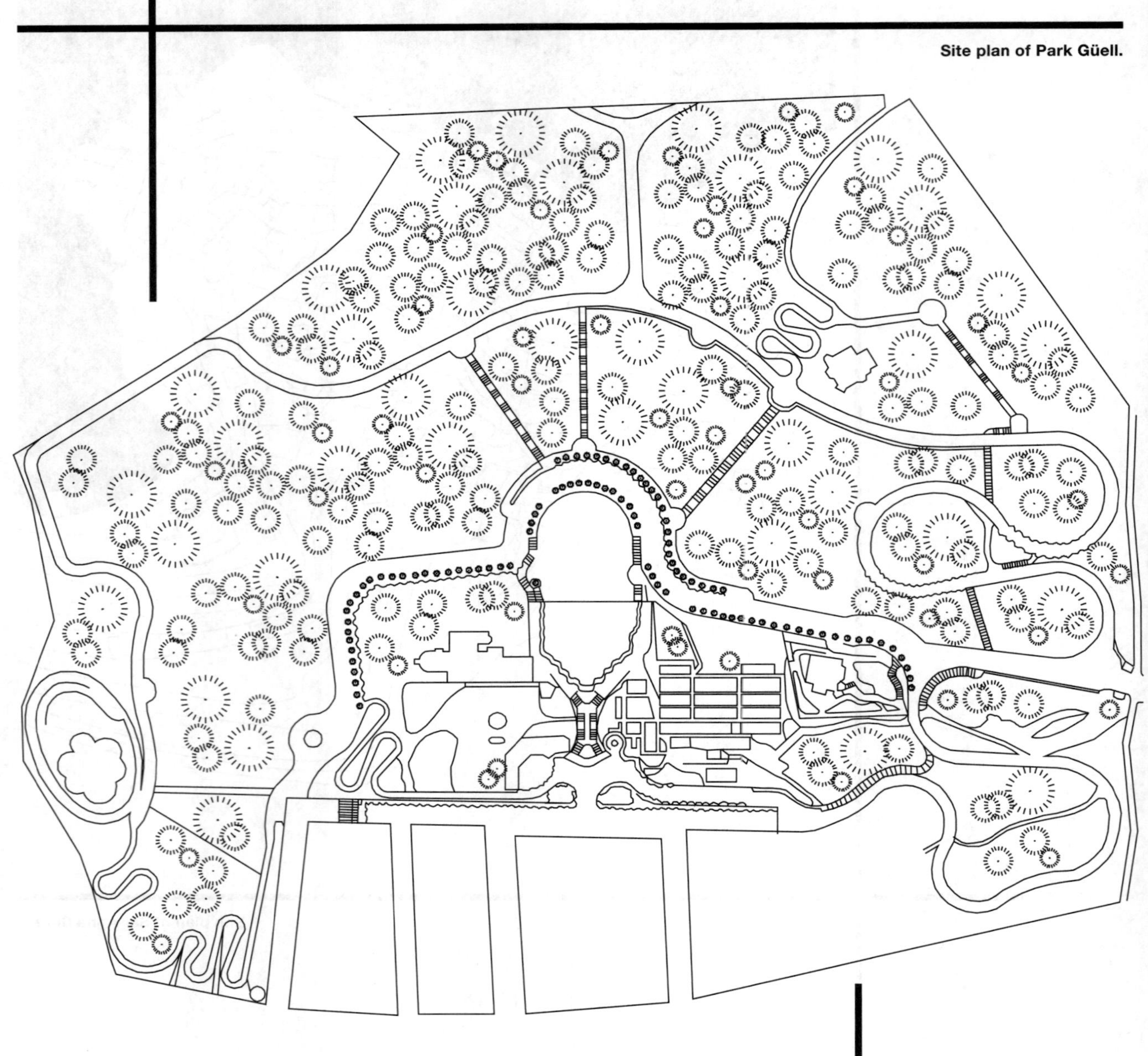

Neither a Spanish *parque*, nor a Catalan *parc*, the name Park Güell hints at an English connection. Park Güell was the brainchild of Count Eusebi Güell, an industrialist with trade links with England, who was inspired by the garden city movement of Ebenezer Howard.

Park Güell was a novelty. Enlightened entrepreneurs had built working-class neighbourhoods in a garden city arrangement elsewhere, but Park Güell was envisioned as a highly exclusive and commercial gated community with lifetime leasehold plots.

Sala Hipòstila, Park Güell, 1907–1909.

Natural stone colonnade.

What also set it apart from the garden city movement was that its architect, Antoni Gaudí, designed and built a garden first, on which wealthy clients would then select a plot and assign their own architect. Out of respect for the landscape, Gaudí analysed the site, a steep and rocky hillside with an impressive outlook and ample water. He started with a topographical study of a road plan. Winding roads were complemented with bridges, viaducts and an underground market hall, the Sala Hipóstila. Infrastructure was built in brick and clad with natural stone to mimic nature and complement indigenous flora.

Viaduct.

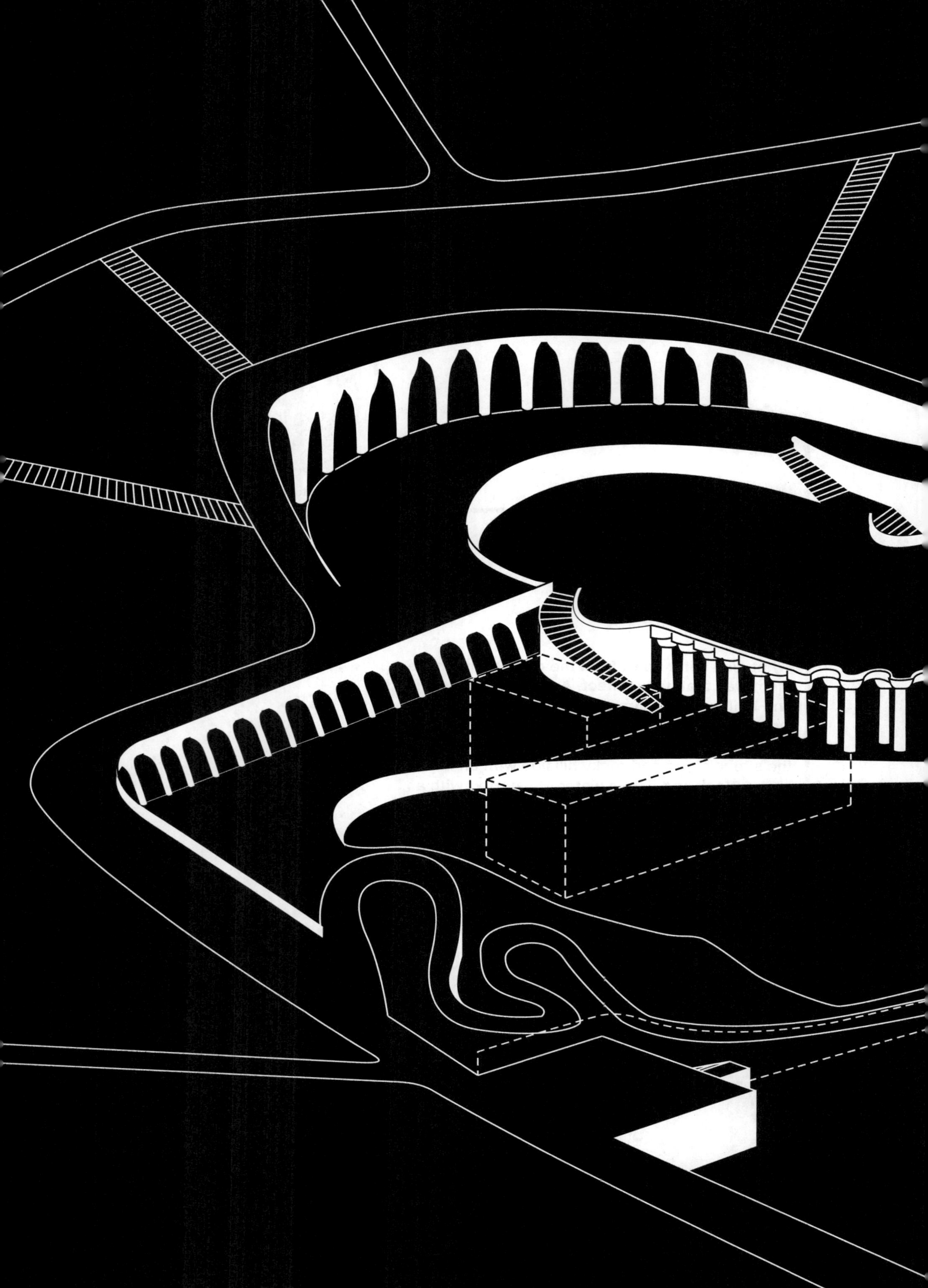

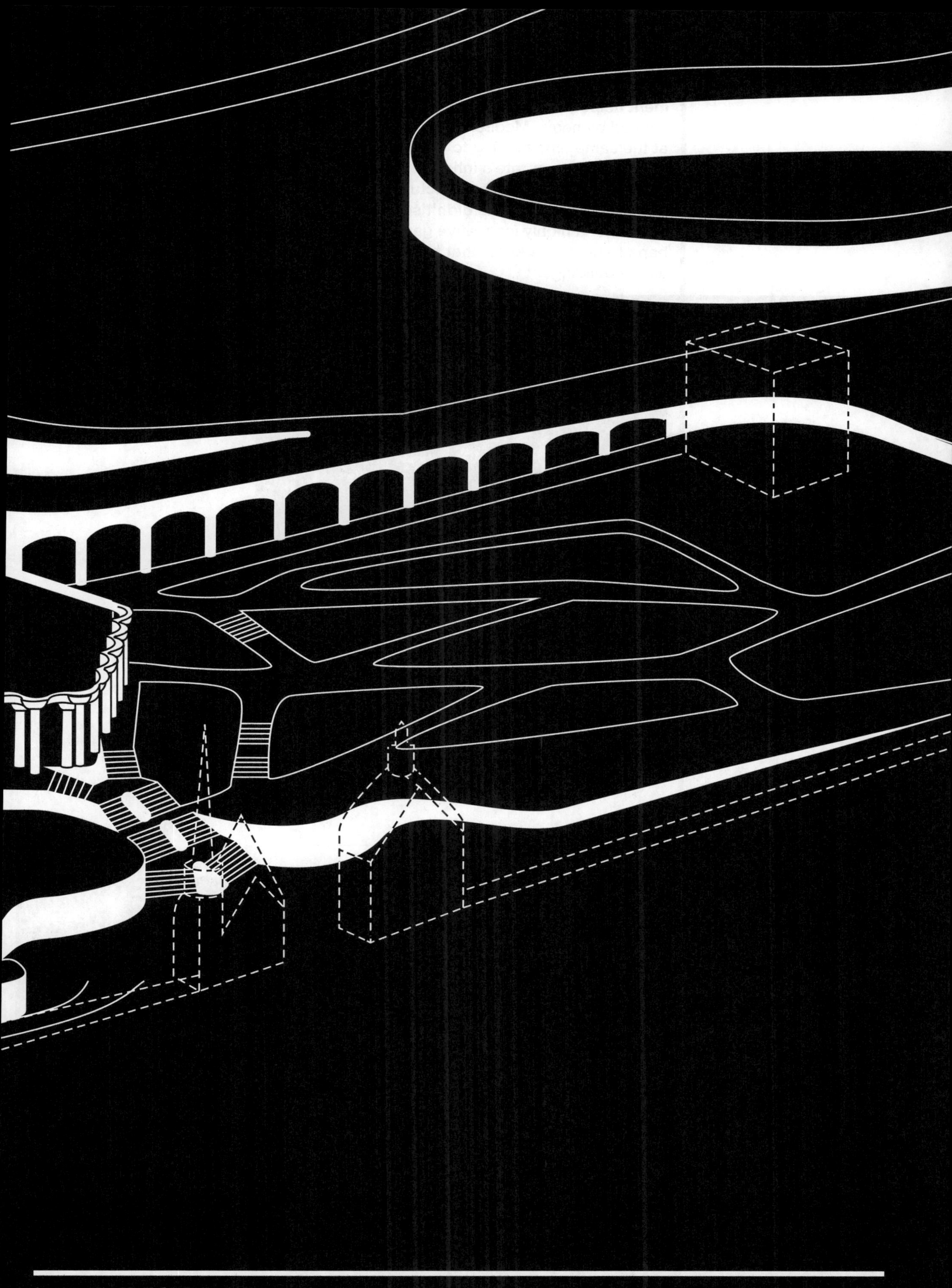

Axonometry of Park Güell showing how the paths and viaducts connect the various levels

Gaudí also designed systems for collecting and storing water. Both vegetation and water management helped to prevent the erosion of the land caused by heavy Mediterranean downpours, while at the same time helping to provide the water needed by the estate's inhabitants.[13] Gaudí is known for his brilliance in structural engineering. But with Park Güell this didn't serve architecture, but rather a highly innovative garden layout, perhaps because he knew that he would not shape all the buildings.[14]

A conduit running inside the famous undulating bench of the square collects rainwater and diverts it to an underground tank.

Section of Park Güell.

Park Güell, c.1910. © Arxiu Fotogràfic de Barcelona.

At the start of World War I in 1914, the general layout of the garden city was complete, but only two houses were built and the development was halted. Güell's heirs offered the park to the city council of Barcelona, who opened it as a municipal park in 1926.[15] Curiously, Count Eusebi Güell's plan for an exclusive residential suburb above Barcelona resulted in a High Line park avant la lettre with elevated infrastructure turned green.

From Seat to City

Van Stoel tot Stad (From Seat to City) is a passionate plea to reconcile rapid urbanization with the human dimension.

Still from the *Van Stoel tot Stad* television series, Jaap Bakema, 1962–1963.

"The story 'From Seat to City' is a difficult story. It is difficult because I do not really want to talk about the chair or the city but about the space in which the chair and the city stand. It has been said that there are two things that one cannot really talk about... I think it was about the fact that you cannot talk about love and about space. But if I tell you I want to talk about love for space then you will understand that the subject is difficult... I feel that we are currently living without the love for space an architect needs. That is why it is worth it to talk about the story from seat to city, and especially about the story of how people have created space to have a seat and to be able to build cities."[16] —Jaap Bakema

Read together, Jaap Bakema and Aldo van Eyck make a powerful plea for design to not just deal with the relative size of objects but to see that they are all connected. From a chair to a house to a city to a landscape to a tree to a leaf. What if we considered architecture as a comfortable, enfolding lounge chair within an infinite landscape? What if we designed it as a supporting element rather than an enclosing body? From a semantic point of view, architecture is about place-making; it is not a static object.

"tree is leaf and leaf is tree – house is city and city is house – a tree is tree but it is also a huge leaf – leaf is a leaf but it is also a tiny tree – a city is not a city unless it is also a huge house – a house is a house only if it is also a tiny city"[17] **–Aldo van Eyck**

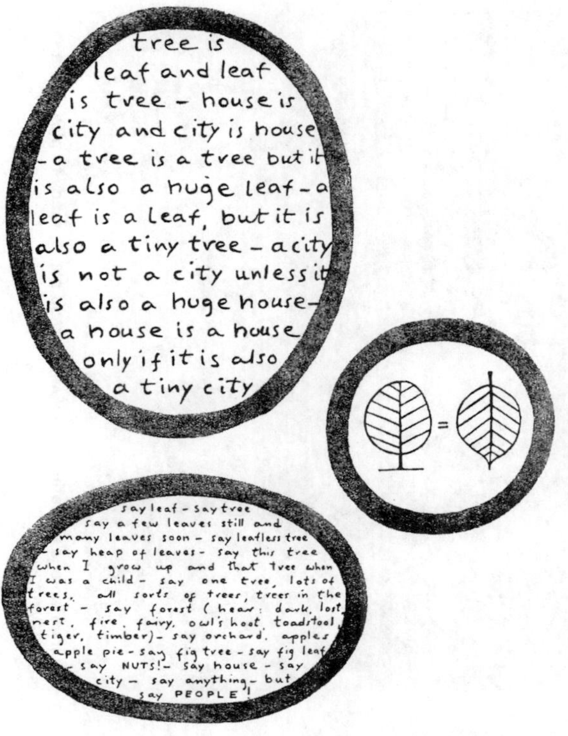

Aldo van Eyck, "tree is leaf and leaf is tree", *Domus*, 1965.

The architects of the projects on the following pages appreciate this more than most. Their work differs both stylistically and theoretically, but what they all share is a profound interest in site-specific design that is not imposed but embedded. It is no surprise that we can tell their story in multiple ways: through the relationships that they forged with each other and by their particular fascination with the chair.

As a relative insider, I know that Miralles was extremely influenced by the Eameses, and in return he especially influenced Alison and Peter Smithson at the end of their career. Their Hexenhaus project is a tribute to Enric Miralles. The deconstructivist nature of the design is reminiscent of his spatially brilliant thinking.

It is probably no coincidence that the Smithsons' client Alex Bruchhäuser leads the furniture company TECTA, and the Eameses worked for the famous Herman Miller. And that Enric Miralles and Benedetta Tagliabue designed the InesTable as a constantly changing object, like a landscape that changes over time, and the Lungomare Bench like a sand dune or wave at sea, a beach in itself.[18]

The InesTable is something between a grand piano, ready to play, and a table, EMBT, 1993.

Lungomare Bench, EMBT, 1997–2000.

Nor is it surprising that Marcel Breuer, Le Corbusier, Pierre Jeanneret, Mies van der Rohe and Gio Ponti are for ever immortalized in the furniture of Thonet, Knoll and Cassina. As are architects like Gerrit Rietveld with his cabinetmaker Gerard van de Groenekan, and Arne Jacobsen for Fritz Hansen. Sigurd Lewerentz almost completely turned away from architecture and started a factory that produced windows and architectural fittings.

Le Corbusier on his Chandigarh series chair with Pierre Jeanneret, 1950s.

Arne Jacobsen on his Swan Chair, 1950s.

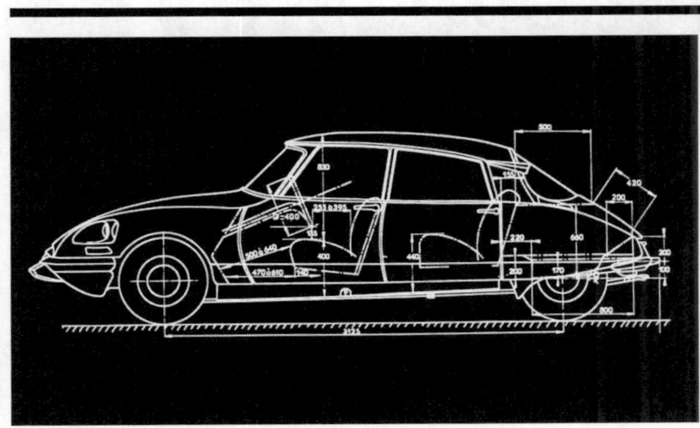

Section of the Citroën DS from Alison Smithson.

Nigel Henderson, Eduardo Paolozzi, Alison and Peter Smithson, seated in a street, c.1956.

Jean Prouvé on his Cité Lounge Chair, 1950s.

Jean Prouvé proved to be a real genius in material innovation and made a stunning series of furniture with his own Ateliers Jean Prouvé. But the most versatile and by far most successful furniture makers were the Eameses. On a global scale, corporate bosses sit on their aluminium chairs, swivelling during long meetings and rolling behind their desks. In their lifetime they will have had more architecture under their bottoms than they will ever have had over their heads.

Gerrit Rietveld on his Rietveld Chair, black model, 1919.

Gio Ponti with his Superleggera Chair, 1960s.

Charles and Ray Eames caught by LCM chair frames, late 1940s.

An embedded architecture all starts with sitting down. And maybe it ends with that too.

Mies van der Rohe on his tubular chair, 1964.

From Seat to City

—

Fallingwater
Mill Run, USA
Frank Lloyd Wright
1936–1939

In Oscar Wilde's *The Decay of Lying*, the character Vivian babbles about nature's lack of design, its crudities and its good intentions, which it is unable to carry out.[19] In her eyes, nature is uncomfortable. It seems we either trust or distrust nature, embrace or escape it. In the struggle to find the right balance, humankind's relationship with nature becomes highly polarized.

Axonometry of Fallingwater.

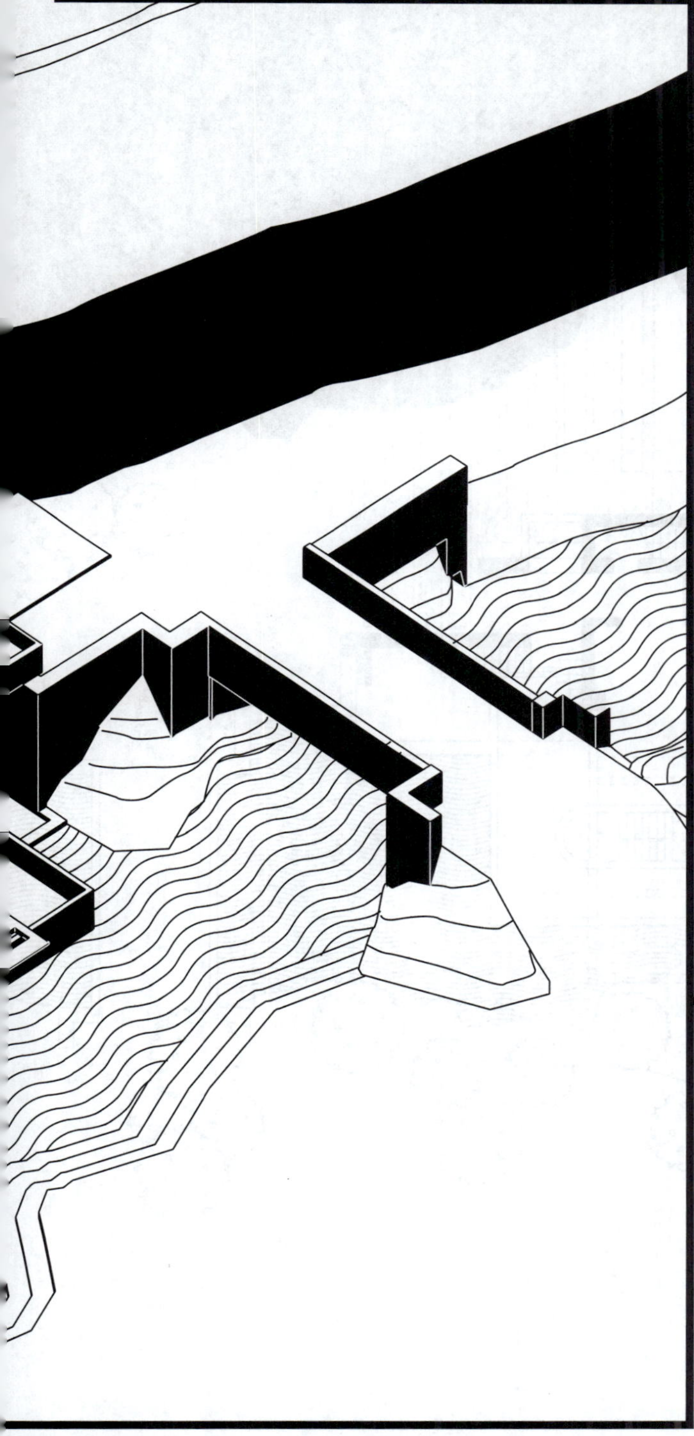

Frank Lloyd Wright's Fallingwater is often described as embracing nature. The Kaufmann family expected a design that faced the beautiful waterfall, but instead Wright put the celebrated house atop the waterfall, almost smothering nature. He was lauded and lambasted for this decision, but it made history and remains one of the most iconic images of modern architecture.

The Fallingwater Cam posts real-time images of the house online, so fans can keep an eye on it.

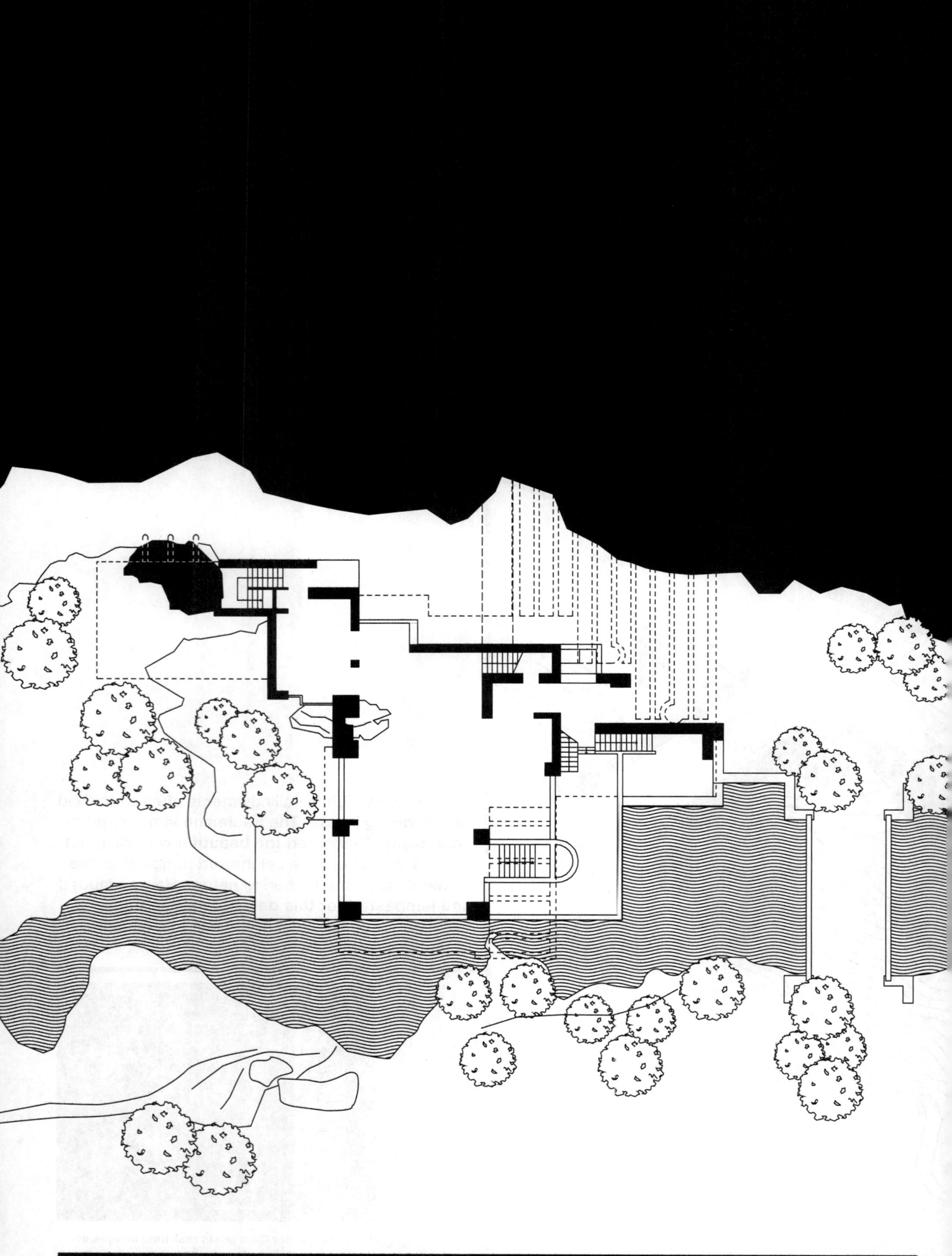

Plan of Fallingwater.

It is such a bold image that it almost taunts the waterfall. “Magic mirror on the wall, who is the fairest one of all?” Attention is focused on the house, not the breathtaking beauty of the waterfall that the house was supposed to face. The waterfall is actually invisible from the interior of the house.

Concrete beams embedded in rock.

Stepping down to the stream.

But nature is not merely a stage in service of the architecture; it is also an active element incorporated within. Stairs flow down towards the stream below, echoing the movement of the falls, and a natural spring drips inside before being channelled outside again. The sounds of crashing water and melting snow are experienced throughout the entire house, which is visibly and physically anchored to the rocky terrain. A boulder juts through the floor of the living room to form the hearth of the fireplace, and large horizontal slabs embed themselves in the banks.

Terrain continues within the interior.

Section of Fallingwater.

Edgar J. Kaufmann Jr's description of the house's closed back and open view crystallizes how Fallingwater is rooted to its site. "He [Frank Lloyd Wright] understood that people were creatures of nature, hence an architecture which conformed to nature would conform to what was basic in people… although all of Falling Water [sic] is opened by broad bands of windows, people inside are sheltered as in a deep cave, secure in the sense of the hill behind them."[20]

For Wright, "No house should ever be on a hill… It should be of the hill. Belonging to it. Hill and house should live together, each the happier for the other."[21] With nature and architecture so entangled, the question remains whether it embraces you or makes you feel like a third wheel.

From Seat to City

—

The Eames House
Los Angeles, USA
Charles & Ray Eames
1945–1949

Although World War II halted the construction of architecture on both sides of the Atlantic, its contribution to the modern movement was profound. Architects from the Bauhaus school like Breuer, Gropius and Mies van der Rohe spread around the world as they fled the Nazi regime and landed on fertile soil that appreciated their talent.[22] A shortage of supplies drove a resourcefulness and material optimization which for ever altered construction.

Axonometry of the Eames House.

Luckily, some good did come from this devastating time, as wisely put by Plato: "Necessity is the mother of all invention."

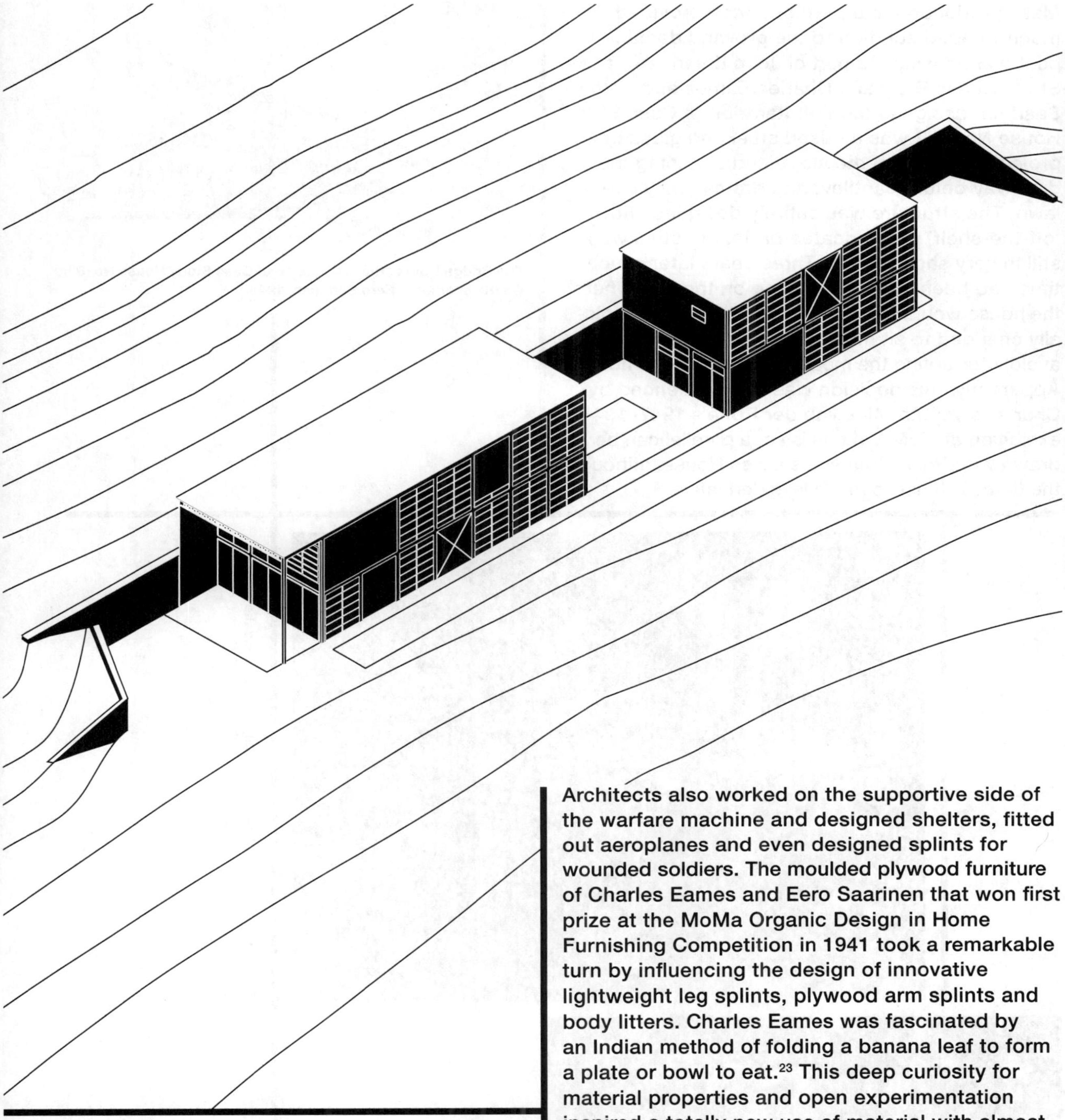

Architects also worked on the supportive side of the warfare machine and designed shelters, fitted out aeroplanes and even designed splints for wounded soldiers. The moulded plywood furniture of Charles Eames and Eero Saarinen that won first prize at the MoMa Organic Design in Home Furnishing Competition in 1941 took a remarkable turn by influencing the design of innovative lightweight leg splints, plywood arm splints and body litters. Charles Eames was fascinated by an Indian method of folding a banana leaf to form a plate or bowl to eat.[23] This deep curiosity for material properties and open experimentation inspired a totally new use of material with almost unlimited potential.[24]

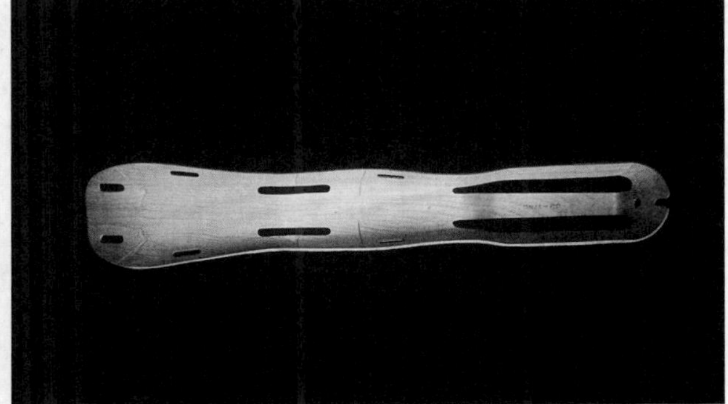

Moulded plywood leg splint, Charles and Ray Eames, 1941.

Mass production and prefabrication provided a much-needed solution to the growing demand for post-war housing. As part of John Entenza's Case Study House Program, Charles Eames and Eero Saarinen designed the first iteration of Case Study House No. 8. It was a raised steel and glass box projecting out from the slope and spanning the driveway before cantilevering dramatically over a lawn. The structure was entirely designed with 'off-the-shelf' prefabricated parts, but steel was still in very short supply. Three years later, much time had been spent picnicking on the plot where the house would stand, and the scheme was radically changed to sit more gently on the land and avoid interrupting the meadow in front of the house. Apparently, this decision was also influenced by Charles's visit to Mies van der Rohe's 1947–1948 exhibition at MoMA. If this is so, a parallel can be drawn with Philip Johnson's Glass House, although the Eames House is much less derivative.[25]

The Bridge House, the first design of Case Study House No. 8 by Charles Eames & Eero Saarinen, 1945.

The house is tucked between the eucalyptus trees and the hillside.

The new design tucked the house sidelong into the slope. Two glass and steel structures run the length of a 60-metre-long retaining wall. House, studio and a series of patios combine to form a single linear volume, hemmed in by hillside and eucalyptus trees. Nature, Charles Eames said, was a shock absorber for a life in work.[26]

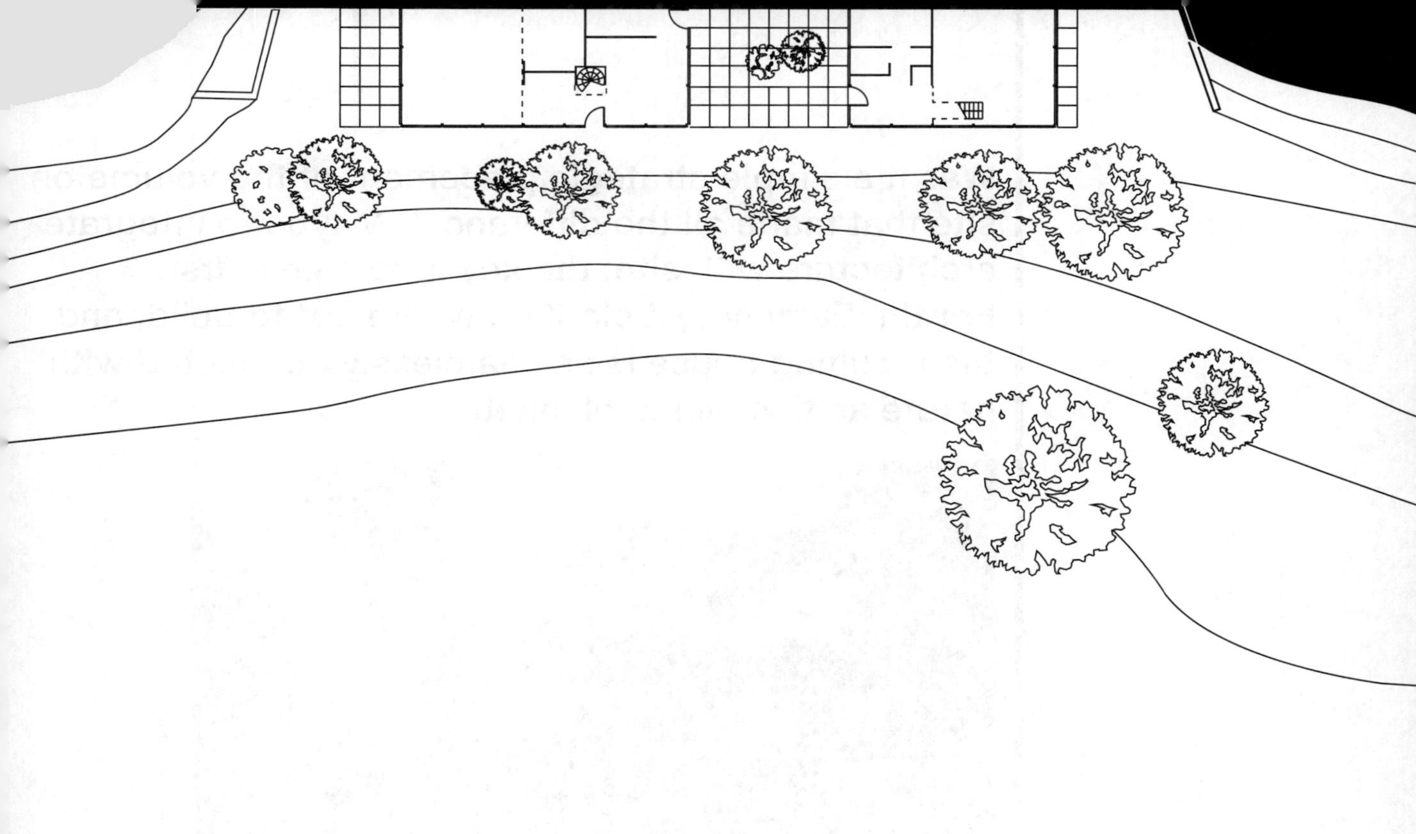

Plan of the Eames House.

Like so many of the other Case Study Houses, the Eames House embraces industrialized construction. But here the wiry trees and the regularity of the structural elements play off against each other. Glass successfully dissolves inside and outside rather than reflecting all that surrounds it. Inside, the house is not stark and minimalist, devoid of human use. Instead, it is filled with the domestic clutter of a humanized modernism.

Was it a simple strategic placement of the volume on site that made all the difference? Maybe to integrate architecture with site, the key is to picnic first. For the Eameses, it clarified where *not* to build, and the resulting house is as seamlessly connected with nature as this picnic blanket.

Ray Eames with John Entenza standing on-site.

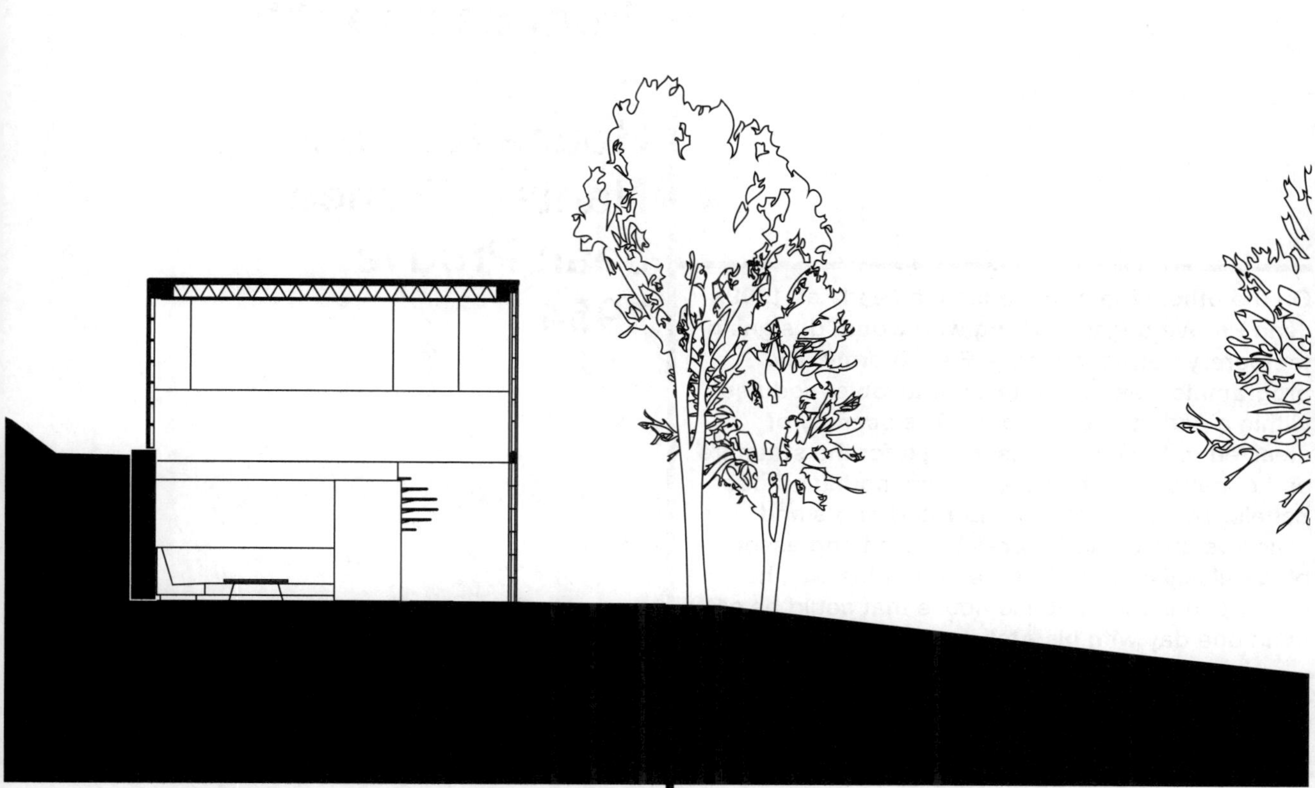

Section of the Eames House.

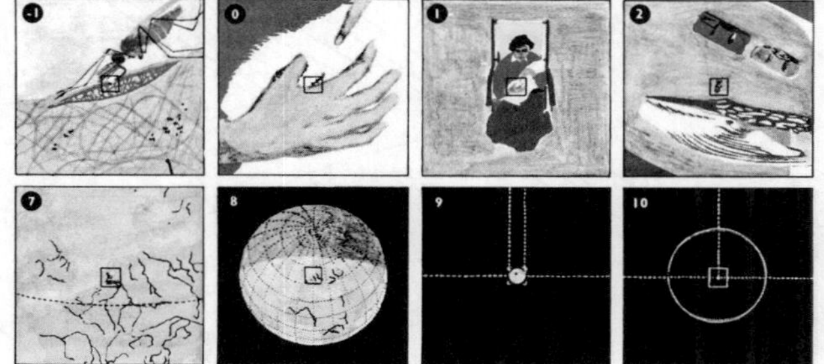

Cosmic View: The Universe in 40 Jumps by Kees Boeke, 1957.

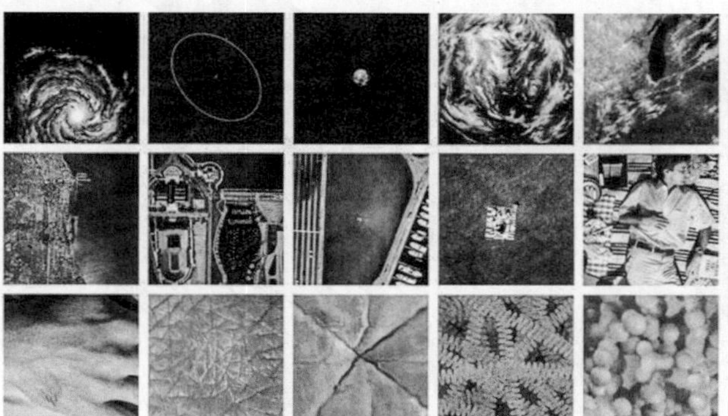

Powers of Ten by Charles and Ray Eames, 1977.

The picnic scene was also used in their 1977 film *Powers of Ten*. The film, based on a book by Dutch educator Kees Boeke, dealt with the relative size of things in the universe by zooming out by a factor of ten from a one-by-one-metre picnic blanket to the universe and then zooming back in to the level of an atom. As with all their work, the development of the Eames House was an iterative process instead of an end that justified its means.

From Seat to City

—

House & Studio
Nantes, France
Jean Prouvé
1954

On the other side of the ocean, as early as 1939, Jean Prouvé began working with wood, designing temporary barracks for the French army. The programme was to create 275 movable modules within a period of one month. The scarcity of steel led to the idea of reserving it for the structure and constructing the facade from modular timber panels. These panels incorporated doors and windows and could be prefabricated and assembled quickly on site.[27] At the end of the war, he developed a demountable house that could be set up in one day with his Ateliers Jean Prouvé.

Axonometry of Prouvé's House & Studio.

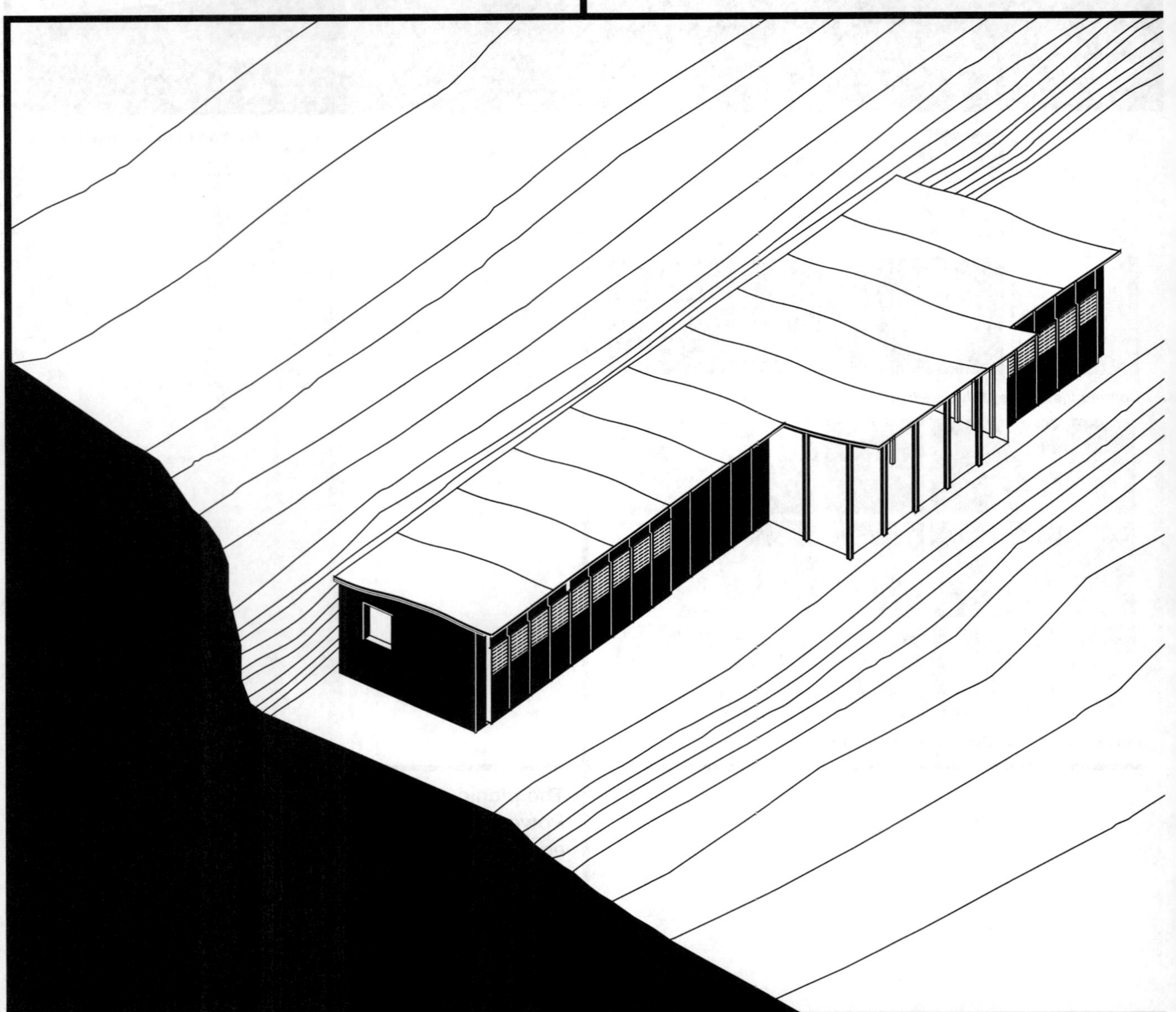

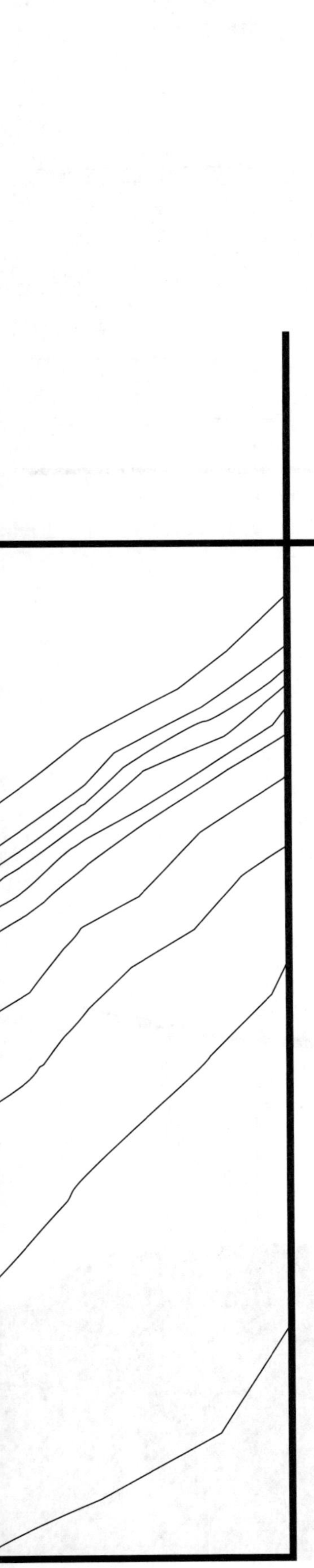

Transporting prefabricated elements to site, as if pitching a tent. Construction of House & Studio, 1954.

After the war, Prouvé continued to experiment, patenting several components between 1955 and 1957. For Prouvé, the building was first and foremost a technical object, focused on the proper use of material for different functions. But second to this comes a great sensitivity to site and climate in his work. The self-contained quality of his designs should not obscure the fact that they were nothing less than a means, with their very permeable skin, to fully enjoy the natural environment.

Prouvé's private House & Studio, built during this highly innovative period, sits on a hillside overlooking Nantes. The first sketches show a barracks dug into the slope with a symmetrical section. A second sketch shows one edge of the roof tilted upward to create more free height with a thin facade underneath, while the other side has much more body. The bent-up roof is held together with sinusoid steel tubes, like a tent construction, and was brought to site by jeep, as if they were looking for an ideal camping spot.

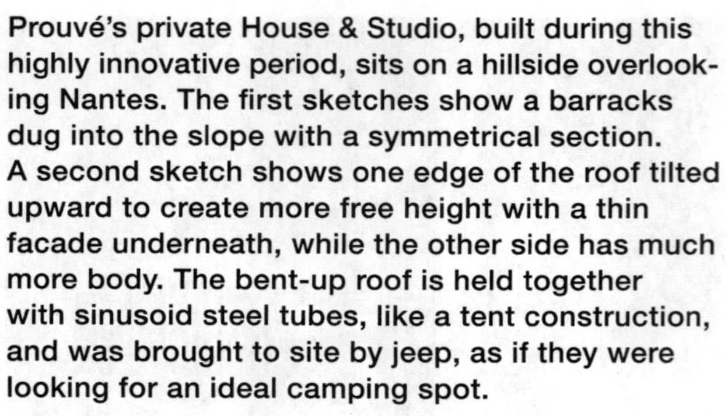

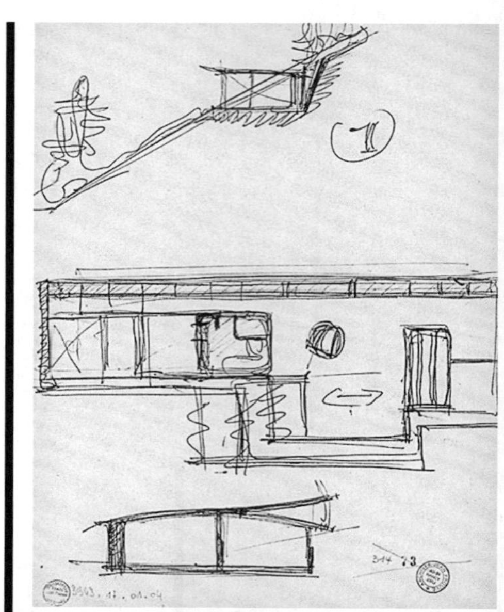

Sketches by Prouvé.

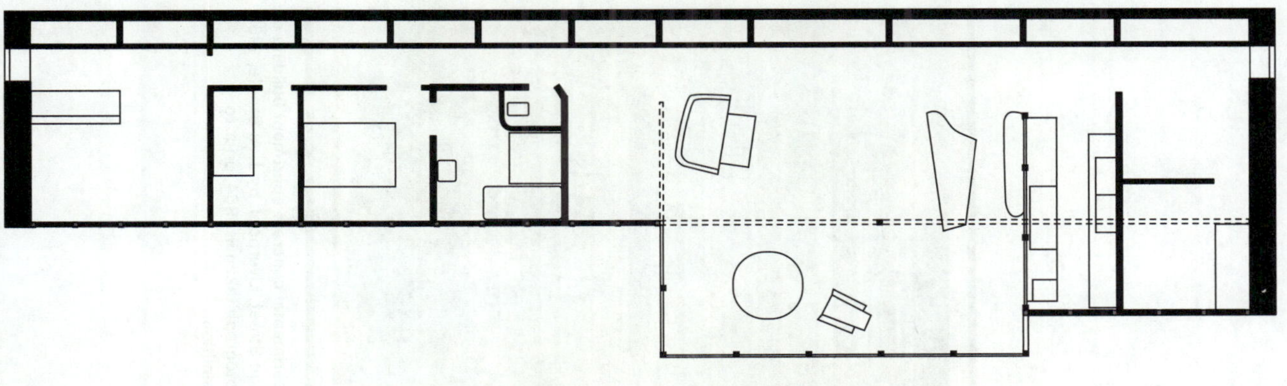

Plan of Prouvé's House & Studio.

Section of Prouvé's House & Studio.

His innovative work prefigured the industrialization and mass production of building components. Unfortunately, they remained prototype units in low-quantity batch production, built in a careful or pre-industrial way where everything exuded enormous tactility. This did not lead to the industrialization of the construction as might be imagined.[28]

Experimental concrete apartment building on Eldon Street, Liverpool, by J. A. Brodie, 1903. Photograph taken in 1964, prior to demolition.

Housing in Pont de Sèvres, Boulogne, Bernard-Henri Zehrfuss, Jean Sebag & Marcel Faure, 1951–1953.

With a little help from pioneers François Coignet, a French industrialist around 1856, and John Alexander Brodie, an English engineer around 1905, Raymond Camus patented a concrete heavyweight panel system in 1948. It soon became the absolute standard in mass housing and 170 million units were supposedly built during the second half of the twentieth century.[29] This includes the Soviet Union, since it was the only system that the Russians purchased licensing rights for, transforming their housing production from Stalinkas (brick buildings) to Khrushchyovkas during the mid-1950s. These standardized designs with large-panel prefab concrete housed sixty million Soviet people within twenty years.[30] It is said that Prouvé once credited Coignet for overwhelmingly winning the battle of prefabrication. It was a victory with very mixed feelings, because another battle was lost.

The Soviet Union operetta *Cheryomushki*, composed by Dmitri Shostakovich and adapted into a colour film in 1963 by Gerbert Rappaport, is a highly satirical piece of propaganda. The film closes with an infatuated explosives expert being catapulted to his lover on the balcony of the new high-rise after blowing up the last remaining *datcha*, or cottage. Shostakovich himself wrote to an acquaintance days before the original opening in 1956: "I am behaving very properly and attending rehearsals of my operetta. I am burning with shame. If you have any thoughts of coming to the first night, I advise you to think again. It is not worth spending time to feast your eyes and ears on my disgrace. Boring, unimaginative, stupid. This is, in confidence, all I have to tell you."[53] This is, in all irony, the Russian equivalent of Jacques Tati's *Playtime*.

From the middle of the twentieth century onward, the building of mass housing dictated the planning of cities. The large-panel prefab concrete system bulldozed over large parts of the world, insensitive to local conditions, site and nature. Nobody could argue with its sheer efficiency. Technical engineering and the building industry simply overruled architectural sensitivity. Architects were overwhelmed, and they had no answer to the blunt pouring of one material in massive quantities instead of intelligently combining materials for different uses, depending on their nature.

Scenes from *Cheryomushki* (Cherry Town) by Gerbert Rappaport, 1963.

Urban development meeting farmland in Chongqing, China.

Standardized apartment blocks of The Integrated Housing Development Program, Addis Ababa.

The sheer quantities, the fully enclosed, heavy, load-bearing facades with small windows and tiny balconies, including the fact that they were mostly stacked to mid- and high-rise proportions, resulted in a complete abandonment of rural and natural qualities. For millions of people it was a sudden, shocking transition from a grounded farm to a high-rise flat. Recently, the same formula has been applied in the rapid urbanization of China and Ethiopia, and Kenya and Nigeria seem set to follow.

In the 1970s, the French government tried to transform this extremely productive and efficient construction industry, inspired by the approach of Jean Prouvé, but its monopoly wasn't broken, not even after the first traumas surfaced in these large, brutalist residential complexes.[31] Moshe Safdie's Habitat 67 redefined urban living with its intricate prefab concrete cloud castle, but ultimately it failed to revolutionize affordable housing or launch the wave of prefabricated, modular development that Safdie had envisioned.[32] Jean Renaudie tried again with his Hachette housing plans for Ivry-sur-Seine in Paris, but the later extensions were a far cry from the original.[33] It is only now, forty years later, that a few of these first attempts are gaining recognition, while many of their contemporaries, pushed to the limits by the building industry and the economy, are being demolished.

It is easy to write these schemes off as completely inadequate for the scale of the housing issue, but imagine what could have been had we made the transition less callously. John Entenza tried it, rallying architects with the Case Study Houses Program in America. Aldo van Eyck tried it in Holland, offering up Structuralism. The Smithsons tried it in England, pushing for 'streets in the sky'. Ralph Erskine tried it in Sweden, proposing an Ecological Arctic Town.[34] But in a way they all failed, crushed by the 'heaviness' of the industry.

Jean Prouvé was not immune to this either. He gave us a view of what might have been and, ironically enough, his works have become blue-chip pieces of fine art sold at auction.[35] His design for the Maison Tropicale was deeply connected to local circumstances and the tropical climate, but it was made a plaything of the industry and politics, fetishized or dismissed as colonial pastiche.[36]

Maison Tropicale re-erected outside the Tate Modern, London, 2008.

The House & Studio of Prouvé is still standing strong and has all the ingredients to become a shining example for sustainable and circular innovation in mass-produced housing. In its DNA lies a willingness to solve acute problems with minimal resources and maximal flexibility.

From Seat to City
—
Die Es
Cape Town, South Africa
Gawie & Gwen Fagan
1964–1965

Axonometry of Die Es.

As one of South Africa's most celebrated architects, Gawie Fagan's ideas of connecting architecture with the natural landscape were revolutionary. This may sound odd for a continent where over eighty-five per cent of people lived in rural areas with abundant wildlife, but in the 1960s Cape Town was a thoroughly modern city.

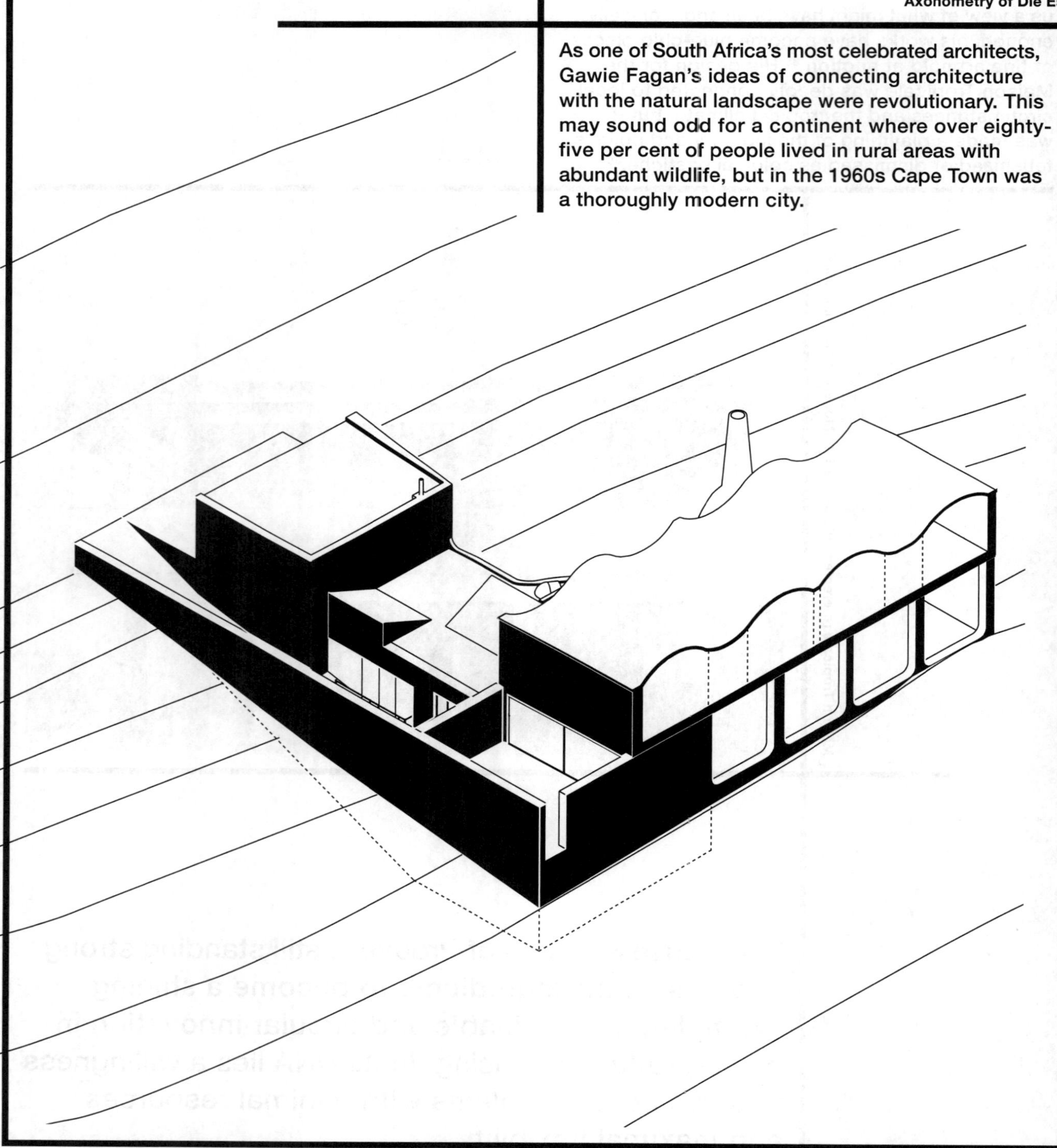

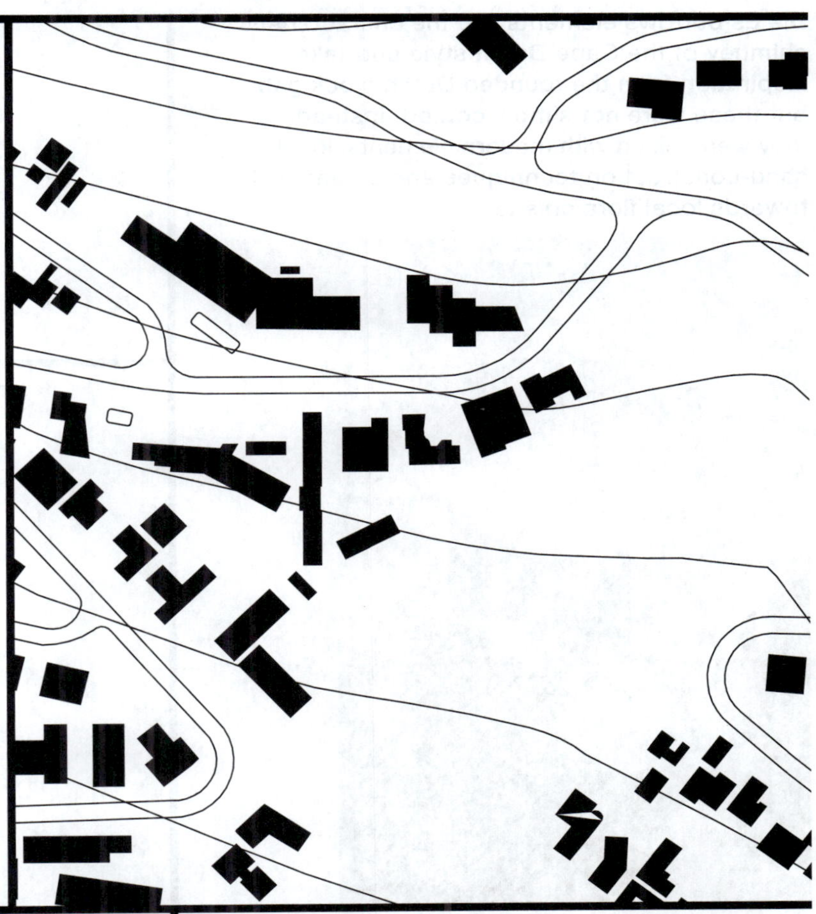

Site plan of Die Es.

Adderley Street, Cape Town, 1967.

Groot Constantia, built by Dutch governor Simon van der Stel, c.1690.

South Africa is known for sharp contrasts and divisions. Waves of colonialism followed by apartheid brought slavery, violence and oppression. Inequality permeated every aspect of society, framing and limiting architectural expression. Colonizers imported and imposed Western architectural and aesthetic ideas. In their eyes, a modern city was a Western city, one that emulated Dutch, Georgian or Victorian traditions. But the real beauty lies in the moments of exchange, where local building traditions and climate considerations drove a new style. Gawie Fagan is beloved for his efforts in developing, "a South African Architecture, which understands the historical vernacular without duplicating it, responds to the site and the particular environment generated by the climate, light, etc., and develops the free plan – an appropriate form to the casual way of life."[37]

Die Es borrows elements like the characteristic chimney of the Cape Dutch style and takes inspiration from the rounded Dutch clock gable, but these were not simply copied. Instead, they were mixed with modern elements, local hand-construction techniques and a sensitivity towards local flora on site.

Die Es means 'the hearth'.

The chimney.

The house turns its back on the vicious wind that comes off the mountain behind and opens out to the ocean to the west. At the back, it has sheltered patios, enclosed by the house and planted retaining walls. The most distinguishing element is the sinusoidal roof, constructed of pine battens set on edge and rocked over a central beam.

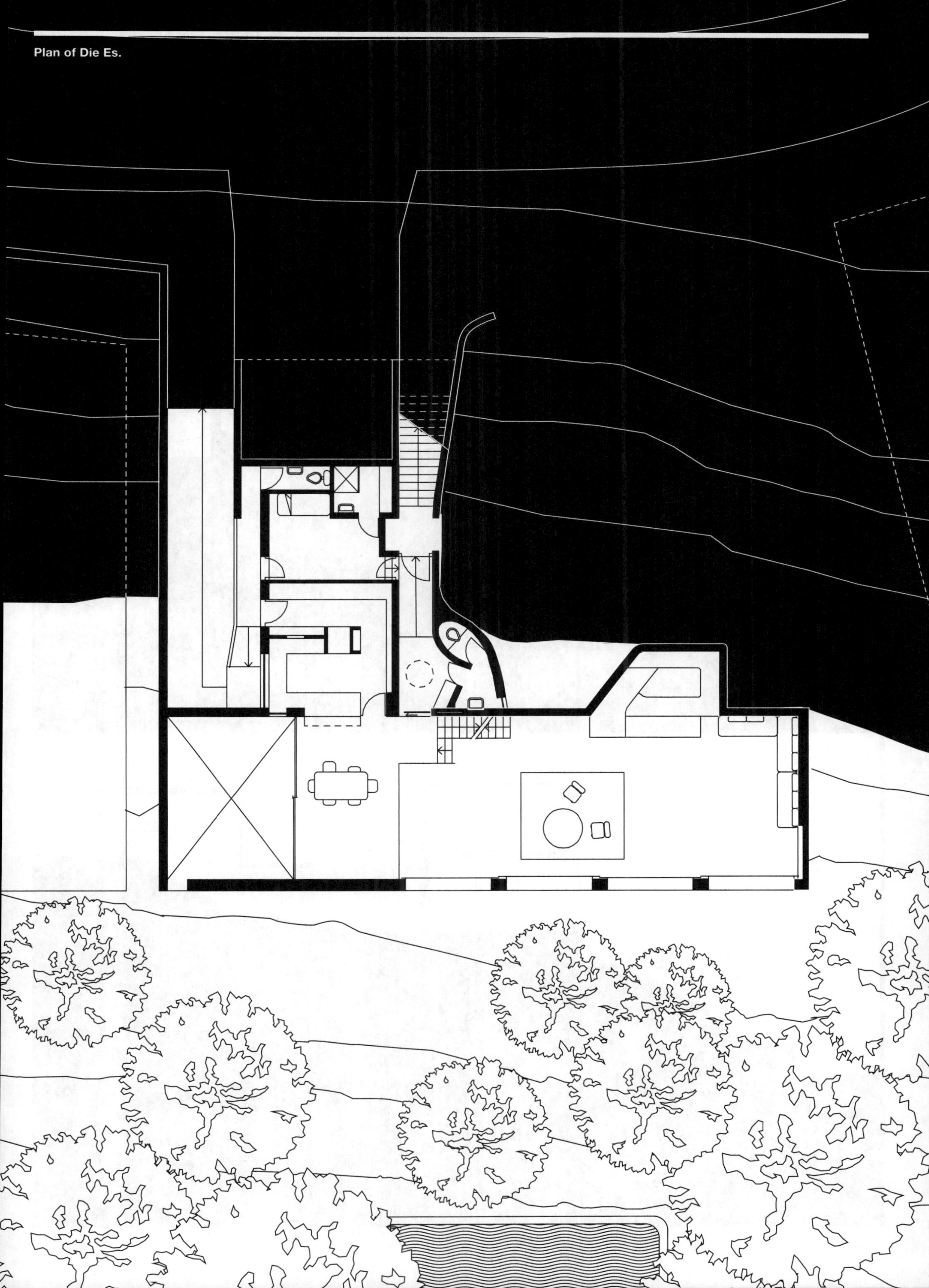
Plan of Die Es.

Long (top) and short (bottom) sections of Die Es house.

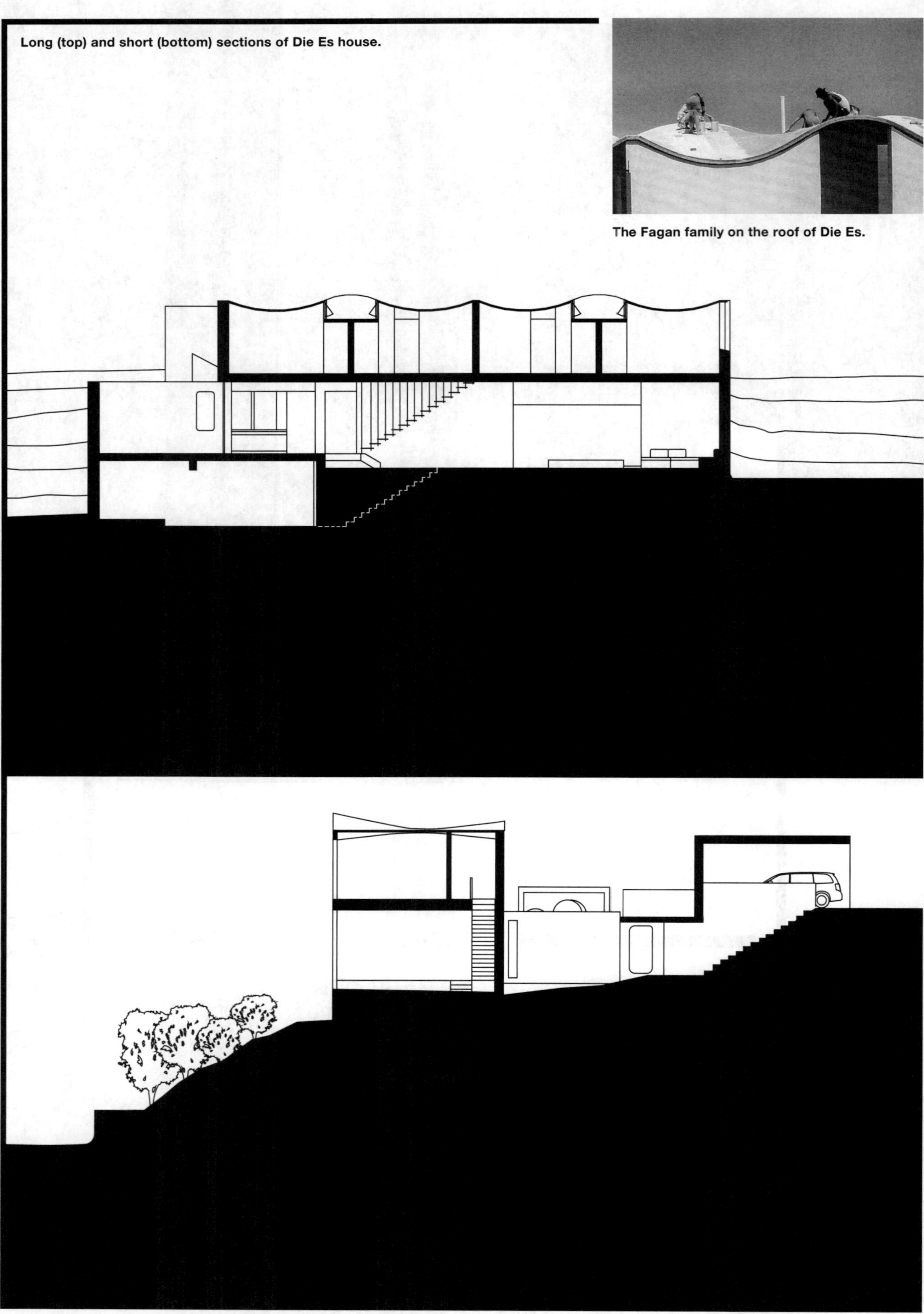

The Fagan family on the roof of Die Es.

Die Es was a truly family affair. Gawie, Gwen and their children hand-built and planted it over five years, and it has a handcrafted character, from the door handles to the oversized chimney.

Gwen received a PhD in landscape design and studied the influence of landscapes from all over the world on the South African landscape. Perhaps this awareness of the tensions and opportunities that exist between indigenous and introduced plant species helped in developing a unique South African style, without trampling over what came before.

From Seat to City

—

Hexenhaus
Bad Karlshafen, Germany
Alison & Peter Smithson
1986–1996

Axonometry of Hexenhaus.

Careful detailing of the Economist building in London, 1964.

Timber oak frame works partially obscuring the big windows of St Hilda's College, Oxford, 1968.

Key proponents of the revolutionary Team 10, Alison and Peter Smithson led the development of 'New Brutalism' in Britain. Their criticism of the modernist approach of CIAM went beyond visual style. In fact, apart from Robin Hood Gardens, little of their work employs the tarnished and oversized rough concrete of brutalism. Instead, their designs have a certain lucidity. Frames with glass or travertine infill, subtle detailing. The latter is not exactly a key element of brutalism.

'Conglomerate ordering' was a term coined by the Smithsons to describe a practice which defines complex relationships on various levels and ensembles of existing and new buildings with imagined activities to complete a place.[61] "One central issue is the idea of territory and the way architecture has a duty to collaborate in constructing this territory ... aspects of 'weaving', 'connecting' and 'interlacing' are looked at again, as well as the bodily experience of architecture and of moving through space."[38]

For the Smithsons it was not about a brutalist aesthetic but about an ethical approach in which building, users and site would connect as an act of 'form-giving'. For them, a building was all about quality of use.[39]

Despite its name, the Hexenhaus ('Witch's House') is by far the most lighthearted and playful project of the Smithsons. It all started with a simple question from the German entrepreneur and TECTA furniture maker Axel Bruchhäuser: can you fix me a door to the garden? In 1986 the Smithsons made the rasterized 'Alex's Porch', the first of a whole series of renovations.

Section of Hexenhaus.

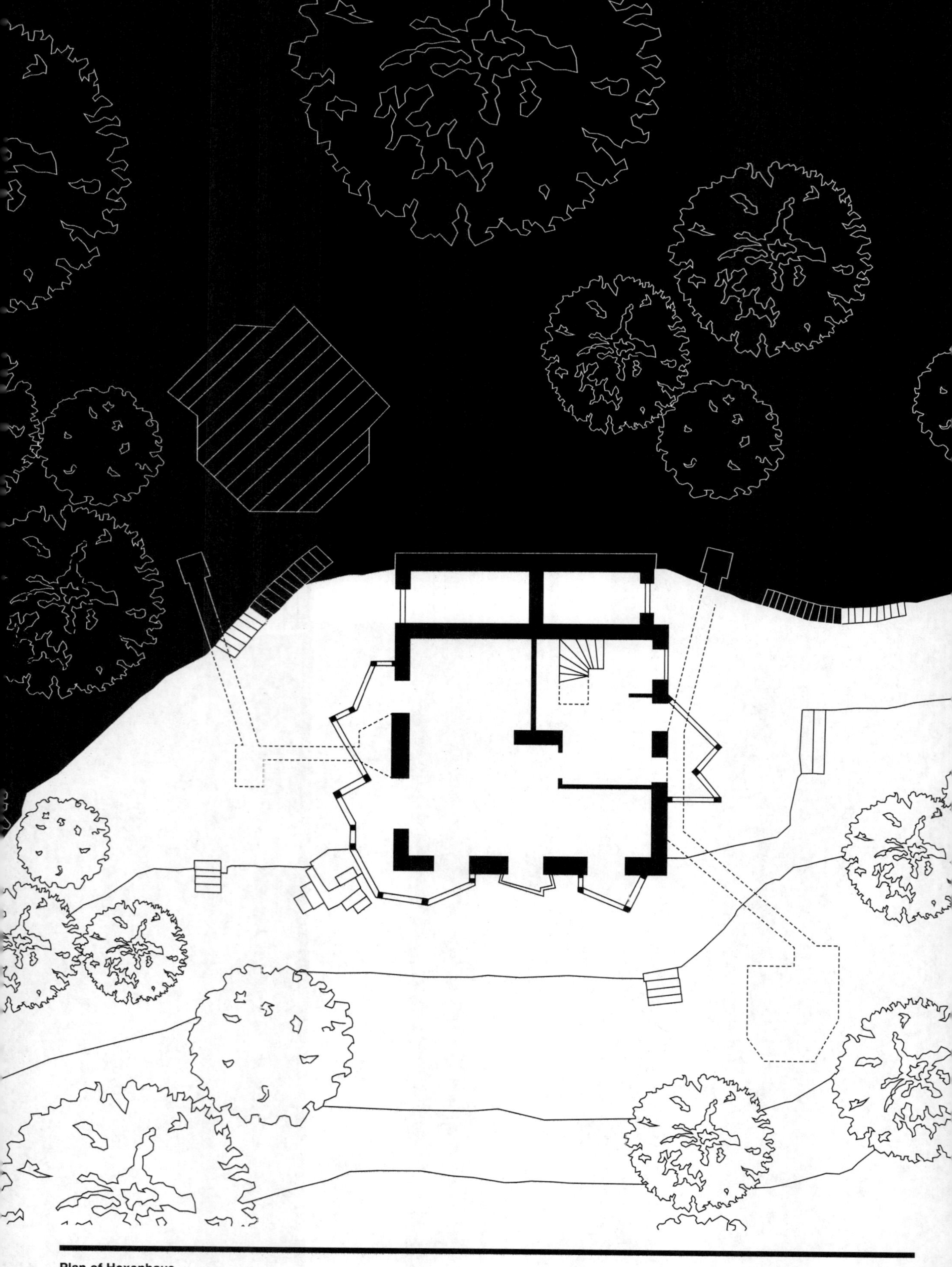

Plan of Hexenhaus.

Another addition is the Hexenbesenraum ('witch's broom room'). This pavilion, built on 11-metre-high poles, is like a tree house. Its elevation makes it safe and protected, while the glass floor keeps you aware of your high position. The Smithsons had an amazing knack of balancing seemingly conflicting elements. In Bruchhäuser's words, "The Smithsons have understood my needs exactly. I don't want the exposure of the Farnsworth House… I want to see out like this, but I need a sense of protection as well."[40] He loved the immersive experience of being in a space in which the surrounding landscape and weather conditions were present.

Bruchhäuser in his Hexenbesenraum.

Sketches of Hexenhaus additions, Alison and Peter Smithson.

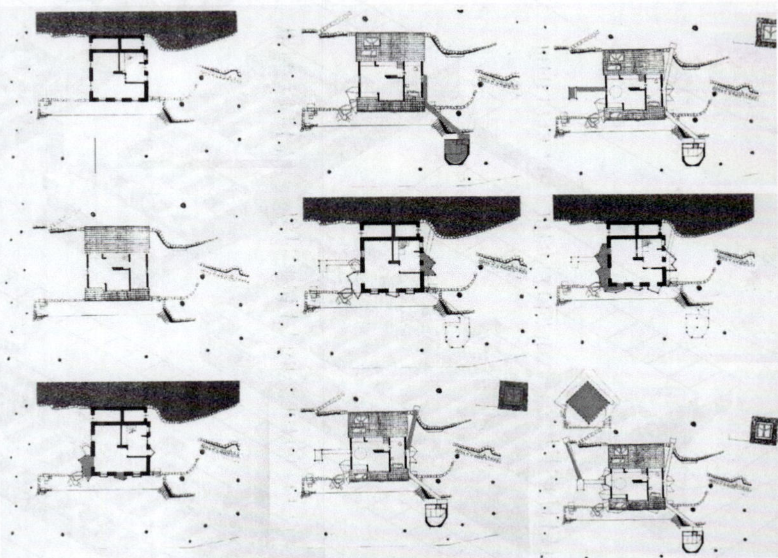

When the Smithsons started the project they found a small house in the woods. First, they heightened the back wall and created a second level with an upper promenade. This connected the house with several freestanding pavilions, built between 1989 and 2001. It is like a spiderweb stretching between the trees and inhabiting the forest in full transparency, instead of a house with solid walls.

Siedlung Halen
Bern, Switzerland
Atelier 5
1955–1961

The ideas that underpin Siedlung Halen extend back to a friendship formed between an architect and a plumber-turned-cook. While Le Corbusier worked at Eileen Gray's Villa E 1027, Thomas Rabutato catered for the team. Over many fine dinners Rabutato invited Le Corbusier to draw up a scheme for holiday homes on his site next door.[41] Concerned that the Côte d'Azur was in danger of being overrun with maisonettes, Le Corbusier devised a plan based on the small hilltop towns nearby. Houses were packed tightly together with their eyes on the infinite horizon.[42]

Axonometry of Siedlung Halen.

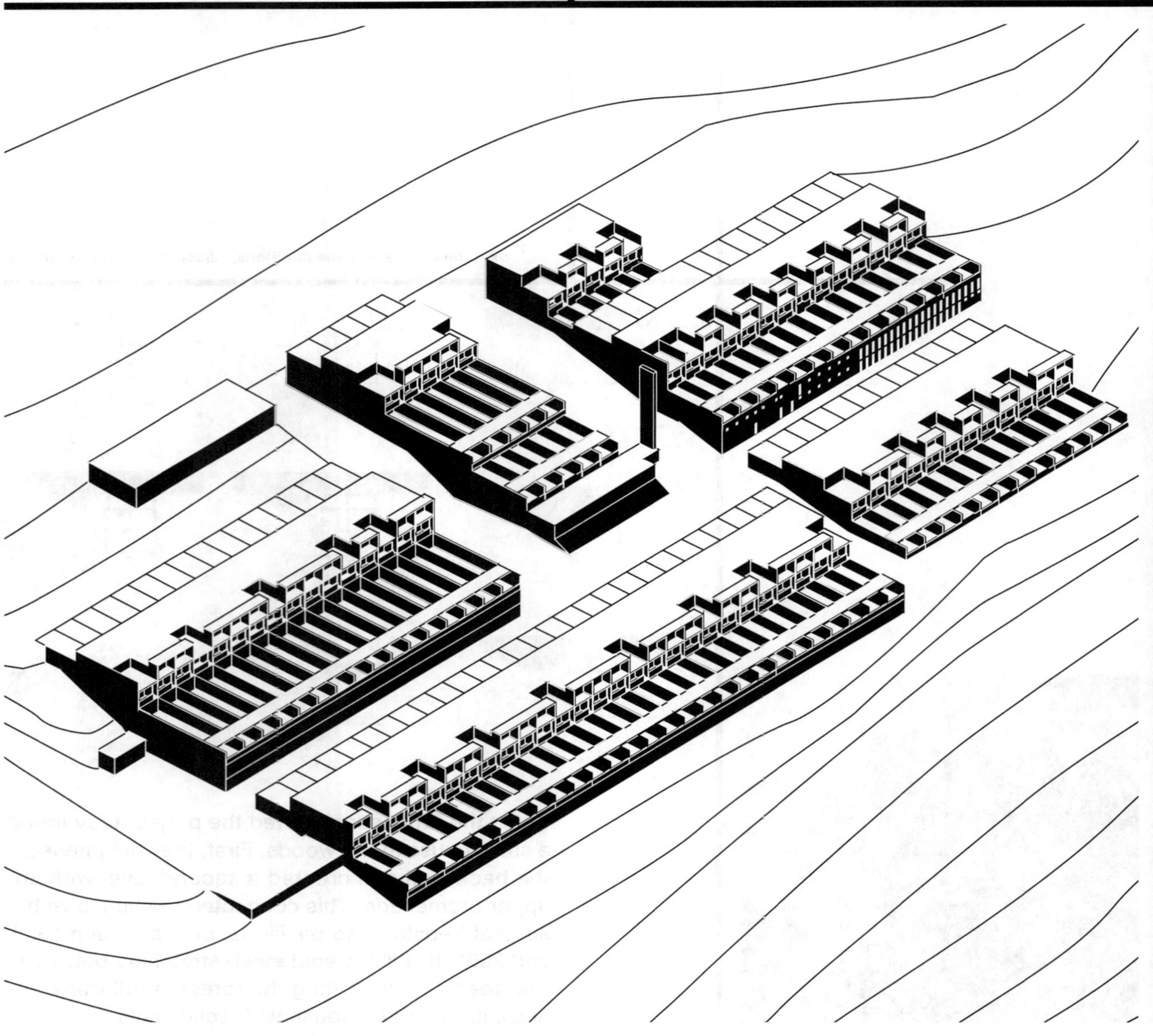

The design of 'Roq' aimed to put Le Corbusier's patent *Le Brevet 226 × 226 × 226* into practice. This easily replicable L-shaped steel profile created cell-like units which could be fixed together in many configurations to a height of three storeys. 'Roq' was an ambitious first study but with 'Rob' the design was downsized substantially. The project slowed and shrunk, and eventually Rabutato agreed that Le Corbusier may build a very small *Cabanon* (cabin) for himself on his land.

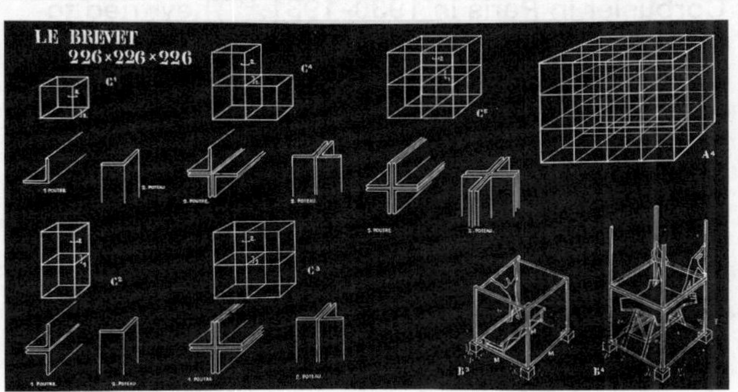

Le Brevet 226 × 226 × 226 was based on a single steel angle with a length of 226 centimetres, the height of a six-foot man with an outstretched arm, the basic unit of Le Corbusier's Modulor.

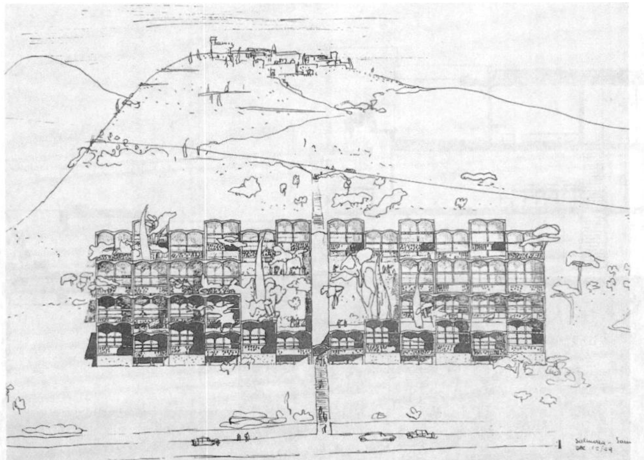

'Roq' seen in relation to the old towns, Le Corbusier, 1949.

Le Corbusier's Cabanon, 1952.

Realizing Siedlung Halen was a struggle, but while Le Corbusier's 'Roq et Rob' shrunk, Halen grew in scale.

The architects of Atelier 5 were all trained in the office of Hans Brechbühler, who worked for Le Corbusier in Paris in 1930–1931.[43] They tried to buy a patch of forest in 1955 to build only five single-family homes, one for each founding partner. Due to costs related to the conditions of the land, they finished 79 units in 1961.[44] Elaborating on Le Corbusier's 'Roq et Rob' schemes, the elongated houses have a strictly linear, terraced arrangement with cavity walls of concrete bricks, partly covered terraces and roof terraces with green roofs.

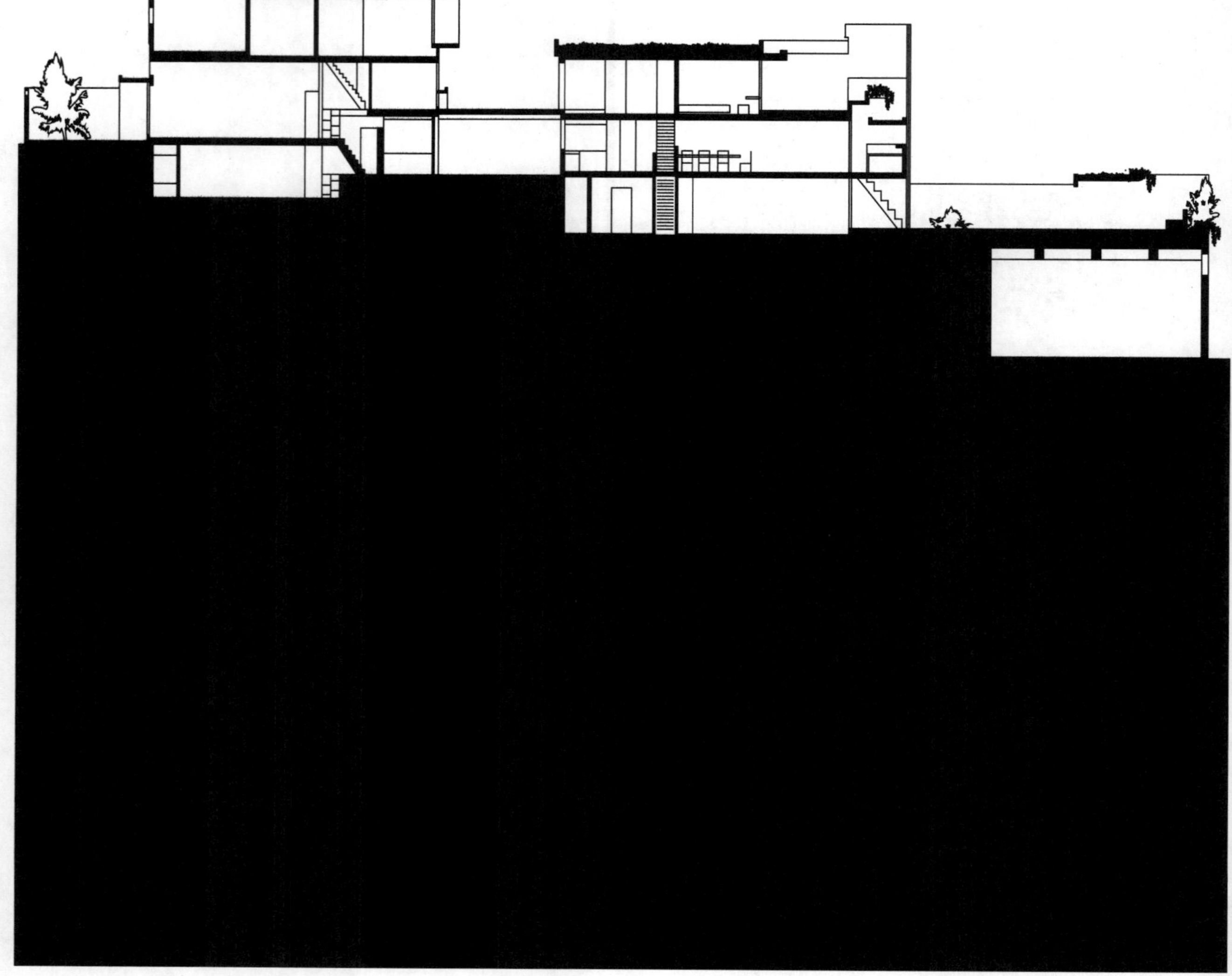

"Siedlung Halen has achieved what so few other estates managed: to provide quality of life for so many people while taking up so little space on the ground. It affords total privacy and social community as you wish."[45] —Urs Heinberg, resident of house 15

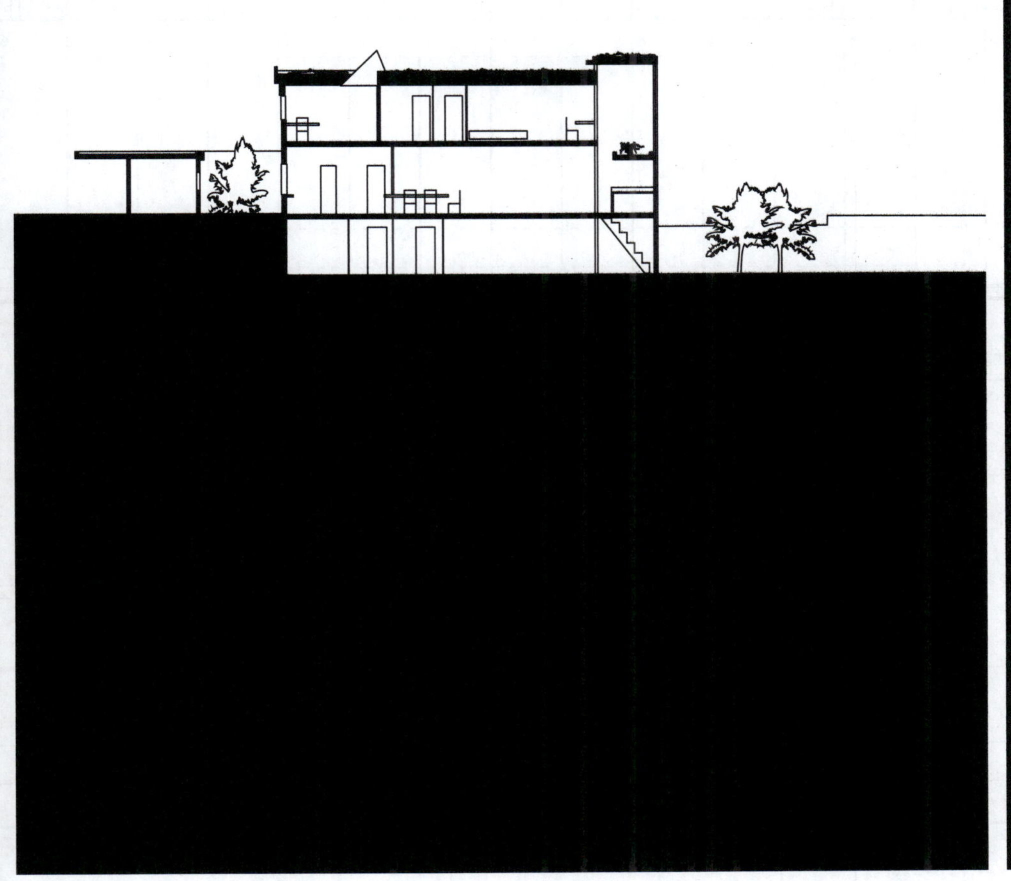

Section of Siedlung Halen.

Upper level plan.

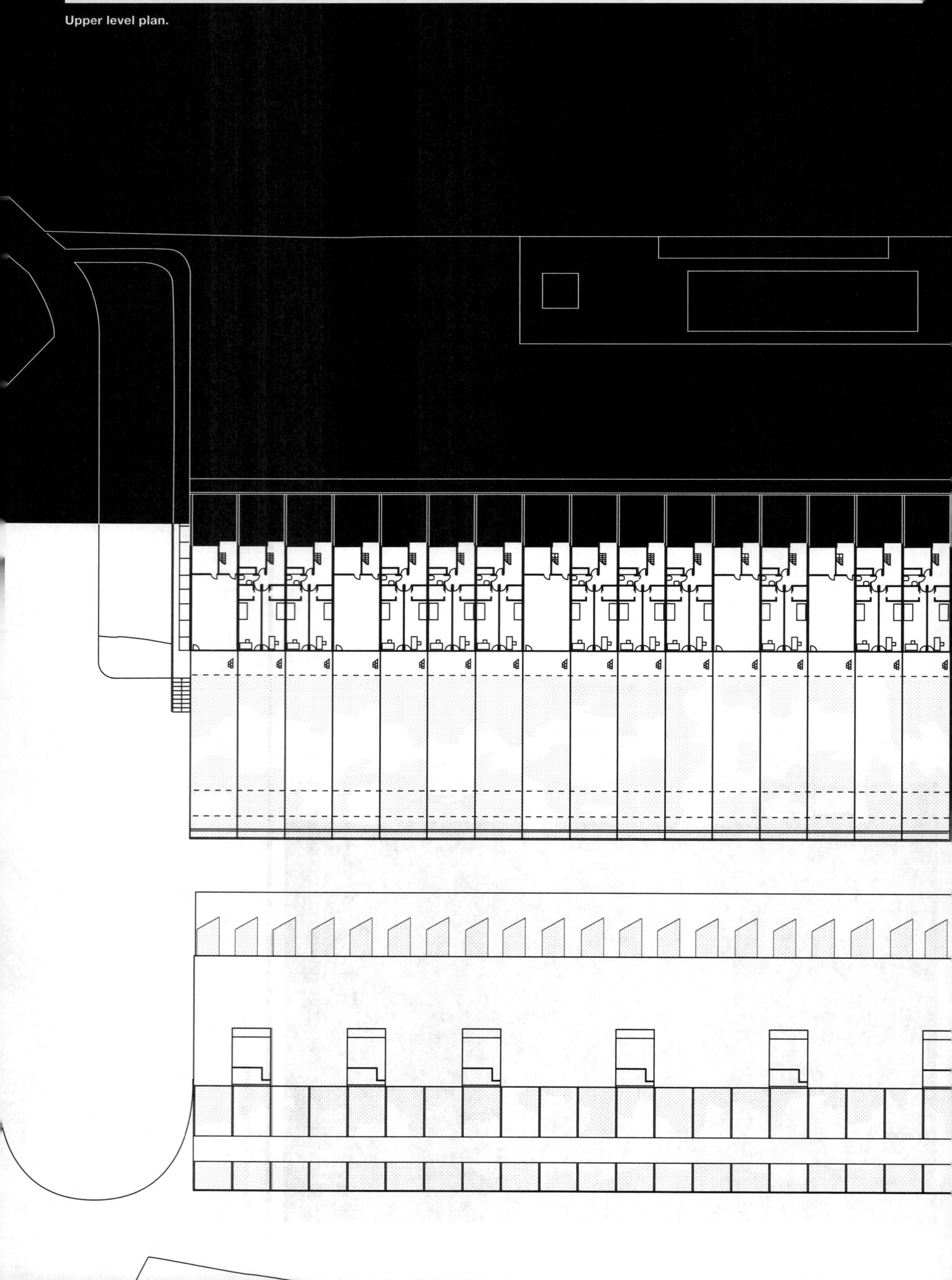

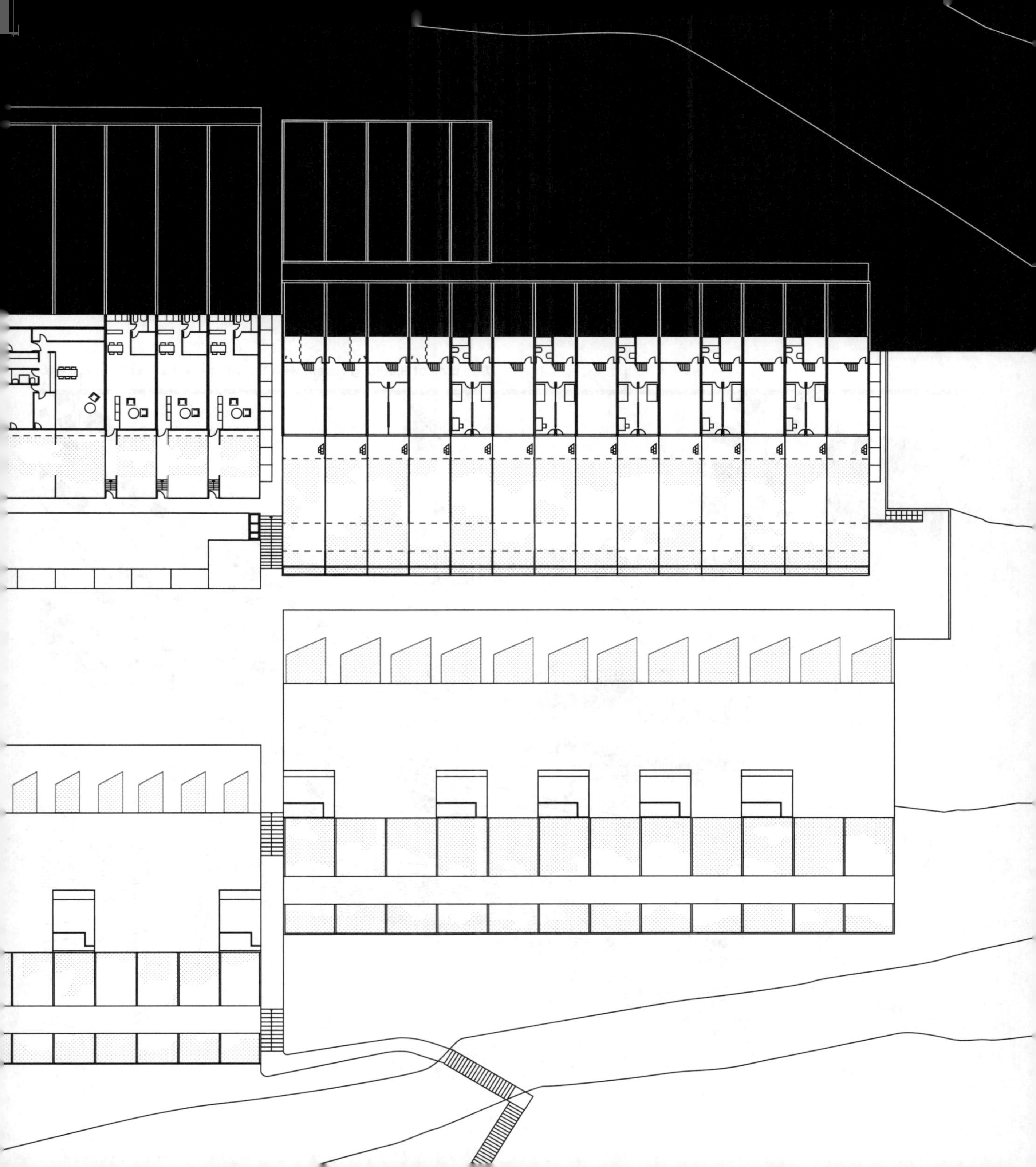

Rotsteinpass, Switzerland (top) and Siedlung Halen (bottom).

It is not a coincidence that this canonical plan was first built in Switzerland. The exposed, brutalist concrete of Halen takes its cues from the rocky Swiss alpine landscape. Small plants slip in between the crevices and flourish in these protected positions. The building is a generous host. Over time it has come to look more like an overgrown rock than rigid terraced housing. Its bold architectonic form challenges the notion that you must mimic nature's softness to embed a building within the land. Like Le Corbusier's 'Roq et Rob', Halen wasn't meant as a suburban project, but as an urban community for like-minded people.

Site plan of Siedlung Halen, with the village of Halen to the top left.

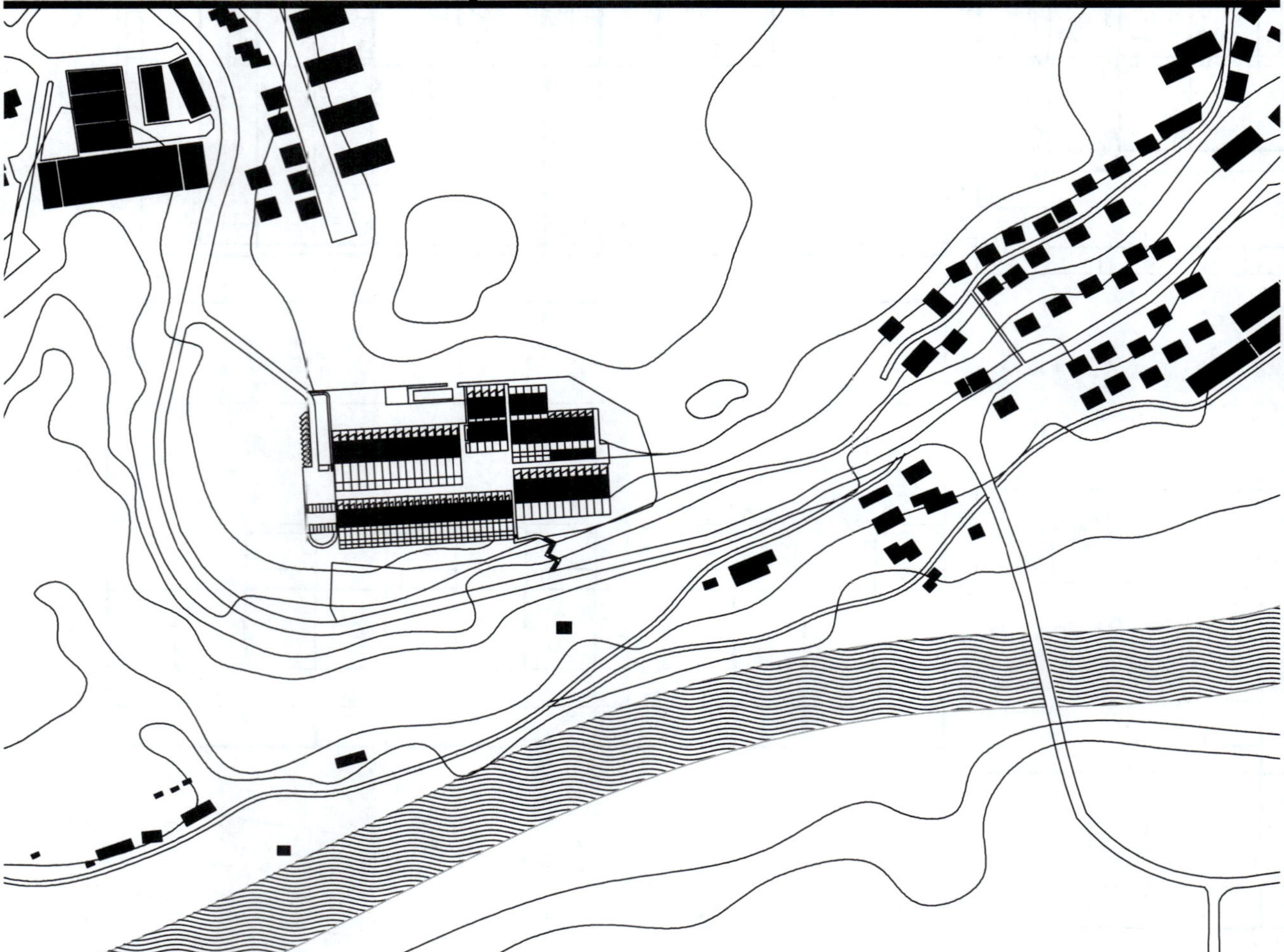

"Nobody has had the courage to replicate the strictness of Halen's design. Details are changed, garden walls are lowered, rooms are widened – but then the effect is diluted and the privacy or sense of community is weakened."[46] – Bernhard Egger, resident of house 75

In the twenty-first century, open space is valued, but private open space is desired. Acknowledging the utter extravagance of suburban sprawl, Western discourse is turning back to a necessary densification, a return to centre, urbanity, amenity and communal services within housing blocks. How can we densify whilst satisfying the suburban ideal? Short answer: it's been done before at Halen.

Athfield House & Studio
Wellington, New Zealand
Ian Athfield
1965–present

The work of Sir Ian Athfield and his magnum opus, the Khandallah project, could easily be downplayed as eclectic illusion. Upon closer study, however, the opposite unfolds. Highly sensitive to site, the Khandallah project pays tribute to several historical references and can be seen as an alternative to the uniformity and norms of detached suburban housing.

Athfield House growing down the hill, 1990.

"It started in '65 and it's still going and it'll never be finished, although I've promised my family I'll finish it. But it's the best example of infill housing in the country. It's good infill housing because it's an appropriate response to how suburbia has to change. You actually have to build on the accidents of the past, on the physical environments which got created because something happened."[47] —Ian Athfield

Ian Athfield and family on the roof.

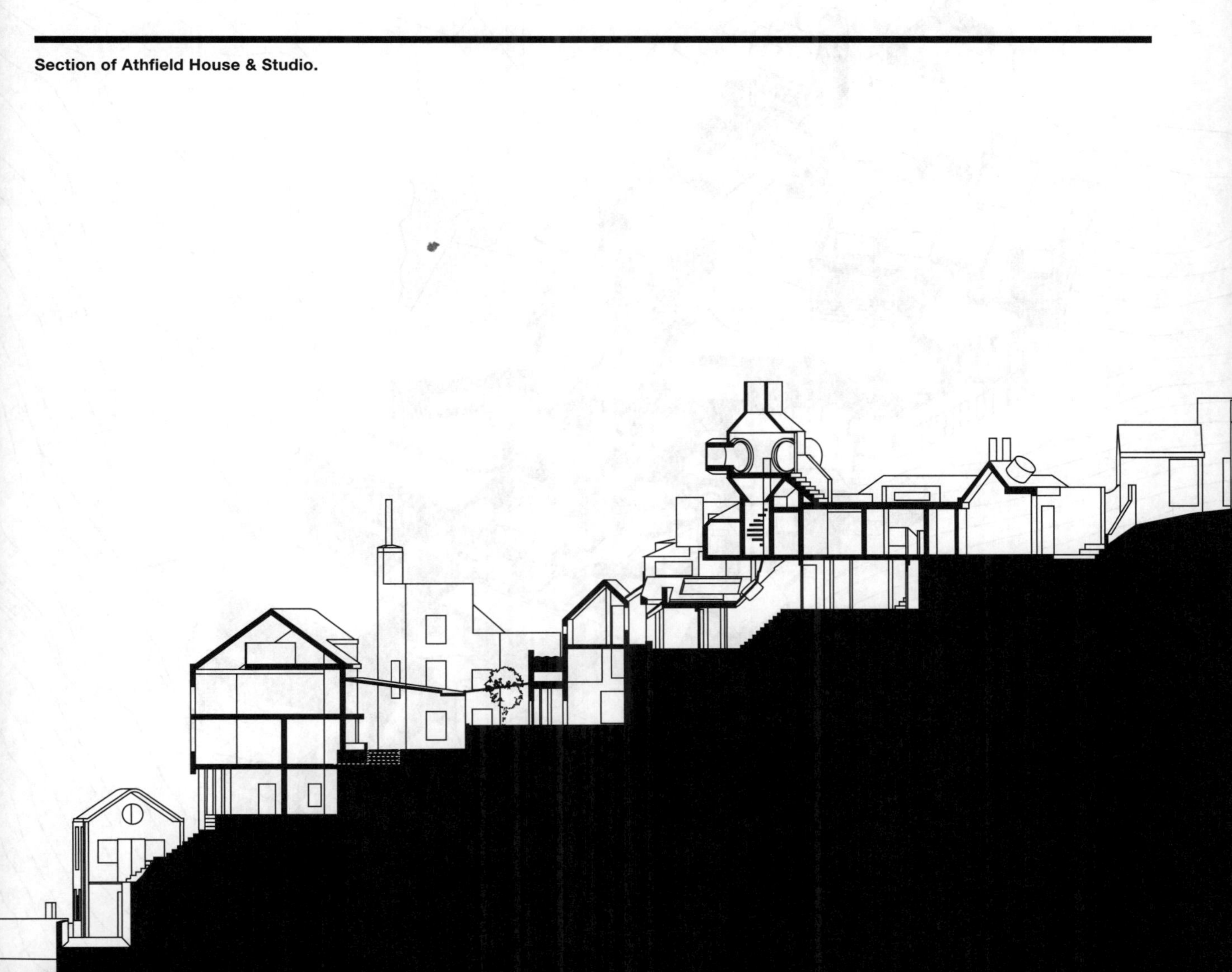

Section of Athfield House & Studio.

Axonometry of Athfield House & Studio, as of 2018.

Athfield House & Studio, lower plan.

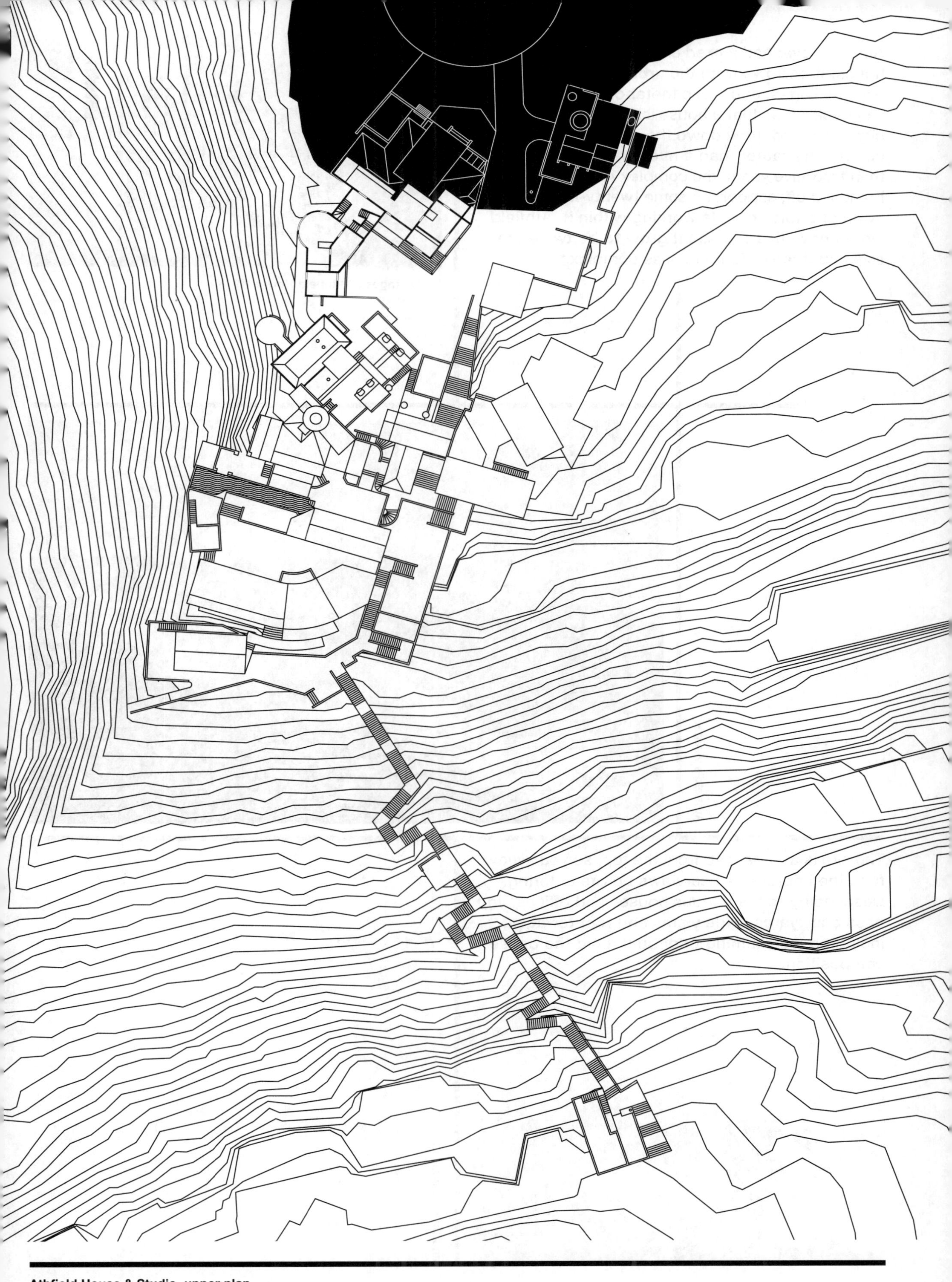

Athfield House & Studio, upper plan.

Athfield never had a fixed end point in mind for the house. It borrows from the urban layout of archaic Greek villages, Japanese Metabolism and Aldo van Eyck's idea that a house is, in fact, a small city.[48] It would grow down the hillside and house a community rather than a nuclear family. After more than forty-five years, the complex has rooted and branched off, supporting some twenty-five people living and forty people working within it. Athfield would have liked to see it grow to be twice the size and three or four times as complex.[49]

Early stages of Athfield House, 1974.

Athfield's village.

The site is approached from the top, so you always face the impressive sea views before entering. Descending to the various houses and offices, you pass courtyards, wide vistas and roof terraces, including a swimming pool built amid the dense composition.

Ian Athfield on his roof.

BUJ186
CCB752

Ath
1940 – 2015

keha pri

Although the site is extremely steep, you are never really detached from the existing landscape. This is because the project was not designed on the drawing board but built intuitively by hand, always immediately responding to existing topography. It is, in the words of his friend Roger Walker, Ath's lifelong doodling, with blocks and concrete, rather than a pen.[50]

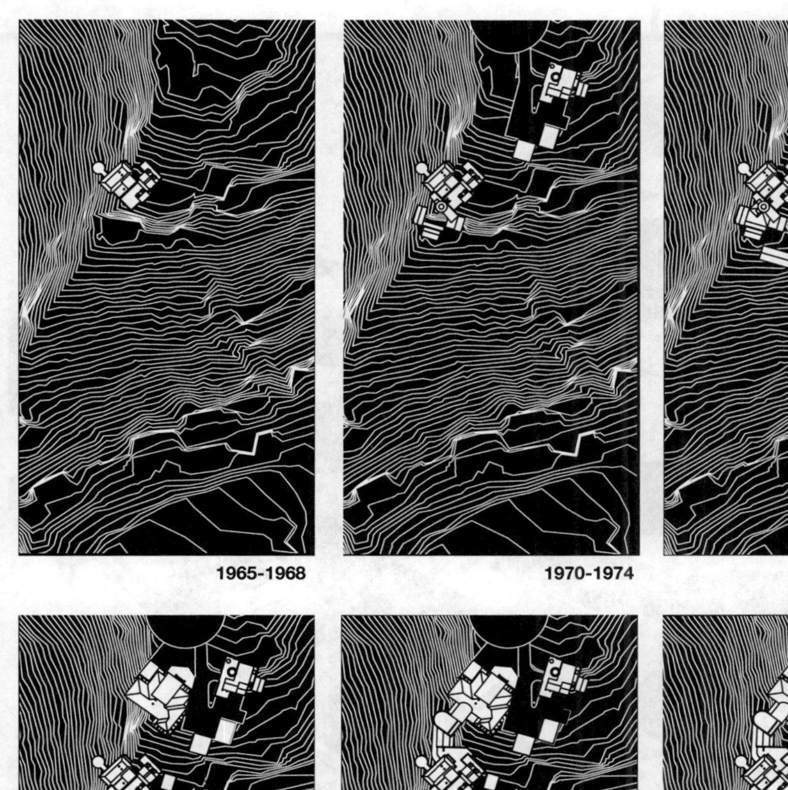

1965-1968 1970-1974 1976-1980

1984-1985 1986-1990 1998-present

The evolution of the Athfield House & Studio.

Later, his son Zac, also an architect, took a crucial role in extending and maintaining the complex. Accurate plans and sections were only recently drawn from the resulting complex and mainly used for restorative purposes and documentation.

Il Magistero
Urbino, Italy
Giancarlo De Carlo
1968–1976

Following the post-war climax of the Congrès Internationaux d'Architecture Moderne (CIAM) a group of plucky youths, known as Team 10, emerged. Criticizing the dogmatism and penchant for clearing a tabula rasa under modernism, Team 10 advocated for a more empathic approach.

Axonometry of Il Magistero.

Disciple and active member Giancarlo De Carlo argued for the pairing of historical and modern elements. With a method referred to as the reading of territory, he described this as an iterative process involving tentative design and feedback. De Carlo completely flipped the top-down CIAM rhetoric into a bottom-up attitude, and his Il Magistero project can be seen as a happy medium, built at the literal midpoint of the Team 10 movement.

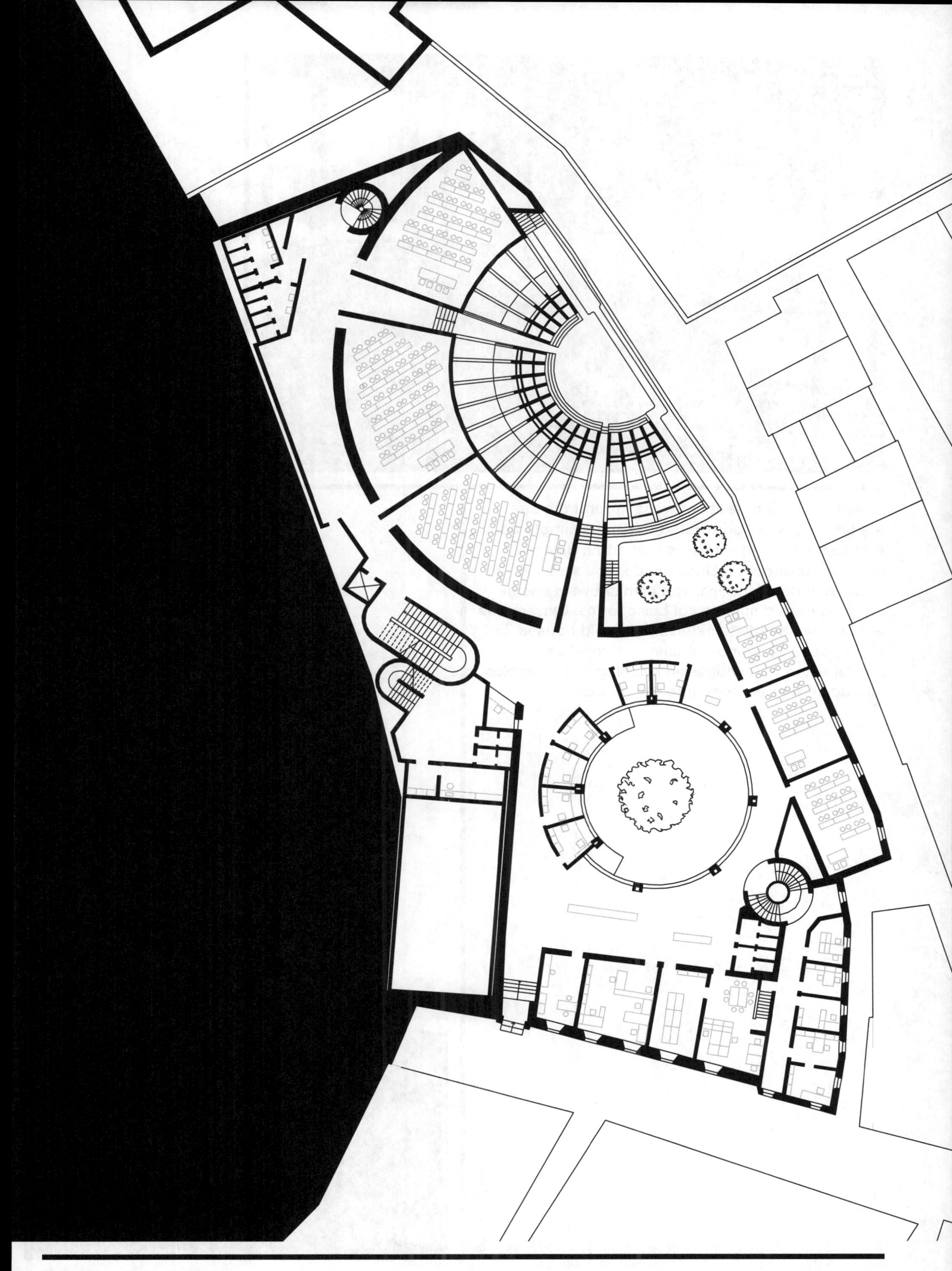

Plan of lower level of Il Magistero.

Circulation space around the circular void.

The almost blind, reticent walls around the site are kept in place, perforated only by a simple door and some existing windows that admit daylight into the classrooms. Once inside, you step into an urban palette of spaces. The plan shows a seemingly haphazard stitching of basic forms. Classrooms are built within the thickness of the old houses, but once past a sequence of alleys, a court and amphitheatre with bridges and sloping ramps unfolds, all dug 14 metres deep into the hillside.

Section of Il Magistero.

The hilltop town of Urbino in 1963, shortly before the design of Il Magistero.

Plan of Urbino today.

Il Magistero burrows into the ground with the same drama with which the Ducal Palace reaches toward the sky.[51] Inside, spaces terrace downwards, following the slope. But at entrance level, one can traverse the smartly set-up cross section to the centre of the skylight that encircles the roof garden. On almost all sides the building is no more than two to three storeys high, although the cross section reveals six levels. The secretive composition of an architecture turned urban with the Aula Magna at the bottom underlines the public importance of this building and can be seen as a continuation of the historic town.

"I lived on the fifth floor of a big building. One day, I think I was just six years old, I was going up the stair, and on the last landing, suddenly, I met an animal. I thought it was a dog, but it had very long legs and the head of a cat. It could have been a lynx, a Siberian hare, or a very big felix serval (an African wild cat). Whichever – and I'm certain this actually happened, even though everyone always denied it – at one point, the animal in my path forced me to measure the surrounding space, to take in its dimensions, comprehend where I was, as I tried to find a way to escape. That was the first time I felt conscious of the height and width of a place, of the horizontal and inclined planes, of going forward and backward, up and down. From then on the idea of stair was impressed in my mind, and it still fills my dreams and my thinking today. I am never so stimulated by flat places as by those on different levels."[52] – Giancarlo De Carlo

Neue Staatsgalerie Stuttgart, Germany James Stirling 1977–1984

James Stirling won the Neue Staatsgalerie competition in 1977 shortly after Giancarlo De Carlo completed his Il Magistero project. Strip away shallow readings of style and it is hard to not see parallels between the two projects. Unfortunately, the international press at the time were far more preoccupied with the postmodern appearance of the building and failed to dig deeper into the matter. Commentary was limited to parallels between the 'Neue' in Stuttgart, 'Altes' in Berlin, and some other golden classics.

Plan of Altes Museum, Berlin, Karl Friedrich Schinkel, 1823–1830.

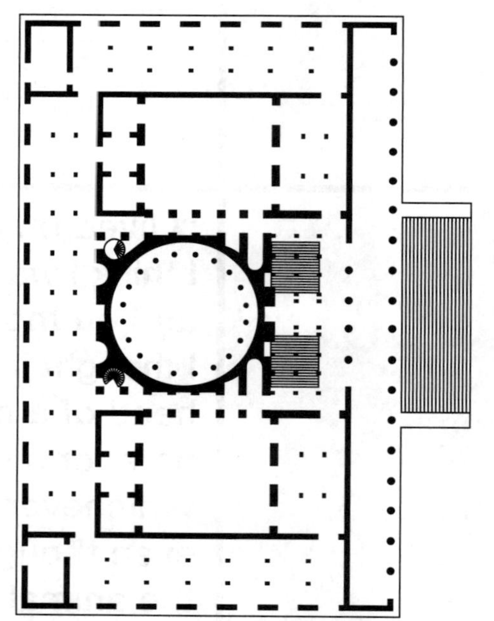

Plan of Il Magistero, Giancarlo De Carlo, 1968–1976.

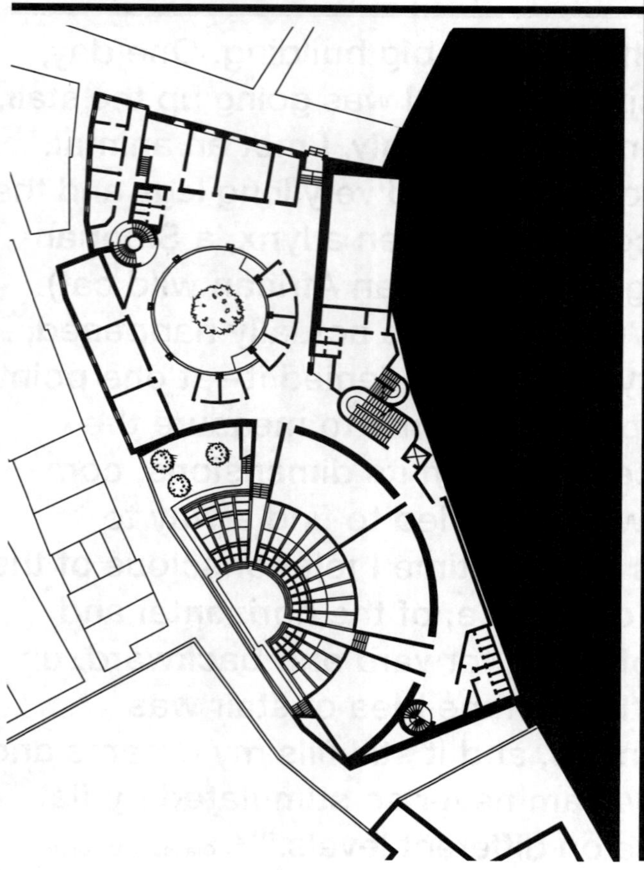

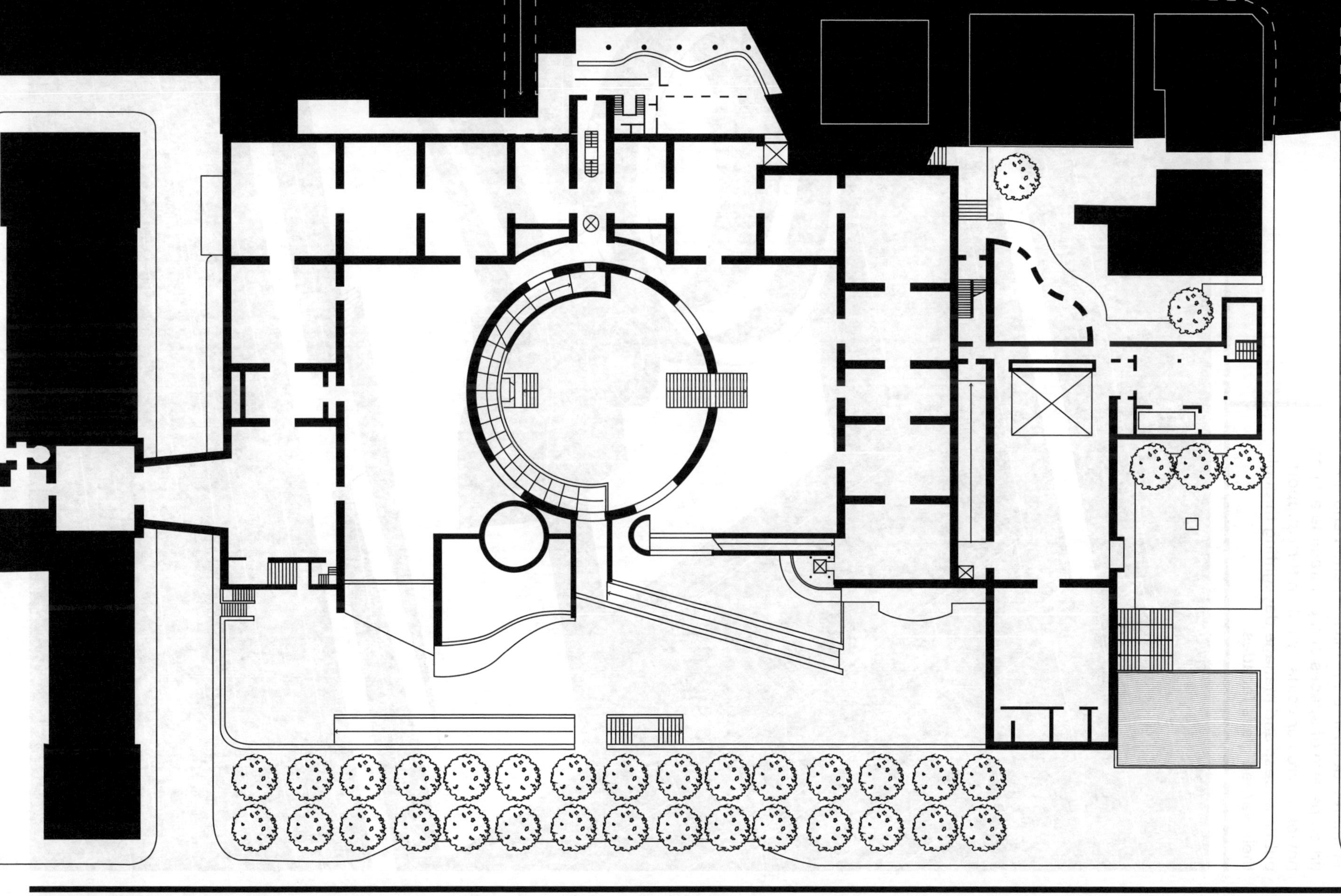

Plan of Neue Staatsgalerie, 1977–1984.

It cannot be coincidental that both schemes dig 14 metres deep into the hillside, and bend an urban palette of spaces and programme around powerful circular voids, which in turn support public access and manage daylighting through their warped glass facades.

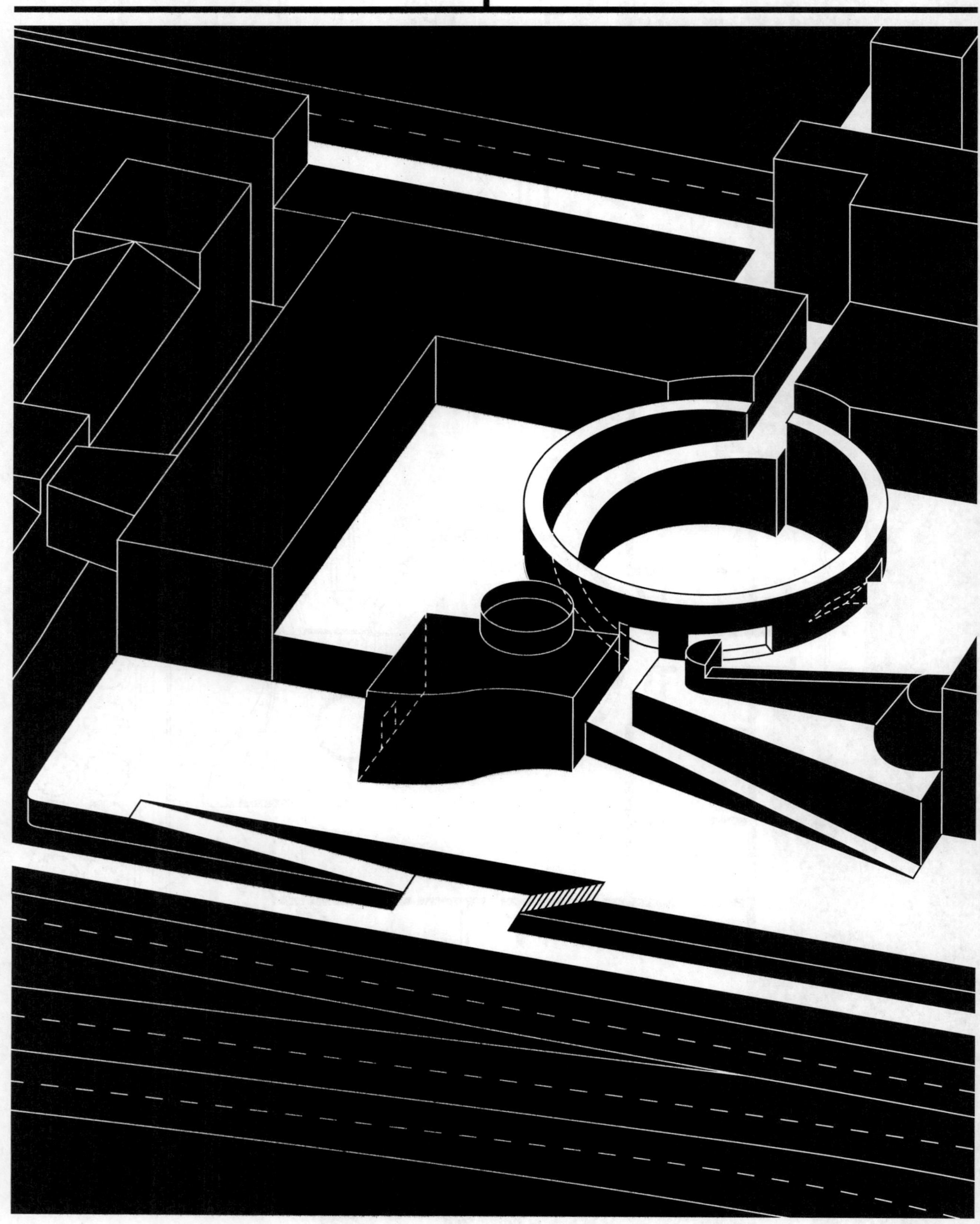

Axonometry of Neue Staatsgalerie.

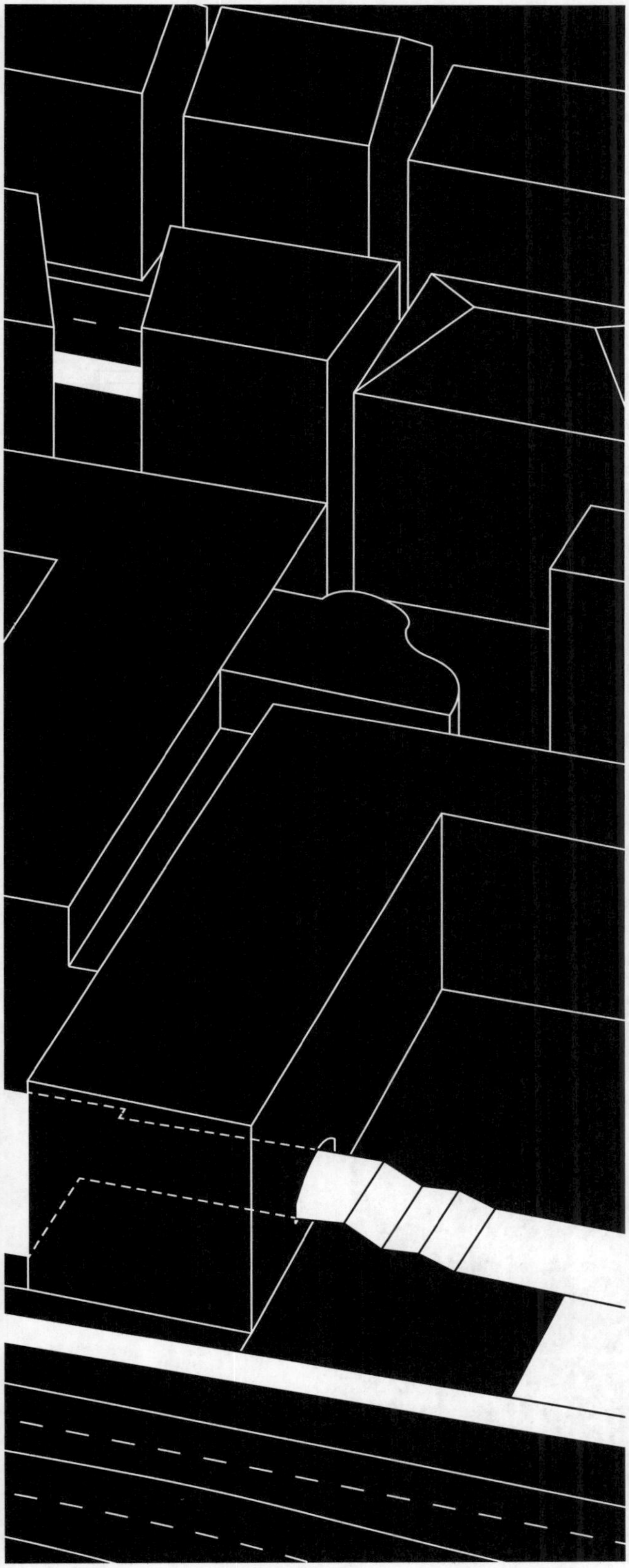

James Stirling must have also undertaken a deep reading of the site, because although the plan of the 'Neue' pays a major tribute to the Altes Museum, the reworking of urban connections overrides the relatively straightforward sequence of museum spaces.

What makes this museum stand out, especially within the postmodern era, is the intricately folded *promenade architecturale*, sculpted in relation to the museum's ancillary spaces.

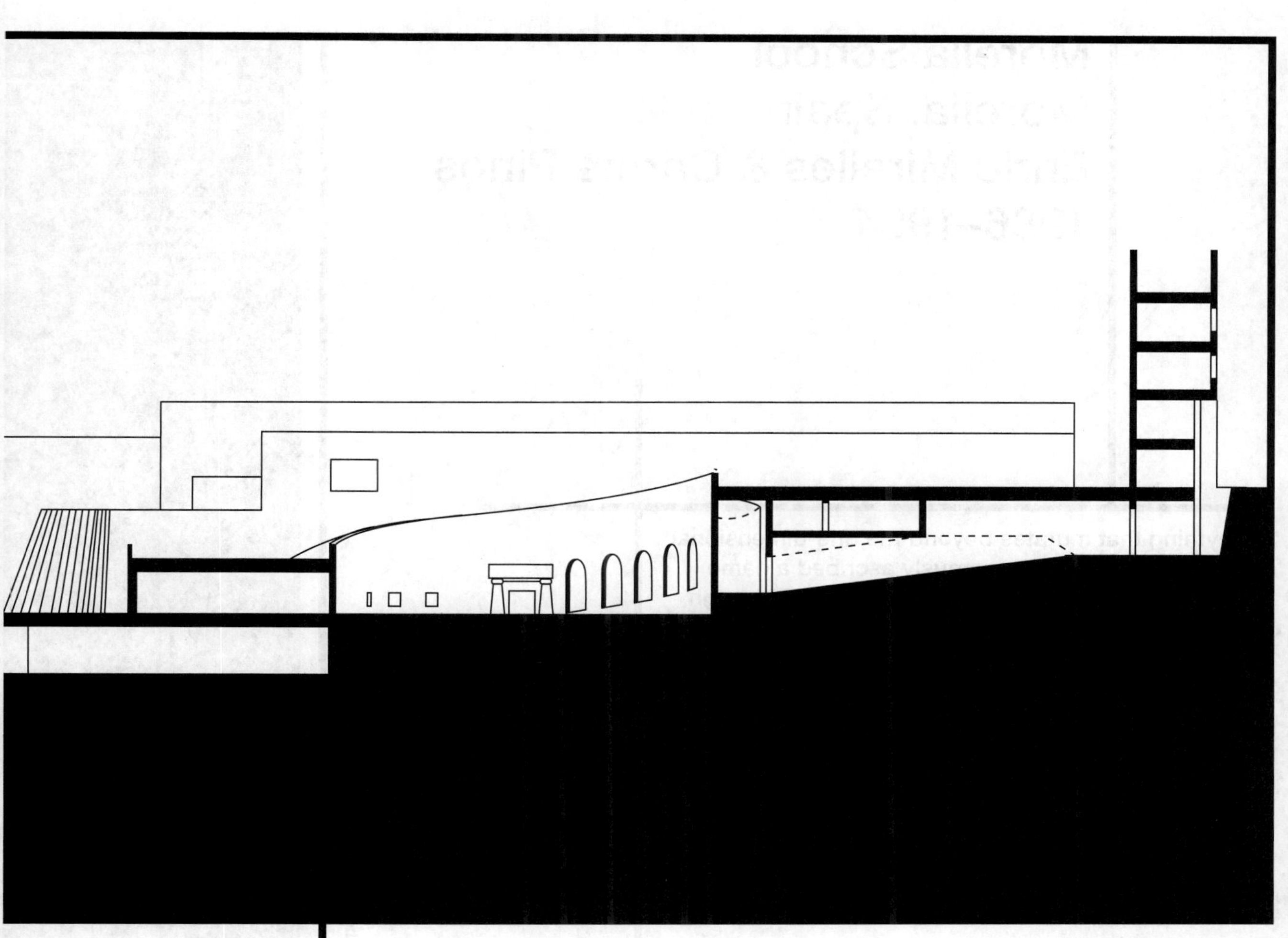

Section of Neue Staatsgalerie.

This route anchors the museum to its immediate surroundings and the postmodern vocabulary is not used as pompous historical reference with mere coquettish architectural rhetoric, but as guiding principle for a building, which offers itself over to the urban realm. This almost goes back to the renaissance play of mass and void within the Parisian hôtel, where ornamented urban void and routing underlined public interest.[53] The building with its art nestles in an almost nomadic way between the monumental buildings and refuses to participate in an all too opulent presentation of style. Not yet finished, or again ruinous, as the ventilation holes of the parking garage suggest with their loose blocks of natural stone in the grass.

Morella School
Morella, Spain
Enric Miralles & Carme Pinos
1986–1994

Anything that mutates beyond the one-dimensional skyscraper is often generously ascribed a name like 'courtscraper' or 'groundscraper'. Although the Morella School has nothing to do with this kind of typological name-dropping, you could very well call it a 'hillscraper'.

Axonometry of Morella School.

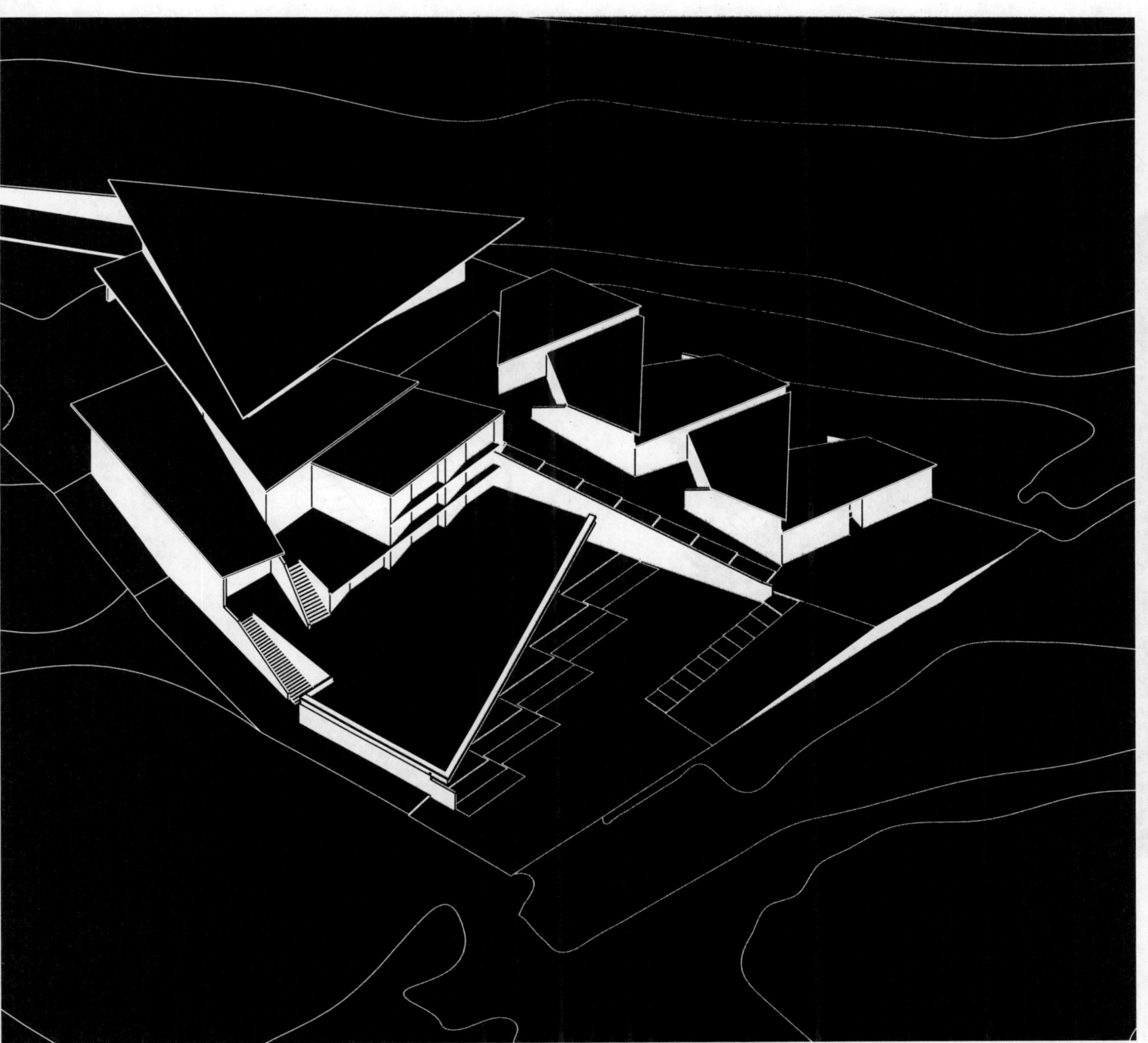

The dormitory folds itself uphill as if it were paper architecture, while the school gouges out the hill for staircases and corridors. These serve three rows of classrooms on top of each other, which jump backwards to form spacious terraces. This intricate reworking of the height lines creates a dazzling spatial play. Although the corridors and staircases are positioned behind the rows of classrooms, the tricky offsetting of walls and roofs creates vertical shafts and clerestory windows, providing an abundance of daylight to these cavernous spaces.

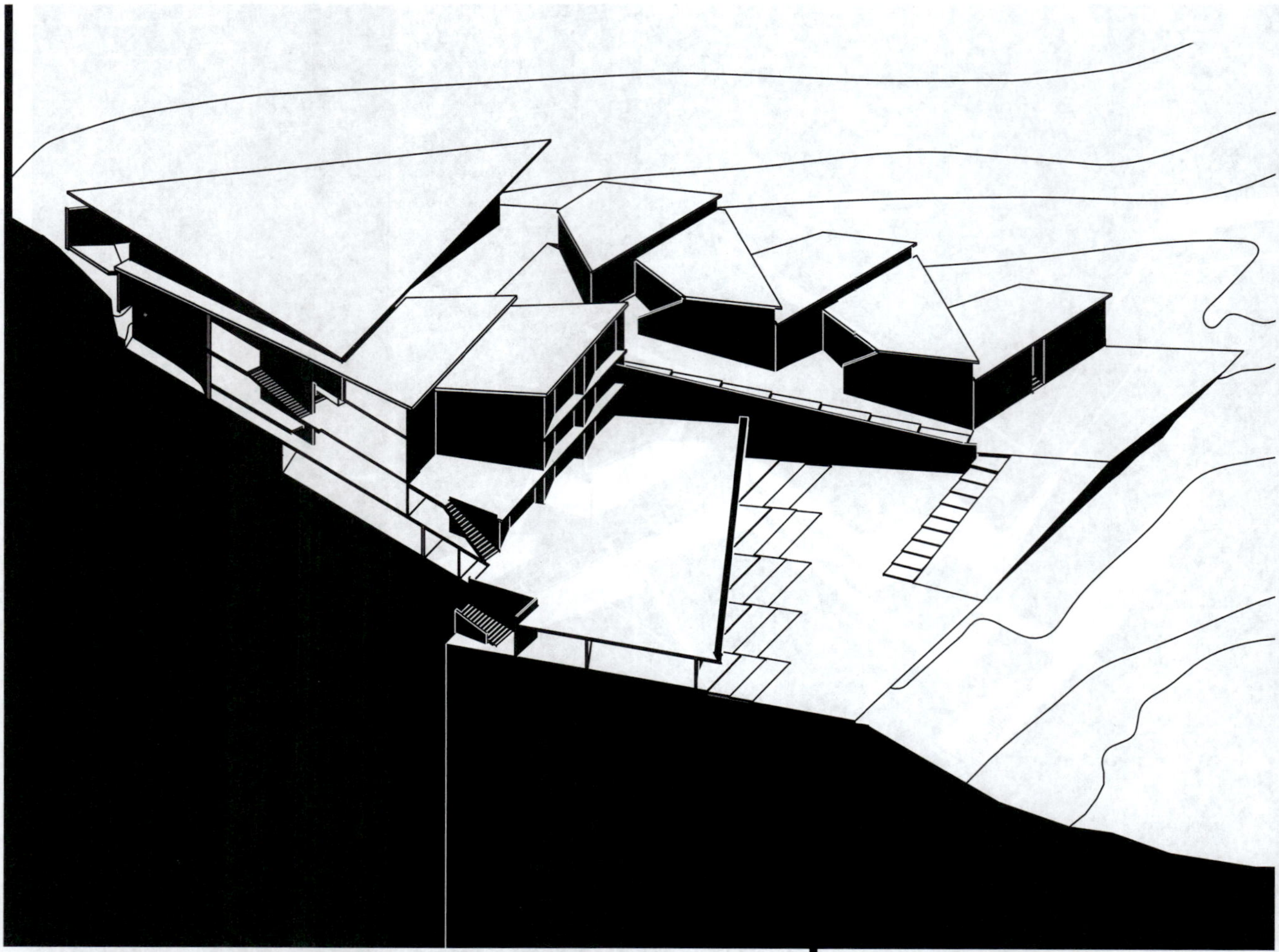

Sectional axonometry of Morella School.

The Glass Mountain Shattered, David Hockney, in *Six Fairy Tales from the Brothers Grimm*, 1969.

In designing the Morella School, Enric Miralles was interested in the link between human activities and preexisting traces in the geographical cultural landscape. He referred to a drawing by David Hockney, which accompanies fairy tales by the Brothers Grimm, where a giant breaks a mountain into crystal pieces. Hockney was fascinated by the challenge of drawing a glass mountain and he tried to make it translucent. The side of the mountain is faceted with triangles. Likewise, Miralles seems fascinated by the challenge of building a translucent geology and talks about the streets of Morella as a sundial, encircling the foot of the castle.

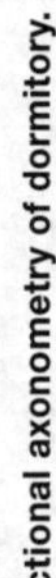

Sectional axonometry of dormitory.

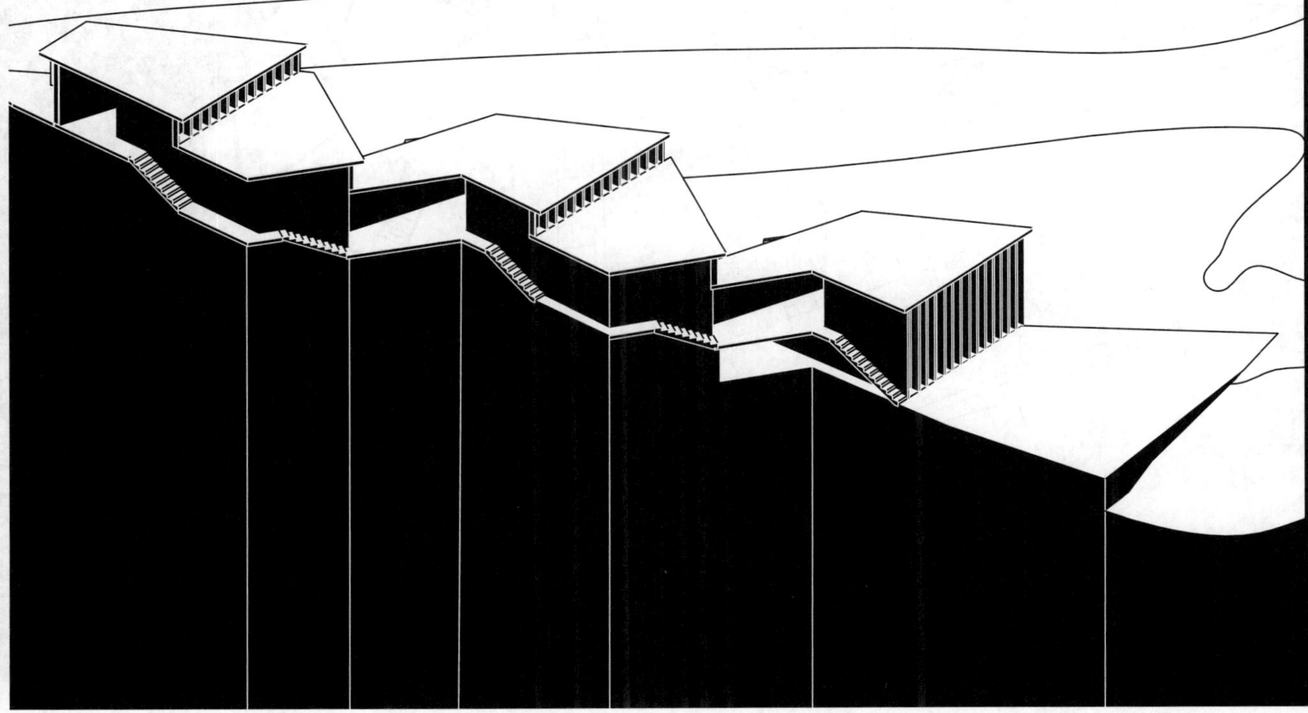

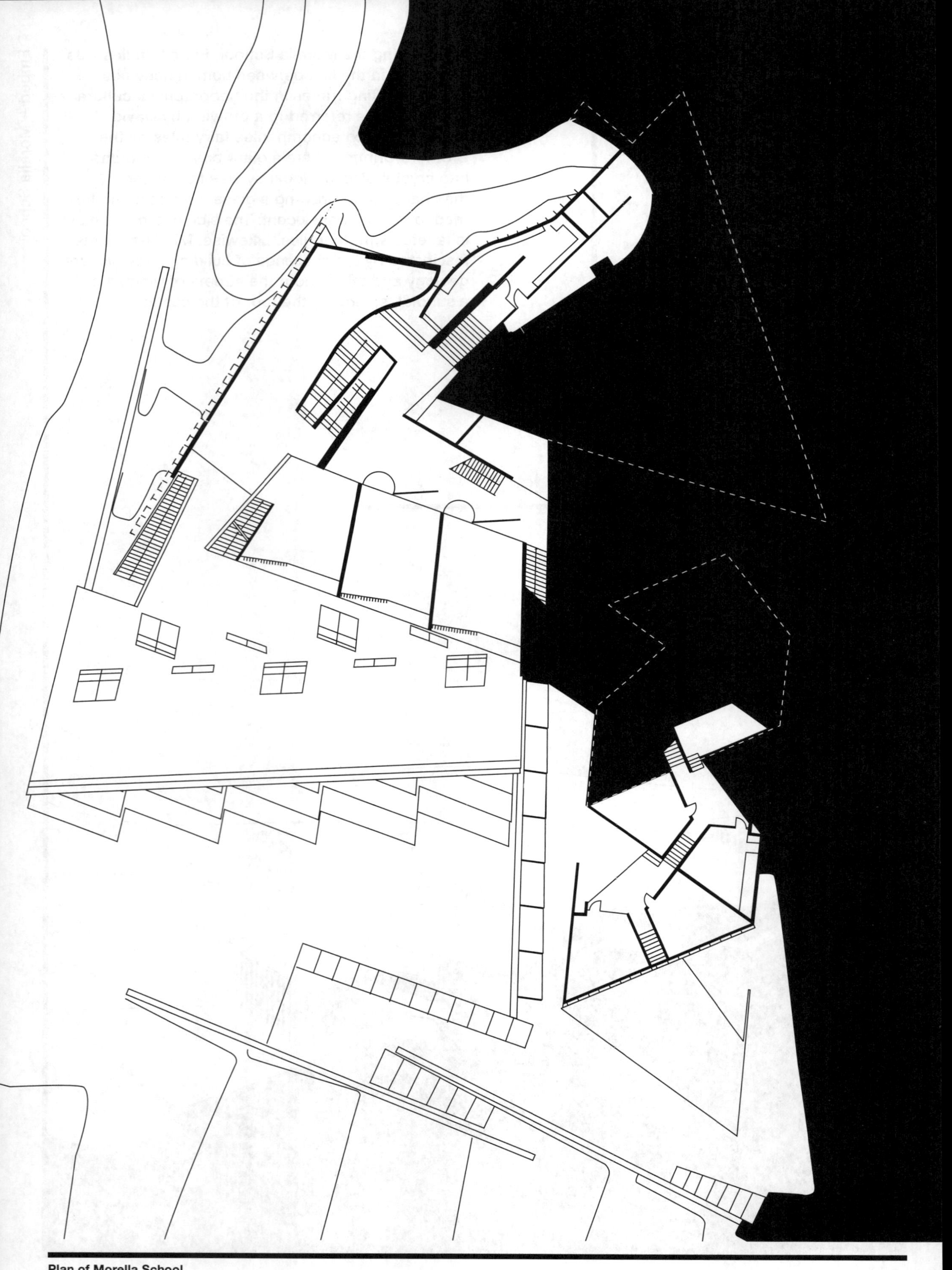

Plan of Morella School.

Morella is surrounded by a terraced agriculture, rarely seen in the Spanish countryside. A zigzagging city wall hems in the town, and the castle at its summit has triangular-shaped bastions and a bent zwinger-like entrance. It is as if the school tries to complete the town's circular outline, punching the missing piece of the fortified landscape into the unprotected western side of the towering castle. The layout of the school condenses the landscaped, urban and architectural structures of the city of Morella all in one go.

This 'deep reading' of site and history has resulted in an overlay of movements, like a piece of origami taking on architectural dimensions.

Castillo de Morella, zwinger and bent entrance, 1300–1400.

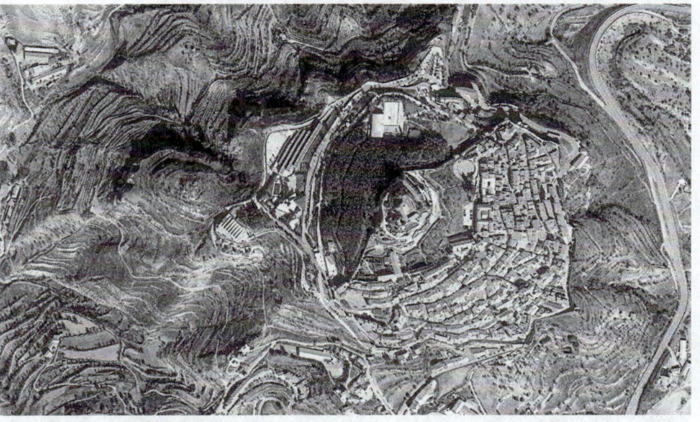

Aerial view of terraced agricultural land, town of Morella and castle.

Olympic Archery Range
Barcelona, Spain
Enric Miralles & Carme Pinos
1989–1991

Archery is one of the oldest forms of hunting, dating back to the Neolithic period, and the humble bow and arrow naturally evolved from a means of survival to a method of warfare. Just a couple of miles away from Morella is the oldest known painting of a battle in the Roure cave at Morella la Vella.[54] It is a tumultuous scene depicting warriors, stumbling over each other as if floating in mid-air.

Axonometry of the Olympic Archery Range.

Hunting, however, was a more grounded activity. Hunters usually fired from the cover of thickets or overhanging branches since the bow and arrow had a shooting range of just 20 metres.

Like the hunter and the warrior, the competitive archer likes to keep his back covered and an open view. Miralles's design for the Olympic archery range exploits the height difference of the site to this end. But what is more interesting is the undulating canopy-like roofscape protruding from the hillside, acknowledging that trees and overhanging branches do create a perfect shelter.

At no point does the building come to a standstill. There is no harsh envelope, and while walls curve to demarcate space, nowhere is it completely enclosed. The pronounced architectural language is more reminiscent of a ruin or a landscape scene, a sheltered place that is really not a building at all.

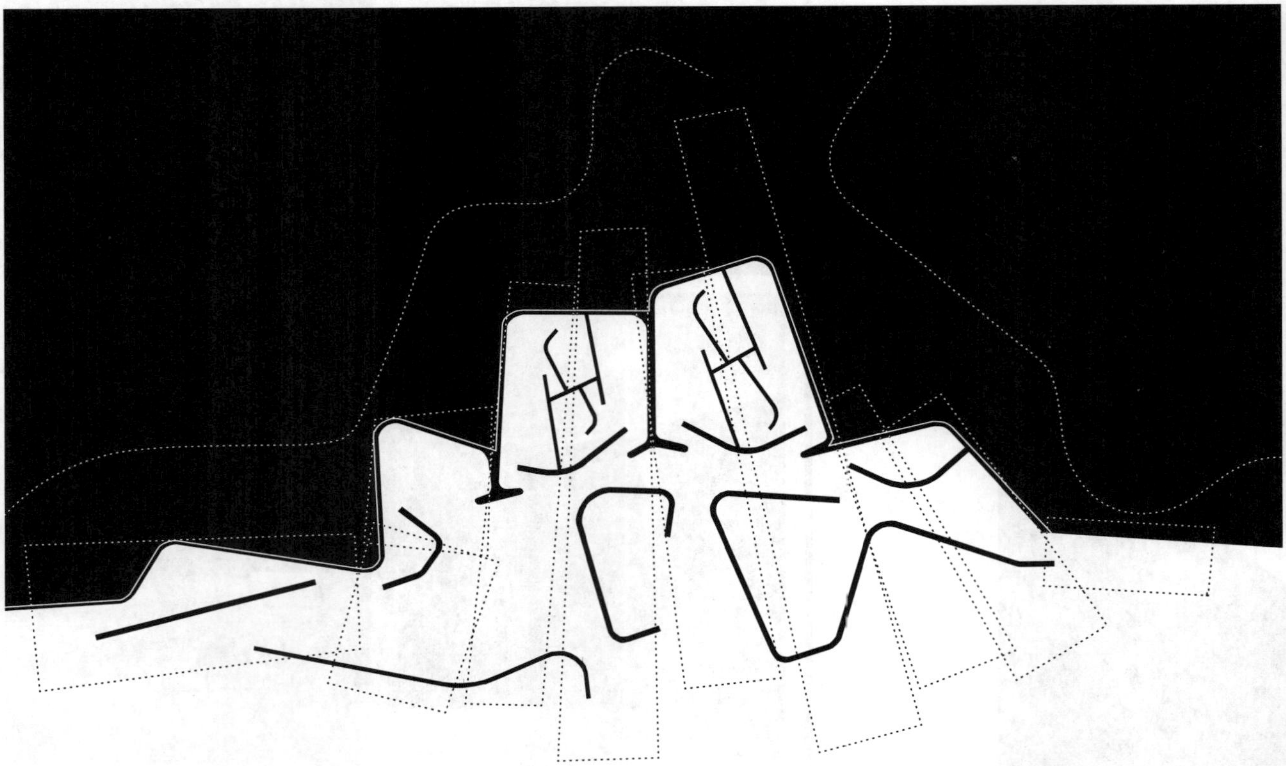

Plan of the Olympic Archery Range.

Equally intriguing is the layout of the training facility. The walls dividing the showers and changing rooms and separating them from the central corridor are almost an exact copy of this early cave drawing with bent bows and arrows, running legs and scattered dots.

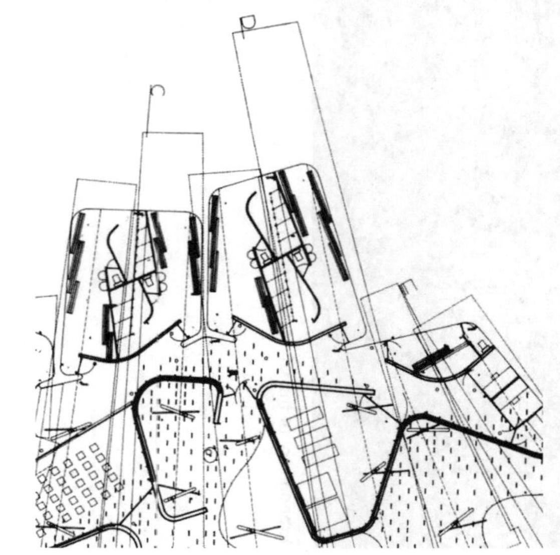

Detail of the floor plan of the Olympic Archery Range.

Painting of a battle between archers dated to the late Mesolithic is the earliest surviving image of combat, in Cueva del Roure, Morella la Vella, Spain.

Miralles also refers to it as "a project that appears and takes form in an instant". The columns stand like arrows, shot in the ground, while concrete beams supporting the higgledy-piggledy roof overhangs have a bow shape.[55]

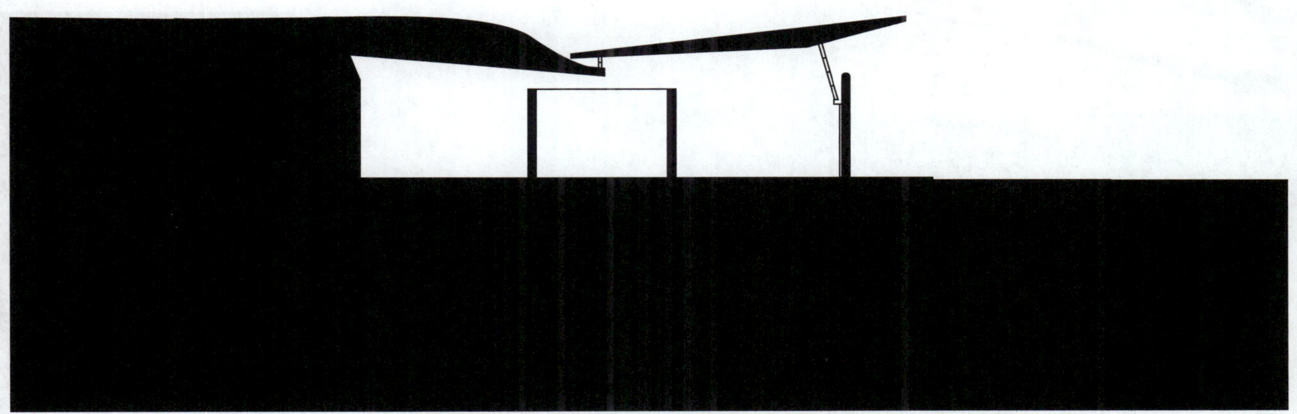

Ten thousand years after it was scratched onto the wall of a Castellón cave, the battle was re-enacted in steel and concrete, a major tribute to the origin of archery.

Therme Vals
Vals, Switzerland
Peter Zumthor
1993–1996

"Mountain, stone, water – building in stone, building with stone, building into the mountain, building out of the mountain, being in the mountain – how to interpret architecturally the meaning and sensuality of the combination of these words, translated into architecture? Along these lines, we designed the building, taking shape step by step." – Peter Zumthor

Giant boulders at an altitude of 2750 metres in Valsertal, near the Dachberg summit.

At first, Zumthor wanted to build a spa into the side of the mountain. Another idea was to carve out giant boulders and to bathe inside, but this was not really feasible. Finally, he settled on disassembling the mountain and building it up again, layer by layer. In the end, his idea to have a spa inside a mountain succeeded.[56] The design was "motivated by the wish to establish a special relationship between the baths and the primal energy and geology of the mountain landscape."

In fact, Zumthor imitated (and significantly sped up) a process, already going on for millions of years in the surrounding landscape. At an altitude of 2800 metres, layers of mica quartzite crumble into massive, remarkably rectangular, blocks of quartzite. This is caused by big fluctuations in temperature and penetrating water that freezes and expands.

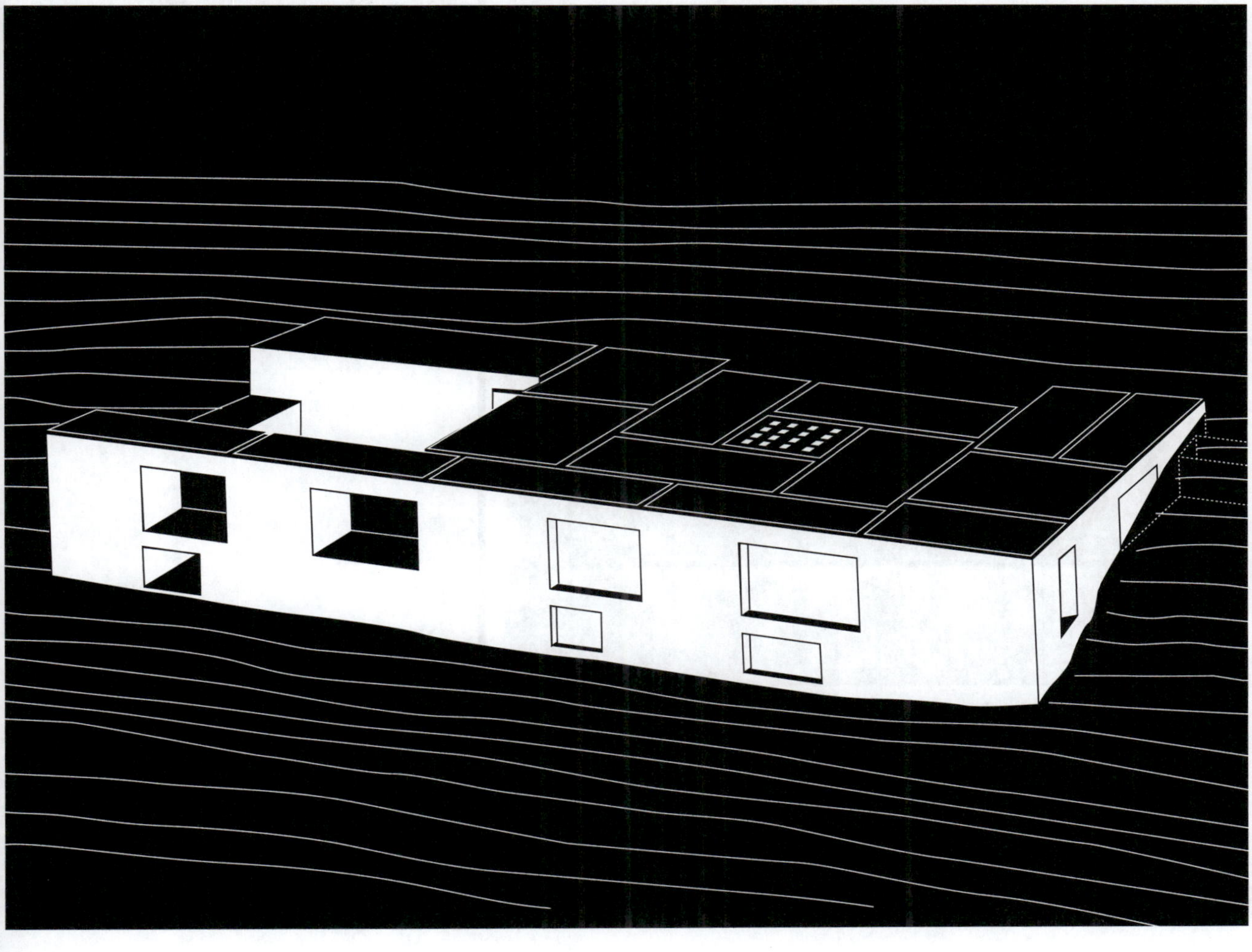

These big boulders lie at short distances from each other and the enclosed deposits of calcite make them appear to be made up of horizontal layers. At Therme Vals, the arrangement of the massive volumes enclosing the different baths, relaxation areas, massage rooms and other service areas have an astonishingly similar set-up to this.[57] What is added is a roof of concrete, where slender recesses control light, giving the space a feeling of depth, of being within the earth.

Early sketch of Therme Vals by Peter Zumthor.

Detail of landscape near Dachberg summit, showing boulders at the same scale as the project in sketch.

Cracks in quartzite stone layers.

It also transcends the idea of a landscape, making it into architecture. Or inversely, as the landscape architect Diana Balmori expressed in one of her last interviews: "I call everything without a roof a landscape".[58] Perhaps here we agree with her.[59] The roof helps to transcend the landscape, joining and enclosing quartz boulders into an architectural space.

Site plan of Therme Vals in the valley.

Summer forest at Peil, the valley directly south of the village of Vals.

Zumthor explains the spatial arrangement as follows: “The meander is a designed negative space between the blocks, a space that connects everything as it flows throughout the entire building, creating a pulsating rhythm. You are walking as if in the woods.”[60] And indeed, when you are in the thermal baths, there is an intimacy that the high alpine mountain landscape lacks. As you come down into the valley, you enter the pine forest with randomly distributed, dense groups of pine trees forming a canopy above your head. This is the meander Zumthor speaks of.

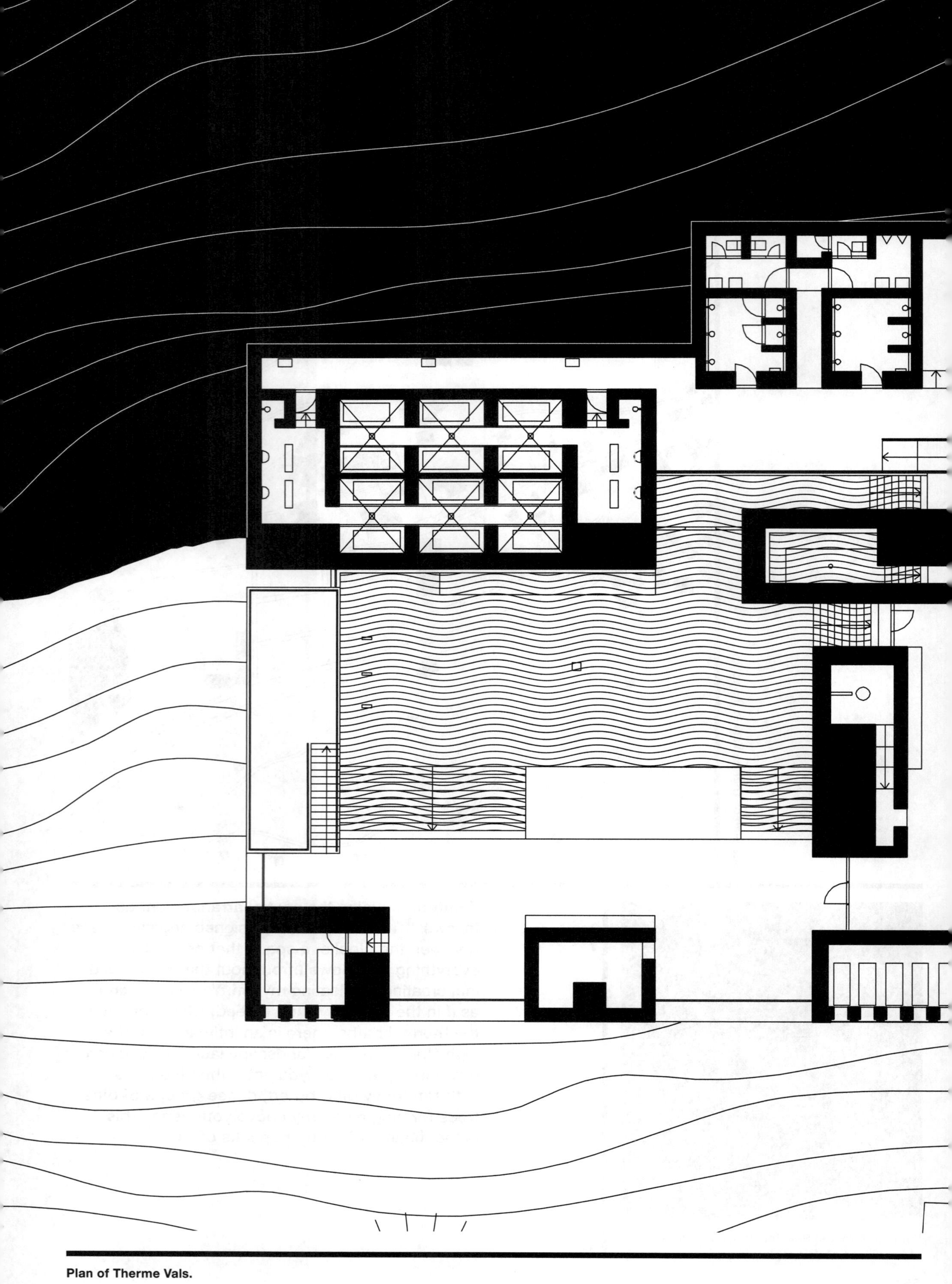

Plan of Therme Vals.

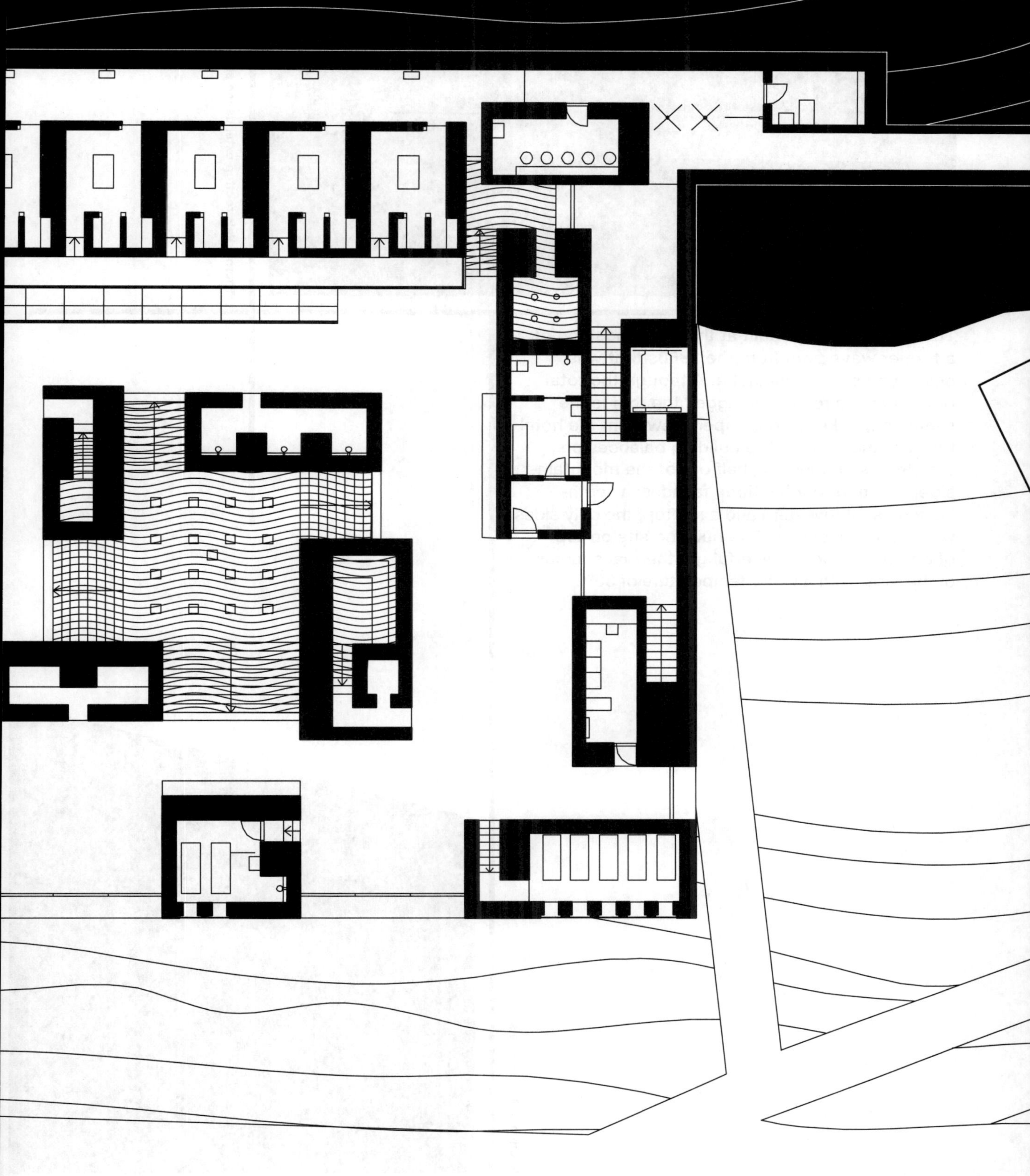

Therme Vals rooftop extends the slope outwards.

The thermal bath is built at the exact position of a former wave pool from the 1960s that was destroyed by an avalanche. Although the total programme is ten times bigger, the roof is the same height, keeping an open view from the hotel towards the village. The building balances on the steep slope, half in, half out of the mountainside, creating roughly three facades: a south-eastern, south-western and a rooftop, the only sides where the sun shines. The building sits on top of one of the most powerful geothermal sources of the Alps, with a water temperature of 30°C.

Section of Therme Vals.

Slender recesses in the roof let light into the centre of Therme Vals.

Connected by an underground tunnel to the hotel, one moves from sparsely lit space towards the light and impressive mountain views. It is almost a visual cleansing, next to a bodily one. As a whole, it seems that the building merely guides and mimics natural processes, creating an immersive experience that transcends the normal, basic relationship between people and buildings. It is not a service-providing object, protecting us from nature, but a revitalizing one, tweaking weatherly conditions, in sync with nature.

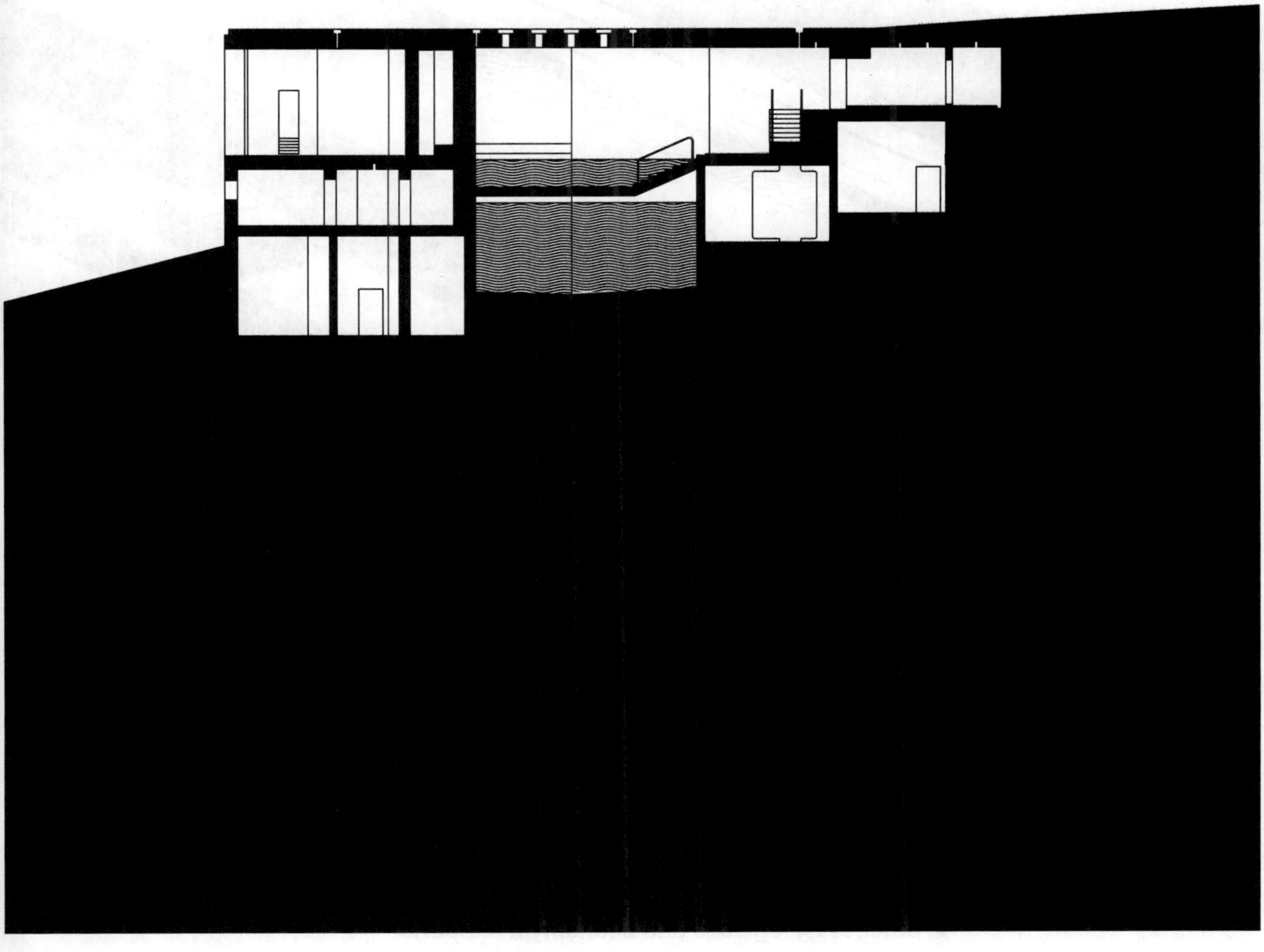

Borneo Housing
Amsterdam, Netherlands
SeARCH & Dick van Gameren
1999

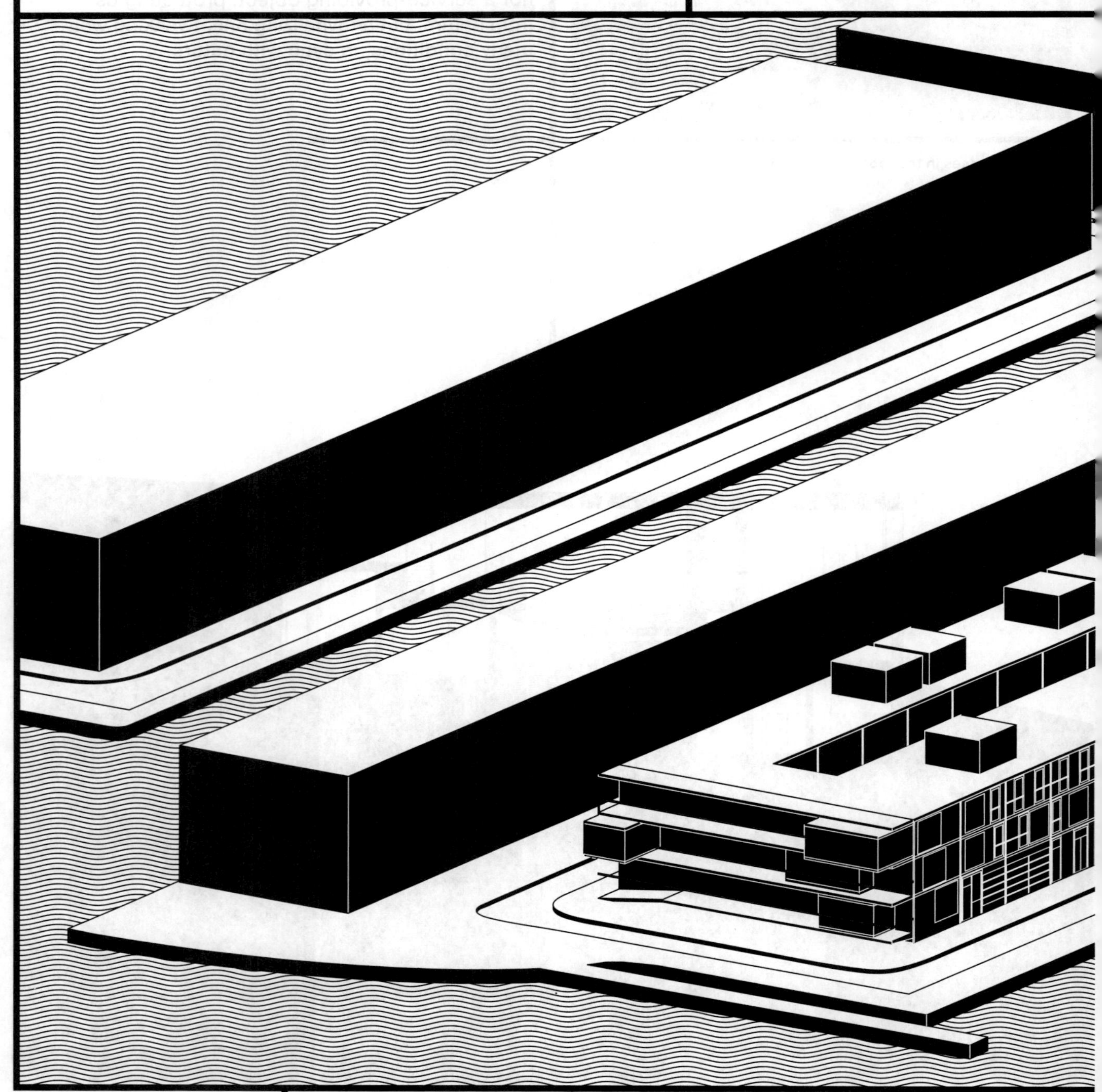

What if there were no landscape reference on site whatsoever? Industrial areas like the eastern docklands of Amsterdam are often artificial. Land is built on water and then filled with repetitive brick and subsequently steel plate warehouses. It is an act that pays homage to the manufacturing processes, logistics and economy it supports.

Likewise, the modern movement was self-referential. Buildings were icons of progress, improved comfort and economic growth. Industrial processes had far more influence over the result than artistic expression, and a tabula rasa mentality ruled. The mantra was: forget the past, build a future! The Rietveld Schröder House clearly shows it was all about an experimental building system and spatial consequences. It was, and is, provocative and somewhat alien, with no reference to the environment or the terraced houses it nudges up against.

Axonometry of Borneo Housing.

From left to right, Borneo, Sporenburg and KNSM island, 1980.

Rietveld Schröder House, Utrecht, Gerrit Rietveld, 1923–1924.

Row of 28 units with an alternative typology at the end.

Borneo Housing tries to mediate between these different worlds. It likes to catch a 'sense of place', using the typology of the superfluous buildings on-site and respecting the laws of the predominant cast-in-place tunnel structures of Dutch housing, an almost unbeatably cheap construction method imposed by the client.

Mathematically, this is taken to the limit, and as a result twenty-eight units are arranged in a line, leaving a little unbuilt piece at the end of the site. As only three-quarters of the standard concrete tunnel structure would fit here, it offered an opportunity to explore an alternative typology.

Concept photo with real Smart cars, 1997.

Site plan of Borneo Housing.

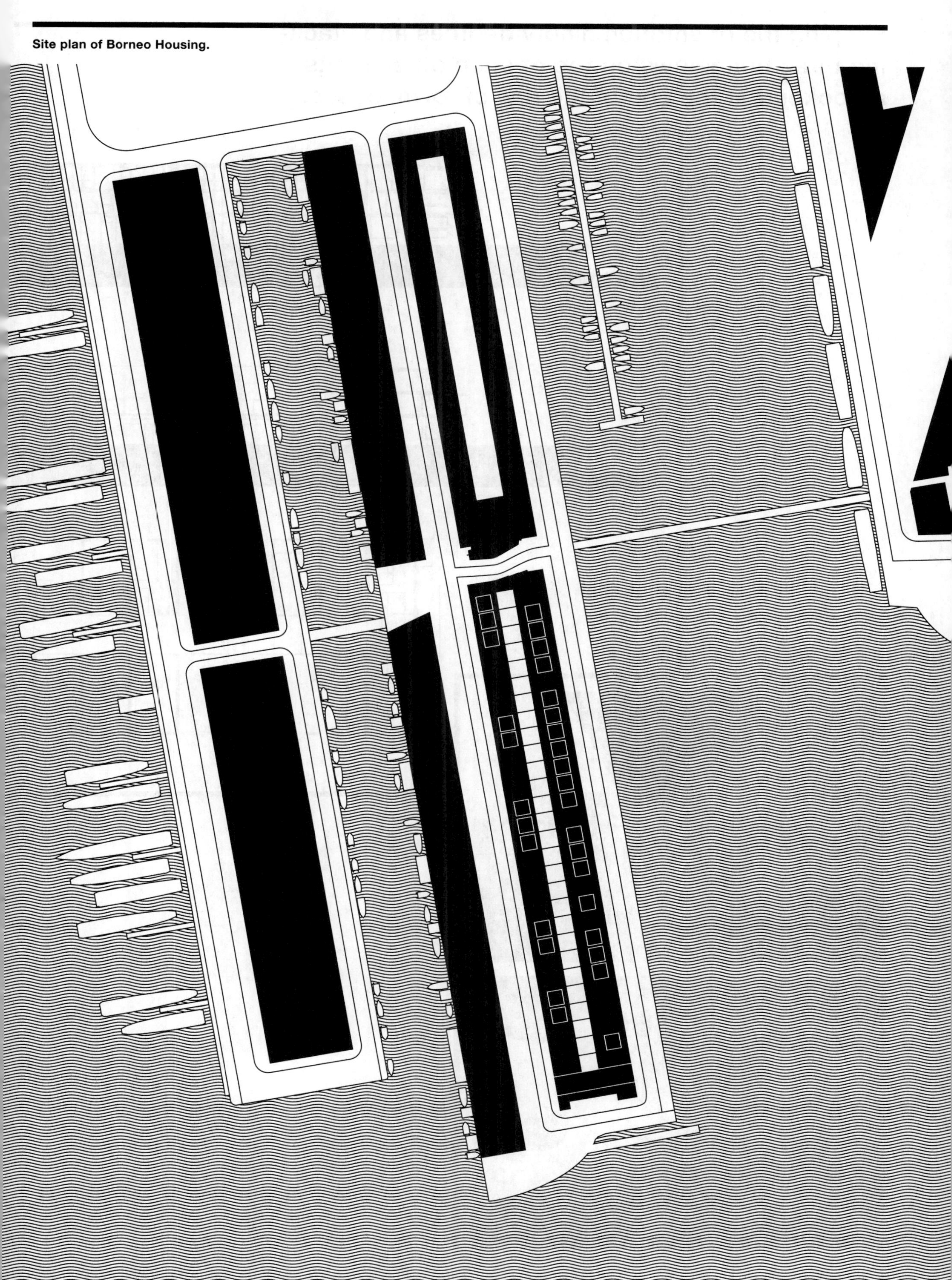

Flipping the orientation ninety degrees and stacking three bungalows on top of each other, it sits like a bookend at the end of the row of townhouses.

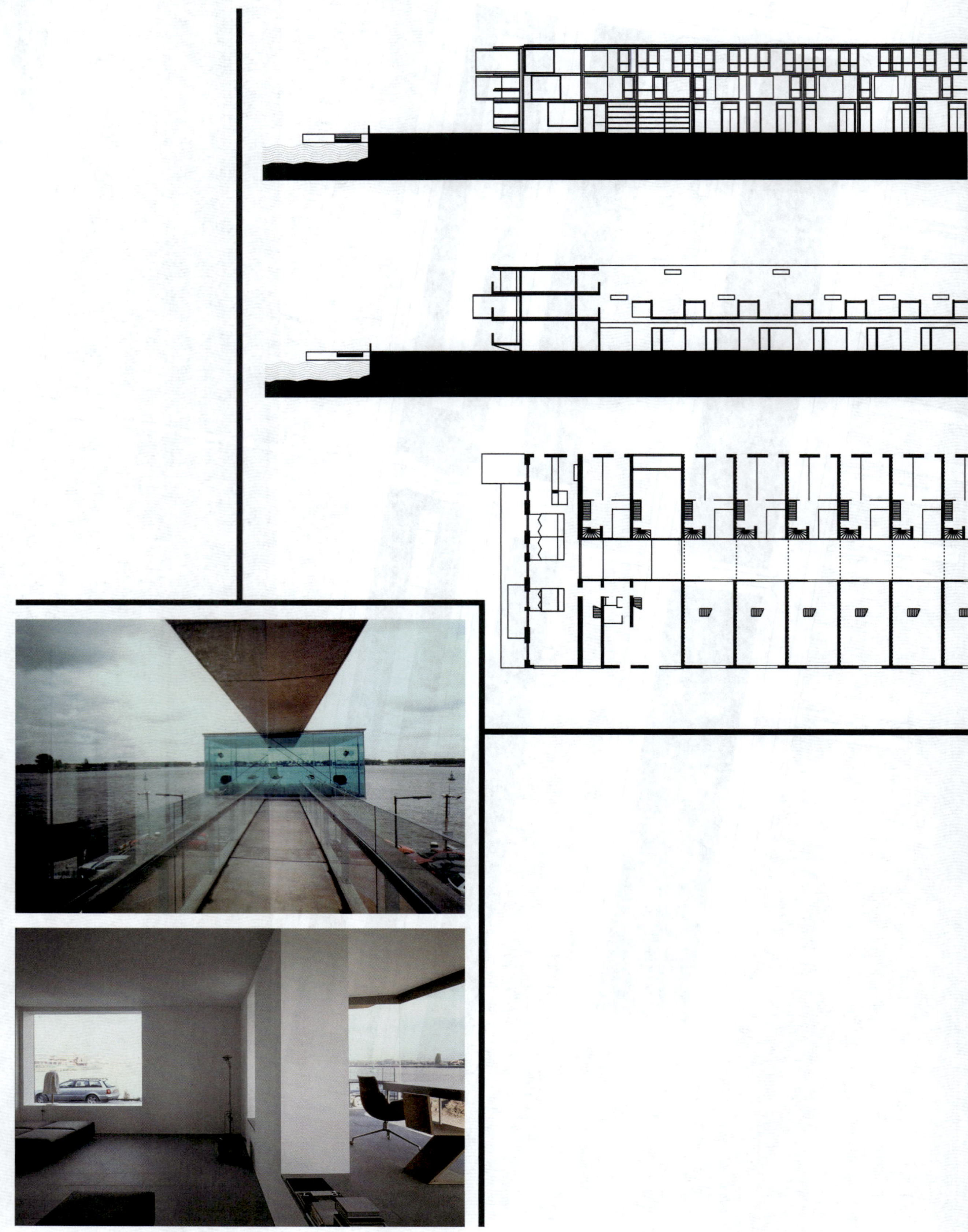

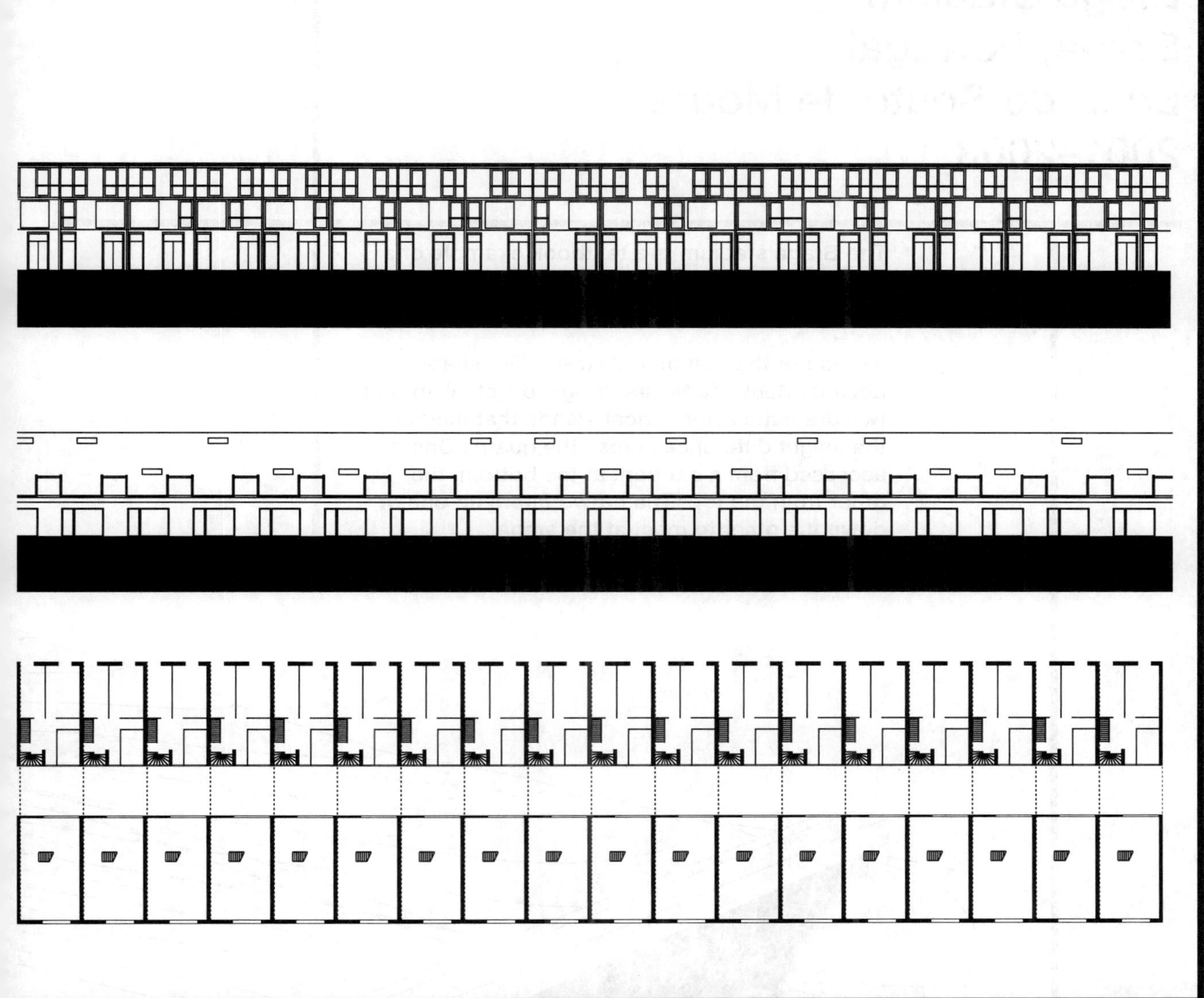

From top to bottom: elevation, long section and floor plan of Borneo Housing.

Instead of the small, often shadowy enclosed patio of the townhouse, the oversized concrete slab of the stacked bungalow functions as a balcony along the full facade, only interrupted occasionally by glazed rooms, which stick out like boxes in a high-rack warehouse. The long walls of the linear apartments create an enclosed feeling, in contrast to the glazed boxes and balconies, which look out towards the Amsterdam-Rhine Canal, one of the most navigated routes in Western Europe. The lowest balcony of the slightly elevated ground floor bends down to street level to create extra private parking, the ultimate luxury in Amsterdam.

Braga Stadium
Braga, Portugal
Eduardo Souto de Moura
2001–2003

The Braga stadium is a textbook example of a project that has made optimal use of a hilly terrain, in this case the abandoned Monte Castro quarry.

Instead of the common cake-tin-like shape, Eduardo Souto de Moura designed a stadium with two dramatic symmetrical stands that mediate the height difference across the quarry. One is accessed from a car park at the bottom, the other from the top. The crowd filters up one or down the other to meet at the arena.

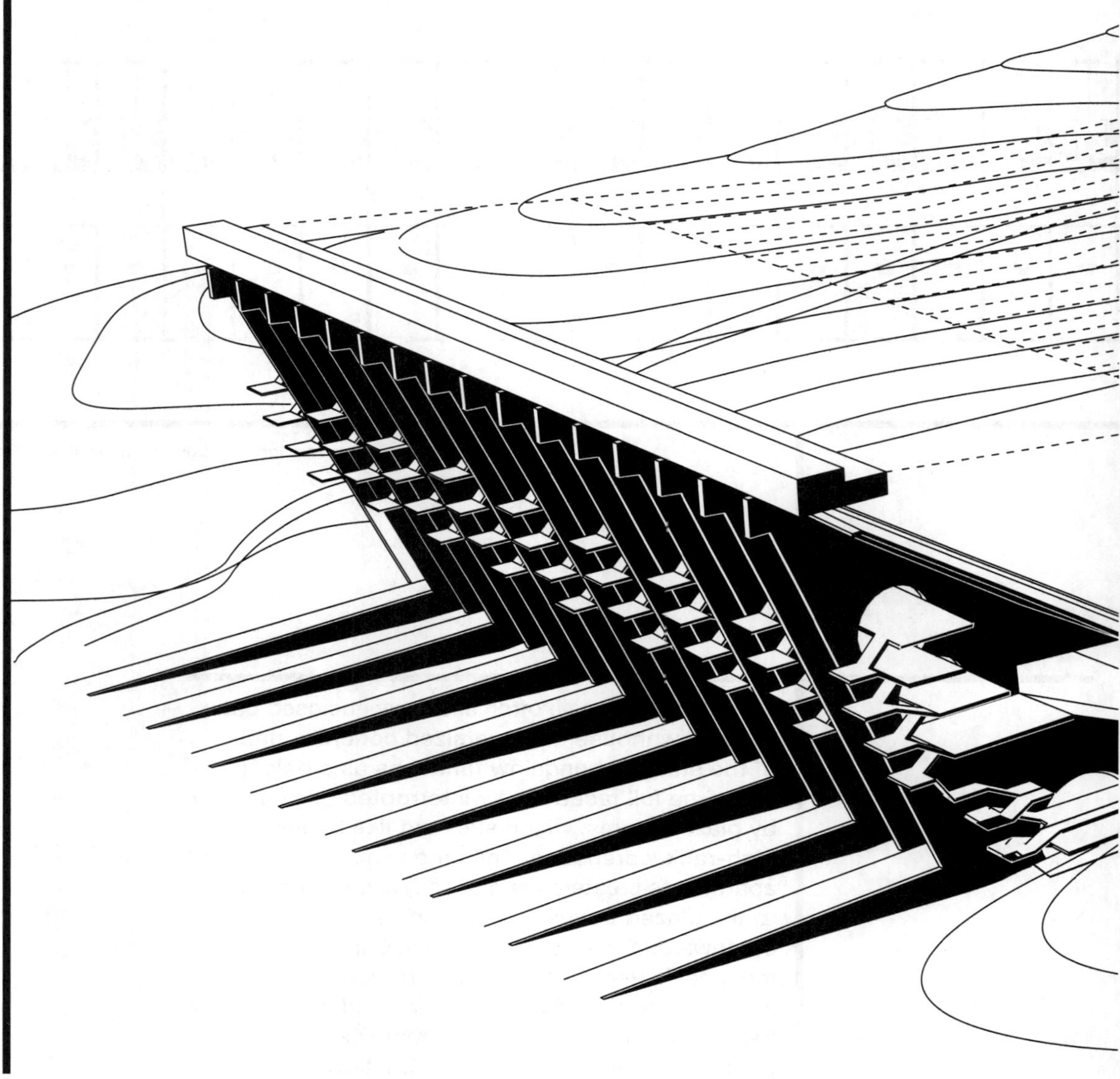

Sectional axonometry of Braga Stadium against the hill.

The two stands face off against each other alongside the pitch. One goalpost opens out towards the city and the other faces the mountainside of the old quarry. It is through this orientation and connection to the site that you realize that by constructing only two sides, Souto de Moura had in fact designed a third. In awarding Souto de Moura the Pritzker Prize, Barack Obama praised the empathic nature of this gesture, which allowed those who couldn't afford a ticket to watch the match from the hillside.[61]

View from the hillside.

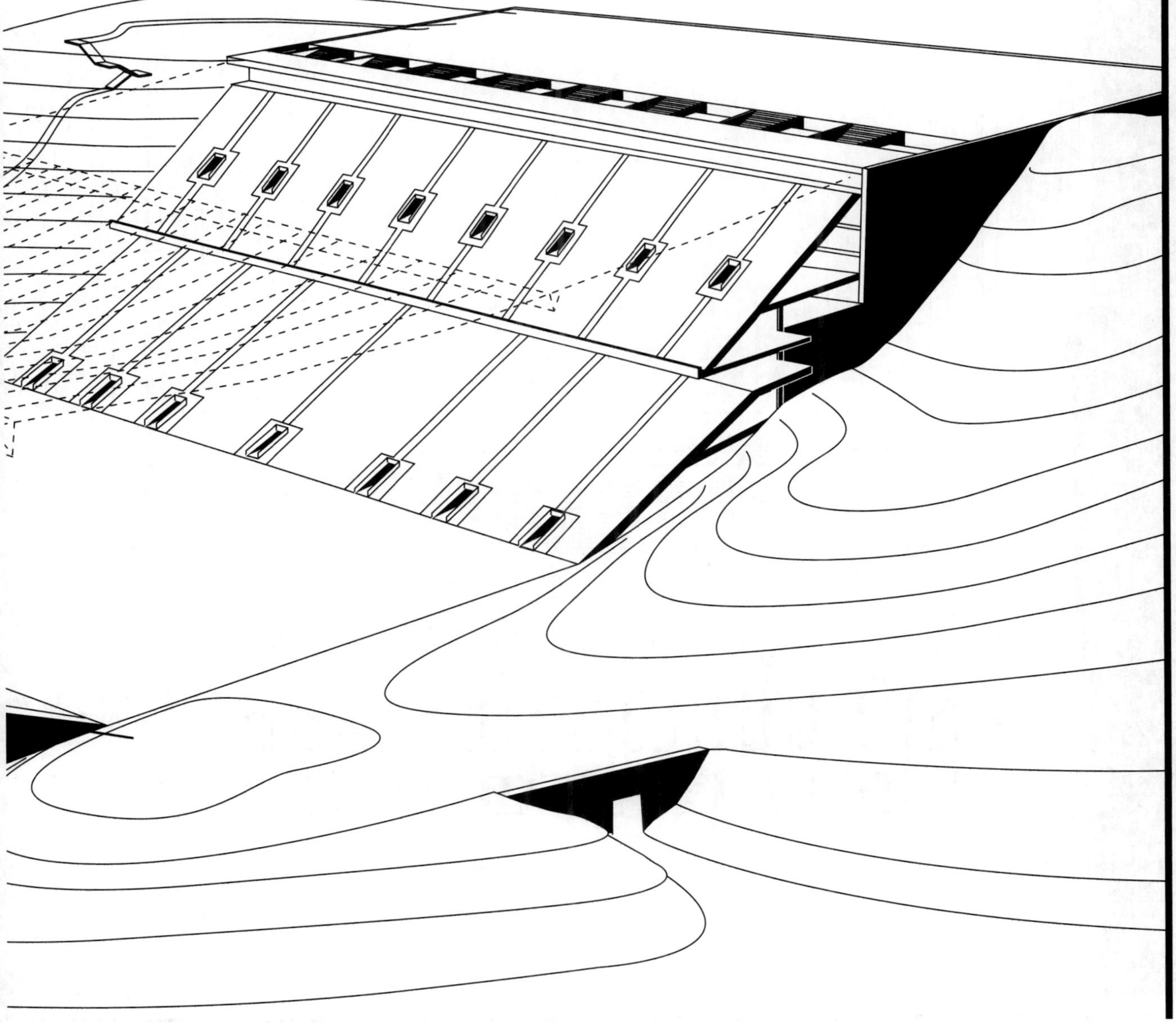

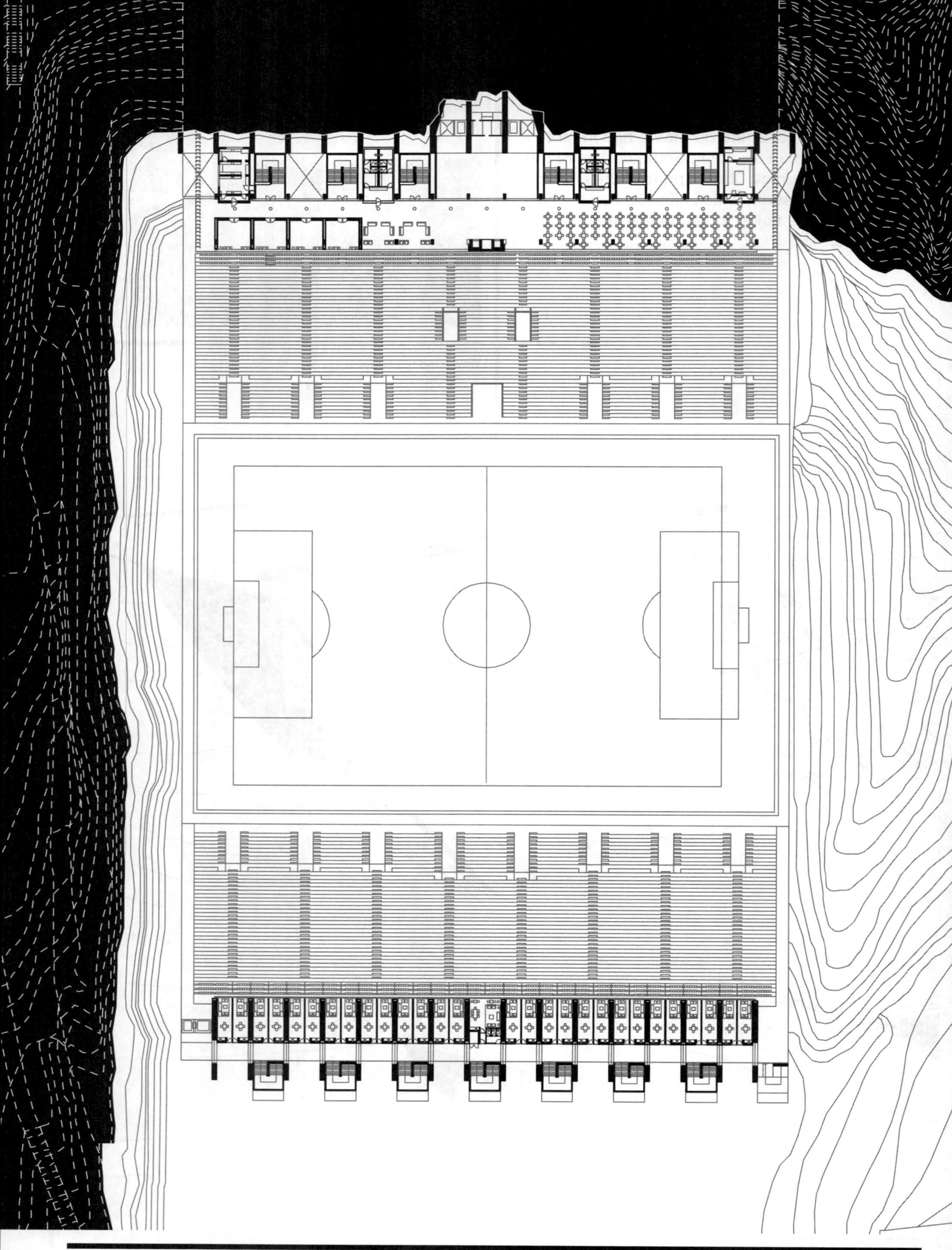

Plan of Braga Stadium.

The Q'eswachaka Bridge has been rebuilt continuously since the time of the Incas.

The Drawbridge by Giovanni Battista Piranesi, 1761.

Inspired by Incan rope bridges, cables stretch between the stands, supporting two much-needed sunshades and giving the canopy its iconic shape. The free-standing, slanted east stand consists of triangular-shaped trusses with huge circular holes. The repetition of these circular cavities creates a tubular space with amazing views over the city of Braga. The opposite western stand offers a completely different spatial experience. A large cavernous space under the stand is exposed to the rugged rock bed, and the galleries and stairs create a Piranesian experience.

To avoid building a costly waterproof screen between hill and stadium, it is set back from the hill and two gigantic rain pipes collect all the water from the enormous sunshades. Water is channelled under the basement to become a stream in an adjacent park. Here, a service road digs into the mountain, providing access to a ground floor of services, circulation and parking, which runs beneath the pitch.

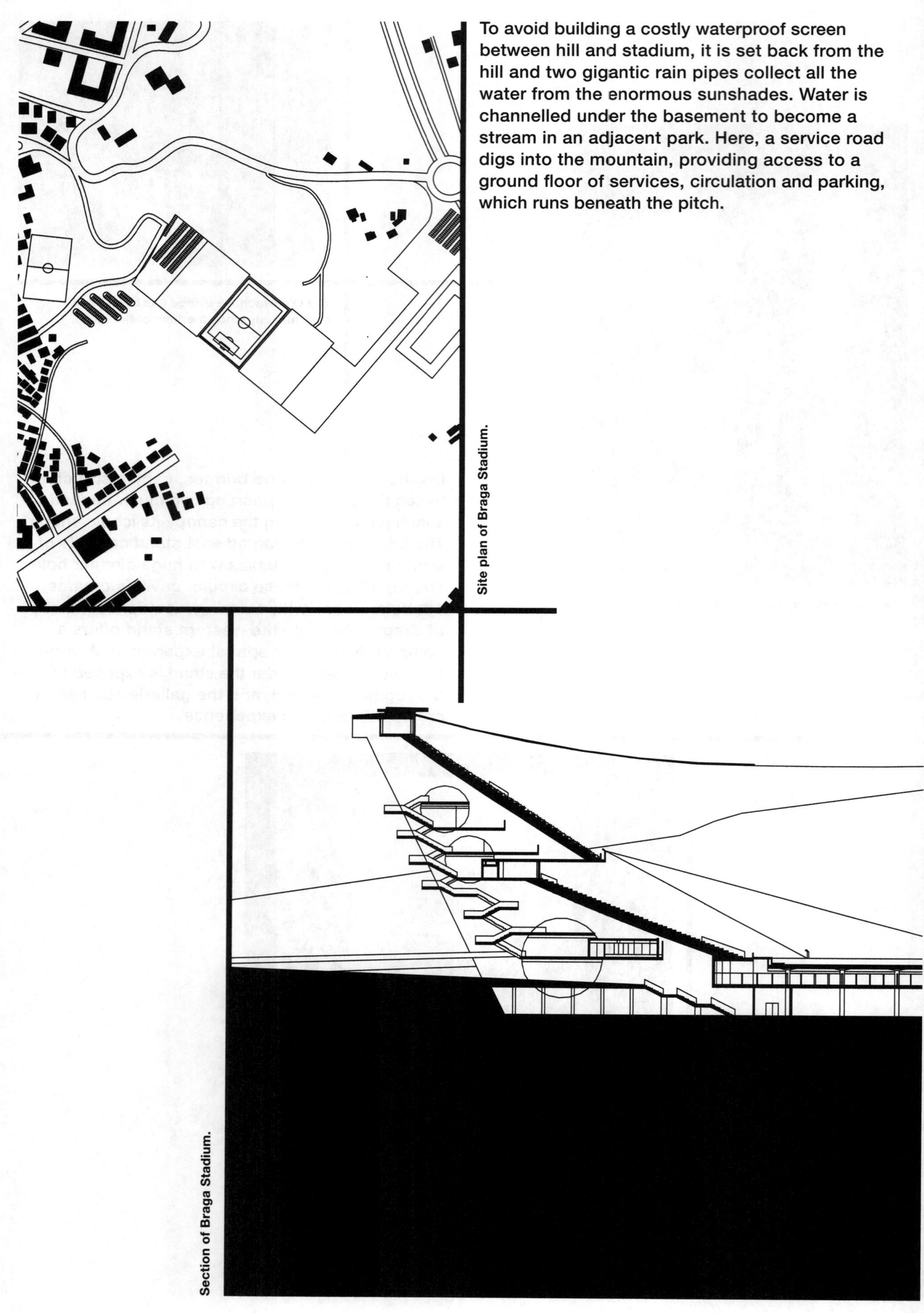

Site plan of Braga Stadium.

Section of Braga Stadium.

This design optimizes its location, using minimal resources for maximum impact. It literally grinds the rock down and pours itself into position.

It is like a giant tree with an invisible root system and overhanging branches. Its effortless natural position on site obscures the enormous forces and torque it handles and the incredible amount of water that runs through its branches and leaves.

Friendship Centre
Gaibandha, Bangladesh
URBANA
2011

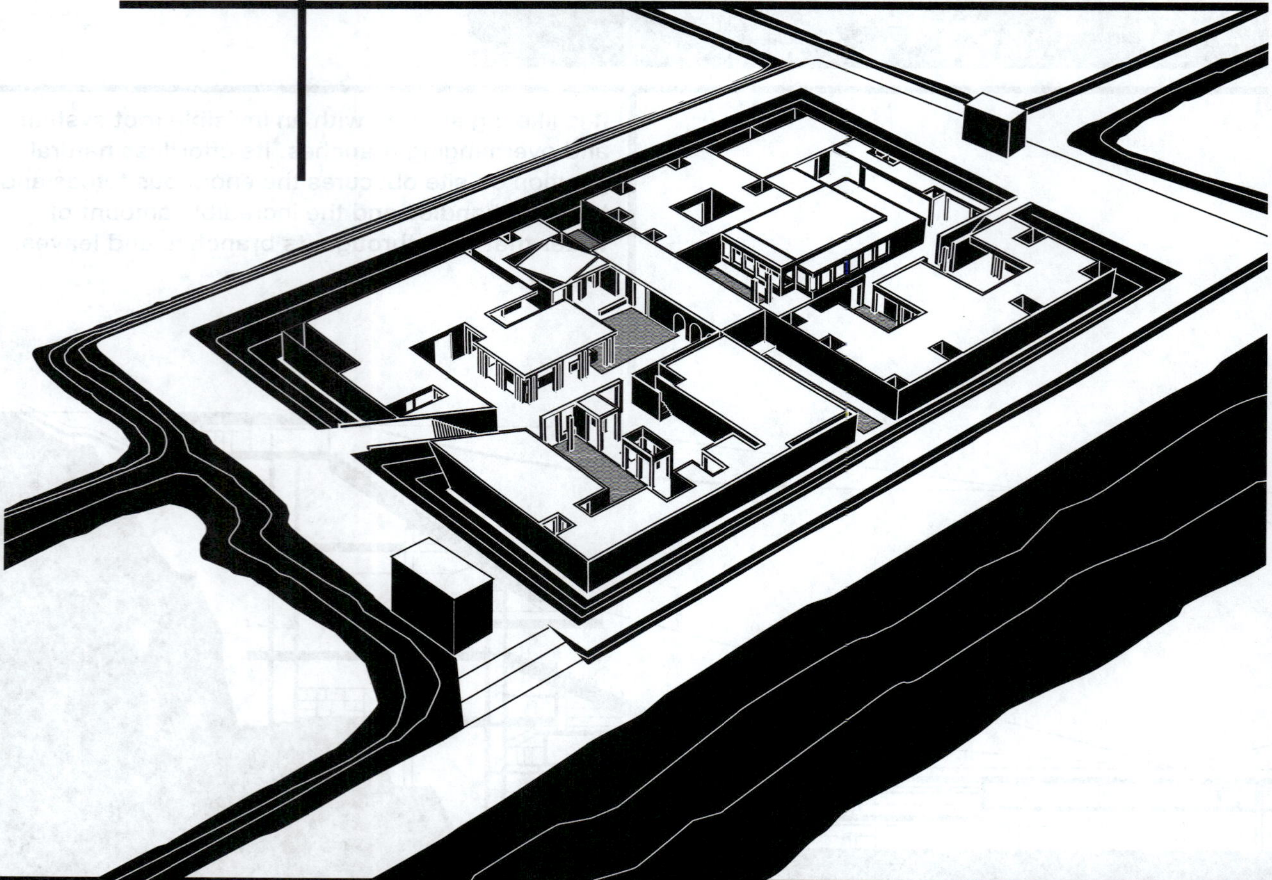

Axonometry of Friendship Centre.

The Friendship Centre by Kashef Mahboob Chowdhury and his practice URBANA is a highly efficient example of the manipulation of levels. Buildings in the low-lying area of Gaibandha can only be secured from flooding when built on stilts. Since the area is also prone to earthquakes, engineering this is fairly expensive, so they made a calculated decision to dig the project another metre down and use the excess earth to build a dike around the centre.

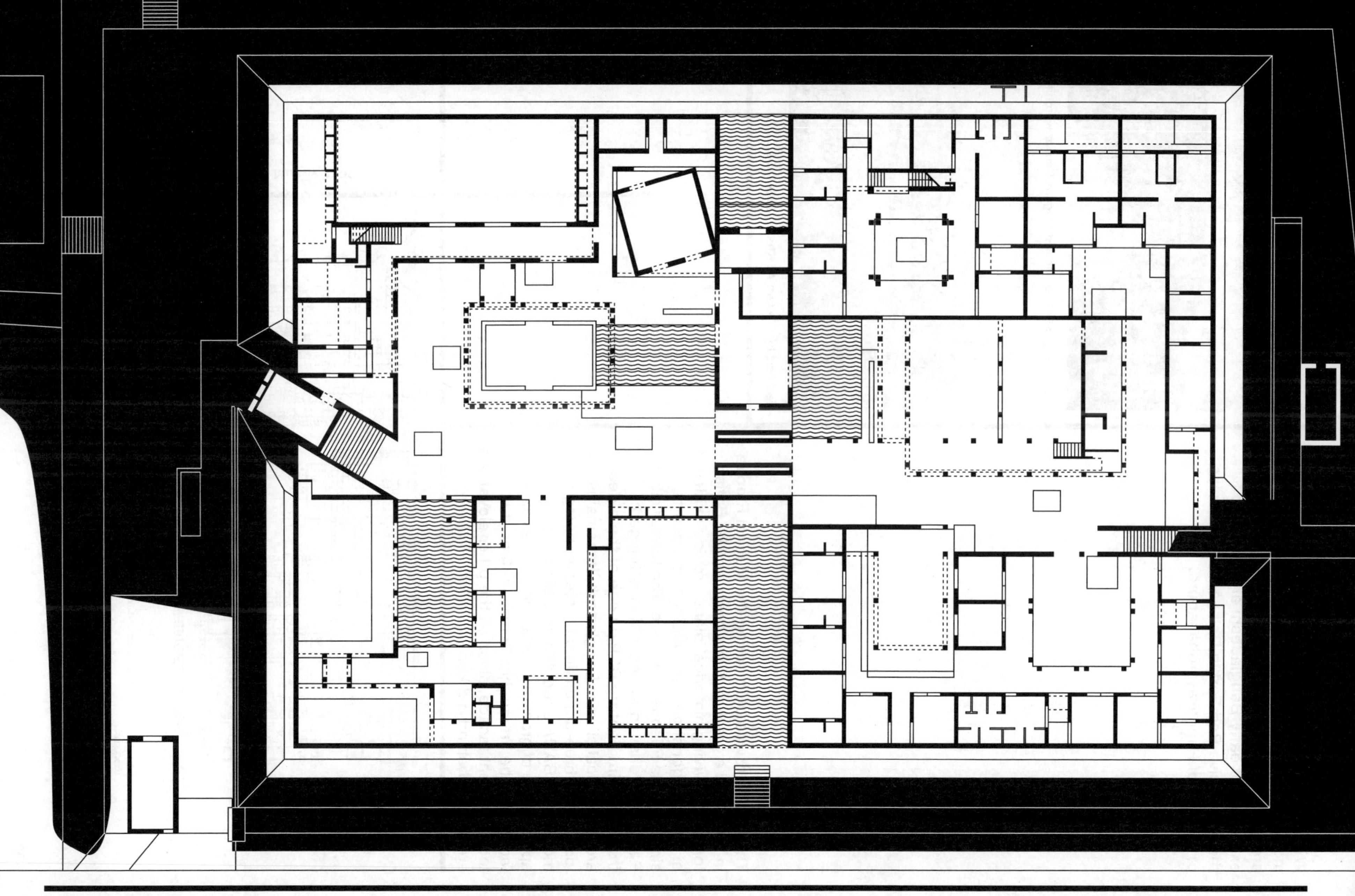

Plan of Friendship Centre.

Within this little polder a dense grid of small buildings is arranged and courtyards and ponds are cut out. It takes its place between two famous examples of early Bangladeshi architecture: the impressive Red Fort in Delhi and the remains of the city of Paundravardhanapura.

Archaeological site of Mahasthangarh, Paundravardhanapura, 300 BCE.

Red Fort by Ghulam Ali Khan, 1852–1854.

The Red Fort was built during the Mughal Empire in 1639, and a great part was destroyed by British forces. Surviving historical plans provide evidence of an orthogonal grid of buildings and courts, similar to the Friendship Centre. The former city of Paundravardhanapura, now Mahasthangarh, from the third century BCE, is one of the oldest archaeological sites in Bangladesh. Its remains look like a three-dimensional raster mapping of a mound. URBANA used this very distinctive appearance of grass-topped brick squares as a fifth facade for the Friendship Centre. In fact, it is the prominent facade, since all the other elevations are hidden behind a dike.

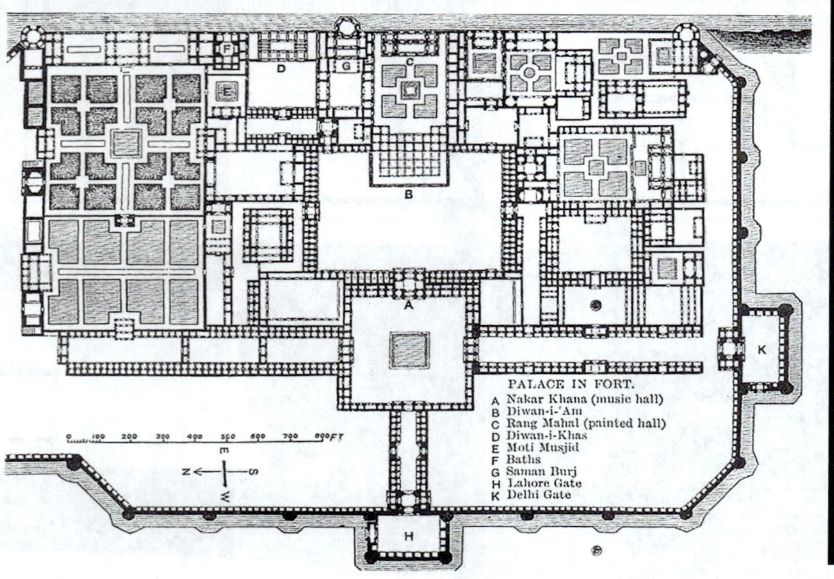

Plan of the Red Fort in Delhi by John Murray, 1901.

The ponds collect rainwater during the monsoon, and excess water is pumped to an excavated pond nearby, also used as a fishery. During summer, the ponds and earthen roofs keep the classrooms and dormitories cool. This safe haven of waterproofness creates an educational Noah's Ark, with the main road as a connecting pier during flooding. Standing on the grass roof, open to the sky, feels like being on deck at sea or in a landscape, a strong concept underlined by its restrained architectural appearance.

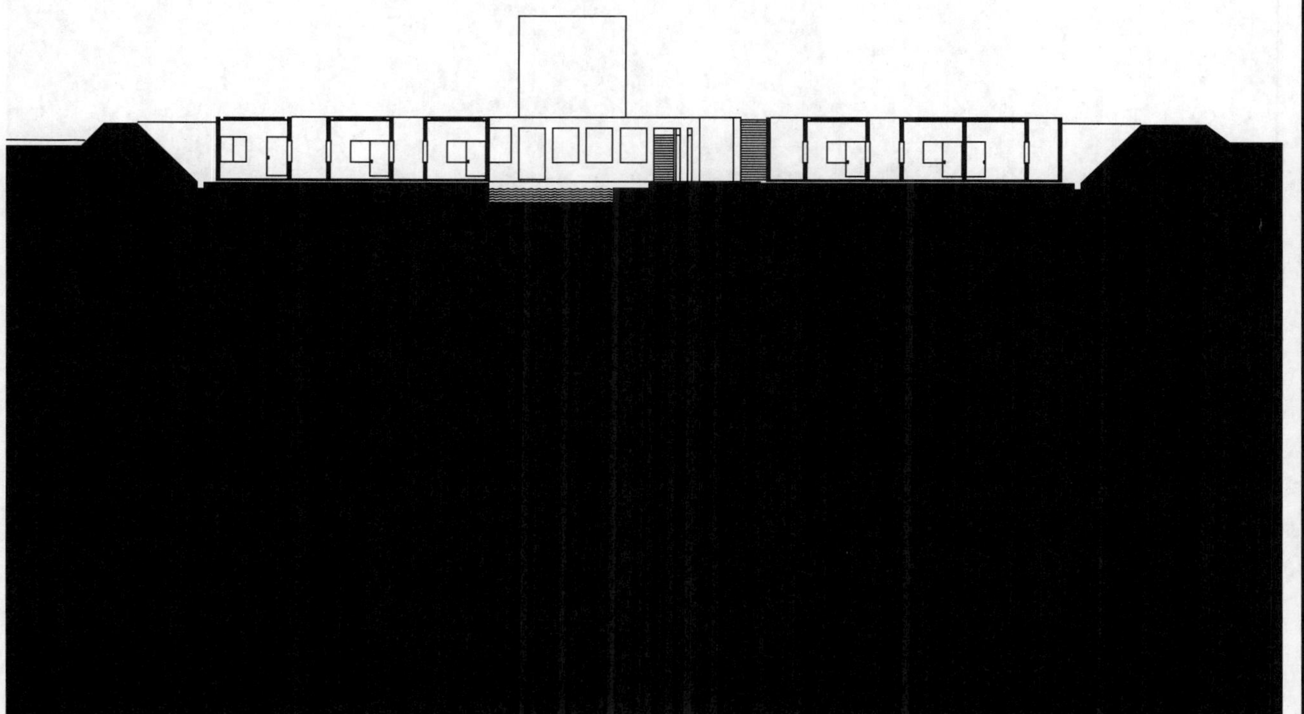

Section of Friendship Centre.

Because of its liberating rather than hindering effect, this reassuring idea while studying at the centre cannot be underestimated.

Chalet Anzère
Anzère, Switzerland
SeARCH
2013–2015

The traditional chalet, originating from *chahtelèt*, meaning 'shepherd's hut', consists of a solid wooden house with shutters and gable roof, resting on a stone foundation. Unfortunately, the chalet has gradually ballooned into a 'multi-gabled' pastiche, as luxury ski-chalets for the rich or into mega proportions in an effort to support the maximum number of apartments and capture the affordable tourism market. Yet the most beautiful examples are still the historic farmhouses found high up in the Swiss Alps, where several families live separately under a single roof in the summertime.

Hotel Zodiaque, a mega-chalet in Anzère.

Multi-gabled chalet, Anzère.

Chalet dissolved to show interaction of levels.

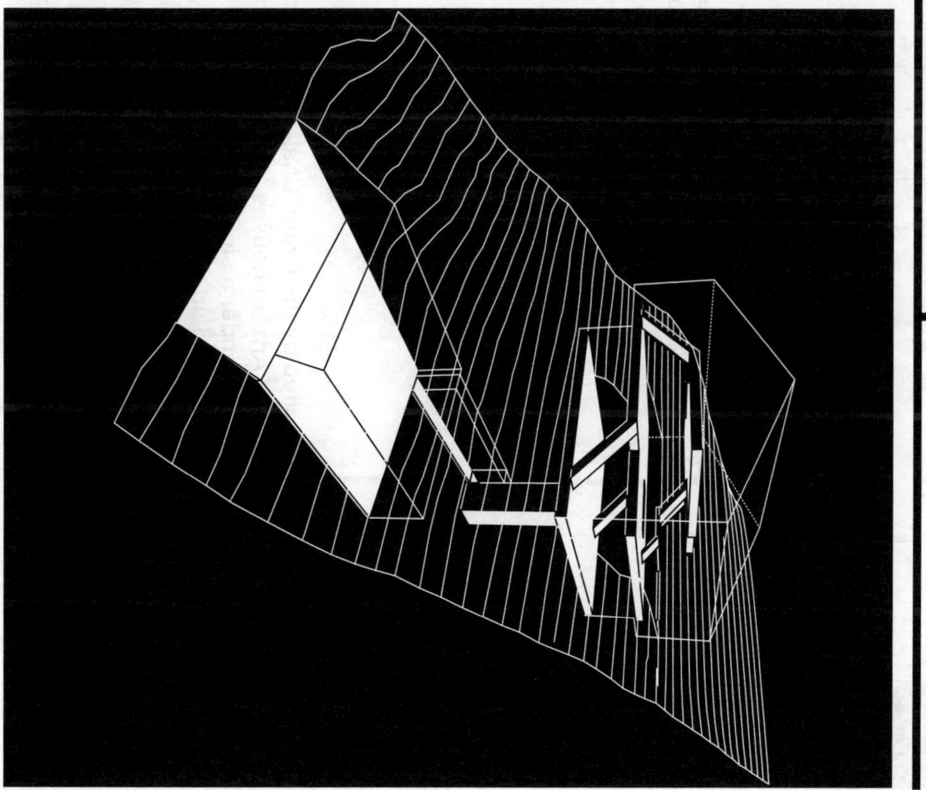

Axonometry of Chalet Anzère.

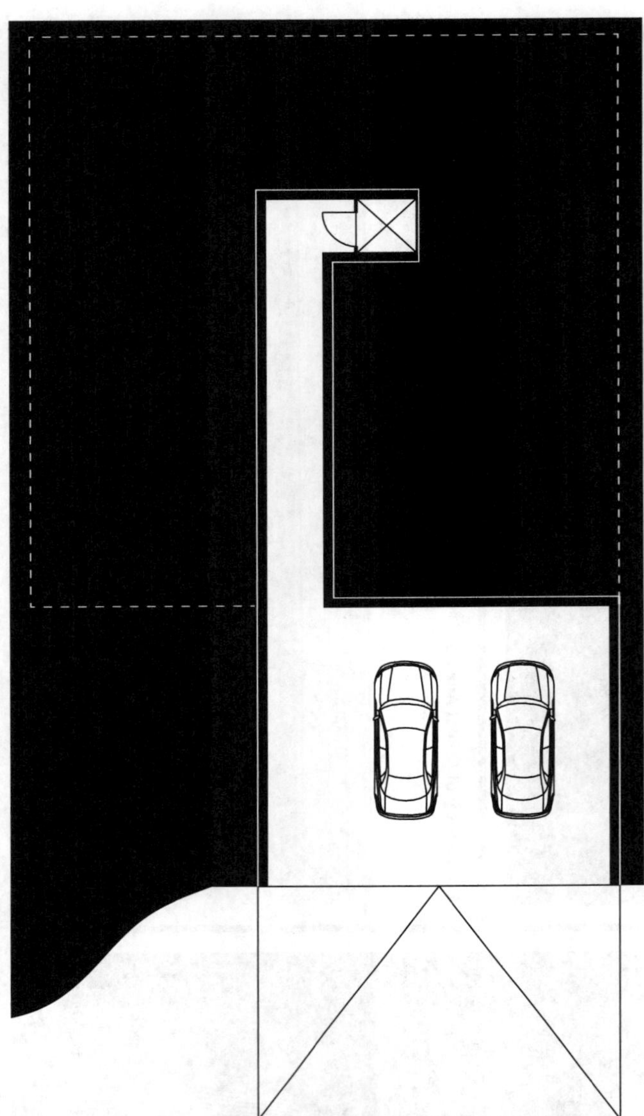

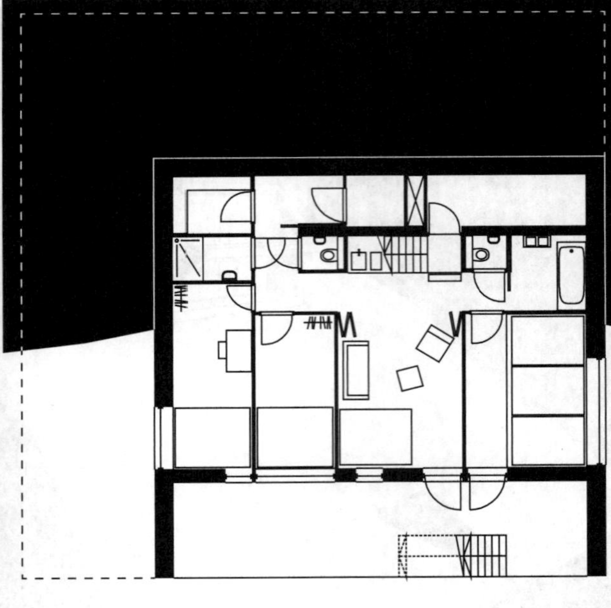

Plan of level -1.

Plan of level 0.

Inspired by the Grand Chalet Balthus in Rossinière, Chalet Anzère houses the many desires of its master under a single roof. Instead of building the cluttered plan offered in the land sale, a more compact and cohesive design was tailored to the piano-playing, race-car-driving entrepreneurial client. Like the Grand Chalet Balthus, the design honours the strong, clear volume of the traditional chalet and exaggerates and abstracts the characteristic overhanging roof.

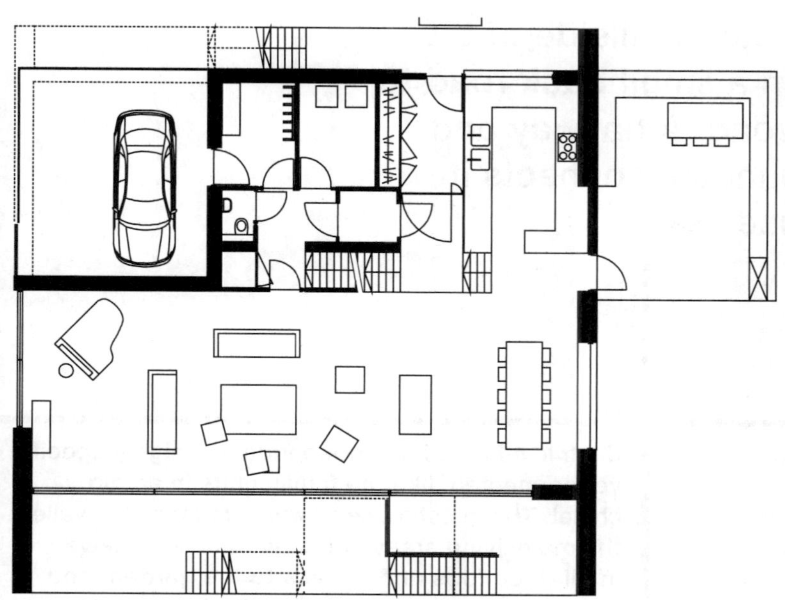

Plan of level 1.

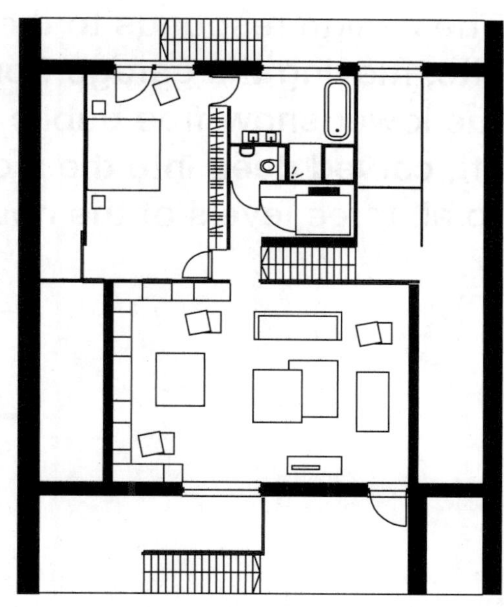

Plan of level 2.

Grand Chalet Balthus, Rossinière, 1752–1756.

The design responds to the steep hillside of the site, moving the garage from a small back road to the lower snow-free public road. A hallway and lift, carved deep into the mountain, connects it to all three levels of the house.

Each level functions independently, highly specific yet connected, like the family units in an old chalet. The guesthouse downstairs faces the valley, the main living areas in the middle have views in all directions and access to the garden, and a secluded apartment in the attic faces north and south. The garage supports the racing hobby and the lofty living room has impeccable acoustics for the Concert Grand Imperial Bösendorfer. All floors have access to sun-drenched terraces, connected by stairs and with a phenomenal view over the Dent Blanche Massif with over 4000 peaks, including the Matterhorn, Dent Blanche, Dufourspitze and Weisshorn.

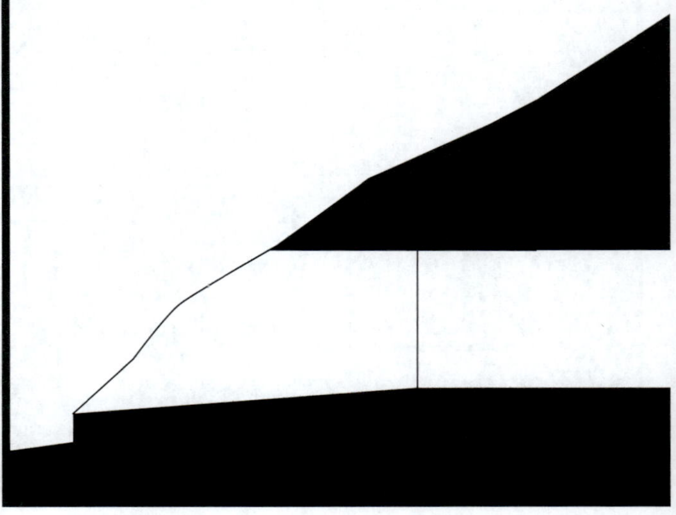

Section of Chalet Anzère.

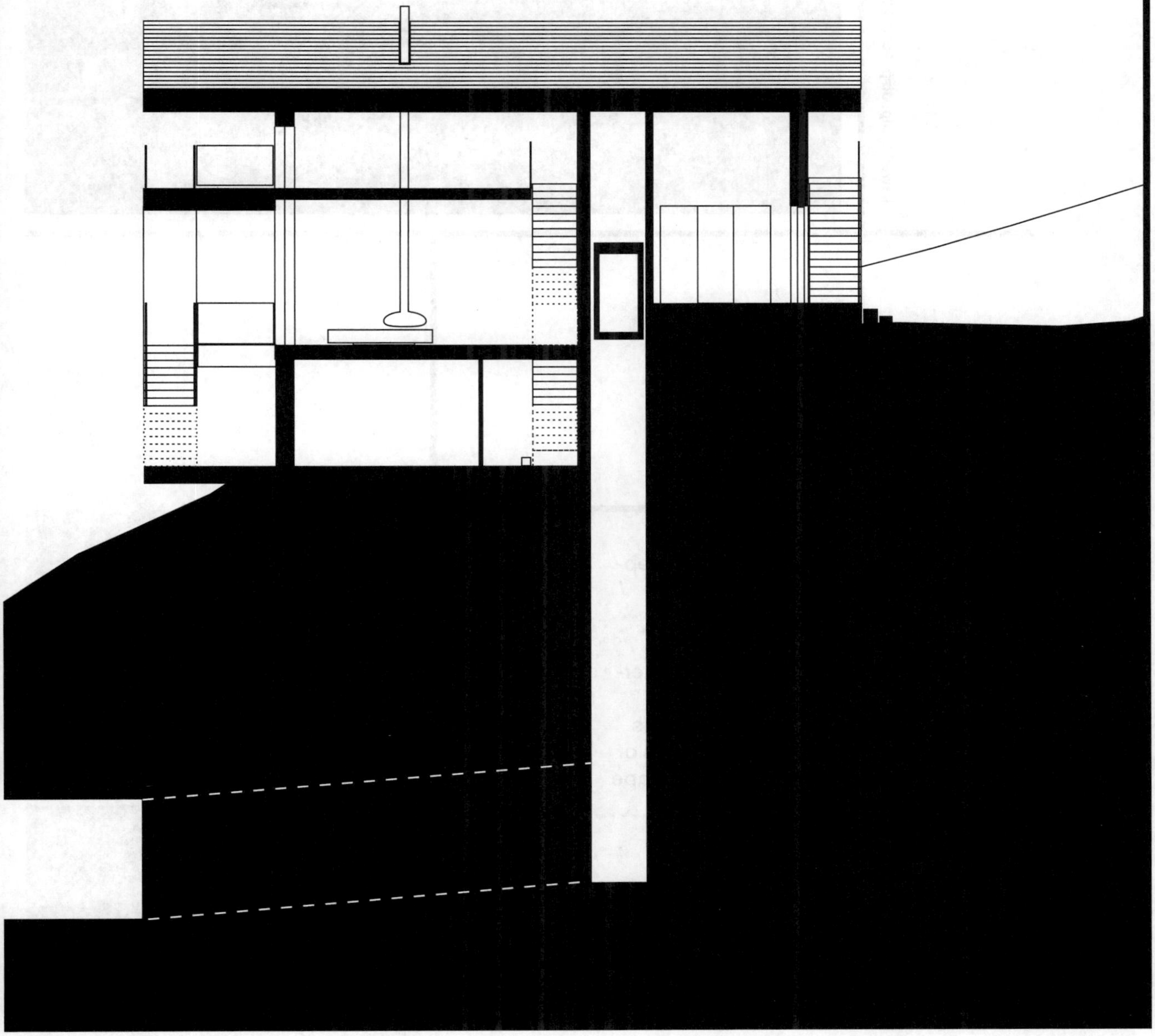

Skewed Stolp
Jisp, Netherlands
SeARCH
2013–2016

Skewed Stolp, Jisp, 2013–2016.

The curious ground level of the Skewed Stolp can be explained by the 150 centimetres that separate Ludwig Mies van der Rohe's Farnsworth House and Phillip Johnson's Glass House.

These iconic houses are often seen as the fraternal twins of modernism. But the genius of their genesis, and the element that sets them apart, is their base. These houses represent two schools of thought, two pathways of how to treat landscape within the modernist canon.

Farnsworth House, Mies van der Rohe, 1945–1951.

Glass House, Philip Johnson, 1948–1949.

Mies van der Rohe designed a house for Edith Farnsworth just as his work was being shown at the Museum of Modern Art. The Farnsworth House is an extremely refined architectural shelter with as few elements as possible and minimal boundaries between inside and outside. Mies chose an unusual spot for the house, not on the higher grounds of the estate but close to the Fox River, one prone to flooding. He lifted the floor 150 centimetres above the lawn, at that time just above the highest flood level. A terrace freely floats between lawn and house. It was a deliberate act to intertwine with the domain of nature.[62]

With heavier rainfall and overdevelopment along the riverbank, the frequency and intensity of flooding at the Farnsworth House has increased.

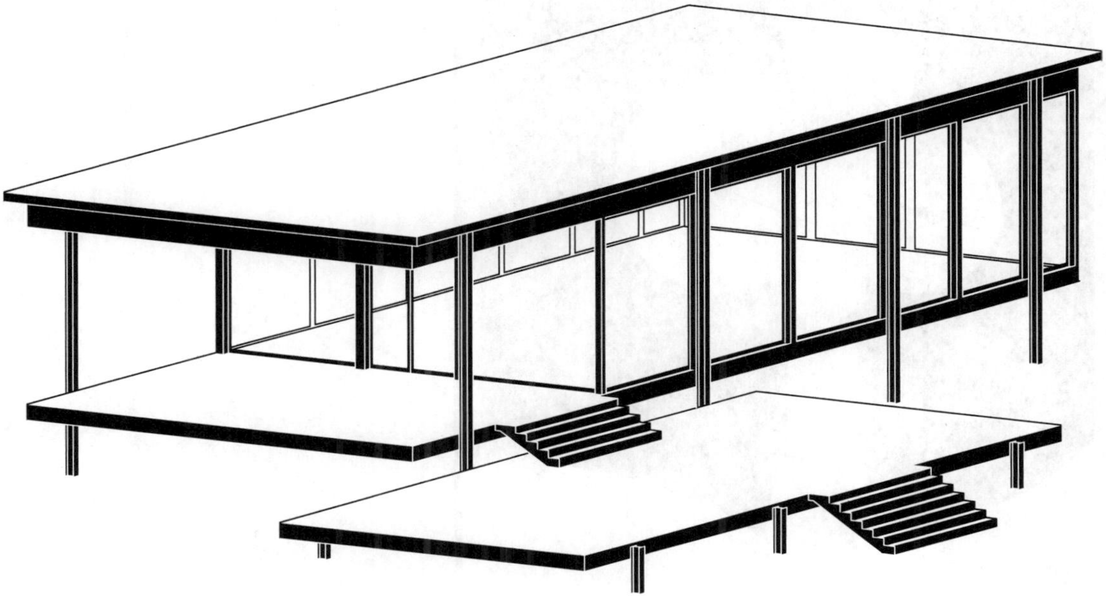

Axonometry of Farnsworth House.

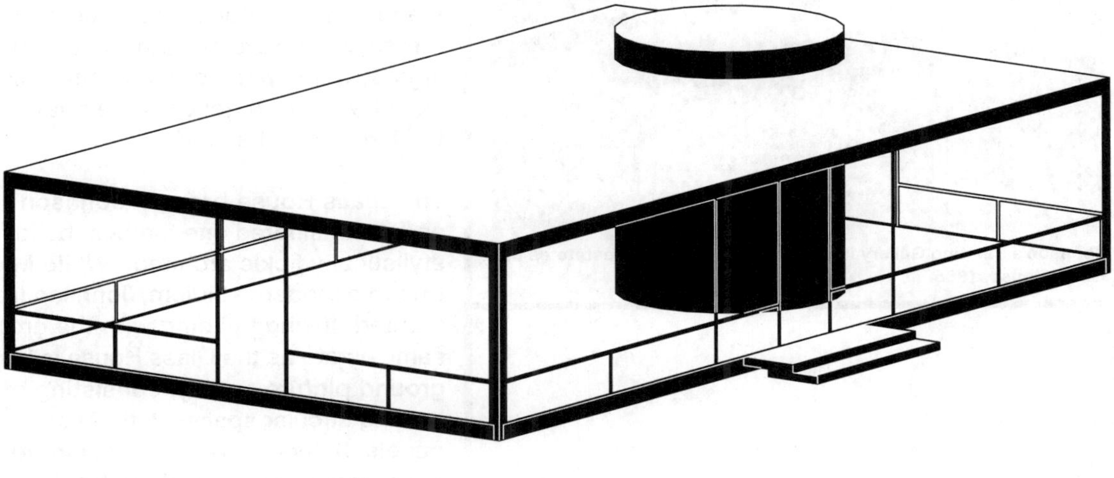

Axonometry of Glass House.

Philip Johnson was clearly impressed, describing the Farnsworth House as an act of 'safe danger', tempting natural forces.[63] Shortly after curating Mies's exhibition, Johnson designed and built an unabashed copy of the Farnsworth House. Johnson flattened Mies's idea and put the house directly on the grass, leaving out the highly orchestrated sequence from inside to outside. The Glass House was crude but effective, snuck in and built while Mies awaited funding to realize his design.

The Glass House was part of the larger commercialization of modern architecture.[64] Stripped of articulation, with simple detailing, the structure hangs nature as 'very expensive wallpaper'.[65] But is the Farnsworth House more convincing than this Machiavellian replica?

Johnson's Painting Gallery is tucked within the same estate as the Glass House, 1965.

While the Glass House's herringbone brick floor sits flush with the earth, the Farnsworth House stands on its tiptoes, detached and floating. Although both are separated from their surroundings by a thin pane of glass, their distance from the ground governs the relationship with the landscape beyond.

The Glass House brought Johnson recognition and is considered one the best buildings of this stylistically fickle architect. While Mies remained true to a modernist idiom, Johnson freely experimented, fusing building with the ground. On the same estate as the Glass House is his underground picture gallery, consisting of three intersecting circular spaces with revolving carpeted panels. It seems Johnson was more interested in experimenting with architectural objects than their relationship with the landscape.

The Dutch have a unique understanding of 'safe danger'. A thousand years ago, a significant part of Holland was land, a little swampy under foot, but land. But with sea-level rise, peat extraction and tidal erosion, land sunk a drastic three to four metres, to be claimed by the Zuiderzee. So the Dutch pinched it back, and the tug of war between wet and dry continues.

The Skewed Stolp lies on a piece of this subsided peat ground in the relatively shallow Wormer, Jisp and Neck Polder. A stable of the old farmhouse, or *Stolp*, sat at the level of the grassland, with the living quarters more than half a metre higher, raising the question: at what level should the extension be?

Historical map of the tidal environment of the Zuiderzee region, Christiaan Sgroten, 1573.

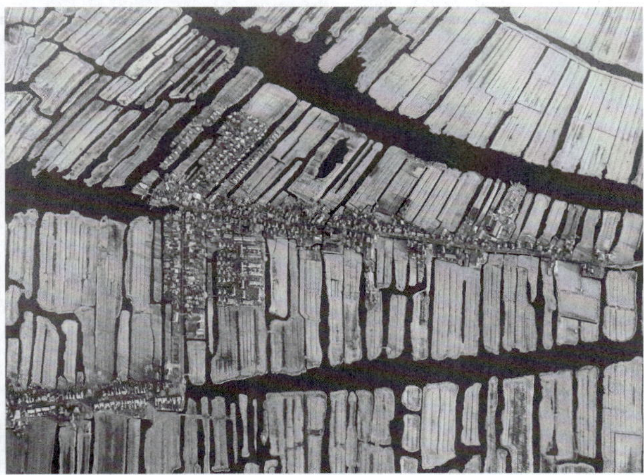

Skewed Stolp within the polder.

Should it follow Johnson and create a seamless connection with the surrounding landscape? Or should it sit proud like Mies, invigorating the stunning polder panorama?

The solution was right under our feet. When jumping up and down on the peat land surrounding the house, we felt the land go up and down and ripple like water.

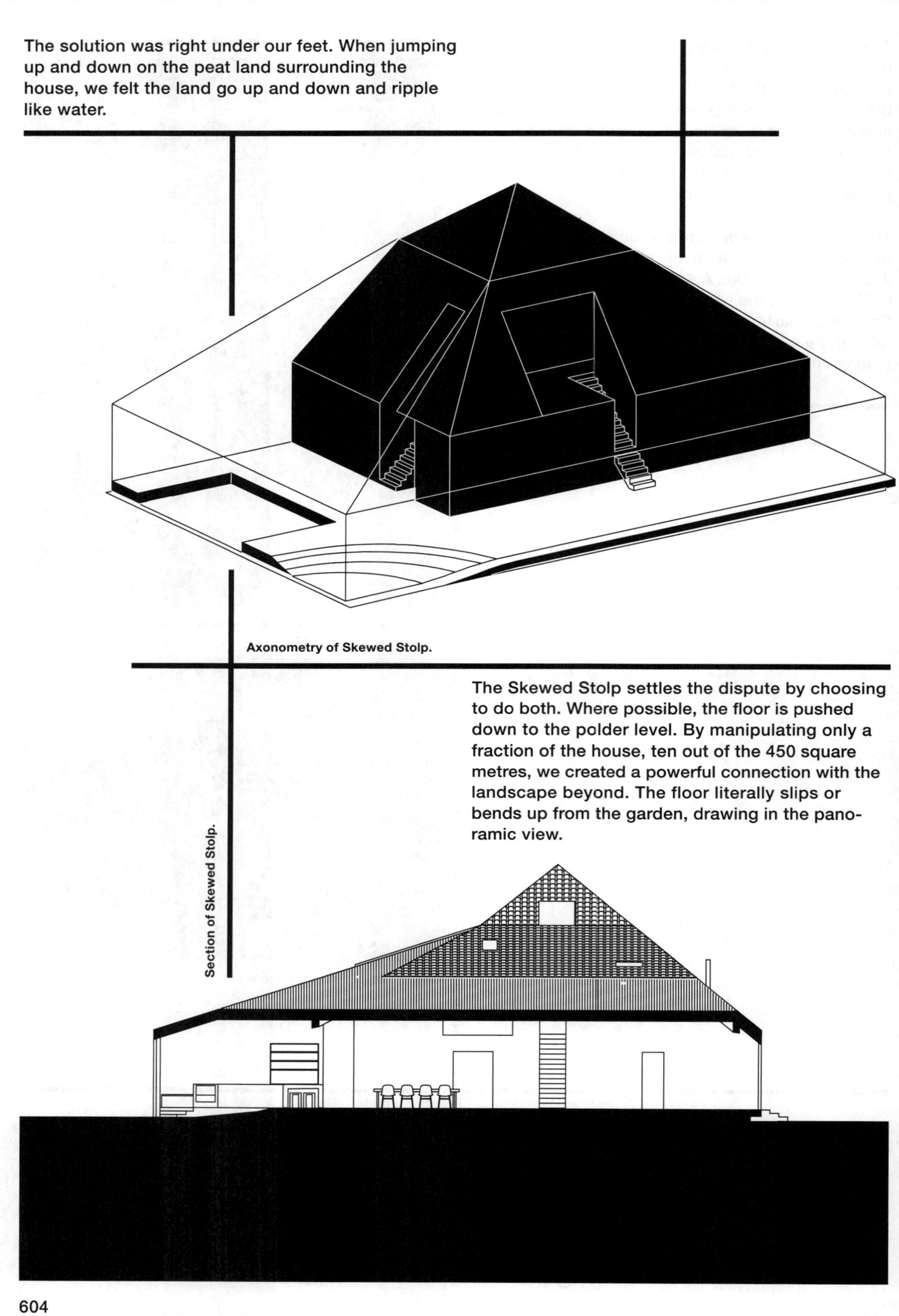

Axonometry of Skewed Stolp.

The Skewed Stolp settles the dispute by choosing to do both. Where possible, the floor is pushed down to the polder level. By manipulating only a fraction of the house, ten out of the 450 square metres, we created a powerful connection with the landscape beyond. The floor literally slips or bends up from the garden, drawing in the panoramic view.

Section of Skewed Stolp.

The next question was how to extend the clear, robust shape of the traditional Stolp, often mutilated by the tacking on of modern extensions. On two sides an extension creates a zone five to seven metres wide, as if glued to the outside facade of the old Stolp. This is where the new living room, kitchen, studio and bedroom are located.

Ground floor plan showing the slab reaching the garden level.

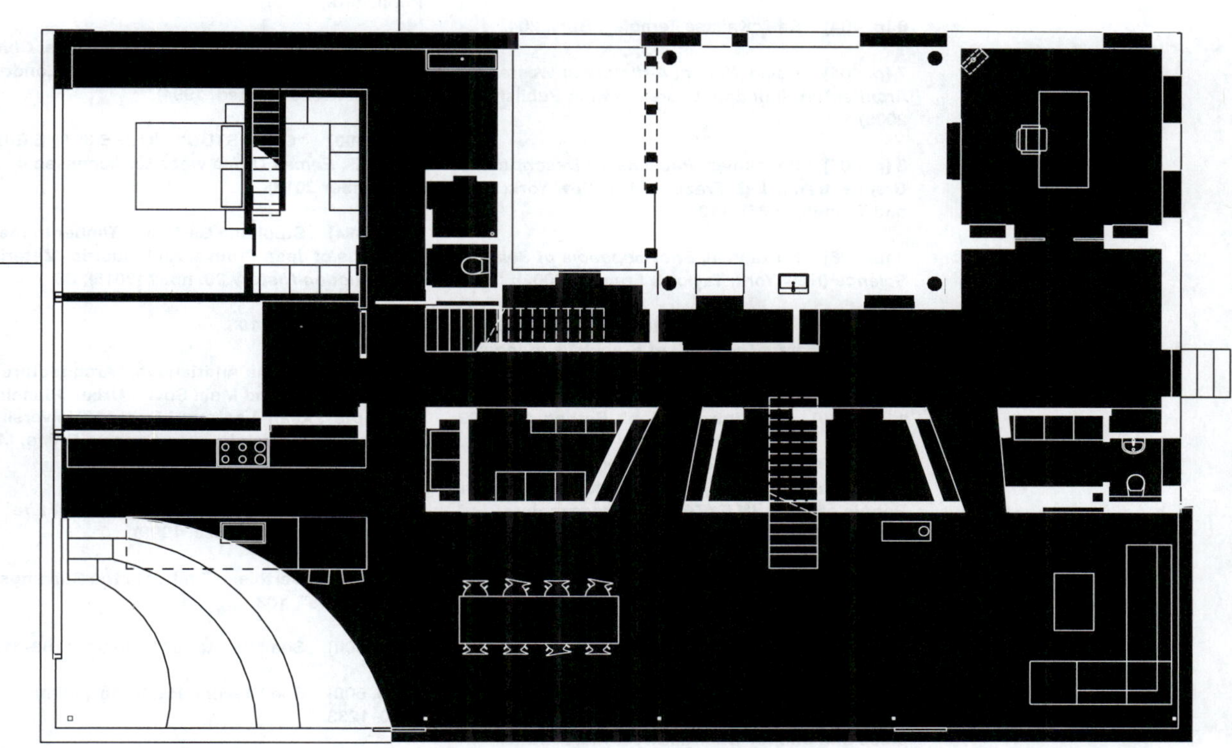

Keeping the high barn door elevation intact, the roofline of the extension is stretched, maintaining the same low eaves on three sides and buffeting the prevailing winds off the polder. It is at this point that the building starts skewing itself towards the landscape.

Existing stolp on the left and skewed extension to the right.

Endnotes:

1 [p. 393] Diana Balmori, "In Conversation", Mimic, 1301–1307.

2 [p. 393] Philip C. Johnson, *Mies van der Rohe* (New York: Museum of Modern Art, 1947).

3 [p. 396] Peter Blake, "Slaughter on Sixth Avenue", *New York Magazine* (May 1969).

4 [p. 396] Annabel Koeck, "Invisible Cities – The Last Remnant of Modernism", *Australian Design Review* (24 October, 2014).

5 [p. 400] Balmori, "In Conversation" (note 1).

6 [p. 404] See "Kailasa Temple", Bury, 204.

7 [p. 404] David Watkin, *A History of Western Architecture* (London: Laurence King Publishing, 2005).

8 [p. 407] Pausanias, *Pausanias's Description of Greece*, trans. J. G. Frazer, vol. 1 (New York: Biblo and Tannen, 1965), 113.

9 [p. 408] Rattan Lal, *Encyclopaedia of Soil Science* (New York: Taylor & Francis, 2002).

10 [p. 410] Morna Livingston and Milo Beach, *Steps to Water: The Ancient Stepwells of India* (New York: Princeton University Press, 2002).

11 [p. 460] See "Introduction", Embed, 393–400.

12 [p. 469] Priska Seisenbacher and Andreas Schörghuber, "Sar Agha Seyed and the Bakhtiari People of Iran", *IN EXTENSO Photography* 12 (October 2017).

13 [p. 474] Gijs Van Hensbergen, *Gaudi: A Biography* (New York: HarperCollins, 2001).

14 [p. 474] The first two houses were designed by architects Francesc Berenguer and Juli Batllevell: a show house commissioned by contractor Josep Pardo i Casanovas to encourage sales and one for Güell's lawyer Martí Trias i Domènech. "Over a Hundred Years of History", Park Güell, *Barcelona de Serveis Municipals S.A* website. Accessed 4 August 2018.

15 [p. 475] Ibid.

16 [p. 476] Jaap Bakema in television lecture series *Van Stoel tot Stad*, Algemene Vereniging Radio Omroep (AVRO) Hilversum, 1962–1963, directed and recorded by Leen Timp, transcribed and translated by Bjarne Mastenbroek; and J. B. Bakema, *Van Stoel tot Stad: Een verhaal over mensen en ruimte* (Zeist: W. de Haan, 1964).

17 [p. 477] See "From Shelter to Shed", Nature's Lack of Design, 47.

18 [p. 478] Enric Miralles and Benedetta Tagliabue, "Lungomare Bench", *Miralles Tagliabue EMBT* website, 2000. Accessed June 2018.

19 [p. 483] William J. R. Curtis, *Modern Architecture Since 1900* (New York: Prentice-Hall, 1983).

20 [p. 486] Frank Lloyd Wright, *Frank Lloyd Wright: An Autobiography* (New York: Duell, Sloan and Pearce, 1943).

21 [p. 487] "Frank Lloyd Wright's Organic Architecture: Green Design Before Its Time", *Britton* (29 July 2014). Accessed March 2018.

22 [p. 488] See the discussion of the Farnsworth House and the Glass House, "Skewed Stolp", Embed, 600–604.

23 [p. 489] Charles Eames, "The Banana Leaf Parable", Problems Relating to Visual Communication and the Visual Environment, Charles Eliot Norton Lecture Series, Harvard University, 1970.

24 [p. 489] John Neuhart and Marylin Neuhart, *Eames Design: The Work of the Office of Charles and Ray Eames* (New York: Harry N. Abrams Publishers, 1989).

25 [p. 490] James Steele, *Eames House: Charles And Ray Eames; Architecture In Detail* (London: Phaidon Press Limited, 1994).

26 [p. 490] "CASE STUDY HOUSE 8: THE EAMES HOUSE", *Eames Office* website. Accessed 4 September 2018.

27 [p. 494] Stéphane Berthier, "Timber in the Buildings of Jean Prouvé: An Industrial Material", *Construction History* 30, no. 2 (2015), 88.

28 [p. 497] Ibid. 103.

29 [p. 498] Ganna Andrianova, "Architecture of Soviet Housing and Main Soviet Urban Planning Concepts", Xi'an Jiaotong-Liverpool University, Department of Architecture, Suzhou, China, May 2015.

30 [p. 498] Laurel Fay, *Shostakovich: A Life* (Oxford: University Press, 1999).

31 [p. 500] Berthier, "Timber in the Buildings of Jean Prouvé", 103.

32 [p. 500] See "Habitat 67", Mimic, 1188–1201.

33 [p. 500] See "Jeanne Hachette", Mimic, 1210–1233.

34 [p. 501] Ralph Erskine's 1963 competition proposal for Svappavaara imagined a new form of housing for the Arctic climate. This model society for miners and workforce would serve as an experiment for future housing planning in northern Sweden, but the whole project was changed and watered down, only to be built in raw concrete. Svappavaara never worked as Erskine had imagined. During the autumn of 2010 half of the building was demolished. Mats Egelius, *Ralph Erskine, arkitekt* (Stockholm: Byggförlaget, 1988), 99.

35 [p. 501] 'Blue chip' refers to art with great value that is expected to hold or increase its economic value, regardless of the general economic ups and downs.

36 [p. 501] "In fact, although it has always been considered that my designs belonged to the company, now that I have no control over how they are interpreted, I cannot allow them to be distorted in a way that would totally detract from their value. Indeed, from the business point of view, should this happen, the very confidence placed in the factory's production by architects could lead to an impossible moral situation, both for the company and for Studal and myself." The

fundamental problem was that Studal, the Société Technique d'Utilisation d'Alliages Légers, as partner in the Ateliers Jean Prouvé, demanded an increase in the use of aluminium in the houses and Aluminum François, as stakeholder in the 'Maison Tropical' development for Africa demanded radical changes. Kathleen O'Day, "Tropical or Colonial?: A Reception History of Jean Prouve's Prefabricated Houses for Africa", master's thesis (Louisiana State University, 2009).

37 [p. 503] Gabriël Fagan, "House Gabriël Fagan – Die Es", *UIA International Architect* 8 (1985), 45.

38 [p. 510] Max Risselada, "Conglomerate Ordering, Growing Houses", in *Alison and Peter Smithson: From the House of the Future to a House of Today*, Dirk van den Heuvel and Max Risselada (eds.) (Rotterdam: 010 Publishers, 2004), 181.

39 [p. 510] Ibid.

40 [p. 513] Axel Bruchhauser quoted in Andrew Mead, "Putting Down Roots", *Architects Journal* (16 August 2001).

41 [p. 514] Joop ten Velden, "Het domein van architect Le Corbusier", *NRC-Handelsblad* (27 August 1990).

42 [p. 514] "Roq et Rob à Cap Martin, 1949", in *Le Corbusier, Oeuvre Complet 1946–1952* (Zurich: Editions Girsberger, 1955) 58ff.

43 [p. 516] Halen, Atelier 5, *Housingprototype* website. Accessed June 2018.

44 [p. 516] Hugo Macdonald, "Estate of the Art", *Monocle* 7, no. 65 (July/August 2013), 238–247.

45 [p. 517] Liga Brammanis, Kelsey Dawson, Zoe Goodman, Elizabeth Lenny and Olivera Neskovic, *The Siedlung Halen Rowhouses*, 2015. Accessed March 2018.

46 [p. 521] Hugo Macdonald, "Estate of the Art".

47 [p. 522] Roger Walker, on the occasion of Sir Ian Athfield (known among his peers as 'Ath') winning the NZIA Gold Medal in 2004, *Architecture New Zealand* website. Accessed 12 March 2018.

48 [p. 528] Julia Gatley, *Athfield Architects* (Auckland: Auckland University Press, 2012).

49 [p. 528] Ibid.

50 [p. 535] Roger Walker, "Portraits of Ath", *ARCHITECTURENOW* (January 2015). Accessed 12 March 2018.

51 [p. 541] John McClean, "Il Magistero: De Carlo's Dialogue with Historical Forms", *Places* 16, no. 1 (2004), 54.

52 [p. 541] Ibid.

53 [p. 547] See "From Public Space to Private Icon", Nature's Lack of Design, 83–86.

54 [p. 554] See "Morella School", Embed, 548.

55 [p. 557] Agustí Obiol, "Miralles & Pinós: Igualada Cemetery & Archery Range", *Transfer* (13 March 2017). Accessed March 2019.

56 [p. 558] "Thermal Springs", *Vals – Das Bergdorf* website. Accessed March 2018.

57 [p. 560] Dale Bechtel, "Stone and Water Temple Delights the Senses", *swissinfo.ch*, 2004. Accessed March 2018.

58 [p. 560] "The moment I can have this infinite dimension of the sky above: that's what I consider landscape. So everything that does not have a roof is landscape; and the moment I have a roof above me, I'm passing into another realm and into another, totally different scale". Diana Balmori, "In Conversation", Mimic, 1301–1307.

59 [p. 560] Balmori, "In Conversation".

60 [p. 561] "Peter Zumthor", *Wordpress* website, 2014. Accessed June 2018.

61 [p. 573] Barack Obama, ceremony speech, Pritzker Architecture Prize, Washington, DC, 2011.

62 [p. 601] Farnsworth House, US National Register of Historic Places, 7 October 2004.

63 [p. 602] "Architecture as an Expression of the Times", Farnsworth House, *architectuul*. Accessed May 2018.

64 [p. 602] See "1964: A Pivotal Moment", Nature's Lack of Design, 105–117.

65 [p. 602] Alexandra Lange, "Philip Johnson's Not Glass Houses", *New York Times Style Magazine* (13 February 2015). Accessed June 2018.

Absorb

Absorb — Architecture as geology

The building sits atop the earth's crust, receiving information from the land below and altering the surrounding landscape. In turn, the landscape dictates the interior.

"Architecture is situated between the biological and the geological – slower than living but faster than the underlying geology."[1] –Stan Allen

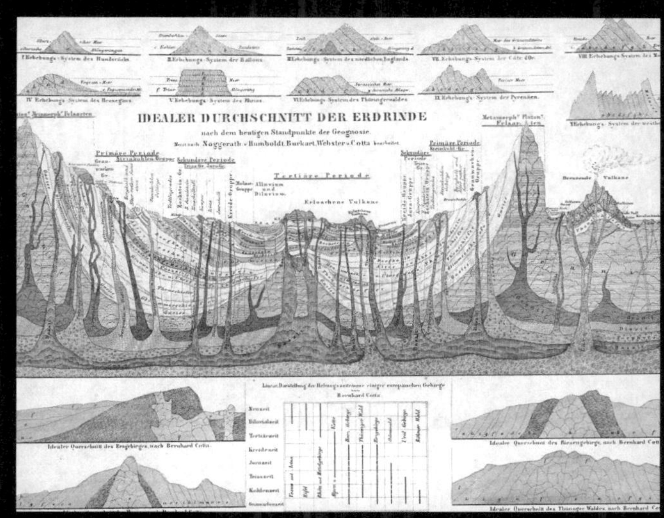

Ideal cross section of the earth's crust. Traugott Bromme, *Atlas zu Humboldt's Kosmos*, 1854.

We are constantly working the ground, mining and reshaping its surface. We literally move mountains, shifting earth from one place to another, grinding it into concrete, firing it into bricks, melting it into glass. We build it up and tear it down, again and again, leaving traces of our presence in its strata. Today this occupation covers almost every square inch of our planet, and our recent urbanization represents a thickening of this anthropogenic crust.[2]

The largest human-made hole in Europe is the Hambach surface mine, Germany.

When considered alongside the earth's geology, architecture is miniscule. Buildings constitute mere lumps on the land, relatively recent additions to a larger process of uplift and erosion. But architecture refuses to be overshadowed by mountains. For centuries it has been preoccupied with raising a visible silhouette against the sky.[3]

One of the first instances of this was fortification, the piling of the ground upwards for protection from harm. Using the material at hand and exaggerating existing topography, the castle positioned itself above the land it controlled. This architecture was both sanctuary and weapon. Passages within extended upwards as they progressed inwards, hindering intruders and denying them contact with their surroundings.

Monastery of Simonos Petra, Mount Athos, founded in 1257.

Driven by a different ambition yet sharing the same genetics, the monastery elevates itself from the rabble below, offering refuge. The modesty of its apertures contradicts its lofty position, withholding the power of panorama from its faithful inhabitants. Instead, the monastery acts as a lens, focusing views, providing relief and mediating the relationship with the environment beyond its walls. Like some mutation of building and rock, the castle and the monastery fuse with their site in such a way that they can no longer be separated. Both turn in on themselves, enclosing the ground on which they sit and facilitating a direct relationship between marked ground and humankind.

Unfortunately, over the last century this tectonic or geologic impulse has lain largely dormant. We are much more interested in using the earth as an inert foundation for rising higher. The earth obligingly carries and offsets the weight of the building above. The greater the mass imposed, the more we sink, consuming the ground.

Section of Monastery of Simonos Petra.

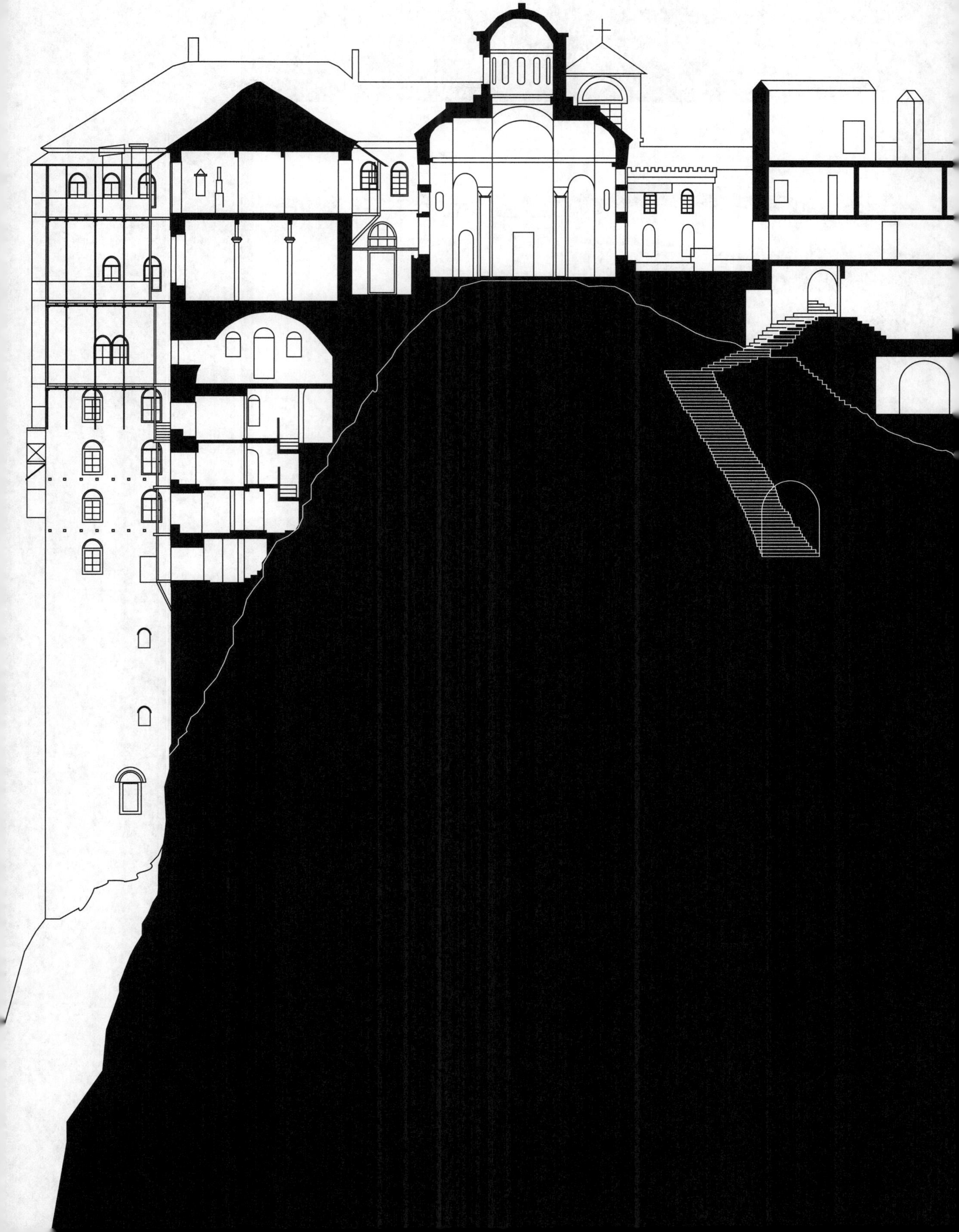

Demolition is often the first act in building, and the first drawing of the construction set, but rarely is the act of manipulating the ground a design tool in itself.[4] Architectural practice and the construction industry often clear a clean, flat, abstract ground plane on which to assemble the building.

Deep foundation pit of IJdock, Amsterdam, 2009.

The concrete piles of Burj Khalifa are driven 50 metres into the ground.

But there are exceptions. Dotted across the globe are buildings that forgo unnecessary excavation. Instead, they draw the ground upwards, into the building, to create an architecture responsive to the skin of the earth. Within some buildings the ground literally erupts into the interior. Geology forms the walls or supports the roof.

A. Fallingwater, Mill Run, USA, Frank Lloyd Wright, 1936–1939.
B. Raymond Loewy House, Palm Springs, USA, Albert Frey, 1947.
C. Casa Prieto-Lopez, Mexico City, Luis Barragán, 1950.
D. Federico Gómez House, Mexico City, Francisco Artigas, 1951.
E. Berggasthaus, Äscher, Switzerland, 1856.
F. Polonatalawa Estate, Nikarawetiya, Sri Lanka, Geoffrey Bawa, 1964.
G. Frey House II, USA, Albert Frey, 1959–1964.
H. Costa Brava Clube, Rio de Janeiro, Brazil, Ricardo & Renato Menescal, 1962–1965.
I. Elrod House, Palm Springs, USA, John Lautner, 1968.
J. Volcano House, Newberry Springs, USA, Harold J. Bissner Jr, 1968.
K. Casa do Penedo, Moreira do Rei, Portugal, 1974.
L. Casa Gerber, Angra dos Reis, Brazil, Paulo Mendes da Rocha, 1973–1975.
M. Fundación de César Manrique, Tahíche, Canary Islands, César Manrique, 1982.
N. Kandalama Hotel, Dambulla, Sri Lanka, Geoffrey Bawa, 1991.
O. Posbank Pavilion, Rheden, Netherlands, SeARCH, 1998–2002.
P. Massaro House, USA, Frank Lloyd Wright & Thomas Heinz, 2008.
Q. The Pierre, San Juan Island, USA, Olson Kundig, 2010.
R. Summer House, Storfjord, Norway, Jensen & Skodvin Architects, 2013.
S. Knapphullet, Sandefjord, Norway, Lund Hagem, 2014.
T. Riverbed, Louisiana Museum of Modern Art, USA, Olafur Eliasson, 2014.
U. Museum Susch, Engadin Valley, Switzerland, Chasper Schmidlin & Lukas Voellmy, 2019.

This architectural act is not about mimicry or camouflage. Architecture as geology looks to the ground to shape space, allowing the site to imprint on its interior. It exhibits a high sensitivity to every little bump and contour, absorbing topographical change or steepness, digesting and internalizing it.

At times, it responds to a harsh cragginess by staying on its tiptoes and encasing the ground. At others, it challenges the geology that supports it, rationalizing topography and smoothing what was once irregular. But a geological architecture always stays faithful to the ground on which it sits. It is informed from below.

Military bunker, Switzerland.

Serpentine Pavilion, London, Herzog & de Meuron and Ai Weiwei, 2012.

From the exterior, these buildings appear like blunt containers. The Costa Brava Clube settles atop a dramatic promontory like an impenetrable bunker. Villa Malaparte extends the cliff on which it sits with its artificial pinkness. In fusing with the ground, both buildings invert and obscure the original topography. To fully understand the dialogue between building and ground within these enclosed volumes you have to get inside.

Within the Costa Brava Clube you enter the building and ascend directly onto the rock. Within Villa Malaparte the ground is imperceptible, yet it controls everything: organizing programme, splitting the building and guiding the inhabitant over a summit they cannot see.

Costa Brava Clube, Ricardo & Renato Menescal, 1962–1965.

Villa Malaparte in *Le Mépris*, Jean-Luc Godard, 1963.

In order to see this articulated ground, we have lifted the roof off. The drawings in this chapter explode buildings vertically, slice volumes in half or dissolve buildings' extremities in an effort to describe the geology that erupts within. Unlike an architecture that buries itself underground or embeds itself within its site, this geological architecture is boldly additive.

Beinecke Rare Book & Manuscript Library, Gordon Bunshaft (SOM), 1960–1963.

It is not interested in draping the building softly over the land. It wants to exaggerate mass, defy gravity and force architecture to confront its role as an 'instrument for configuring the land'.[5]

Boulder Garden Resort, Sri Lanka, Lalyn Collure, 2008.

By treating buildings as strata of occupation rather than discrete objects, we begin to realign architecture with the land on which it sits. Considering architecture as an inseparable extension of the ground opens up further questions for designers. What happens in its crevices? How does it aggregate? And what is its scale or rhythm globally?

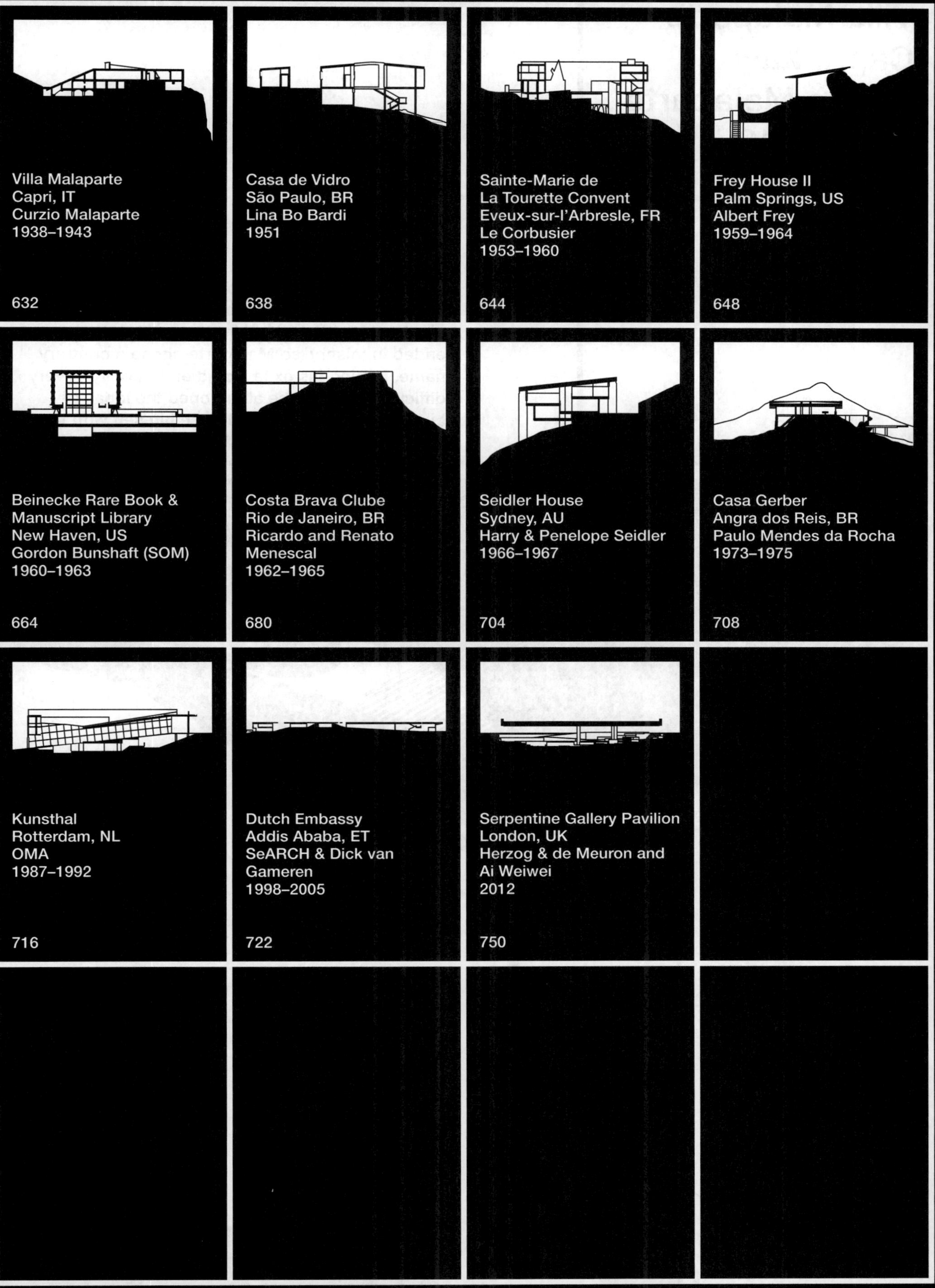

Villa Malaparte
Capri, Italy
Curzio Malaparte
1938–1943

On a mesmerizing spot on a pinnacle on the island of Capri, Curzio Malaparte asked the architect Adalberto Libera to design a house. *Malaparte*, meaning bad part or side, was the pseudonym of Kurt Erich Suckert and a play on *Bonaparte*, meaning good side. Napoleon's exile to Elba, another beautiful island in the Mediterranean, ended in misery, so Malaparte chose a contrary name, hoping his exile would end happily. A very difficult character, he abandoned the ideas of Libera and designed the house himself with the help of stonemason Adolfo Amitrano.

Axonometry of Villa Malaparte.

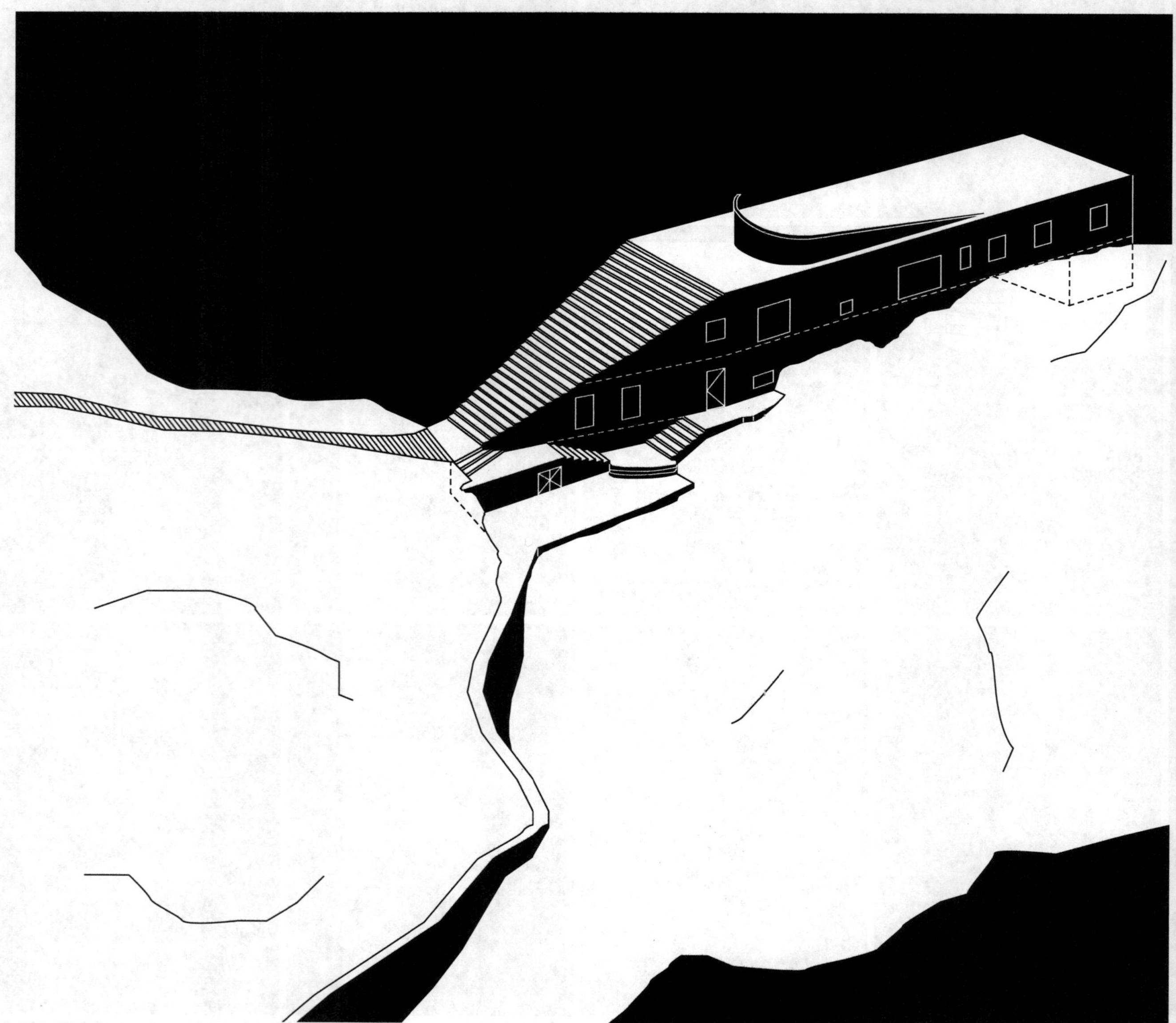

Malaparte's peninsula, Capri, Italy.

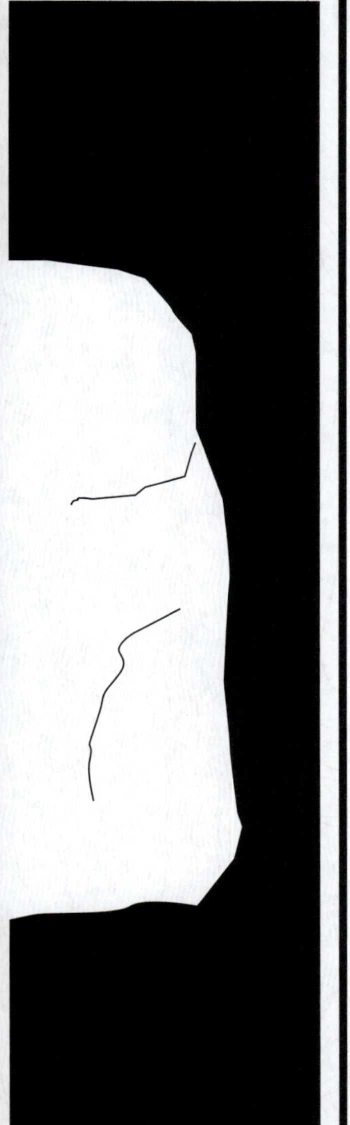

Brigitte Bardot and Michel Piccoli in *Le Mépris (Contempt)*, directed by Jean-Luc Godard, 1963.

Not bothered by lack of knowledge, the client and mason constructed a jewel of unequalled but also unapproachable beauty. Not only is the house inaccessible by car and a tough climb by boat, but it also has an unworldly, unattainable character. Like the serene image of Brigitte Bardot sunbathing on its open roof in the unsettling film *Le Mépris*, it should not be disturbed. And for thirty years following Malaparte's death it wasn't. It was abandoned, left to become a beautiful pink ruin.

Lower plan of Villa Malaparte.

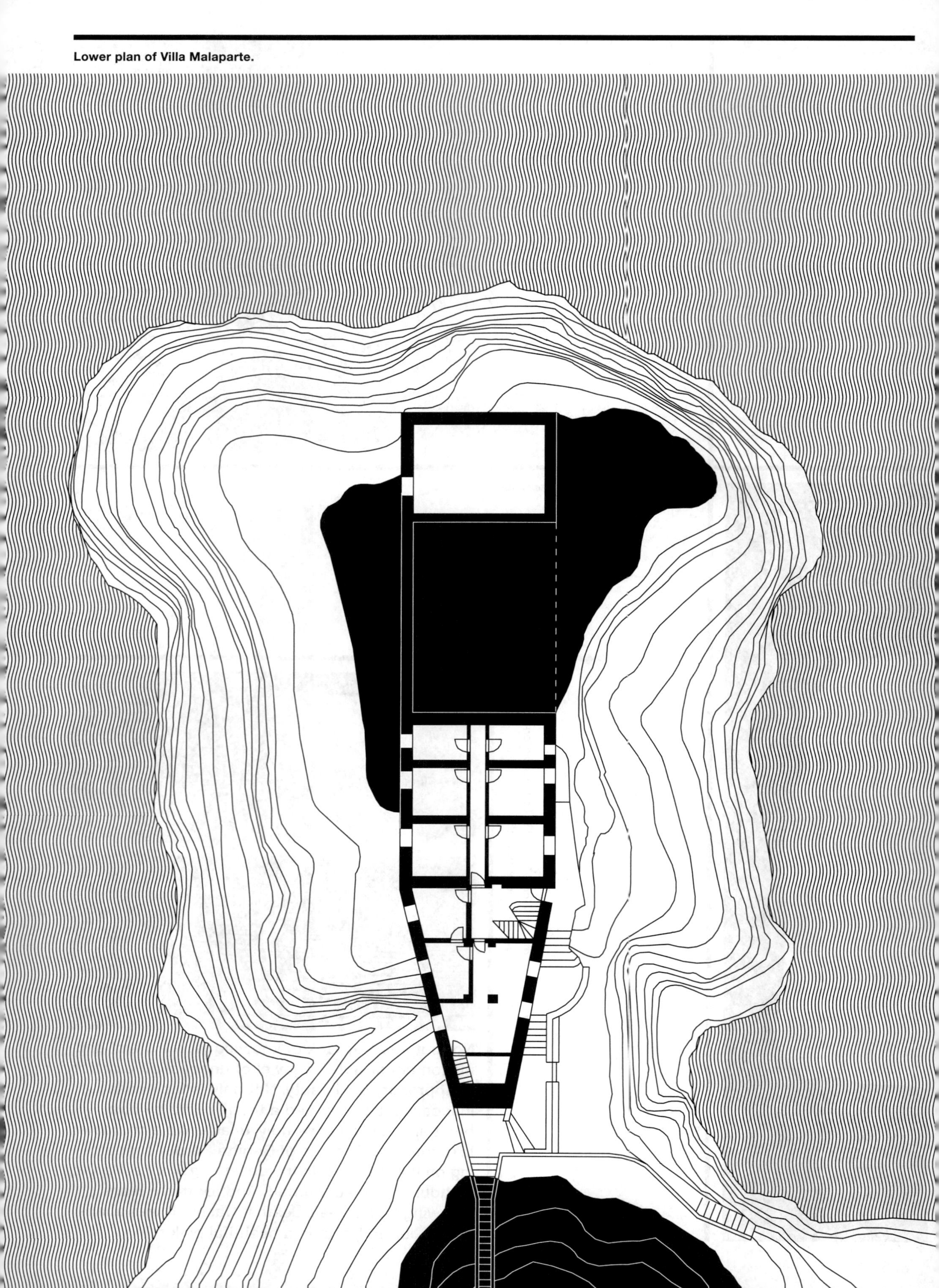

There is something contradictory about the design. On the one hand it is a brutal volume; on the other the building nestles on the rocks, sometimes almost invisible from the sea. At first sight the monumental steps look as if they are facing the wrong way, but on closer inspection you see that the steps extend the cliff, an abstract relief of the promontory. Pinched at the base, they widen as they rise towards the horizon.

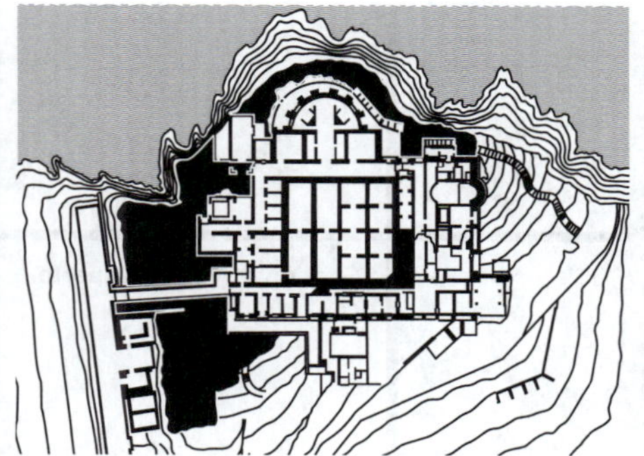

Villa Malaparte is reminiscent of Villa Jovis, a grand palace constructed by Tiberius in 27 CE on a similarly isolated promontory nearby.

Reconstruction of Villa Jovis, C. Weichardt, 1900.

Tapered monumental flight of steps.

The house below is oblivious to this expansive panorama. Small windows punctuate the exterior, directing the view sideways. The house's programme is distributed over three levels that vary in length, responding to the contours of the rock beneath. In places, levels are cut off from each other and occupants are made to walk over a rock they cannot see.

It is an immense house with a strangely proportioned living room that extends the full width of the house, interrupted only by two panoramic windows. But the highlight is a fireplace with a glass back that reveals a landscape of vertical rock formations in the Mediterranean at sunset.

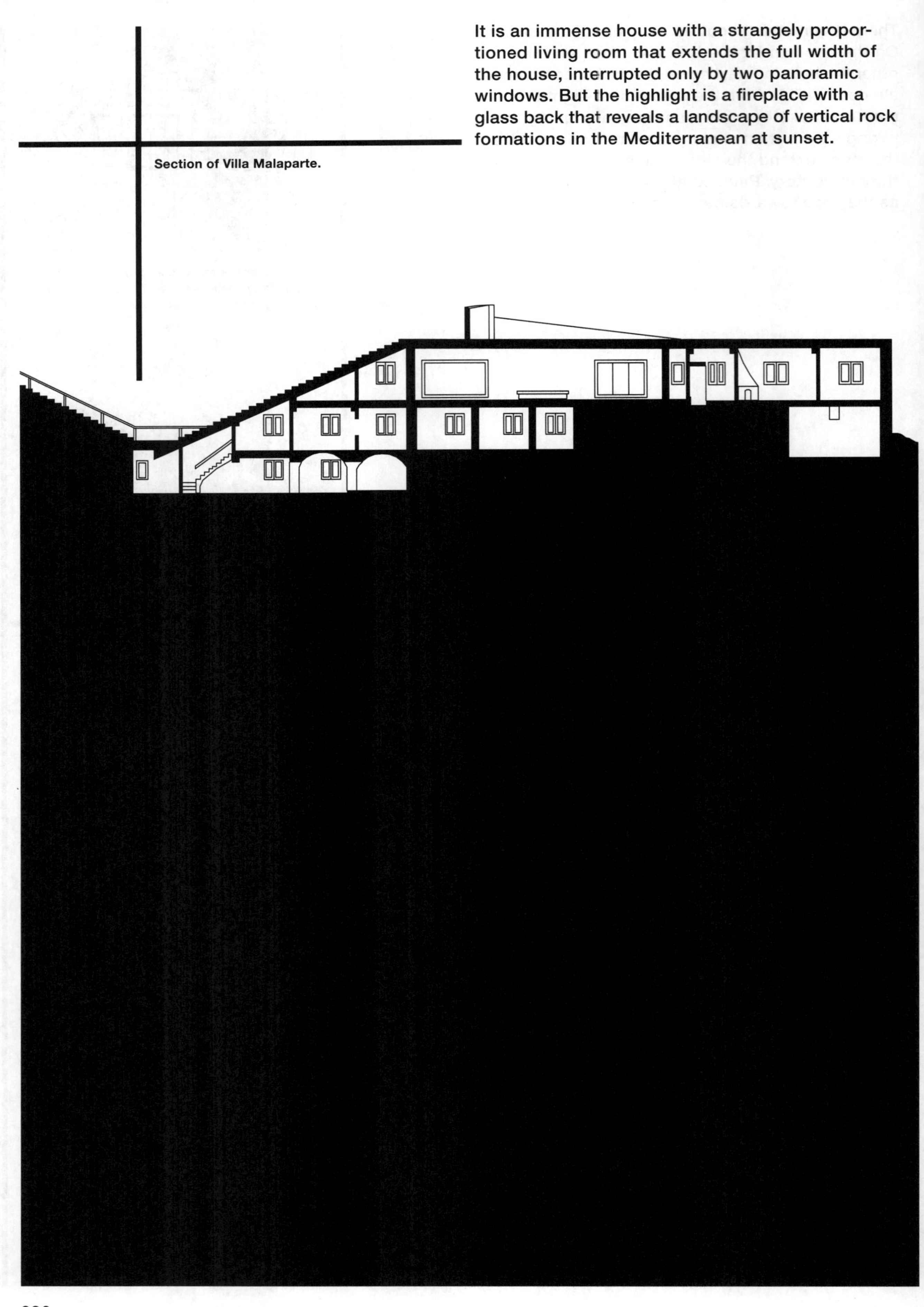

Section of Villa Malaparte.

View through the fireplace and of the living room windows, which direct views sideways.

Villa Malaparte grows from the rock on which it sits, emerging from its own geology. Its pink, plastic geometry both disrupts and fuses with the landscape, creating a duality between the formal and the natural. Is the house's ambiguity a consequence of curious incompetence, rational clarity or true brilliance? Perhaps all three. As John Hejduk noted, Villa Malaparte is a 'house of paradoxes'.[6]

Casa de Vidro
São Paulo, Brazil
Lina Bo Bardi
1951

Before the Casa de Vidro was engulfed by tropical plants, a small forest of slender pilotis supported a glass box in an open landscape. The levitating horizontality is interrupted only by an open-air staircase rising from below and leading directly into the living area. It is very similar to the first design of the Eames House in 1945, which was never built.[7] The back of the house sits on the solid ground of the upper slope. Between these spaces, a central void allows trees to grow through the building, creating conditions for a tropical undergrowth.

Casa de Vidro within the residential district of Morumbi.

Casa de Vidro.

Slender pilotis and tropical plants.

The open-air staircase.

Most of the area around Morumbi was cleared to allow for the construction of villas. But today, the Casa de Vidro is again surrounded by a domesticated version of the Mata Atlantica, the Atlantic rain forest that used to surround São Paulo. Like urban agriculture, this tropical paradise serves the people living within it. It is purposely planted to offer privacy and a sense of nature. The birds and insects return, but all the wild animals are long gone. Casa de Vidro stands out because it minimizes its demands on the land.

Looking through the central void.

Casa de Vidro lifts itself off the ground where possible and hides itself like a tree house. It affirms the statement that uninterrupted nature is the stronger force.

Overgrown Casa de Vidro.

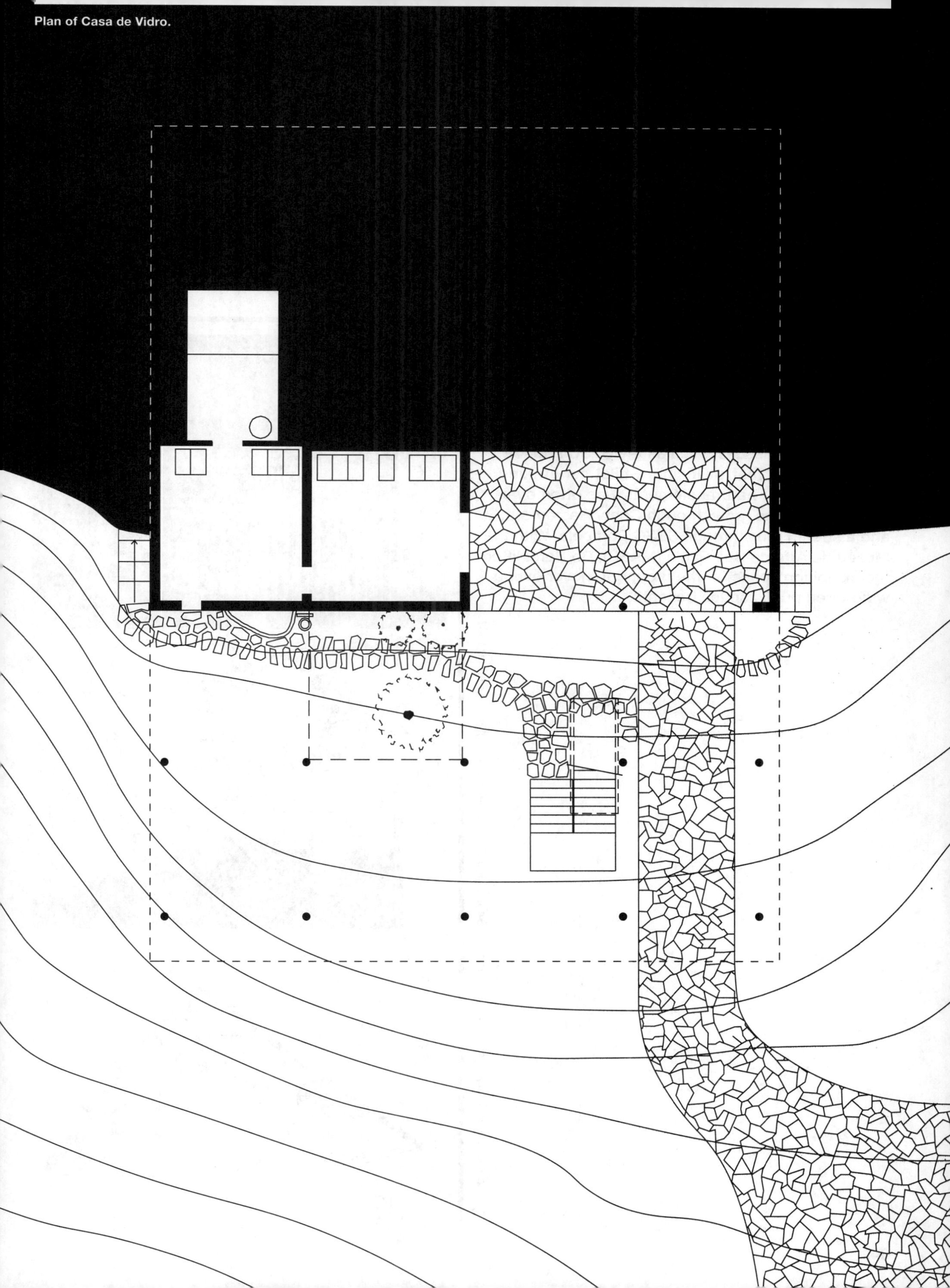

Plan of Casa de Vidro.

Stream within the SESC Pompéia, São Paulo, Lina Bo Bardi, 1977.

Lina Bo Bardi is celebrated for projects that reflect pressing social issues, such as the SESC Fabrica da Pompéia or Teatro Oficina, whilst her striking interpretation of natural elements was often overlooked. Old trees grow through Coaty Restaurant, and a stream runs through SESC Pompéia. With the Museu de Arte de São Paulo (MASP), Bo Bardi lifted the exhibition space off the ground to hover over a wide-open public space beneath.[8]

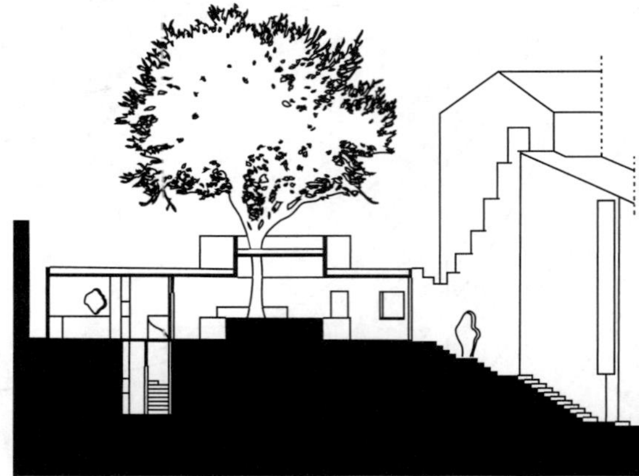

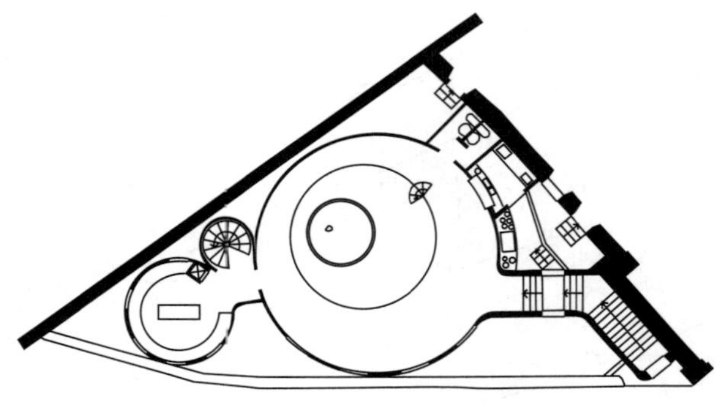

Plan and section of Coaty Restaurant, Salvador de Bahia, Lina Bo Bardi and João Filgueiras Lima, 1987.

The work of Bo Bardi is bold and gentle. Casa de Vidro was her first project and gave a taste of what was to follow. This highly modern glass house floated effortlessly, inviting nature to grow and weave through it. In Casa de Vidro you live between the branches. Nature is within reach, not a distant view framed by the architecture.

Section of Casa de Vidro.

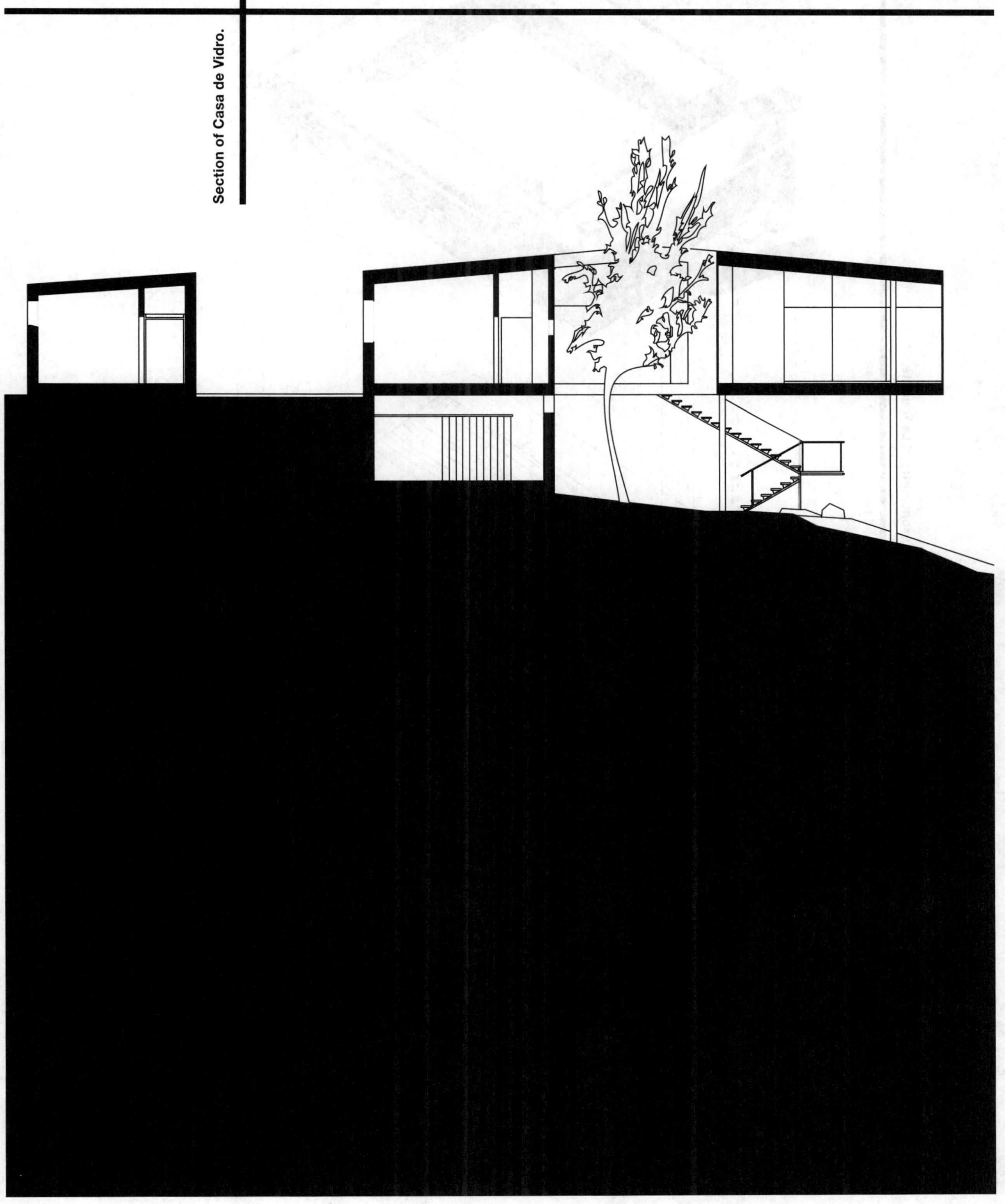

Sainte-Marie de La Tourette Convent
Eveux-sur-l'Arbresle, France
Le Corbusier
1953–1960

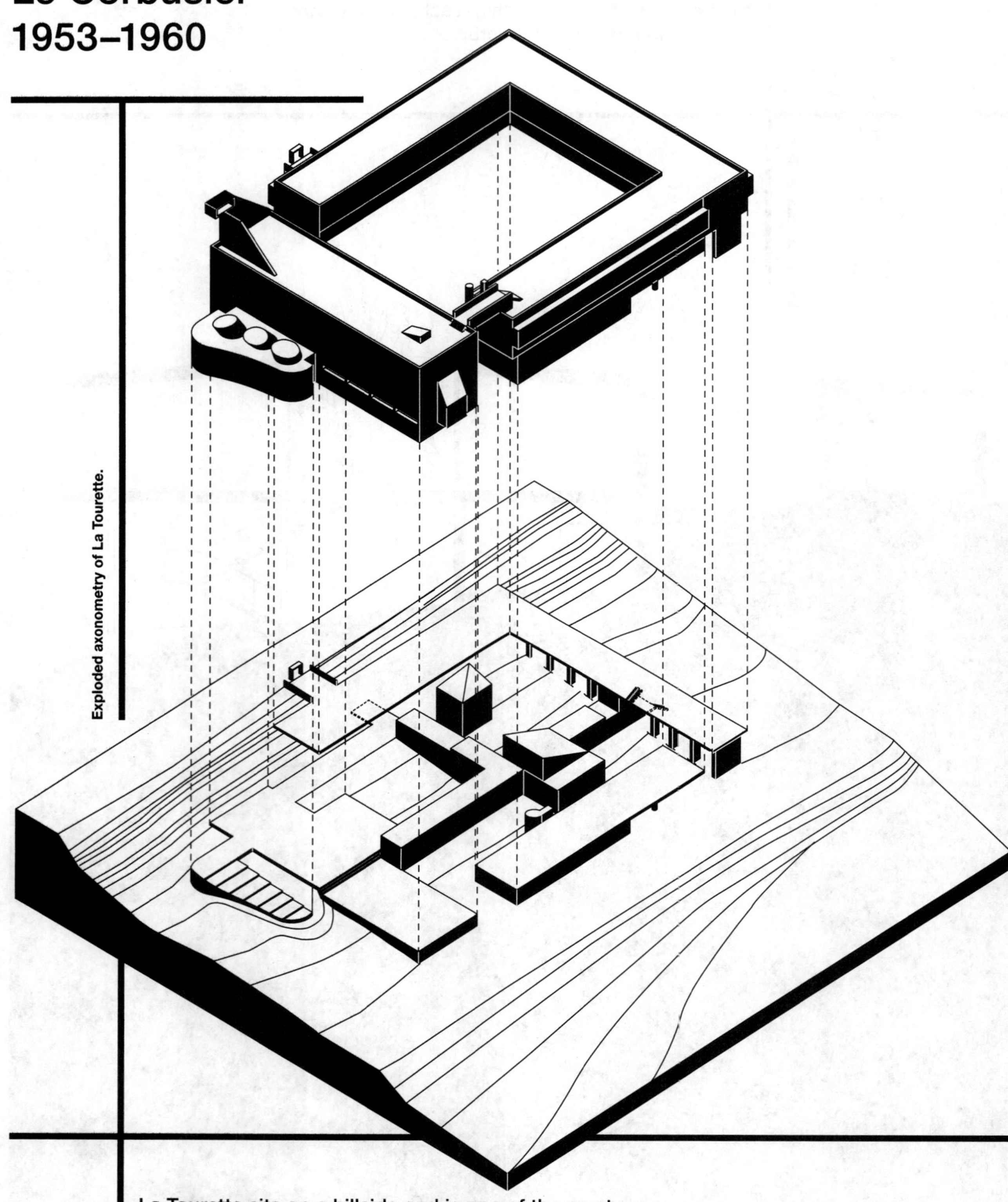

Exploded axonometry of La Tourette.

La Tourette sits on a hillside and is one of the most dramatic buildings in modern architecture in terms of site-specific design. In a most intriguing way the building seems to both ignore and entwine with the slope.

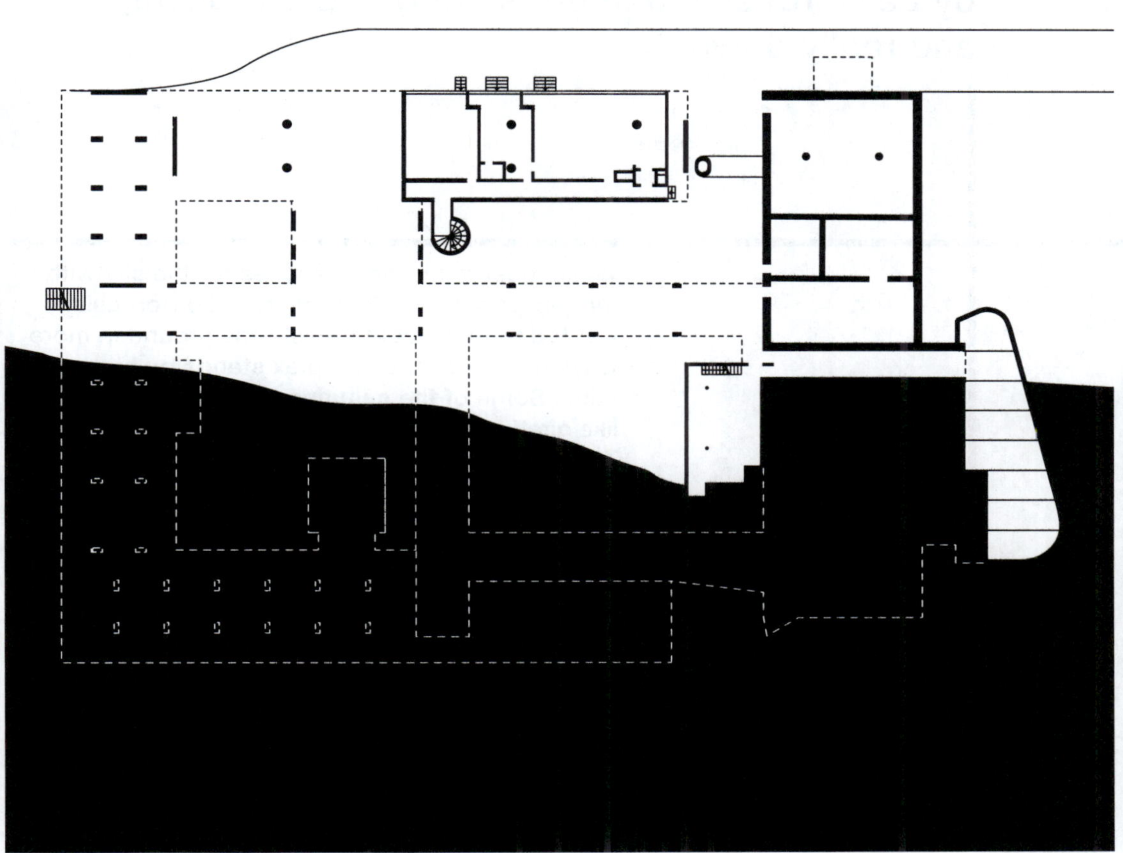

Ground floor plan of La Tourette.

Elephants and giraffes standing on the slope.

There has been endless analysis of how Le Corbusier turned the cloister from a rectangle surrounding a court into a cruciform design with two perpendicular routes, but what is less discussed is the way you enter the chapel. Right after you enter the monastery you have to work your way down via a labyrinthine stairway, from where an underground corridor leads you directly to the high altar of the chapel, which short-circuits the cross. Accessing along the other route, you enter the church nave to find altars on either side of the long central axis, which are connected by an even deeper underground passage. All light in the chapel is indirect and from above, giving a strong sub-terranean feeling.

At La Tourette, unlike all the other designs by Le Corbusier, one does not go up but down, and really down.

While most of his work reaches for the sky with modernist sublime, it seems as if Le Corbusier wanted to make contact with the ground in more ways than one. The complex stands on high stilts. Some of the columns are slender and tall like giraffes, while others are bold like elephant feet. The building stabilizes the ground, a stronghold that keeps the hillside in place, not vice versa.[9]

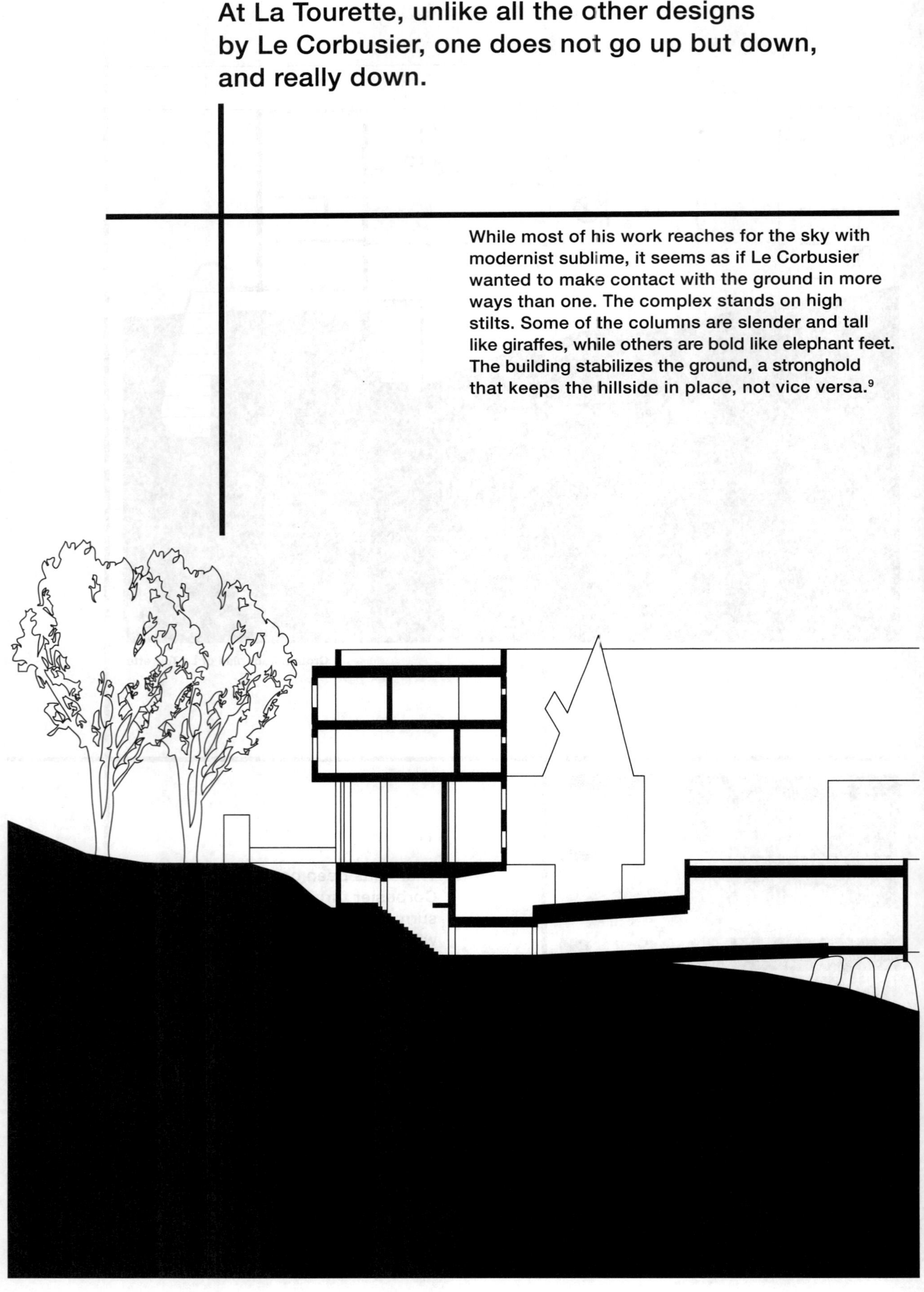

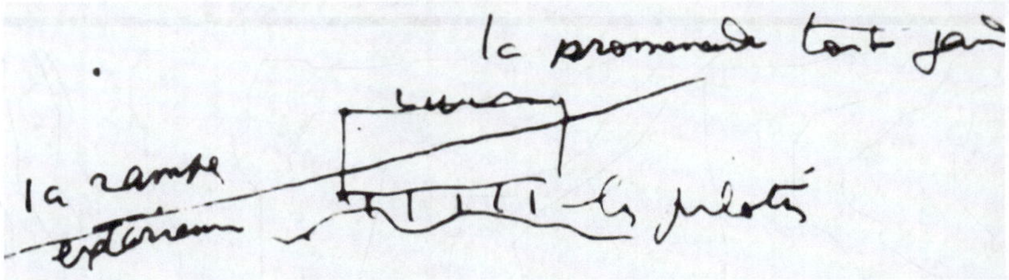

Sketch by Le Corbusier showing downward promenade.

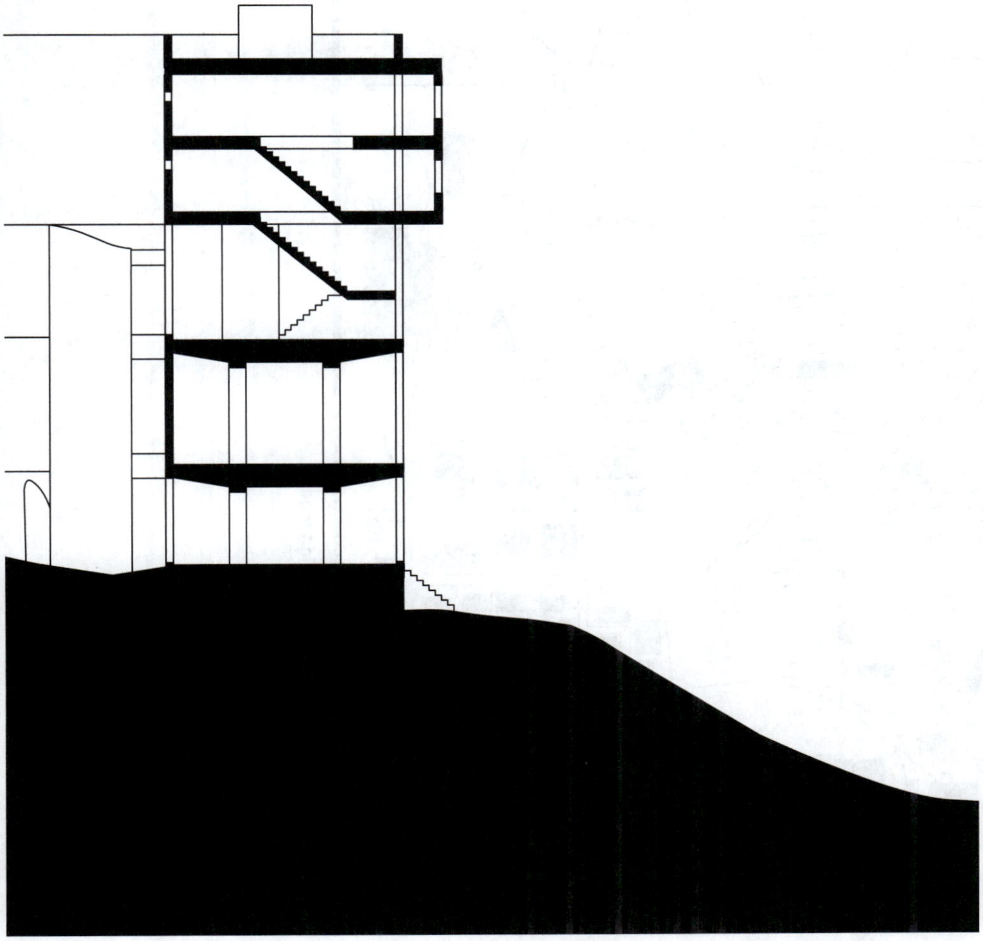

Section of La Tourette.

Frey House II
Palm Springs, USA
Albert Frey
1959–1964

Albert Frey built his house around a rock. Taking five years to find the right position and another year to survey the contours of the site and the movement of the sun, Frey designed a house that carefully responds to climate and terrain. And in a spot like Palm Springs, lucky enough to boast 300 days of sunshine a year, a thin envelope will do.

Site plan of Frey House II (follow the winding road).

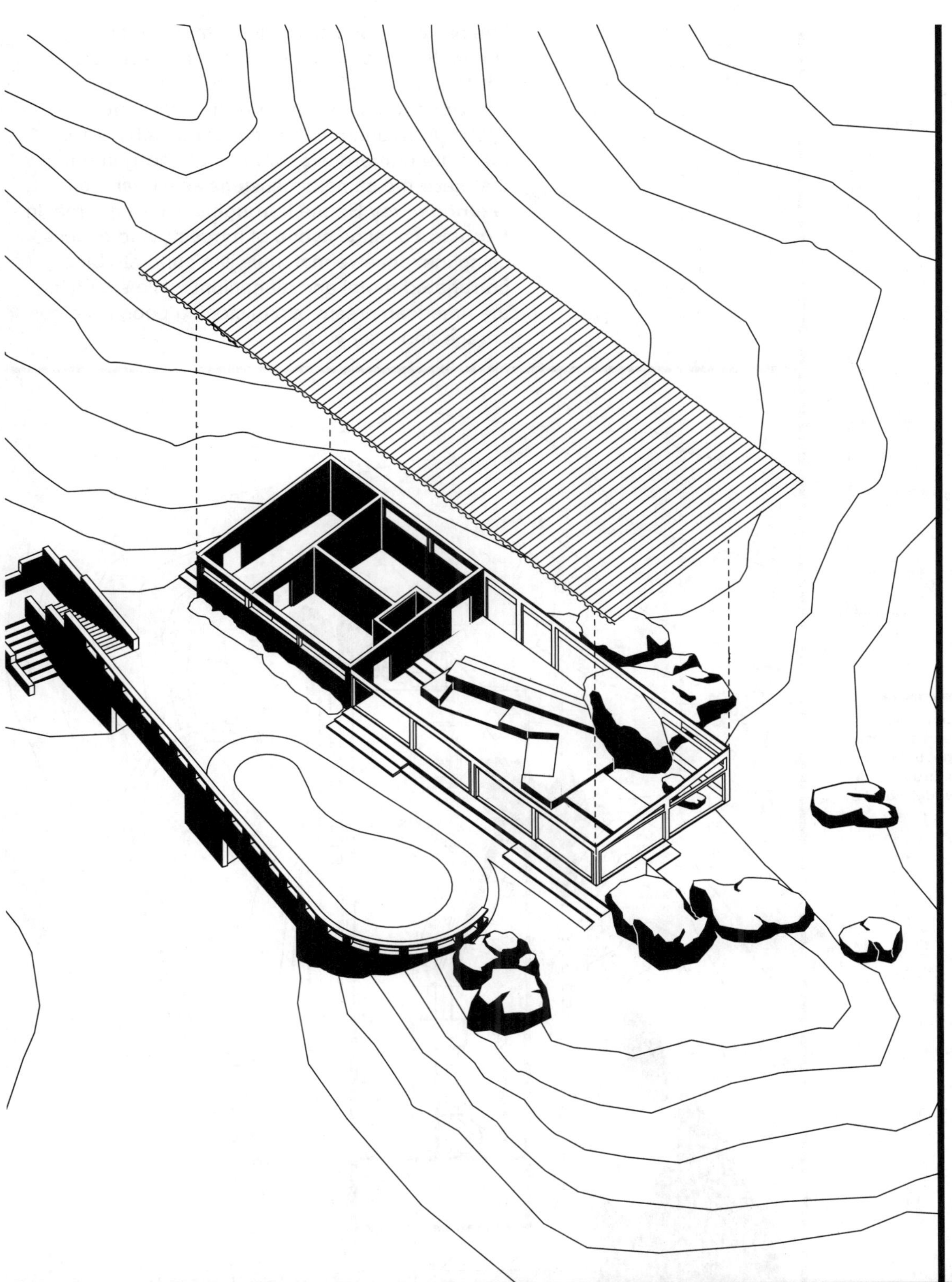

Exploded axonometry of Frey House II.

Taking the 'light touch' to an almost obsessive level, the house gently perches on an enviable elevation above Palm Springs. The ground was not excavated. Instead, a simple steel skeleton encased in glass sits on a concrete block podium nestled into the rock. If you squint, you can almost reduce the house to the single, slightly inclined plane of its corrugated aluminium roof, which follows the slope of the terrain below.

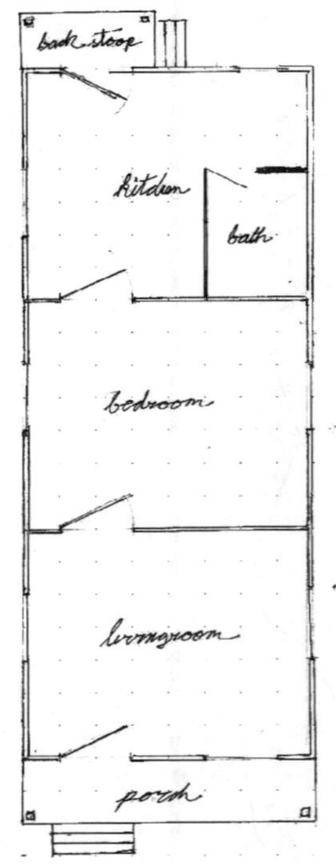

Plan of shotgun house, a narrow volume of consecutive rooms and aligned doors. If a shot was fired through the front door, it would exit the back door.

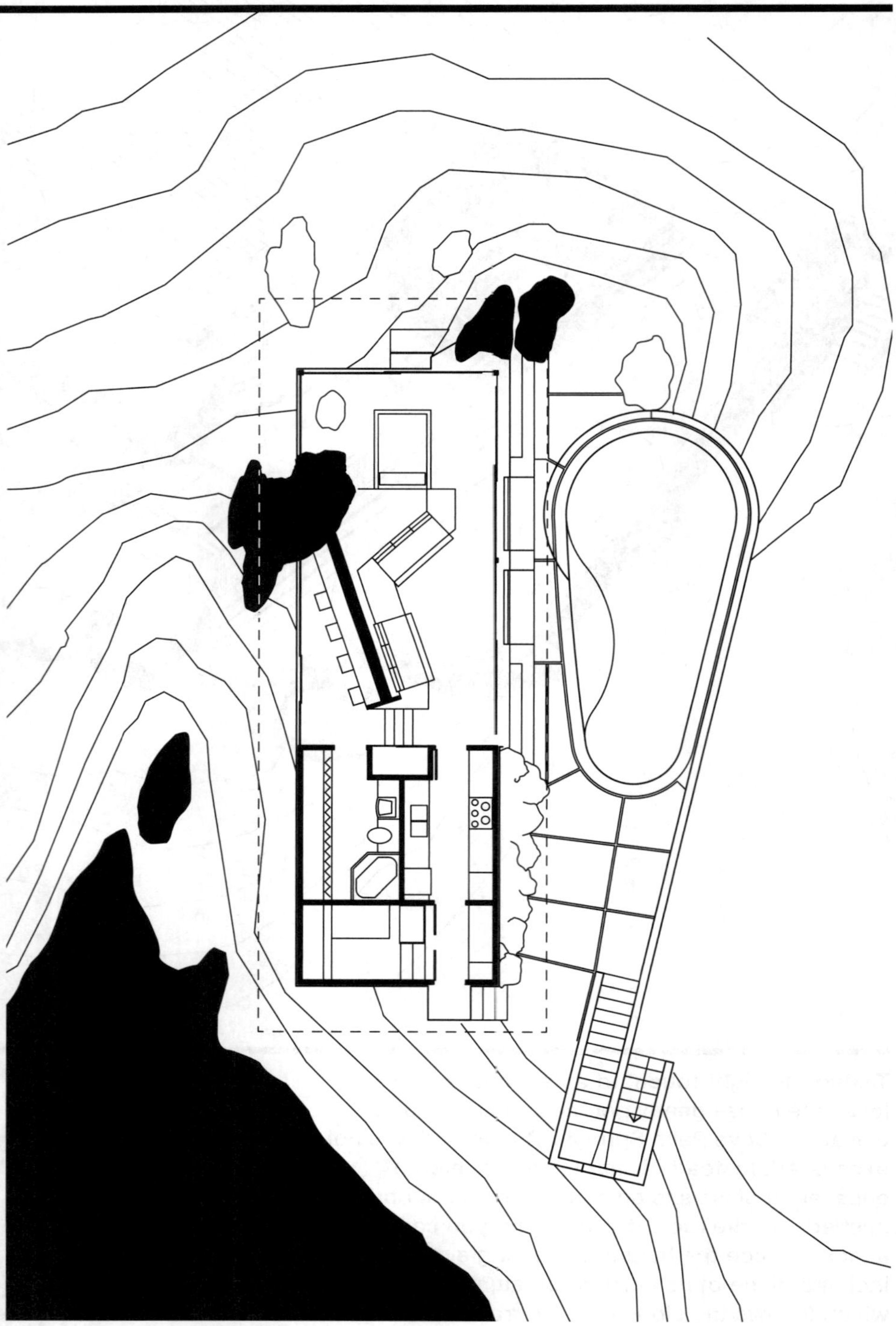

The narrow proportions and simplicity of Frey House II are reminiscent of the now-criticized shotgun house, the most popular style of American housing from the Civil War until the 1920s. Although often as narrow as 3.5 metres, there are numerous examples of shotgun houses that have the same dimensions as the far more luxurious Frey House II, roughly 5 x 16 metres. In fact, it is a strange hybrid of modesty and excess, using inexpensive materials like concrete block, corrugated metal and aluminium while satisfying the American dream of a glistening pool, spacious garage and killer view.

Plan of Frey House II.

STOP

Frey House I, Palm Springs, 1941–1953.

Educated by Le Corbusier and Pierre Jeanneret, Albert Frey translated his modernist roots into a unique desert modernism. Some of Frey's odd metal-clad structures look like they may launch into space at the push of a button.

Section of Frey House II with the boulder protruding through the facade.

Albert Frey leaning against his boulder.

But Frey House II is different. It does not want to leave the ground. A boulder protrudes through the rear facade and interrupts the modern glass house. This rock marks a division between living space and bedroom. Furniture is built around it, the glass was contoured around it, and the roof gently rests on top of it. The building leans on this natural form, depending on it for support, not dominating it. It looks as though without the rock, the house may collapse. The bright yellow curtains add drama to the impressive sunsets, as if the building exists between a trailer and a tent, underlining its temporary character.

Beinecke Rare Book & Manuscript Library
New Haven, USA
Gordon Bunshaft (SOM)
1960–1963

Beinecke Library is like the hat grab scene in *Indiana Jones and the Raiders of the Lost Ark*, where Harrison Ford slides under a giant boulder just before the tomb closes. You enter the building through a narrow horizontal slit formed by a hovering marble mass above an empty square. It's almost like a one-way ticket, with the only possible escape through one of the reading rooms around the sunken patio. You're in open air, but still trapped.

Site plan of Beinecke Library.

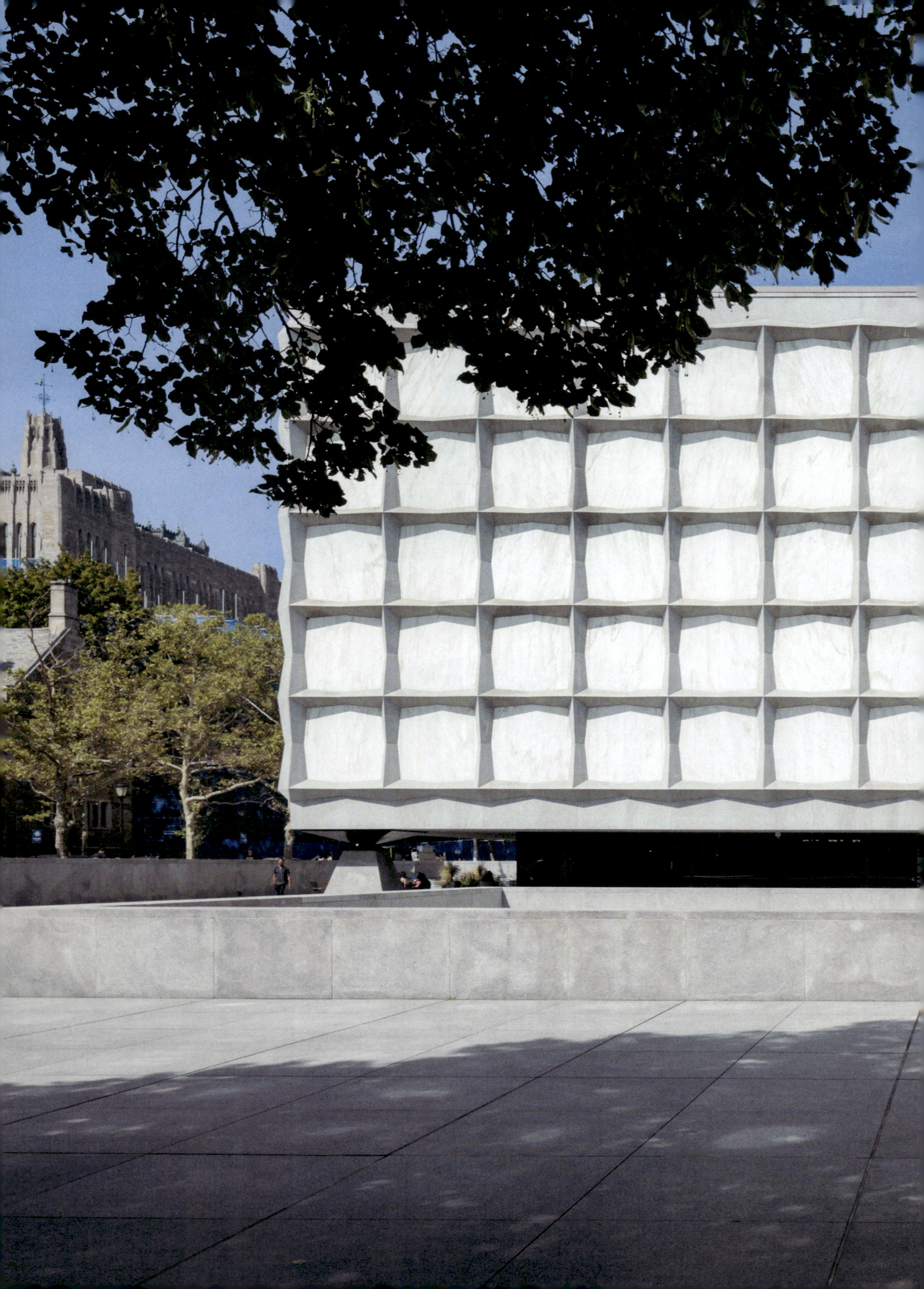

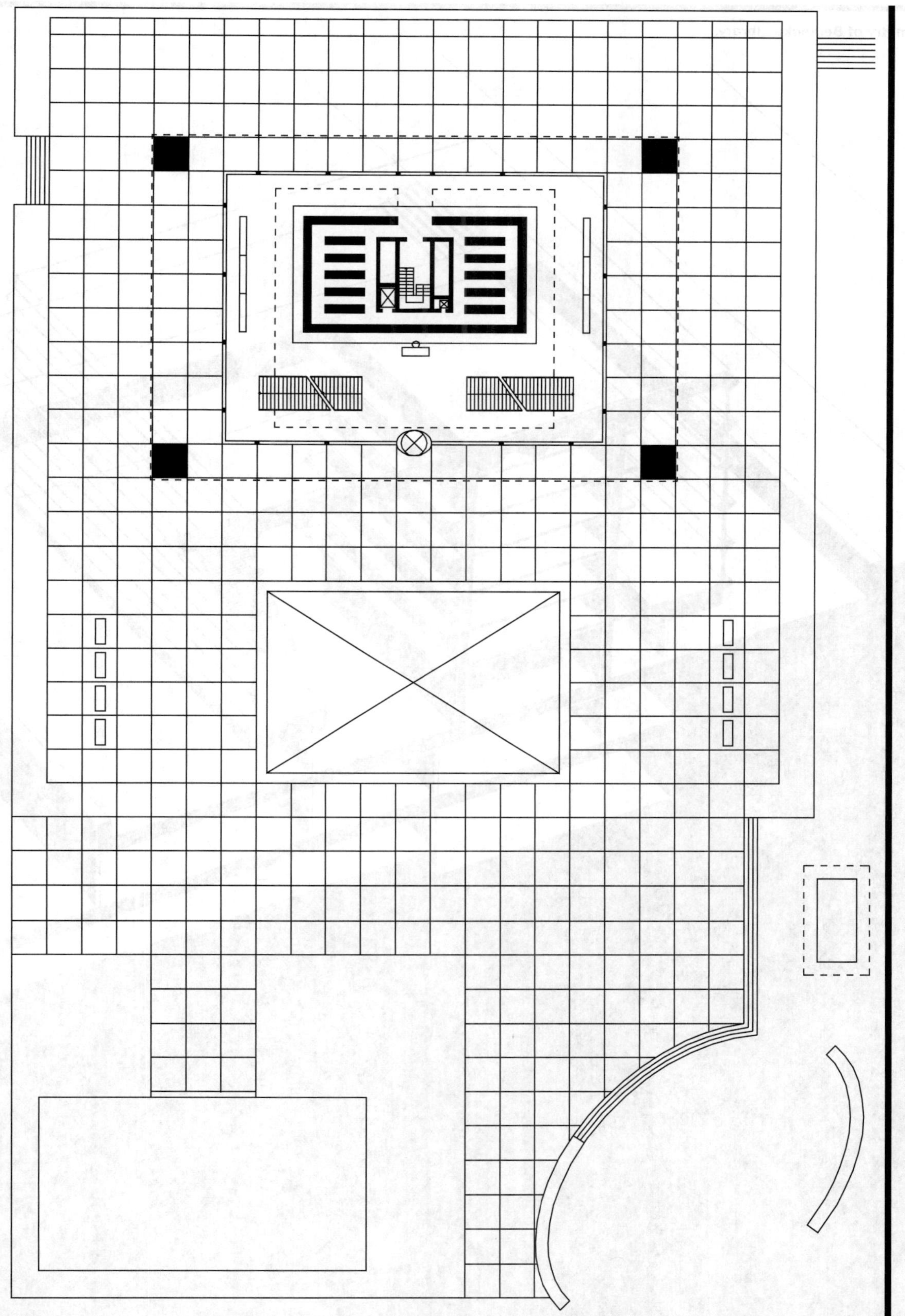

Ground floor plan of Beinecke Library.

By balancing on four points, the ground floor is almost entirely glazed. From the interior, the thin opening is a sliver of natural light. From the exterior, it reads as a dark band, set back and shaded by the building above.

Sectional axonometry of Beinecke Library.

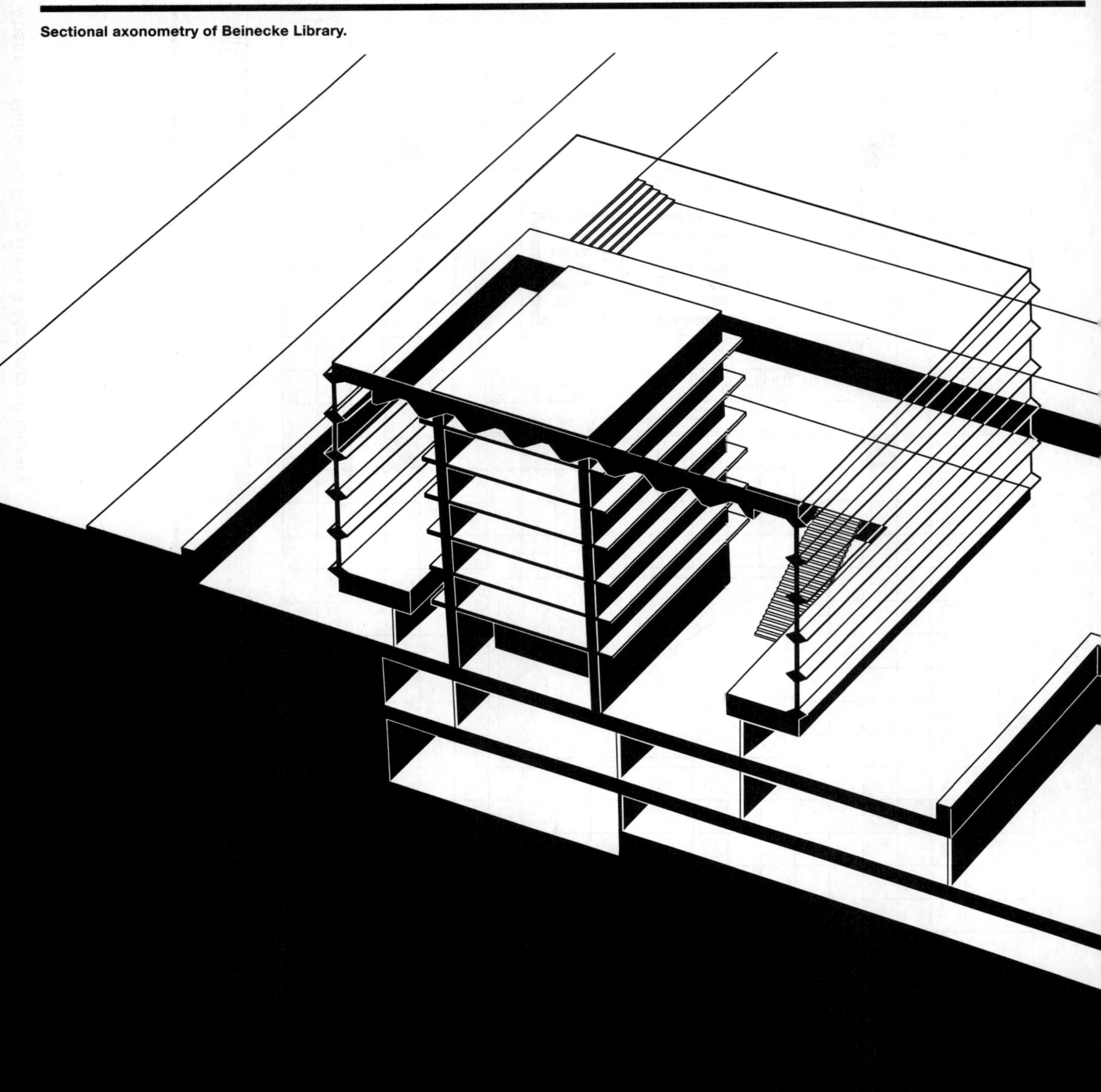

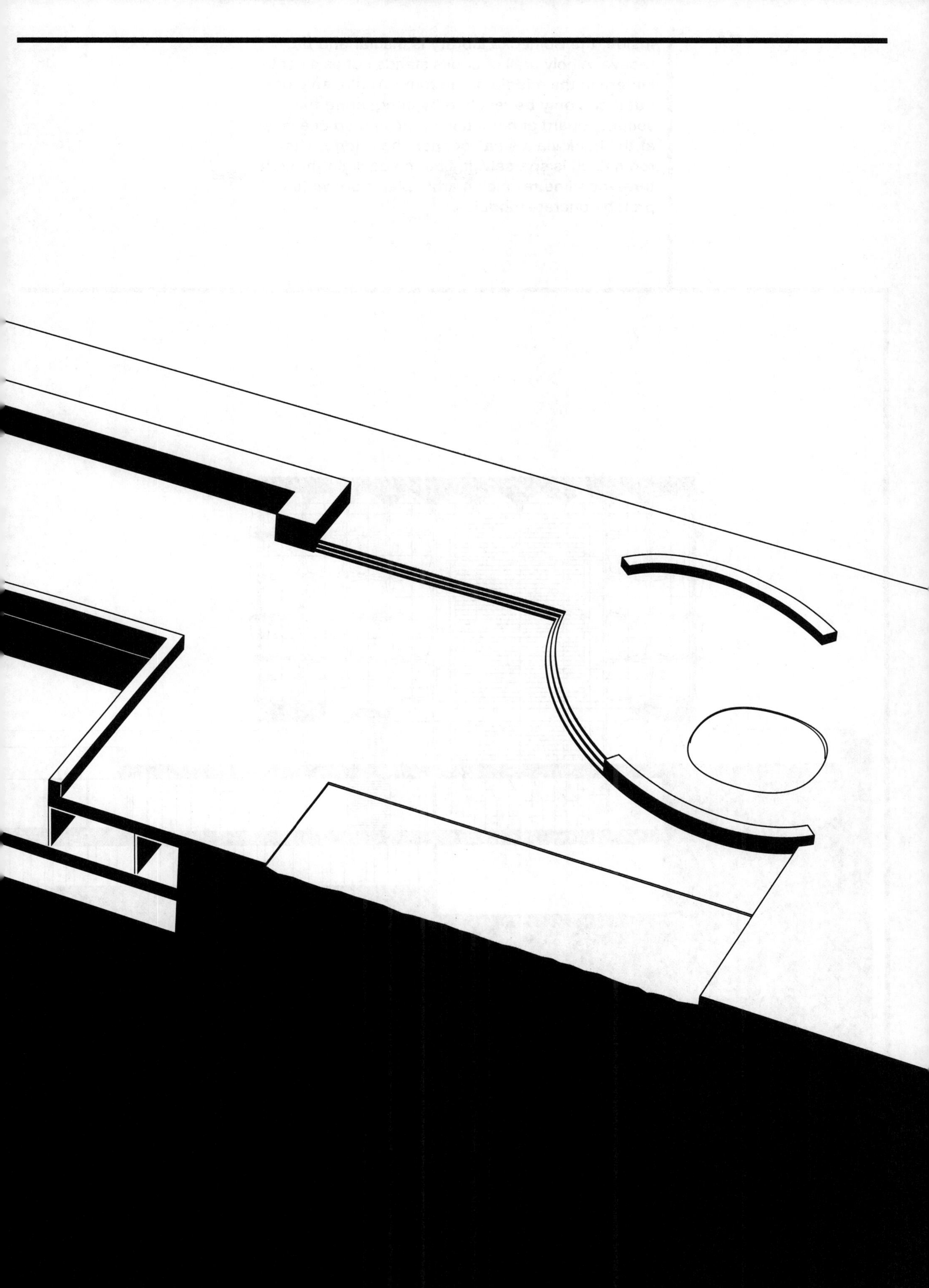

Inside, the Beinecke Library is insular and protective. A holy grail of books stands out as a central lantern in the middle of the room. You're so close, but it can only be reached by conquering the security guard at reception or moving up one level at the back via a small connecting bridge. The room itself is sparsely lit, filtering daylight through three-centimetre-thick marble plates set within prefab concrete modules.

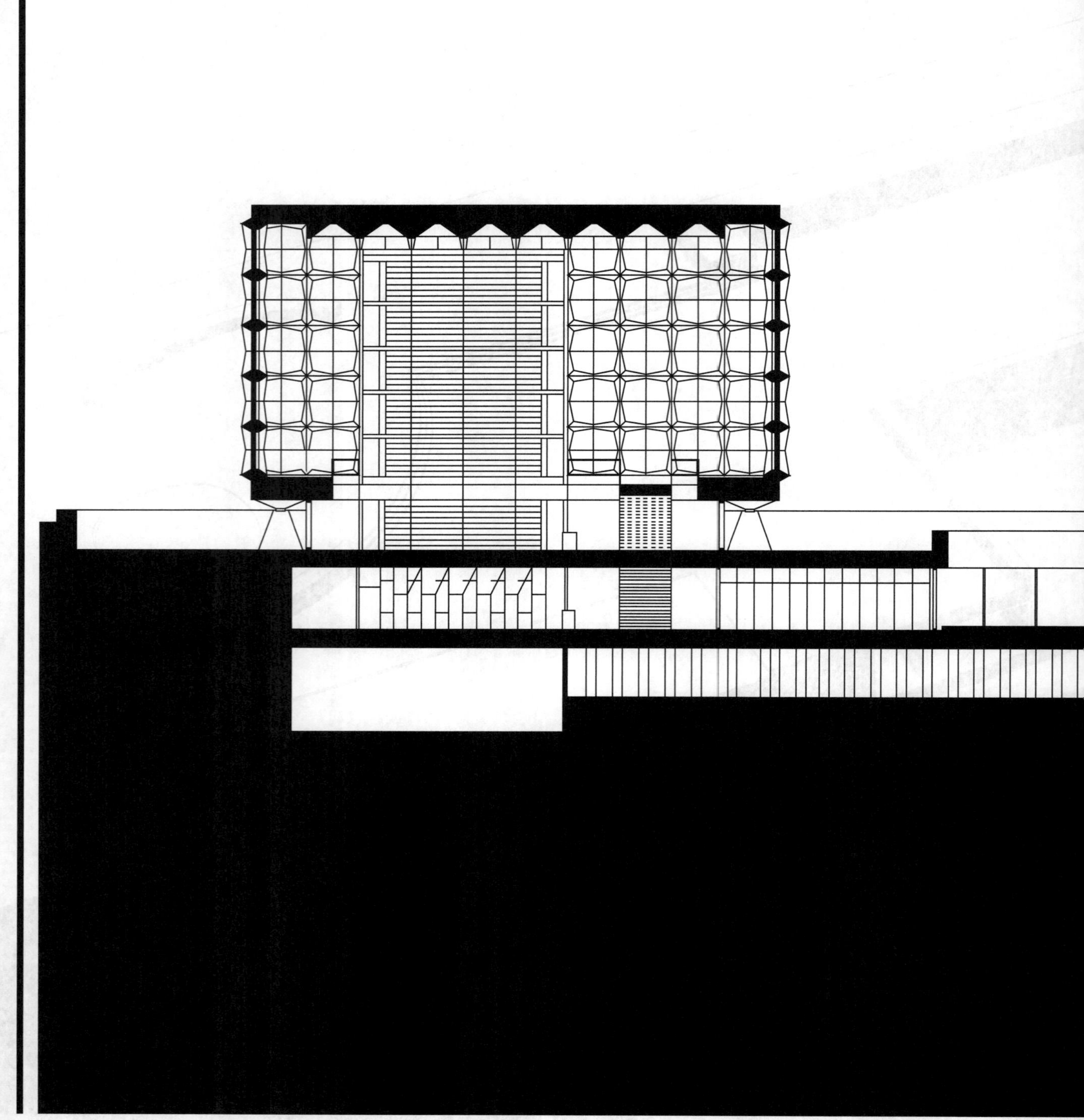

Absorb – Beinecke Rare Book & Manuscript Library

This world-class spatial play is achieved with a minimum of elements and well-calibrated level differences between street, square, entrance, internal book tower and sunken courtyard.

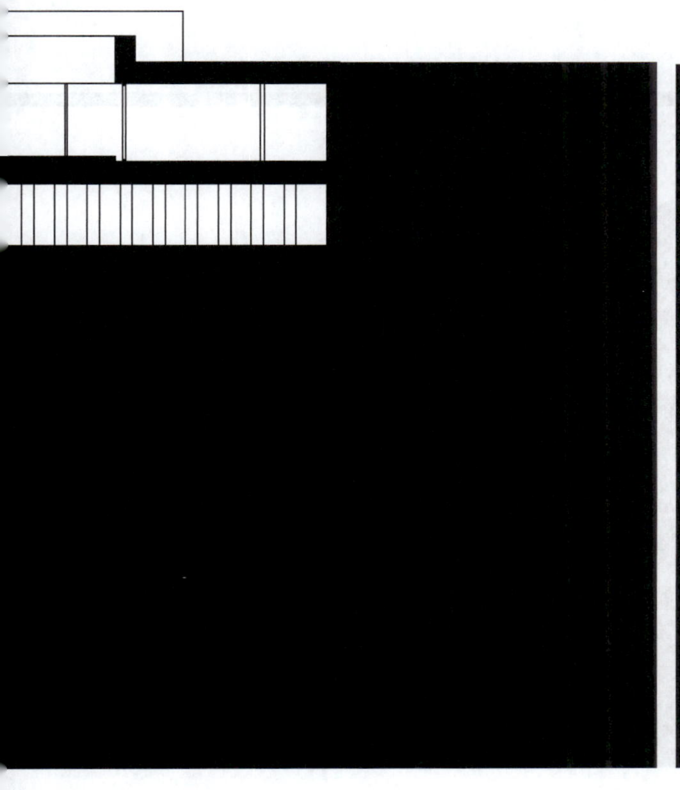

Section of Beinecke Library.

Costa Brava Clube
Rio de Janeiro, Brazil
Ricardo and Renato Menescal
1962–1965

Ponta do Marisco prior to construction.

Costa Brava Clube during construction.

The Menescal brothers chewed on this rocky outcrop for many years. For them the Costa Brava Clube is a work of nature, an evolving rock. But if forced to accept it as a built structure, they describe it as a vessel at sea, its roof a cruise ship quarterdeck with a pool. Sitting atop a rocky outcrop jutting out towards the sea, the Costa Brava Clube magnifies the isolation of the site.

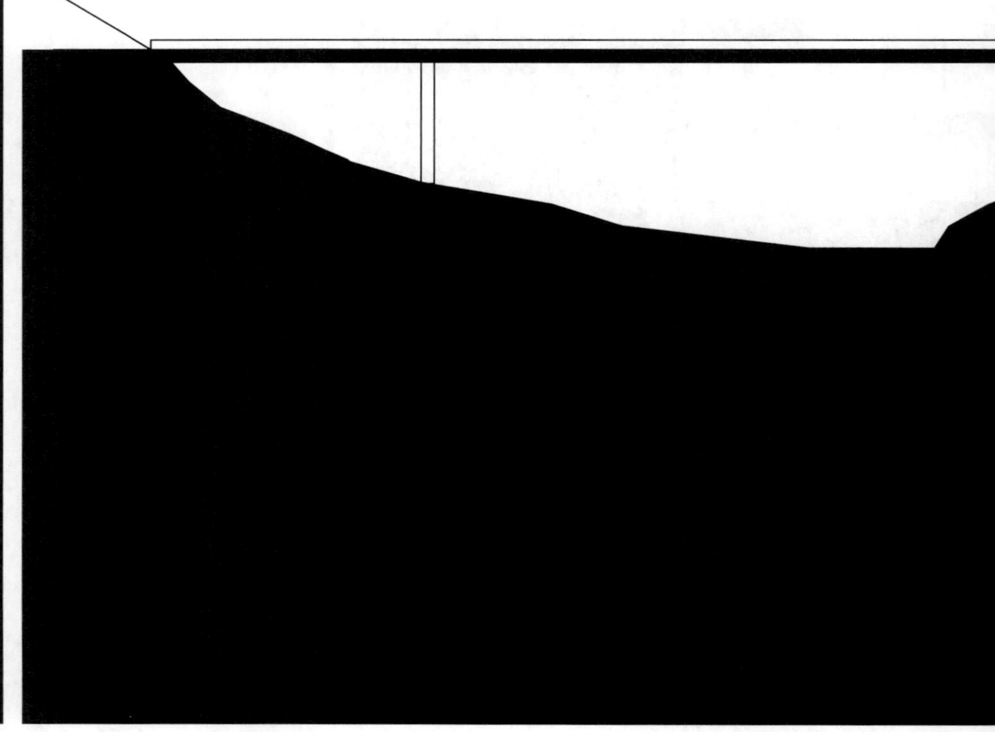

Section showing journey along bridge, into the building and up onto the rock.

Perspective by Ricardo & Renato Menescal.

It started with a much smaller clubhouse in 1962, and was subsequently enlarged seven times between 1964 and 1982 with saltwater pools, event halls and wellness and sports facilities. Originally, steep pathways leading up to the building were hewn into the rock, while later a simple horizontal bridge over the dramatic gorge created a shortcut.

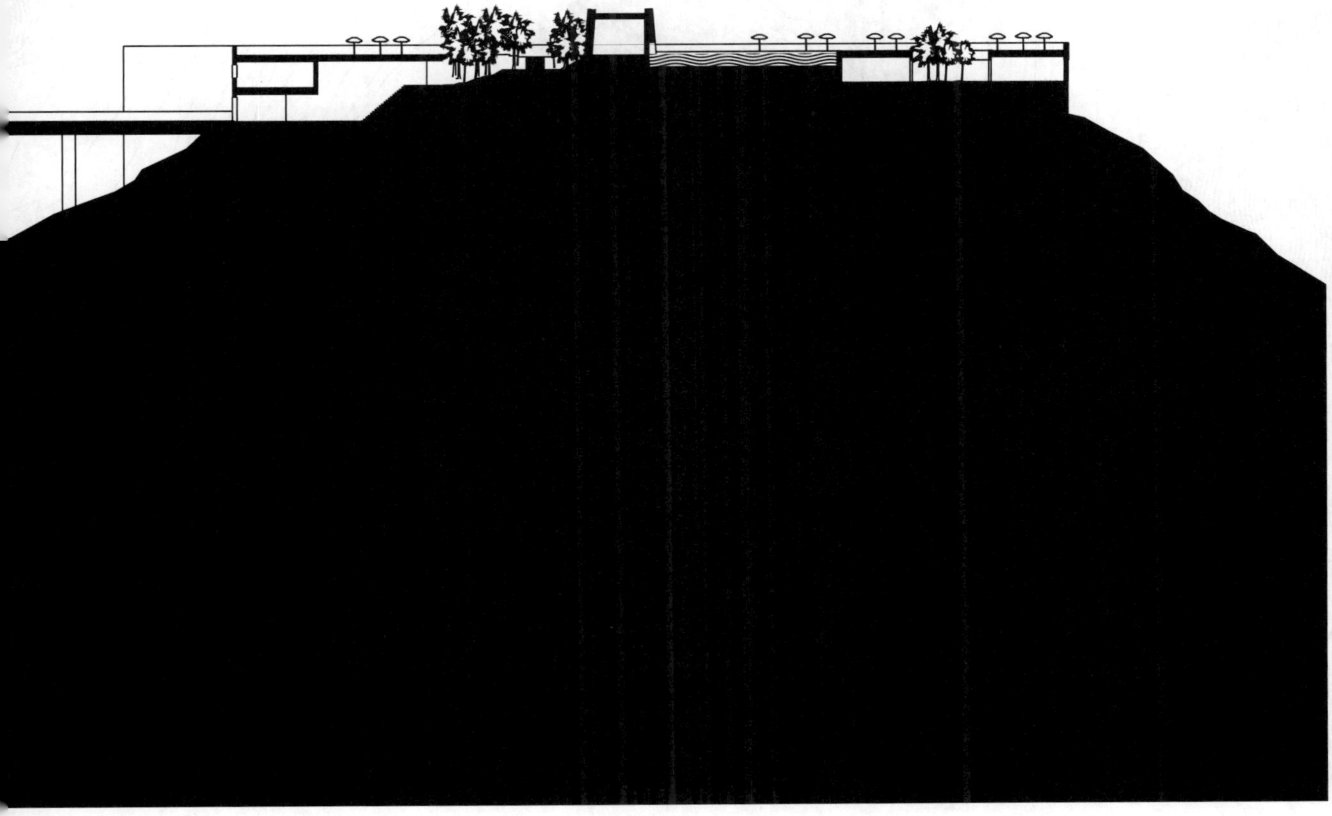

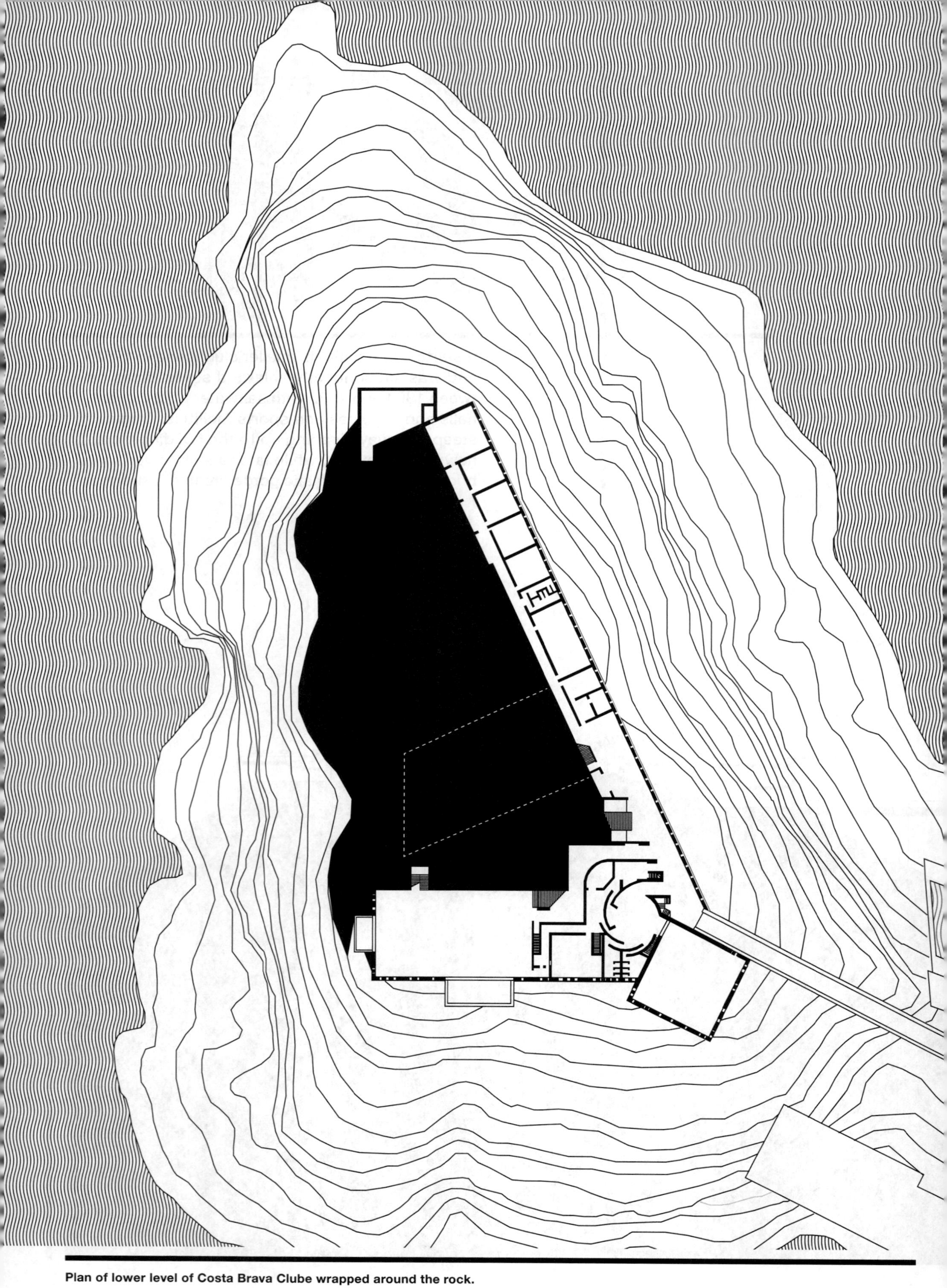

Plan of lower level of Costa Brava Clube wrapped around the rock.

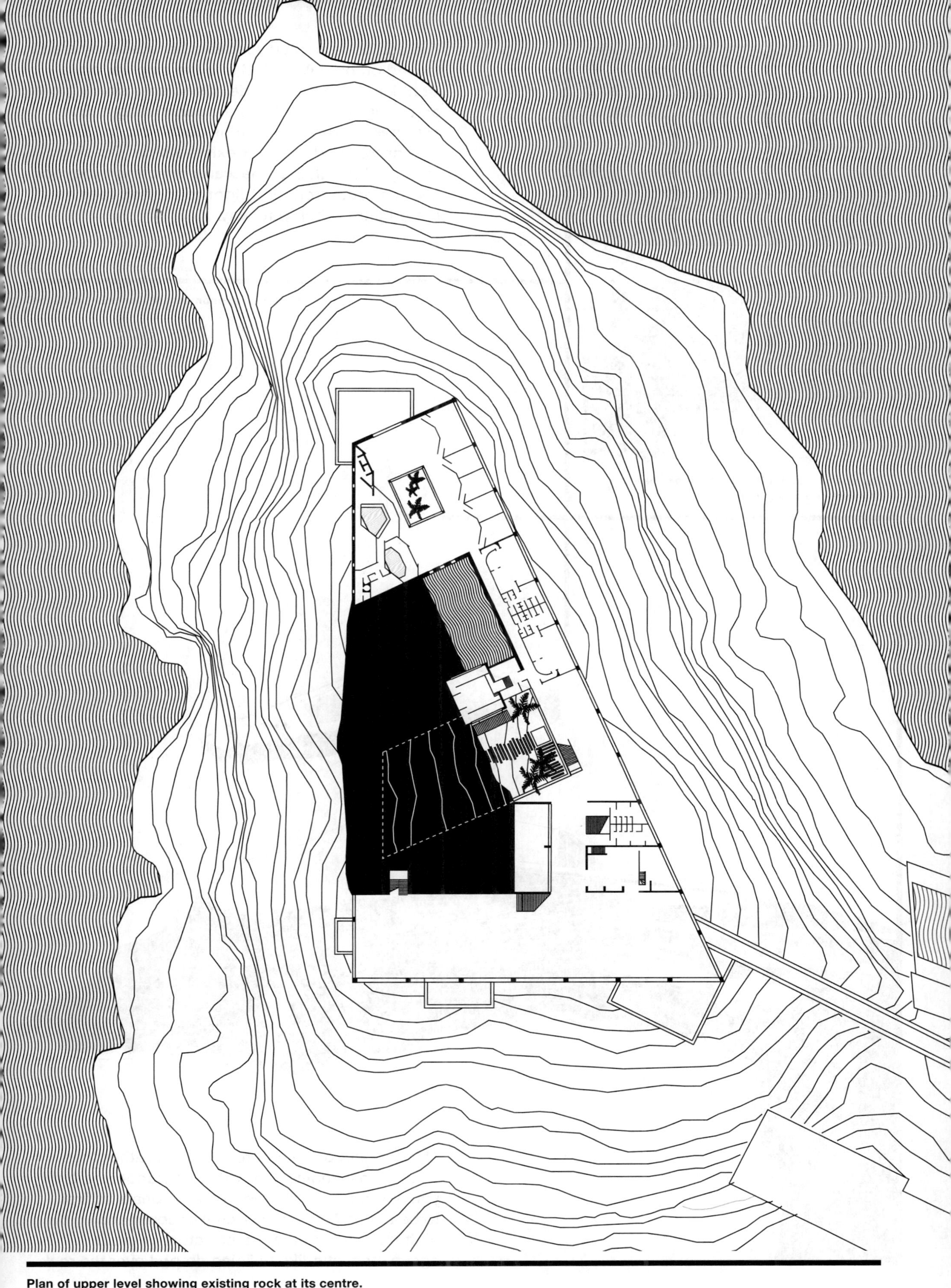

Plan of upper level showing existing rock at its centre.

Traversing the rock.

The pool bar is hidden in what looks like the chimney of a cruise ship.

The additions aren't discernible because they aren't tacked on but integrated into the singular brutalist block. From the outside this volume slowly grows on top of the rock, ultimately dominating it. But external appearances can be deceiving, for the core is kept free and the rock exists within. Passing through the building, one walks directly on the rock, and the route from first floor to rooftop follows the original hilltop pathway.

Exploded axonometry of Costa Brava Clube.

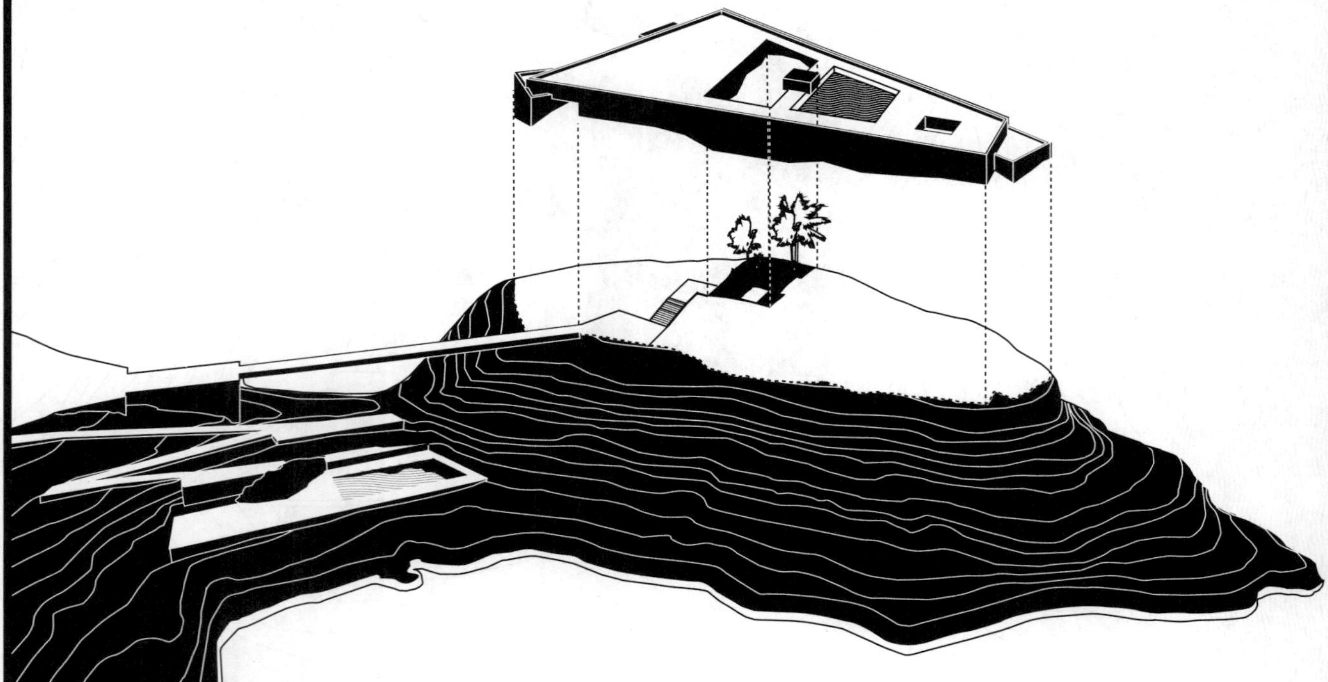

The connection to nature is mental rather than visual, postponing the dramatic panorama until you emerge onto the roof. What appears at first to be a brutalist concrete bunker commanding the highest point is in fact a structure without ego: a monastic-like building draped over the rock.

The craggy topography is integral to the architecture. All parts derive their identity from what happens underneath. What impresses most is the saltwater pool at sea level. Viewed from the bridge, the bedrock seems to have turned into a giant sperm whale.

The ocean pool.

Site plan of Costa Brava Clube.

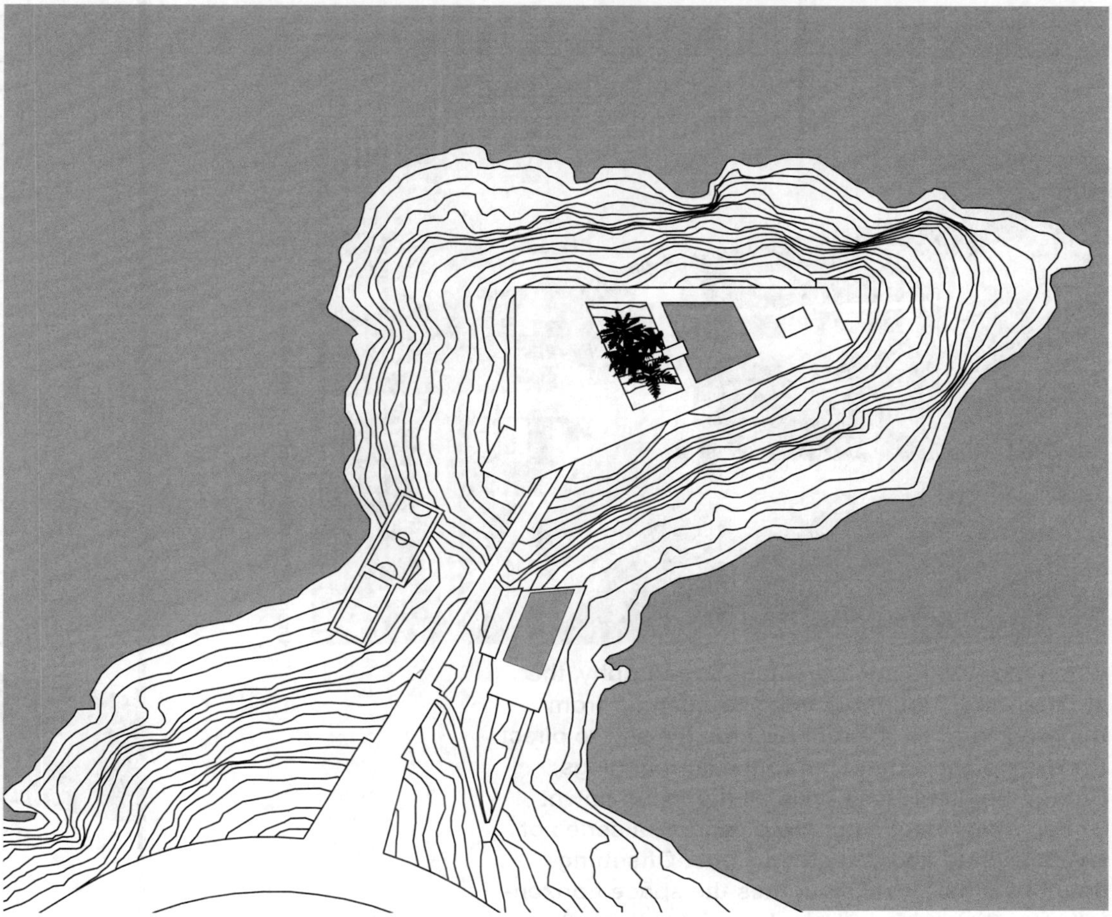

Costa Brava Clube's stern.

Facing the Atlantic, you look down on a small extension, attached to the quadrilateral form, which resembles the stern of a ship. It is intriguing to realize that while nothing in the building mimics naval architecture, it feels quite like sailing away with an encapsulated piece of nature.

Seidler House
Sydney, Australia
Harry & Penelope Seidler
1966–1967

Dramatic roof pitch follows the slope.

When faced with such dramatic topography, the architectural instinct is often to push up from the ground, to tilt the roof towards the sky, to direct the eye up and extend out to the surroundings. But the Seidler House pulls all the focus down. Under an enormous concrete canopy, a series of levels levitate above a steep slope. Offsetting floors by a half-level elongates the space horizontally, creating wide but pinched views through a shaded quiet back to a sunny active front.

Levels hung below the roof.

As noted by Penelope Seidler, “There's a medieval quality to the masonry walls, and the texture of timber all around, it's like my castle. Harry liked things tough; he always said this house was indestructible, and he's absolutely right.”[10] But the Seidler House does not wall itself in like the medieval fortification. The exposed concrete floor and ceiling are treated the same inside and outside, only interrupted by a thin glass envelope.

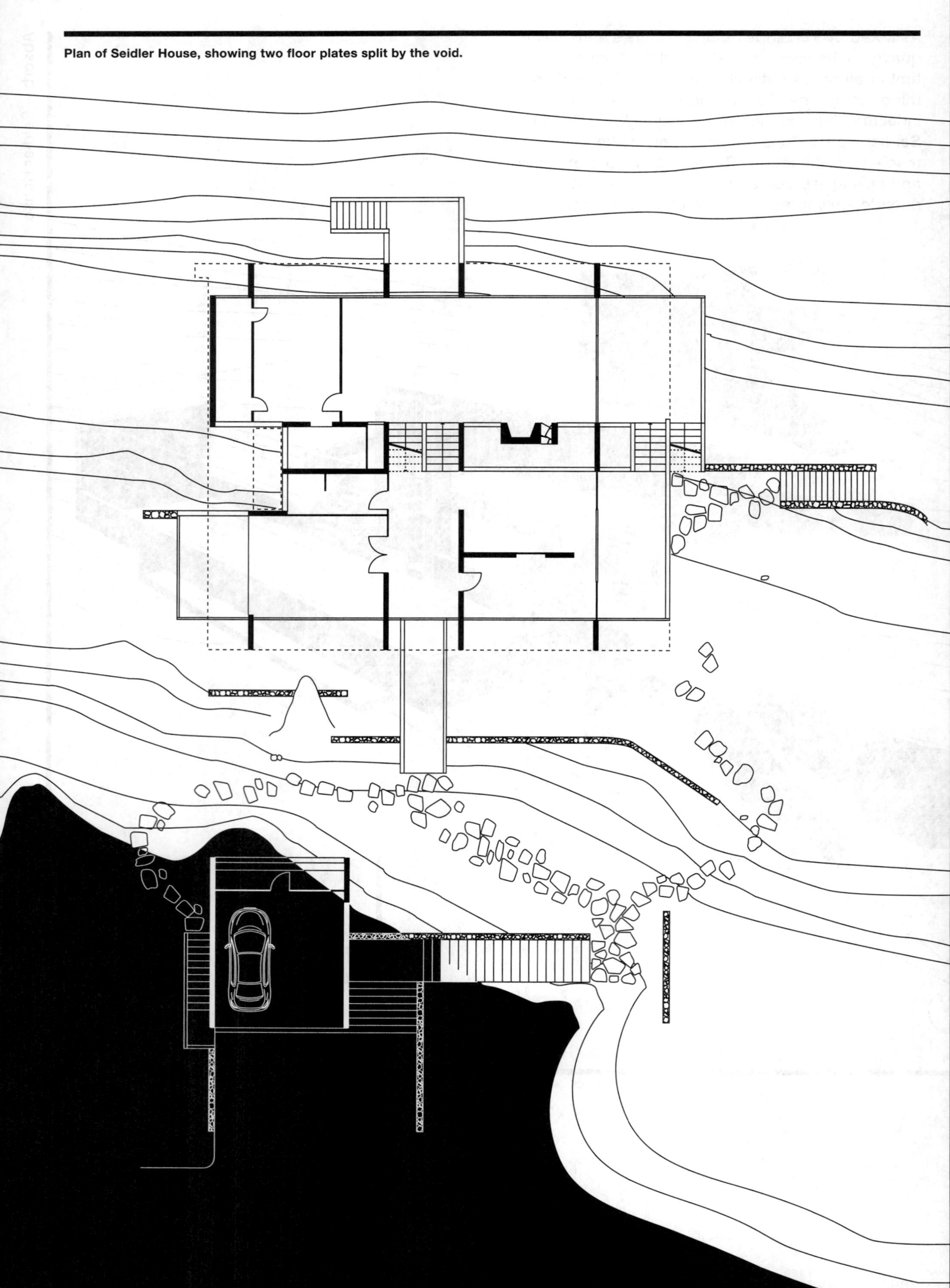

Plan of Seidler House, showing two floor plates split by the void.

Looking across levels.

Moving through the house from top to bottom, from living space to private bedrooms and studio, you cross a two-and-a-half-storey open shaft that extends through the centre of the house. The enormous roof compresses the space and weighs it down, while the levels of the house pull up towards it.

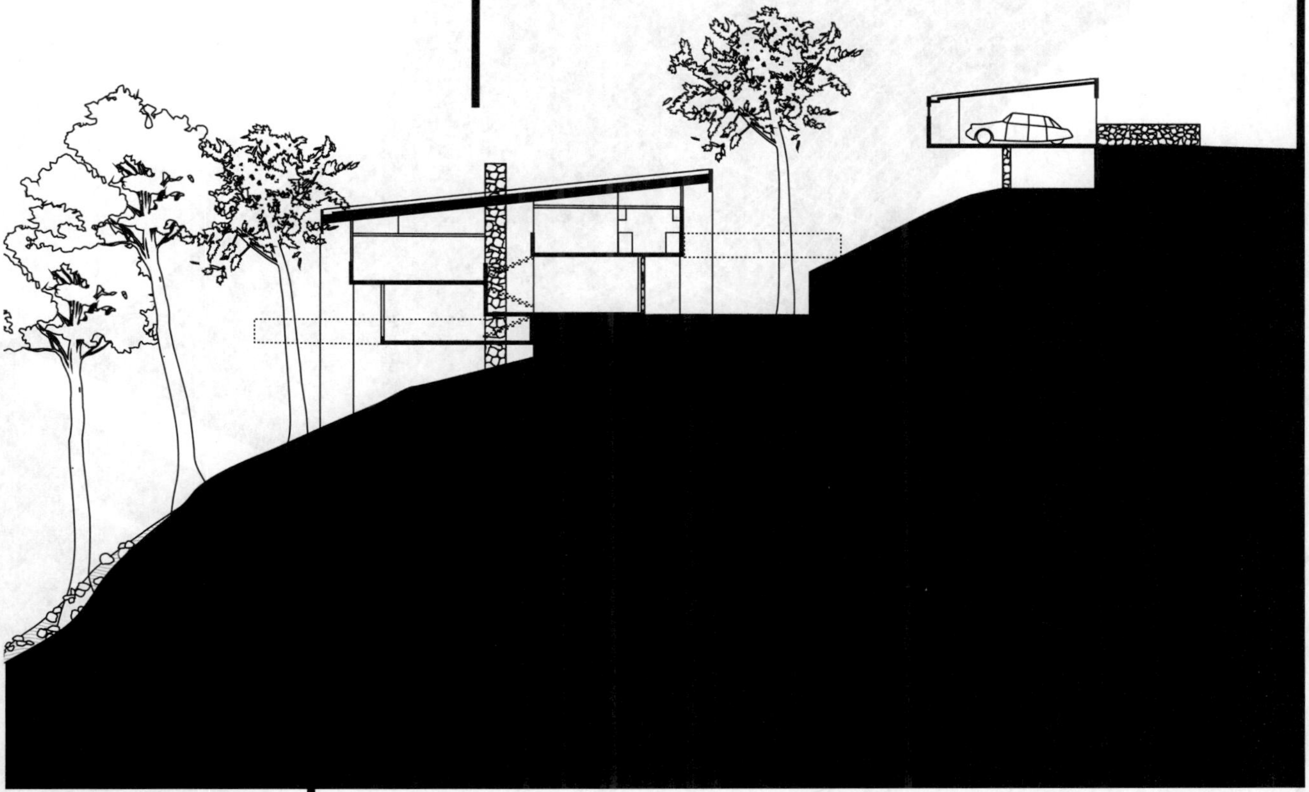

Section of Seidler House.

There is a seismic quality to this opposition of topography, as if the house is balancing forces, pushing down and pulling up on either side of the fissure of the void.

Penelope Seidler below her canopy.

Casa Gerber
Angra dos Reis, Brazil
Paulo Mendes da Rocha
1973–1975

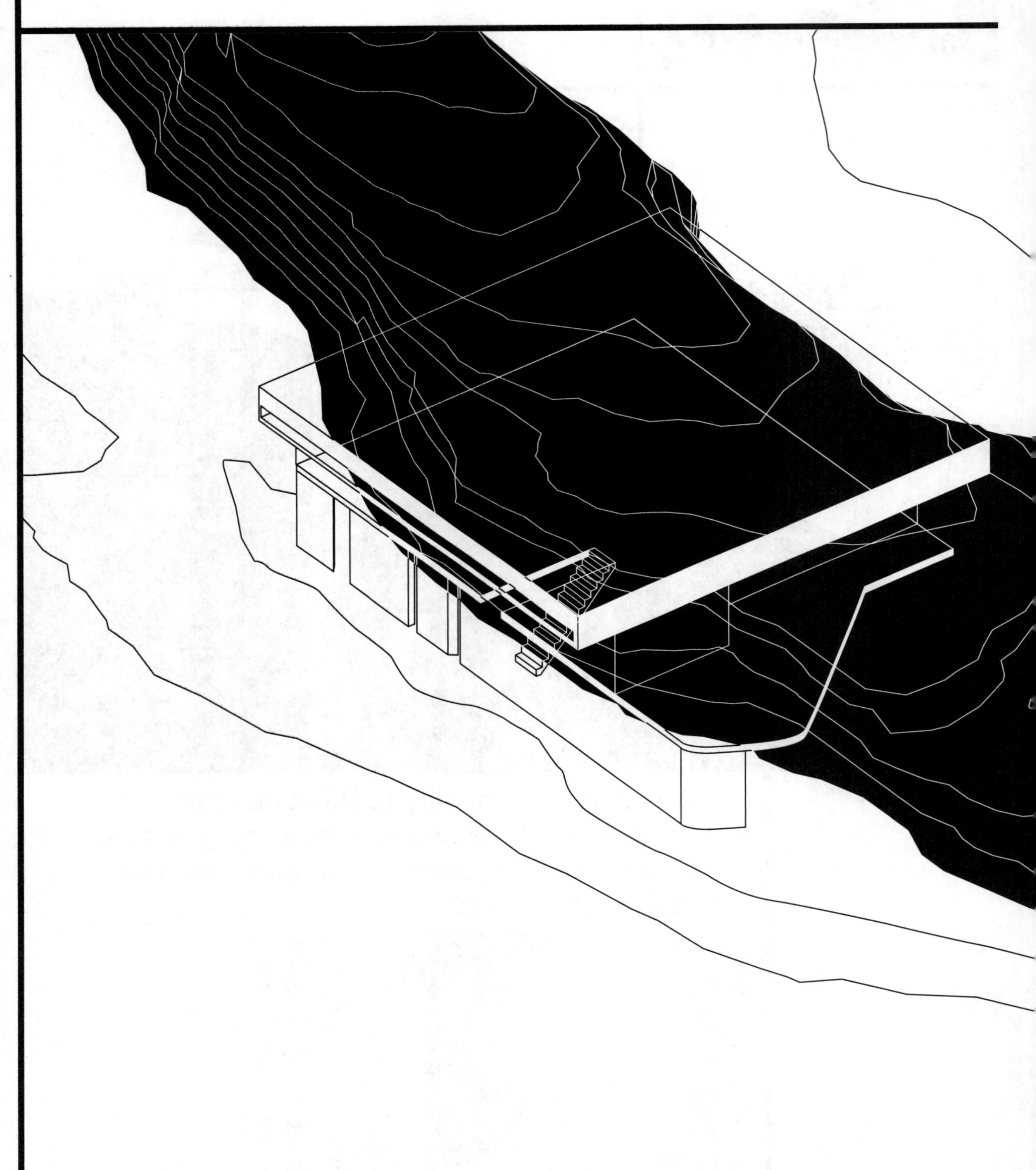

Paulo Mendes da Rocha regards architecture as an instrument for configuring the land. His work reveals a fascination for an uninterrupted horizontal space between roof and ground.

Massive concrete structures are raised up or pushed below grade to liberate the earth's surface as a continuous democratic public realm.[11]

Axonometry of Casa Gerber on the rocks.

The gravity-defying cantilever under construction.

His design for the Brazilian pavilion at Expo '70 in Osaka appeared to balance on a single point of terrain. The original design of the Paulistano Athletic Club in São Paulo pushed the court and stands into the ground and perched a circular concrete canopy above, allowing free movement of air, light and people, removing the threshold between interior and exterior.

Brazilian pavilion at Expo '70 in Osaka, Japan.

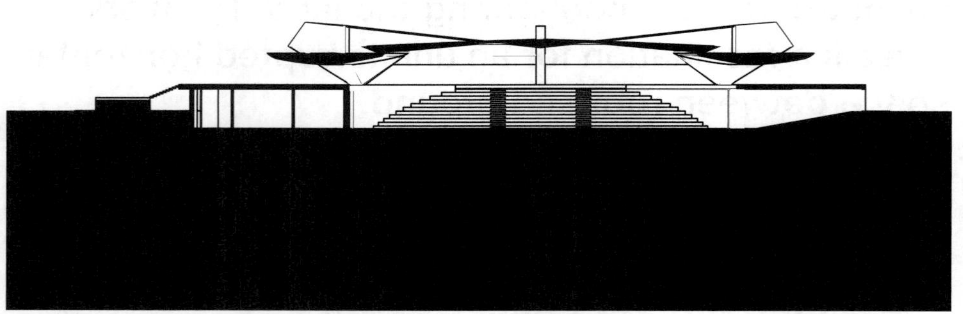

Section of Paulistano Athletic Club in São Paulo, Brazil, 1957.

Unfortunately, what started out below grade slowly rose out of the ground during design realization. The final blow was the subsequent enclosure of the open air court.

Section of Casa Gerber.

The dense Amazon canopy. Earth Innovation Institute.

It is almost as if Mendes da Rocha found the wall obsolete. Perhaps this is a Brazilian sensibility. The Amazon's canopy is so thick it provides all the necessary shelter for life below to thrive. Buffeting abundant rainfall and thinning out towards the ground, nature offers up all the ingredients for architecture to play with.

Lower level plan, wrapped around the rock.

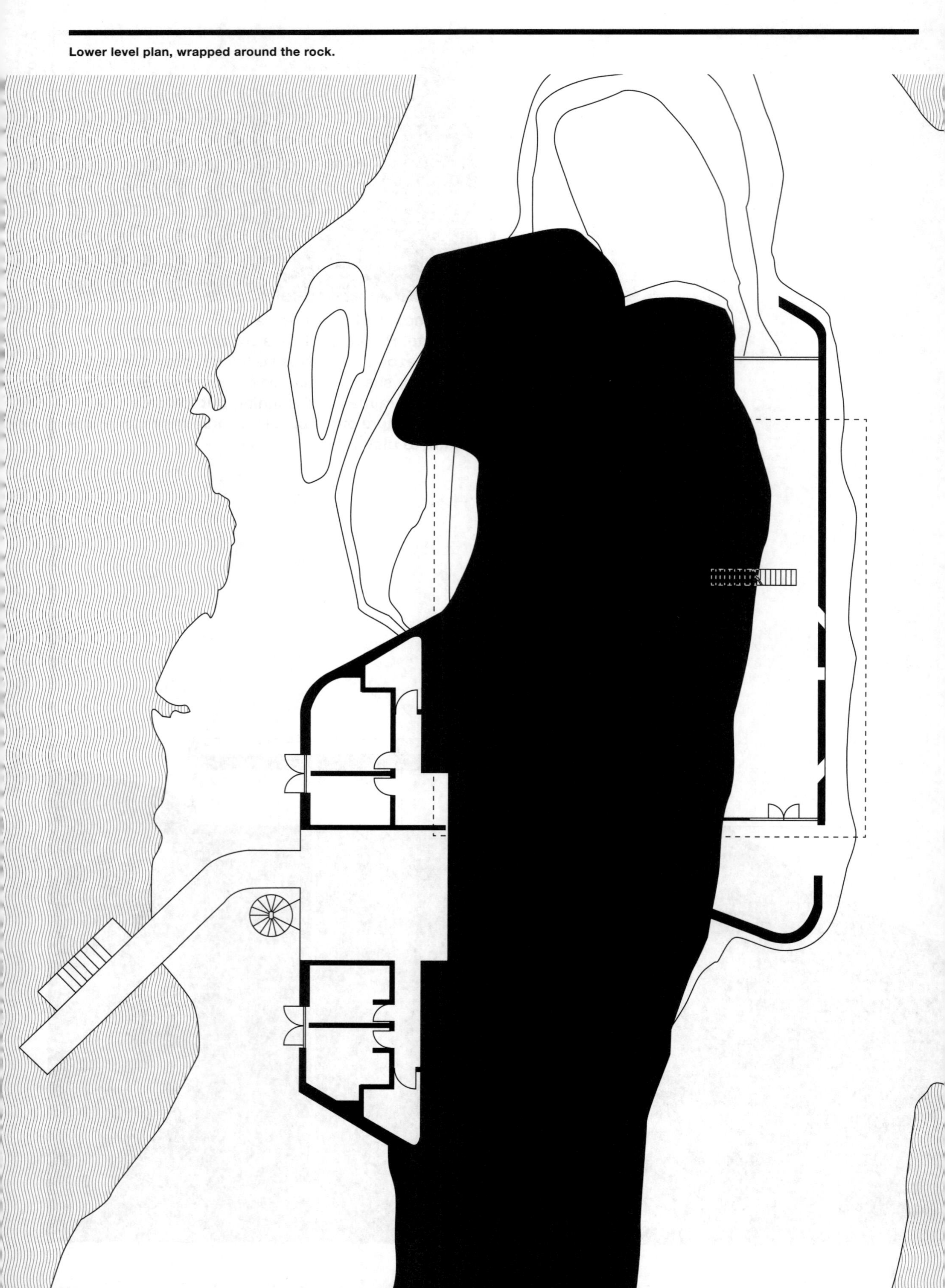

Upper level plan. Note the rock protruding through the floor.

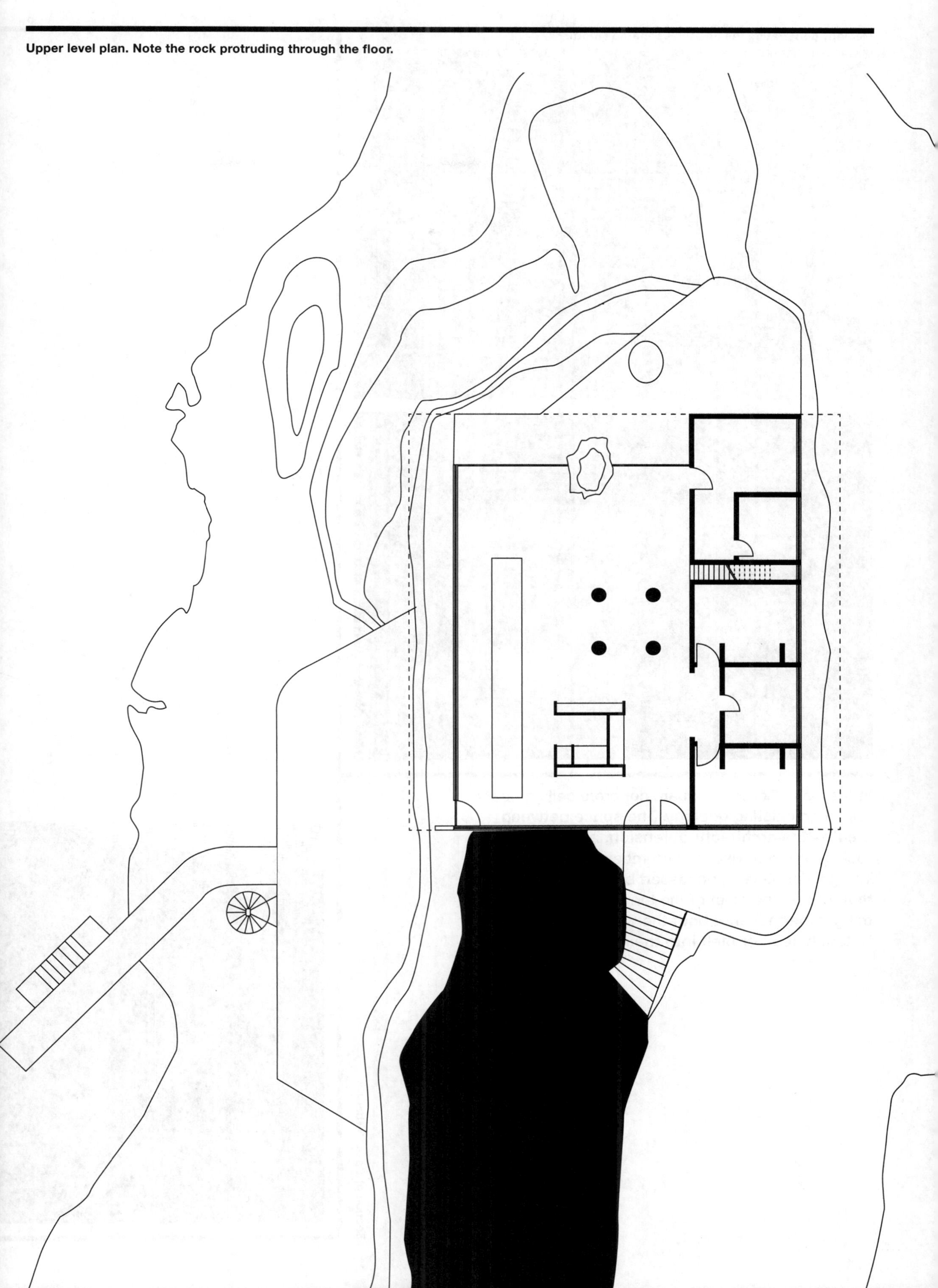

Geology penetrating the interior, Leonardo Finotti.

In the Casa Gerber a square concrete ceiling floats above an existing geology. The space between creates the architectural tension, as though the rock is trying to rise up and meet the ceiling. The ground level is accessed by a ladder-like stair that follows the relief of the terrain. There is something impermanent about the way the stair refuses to touch, lean or melt into the rock below it.

Section of Casa Gerber.

This thin horizontal living plane is accentuated by keeping the perimeter free of enclosure. Like some enormous tree, Casa Gerber's canopy is supported by four central columns.

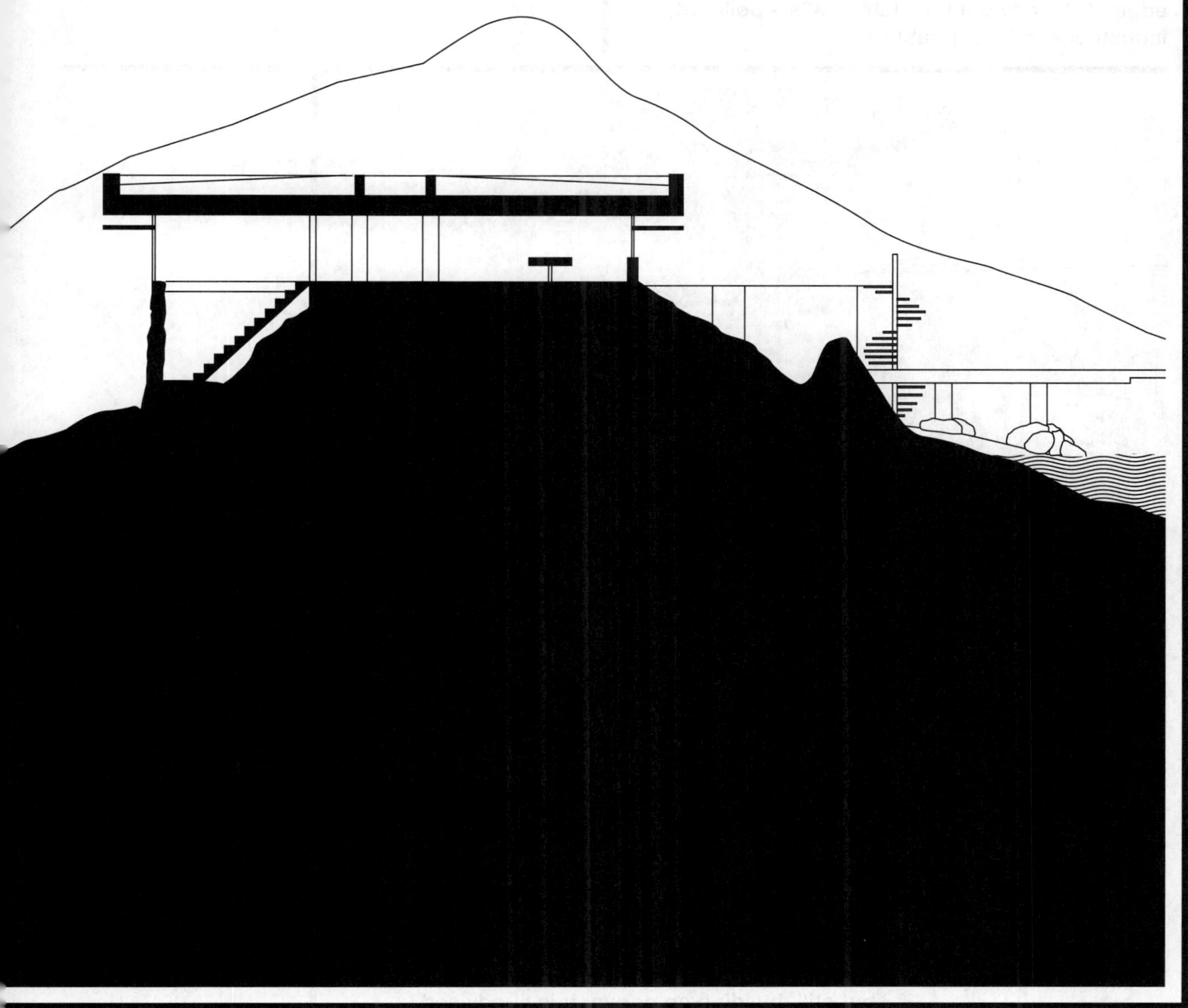

Kunsthal
Rotterdam, Netherlands
OMA
1987–1992

Houses behind a dike, Uitdam.

There is little that is more Dutch than a dike. Dikes are the essence of existence in the lowlands and their sole purpose is to keep the water out. In the Netherlands water has always been a necessary evil, both respected and avoided. It did not always ensure the safe return of fishermen or sailors, and in cities like Rotterdam the port was the dirty edge of the city until the late 1980s – polluted, industrial and inhospitable.

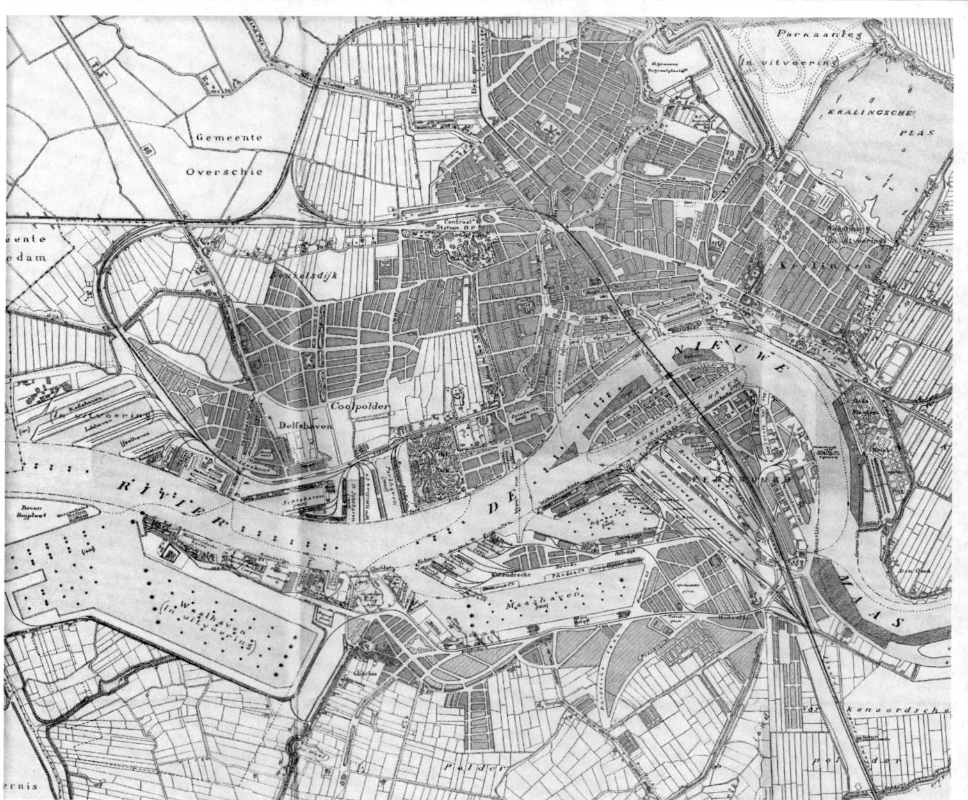

Map of Rotterdam, 1912, Coolpolder at centre left.

It took until far into the twentieth century before property with a waterfront was desired for its quality of living. Where it first stood for danger and uncertainty in the form of sewer stench, dike breaches and storm floods, it has now come to guarantee space, openness and unobstructed views. The Dutch have turned to face the water, but still, building on or over it is ill-advised.

The Kunsthal is built in the Coolpolder of Rotterdam, land protected by the Westzeedijk. Today this grass verge looks more like a road embankment than a vital force against nature.

Sectional axonometry of Kunsthal.

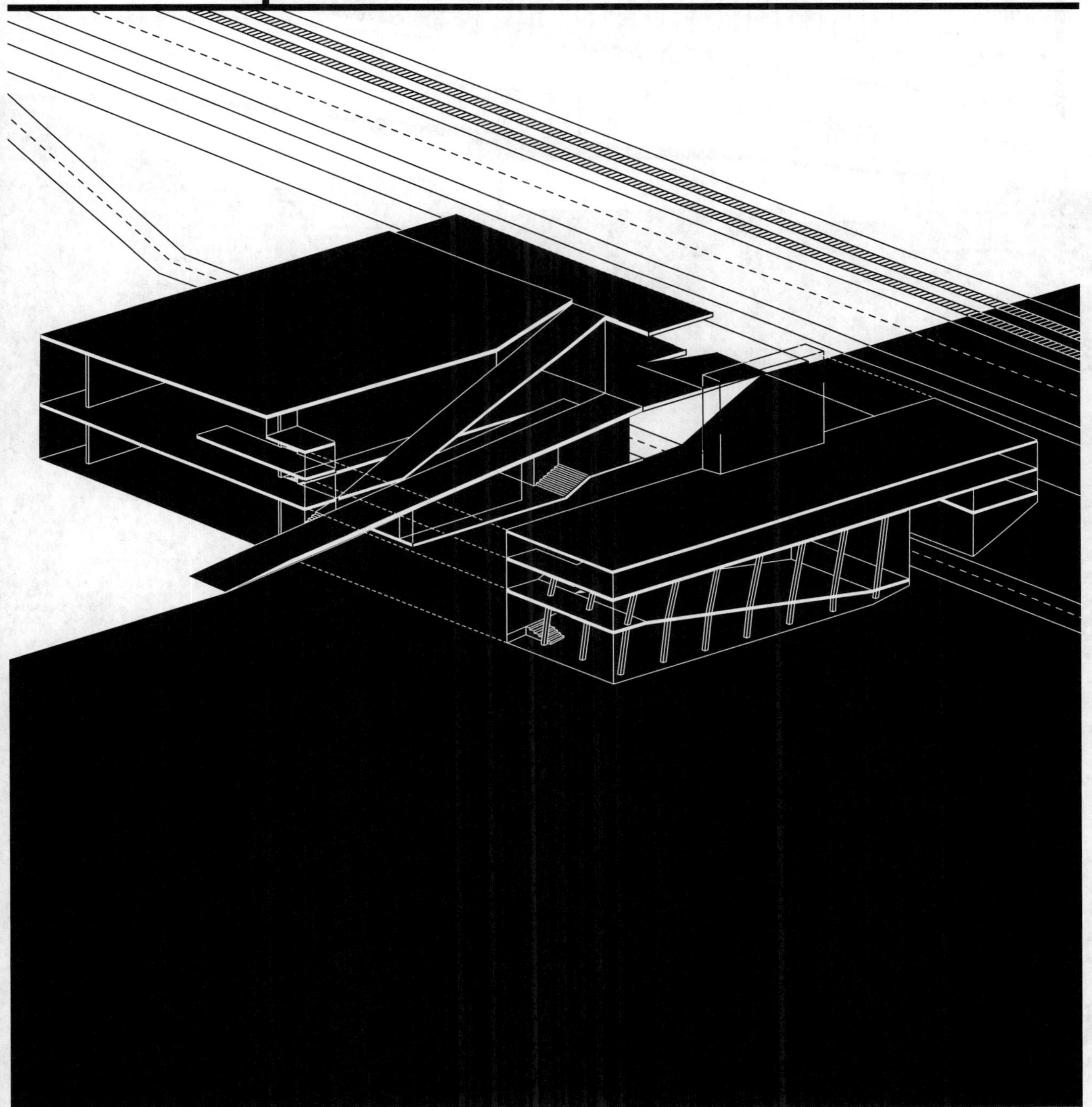

Section of the Kunsthal, with the dike on the right.

The Kunsthal seems closely linked to the dike, but this is an optical illusion. The built mass of the Kunsthal sits at the bottom of the dike and leans towards it as much as it can. Only a thin metal grid floor bridges the road below to lightly touch the top of the dike.

The Kunsthal desecrates and celebrates the dike by tilting its floors. The entrance is not an obvious door on the perimeter but located at the heart of the building, halfway along a ramp that connects dike and polder. This ramp continues inside. The auditorium is tilted in the opposite direction, meeting the entrance level halfway, and here starts a journey inside the museum, spiralling around the public ramp that bisects the whole building. It is a boxy version of Le Corbusier's Carpenter Center, but OMA takes it to the next level in spaciousness with a series of sloped floors and switchback ramps, which combine to connect multiple flows and programmes.

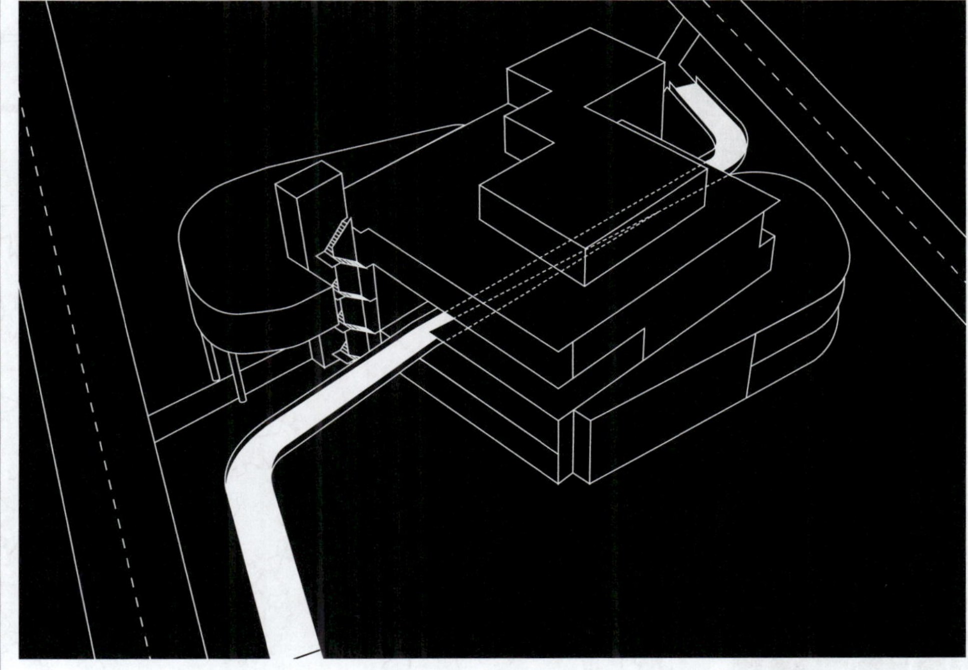

Axonometry of the Carpenter Center for the Visual Arts, Cambridge, Massachusetts, Le Corbusier, 1963.

Plan of the Kunsthal.

Central ramp that bisects the Kunsthal.

Level changes, parallel movements and an interplay of transparent materials create a sequence of contradictory experiences. A glass wall splits the central ramp so that visitors inside and public outside rub shoulders on their separate routes through. It seems as if the building should have been on the other side of the dike – not in a secured polder landscape but rocking on the waves of the North Sea. As if once stable floors have been unmoored.

Section of the Kunsthal auditorium.

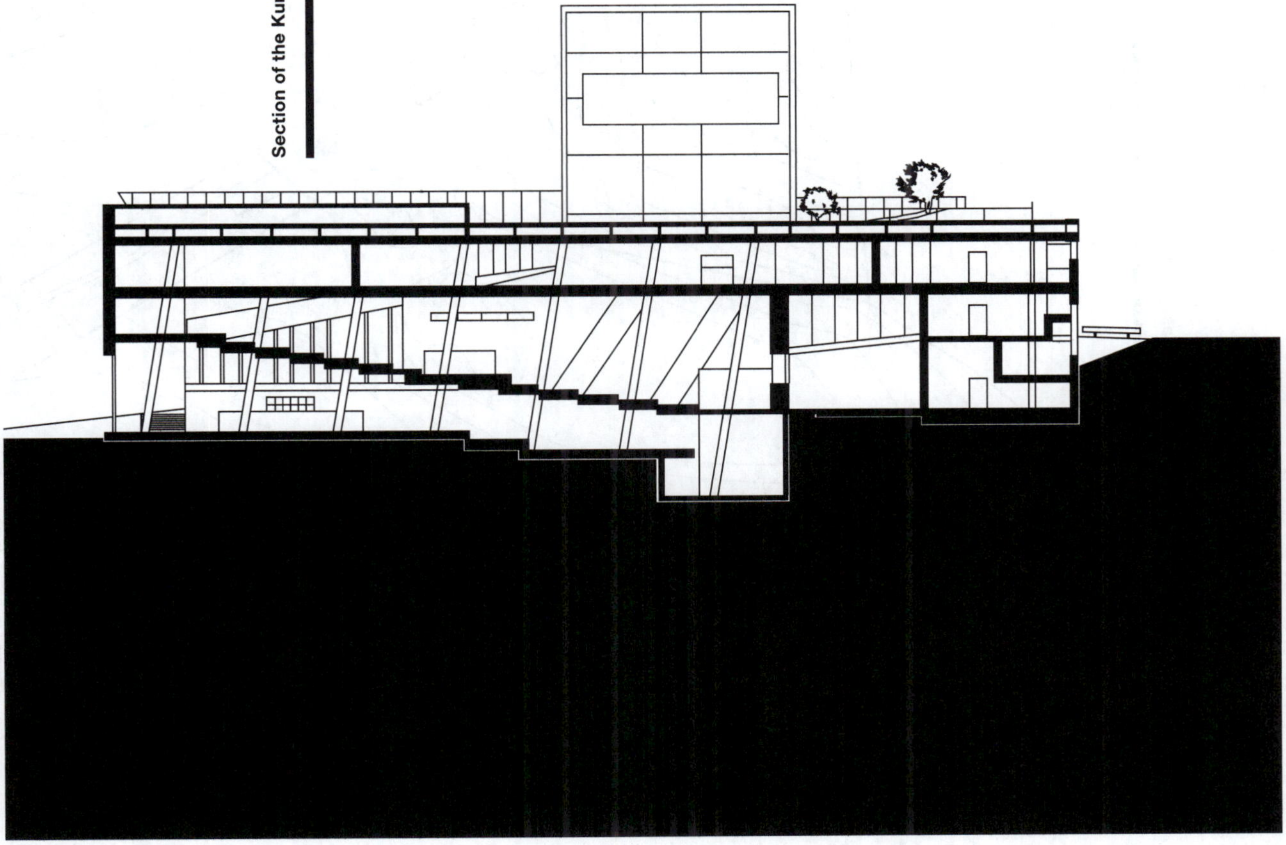

Dutch Embassy
Addis Ababa, Ethiopia
SeARCH & Dick van Gameren
1998–2005

There are two landscapes on an embassy compound. The physical one of the host country, and an invisible one of the guest on site. A building can only connect with or react to the first, but it can reflect the latter.

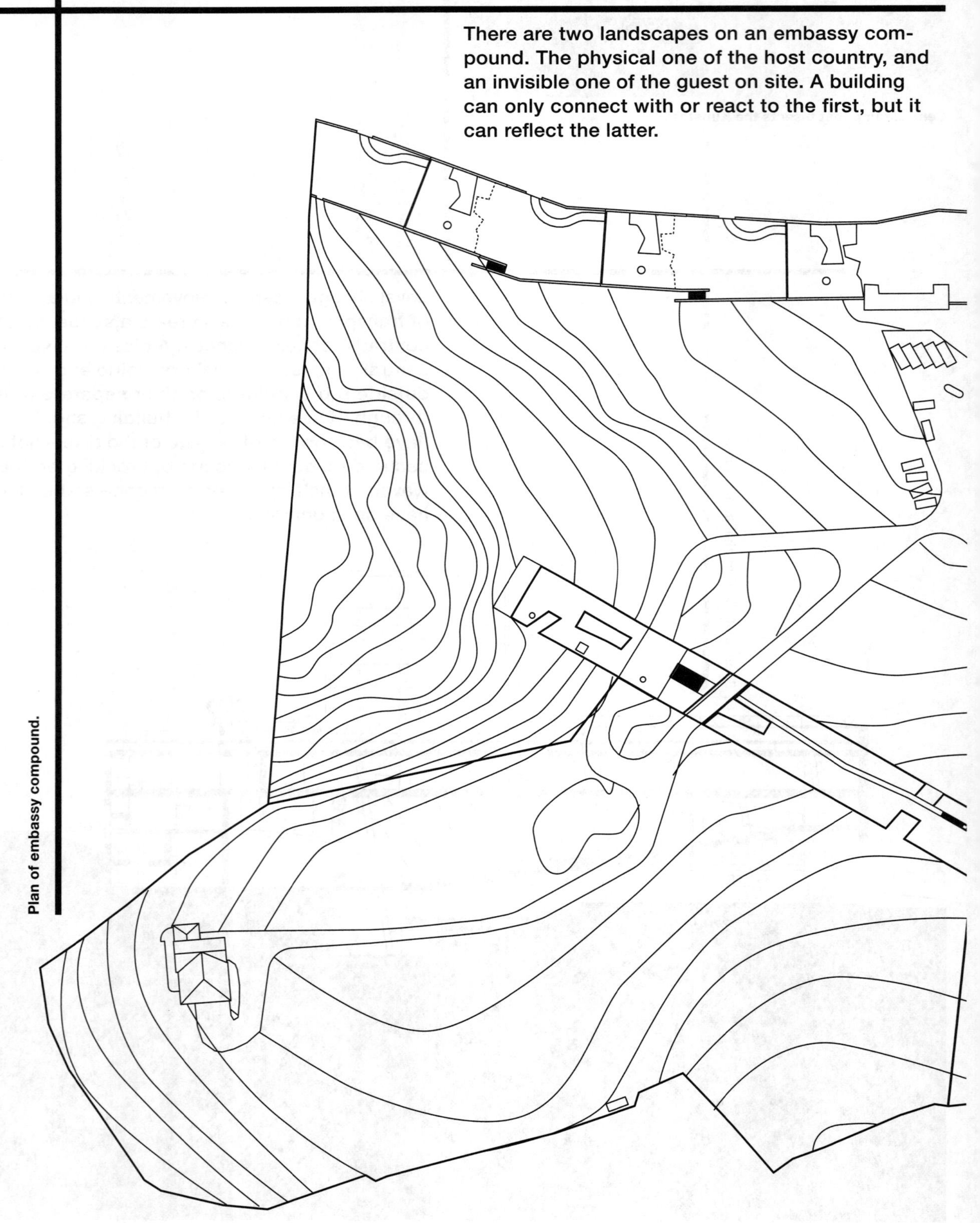

Plan of embassy compound.

Villager in the Gheralta Mountains, Ethiopia.

There couldn't be two countries more different than Ethiopia and the Netherlands. The latter is as flat as a pancake, and more than half of the population lives below sea level. The Ethiopian landscape, in contrast, ranges from rugged alpine terrain to one of the hottest, driest deserts in the world, the Danakil Depression. Its capital, Addis Ababa, is fourth in the world when it comes to altitude, lying 2400 metres above sea level.

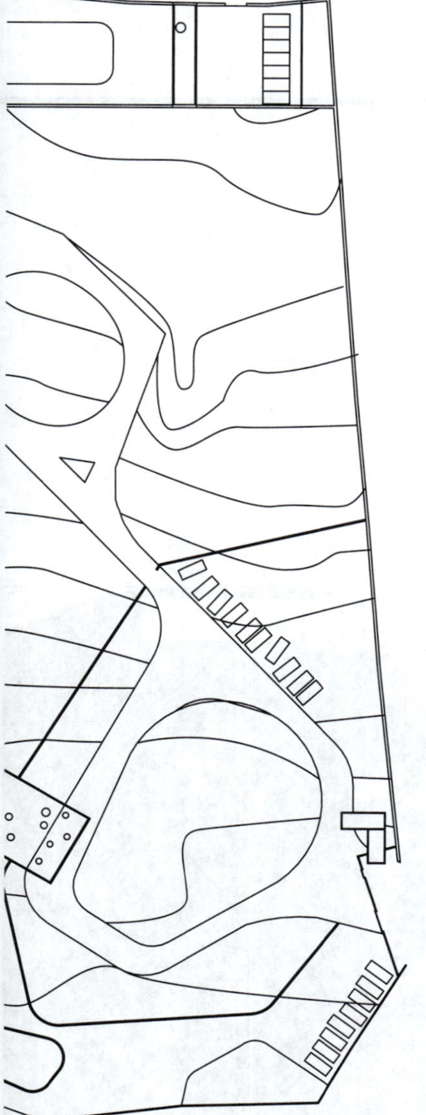

Without dikes, much of the Netherlands would be inundated with water.

The Dutch embassy and residence building could be seen as a re-enactment of Dutch conditions within an Ethiopian landscape.

The roof is a singular horizontal plane that collects rainwater.

The embassy building is visible at both ends and, as the landscape slopes gradually upwards, it disappears temporarily from view, transforming into a pool among the eucalyptus trees. The roof's shallow pool acts as a unifying element, combining the Dutch tradition of water management and landscape technology with the natural craggy countryside of Ethiopia.

Employees work and live under this artificial water level, just as the Dutch do. The collected rainwater can irrigate the gardens during the dry season, avoiding the need for precious borehole water.

The ground floor follows the natural topography of the site.

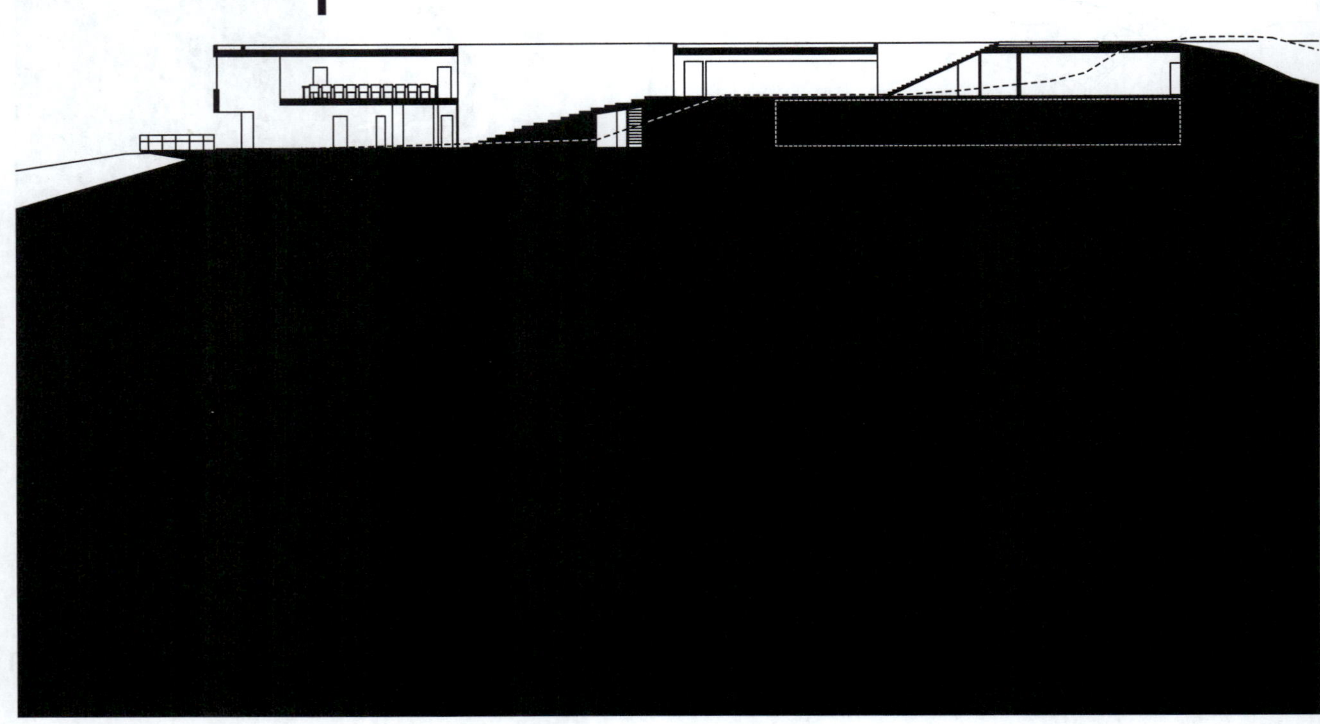

Flight of steps to embassy residence.

While the roof is strictly horizontal, the interior programme undulates in response to the existing sloping terrain. These two landscapes, the technical and the natural, meet at a point in the middle. Here all programme is squeezed out by the terrain. The hill naturally divides the building into two units, public chancellery and private residence. The long sloping corridor of the chancellery culminates in a patio on one side of the hill and the residence sits on the other, accessed by descending a grand flight of steps.

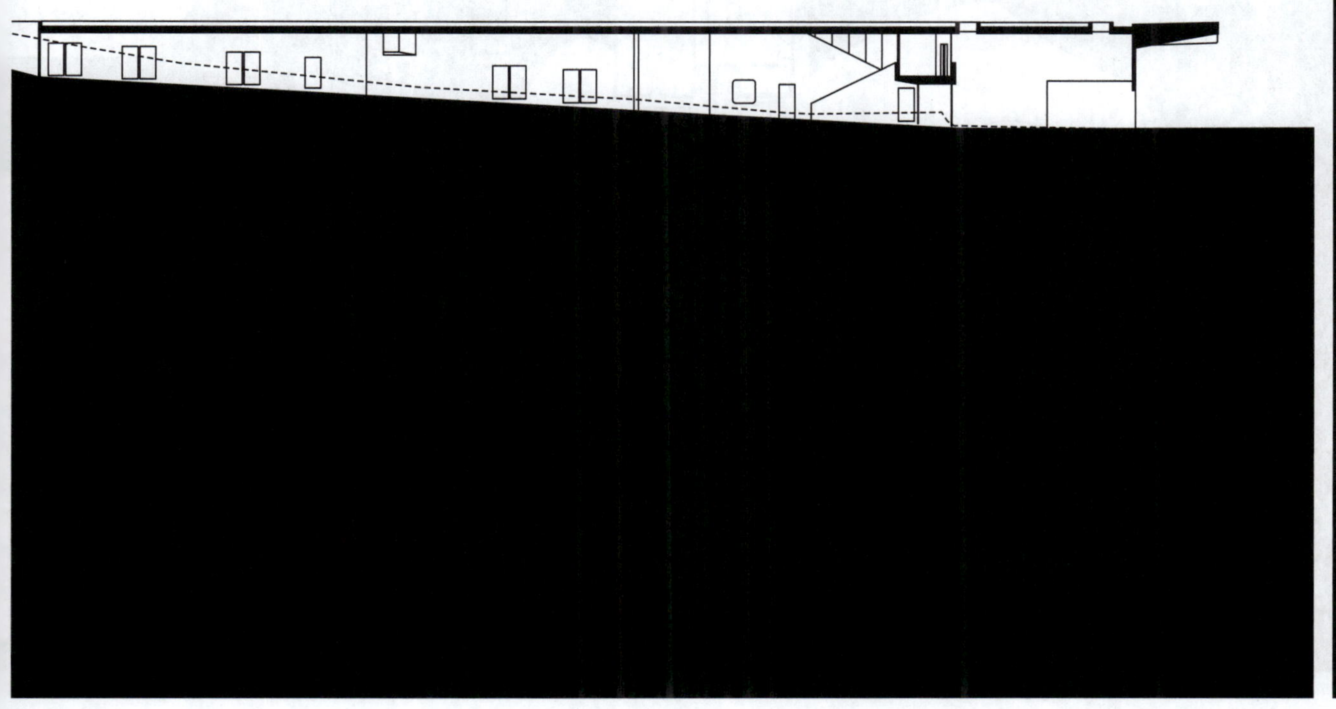

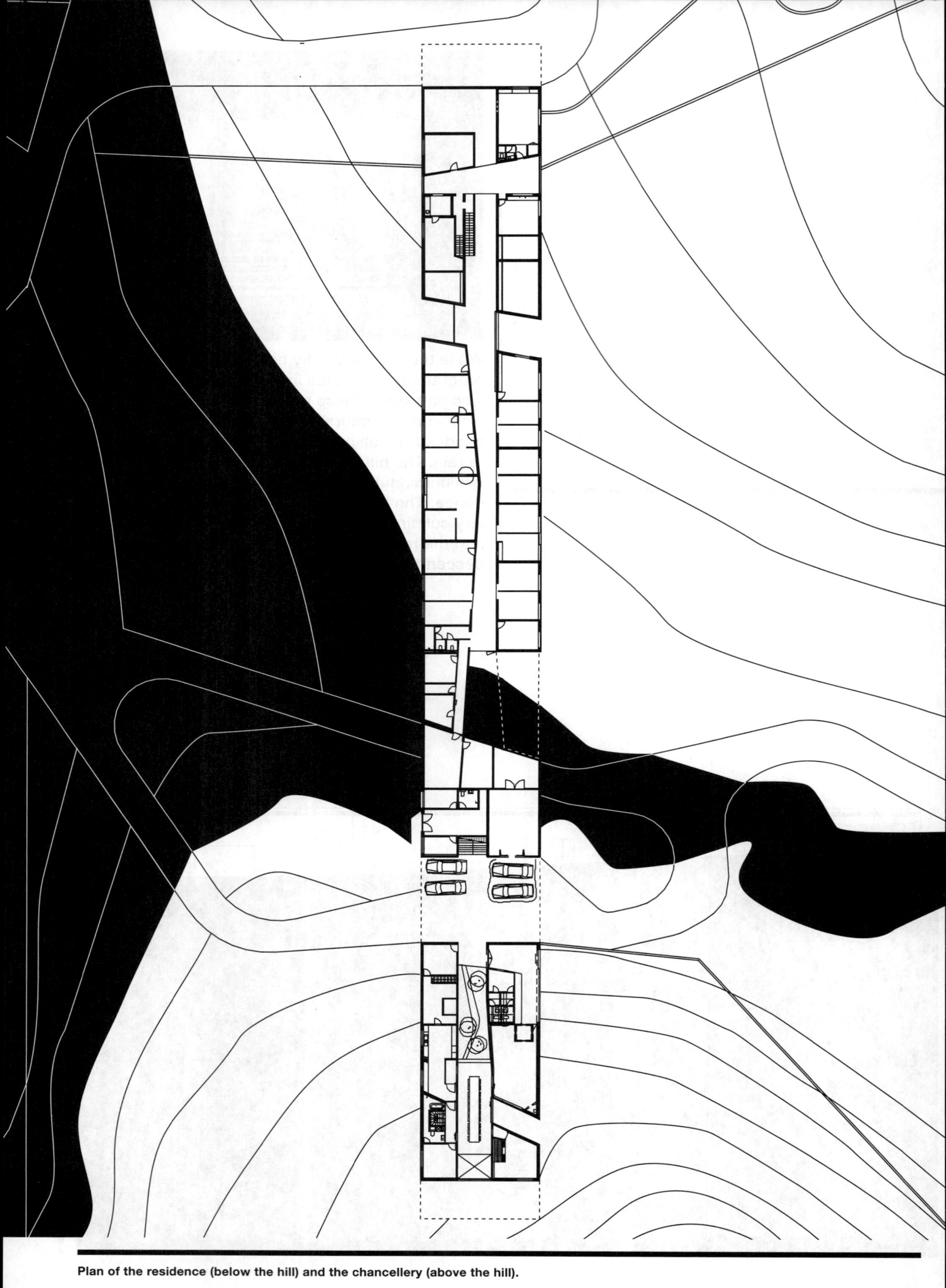

Plan of the residence (below the hill) and the chancellery (above the hill).

A road loops over and through the building. This covered space at the base of the stairs serves as a dry entrance during heavy rains. It also accommodates the customary coffee ceremony, where coffee beans are roasted on the spot. Welcoming guests with coffee is where Ethiopian and Dutch traditions come together.

Watery landscape of the 'Realm of a Thousand Islands'.

Axonometry of chancellery and residence.

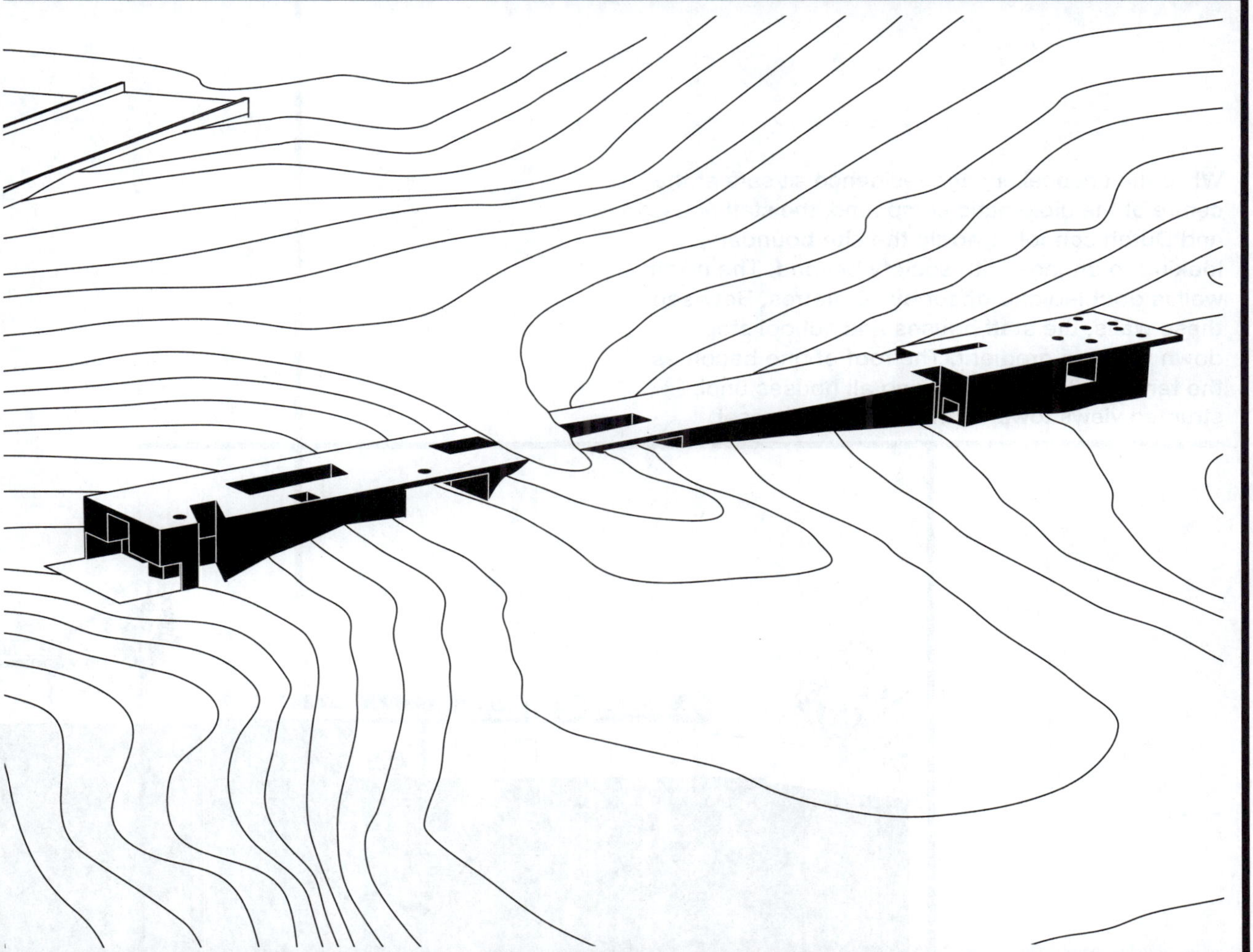

Coptic cross of Ethiopia.

The elongated volume is evocative of the traditional rock-cut churches of Ethiopia that are sculpted from the earth. The facades are made of untreated concrete in the same tint as the red-purple cotton soil of the Ethiopian Highlands.[12] The relief on the roof slowly transitions from an intricate Coptic cross to a map of the 'Realm of a Thousand Islands' north of Amsterdam. These represent host and guest.

The essence of the design lies in the juxtaposition of two seemingly incompatible landscapes, creating a world of its own.

While the chancellery and residence sit safe at the centre of the diplomatic compound, the staff houses and Dutch school straddle the site boundary, looking to engage with society beyond. The north wall is doubled and offset by 20 metres. Between these walls, the staff houses and school step down with the gradient. The roof of one becomes the terrace of the next, giving all houses unobstructed views towards the valley and sunset.

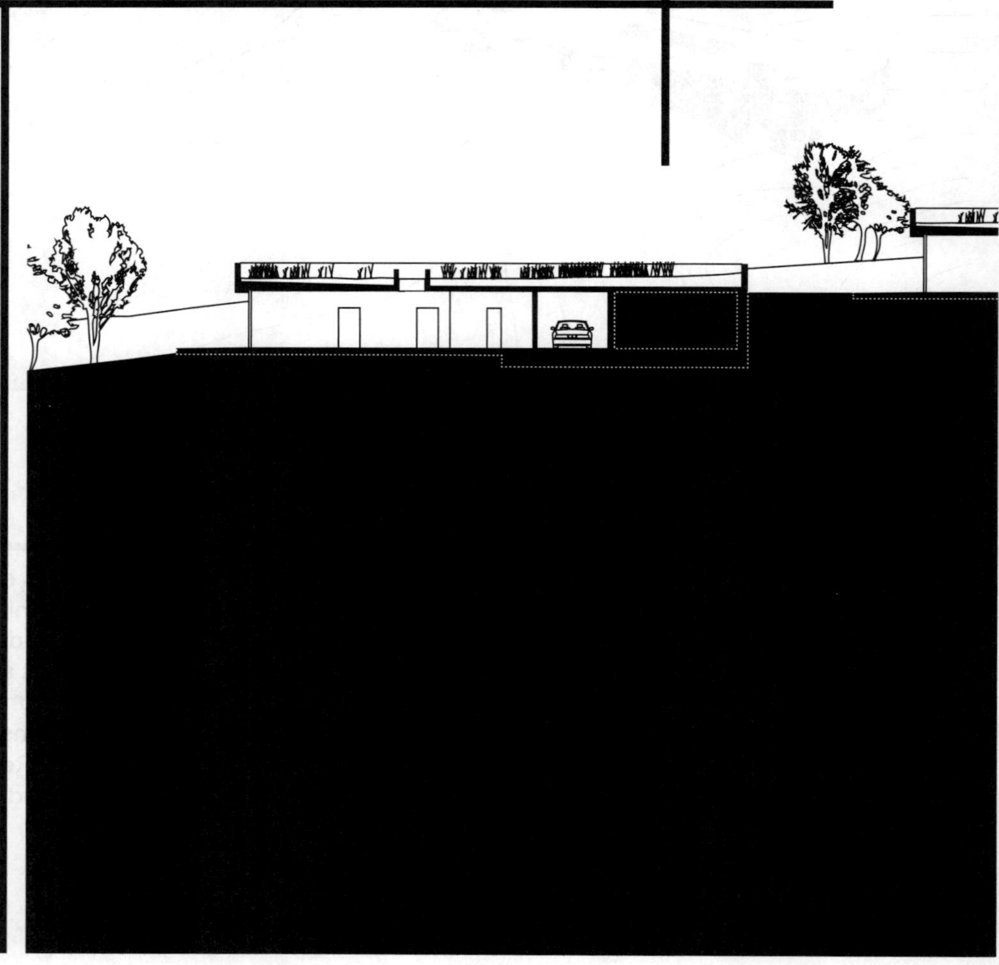

Section of terraced staff housing.

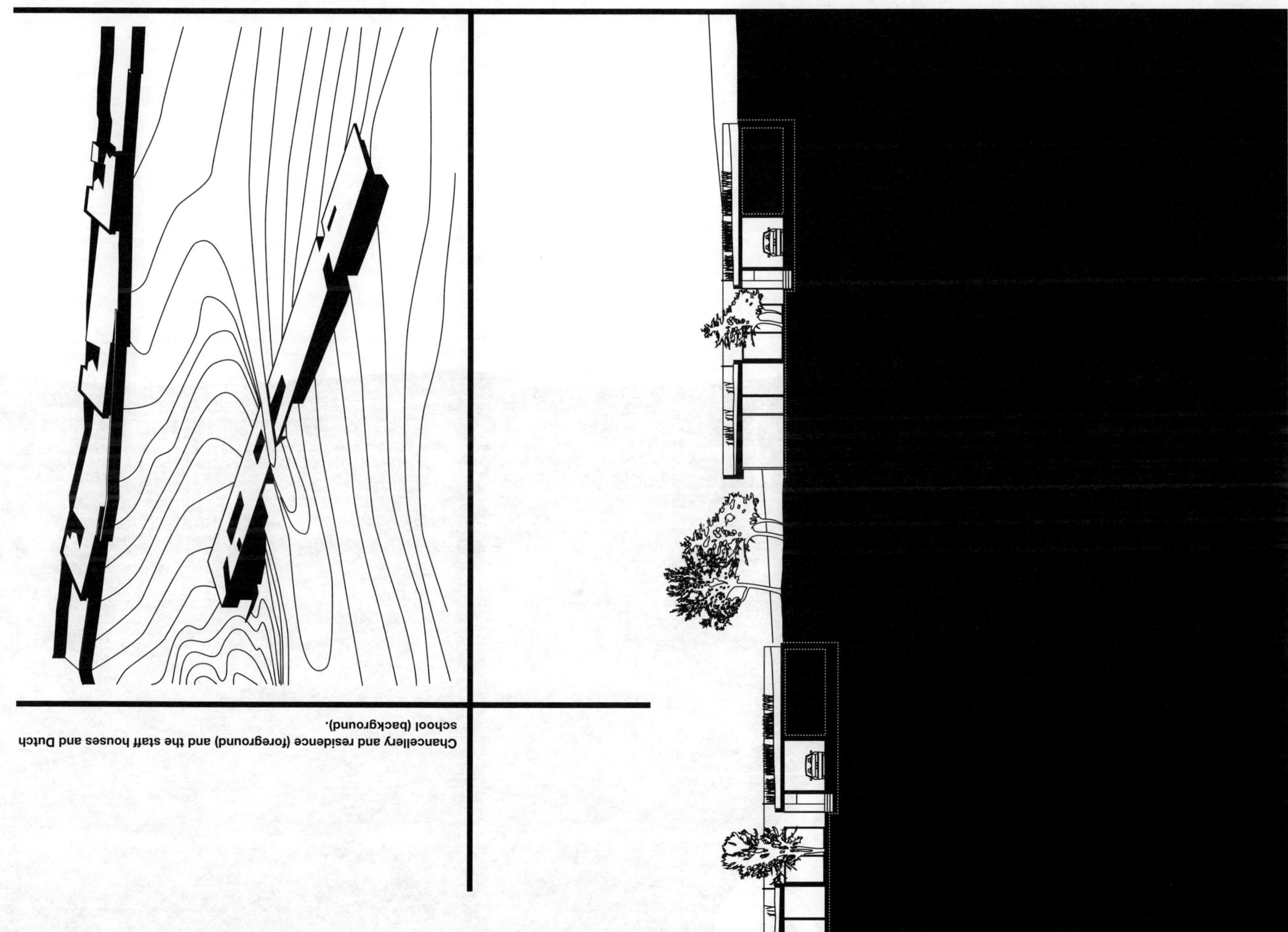

Chancellery and residence (foreground) and the staff houses and Dutch school (background).

Lower plan of terraced staff housing.

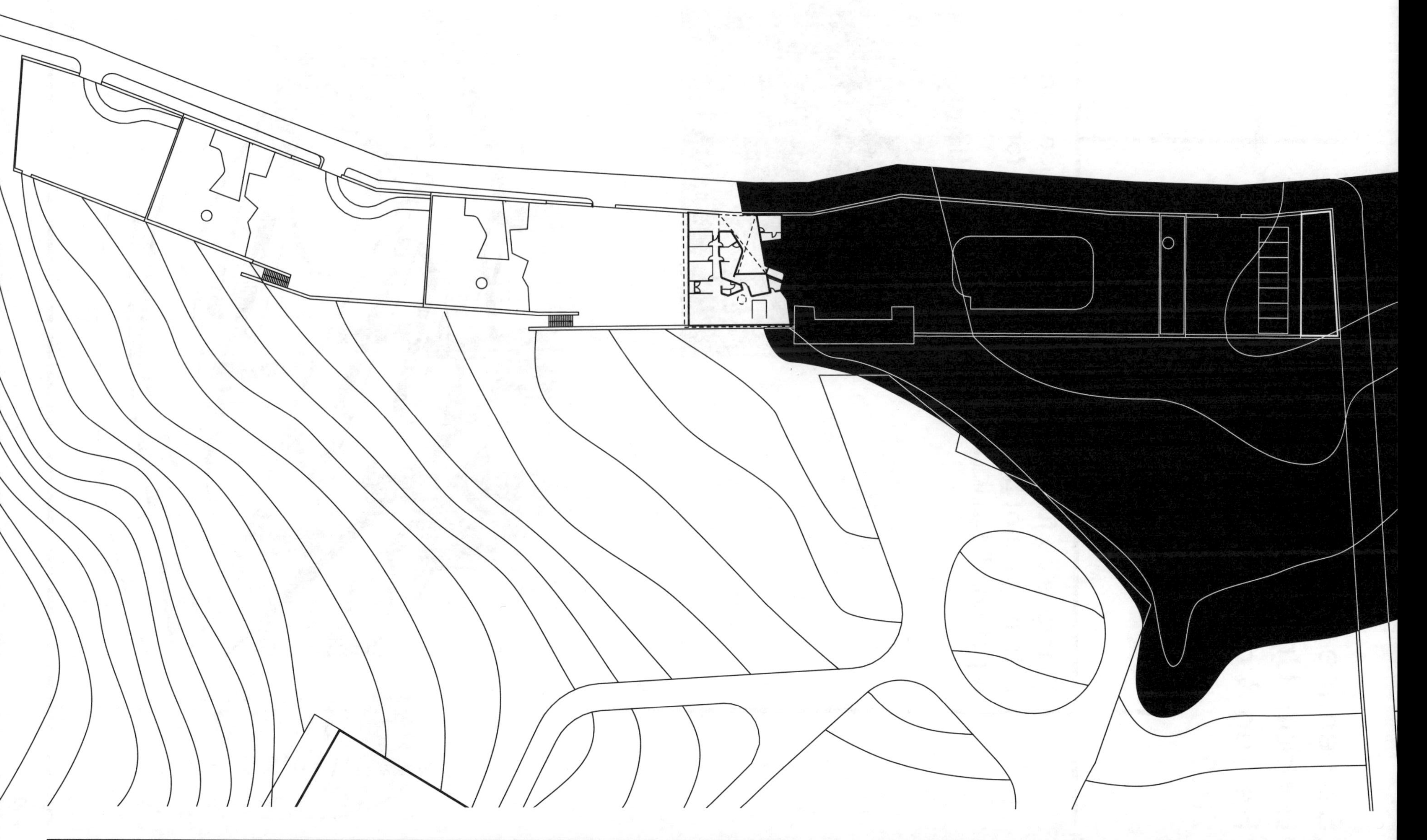

Upper plan of terraced staff housing.

Serpentine Gallery Pavilion
London, United Kingdom
Herzog & de Meuron and Ai Weiwei
2012

"There is no future without a past, because what is to be cannot be imagined except as a form of repetition."[13] —Siri Hustvedt

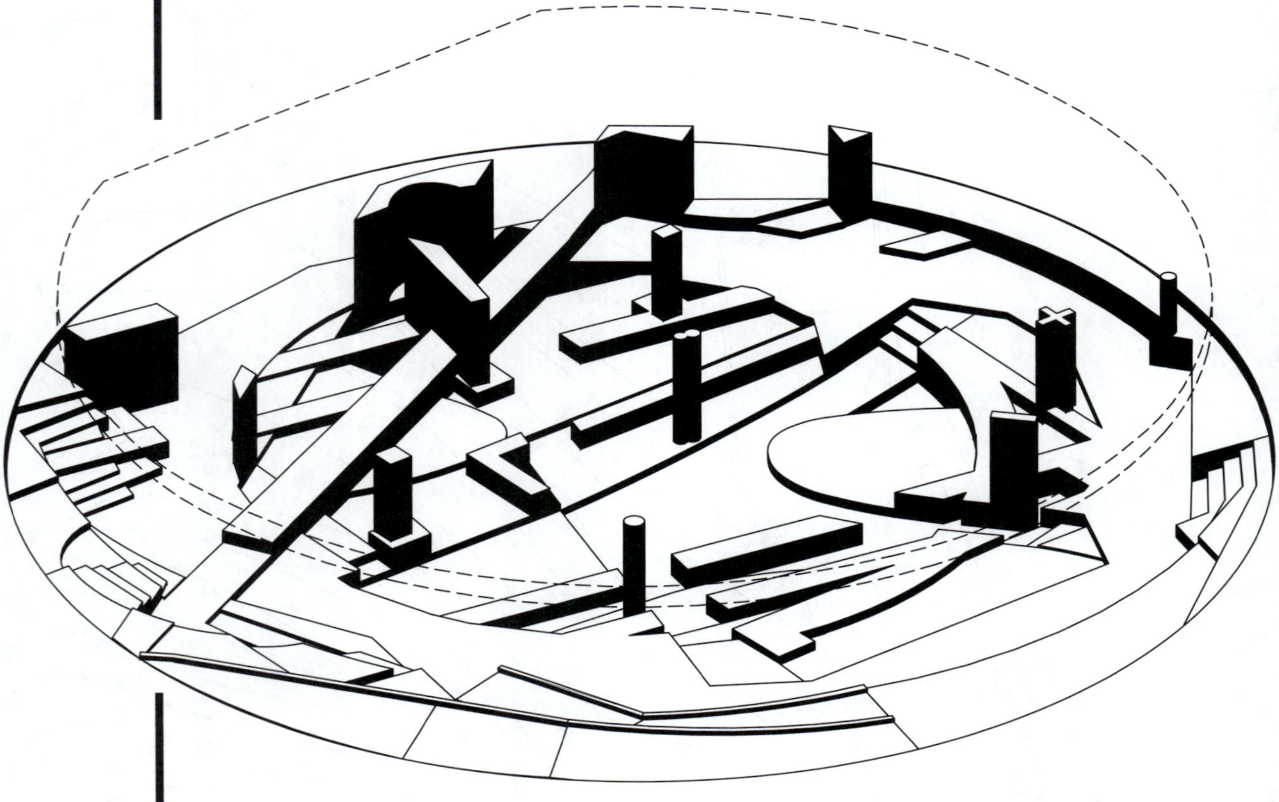

Axonometry of Serpentine Gallery Pavilion.

Parchment was once made from the skin of domesticated animals, and the finer version, vellum, specifically from the skin of calves. Due to its high price it was often reused by the Romans, who scraped off or washed away text that was often visible as 'scriptio inferior', the writing beneath. The cheaper papyrus used since the fourth millennium BCE was also reused by washing away the ink. Either still visible or resurfacing later, two or more overlaid texts create a palimpsest.

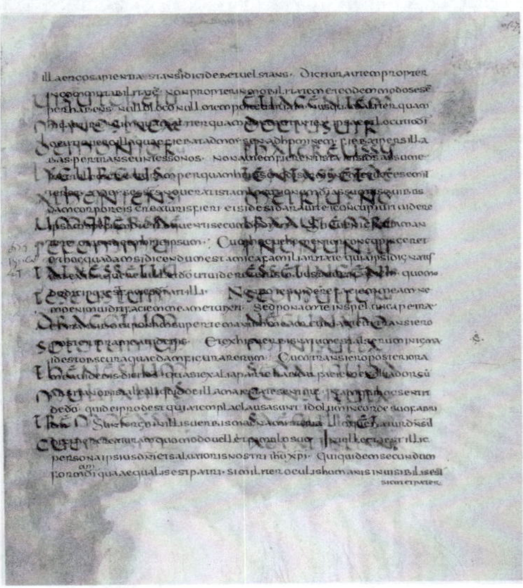

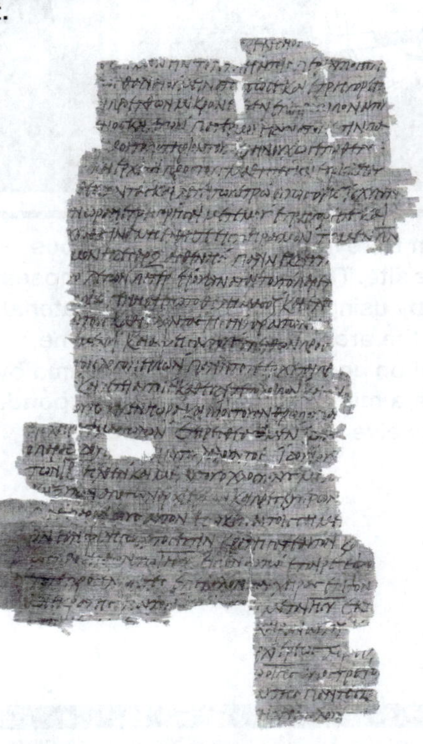

Fragment of *De re publica* by Cicero, 400–500 BCE (left) and papyrus palimpsest made from the pith of the papyrus plant, 260 BCE (right).

From 2000 to 2011, eleven architects constructed a pavilion on the perfectly manicured lawn of Kensington Gardens next to the Serpentine Gallery. In 2012, Herzog & de Meuron with Ai Weiwei were the twelfth, and their proposal was to create a palimpsest, this time with the earth as a medium.

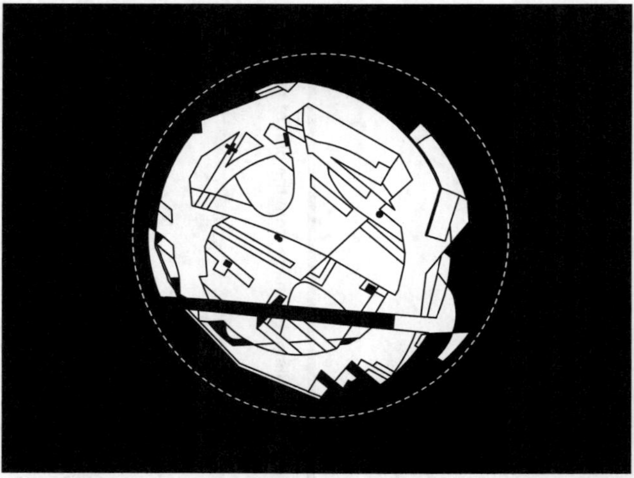

They dug down to reveal traces of all previous pavilions on the site. The traces mimic a palimpsest-like earthwork by using warm-brown cork material. The only thing the architects added was some cuts for circulation and some cavernous drama by covering it with a mirroring, almost circular pond, supported by twelve uniquely shaped columns.

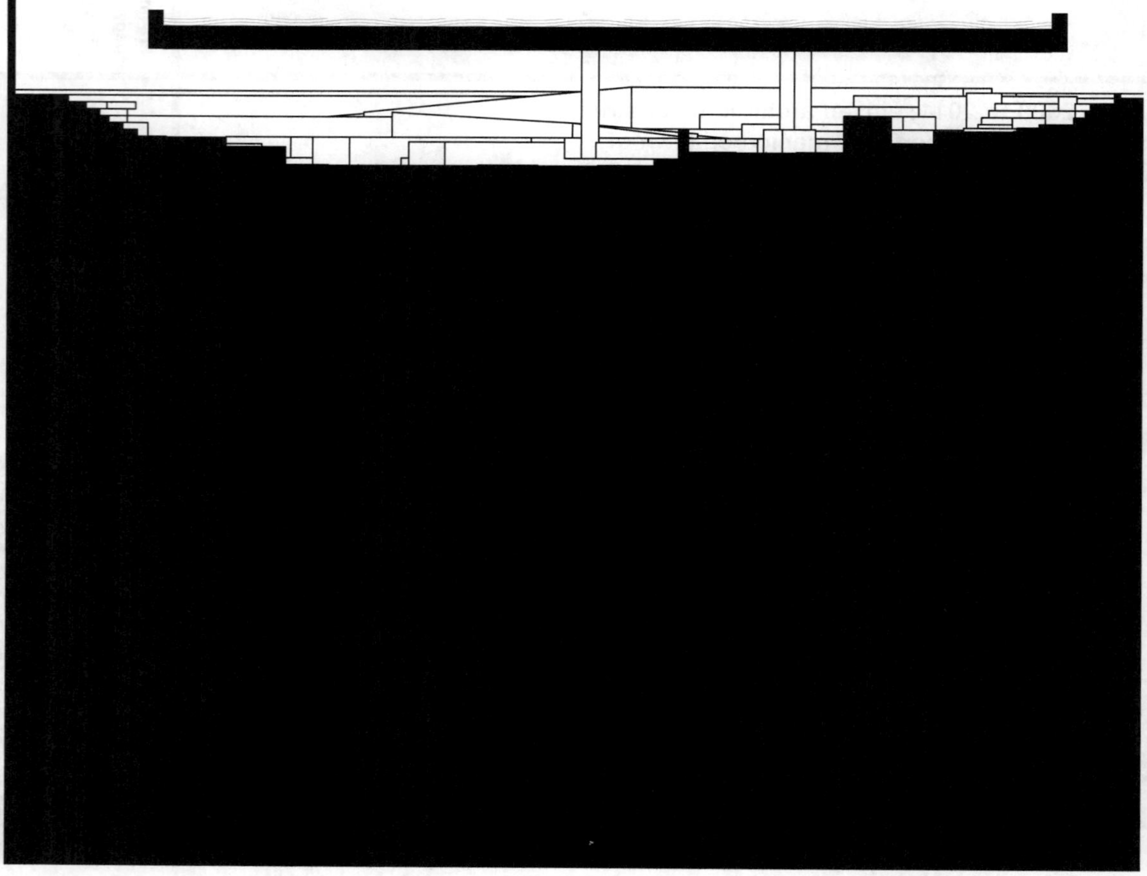

Section of the Serpentine Gallery Pavilion.

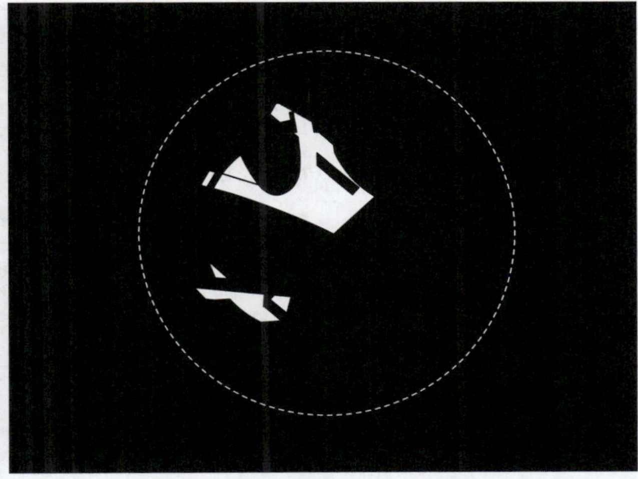

Layers of the plan.

Sometimes referred to as the Archeological Pavilion, it expresses the memory of the earth's crust. Memorializing the past is almost an obsession today, while in ancient times, as the palimpsests demonstrated, it was simply an unavoidable side effect.

Endnotes:

1 [p. 623] Stan Allen and Marc McQuade, *Landform Building: Architecture's New Terrain*, Princeton University School of Architecture (Zurich: Lars Müller Publishers, 2011).

2 [p. 623] Beatrix Colomina and Mark Wigley argue that the planet itself has been completely encrusted by design as a geological layer in *Are We Human? Notes on an Archeology of Design* (Zürich: Lars Müller Publishers, 2016), 9.

3 [p. 624] Allen and McQuade, *Landform Building*, 264.

4 [p. 626] Keller Easterling, "Subtraction", *Perspecta* 34 (2003), 80.

5 [p. 630] Oliver Wainwright, "One Never Builds Something Finished: The Brutal Brilliance of Architect Paulo Mendes da Rocha", *The Guardian* (4 February 2017).

6 [p. 637] John Hejduk, "Adalberto Libera's Villa Malaparte", *Domus* 605 (1980).

7 [p. 638] See "The Eames House", Embed, 488–493.

8 [p. 642] See "MASP", Carve, 1006.

9 [p. 646] Alejandro Virseda, "Reversing the Promenade: Homage to Le Corbusier after UNESCO World Heritage Site Listings", *Bigmat International Architecture Agenda* (8 September 2016). Accessed March 2018.

10 [p. 705] Penelope Sielder in conversation with Peter Salhani, "Revisited: The Seidlers' Killara House", *Architecture AU* (1 October 2011). Accessed February 2018.

11 [p. 709] Wainwright, "One Never Builds Something Finished".

12 [p. 737] See "Biete Ghiorgis", Bury, 222–255.

13 [p. 750] Siri Hustvedt, *The Summer Without Men* (London: Hodder & Stoughton, 2011).

Spiral

Spiral — Circulation as ceremony

The spiral twists the ground upwards or downwards, multiplying the building's surface area without breaking it into discrete floors. The fluidity of movement and continuity of surface offer a way of unifying building, infrastructure and landscape.

It took over two millennia for humankind to overcome significant height differences without barriers. As far back as 236 BCE, Vitruvius reported that Archimedes had built his first elevator. A thousand years later Alī Ibn Khalaf al-Murādī described the use of a lifting device with a large battering ram to destroy a fortress in *The Book of Secrets in the Results of Ideas*,[1] and in the Late Middle Ages, an elevator-like lifting device was drawn in Konrad Kyeser's *Bellifortis*, an illustrated manual of military technology.

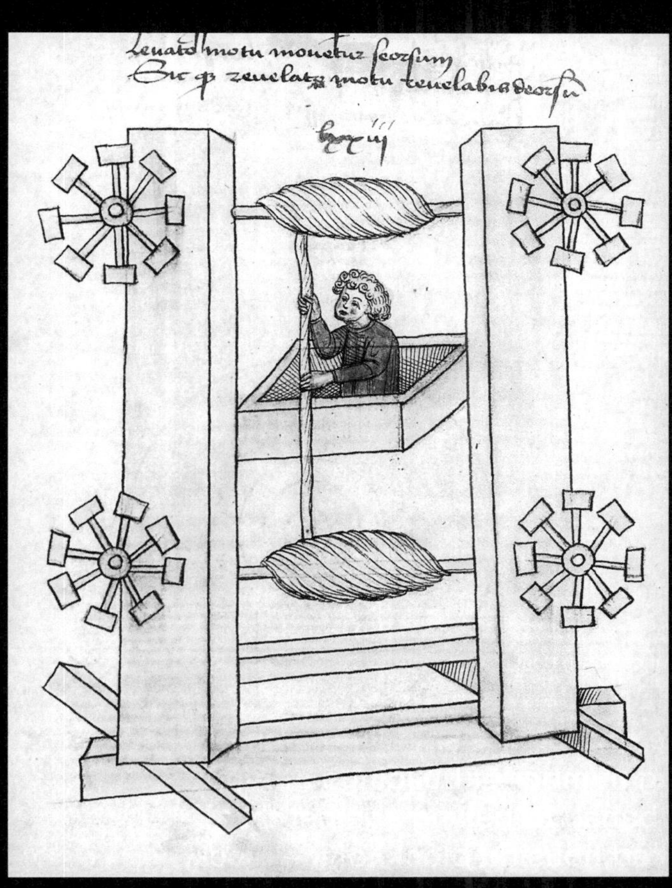

Elevator-like lifting device in Konrad Kyeser's *Bellifortis*, 1402–1405.

Military engineering fuelled the development of basic lifting equipment, but the continuous pathway held its ground. A winding road, or a steep ramp in case of limited space, was the dominant means of carrying goods, horse and carriage, or large groups of people upwards. The spiral was a powerful, functional geometry, used as a ceremonial ascent to the top of a minaret, a means to overpower the enemy in the medieval castle and an element of pageantry and sophistication at the entrance to the Renaissance palace. But with Elisha Otis's steam-propelled safety elevator of 1852 and Werner von Siemens's electric powered lift of 1880, all of this became obsolete. A little metal box in the middle of our buildings became the new connector of levels.

A funeral ramp, used for bringing down coffins in Hong Kong before 1912.

But today we are witnessing the revival of a spiralling architecture, in all its glory. A growing number of buildings attempt to elevate themselves from the banal. Rebelling against the blind proliferation of the pancaked housing block, office block, civic block; each indistinguishable, skewered by a lift, fire stairs and a bit of void.

Aided by modern prefabrication techniques, mechanical transport systems and the market demanding ‘connectivity’ (whatever that might be exactly), the slanted floor has made a comeback. Adopting terms that have previously been used to justify the blunt stacking of storeys, a spiralling architecture is redefining economy, efficiency and flexibility. Circulation no longer needs to be a separate system, tacked on. Space can now expand and contract vertically, responding to fluctuating demands.

A. Reichstag Dome, Berlin, Germany, Foster + Partners, 1999.
B. Mole Antonelliana, Turin, Italy, Gianfranco Gritella & associates, 2000.
C. Turning Torso, Malmö, Sweden, Santiago Calatrava, 2001.
D. City Hall, London, United Kingdom, Foster + Partners, 2002.
E. ARoS Art Museum, Aarhus, Denmark, Schmidt Hammer Lassen, 2004.
F. CosmoCaixa Science Museum, Barcelona, Spain, Robert Terradas, 2004.
G. Cocoon, Zurich, Switzerland, Evolution Design, 2005.
H. Serpentine Gallery Pavilion, London, United Kingdom, Olafur Eliasson & Kjetil Thorsen, 2007.
I. BMW World, Munich, Germany, Coop Himmelb(l)au, 2009.
J. Andalucía's Museum of Memory, Granada, Spain, Alberto Campo Baeza, 2010.
K. Automobile Museum, Nanjing, China, 3Gatti Architecture Studio, 2010.
L. F&F Tower, Panama City, Panama, Pinzón Lozano & Asociados Arquitectos, 2011.
M. Hanoi Museum, Vietnam, Gerkan Marg and Partners, 2011.
N. Hellenic Motor Museum, Athens, Greece, 2011.
O. Ribbon Chapel, Hiroshima, Japan, Hiroshi Nakamura & NAP, 2013.
P. Audemars Piguet Museum, Vallée de Joux, Switzerland, BIG, 2014.
Q. Şışhane Park, Istanbul, Turkey, SANALarc, 2014.
R. Central Station, Arnhem, Netherlands, UNStudio, 2015.
S. United Tower, Manama, Bahrain, Ahmed Al Qaed Construction, 2016.
T. Heli-stage, Shaoxing, China, ATAH, 2018.
U. Shanghai Grand Opera House, Shanghai, China, Snøhetta, 2019.

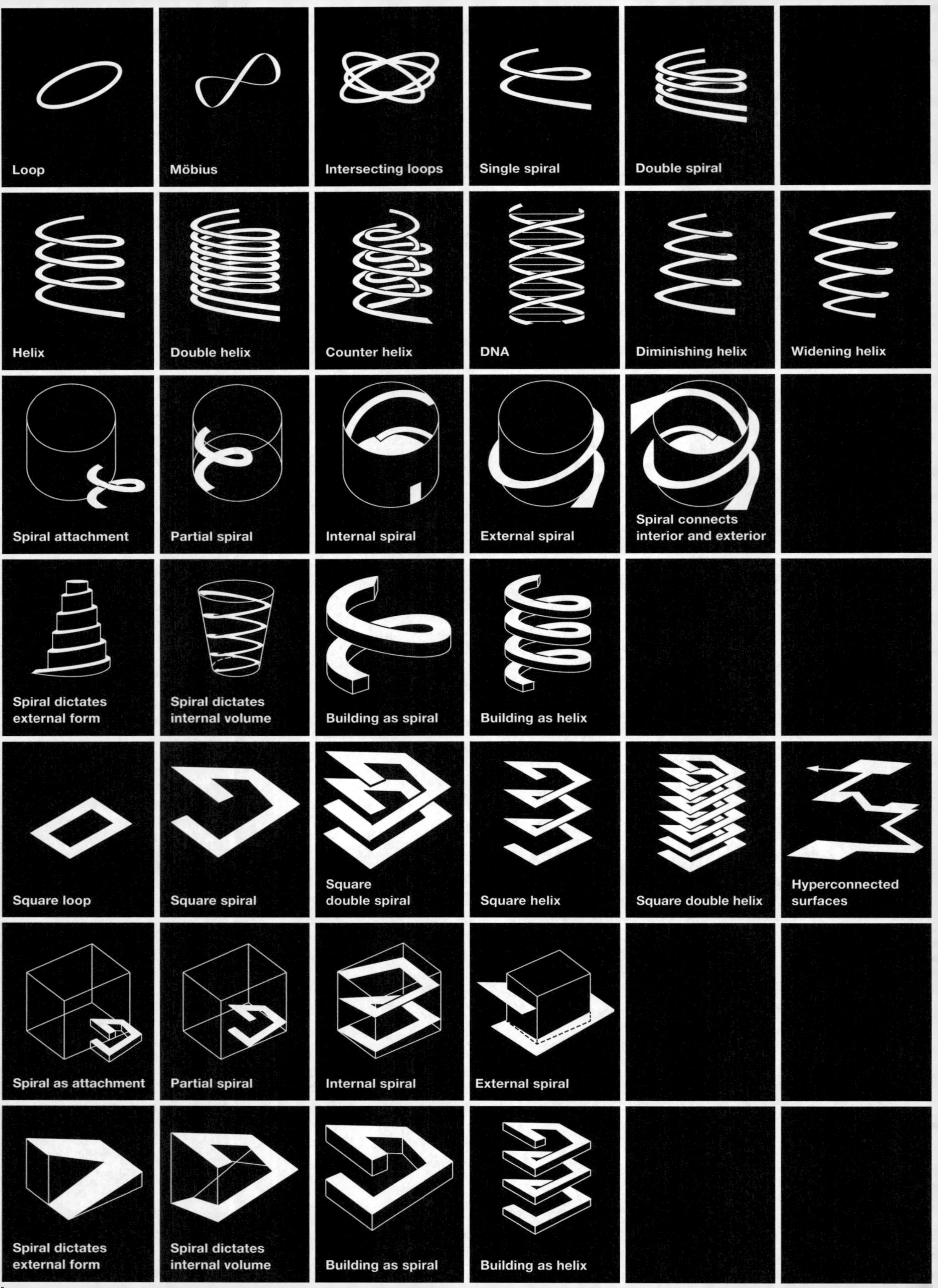

Loop
Möbius
Intersecting loops
Single spiral
Double spiral
Helix
Double helix
Counter helix
DNA
Diminishing helix
Widening helix
Spiral attachment
Partial spiral
Internal spiral
External spiral
Spiral connects interior and exterior
Spiral dictates external form
Spiral dictates internal volume
Building as spiral
Building as helix
Square loop
Square spiral
Square double spiral
Square helix
Square double helix
Hyperconnected surfaces
Spiral as attachment
Partial spiral
Internal spiral
External spiral
Spiral dictates external form
Spiral dictates internal volume
Building as spiral
Building as helix

Contemporary architecture boasts the helix, double helix, loop, trefoil and Möbius. At times boldly formal, the spiral building twists and turns with muscular energy. At others, the spiral hides within, acting as the organizer of programme, circulation and structure. The articulation of the surface offers the potential to choreograph multiple spatial experiences, to accommodate different speeds and motions and create greater continuity between interior and exterior. This new richness in spiralling species is not accidental. It is not pure fashion or gimmick. There's something more elemental at work.

A spiralling architecture symbolizes our ascension to a higher state. It was not born out of necessity, like shelter. It was introduced to architecture as a ceremonial element. Humans built artificial mountains on the vast plains of ancient Mesopotamia. These early attempts to reach a higher plane were constructed out of the earth. The ground was baked, stacked and pulled upwards to form the stepped pyramid of the ziggurat, a momentous effort to get closer to the heavens.

Etemenanki Ziggurat, Babylon (north of Hillah, Iraq), 604–562 BCE (left) and Minaret al-Malwiya, Samarra, Iraq, 848–852 CE (right).

Ancient Mesopotamians wound upwards in the quest for wisdom, traversing a series of stepped platforms, each receding inwards towards the summit. The external spiralling circulation was not purely a route. It shaped geometry, defining the fundamental form of the building. While the ziggurat was orthogonal, the Islamic minaret's circular form offered a fluid spiralling procession. From this conic tower, the gate between heaven and earth, humankind was summoned.

The initiation well of Quinta da Regaleira was never intended for water. It was a processional space honouring tarot mysticism and masonic principles.

Although many of these monumental structures have long since eroded away, the spiral continues to inspire symbolic proclamations. Ascending to heaven or descending deep into the earth has obvious biblical connotations. The rhythm and gradient of the spiralling rotations is suggestive of time passing, of orbiting an invisible clock. And the ever-increasing or decreasing geometry of the spiral conjures limitless, endless space.

The elevation of the citizen in the Reichstag, Berlin.

The universal access provided by the spiralling ramp has been conflated with the transparency of the democratic process or the citizen's position of power within government. In London City Hall, a ramp encircles the debating chamber. Within Berlin's Reichstag, the public ascend two helical ramps above their representatives in the chamber.

The radical headquarters of the Third International would have loomed 400 metres over St Petersburg had it been built. In this monument to the Bolshevik Revolution, two dynamic centripetal spirals encircle four internal glass volumes, each revolving at a different speed. It was a physical and literal translation of communist ideals: elevating and enlightening the masses.[2]

Still from Takehiko Nagakura's 1999 film *Tatlin's Tower*, depicting the speculative St Petersburg skyline.

Similarly, the elegantly coiled El Helicoide was conceived as an embodiment of Venezuela's wealth and confidence. A mammoth mall in the form of an interlocking helix, a modern high street of spiralling ramps. But here the utopian image of the spiral is inverted. Now a political prison and intelligence headquarters, this symbol of progress is described as 'hell on earth'.[3]

El Helicoide, Caracas, Arquitectura y Urbanismo C.A., 1955–1961.

The Vatican's Bramante staircase designed by Guiseppe Momo allows visitors to ascend and descend simultaneously without meeting.

We modern heathens no longer build monuments to the gods we admire, but we do construct buildings in our own image. The Seattle Central Library is a temple of information, arranging a collection of media in a continuous ribbon. The Mercedes-Benz Museum is not just a temple to automotive design but a celebration of movement, where a culture of consumerism is curated along a double helix.

***Inferno*, from Dante's *Divine Comedy*, Bartolomeo Di Fruosino, 1430–1435.**

The weighty associations and iconography of the spiral are inescapable. There is an inherent power to this geometry, positioned between Dante's inferno and paradise. But if we are to worship the spiral, perhaps we need to better understand what it could offer.

The spiral building has mutated into endless variations. It has been inverted, flipped over, turned in on itself, bent, twisted and elongated, but always a continuous flow is preserved. The spiral condenses horizontal distance, carrying humans and our vehicles between levels within a tight space. But the spiral is not some impotent pathway; it is not just a staircase or a car park ramp. It is an organizer and generator of space.

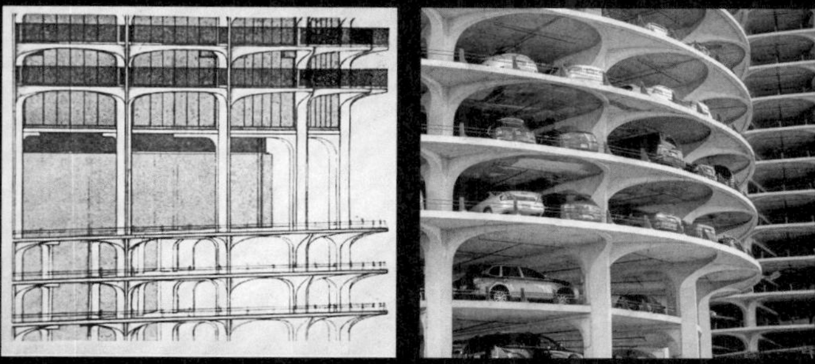

A spiral parking ramp extends across nineteen floors of Marina City, Chicago, Bertrand Goldberg, 1961–1968.

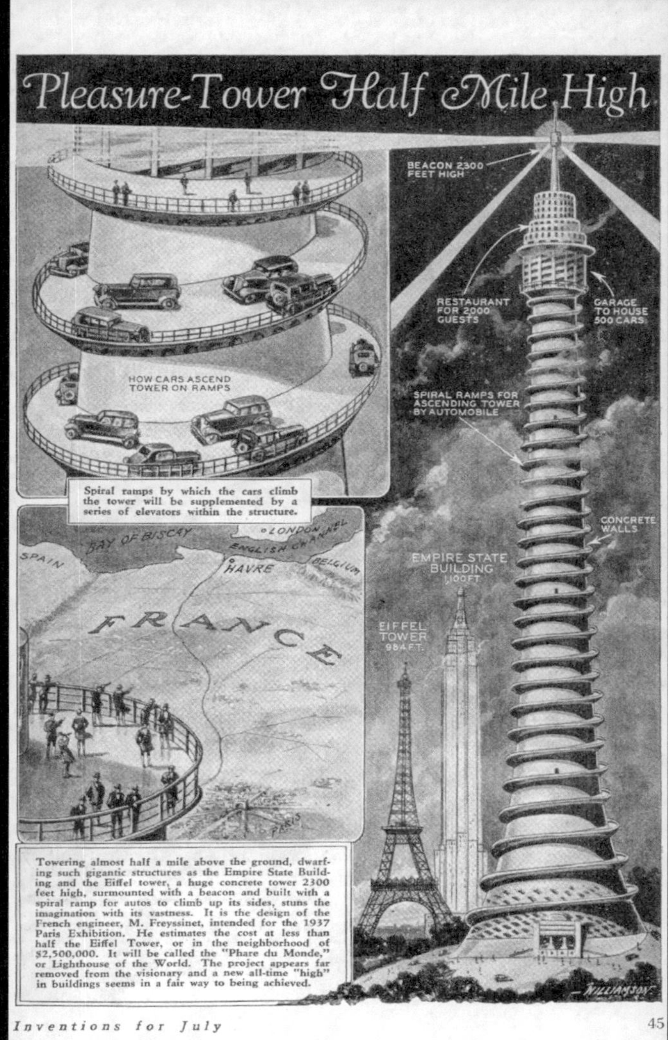

Pleasure-Tower Half Mile High

Spiral ramps by which the cars climb the tower will be supplemented by a series of elevators within the structure.

Towering almost half a mile above the ground, dwarfing such gigantic structures as the Empire State Building and the Eiffel tower, a huge concrete tower 2300 feet high, surmounted with a beacon and built with a spiral ramp for autos to climb up its sides, stuns the imagination with its vastness. It is the design of the French engineer, M. Freyssinet, intended for the 1937 Paris Exhibition. He estimates the cost at less than half the Eiffel Tower, or in the neighborhood of $2,500,000. It will be called the "Phare du Monde," or Lighthouse of the World. The project appears far removed from the visionary and a new all-time "high" in buildings seems in a fair way to being achieved.

Inventions for July 45

Intended for the 1937 Paris Exhibition, the *Phare du Monde*, or 'lighthouse of the world', by Eugène Freyssinet, was an enormous concrete minaret for automobiles.

The railway between Bergün and Preda spirals five times within the Swiss Alps to climb 400 metres over a journey of five kilometres. It was constructed in just five years, 1898–1903.

Within Frank Lloyd Wright's Guggenheim Museum, the spiral dictates everything. You exist within the spiral. It is the generator of a central void, of the iconic facade. It organizes the artwork and your passage through. The continuity of the slanting floor allows a continuity of experience, while the spiral represents an incredible moment of liberation for the gallery. A sinuous, unbroken journey through art, it is equally chastised for the control it exerts on those who experience it.

Brothers in arms, the Musée Gallo-Romain and the Mercedes-Benz Museum adapt the elemental spiral to subdue its dominance. Within the double helix of the Mercedes-Benz Museum, two spiralling trajectories are interwoven to allow the visitor a degree of self-orientation. A large triangular void within allows visual crossovers, and the 'twist' acts as both structural support for the exhibition levels and a bridging device between the two routes.

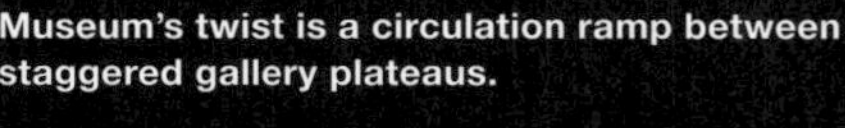

The curved top surface of the Mercedes-Benz Museum's twist is a circulation ramp between staggered gallery plateaus.

Within the 'paper clip' of Musée Gallo-Romain, Lyon, 1966–1975.

In the Musée Gallo Romain, exhibition spaces are terraced alongside the paper clip–like spiral ramp, offering moments of relief. Space expands and contracts as you are guided through enormous porticos and gradually led downwards. Running parallel to the contours, the internal ramp mimics how one might navigate the steep slope above.

We see the slope or gradient of the ramped architectural promenade as a rigid metric, a standard we must conform to, but there is room enough for expansion in a highly advanced commercial market.

Defying convention, Claude Parent and Paul Virilio proposed inhabiting the 'oblique' to escape the rationality of modern space. "Objecting to the vertical city, (they) imagined inclined sites, oblique cities where inhabitants, like mountain dwellers, essentially live on slopes in a new organization of space based on health and the pleasure of the body in movement."[4] This proposition has undoubtedly shaped a contemporary fascination with continuous topographies and fluid form. But a reconsideration of how the inclined surface could alter behaviours, senses and interpersonal dynamics is only just igniting.

Claude Parent's apartment, Neuilly-sur-Seine, Paris, 1973.

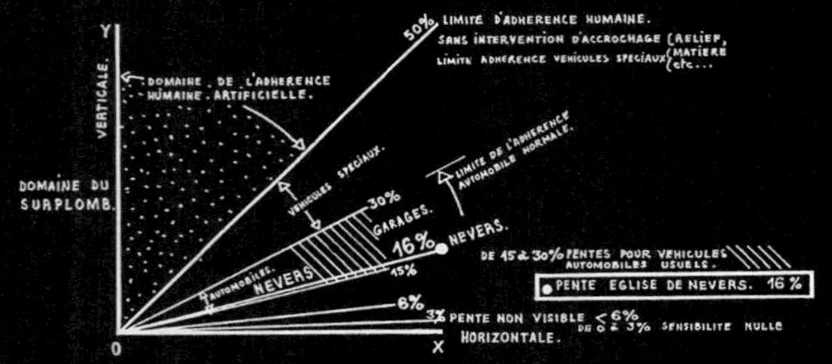

Function of the Oblique, Claude Parent & Paul Virilio, 1966.

The fluctuating demands of growth and contraction contrast with the steadfast bygone era of the high-rise. Flexibility was once restricted to discrete floor plates. The open plan and easily re-organizable floor neatly stacked up. The Fordist hierarchy of many divisions conducted from the top is now seen as heavy, slow and in need of a shakedown. Unfortunately, this has gifted us tacky fads such as 'bump' space and hotdesking, but beneath this thin veneer of bullshit there is a recognition that a compartmentalization of space goes against our natural disposition. Now we need more than a lift for connection. We require gradients of programme, less division, greater cross-pollination. We need the continuous, storey-less spiralling building.

Accessible ramp gradients and vehicle ramp gradients, *Metric Handbook*.

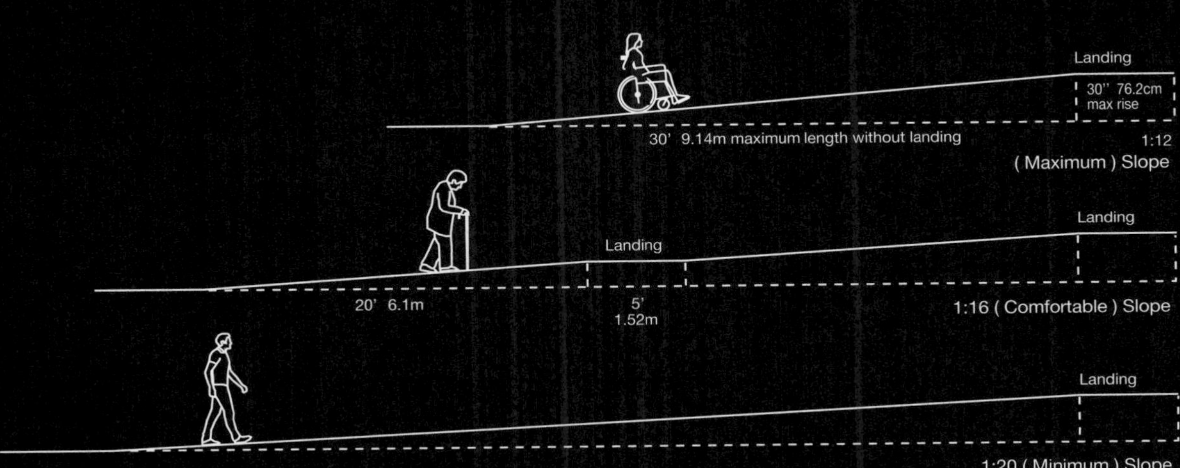

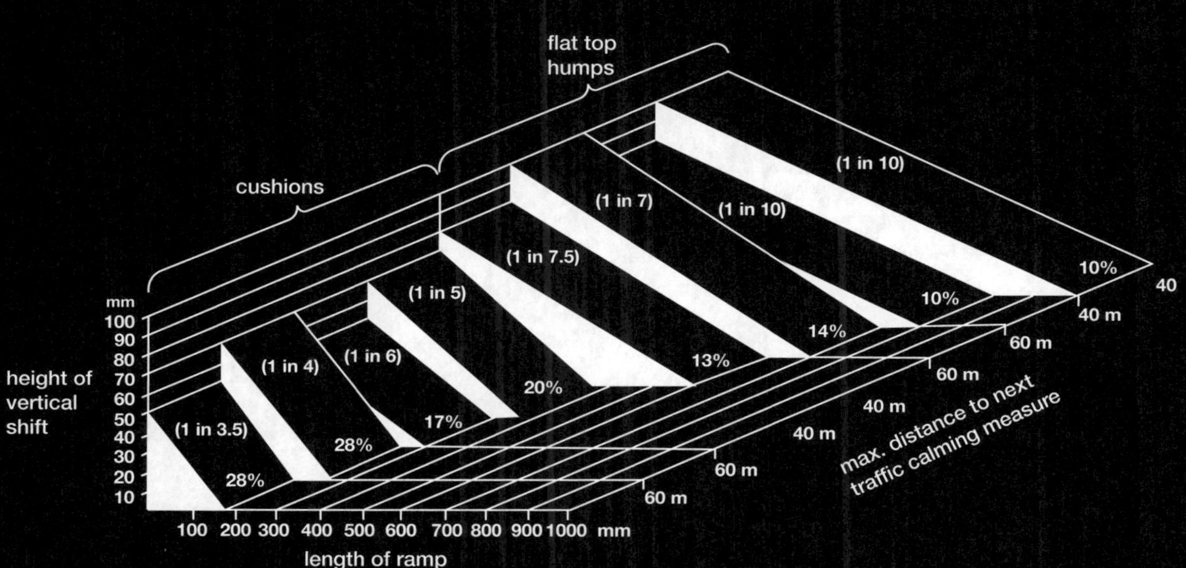

Within SeARCH's Junior College, three education blocks were wrapped around an elongated, rising spiral-shaped hallway. This continuous strip of programme allowed each block to expand and shrink as necessary, something unattainable as stand-alone blocks.

A spiral ramp coils around the atrium of Junior College, Julianadorp, SeARCH, 2004–2008.

The spiral has ripped the frontage off trusty structures and trashed the modernistic glass facade. The two-dimensional seamless transition between interior and exterior has been stretched into a three-dimensional membrane and filled with light, air and activity. Seattle Public Library can be seen as an almost seismic, unstable precursor, challenging the regular wrapping of ascending floors. It visually and physically pulls the ground and sky into the building, offering new interstitial spaces to grapple with.

Seattle Central Library, OMA, 1999–2004. Philippe Ruault.

The twisted surfaces of a spiralling architecture allow interlocking levels and spatial programmes. Sinking one edge of a spiral building into the site creates a fluid transition from ground to roof. The pinched loop of the Danish Pavilion at the Shanghai Expo slips effortlessly between interior and exterior space, bridging the ground level and the elevated promenade of its own upper surface.

The spatial logic of this continuous double loop is highly adaptive, a reoccurring element in BIG's work.

With the spiral we can bring the ground up. We can extend the ground floor while continuing both surface and experience. With the spiral we can pull landscape inside and restore a connection to our surroundings.

Acacia parquet of the Posbank Pavilion. Rheden, SeARCH, 1998–2002.

The spiral building offers a way to relate more to the pliable surface of the earth. The incongruous contours of the site can, and should, morph with the building, instead of being smoothed and levelled to make way for a flat slab. Through a hyper-connected floor surface, such as that of the Posbank Pavilion, the outdoors can be acutely experienced from indoors. The spiral allows us to wrap ourselves in our surroundings, to create a continuity of experience from context to building. A connection that goes beyond a bit of indoor-outdoor flow.

And by inviting nature inside can we indoor creatures mitigate our own devastating impact? Can nature recuperate in the interior comfort we have designed? Some call it 'Hedonistic Sustainability' (Bjarke Ingels), others 'Next Nature' (Koert van Mensvoort), but what would it really take to realign and reconnect with our surrounding landscape?

The spiral across scales: DNA, shell, plant, hurricane, galaxy.

The more we study the environment, the more the spiral presents itself. It exists in the structure of our DNA, the phyllotaxis of plant life, the flows and forces of the atmosphere and the distribution of stars within our galaxy. When you consider how prevalent the spiral is in nature you realize that the project of harnessing its logic at the human scale has only just begun.

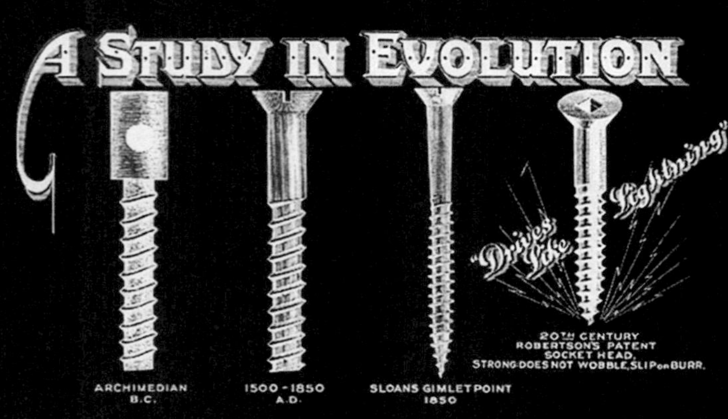

To fasten: Screw patent, P. L. Robertson, 1909.

Often without realizing it, we inhabit a more comfortable world thanks to the spiral. It is invaluable for transporting water and ships, for damping unwanted shocks while we are moving, and even for ensuring a good night's sleep in our beds. It has been crucial for fastening, writing, driving and lighting. It plays a role in the propulsion of every engine or machine

To raise water: Archimedes' screw, 250 BCE, still in common use for hydro power and water turbines.

To fly: Spiralling Ornithopter, Leonardo da Vinci, 1485.

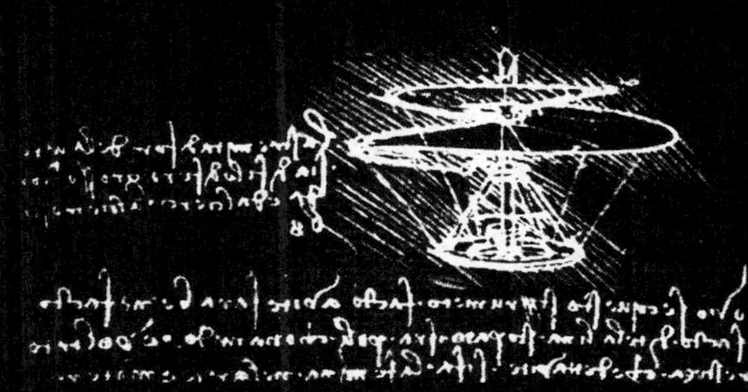

To define theory of elasticity: Coil sprint experiments, Robert Hooke, 1678.

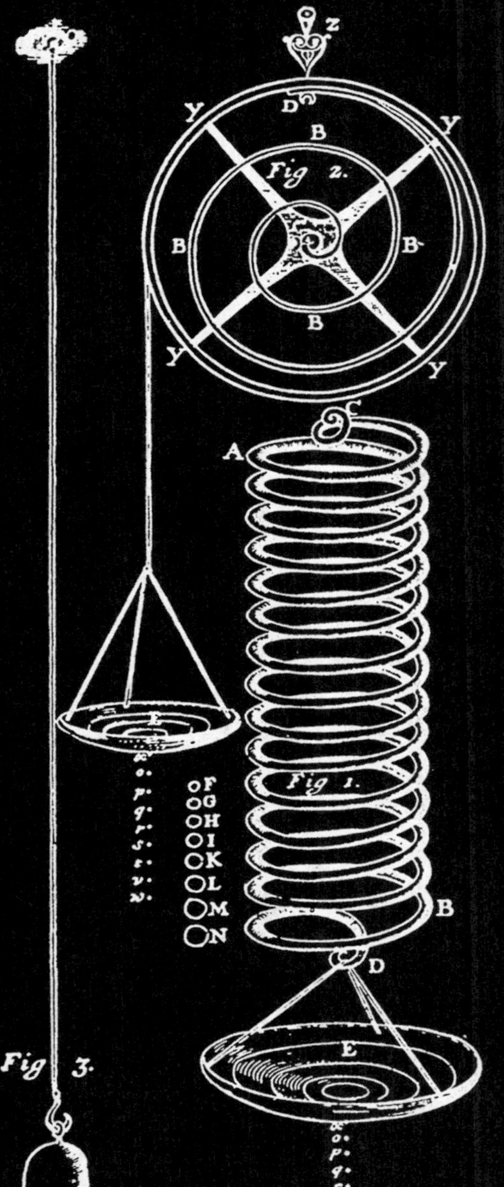

To propel: Screw propeller, Francis Pettit, 1836.

(No Model.)

W. THOMPSON.
SCREW PROPELLER.

No. 543,909. Patented Aug. 6, 1895.

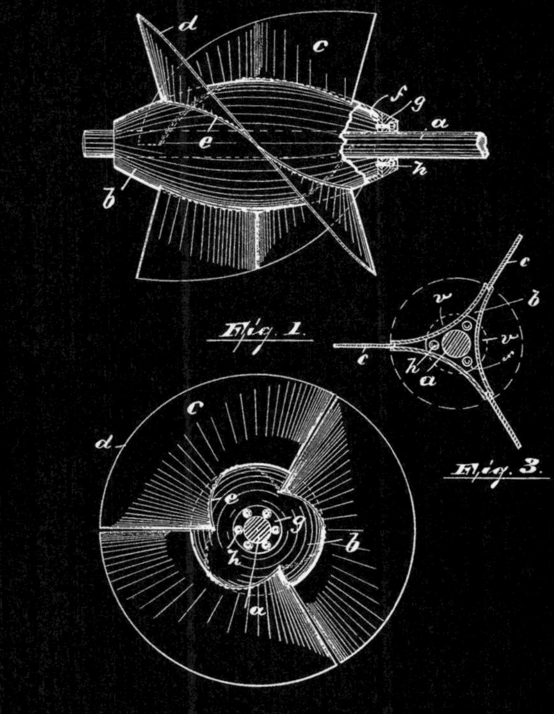

WITNESSES: INVENTOR:

Walter Thompson

BY

ATTORNEYS

To sleep: Bed spring patent no. 16972A, 7 April 1857.

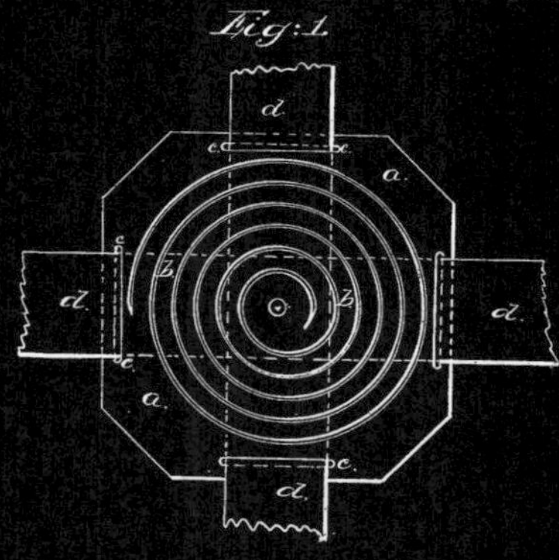

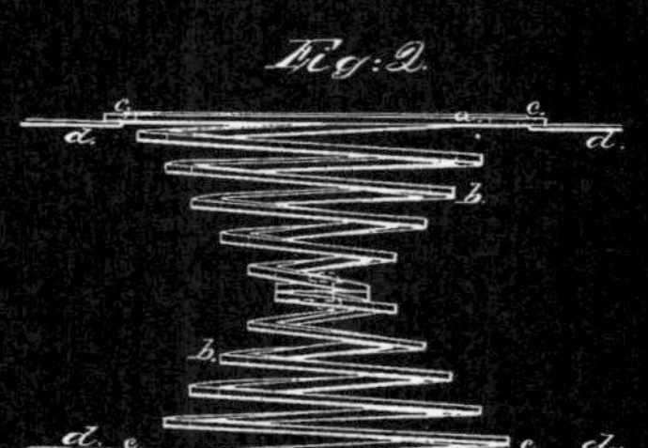

To light: Bulb patent no. 223898 with a coil as glowing tip, Thomas Edison, 27 January 1880.

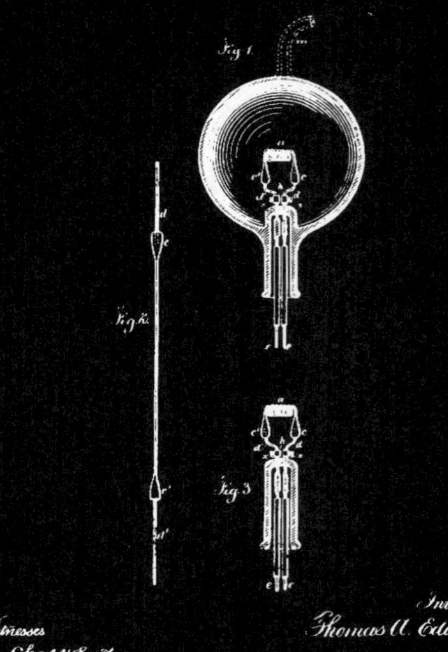

To write: Stylographic Pen patent no. 232804, Alonzo T. Cross, October 1880 (the spring was not for releasing the tip but for forcing ink into the tip of the pen).

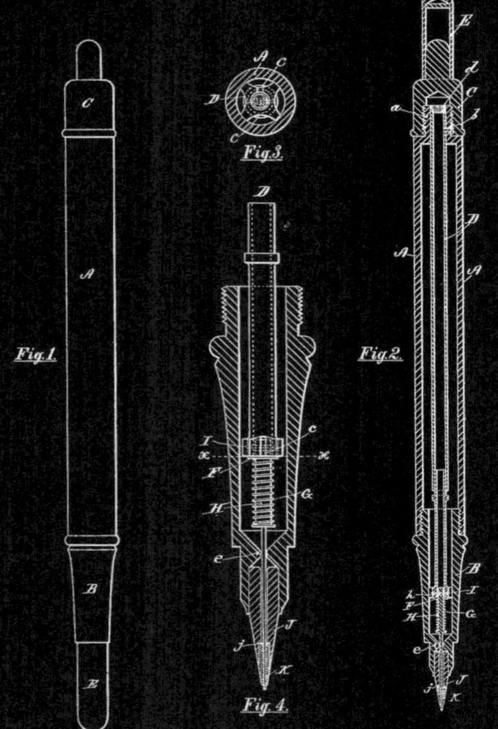

To drive (electric): Elektro Magnetic Motor, Nikola Tesla, 1 May 1888.

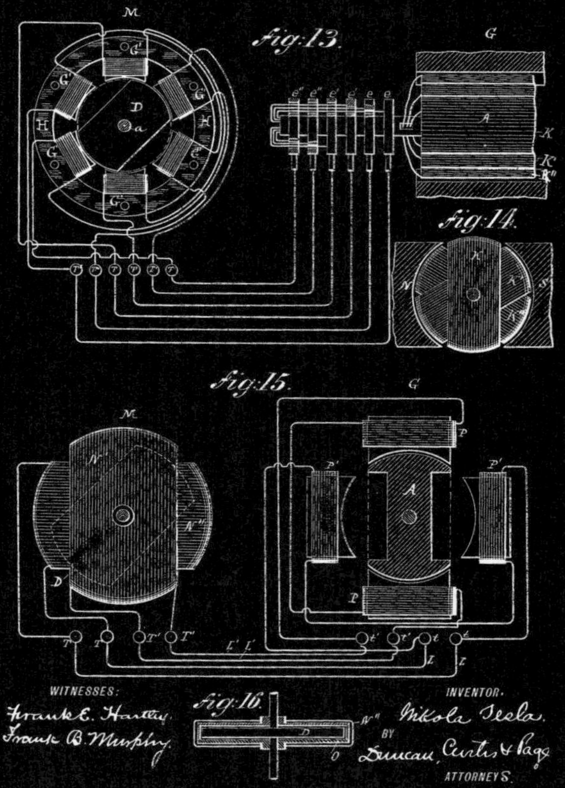

The incredible omnipresence of the spiral for almost every living species and every working machine makes you wonder why it does not hold a similar fundamental position within architecture?

Looking back with twenty-twenty hindsight, we see that although the lift was a highly efficient connector of floors, it resulted in absolute disconnection. By contrast, the spiral, pushed aside as a space-consuming and laborious element, offers fluidity and continuity.

In a world of increasing complexity and densification, there is a renewed desire to be physically connected and the spiral does this with ease, creating new connections between building, infrastructure and landscape.

The Ziggurat
—
Nanna Ziggurat
Ur (present-day Tell el-Muqayyar, IQ)
2100–2050 BCE

782

The Ziggurat
—
Dur-Sharrukin Ziggurat
Dur-Sharrukin (present-day Khorsabad, IQ)
722–605 BCE

784

The Ziggurat
—
Etemenanki Ziggurat
Babylon (north of Hillah, IQ)
604–562 BCE

788

Minaret al-Malwiya
Samarra, IQ
848–852 CE

794

The Limitless Museum
—
Silkeborg Museum
Silkeborg, DK
Jørn Utzon
1963 (unbuilt)

830

The Limitless Museum
—
Musée Gallo-Romain
Lyon, FR
Bernard Zehrfuss
1966–1975

836

The Limitless Museum
—
Neanderthal Museum
Mettmann, DE
Günter Zamp Kelp, Julius Krauss and Arno Brandlhuber
1994–1996
856

The Limitless Museum
—
Museum aan de Stroom (MAS)
Antwerp, BE
Neutelings Riedijk Architects
2000–2010
860

Seattle Central Library
Seattle, US
OMA
1999–2004

912

Junior College
Julianadorp, NL
SeARCH
2004–2008

926

Danish Pavilion
Shanghai Expo, CN
BIG
2010

938

Katendrecht
Rotterdam, NL
SeARCH
2016 (unbuilt)

950

The Ziggurat
Mesopotamia
(present-day Iraq, Iran, Syria and Turkey)
2500–500 BCE

Chogha Zanbil, Khuzestan Province, Iran, 1250–640 BCE. © 2019 CNES, Google Earth.

On the flat terrain of Mesopotamia, elevation signalled monumentality. Palaces and administrative buildings of an elite class were raised above those they controlled, supported by terraced earth substructures.[5] Above these centres of wealth and power sat the gods and, in their honour, humans built artificial mountains called ziggurats.[6]

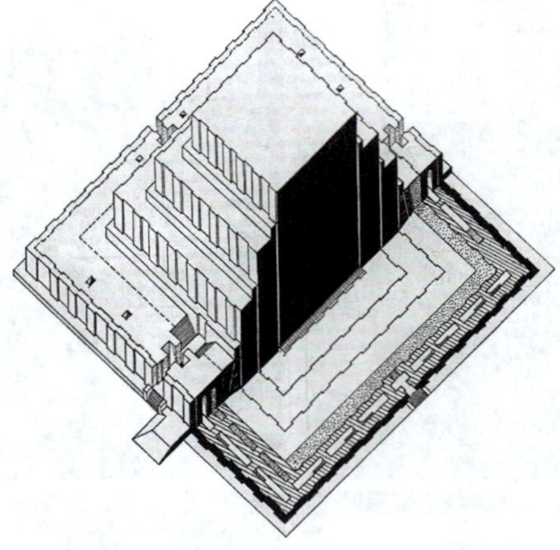

Chogha Zanbil drawn by J.-H. Sixtus, 1966.

The enormous stepped structure of the ziggurat was the link between heaven and earth. Built with a solid core of mud brick and an exterior covered with baked brick, levels slowly diminish in size until one reaches an elaborate temple or shrine, honouring the patron of the city at the summit. The diminishing height of each tier and the sharp slope of the stairways were calculated to accentuate the impression of height of the ziggurat for those standing at its feet.

View from the base of Nanna Ziggurat.

Eanna Ziggurat at Warka, Iraq, 2018.

Axonometry of Anu Ziggurat, Uruk (present-day Warka, Iraq), 3500–3300 BCE.

The Ziggurat

—

Nanna Ziggurat
Ur (present-day Tell el-Muqayyar, Iraq)
2100–2050 BCE

By the third millennium BCE the column, arch, vault and dome had made their appearance in Sumerian architecture. The well-preserved Nanna Ziggurat at Ur exhibits this growing sophistication. Each wall from base to top and from corner to corner is a convex curve.

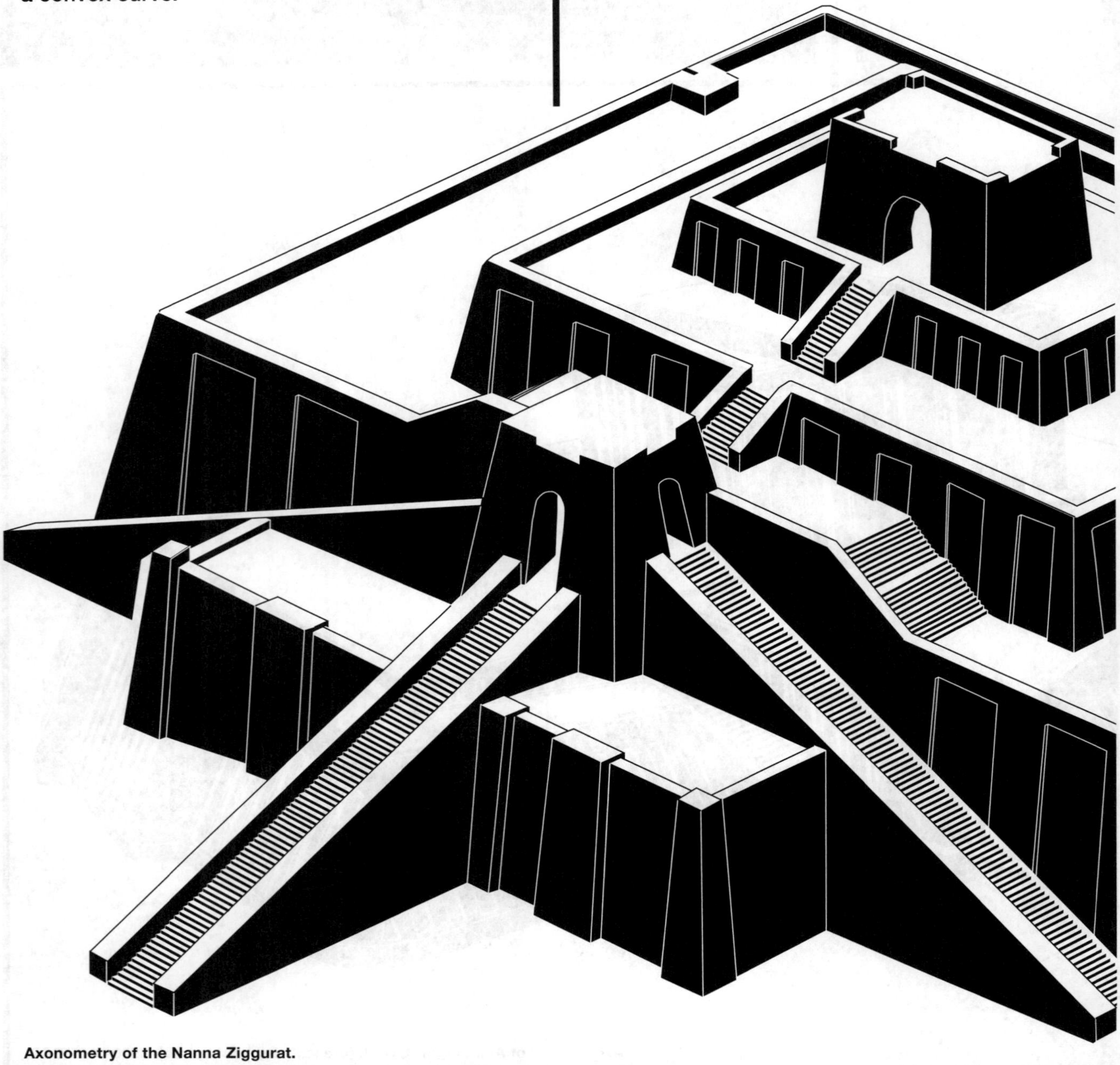

Axonometry of the Nanna Ziggurat.

Tell el-Muqayyar, Iraq. © 2002 Digital Globe, Google Earth.

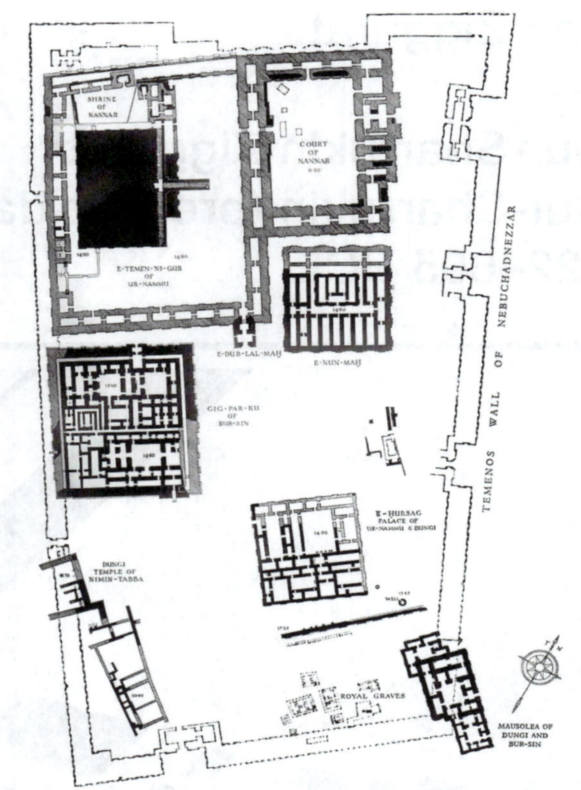

Plan of Nanna Ziggurat within the palace structure.

Archaeologist Sir Leonard Woolley believed this was carefully calibrated to give the illusion of solidity, where a straight line might have seemed to sag under the weight of the superstructure, a principle the Greeks would later call *entasis.*[7]

The Ziggurat

—

Dur-Sharrukin Ziggurat
Dur-Sharrukin (present-day Khorsabad, Iraq)
722–605 BCE

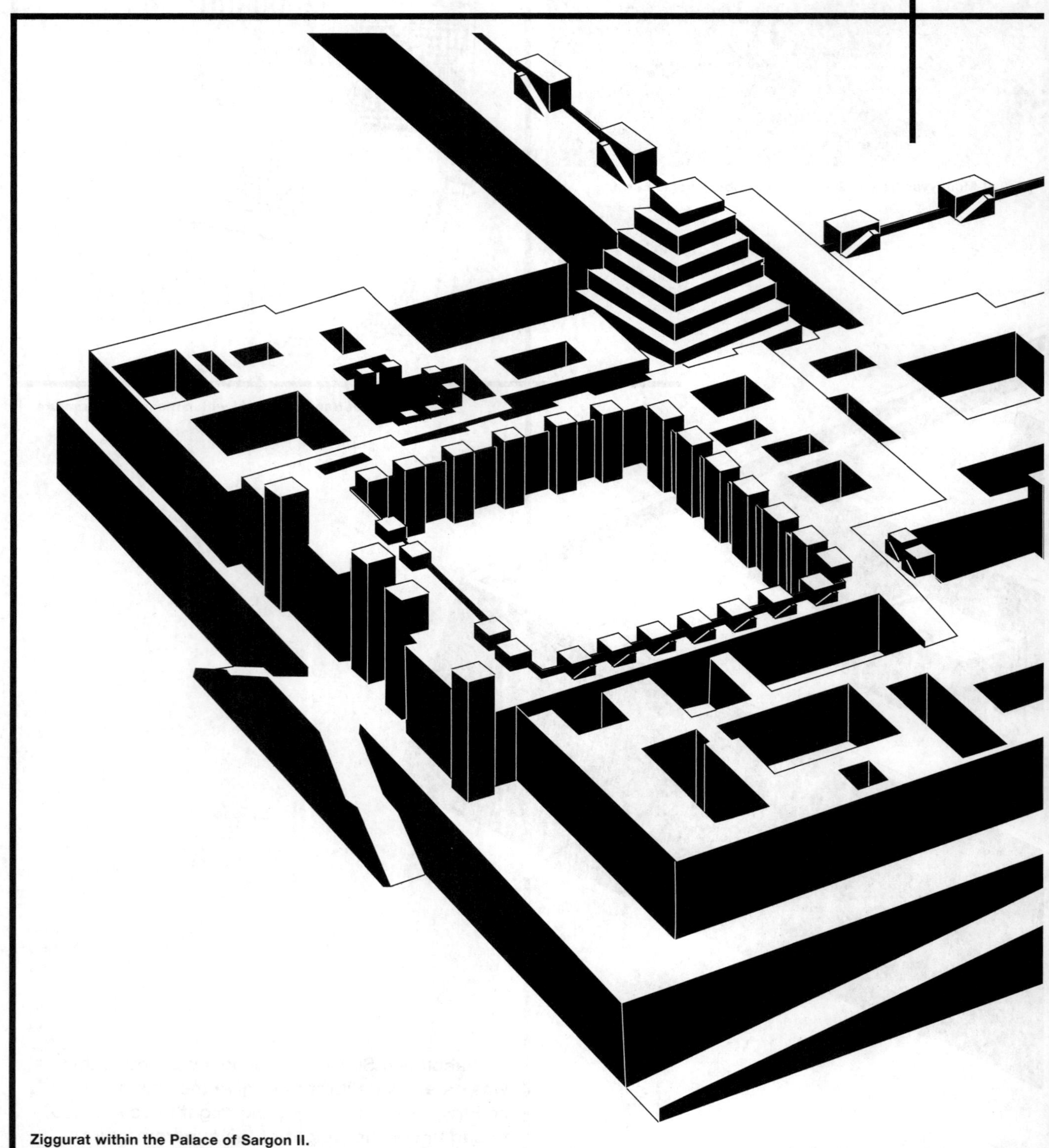

Ziggurat within the Palace of Sargon II.

Unlike the Egyptian pyramid, the ziggurat was accessible. A series of steps and ramps allowed people to humbly approach divinity. Over its 1000 years of development, this passage up to the heavens grew in complexity, from straight to tripartite to zig-zag. In the vast majority of ziggurats, stairs were set at right angles to their sides, but in Dur-Sharrukin stairs wrap around each level to form a spiralling route.[8]

Plan of the Palace of Sargon II, Dur-Sharrukin.

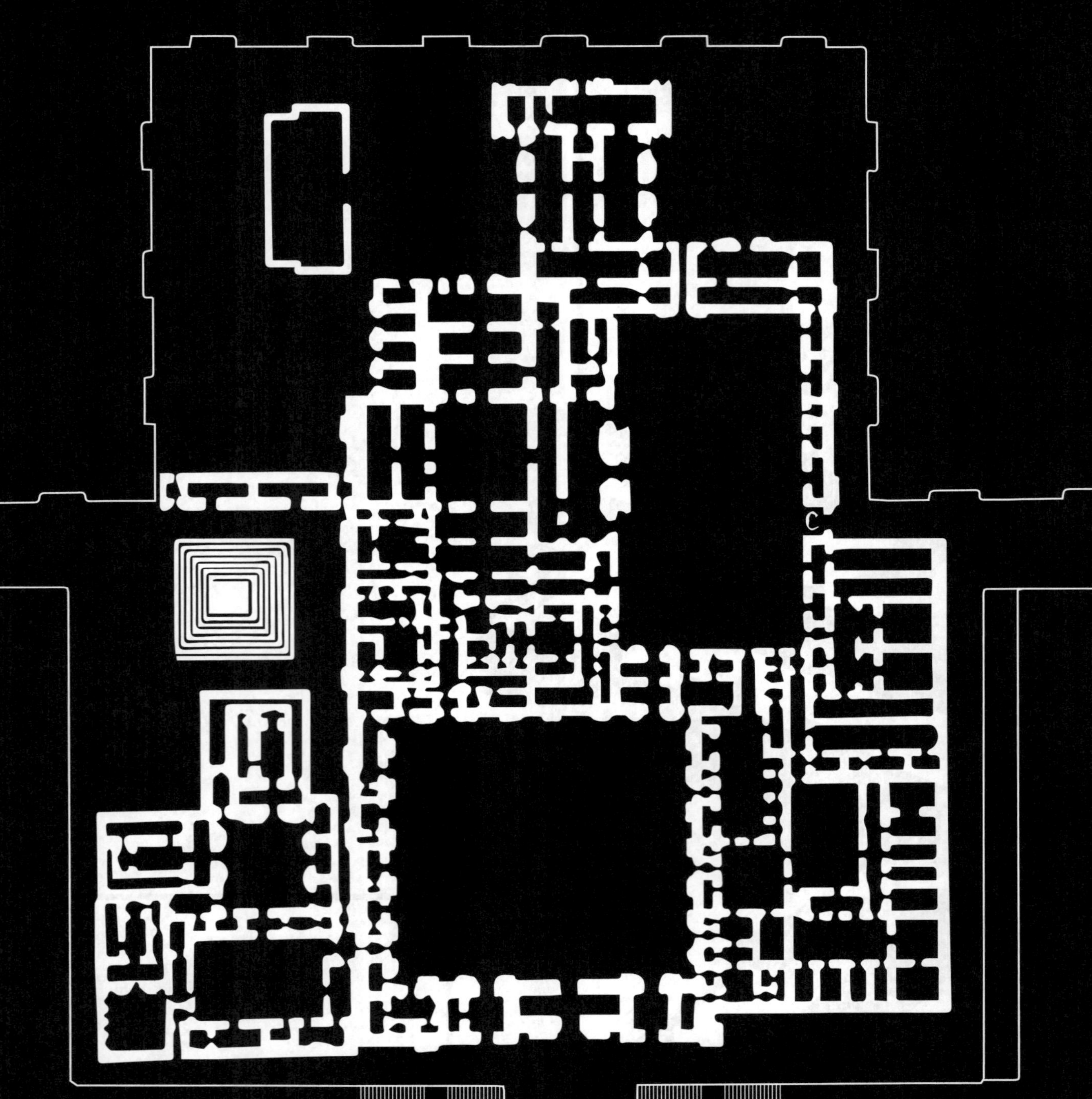

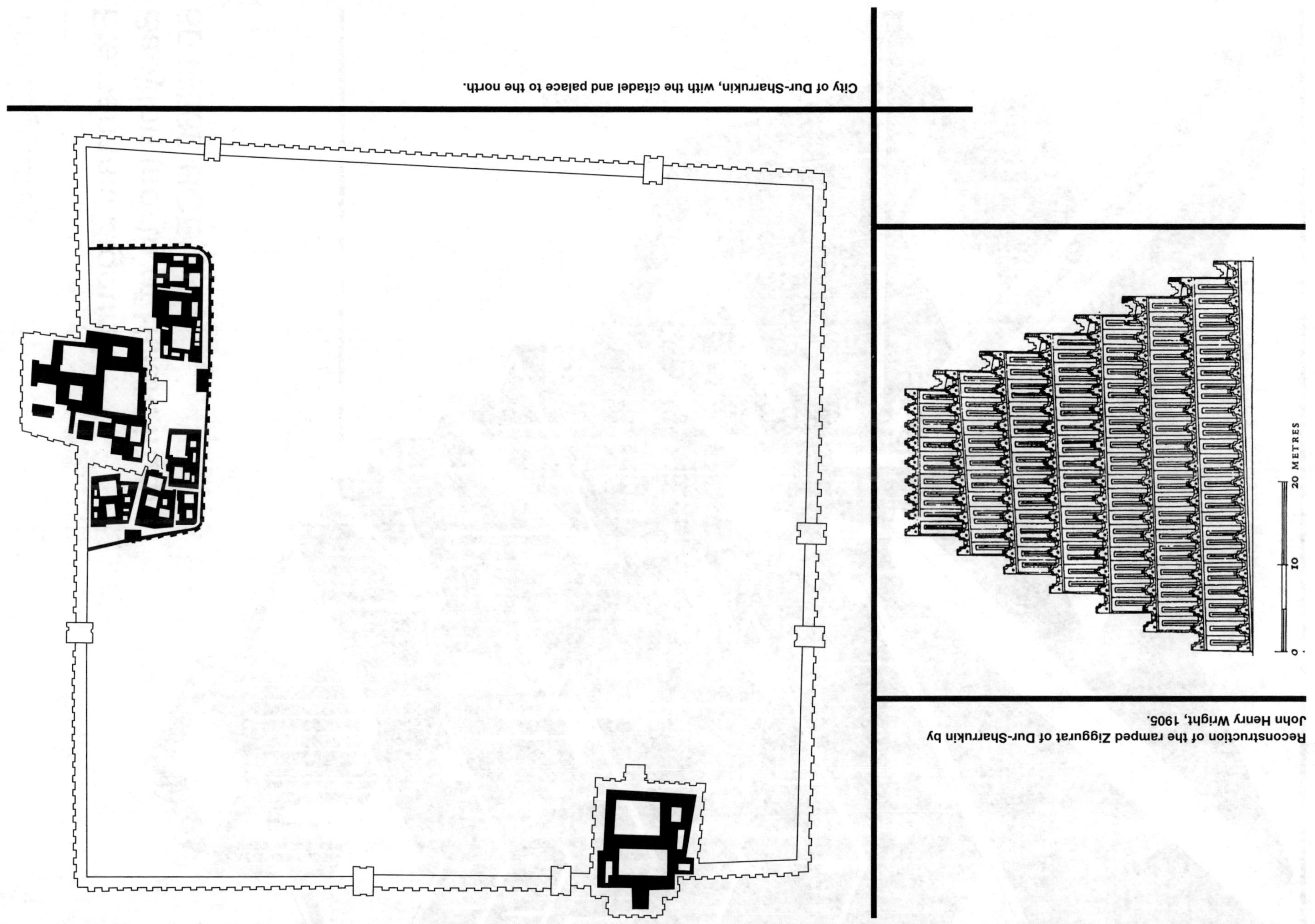

City of Dur-Sharrukin, with the citadel and palace to the north.

Reconstruction of the ramped Ziggurat of Dur-Sharrukin by John Henry Wright, 1905.

The Ziggurat

—

Etemenanki Ziggurat
Babylon (north of Hillah, Iraq)
604–562 BCE

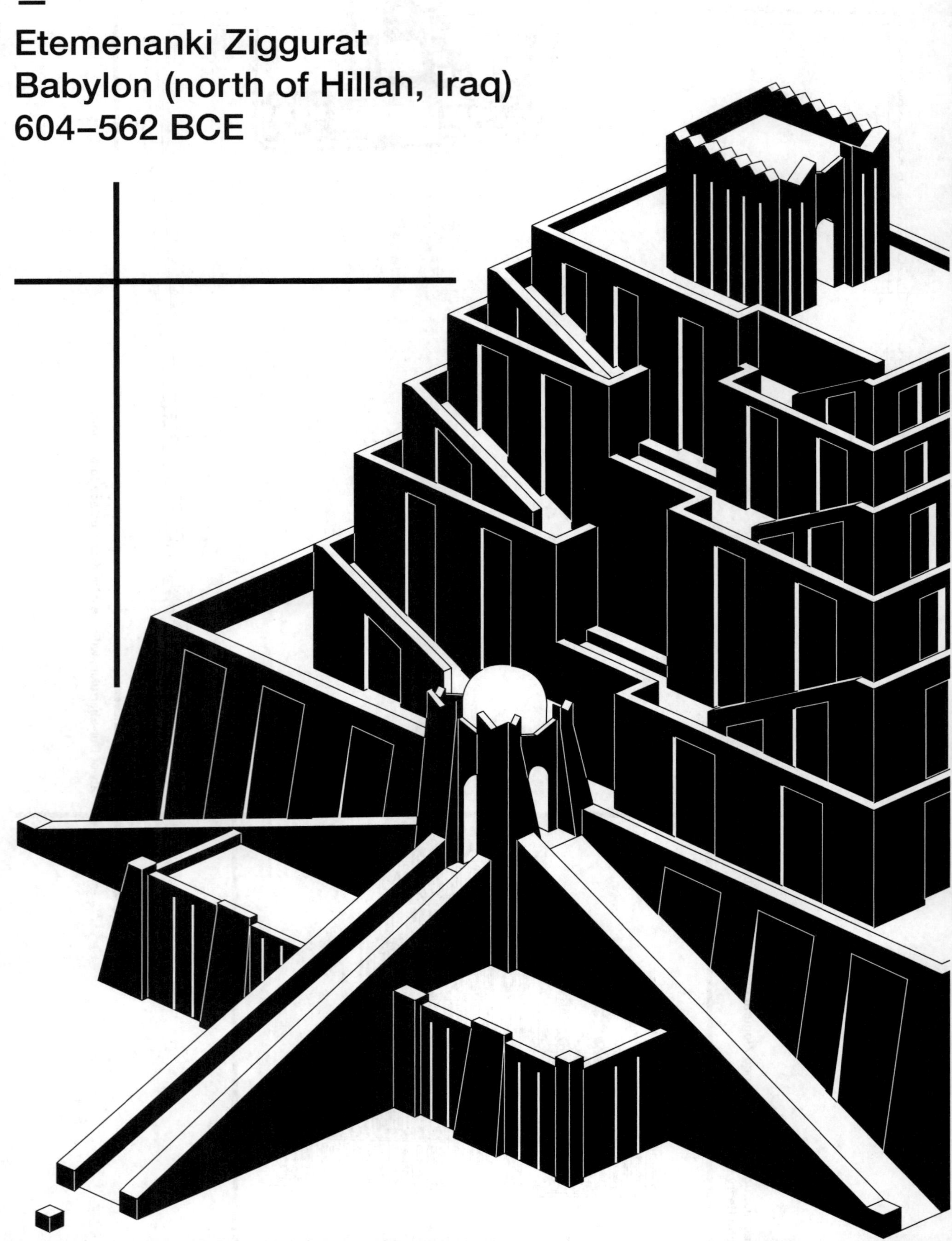

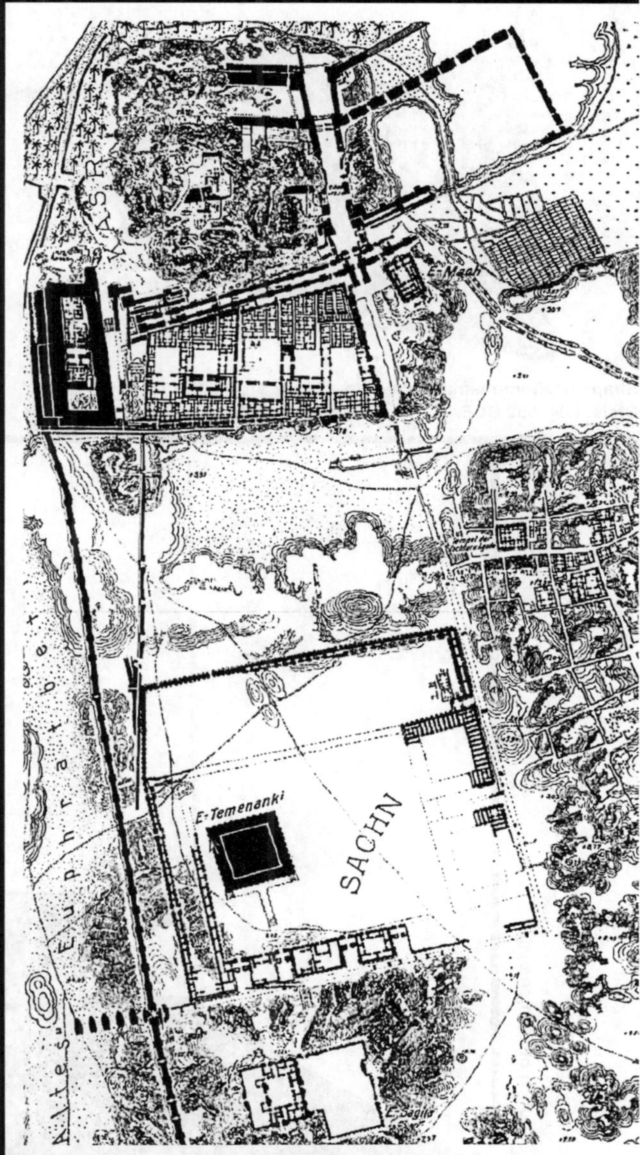

Plan of Etemenanki Ziggurat within city of Babylon.

No ziggurat is preserved to its original height, and the conflicts in Iraq and Syria have seen the deliberate destruction of archaeological remains.[9] As evidence we rely on inscriptions on Sumerian tablets, the tall tales of travelling historians, artistic reproductions of biblical passages and reconstructions by archaeologists. The most infamous (and most misunderstood) is the Etemenanki Ziggurat in ancient Babylon.

Ancient clay tablets tell of a colossal ziggurat of seven successively receding storeys, which once reached a height of 91 metres.[10] At its summit sat the temple of Marduk, patron of the city of Babylon, described by its creator Nebuchadnezzar II as the 'House of the Seven Lights of the Earth'.

Shape of Etemenanki carved on a black stone, the Tower of Babel Stele, 604–562 BCE.

Section of Etemenanki.

Reconstruction by Zénaïde A. Ragozin, 1889.

Reconstruction by Robert Koldewey, 1913.

Reconstruction by Hans-Jörg Schmid, 1999.

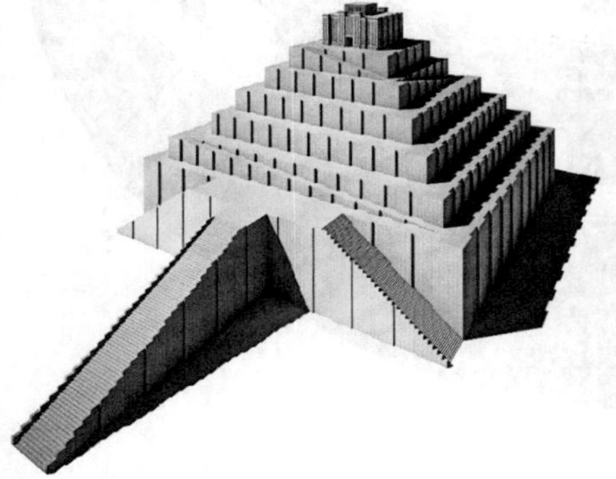

Reconstruction by J. L. Montero Fenollós, 2013.

Plan of Etemenanki.

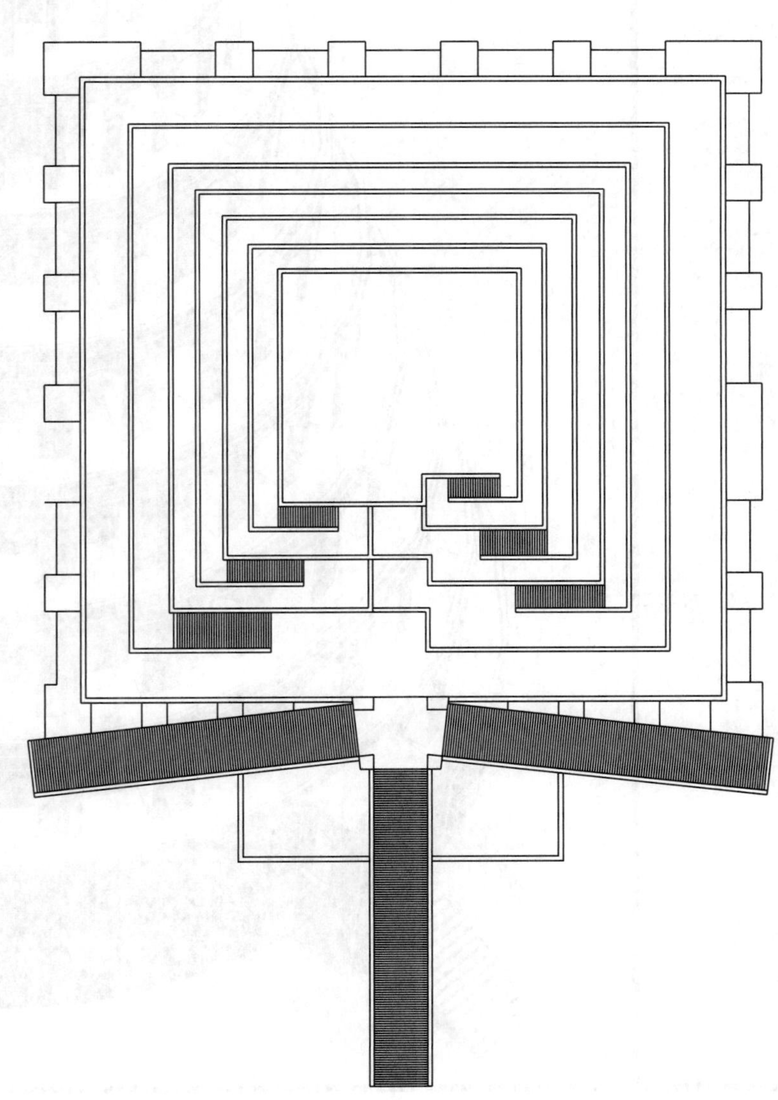

In 460 BCE Herodotus, a Greek historian with a penchant for exaggerating, described Etemenanki as an eight-tiered structure ascended by a spiralling way. This inspired countless accounts, reproductions and narratives, the most famous of which was the Tower of Babel. This powerful image has taken on a life of its own, but the more measured opinion is that the ascent was by a triple stairway that wound its way up the sloping sides of each tier in a similar fashion to the Ziggurat of Dur-Sharrukin.[11]

Imagined biblical Tower of Babel.

A.

B.

C.

D.

E.

F.

G.

H.

I.

J.

A. *The Tower of Babel*, Cornelis Anthonisz, 1547.
B. *The Tower of Babel*, Pieter Bruegel the Elder, 1563.
C. *The Tower of Babel*, Lucas van Valckenborch, 1568.
D. *The Tower of Babel*, Abel Grimmer, 1585–1600.
E. *The Tower of Babel*, Tobias Verhaecht, 1585–1600.
F. *The Tower of Babel*, Lucas van Valckenborch, 1594.
G. *The Tower of Babel*, Marten van Valckenborch, 1595.
H. *The Tower of Babel*, Abel Grimmer, 1604.
I. *The Tower of Babel*, Jan Micker, 1650.
J. *The Tower of Babel*, Athanasius Kircher, 1679.

For two paintings depicting a rectangular version of the Tower of Babel see the project Katendrecht on page 951.

Minaret al-Malwiya
Samarra, Iraq
848–852 CE

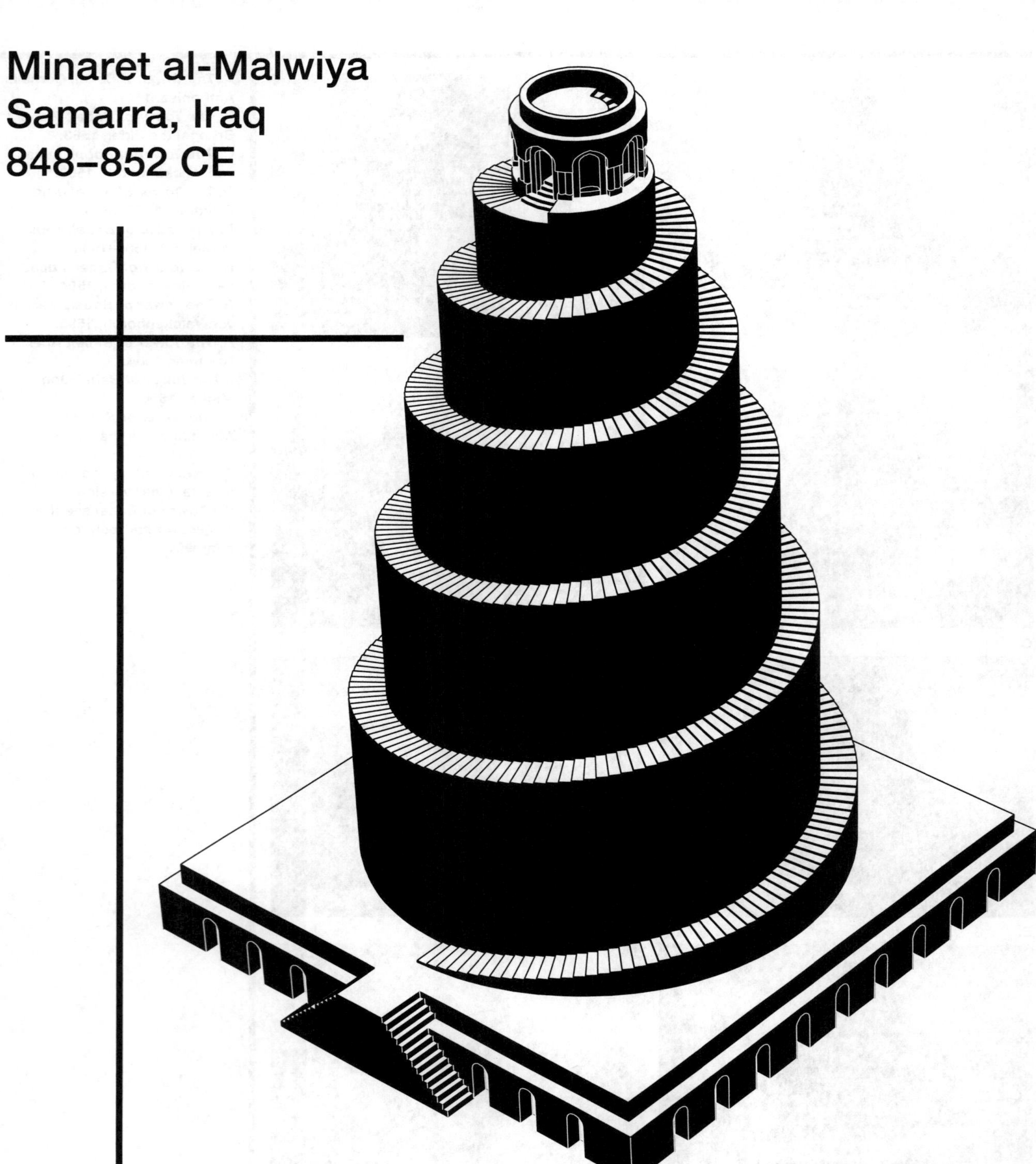

The minaret is a powerful vertical edifice, signalling the presence of Islam and calling the faithful to prayer. In a ritual practised since 624 CE, the muezzin winds upwards five times daily to announce the prayer from this dramatic open pulpit.

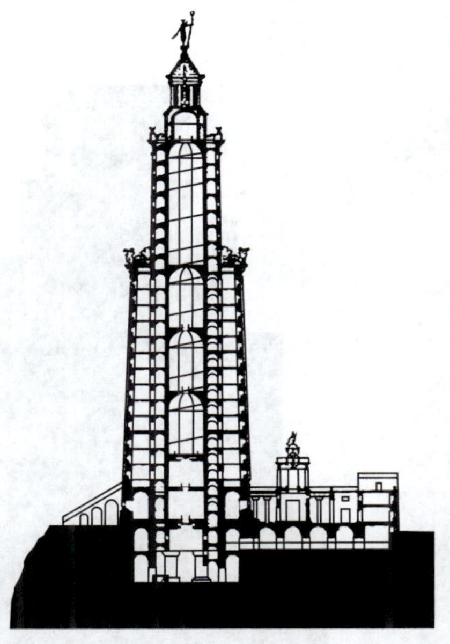

Reconstruction of the Pharos of Alexandria lighthouse, 280 BCE–1320 CE, H. Thiersch, 1909.

The term minaret is derived from two Arabic words: *ma'dhana*, denoting the place from which the faithful are called to prayer, and *manār* or *manāra*, meaning place of fire or light, inspiring parallels between the minaret and the Pharos of Alexandria lighthouse, which guided humankind to safety for seventeen centuries.[12]

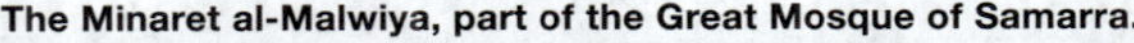

The Minaret al-Malwiya, part of the Great Mosque of Samarra.

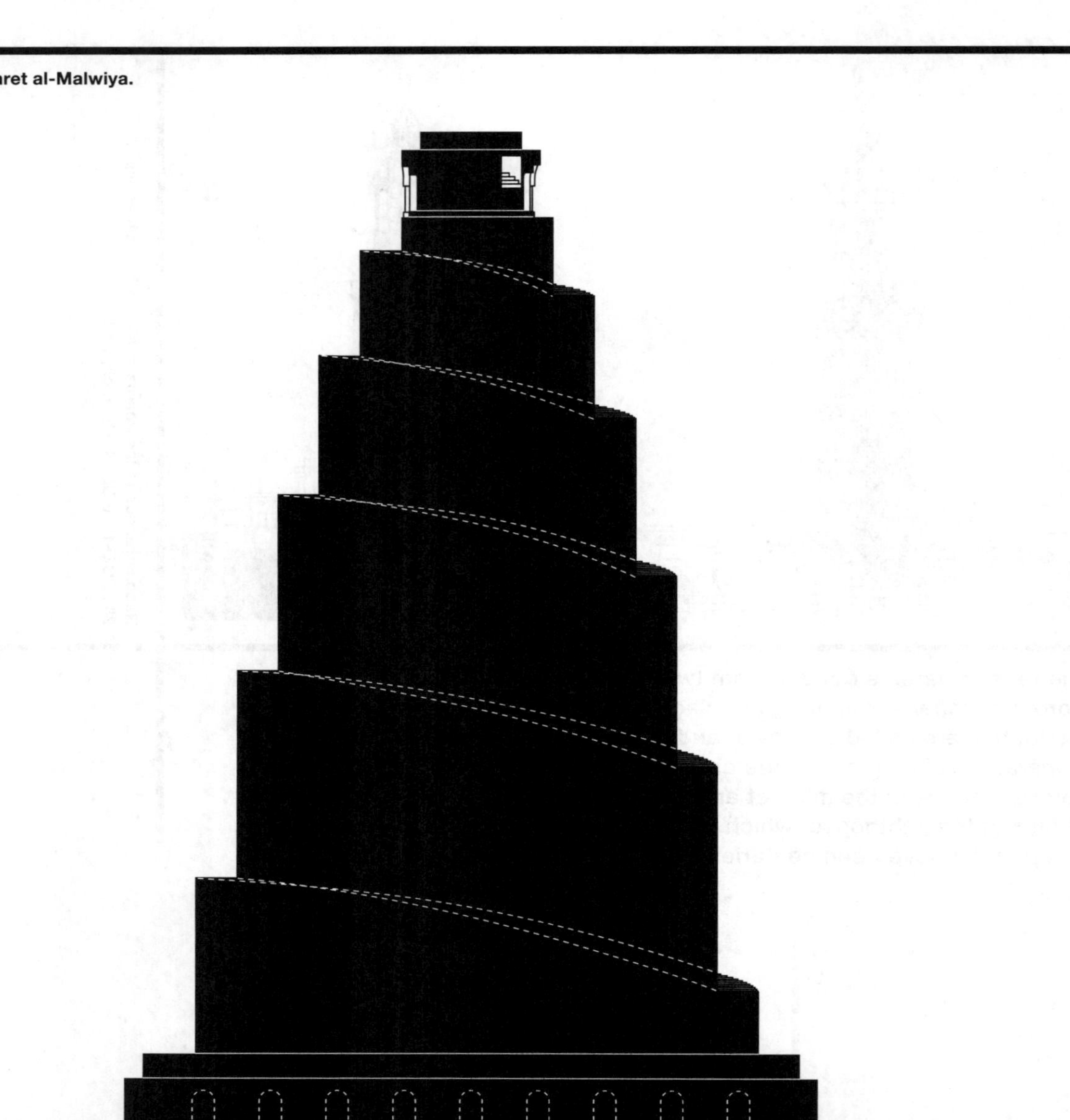

Section of Minaret al-Malwiya.

Depiction of the Minaret al-Malwiya in *The Confusion of Tongues* by Gustave Doré, 1865.

While the Pharos of Alexandria goes some way to explain the multi-storeyed towers of Egypt, and the octagonal or square minarets of North Africa and Spain can be traced back to the square church towers of Syria, the roots of the cylindrical minaret puzzle historians.

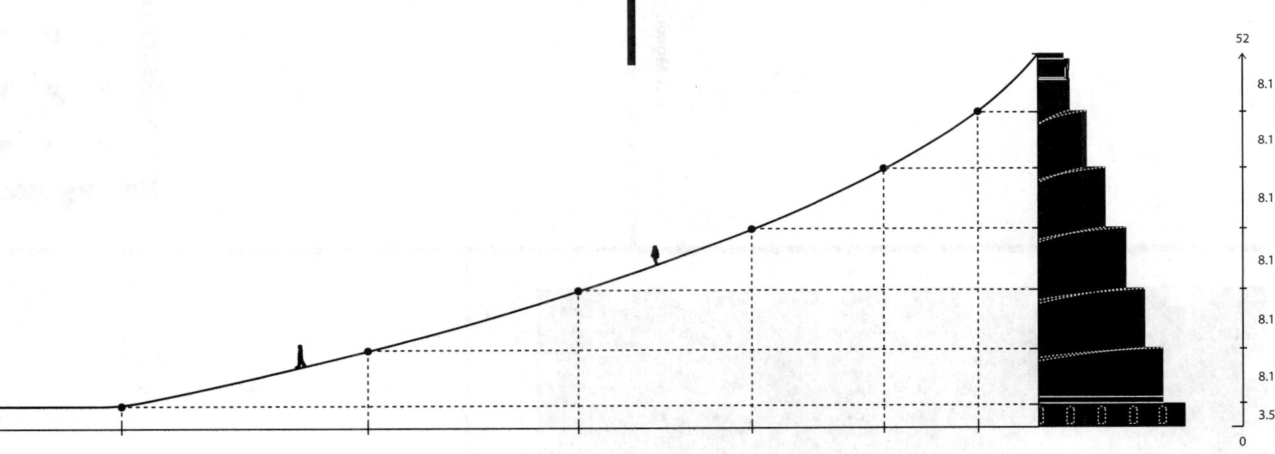

Minaret al-Malwiya unrolled.

Like the ancient ziggurat, the Minaret al-Malwiya is solid at its core, expressing its spiralling way externally. Circling the cone-shaped minaret five times, a helicoidal ramp ascends to a round vestibule at the peak, 52 metres above the ground. This external ramp gets steeper as it rises, the result of rotations around an ever-decreasing conic form. By unrolling the section of the Minaret al-Malwiya, we can visualize the gradient of this procession.

Although al-Malwiya uses the earth to raise people towards the heavens, it is unlikely that it was modelled on the ziggurat. With the ascension of the Abbasid Caliphate during the Islamic Golden Age, the ziggurat was associated with idol worship and seen as an inappropriate addition to an Islamic mosque.[13]

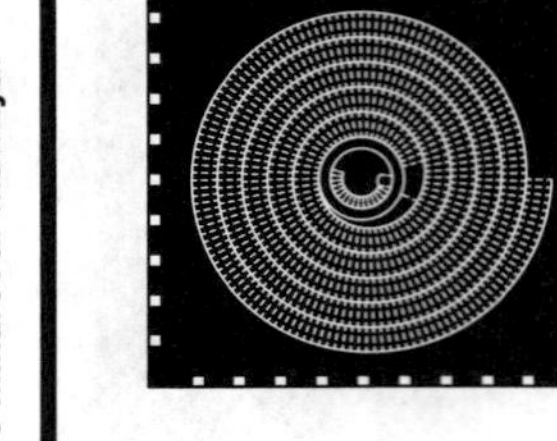

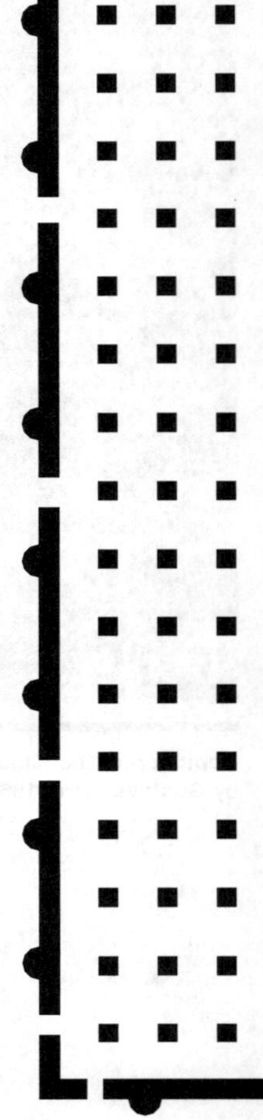

Plan of the Great Mosque of Samarra and the Minaret al-Malwiya.

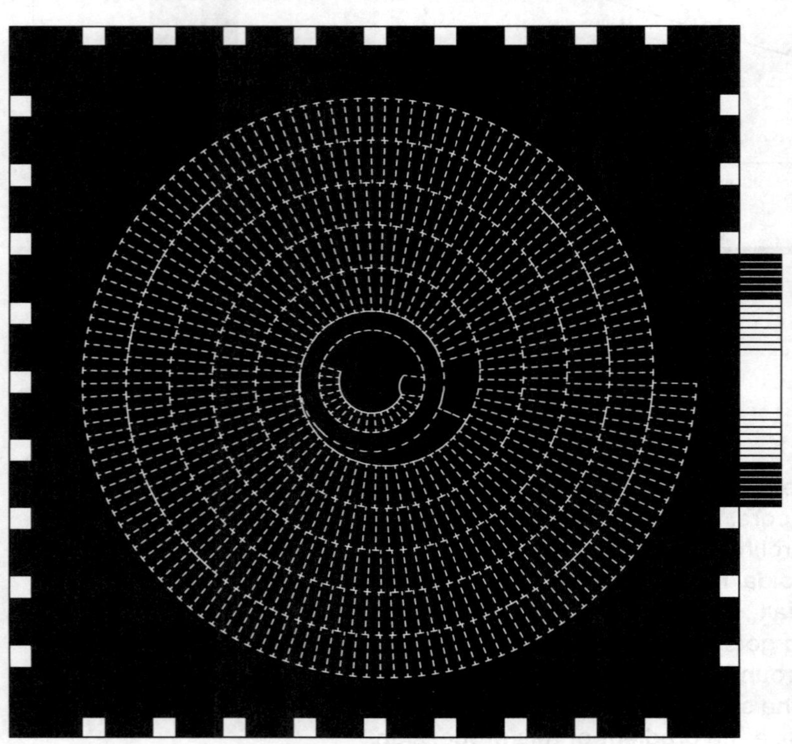

Plan of the Minaret al-Malwiya.

The city of Samarra in Iraq. © 2005 Digital Globe, Google Earth.

Minaret al-Malwiya is a monumental geometry, but it is an emblem of faith, not power. While the Abbasid palace of Al-'Ashiq (877–882 CE) and the Great Mosque of Samarra (847–851 CE) are immense, they were predominantly low-rise structures, offering the towering minaret an exclusive claim to height.[14] There is an elemental simplicity to al-Malwiya's spiral form. Its mass and height are in perfect balance with the bare steppe that surrounds it.

Rundetårn
Copenhagen, Denmark
Hans van Steenwinckel the Younger
1637–1642

Why precisely this spiral tower was constructed is unknown. Was it a Danish tower of Babel or an appropriately comfortable way in which the king could climb to an elevated chamber? Whether it was for beauty, oddity or practicality remains largely unknown. But conveying astronomical instruments to an observatory at the top or carrying books to the library seem the most obvious reasons.

Banked slope of the Rundetårn spiral ramp.

The 209-metre-long spiral corridor wraps around the hollow core of the tower, climbing 3.74 metres per revolution to reach a height of 34 metres. It forms the only connection between the observatory above and the bell loft, church and library alongside. The banked slope of the floor is three times steeper at the centre than at the outer wall, which combined with the radiating brickwork, gives the space its fluid motion.

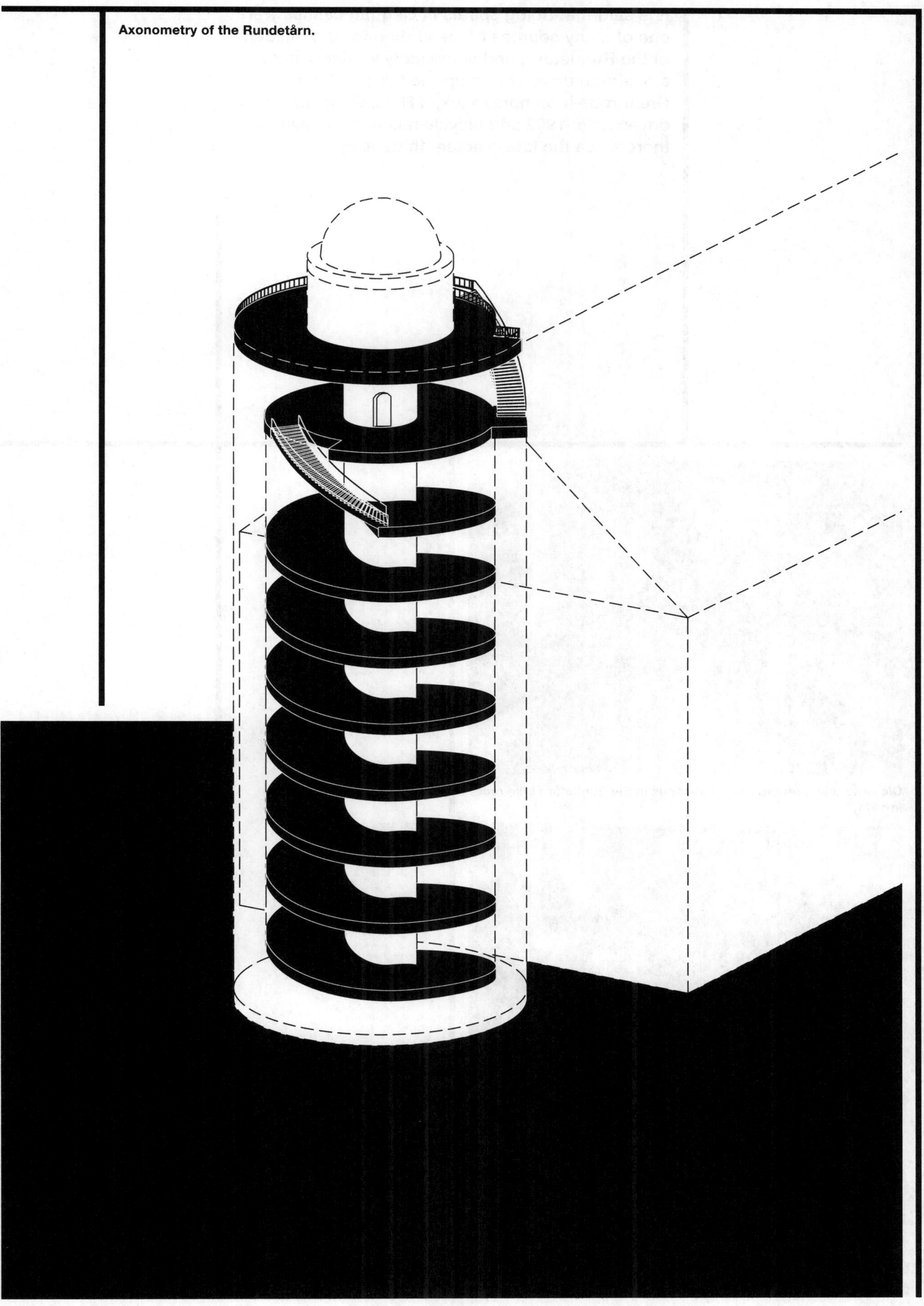

Axonometry of the Rundetårn.

It is said that riding spirals in German castles were one of many sources of inspiration for the builders of the Rundetårn, and some early writings mention a desire to drive or ride up the tower.[15] Peter the Great rode it on horseback, a Benz Gaggenau was driven up in 1902 and bicycle races have been held there since the late-nineteenth century.

Ole Ritter set a record of 55.3 seconds in the Rundetårn bike race in 1971.

Kids during the Uniracer Rally, held since 1982, with a record time in 1989 of 1 minute 48 seconds.

Plan of Rundetårn.

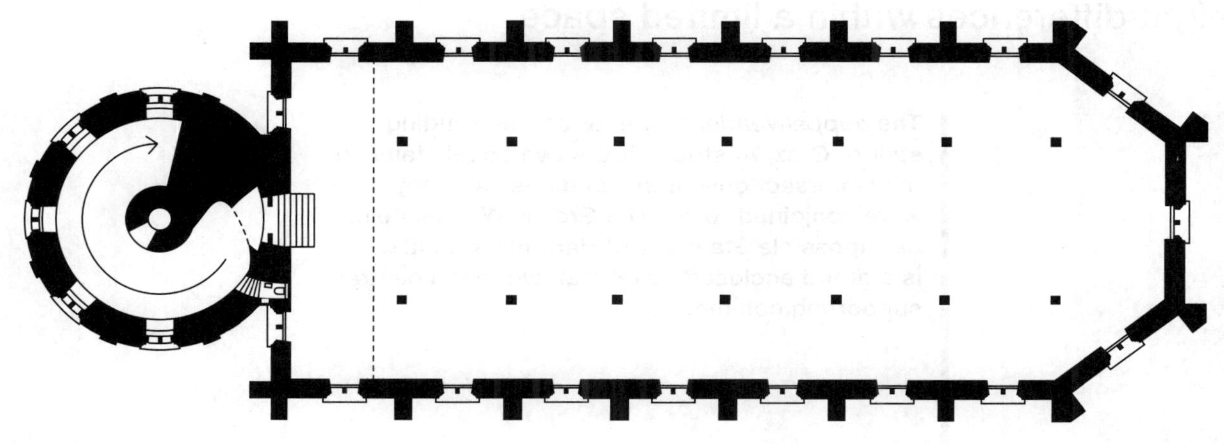

Section of Rundetårn.

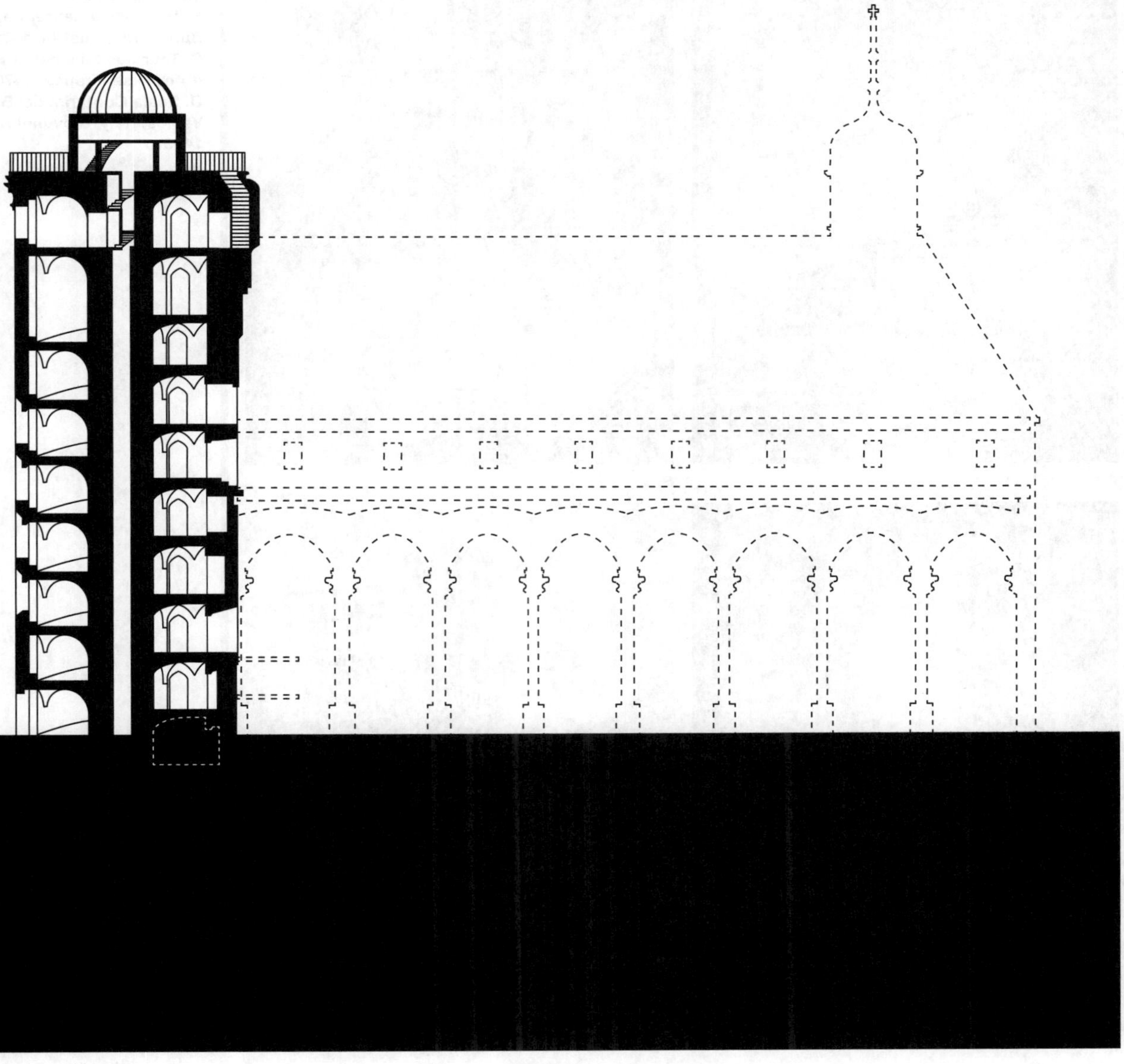

The Rundetårn is part of a long lineage of ingenious spiralling staircases and ramps that bridge serious height differences within a limited space.

The *doppelwendeltreppe*, or double winding stair of Graz, Austria, mirrors two spiral stairs so they intersect only at the landings as if they were conjoined twins. The Grosse Wendelstein, or Impossible Staircase of Hartenfels Castle, is a grand enclosed spiral stair without a central supporting column.

A.

B.

C.

D.

A. Mule ramp, White Tower of Thessaloniki, Greece, reconstructed in 1430.
B. Doppelwendeltreppe, the Burg, Graz, Austria, 1439.
C. Tour des Minimes, Chateau d'Amboise, France, 1470–1498.
D. Scala Contarini del Bovolo, Venice, Italy, Giovanni Candi, 1499.

E.

F.

G.

H.

I.

J.

E. Spiral staircase of François I, Château de Blois, France, 1515–1524.
F. The Grosse Wendelstein, Hartenfels Castle, Germany, 1533–1537.
G. Double Helix Staircase, Chateau de Chambord, France, 1520.
H. Painted spiral stair, Melk Abbey, Austria, 1702–1736.
I. Spiral road, Hohenzollern Castle, Germany, 1846.
J. Spiral horse ramp, Palau Güell, Spain, 1886–1888.

The core of Tour des Minimes, Château d'Amboise.

At the Chateau d'Amboise, the Tour des Minimes ramp is negotiable on horseback. Spiralling five times, it bridges the height difference between the town on the bank of the River Loire and the elevated castle grounds 27 metres higher. On the other side of the garden, the Tour Heurtault spirals down into town again.

Château d'Amboise above Amboise, France.

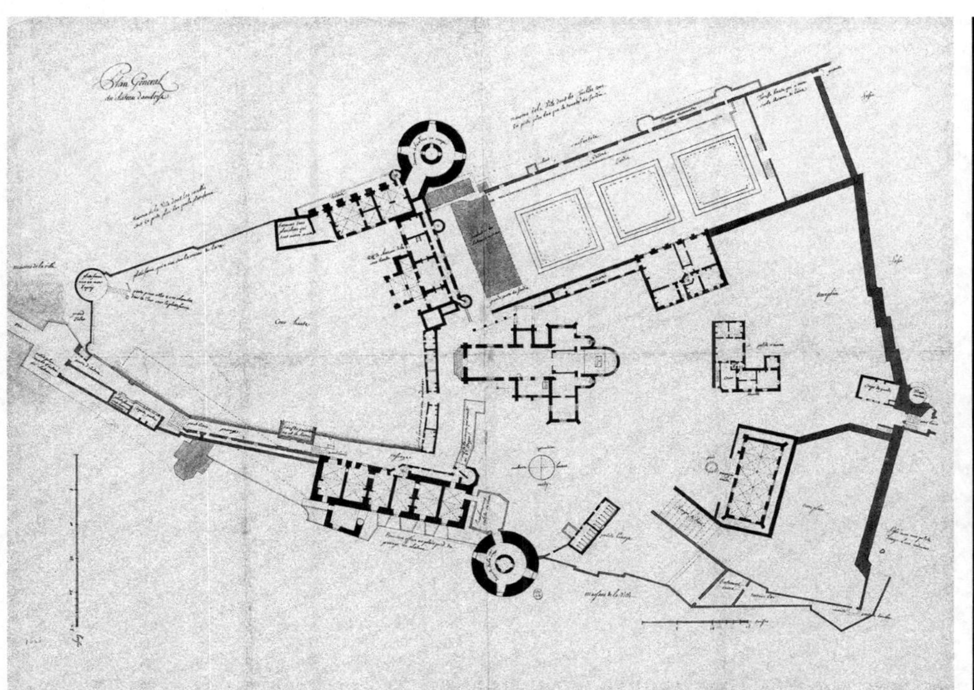

Plan of Château d'Amboise, Tour des Minimes above and Tour Heurtault below.

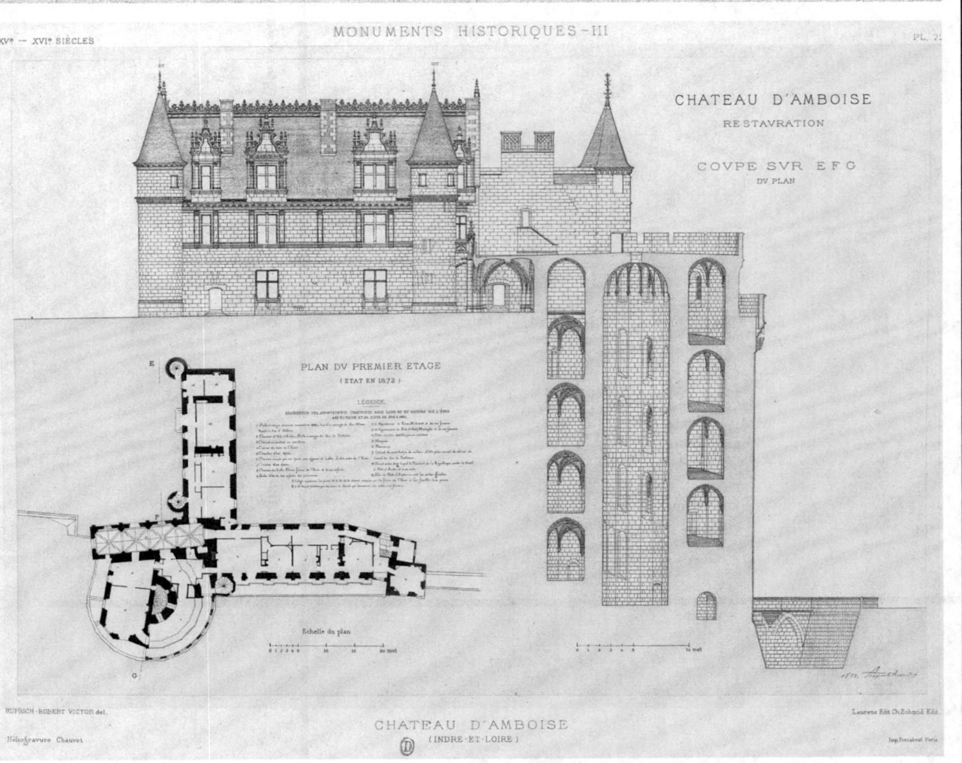

Plan and section of Tour des Minimes.

Between the castle and Clos Lucé, Leonardo da Vinci's home at the time, a 300-metre-long secret tunnel was built under the city of Amboise so that the artist could visit the king in total privacy. It is said that da Vinci is the author of the double helix staircase at Château Chambord, located just 50 kilometres from the Château d'Amboise.

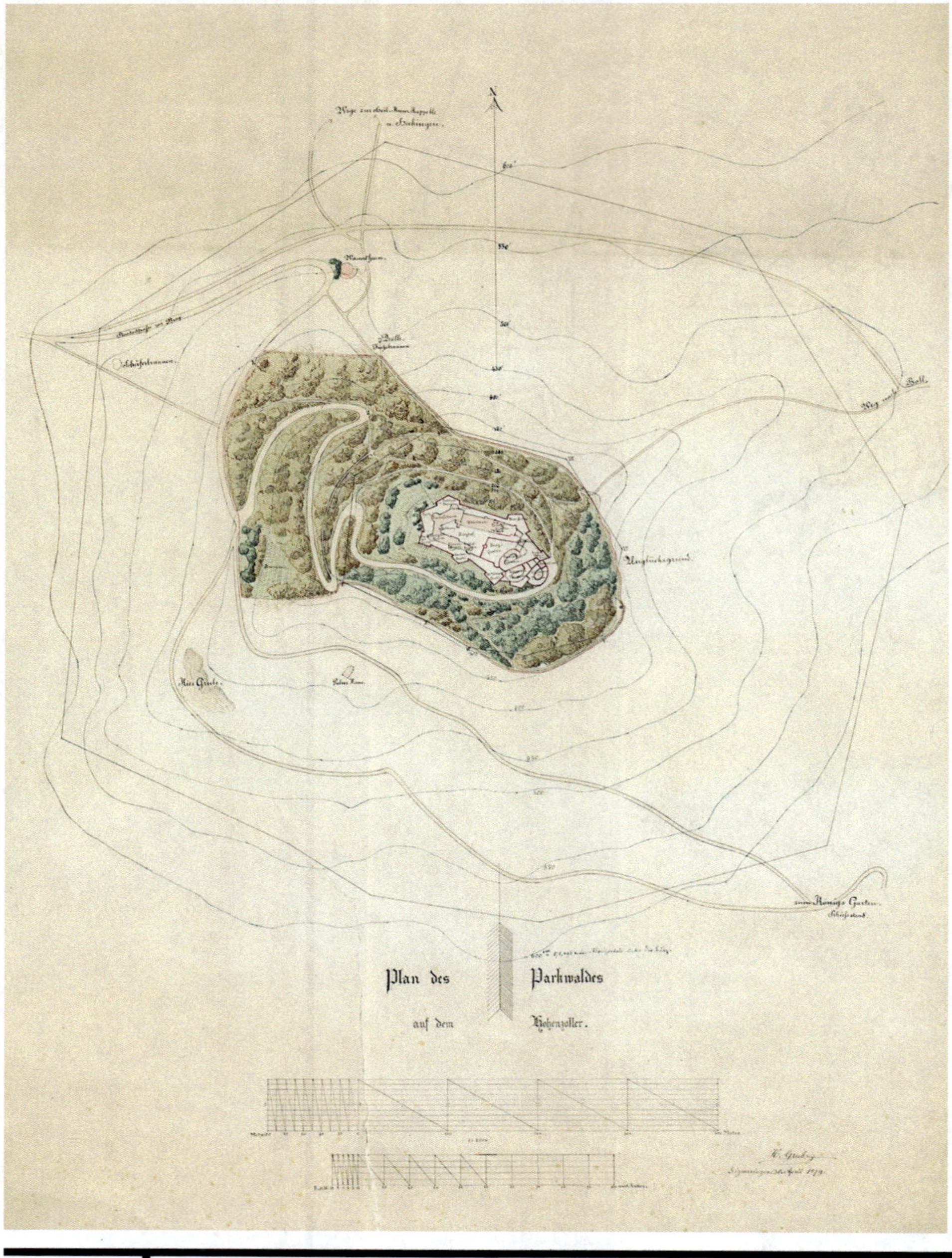

Plan des Parkwaldes auf dem Hohenzoller.

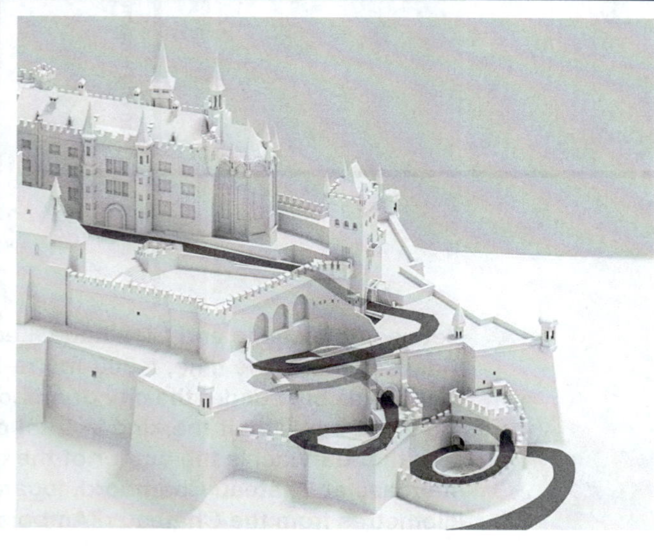

The spiralling approach to Hohenzollern Castle, Hechingen, Germany, 1846.

Late examples can be found at Hohenzollern Castle, where King Frederick William IV had a partially covered, quadruple-spiralling road built in 1846 to allow horse and carriage to reach the castle with ease, and at Pena Palace in Sintra, where Wilhelm Ludwig von Eschwege, a German amateur architect with knowledge of several castles along the River Rhine, designed an impressive spiral road under the palace forecourt.[16] It was finished around 1852, the year Elisha Otis introduced the safety elevator. With this invention these continuous, step-less connections in use for millennia became obsolete.

Pena Palace, Sintra, Portugal, 1852.

Initiation Well of Quinta da Regaleira
Sintra, Portugal
Luigi Manini
1904–1910

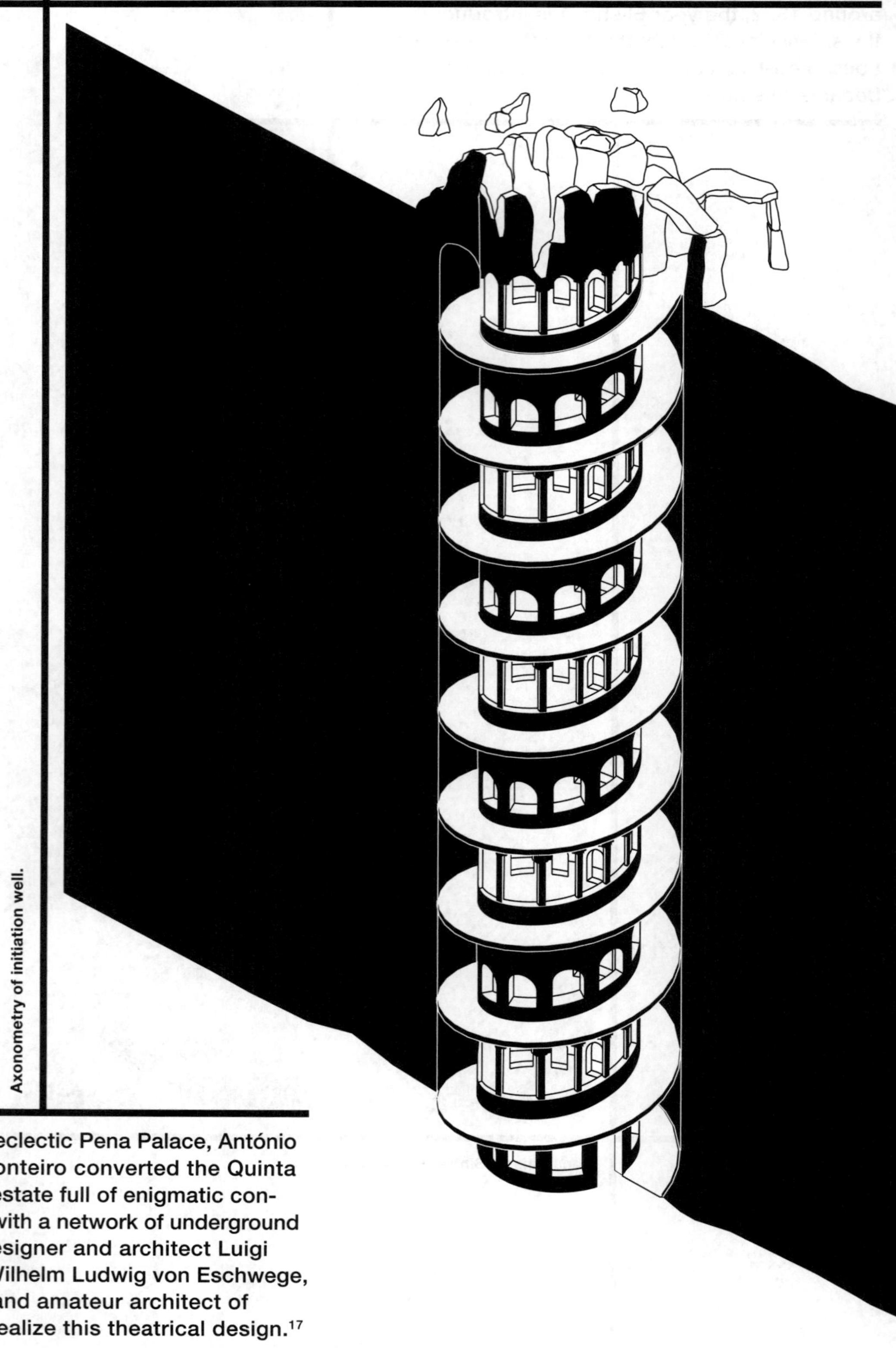

Axonometry of initiation well.

Next door to Sintra's eclectic Pena Palace, António Augusto Carvalho Monteiro converted the Quinta da Regaleira into an estate full of enigmatic constructions, complete with a network of underground tunnels. Italian set designer and architect Luigi Manini worked with Wilhelm Ludwig von Eschwege, the mining engineer and amateur architect of the Pena Palace, to realize this theatrical design.[17]

View from the bottom of the initiation well.

At Regaleira, the most striking elements are the initiation wells, or inverted towers. It is almost as if someone took the Rundetårn (or classic spiral stair), hollowed out its centre and plunged it 27 metres deep into the ground. At the bottom of the well it connects to a larger tunnel system and another unfinished well.

These wells never served as water sources but were apparently built for ceremonial purposes like tarot initiation rites at the bottom of the shaft.

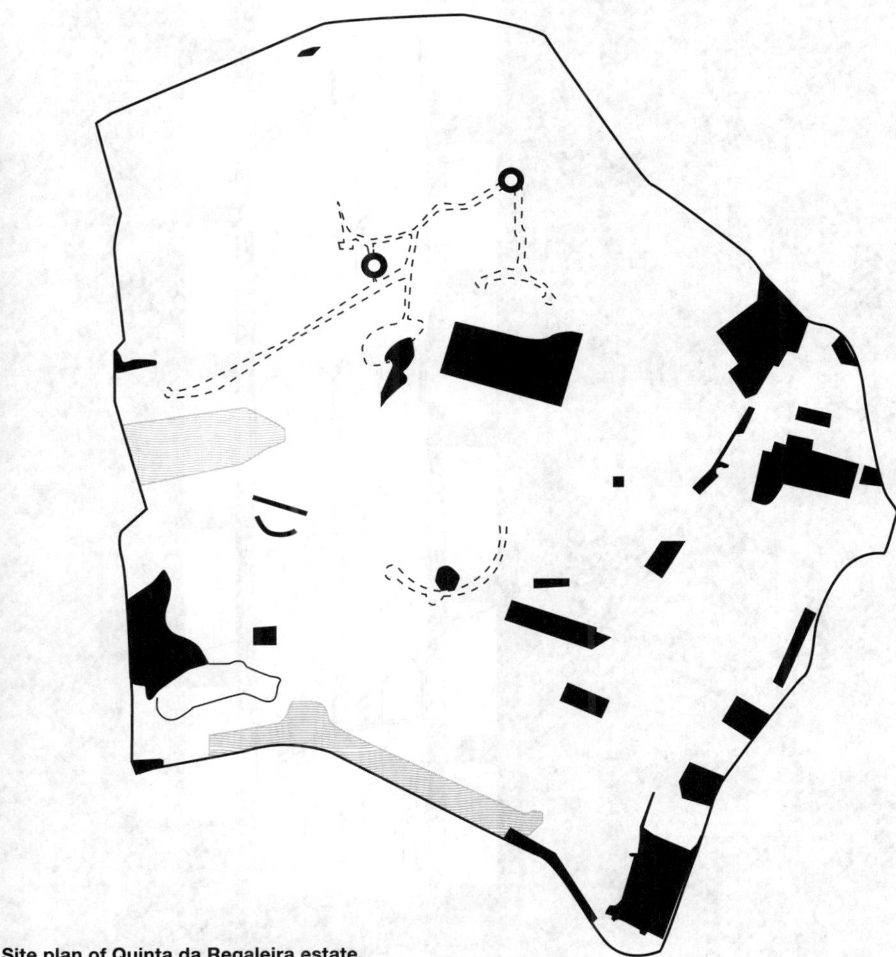

Site plan of Quinta da Regaleira estate.

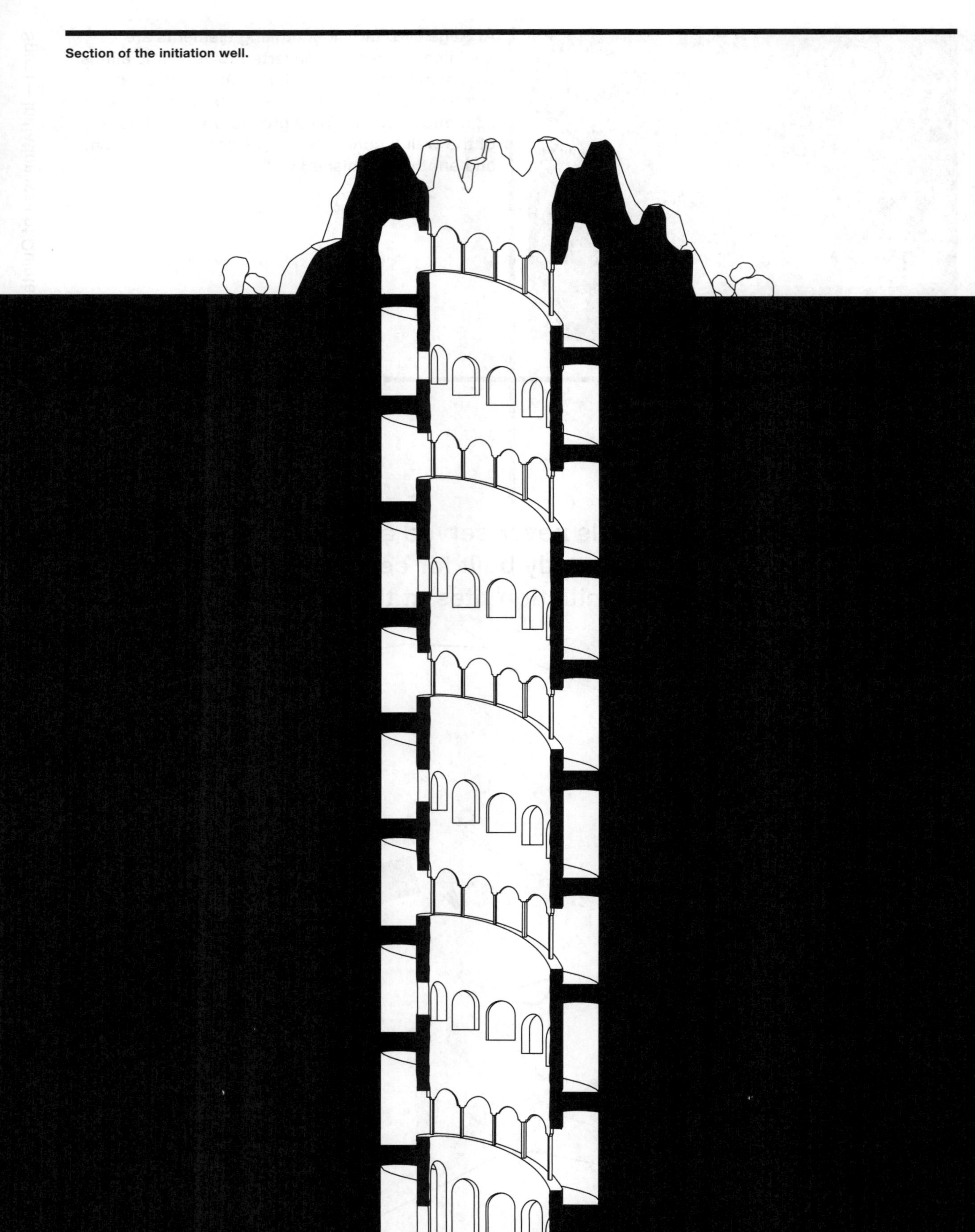

Section of the initiation well.

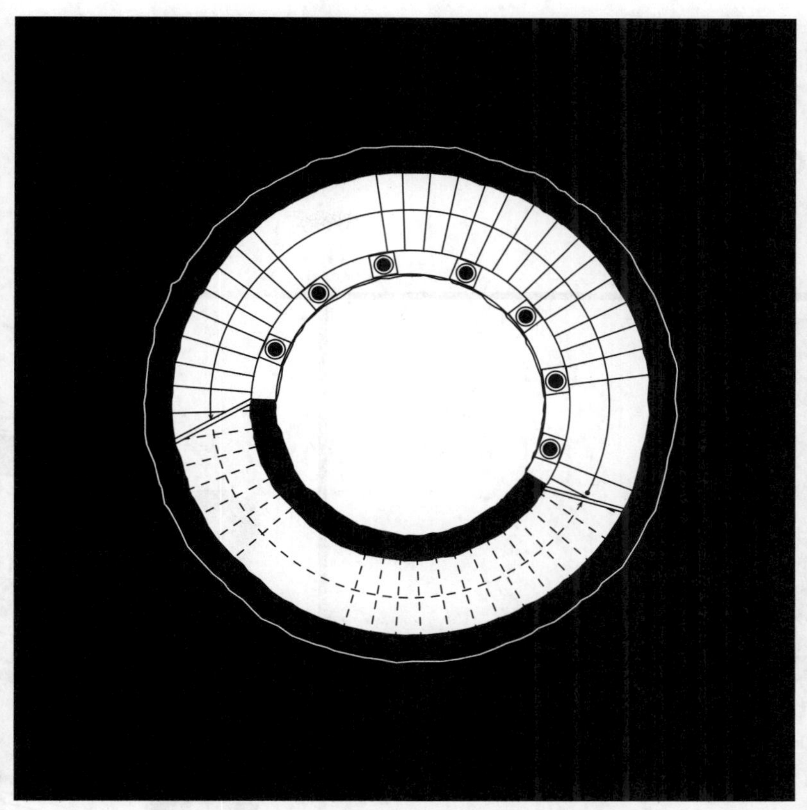

Plan of the initiation well.

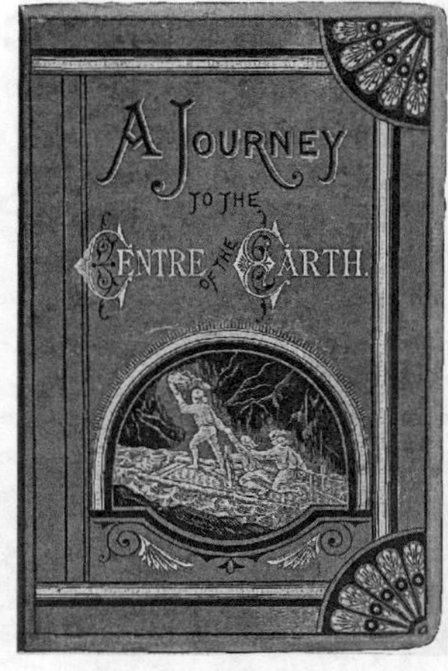

Subterranean fiction novel *A Journey to the Centre of the Earth* by Jules Verne, 1864.

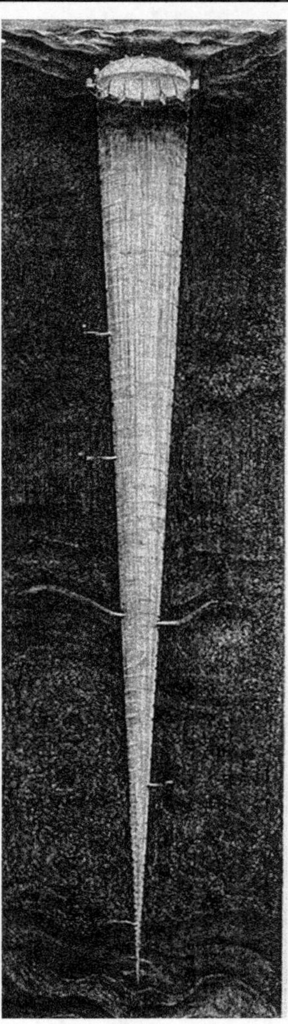

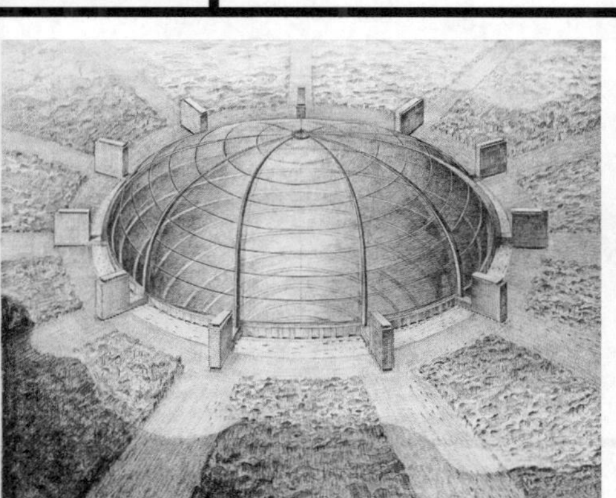

Plan the Impossible, Hendricus Theodorus Wijdeveld, 1944.

Manini's well without water joins a multitude of highly sophisticated and laborious works with no direct practical use. It seems the journey to the centre of the Earth is an end in itself. Perhaps the inverted tower served as an early prototype for the bold utopian vision of Hendricus Theodorus Wijdeveld. His self-professed 'impossible' plan for a shaft '15 Miles into the Earth' was made during a particularly harsh winter in World War II and depicts a ritual scene of human and nature colliding at the base of the shaft.[18]

Lingotto Factory
Turin, Italy
Giacomo Mattè-Trucco
1916–1923

The Lingotto Factory of Fiat was the first example of modular construction in reinforced concrete and a celebration of an industrialized future.

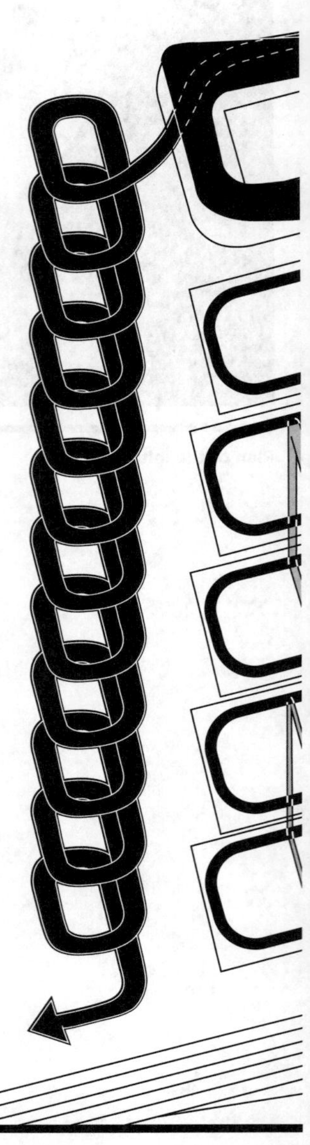

Site plan.

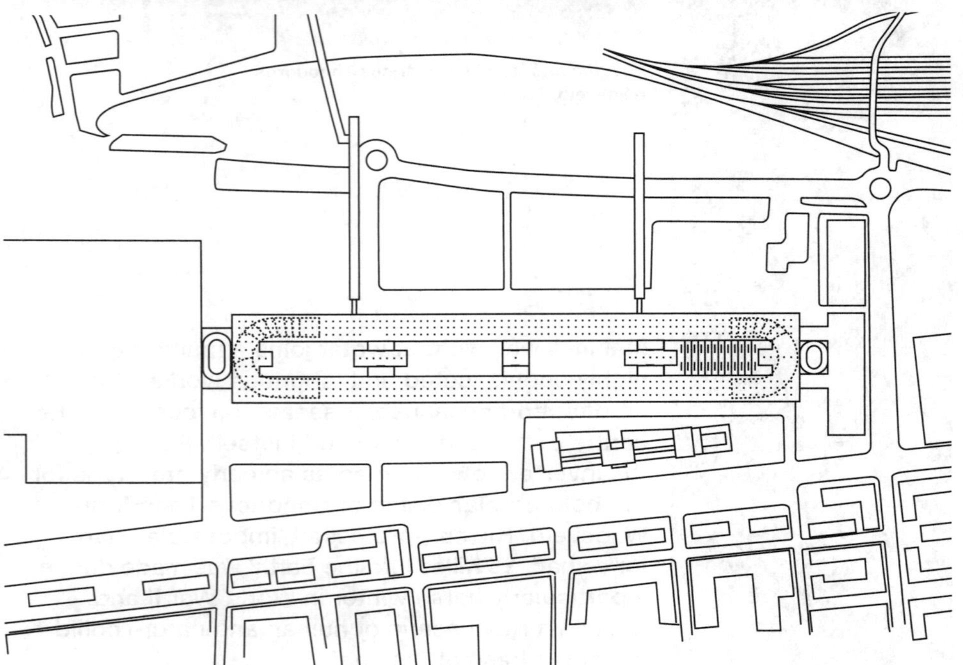

Production process of the Fiat Lingotto Factory.

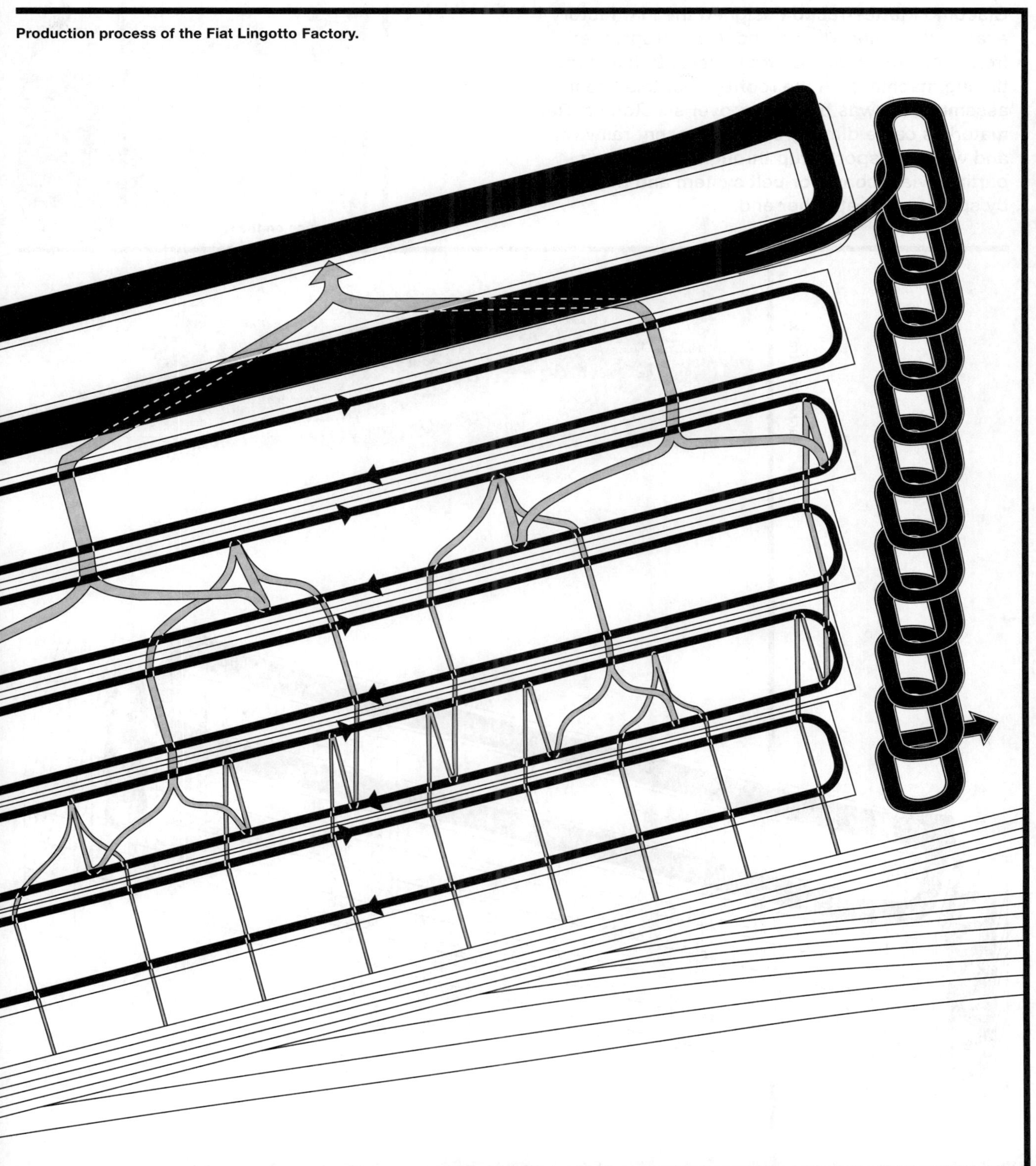

Production was organized according to the principles of Albert Kahn, the chief architect behind Henry Ford's factories and an automotive factory inventor completely dedicated to the pragmatism of the assembly line. At the Ford Motor Company plant in Michigan, which Kahn designed in 1903, production started on the top floor and used gravity and large openings in the floor to move components downwards and deliver a finished car on the ground floor.[19]

Giacomo Mattè-Trucco designed the Fiat factory exactly the other way around. Cars progressed from basic materials at ground level to fully functioning machines on the rooftop, but this linear assembly line was broken up over six storeys. Raw materials came directly off the adjacent railway and were transported up through the building, partially via a conveyor belt system and partially by spiral ramps at either end.

Vespa race on the roof, 2011.

Banked test track.

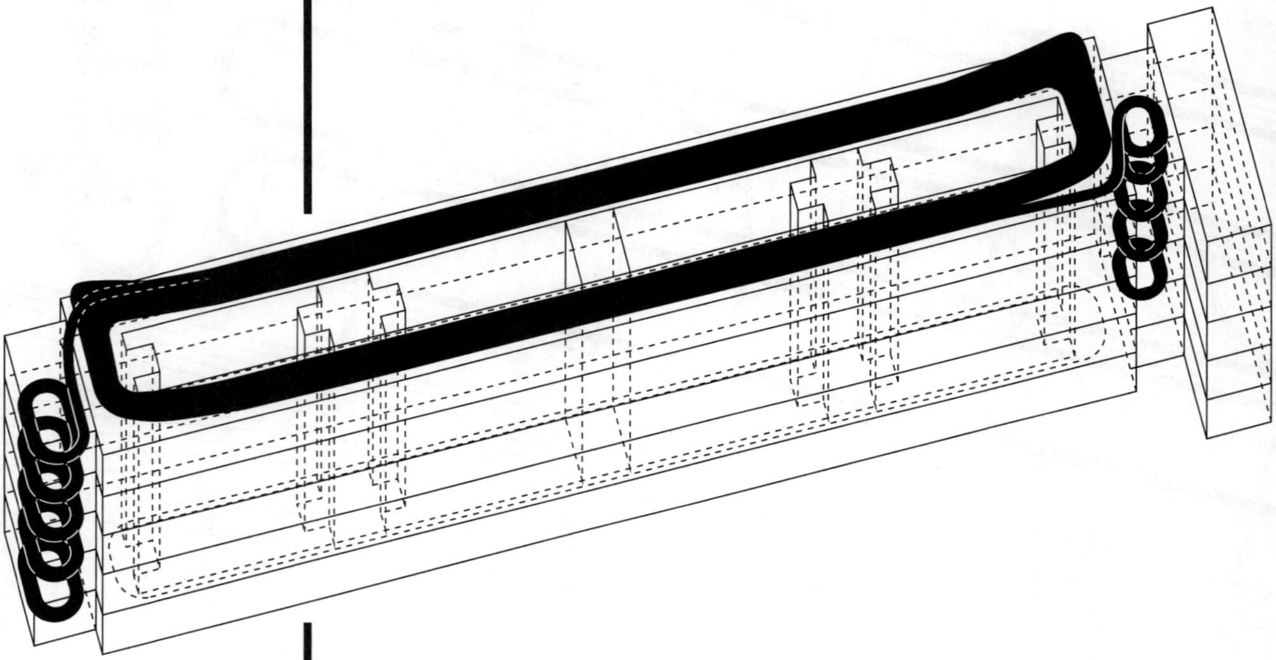

Axonometry of Lingotto Factory.

Like a temple on top of a ziggurat, this colossal ark is crowned by a banked test track. A celebration of the automobile's speed and power. Although manufacturing moved out in 1982, the track was used for races up until 2011.

Lily pad–like radial concrete structure by engineer Vittorio Bonadè Bottino. Gabrielle Basilico, 1915.

While the structure of this 500-metre-long elongated box was highly modular, the two spiral ramps (completed in 1926) have a unique lily pad–like form, with a central column and concrete ribs that radiate outwards. This composition expresses the structural forces within, echoing a marvel of engineering built 550 years earlier and anticipating an entirely new building method.[20]

Section of spiral ramp.

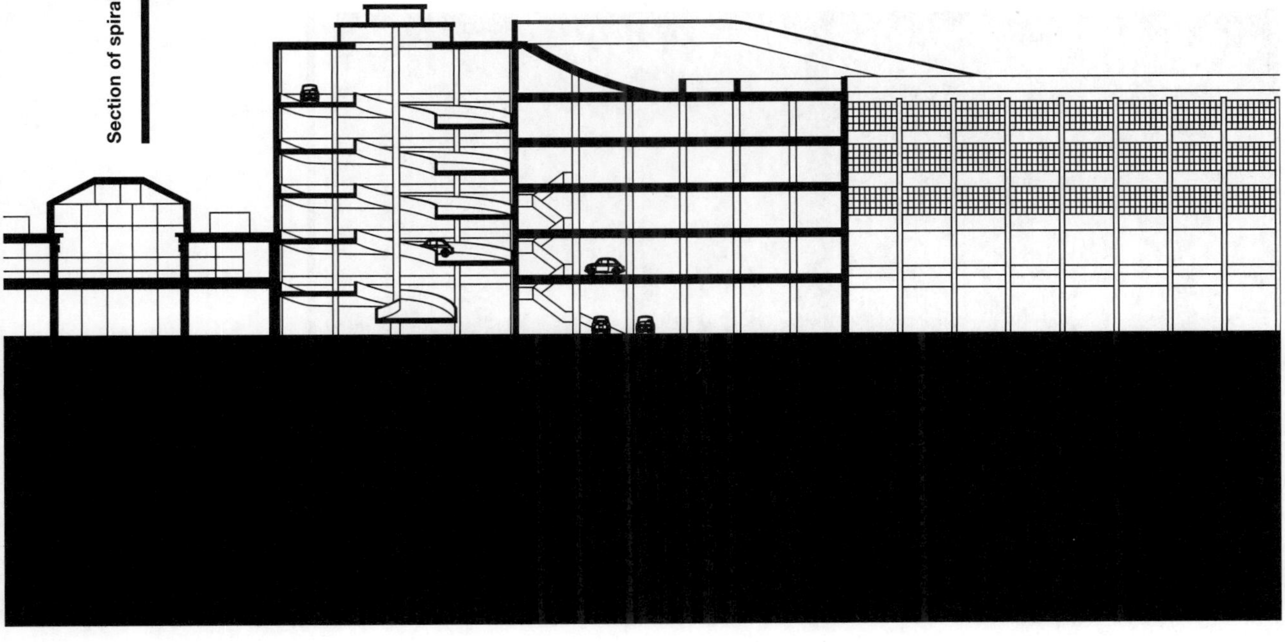

Lingotto's spiral ramps bear a striking resemblance to the rib-and-fan vaulted ceilings of English Gothic structures, like the cloisters of Gloucester or the Chapter House of Wells Cathedral. And they can also be seen as part of a lineage that leads to the ferrocemento method of Pier Luigi Nervi some thirty years later: a prefabricated system using precast concrete units as formwork, nesting reinforcing bars within voids and then pouring concrete to make the system act as one unit.[21]

Rib-vaulted ceiling of the Chapter House of Wells Cathedral, Somerset, England, 1286–1310.

Reinforced concrete slabs with isostatic ribs in the Palazzo del Lavoro (Palace of Labour), Turin, Pier Luigi Nervi, 1961.

The corrugated vaulted roof of the Turin Exhibition Hall is made of a series of ferrocement components, Pier Luigi Nervi, 1947–1954.

The fan-vaulted ceiling of Gloucester Cathedral cloisters dates back to 1351–1377.

Vertical letter file of the Central Social Insurance Institution, Prague, 1936.

Rapid mechanization, increasing administration, and the desire of industrialists to streamline buildings like they do the industrial processes led to many multilevel inventions. In 1936, the Czech Social Insurance Administration in Prague used bidirectional lifts to move administrators and their desks along a huge wall of personal data files. And the director of the Bata shoe factory built his office within a lift, complete with running water, ventilation and communication, so he could work from all sixteen floors.

The director's office within a five-by-five-metre lift, Bata Headquarters, Zlin, 1937.

The space occupied by manufacturing and living has grown exponentially, but the two have also drifted further and further apart. No longer are factories built near housing to ensure the proximity of workers. Factories have been removed from cities. While workers continue to flock together within the vertical office tower, industry has been pushed to the periphery, where it occupies an unprecedented amount of the earth's crust. This is a cold case begging to be picked up again.

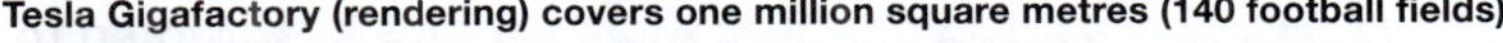

Tesla Gigafactory (rendering) covers one million square metres (140 football fields).

The Limitless Museum

"The museum is bad because it does not tell the whole story. It misleads, it dissimulates, it deludes. It is a liar."[22] —Le Corbusier

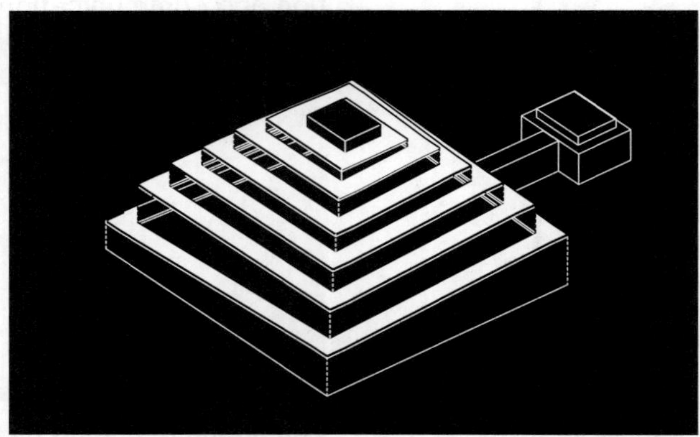

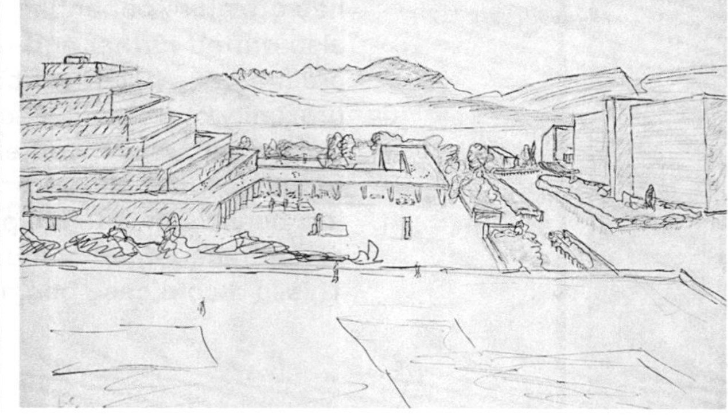

Mundaneum, *Musée Mondial* (World Museum), Geneva, Switzerland, Le Corbusier, 1929.

As the son of a textile engineer, I witnessed the obsession of my father trying to solve the challenge of yarn spinning and its non-linear limitations. A spun thread (yarn) was coiled on a spool and at a certain time, depending on its size, it had to be replaced by a new spool. The preferably continuous process of spinning had to be interrupted to exchange the full (or empty) spool.

In the 1960s and 1970s, patents on high-speed spinning were submitted, all with their pros and cons, but the most important subject was how to achieve an uninterrupted and thus endless industrial process. Shooting yarn with air, water or oil drops, using adhesive fluids that could be washed out when the yarn was woven and other no-twist spinning methods (a contradiction in terms) were invented. I don't know if they ever succeeded because my father retired. But as far as I can judge, the spool is still part of the process. It is probably comparable to the quest for perpetual motion. There is no such thing.

It is interesting to see the same struggle in architecture. The idea of the endless museum has always boiled down to one crucial issue: how to start or end the sequence.

Le Corbusier viewed the museum as a wall, continuously folded in on itself.[23] For Le Corbusier, the museum was a temple to humankind's achievements, where art or artefact was to be curated into a sequence or story for the viewer. The architect's job was to guide the visitor through this sequence, and keeping a tight grip on this procession through space was fundamental. According to Beatriz Colomina, Le Corbusier's thirty-year obsession with building a limitless spiral museum all stemmed from the Villa Savoye, and essentially involved the scaling up and internalizing of the domestic *promenade architecturale*.

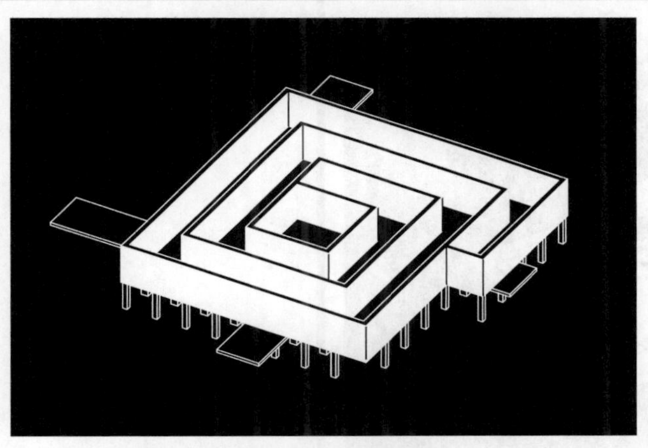

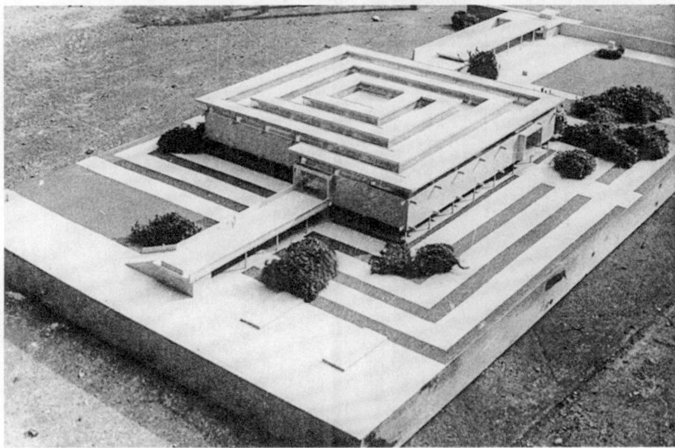

Flattened spiral of the *Musée à croissance illimitée* (Museum of Unlimited Growth), Le Corbusier, 1939.

For Le Corbusier, the problem of the museum was its finite limitations. Unless it was endless, how could it possibly tell the complete story and fully encapsulate the entire image and significance of the world?

For the Musée Mondial in Geneva, Le Corbusier designed the Mundaneum. It was a square spiral, a ziggurat-like structure where the visitor would take a lift to the top (the beginning of civilization) and walk down a spiral ramp to meet the ground (present day).[24] To take the traditional enfilade set-up of the museum and coil it up over many levels was brilliant, and this strategy has been repeated in countless museums by many architects ever since. Le Corbusier even managed to build a spiral himself in the National Museum of Western Art in Tokyo.

The National Museum of Western Art, Tokyo, Le Corbusier, Kunio Maekawa, Junzo Sakakura and Takamasa Yoshizaka, 1959.

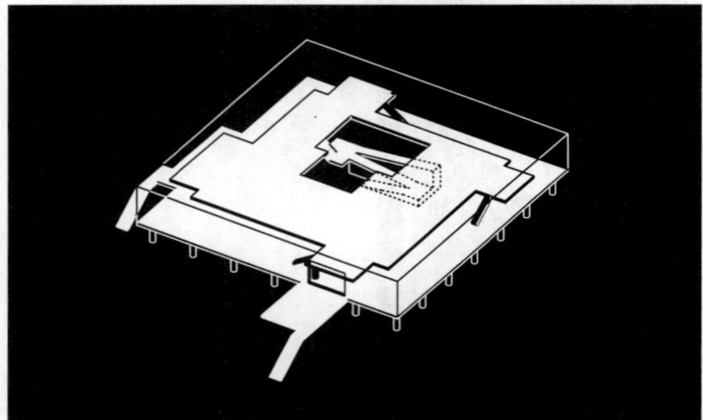

Within the world of modern art, the blind box lifted off the ground, where the architect has total control of the visitor's procession and experience, became the standard. The architect's job was to provide a neutral container, a white wall for maximum contrast, a flexible ground plan and moveable partitions.

Today, contemporary art challenges the confines of the traditional white cube and gallery wall with installations, performance art and scatter art. Artists often take full control of the exhibition experience, and the role of the curator has shifted from designing the viewing of artwork to designing the intellectual space or shaping the wider theoretical framework of the exhibition.[25] This has had interesting repercussions for the museum building. No longer is the pristine white box desired. The architect enjoys a new-found freedom.

Sunflower Seeds by Ai Weiwei, 2010. The Turbine Hall of the Tate Modern is one of the most prominent contemporary art spaces.

Installation view of *You* by Urs Fischer at Gavin Brown's enterprise, New York, 2007.

The museum spiral has become less and less hermetic. It has transformed from a single spiral, a singular experience and choreographing of what is viewed, to a more dynamic spiral, offering multiple experiences and multiple spaces for art. The Guggenheim's spiral was stretched into the the Musée Gallo-Romain's paper clip; Utzon cloned spirals and pulled them off the building envelope to make them the focus of an interior; and UNStudio twisted helixes around each other to create two intersecting journeys.

In *The Delirious Museum*, Calum Storrie proposes that the museum should be both a repository of the artefacts of the past and a continuation of the city street in the present.[26] Perhaps the museum can someday be limitless if it learns to connect to the world around it.

The Limitless Museum

—

Solomon R. Guggenheim Museum New York City, USA Frank Lloyd Wright 1943–1959

The Guggenheim's spiral is a powerful driver of form, flow and programme. By un-stacking floors and breaking away from conventional geometry, the gentle slope of the descending helix redefines the relationship between the content and the container.

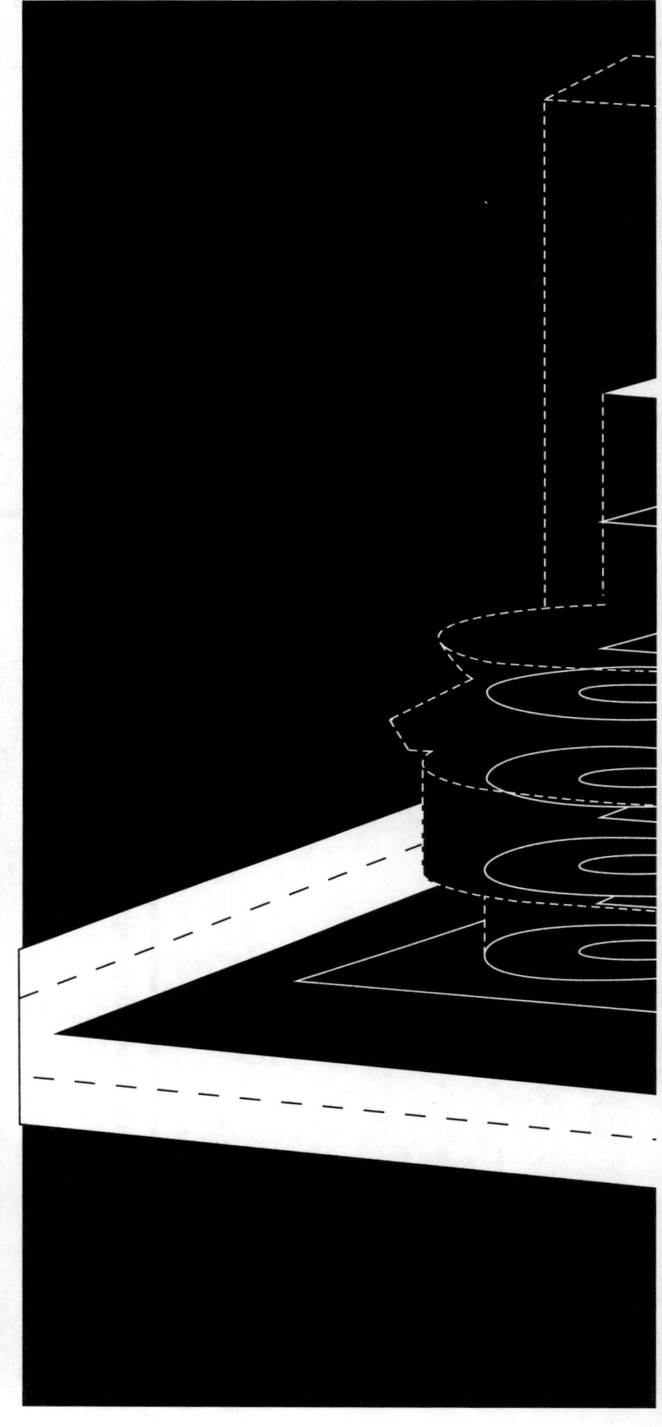

Axonometry of Solomon R. Guggenheim Museum.

Guggenheim Museum under construction, 1957.

Iconic facade, 2004.

"No, it is not to subjugate the paintings to the building that I conceived this plan. On the contrary, it was to make the building and the painting a beautiful symphony such as never existed in the world of Art before."[27] —Frank Lloyd Wright

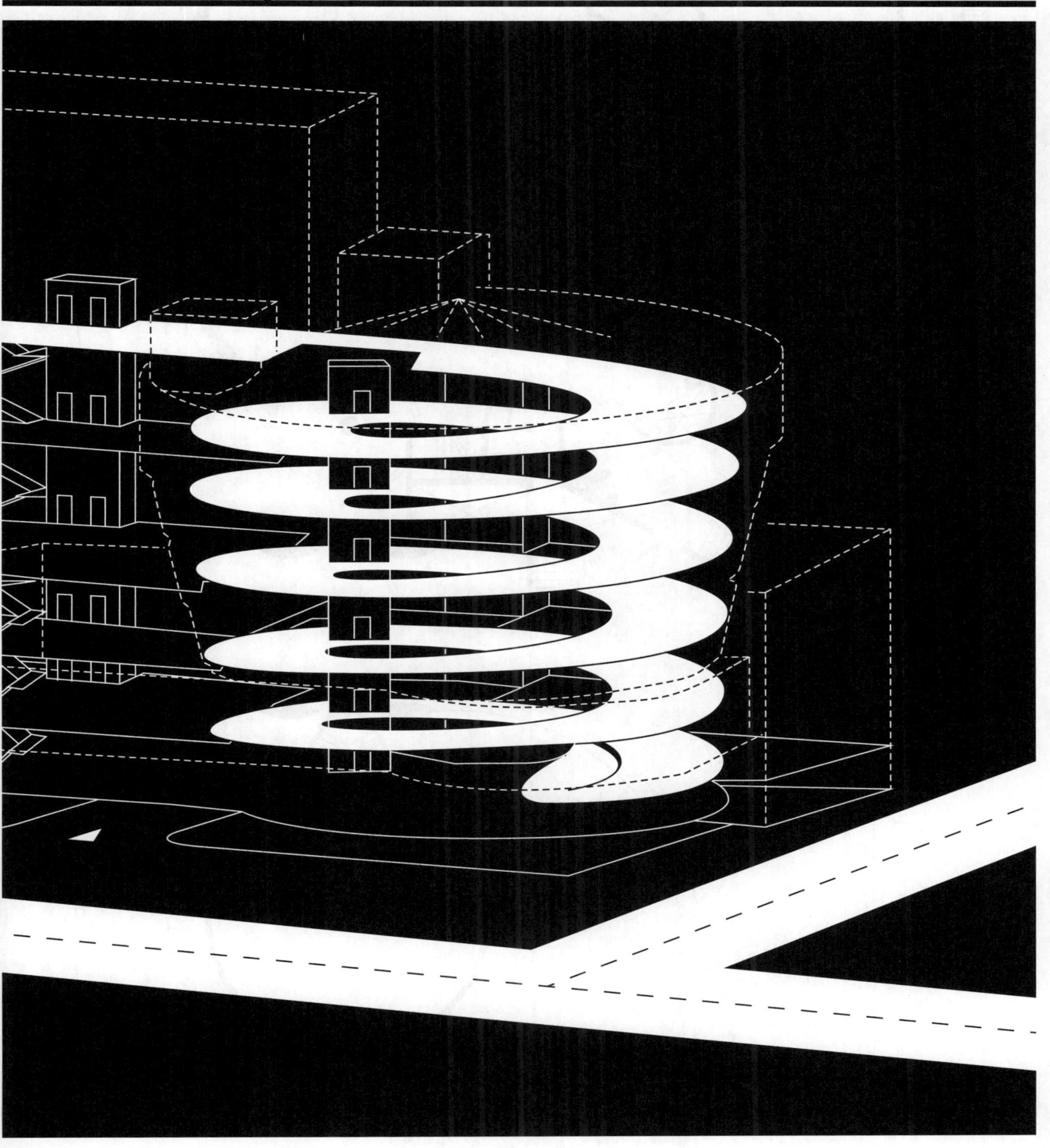

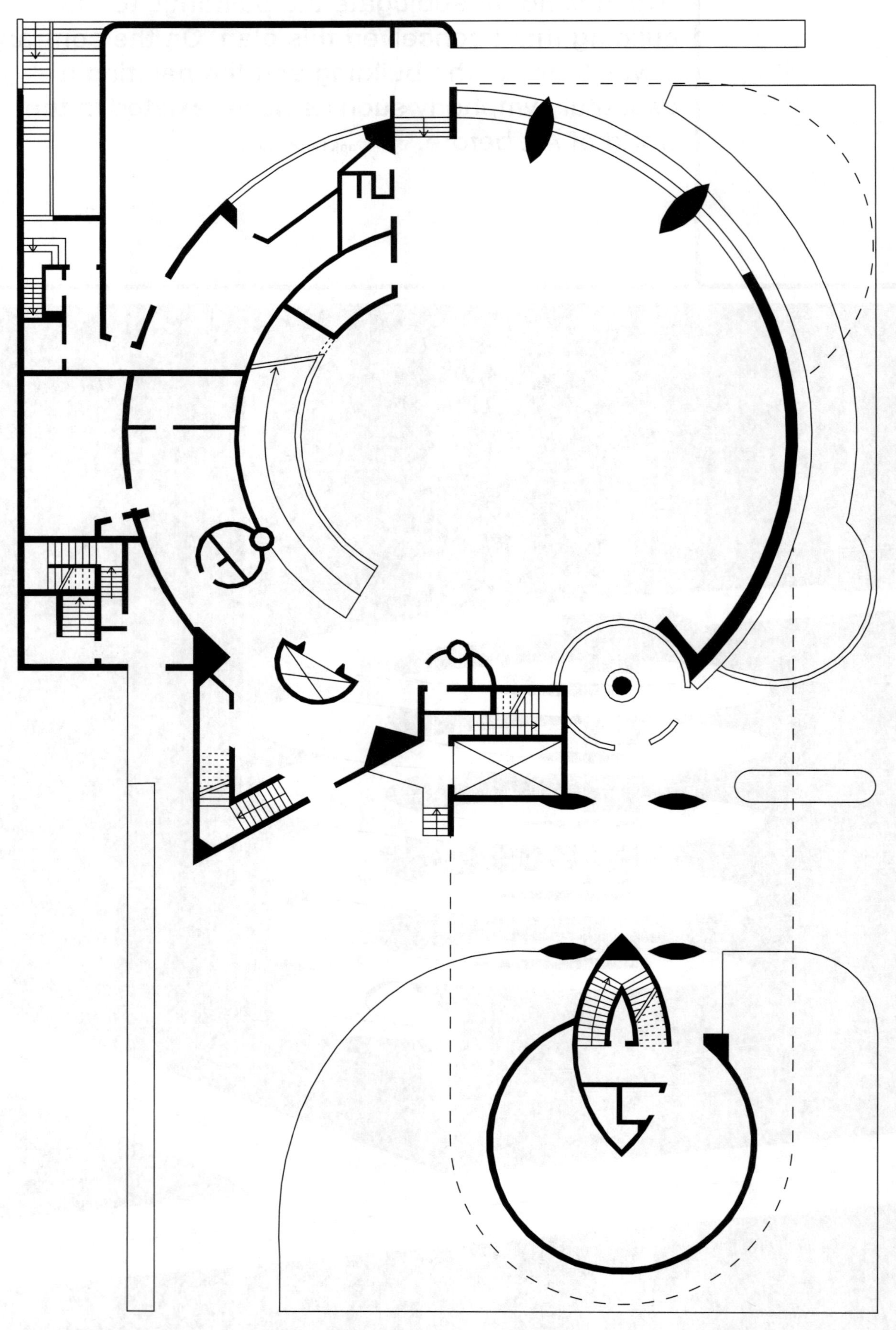

Ground floor of the Guggenheim Museum.

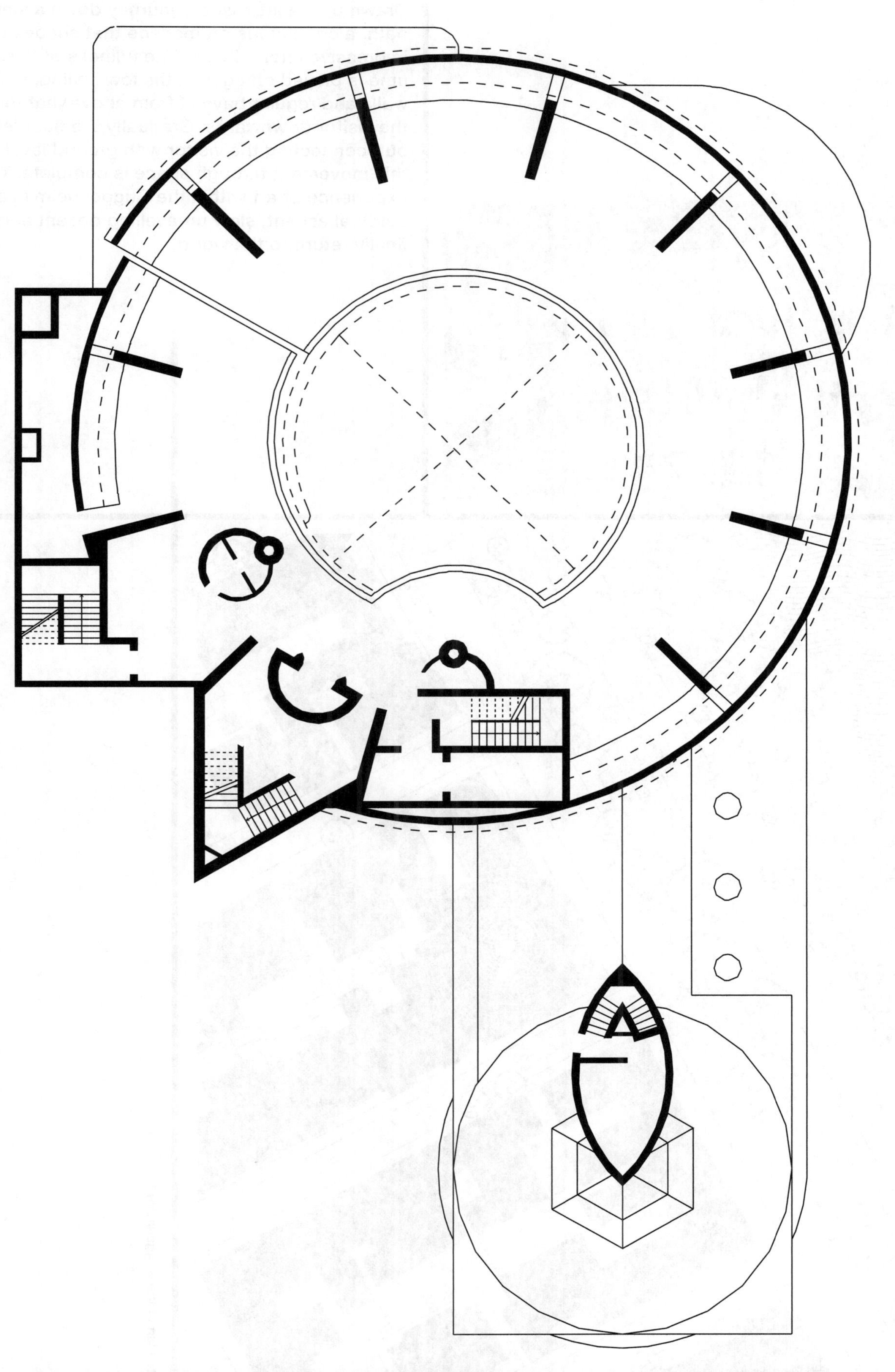

Level 4 of the Guggenheim Museum.

Drawn up via lift, visitors journey down a sinuous path, a continuous promenade that shapes the impressive internal void. The fullness of this volume is played off against the low ceiling, banked walls and regular bays lit from above that follow the visitor downwards. Gradually the floor levels out, connecting the visitor with ground level once this movement through space is complete. The experience of art within the Guggenheim is of a spiritual ascent, slow unravelling decent and finally return to the world.

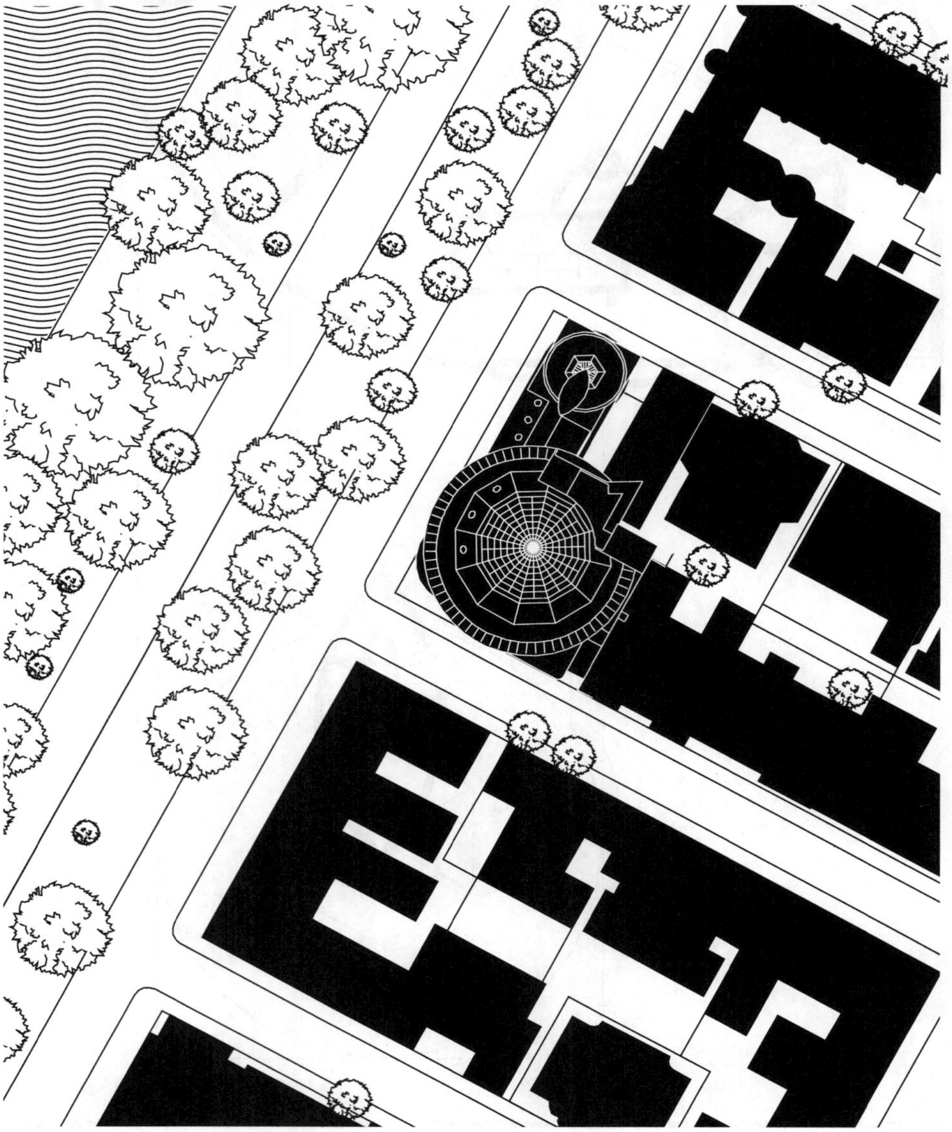

Site plan of the Guggenheim Museum.

Looking up from the centre.

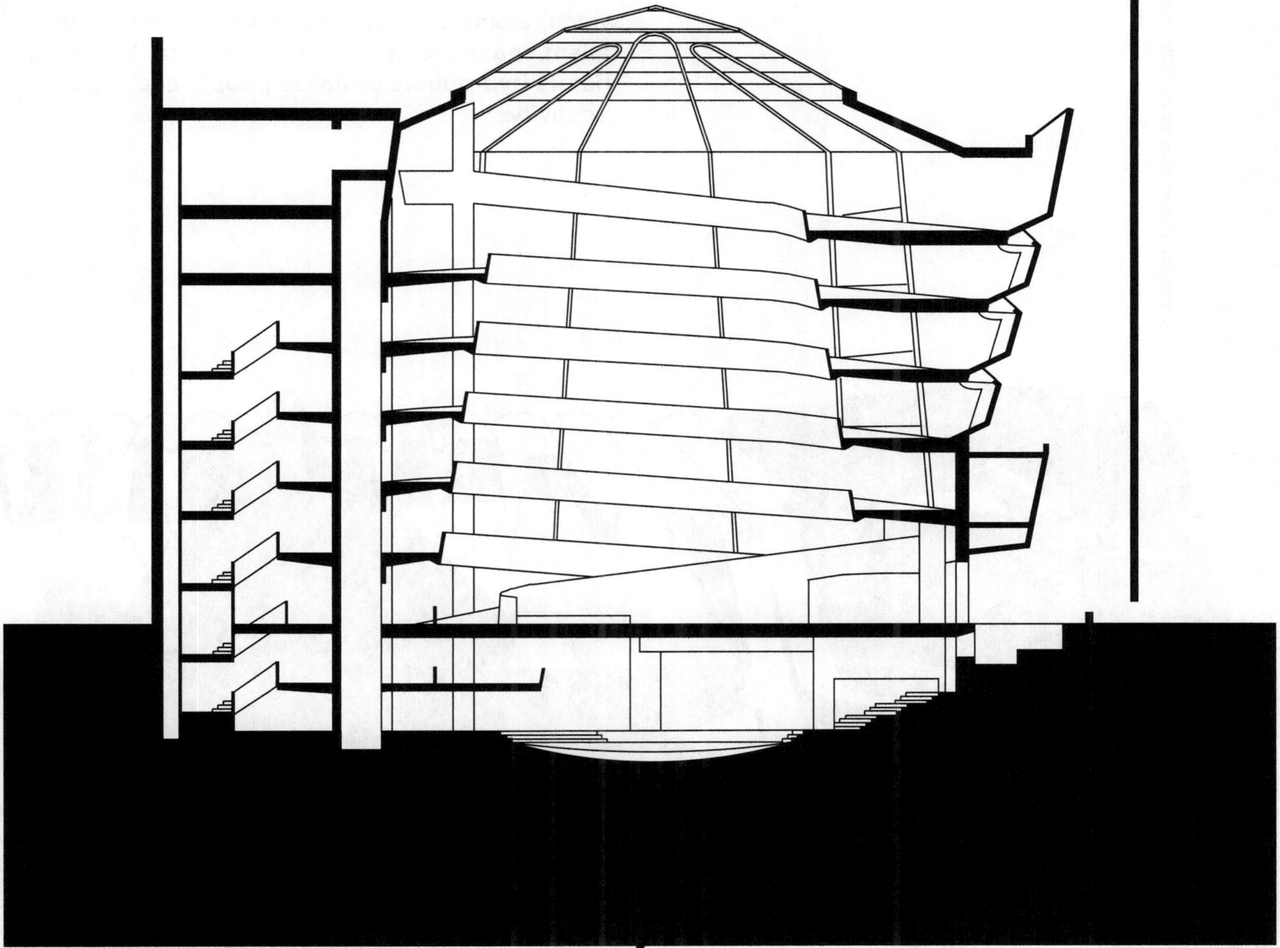

Section of the Guggenheim Museum.

That was the 1950s. Now the Guggenheim spiral is often seen as a tool to enable the mass consumption of art. The gradient of the floor keeps you moving on a mall-like stroll past regular cubicles of art. These bays are dwarfed in size by the monumental dimensions of the central void, which grabs all attention. If Wright did not want to subjugate the paintings, then why hang them around the perimeter, invisible if you stand in the centre of the space?

The Limitless Museum

—

Silkeborg Museum
Silkeborg, Denmark
Jørn Utzon
1963 (unbuilt)

Jørn Utzon was asked by Asger Jorn to design a museum for the collection he donated to the city of Silkeborg. Asger Jorn was a key figure of the avant-garde CoBRA movement (1948–1951) and the Situationist International movement (1957–1972), which rejected the ideologies of advanced capitalism, mass media and consumerism, believing that its byproducts brutalize people and crush creativity.[28]

Sectional axonometry of the Silkeborg Museum.

"It is not just a matter of creating an organic, living and cohesive architectural style, but also of creating a living lifestyle, an organic collaboration between human beings – an organic society in effect."[29] –Asger Jorn

The Situationist International movement believed the best way to combat this was to respond with 'alternative life experiences'.[30]

The Situationist Times comes with a fabulous disclaimer: "All reproduction, deformation, modification, derivation, and transformation is permitted."

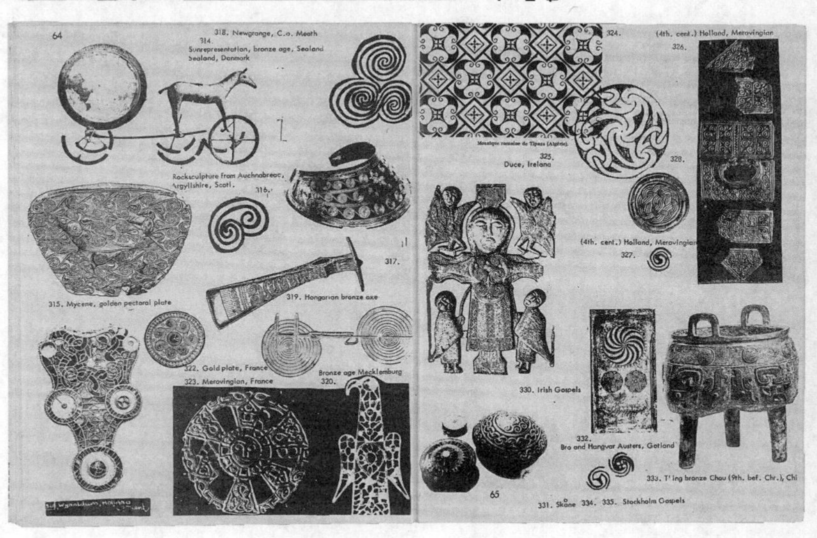

Spiral imagery in *The Situationist Times* 3, 1963.

Section of the Silkeborg Museum.

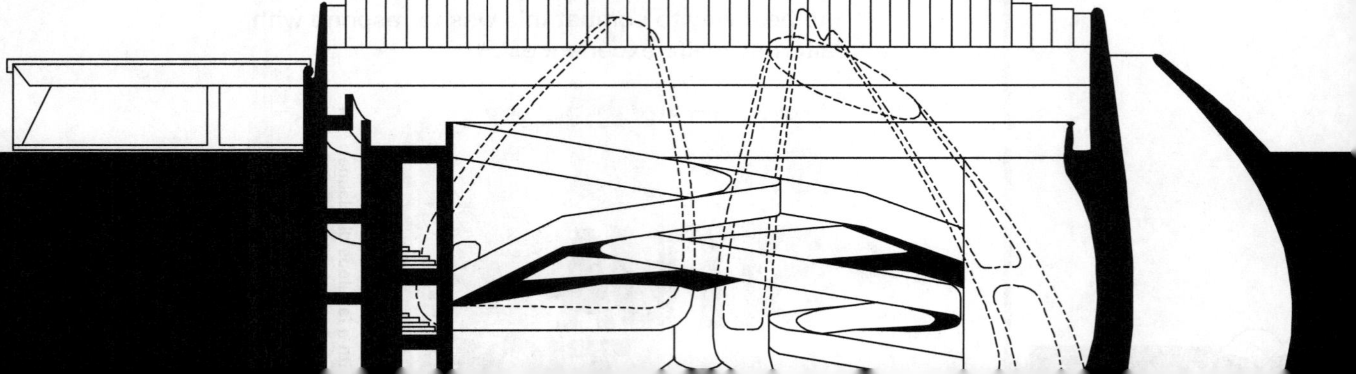

Section of the Silkeborg Museum.

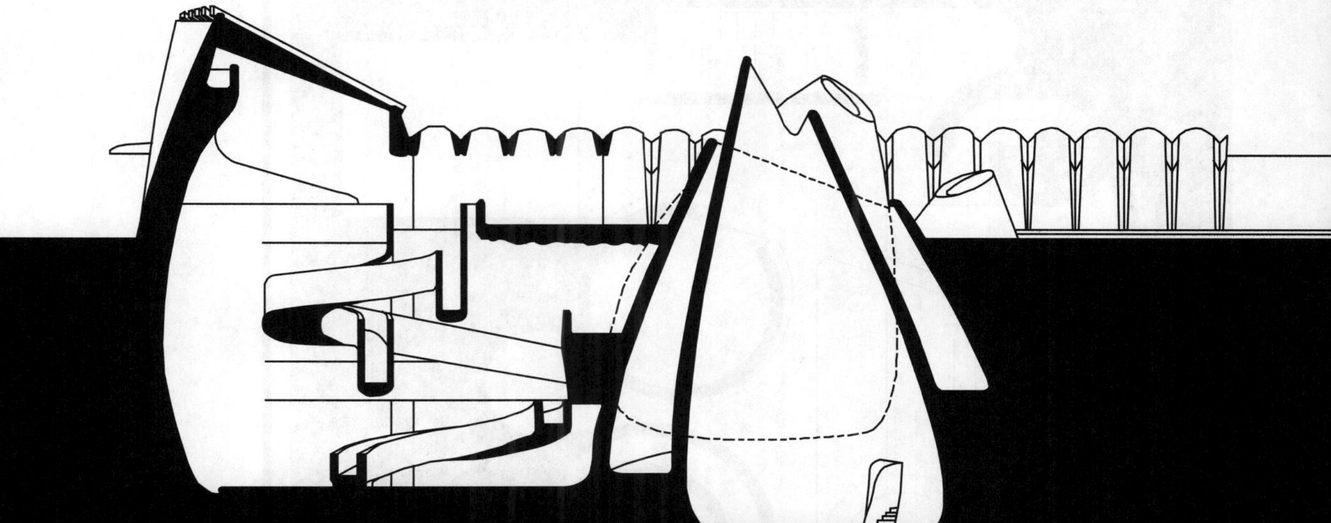

The speculative Silkeborg Museum is an almost mythical space, a great meeting of minds, and a synthesis of art and architecture. It was not intended to purely house art, but to create a new, mutual space of experience. Understanding this, Jørn Utzon buried most of the museum below ground in order to not intervene with the existing environment, and then designed a geometrically rigorous, voluptuous interior to encourage a bodily experience.

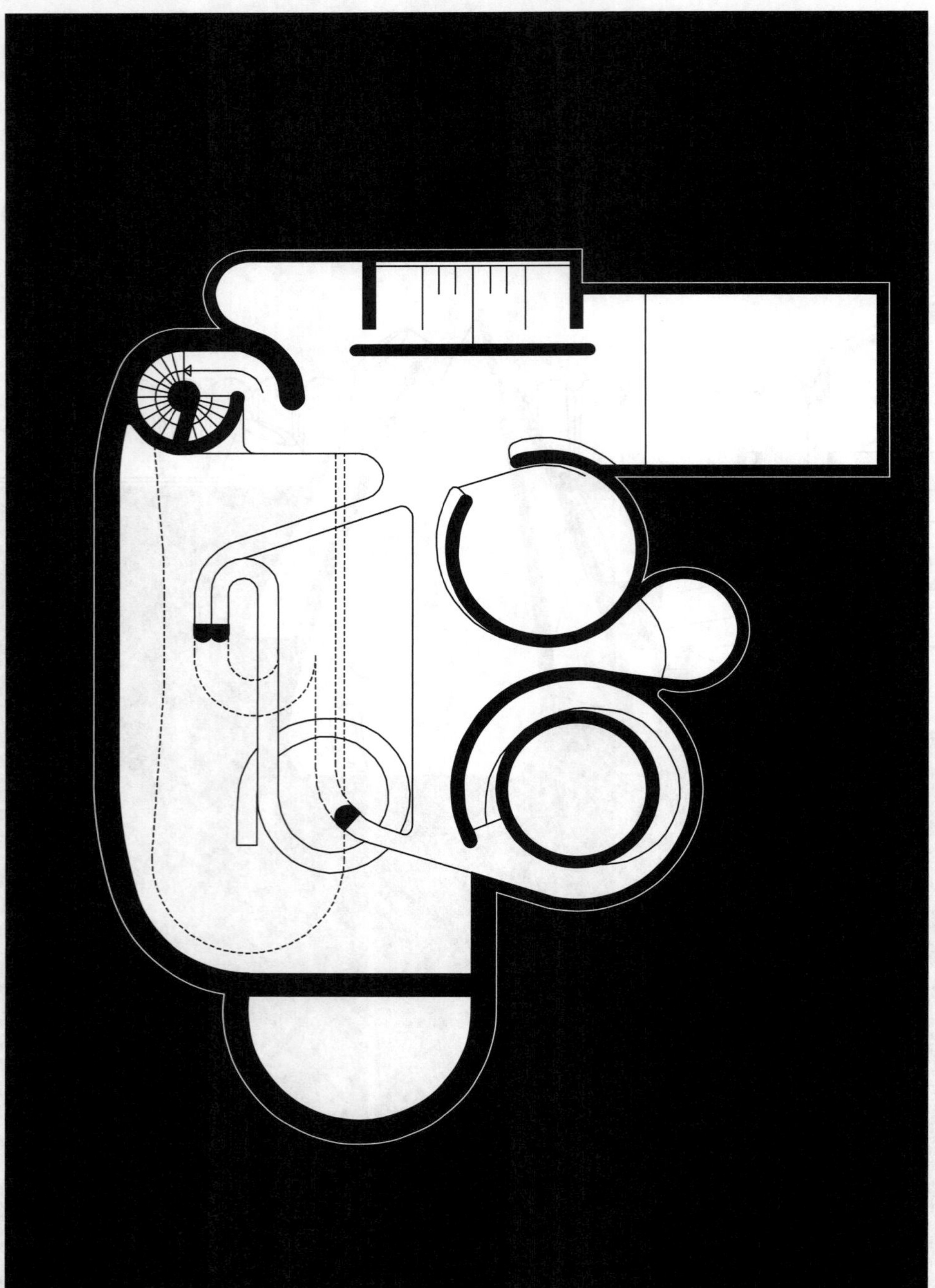

Plan of the Silkeborg Museum.

Multiple spiralling ramps descend and turn at different heights, filling a large open space beneath ground. Bulb-like enclosed spaces sit within, each layer ramping towards the next. The spiralling ramps give a strong non-linear dynamic to the space while descending into these sky-lit spaces.

The design of the Silkeborg has a sculptural quality. The right angle is substituted for a myriad of curves, drawing inspiration from ancient Yungang, Tatung or Datong caves in China, ship hulls, sculpture and Nordic earth and nature.

Yungang Grottoes, Shanxi, China.

Jørn Utzon's design for the National Opera House competition, Sydney, 1957.

The bulb-like forms of the museum spaces are reminiscent of the scooped-out alcoves of the Yungang grottoes, and although we never saw them built at Silkeborg, a somewhat similar broken shape was built in the Sydney Opera House scheme. Although many people see these petals as sails of a tall ship, Utzon imagined them encapsulating and protecting people.

The Limitless Museum
—
Musée Gallo-Romain Lyon, France Bernard Zehrfuss 1966–1975

Early in his career, Bernard Zehrfuss worked on the post-war reconstruction of Tunisia and was inspired by the semi-subterranean structures of Bulla Regia. Not to be confused with the vernacular troglodyte dwellings of Matmata, which sit fully below ground, the late Roman dwellings of Bulla Regia sat above ground with a subterranean level arranged around a peristyle from which daylight could enter.[31] Only these underground spaces remain among the ruins of the old city.

Maison de la Pêche, Bulla Regia, Tunisia, 100–200 CE.

Axonometry of Musée Gallo-Romain.

Postcard of La Maison de l'UNESCO, Paris, with the main building on the right and subsequent extension under the plaza on the left.

Zehrfuss appreciated this idea of an invisible architecture. The first time he used the Tunisian approach was for an extension to the UNESCO headquarters in Paris. Zehrfuss, along with Pier Luigi Nervi and Marcel Breuer, had designed the original headquarters, but upon completion in 1958 it was already too small. Zehrfuss buried the extension below the main plaza so as not to compete with the iconic headquarters and then perforated it with patios to bring in daylight.

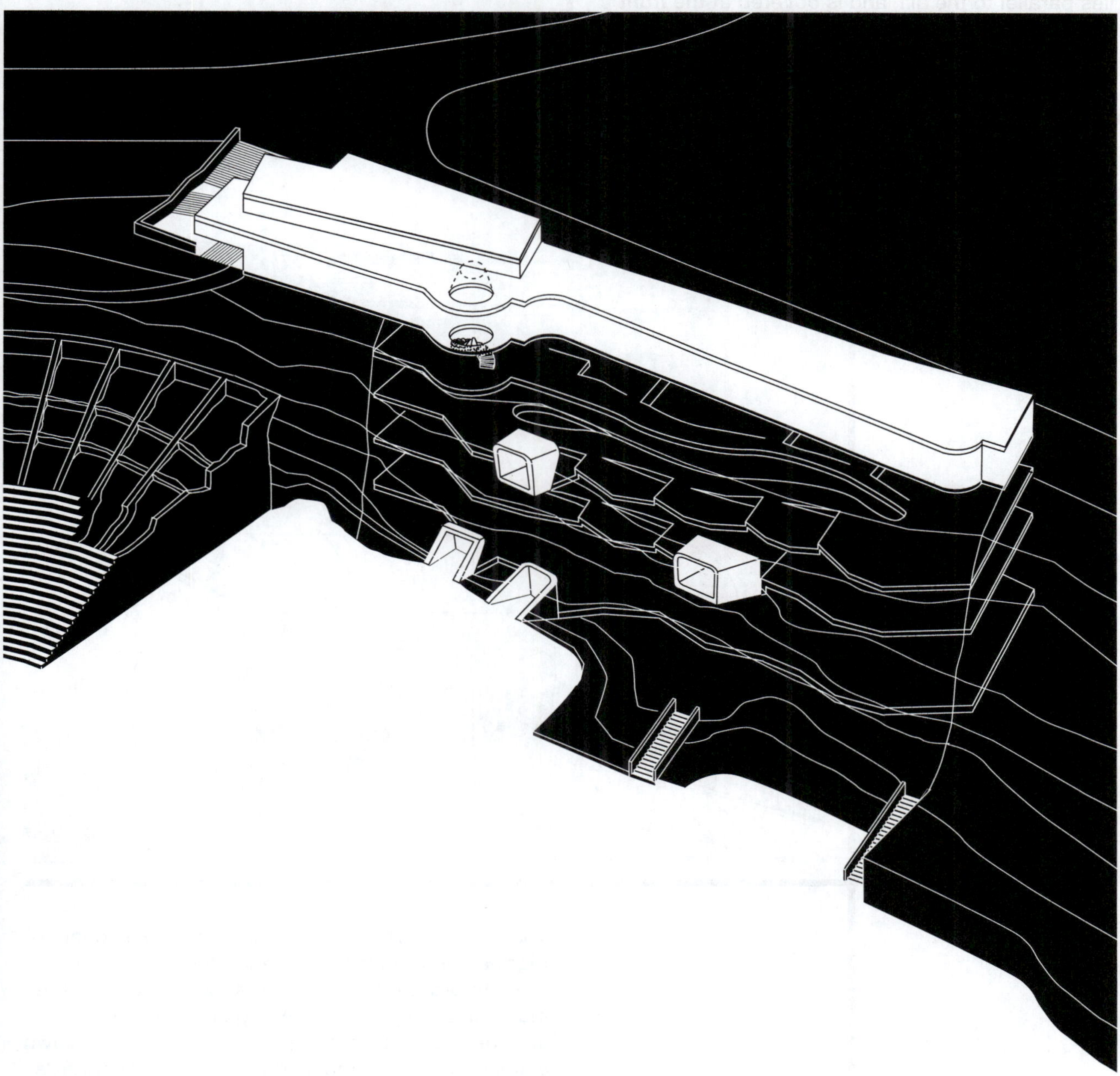

Likewise, the Musée Gallo-Romain respects the adjacent archaeological site by submerging itself into the hillside. In doing so, Zehrfuss had complete freedom over the interior. "I immediately thought that the underground structure could only be reinforced concrete. The knowledge of this method of construction allowed me, thanks to the flexibility of formwork, to imagine the creation of various forms and to find in the raw cement a material that could highlight the rich lapidary collection which was to be one of the main elements of the museum."[32]

The main concept was to bury a Gothic cathedral with flying buttresses to show the power of retaining the hillside it is built against. The museum lies parallel to the hill, and is covered at the front by a rippling wall, broken only by bay windows that punch through the mantle of the earth.

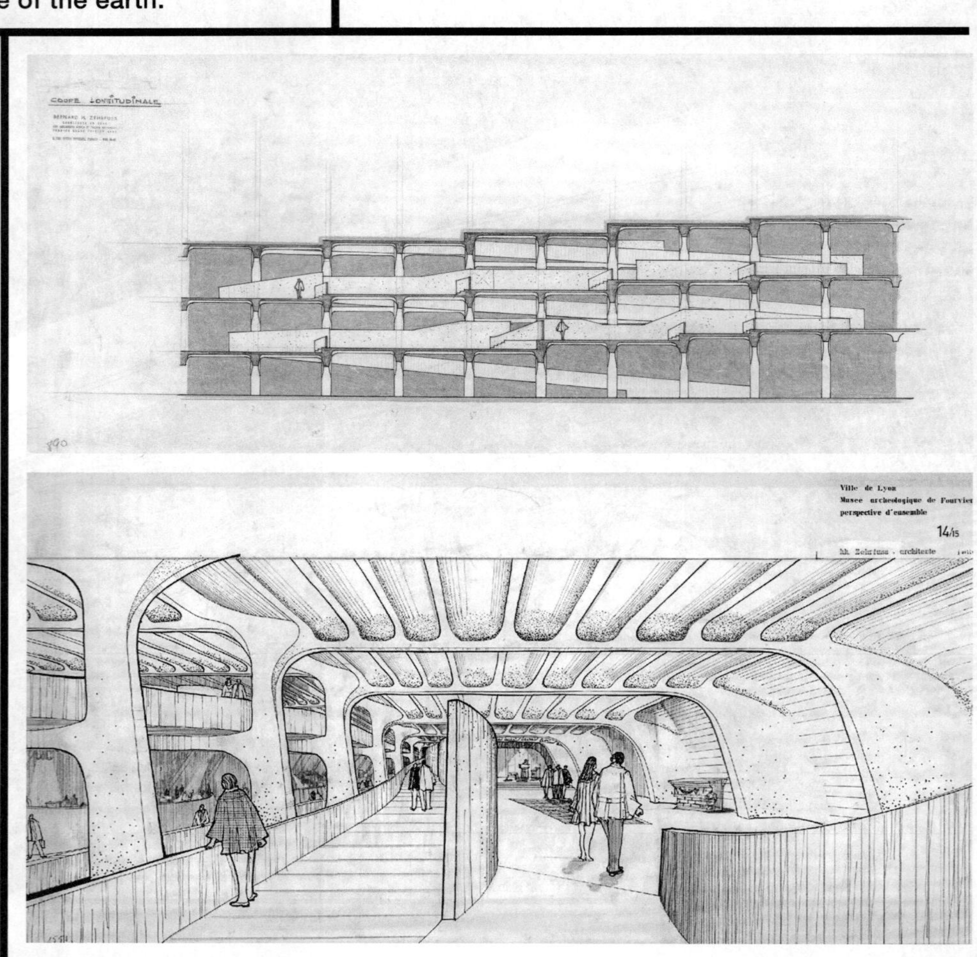

Original sketches, Bernard Zehrfuss, 1968.

The Musée Gallo-Romain's paper clip–like spiral integrates programme, circulation and landscape. It is the pragmatic means of accommodating the museum's weighty archaeological collection and the spatial organizing device of a descent down a slope. A gentle ramp leads the visitor downwards, following the chronology of the work within, to the exit at the base of two Roman amphitheatres.

MUSÉE
ENTRÉE
GRAND LYON

MUSÉE
ENTRÉE

A *promenade spatiale* takes the form of a gently ramping descent bordered by terraced exhibition spaces. Space expands and contracts as you are guided through enormous porticos. An irregular structural grid and variation in the height of pillars generate long, short and framed views into the exhibition spaces. Viewing shafts penetrate the floor level and frame a view of mosaics laid out below.

Sketch of main organizational principle by Zehrfuss.

Short section of spiral ramp in Musée Gallo-Romain.

Building during construction and landscaping.

Zehrfuss's desire for an invisible architecture is not about shyness or shrinking away from the strong form of the amphitheatre. Musée Gallo-Romain pays tribute to the existing, while matching its boldness and permanence with only a few visible elements.

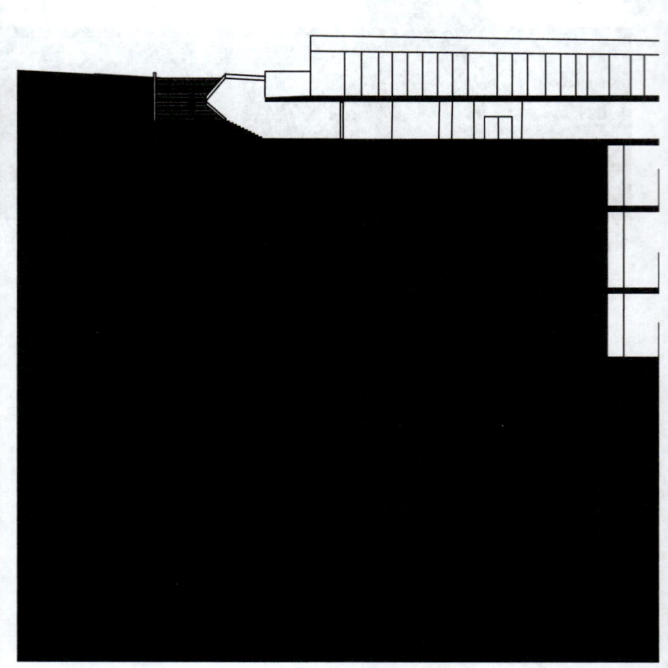

One would imagine that burying a spiral in a hill would only increase its hermetic nature, but the experience within is the opposite. Somehow the earth subdues its dominance.

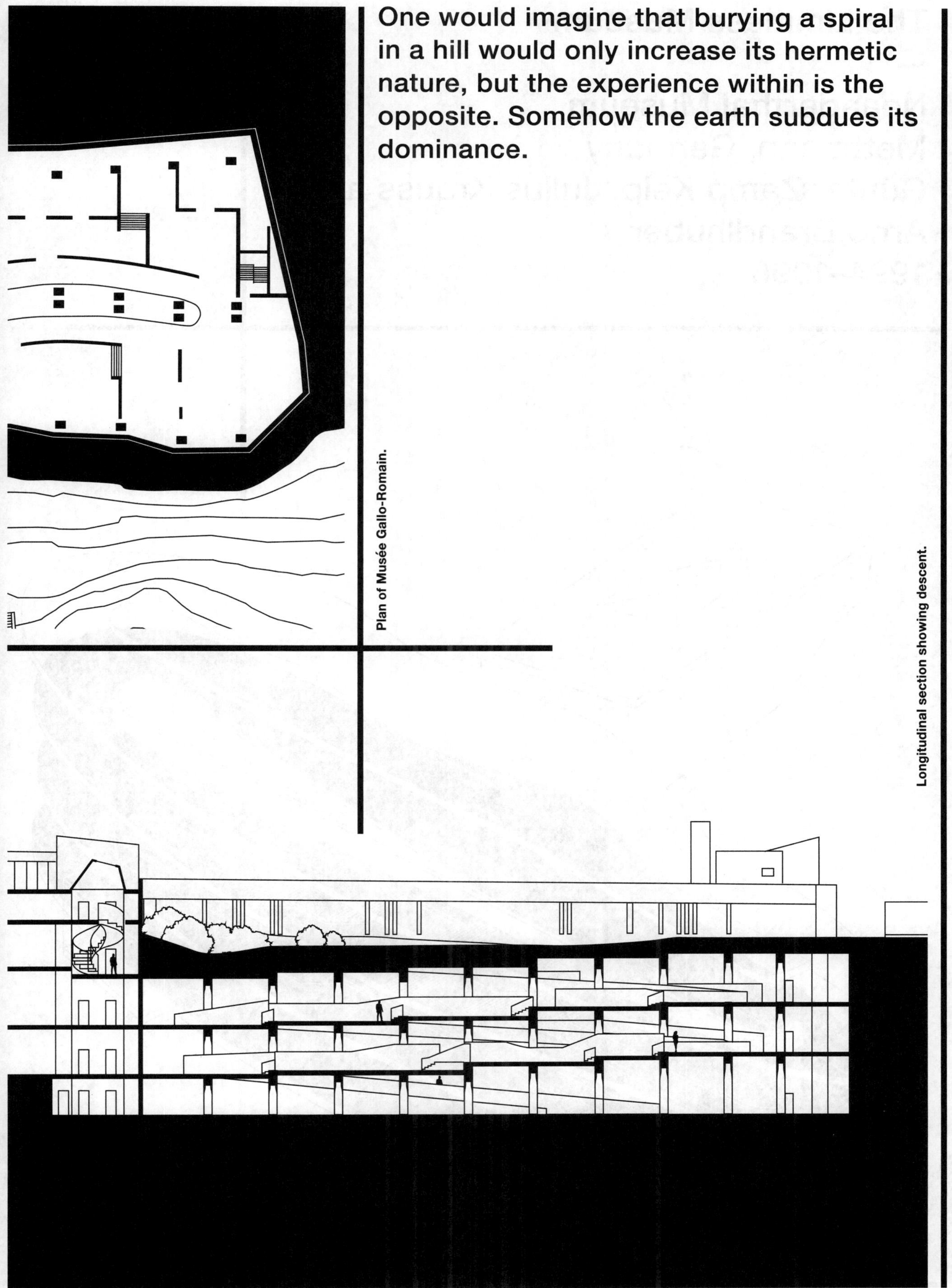

Plan of Musée Gallo-Romain.

Longitudinal section showing descent.

The Limitless Museum
—
Neanderthal Museum
Mettmann, Germany
Günter Zamp Kelp, Julius Krauss and Arno Brandlhuber
1994–1996

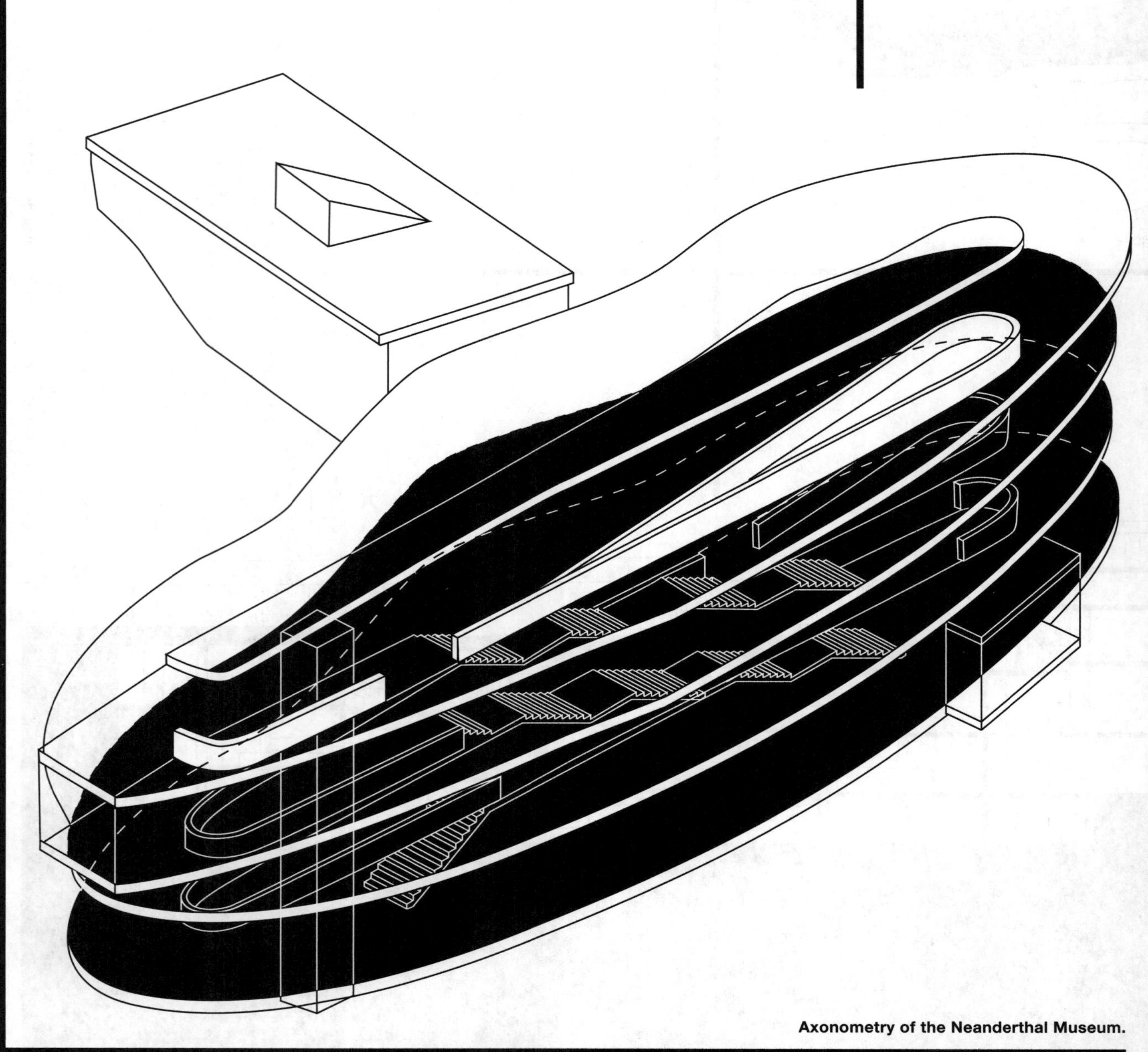

Axonometry of the Neanderthal Museum.

The circulation route through the Neanderthal Museum winds its way upwards in a spiral, following the historical sequence of the exhibition. This spiralling walkway ends in the 'present time' by reaching a large window on top of the building overlooking the surrounding forest.

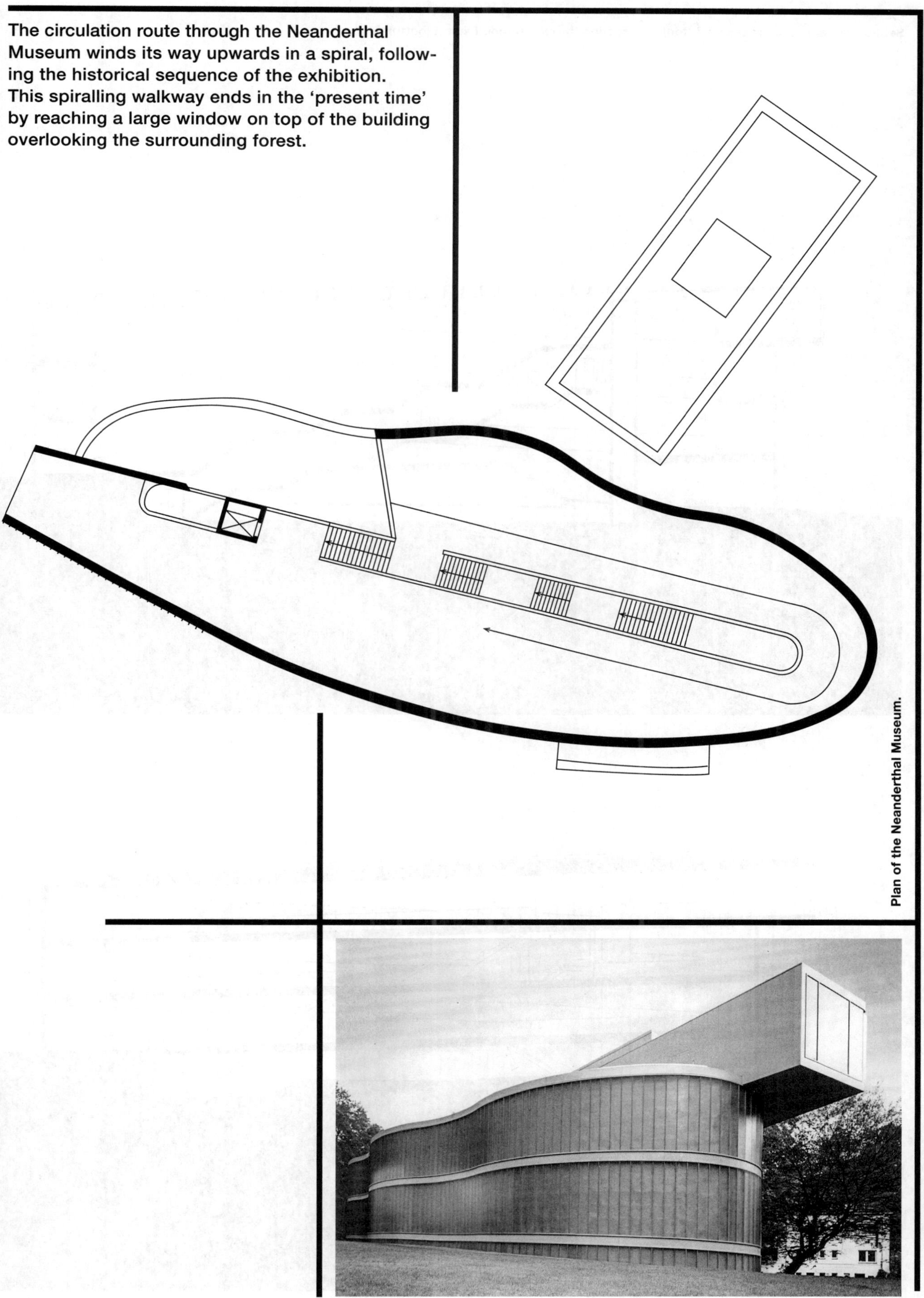

Plan of the Neanderthal Museum.

Section of central staircase void (top) and section through ramped spiral (bottom).

A hollow body that runs diagonally across the building fulfills four functions: immediate staircase access, second fire escape, ventilation system and structural reinforcement. This is an example of a straightforward spiral with limited effect on its architectonical expression.

The Limitless Museum

—

Museum aan de Stroom (MAS) Antwerp, Belgium Neutelings Riedijk Architects 2000–2010

An *entrepôt* (*entre* + *poser*, meaning to place 'in between') is a customs house where merchandise is processed for import or export. In Flemish it is called a *stapelhuis* (stacking house, house with stacked floors), a common typology in port cities from the seventeenth to the nineteenth century. Neutelings Riedijk Architects' competition entry for the Museum aan de Stroom (MAS) was entitled Stapelhuis. It stands on the site of the former Hanseatic trading house and on the edge of Antwerp port, still one of the busiest in the world.

The MAS recreated at the museum bookshop.

Instead of stacking floors on top of each other and then servicing them from one side via hoists from a quay, the architects rotated each floor of the MAS ninety degrees, twisting this service space to create an abundantly lit helical gallery along the facade.

Diagram of a stapelhuis (A), single module of MAS rotated three times (B), this block is then stacked up to create the twisted stapelhuis of MAS (C).

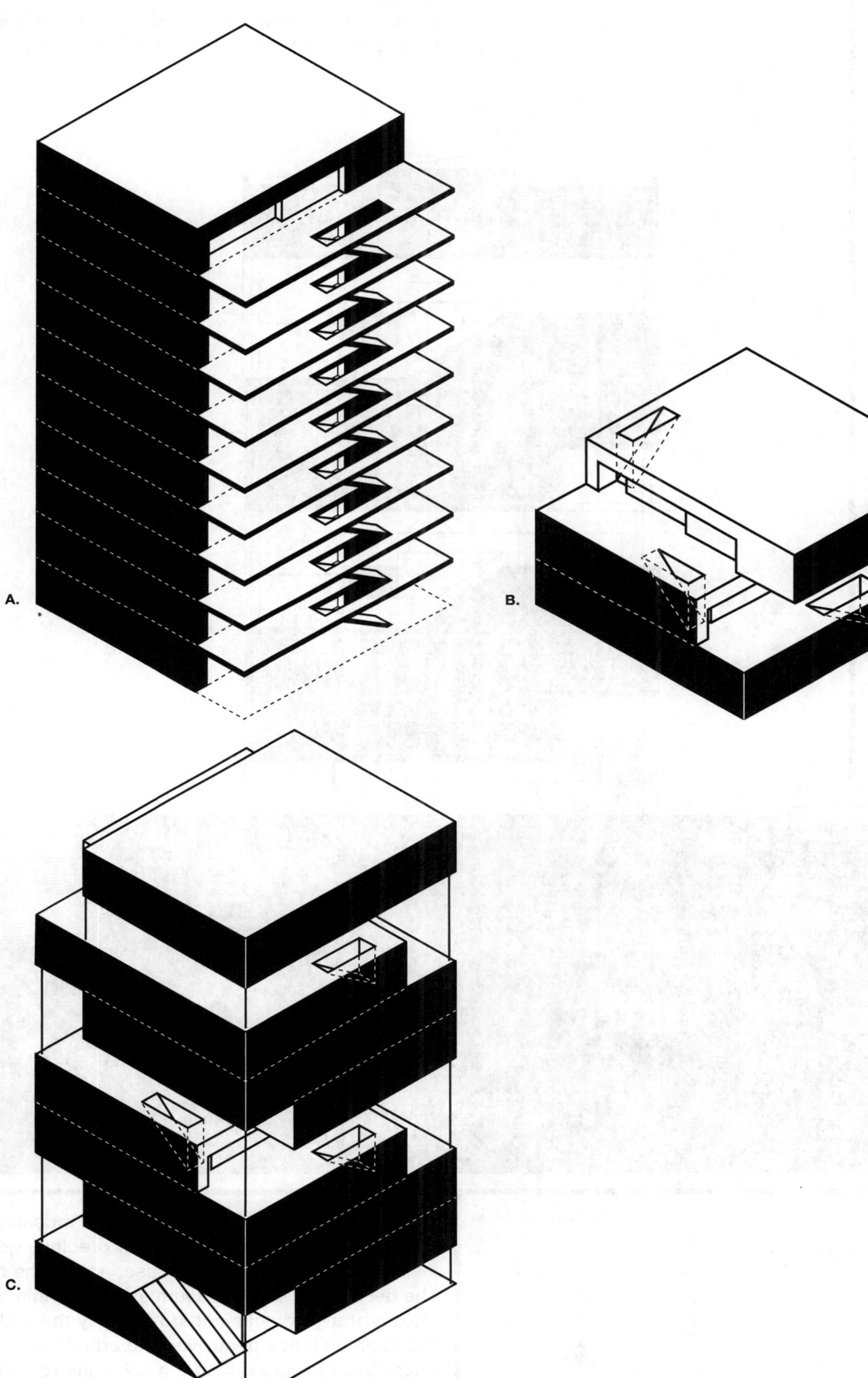

A striking feature is the way you move from floor to floor. A small opening in the sandstone volume sucks you up an escalator, and a little while later you pop up through the floor of the next open gallery.

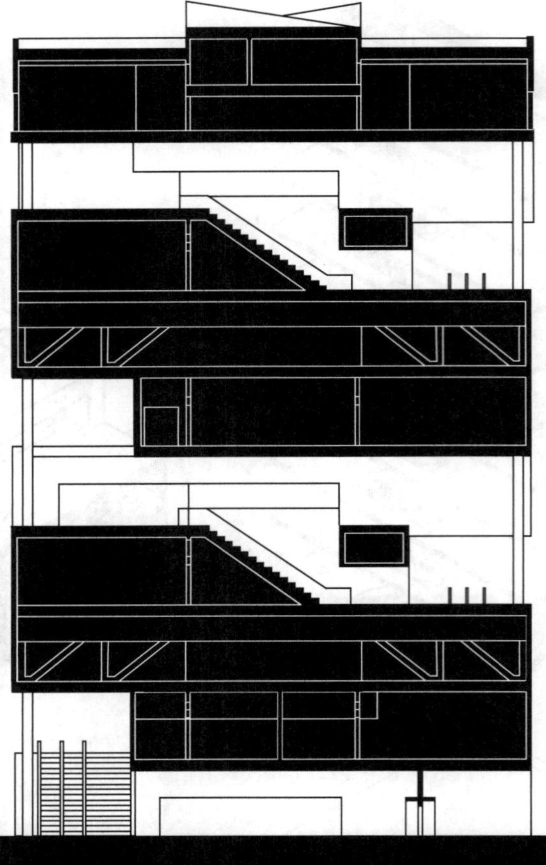

Section of MAS.

Unfortunately, stapelhuis traders and museum curators are alike, preferring their precious goods inside a well-secured warehouse, not on the quay. The decision to keep museum exhibits within the closed orange blocks and not display them along the open galleries destroyed the architect's intention of programming the spiralling route and neutered the potential of the spiral as a connector.

Like some kind of architectural *Groundhog Day*, the spatial experience repeats up the building. Your choice is always the same: continue along the corrugated glass facade or disappear into the block to see the exhibition inside.

A giant, empty spiral has become a public street in the air, a continuous path from public ground to tower roof, but its programming is sorely missed.

Within the spiral void.

The Limitless Museum

—

Mercedes-Benz Museum Stuttgart, Germany UNStudio 2001–2006

When four of the ten architecture firms in the running for the Mercedes-Benz Museum competition submitted a spiralling design, it was more than coincidence. Mercedes-Benz, the holy grail of automotive design, had done their homework. Two years earlier they enlisted architect HG Merz to devise an overall concept for the museum and the competition brief, which revolved around two thematic ideas: chronology and myths.

Interpreting this, a few architects furled a continuous walk through Mercedes-Benz fame within a museum box, while Alberto Campo Baeza's design created a spiralling flyover motorway.

Renderings of the competition design by Alberto Campo Baeza.

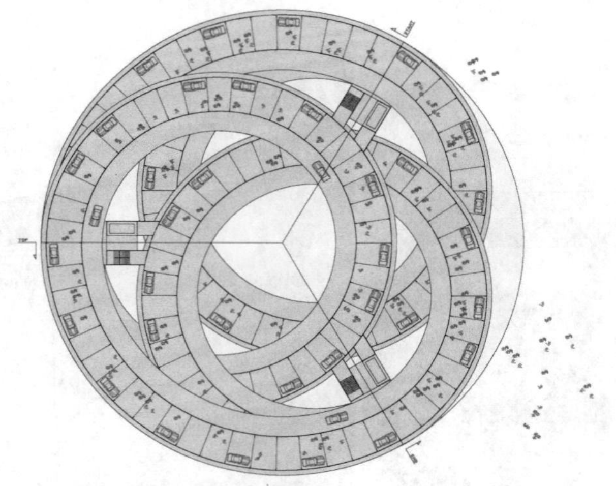

Competition plan by Alberto Campo Baeza.

Plan of the Mercedes-Benz Museum by competition winner UNStudio.

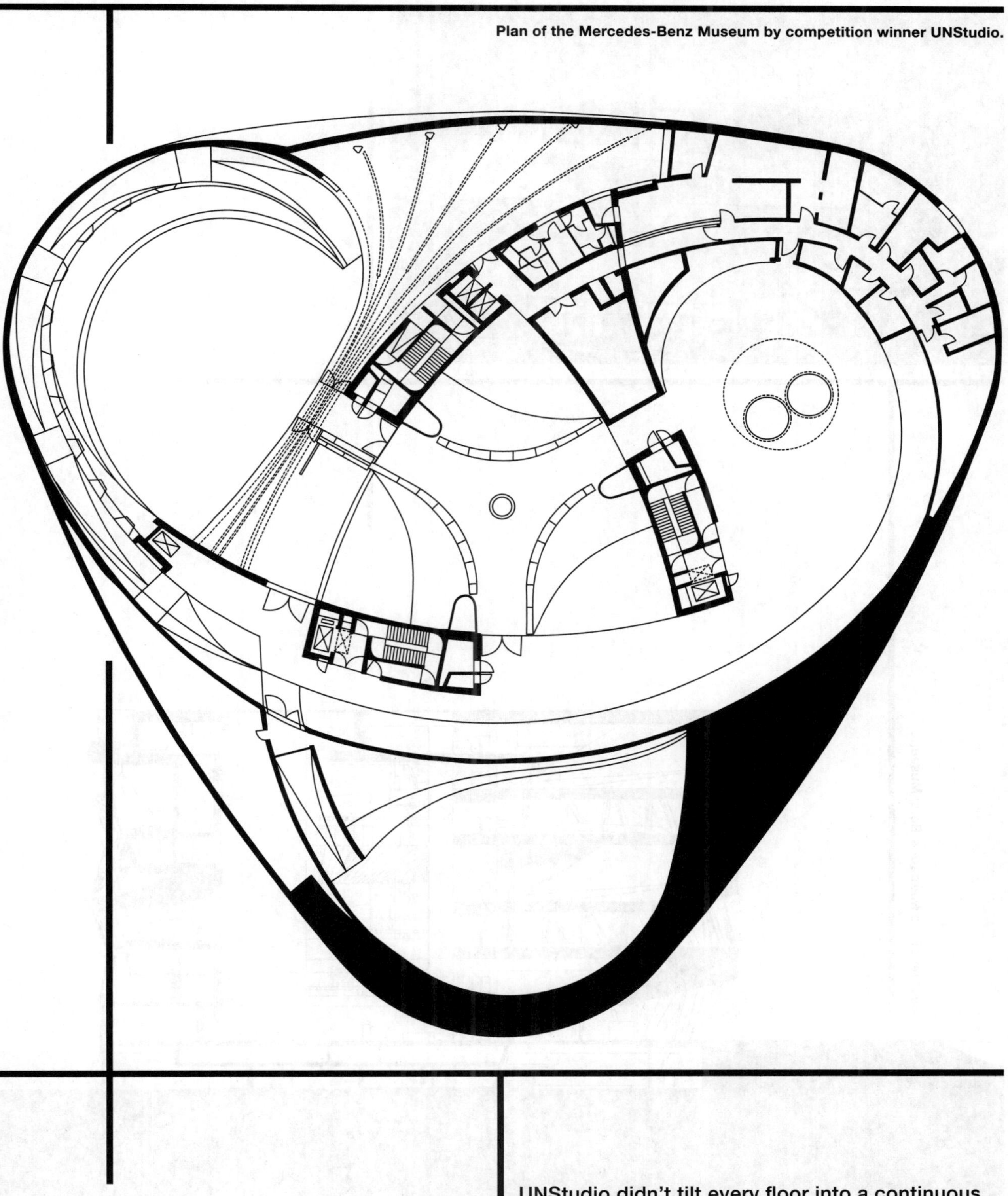

UNStudio didn't tilt every floor into a continuous spiral. Instead, floors for the collection level out, while the circulation manipulates their edges to manage the height difference between floors. The chronological collection is bathed in bright daylight. Stacked between these floors are closed museum boxes that highlight the myths of the first car manufacturer in the world. Mercedes-Benz and HG Merz revised their ideas to support this efficient set-up that allows visitors to take two different routes, the chronological or the mythical.

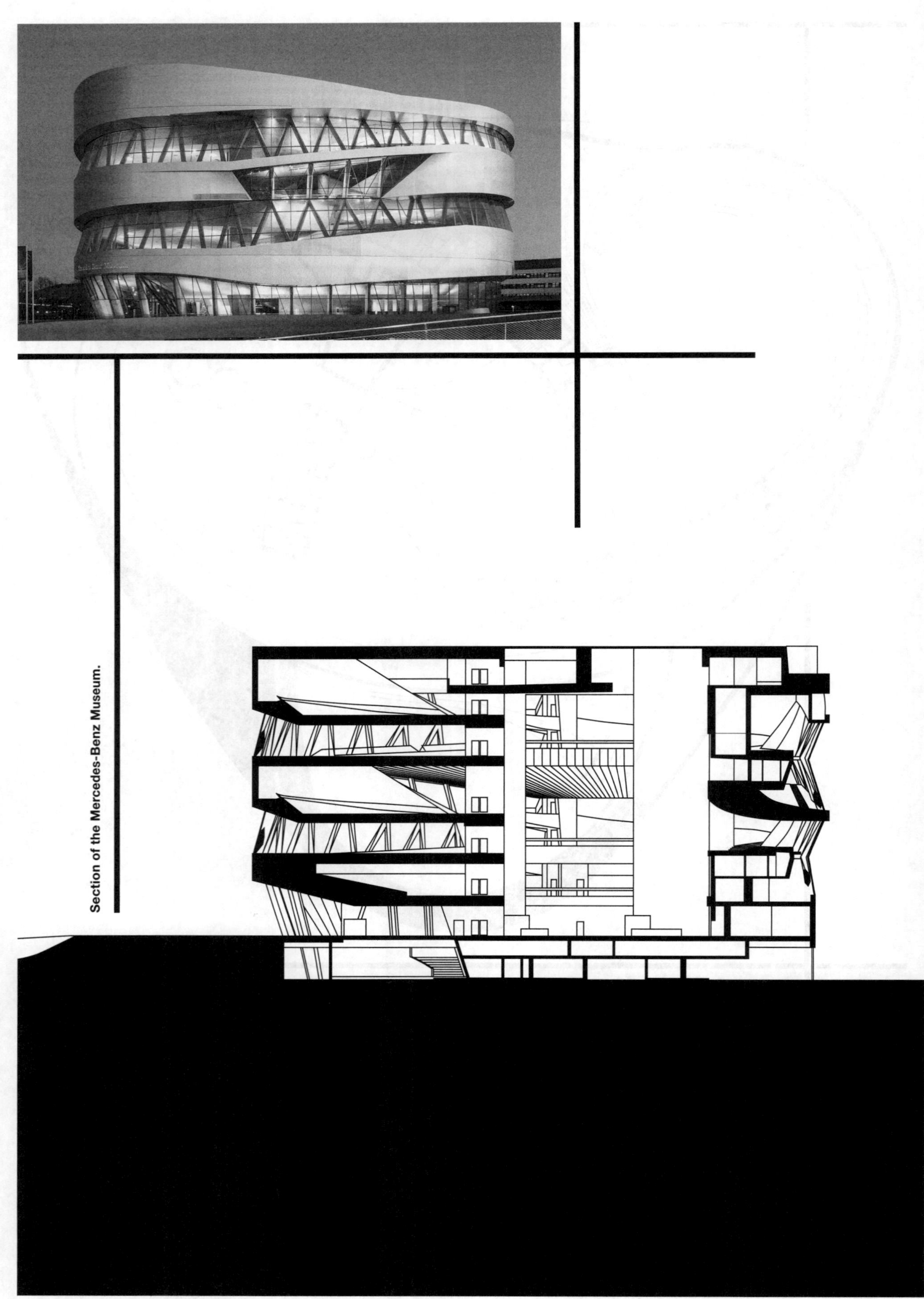

Section of the Mercedes-Benz Museum.

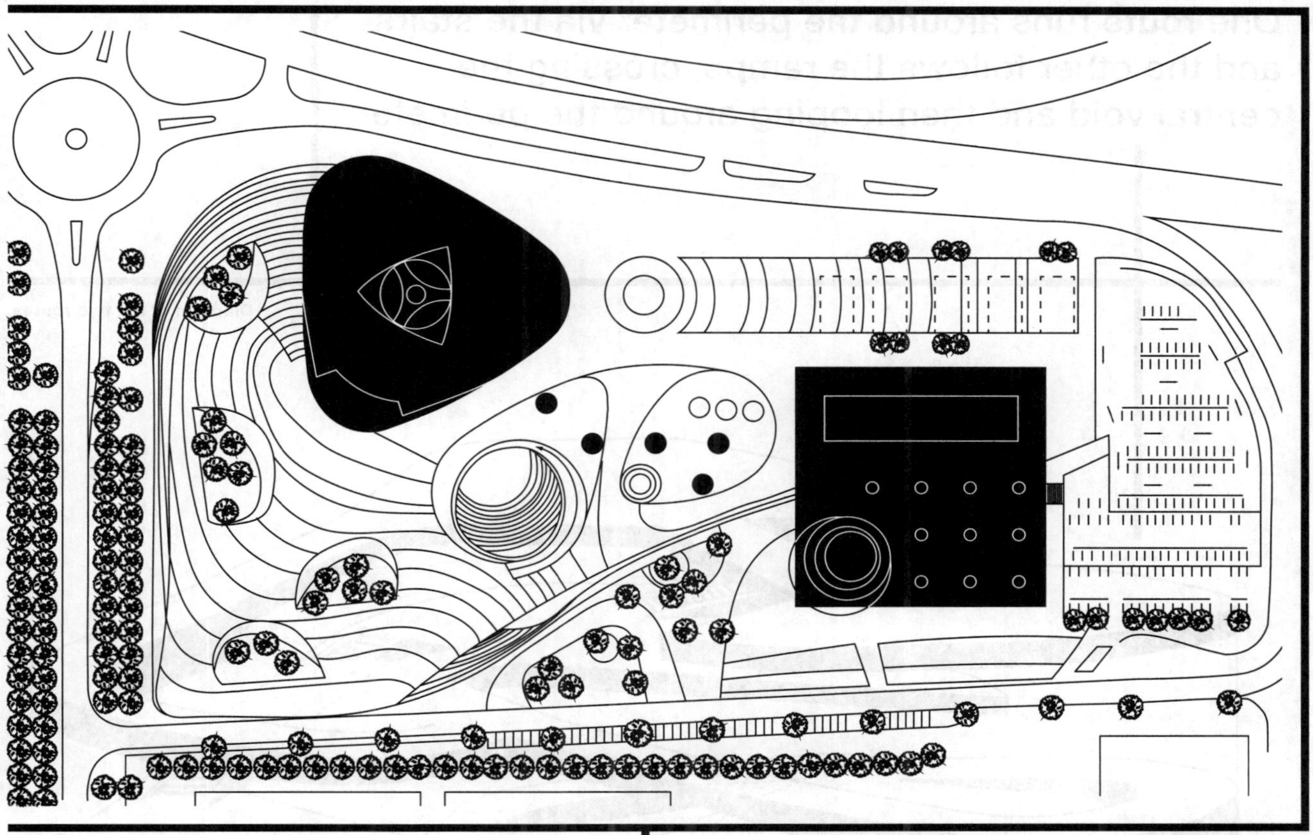

Site plan of the Mercedes-Benz Museum.

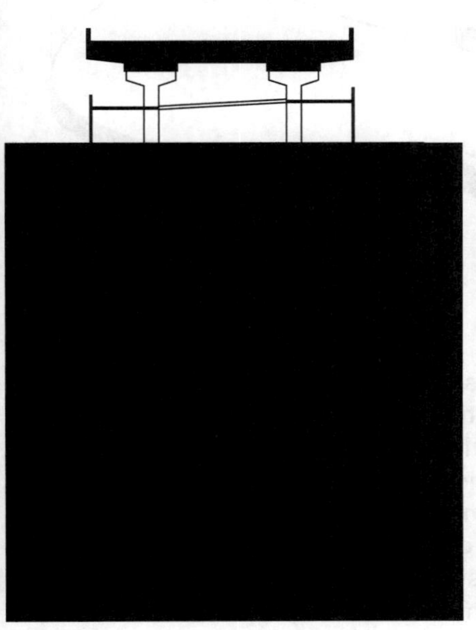

The double helix intricately combines structure and content. Like the Guggenheim, the visitor is transported by lift to the uppermost level of the museum. From here, two chronological routes spiral downwards. These trajectories are interwoven around a central triangular atrium that visually connects the two narratives. A 'twist' in the structure acts as a bridging device between the two routes, allowing visitors a high degree of self-navigation and concealing the simple and conventional enfilade set-up.

One route runs around the perimeter via the stairs and the other follows the ramps, crossing the central void and then looping around the perimeter.

Diagram of the two routes.

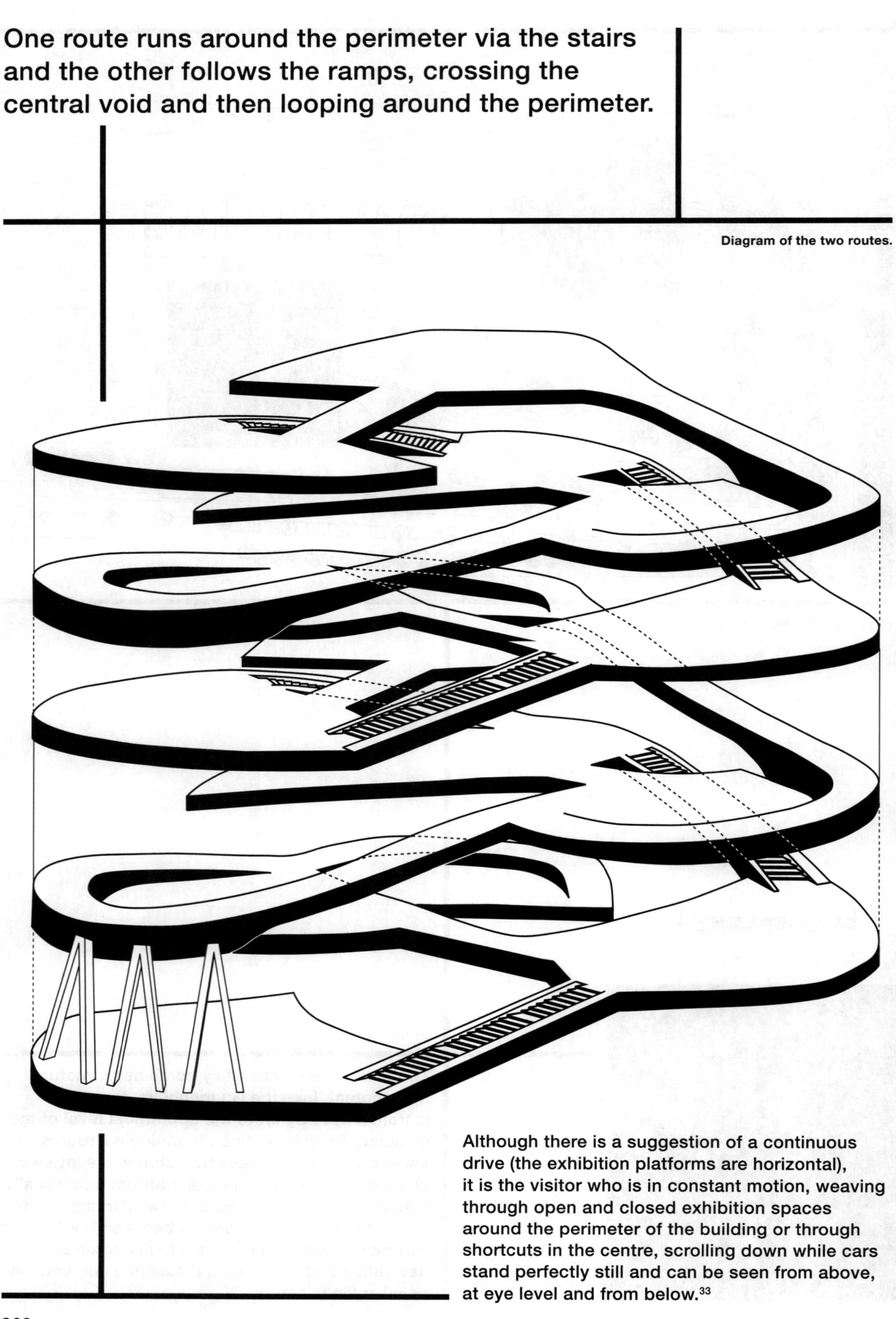

Although there is a suggestion of a continuous drive (the exhibition platforms are horizontal), it is the visitor who is in constant motion, weaving through open and closed exhibition spaces around the perimeter of the building or through shortcuts in the centre, scrolling down while cars stand perfectly still and can be seen from above, at eye level and from below.[33]

Looking up through central void.

As we sometimes see with really good architecture, client, consultant (HG Merz) and architect (UNStudio) shared common ground, fully understanding what was necessary to communicate the story of an automotive collection in a new way. UNStudio's design is the only version where the spiral is more than a tilted road through time. It is three-dimensional and dynamic.

Vehicles on level platforms, visitors spiralling around.

El Helicoide
Caracas, Venezuela
Arquitectura y Urbanismo C.A.
1955–1961

"Historically, roads have been a prime factor in the development of civilizations. Materials and technical ability have determined engineering possibilities in each era, but the well-designed road has always reflected an essential beauty of form linked with function."[34] –MoMA

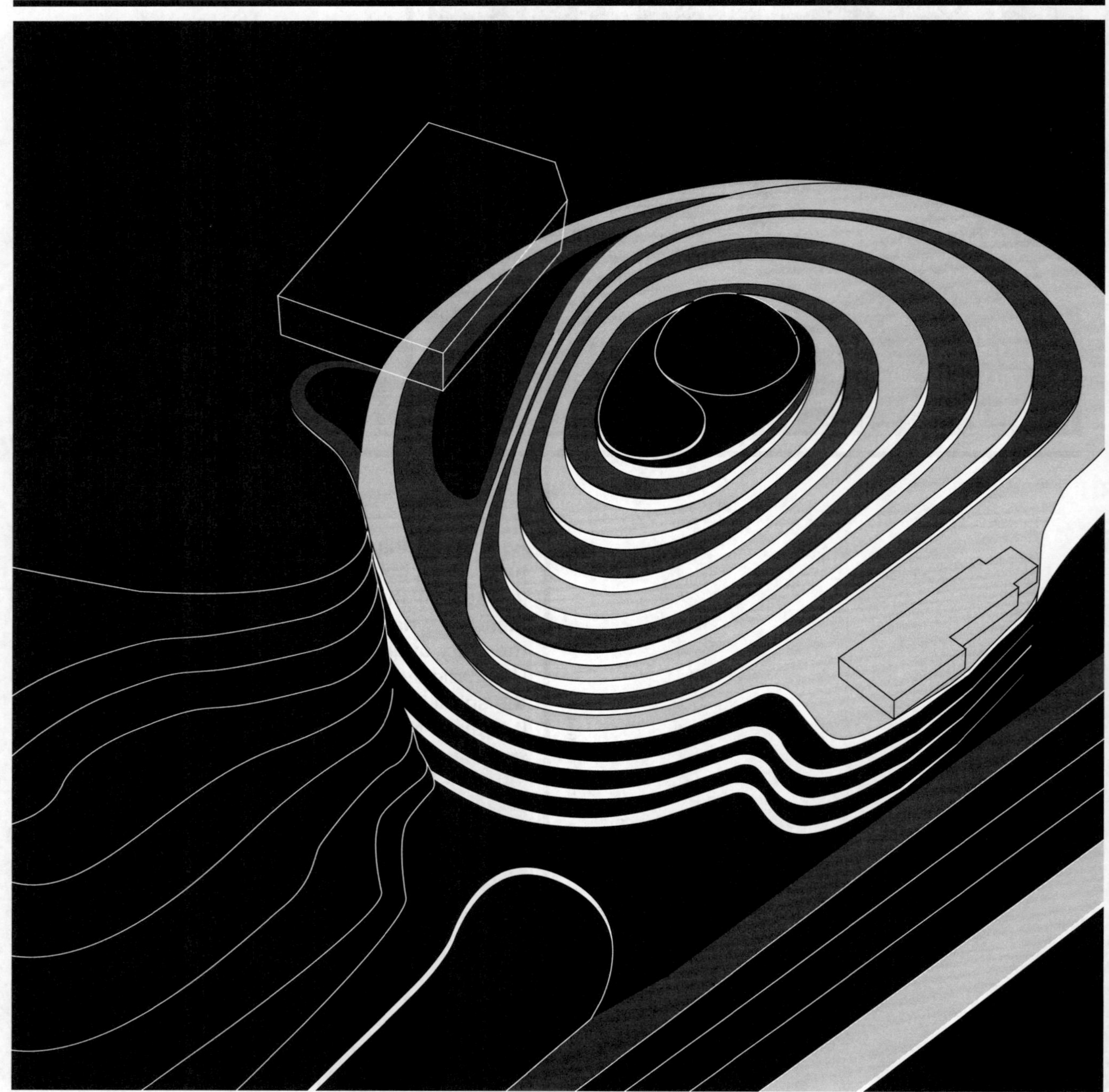

"[The ROADS exhibition] illustrates the complexity of recently built highways and suggests that we may presently see a wholly new kind of architecture, road-inspired and road-conditioned… The most recent example of this trend is the Helicoide now under construction in Caracas. Designed by Guitierrez, Neuberger and Bornhost, it consists of a spiral road which envelops an entire hill, providing automobile access to a continuous chain of shops."[35] —Bernard Rudofsky & Arthur Drexler

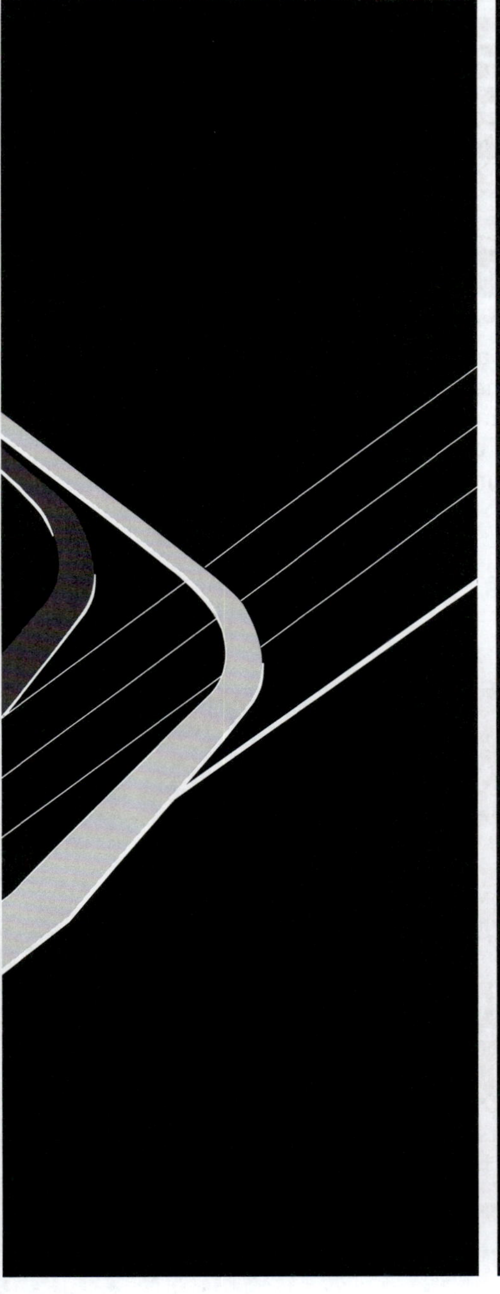

Axonometry of El Helicoide.

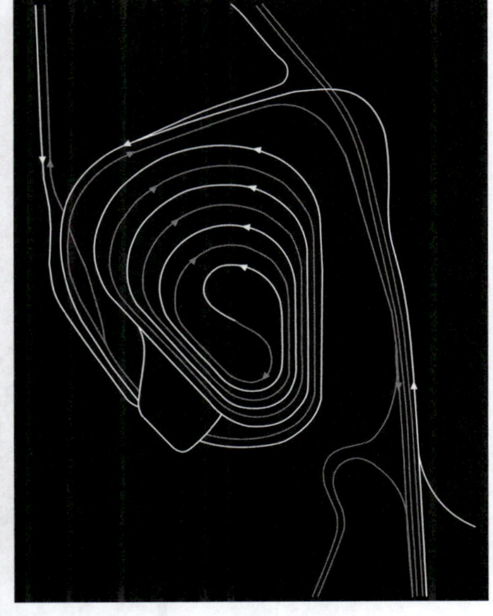

Diagram of ascent and descent.

Conceived during Venezuela's oil boom, El Helicoide embodied a progressive, modernist future.[36] This mall designed for the automobile received immediate worldwide attention and a prominent position in the MoMA exhibition *ROADS* in 1961. Salvador Dalí offered to decorate it with art and the poet Pablo Neruda wrote that it was "one of the most exquisite creations ever to have sprung from the mind of an architect."

El Helicoide under construction. Paolo Gasparini.

The spiral road of El Helicoide de la Roca Tarpeya consumes the hill on which it is built. Alternating ascending and descending levels of this colossal double helix coil smoothly, reflecting the rhythm of the surrounding topography.

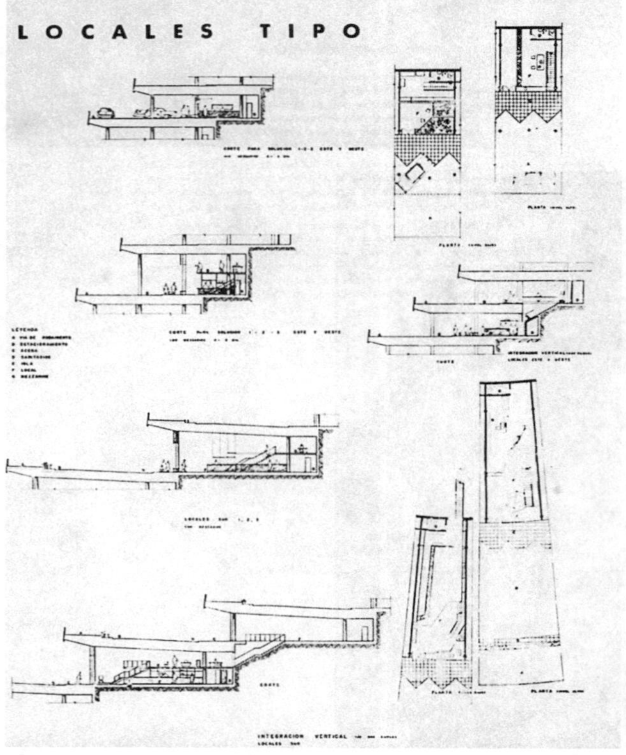

Plans and sections of commercial mall spaces and parking, 1958.

TOYOTA

Short section of El Helicoide.

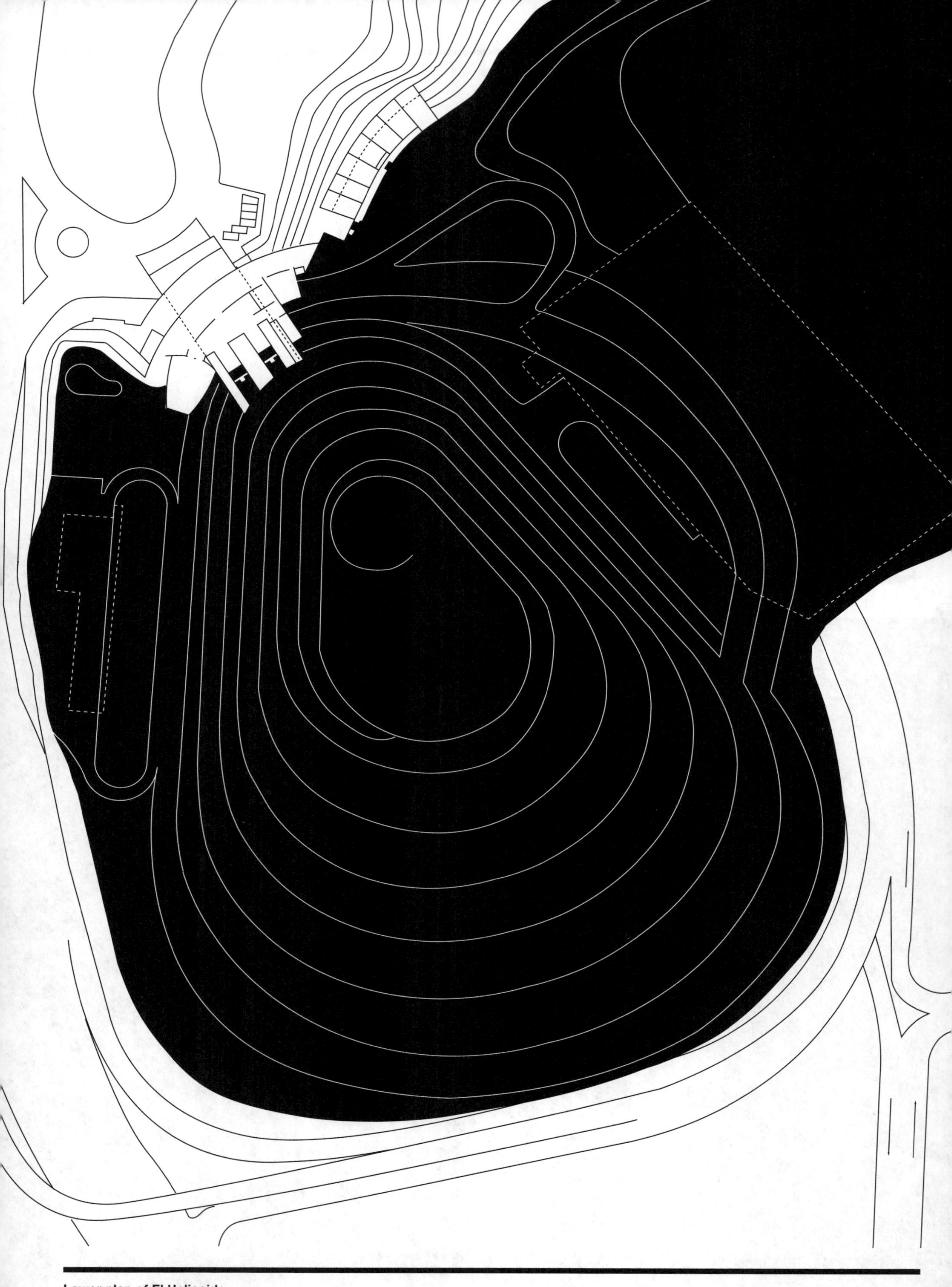

Lower plan of El Helicoide.

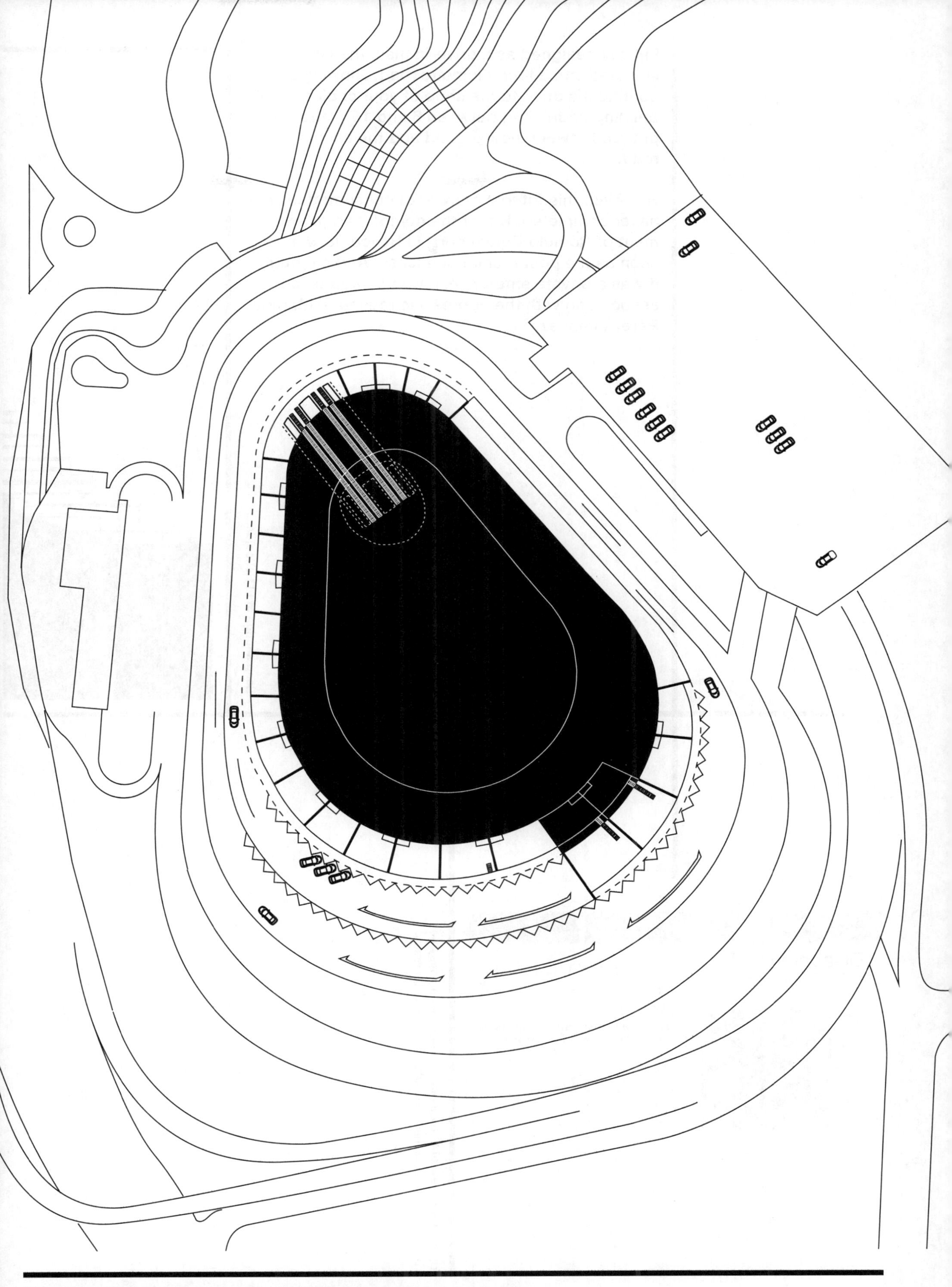

Upper plan of El Helicoide showing thin ribbon of shops wrapped around the hill.

Initially designed as a drive-in mall, the land was sculpted into a four-kilometre road, allowing a continuous drive to the shop of your choice. A thin building undulating between 6 and 15 metres was poured between new ground and the encircling road.

However, this futuristic tower of consumption was never completed. Under the democratic government of Rómulo Betancourt, El Helicoide was seen as the poster child of excess. And although it was a private enterprise, it was tainted by an association with the oppressive regime of Marcos Pérez Jiménez.[37]

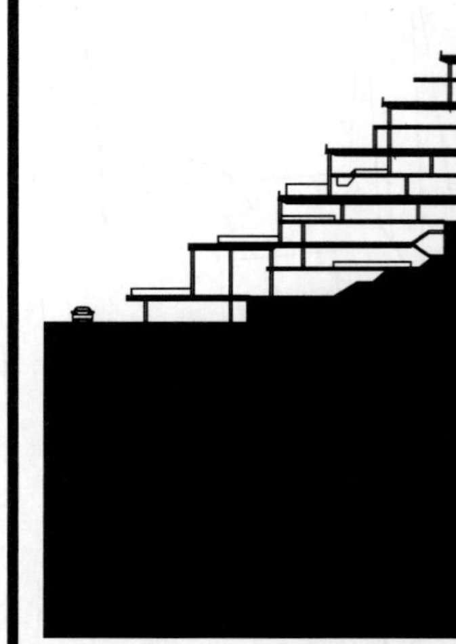

Long section of El Helicoide.

tripadvisor SOUTH AFRICA

"Disappointing"

Review of El Helicoide

1 photo

El Helicoide

Avenida Fuerzas Armas con Calle Helicoide, Roca Tarpeya, Caracas, Venezuela Website Improve this listing

Reviewed 17 August 2014 via mobile

Disappointing

Looks interesting from distance but once you get closer you notice it's ugly and pretty much a ruin. Also it is locked down so there is no way to really get there. All the walking for nothing. Not recommendable.

26 24

Tripadvisor review of El Helicoide. 'Disappointing' may be a bit of an understatement considering its violent history.

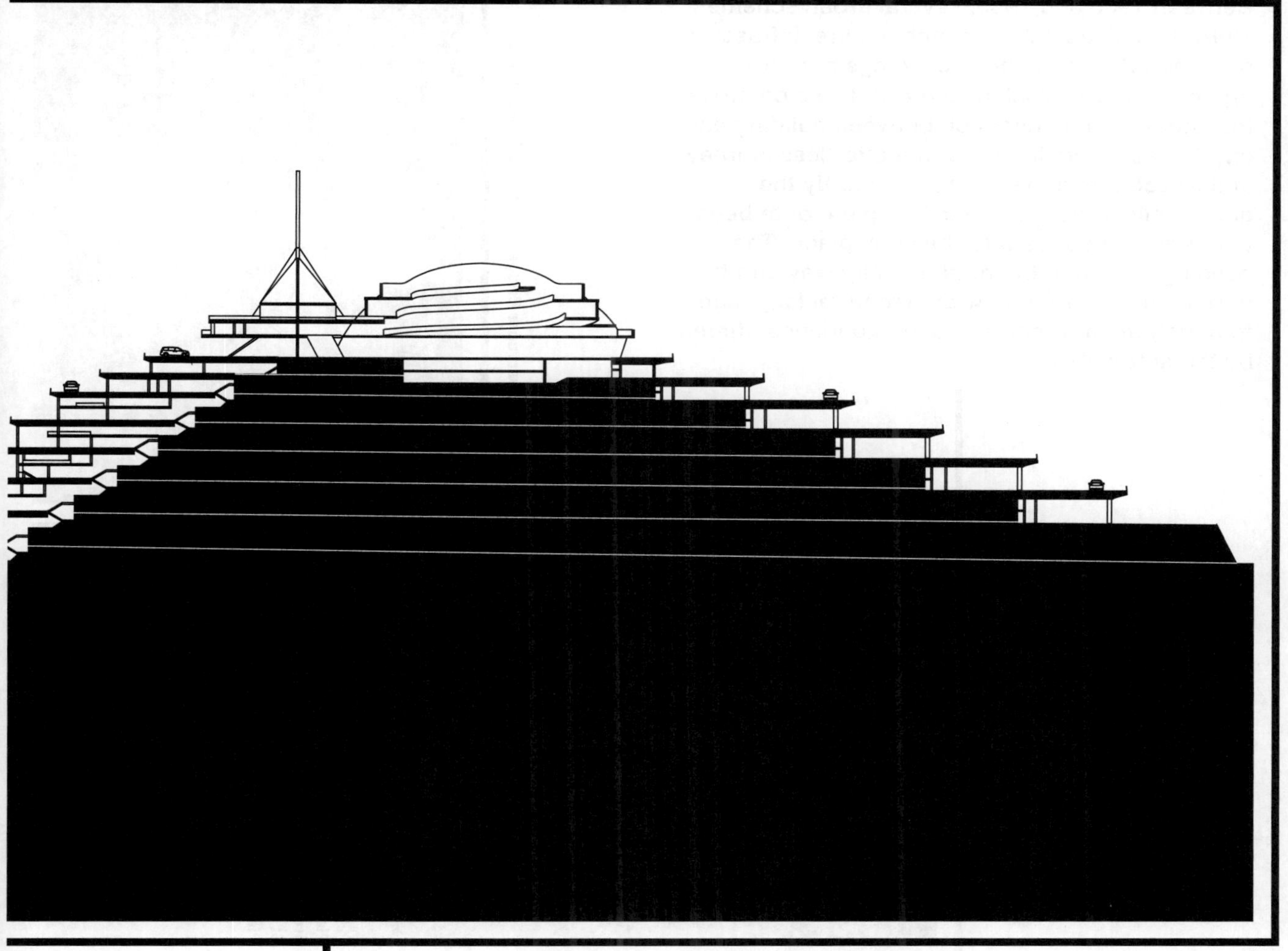

"...the world's most remarkable drive-in mall... El Helicoide did not remain Caracas's symbol of progress for long."[38] —Celeste Olalquiaga

"The three-dimensional city was undoubtedly naive, but the implications of its disappearance are profound."[39] —Douglas Murphy

The project stalled. It was abandoned, unsuccessfully resurrected (multiple times), occupied by the dispossessed (refugees of the 1979 landslide), and more recently used as an appalling torture chamber for political prisoners, again under dictatorship. There seems to be a very unfortunate correlation between mind-blowing utopian, hermetic schemes and totalitarian regimes.

Between 1930 and 1955, several urban schemes blurred the lines between architecture, infrastructure and urbanism. These buildings not only organized the internal functions but also controlled the access and connection between building and city. It was an era in awe of the effortless journey and freedom of movement provided by the automobile. A concern with being en route began to overtake a concern for being in place. The building emulated the road, the highway and the bridge, looking for a new architectural language to match the new and exciting experience offered by the automobile.

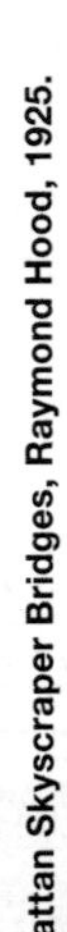

Manhattan Skyscraper Bridges, Raymond Hood, 1925.

Plan Obus A, B, C, H for Algiers, here with project C in the front as a connector between St Eugène and Hussein-Dey, Le Corbusier and Pierre Jeanneret, 1930.

Cities of the Future, Harvey Wiley Corbett, 1913.

Harvey Wiley Corbett believed the roads would be stacked up like a high-rise and Raymond Hood envisioned a hybrid of bridge and skyscraper crossing the Hudson River. Le Corbusier with Pierre Jeanneret designed an elevated express route between St Eugène and Hussein-Dey in Algiers. This sweeping infrastructure would sit between 60 and 90 metres above the terrain, supported by housing for 180 000 people. Here the two functions still seem completely disconnected, since the expressway is not connected by car ramps, stairs or lifts to the houses below.

While these utopian visions of modernist masters remain unbuilt, more realistic versions were realized in South America. Alfonso Reidy's Pedregulho project connects the top of a hilly terrain with a large winding block at mid-level with over 300 apartments, all with a magnificent view over Guanabara Bay. The terrain below is almost untouched. It is a successful version of a dissected and reconstructed Unité d'Habitation.

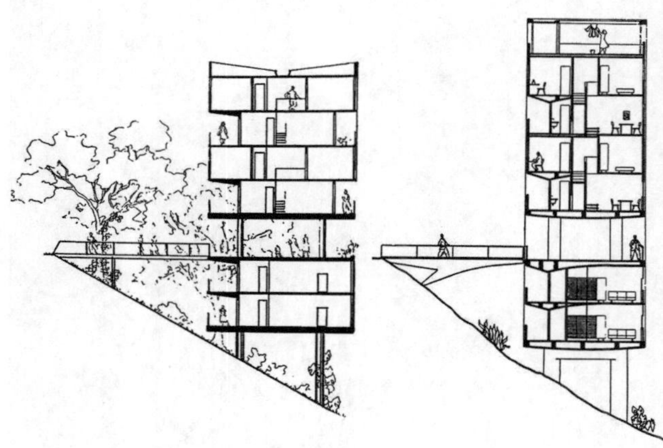

Alfonso Eduardo Reidy, Pedregulho housing development, Rio de Janeiro, 1947–1955.

El Helicoide could have been a winding South American variant of optimistic modernism, but it became a prison. Directly next to it the raw economic reality of Caracas drove a completely different reshaping of the same rolling hills as the one from which El Helicoide was carved. Here we see a bottom-up development, an enormous slum with almost no space for infrastructure.

El Helicoide & Metro Cable above the sprawling barrios of Caracas.

Today the three hilltops in the middle of this huge favela are connected by a gondola lift system, known as the Metro Cable, that provides transport for tens of thousands of people who intelligently stroll down once they have arrived at their hill. They can leave by again walking down the hill and taking public transport at the bottom.[40]

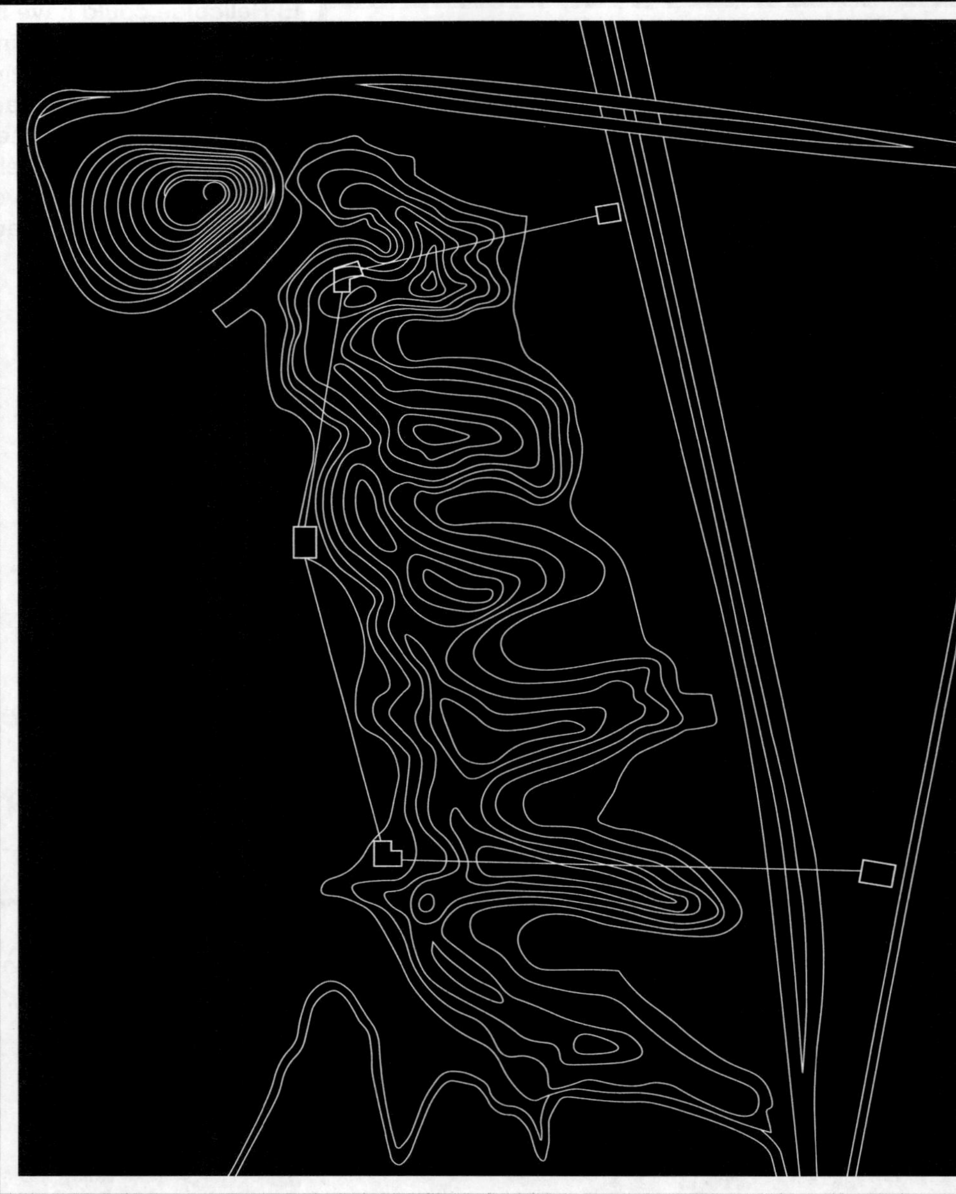

Site plan of El Helicoide and Metro Cable, Caracas.

At first glance, these two realities, El Helicoide and its surrounding favela, couldn't be more different, but a closer look reveals that they share more than you would imagine when it comes to merging building and interconnecting infrastructure.

In Conversation

In 2014 Bjarne Mastenbroek interviewed the founding partners of Urban Think Tank, Hubert Klumpner and Alfredo Brillembourg, about the informal city, informal architecture and forms of spontaneous appropriation of the built environment in Caracas, Venezuela.

[Bjarne Mastenbroek] In Caracas, your primary field of action, a spatial urban disconnection reflects an economic and social division. There is the formal city and the informal city. As an answer to this division you call for hybridization. Why? And what would be the results?

[Hubert Klumpner and Alfredo Brillembourg] We see the built form of the city as frozen politics. The shape and distribution of urban development is determined by large systems and social processes. To speak about a city, one must take into account the complex and interconnected reality of micro and macro decisions made by human beings. The divide between the wealthy and the poor is sometimes so extreme in appearance that one forgets to question its inherent complexity. While we initially became interested in slums by trying to study their phenomenology, we have increasingly come to see that there is a false binary between the formal and informal. The ways that cities grow and change, and under which political, social and economic systems, are often so interdependent that a deeper analysis blurs boundaries. Therefore we embrace the inherent syncretism of cities and we seek to work with remixing and hybridizations. In short, we think architects and designers have to get messy in order to get real.

[BM] We could define the natural hills on the border of Caracas and Torre David's skeleton in the core of the city as the original contexts where informal communities built their homes. What are the main differences and similarities in the appropriation of such different morphologies?

[HK + AB] In some respects, one can see Torre David's antecedents in the barrios: makeshift solutions in the absence of an infrastructure in the high-rise, in the absence of municipal services in the barrios, and the use of bricks and found materials in both; certain elements of the architectural vernacular. Yet despite the precariousness of the occupation and because Torre David is structurally sound and durable, one sees in the construction of many of the family apartments a greater striving for permanence and a different kind of aspiration. The physical fragility of the barrios appears to be a greater obstacle to a sense of ownership than Torre David's tenuous occupancy. And while the living quarters in the latter are, like barrio dwellings, in an ongoing state of creation, expansion and enhancement, many residents are explicitly and purposefully moving toward a middle-class lifestyle. They are emphatically not looking to the hillside barrios for inspiration.

[BM] How did people respond to living in a vertical structure instead of in a horizontal favela?

[HK + AB] Torre David's physical structure and the needs of its occupants are clearly at odds. While the extreme verticality is accompanied by the kind of density we recognize as valuable for certain kinds of efficiencies and for a desirable social concentration, it also constrains the spatial mobility of residents. Yet in defiance of the physical limitations of the building, they have fostered a remarkable degree of social exchange, evident in the disciplined leadership structure, democratic processes, and religious bonds. Even more telling is the fact that without a working elevator, the community's leadership decided to limit access to the upper floors for reasons of safety. Nevertheless, even given the physical burden of the long climb, the upper floors are considered desirable by those seeking to move in.

[BM] One of the main problems in informal settlements is the lack of infrastructure. How was the condition of the barrio of San Agustín before the introduction of the Metro Cable?

[HK + AB] San Agustín is situated on a large hill that for decades limited the social and economic vitality of the neighbourhood, and whose distance fostered a sense of physical and psychological isolation

Metro Cable, Caracas, Urban Think Tank, 2006–2010.

amongst residents. Through careful mapping and diagnosis, we drew the necessary conclusion that the people living in the barrio needed an 'elevator', as many residents were relatively incapable of trekking down or up the 89-storey hill due to health concerns and lack of resources. Less obvious was the opportunity for transportation infrastructure to permeate the informal settlement with a multitude of other services, in this case garbage collection, water and electricity bundled with social functions.

[BM] The informal city is a very dynamic entity in continuous transformation. Therefore the barrio will react to the increase of internal and external connectivity. What did you expect to provoke?

[HK + AB] The Metro Cable was the result of a simple question: how to create access to the top of a slum on a steep hillside if there are no roads for public transport and the inhabitants are opposing government plans for road construction that would displace thirty per cent of the population? In this context, our strategy was to read the neighbourhood carefully, engage in participatory design with residents, develop thoughtful and novel mapping techniques, and ultimately to propose an infrastructural intervention. What we sought, was to put in place the means for change in relation to the fundamental needs of the barrio, identified by inhabitants themselves: safe, accessible, and cost-effective public transportation for residents; the growth of work opportunities and of the economy of the barrio; the development of a sustainable infrastructure to give permanence and stability to the community; improvement of the health, education, employment opportunities, and quality of life for barrio dwellers; and improved safety and reduction in crime. The mobility infrastructure is not meant to be a definitive solution, but rather a catalyst to even more meaningful change. We strive to build for change, not for static conditions – those don't exist!

[BM] Your architecture adapts to what it finds in situ with careful attention not only for the social and economic dynamics but also for the actual physical conditions. We find it very interesting how you took the form of the barrio and built the Metro Cable almost without touching the existing fabric. Could you explain the idea of a retrofitting intervention?

[HK + AB] While the city made an automobile-centred proposal to integrate San Agustín with the rest of Caracas, we saw the opportunity to implement a sensitive form of infrastructure that would act as urban acupuncture. By inserting an above-ground cable car system, integrated with new housing, community recreational centres and spaces for commercial developments, the barrio would not have to sacrifice its existing fabric or a third of its inhabitable space for mobility. The Metro Cable's structural backbone permitted us to speculate about the neighbourhood's future, but it also allowed community residents to independently adapt their environment and create new spaces of growth.

[BM] How do you read the fact that Torre David is a vertical community with a big handicap – the lack of an apparent vertical connection, while barrio San Agustín is a horizontal settlement with an extra feature – the Metro Cable?

[HK + AB] We might disagree with the premise of the question. San Agustín is not a horizontal settlement; it is a house the size of a mountain.

[BM] What are the factors that produce in Torre David such intense social activity? Is this density one of the elements that keeps disconnected levels together and makes us read the tower not like a simple residential building but as a vertical city?

[HK + AB] It may be partly spatial, but at the same time the organization, invasion and settlement of Torre David, as well as the development of social structures and implementation of infrastructural improvements, have all emerged from the community, working in concert. Residents have an uncommon cohesiveness and solidarity with one another, understanding only too well the necessity of their interdependency for the maintenance of stability and order. At the same time, there is a diversity of professions, programming, cultural practices, nationalities, financial wealth, and political views within Torre David. The dynamism that typifies a city can be found inside Torre David, which leads us to view it as a slice of the city rather than a homogenous unit.

[BM] It sounds impossible to live in a 45-storey tower without any lift, yet in Torre David the problem seems to have been overcome. How? What's the role of parking and the stairs?

[HK + AB] The tower's use of a ten-storey car park provides a vertical transport solution. Residents built their homes up to the 28th floor – a high climb in a tower without a lift. They then transformed the car park into an informal entry ramp to the high-rise. For security reasons, the original design excluded any direct access from the parking structure to the other buildings apart from the lobby. But today the ramp of the parking structure serves as an informal access solution for the complex. Moto-taxis and drivers queue up every day to ferry people, goods and building materials up and down the ten floors for a small fee. In order to move between the parking garage and the central housing complex, occupants have broken through the reinforced concrete walls, creating openings from which small footbridges on each floor lead into the tower. The garage was intended to accommodate immobile vehicles at the end of a journey, but it has become an essential part of residents' last mile home.

[BM] Is it this absence of a quick vertical transport that strengthens the physical connection with the ground floor and within the different levels of the towers? Is it the slow experience of 'meeting with everybody' on the stairs that transforms the stairs into a vertical street and consequently the tower in a vertical city?

[HK + AB] Residents use unoccupied or common spaces where they stop and talk, exchange news and cement the bonds of proximity. The stairs are, of course, a primary informal meeting place and the physical manifestation of a community grapevine. Since the one accessible stairway in the high-rise is the only means of vertical circulation within that structure, sooner or later everyone passes everyone else.

[BM] Another very interesting element that we can recognize both in a favela and in the tower is the blurred boundary between the dwellings and the street, the private and the public, the individual and the community. How did people build their homes in the tower?

[HK + AB] Despite certain immovable and unalterable features, much of Torre David is in a near constant state of evolution and modification – physically and socially. Early in the occupation, only the ground floor was electrified and many residents still lived in tents. Almost all spaces and services were shared. As an informal communal organization began to emerge, spaces were systematically divided and

allocated to each family. Over time, this distribution of space eroded the strictly collective organization, giving rise to greater individuality with respect to one's own habitation.

[BM] How did the appropriation of Torre David influence its immediate surroundings?

[HK + AB] Torre David is situated in what was once meant to be South America's Wall Street. However, the banking crisis of 1993 dampened not only Torre David's intended future, but also its urban context. The neighbourhood depreciated in property value and the next two decades of political and economic instability dampened much of the domestic and foreign investment in both real estate and the nation's financial sector. However, to this day Torre David is located across the street from two of Venezuela's largest banks, which both have their own skyscraper headquarters. On the other side of Torre David is a small barrio of single- and double-storey brick structures. Torre David can perhaps be viewed as a spatial mediator between these two morphologies.

[BM] We can see that the only pedestrian access to the tower is a very small door and that non-residents are not allowed in. What if Torre David would be more accessible and have public programmes on its lower floors? Wouldn't they 'ground' it more in its surroundings, and in Caracas in general?

[HK + AB] We need to bear in mind that Caracas is a violent and unpredictable city, and security is a top priority for all citizens. In this sense, residents of Torre David are no exception. Similarly, given the precariousness of their occupancy, the residents remain understandably alert and guarded against outsiders whose intrusion may rock the delicate stability they have managed to create. We do realize that it is an oxymoron of sorts – a barrio that is also a gated community. But this is increasingly a defining quality of global urbanism today – inequality increases insecurity at all levels of society.

[BM] What did you learn from working with the informal? Are there elements, tactics or strategies that we could bring into the formal city?

[HK + AB] While careful not to treat the ad hoc, self-built environment as a romantic idea, we also reject the conventional depiction of slums as tumours on the civic body. Architects and designers worldwide have much to learn from these zones of instinctive innovation – the infinite adaptability and resourcefulness of bottom-up, organic urbanism. And far from stifling the maverick spirit of the informal, it is our role to contribute to a more fundamental vision of the city as a place of equal opportunity. After all, we cannot forget that these solutions have emerged from crisis. Individuals have been forced to respond to problems of sanitation, shelter, energy and water with improvisational survival tactics. For architects and designers working across formal and informal contexts alike, scarcity should function not as a survival state, but as a design tool.

[BM] What did the municipality learn from these experiences? Are there plans for interventions in other favelas, or even new radical vertical settlements?

[HK + AB] In the case of Torre David, the occupation is an extreme example of adaptive reuse, and the tower's monumental qualities, in terms of volume, layout and verticality, limit the possibilities of becoming a generic model for other sites in Caracas or elsewhere. With this in mind, we actually identified the parking structure in the tower as a common, universal element of the modern, global city that shares a similar potential to transpose informal and incremental growth. The local government has treated Torre David inconsistently, sometimes indicating a willingness to work with the residents to improve their living conditions, other times promising to provide them with social housing elsewhere in the city, and occasionally also suggesting forceful eviction. Recently, new municipal leaders have visited Torre David and pronounced a willingness to work with residents to redevelop the complex. We, along with everyone else, are eager to see what might come from this renewed interest.

[BM] You describe the function of the architect as a connector, a bridge between top-down and bottom-up and between all the different disciplines involved. How, as you say, is contemporary architecture shifting the emphasis from form-driven to purpose-oriented? Can we say that U-TT is filling the gap between social processes and physical forms?

[HK + AB] We are convinced that design and architecture have the potential – and obligation – to contribute to positive social change. The challenging dynamics shaping everyday realities in informal settlements across the global South are largely systemic. Any attempt to address the quality of life and access to opportunities of residents must operate simultaneously on a number of levels. Changes to the built environment are part of that equation, but cannot achieve real change in isolation. From our beginnings in Caracas to our more recent activities in South Africa, Colombia and elsewhere, we have sought to work with communities and partners to reimagine the possibilities of life in the informal city.
We believe it is our responsibility to identify common ground between diverse players defining and shaping the long-term urban fabric of cities, capitalizing on our unique position at the juncture of the formal and informal to bridge bottom-up and top-down processes. The missing thread in discussions of form, style and urban development is accountability to those whose lives are directly affected.

[BM] U-TT is a lot about connecting and merging, about continuity and adaptation. We find these themes in your research, in the subjects of your studies, in the processes you initiate and in your architecture. Why should architects, as you put it, build bridges, not walls; networks, not moats?

[HK + AB] It is not enough to deliver projects if there is no mediation between city dwellers and city governance. Successful projects need the energy of bottom-up, grassroots actors, but they must also be connected to top-down agencies, institutions and processes to achieve deeper impacts. We remain committed to the idea of design as a collaborative and participatory act.

Posbank Pavilion
Rheden, Netherlands
SeARCH
1998–2002

The Netherlands has no mountains, so the rolling hills in the east are quite an attraction. During the last ice age, glaciers pushed sand up more than 100 metres above sea level (some achievement by Dutch standards). The deep-lying moraine was carried all the way from Scandinavia.

Kummakivi rock formation, Ruokolahti, Finland, accidentally created by the receding ice, 10 000 BCE.

Hunebed D27, Borger, Netherlands, 4000–2000 BCE.

Kjeragbolten wedged in a mountain crevasse, Norway, 50 000 BCE.

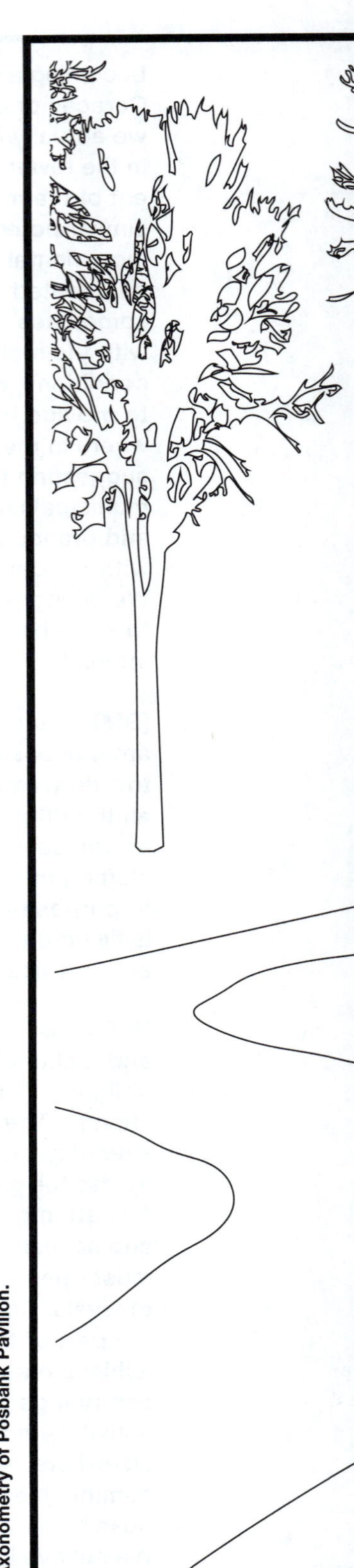

Axonometry of Posbank Pavilion.

These so-called 'erratics' (*errare* in Latin is 'to wander') are found further north in the Netherlands as tombstones. Erected in megalithic times, the Dutch *Hunebedden* are akin to the English dolmen. In Scandinavia, these perfectly balanced rock formations occurred naturally, the result of retracting ice as the earth warmed.

Owned by one of the oldest and largest nature preservation societies in the world, the Vereniging Natuurmonumenten of 1902, and located on one of the elevations of the undulating Veluwezoom National Park, the Posbank Tea Pavilion visually dramatizes the workings of a glacier and the astonishing wandering of boulders over a thousand kilometres.

Site plan of Posbank Pavilion within the Veluwezoom National Park.

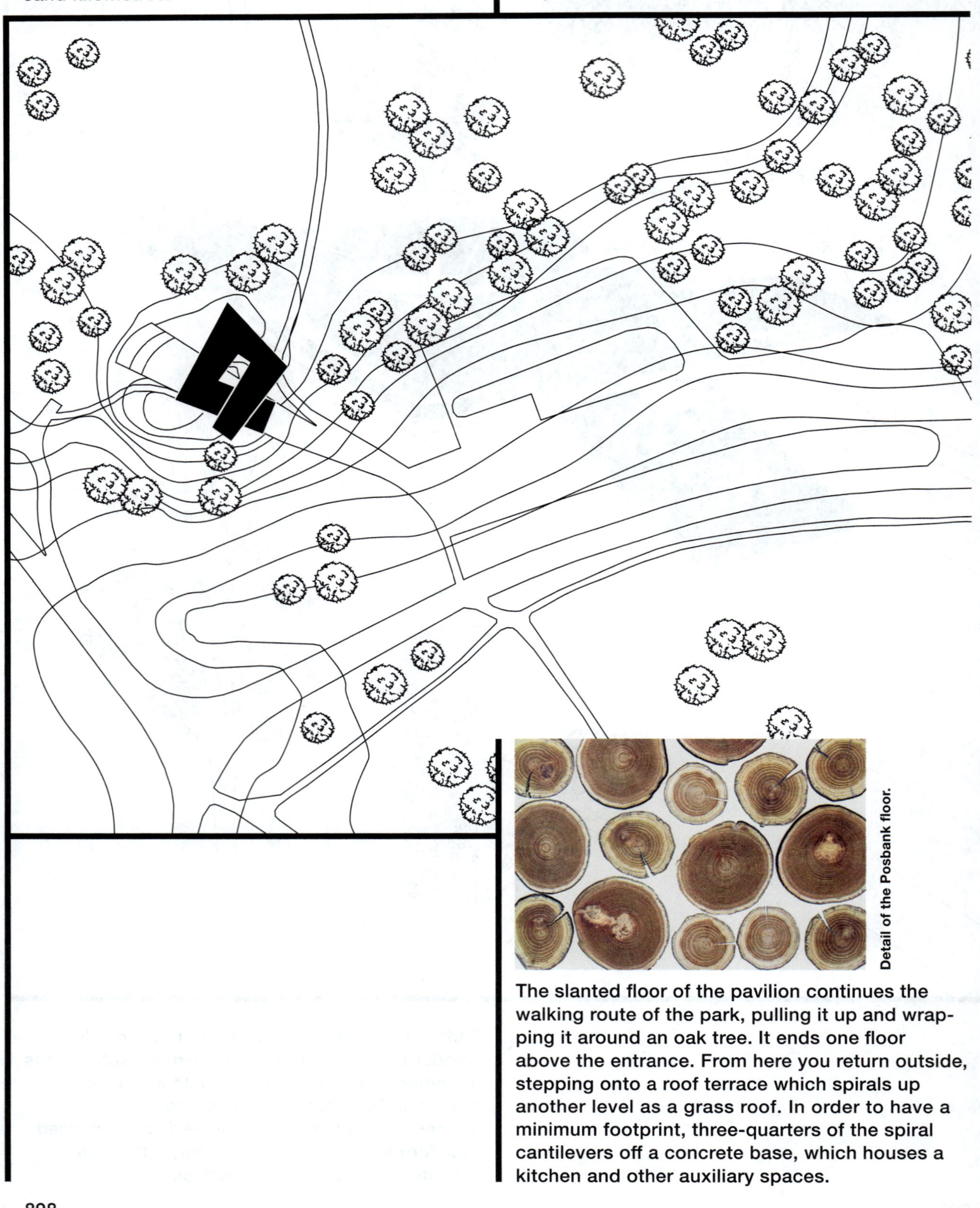

Detail of the Posbank floor.

The slanted floor of the pavilion continues the walking route of the park, pulling it up and wrapping it around an oak tree. It ends one floor above the entrance. From here you return outside, stepping onto a roof terrace which spirals up another level as a grass roof. In order to have a minimum footprint, three-quarters of the spiral cantilevers off a concrete base, which houses a kitchen and other auxiliary spaces.

Plan of Posbank Pavilion.

Big trusses spanning between floor and ceiling make this possible, and are a hybrid of unprocessed solid oak trunks for compression and steel rods for tension. The six per cent grade floor at the perimeter along a panoramic glass facade gives access to several smaller platforms with seating. At its most pivotal point, all of this is stabilized by two big boulders on top of each other, as if the melted ice had put them in place.

The building emphasizes the value and power of natural resources and demonstrates the continuing dominance of nature over culture. At the same time, what remains of nature can no longer be experienced without cultural intervention.

Section of Posbank Pavilion.

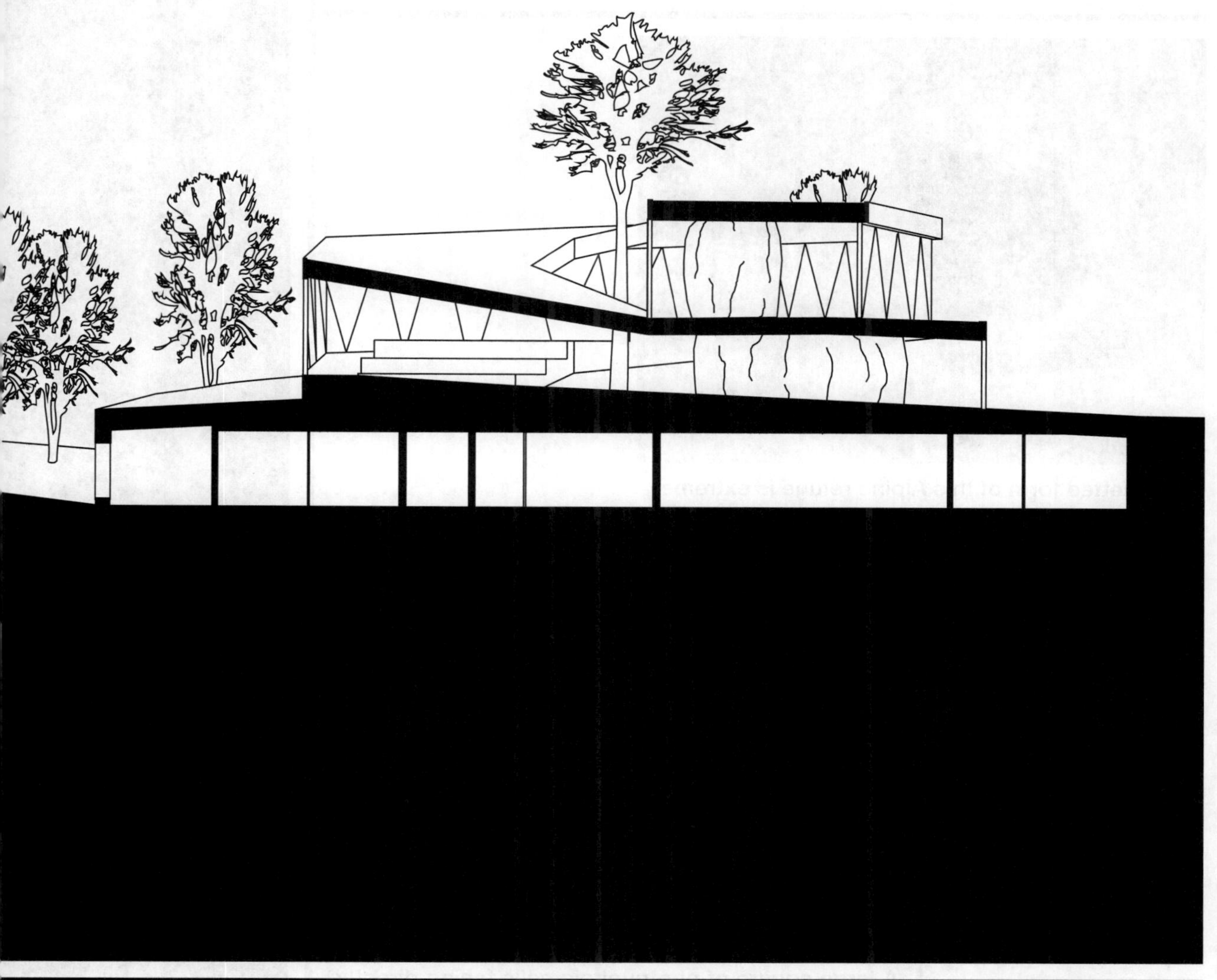

Although it is possible to preserve nature by purchasing it, as the Dutch Nature Conservancy does, the real challenge is in changing human behaviour. The medium of building has a role to play in raising awareness of both the power and vulnerability of nature.

Monte Rosa Hütte
Zermatt, Switzerland
ETH Zürich and
Bearth & Deplazes Architekten
2004–2009

The facetted form of this Alpine refuge is extremely compact, as if all excess has been sliced away. Inside, the layout is equally efficient, as the extreme conditions and inhospitable landscape of the Alps demand maximum sobriety.

A large square of photovoltaic cells facing directly south makes the building look like a one-eyed pod. The stairway and corridor of Monte Rosa Hütte merge into glazing spiralling across the facade, like the path of the sun, cutting right through the photovoltaic surface while bringing in passive heat from sunlight.

Building facade dissolved to show spiral circulation.

This large stair connects all floors. From the central landings, tapered sleeping quarters and bathrooms fan out to the facade, making further corridors or circulation unnecessary. Designing with efficiency in mind has had a generous outcome: small spaces open out to air, light and views.

The Monte Rosa Hütte is a complete inversion of the Guggenheim spiral, not extravagant but spot-on. Like an elastic band, it tightens the programme, whereas the omnipresent ramp in Frank Lloyd Wright's circular design from the 1950s works as a centrifugal force, pivoting out from an empty void. It is astonishing to see that a spiral staircase at an altitude of 2800 metres easily beats its world-famous forerunner when it comes to functionality.[41]

Solomon R. Guggenheim Museum, 1943–1959 (left); Norman Lykes House, Frank Lloyd Wright, 1959–1967 (middle); David and Gladys Wright House, Frank Lloyd Wright, 1952 (right).

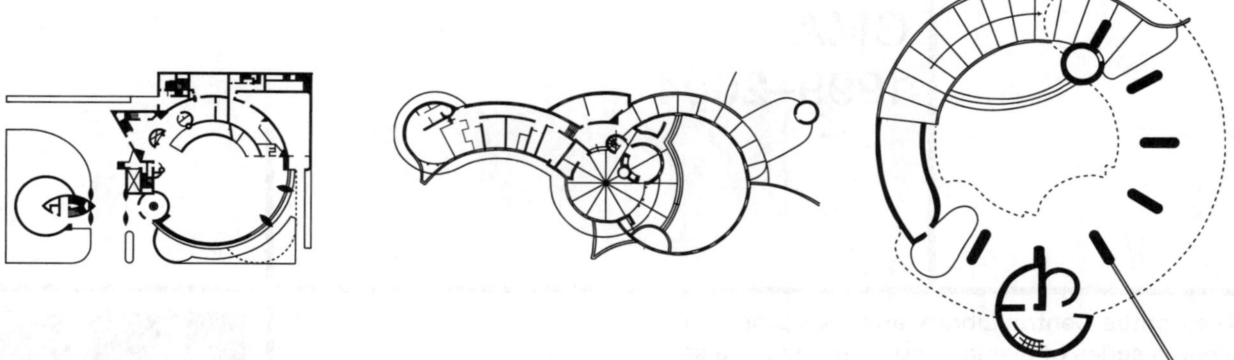

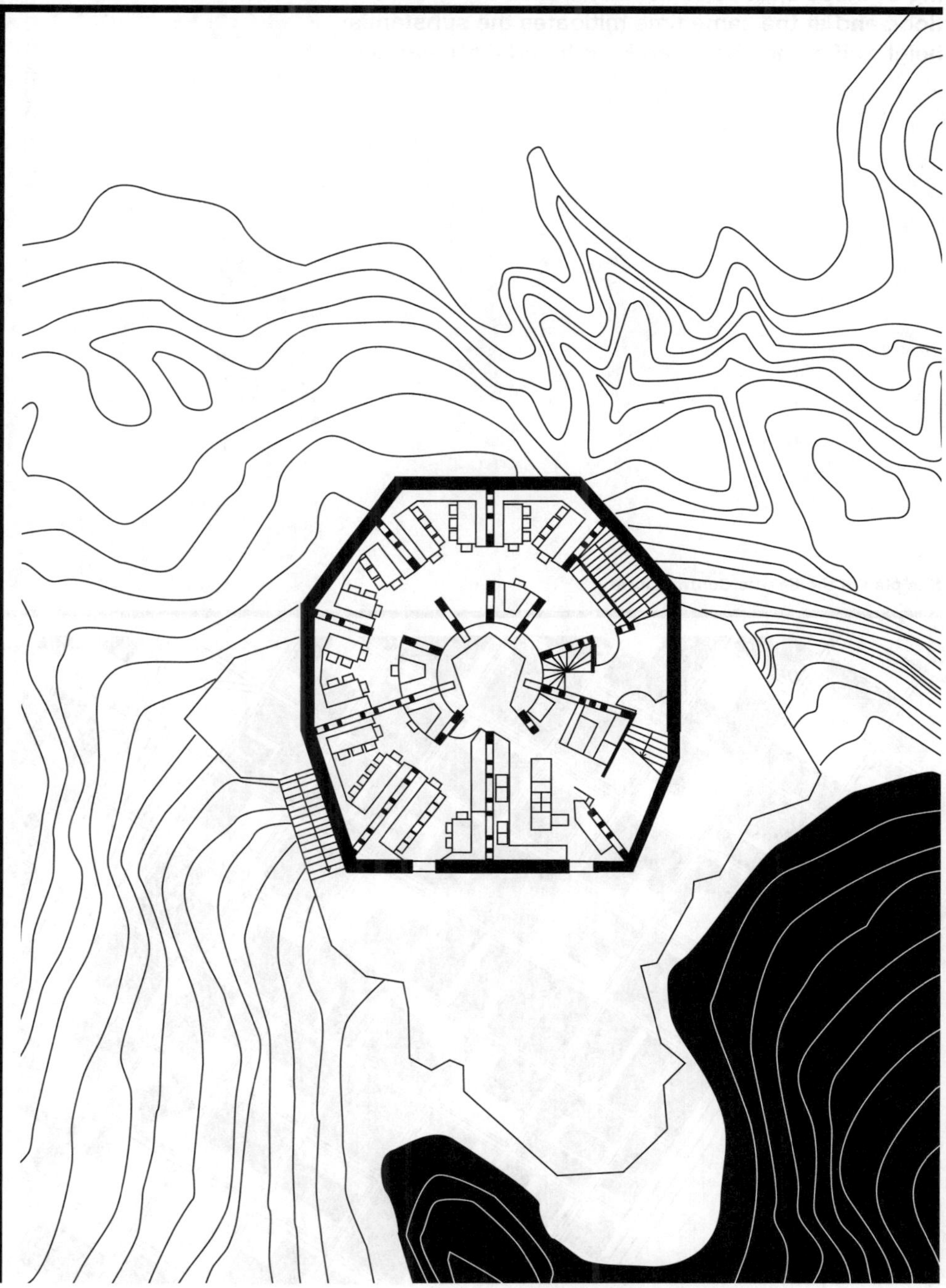

Plan of Monte Rosa Hütte.

Seattle Central Library
Seattle, USA
OMA
1999–2004

The Seattle Central Library arranges programme along a series of overlapping platforms. The stacking of these spaces effectively triples the ground floor, and at the same time mitigates the substantial height difference between Fourth and Fifth Avenue.

Axonometry of the Seattle Central Library.

Site plan of the Seattle Central Library.

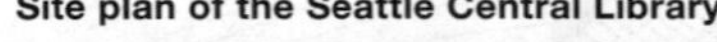

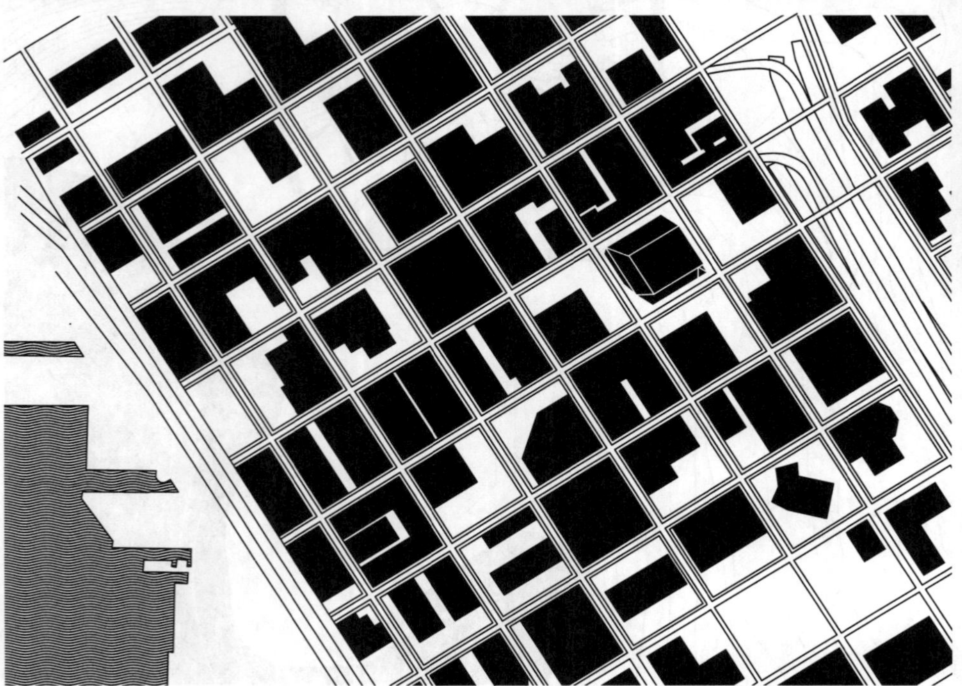

Irony is OMA's middle name, and they seem to take great pleasure in playing with contradictions inherent in both the structure and programme. Despite being situated in an earthquake-prone area, OMA stacks and offsets a series of volumes in a highly unstable fashion. These masses are then tied down to shaky ground by a large net. The thin continuous mesh of beams that makes up the facade gives the building its structural stability.

Section of the Seattle Central Library.

ck-out

library cards

ry a. ackerley
collection

Bookstacks along the ramped spiral walkway.

As for the library programme, OMA has taken a typology synonymous with private study and turned it into a public space. A series of interstitial spaces flow together to form one continuous experience with an abundance of daylight. This building overwhelms anybody who enters.

The ambiguous flexibility of the undefined, generic space of the public library is transformed into a fine-grained programmatic complexity. Arranging multiple spatial compartments along a ramping spiral means that each space is connected without the threat of one section hindering others. This is mirrored in the 'book spiral', a continuous ramp of shelving, allowing categories in the collection to grow and shrink in relation to each other.

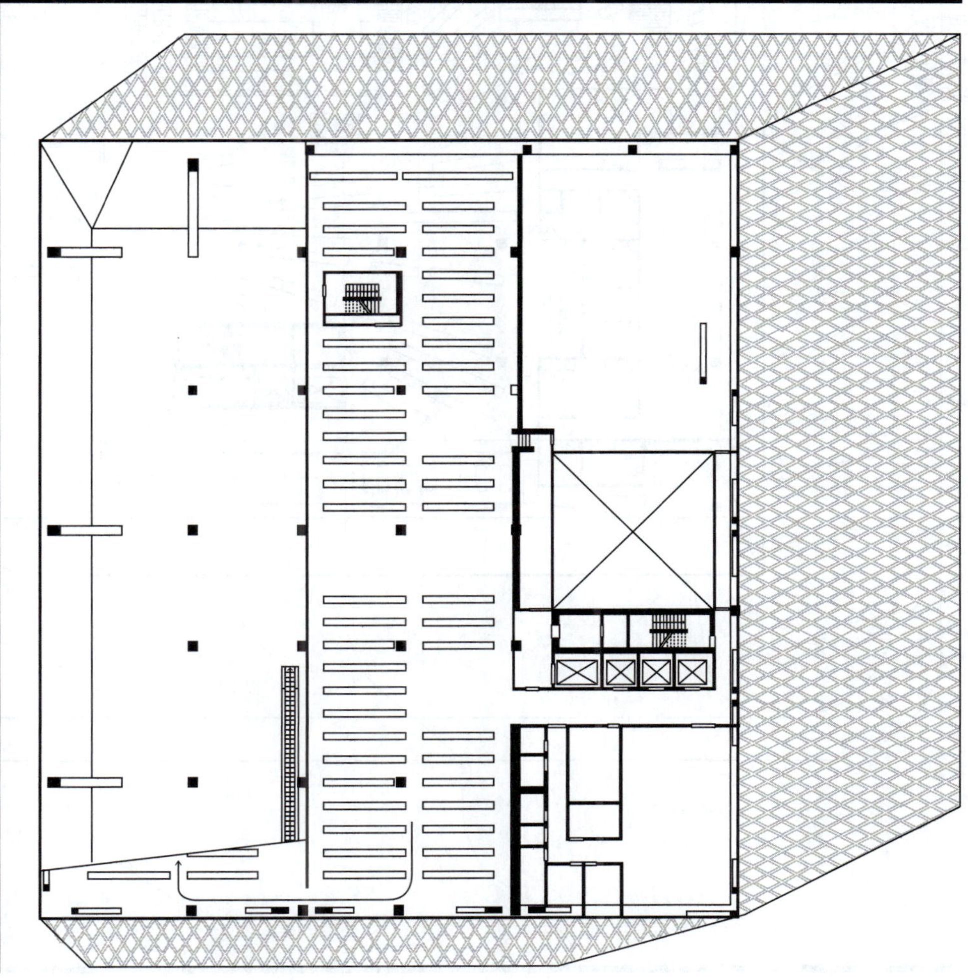

Plan of level 7, the 'book spiral'.

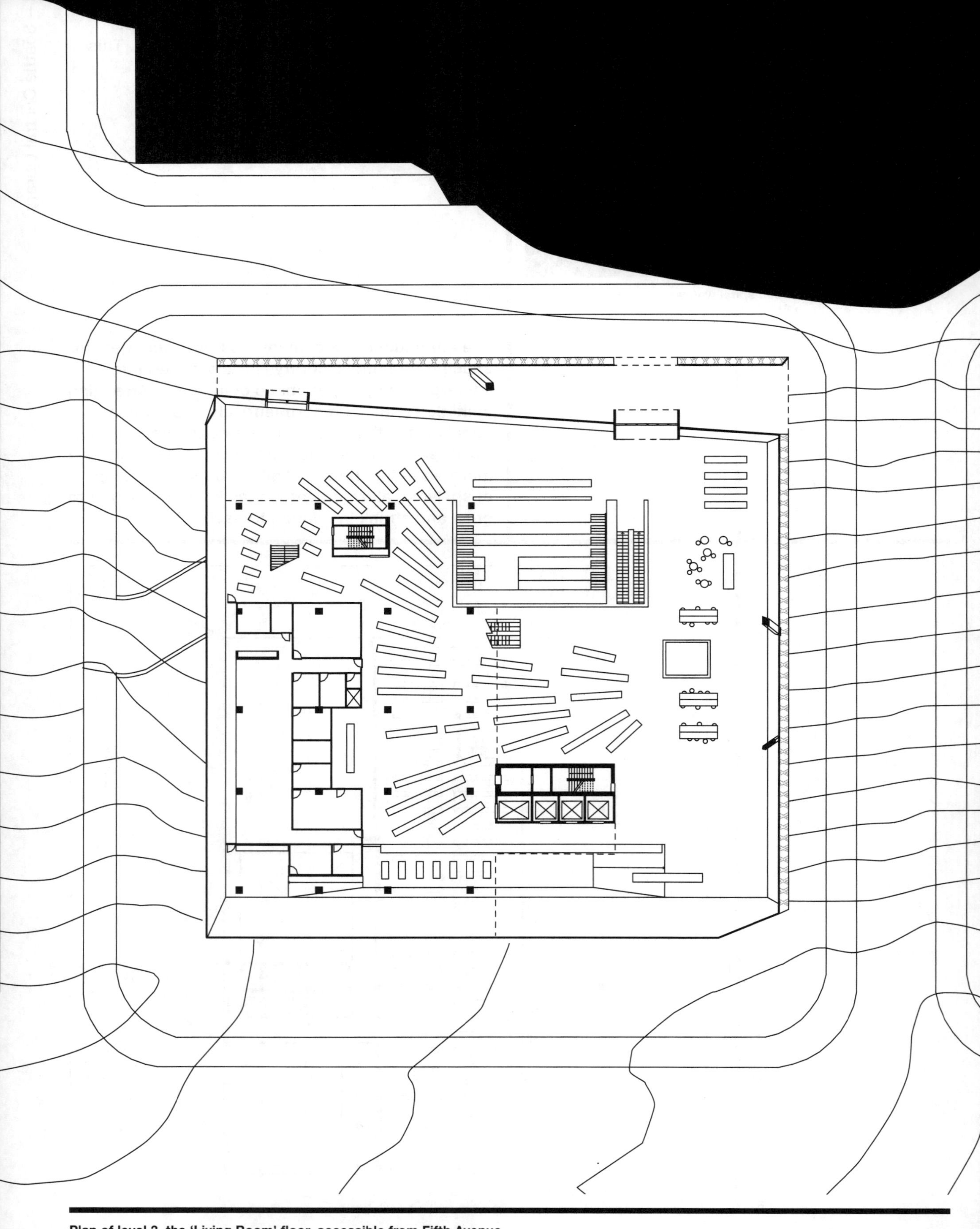

Plan of level 3, the 'Living Room' floor, accessible from Fifth Avenue.

Space is connected visually and physically, drawing the urban fabric into the building. Newly blind people have actually used the library to practise moving through public space as it mimics the urban environment without its perils.

This building is proof that the spiral has a bright future in architecture as both an organizer, conveyor and connector.

Junior College
Julianadorp, Netherlands
SeARCH
2004–2008

The main idea behind the spiralling set-up was to eliminate separate floors and the need for something to connect them.

In the Junior College a continuous ramp is the main connector. It spirals up four (traditional) levels and eliminates the need to use the lift. Classrooms and a ramp enclose an atrium, topped with a double membrane roof. This atrium acts as an in-between space and gives a sense of the outdoors; a novel schoolyard sheltered from the harsh North Sea winds and rainy days.

Exploded axonometry of the Junior College.

Plan showing staggered classrooms.

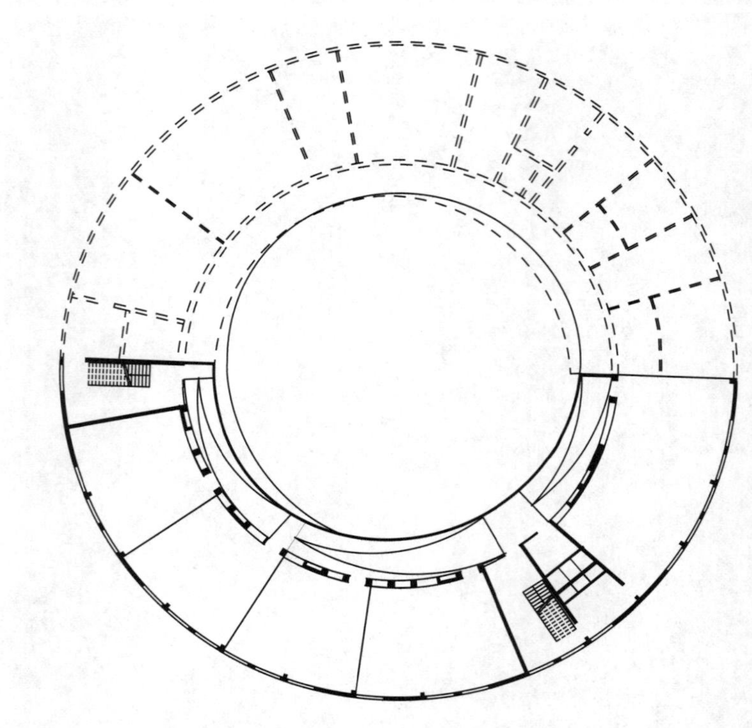

Ground level plan of the Junior College.

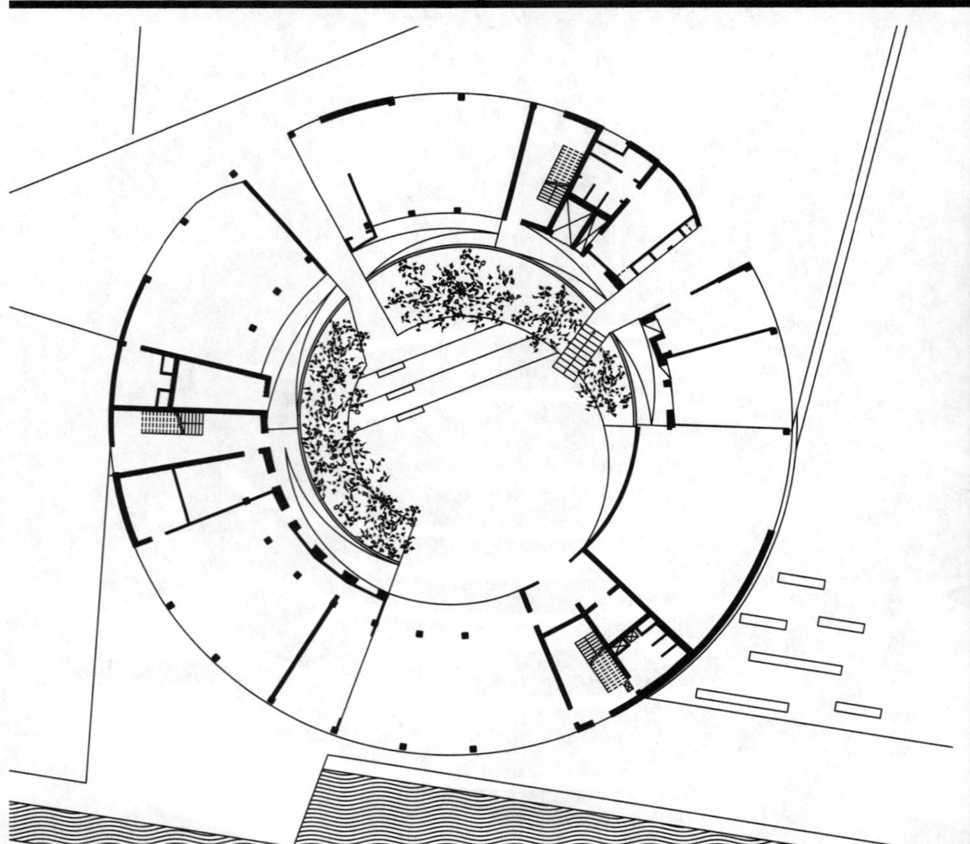

The classrooms of three different levels of secondary education are organized as one linear strip in a non-hierarchical structure. This offers maximum flexibility by allowing classes and levels to expand or shrink in size without being pushed to the next floor. It also offers a way to keep levels connected to one another through their adjacency.

Section of the Junior College.

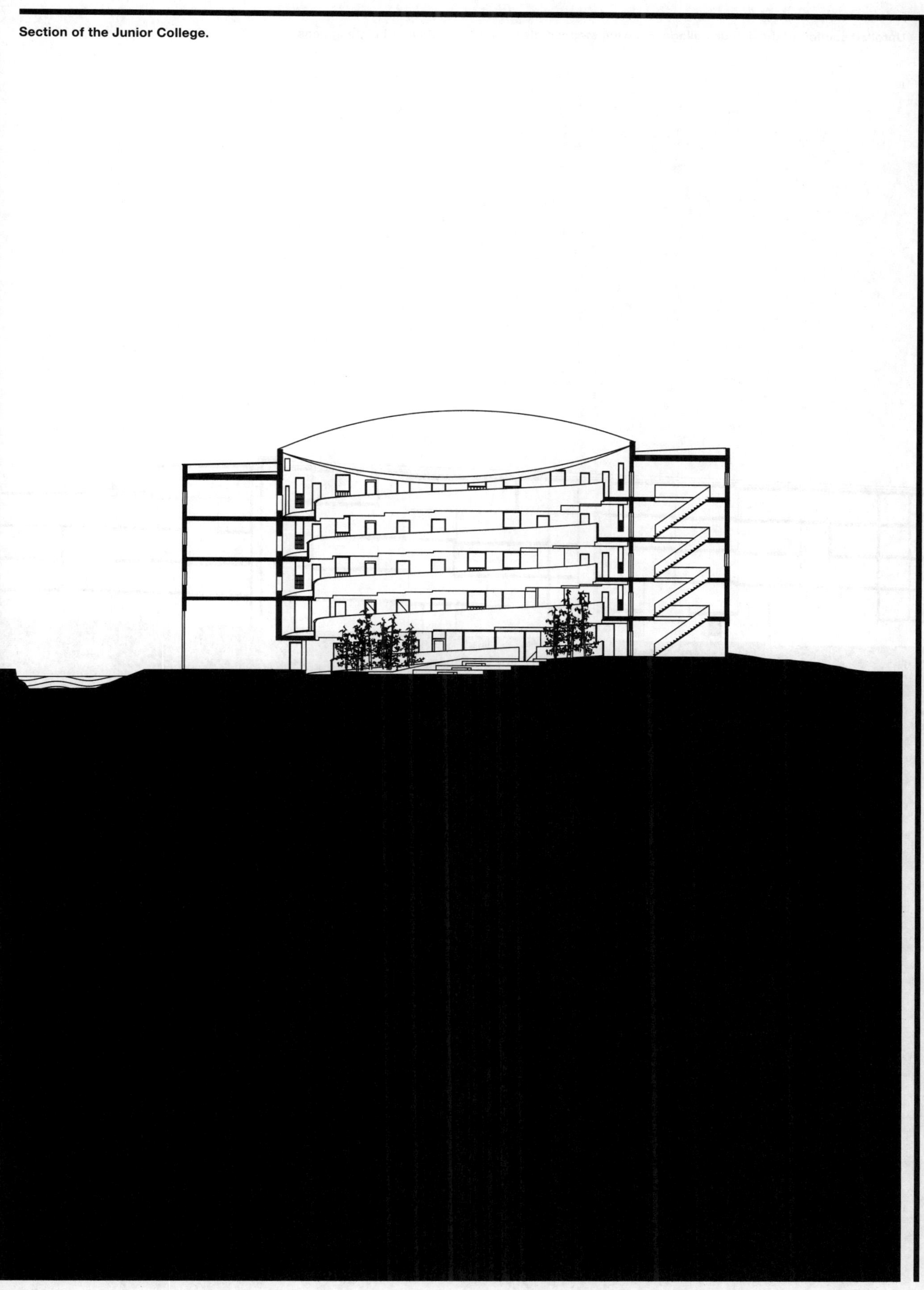

Unrolled section of the Junior College, showing stepped classrooms and double-height spaces.

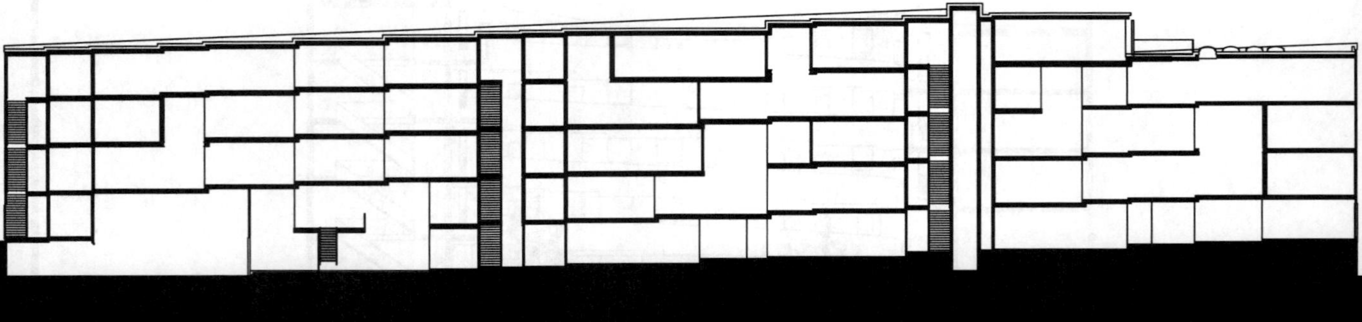

Unlike the Guggenheim Museum, where visitors are supposed to rise to the top by lift and stroll down at a leisurely pace, this 'Guggenschool' challenges pupils to climb the path of learning on their own.

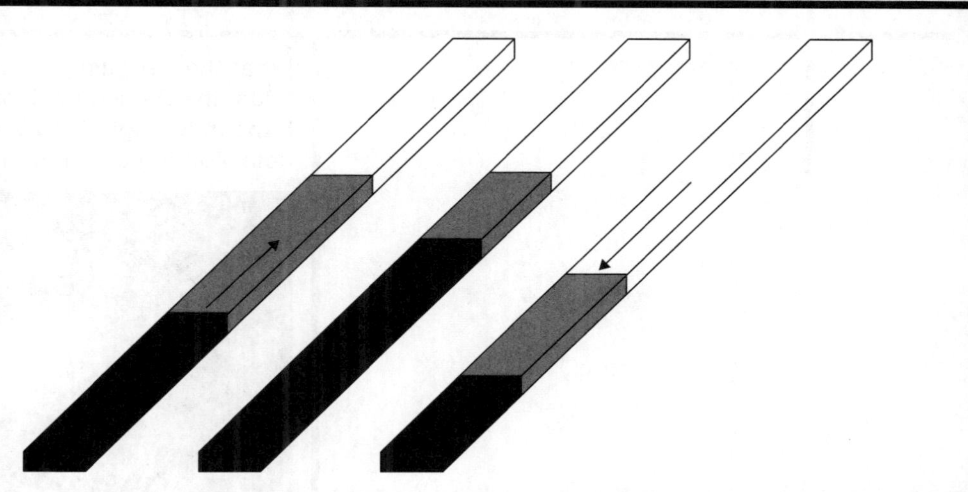
Diagram of traditional fluctuating classroom size.

Since education in the Netherlands is constantly subject to innovation, the Junior School's director wanted to forge better connections to higher professional education within the school, including lecture rooms he couldn't afford. An unintended side effect of the spiral was that classrooms had to be stepped so that they are all on the same level as the inclined gallery to ensure accessibility. The director got exactly what he wanted, though not the way he expected.

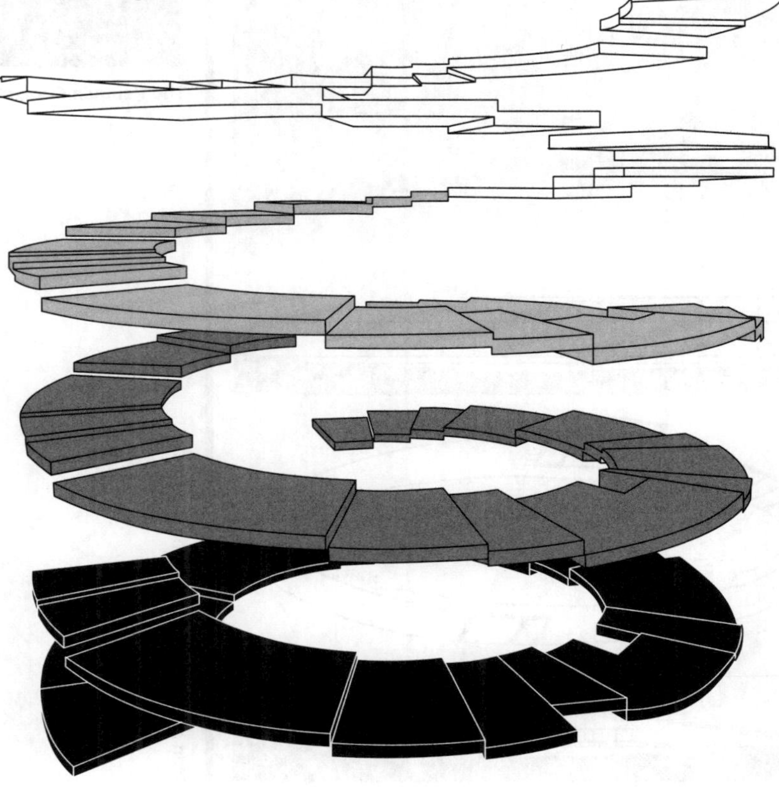
Spiralled solution of the Junior College.

Danish Pavilion
Shanghai Expo, China
BIG
2010

What the penguin pool was for London Zoo in 1934, the Danish Pavilion was for the World Expo in Shanghai in 2010: a spectacular double helix floating over a pond.

The Penguin Pool, renovated by Avanti Architects, 2017.

Berthold Lubetkin, Penguin Pool, London Zoo, 1934.

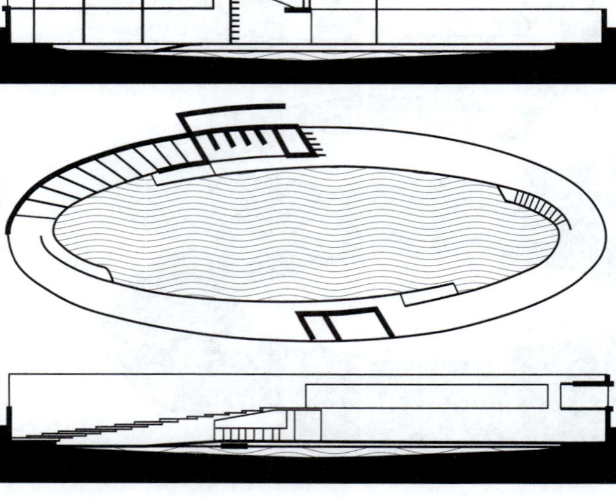

Plan and section of the Penguin Pool.

Sectional axonometry of Danish Pavilion showing intersecting pathways.

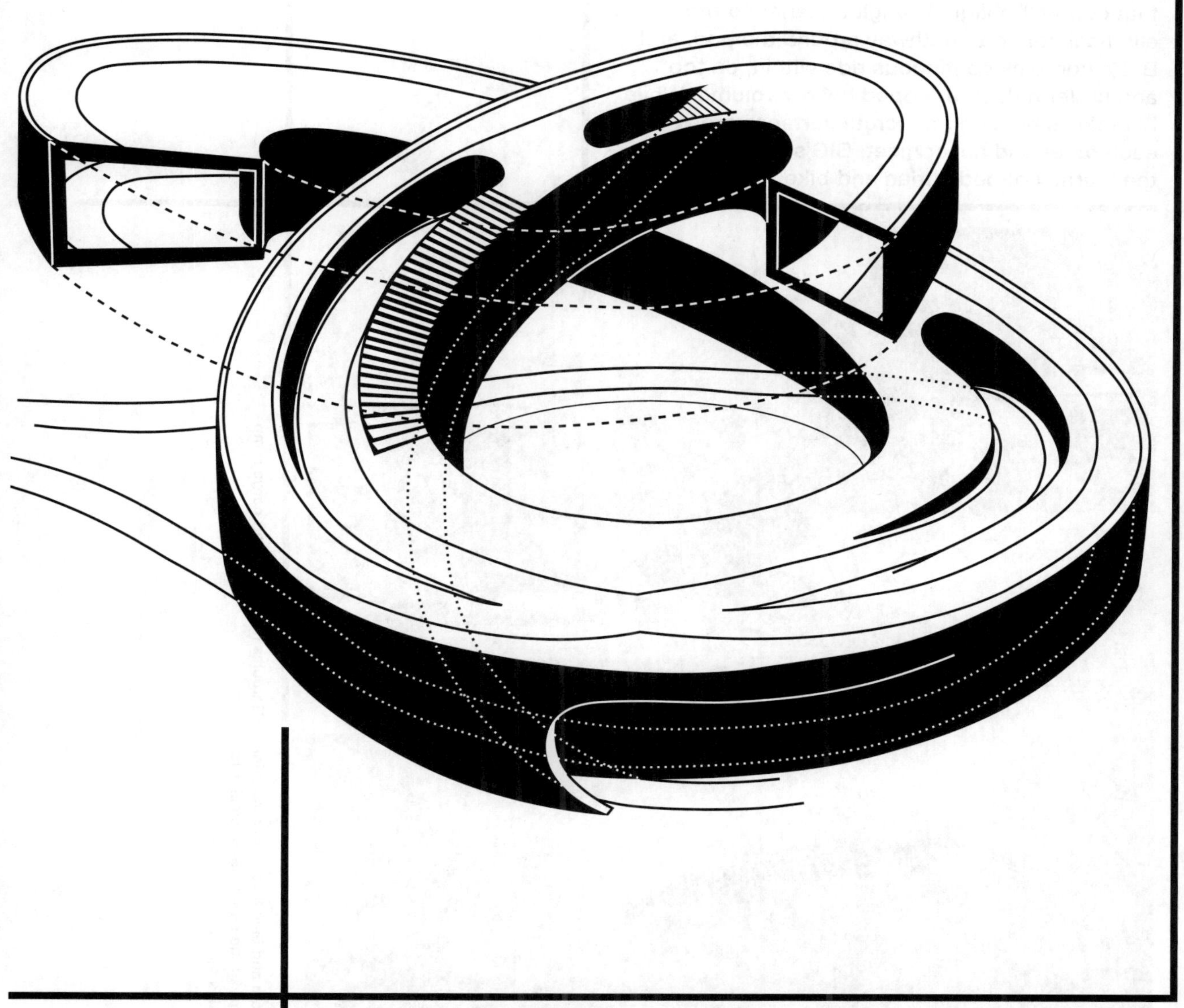

In London, the spiral pivots around the penguins' antics as they waddle over the ramps while people watch through long horizontal windows. In Shanghai, the penguins become people on bikes, cycling along interlocking loops that are short-circuited at both ends. At the centre is not a fountain, as in London, but the Little Mermaid statue, brought over from Copenhagen harbour.

Both projects, engineered by Arup in 1934 and 2010, show the increasing sophistication of a spiralling architecture. While they share a fluid circular geometry, there is a significant distinction between Berthold Lubetkin's interlocking loops that connect obliquely angled planes to the elliptical concrete pathway around the pool and BIG's complex continuous ride within, on top and under a double-looped hollow volume. While Lubetkin's hovering concrete surfaces cross each other and never meet, BIG's spiral weaves the journey of pedestrian and bike together.

Hercules military aircraft cargo ramp.

A striped pedestrian path and blue bike path run under the tilted circular volume of the double loop, similar to the bent tail of a Hercules cargo plane.

Bikes enter via a ramp that is reminiscent of a military plane cargo ramp. Once inside, the bike ride continues until a second ramp brings you to the top of the tube. After another round on the deck, one passes the previous exit ramp from below and crosses the bike lane to take a third ramp, bypassing the interior of the tube and ending directly under the circular shape onto the square. Exhibition spaces, seating and a pedestrian path run parallel with a bike path for most of the route.

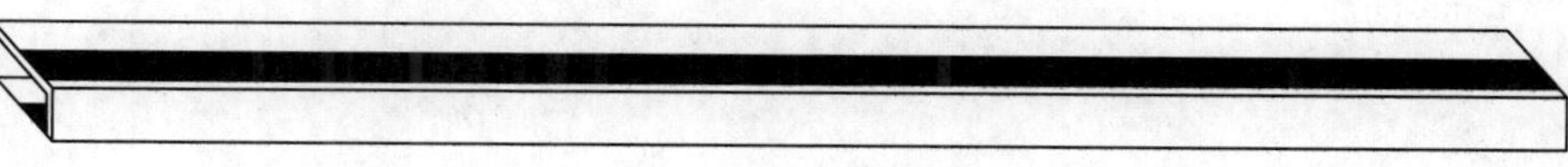

Tube with a path within and path above.

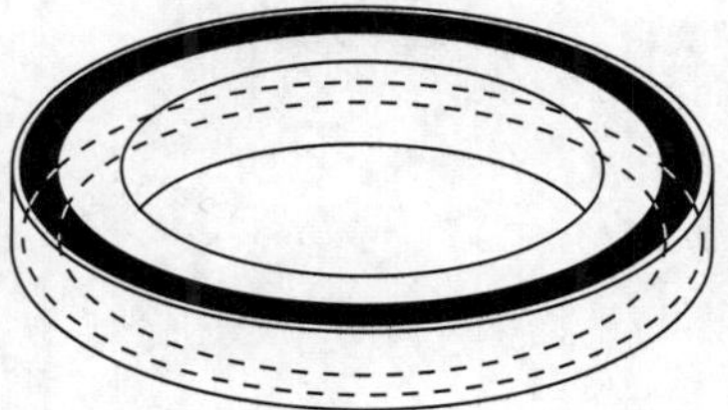

Make a closed loop.

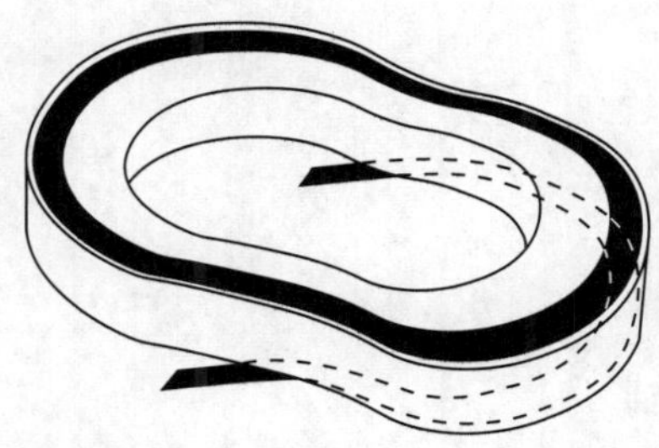

Lift loop and cut it to make an entry and exit.

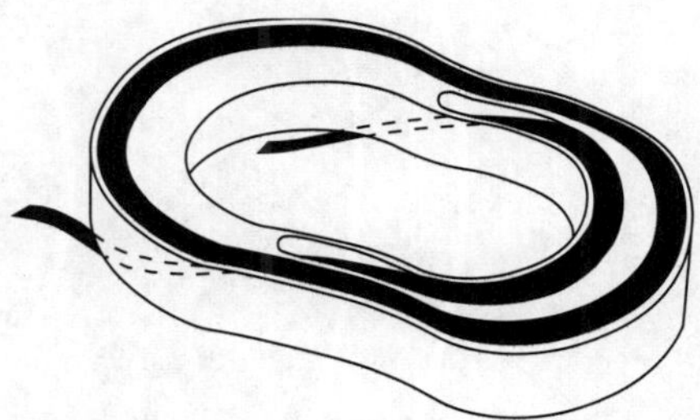

Cut loop to connect path inside with path above.

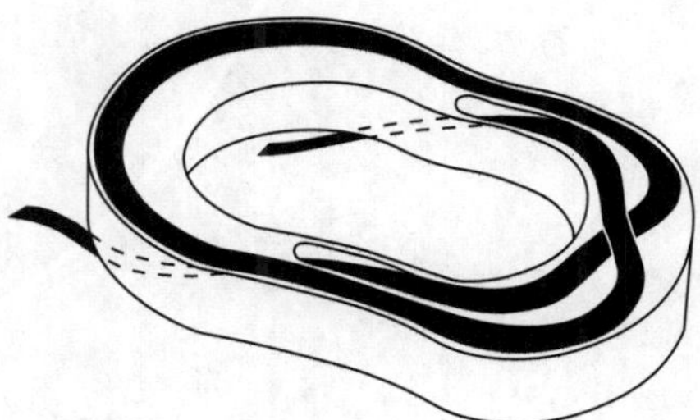

Weave the pathways together.

Pinch and fold loop over itself.

Plan of Danish Pavilion.

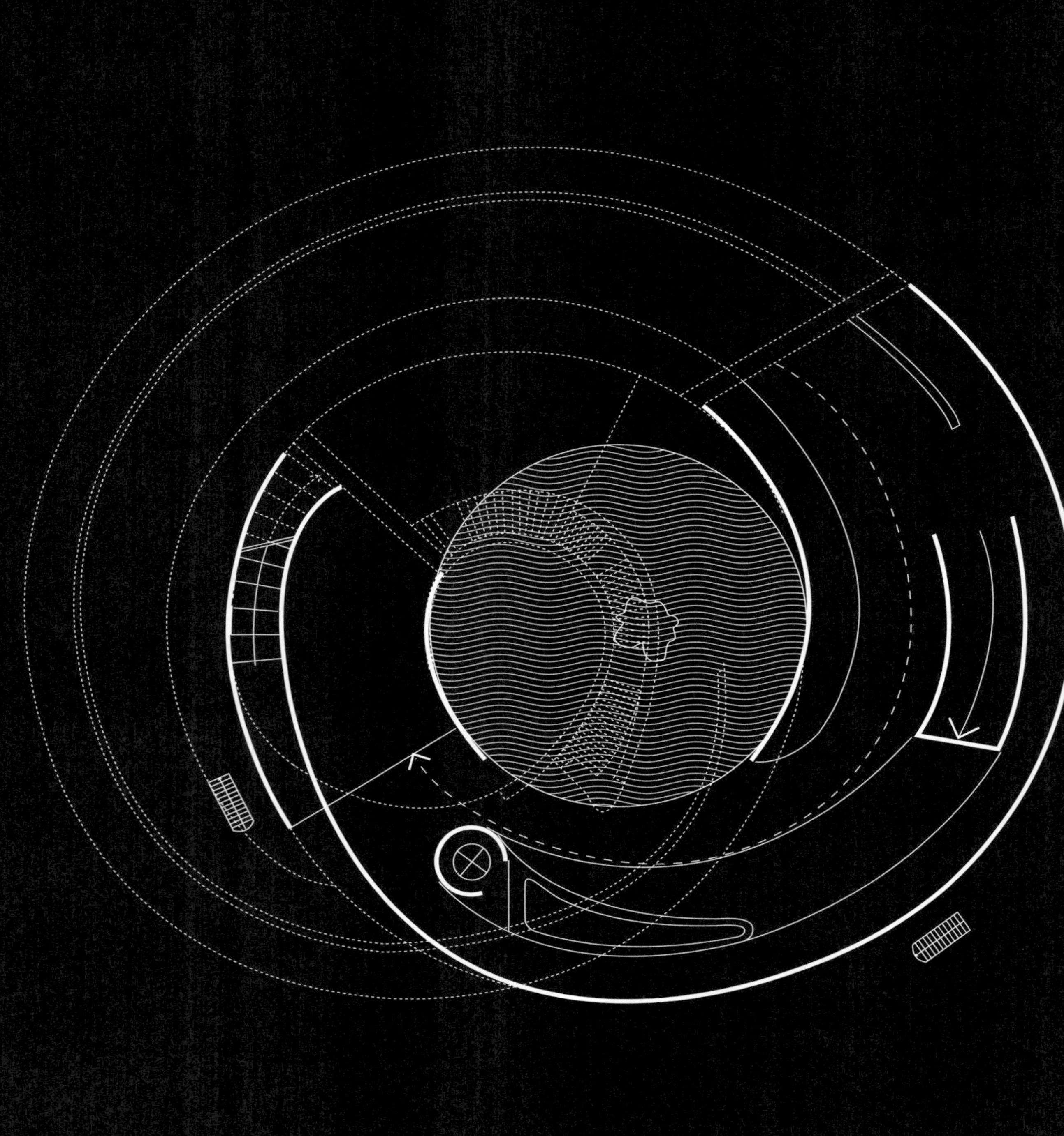

Coca-Cola

EURO E

WELCOME

Bjarke Ingels entering and exiting the journey.

There is no bike lane inside a section of the tube. This is the section between entering and exiting, and here a sweeping stair brings pedestrians from the circle's outer wall to the inner wall, straight up to the highest point of the double helix. It is exactly at those moments where the incline is too steep that a ramp bridges the height differences between the interior and exterior bike lanes.

These moments of tangle within a highly ingenious fluidity are obscured by, and sandwiched between the layered double helix, creating an almost magician-like spatial play.

Section showing the full journey through the pavilion.

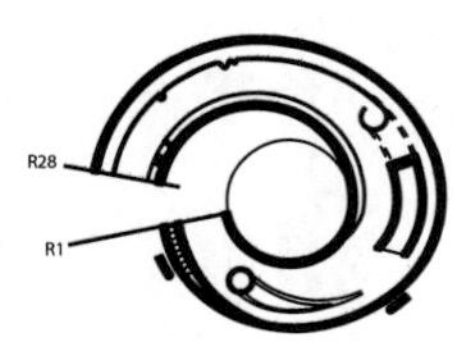

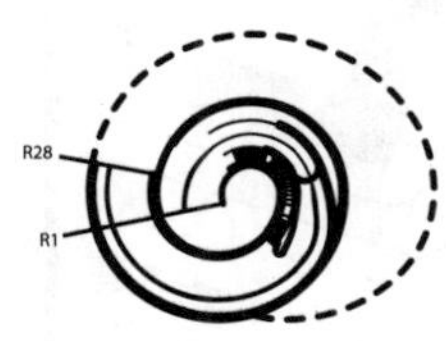

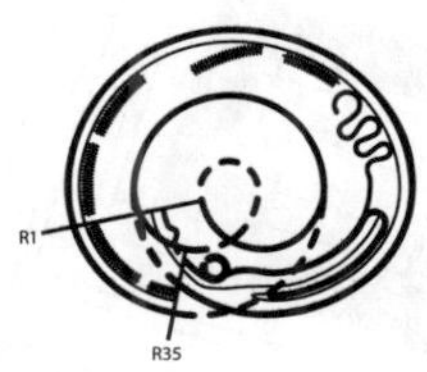

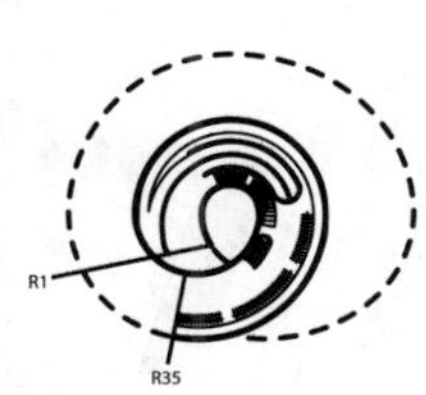

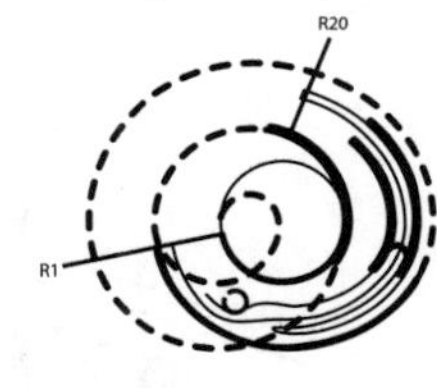

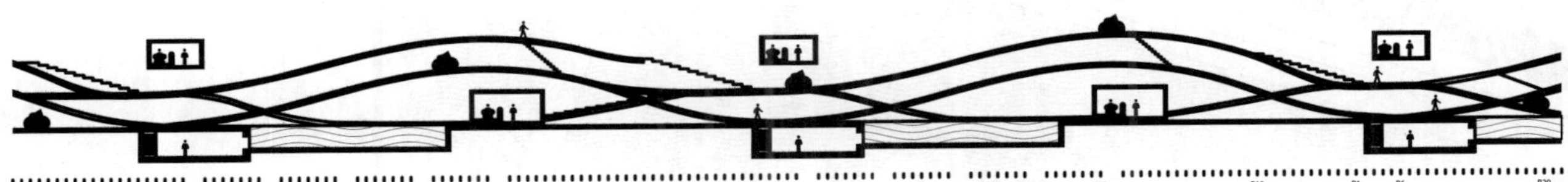

Katendrecht
Rotterdam, Netherlands
SeARCH
2016 (unbuilt)

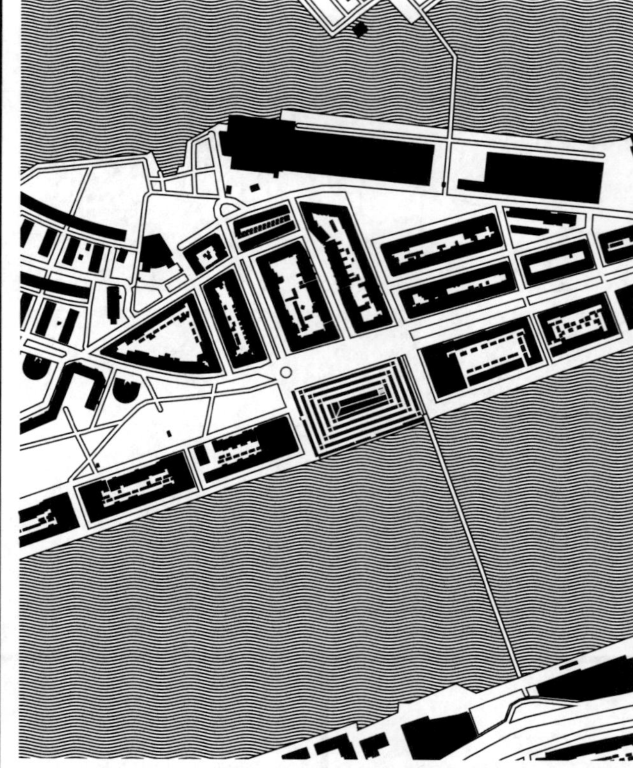
Site plan of Katendrecht.

The biblical story of Genesis speaks of a confusion of tongues, resulting in a human diaspora, leaving the Tower of Babel unfinished. In contrast, the story of Rotterdam is one that involves the collaboration of post-war generations of multicultural citizens. The city has been rebuilt with a hands-on, no-nonsense approach.

Plan of Katendrecht.

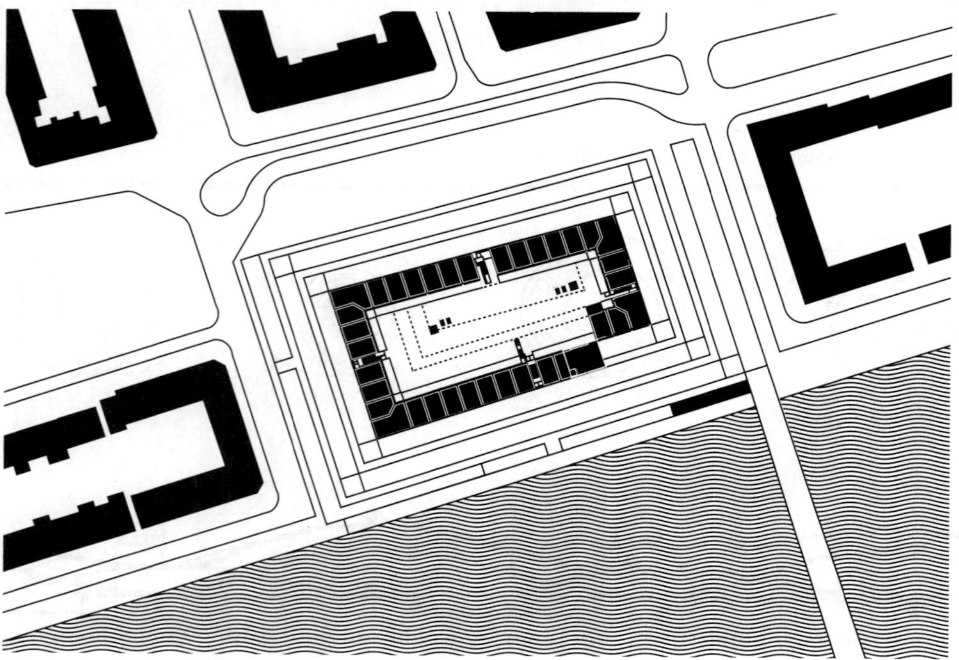

SeARCH's contemporary Tower of Babel is a tribute to this spirit, as if Rotterdam can pull off what others apparently abandoned.

Sketch of connection between pedestrian bridge and Katendrecht.

The Building of the Tower of Babel, Marten van Valckenborch, sixteenth century.

The Construction of the Tower of Babel, Hendrick van Cleve III, late-sixteenth century.

One of the most iconic paintings of the fictional Tower of Babel was made by Pieter Bruegel the Elder around 1560, and it hangs in Museum Boijmans van Beuningen, not far from the Katendrecht site.

Interestingly, most paintings of this imaginative tower depict a circular set-up, while the minimal historical evidence available suggests that the Tower of Babylon was a rectangular ziggurat.[4] That suits Rotterdam's post-industrial harbour site far more.

The sixteenth-century painters Marten van Valckenborch and Hendrick van Cleve painted a rectangular version, although Cleve's tower morphs back to a circular form halfway up. His painting proved particularly useful as it offers a solution for how a pedestrian bridge could span the vast Maashaven dock with a clearance of eight metres and land on this Katendrecht site.

Sketch of spiral path and front gardens.

Katendrecht is a highly egalitarian ziggurat. While the ancient ziggurat had only one habitable space, a temple for the gods at its peak, Katendrecht wraps 200 townhouses around a substantial heap of auxiliary space. A ground-floor hardware store with two floors of car parking, self-storage cubicles and a rock-climbing gym fill the core of this ziggurat. The outer spiral of Katendrecht is a 1300-metre-long communal path that runs along the front gardens of the townhouses.

Section of Katendrecht.

Rendering of Katendrecht.

Katendrecht inverts the urban courtyard typology around it, pulling the garden from the dark interior and placing it on the perimeter, where everyone can enjoy generous light and an expansive view.

Roy and Diana Vagelos Education Center
New York City, USA
Diller Scofidio + Renfro
2013–2016

This building could be described as the amputated end of the Lingotto Factory in Turin. It is as if a piece of the elongated volume that contains a large spiral ramp and a tiny section of the assembly floors with the tilted test track on top was lopped off and transported to New York. Or perhaps it's more of a modern process of genetic selection, where DNA is spliced together without the generic middle part.[42]

In this education centre, a spiralling, twisting string of spaces and interior connectors feed the thin tower of regular slabs next to them.

In general, within a building you'll find an emergency staircase at both ends of a vertical slab, ensuring your safe descent by the shortest route. Here, one of these staircases is turned into an artery with an irregular pulse. As Columbia University states, the cascading staircase that weaves social space and study space reflects how medicine is taught, learned and practised in the twenty-first century.[43]

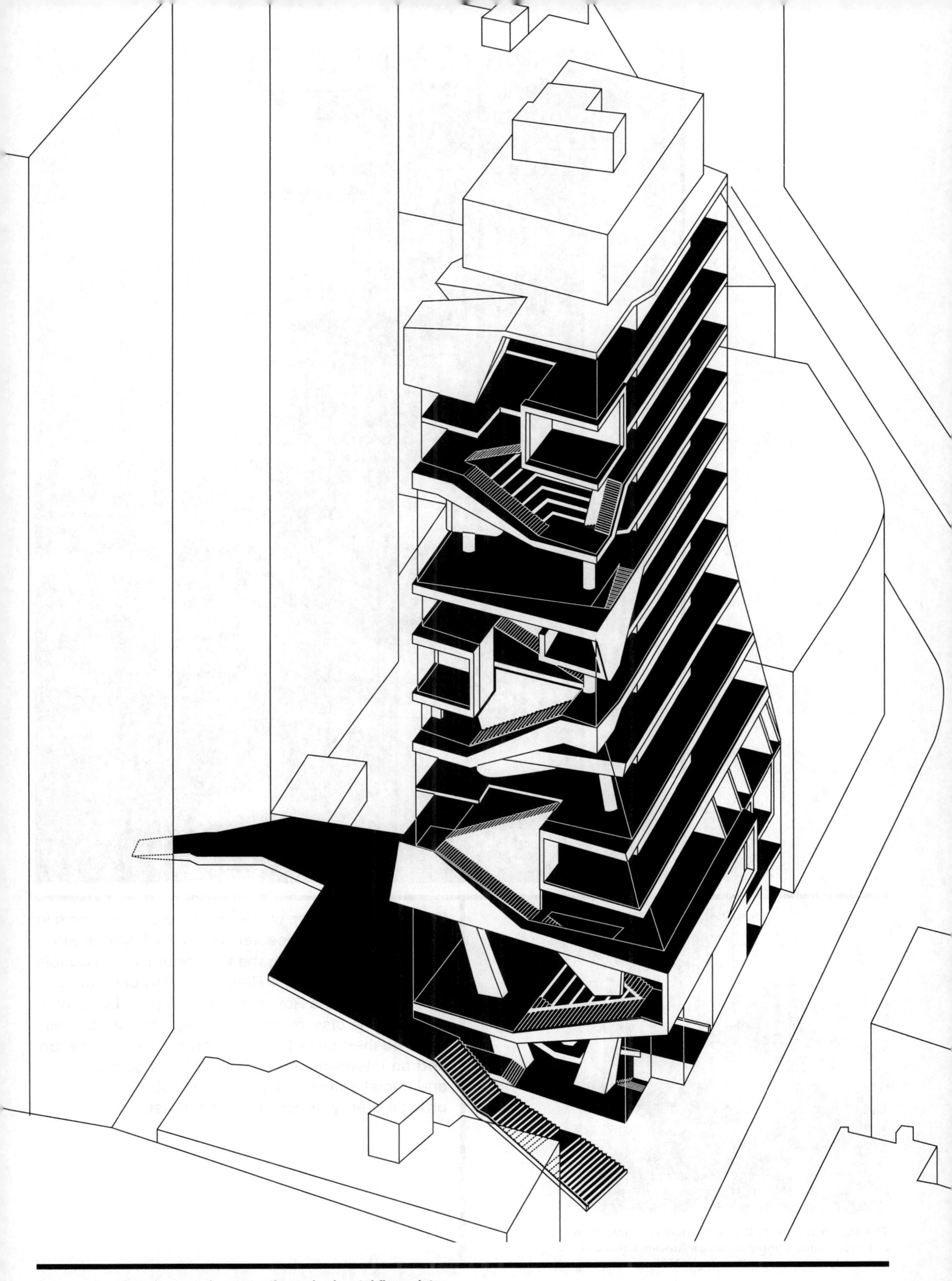

Axonometry of study cascade connecting to horizontal floor plates.

The angled volume of the auditorium is visible from outside. James Stirling & James Gowan, Leicester University Engineering Building, 1959.

While James Stirling chose to express programme in his design of the Leicester University Engineering Building by presenting the auditorium as a readable mass, Diller Scofidio + Renfro express circulation. All the guts of the Roy and Diana Vagelos Education Center – the classrooms, anatomy labs and offices – are pushed back from the south-facing elevation and an interconnected series of staircases and social spaces, known as the 'Study Cascade', provide plenty of pomp and circumstance.

This cascade shows the level of complexity now achievable with the spiral. An enormous variety of spaces – open atria, small study areas, lecture theatres, cafeteria, mini amphitheatres, outdoor balconies and a roof terrace – are woven together in one continuous sweep.

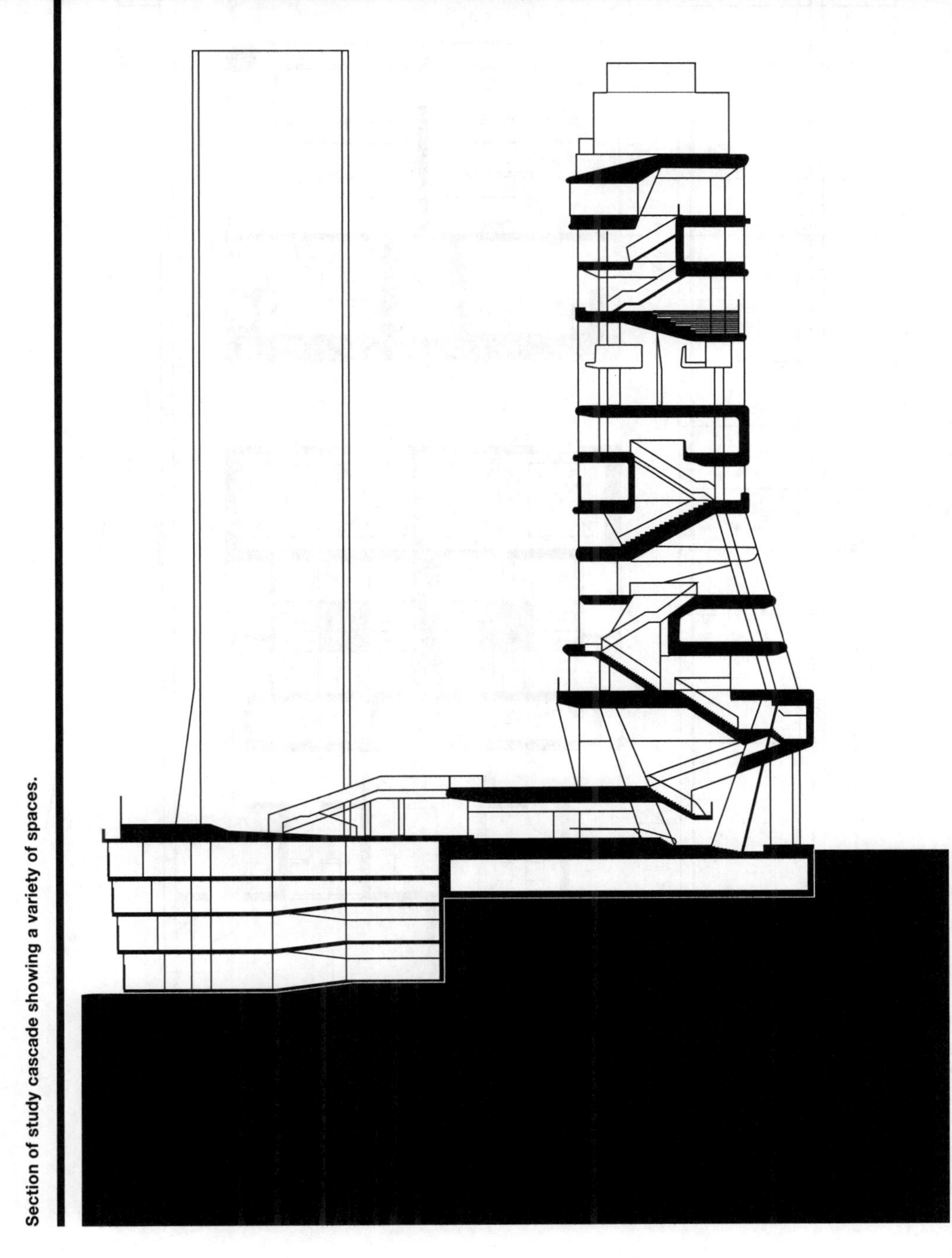

Section of study cascade showing a variety of spaces.

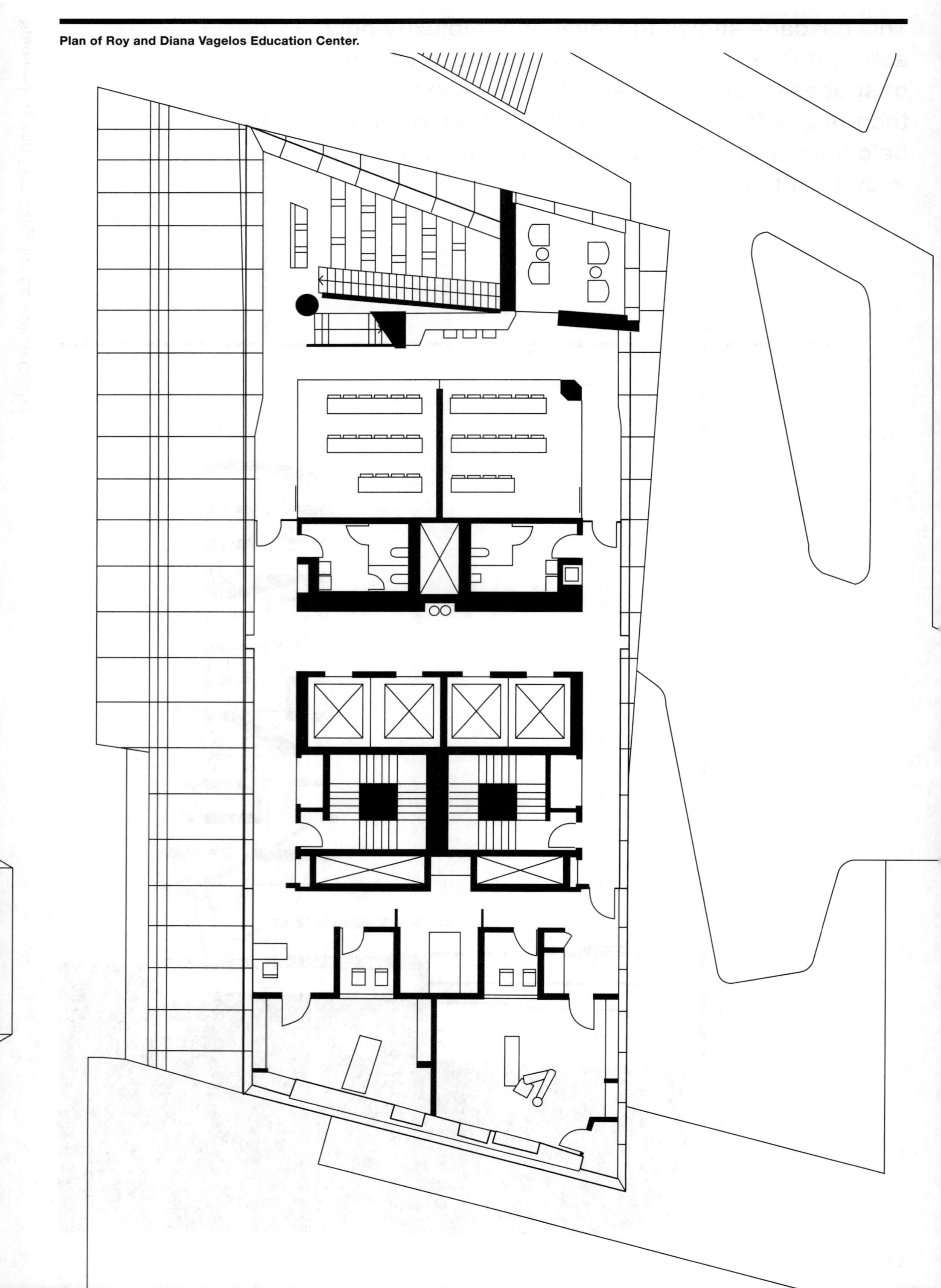

Plan of Roy and Diana Vagelos Education Center.

Endnotes:

1 [p. 759] Alī Ibn Khalaf al-Murādī, *Kitāb al-asrār fī natā'ij al-afkār* (1000 CE) / *The Book of Secrets in the Results of Ideas*, trans. Soha Bayoumi and Ahmed Ragab (Milan: Leonardo 3, 2009).

2 [p. 765] The Third (Communist) International, 1919–1943, was an organization of communist parties dedicated to overthrowing capitalism and revolutionizing work.

3 [p. 765] Quote from Rosmit Mantilla, an LGBT activist and opposition politician in "Downward Spiral: How Venezuela's Symbol of Progress Became Political Prisoners' Hell", Emma Graham-Harrison, *Guardian* (15 September 2017).

4 [p. 770] Joseph Giovannini, "Claude Parent, Visionary Architect of the Oblique, Dies at 93", *New York Times* (29 February 2016). Accessed February 2018.

5 [p. 780] See "From Compound to Community", Nature's Lack of Design, 48–56.

6 [p. 780] The ziggurat represents the replacement of the natural mountains known by the inhabitants of northerly Mesopotamia, near the Caspian Sea. Fernando Vegas & Camila Mileto, "La cultura de la montaña sagrada", *Publicat a Asimetrías* (Valencia: Universidad Politécnica de Valencia, 2006).

7 [p. 783] The principle of entasis was discovered, or perhaps rediscovered, by the builders of the Parthenon at Athens a thousand years later. Leonard Woolley, "Ur: Ancient City Iraq", *Encyclopædia Britannica* website (29 August 2017).

8 [p. 785] Fatema AlSulaiti, "Minaret", *Ancient History Encyclopedia* website (6 February 2013). Accessed 12 October 2018.

9 [p. 789] The Iraqi Ministry of Tourism and Antiquities have reports that the ancient capital of Dur-Sharrukin outside of Khorsabad has been destroyed, March 9 2015. Andrew Curry, "Here Are the Ancient Sites ISIS Has Damaged and Destroyed", *National Geographic* (1 September 2015). Accessed 4 November 2018.

10 [p. 790] The height of Etemenanki is described as seven stocks (91 metres) with a square base of 91 metres in a cuneiform tablet from Uruk from 229 BCE.

11 [p. 792] Juan Luis Fenollós, "La ziggurat de Babylone: un monument à repenser", in *La Tour de Babylone*, Béatrice André-Salvini (ed.), *Documenta Asiana* 10 (2013), 127–146.

12 [p. 795] Fatema AlSulaiti, "Minaret".

13 [p. 798] Jonathan M. Bloom, "The Minaret: Symbol of Faith and Power," *Saudi Aramco World Magazine* 53, no. 2 (March/April 2002), 31.

14 [p. 799] Ibid. 33.

15 [p. 802] See official website of the Rundetårn; and Jens Lauridsen Wolf, *Diarium sive Calendarium ecclesiasticum politicum et occonomicum* (Ecclesiastical, Political and Household Management Calendar), 1648.

16 [p. 809] See "Initiation Well of Quinta da Regaleira", Spiral, 810–813.

17 [p. 810] Both Monteiro and Von Eschwege had strong connections with Brazil where they worked and traded.

18 [p. 813] Hendrik Wijdeveld, "15 Miles into the Earth" (design), NAI Collection and Collection Het Nieuwe Instituut, 1944.

19 [p. 815] Analysis of Fiat Lingotto and the influence of Albert Kahn in *The Path of Kahn* (digital exhibition), Claire Zimmerman, Derek Chang and James Joslin, Taubman College of Architecture & Urban Planning, 2014.

20 [p. 817] While stone ribs carry the vaulted surface in the rib vault, the fan vault is a secondary decorative skin which distributes self-loads throughout its rotated curved surface. Peter Salter, "The Romantic and Pragmatic History of the Fan Vault Has Lessons for Contemporary Structures", *Architectural Review* (21 December 2010).

21 [p. 818] Bjorn Sandaker, Arne Eggen and Mark Cruvellier, *The Structural Basis of Architecture* (London: Routledge, 2011), 176.

22 [p. 820] Le Corbusier quoted in Calum Storrie, *The Delirious Museum: A Journey from the Louvre to Las Vegas* (London: I.B. Tauris, 2006).

23 [p. 821] Beatriz Colomina, "The Endless Museum: Le Corbusier and Mies Van Der Rohe", *Log* 15 (2009), 56.

24 [p. 822] Ibid. 55.

25 [p. 823] Niklas Maak, Charlotte Klonk and Thomas Demand, "The White Cube and Beyond", *Tate* 21 (Spring 2011).

26 [p. 823] Calum Storrie, *The Delirious Museum: A Journey from the Louvre to Las Vegas* (London: I. B. Tauris, 2006).

27 [p. 825] Frank Lloyd Wright to Harry Guggenheim, 15 July 1958, quoted in *Frank Lloyd Wright: From Within Outward* (New York: Solomon R. Guggenheim Foundation, 2009), 268.

28 [p. 830] Guy Debord's *Report on the Construction of Situations*, the founding manifesto of the Situationist International revolutionary organization, talks about the imbecilization of young people and trivialization and sterilization of the subversive, resulting in an emptiness of an art separated from politics. Guy Debord, *Report on the Construction of Situations and on the International Situationist Tendency's Conditions of Organization and Action* (Italy, June 1957).

29 [p. 831] Asger Jorn, "What Is an Ornament?" (1948), in Ruth Baumeister (ed.), *Fraternité avant tout: Asger Jorn's Writings on Art and Architecture, 1938–1958* (Rotterdam: 010 Publishers, 2011), 206; and Asger Jorn, "Formsprakets Livsinnehåll", *Byggmåstaren* 26, no. 17 (1947).

30 [p. 831] Simone Hancox, "Contemporary Walking Practices and the Situationist International: The Politics of Perambulating the Boundaries Between Art and Life", *Contemporary Theatre Review* 22, no. 2 (2012), 237–250.

31 [p. 836] For comparison see the troglodyte dwellings of Matmata, Tunisia in Bury, 158–159. For further information on peristyle Roman dwellings of Bulla Regia and new forms created due to densification in the second and fifth century see Anna Leone, *Changing Townscapes in North Africa from Late Antiquity to the Arab Conquest* (Bari: Edipuglia, 2007).

32 [p. 838] Bernard Zehrfuss speaking at the Ecole du Louvre, 18 May 1981, in Christine Desmoulins, "Bernard Zehrfuss – le Musée Gallo-Romain de Lyon (1969–1975)", *AMC* 23 (December 2015).

33 [p. 868] Per a telephone conversation with HG Merz on Monday 25 March 2019 in which he stated that the set-up, designed by UNStudio, was unanimously seen as the best concept.

34 [p. 870] Press release no. 75, MoMA, New York, 1 July 1961.

35 [p. 871] "ROADS, New Exhibition at Museum Of Modern Art", press release no. 91, MoMA, New York, 15 August 1961.

36 [p. 872] With 300 billion barrels, Venezuela still has the largest confirmed oil reserves in the world.

37 [p. 886] Celeste Olalquiaga, "Tropical Babel", *Failed Architecture* (11 September 2014).

38 [p. 887] Ibid.

39 [p. 887] The 1963 Buchanan Report, later published as *Traffic in Towns*, is discussed in Douglas Murphy, "Notopia: The Fall of the Streets in the Sky", *Architectural Review* (9 June 2016).

40 [p. 890] Alfredo Brillembourg and Hubert Klumpner, "Metro Cable Caracas / Urban-Think Tank", trans. Lorena Quintana, *ArchDaily* (23 September 2013). Accessed 4 October 2018.

41 [p. 910] See "Solomon R. Guggenheim Museum", Spiral, 824–829.

42 [p. 954] See "Lingotto Factory", Spiral, 814–819.

43 [p. 954] "Roy and Diana Vagelos Education Center", Capital project, *Columbia University* website. Accessed 18 January 2019.

Carve

Carve — Encapsulating the void

Space is carved out of the centre of the building to form a new interior landscape. Natural elements of air and light are invited inside and enclosed.

"Space is nothing, yet we have a kind of vague faith in it."[1] —Robert Smithson

Constructing a large open space within a building – be it a grand nave for congregation, a slick atrium to impress those who enter it or a lightwell or courtyard within an urban block to aid ventilation and circulation – has always held a special place in building culture. While a desire to congregate sits at its roots, both the motivation for constructing collective space and the method of doing so make for a tangled tale, where only briefly does the open (yet enclosed) space of a 'void' and the 'mass' of the structure that encapsulates it come into balance before tipping over once again.

This chapter goes back through time to illustrate how small voids once carved from heavy structures transformed into vast voids covered by almost weightless structures. Once weight and span were conquered, the mass of buildings that was once represented by bricks and mortar became synonymous with dense programme. The open space, or public space, of the void was squeezed out in the name of economy and efficiency, and only recently is it being carved back out of buildings.

Treasury of Atreus, Mycenae, 1250 BCE.

In ancient structures of worship, ritual and death, the pragmatic rules of the dwelling simply did not apply.[2] Efficiency was not at stake. On the contrary, the building had to express profound dedication and sacrifice.

The building's performance was a matter of space and light. Its purpose, if any, was to support the gathering of people, and thus providing an unobstructed, large open space – a void within a built structure – was fundamental.

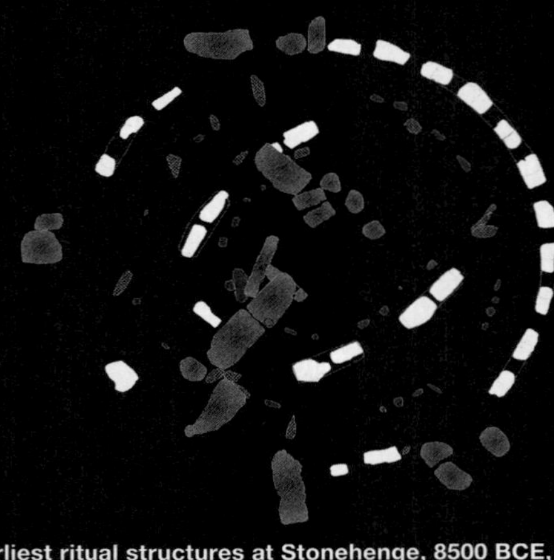

Earliest ritual structures at Stonehenge, 8500 BCE, inner stone pillars and lintels erected c.2100–2000 BCE. Derived from the work of Anthony Johnson.

Constructing a large space that might inspire, amaze, calm or comfort was not simple. Although we built enormous monumental temples as early as 11 500–9000 BCE, it is unlikely we fashioned a structure to span the space they contained. Despite suggestions that the pillars of Göbekli Tepe or Stonehenge may have served as supports for a timber roof, the general consensus is that these ancient ritualistic structures were open to the sky.[3]

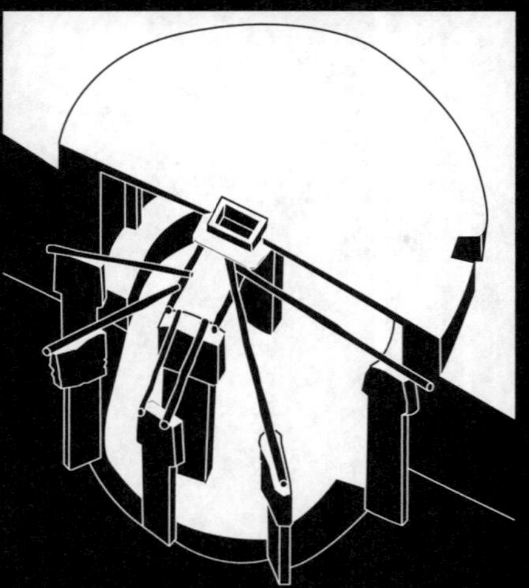

Göbekli Tepe, reconstruction of a wooden roof over structure. B. D. Kurapkat, 2014.

Plan of six structures of Göbekli Tepe, 11 500–9000 BCE. Derived from the work of A. Collins and R. Hale.

Most of the voids within enclosed ancient structures are domestic in scale: a series of small rooms within heavy constructions. The epitome of this is the Great Pyramid of Giza, an almost entirely solid mass with small tombs housed within.

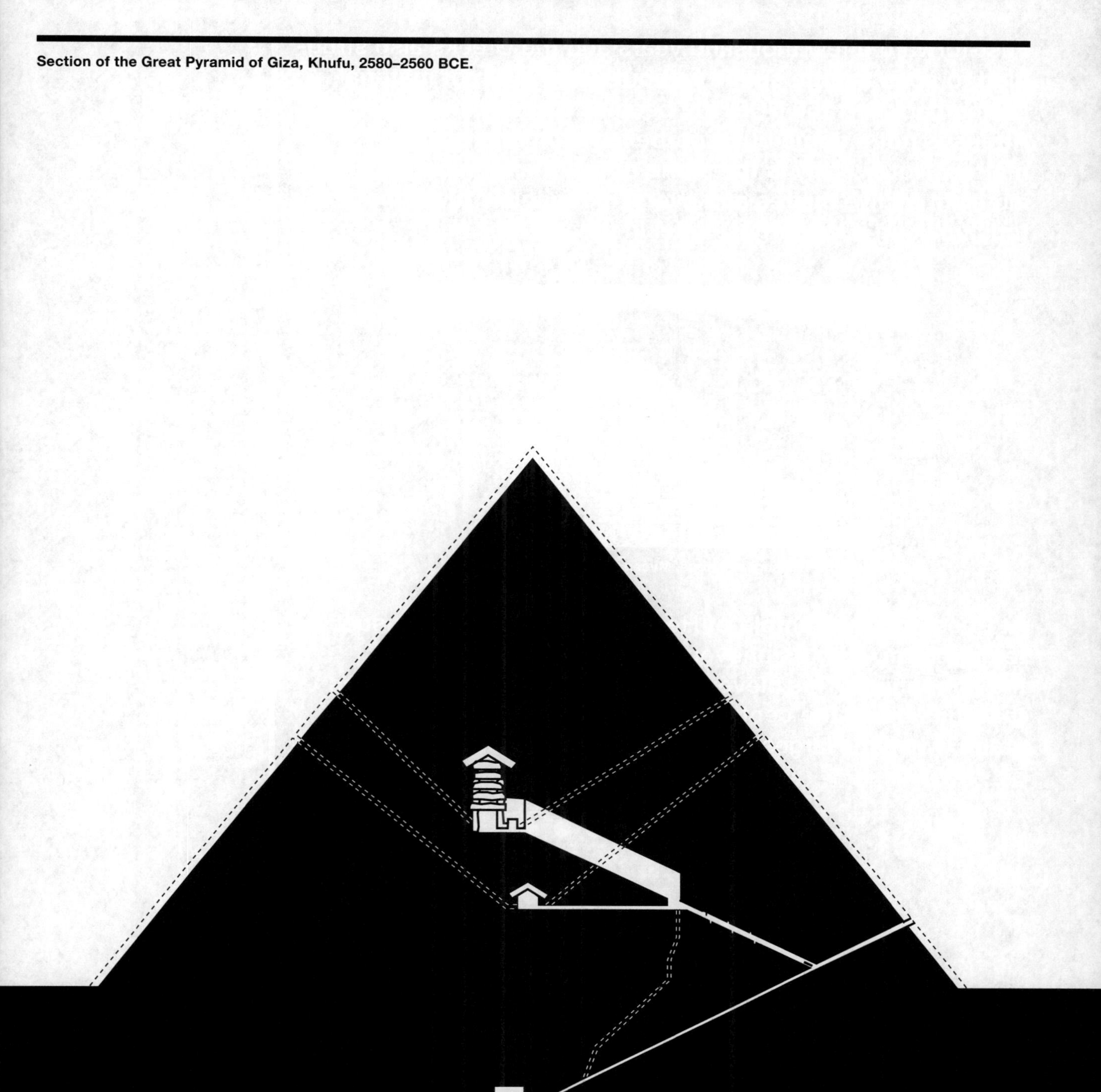

Section of the Great Pyramid of Giza, Khufu, 2580–2560 BCE.

Fast-forward a few thousand years and the Greeks also struggled to span a large space without using a ton of material. Dating back to 1250 BCE, the beehive tomb of the Treasury of Atreus is not a dome but a corbelled arch that spans 14.6 metres. Noteworthy is the stone above the entrance, measuring eight by five metres and over a metre thick. It weighs 120 tons, making it the largest lintel in the world.

Section of the Treasury of Atreus, Mycenae, 1250 BCE.

At Paestum, the Temple of Hera I deviates from the usual temple form, with its uneven number of columns under the tympanum. This cleverly disguises the row of columns that runs down the centre and makes the temple appear grand, when the largest span within is only around five metres.

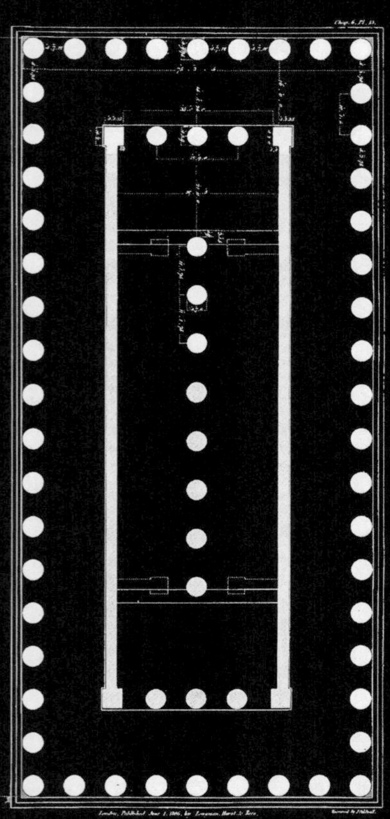

Plan of the Temple of Hera I at Paestum, 550 BCE.

Temple of Hera I from the East. The uneven columns negate the traditional central door.

A few hundred years later, the Romans learned to use mass to their advantage by optimizing the vault, the beam and the lintel. Around 100 BCE, the dome of the Temple of Mercury set an impressive record diameter of 21.7 metres.

The Temple of Mercury at Baiae, Naples, c.100 BCE, held the record for the largest dome until the Pantheon was built.

Photo from the top of the Temple of Mercury's dome.

Section of the Pantheon, S. R. Koehler, 1879. First construction by Hadrian & Apollodorus of Damascus, 29–19 BCE. Rebuilt 113–125 CE.

But nothing really came close to the wonder of the Pantheon. Its record-setting diameter of 43.5 metres stood for more than 1750 years before it was surpassed by a mere 70 centimetres. Undeniably, the Pantheon was a triumph of the Roman concrete revolution. It successfully balances mass and void. The great pressure of material kept the constructive arch in place and in shape, achieving a truly monumental void. It is still the largest concrete dome in the world without reinforcement. Beat that!

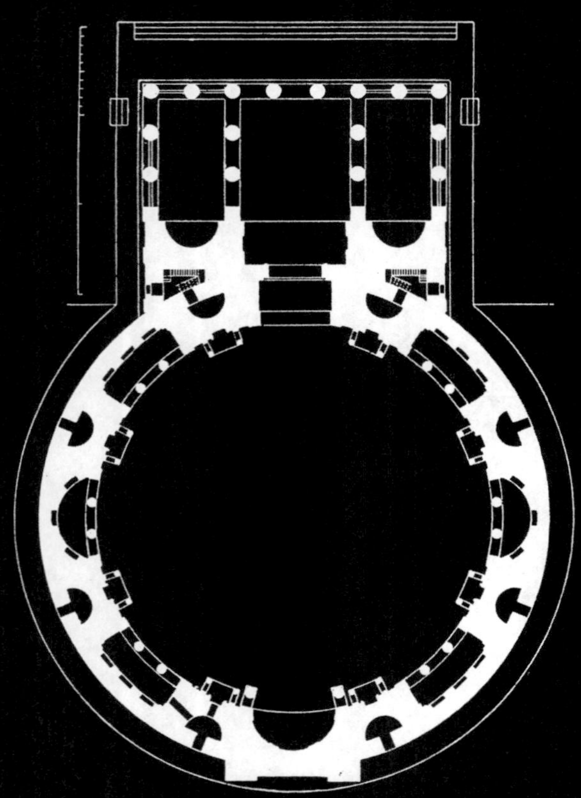

Plan of the Pantheon, Rome.

Interior of the Pantheon, Rome, Giovanni Paolo Panini, 1734.

Surprisingly, many of these buildings had no religious function. The Temple of Hera I was a civic hall, the Temple of Mercury was a public bath and the immense 2000-square-metre column-free space of the Basilica of Maxentius and Constantine was used as a courthouse, council chamber and meeting hall. However, the Romans' successful balancing of mass and void undoubtedly communicated a level of power and resilience. Under Hadrian's reign the Pantheon served as an assembly hall where the public could gather and be reminded of the greatness of Empire (and emperor), satisfying both a symbolic and pragmatic function.

Basilica of Maxentius and Constantine, Rome, c.312 CE. Auguste-Rosalie Bisson, 1861.

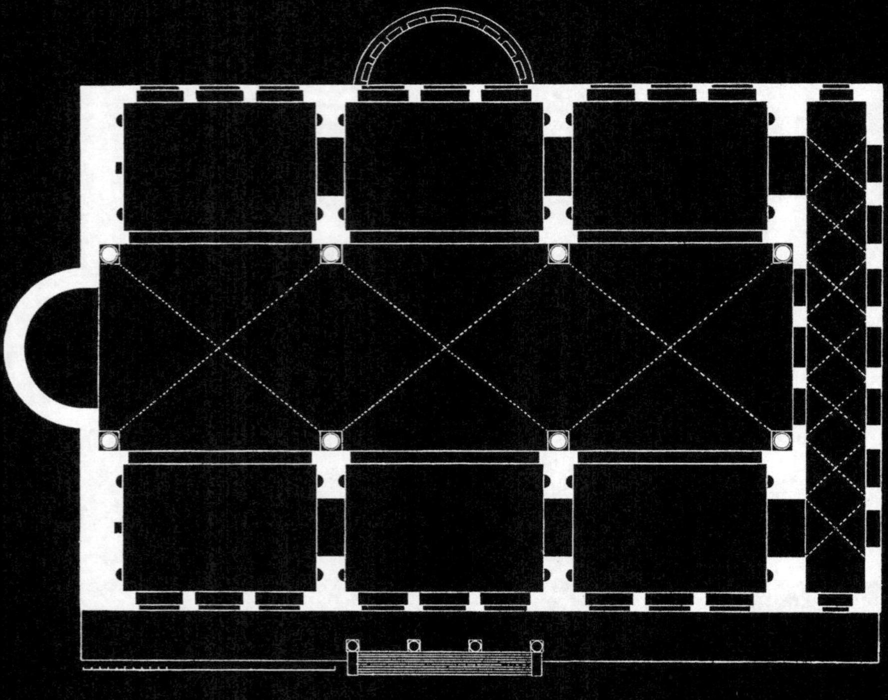

The nave of the Basilica of Maxentius and Constantine is 25 metres wide and 80 metres long.

Just after the first Pantheon was built, Emperor Tiberius had the Villa Jovis built on Capri and appropriated the immense and hypnotic Grotta Azzura nearby as a swimming pool.[4] Perhaps Tiberius knew humankind was no match for master-builder Mother Nature. The spans of dome-shaped caves and overhanging cliffs, created by geological formation in the crust of the earth, amply surpassed human-made constructions. Interestingly, many of the largest-known caves in the world, formed millions of years ago, have only been stumbled upon in recent history. The stunning Son Doong Cave in central Vietnam runs underground for over nine kilometres and could easily fit a sixty-storey building within it. Yet somehow, we failed to notice it until 1991.

Section of Grotta di Seiano, a cave excavated into a 770-metre-long tunnel, Naples, 37 BCE.

Depiction of Grotta di Seiano, Gustaf Söderberg, 1820.

Son Doong Cave, Phong Nha-Kẻ Bàng National Park, Vietnam.

Grotta Azzurra (Blue Grotto), Anacapri, Italy, c.27 CE.

Likewise, a huge cave along the cliffs of Mokattam in Cairo was only rediscovered during groundwork in 1974. Coptic Christians saw this as a godly gift and excavated it, transforming it into a magnificent church, the largest in Africa. Its presence gave inhabitants, known as the *Zabbaleen* ('rubbish collectors of the Cairo megalopolis'), the reassurance to build more permanent houses. Today, 60 000 people live in conditions that are beyond belief, surrounded by piles of waste up to six metres high.[5] It is sobering to witness the stark contrast between the shadowy and spartan spaces in which people live and the grandeur of nearby places of worship.

Upper level of Saint Samaan the Tanner Hall, Mokattam.

Saint Mark's Church, below Saint Samaan the Tanner Hall, Mokattam, 1993.

Rooftops of the high-density slum of Mokattam in Cairo.

Mokattam home, with piles of rubbish out the window.

Each of these fascinating naturally formed spaces reaffirms what the Romans learnt by building the Pantheon. No span without weight.

The quest for large indoor spaces to inspire awe continued during the High and Late Middle Ages, but it wasn't until the Industrial Revolution that the game changed entirely. The hammerbeam roof of Westminster Hall and the flying buttresses of the Gothic cathedral can be seen as the first testing of these skeleton-like structures, as if society had a suspicion enormous spans could be achieved with trusses but lacked the material to carry it out.

Westminster Hall, London, 1097. The present-day roof was built in 1393. Drawn by Thomas Rowlandson and Augustus Pugin for R. Ackermann. *Microcosm of London*, 1808–1811.

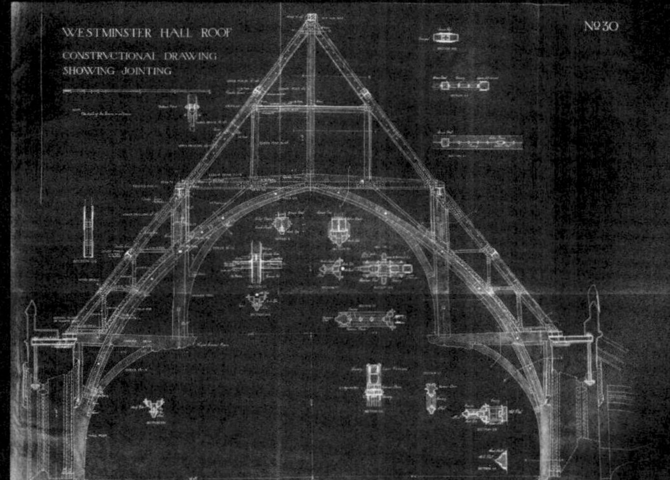

In 1923, Frank Baines of the Ministry of Works saved the roof of Westminster Hall by inserting steel trusses and largely relieving the medieval timber roof of its structural function.[6]

Westminster Hall, one of the oldest surviving structures still in use in Europe, was first erected in 1097. How the roof was supported in the first three centuries is unclear, but in 1393 King Richard II commissioned its hammerbeam roof, which spanned a length greater than the length of any individual piece of timber used.[7] Shorter hammerbeams are supported by arches and greatly depend on the stiffness of their supporting walls. Again, considerable weight is necessary and often the timber structure is distorted by the weight it supports.

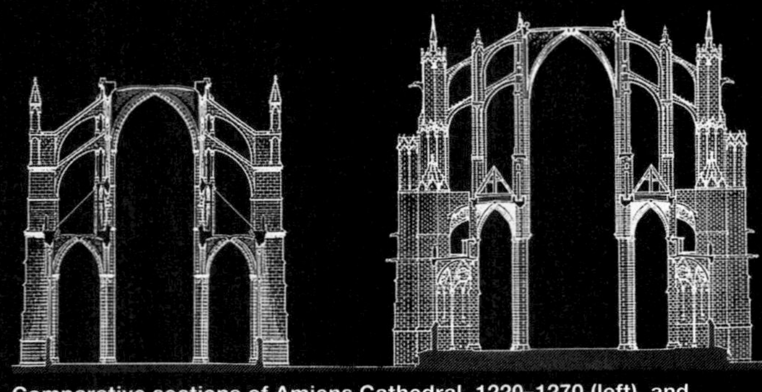

Comparative sections of Amiens Cathedral, 1220–1270 (left), and Beauvais Cathedral, 1225–1284 (right).

Cathedral builders in Amiens and Beauvais competed for the tallest structure, reaching for the heavens with highly experimental works of engineering. Beauvais would have been the tallest structure, if completed, but parts collapsed and the wider central nave was never built. Many Gothic churches showed major defects soon after construction because the lateral forces were not evenly spread over the flying buttresses, vaults and arches. This resulted in collapses, repairs and strengthening with extra flying buttresses and iron reinforcements.

North transept with stained-glass window, Amiens Cathedral, France.

Plan of Amiens Cathedral.

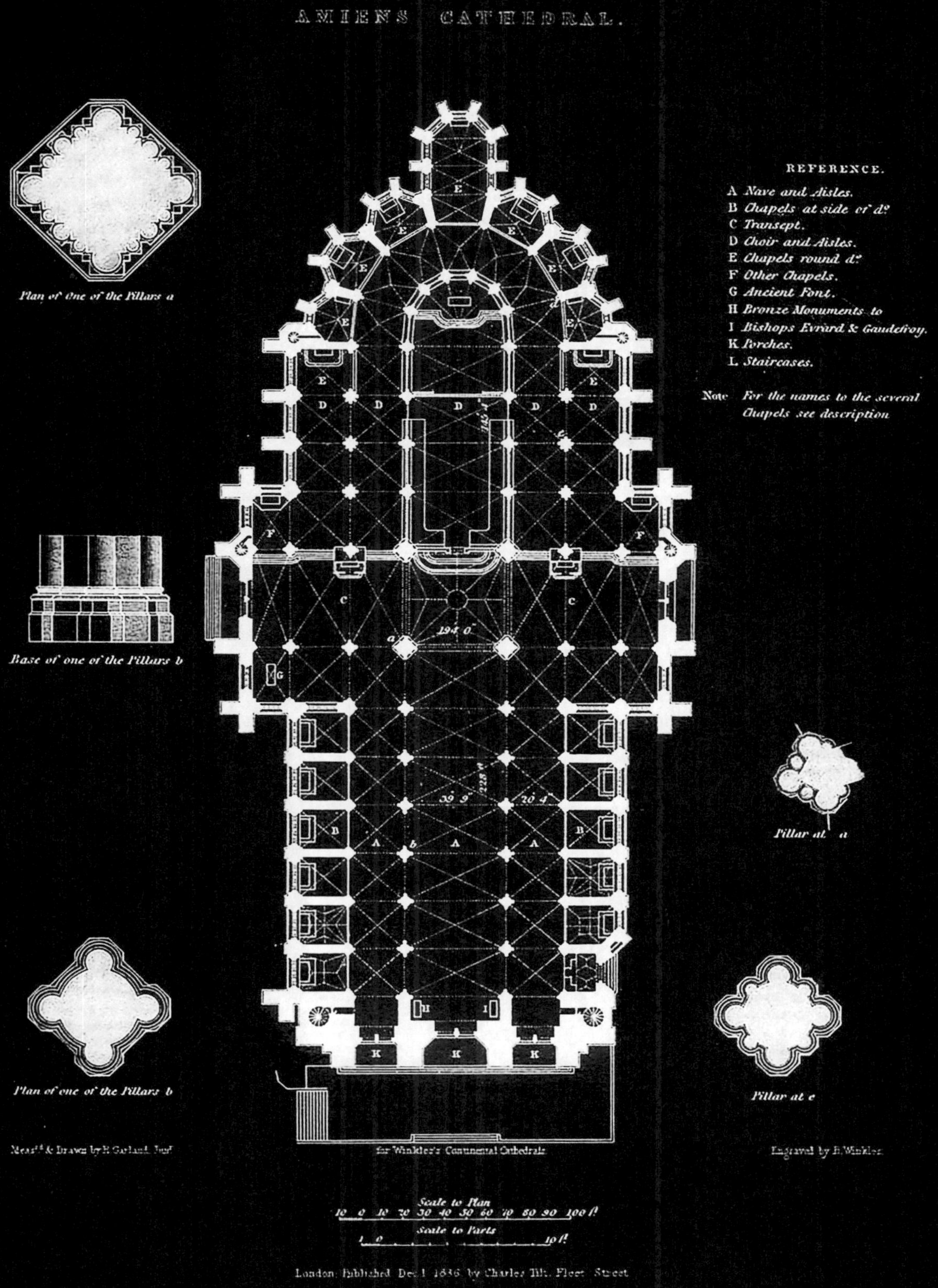

AMIENS CATHEDRAL.

Plan of One of the Pillars a

REFERENCE.

A *Nave and Aisles.*
B *Chapels at side of d°*
C *Transept.*
D *Choir and Aisles.*
E *Chapels round d°*
F *Other Chapels.*
G *Ancient Font.*
H *Bronze Monuments to*
I *Bishops Evrard & Gaudefroy.*
K *Porches.*
L *Staircases.*

Note *For the names to the several Chapels see description*

Base of one of the Pillars b

Pillar at a

Plan of one of the Pillars b

Pillar at c

Meas^d & Drawn by R. Garland, Junr

for Winkler's Continental Cathedrals

Engraved by B. Winkles

Scale to Plan
10 0 10 20 30 40 50 60 70 80 90 100 ft
Scale to Parts
1 0 10 ft

London: Published Dec 1 1836 by Charles Tilt, Fleet Street

During the Renaissance and Baroque periods, architects lost their nerve, reverting to more conventional Greco-Roman structural engineering. Airy, experimental Gothic architecture was abandoned in exchange for more classical certainties.

While inquisitive minds like Leonardo da Vinci, Galileo Galilei and Isaac Newton opened Pandora's box and questioned the foundations of science and mathematics, the engineering of buildings didn't make quantitative progress.[8] Despite the incredible advancements made in this Age of Discovery, architects struggled to achieve a span larger than 20 to 30 metres. The diameter of the Pantheon remained an unsurpassable boundary, and although technologically more advanced, not even Brunelleschi's double-shelled dome in Florence could beat it in 1436.

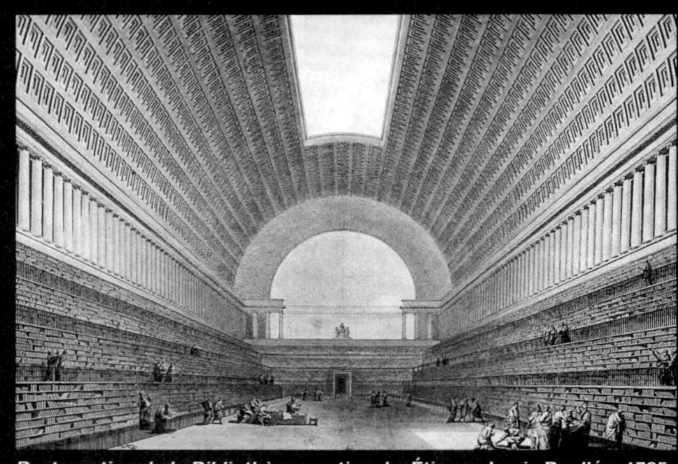

Restauration de la Bibliothèque nationale, Étienne-Louis Boullée, 1785.

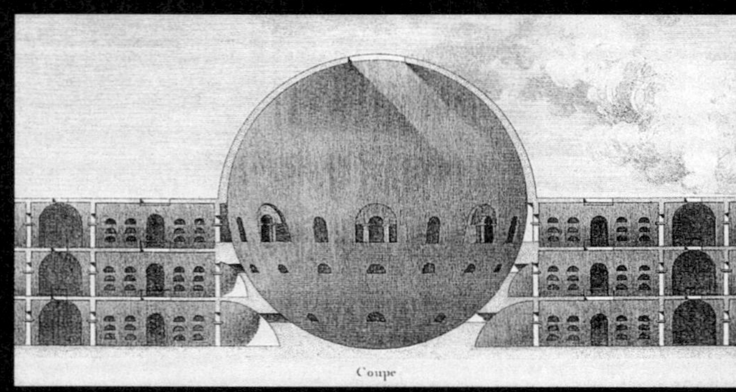

Coupe du Cimetière de la Ville de Chaux, Claude-Nicolas Ledoux, 1773–1806.

However, the neoclassical designs of Claude-Nicolas Ledoux and Étienne-Louis Boullée, among others, lightly skipped 1800 years.[9] Although inspired by the Pantheon, these buildings were not shackled by it. They boldly dreamt of barrel-vaulted ceilings and domes spanning 150 metres. Yet it still took another fifty years before what they knew was possible finally took off.

Interior of the transept of Crystal Palace, Joseph Paxton, 1851.

Nineteenth-century ironwork construction can be seen as a huge leap forward, both technically and aesthetically. The mechanical properties of iron made it possible to span great widths, and the standardization of building components and mass production made it possible to fabricate everything offsite. The most convincing proof of this was Joseph Paxton's Crystal Palace, designed for the Great Exhibition of the Works of Industry of All Nations. It took him less than a year and just under £86 000 to build a greenhouse of almost 72 000 square metres. It was one quarter of the construction budget and twelve times bigger than the brick structure proposed by the exhibition building committee![10]

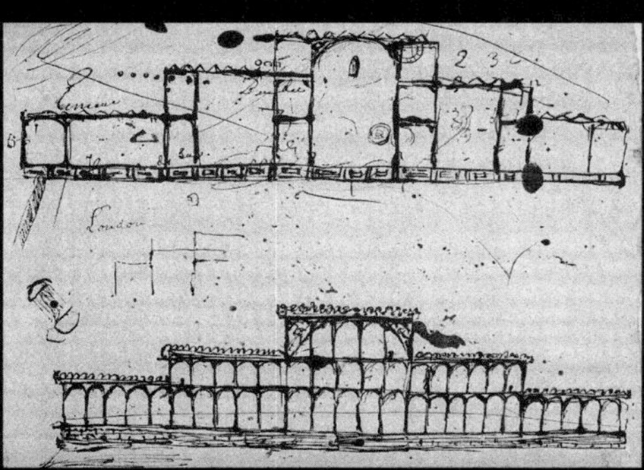

First sketch of Crystal Palace, Joseph Paxton, 11 June 1850.

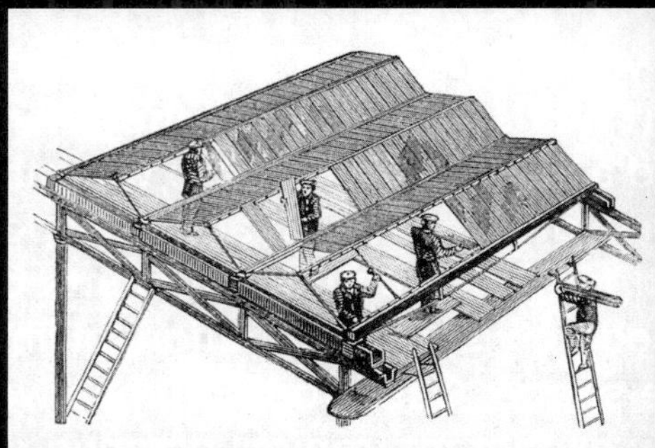

Paxton's patented 'ridge-and-furrow' system has become the standard covering for atria ever since.

Between 1850 and 1900, the free-span race really took off. The maximum span of Paxton's Crystal Palace was 25 metres. By 1869, St Pancras Station conquered 74 metres, and in 1889 the Galerie des Machines reached more then 110 metres.[11] These houses of glass became the basis for twentieth-century modern architecture, for ever altering our conception of space.[12] No longer was the demarcation of space limited to load-bearing walls.

The Great Stove, Chatsworth, Joseph Paxton, 1836–1841.

The privately funded tropical gardens, Jardin d'Hiver, stood south of the largely empty Champs-Élysées, Paris, Meynadier & Rigolet, 1847–1952.

When Charles Darwin visited the Great Stove at Chatsworth he proclaimed that "Art beats nature altogether there".[13] The glasshouse created a new environment of warmth or humidity which could sustain exotic vegetation and transport its visitors to tropical antipodes. Structural elements became so small that they posed no visual obstruction, giving the sensation of one large space. Cast-iron columns were completely camouflaged by exuberant tropical planting or even detailed to mimic palm trees.

Palais de l'industrie, Exposition Universelle, Paris, 1854.

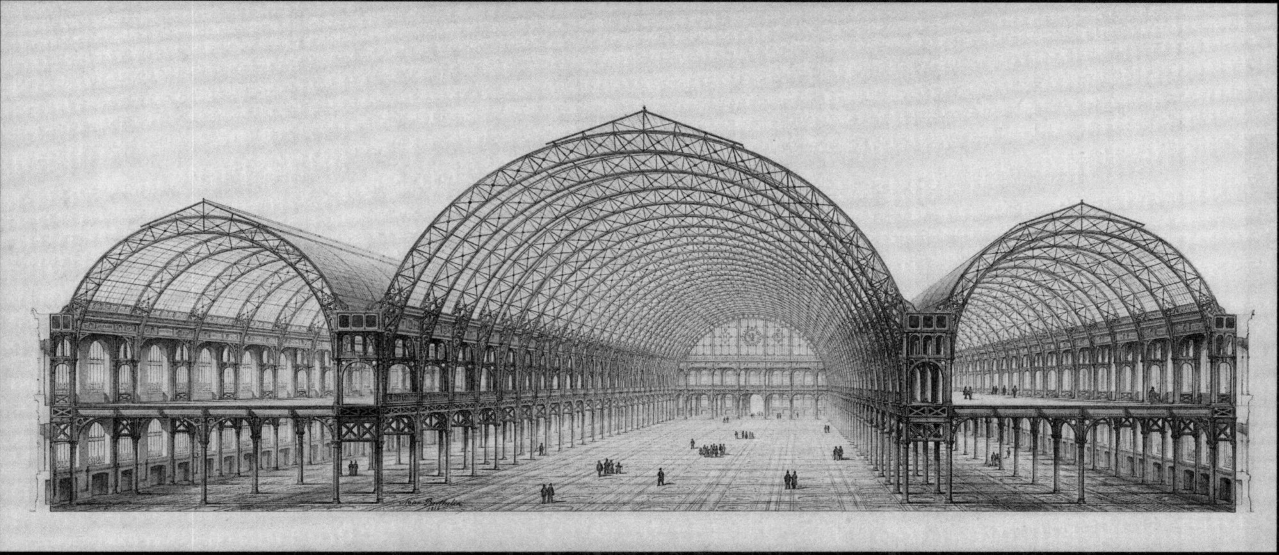

Galerie des Machines, Ferdinand Dutert & Victor Contamin, 1889.

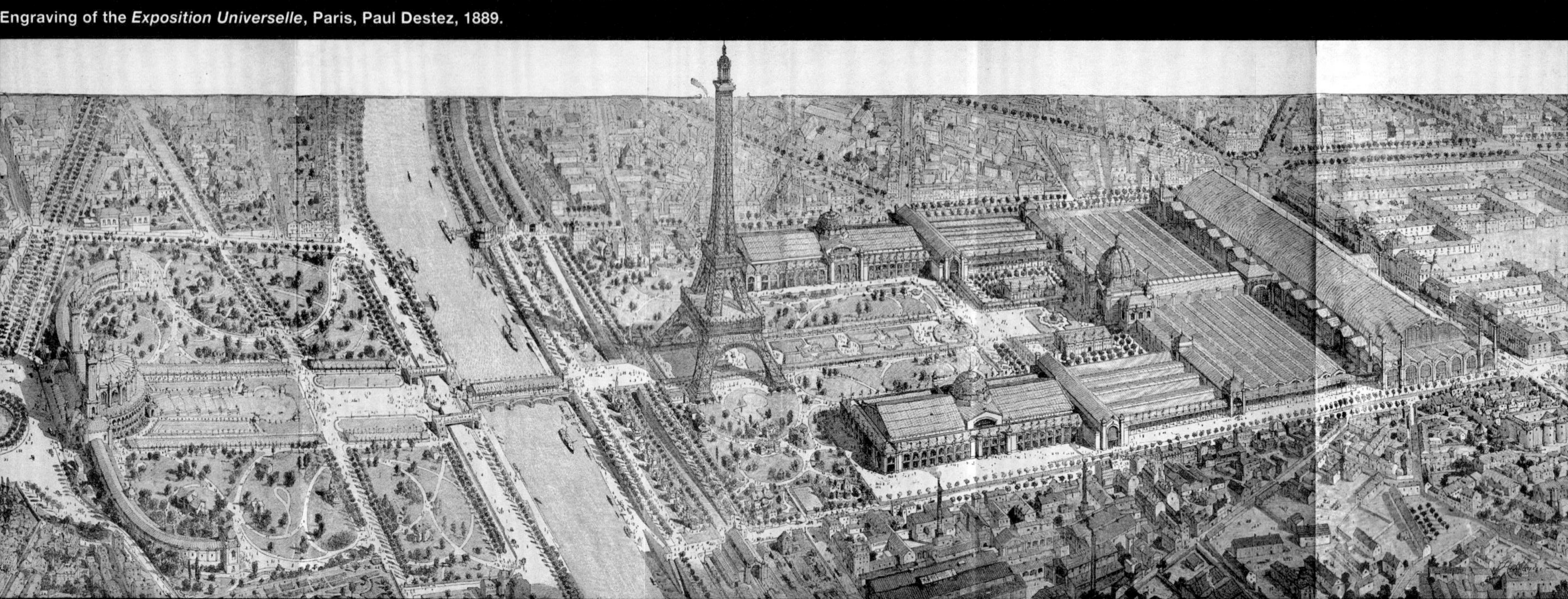

Engraving of the *Exposition Universelle*, Paris, Paul Destez, 1889.

It was the first historic appearance of a space completely filled with light, "a spatial vacuum and yet a room".[14] In solving the 'problem' of mass, architecture had developed a way to gently cover a part of the earth, interiorizing outdoor space with the thinnest transparent membrane.[15]

Sigfried Giedion refers to these buildings as being limitless, and in many ways they were.[16] These endlessly repeatable structures could cover vast distances. The accumulated buildings of the *Exposition Universelle* in Paris between 1850 and 1900 represented the largest amount of free-span interior space at that time.

The efficiency achieved in the construction of the Eiffel Tower shows the incredible sophistication reached by the end of the nineteenth century. If you take all the iron of the Eiffel Tower and spread it over the surface occupied by the tower on the ground, you would have a plate of just five centimetres in height. It is the complete inversion of the Pyramid of Giza, almost all void and no mass. In fact, the air encompassing it weighs more than the Eiffel Tower itself!

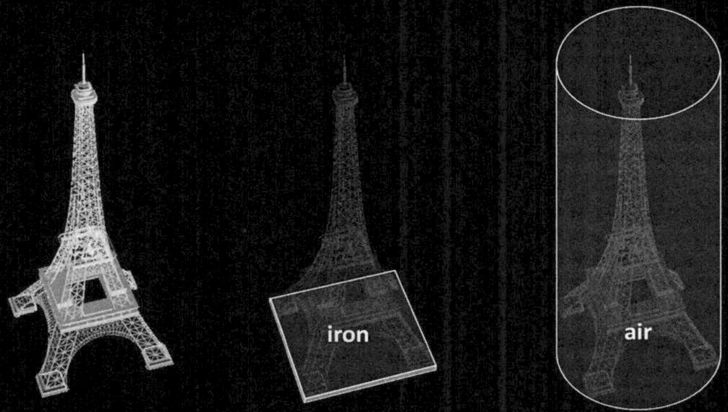

Eiffel Tower, Gustave Eiffel, 1887–1889, measures 124.9 × 124.9 metres in surface area, is 324 metres high, and contains 7300 tons of iron.

The Eiffel Tower marked both the climax and the conclusion of a long development. The great exhibition buildings of England and France had conquered gravity with their almost floating constructions.[17] But enclosing such a large open space with a vast cast-iron structure was expensive. The survival of these exhibition buildings relied on temporary spectacle and the millions of people that might pay to consume their internal world. Gradually, these large structures sought programme to fill their void and prop up their business model. The last exhibition buildings built at the cusp of the twentieth century had lower side wings with commercial facilities and restaurants, almost like a bloated shopping mall.

Throughout the twentieth century, the ancient principle of no void without mass morphed into no void without programme. With steel and concrete and a modernist, functionalist mind-set, large, open public spaces could be built within a building, but a use or function should support this void financially and potentially wrap around it physically. Architecture began experimenting again with the interplay of volumes, but this time the volumes weren't numb masses without interior programme (like the Ziggurat) or bound by massive load-bearing walls (like the Roman Pantheon).[18]

As the light structure was filled with programme, mass and void had to renegotiate.

Österreichische Postsparkasse (Austrian Postal Savings Bank), Otto Wagner, 1906.

At first glance, Otto Wagner's Österreichische Postsparkasse (Austrian Postal Savings Bank) looks like a traditional Viennese building block, perforated by five big light courts in a very functionalist way. But on closer inspection, one sees that it has swallowed a miniature Crystal Palace. The luminous public banking hall intrudes on the adjacent office wings on all sides, while from within, its translucent skin conceals the surrounding mass.

Section showing the relationship between banking hall and surrounding offices in the Österreichische Postsparkasse.

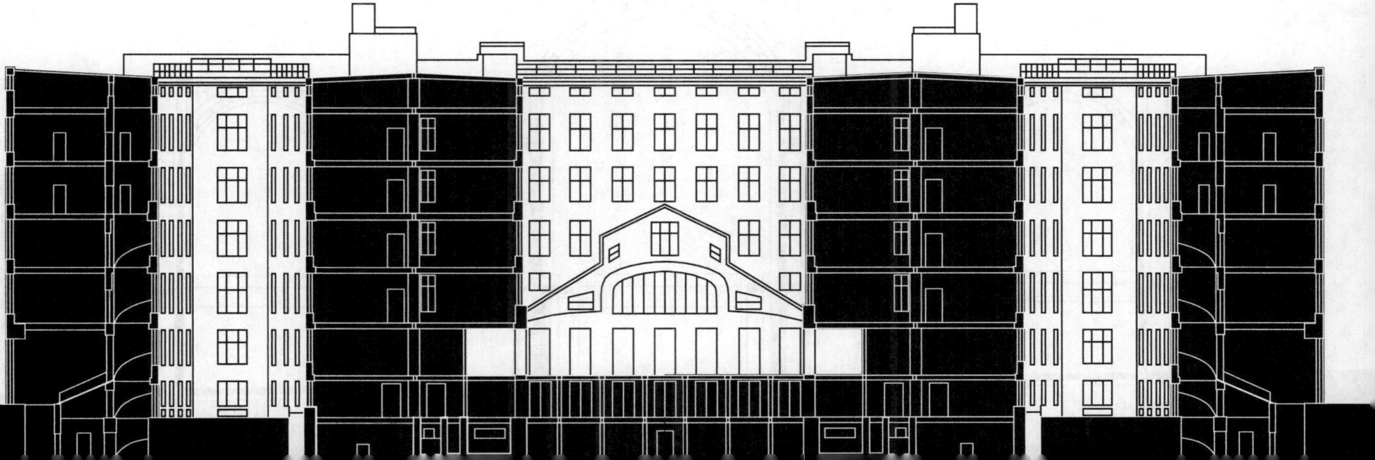

Section of Mercado de Abasto, Buenos Aires.

Mercado de Abasto, Buenos Aires, Viktor Sulčič with José Luis Delpini and Raúl Bes, 1931–1934.

Both the Mercado de Abasto of Buenos Aires and the Great Workroom of the Johnson Wax Headquarters represent a highly innovative approach to the balancing of mass and void. Mercado de Abasto is a fusion of a Gothic cathedral and the Crystal Palace, with light filtering through its vaulted rib-like canopy. It sits atop three layers of infrastructure with streets, loading bays and parking. The Great Workroom of the Johnson Wax Headquarters is naturally lit from clerestory windows above a series of concrete columns, which Frank Lloyd Wright referred to as 'a glade of trees'.[19] At their base, each dendriform column is only 23 centimetres wide, fanning out to 5.5 metres at the ceiling two storeys above.

The Gothic vaulted ceiling of Bath Abbey built by George Gilbert Scott in 1539 (left), and the glazed ceiling of the Mercado de Abasto, Viktor Sulčič, 1931–1934 (right).

The Great Workroom sits within an almost blind brick box of the Johnson Wax Headquarters.

The Great Workroom of Johnson Wax Headquarters.

In his book *The Radiant City*, Le Corbusier lamented that everything was driven by money, but he refused to accept that the cramped, polluted, inefficient urban realm was the natural habitat of machine-age human beings. For Le Corbusier, the troublesome city centre should be radically rebuilt to support new growth. Buildings should be taller and spread out, so the city could be as green as the countryside. The equation was simple: more height for more space.

These ideas were adopted, though not as Le Corbusier predicted. While buildings rose skywards, the dense city centre remained intact. Open space was not carved out of the city centre and the countryside was not let in. On the contrary, new suburbs spread outward, hemming in and choking the city centre.

Furthermore, an unprecedented growth in infrastructure and technology made the city infinitely more complex. Commercial and leisure spaces diversified and cinemas, theatres, swimming pools and sports halls, along with parking garages and metro stations, were squeezed into the city centre. The modernist principle of separating functions started to look bizarre, and so architects (and developers) began searching for a way to economize all of these new programmes within limited space.

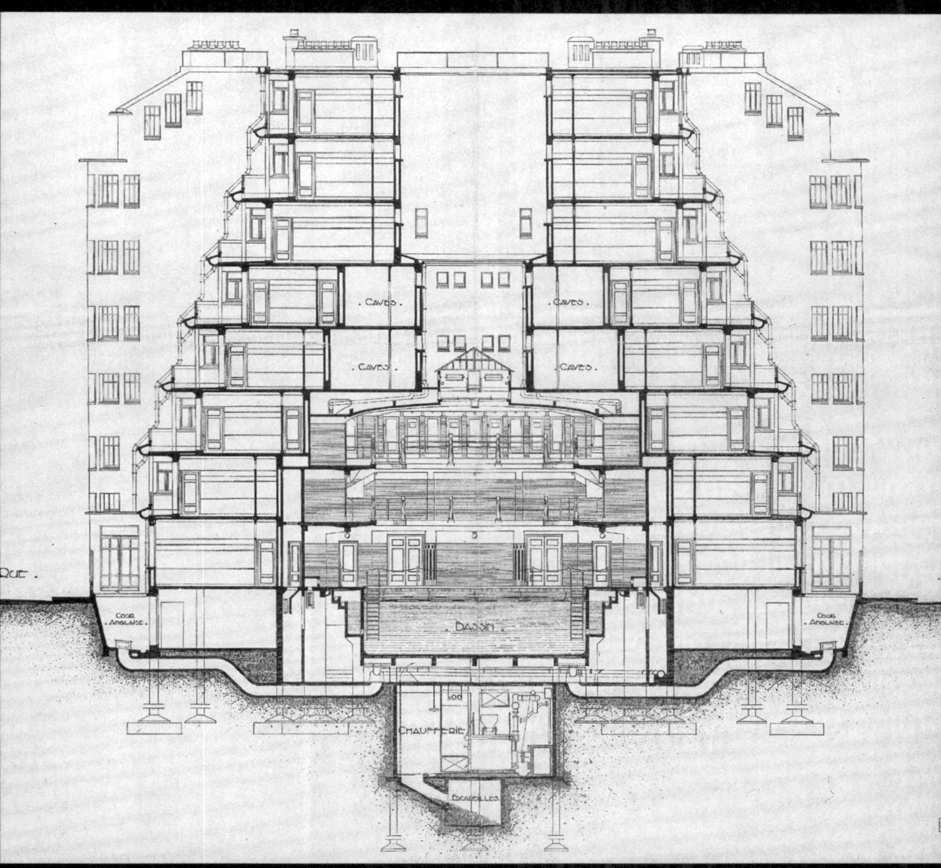

Section of Piscine des Amiraux, Paris, Henri Sauvage, 1922–1927.

The best version of this involved combining different programmes within a single building. A perfect example is the Piscine des Amiraux, where a set-back housing typology and a public pool are merged within a Parisian block to maximize light, air and floor area. Here, mass and void negotiate a mutually beneficial exchange. One programme is carefully sculpted around another to optimize space and satisfy the spatial needs of both.

Economizing space and programme was not always so well considered. If you take the articles of Ada Louise Huxtable, legendary architecture critic of *The New York Times*, as a litmus test for the zeitgeist, commercial forces through the mid-twentieth century waged an unrelenting war. In the name of economy and efficiency, airy iron and steel structures were simply filled with maximum programme. Buildings became tighter and tighter as developers squeezed out all the void to maximize rentable space. The peak modern building was reduced to a blunt stacking of floors, reaching as high as planning permits and budget would allow.

Five stages of the One Times Square building, later the Allied Chemical Corporation building (left to right): under construction in 1903, unveiling in 1905, recladding in 1964, unrealized proposal in 1985 by the artist Christo, and finally fully billboarded in 2003. A perfect showcase of the real forces in the development of cities.

Luckily, there was acknowledgement that the extreme quantities and densities that this model represented were not sustainable, and as the pressure on space within the city became so great, something snapped. Buildings began to compensate for a spaciousness once lost. Large atriums, central courtyards and vertical glasshouses were carved out of buildings. Though there were compromises and negotiations along the way, mass and void have been coming back into balance ever since.

The Ford Foundation, New York City, Kevin Roche John Dinkeloo and Associates, 1963–1968.

The projects on the following pages engage mass and void in various ways and to varying degrees. While some voids sit within a hermetic mass, others are physically cut from the building envelope to create a semi-outdoor space of ample shade and ventilation. The carving of void can be both physical and programmatic. It can be an open space punctured directly through the centre of a building, or it can be the central collective space to congregate in, with a mass of private programme carefully sculpted around it.

The Whitney Museum, New York City, Marcel Breuer, 1964–1966.

Today, projects levitate mass, using the full potential of the airy frame to pull the building off the ground, as Le Corbusier had once intended. The multilevel connections between building and ground, the covered plazas, the bold cantilevers and urban porousness that struggled under Brutalism are now being celebrated.

More and more, we see that the real quality of the carved building lies in how it manages the threshold between inside and outside and between building and ground.

Piscine des Amiraux
Paris, FR
Henri Sauvage
1922–1927

996

MASP
São Paulo, BR
Lina Bo Bardi
1956–1968

1004

Indian Institute of Management
Ahmedabad, IN
Louis Kahn
1963–1974

1012

The Ford Foundation
New York City, US
Kevin Roche John Dinkeloo and Associates
1963–1968

1018

Westin Bonaventure
Los Angeles, US
John C. Portman
1974–1976

1054

Villa KBWW
Utrecht, NL
SeARCH & MVRDV
1994–1998

1072

IJdock
Amsterdam, NL
SeARCH
1999–2013

1076

Synagogue LJG
Amsterdam, NL
SeARCH
2005–2010

1088

Piscine des Amiraux
Paris, France
Henri Sauvage
1922–1927

In many ways the Piscine des Amiraux is a great little modernist machine. Highly functionalist, it takes two programmes and combines them for economy and efficiency. Housing takes the prime spot on top, with each floor receding in size and stepping backwards to maximize light, air and a feeling of space. Wrapping housing around the perimeter of the urban block left a large void at its core, a fine spot for all the new technology now available, like the lift, personal storage, automatic trash chutes, central heating or perhaps a function to support a truly modern residential building. This central space could have been a cinema, a theatre or shops, so why choose a swimming pool?

Site plan of Piscine des Amiraux.

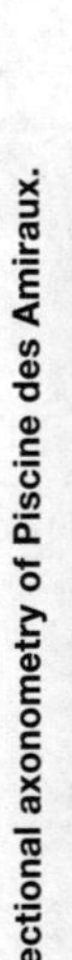

Sectional axonometry of Piscine des Amiraux.

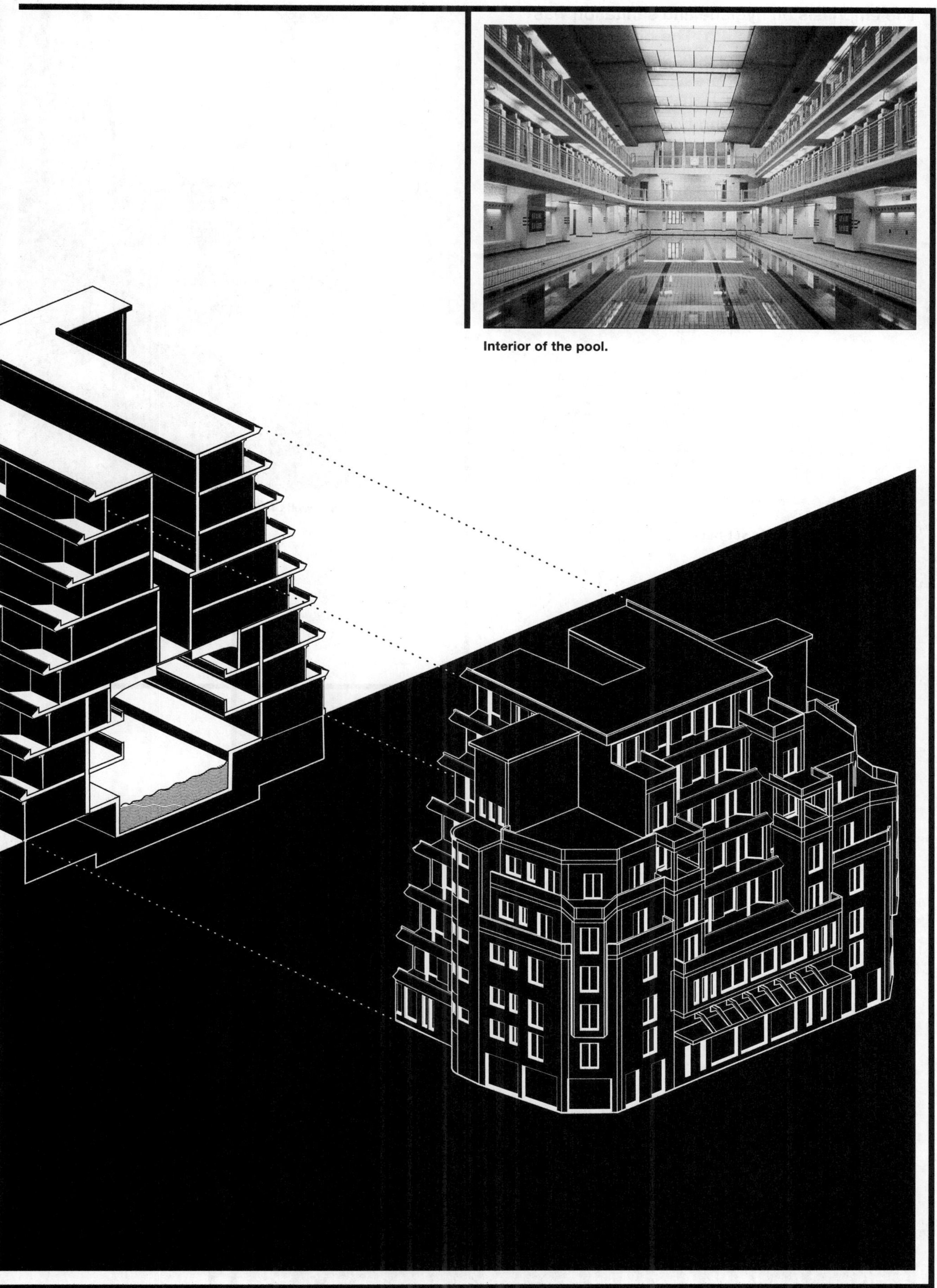

Interior of the pool.

The emphasis on hygiene and sanitation was representative of the era. The beginning of the twentieth century saw a concerted effort to reform or cleanse the oppressively filthy and congested industrial city.[20] Housing was a machine and the set-back building type developed by Sauvage and Charles Sarazin was a great example of technology that could raise living standards. Sauvage and Sarazin were so confident in the value of their set-back building method that they patented it in 1912.

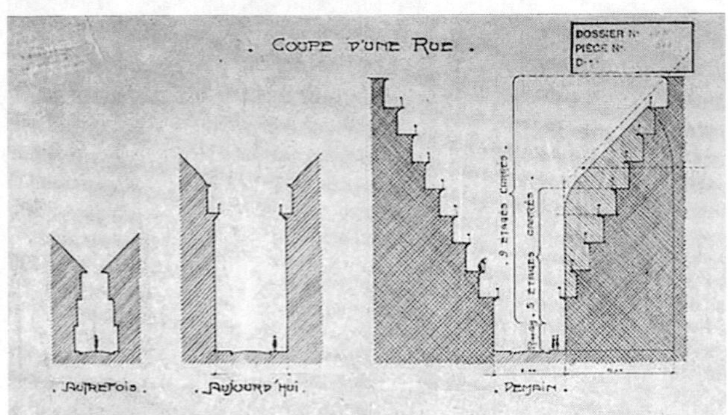

Street section illustrating set-back.

Light well of Piscine des Amiraux.

In its section, the central leftover space created by stepping floors backwards stands out. What makes the Piscine des Amiraux interesting is how Sauvage optimizes this potentially dead space. The apartments and the pool are not numb masses; there is an interplay and mutually beneficial relationship between the two volumes.

Balconies of Piscine des Amiraux.

Short section of Piscine des Amiraux.

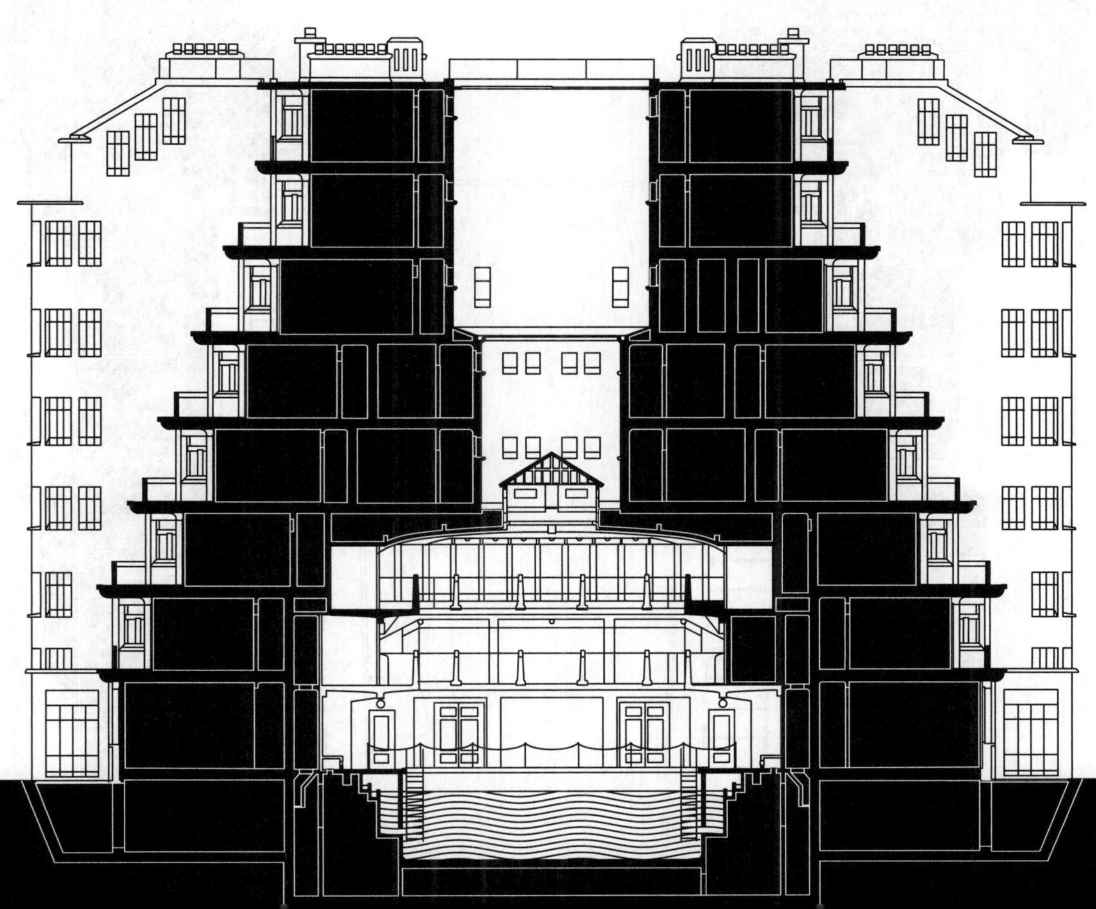

Lower plan of Piscine des Amiraux.

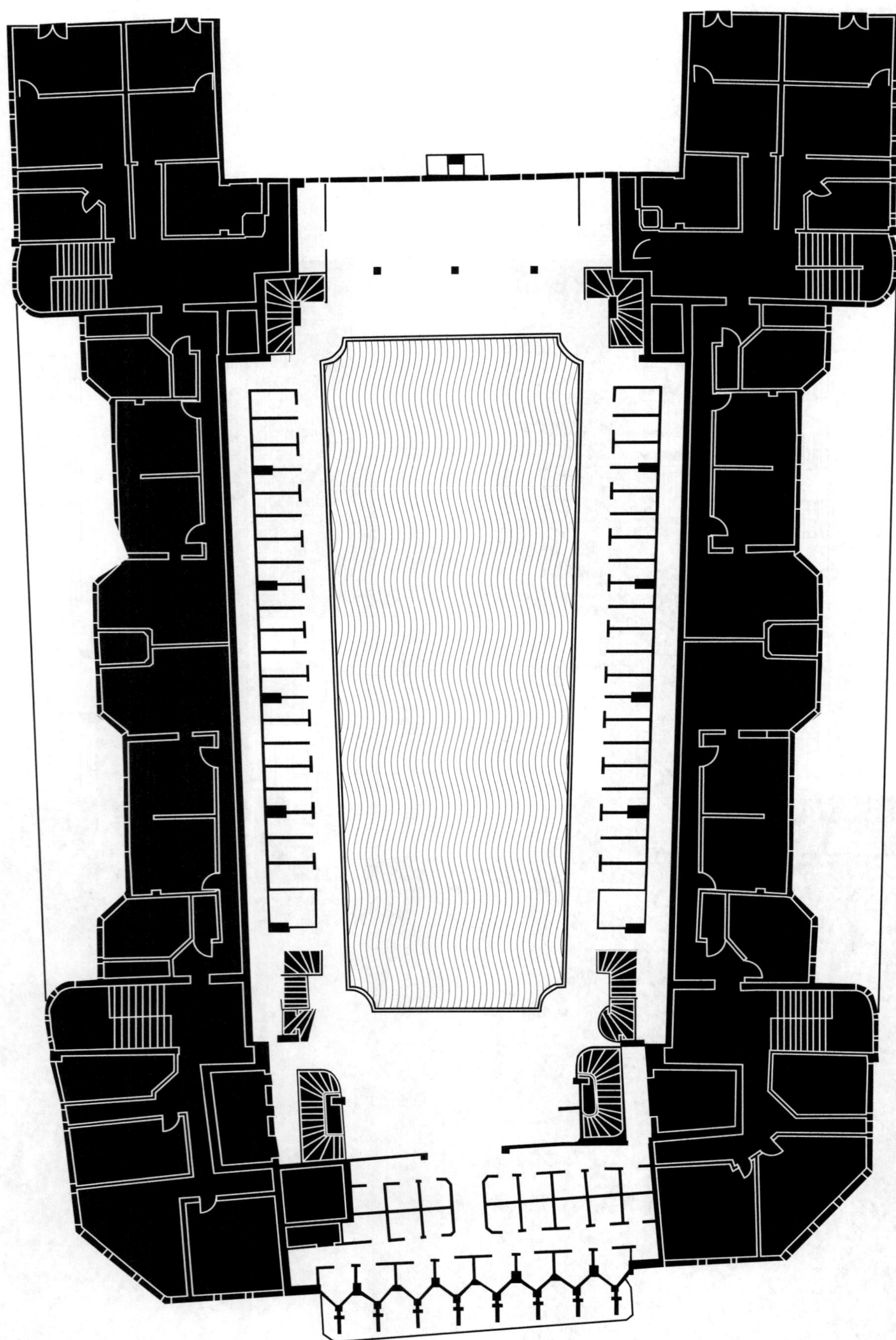

Upper plan of Piscine des Amiraux.

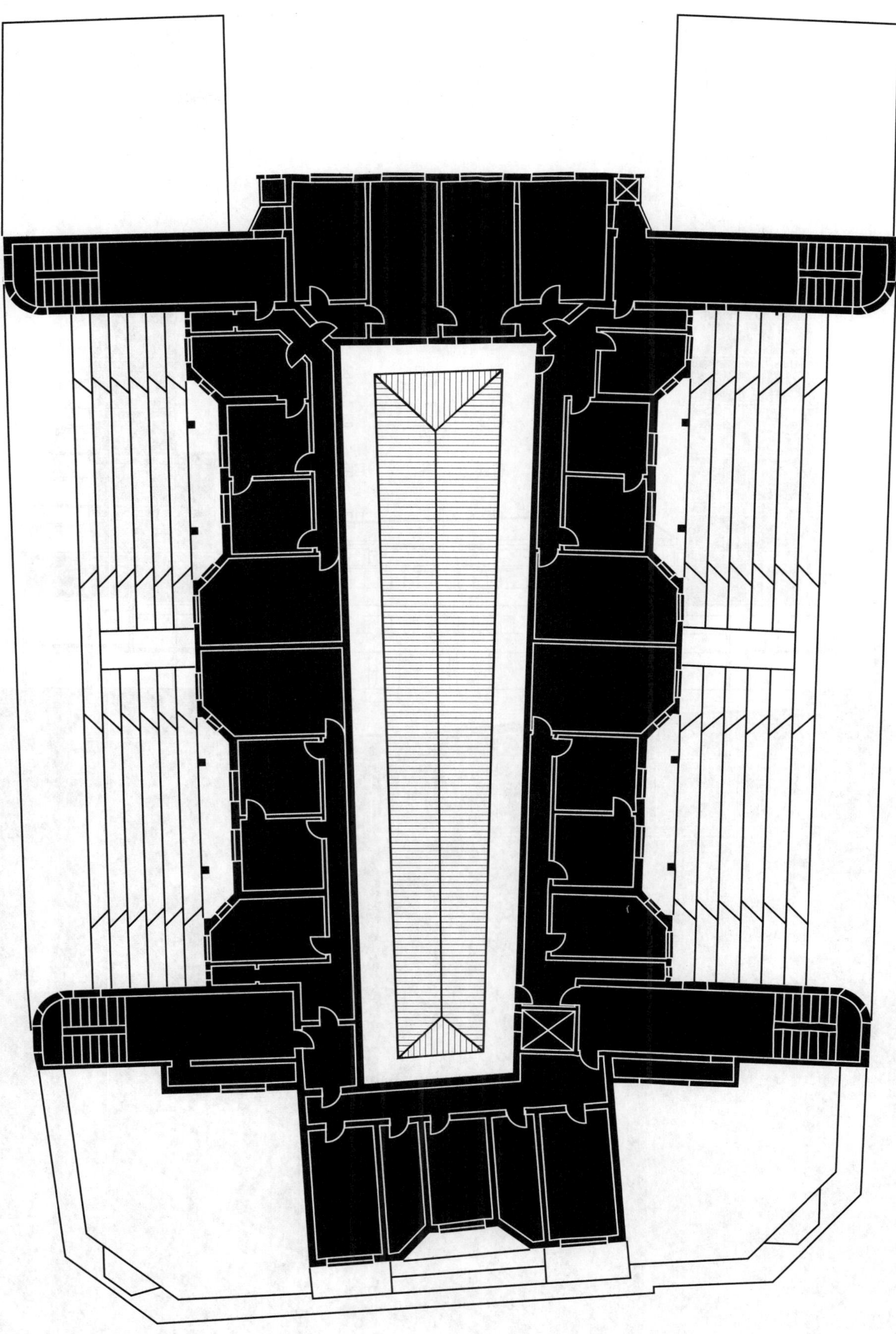

Long section of Piscine des Amiraux.

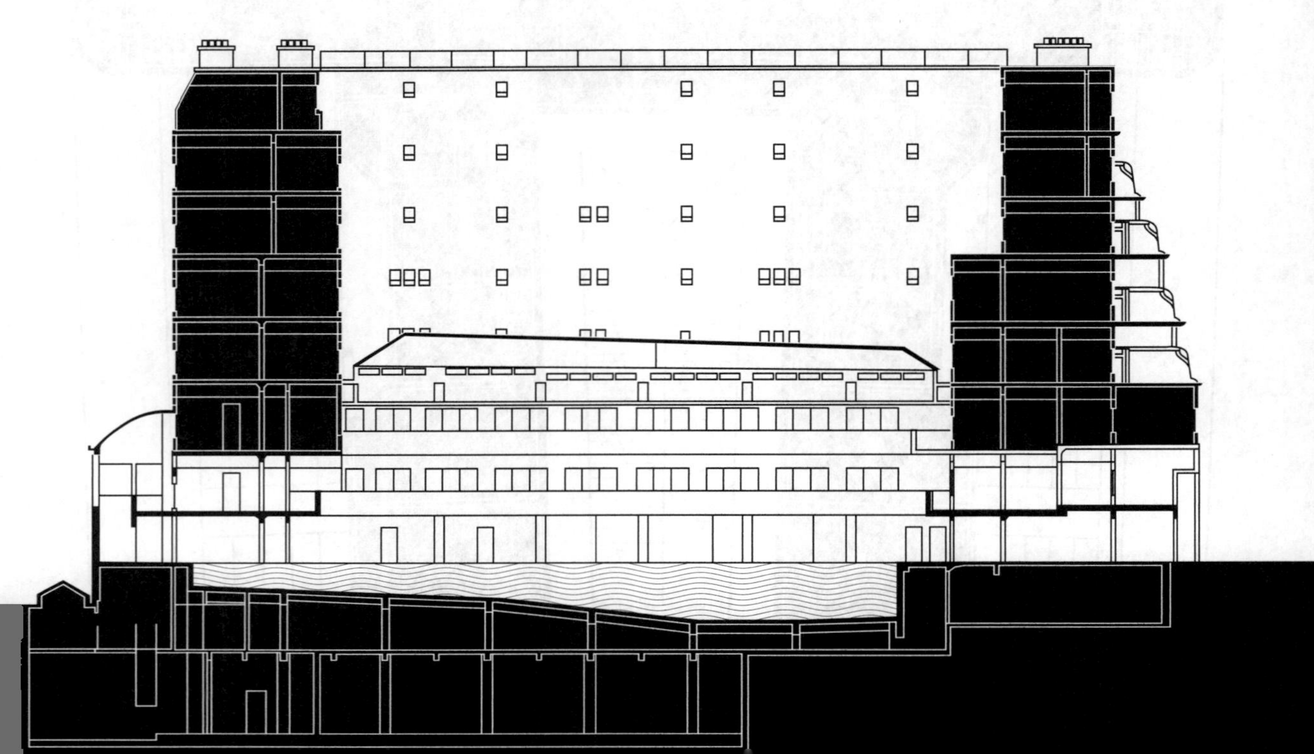

Soon after being developed, this building typology was blown up to utopian proportions. Adolf Loos designed the Grand Hotel Babylon, a double pyramid with two vaulted spaces carved from the centre. This inspired Sauvage to dream up two more mountains with treasures hidden in their walls. This giant hotel would have been 70 metres high with 1300 rooms, six restaurants, four tennis courts, a hammam, an Olympic swimming pool and a theatre or cinema.

Grand Hotel Babylon, Nice, Adolf Loos, 1923.

Giant Hotel, Paris, Henri Sauvage, 1927.

University of East Anglia, Halls of Residence, Sir Denys Lasdun, 1964–1968.

This typology is revived now and again. In the 1960s, Denys Lasdun related buildings to 'hills and valleys' with towers, terraces and platforms forming the generic features of an 'urban landscape'. Today, architects and developers are warming to the intrinsic value this typology offers. Maybe architecture is becoming sculpted again.[21]

MASP
São Paulo, Brazil
Lina Bo Bardi
1956–1968

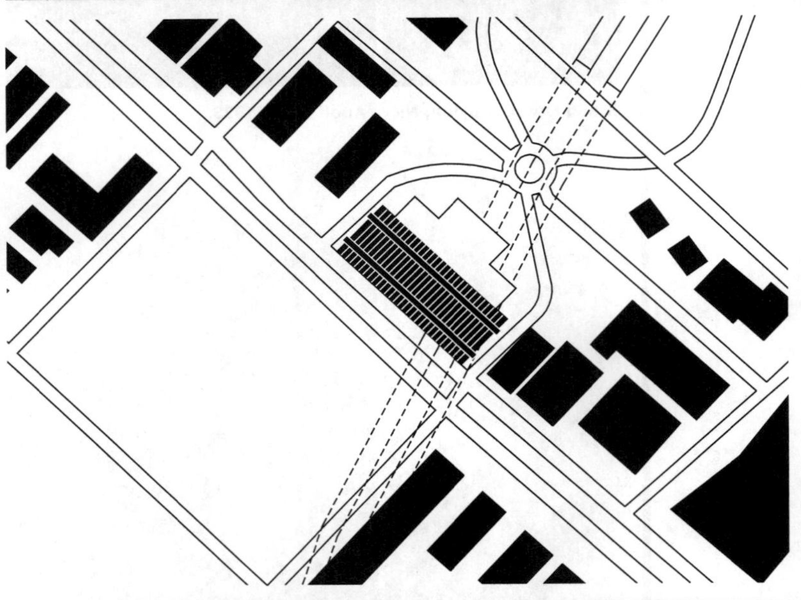

Site plan of MASP.

Axonometry of MASP.

The works of Lina Bo Bardi exhibit one of two highly distinctive features: either a modernistic, levitating airiness or a rocky, *béton brut* appearance which intertwines with the urban roughness or lush vegetation of its context. Her house Casa de Vidro hovers above, while SESC Pompéia or Coaty Restaurant bears downwards, incorporating natural elements of water and greenery.[22]

But the São Paulo Museum of Art (MASP) is a combination of the two. Modernist, open-plan floors and fully-glazed facades combine with a brutalist concrete structure that has a massive split through its midsection. Half the building is buried below the Trianon Terrace and the other half is lifted into the sky, making use of a substantial height difference across the site.

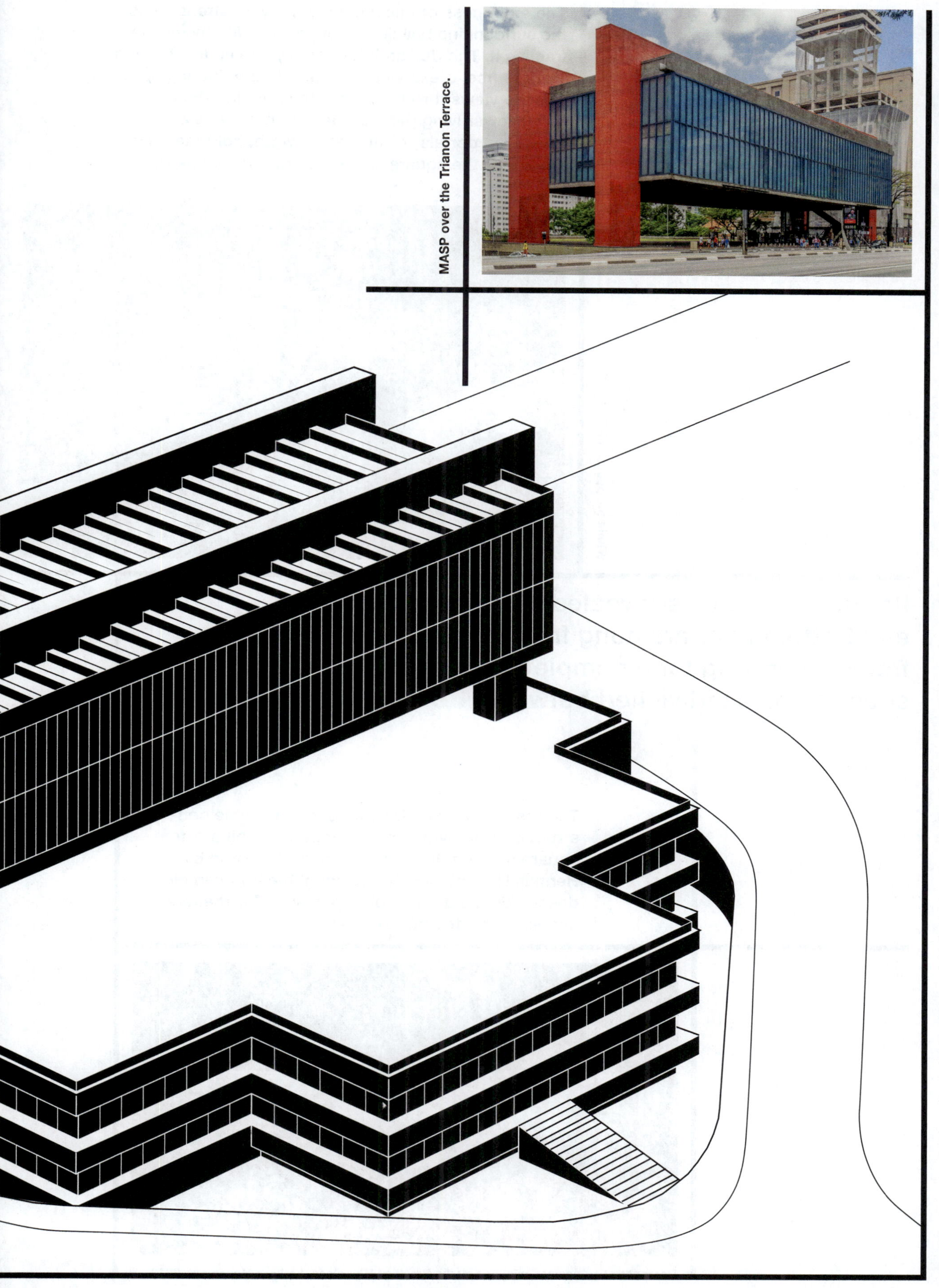

MASP over the Trianon Terrace.

The emptiness of this monumental void strengthens the surrounding buildings, connecting with the city by framing it. The design intentionally leaves the Trianon Terrace free, preserving this important gathering space and the views through it from the Avenida Paulista to the lower-lying parts of the city. Two oversized, bright-red portals, 70 metres in width, hold the building above the square like an enormous billboard.

Within the public void of MASP.

Its true ingenuity is revealed in section. The roof and bottom floor are hung from the two portal frames, allowing for a completely open exhibition space to be sandwiched between.

The result is a complete absence of visible construction from within and a generous column-free square under a flat canopy below. As noted by Herman Hertzberger, the weight of the levitated block doesn't create a sense of oppression.[23] It shelters and supports the human scale.

Demonstration against evictions by the Brazilian Homeless Workers Movement, 2013.

Long section of MASP, showing the hovering mass.

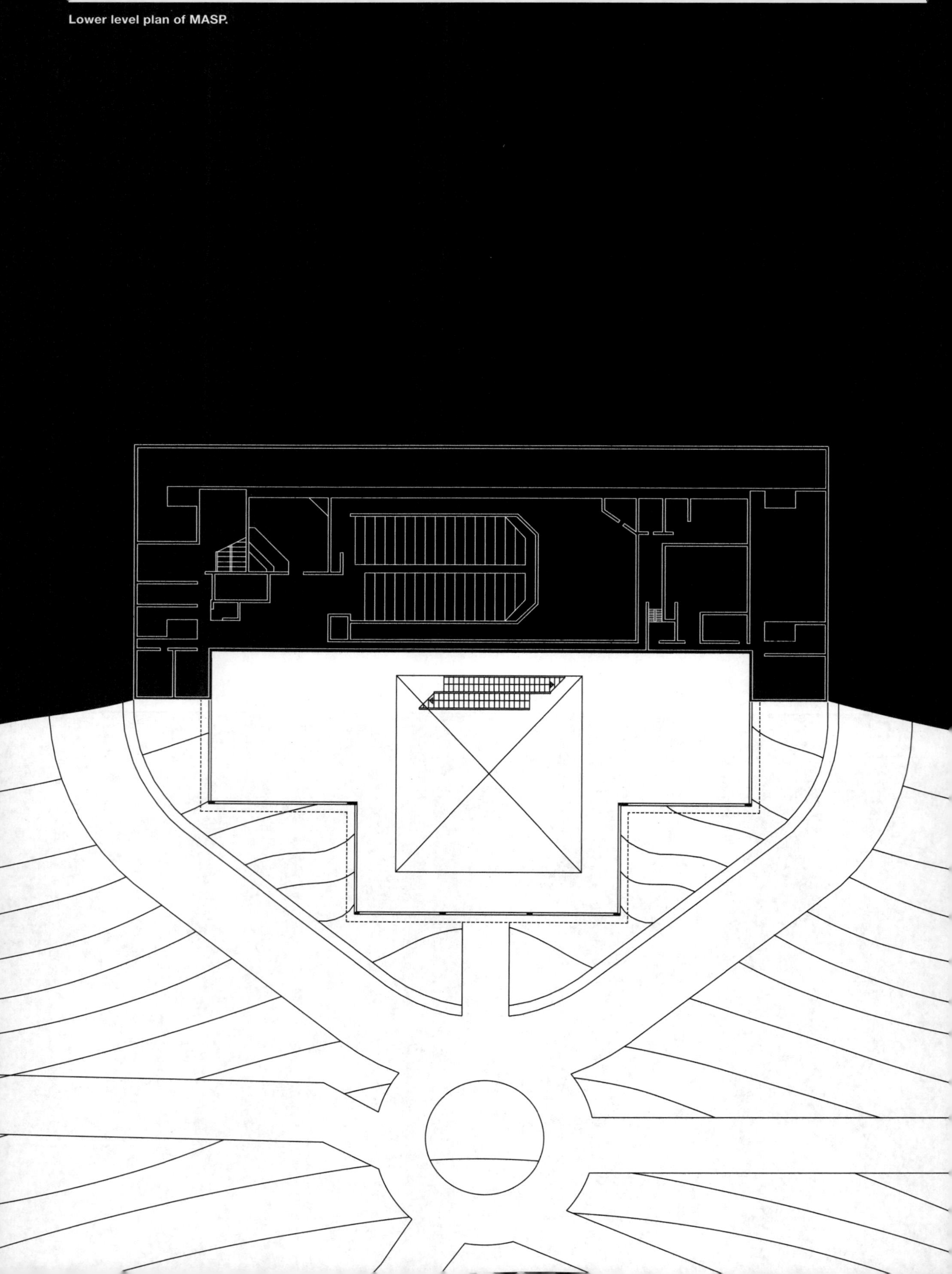

Lower level plan of MASP.

Lina Bo Bardi was as concerned with this urban space as she was with the museum itself. In one of her paintings is a circus-like set-up on the terrace, bordered with plants. They are the only elements that have colour, while the museum acts as a neutral background, a huge gate giving access to a place with endless possibilities.

Lina Bo Bardi's watercolour painting of the Trianon Terrace, 1965.

Within the levitating block.

There is a deliberate absence of institutionalized culture on the square. It is a space for overlapping informal programmes, occupied by market hawkers, protest marches and dawdling tourists. In many ways the museum is subservient to the void. Bo Bardi pushes the museum's programme above and below, giving over the largest space to the city. The only interference is when museum visitors are pulled back into the city for a few seconds while they take the glass lift between the two parts.

Located just three kilometres away and completed two years before Lina Bo Bardi received the MASP commission is Ibirapuera Park by Oscar Niemeyer. Here, Niemeyer went against a modernist desire to name, organize and maximize space. Instead he tucked a series of small volumes, like the Museu de Arte Moderna, under a gigantic curvy canopy, letting public life flow through.

The curved canopy of Ibirapuera Park, Oscar Niemeyer, 1954.

Spider sculpture by Louise Bourgeois in the Museu de Arte Moderna de São Paulo (MAM).

Ibirapuera Park can be seen as an interesting precursor, in that Bo Bardi's design comes very close and then flips the two elements completely. It shows that the modernist dream of an open, boundless space could be pushed further by inverting building and void and pulling all of the museum's programme off the ground.

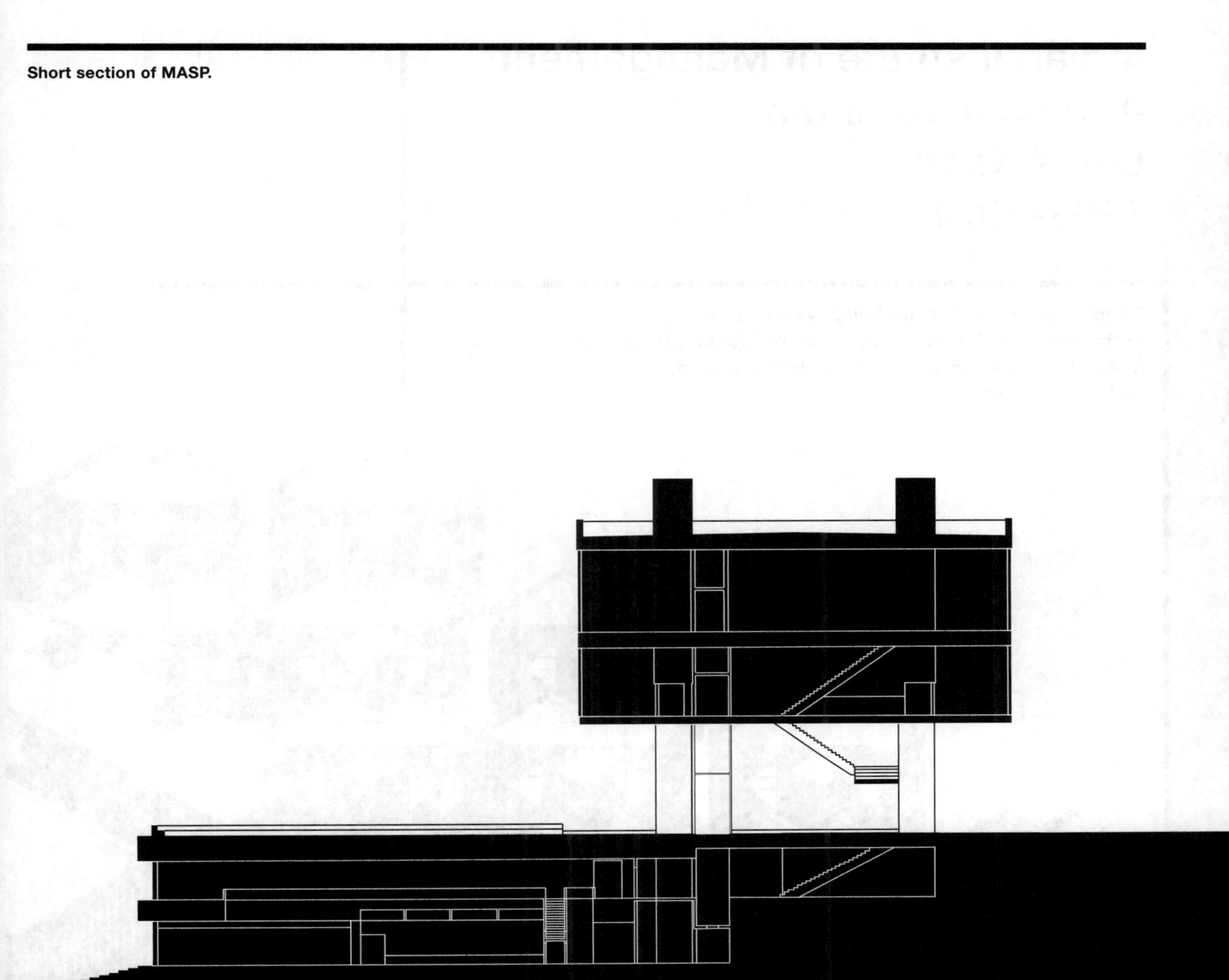
Short section of MASP.

Indian Institute of Management
Ahmedabad, India
Louis Kahn
1963–1974

A high degree of permeability is crucial to the architecture of Louis Kahn. He often spoke about a layered architecture, as if you have buildings within buildings.

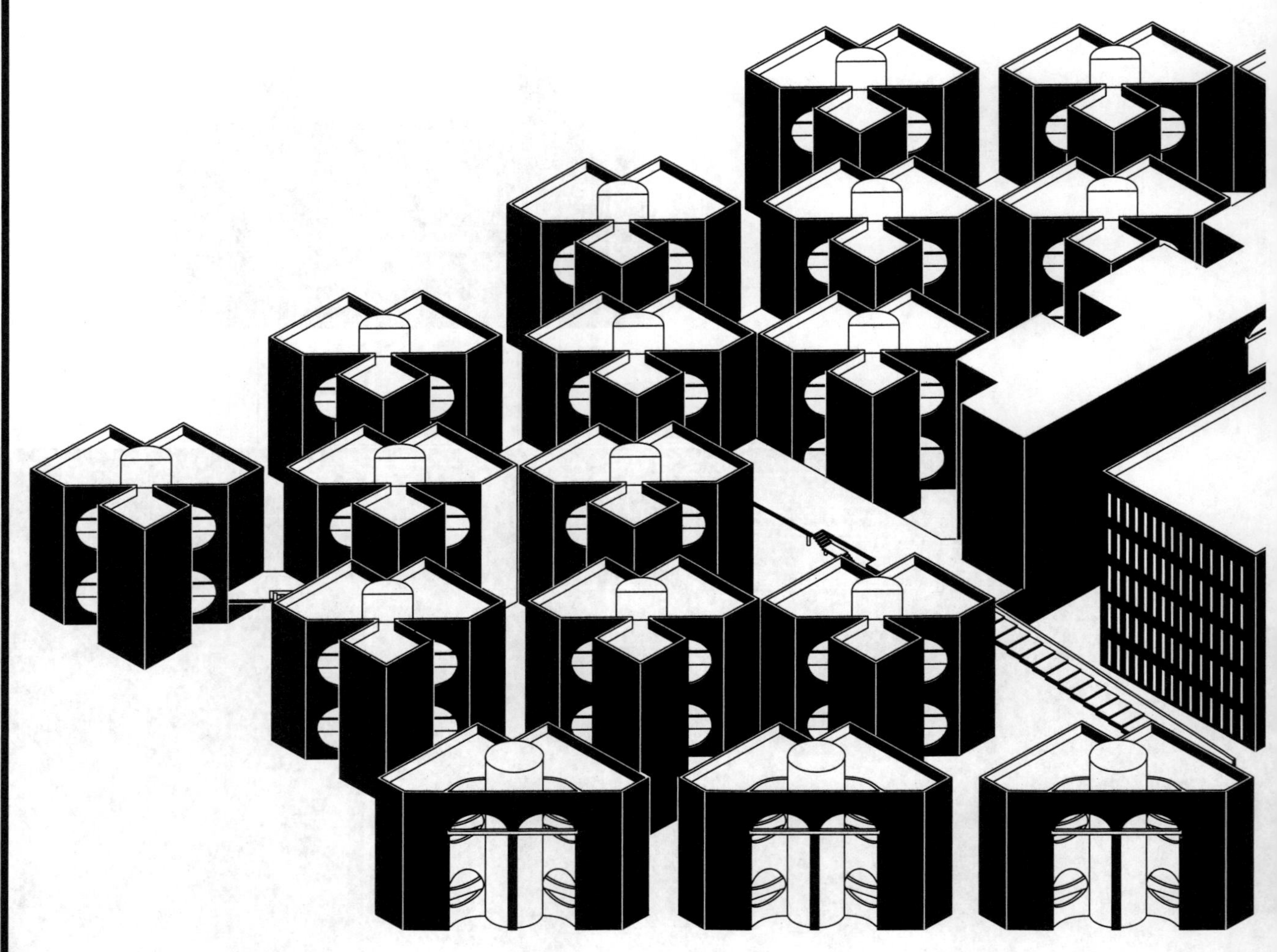

Axonometry of the Indian Institute of Management.

In the Exeter Library, which he designed in parallel with the Indian Institute of Management, you are confronted with a second and third facade while moving towards its centre. The outer volume is made up of library cubicles, designed as if you are sitting outside. The high windows act like a sky, flooding the desks with natural light. A mass of books in the middle forms the second volume, while the third and innermost volume is a large atrium with diffuse light.

Diffuse light in the atrium of Phillips Exeter Academy Library, New Hampshire, Louis Kahn, 1965–1975.

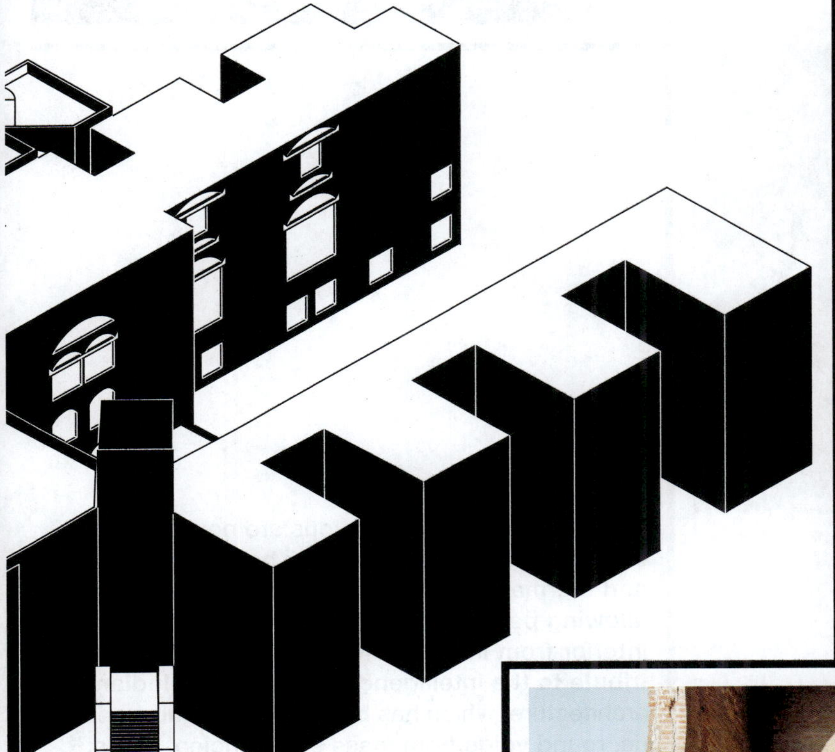

Natural light in reading spaces along the perimeter of Phillips Exeter Academy Library.

In the Indian Institute of Management, the overlap of interior and exterior space goes further. Omnipresent circular openings cast light on the interior walls like giant suns, connect different floor levels and create low vaulted corridors and curvy voids in a three-dimensional interplay with the imposing brick walls.

It is an interesting contradiction to see the buildings literally decompose despite their monumental character. Deep cuts deconstruct heavy brick volumes into plate-like facades.

In the Indian Institute of Management, the classrooms or dormitories are pushed far back from the facade and windows are removed completely. The generous scale of this space is not by accident. Kahn envisaged these hallways and intermediate spaces as the centres of learning.[24]

Ajanta Cave 26, Maharashtra, India.

These large facade omissions are not just formal or programmatic; they cleverly balance light, shade and thermal mass, minimizing direct sunlight, allowing passive ventilation and protecting the interior from India's harsh desert climate. A true tribute to the intelligence of vernacular Indian architecture, which has been cutting highly geometric, round voids from mass since ancient times.[25]

Exploded axonometry of the dormitory.

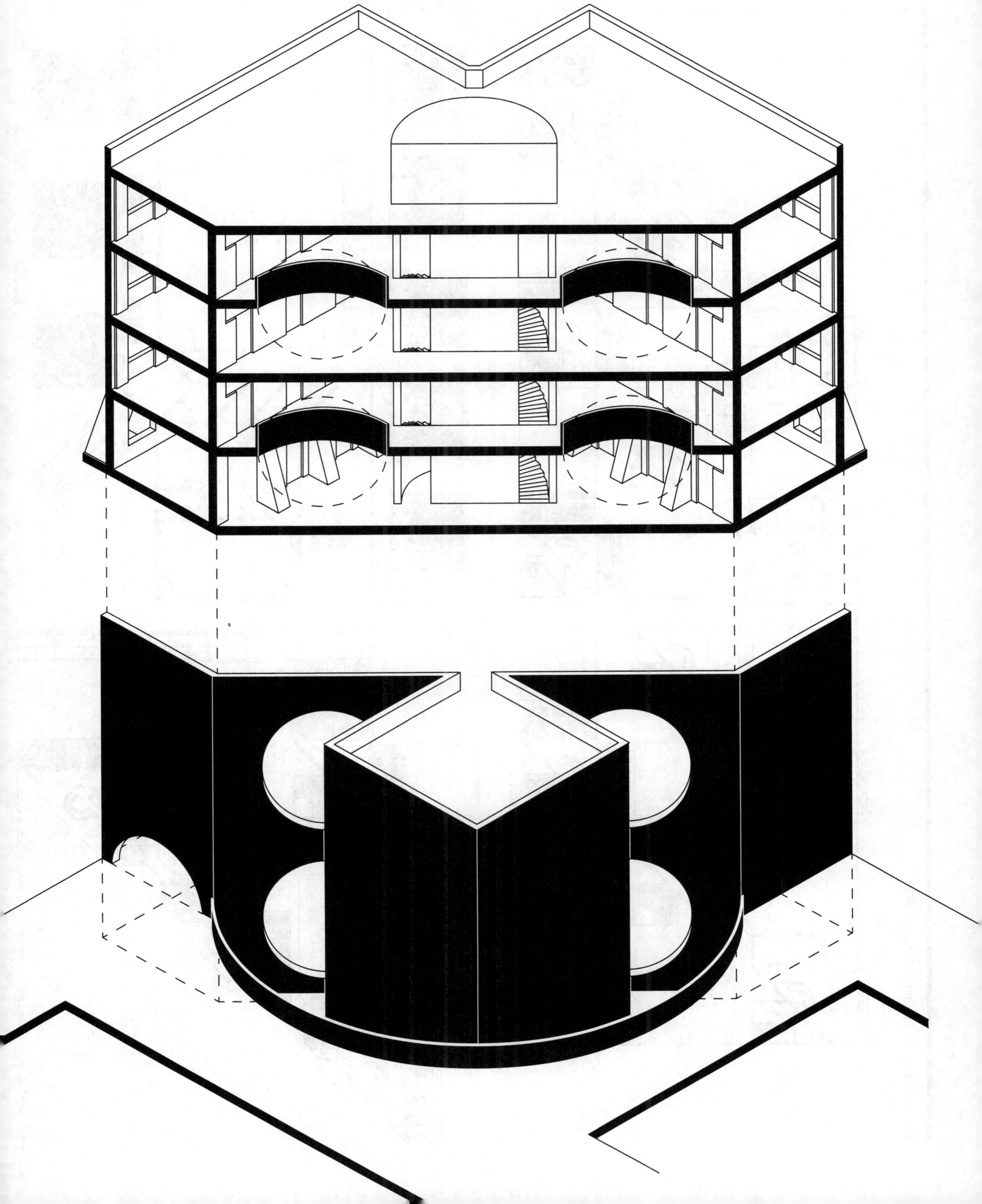

Plan of the Indian Institute of Management.

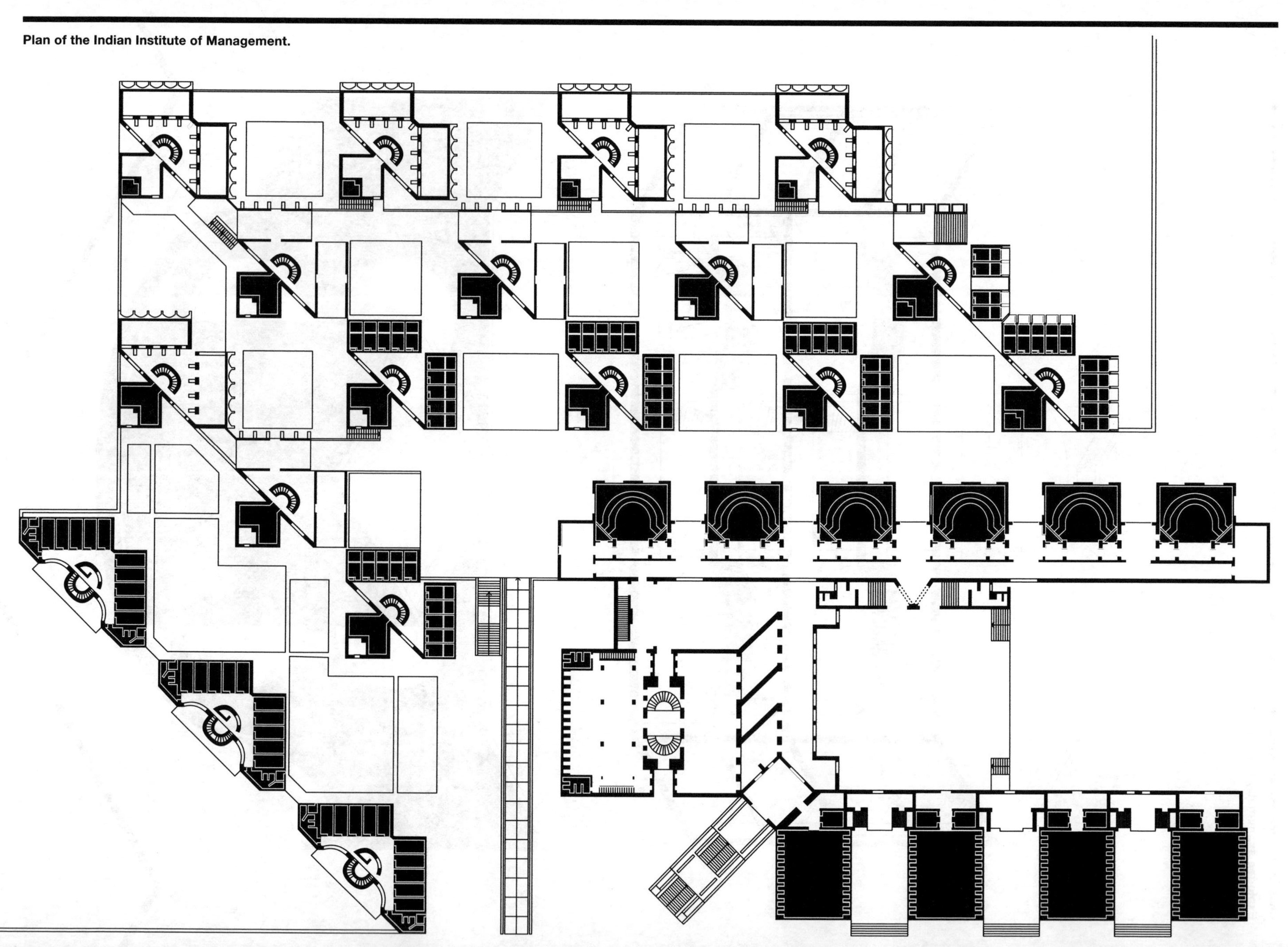

Conical Intersect, Gordon Matta-Clark, Paris, 1975.

Just following the Institute's completion, architect-turned-artist Gordon Matta-Clark made his *Conical Intersect* in Paris. It is a perfect artistic pendant to Kahn's project and also a deconstruction, this time consisting of existing structures about to be demolished to make way for the new Centre Georges Pompidou. Both Matta-Clark and Kahn were interested in questioning the static, inert built environment, uncomfortable with the direction that modern architecture was taking society.[26]

Cutting an opening or deconstructing a building to challenge an assumed or prevailing style remains a powerful architectural act. Atelier Bardill by Valerio Olgiati has an unobtrusive archetypical shape to blend with its neighbours, but if you catch a glimpse at the right angle you see it is mostly an empty shell. The perimeter wall mimics a gabled roof, and what would be the attic floor is punctured with a big round skylight. This carved-out space regulates privacy and daylight. Most of the house is a garden in disguise.

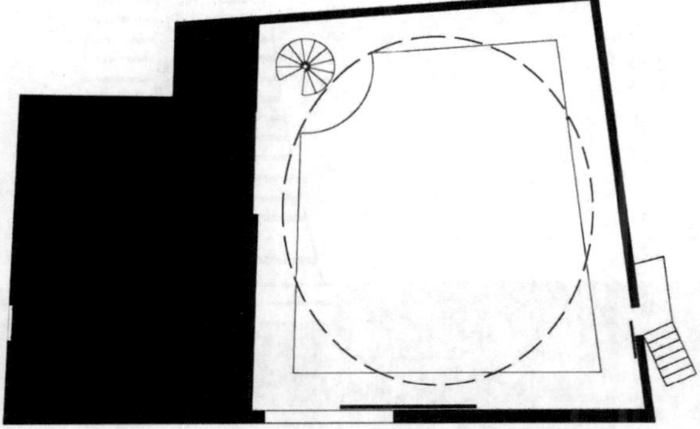

Plan of Atelier Bardill, Scharans, Valerio Olgiati, 2007.

Exterior of Atelier Bardill.

Within the void of Atelier Bardill.

The Ford Foundation
New York City, USA
Kevin Roche John Dinkeloo and Associates
1963–1968

Critic Ada Louise Huxtable was lyrical about the Ford Foundation. Rather than building a high-rise on a landscaped plaza, it respects the continuity of the street, by occupying the whole urban plot.

"It is a horticultural [spectacle] and probably one of the most romantic environments ever devised by corporate men... The building reveals itself totally from the street; the Ford Foundation has built itself a splendid, shimmering Crystal Palace."[27] —Ada Louise Huxtable

Receding facade of 9 West 57th Street (Solow Building), New York City, Gordon Bunshaft (SOM), 1974.

Just six years later, Huxtable ranted against Gordon Bunshaft for surrendering to commercial developers, believing the twin W. R. Grace and Solow Buildings to be a slap in the face to the New York street and street-goer.[28] But there is something illogical in this. Why praise a building that greedily takes all the urban space at ground level and pulls it into a lush garden for private use, while criticizing a gesture to give the urban space next to a skyscraper back the public?

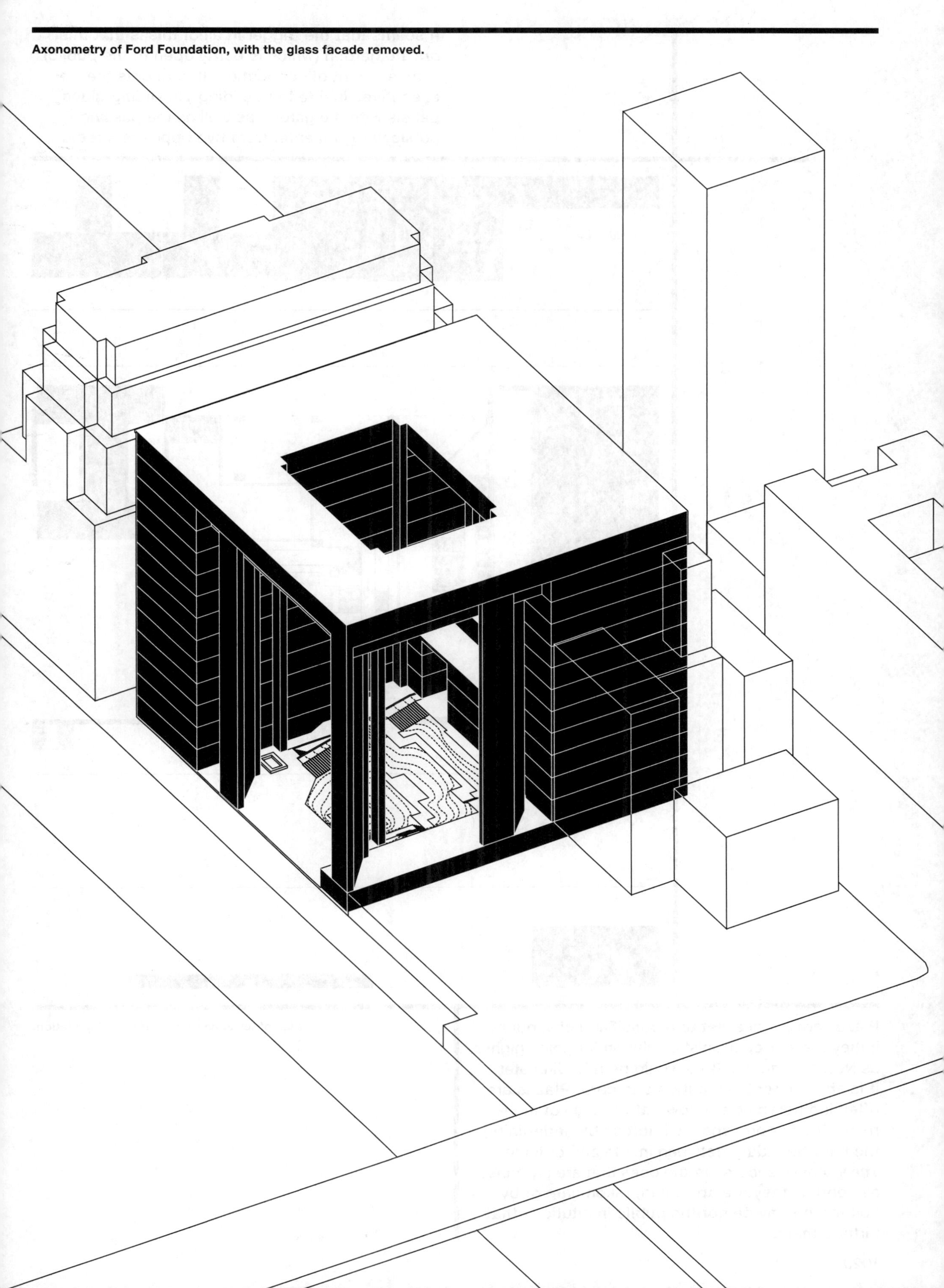

Axonometry of Ford Foundation, with the glass facade removed.

It seems that the trigger in all of this is that this *private* garden (which is partly open to the public) is an element of connection. It connects the executives inside the building via sliding glass panels with the garden as well as the passing public who can enter from two opposite streets.

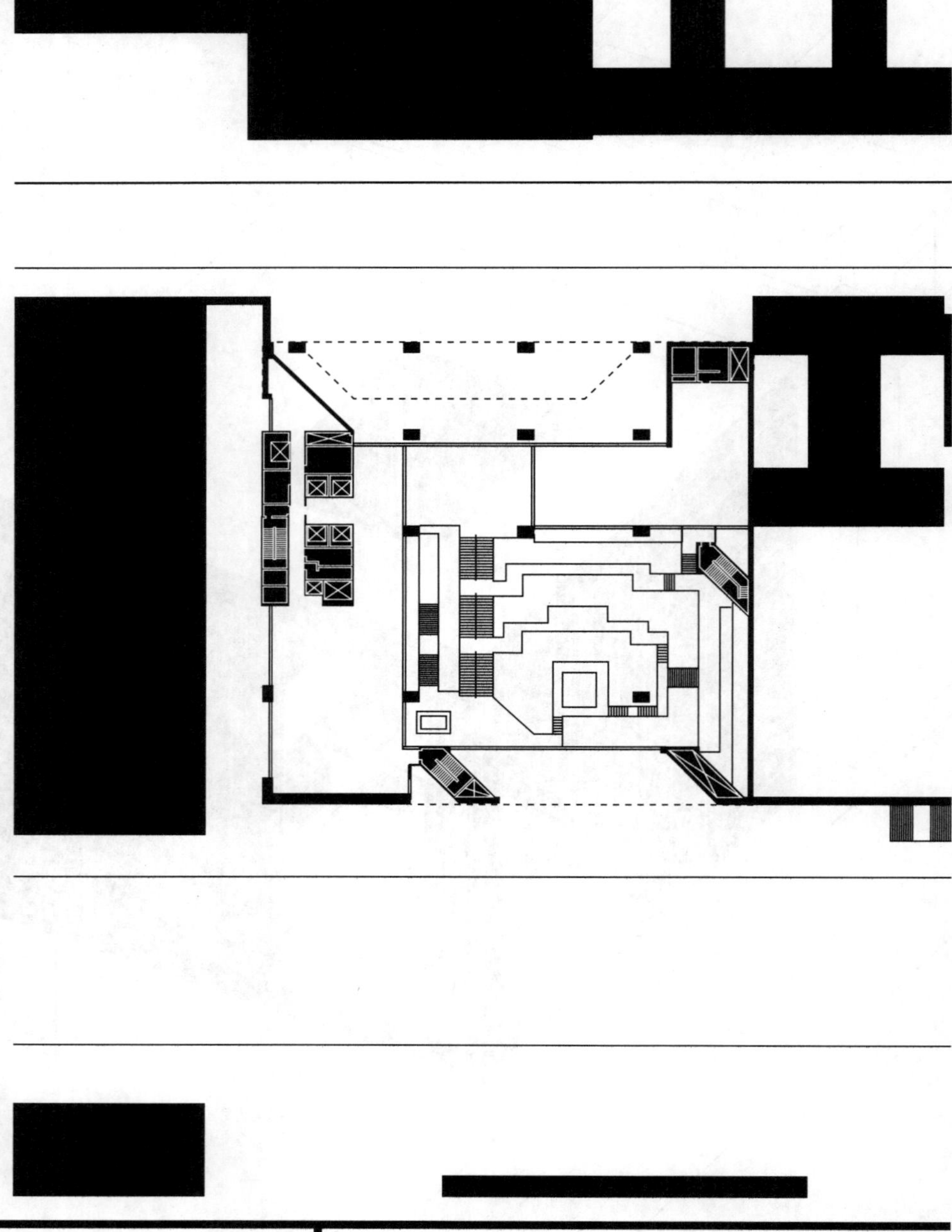

Plan of terraced ground of Ford Foundation.

Plazas are a real asset to a densifying city, but not if they are an opportunistic solution for going higher, as New York zoning laws would permit. Ultimately, it is about intent, execution and care. Plazas are often indifferently laid down at the toes of high-rises. These open spaces impress by underlining the hard boundary between inside and outside. The worst offenders are the ones that are orphaned as soon as they are approved, taken care of by neither the private nor the public institutions that birthed them.

The Ford Foundation builds out to the site boundary and carves a generously forested living room from one corner of this square office block. The building's strong form and distinct boundaries make it utterly clear who owns and takes care of this space. There are many precedents that perforate the self-contained office building, but most are driven by aesthetic or architectonic reasoning and less by beautifully clear functionality. When not done well, these spaces don't mitigate or connect but merely stand in the way.

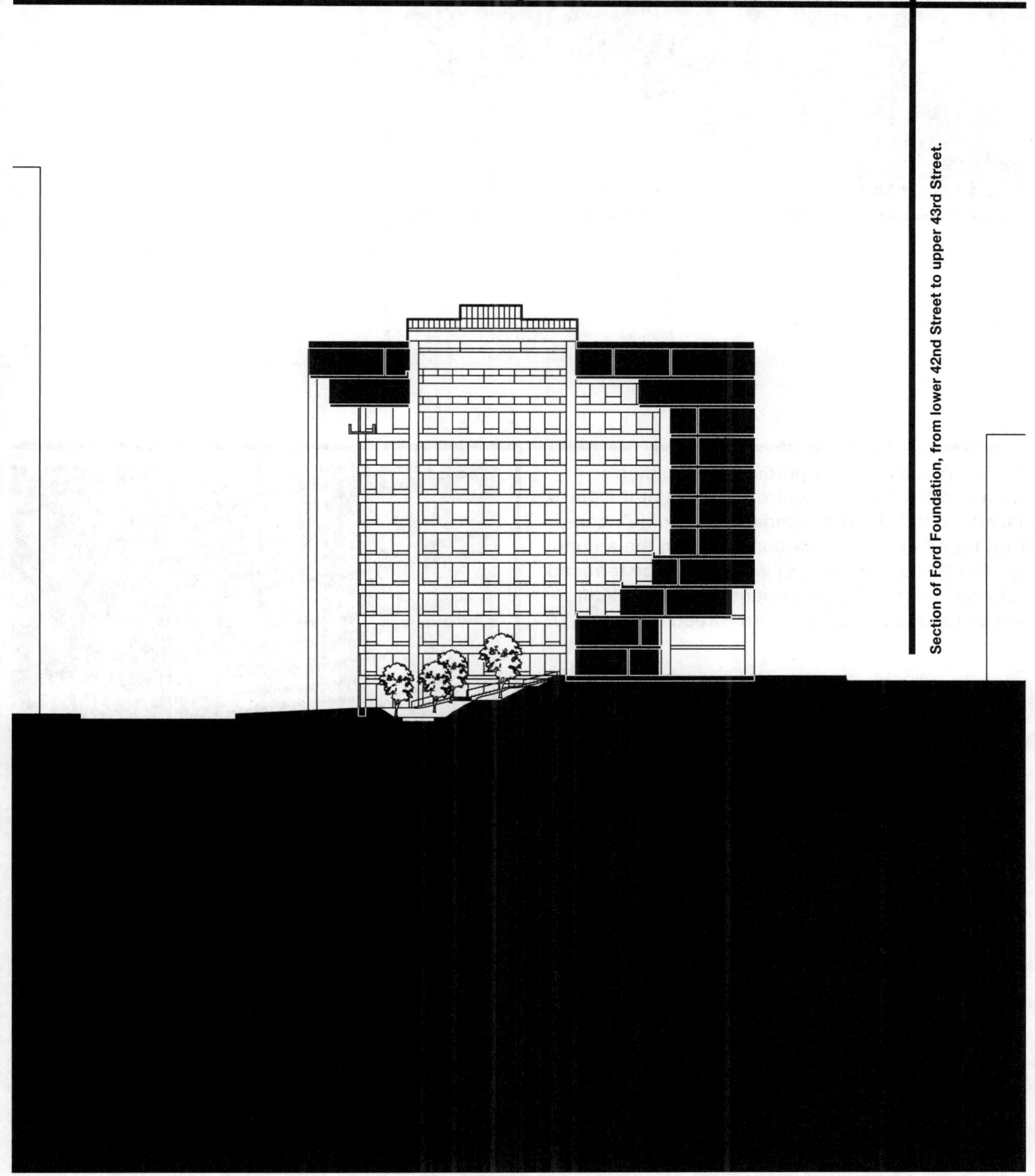

Section of Ford Foundation, from lower 42nd Street to upper 43rd Street.

Kevin Roche holding a model of the Ford Foundation facade.

The entrance provides proof of the building's permeability. The main entrance is not at the glass facade to the street but under the building's canopy, found once one has gone through the atrium garden and up one fight of lazy stairs. The terraced ground floor intelligently mitigates the level differences between 42nd and 43rd Street.

Lazy steps between 42nd and 43rd Street.

Office wings line two sides of the building, creating an L-shape that faces the open view down 42nd Street. Together, the two Tudor-style apartment blocks flanking the street and the flyover between them frame the East River beyond.

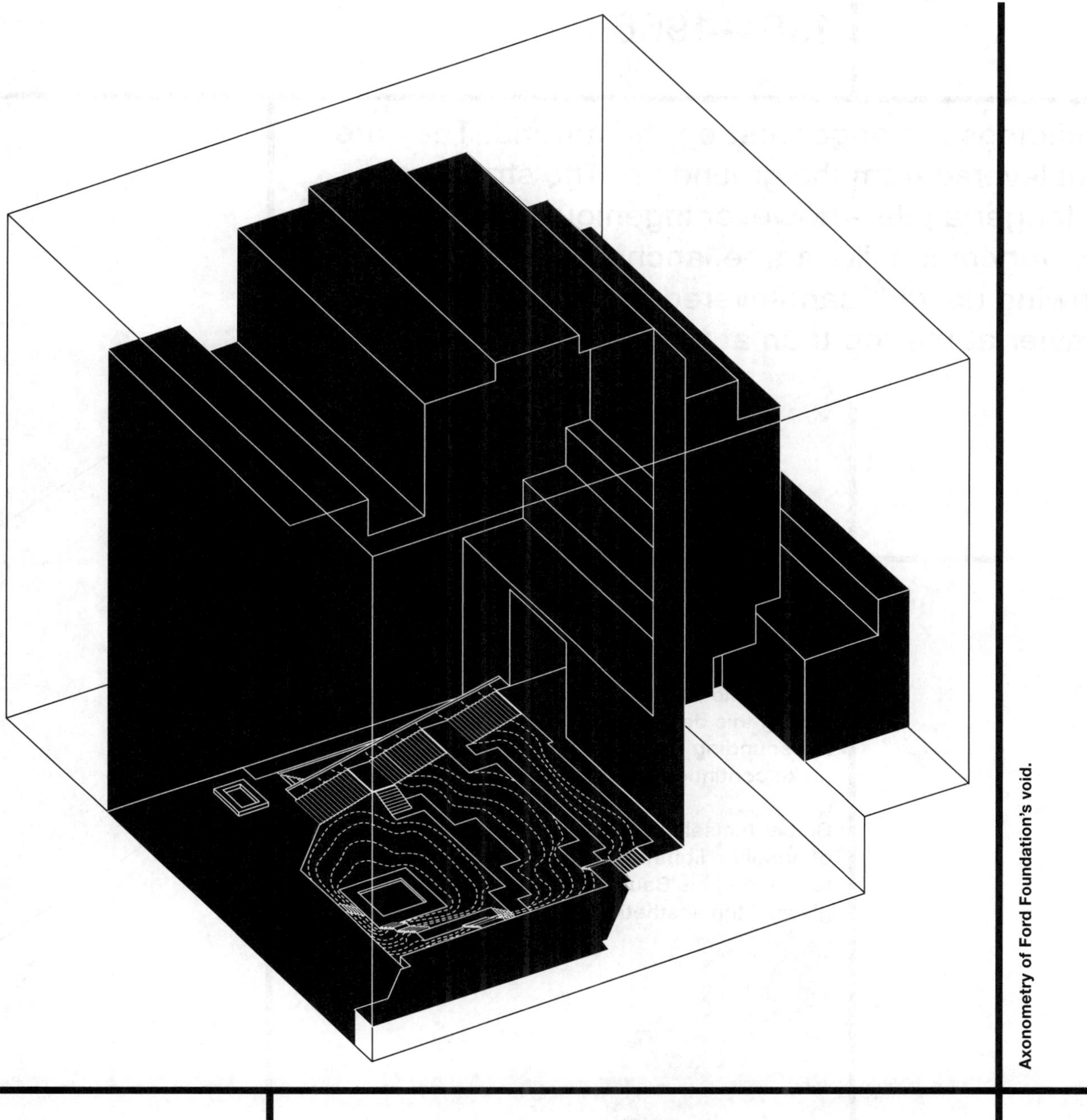

Axonometry of Ford Foundation's void.

When all seen together, you fully understand why Roche Dinkeloo builds the full volume and then carves away this carefully considered void.

The Whitney Museum
New York City, USA
Marcel Breuer with Hamilton P. Smith
1964–1966

"Buildings no longer rest on the ground. They are cantilevered from the ground up. The structure is no longer a pile – however ingenious and beautiful – it is very much like a tree, anchored by roots, growing up with cantilevered branches, possibly heavier at the top than at the bottom…"[29] –Marcel Breuer

In 1959, gravity was challenged when the moon was reached in an unmanned mission. In 1969, humankind planted their feet on the moon. This effort to defeat gravity was less about leaving the crust of the earth and more about liberating it. During this decade, within architecture, there was a resounding wish to build levitating masses and make continuous, open ground floors.[30]

Breuer himself made a transition from the pursuit of absolute lightness with his tubular steel furniture during his Bauhaus period (1920s) to a form-giver of the aesthetics of heaviness.[31]

"Today's structure in its most expressive form is hollow below and substantial on top – just the reverse of the pyramid. It represents a new epoch in the history of man, the realization of his oldest ambitions: the defeat of gravity."[32] –Marcel Breuer

New York's 'Whitney', as it is lovingly called, has had many lives.[33] Its third, designed by Marcel Breuer, was the home of Gertrude Vanderbilt Whitney's vast collection of twentieth-century American art that more-established museums had refused to exhibit. Honouring this boldness, Breuer wanted a building that looked like an independent, self-reliant unit, transforming the vitality of the street into the sincerity and profundity of art.[34]

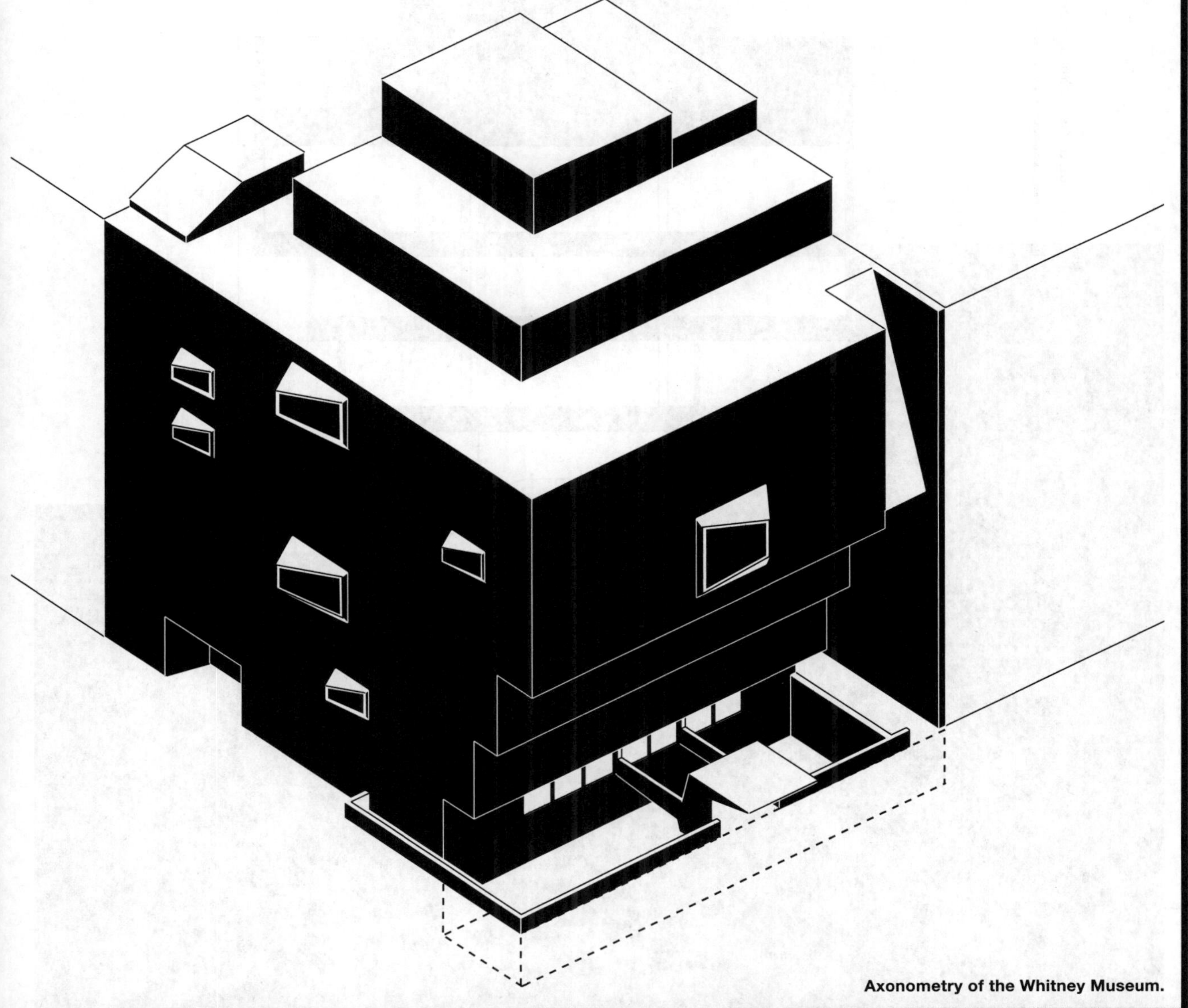

Axonometry of the Whitney Museum.

The recessed facade and lowered entrance hall patio.

Section of the Whitney Museum.

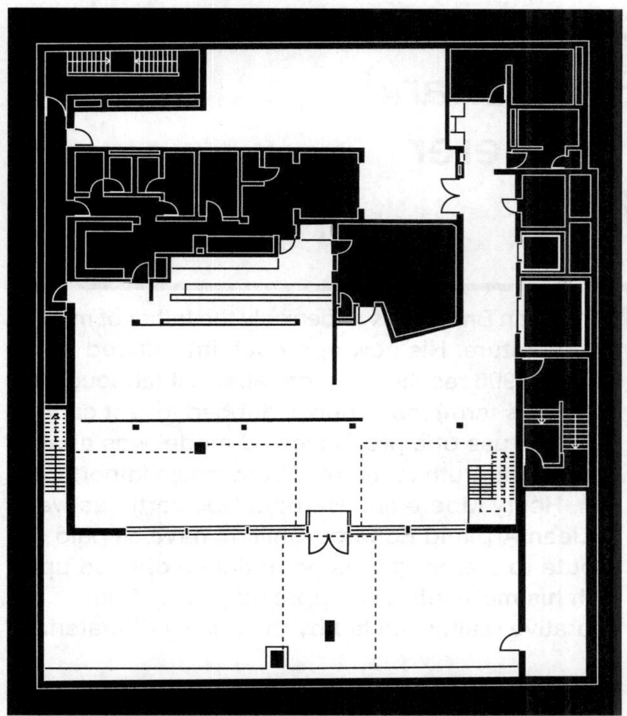

Ground floor plan of the Whitney Museum.

The facade is almost completely windowless and closed, yet the increasing recession of lower floors and the sidewalk-level void creates a dramatic outdoor space. Seldom is a building so generous, embracing public space by inverting an exterior entrance into a sheltered urban interior.

It was the perfect antipode, maybe even antidote, to the prevailing trend within corporate architecture. The Whitney is living proof that in order to be welcoming, one doesn't need transparency, a corporate deceit too often used.

Breuer's work often resembles sculpted volumes of stone and concrete. His use of concrete as a finished exterior surface was an inversion of the traditional American skyscraper. Instead of internalizing structure to allow the building to be clad in a non-load-bearing enclosure, Breuer's externalized concrete frame took structure to the exterior to free up interior space.[35]

View from under one of two treelike columns with twelve branches which hold up the whole roof of St John's University Alcuin Library, Marcel Breuer, 1966.

Holy Cross Church
Chur, Switzerland
Walter Förderer
1966–1969

Constantin Brâncuși is undeniably the father of modern sculpture. His new approach introduced around 1906 resulted in more abstract (although he hated this term) forms and is dubbed 'direct carving'. The use of a preconceived model was abandoned, and truth to material became an important aim. Henry Moore and Barbara Hepworth, as well as Jean Arp and Eduardo Chillida have all paid tribute to the enormous potential he opened up with his more intuitive approach, away from figurative reality and led by the quality of material.

Portrait of Mlle Pogany, Constantin Brâncuşi, 1912.

Barbara Hepworth at Trewyn Studio, 1961.

Two Piece Reclining Figure No. 5, Henry Moore, Kenwood House, London, 1963.

Knife Edge Two Piece, bronze, Henry Moore, opposite House of Lords, London, 1962.

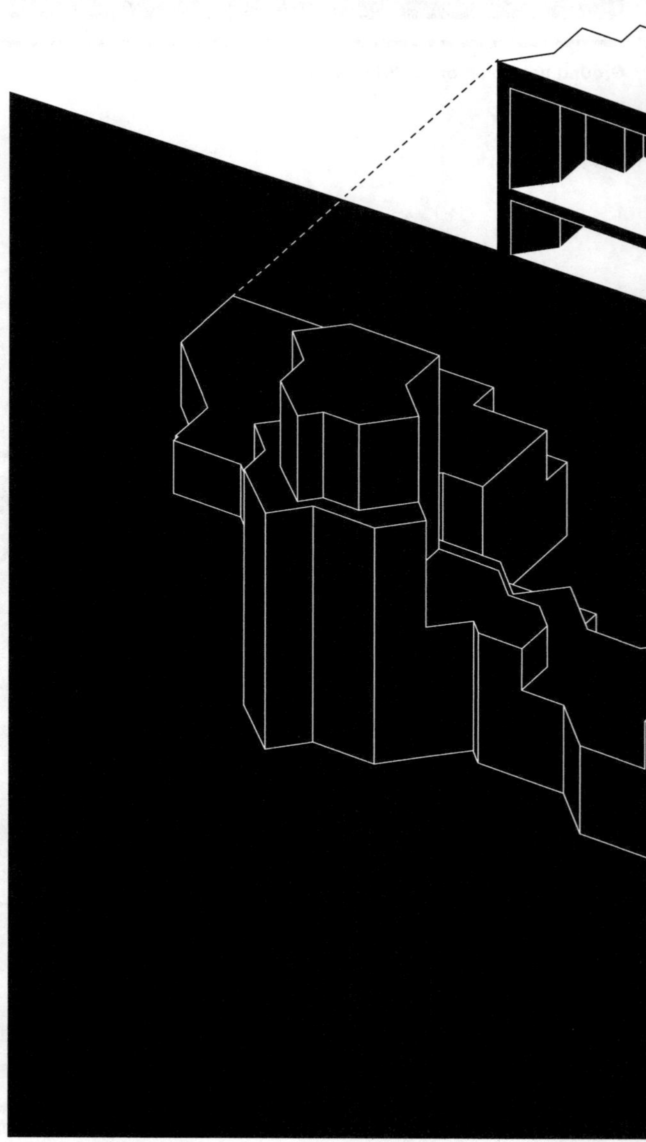

Sectional axonometry of the Holy Cross Church.

These exquisite artists mostly knew each other and shared ideas; Henry Moore dubbed 1932 'The Year of the Hole', just a year after Barbara Hepworth made her first pierced form.[36] Their experimental work paved the way for a slower form of art: architecture. During the 1950s and 1960s, architects drew inspiration from sculpture. An emphasis on carving voids and visualizing negative space is present in the work of Gordon Bunshaft, Marcel Breuer and Bernard Zehrfuss, among uncountable others.

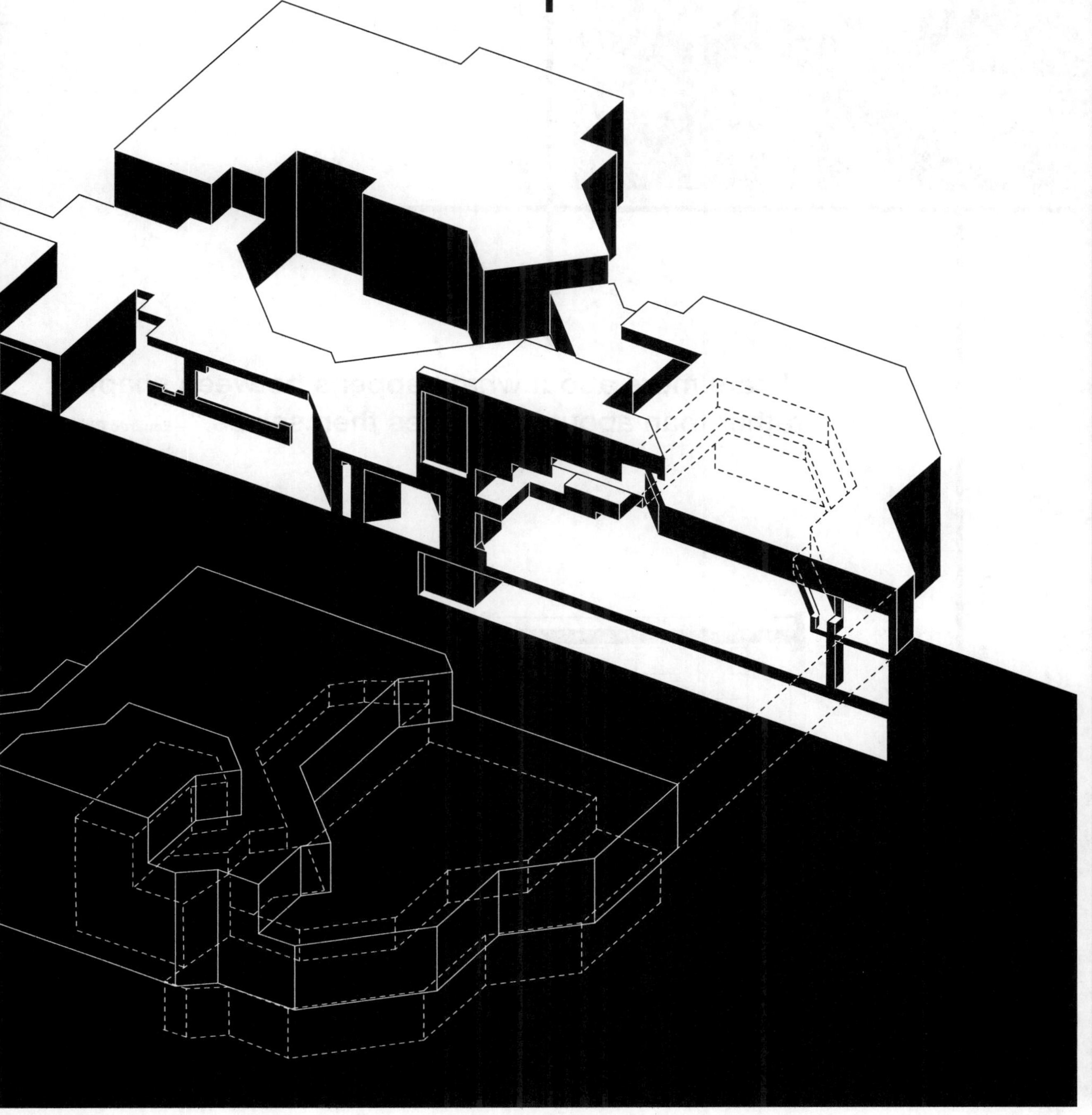

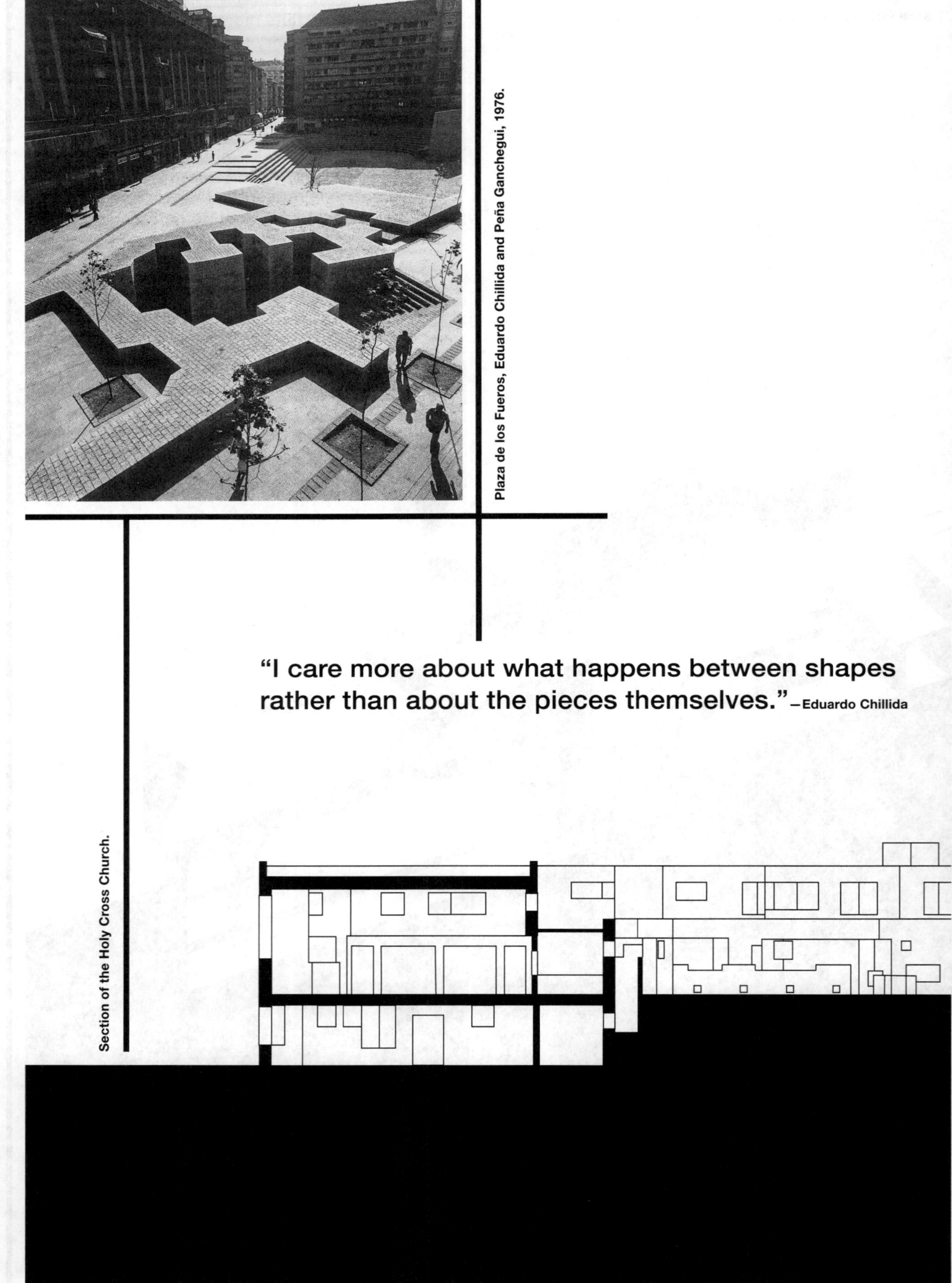

Plaza de los Fueros, Eduardo Chillida and Peña Ganchegui, 1976.

"I care more about what happens between shapes rather than about the pieces themselves." —Eduardo Chillida

Section of the Holy Cross Church.

Architect and devout Catholic Walter Förderer belongs to this tribe. Trained as a sculptor, Förderer began his architectural career at the office of Hermann Baur, a church architect. Förderer only practised for twenty years, between 1959 and 1979, and although his design of the University of St. Gallen brought him recognition, it is his many churches, the first of which was the Holy Cross Church in Chur, that show his capacity to sculpt space.

Standing within the Holy Cross Church is like being immersed in a Chillida sculpture blown up in scale. The omnipresent concrete gives the impression of a cave. In places, the crust of the earth bursts open to let daylight beam in. The church is sparsely lit, adding to the drama and subtle height differences, including hidden stairs that give access to a balcony and an organ that creates a rocky landscape.

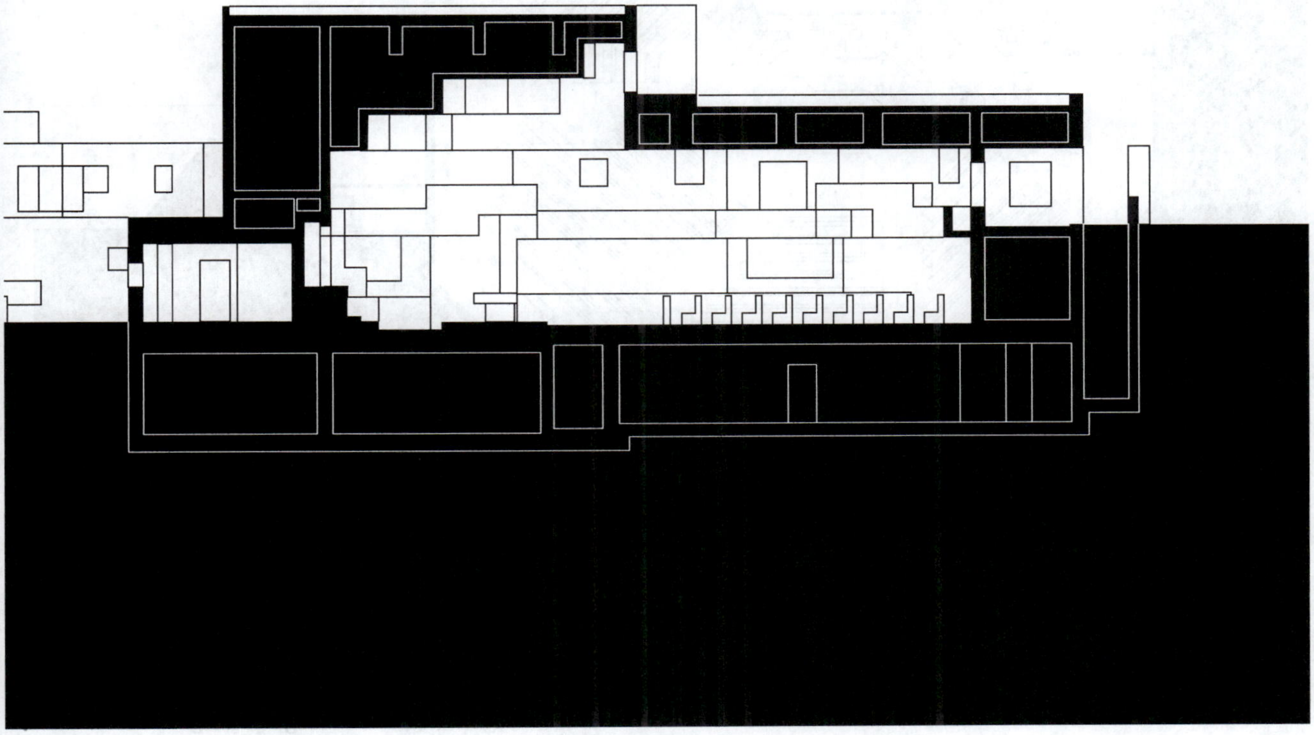

Förderer spoke about a continuation of topography. A building should work on all sides and relate to its surroundings. Like a sculptor who respects and connects to the material he works with, Förderer listened to site, and ground.

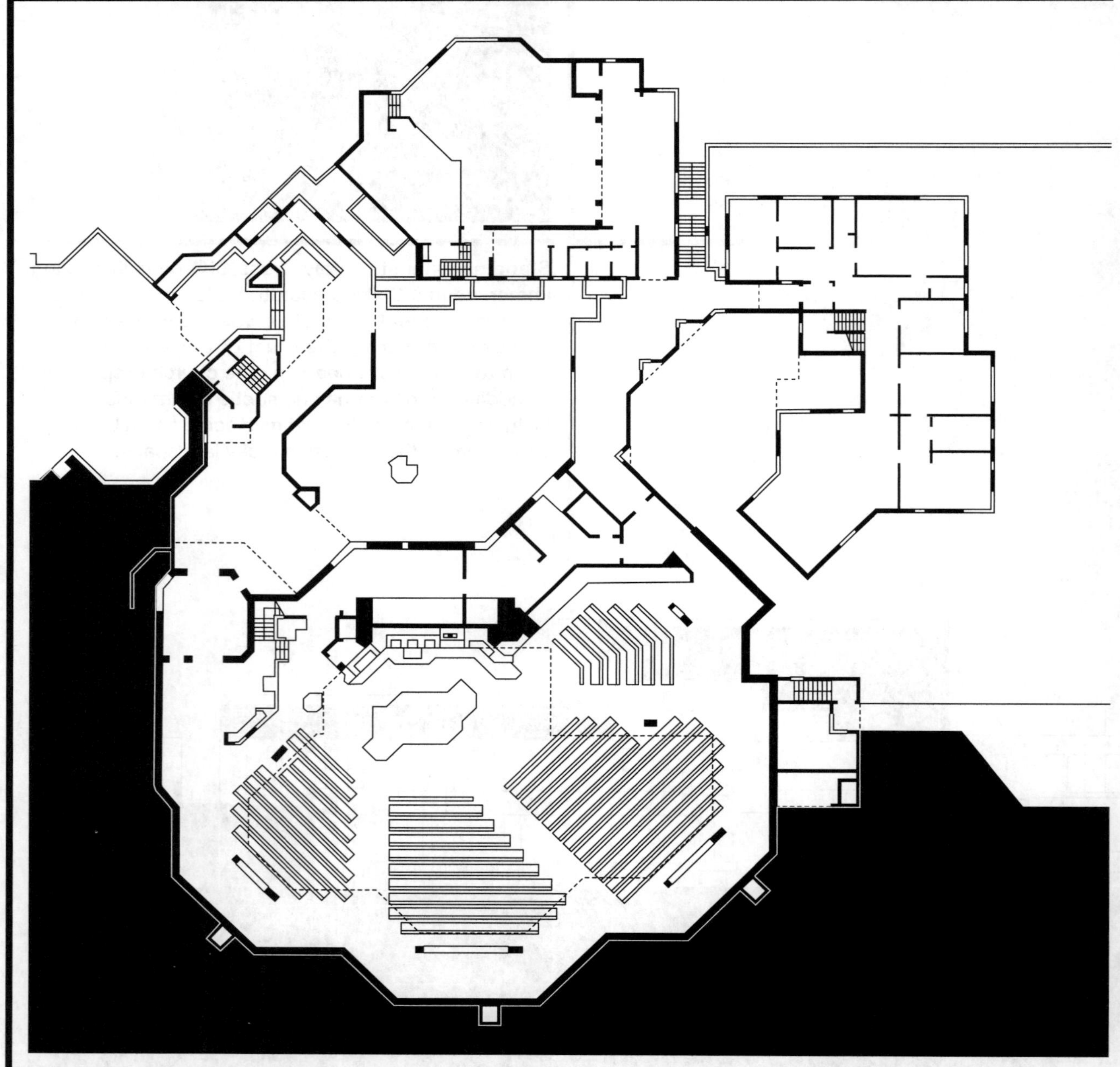

Plan of the Holy Cross Church.

This brutalism taken to the extreme is remarkable when you consider how, during the same era, efficiency, economy and profitability were squeezing all the expression out of buildings in favour of a blunt stacking of floors and a generic ground level.[37]

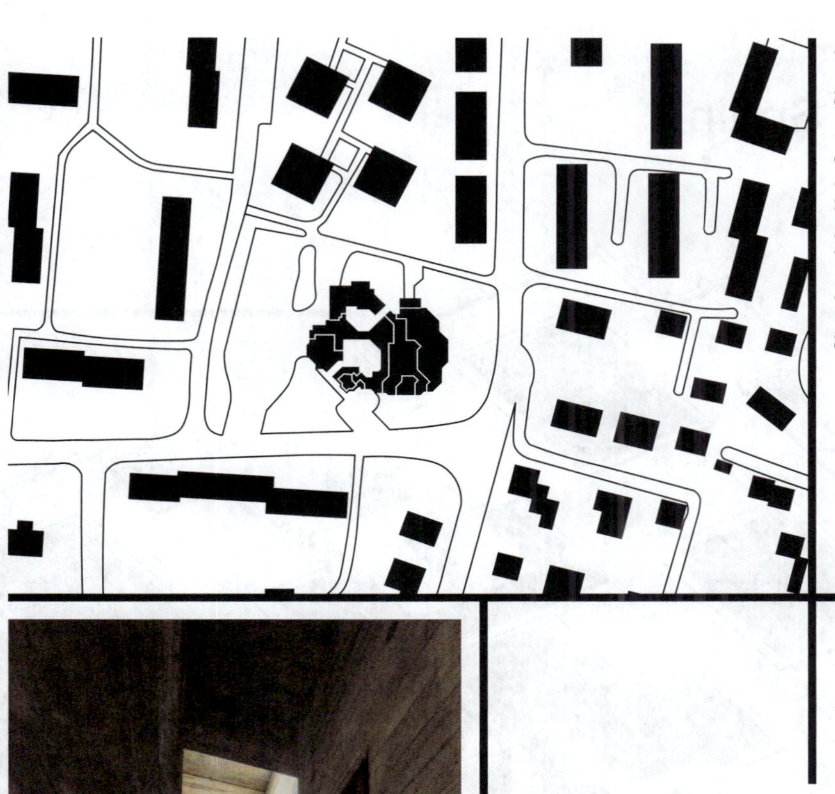

Site plan of the Holy Cross Church.

The building does what you expect of a church building. It calms you down with a sacred feeling. Even the greatest religious sceptic (or the most hardened modernist) is able to drift away in thought, as you can do within a dramatic landscape or in front of an open fire, looking at the never-ending twists of forms.

Walden 7
Sant Just Desvern, Spain
Ricardo Bofill
1972–1975

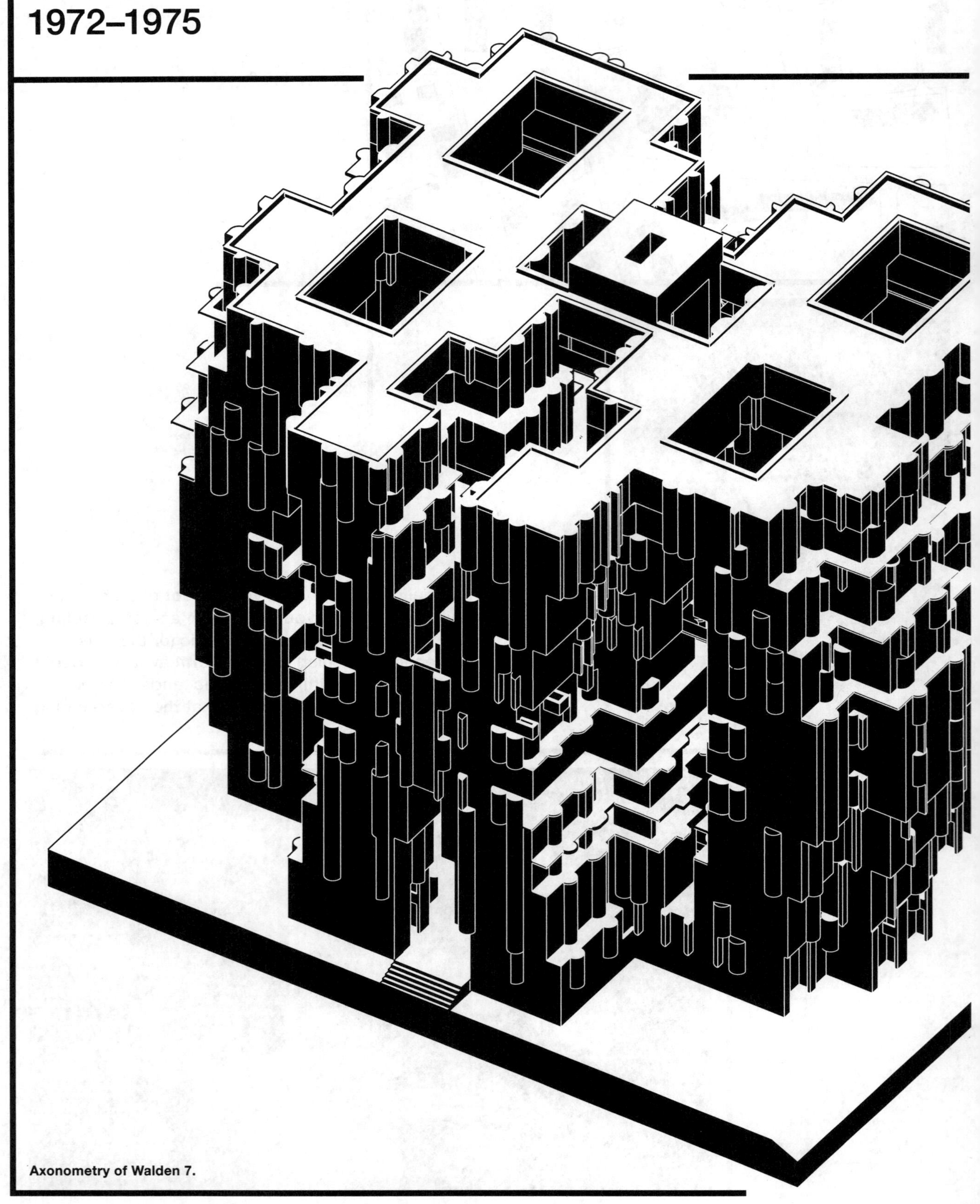

Axonometry of Walden 7.

Probably the most interesting story behind this project is its name, Walden 7. Ricardo Bofill's Walden is part of a strange literary lineage that begins with Henry David Thoreau's novel in 1854, *Walden; or, Life in the Woods*, and ends with B. F. Skinner's novel *Walden Two*, published almost a hundred years later in 1948.

While the first Walden is a call for living simply and immersed in nature, Skinner's Waldens two to six are utopian communities driven by a kind of scientifically induced altruism.[38] In his controversial novel, Skinner rejects the idea of a free will, believing that human behaviour is determined by the environment, and further speculates that by altering environmental variables, a new sociocultural system, a utopia of greater social justice and human well-being could be generated.[39] The hope, as in *Animal Farm*, is to create citizenry who eventually can conceive only of actions that benefit everyone in society.

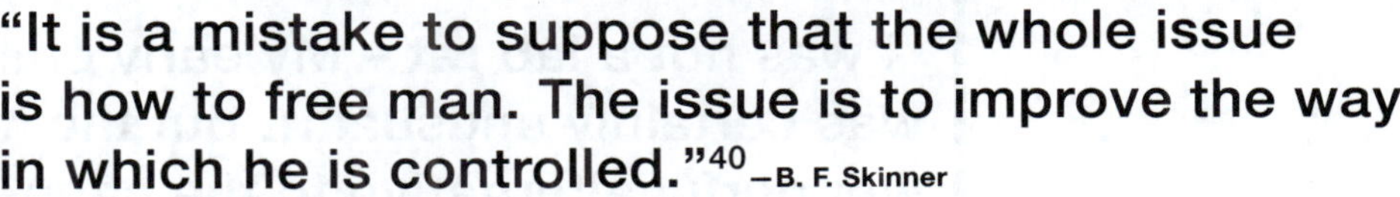

"It is a mistake to suppose that the whole issue is how to free man. The issue is to improve the way in which he is controlled."[40] – B. F. Skinner

"We can no longer afford freedom. We must design our culture to shape the behavior needed for survival."[41] – B. F. Skinner

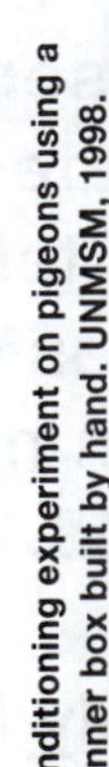

Conditioning experiment on pigeons using a Skinner box built by hand. UNMSM, 1998.

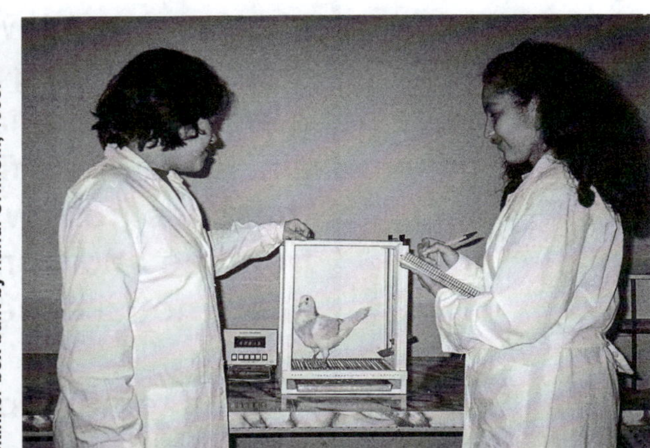

Skinner's work was not purely science fiction. He was a behavioural scientist and his theories stemmed from his experiments and inventions. The 'Skinner Box' was a laboratory box to study animal behavioural conditioning, and the 'Air Crib' was a kind of human version of this, although not as sinister. It was designed to minimize time-consuming activities and provide a baby with maximum comfort, all for the sake of improving the quality of life for mother and baby.

The Air Crib, B. F. Skinner, c.1945.

"I was not a lab rat – My early childhood, it's true, was certainly unusual ... but the 'aircrib' was a wonderful alternative to the cage-like cot, based on removing what he and my mother saw as the worst aspects of a baby's typical sleeping arrangements: clothes, sheets and blankets.

I had a clear view through the glass front and, instead of being semi-swaddled and covered with blankets, I luxuriated semi-naked in warm, humidified air. The air was filtered but not germ-free, and when the glass front was lowered into place, the noise from me and from my parents and sister was dampened, not silenced.

I was a remarkably healthy child... I didn't have a cold until I was six."[42] – Deborah Skinner Buzan (daughter of B. F. Skinner)

Knowing all this, you see that Walden 7 is far closer to Skinner's vision than Thoreau's. It is an experiment in human behaviour, this time at an urban scale, hoping to mould its inhabitants into a utopian community by improving their environment.

Bijlmermeer, Amsterdam, 1975.

The early 20th century was a romantic and naive period in which the quality of housing was about the new revelations of light, air and space. Now, in hindsight, we see it was much more about behavioural change and control. It was about keeping society, radically changing from rural to urban, under control.

Countless people who used to live in a rural setting with menial jobs were relocated to high-density living environments with alternative indoor-outdoor connections, elevated circulation and communal facilities within building volumes. These new connections were both physically and socially an imperfect, surrogate replacement for their earlier structures, which were natural, hyper-social and grounded.

La Cité de la Muette, Drancy, Paris, Eugène Beaudouin & Marcel Lods, 1929–1946.

The progressive changes designed from a social point of view could not provide these qualities. Top-down, insufficiently empathic and pedantic, these projects provided quality of shelter but lacked quality of living. They were completely detached from people's original habitat. The changes were in fact a condensed version of what hunter-gatherers had experienced when changing from a nomadic lifestyle to settled farming.
It was not a choice but rather an evolution from a high quality of life in smaller numbers and with higher mortality rates to a less healthy and lower quality of existence, in much larger numbers and with lower mortality rates. Or, as B. F. Skinner would say, "We can no longer afford freedom."

Walden 7 is a collection of individual cells, all 30 metres square and holding all necessary facilities for independent living.[43] The project is often referred to as a series of eighteen towers leaning against each other to form ellipse-shaped voids and courtyards. Look closer and examine construction photos and you will see it is more of a two-way-joist concrete slab floor system (waffle slab) with columns. Every floor is perforated, and this perforation shifts per floor, creating the expanding and contracting voids.

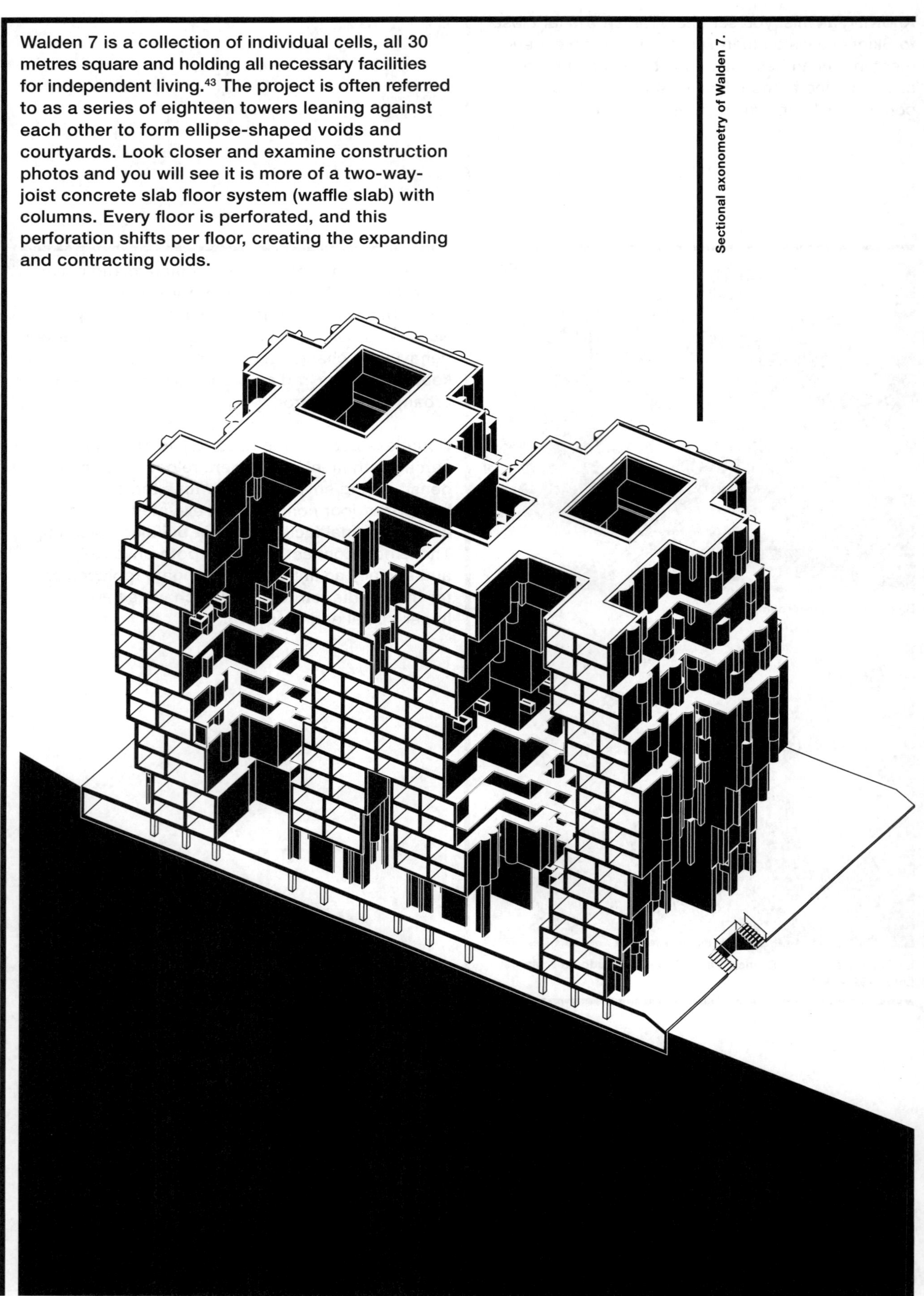

Sectional axonometry of Walden 7.

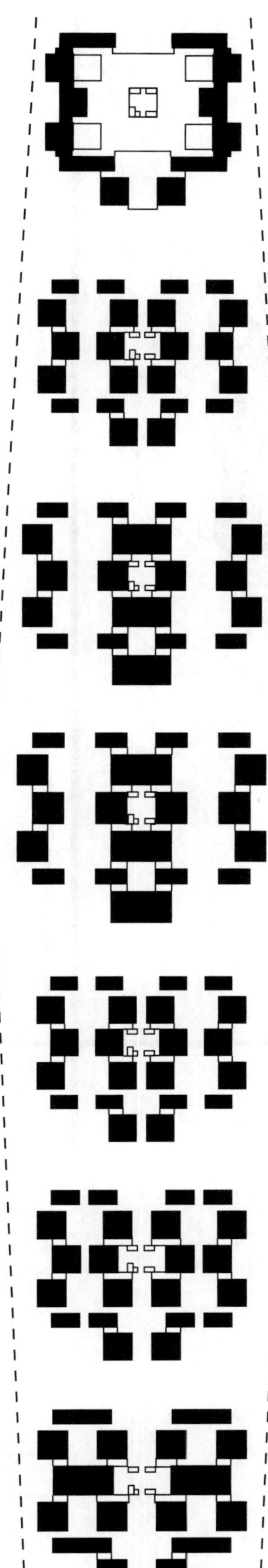

Series of plans showing how the building expands and contracts.

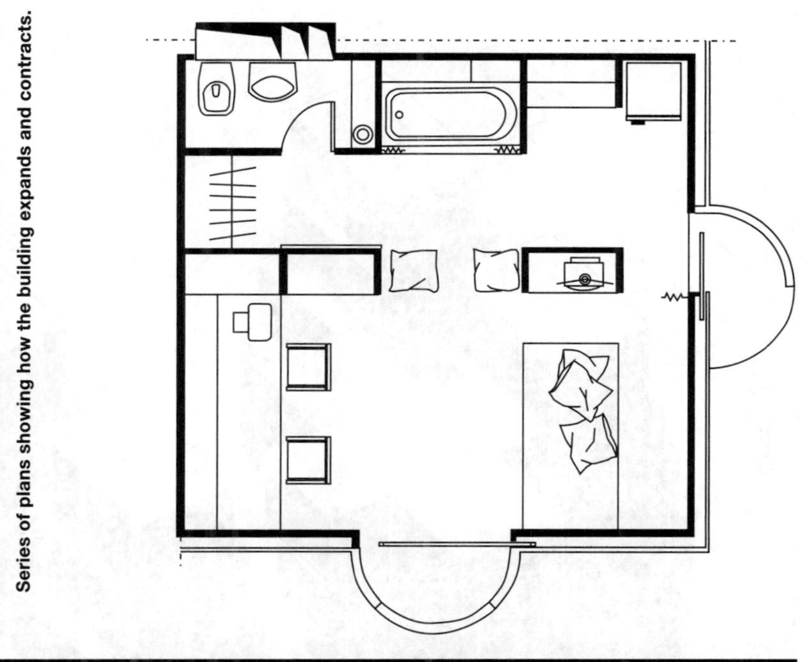

Plan of an individual cell within the Walden 7 project.

La Ciudad en el Espacio (City in Space), Ricardo Bofill, 1970.

Ricardo Bofill firmly believed that the smallest social cell is not the family but the individual. But rather than divide a large slab into many equal units, Bofill tried to aggregate individual units to create a larger 'communal hive'.[44] Although Walden 7 does not quite achieve the variety and juxtaposition described in his speculative manifesto, City in Space, the intent is clear. Modular units don't have to be packed tightly together. Instead they should have maximum contact with the exterior to create open, porous urban living.

Axonometry of Walden 7's voids.

Within the void looking out.

Walden 7 is only the first part of a larger scheme that also included part of a cement factory converted into a studio and home for Ricardo Bofill himself. The other high-rises, parts two and three of the scheme, were never built, but the model looks like a fortified city-state with a palace surrounded by housing for the plebs. The converted cement factory and silos with their royal dimensions seem like a grunge-look castle for a modern king. This is underlined by the way Ricardo Bofill talks about it.

Model of the larger scheme with Walden 7 in the foreground.

"I have the impression of living in a precinct, in a closed universe which protects me from the outside and everyday life. The Cement Factory is a place of work par excellence. Life goes on here in a continuous sequence, with very little difference between work and leisure."[45] –Ricardo Bofill

La Fábrica, Ricardo Bofill, 1973.

In the end, the project, like its socially engaged flower-power description, is somewhat deceitful. Indeed, it is somewhat Orwellian in character. "All animals are equal, but some animals are more equal than others."

Doña Maria Coronel Apartments
Seville, Spain
Cruz y Ortiz
1973–1976

Looking up within the central void.

With this small housing project, the very first project Cruz and Ortiz designed the year they graduated, they presented their credentials and it catapulted them immediately into the international spotlight.

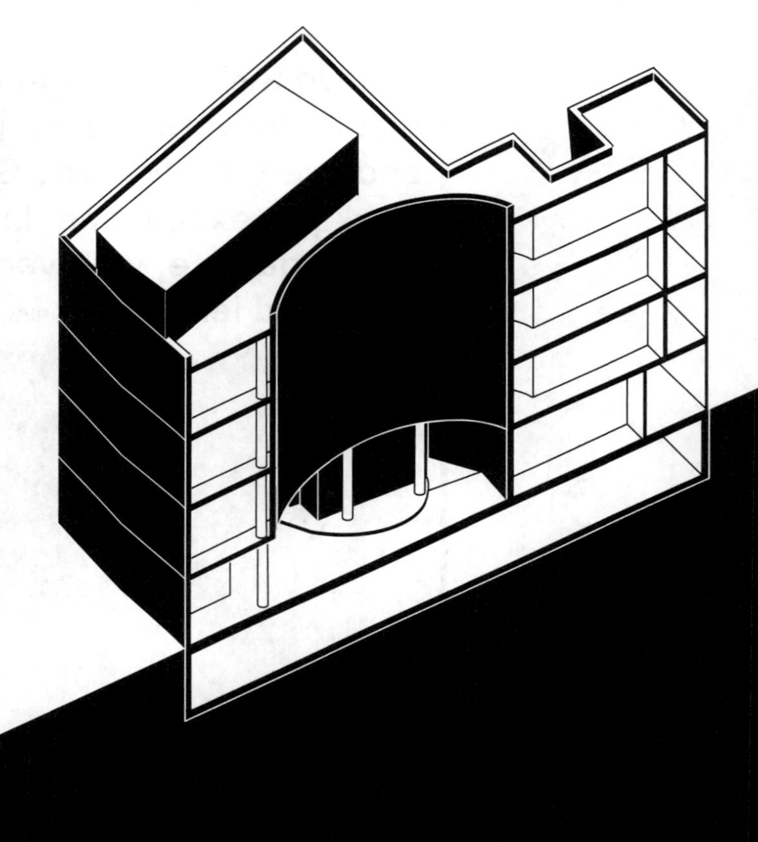

"We like ideas not to be in the foreground... We often have the feeling of practising an art that is already antiquated; whose essence is shared less and less.

Sometimes we have said that we prefer to design single family dwelling rather than a general plan... its results are usually so ungratifying."[46] – Cruz y Ortiz

Sectional axonometry of Doña Maria Coronel Apartments.

Axonometry of the void.

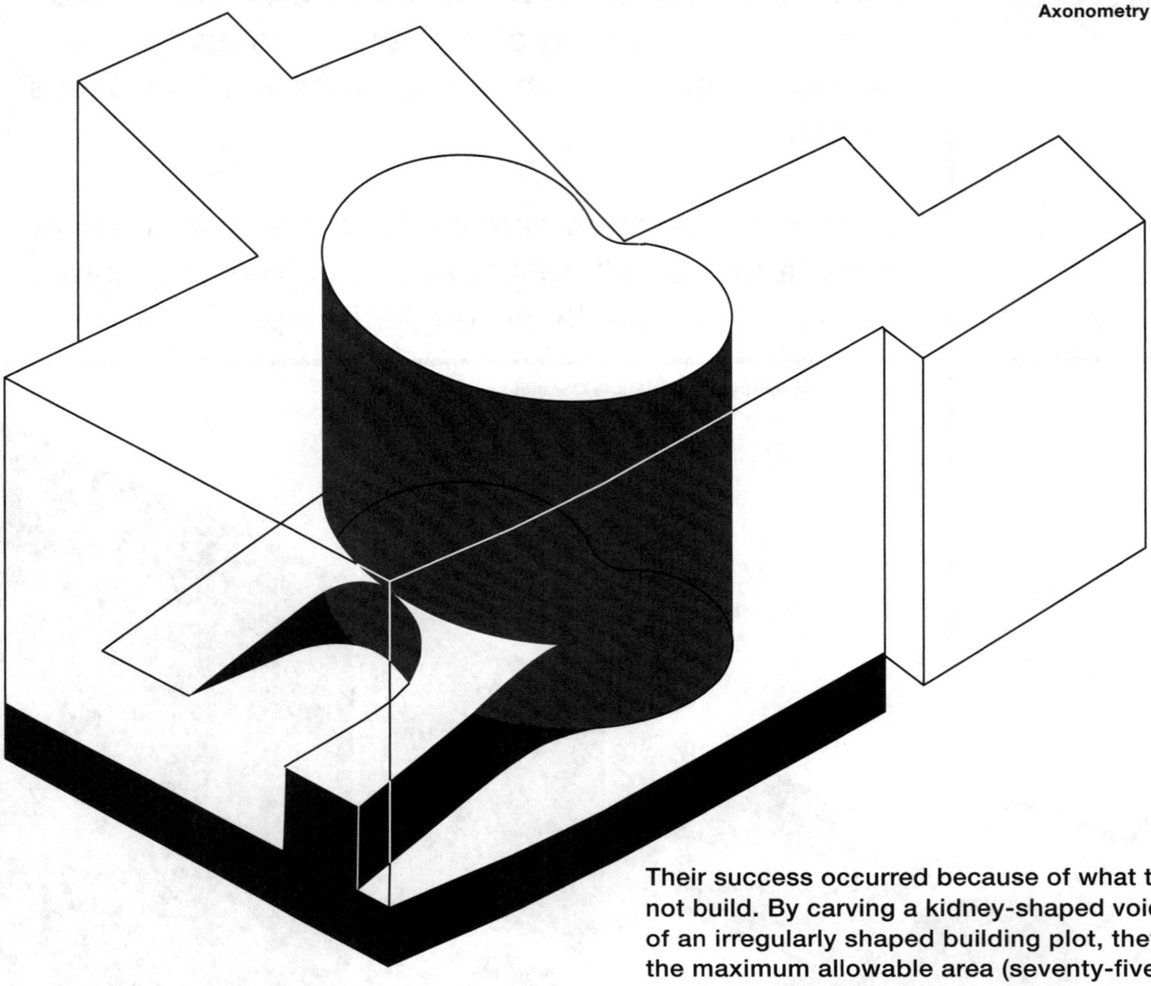

Their success occurred because of what they did not build. By carving a kidney-shaped void out of an irregularly shaped building plot, they filled the maximum allowable area (seventy-five per cent) with absolute grace.

Plan of Doña Maria Coronel Apartments.

The accompanying model says it all. Cruz y Ortiz didn't bother following the site boundary. Instead, they made a model of the central void within a simple cube of wood. The dent in this kidney shape does not justify itself through the protruding corner of the plot. The major limitations of the site have been neutralized and converted into something that has become much stronger.

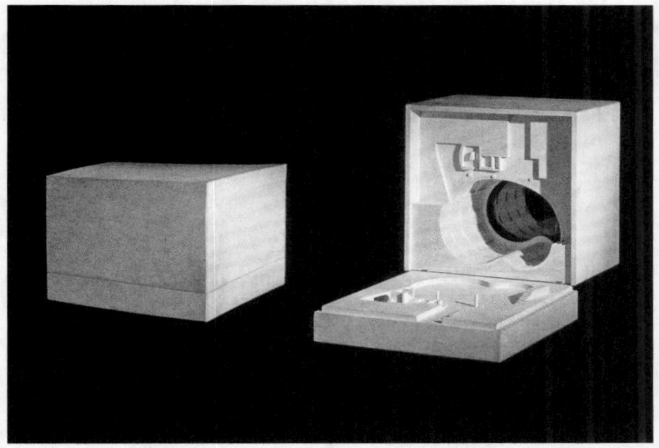

Model of Doña Maria Coronel Apartments.

The design is conceived as a late-renaissance solution to the dense fabric of inner-city Seville. All irregularities are smoothed out by diverting attention from the object to the void. The kidney-shaped courtyard pulls the focus inwards, apartments turn to face it and are accessed from it. The inverted element being a *poché* between the patio and the perimeter walls is parcelled into apartments. It opens up an array of possibilities to orientate the different apartments according to their position within the *poché*. The street facade obscures all of this, only to be revealed once you enter the gate to the central patio. In all its modernity it does exactly what good buildings have done for millennia; creating the best possible background for a maximum quality of everyday life.

Site plan of Doña Maria Coronel Apartments.

The Westin Bonaventure
Los Angeles, USA
John C. Portman
1974–1976

John Portman is the Renaissance man of the late-twentieth century, the living embodiment of the architect-entrepreneur and painter-sculptor, and responsible for many of the artworks incorporated in his designs.[47]

He understood that the commercial exploitation of architecture and development could be a remedy for the deterioration of downtown areas in cities such as Atlanta. They lacked one crucial component and he didn't care: urban planning. This had never been America's biggest forte, but Portman pulled all the tubes from a dying patient and literally connected the buildings with elevated walkways and tubular corridors. Instead of revitalizing the urban realm, he sucked all urbanity in, with the result that a deaf-mute urban space remained.

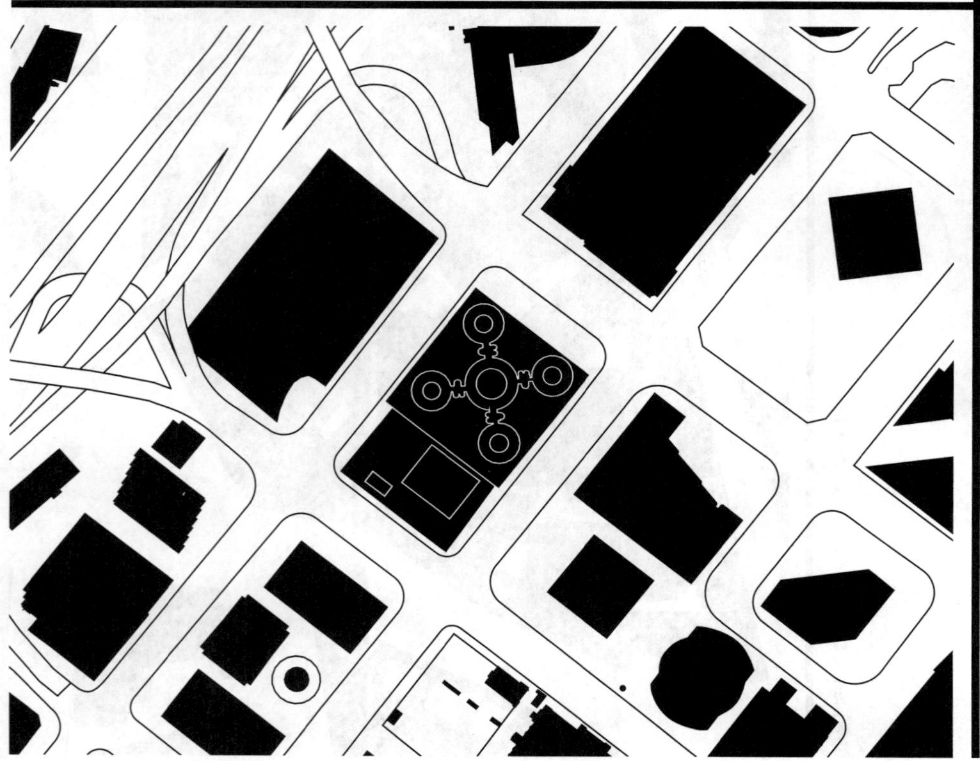

Site plan of Westin Bonaventure.

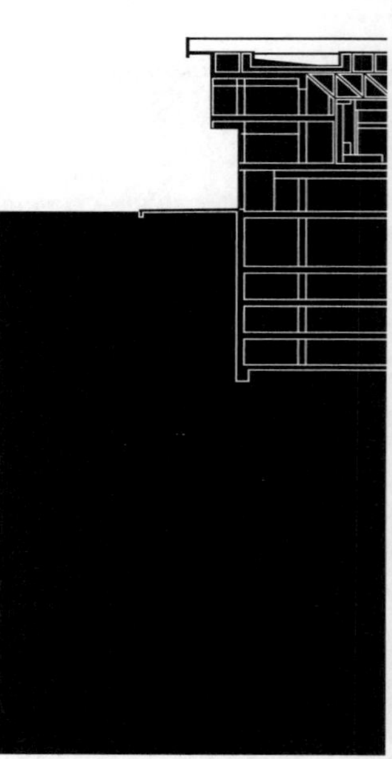

Section of Westin Bonaventure.

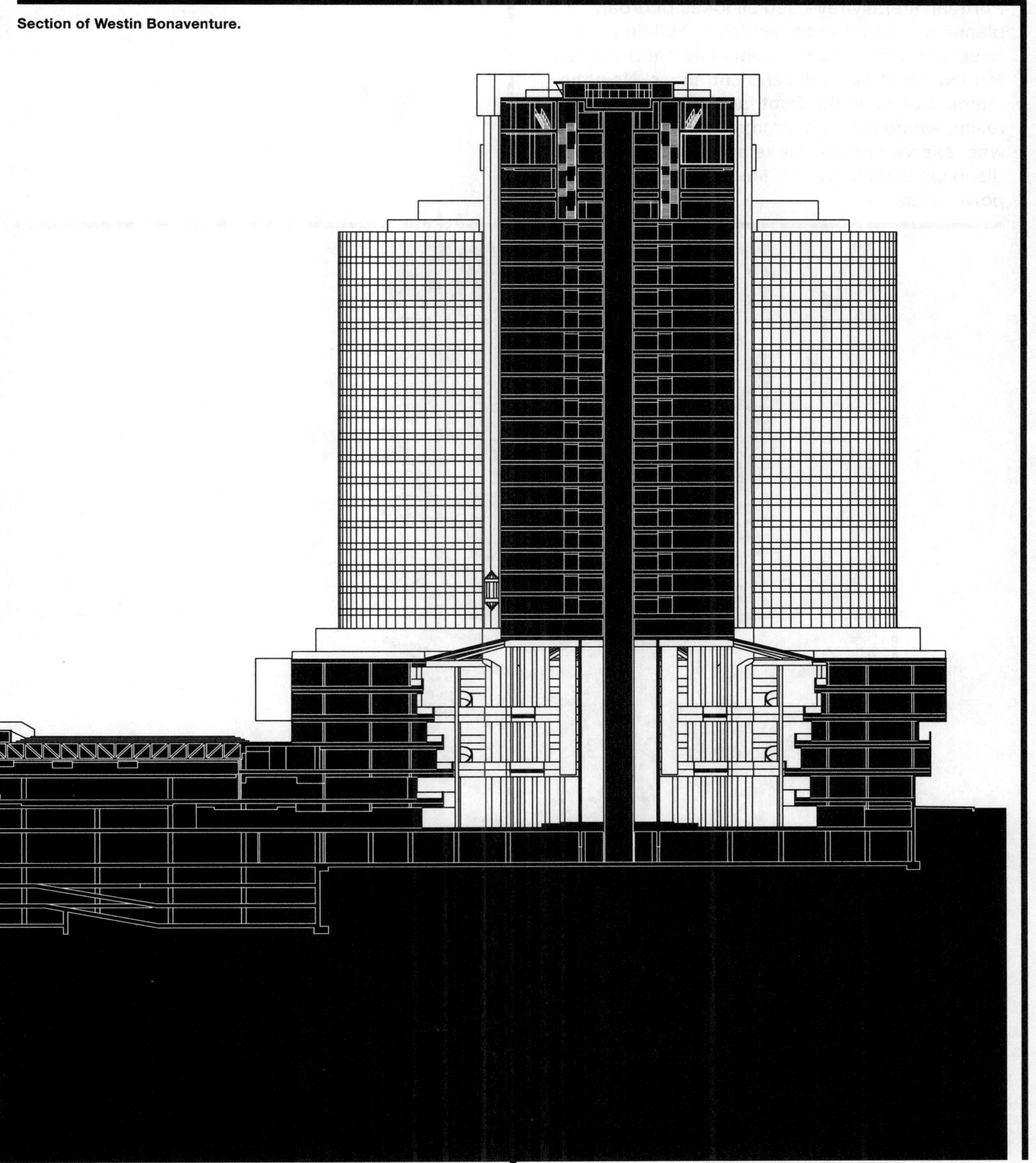

In Atlanta, between 1961 and 2018, Portman designed and developed a whopping two million square metres, but even more important were the carved-out spaces, the voids and atria. Interiorizing public space and controlling temperature and humidity in the hot Georgian summers seemed good enough of a reason. But it created a complete inner-city public life detached from the streets outside.

Portman literally reversed all ideas of urban planning, where the backsides of buildings used to service them and the fronts and shop windows formed the street walls and entrances. Now the interiors became the front face, and the urban realm, where local governments used to reign, was reserved for car parks and entrances, waste disposal, loading docks, fire escapes and power stations.

Marriott Marquis, Atlanta.

The Marriott Marquis, built in 1985, shows an obese slab, bulking out at the lower floors. Hidden inside is an atrium, overwhelmingly high, like looking through the ribs of a centipede. The problem is certainly not the undeniable quality of the interior spaces. It is the shameless lack of ambition to connect and contribute to the city as a whole.

Portman proved that developers didn't need to build in city centres at all. As Rem Koolhaas argues: "At first, the atrium seemed to help rehabilitate and stabilize Atlanta's downtown, but it actually accelerated its demise … with atriums as their private mini-centres, buildings no longer depend on specific locations. They can be anywhere. If they can be anywhere, why should they be downtown?"[48] They had become completely site-less, completely groundless. They might as well be floated off into space.

The atrium of the Hyatt Regency, San Francisco.

Within the oeuvre of John Portman there are also jewels. The intriguing pyramidal volume of San Francisco's Hyatt Regency, with the oversized living room of its atrium, seems to have an appropriate monumentality. It is among the biggest hotel lobbies in the world.

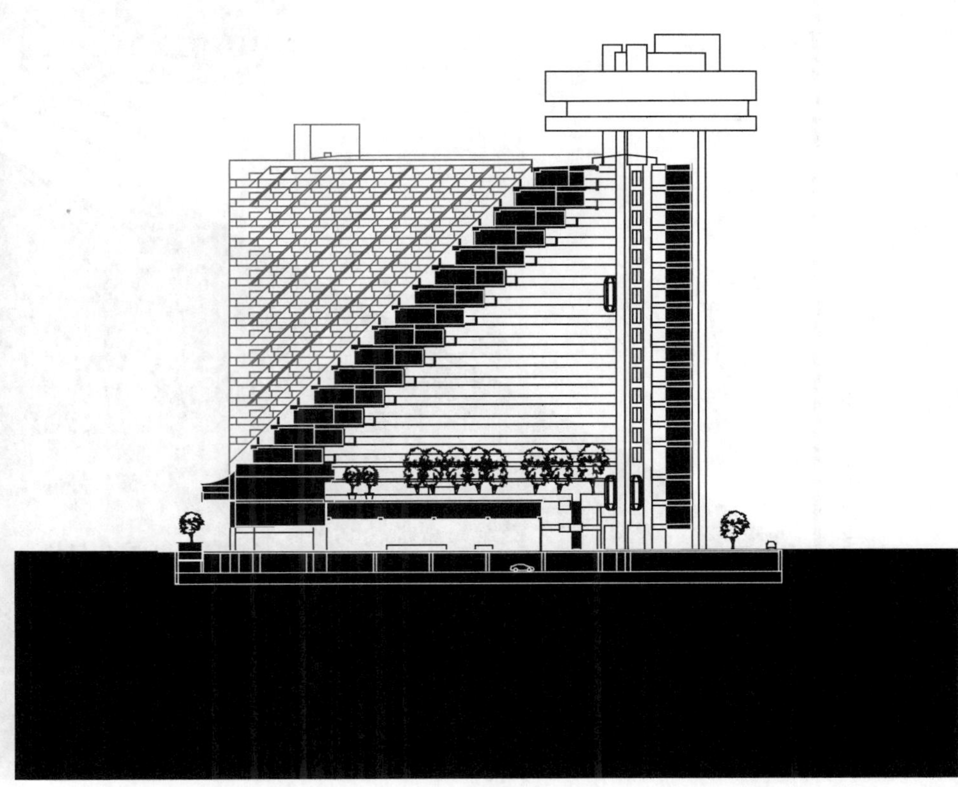

Section of the Hyatt Regency, San Francisco, John C. Portman, 1973.

The Westin Bonaventure Hotel is less a single carved-out space from one big volume, or less one open space between hotel slabs, and more a hybrid space, or as Portman himself describes it, a kinetic or centrifugal sculpture.

At the root of five round towers, set up like the quincunx on a die, an elaborate network of walkways, floating seats, water gardens, fountains, trees and surging lifts creates an urban jungle. The multi-circular set-up disorients completely, strengthening the closed-circuit feeling of a world turning into itself. Sunlight pops in through the glass roof that circles the central tower and between the four corner towers and their base.

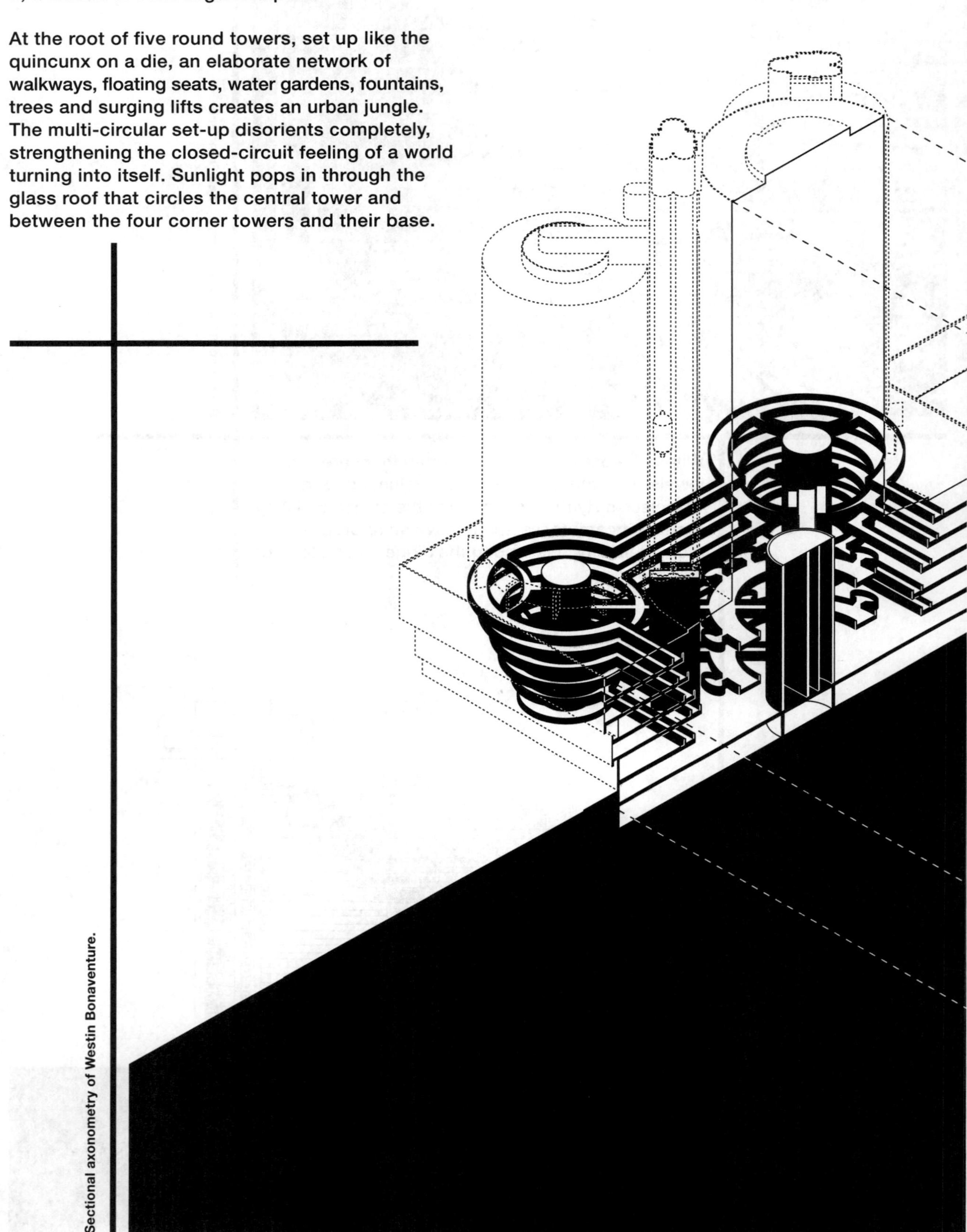

Sectional axonometry of Westin Bonaventure.

But the most curious thing is the base itself. It is a completely numb block of concrete, 90 x 90 metres wide, with not a single opening on West Fourth Street. For a complex this big, managing all the necessary movement of goods and people, it is clearly deliberate.

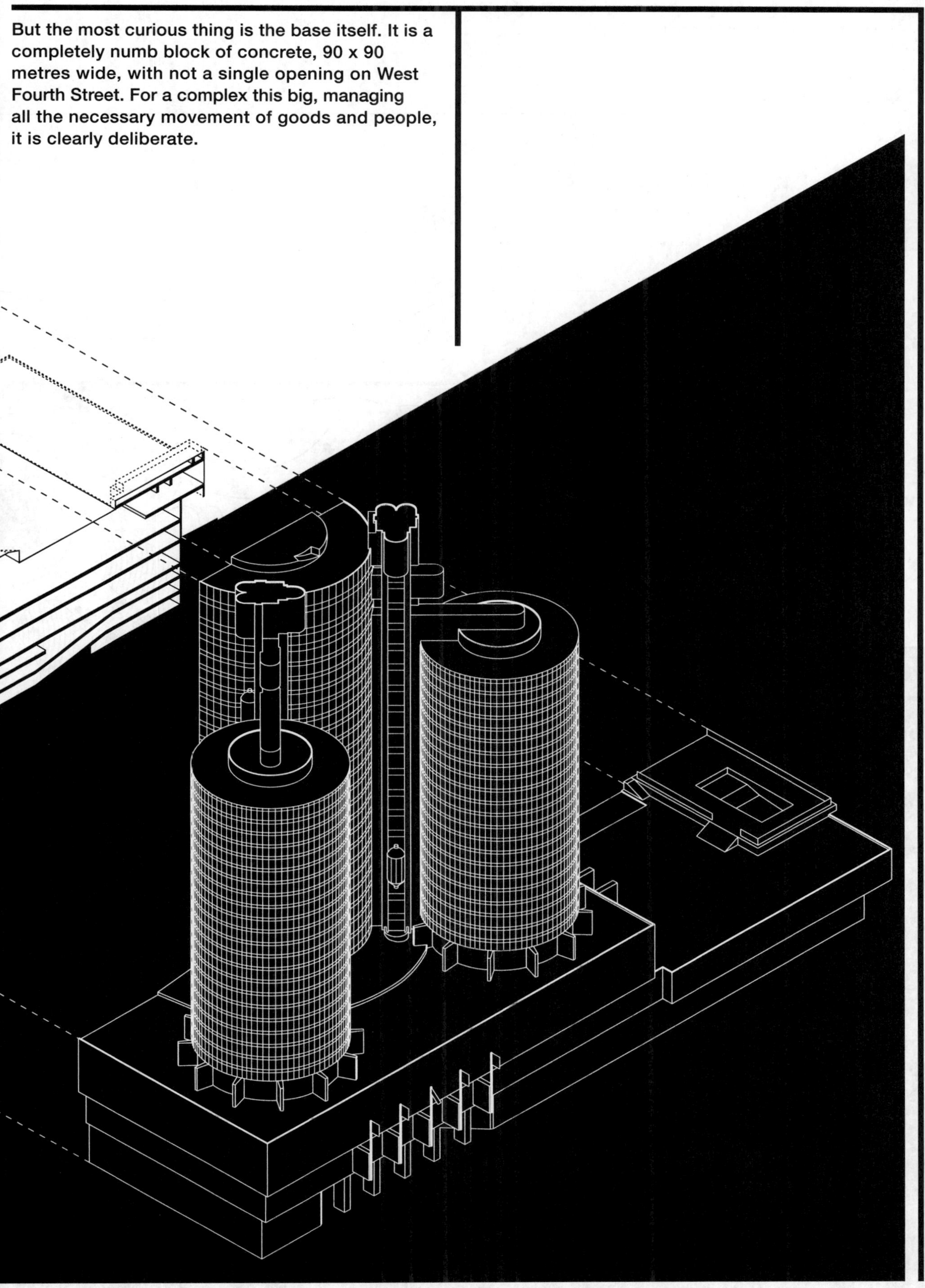

Ground floor plan of Westin Bonaventure.

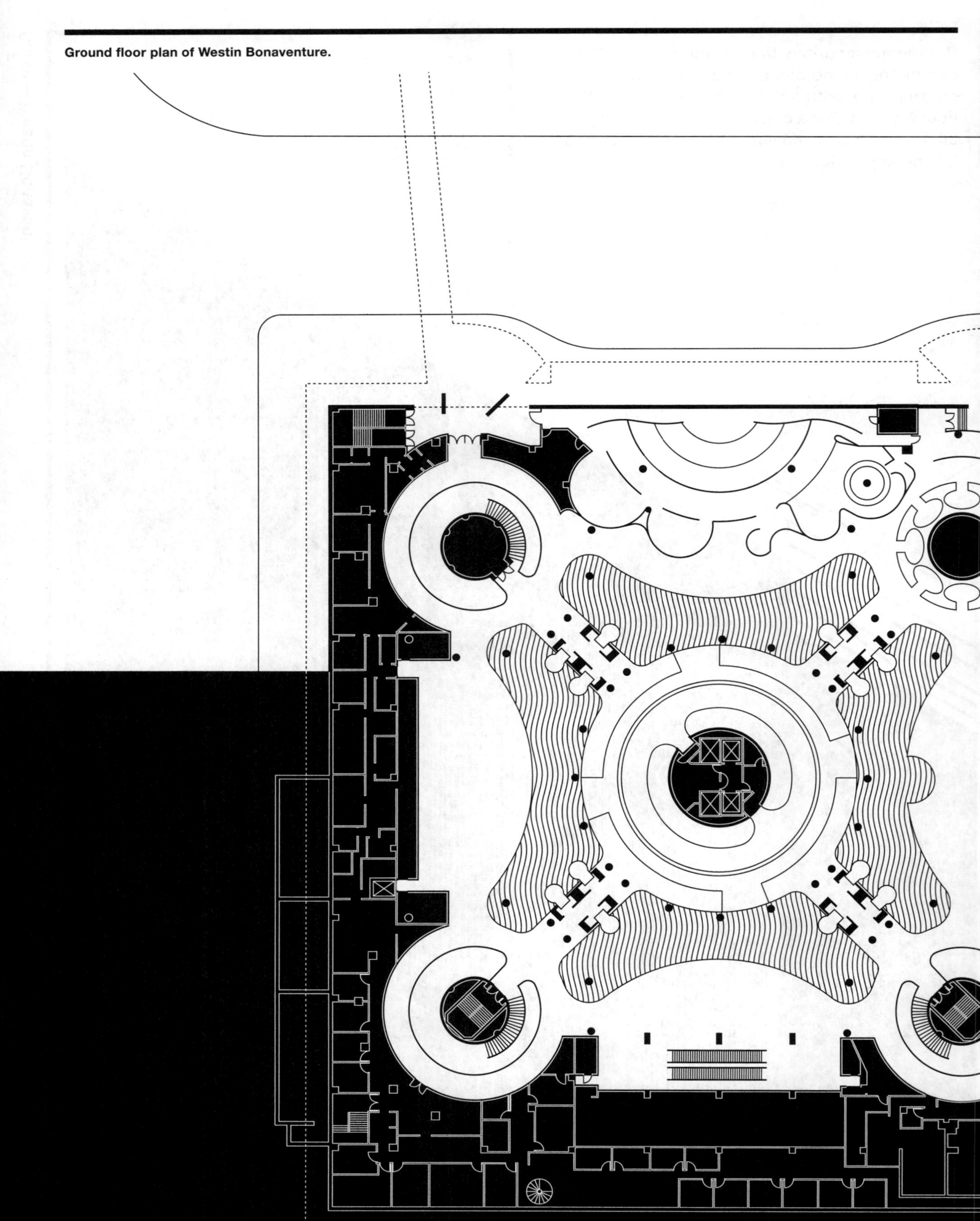

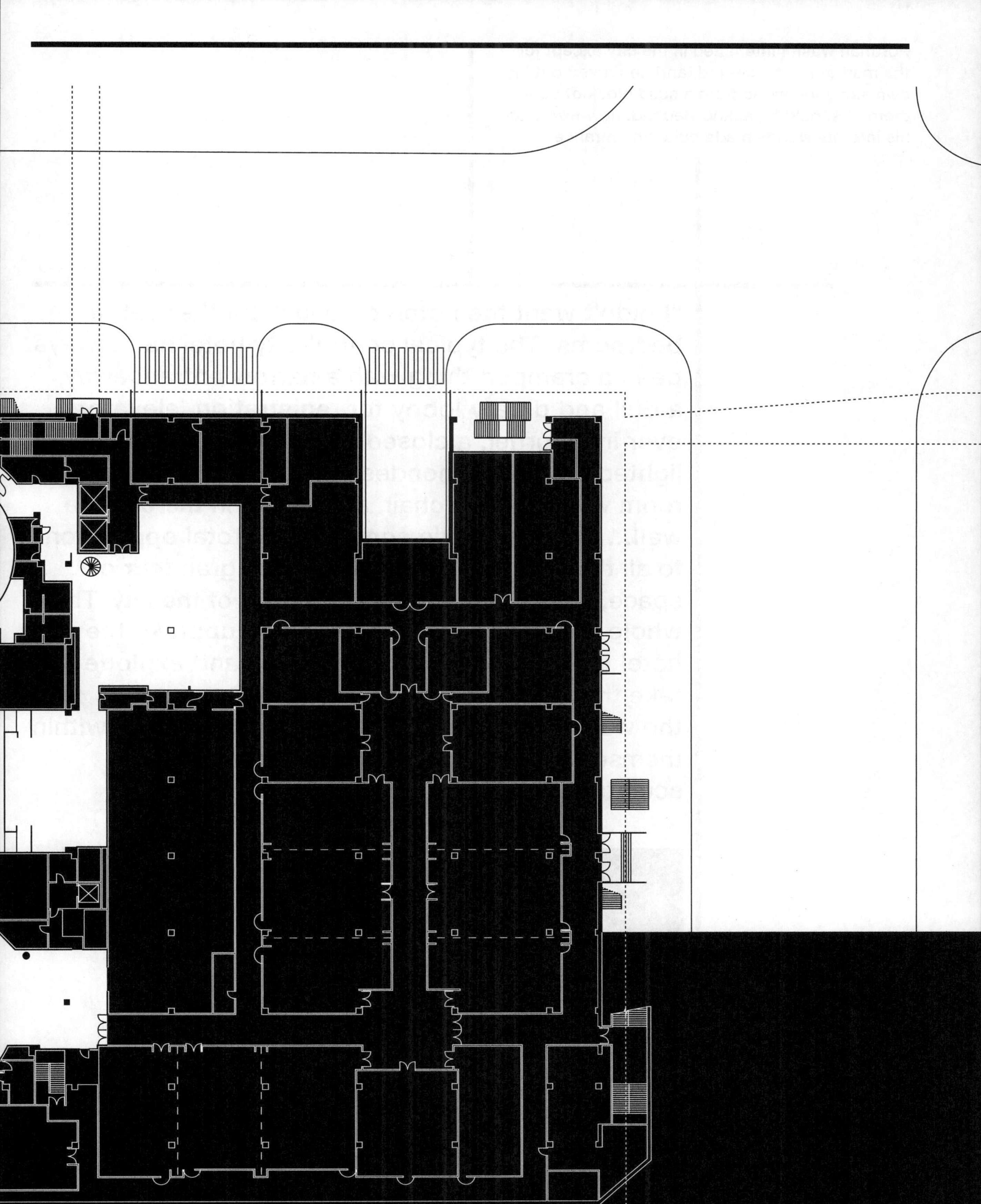

Portman wasn't interested in the city except for the market it represented, and he carved out his own secluded world from a solid block of concrete. It should be acknowledged, however, that his internal worlds made quite an entrance.

"I didn't want the hotel to be just another set of bedrooms. The typical central-city hotel had always been a cramped thing with a narrow entranceway, a dull and dreary lobby for registration, elevators over in a corner, a closed elevator cab, a dimly lighted corridor, a nondescript doorway, and a hotel room with a bed, a chair, and a hole in the outside wall... I wanted to do something in total opposition to all this, to open it up; to create a grandeur of space, almost a resort, in the center of the city. The whole idea was to open everything up; take the hotel from its closed, tight position and explode it; take the elevators and literally pull them out of the walls and let them become an experience within themselves, let them become a giant kinetic sculpture."[49] —John Portman

Westin Bonaventure atrium.

LuxBus AMERICA

BREWERY
3
3

6

The most cynical aspect is that Portman built himself a private residence called Entelechy I, where nature and the built environment merge to form a utopian paradise. And this was as early as 1964! In 1986 he built himself another paradise, creatively named Entelechy II, which is a flabbergasting mix of lush vegetation, air, water and art under a single canopy.[50]

Entelechy I, Atlanta, John C. Portman, 1964.

Entelechy II, Sea Island, John C. Portman, 1986.

Portman perfected the adage that spending money is the opposite of making money. While his private houses were a paragon of exterior permeability, his colossal urban hotels completely excluded the outside world. The often dysfunctional American downtowns of Atlanta, Los Angeles, San Francisco and Detroit received a dystopian counterpart. Not surprisingly, his buildings became the backdrop for several apocalyptic movies.[51] No film set or computer animation was needed. It was already there, a twenty-minute drive from Hollywood and, let's face it, extremely well made.

Street elevation of Villa KBWW.

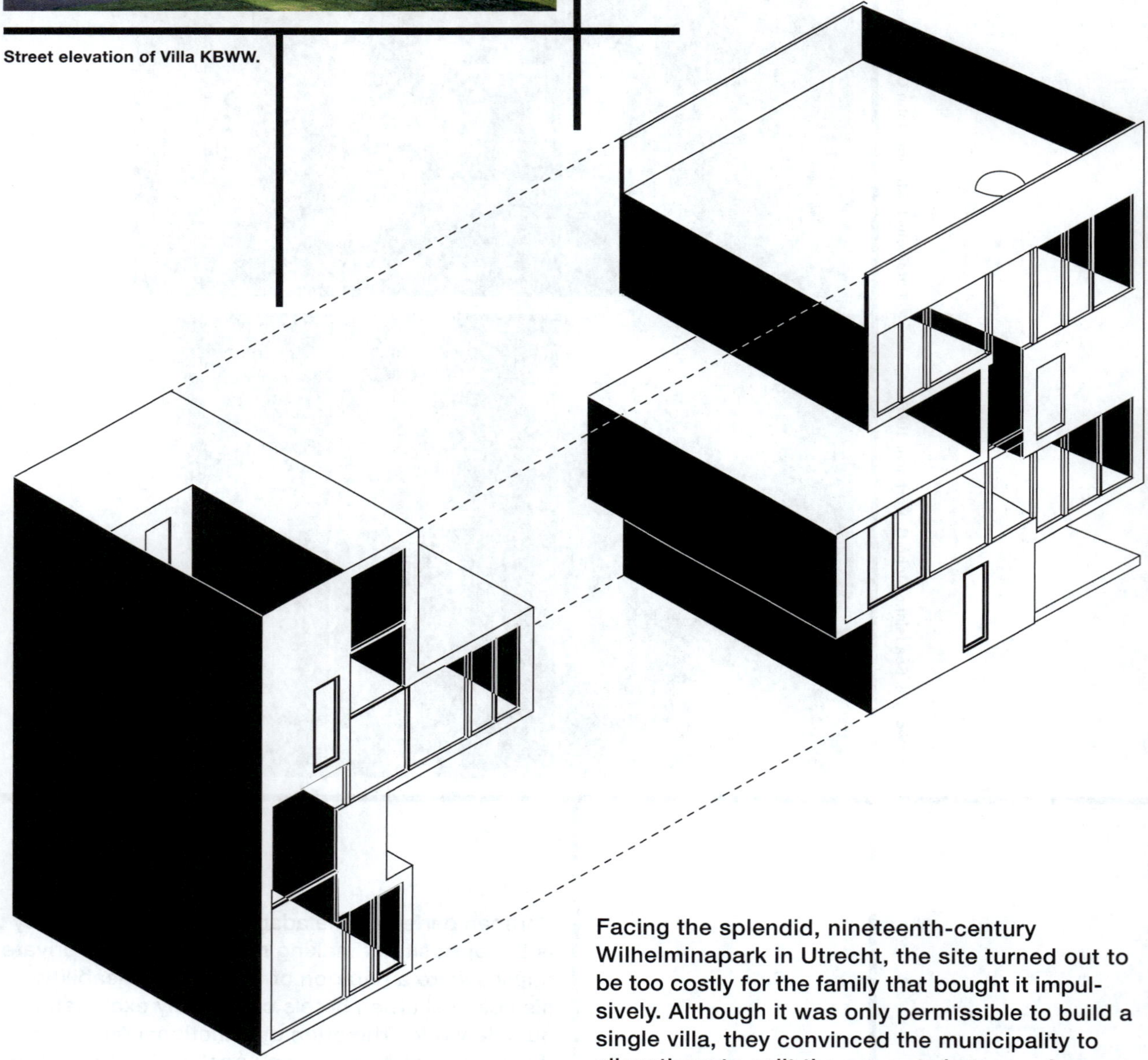

Villa KBWW
Utrecht, Netherlands
SeARCH & MVRDV
1994–1998

Axonometry of Villa KBWW.

Facing the splendid, nineteenth-century Wilhelminapark in Utrecht, the site turned out to be too costly for the family that bought it impulsively. Although it was only permissible to build a single villa, they convinced the municipality to allow them to split the property in two as long as they continued the row of adjacent monumental villas. Villa KBWW respects its neighbours by obscuring the boundary between the two houses (KB and WW) and presenting itself to the street as a single entity.

Hôtel de Carnavalet, Paris, France.

Fourteenth-century Chalet, Engadin, Switzerland.

Chalet, Graubunden, Switzerland.

Combining dwellings into a single volume is common in French hôtels and Swiss chalets, which are often designed as multi-family houses.

For both homes there was a desire to combine the best views of the park with easy access to the garden at the back. Keeping the depth of the house to an absolute minimum meant that every room in the house could have both, and the programme could be 'stretched' upwards to four or five storeys, making the garden as large as possible.

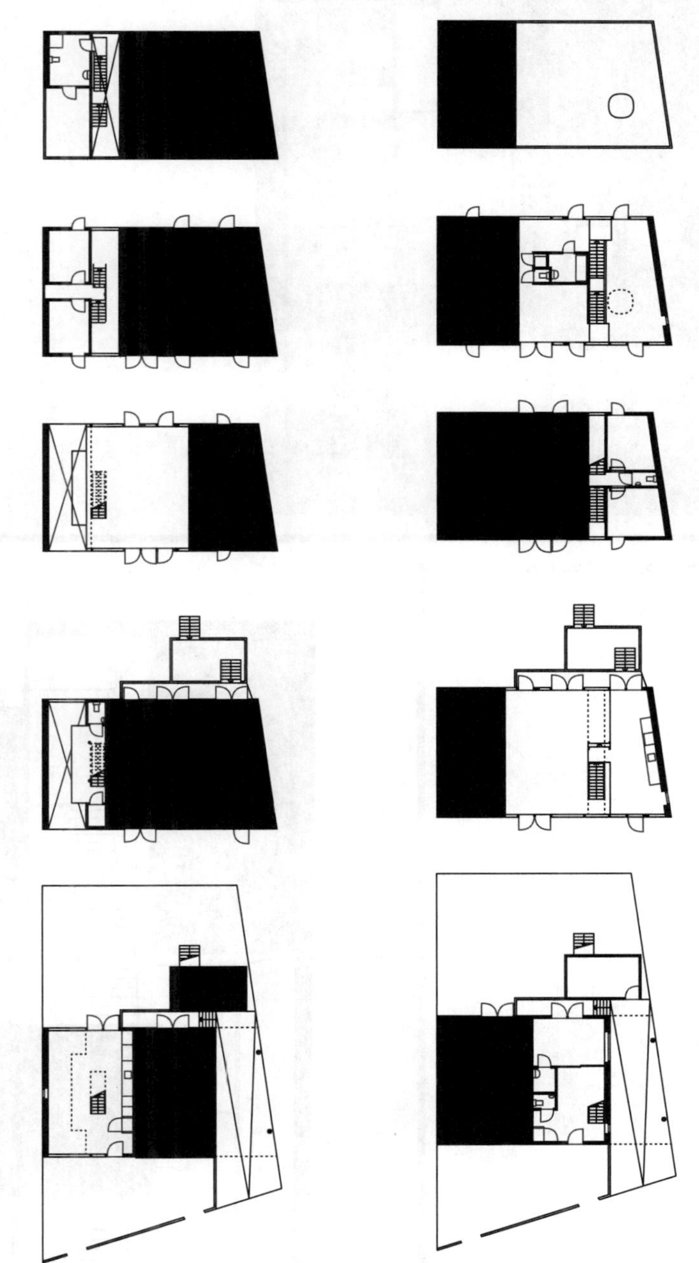

Plans of Villa KB (left) with kitchen on ground floor connected via a library landing with the second-floor living room. Plans of Villa WW (right) with living and kitchen on the first floor connected to a study and open master bedroom on the third floor.

The two interlocking volumes of KB & WW give a distinct character to each of the houses. One volume intrudes on the other, acting as a form of *poché* and enriching the spatial character of what are essentially two terrace houses side by side.

Living space of Villa KB.

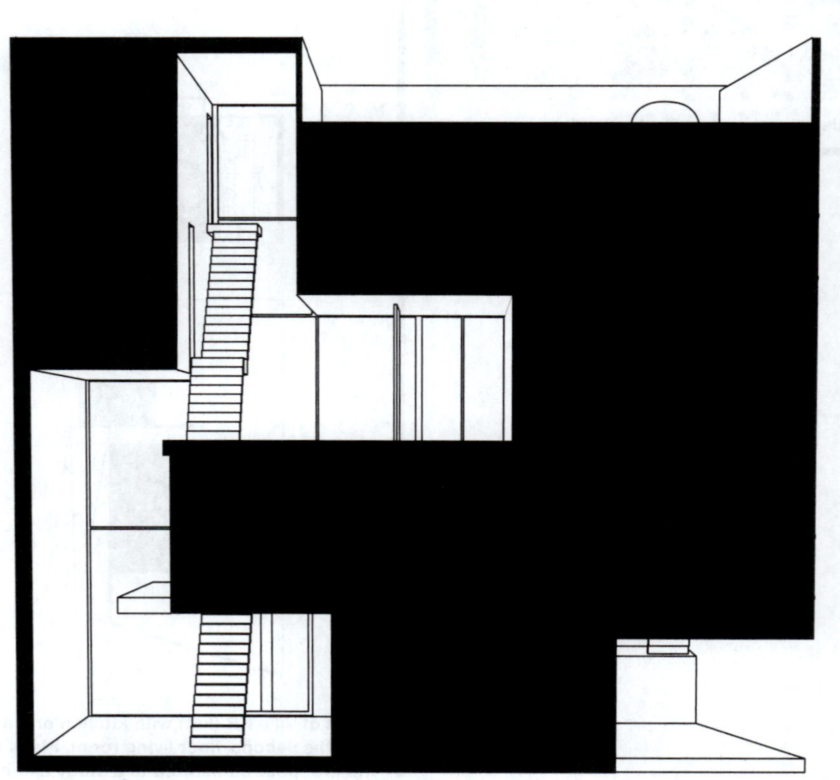

The partition wall between apartments was used as a 'therapeutic stick', which was moved backwards and forwards during negotiations between the neighbours to satisfy their sometimes conflicting wishes. Here, various interpretations can coexist. One occupant wants to be surrounded by the garden, another withdraws to the *piano nobile*, one chooses a salon just past the children's playrooms, another opts for a work-cum-bedroom upstairs, and so on. Levels of privacy play out in a different way here. All services and clearly secluded spaces are arranged around the two interlocking main spaces, while the bedrooms of both families 'float' above as houses-in-a-house.

While the house fulfils its obligation as a dutiful monumental villa, it has a playful, spatially complex interior world. When ringing the doorbell on the right, you might notice that a window opens on the left on the second floor, creating a Tati-esque entanglement.

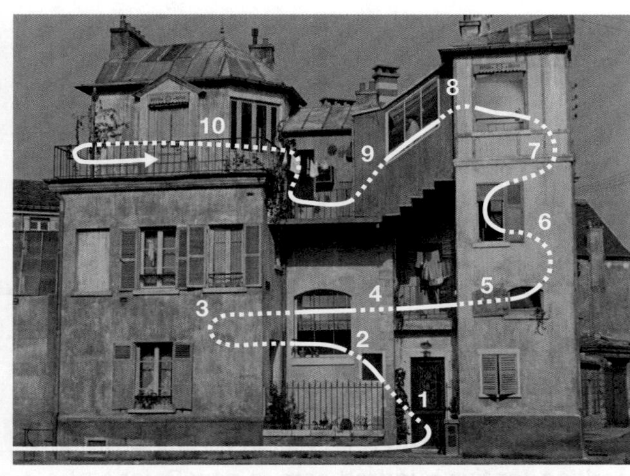

Monsieur Hulot weaving through his apartment building. ***Mon Oncle*****, Jacques Tati, 1957.**

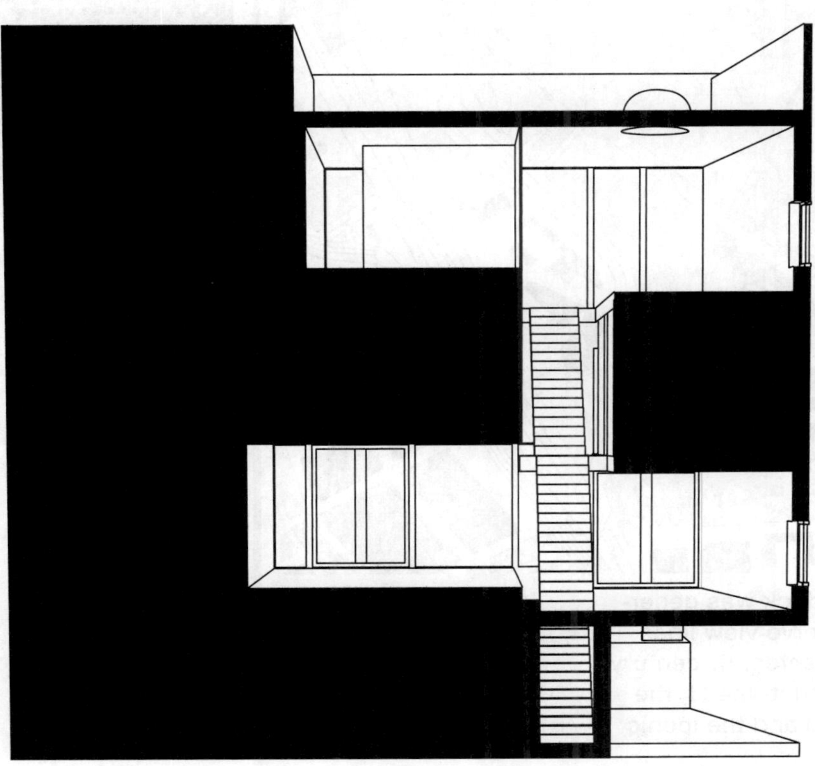
Sections of Villa KB (left) and Villa WW (right).

IJdock
Amsterdam, Netherlands
SeARCH
1999–2013

In the booming mid-1990s there was an ambitious plan to develop a multifunctional urban complex of 90 000 square metres on the southern quay of the IJ waterway, a short distance from Amsterdam Central Station. The brief called for underground parking for five hundred cars, a new Palace of Justice, a five-star hotel, apartments, a new office for the water police, commercial space and a new marina. In short, an enormous mass on a high-profile and highly visible site.

Site plan of IJdock.

The unique form and skyline of IJdock was generated by carving out space to preserve view lines and connections between the seventeenth-century UNESCO world heritage canal district, the IJ, the western docks, the Central Station and the iconic Shell tower on the northern shore.

Mitre block, a woodworking tool.

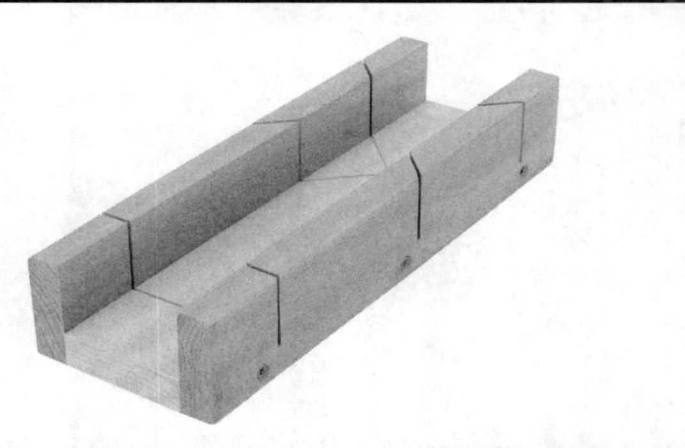

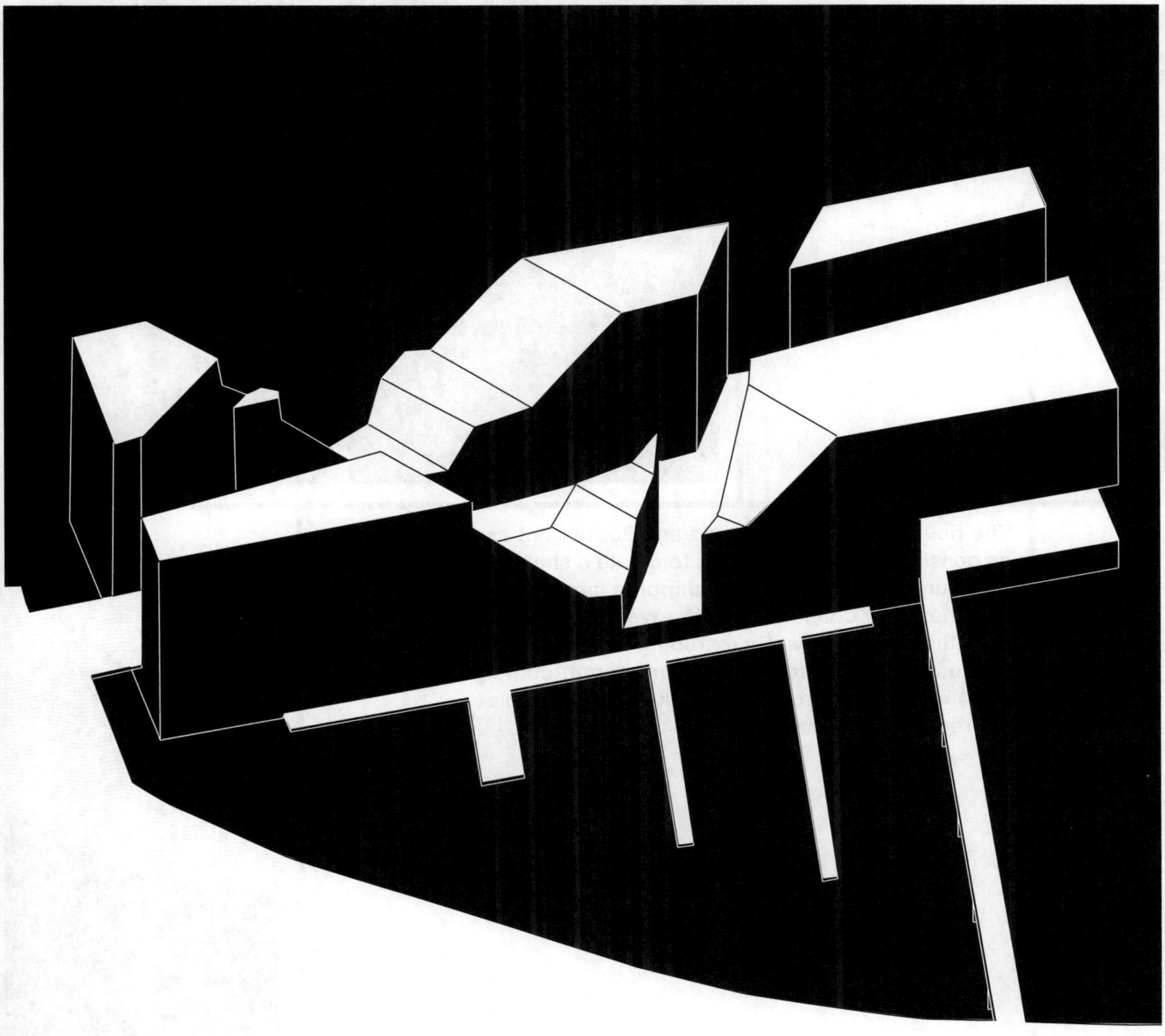

The resulting building came out of a process of 'reverse negotiation' with the twenty-six client bodies and external parties such as the 'Friends of the Inner City', who oppose most new initiatives on principle. But instead of creating a volume only to chip away at it with endless compromises, the making of IJdock considered the sound advice of Monty Python: *how to not be seen.*

Axonometry of IJdock.

The development was flipped and floated out as far as possible from the dockside to create a sheltered harbour for the marina. The shipping lanes of the IJ and the water connection to the Westerdok formed the other boundaries. By extruding the 60-by-180-metre footprint up to its maximum permitted height of 44 metres, we produced a volume with double the required floor area.

This allowed half of the mass to be cut, carved away or excavated. The unique form and skyline was generated by intersecting lines of sight and the specific stipulations of the many parties involved. Site conditions (footprint), programme (volume) and the urban interventions (void) come together to form a genuine 'polder model' design.

Section of IJdock.

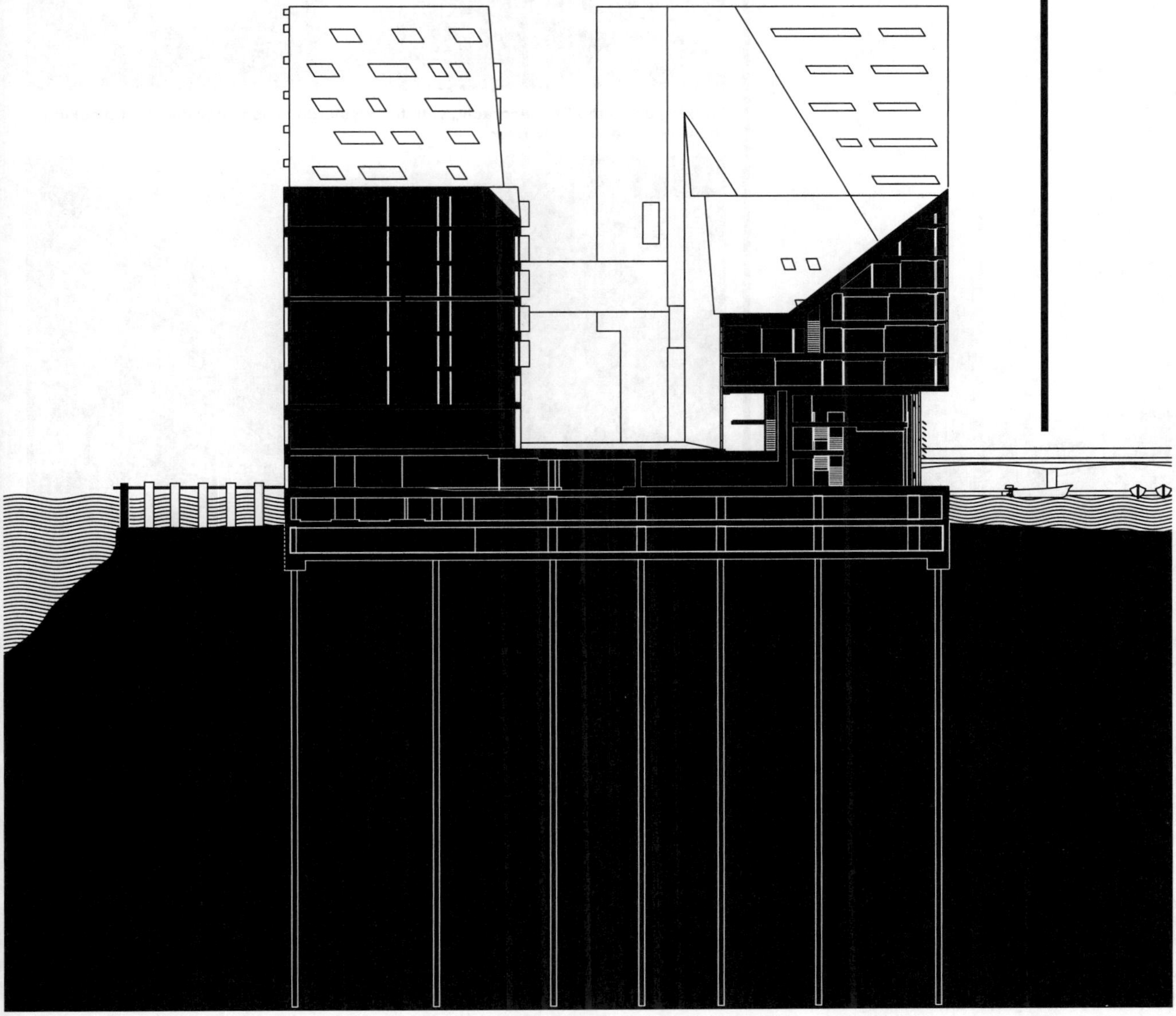

The ‘Caesarean cut’ (with a view to Keizersgracht) and the Central Station cut (with a station view) are the most important and prominent. In the last century, three of the four canals that originated from the Haarlemmerdijk were visually cut off from the IJ, most recently when the Westerdok was redeveloped. Dramatically lowering the height of IJdock in the middle preserves the view down the Keizersgracht and the seventeenth-century profile of the Brouwersgracht canal house.

Looking down the Prinsengracht, with the Westerdok Island development blocking the view towards the IJ river.

Looking down the Keizersgracht towards the lower canal houses of the Browersgracht. The IJdock is not visible due to its lowered profile.

From left, Prinsengracht and Keizersgracht, 1974.

A cut inspired by Michael Heizer's *Double Negative* branches off from the quay and opens up the block towards central station. Where Heizer's cut reaches over the canyon to the other side, the IJdock cut leaps a bend in the River IJ to look directly into the vaulted space above the railway tracks. As with Heizer's work, the IJdock celebrates what is not there, the mass of what remains is strengthened by what has been removed.

Double negative, **Nevada desert, Michael Heizer, 1969.**

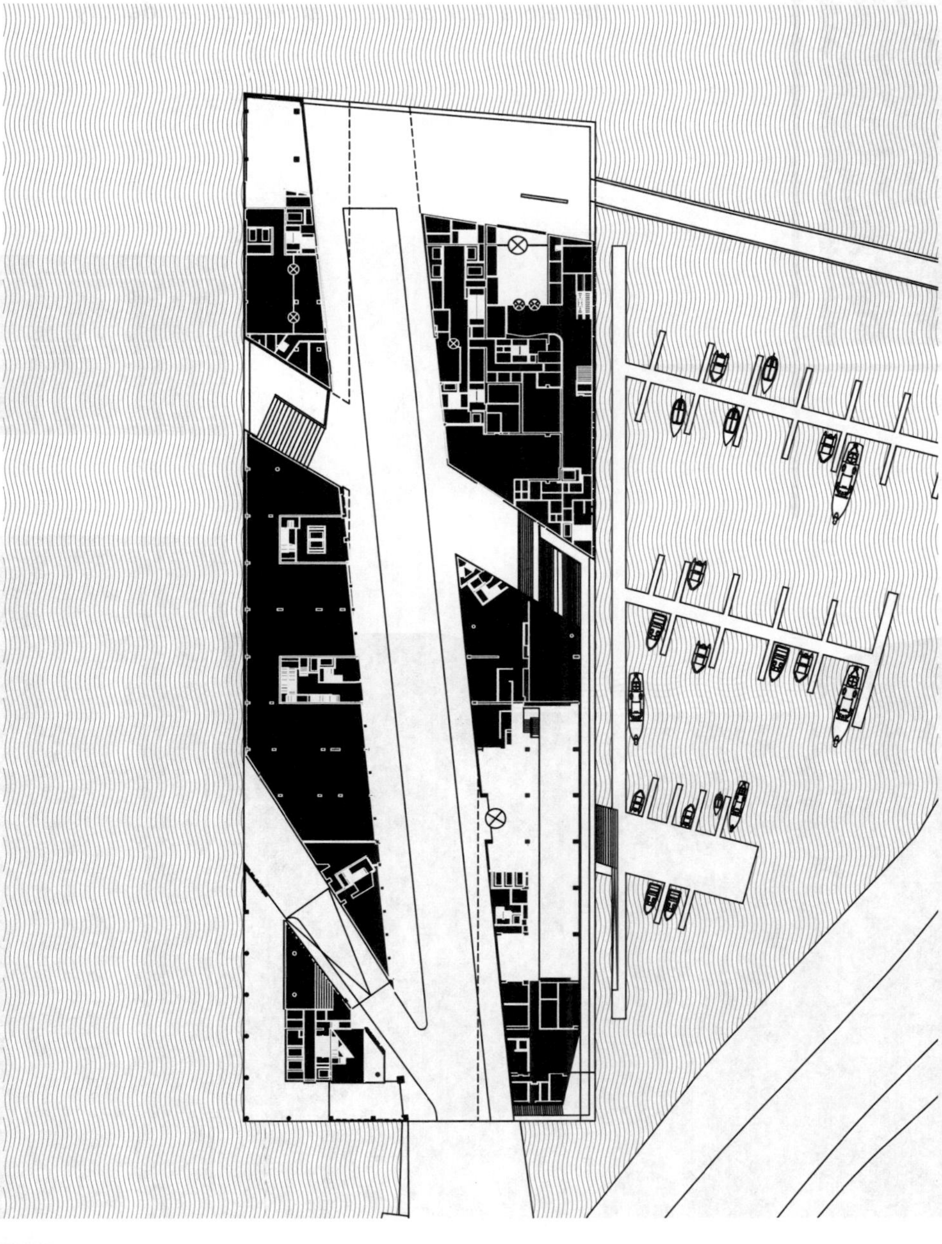

Ground level plan of IJdock.

Synagogue LJG
Amsterdam, Netherlands
SeARCH
2005–2010

Traditionally cathedrals, mosques and temples are strong, recognizable typologies with prominent silhouettes, while synagogues can be more diverse in their appearance and often even unremarkable. In part due to the diasporic existence of the religion, there is no set blueprint for a synagogue, and the ceremonial traditions and rituals present few recognizable reference points for the synagogue's physical expression. They are usually built in the prevailing style of their time and place, and therefore lack a unified architectural identity.

Section of Synagogue LJG showing both void and raised platform.

The cathedral, mosque and temple are distinguished by external silhouettes; the synagogue is recognizable by elements housed within.

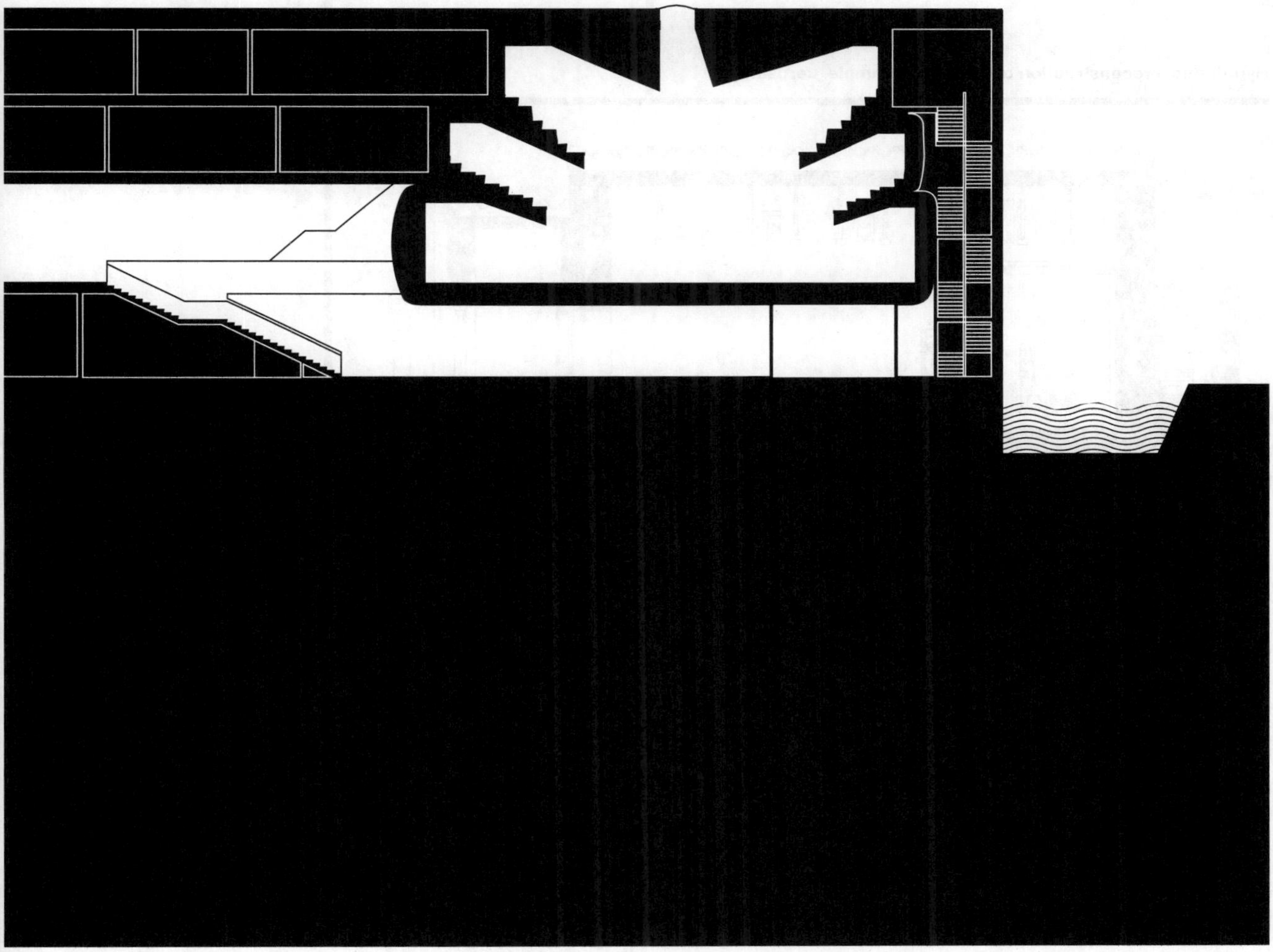

The need for abundant natural light and the customary positioning of the benches opposite each other and parallel to the axis between the *bimah* (platform for Torah reading) and the ark (depository for the Torah scrolls) were the most important starting points for the design process.[52] The orthogonal shape of the synagogue for the Liberal Jewish Congregation of Amsterdam is a reference to the descriptions of the first temple, the Temple of Solomon, which presumably stood in Jerusalem from 974 to 587 BCE. Highly symbolic gestures integrated within the building and on the facade reflect the beliefs central to Judaism.

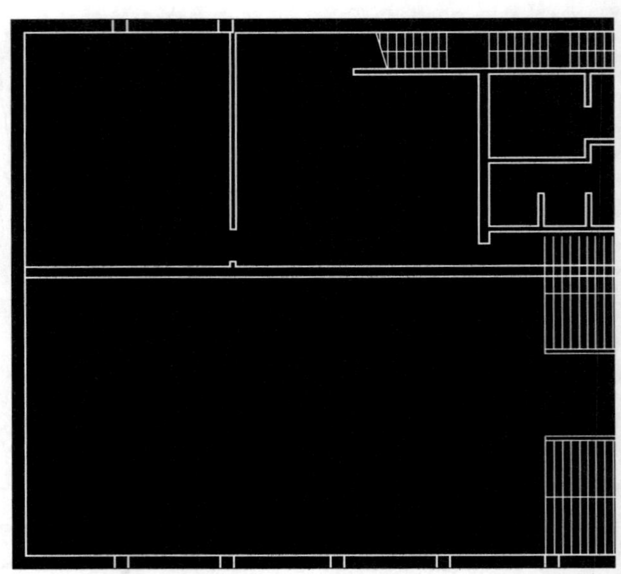

Plan of the Synagogue LJG.

Hypothetical reconstruction of Solomon's Temple, Jerusalem.

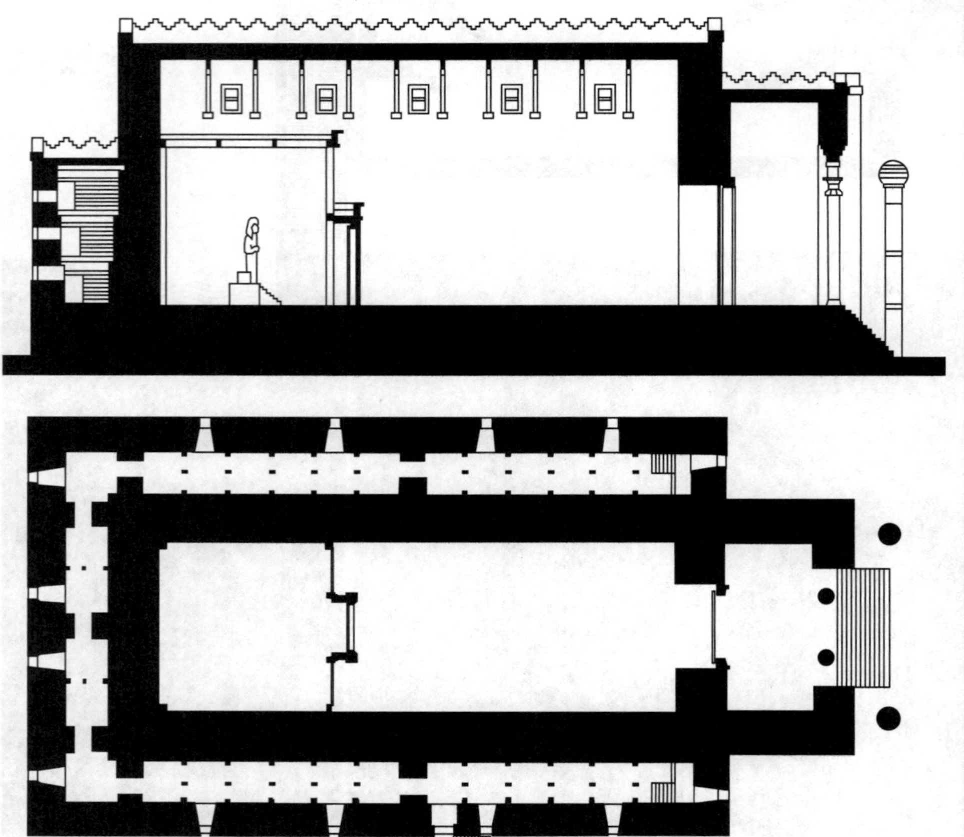

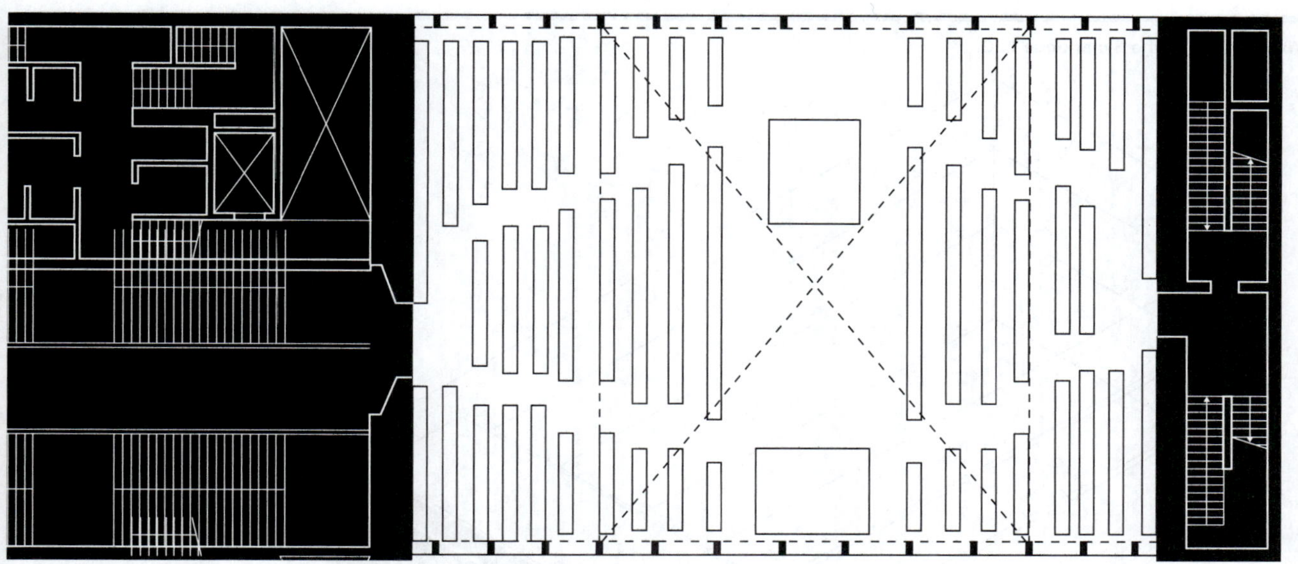

The hollowing out of a mass, to form the 'emptiness' of the great ceremonial hall, or shul, lends the building its identity.

Axonometry of the Synagogue LJG.

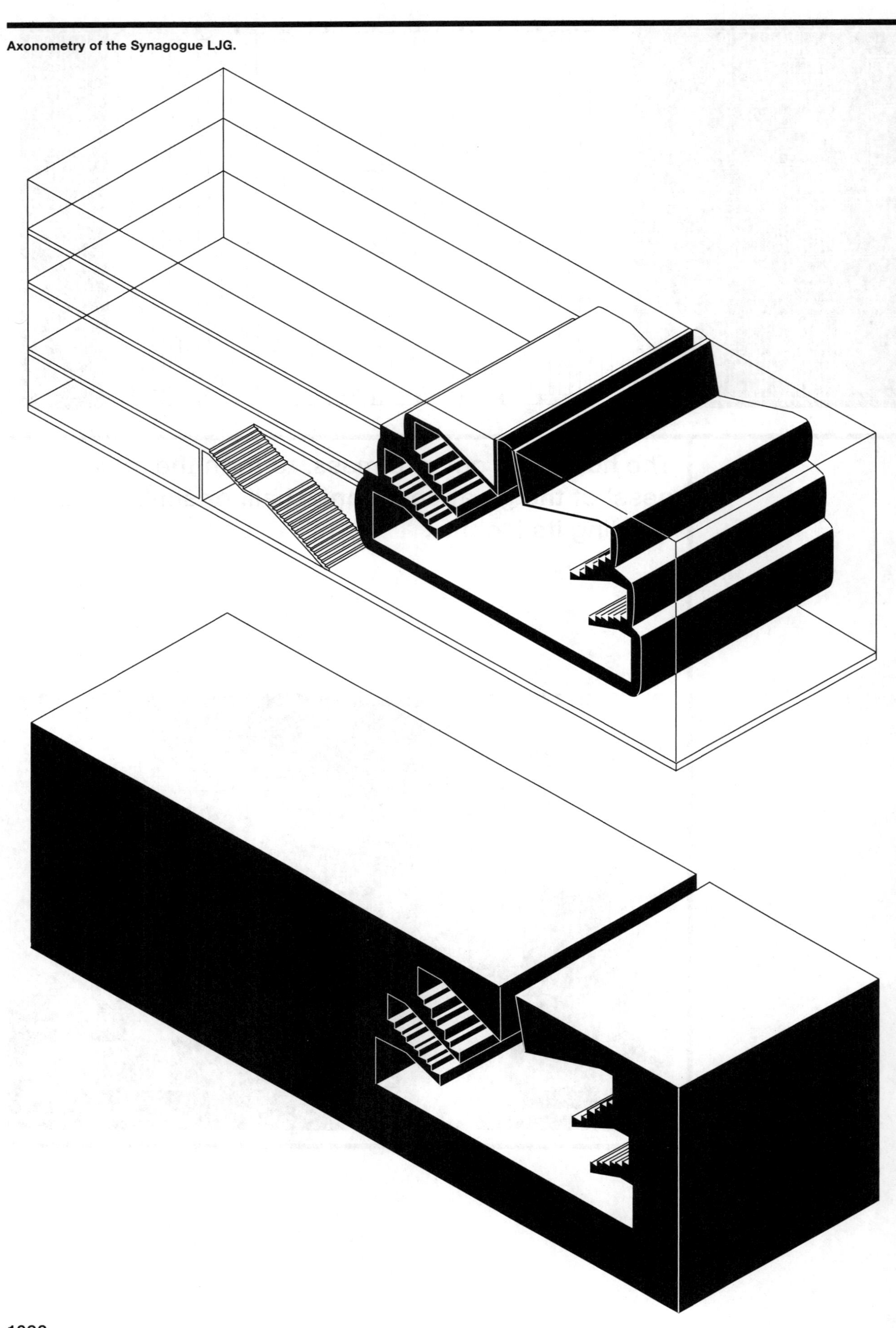

Two side wings under the balconies, two balconies on each side of the shul and a skylight right above the axis between *bimah* and ark make up a seven-fingered void that erupts from within, a central space open to the heavens. This void perforates the rather closed-box shape from west to east, marking the direction toward Jerusalem. This menorah shape, the seven-armed candelabrum and symbol of the burning bush revealed to Moses on Mount Sinai, is the oldest and most revered symbol of Judaism.

All other programmatic elements enclose this sculpted form, completely wrapping it in a warm oak finish. Like in Solomon's temple, the only extravagance permitted are the golden doors that provide access to the shul. The route from the main entrance to the shul is designed as a procession along spaces that have a strong outdoor connection. A grand staircase brings you to a raised platform, often an open courtyard, or *azarah*. This is named after Anne Frank, who was part of this congregation between 1933 and 1942. As with the Temple Mount in Jerusalem, the act of ascending to a raised temple, church, mosque or shul offers a new ground for contemplation.

Markthal
Rotterdam, Netherlands
MVRDV
2009–2014

The new covered market hall of Rotterdam is at first glance a clear example of negotiating a mutually beneficial relationship between two programmes. The ideas of Henri Sauvage's terraced housing in Paris and John Portman's Hyatt Regency in San Francisco run through its veins, lightly skipping a few generations.[53] And further back in its bloodline, two distant relatives, the Pantheon in Rome and the Santa Maria del Fiore in Florence, exert their influence.[54]

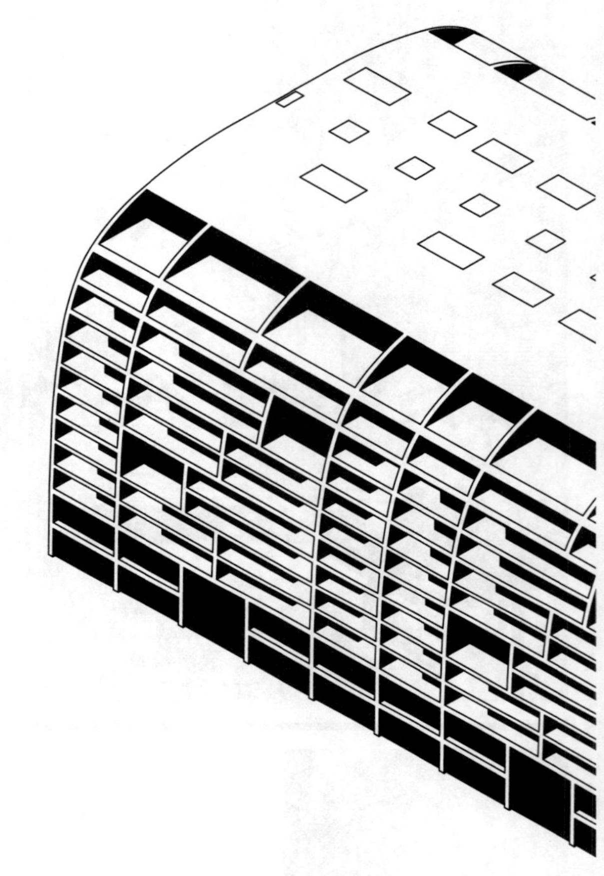

Sectional axonometry of the Markthal.

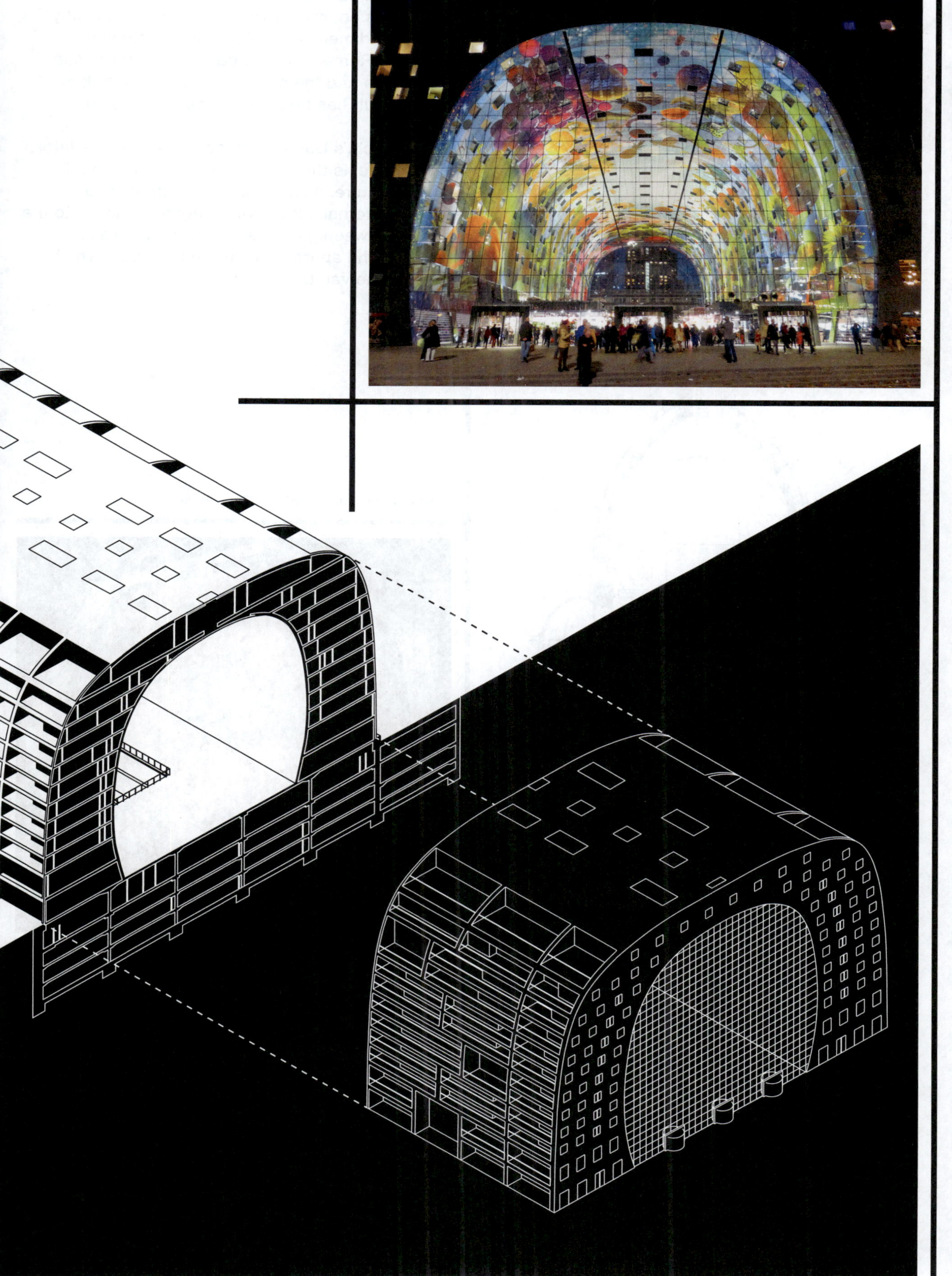

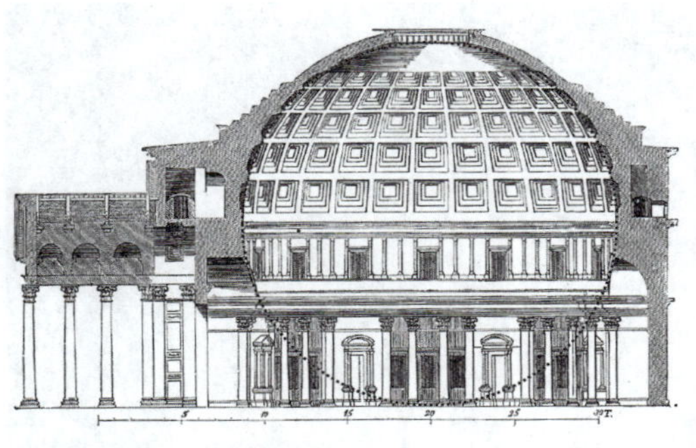

Pantheon, Rome, rebuilt 113–125 CE, 43.5 metres in diameter.

The perfect dome of the Pantheon and the Markthal's enormous vault have almost exactly the same dimensions, although the circular set-up in Rome is stretched into a linear one in Rotterdam and the concrete mass that makes up the vault has been activated as housing.

Brunelleschi's Dome, built some 1400 years later in Florence, is the earliest example of a double-shell structure. A lighter external cupola and heavier internal cupola work together thanks to the ribs in between, just like the structural walls between the apartments in the Markthal, which hold up the vault.

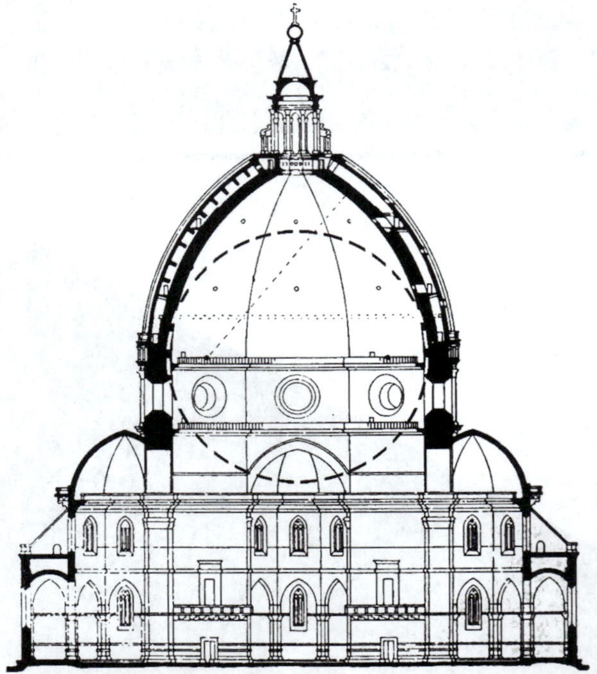

Santa Maria del Fiore, Florence, Filippo Brunelleschi, 1296–1436, 42 metres in diameter.

Cupola of the Santa Maria del Fiore, Florence.

And there are more striking similarities. Both buildings have a cornucopia painting covering the vault and dome, including little punctures enabling people to look down while climbing the narrow stairs in between the two shells in Florence's dome. In Rotterdam, these holes are windows from the apartments into the huge market space.

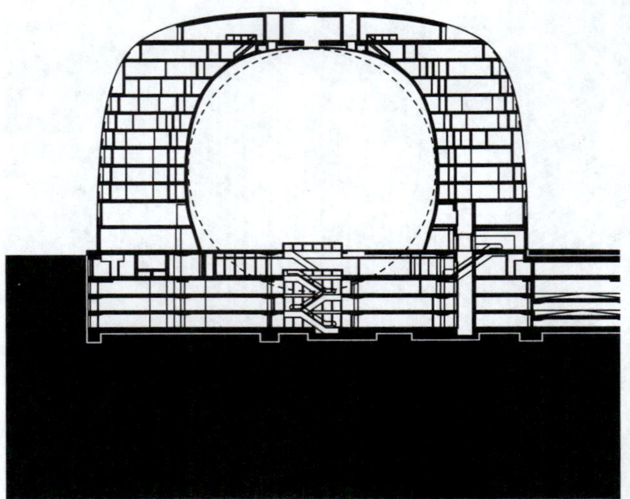

Section of Markthal, 42.5 metres in diameter.

MVRDV took the idea of a continuous public ground floor literally by cladding (or wrapping) the whole volume with the same concrete paving tiles that you find on the Binnenrotte Square around the building. Many other elements have been taken to the extreme. The bluntness of the overall form, bulging on both sides to allow for more commercial floor space, contrasts starkly with the glass facade at both ends. Joseph Paxton would lick his fingers were he to see this gossamer spectacle.

Only a few decades ago, the grand void of Pennsylvania Station collapsed under the weight of commercial forces.

"Not that Penn Station is the Parthenon, but it might as well be because we can never again afford a nine-acre structure of superbly detailed travertine, any more than we could build one of solid gold... The tragedy is that our own times not only could not produce such a building, but cannot even maintain it."[55] —Ada Louise Huxtable

Pennsylvania Station, New York City, Charles McKim, 1910.

Plan of level 4 of the Markthal.

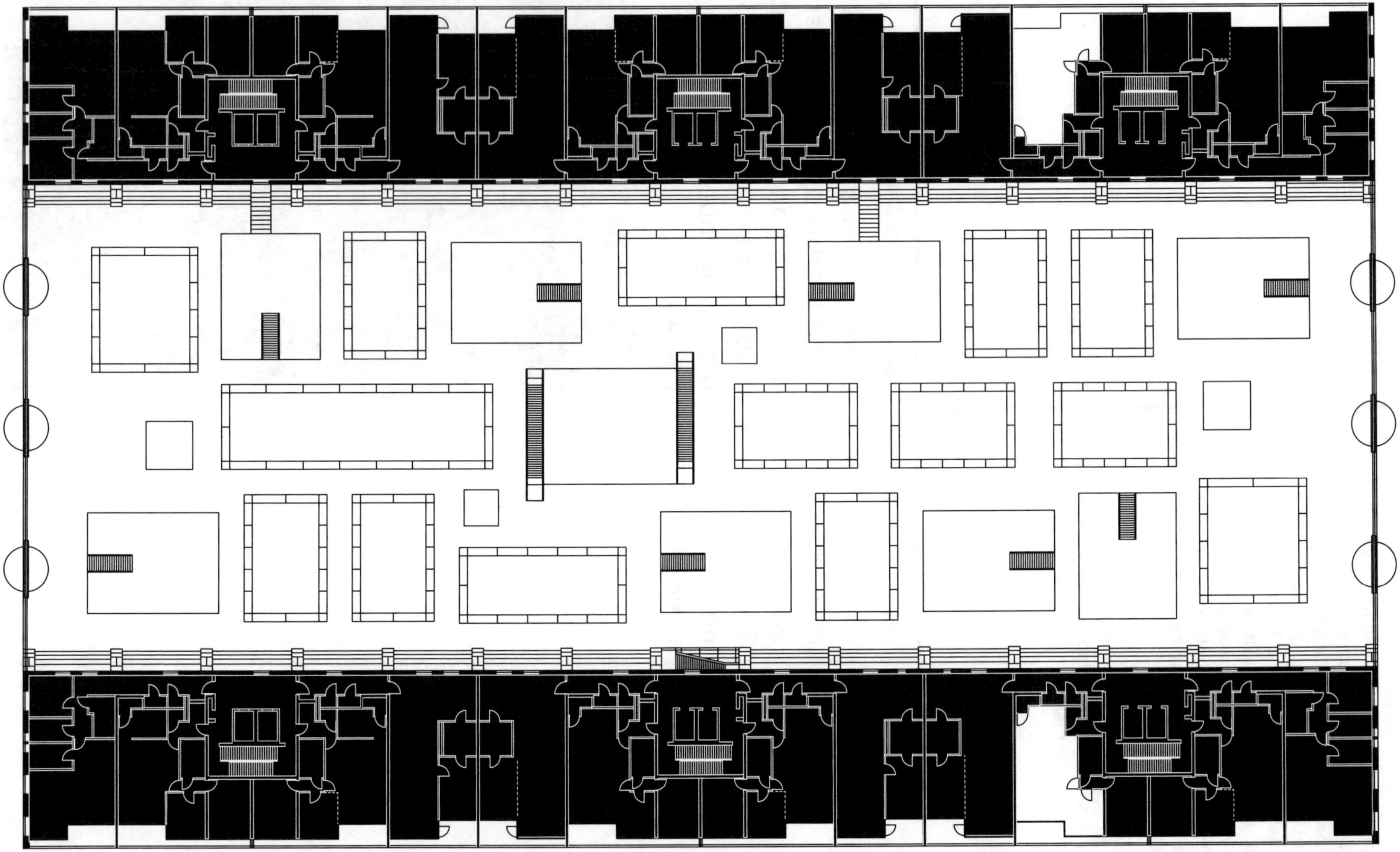

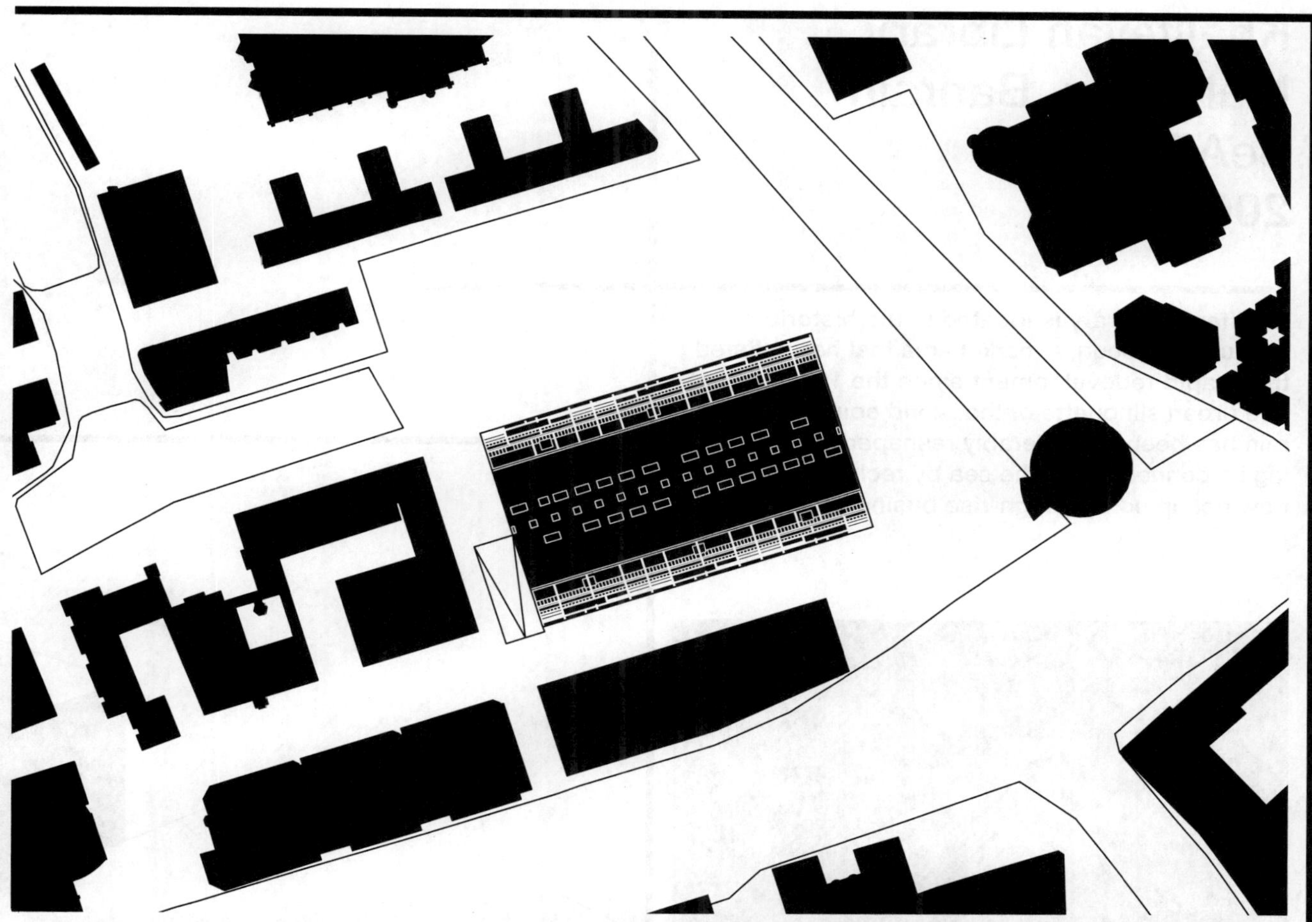

Site plan of the Markthal on Binnenrotte Square.

MVRDV made an optimistic attempt, but at what price and at whose cost? Today mass and void, public and private, battle it out on unstable grounds. As the city densifies, we build more and more housing to support a growing population, and at the same time try to hollow out public (often commercial) spaces.

The Markthal cleverly does both in one; drilling a public market though the core of a housing block. But commercial forces were at work here too, and to support such a large open space in the heart of Rotterdam, public space morphed into a luxurious food mall. Rotterdam got a spectacular tourist attraction, but only time will tell whether this is such a blissful marriage.

After all, as public and private interests jostle for space, it all comes down to one thing: the success of their encounter.

Khalifeyah Library
Muharraq, Bahrain
SeARCH
2009–2016

Khalifeyah Library is located in the historical Al-Muharraq souq, a market area that has suffered from rapid redevelopment since the 1980s. The urban silhouette of the island country of Bahrain has been considerably reshaped, destroying its connection to the sea by reclaiming land now occupied by a high-rise business district.

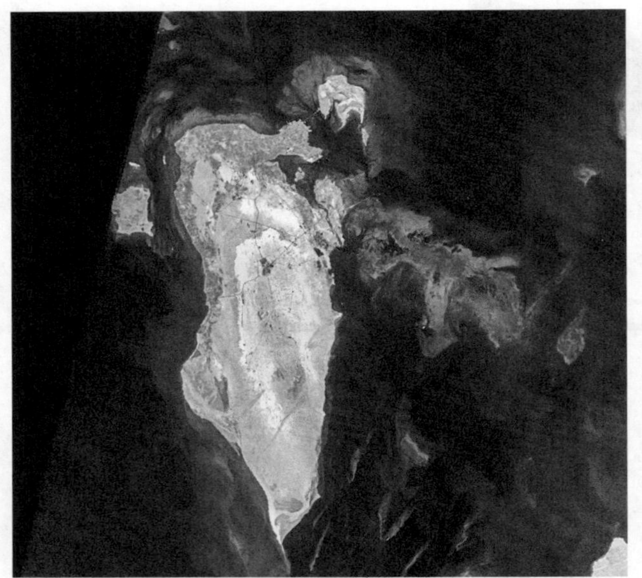

It took less than two decades for Bahrain to increase by about 40 square kilometres, 1972 (top) and 2018 (bottom).

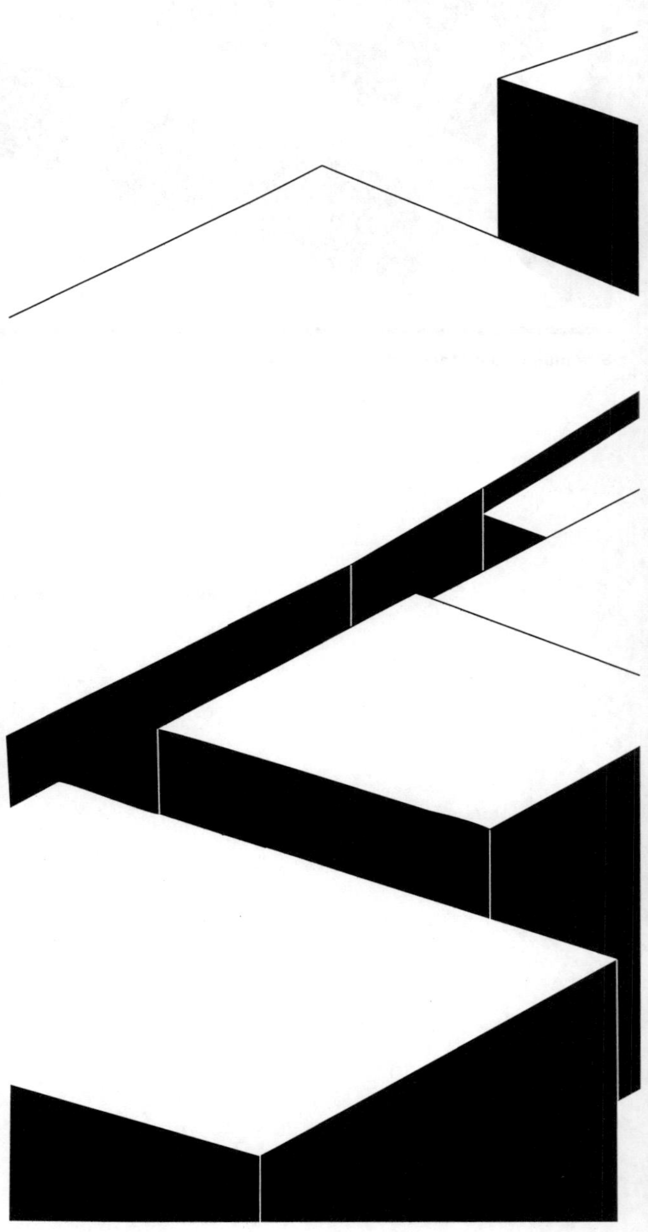

Taking cues from the traditional houses around it, the Khalifeyah Library both embeds itself in the existing neighbourhood and commands a strong public presence.

Axonometry of Khalifeyah Library.

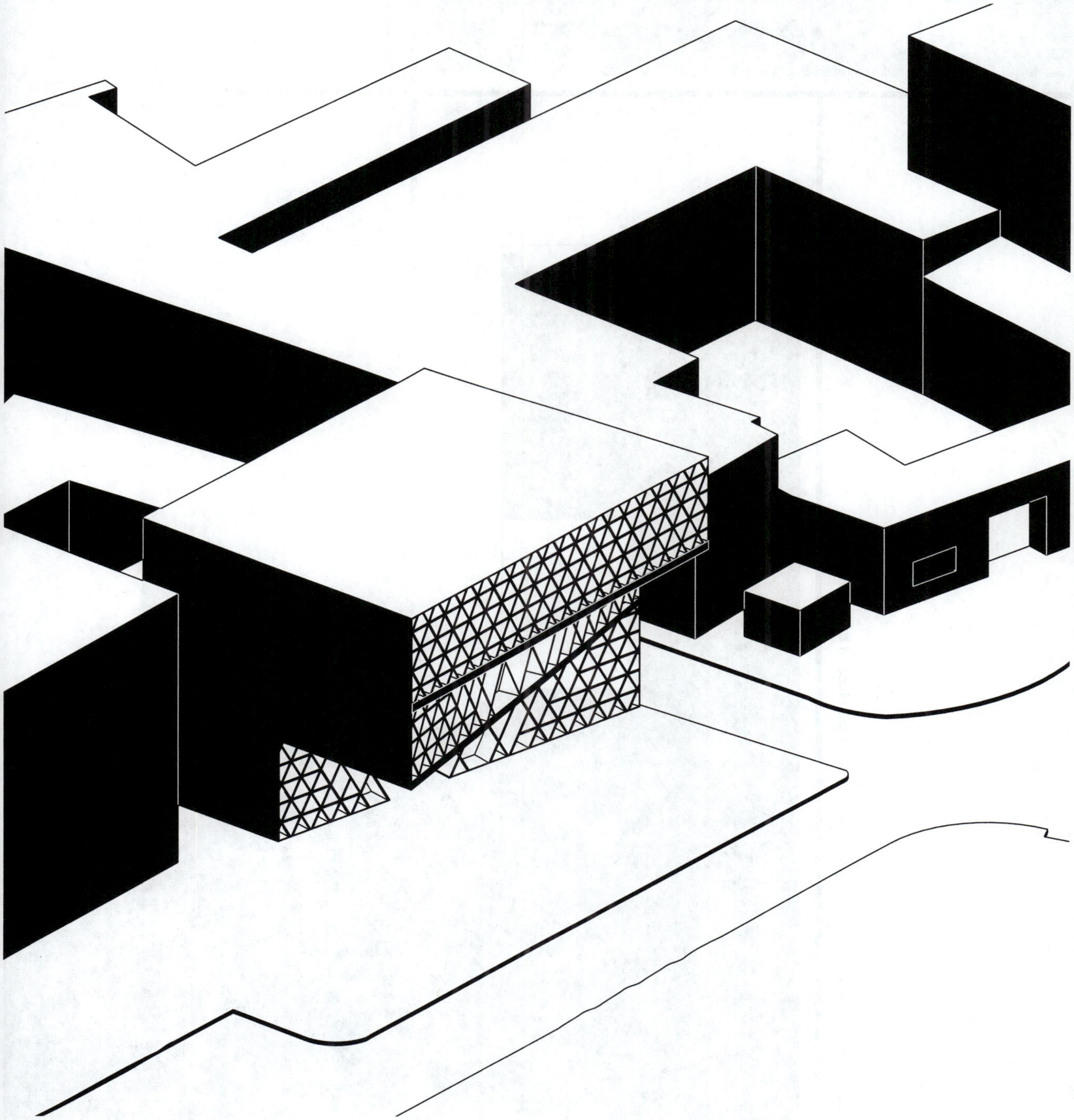

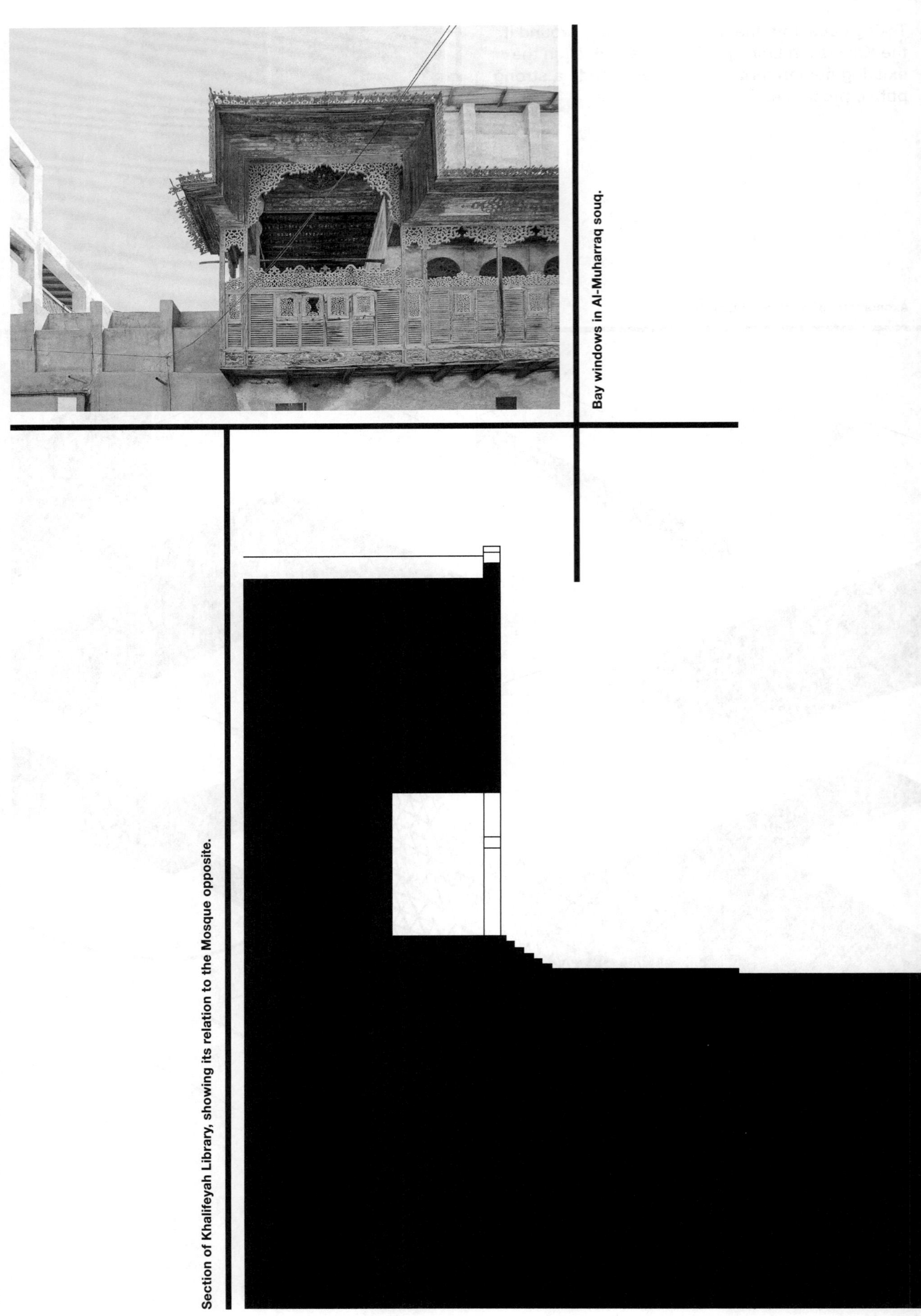

Bay windows in Al-Muharraq souq.

Section of Khalifeyah Library, showing its relation to the Mosque opposite.

The walls and houses that line the Al-Muharraq souq are porous. Often a central gate opens up to a portico, followed by an entrance room used for the reception of guests. Tall palm trees towering above clearly show that it is not just a building behind closed walls. One of the most intriguing elements is the perforated timber bay windows that protrude through or over these walls. By popping outwards, they keep the sunlight away from doors and windows and give residents an overview of the narrow streets without being seen themselves. Here, private space discreetly overhangs public space without disturbing traffic flows and providing always welcome shade.

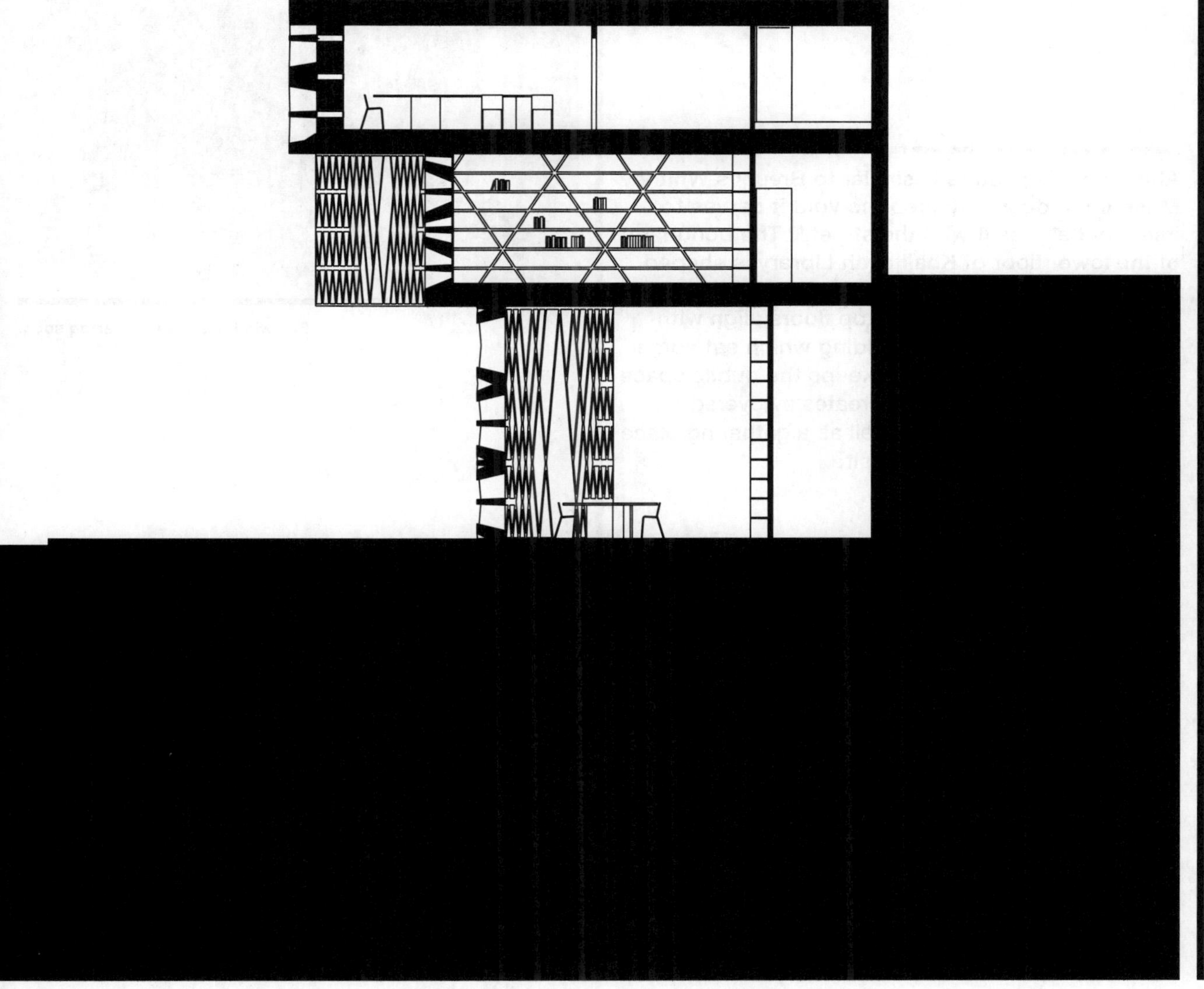

Reinterpreting this bay window, the Khalifeyah Library cantilevers outwards, negotiating itself into the public space.

Bay windows in Al-Muharraq souq.

Although this gesture is similar to Breuer's Whitney Museum, it does not keep the void it carves to itself, but shares it with the street.[56] The boundary of the lower floor of Khalifeyah Library is shaped by the footprint of the existing site, while the cantilevering volumes of the two top floors align with the ghost of the original building which sat some seven metres forward. This keeps the public space intact and at the same time creates a covered entrance for the library as well as a gathering place in front of the mosque opposite.

Whitney Museum, New York City, Marcel Breuer, 1964–1966.

STOP

GROPPI
AL-Wafa
Mob: 39150863 - 33869293
Welcome To AL

ONE WAY
TOYOTA
482403

دلوني
نظارات النور
نظارات النور
AL NOOR OPTICAL
فحص النظر بالكمبيوتر - تركيب عدسات لاصقة
COMPUTER EYE TEST - CONTACT LENS FITTING
1734 2124
دلوني
SALE

127429

242519
البحرين
BAHRAIN

SMARTECH
SMARTECH
PEST CONTROL
39453595
ROOM FOR SHARING (ONLY FAMILY) 33965861
HOUSE SHIFTING
PEST CONTROL
34117522
34486099
ROOM FOR RENT
35973779
38861712

نظارات النور
نظارات النور
AL NOOR OPTICAL
COMPUTER EYE TEST – CONTACT LENS FITTING
فحص النظر بالكمبيوتر - تركيب عدسات لاصقة
BIG SALE
اشتري واحد و احصل على الثاني مجانا !!
Buy one get one free on all sunglasses and frames !
054

BRARY
CHEVROLET
419671

جميلة
JAMEELA
NOOR OPTICA

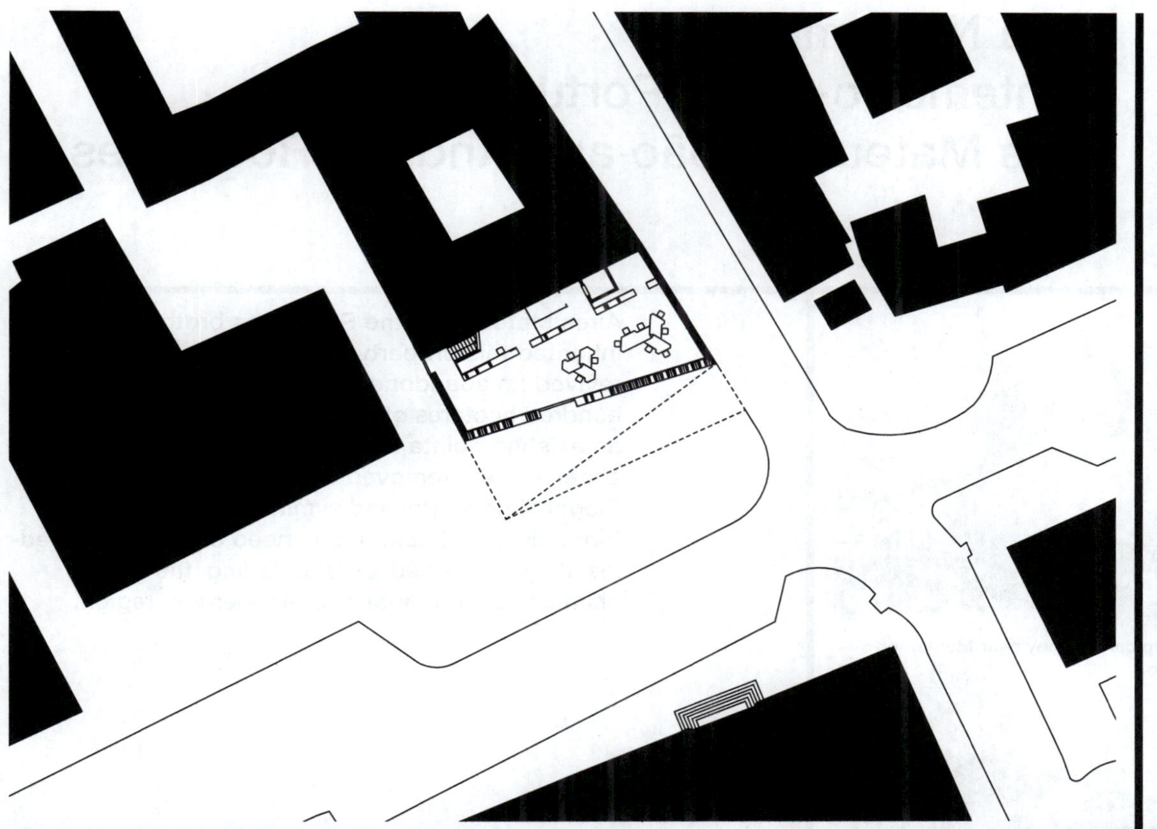

Plan of Khalifeyah Library, showing the cantilever aligned with the surrounding built fabric.

Overlaying the shadows created by the typical shapes of the cantilevers, an interesting pattern emerges. This informed the design of a diagonal grid of louvres projected on the facade. Rather than being defined by structural logic or the repetitive array of traditional Arabic shapes, this pattern regulates incoming sunlight by varying the density of the grid. This leads to an abstract sculptural facade that changes its appearance under different viewing angles. Sometimes it seems solid and closed, but it opens up to passers-by.

Casa No Tempo
Montemor-o-Novo, Portugal
Aires Mateus & João and Andreia Rodrigues
2014

Quinta with typical chimney near Montemor-o-Novo, Alentejo.

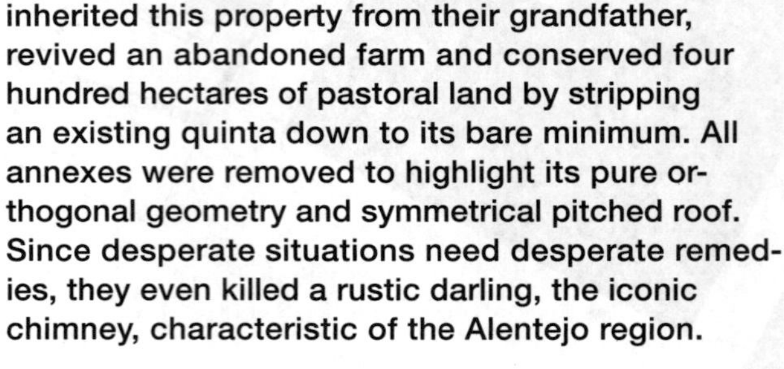

Aires Mateus and the Rodrigues brothers, who inherited this property from their grandfather, revived an abandoned farm and conserved four hundred hectares of pastoral land by stripping an existing quinta down to its bare minimum. All annexes were removed to highlight its pure orthogonal geometry and symmetrical pitched roof. Since desperate situations need desperate remedies, they even killed a rustic darling, the iconic chimney, characteristic of the Alentejo region.

Existing quinta with roof and annexes removed.

Sections of living space (top), and portico and hidden chimney (bottom).

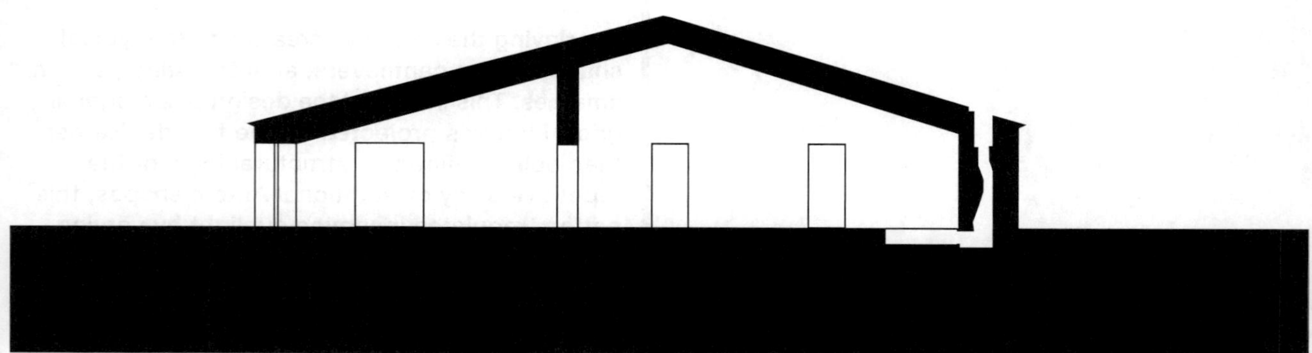

Axonometry of Casa No Tempo.

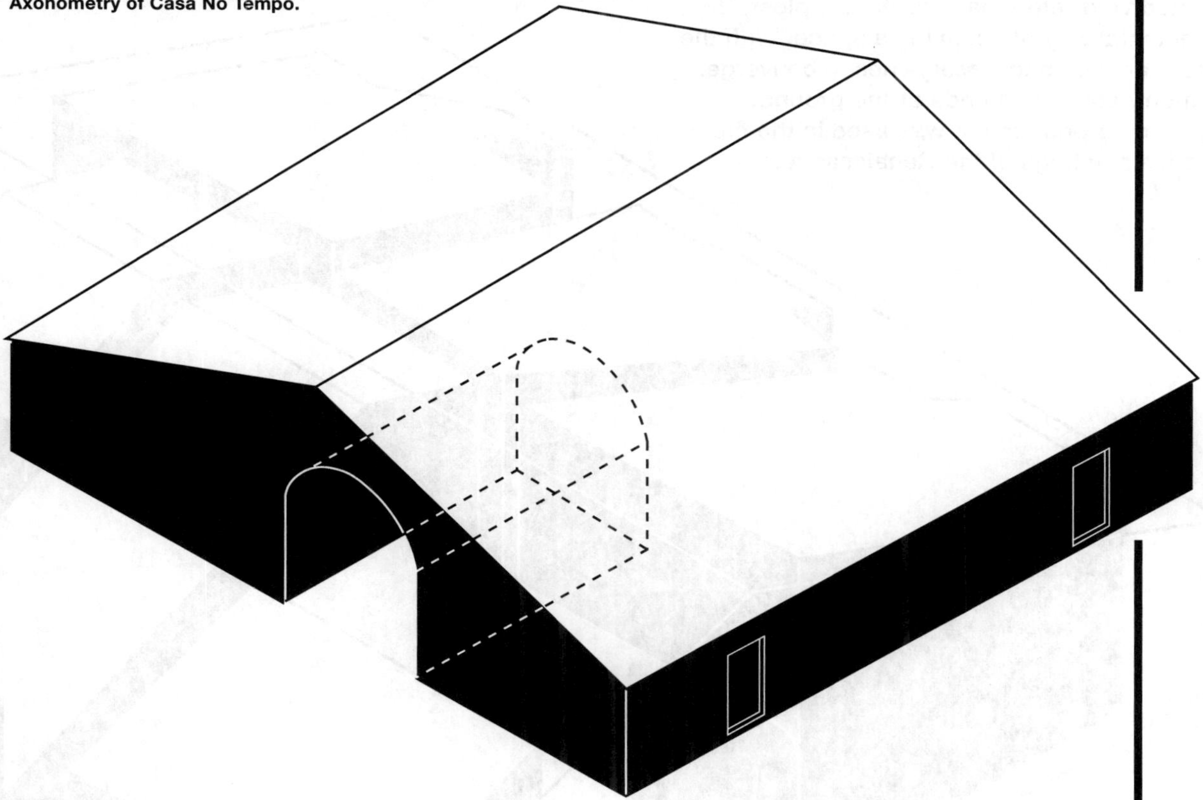

The remaining archaic form is perforated with two spaces positioned perpendicularly to each other: a suite for living and a vaulted portico. The rest of the built mass is like a *poché*, enclosing four bedrooms and a kitchen. All the bathrooms and storage spaces are cavities within the ultra-thick outer walls.

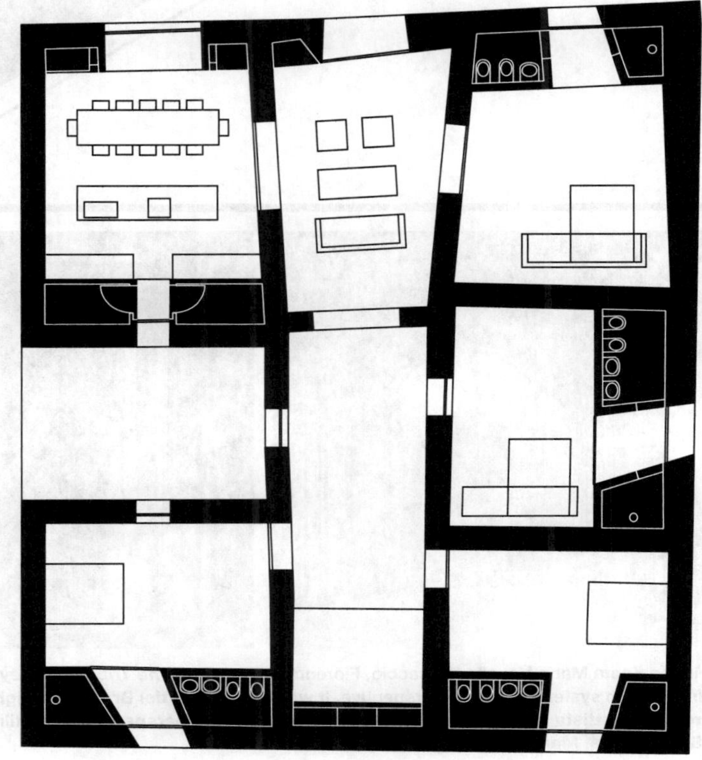

Plan of Casa No Tempo. A suite for living runs top to bottom and a vaulted portico from left to right.

The vaulted void refers back to the simplest, most elemental way of spanning a space. With the vault there are no unnecessary lines to converge. Its geometry starts and ends at the ground, making it no surprise that it was used in the first perspective paintings of the Renaissance.

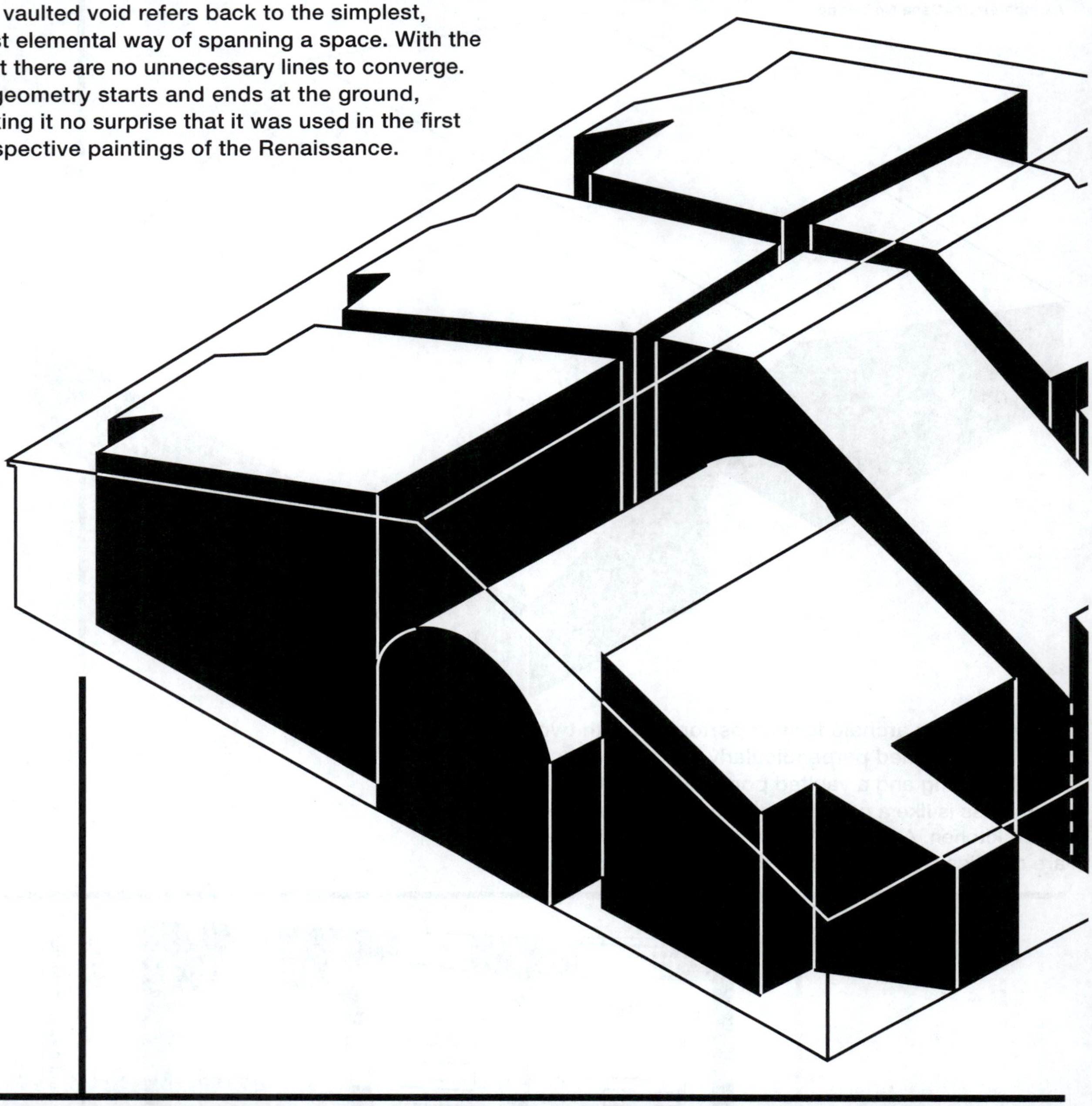

Holy Trinity fresco (left), in the Santa Maria Novella, Masaccio, Florence, 1427, is the first known fresco with systematic linear perspective. It was painted fifty years before Leon Battista Alberti built the monumental vault of the Basilica of Sant'Andrea, Mantua, 1472–1790 (right).

Detail of *The Tribute Money* fresco (left) by Masaccio, in the Cappella dei Brancacci (right), Florence. It is the first painting with proper perspective that still exists. c.1425.

Axonometry of voids within.

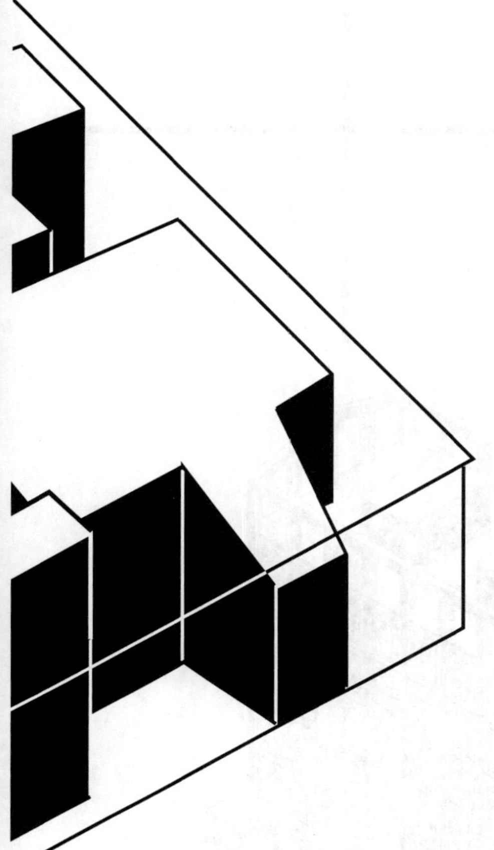

The two voids are oriented towards the pool and the valley. In stark contrast to the conventionally small windows that punctuate the white mass, these spaces open out to landscape with large pivoting doors. The 20 x 20 metre white concrete platform is a brilliant merger of beach and infinity pool. It seems as if the surrounding landscape is served on a silver platter, leaving the abstract white volumes in complete silence. The simplicity of this pared-down architecture puts the landscape in the spotlight.

Zeitz MOCAA
Cape Town, South Africa
Heatherwick Studio
2014–2017

At first glance it looks as if someone opened a beehive and scooped out the honeycomb. The idea behind the conversion of an abandoned grain silo is as simple as it is overwhelming. Thomas Heatherwick describes it as some sort of "archaeology, like excavating out gallery spaces, but not wanting to obliterate the tubularity completely."[57]

Sectional axonometry of Zeitz MOCAA.

However, this excavation isn't what it appears, as we often see in architecture. Prosaic building decisions intrude to shape the end result. Over seventy per cent of this abandoned grain silo was demolished and the remaining tubular structure was reinforced with a 40-centimetre-thick lining of structural concrete. In the end, the equation came down to removing 10 000 cubic metres of concrete and inserting some 9000 cubic metres.[58]

Zeitz MOCAA under construction, 2015.

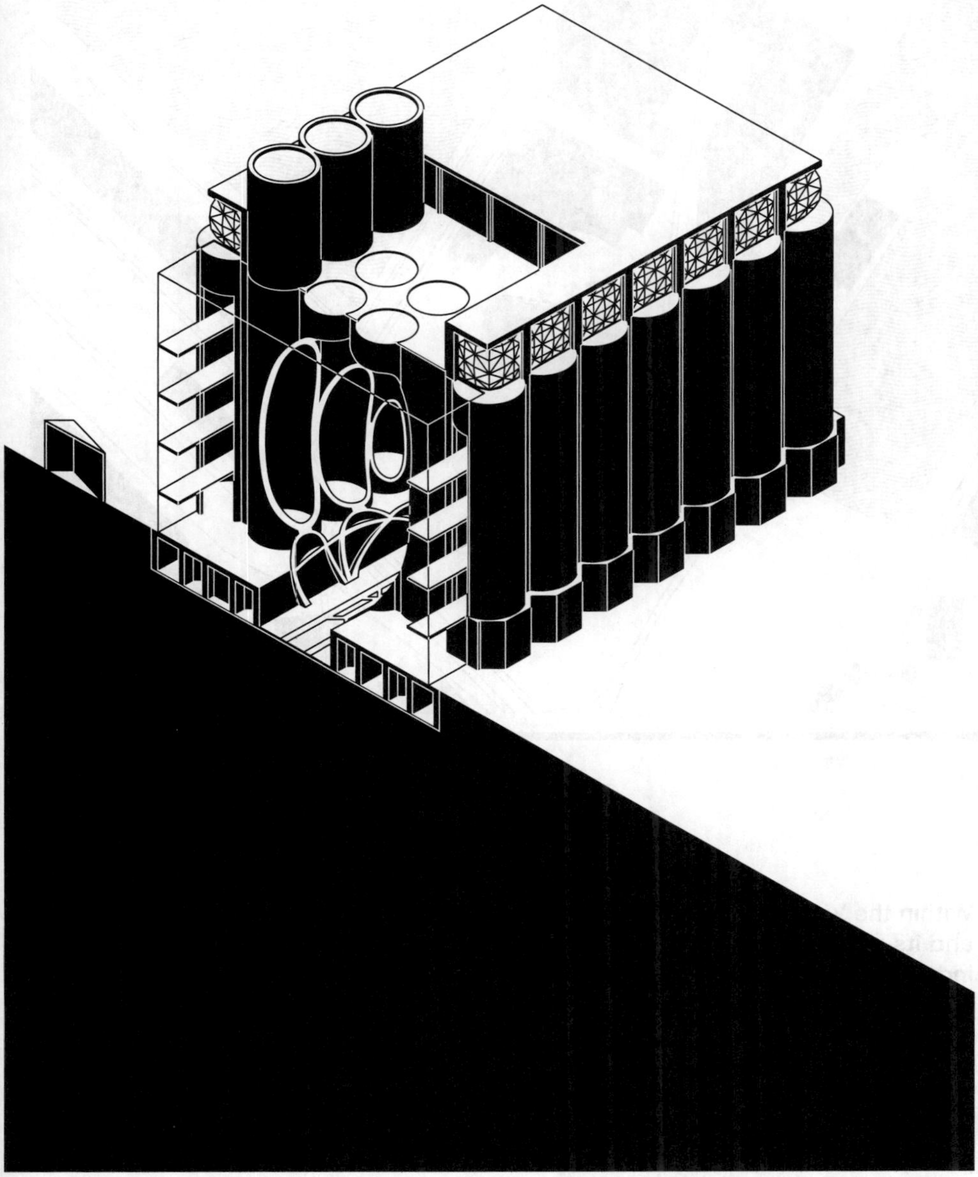

In archaeology or monument conservation, uncovering the truth is vital, so you don't mess with evidence. In architecture, archaeology is often limited to a conceptual framework. Here it went from a silo complex, from where grain was exported to the rest of the world, via the idea to establish the first museum in Africa, solely dedicated to contemporary African artists and the diaspora, to creating a collective space in the heart of the building that a series of exhibition spaces pivot around. Transforming the silo was a conscious act of processing the site's history, rather than memorializing it. As Heatherwick states, they were interested in, "(d)estructing rather than constructing, but trying to destruct with a confidence and an energy."[59]

Site plan of Zeitz MOCAA.

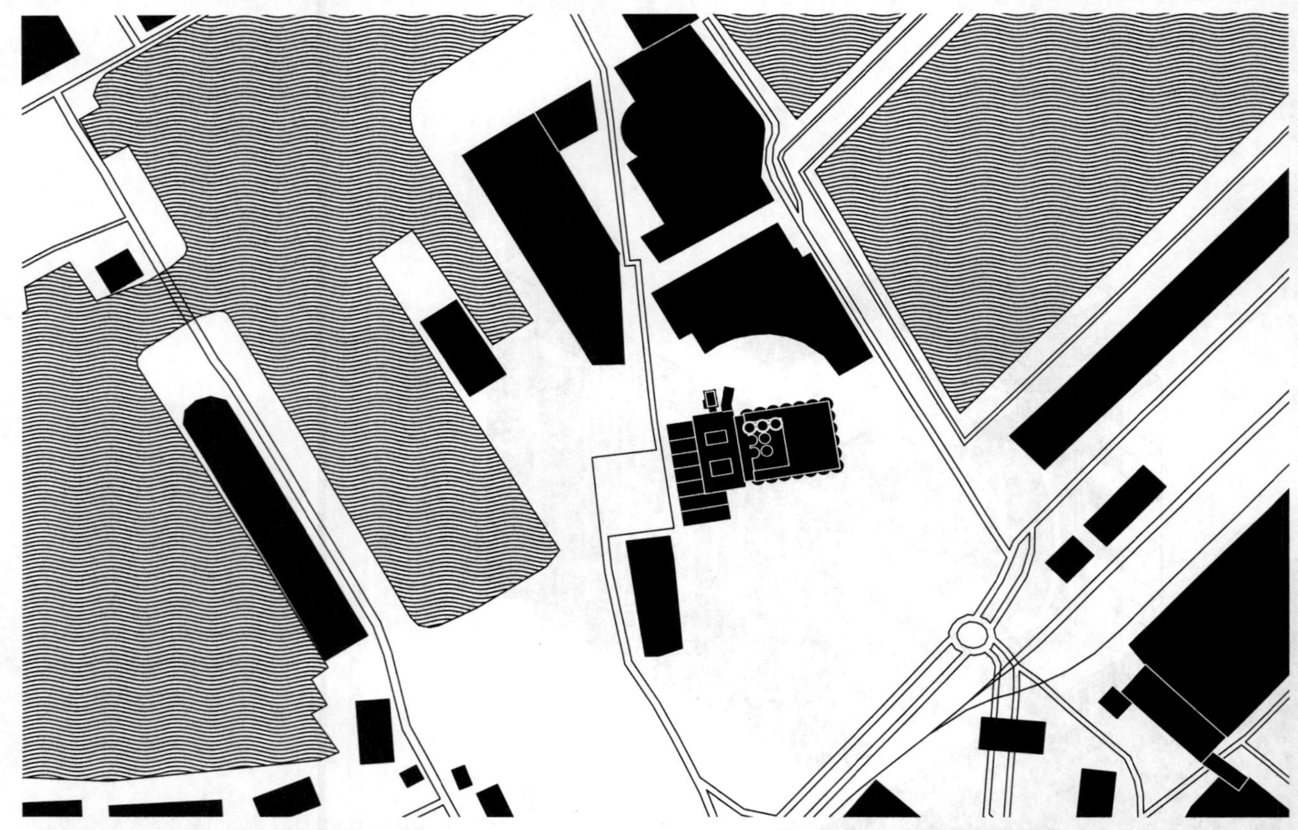

Within the Victoria & Alfred Waterfront development and its predictable shopping mall and post-industrial harbour clichés, the Zeitz MOCAA stands like a cathedral at the centre of a circular square. The original facade is almost entirely preserved and gives no hint at all of the dramatic vaulted space inside. This building will link to Cape Town, South Africa, and the continent entirely through its contemporary African art collection inside.

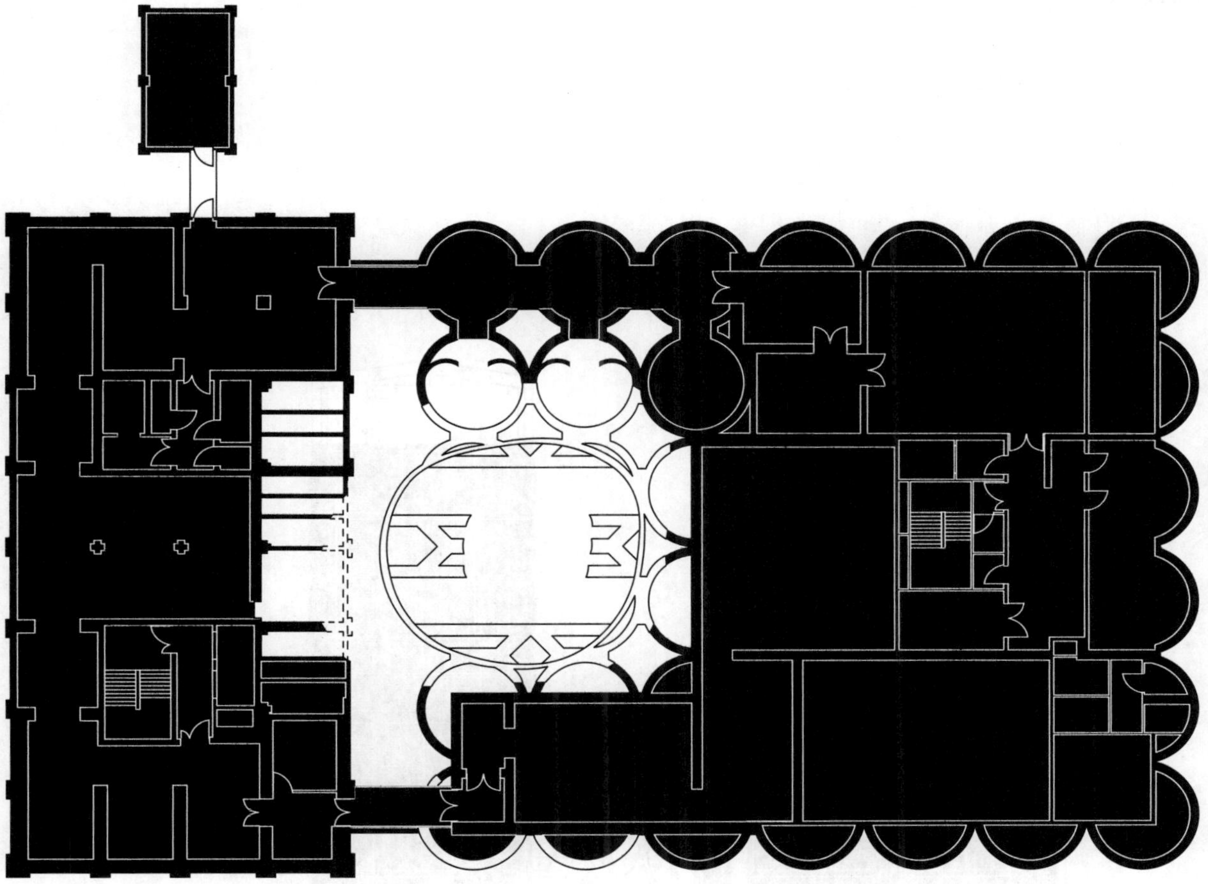

Level 1 Plan of Zeitz MOCAA.

Section of Zeitz MOCAA.

Seatrade
MEDIA

TUNNEL
TUNNEL
6A
75-87

EXIT

The Barion cut.

The bulging windows that crown the nave and tower are shaped like square-cut diamonds. The Barion cut was one of the first mixed cuts invented by South African diamond cutter Basil Watermeyer and named after him and his wife Marion. It could be purely coincidental, but there's something in the stark contrasts of its imagery, a diamond-encrusted, industrial concrete mass that conceals a cathedral within, that make it a truly South African building.

The Zeitz MOCAA facade.

Today, the void is a highly desired commodity that adds value to a building's mass. The Zeitz MOCAA shows just how far this has come. The mass of the existing silos would once have been considered dead space if kept and expensive to demolish, but now they are carved like butter to become the star attraction.

Endnotes:

1 [p. 965] Jack Flam, *Robert Smithson: The Collected Writings* (Los Angeles: University of California, 1996), 6.

2 [p. 965] Within the ancient dwelling or granary, need and scarcity drove efficiency, and every element, be it the floor, roof, wall, window or door, had a clear function, size and material. See "Domesticating Nature", Nature's Lack of Design, 32–35.

3 [p. 966] Regarding Göbekli Tepe, see Dietmar Kurapkat, "Bauwissen im Neolithikum Vorderasiens", in *Wissensgeschichte der Architektur. Band I: Vom Neolithikum bis zum Alten Orient*, Jürgen Renn, Wilhelm Osthues, Hermann Schlimme (eds.) (Berlin: Open Access, 2014); and on Stonehenge, see research of architect Sarah Ewbank.

4 [p. 973] The impressive structure of Villa Jovis atop the extreme relief of a protruding cliff bears a striking resemblance to Villa Malaparte, built nearby. See "Villa Malaparte", Absorb, 632–637.

5 [p. 975] Coptic Christians suffer abduction, forced conversion and violence. Their religion is not legally recognized, and they have been resettled multiple times by the Egyptian government. Many in Mokattam had lived in tin houses since the 1970s.

6 [p. 977] Patrick Duerden, "Great Detail: Duerden on Baines' Westminster Hall Roof Repair", *Architects' Journal* (9 December 2016).

7 [p. 978] It may have had two rows of wooden columns to support it, but there are also traces of poor structural condition, maybe due to faulty calculations at the time of construction, since the roofing material science of the 12th century was perhaps not enough to handle a span of 20.7 metres. Herbert Cescinsky and Ernest R. Gribble, "Westminster Hall and Its Roof", *Burlington Magazine for Connoisseurs* 40, no. 127 (February 1922), 76.

8 [p. 980] Although there was little quantitative progress in span, the establishment of completely new religious and social orders had an enormous impact on the relationship between building and landscape. Medieval fortifications changed the way a building connected to its surroundings, with relief and level differences (see pages 32–35). Gunpowder increased both the size and the distance between settlements while blurring the boundary between the built realm and the landscape (see pages 73–80, and within the Western city the private sphere began to outstrip the public, see "From Public Space to Private Icon", Nature's Lack of Design, 81–94).

9 [p. 980] Véronique Patteeuw, "Delirious Architects and Globes", The Ball, *MacGuffin: The Life of Things* 6 (2018).

10 [p. 981] The building committee refused all 233 competition entries and then recommended their own design for a structure to house the Great Exhibition: a brick structure which was ridiculed publicly. Jeffrey Auerbach, "Victorian Prism: Refractions of the Crystal Palace", *Victorian Studies* 50, no. 3 (Spring 2008), 508–510.

11 [p. 982] Sigfried Giedion, *Space, Time and Architecture: The Growth of a New Tradition* (Cambridge: Harvard University Press, 1941), 270.

12 [p. 982] However, it took a while for this building method to become commercially viable, because traditional manufacturing methods profited from cheap labour in what was still a feudal period.

13 [p. 982] Kate Colquhoun, *The Busiest Man in England: A Life of Joseph Paxton, Gardener, Architect & Victorian Visionary* (Boston: David R. Godine, 2006).

14 [p. 985] Georg Kohlmaier and Barna von Sartory, *Houses of Glass: A Nineteenth-Century Building Type* (Cambridge: MIT Press, 1986), 2.

15 [p. 985] Sigfried Giedion, *Space, Time and Architecture*.

16 [p. 985] Ibid. 271.

17 [p. 986] Ibid. 249.

18 [p. 985] See "The Ziggurat", Spiral, 788–792, and the intriguing poché plans of Dover Castle, "The Age of Gunpowder", Nature's Lack of Design, 73–76.

19 [p. 989] At the Johnson Wax Headquarters' Great Workroom, Frank Lloyd Wright had to prove that a column could support 12 tons and, when tested, it took 60 tons to crack one. He referred to their tops as 'lily pads' and the ensemble as 'a glade of trees'.

20 [p. 998] See "The City in the Garden", Nature's Lack of Design, 95–104.

21 [p. 1003] William J. R. Curtis, *Denys Lasdun: Architecture, City, Landscape* (London: Phaidon Press, 1994).

22 [p. 1004] See "Casa de Vidro", Absorb, 638–643.

23 [p. 1006] Herman Hertzberger, *Space and the Architect: Lessons in Architecture 2* (Rotterdam: 010 Publishers, 2010).

24 [p. 1014] The brief was set by a group of industrialists, supported by the Harvard Business School. In order to keep up with India's rapid industrialization and modernization they believed it was necessary to take students out of the traditional classroom into a more participatory way of studying.

25 [p. 1014] See "Kailasa Temple", Bury, 204–221.

26 [p. 1017] Label for the artwork *Conical Intersect* in the exhibition *9 + 1 Ways of Being Political: 50 Years of Political Stances in Architecture and Urban Design*, MoMA, 12 September 2012–25 March 2013.

27 [p. 1018] Ada Louise Huxtable, "Ford Flies High", *New York Times* (26 November 1967).

28 [p. 1018] Ada Louise Huxtable, "Anti-Street, Anti-People", *New York Times*, 10 June 1973.

29 [p. 1032] Barry Bergdoll, "Marcel Breuer and the Invention of Heavy Lightness", *Places* (June 2018); Barry Bergdoll and Jonathan Massey, *Marcel Breuer: Building Global Institutions*

(Zürich: Lars Müller Publishers, 2018), and in part Ruth Verde Zein, *Brutalist Connections* (São Paulo: Altamara, 2014).

30 [p. 1032] Natalie de Blois's recollections of herself and Gordon Bunshaft in Detlef Mertins, "Cracking the Glass Ceiling: A Look Back at the Career of Trailblazing Architect Natalie de Blois", *SOM Journal* 4 (2006).

31 [p. 1032] Barry Bergdoll, "Marcel Breuer and the Invention of Heavy Lightness", in Bergdoll and Massey, *Marcel Breuer: Building Global Institutions* (Zürich: Lars Müller Publishers, 2018). See Breuer's tubular furniture in "From Seat to City", Embed, 476–481.

32 [p. 1033] Bergdoll and Massey, *Marcel Breuer: Building Global Institutions*.

33 [p. 1033] First Whitney Museum of American Art on West 8th Street, 1931, Expanded Whitney on West 54th Street in 1954, Breuer's Whitney at the corner of Madison Avenue and 75th Street, 1966, and finally Renzo Piano's Whitney at 99 Gansevoort Street, 2015.

34 [p. 1033] Marcel Breuer and Tician Papachristou, *Marcel Breuer: New Buildings and Projects* (New York: Praeger, 1970), 14–15.

35 [p. 1035] Bergdoll and Massey, *Marcel Breuer: Building Global Institutions*.

36 [p. 1037] Jeanette Winterson, "The Hole of Life", *Tate Magazine* 5 (1 June 2003).

37 [p. 1040] See "1964: A Pivotal Moment", Nature's Lack of Design, 105–117.

38 [p. 1043] Richard Sennett, "Beyond Freedom and Dignity", *New York Times* (24 October 1971).

39 [p. 1043] B. F. Skinner, "Some Thoughts about the Future", *Journal of the Experimental Analysis of Behaviour* 2 (1986), 228.

40 [p. 1043] B. F. Skinner, *Walden Two* (Indianapolis: Hackett Publishing Company, 1948).

41 [p. 1043] B. F. Skinner, *Beyond Freedom & Dignity*, Indianapolis: Hackett Publishing Company, 1971.

42 [p. 1044] Deborah Skinner Buzan (daughter of B. F. Skinner), rebutted false rumours and criticisms of the 'Air Crib'. Deborah Skinner Buzan, "I Was Not a Lab Rat", *Guardian* (12 March 2004). Accessed 4 November 2018.

43 [p. 1046] José María Carandell, "The Peculiar Charm of Walden 7", *Archisearch* (8 March 2016). Accessed 18 January 2019.

44 [p. 1047] Ricardo Bofill, "Walden 7 project text", *Ricardo Bofill Taller de Arquitectura* website. Accessed 9 January 2019.

45 [p. 1049] Ricardo Bofill, "La Fábrica project text", *Ricardo Bofill Taller de Arquitectura* website. Accessed 3 January 2019.

46 [p. 1051] Excerpts from an interview between Richard C. Levene, Fernando Marquez Cecilia, Antonio Cruz and Antonio Ortiz, *El Croquis* 48 (1991), 6–7.

47 [p. 1054] Speaking of which...the biggest commercial development at its time worldwide was Portman's Renaissance Center in Detroit.

48 [p. 1056] Quoted in Irene Holliman Way, "'Creating a City within a City': John Portman's Peachtree Center and Private Urban Renewal in Atlanta," Kennesaw State University, www.atlantastudies.org (15 January 2019). Originally in Rodolphe El-Khoury and Edward Robbins, *Shaping the City: Studies in History, Theory, and Urban Design, about Atlanta* (London: Routledge, 2013).

49 [p. 1062] Quoted in August McIntyre Dine, "Identifying Atlanta: John Portman, Postmodernism, and Pop-Culture", Bard Undergraduate Senior Projects, Spring 2017, 28.

50 [p. 1071] See "Entelechy II", Mimic, 1248.

51 [p. 1071] Jenny Xie, "Meet John Portman, the Architect Behind the Dystopian Backdrops of 'The Walking Dead' and 'The Hunger Games'", *Curbed Magazine* (2 April 2015).

52 [p. 1090] Natural lighting is preferred as the handling of switches is not allowed on Shabbat.

53 [p. 1094] See "Piscine des Amiraux", Carve, 996–1003 and "Westin Bonaventure", Carve, 1054–1071.

54 [p. 1094] See "Introduction", Carve, 970.

55 [p. 1097] Ada Louise Huxtable describing the upcoming demolition of Penn Station in "How to Kill a City", *New York Times* (5 May 1963).

56 [p. 1104] See "The Whitney Museum", Carve, 1032–1035.

57 [p. 1120] Amy Frearson, "Thomas Heatherwick Reveals Zeitz MOCAA Art Galleries Carved Out of Cape Town Grain Silo", *Dezeen Magazine* (15 September 2017).

58 [p. 1121] Cristina Ruiz, "Inside Zeitz Mocaa: Our Guide to Cape Town's New Mega-museum", *Art Newspaper*, 15 September 2017.

59 [p. 1122] Amy Frearson, "Thomas Heatherwick Reveals Zeitz MOCAA".

Mimic

Mimic — (Re)constructing the landscape

The building learns from the landscape. It mimics and simulates natural features and systems, terracing, branching and growing. Building and landscape have begun to merge.

"The earth doesn't share our prejudice towards plastic. Plastic came out of the earth. The earth probably sees plastic as just another one of its children. Could be the only reason the earth allowed us to be spawned from it in the first place. It wanted plastic for itself. Didn't know how to make it. Needed us. Could be the answer to our age-old egocentric philosophical question, 'Why are we here?' Plastic ... asshole."[1] —George Carlin

As we write this book, geologists and environmental scientists are bickering over whether or not humankind now lives in the Anthropocene. Labels aside, society is recognizing that our actions have irrevocably altered the planet, so much so that our waste has begun to merge with our geology to create the fossil of the future.[2]

Plastiglomerate, the Anthropocene's new stone.

In an age when only twelve per cent of the world's surface remains unaltered wilderness, there is a need to come to terms with the fact that (unless you are one of the fortunate few who live in the Siberian Taiga or the Northern Territory of Australia), your nature, your habitat is synthetic. The trees around you have been planted, the green surfaces have been cultivated and the contours of the ground have been sculpted. And this is no small undertaking. In fact, in the United States, the unassuming green carpet of residential lawn occupies more land than fields of wheat, corn or tobacco.[3]

A man vacuums his artificial lawn.

Geometrical Gardens, Herning, Denmark, Carl Theodor Sørensen, 1983–1984.

We live in a strange yet exhilarating time when false dichotomies and past assumptions are being challenged. Nature is not the green stuff. Intensive agriculture removes biological competition to increase efficiency, creating a synthetic pasture. And the concrete jungle of the city is a living entity, an amazing collection of natural systems. Both the rolling pastoral landscapes and the junkspaces of big-box retail on the urban periphery are monocultures in their own right. Constructing landscape is a cultural act, and by studying how we make and remake our environment we can better understand humankind's position within it.[4]

Rich natural variation of an alpine meadow (left) versus monoculture of agricultural pasture (right).

The made and the born are fusing, and as Koert van Mensvoort argues we should embrace the fusion. Nature is not a static entity but a dynamic force that evolves with us.[5] This is a compelling thought, but unfortunately, the examples and experiments illustrated in his books are all style and no substance. To solve the issue of meat consumption, which has proven to be detrimental to the environment, *The In Vitro Meat Cookbook* grows meat in a lab rather than a field. Sounds good, until you realize there is no real negotiation with nature, no challenging of our cravings or changing of our culture. Human beings are trying to engineer nature, and not in a particularly clever fashion, as growing fake meat is typically done with serums made from animal blood.[6]

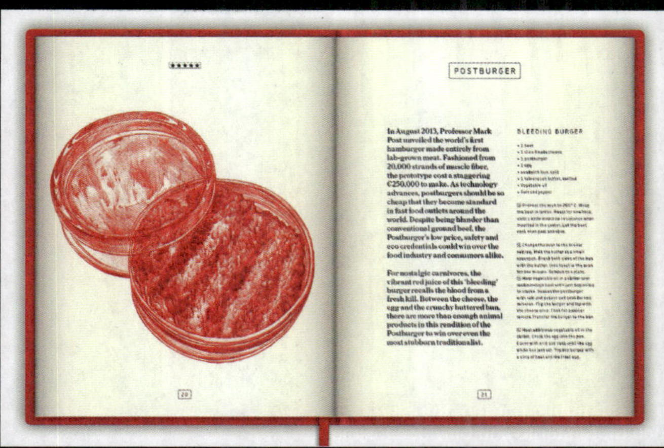
POSTBURGER

In August 2013, Professor Mark Post unveiled the world's first hamburger made entirely from lab-grown meat. Fashioned from 20,000 strands of muscle fiber, the prototype cost a staggering €250,000 to make. As technology advances, postburgers should be so cheap that they become standard in fast food outlets around the world. Despite being blander than conventional ground beef, the Postburger's low price, safety and eco credentials could win over the food industry and consumers alike.

For nostalgic carnivores, the vibrant red juice of this 'bleeding' burger recalls the blood from a fresh kill. Between the cheese, the egg and the crunchy buttered bun, there are more than enough animal products in this rendition of the Postburger to win over even the most stubborn traditionalist.

BLEEDING BURGER

20

21

45 speculative recipes for lab-grown meat in ***The In Vitro Meat Cookbook***.

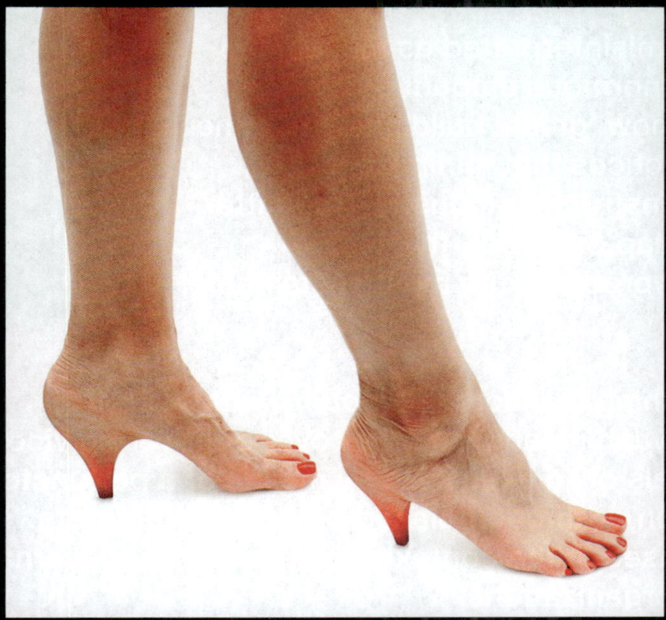
Overstepping, Julie Rrap, 2001.

These ideas have a tongue-in-cheek Instagram appeal, because they mimic what we already have and already know. But since when did radical ideas rely on tired traditions and stereotypes?

Within the built environment, the same shallow thinking exists, when we greenwash our buildings. The architectural rendering glows an almost nuclear green, greenhouses crown towers, and vertical parks creep up skyscrapers, leading from nothing to nowhere. The 'living' wall is widely tolerated in buildings, which see no value in natural light or natural ventilation. They are a token gesture that take up surprisingly little space and end up looking much like a forgotten vegetable garden.

Despite being sold to London City as a lush public garden, the Sky Garden atop the 'Walkie-Talkie', is much more sterile and only accessible by appointment.

Shallow experiences are often misinterpreted as meaningful contributions to progress. An enormous amount of time and money is spent promoting how 'green' buildings are, rather than actually implementing practices that minimize the environmental impact of the construction industry. No matter how much urban farming you slap on a roof, the simple fact is that not building at all is probably the most sustainable, ecological action.

> whitewashing (censorship): *noun* /ˈwaɪt.wɑː.ʃɪŋ/
> To whitewash means "to gloss over or cover up vices, crimes or scandals or to exonerate by means of a perfunctory investigation or through biased presentation of data."[7] It is especially used in the context of corporations, governments or other organizations.
>
> The first known use of the term is from 1591 in England. Whitewash is a cheap white paint or coating of chalked lime that was used to quickly give a uniform, clean appearance to a wide variety of surfaces, for instance, the entire interior of a barn.

A. Garden Library, Stockholm, Sweden, JDS, 2006.
B. New York Tower, New York City, USA, Daniel Libeskind, 2008.
C. Urban plan, Ansan, South Korea, BIG, INABA, MAD & Mass Studies, 2008.
D. Urban Forest, Chongqing, China, MAD, 2009.
E. The Berg, Berlin, Germany, Jakob Tigges, 2009.
F. International Investment Square, Beijing, China, UNStudio, 2009.
G. Caohejing Hi-Tech Park, Shanghai, China, Massimo Roj, 2010.
H. Permeable Lattice City, Singapore, WOHA, 2011.
I. Positive Island, Istanbul, Turkey, Dror Benshetrit, 2012.
J. City Garden, Aberdeen, Scotland, Diller Scofidio + Renfro, 2012.
K. Vankely, Xiamen, China, NL architects, 2014.
L. Smart City 2050, Paris, France, Vincent Callebaut, 2015.
M. Forest City, Liuzhou, China, Stefano Boeri, 2015.
N. Diamond Lotus, Ho Chi Minh City, Vietnam, Vo Trong Nghia Architects, 2015.
O. In Vivo, Paris, France, XTU architects, 2016.
P. Jaarbeurskwartier Utrecht, Netherlands, SeARCH, 2016.
Q. Green City Hall, Bac Ninh, Vietnam, Vo Trong Nghia Architects, 2016.
R. 1000 Trees, Shanghai, China, Heatherwick Studio, 2017.
S. Digbeth Hanging Gardens of Babylon, Birmingham, United Kingdom, Architects of Invention, 2017.
T. Triango, Paris, France, Rau & SeARCH, 2017.
U. Zhangjiang Future Park, China, MVRDV, 2018.

Mimicking nature is nothing new. There have been countless attempts in history not only to mimic nature and landscape but also to outshine and surpass it. It is almost as if once agricultural humans removed themselves from a natural and precarious state, they began to look back and romanticize it.

Lower gardens of Villa di Pratolino, Giusto Utens, 1599.

Apennine Colossus, Villa di Pratolino, Giambologna, 1580.

After about ten centuries of killing and conquering one another during the Middle Ages, Europe entered the Renaissance. In this comparatively peaceful era, fortifications no longer held such prominence, and estates that would once have been hidden behind great walls began to spill outwards into the surrounding landscape. The Italian Renaissance garden broke down the wall between house, garden and surrounding landscape, integrating natural elements.[8]

The first botanical garden was established in 1543 in Padua, and in 1552 Pier Francesco Orsini violated all the rules of the Renaissance garden in the Sacro Bosco gardens. Order, axis and symmetry were abandoned for a more organic, mannerist composition. Figural statues melted into grottos and fantastic animals were sculpted from volcanic rock.

The Mouth of Hell, Sacro Bosco, Bomarzo, Pier Francesco Orsini, 1552.

Although there was a desire to inhabit nature, it took a while for Europeans to loosen their grip. The French Renaissance garden of the mid-seventeenth century was geometrical in layout and separated itself from the surrounding landscape. The level of control exerted on this garden became even greater with the formal symmetry of the *Jardin à la Française*. At the Château de Versailles, André Le Nôtre constructed impressive panoramas and played with perspective to exaggerate the expanse of the gardens.

View towards the Grand Canal, Château de Versailles.

General plan of the gardens of Versailles, Nicolas de Fer, 1700.

In the eighteenth century, the English landscape garden began to replace these formal predecessors. The English garden designer became the composer of an idealized, pastoral countryside of rolling lawns, groves of trees, and winding streams and lakes that made the landscape seem even larger. At Blenheim Palace, Capability Brown turned a marshy area into a sweeping landscape, featuring a small stream that flows under a monumental bridge into a large lake. Perfecting the pictorial composition of this landscape was so important that Brown flooded the lower levels of the existing bridge, transforming it from a 'habitable viaduct' to non-functional folly.[9]

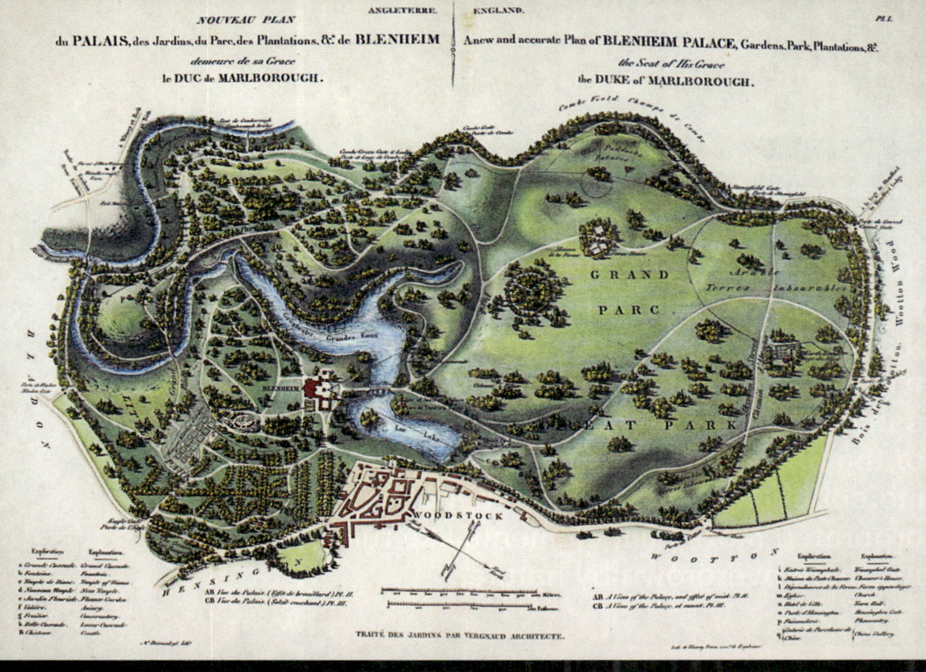

Blenheim Palace grounds redesigned by Capability Brown around 1765. Drawn by Nicolas Vergnaud, 1835.

Blenheim Palace grounds, 1705.

Apollo and the Muses on Mount Helion (Parnassus), Claude Lorrain, 1680.

These ideas were exported across Europe, but although the French landscape garden developed from its English predecessor, it remained more of a garden, inspired by romantic paintings instead of the observed natural environment. The greatest contradiction is that the manicured lawns and precisely positioned vegetation of the English model was actually far more constructed and contrived than the French model. The French garden incorporated more built elements like ruins and bridges, only to have them overgrown by nature.

Marie Antoinette's Hameau de la Reine at Versailles, 1783.

In 1774, Marie Antoinette had a garden built at Neuilly in an Anglo-Chinese style with grottoes and follies. Some ten years later, she ordered the construction of the Hameau de la Reine at Versailles, a completely fake farm with a mill and cottages. Marie Antoinette even took to dressing up with animals and peasants and re-enacting pastoral life in a *tableau vivant*.

Up until this point, built elements like temples, follies, ruins or bridges had been incorporated as part of the landscape within all these styles. Such elements were modest in position, enhancing and underlining the natural setting and drama. Things were changing, however.

Der Stein zu Wörlitz. Wilhelm Friedrich Schlotterbeck, 1797.

Probably the most wacky example of a constructed landscape is the mountain of Wörlitz. After completing his Grand Tour to Italy, the Netherlands, England, France and Switzerland, Leopold III Frederick Franz constructed an artificial volcano in the image of Pompeii's Mount Vesuvius. With this structure, over five storeys tall and fitted with water tanks and fire pits, he could simulate volcanic eruptions for spectators. The Grand Tour was highly valuable (for upper-class European men) in acquiring and dispersing new ideas and styles in architecture and art.[10]

Eruption of Wörlitz volcano in 2010 after the restoration.

Interior of the Temple of Neptune, Giovanni Battista Piranesi, c.1777/78.

Giovanni Battista Piranesi shared the Grand Tourist fascination with antiquity, travelling to Rome to draw its treasures.[11] His etchings show a world beyond imagination. Architectural models, built and ruined, merge with the landscape. Natural and built elements are presented in equilibrium. Grand temples are overgrown, and classical columns stand like dead trees, under which cows and herders rest. His depictions of Rome in ruins, part real, part recreated, were an important source for the neoclassical revival in Europe.

Cenotaph for Newton, Étienne-Louis Boullée, 1784.

Although neoclassicists Claude-Nicolas Ledoux and Étienne-Louis Boullée experimented with natural phenomena and landscape elements, nature was subservient to strong classical architectural forms. Boullée interiorized the universe within the Cenotaph for Newton by perforating an enormous orb with constellations, and Ledoux imagined a river rushing directly through a house in his Ideal City. But in both cases, the building only lets in what it wishes, always in control of nature, and not at all willing to be overgrown like Piranesi's ruins.

Inspector's House at the Source of the Loue, Claude-Nicolas Ledoux, 1773–1779.

The introduction of cast iron during the same period ignited a revolution in building technology.[12] Cast-iron building components resembled Acanthus leaves and palm trees, mirroring classical orders, but since the dimensions were much slimmer, these elements merged into an airy fusion of construction and exotic floral abundancy. Henri Labrouste's library reading room looks like a palm grove with an infinite vista beyond the bookshelves, and Victor Horta's art nouveau houses transport you to a tropical world with their winding stairs and wallpapers full of abstractions of overgrown tendrils. At the dawn of the twentieth century, architects were still mimicking, replicating and romanticizing an image of nature rather than truly engaging with it.

Reading room of the Bibliothèque Nationale Richelieu, Paris, Henri Labrouste, 1860.

Stairway of art nouveau–style Tassel House, Brussels, Victor Horta, 1892–1894.

The structural possibilities and freedom of the twentieth century brought with them the idea of a floating city on stilts. This was commonly based on a treelike structure that could hover over any landscape, flat or rugged, water or existing urban fabric, to create a new human canopy of multiple horizontal levels or new grounds.

Wolkenbügel, El Lissitzky, 1925.

El Lissitzky experimented with horizontal skyscrapers, the Wolkenbügel, or cloud-irons. He believed that moving horizontally (as human beings do on the ground) was natural and flying was not, so he tipped the skyscraper over and propped it up on three legs like a tripod. This created a highly stable building block that could be multiplied and connected. Large constructions could be built without consuming all the ground beneath them.[13] Lazar Khidekel, a student of Lissitzky, continued this experiment, imagining radical urban futures such as the Aero-City, Garden City, City above Water, Floating and Flying City.[14]

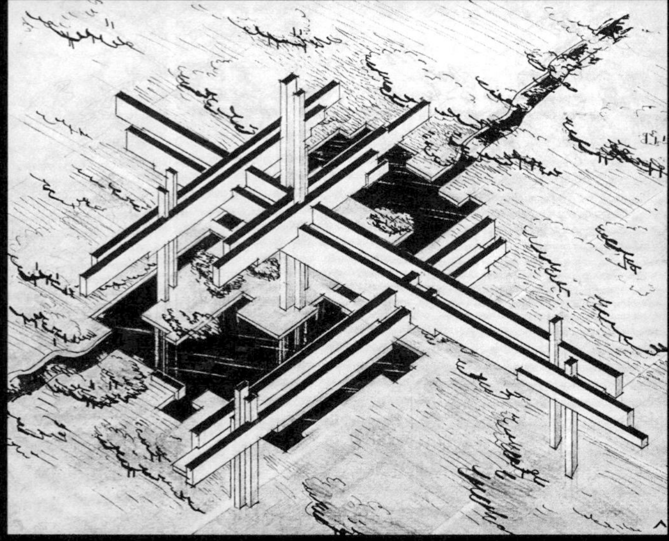

Sketch for a futuristic city (on poles), Lazar Khidekel, 1926–1928.

The Wolkenbügel was a three-storey, 180-metre-wide slab raised 50 metres above street level and resting on three pylons.

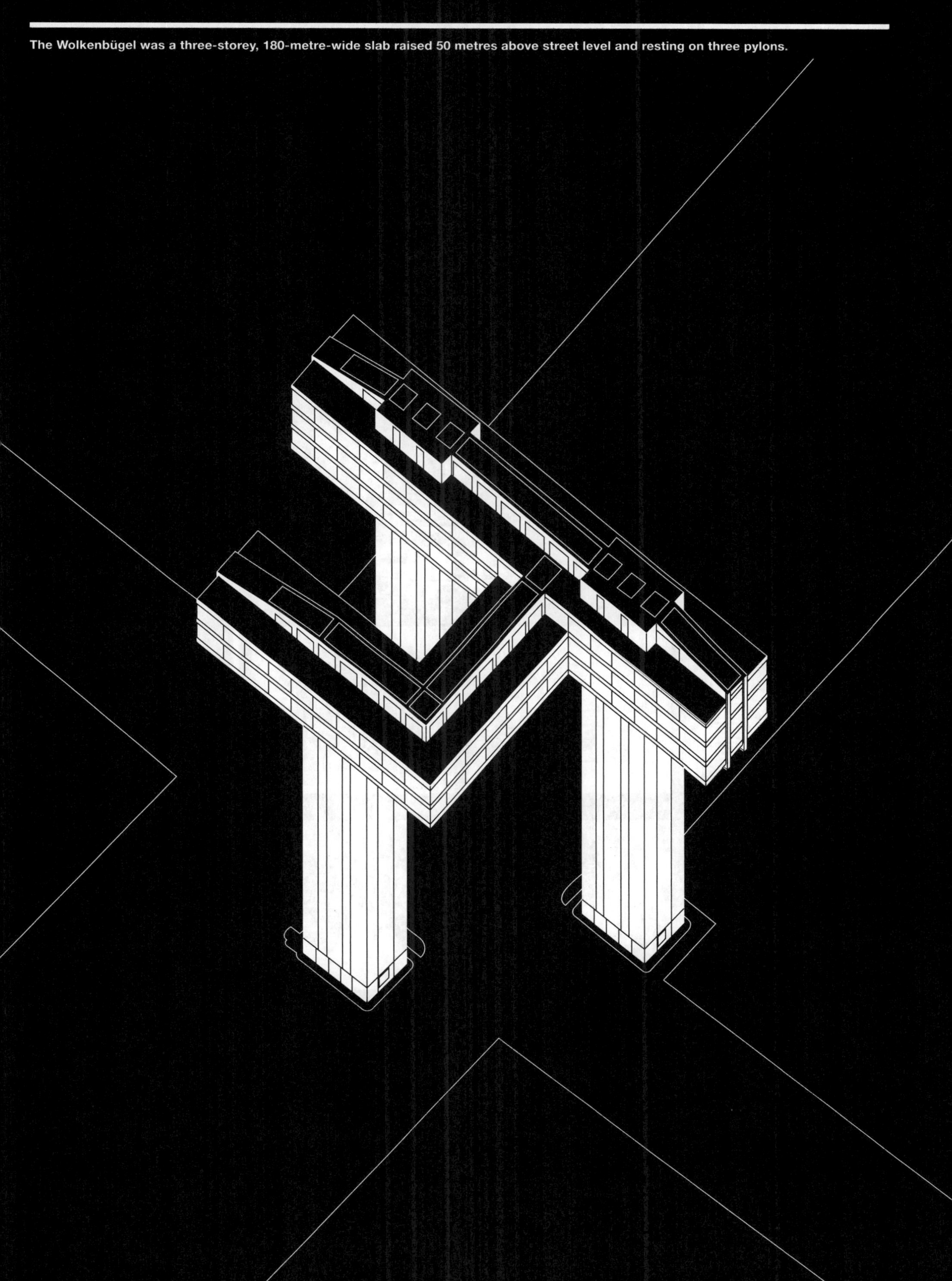

While Suprematist architects and artists pursued an unstable and tilting, almost floating city, Henri Sauvage and Adolf Loos experimented with the pyramidal form, the ultimate secure construction. Both involved a radical challenge to the skyscraper in the pursuit of a solution to the problem of increasing density. For reasons of economy, both extremes turned out to be equally unstable.

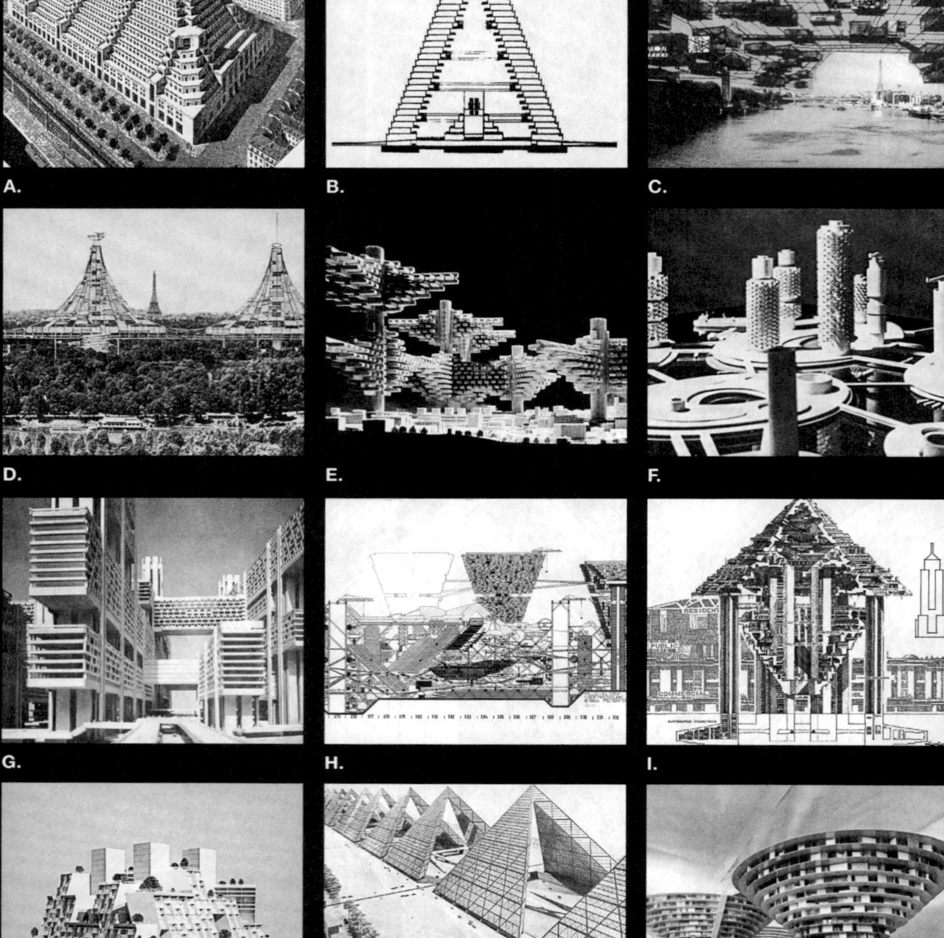

A. Giant Hotel, Paris, France, Henri Sauvage, 1927.
B. Wohnberg, Walter Gropius, 1928.
C. Spatial City, Yona Friedman, 1958.
D. Ville Flottante, Paul Maymont, 1959.
E. Shibuya Project: City in the Air, Arata Isozaki, 1962.
F. Marine City, Kiyonori Kikutake, 1963.
G. Proposal for Tsukiji District, Tokyo, Kenzo Tange, 1963.
H. Plug-in City, Peter Cook, Archigram, 1964.
I. Hexahedron, Paolo Soleri, 1964.
J. Triton, Buckminster Fuller, 1967.
K. Instant City, Stanley Tigerman, 1968.
L. Intrapolis, Walter Jonas, 1968.

These models were the progenitors of Yona Friedman's Spatial City (1958), Constant Nieuwenhuys's New Babylon (1959–1974), Archigram's Plug-in City (1964) and the Metabolist designs of Japanese architects like Kenzo Tange and Arata Isozaki. These utopian cities float, branch, grow and walk across the land. Like their influencers, however, they never saw their own ideas rise from paper or model to reality. It was close, but they were just a few years short.

These ideas (and architects) were often criticized as being anarchistic and anti-capitalist, or they were written off as utopian and unrealistic. Yet, frustratingly, these models were already implemented in two parallel realities, war and industry. By the 1940s, the sea fortress and the oil rig had already reached megastructure scale.

Maunsell sea fort in the Thames Estuary, 1939–1945.

Offshore mobile oil drilling platform "Mr. Gus II," in the Gulf of Mexico, 1957.

Sea fort in the Thames Estuary, 1939–1945.

It is still a miracle that Moshe Safdie's Habitat 67 slipped through the sieve of economy and was built. Safdie called it "a fairy tale, an amazing fairy tale".[15] He had the advantage that it was a government-funded project for the 1967 Expo, which needed some cutting-edge pavilions. Even so, it was sheer luck that a twenty-five-year-old architect who just graduated got his thesis project built. It was the very first cloud concept realized. Safdie received many more commissions to replicate the design worldwide, though none came to fruition.

In 1974, Gyorgy Chakhava, architect and deputy minister of road construction in Georgia, combined his influence and training to realize his Space City method, an idea he even patented.[16] Chakhava said, "With the Space City approach we are able to build over any terrain and not destroy the life which exists there ... as we know forests cover most of the earth. A forest consists of different trees, which have crowns separated from the earth, connected by tall communicating trunks to the roots... Space City gives the possibility to construct buildings in areas of complicated terrain or on the coast – and to not be afraid of natural calamities."[17]

Former Ministry of Transportation, Tbilisi, Georgia, Gyorgy Chakhava and Zurab Jalaghania, 1974.

Unrealized hotel, Yalta, Crimea, Gyorgy Chakhava, 1967.

All these historical examples show that buildings as landscape are not a new phenomenon. Spurred by an effort to realign architecture with the dictates of the environmental movement from the late 1960s, building and landscape began to merge.[18]

Increasing density without seizing pristine landscapes was a noble ambition, but in reality these landscapes are either so protected that building in them is out of the question, or it is seen as a necessary resource, bulldozed and used for a suburban typology of low- and mid-rise housing.[19] Within urban settings, most contemporary 'green' development is wrapped in a continuous coat of synthetic green without a serious commitment to connecting with their surroundings.

Don't be distracted by this green artifice. It is just whitewashing with a green brush. A shallow sprinkling of plants is no substitute for a serious engagement with natural systems. Mimicking nature is not enough. It is about integrating nature in all its aspects, not just the parts that we fancy. As Gyorgy Chakhava stated, "between the earth and the crowns – columns – there are a lot of free spaces for other sentient beings to create a harmonious, balanced world with the forest."[20]

Biosphere 2, Oracle, Arizona, 1987–1991.

Unfortunately, science seemed more focused on leaving the earth rather than fully understanding its true workings. Only twenty years after we first landed on the moon, the first attempt was made to mimic life on earth within a completely closed ecosystem. Biosphere 2 was built in the Arizona desert in an attempt to mimic biosphere 1, the earth.[21] It was the most airtight system ever built, thirty times more tightly sealed than the space shuttle sent out a couple of years earlier.[22]

From the very start, this modern Noah's Ark faltered. Secret deliveries were made, including extra oxygen, compromising the true closed ecosystem. Birds and bees died, leaving crops unpollinated and cockroaches reigning.[23] The crew inside became irritated and lost a dramatic amount of weight.[24]

Agriculture inside Biosphere 2.

The crew inside.

The inability to generate enough breathable air, potable water and adequate food for just eight humans, despite a $200 million investment and over 8350 square metres of biomes, was seen by many scientists as a colossal failure. Others wrote, "No one yet knows how to engineer systems that provide humans with the life-supporting services that natural ecosystems produce for free".[25] It is amazing to realize that so few scientists really studied how human behaviour fundamentally transformed the biosphere, just as the biosphere has fundamentally changed the geosphere (all inanimate matter).

In the nineteenth century Charles Darwin showed that plant and animal species were not fixed, but instead evolved in relation to the environment. Around 1925, Russian geochemist Vladimir Ivanovich Vernadsky was the first to argue that living matter was a major geological force, that the biosphere could alter the physical and chemical nature of the earth. In the 1970s, Ken Wilber introduced the concept of the Holon, which visually depicted the interrelated nature of our existence. Everything depends on the elements that precede it.[26] Yet only now are we really acknowledging the complex interrelation of species and that the biosphere, geosphere and atmosphere are not discrete systems.

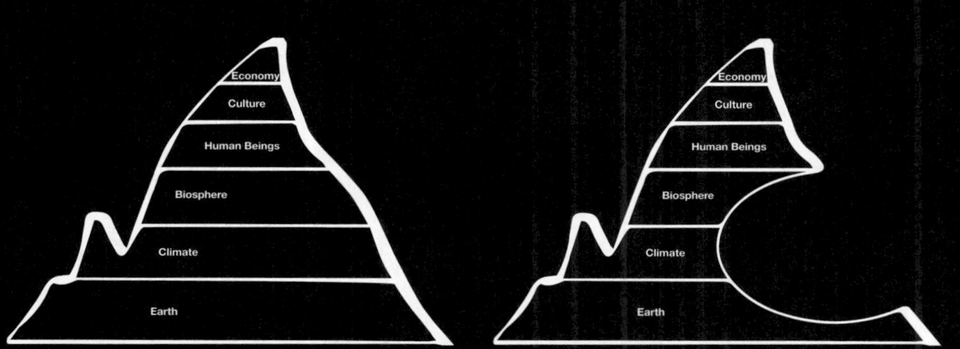

Holon diagram, Ken Wilber, 1970.

> "A free massive multibillion-dollar insurance policy is provided by nature for us, and yet year by year we destroy it in the name of economic development."[27] —Tony Juniper

In fact, the only all-inclusive, most protective and most reliable home we have is still the nature we are fully dependent on. Buildings are no more than a protective layer against unpleasant weather conditions, animals and other people, and while they can offer us some comfort and privacy, closing ourselves off in a bubble is pointless, expensive and dangerous. As Biosphere 2 illustrated, there is no bubble big enough for all seven billion of us and we'd likely suffocate within a few months.

"You don't imitate the surface or looks of the landscape, but you imitate how it works. This is embedding the city in nature."[28] —Diana Balmo

The line between human and nature, urban and rural, architecture and landscape was entirely humankind's invention. Now, with our eyes open, we can see the blur. And curiously, it is the point of interface that holds a certain allure. Take, for instance, the unbelievably architectonic form of natural systems like Northern Ireland's Giant's Causeway or the artificial smoothing of an enormous geographical feature with France's Col du Chaussy Pass.

Giant's Causeway, Northern Ireland.

Hairpin bends of the *lacets de Montvernier*, Col du Chaussy.

Today we discuss the city in the same language as we do landscape. It is a space of forces and flows that we manage, manipulate or direct through building. Our cities are an amazing (and largely untapped) repository of systems, networks and infrastructure we can repurpose and reinvent. 'Site' and 'building' are not just morphing into each other but marrying into reciprocity. Site goes over, gets under and is stretched within the building.

This marriage of made and born, building and site is far from stable, both are snogging and tearing each other's clothes off like teenagers, unaware of what their future will bring.

As the natural world reaches crisis point, with sea-level rise, shrinking lakes and growing deserts, strange plastic alternatives are being constructed. Around the Dead Sea, resorts continuously add storeys to their complexes. Not on the top but at the bottom, as the Dead Sea level is dropping by an astonishing metre per year.

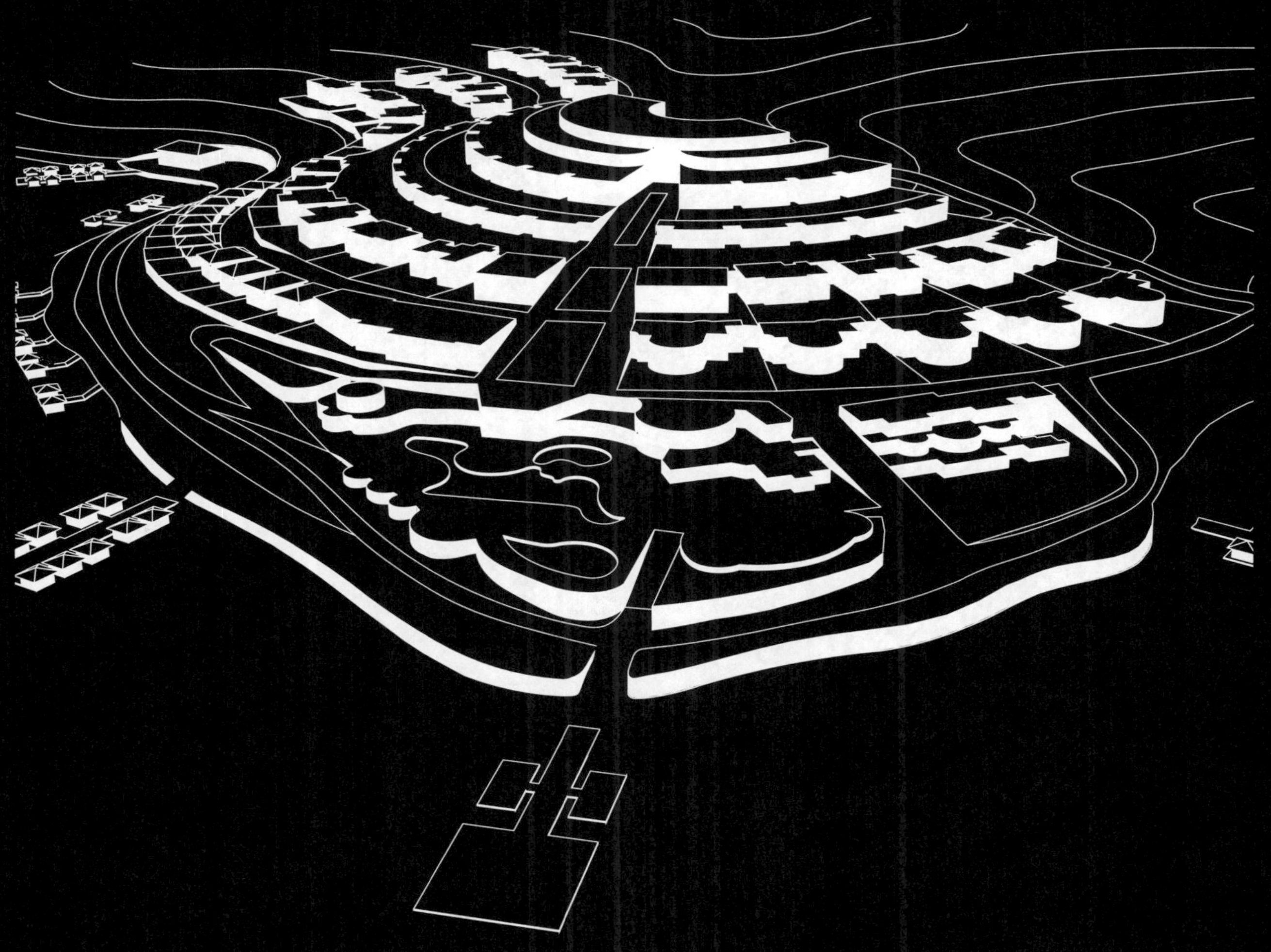

Axonometry of the Bodrum, Turkey, 2014.

Resorts like the Bodrum on the south-western Turkish coast build a new topography of luxury villas, subtropical gardens and themed swimming pools in all shapes and sizes that resemble the rear end of a cruise liner more than anything nature has ever conjured up. It is plastic nature without the discomforts, any signs of nature's unpredictability are swept away every morning before the guests wake up.

These places of leisure and luxury show our desire to escape to a natural paradise is very real. So much so that a synthetic nature is being packaged up as a product to be consumed.

The Bodrum, Torba, Turkey.

World's largest cruise liner *Harmony of the Seas*.

Roof of the Unité d'Habitation, Marseille, Le Corbusier, 1945–1952.

But don't despair, we are also witnessing a resurrection of ideas once dismissed as utopian, expensive, uneconomical or impractical. As early as 1952, Le Corbusier pulled communal space from an apartment block and placed it on the roof in the Unité d'Habitation in Marseille. But it has taken over fifty years for the fifth elevation, the roof, to become a highly coveted surface. Today, the roof is experiencing a renaissance, and luckily capitalizing on its added value is not about rolling out a green carpet, but about creating complete and complex landscapes.

A. Orquideorama, Medellín, Colombia, Plan B & JPRCR, 2006.
B. Opera House, Oslo, Norway, Snøhetta, 2007.
C. Ewha Womans University, Seoul, South Korea, Dominique Perrault, 2008.
D. Ahmet Baba Library, Timbuktu, Mali, DHK Architects & Two Think Architecture, 2009.
E. Holocaust Museum, Los Angeles, USA, Belzberg Architects, 2010.
F. Rolex Learning Centre, SANAA, Lausanne, Switzerland, 2010.
G. Giant Interactive Group Corporate Headquarters, Shanghai, China, Morphosis, 2010.
H. Marcel Sembat High School Sotteville-lès-Rouen, France, archi5, 2011.
I. Metropol Parasol, Seville, Spain, J. Mayer H Architects, 2011.
J. Groupe scolaire Aimé Césaire, Nantes, France, Mader, Mabire & Reich, 2011.
K. Primary School for Sciences and Biodiversity, Paris, France, Chartier Dalix Architect, 2014.
L. National Taiwan University Library Taipei, Taiwan, Toyo Ito, 2014.
M. Thread, Tambacounda, Senegal, Toshiko Mori, 2015.
N. Lycée Schorge, Koudougou, Burkina Faso, Francis Kéré, 2016.
O. Hotel Jakarta, Amsterdam, Netherlands, SeARCH, 2014–2018.

Jeanne Hachette, Ivry-sur-Seine, France, Jean Renaudie, 1969–1975.

This chapter looks beneath the green artifice to reveal how we have tried to construct nature. It shows how a building can act as a plateau, a raised pediment offering remoteness or vastness within the dense urban realm, a tree whose roots and branches connect disparate structures or a landform rising up from the earth's surface with sloping, terraced facades that offer a socialized outdoor space where everyone gets a bit of green and a view to boot.

Exquisite examples like Jean Hachette in Ivry-sur-Seine terrace down to ground level to become fully navigable terrains connected to the urban fabric. Air, light and open green space are paramount, and the inferior yet necessary programme like parking is used to prop this space up. Repetitive, aggregate structures such as these challenge the standardization of housing, offering a model far more sympathetic to the diversity of society and its desire to reconnect mentally and physically with the natural environment.

Sirius Building, Sydney, Tao Gofers, 1980.

Like Diana Balmori's concept of the 'thick line'[29], the buildings in this chapter represent a thickening of the earth's crust, stretching and pulling the surface and transforming the ground into something malleable. This plastic condition seeks to double or triple the earth's surface, to do more with less. It is an acknowledgement that we humans take up far too much space, but we are unlikely to return to our once-natural state.

Sydney Opera House
Sydney, AU
Jørn Utzon
1957–1973

1174

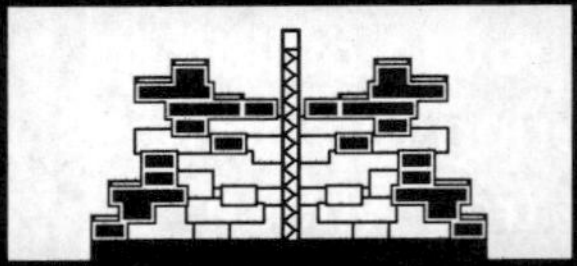

Habitat 67
Montreal, CA
Moshe Safdie
1967

1188

Centraal Beheer
Apeldoorn, NL
Herman Hertzberger
1968–1972

1202

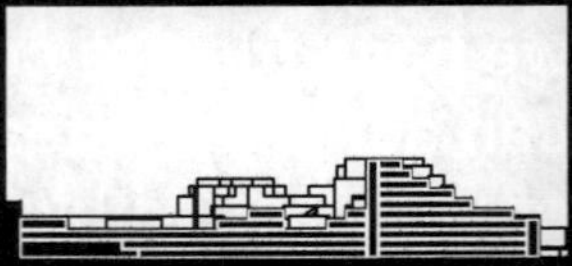

Jeanne Hachette
Paris, FR
Jean Renaudie
1969–1975

1210

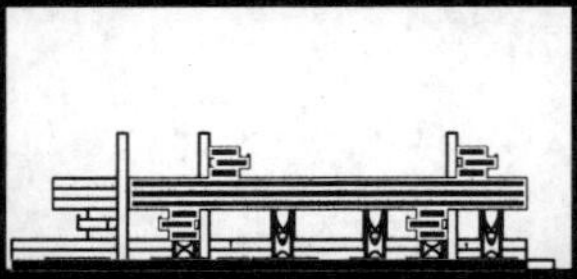

Árbol para Vivir
Lechería, VE
Fruto Vivas
1990

1274

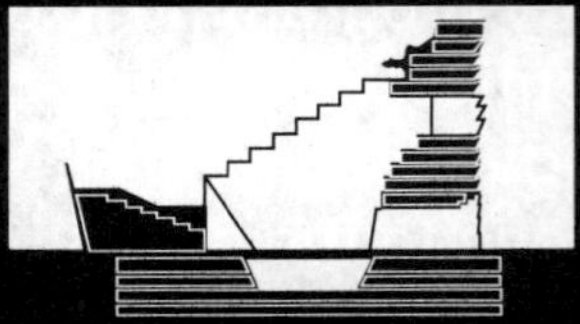

ACROS
Fukuoka, JP
Emilio Ambasz
1995

1278

Scherf 13
Leidsche Rijn, NL
SeARCH
2000–2006

1282

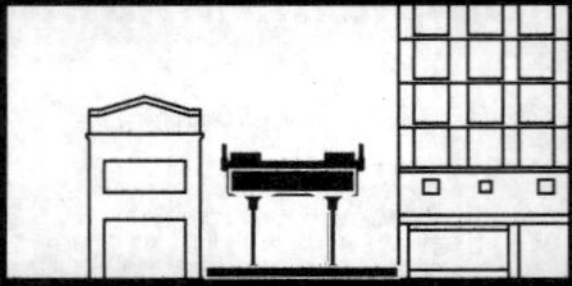

The High Line
New York City, US
Diller Scofidio + Renfro,
James Corner Field
Operations & Piet Oudolf
2003–2014

1294

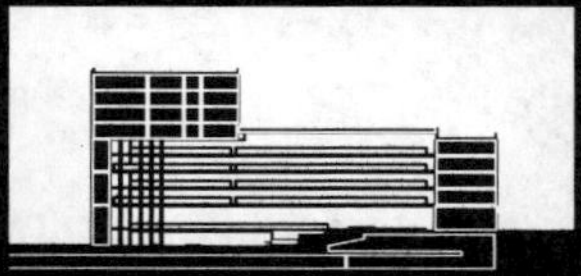

Hotel Jakarta
Amsterdam, NL
SeARCH
2014–2018

1346

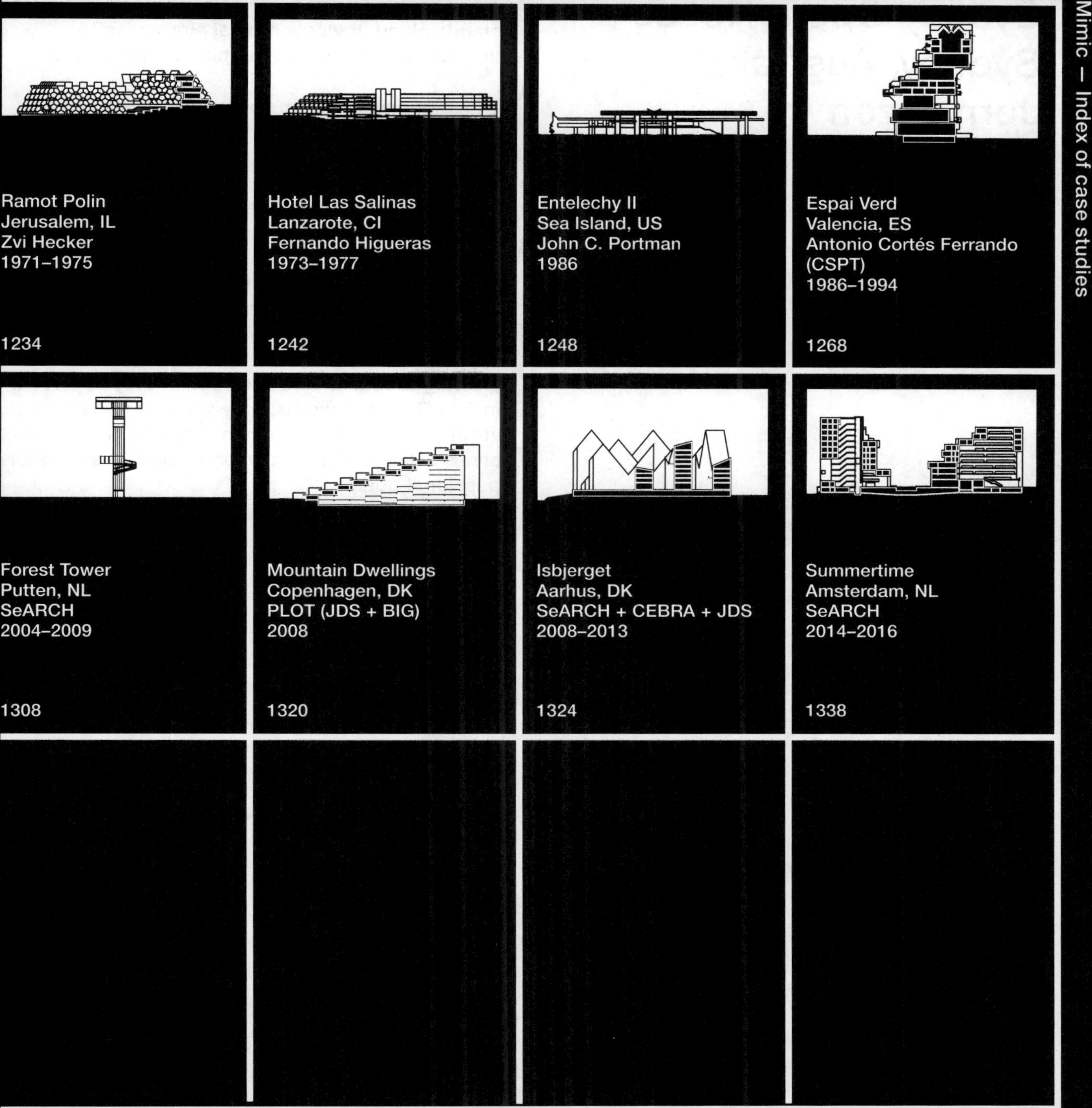

Sydney Opera House
Sydney, Australia
Jørn Utzon
1957–1973

Jørn Utzon's design for the National Opera House stands alone. It was a radical alternative to the mainstream modern architecture of its era.

The relationship Utzon formed with Asger Jorn during their collaboration on the (unbuilt) Silkeborg Museum had a considerable influence on his architectural perspective.[30] Asger Jorn, and the avant-garde Situationist International movement that he founded with Guy Debord, rejected the doctrine of progress that held technological advancement and economic growth as the tools and measures of a successful society. Instead, they pushed for constructing authentic experiences or situations that could combat the growing alienation and dysfunction they observed. In Guy Debord's words, they were interested in "the concrete construction of momentary ambiances of life and their transformation into a superior passional quality."[31]

Section of the Sydney Opera House.

Plan of the Sydney Opera House.

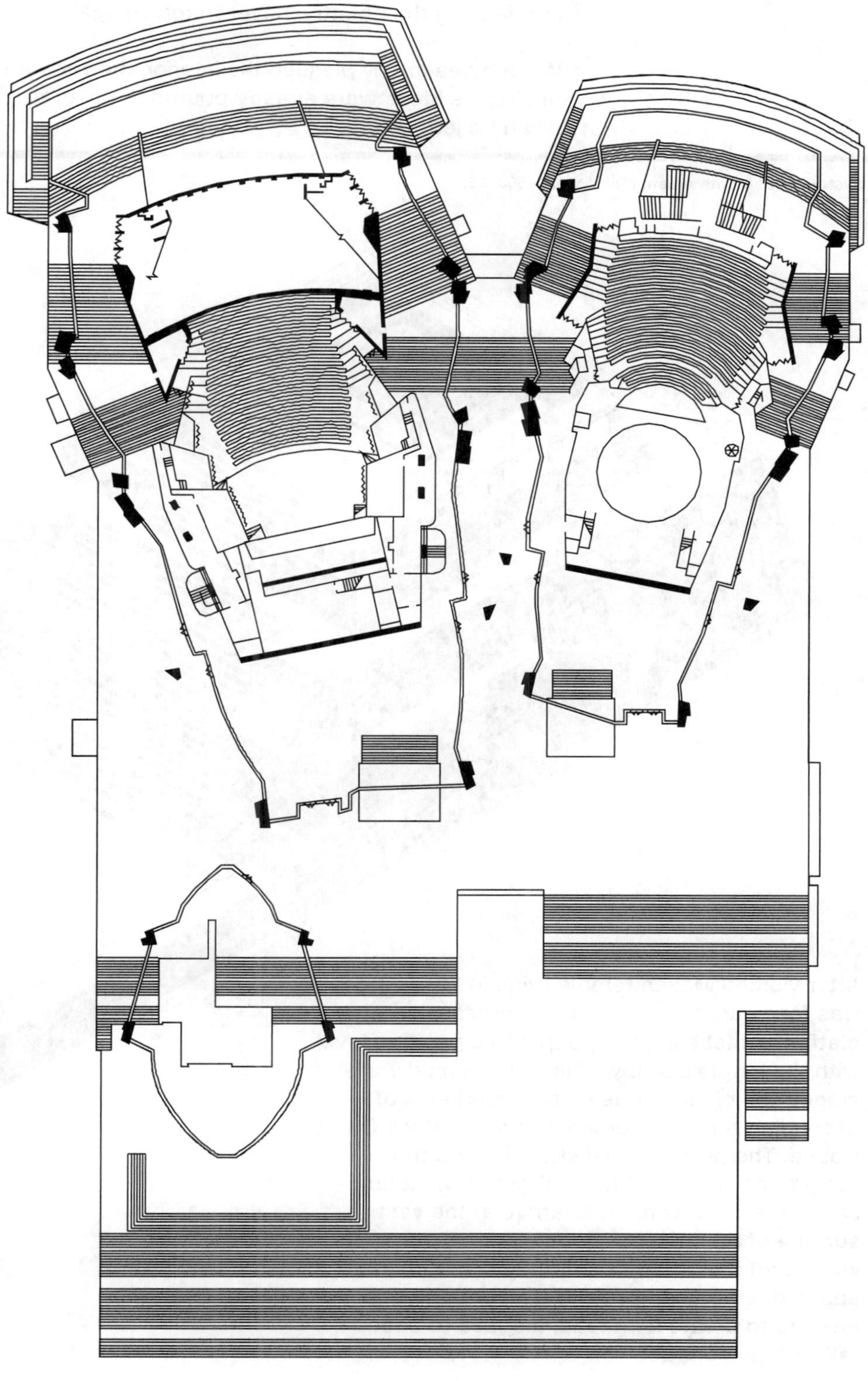

Utzon's approach ran parallel to this. He rejected universal solutions in favour of personal expression. His designs went beyond pure functionalism and did not shy away from the poetic, often drawing on nature, other cultures and personal experience. These references were not easily graspable, nor particularly easy to negotiate for the client. A fundamental difference in mindset, made crystal clear by the words "Here in Australia you do what your client says", was ultimately responsible for Utzon's resigning from the Opera House commission and leaving the country, never to return again.[32]

While bureaucracy plagued the interior, the strength of Utzon's ideas were already poured in concrete when he left.

System IV of Monte Albán, Mexico. 450–500 CE.

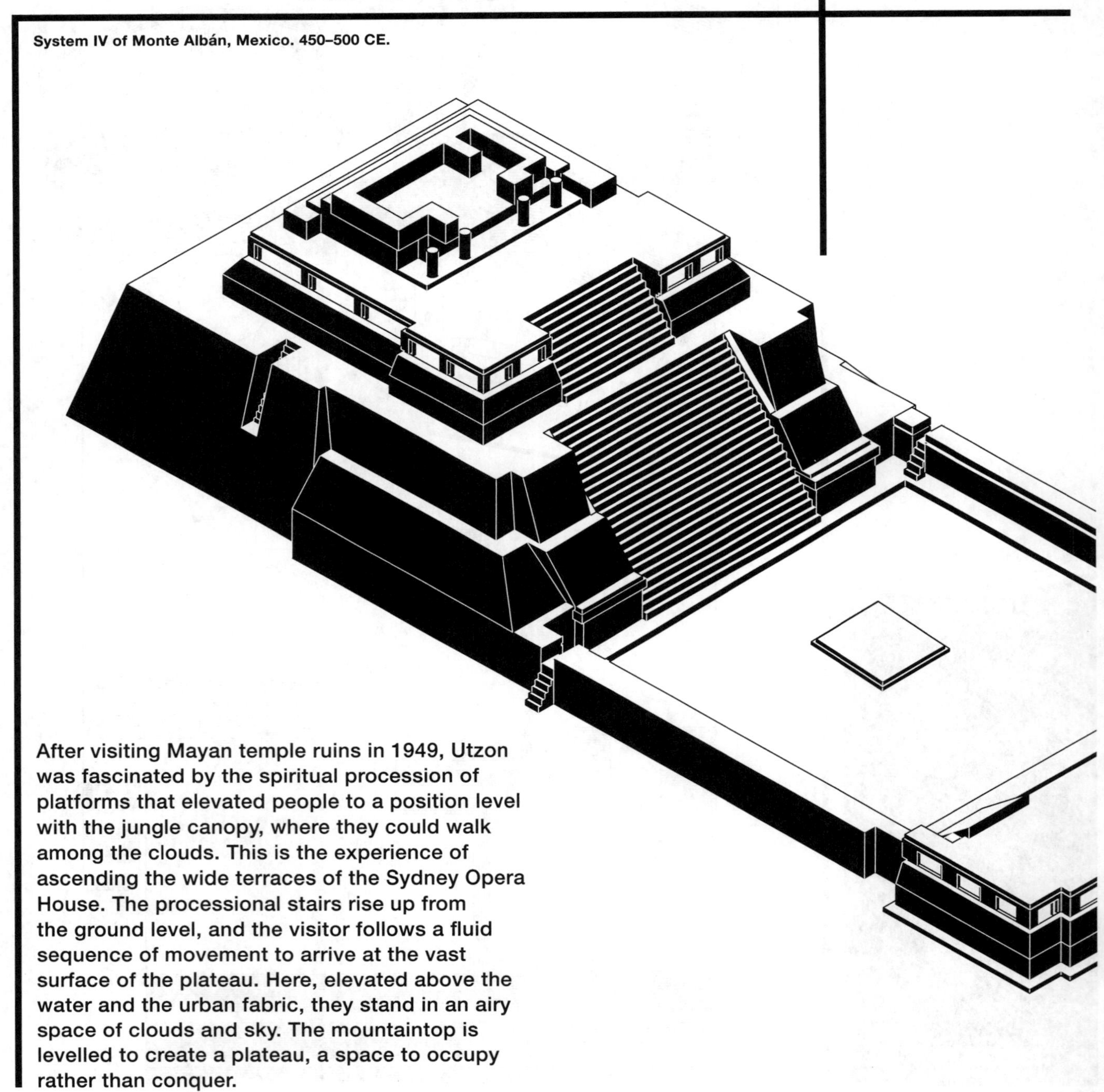

After visiting Mayan temple ruins in 1949, Utzon was fascinated by the spiritual procession of platforms that elevated people to a position level with the jungle canopy, where they could walk among the clouds. This is the experience of ascending the wide terraces of the Sydney Opera House. The processional stairs rise up from the ground level, and the visitor follows a fluid sequence of movement to arrive at the vast surface of the plateau. Here, elevated above the water and the urban fabric, they stand in an airy space of clouds and sky. The mountaintop is levelled to create a plateau, a space to occupy rather than conquer.

Aerial view of Monte Albán complex, Mexico.

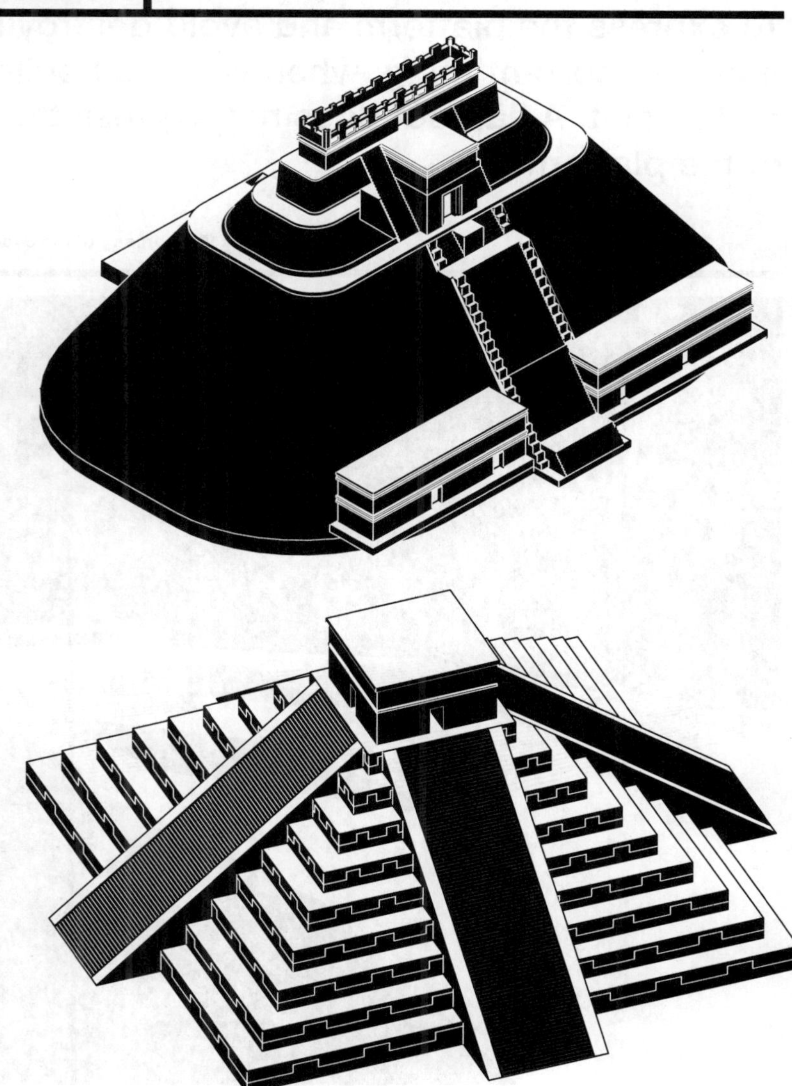

Pyramid of the Magician, Uxmal, 600–1000 CE.

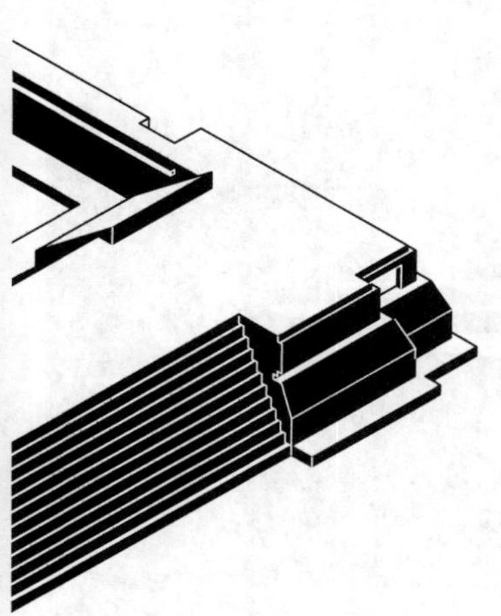

Kukulkan temple of Chichen Itza, Mexico, 800–1200 CE.

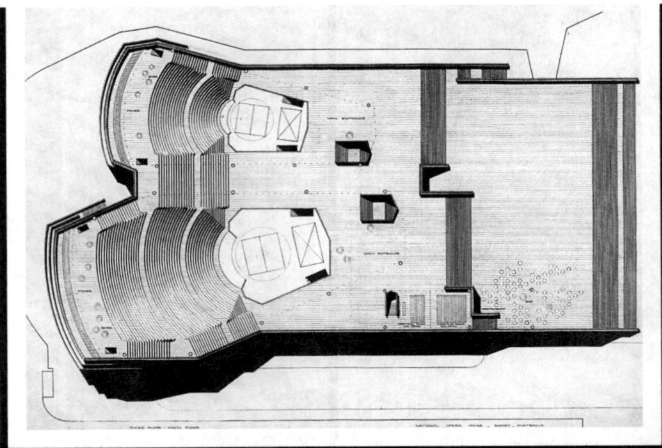

Competition plan of the Sydney Opera House plinth, 1956.

"In the Sydney Opera House scheme, the idea has been to let the platform cut through like a knife and separate primary and secondary functions completely. On top of the platform the spectators receive the completed work of art and beneath the platform every preparation for it takes place. To express the platform and avoid destroying it is a very important thing, when you start building on top of it. A flat roof does not express the flatness of the platform."[33] —Jørn Utzon

Axonometry of the Sydney Opera House.

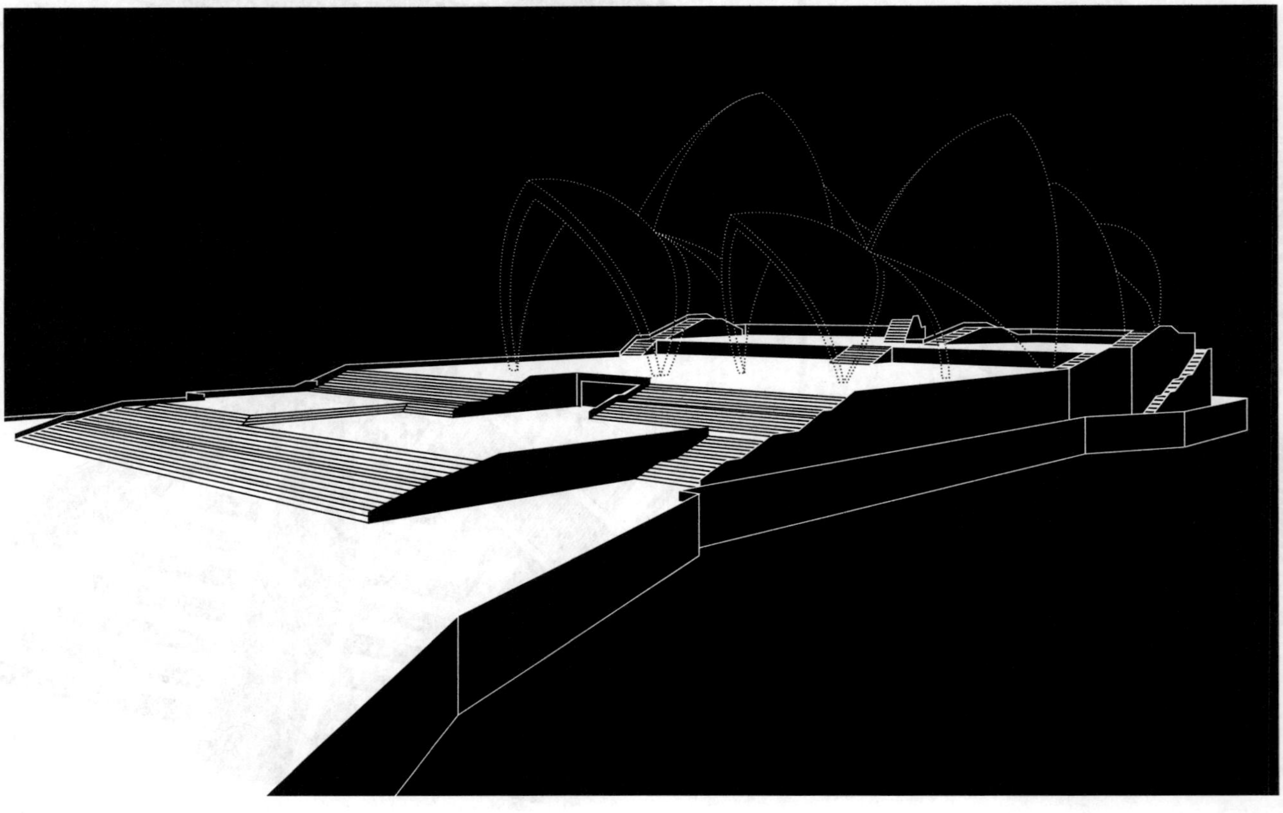

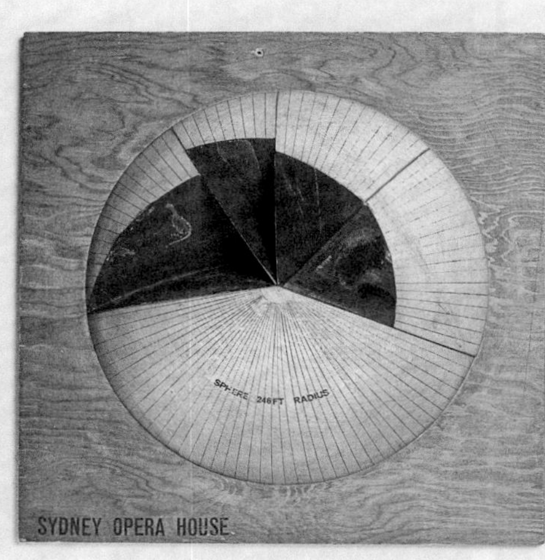

Model of the roof shell concept as built. The meridian lines allowed the ribs to be identical, only to be shortened to the appropriate length, making the construction of the shells much more economical.

Utzon's concept of 'additive architecture' is based on systems and growth patterns observed in nature. This was not a literal translation, it was a transformation of nature. Within the design for the Sydney Opera House, elements of nature recur in materialization and form; the fourteen outer shells that make up the iconic roof form a perfect sphere if pieced together. Utzon worked on it like a sculptor, without detailed drawings. And together with structural engineers Ove Arup and Partners, he came up with at least twelve different proposals over six years until it was resolved.

The opera house was designed as a collection of experiences or a construction of situations, rather than one singular, clear-cut concept. Utzon worked from a boathouse north of Sydney, surrounded by sailboat hulls and naval wood details. He trusted the strength of his personal interpretations, immersing himself in Australia's natural and cultural environment. The white, semi-glazed tiles were chosen for their reflective quality, an idea that came to Utzon while swimming at the Great Barrier Reef.[34]

Shells of the Sydney Opera House.

Just like the busy harbour it sits in, the Sydney Opera House is in constant motion. Non-stop activities, seasonal maintenance and ongoing renovations make it seem like a living being rather than a static monument. In Utzon's words, "You never finish with it while you move around it or see it against the sky… This interplay, with the sun, the light and the clouds, is so important that it makes the building into a living thing."[35]

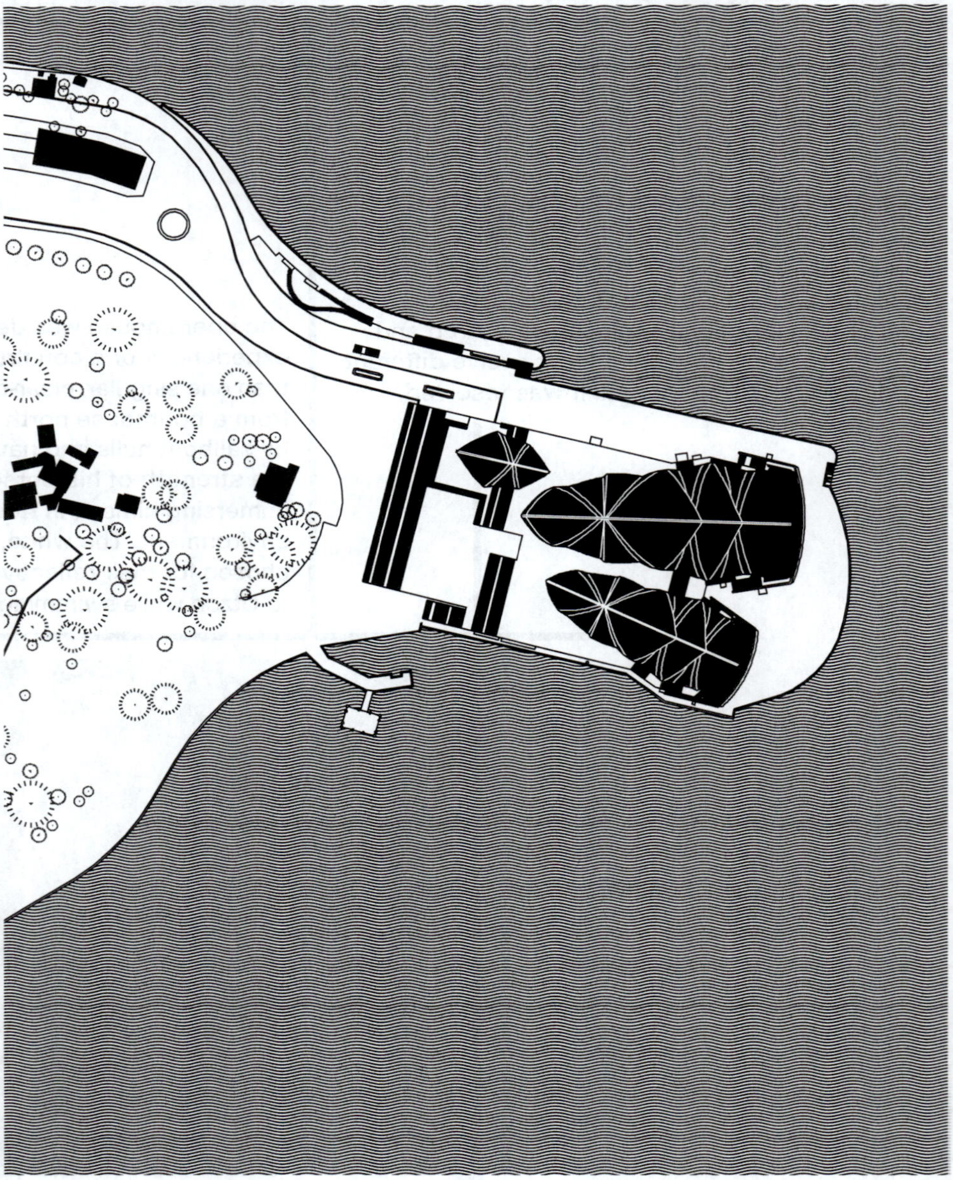

Site plan of the Sydney Opera House.

When Eero Saarinen rescued Utzon's design from a pile of discarded competition entries in 1957, Guy Debord and Asger Jorn were busy working on a map called the *Naked City*. They remapped Paris by considering the relationship between spaces and emotions. As Guy Debord stated, "spatial development must take into account the emotional effects." It was inspired by the *Carte du Pays de Tendre* ('Map of the Land of Tenderness'), from 1654, which was made for Madeleine de Scudéry's novel *Clélie*. The map depicts a fictional land with places and landscapes as a geographical allegory of emotions and virtues.[36]

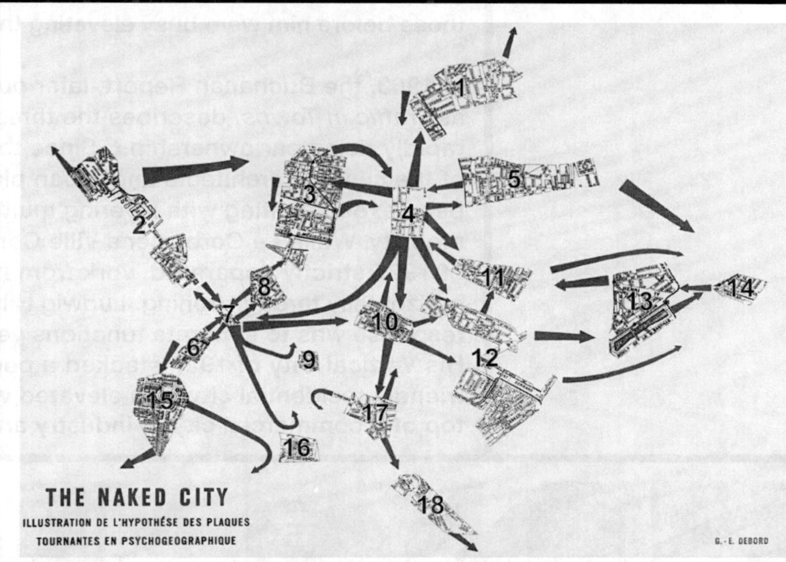

Guy Debord and Asger Jorn, *The Naked City*, 1957.

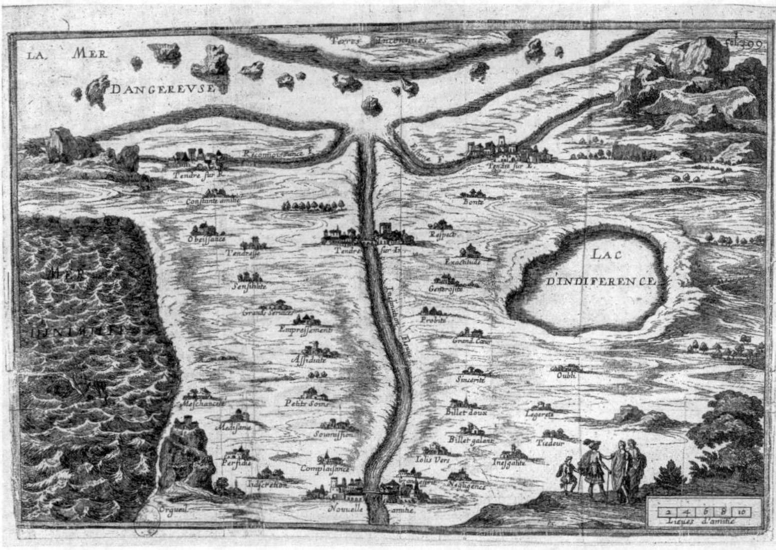

Carte du pays de Tendre, Francois Chauveau, 1654.

Stunningly, it is as if the places marked on this map gather all the thoughts and attitudes that swirl around the Sydney Opera House: the Dangerous Sea, the Unknown Land, Tender on East, Accuracy, Respect, Warmth, Lightness, Kindness, Lake of Indifference, Forgetfulness, Friendship, Sincerity, Submission, Complacency, Caregiving, Attendance, Pride, Mechanism, Eagerness.

Habitat 67
Montreal, Canada
Moshe Safdie
1967

Before Moshe Safdie could lift a suburb into the sky, those before him were busy elevating the city street.

In 1963, the Buchanan Report, later published as *Traffic in Towns*, describes the threat posed by rapidly rising car ownership.[37] Since the turn of the century, architects and urban planners had been experimenting with layering multiple forms of mobility. While Le Corbusier's Ville Contemporaine of 1925 strictly separated work from housing horizontally through zoning, Ludwig Hilberseimer's response was to separate functions vertically. His Vertical City of 1927 stacked a pedestrian-friendly residential city with elevated walkways on top of a commercial city of industry and cars.

Illustration from *Traffic in Towns*, England, Colin Buchanan, 1963.

***The Vertical City*, Ludwig Hilberseimer, 1927.**

Short section axonometry of Habitat 67.

Later, in the 1960s, Hilberseimer himself criticized his project for being too sterile, lacking green space and being more of a necropolis than a metropolis. But surprisingly, one of the earliest examples of an elevated street, built in 1922, has functioned relatively well for almost a century.

The ground-floor and first-floor apartments of Michiel Brinkman's Justus van Effen complex in Rotterdam have their front doors at street level, and the 140 maisonettes above have their own one-kilometre-long looped upper street. Intermittent staircases and a lift at each end connect this elevated street to the main street below.

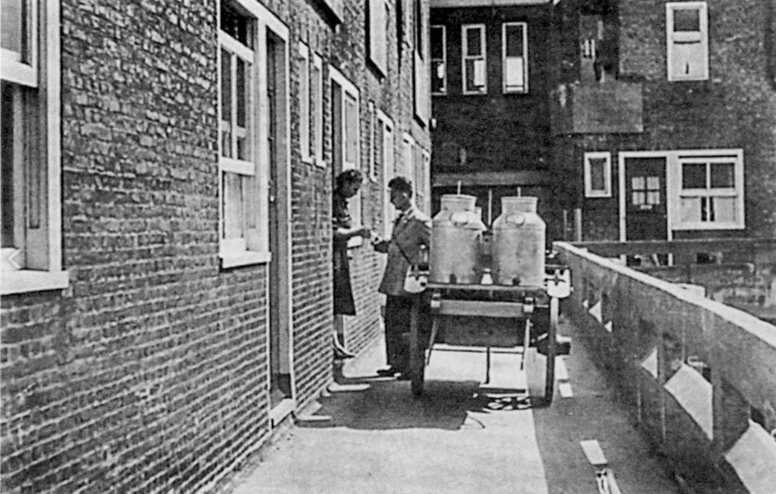

Upper street of the Justus van Effen complex, Rotterdam.

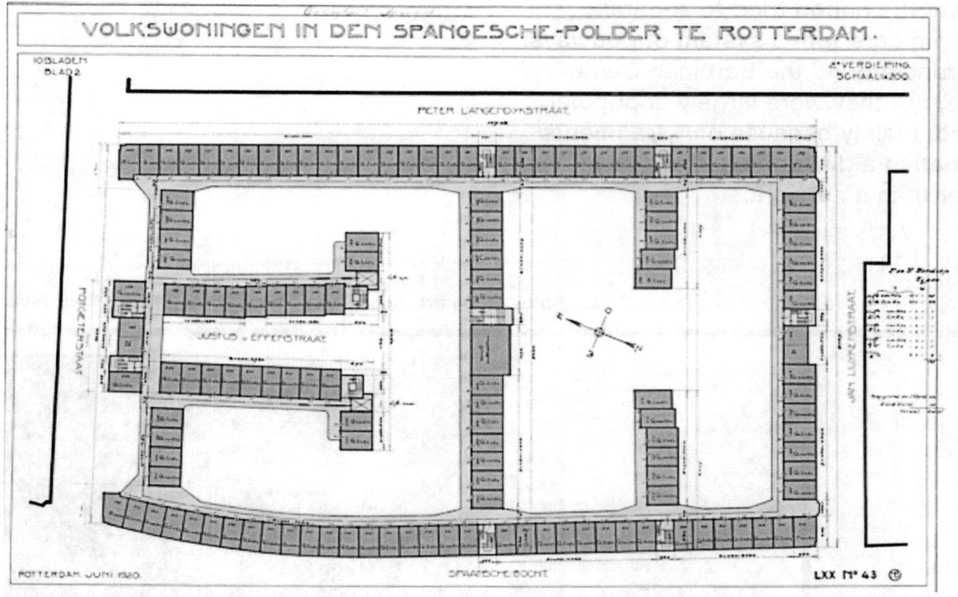

Plan of the Justus van Effen complex by Michiel Brinkman, 1922.

What separated Brinkman's idea from many other versions like Moisei Ginzburg's Narkomfin, Le Corbusier's Unité d'Habitation and the Smithsons' Robin Hood Gardens was that he attached the street loosely against the facade of the housing block while the others carved streets out of it, making the street more of an interior walkway. The success of Brinkman's project lies largely in the continuation of widely accepted social relationships within the block. The postman passes by with his pack and the gallery functions as a sidewalk where neighbours meet.

But this functional clarity can only partly explain why this elevated walkway worked, when so many others failed.

After World War II, London tried to separate pedestrians from cars with a system of pedways. The one that runs around the Barbican Centre was elaborate, but they were largely unpopular and underused, mainly because only fragments were built, creating a disconnected series of bridges, rather than a network.[38]

Barbican Centre, London, Chamberlin, Powell and Bon, 1982.

Elevated walkway, Barbican Centre, London, Chamberlin, Powell and Bon, 1982.

Many of the brutalist complexes built throughout England and France after the war also had exposed elevated walkways, but as with the London pedways over-complexity, a lack of functional clarity and a lack of connection with the context they were in led to their ultimate failure.

Walk between the glassy offices and tucked-away churches of the City of London along the thundering roads down by the Thames and you can occasionally find staircases embedded in the sides of buildings. These are small remaining fragments of the pedway, a relic of the idea – once popular, now largely discredited – of the 'three-dimensional city': urbanism that abandoned the primacy of the ground plane in favour of a rich spatial interplay of different layers of activity.

The 'three-dimensional city' was undoubtedly naive, but the implications of its disappearance are profound.[39]

Thamesmead Housing Estate, London, 1968.

While its intention was to humanize the modern city and give it a picturesque or even romantic feel by adapting elements of the 'townscape', such as the village green, laneway or town square, planners and architects largely achieved the opposite.[40] Stanley Kubrick used the Thamesmead Estate in London, just a few years after its completion, as a backdrop for a felonious and sadistic movie. In *A Clockwork Orange*, littered stairwells and walkways are taken over by a rampaging gang, leaving little room for a positive interpretation.

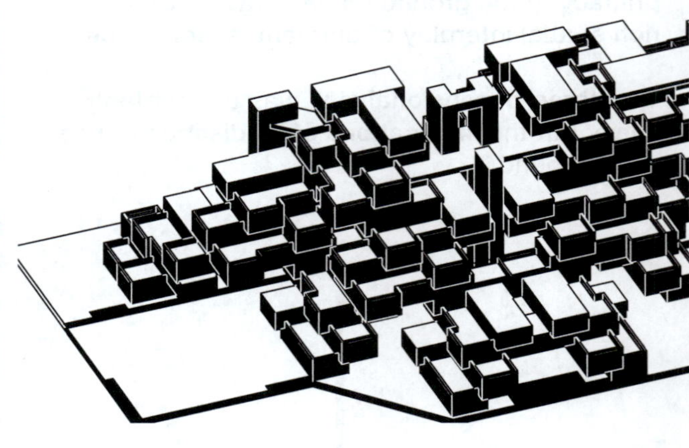

View of Habitat 67 from the west, showing the cascading terraces and gardens.

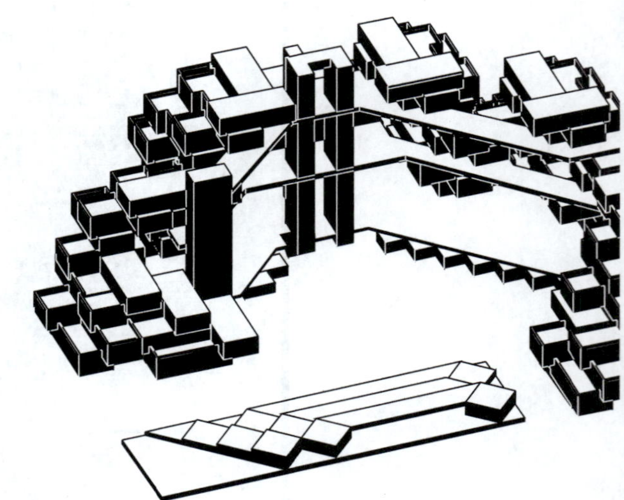

View of Habitat 67 from the east, showing the vertical circulation and pedestrian streets.

This cynicism had not quite crossed the Atlantic. Habitat, the brave thesis project of the young Moshe Safdie, did not give up on this idea of merging the, a semi-detached house with a garden, with a layered, three-dimensional urban block.

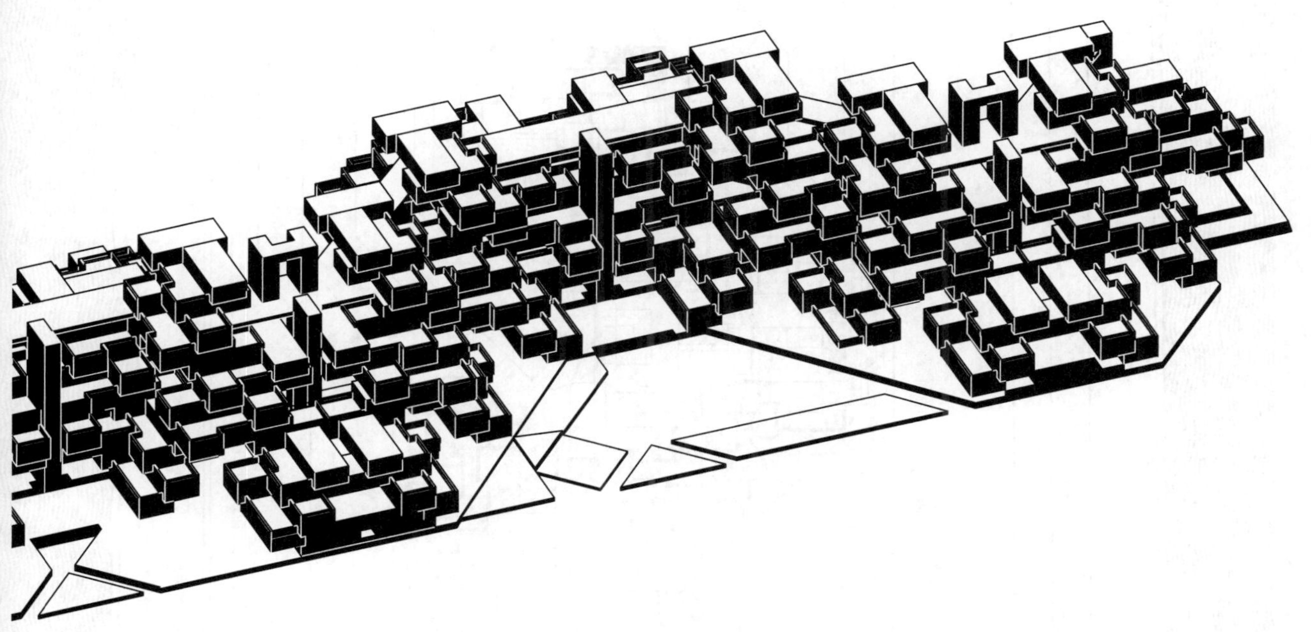

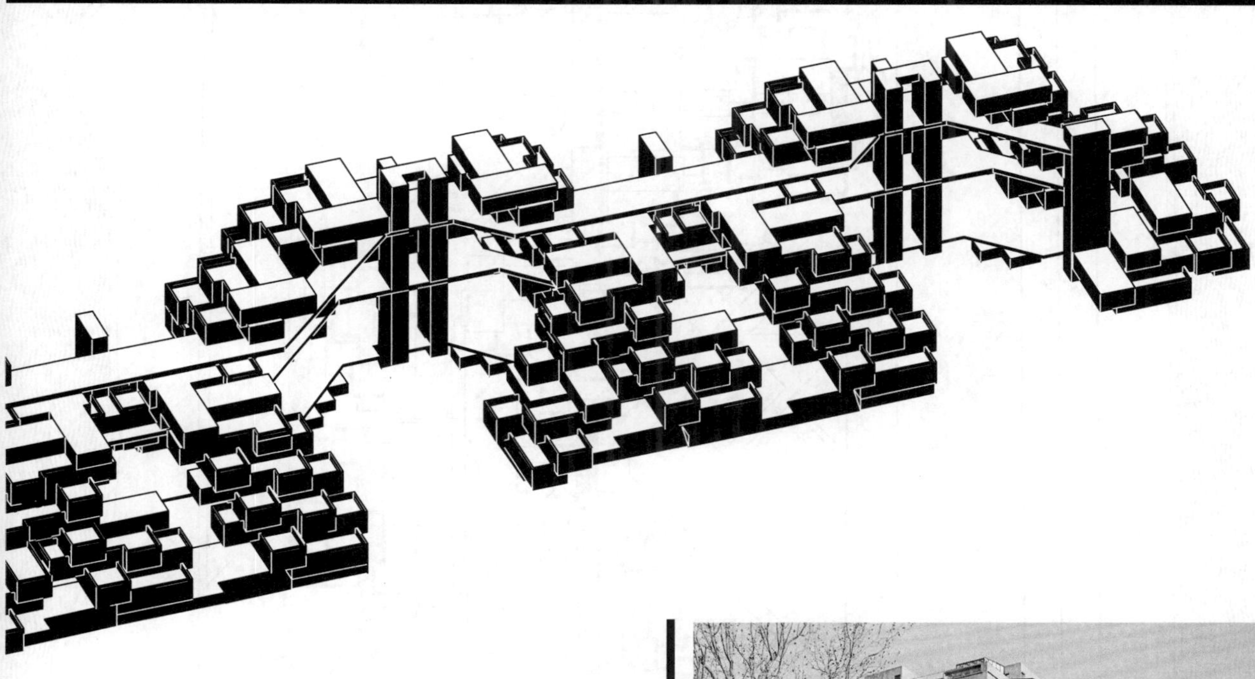

Instead of treating the housing block as a solid mass, Safdie made it multifaceted, open and light. Its porosity is unmatched. Elevated streets run its full length, shifting from covered to completely exposed. It asymmetrically stacked detached suburban homes in the sky, making use of setbacks and voids to stretch distance between dwellings and maximize privacy, airflow and exposure to light – qualities unprecedented in a twelve-storey building of 158 homes.

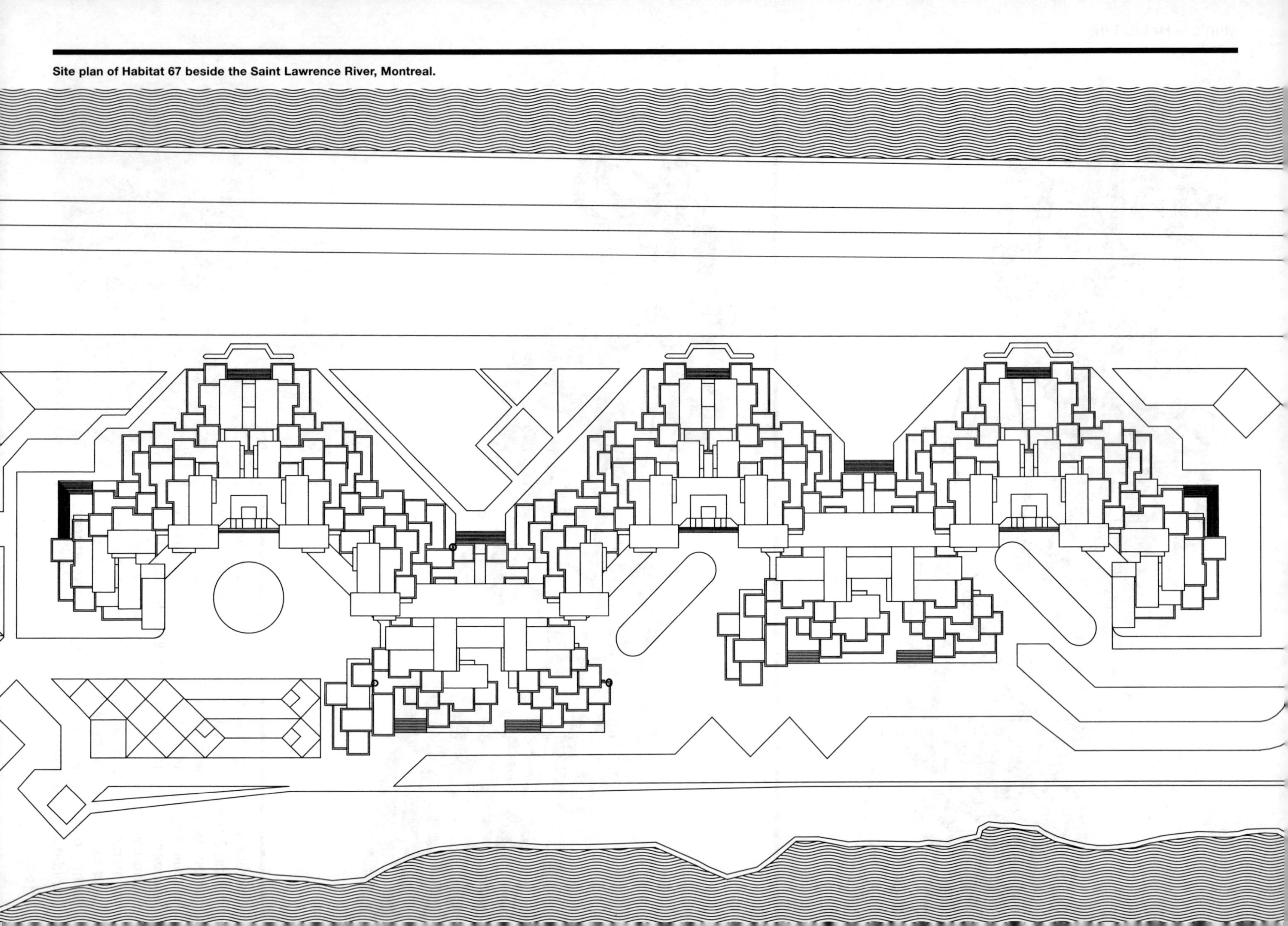

Site plan of Habitat 67 beside the Saint Lawrence River, Montreal.

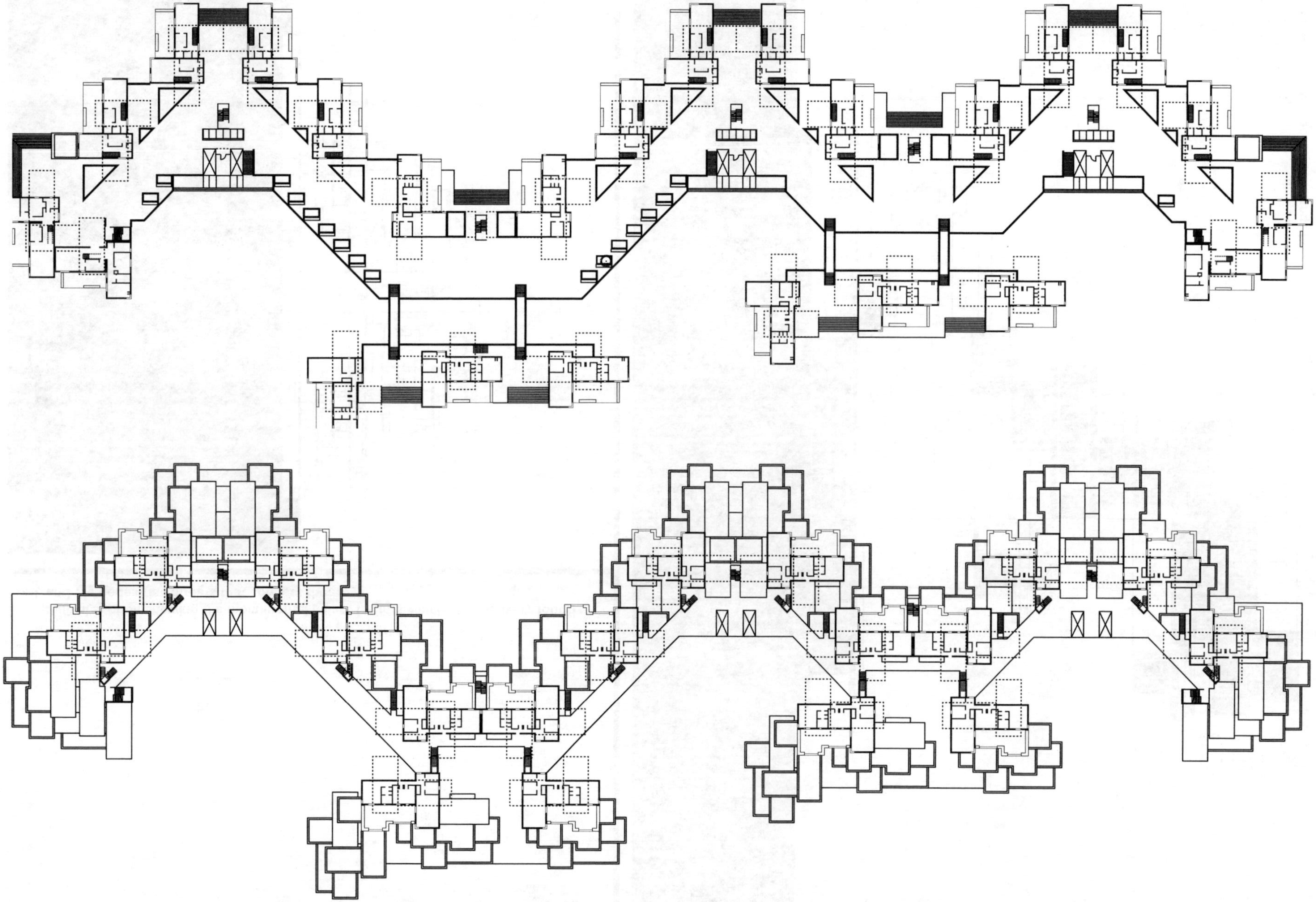

Level 1 and level 5 plans.

Short section showing the porosity of the suburb.

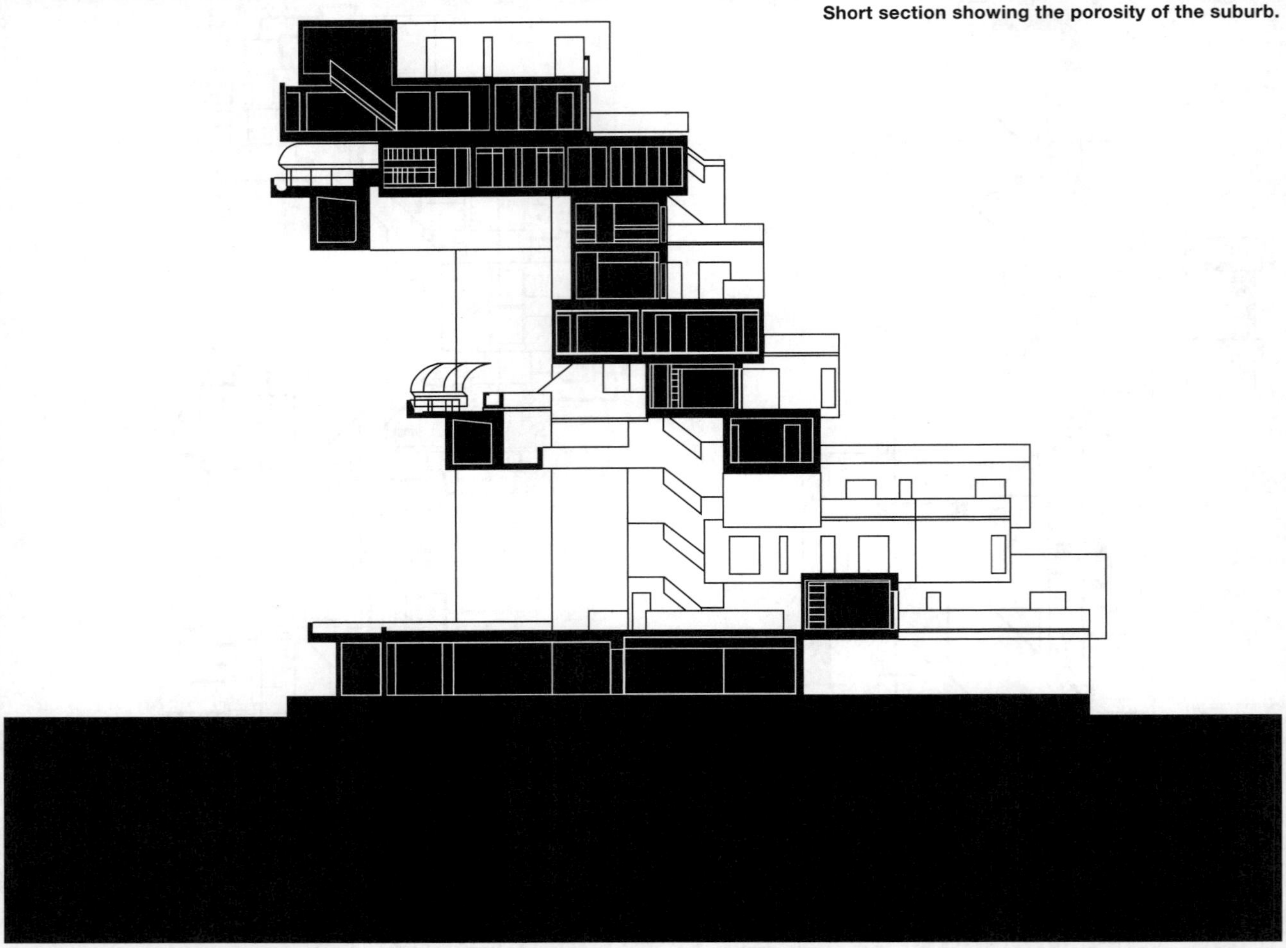

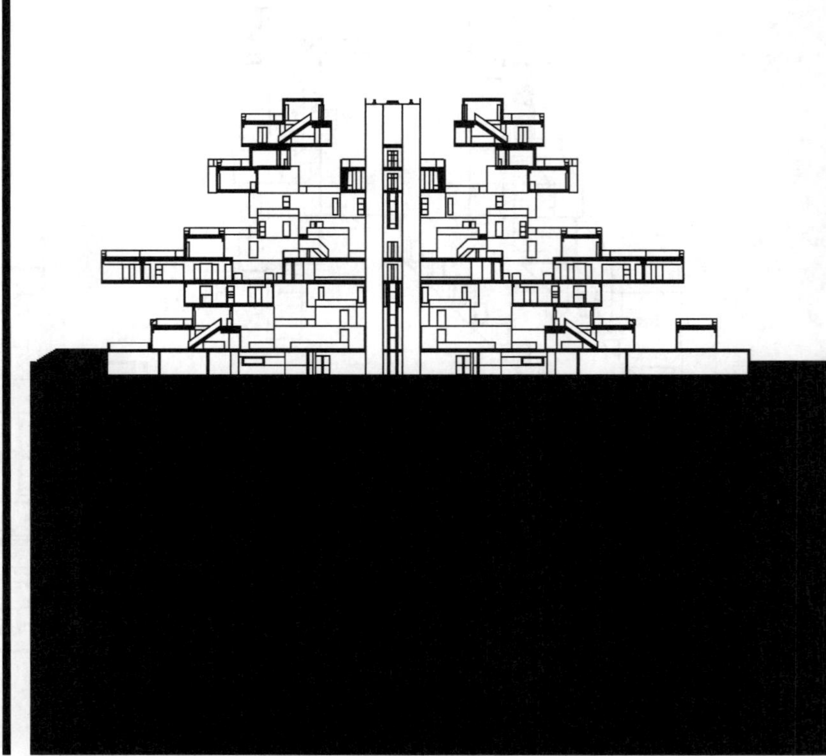

Longitudinal section showing the monumental pillars for lifts which stop at every fourth level, and the pedestrian streets that connect them.

> "If I'm asked what inspires me most as an architect, I'd say, at this point, it's not any particular building. It's nature and how nature designs, and what I as an architect might be able to learn from it. Which is perhaps, for architecture, the ultimate humility."[41] —Moshe Safdie

Habitat 67 under construction.

The idea was simple, but the execution was overcomplicated. In the 1960s there was a romantic idea (or myth) that industrialized processes would result in affordable objects. A reliance on technology to simplify construction methods resulted in a project that was far more complex and expensive to build and maintain than if built using conventional methods.[42]

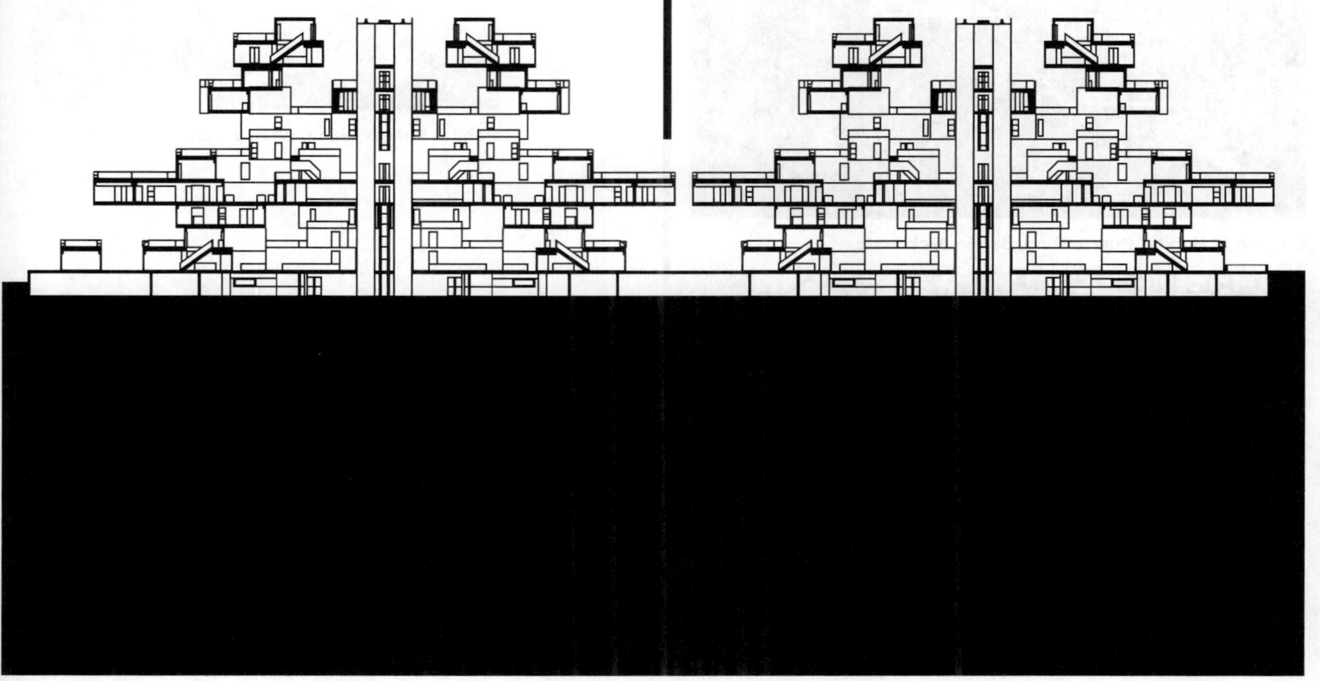

Attempts to replicate Habitat 67 were unsuccessful. Safdie's Habitat New York (1967), Israel (1969), Rochester (1971) and Tehran (1976) remained speculative designs. Only once in Puerto Rico did a Habitat scheme break ground, but after the first thirty units were constructed the project was abandoned, left to be invaded by nature.

Model of Habitat Puerto Rico, Safdie Architects, 1968–1970.

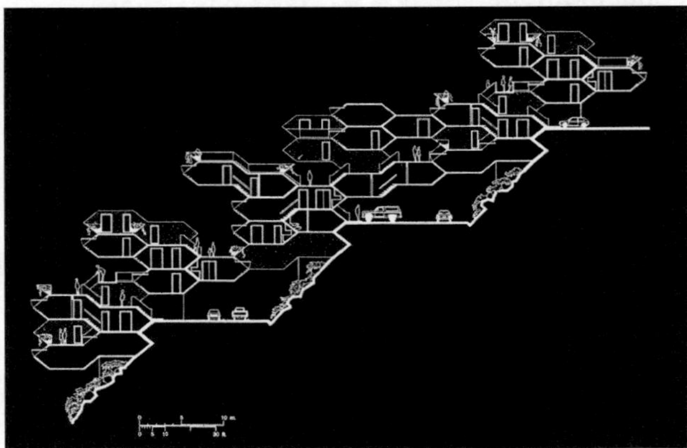

Section of Habitat Puerto Rico, Safdie Architects.

Habitat Puerto Rico model, Safdie Architects.

Caricature of Habitat Puerto Rico, Enver Azizi, 1969.

Overgrown Habitat Puerto Rico.

But Safdie's vision doesn't seem so radical today. The desire for high-quality private outdoor space never really disappeared. The suburbs have dominated for the last half century, but now as money and development move back to the city centre, providing a sky-high house with a garden is a lucrative endeavour. You can take people out of their rural habitat, but it's not so easy to take rural habits out of people.

Unfortunately, nothing quite lives up to the title of Habitat 2.0, where the pixilation of dwellings has become much denser to squeeze as much profit as possible out of the scheme.

Proposed Habitat 2.0, Toronto, BIG, 2016.

Centraal Beheer
Apeldoorn, Netherlands
Herman Hertzberger
1968–1972

Axonometry of Centraal Beheer.

The design or planning of collective workspace began roughly in the eighteenth century. Up until then, people mainly worked individually and from home.[43] An exception to this is the medieval scriptorium where monks would write and illustrate illuminated manuscripts within cubicle-like recesses of the cloister.

St Augustine in His Study, Sandro Botticelli, 1490–1494.

Ezra the Scribe, Codex Amiatinus, 692–710 CE.

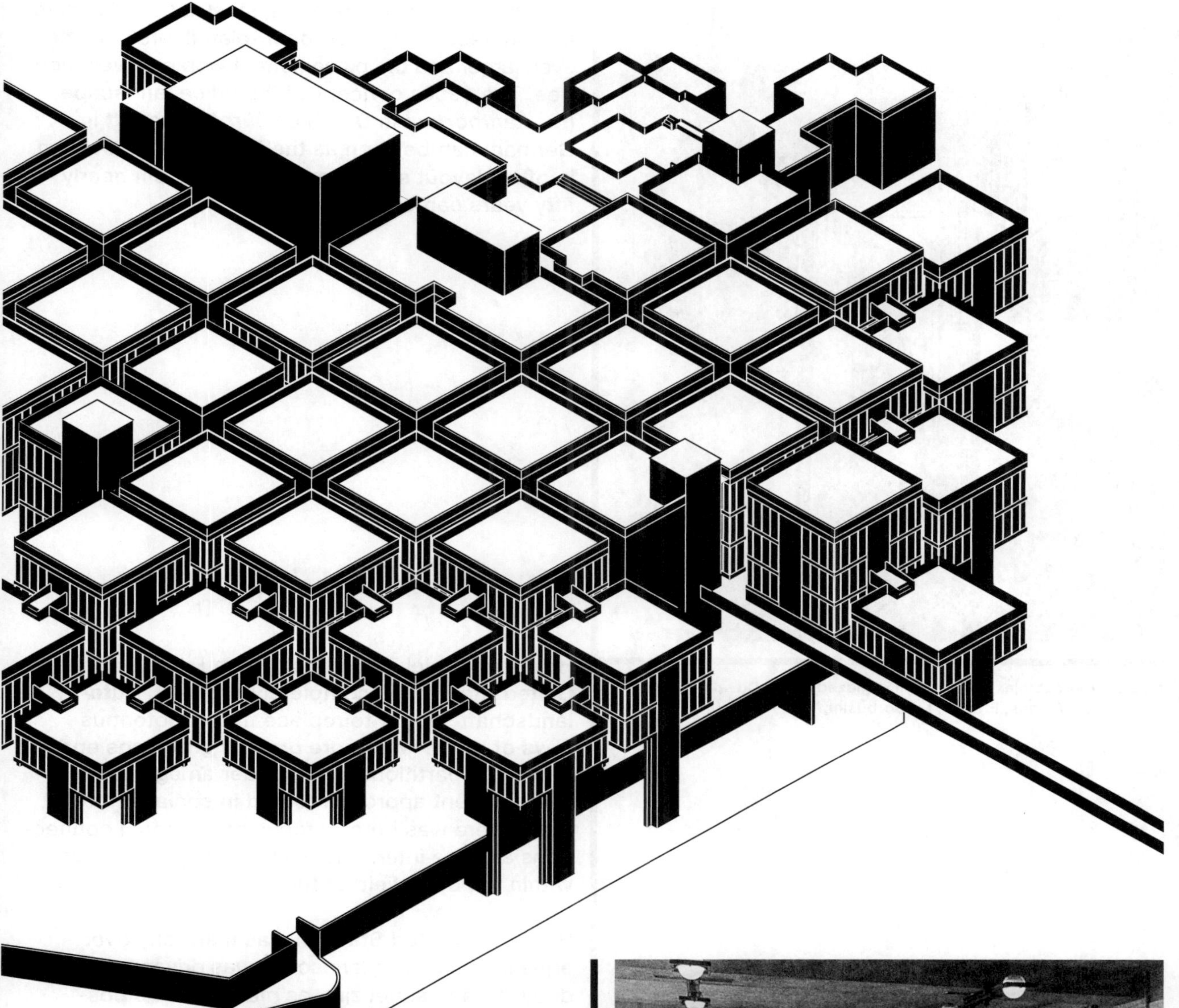

Larkin Administration Building, Buffalo, Frank Lloyd Wright, 1903–1906.

In the early twentieth century, modernist architects such as Frank Lloyd Wright saw walls and rooms as downright fascist.[44] After the 'cast-iron revolution' there was no need for load-bearing walls.[45] An office could be truly open, but the question of how to organize a large number of workers in the same place remained. The Larkin Administration Building was the first commercially viable Taylorist office, with 1800 workers seated at long rows of desks like a white-collar assembly line.[46]

Like a fixed cubicle, half the wall is glazed at the Duval Factory, St-Dié-des-Vosges, France, Le Corbusier, 1946–1951.

With the introduction of glass, steel, air conditioning and fluorescent lighting, open-plan floors became even larger and the placement of workers even more free. The 1950s concept of the office landscape (the *kantoortuin* in Dutch or *Bürolandschaft* in German) can be seen as the first major innovation in office layout since American Taylorism nearly fifty years earlier.

How this model played out within Europe and the United States was completely different. Bürolandschaft sought to replace the monotonous rows of desks with more organic groupings and moveable partitions to engender an egalitarian management approach rooted in social democracy. There was greater focus on personal connections and the interactions and dynamics of staff within the open field of the office.

But in the United States it was hierarchy over equality. The office landscape was driven by productivity, and squeezing as many staff as possible into a large room was key. In 1964, Robert Propst invented the Action Office for Herman Miller. Although his intention was to improve privacy and communication within the open-plan office, it morphed into the monotonous cubicle farm still present (and loathed) today.

Office cubicles in Gulf Worldwide, Dubai, 2012.

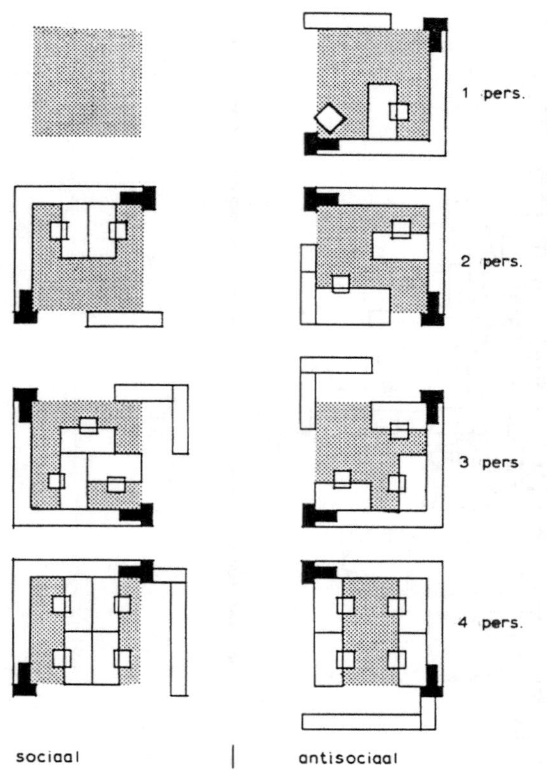

Examples of making places as primary building components, Atelier Herman Hertzberger.

Architect Francis Duffy described office design as having gone through three phases: Taylorist, Social Democratic and Networked.[47] While the Taylorist model still exists alongside the highly mobile twenty-first-century office, Herman Hertzberger's Centraal Beheer was deeply rooted in the second, pushing for a socially-minded, egalitarian office set-up.

Space for family and work within Centraal Beheer.

Hertzberger believed that the architect's role was not to provide a complete solution, but to provide a spatial framework to be filled in by the users.[48] It was common during the 1970s to build your own habitat, personalizing your workspace environment not with studio photos of family, trophies, certificates and diplomas but with sling plants and succulents, ugly mugs and kids' drawings, including notorious bottles of liquor and packs of cigarettes.

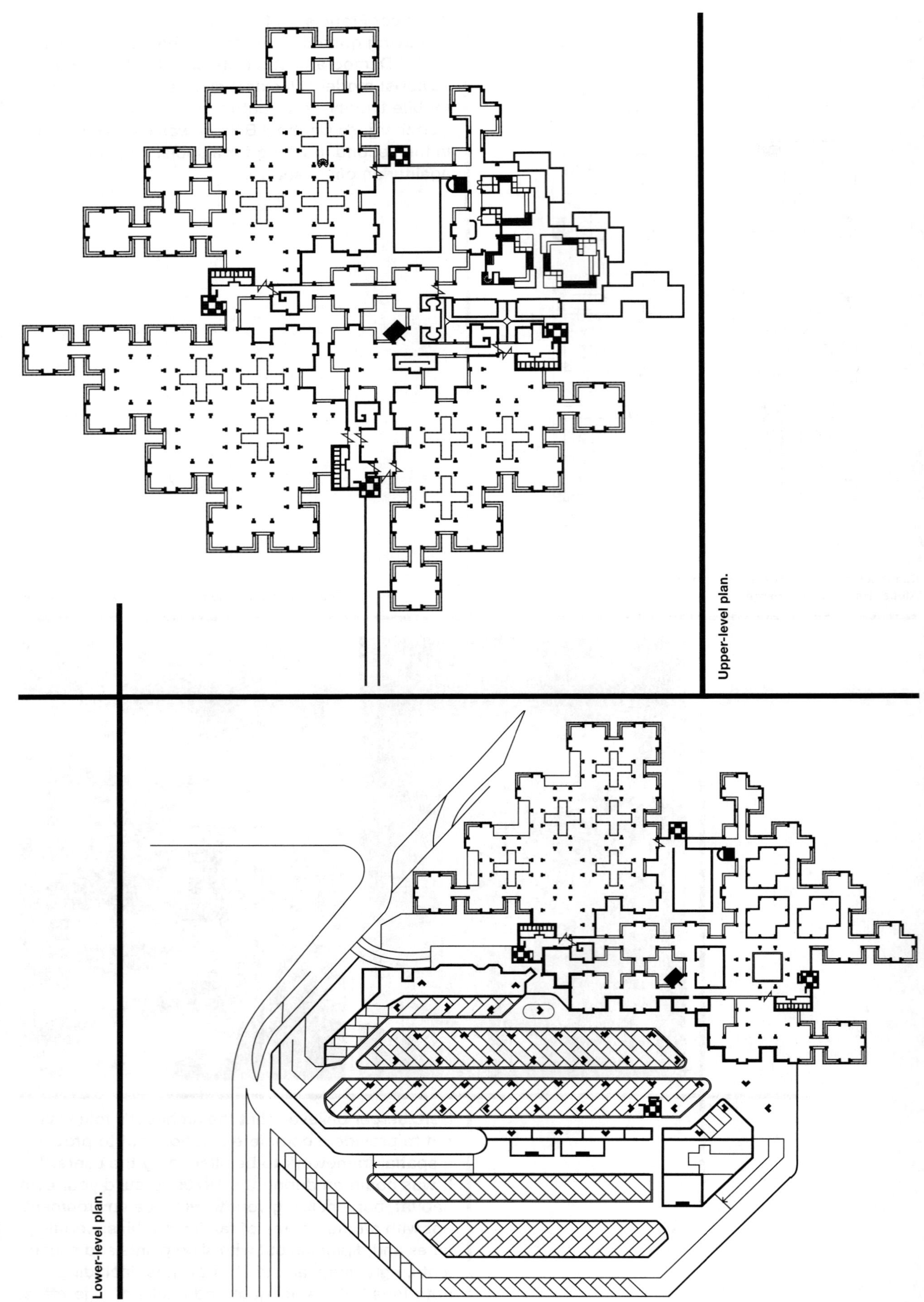

Upper-level plan.

Lower-level plan.

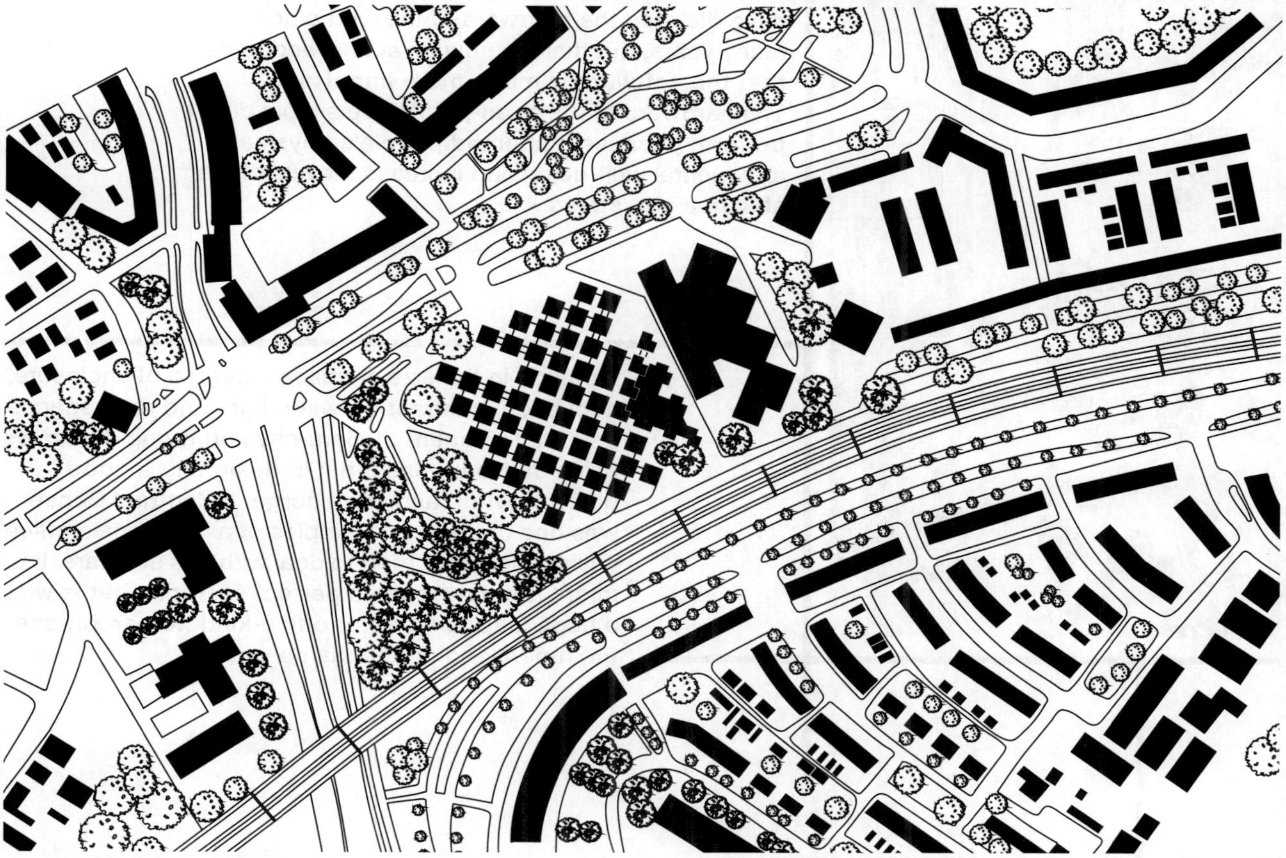

Site plan.

Centraal Beheer is made up of sixty tower-like cubes connected on each floor by bridges. Similar units of nine square metres are clustered together to form a 'worker's village', allowing for both individual and group working space.[49] The building is remarkably structured and repetitive, yet the system permits deviations like a central street, open squares on the ground floor and bigger voids.

Central street inside Centraal Beheer.

Along the extensive central street, space is equally developed in vertical and horizontal directions.[50] In plan it calls to mind the street pattern of a medieval town, while the light slipping through small voids on all sides of the square units creates a condition more similar to a forest, as if open space is punctured by the dense foliage of the working spaces above.

The dynamics of working individually or in teams have dictated the hardware of the workplace for many years, but there is now an acknowledgement that the software is much more important. The hardware of the open-plan office simply didn't perform because it affected people's physical and mental well-being and increased levels of staff absence and stress.[51]

Variation in the size of spaces, degree of enclosure, acoustics, contrast between light and dark spaces and the treatment of hierarchy and group dynamics turns out to be essential in designing a good place of work, and Hertzberger's Centraal Beheer was one of the first examples of a large-scale office environment that tried to deal with this software. It might not have been a perfect example, but is was a huge leap forward for office-kind (to paraphrase the moon landing that same year).

Section of Centraal Beheer.

Centraal Beheer liberated the office desk from the confinement of walls and the discomfort of complete openness at the same time. Today it seems as if we have almost come full circle, returning to a workspace with domestic comforts, like Saint Augustine in his small study with a curtain for privacy and concentration.

But perhaps we haven't regressed far enough. It would be interesting to explore the role that landscape could play in the twenty-first-century workspace, as that was humankind's very first office.

The networked office space – work is where the Wi-Fi is.

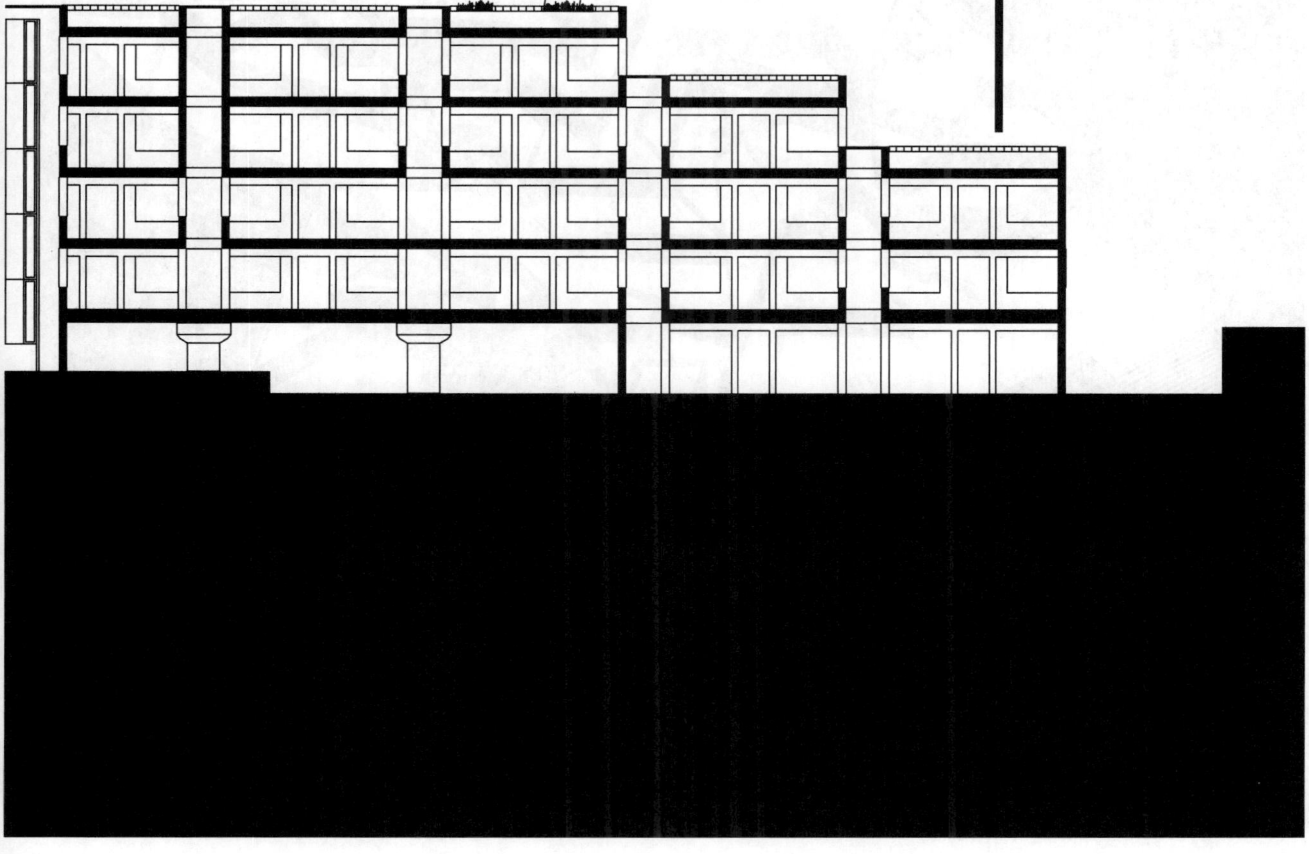

Jeanne Hachette
Paris, France
Jean Renaudie
1969–1975

"In the city, there are no simple objects. There are probably no objects at all. Each element only makes sense in its combination with a larger whole, itself involved in the deepest part of the bigger element."[52] —Jean Renaudie

Axonometry of Jeanne Hachette.

A.

B.

C.

D.

E.

F.

G.

H.

Les Grands Ensembles:
A. Cité de l'abreuvoir, Bobigny, Émile Aillaud, 1952–1968.
B. Les Courtillières, Pantin, Émile Aillaud, 1956–1960.
C. Ensemble La Pierre-Collinet, Meaux, Doignon-Tournier, 1958–1963.
D. Cité du Wiesberg, Forbach, Émile Aillaud, 1959–1972.
E. La Grande Borne, Grigny, Émile Aillaud, 1967–1971.
F. Cité Pablo Picasso, Nanterre, Émile Aillaud, 1973–1981.
G. Cité Curial-Cambrai, Paris, André Coquet, 1966–1969.
H. Grand ensemble de Lochères, Sarcelles, France, Jacques Henri-Labourdette, 1959–1961.

After World War II, an unprecedented amount of standardized housing was built across Europe, stretching from Russia to France.[53] In France these highly repetitive housing estates were called *Les Grands Ensembles*. Each ensemble is a collection of identical shapes, a single tower cloned many times and scattered over the land, or long slabs of housing extruded to the same height, resembling whipped cream sprayed over a site.

Like Jørn Utzon and other rebels to come in this chapter, Jean Renaudie resisted the standardization of the modernist approach. In the midst of the turbulent civil unrest of 1968, Renaudie parted from his colleagues at l'Atelier Montrouge. While Pierre Riboulet, Gérard Thurnauer and Jean-Louis Véret continued to focus on a modernism-light, introducing regional influences, Renaudie radically broke with the fashionable ideas of CIAM. For the new town of Le Vaudreuil, Riboulet, Thurnauer and Véret came up with a grid-like arrangement in the valley, whereas Renaudie made hallucinatory drawings of a molecular structure draped over the hills overlooking the valley.

Holiday village of 180 houses, Gigaro, France, 1964.

It is no coincidence that all of Renaudie's projects were commissioned by like-minded, communist-led municipalities, sharing similar anti-capitalist ideas and distancing themselves from the ideas behind Les Grands Ensembles. The idea that a new city can be manufactured by providing a dozen functions and stacking identical apartments to satisfy housing demand didn't do justice to the infinite complexity of people and their need to connect with one another and the space they inhabit.

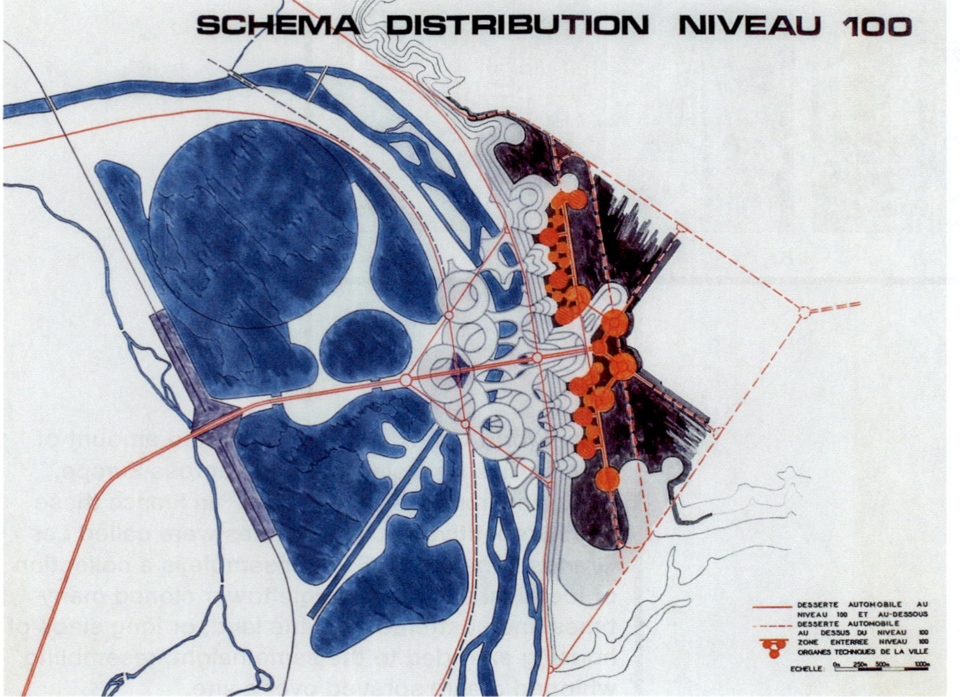

Le Vaudreuil, France, Jean Renaudie, 1967–1968.

Jean Renaudie's ideas were influenced by an organic approach. He would certainly agree with Moshe Safdie that looking to nature for inspiration is the ultimate humility for an architect, but the lens through which he looked at architecture was a social one.[54]

Conceptual drawing of a new city, Jean Renaudie.

Passionate about philosophical and scientific debates, Renaudie sought to create an architecture and a city whose formal novelties are part of the renewal of social relations. Architecture should never reduce society to averages because this leads to a closed and alienating urban realm. Moreover, construction methods or economics should never be an excuse to build mediocre spaces. For Renaudie, form was of the utmost structural importance. To him, there was no such thing as an innocent or apolitical architecture, so the architect had to bring out new, daring ideas.[55] Although this sounds a lot like an architect playing god, his ultimate aim was to build a piece of city fabric that could be appropriated by its citizens.[56]

The mixed-use building Jeanne Hachette is a wildly stacked and twisted pyramid. Geometrically and programmatically, it rails against the large ubiquitous modern housing blocks composed of load-bearing prefabricated partition walls and facades with often small windows. The fact that he used a columnar structure based on the parking grid below gave him much more freedom of form, allowing for a complex triangulation of space and ensuring that there was very little standardization on each floor. And all apartments were unique.

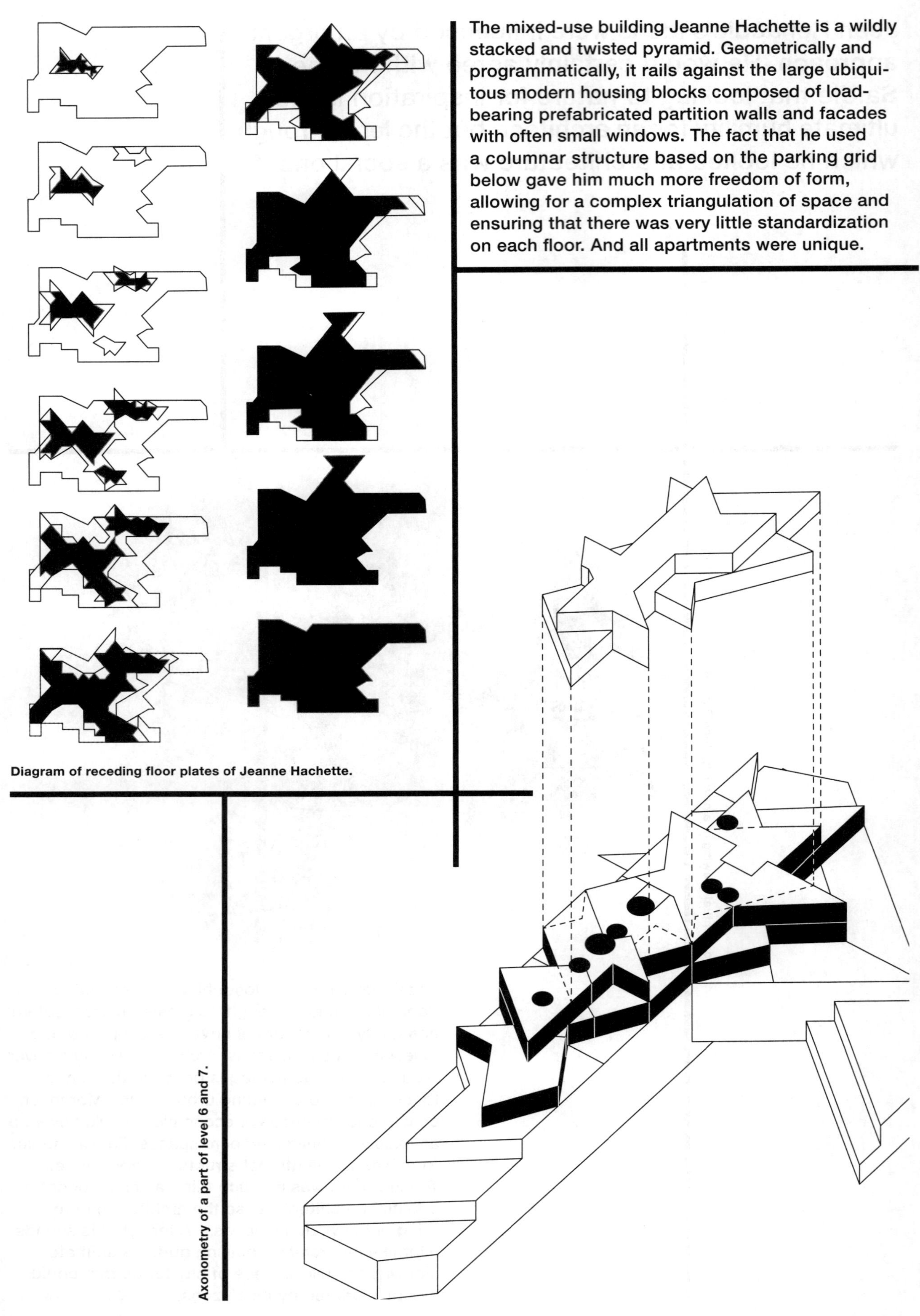

Diagram of receding floor plates of Jeanne Hachette.

Axonometry of a part of level 6 and 7.

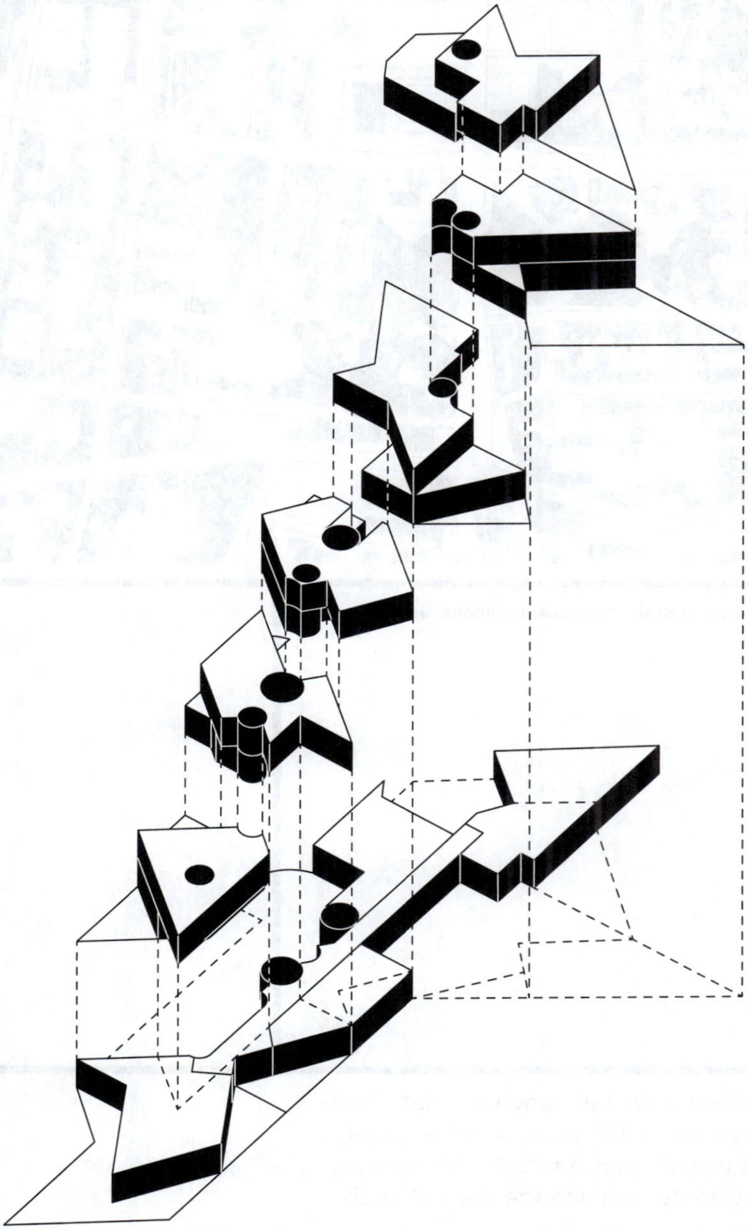

Exploded axonometry of the double-level apartments of levels 6 and 7 to show their uniqueness and how they interlock.

Site plan of Ivry-sur-Seine complex. Renaudie designed three of the ten housing blocks, and Renée Gailhoustet designed the other seven.

Studying the plans, one can conclude that apartment layout was the last thing to resolve, though not because it wasn't important. On the contrary, a few simple rules determined the DNA of each apartment.

A central spiral staircase and a lift give access to a short corridor on the lower levels and a compact hallway on the upper ones. Apartments fan out from the central access points. The apartments above have their terraces and gardens on top of these outgrowths.[57]

Level 7 of Jeanne Hachette.

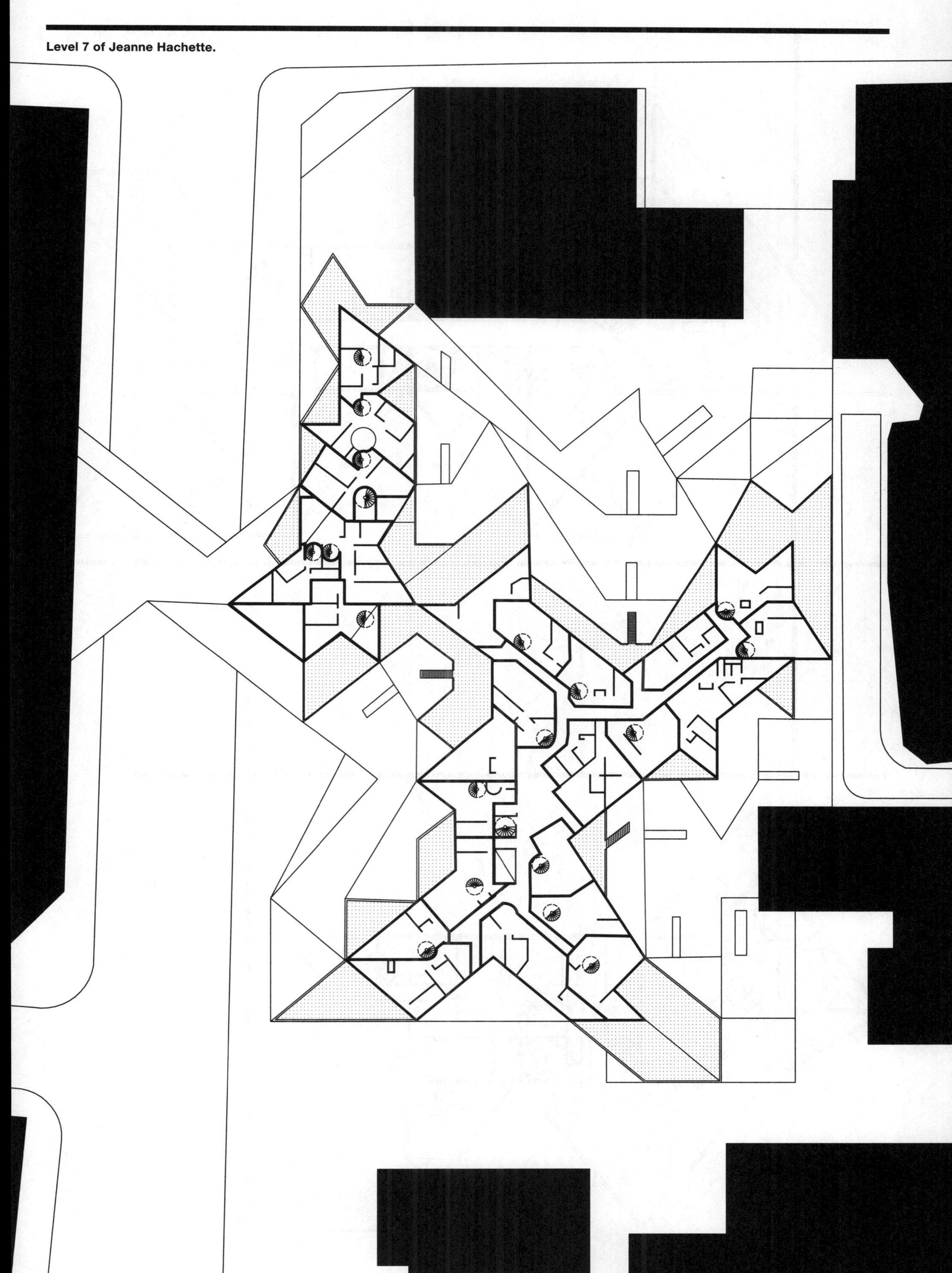

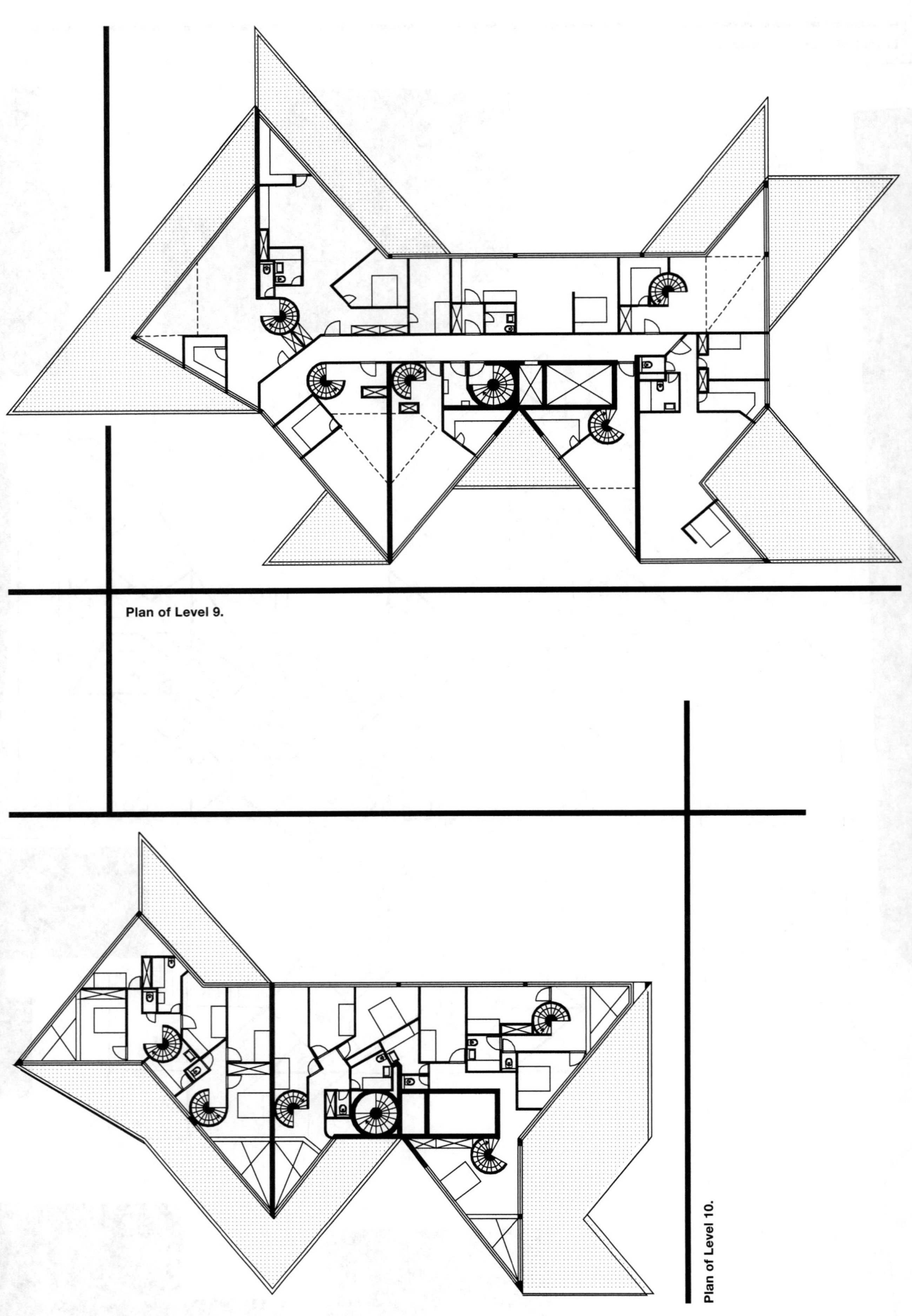

Plan of Level 9.

Plan of Level 10.

ROC-ECLERC
Tél : 01 49 60 75 63
Pompes Funèbres
ROC-ECLERC
Marbrerie
Contrat Obsèques

BUS

QUE POPULAIRE RIVES DE PARIS
RESTAURANT PIZZERIA
La Taverne Des

FÊTE
FAADA
FREDDY

Although originally disliked because of its brutalist aesthetics, many people appreciate the abundant greenery and the fact that the internal circulation groups up to ten apartments together. This means there is no anonymity within the building, as one inhabitant commented, "People know everybody and greet everybody."[58]

Jeanne Hachette is a superlative example of a utopian and diverse social housing complex, driven by a strong belief that variation is vital because human beings are diverse. While modernism designed for a standard or average person that simply does not exist, Renaudie knew better.[59]

Ramot Polin
Jerusalem, Israel
Zvi Hecker
1971–1975

Ramot Polin, Jerusalem, Israel, 1975.

Nature is an inspirational horn of plenty for many architects. Deriving meaning and inspiration from her seems simple enough, but interpreting her methods is not. Mimicking nature can be an intelligent way to realign domestic architecture with a more elemental existence, to cut through the noise and challenge assumed spatial, practical or economic constraints. Or it can be a token gesture, a literal translation of nature's shape, like some awkward kind of form follows sixty-million-year-old geological formation. When done right, eyebrows are lifted in delight. When not, eyes are rolled in contempt.

Axonometry of one of the five fingers.

Pentagonal basalt formations of the Giant's Causeway, Northern Ireland.

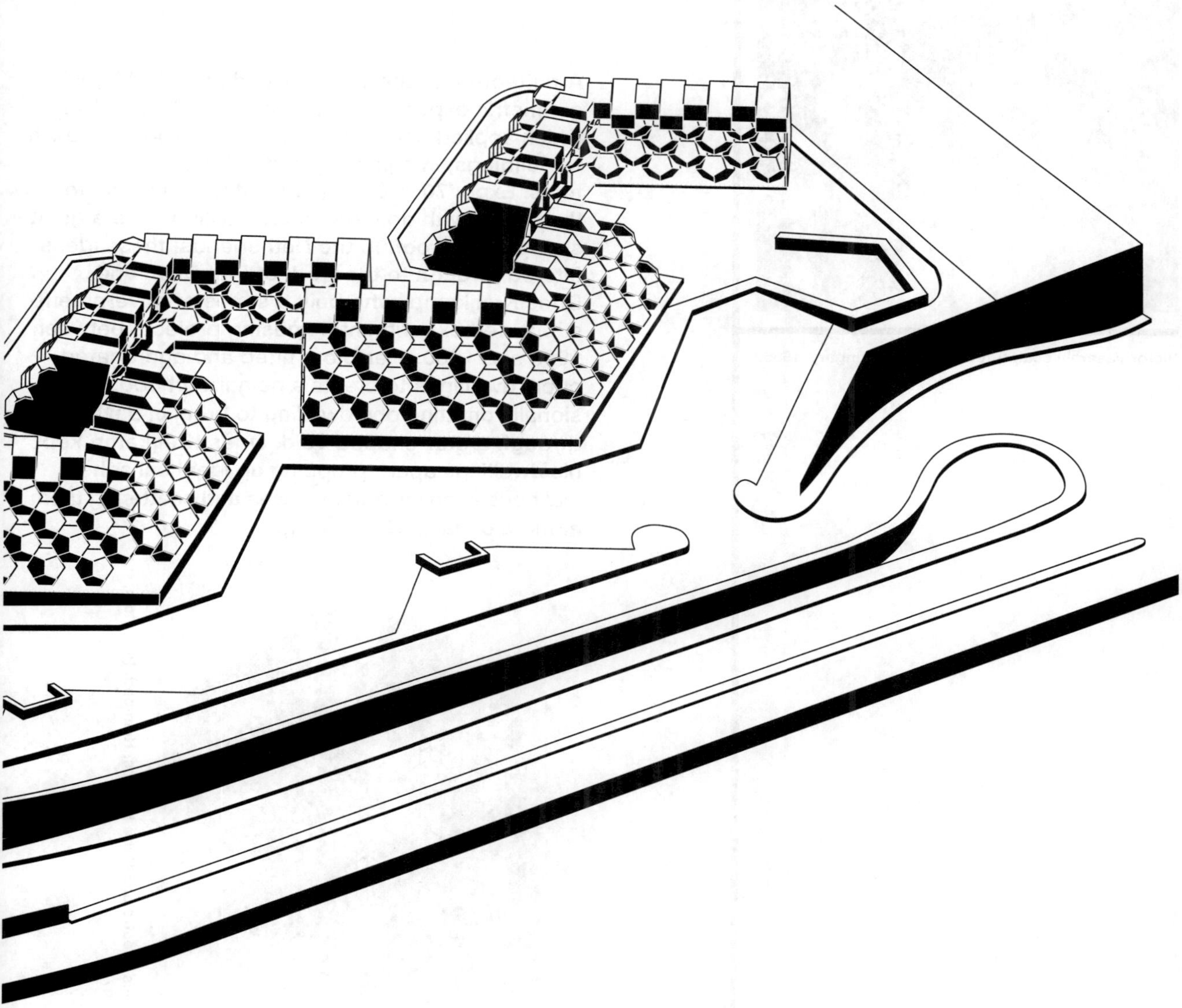

Postcard of Expo '70.

Victor Vasarely sculpture, Budapest, Hungary, 1986.

Architecture in the 1970s was dominated by wild geometric experiments, among them Metabolism, which applied principles of organic biological growth to buildings, imagining grand cellular megastructures. Expo '70 in Osaka presented this vision to the world, with dome-shaped pavilions and a giant space-frame roof. In the Netherlands, these ideas filtered through to the work of Piet Blom and Dries Kreijkamp, who built a series of government-supported experimental housing projects between 1968 and 1980. Piet Blom tilted and aggregated cubic dwellings to create a neighbourhood, occasionally omitting one dwelling to bring in daylight through a star-shaped void. Dries Kreijkamp kept his dwellings apart, propping up identical spherical houses on cylindrical bases and scattering them along a canal in Den Bosch.

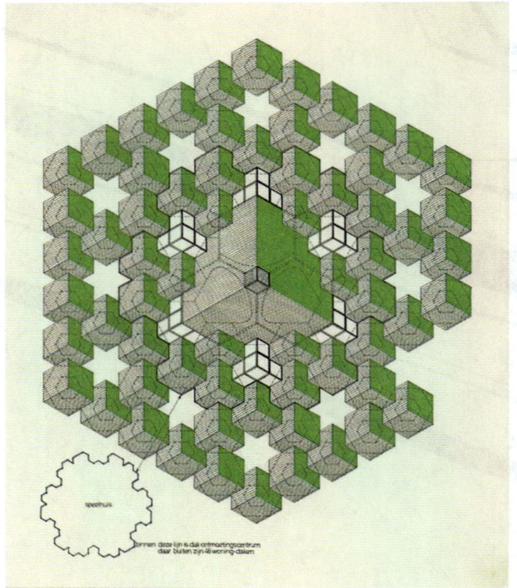

Speelhuis Theatre and Cube Houses, Helmond, Piet Blom, 1972–1974.

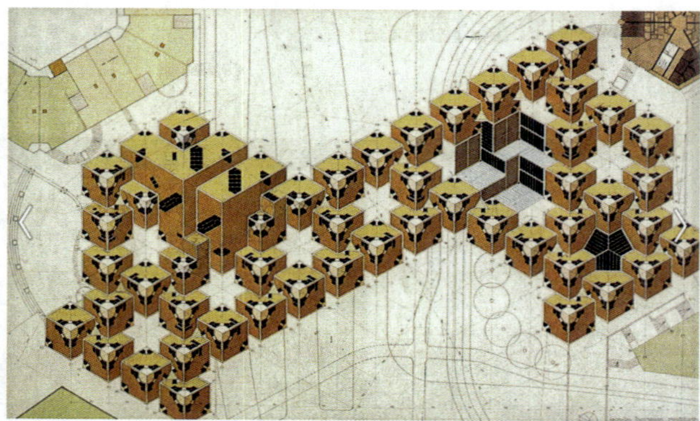

Roof plan of Cube Houses, Rotterdam, Piet Blom, 1982–1984.

Cube Houses, Rotterdam, 2013.

Sphere Houses, Den Bosch, Netherlands, Dries Kreijkamp, 1970–1984.

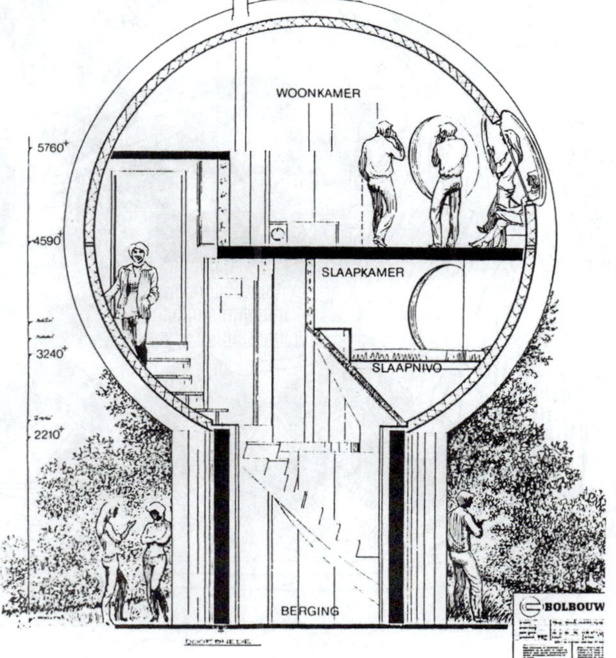

Section showing the unique yet narrow interior of a sphere house.

Ramot Polin is a series of unorthodox apartment buildings, inhabited by Orthodox Jewish families on the outskirts of Jerusalem, that look like they are trying to swallow or are being swallowed by a wall of dodecahedrons.

Site plan of Ramot Polin.

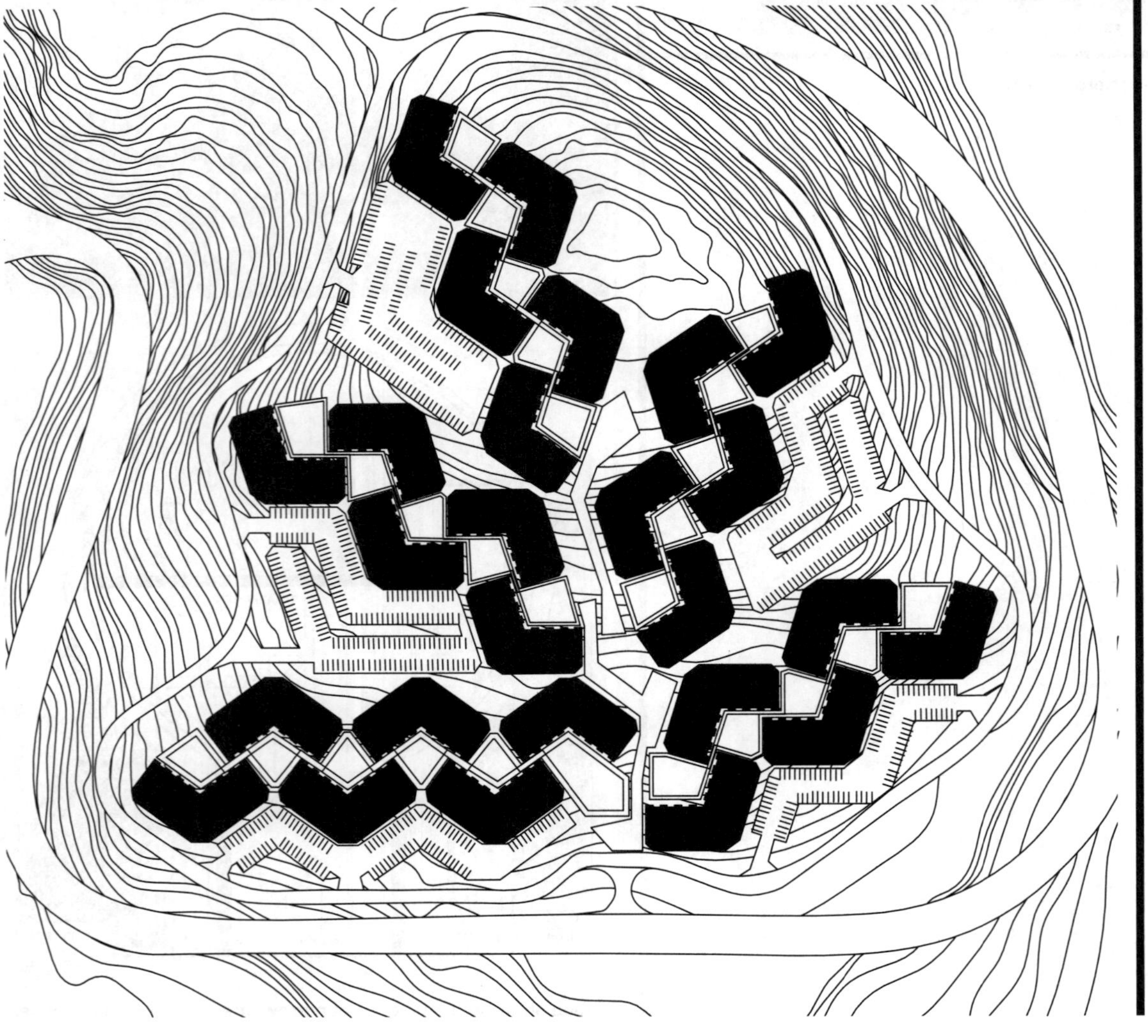

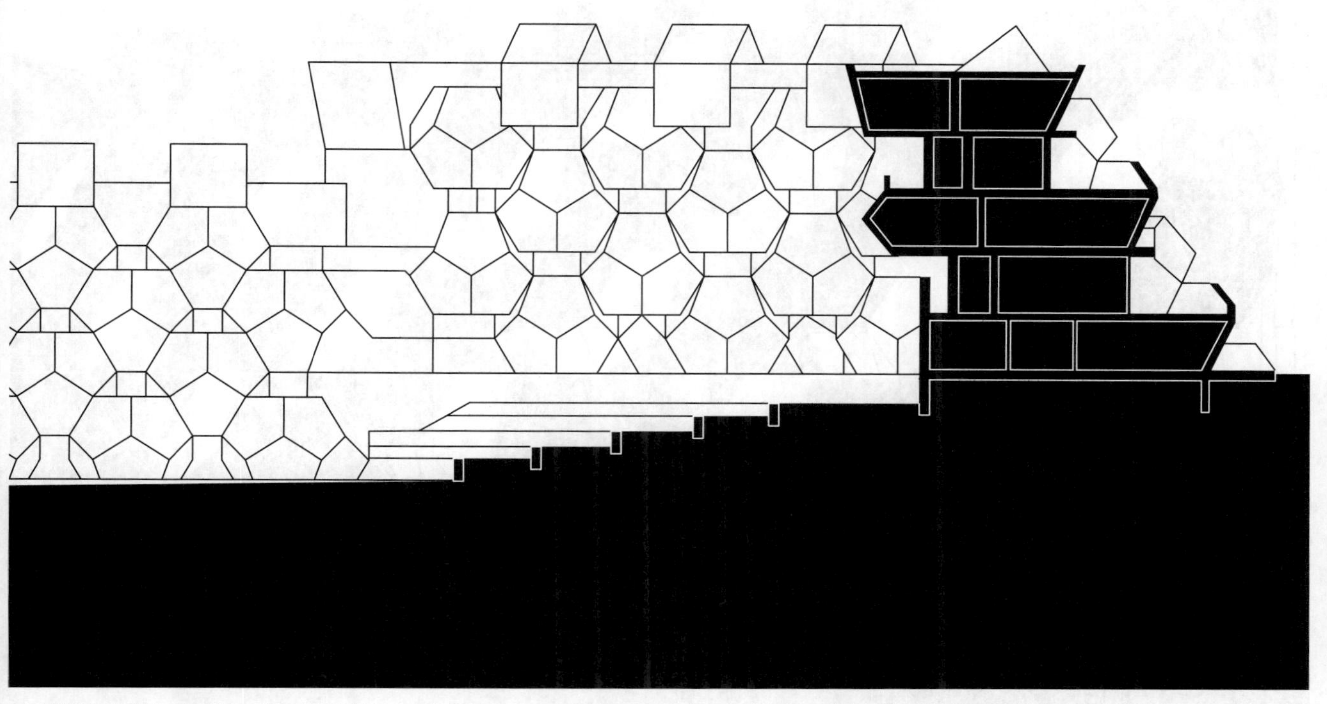

Long section of Ramot Polin.

Although constructing housing seems innocent enough, many of the settlements like Ramot Polin were built to cement the Jewish occupation of Palestinian land captured after the 1967 Six-Day War.[60] Putting aside this problematic foundation, the Ramot Polin scheme is overly concerned with the formal geometry of the module, rather than the functional space inside.

Aerial view of Ramot Polin, c.1975.

Zvi Hecker describes the general plan of Ramot Polin as the palm of an open hand, with five fingers splayed out, supporting the slope of the hill.[61] Only two (little finger and thumb) were built in the clustered dodecahedron fashion, while the others became more rectangular and snake-like.

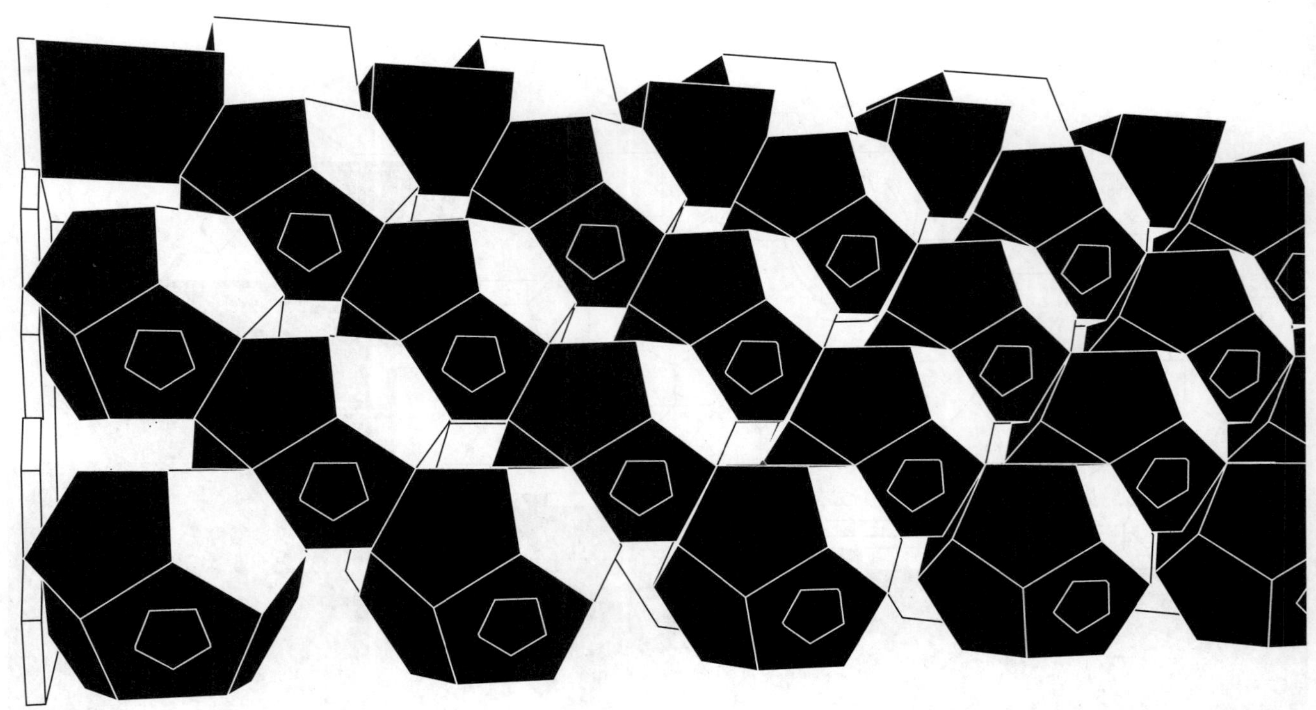

The original polyhedral (dodecahedral) geometry.

Ramot Polin as built.

Ramot Polin has been compared to beehives, to a chemical structure, and to a Star Wars settlement on Tatooine. Zvi Hecker himself likens them to stone walls found in and around Jerusalem. All these references denote a fascination with geometry over habitation. Hecker's interpretations tied him up in constraints rather than freeing him from them.

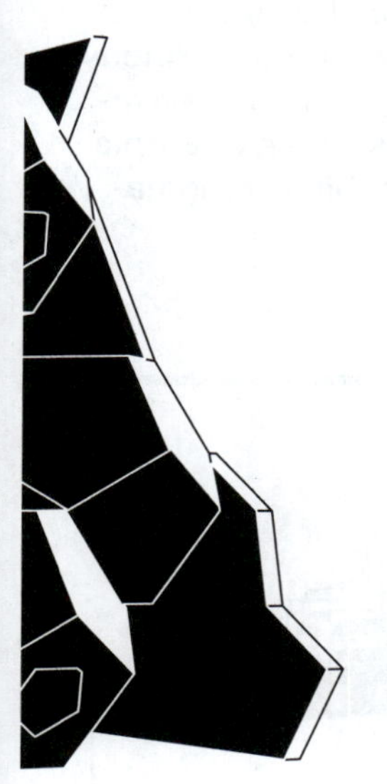

Ramot Polin is a curious example of the Metabolist doctrine. The building evolved organically, although not in the way the architect intended. The rigid geometry of the dodecahedron units led tenants to acts of 'creative coping'.[62] They righted slanted pentagonal walls, widened tight corners and narrow balconies and added air conditioning units, privacy screens and shading elements to the facade. The epiphytic and parasitic character of these extensions didn't kill the building. In fact, they brought the project to life.

The reworking of the geometry by the inhabitants.

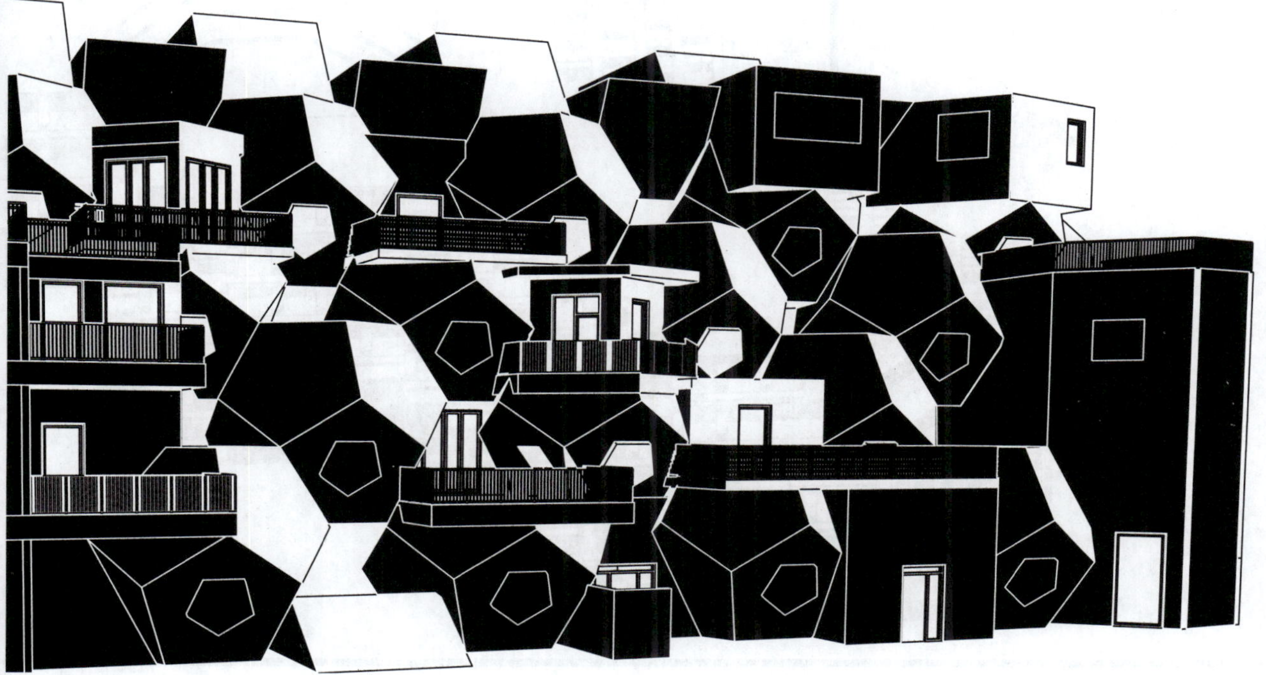

Hotel Las Salinas
Lanzarote, Canary Islands
Fernando Higueras
1973–1977

For Fernando Higueras, housing should resemble living in a cave, so he built himself a subterranean studio in Madrid and named it the Rascainfiernos, or Hellscraper. Perhaps a strange choice of name for something he believed promoted the harmony between the human habitat and its natural environment, but then again Higueras's idea of utopia was an unusual blend of sustainability, pragmatism and hedonism.[63]

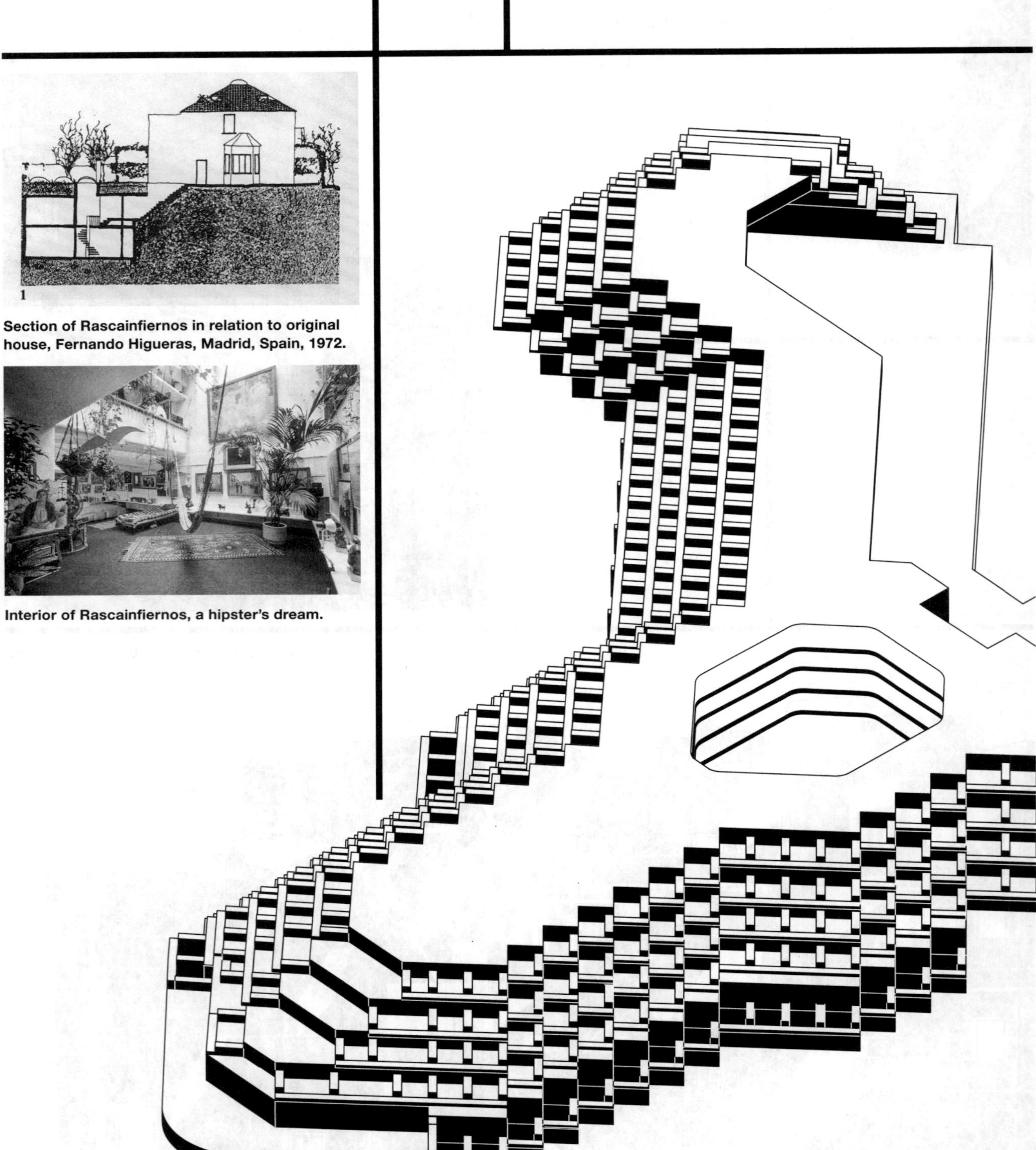

Section of Rascainfiernos in relation to original house, Fernando Higueras, Madrid, Spain, 1972.

Interior of Rascainfiernos, a hipster's dream.

Fernando Higueras at Hotel Las Salinas in the 1970s.

Higueras was a megalomaniac who sacrificed friendships and ruined clients in his drive to produce the best building he could, so it is not that surprising that 'the sinner' felt so at home in the volcanic Lanzarote, where if you dig down you can cook using the heat of the earth.[64]

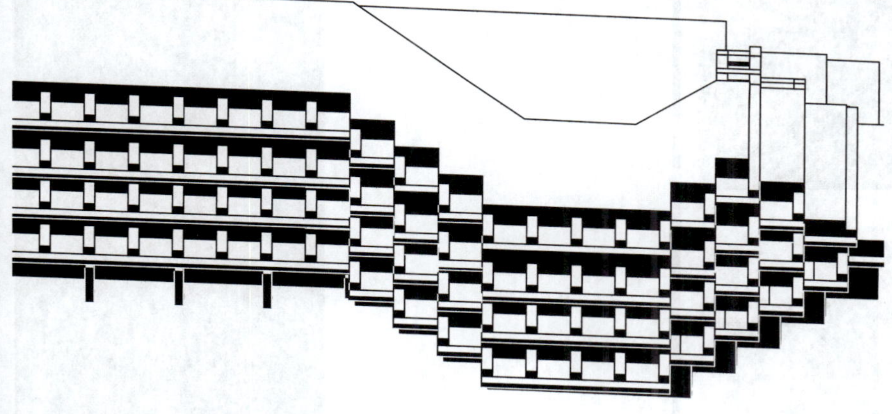

Axonometry of Hotel Las Salinas.

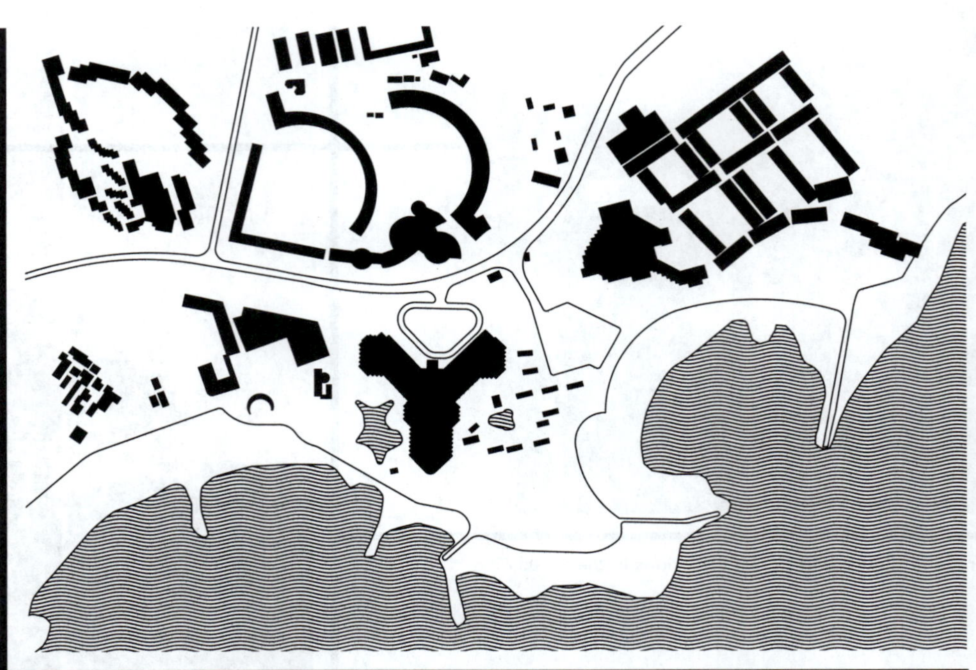

Site plan of Hotel Las Salinas.

In 1963 Higueras travelled to Lanzarote to complete an urban plan for Playa Blanca and was struck by the drama of its lunar landscape: black soil, sharp light, deep blue water and porous volcanic rock formations. In particular, the viticulture unique to the island inspired Higueras.[65] Vines grow in *gería*, or conical depressions, up to three metres deep and five metres wide dug into the arid soil. Stones are arranged in a horseshoe shape to protect the vines from harsh winds and to collect dew for irrigation.

Gería.

Urban development plan, Playa Blanca, South Lanzarote, 1963.

Hotel Las Salinas scales the intelligence of the *gería* up to that of a megastructure. From above it is immense, but in section you can appreciate how it nestles down into the ground for shelter. Its three branches stretch out, and the repetition of balconies loosely follows the outlines of the concave forms in the Playa Blanca master plan.

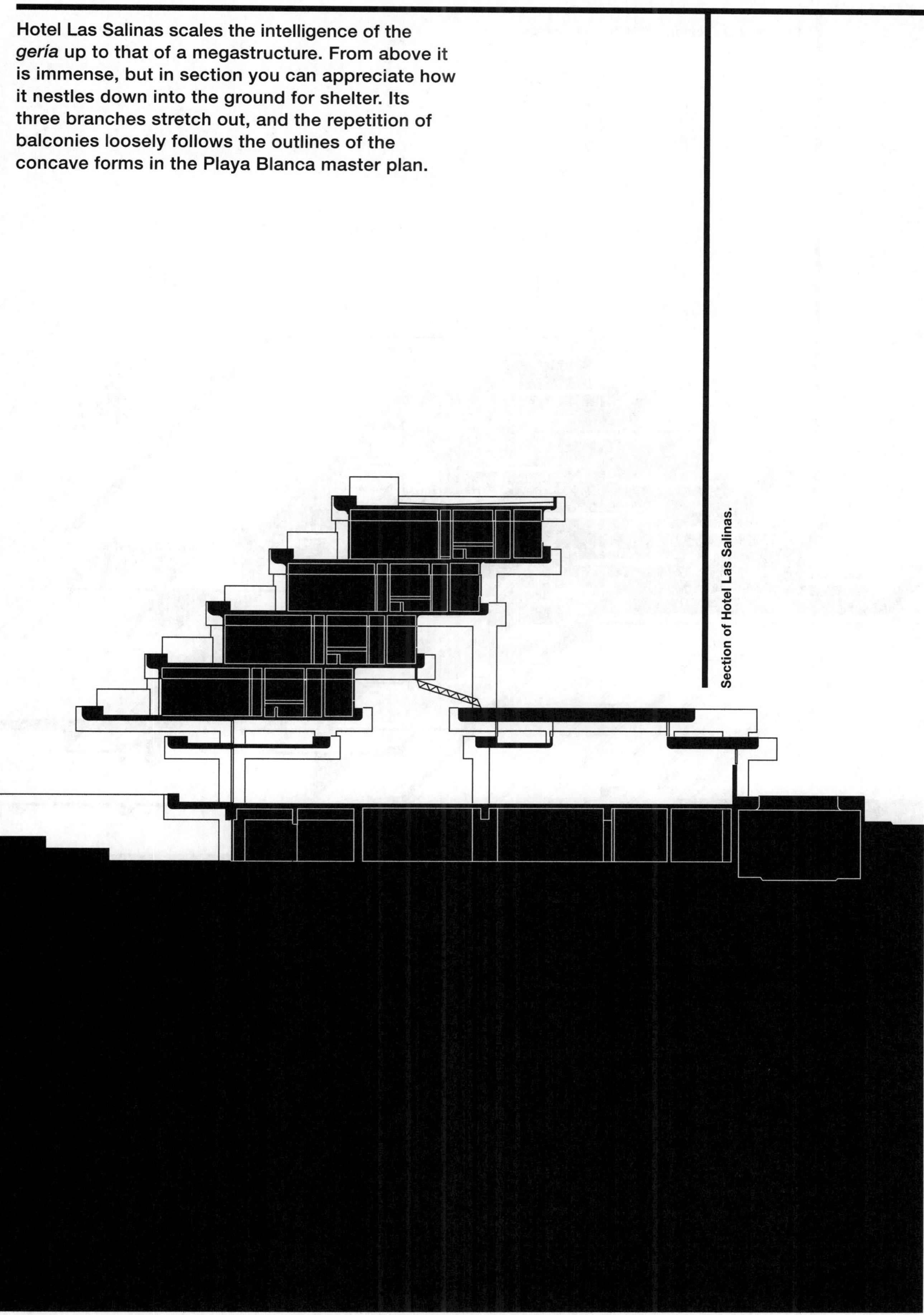

Section of Hotel Las Salinas.

Sectional axonometry of Hotel Las Salinas.

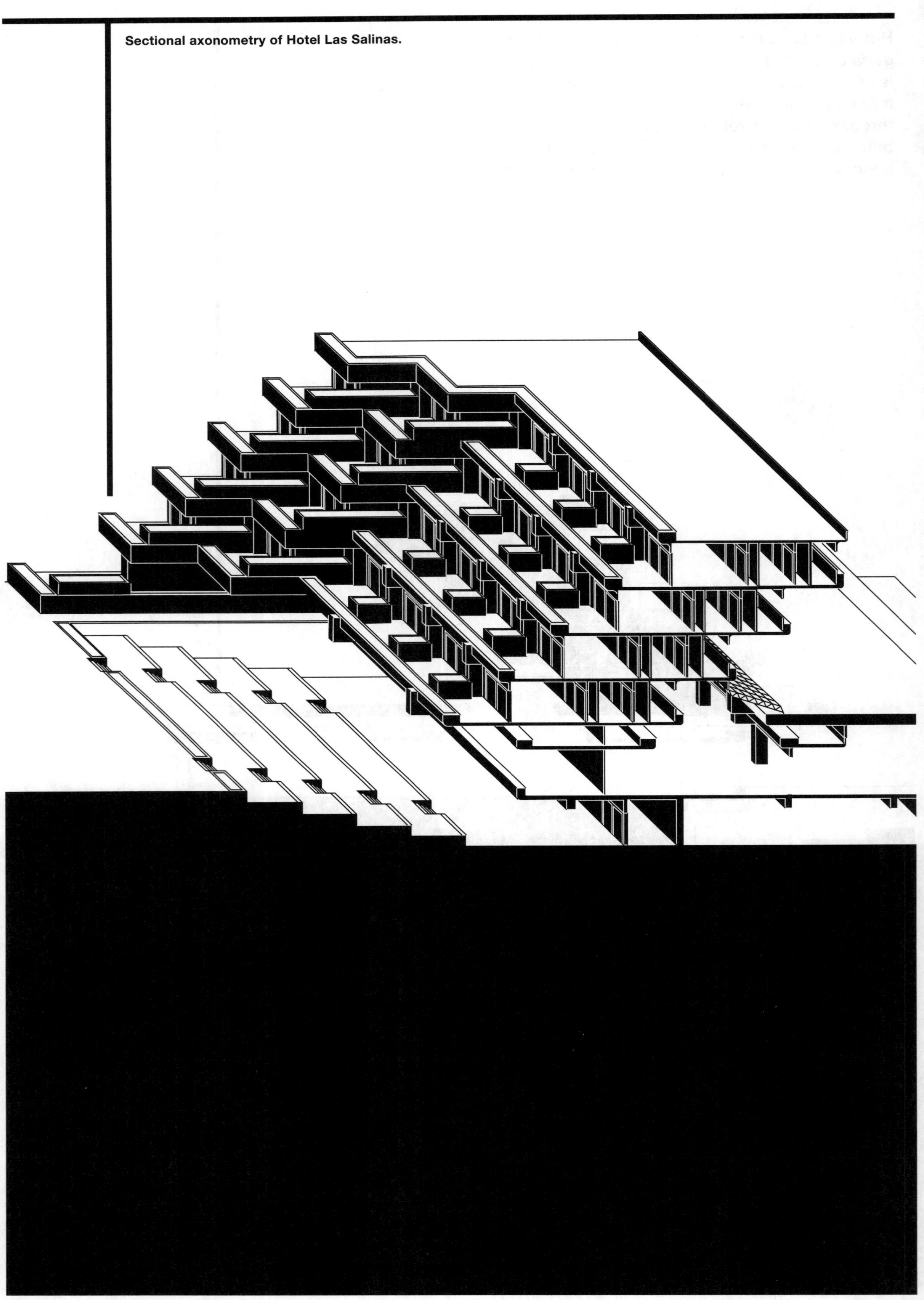

The exterior and interior is raw bright white concrete, like a challenge to the sharp white light of the island. And at the centre, in a reprieve to all this contrast, a cenote-like void is filled with abundant plants and water.

It seems as if Hotel Las Salinas pivots around the soil and the sun, two ingredients abundantly available on Lanzarote.

Interior of Hotel Las Salinas.

The cenote-like void of Hotel Las Salinas.

Entelechy II
Sea Island, USA
John C. Portman
1986

Travelling along Sea Island Drive, you see what looks like an oversized petrol station, impeccably white and overgrown with ivy. Beneath a broad canopy sit three shoebox-shaped volumes and a series of cylindrical columns lined up like petrol pumps. This is the private holiday home of John Portman, closer in size and grandeur to a commercial showroom than a domestic house.

Canopy, shoebox-shaped shop and garage of a typical petrol station.

Exploded axonometry of Entelechy II.

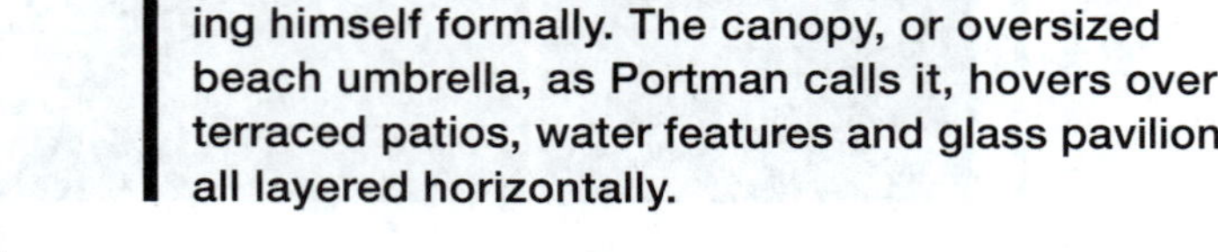

It must be acknowledged that Portman had guts. He seems to have had no fear whatsoever expressing himself formally. The canopy, or oversized beach umbrella, as Portman calls it, hovers over terraced patios, water features and glass pavilions, all layered horizontally.

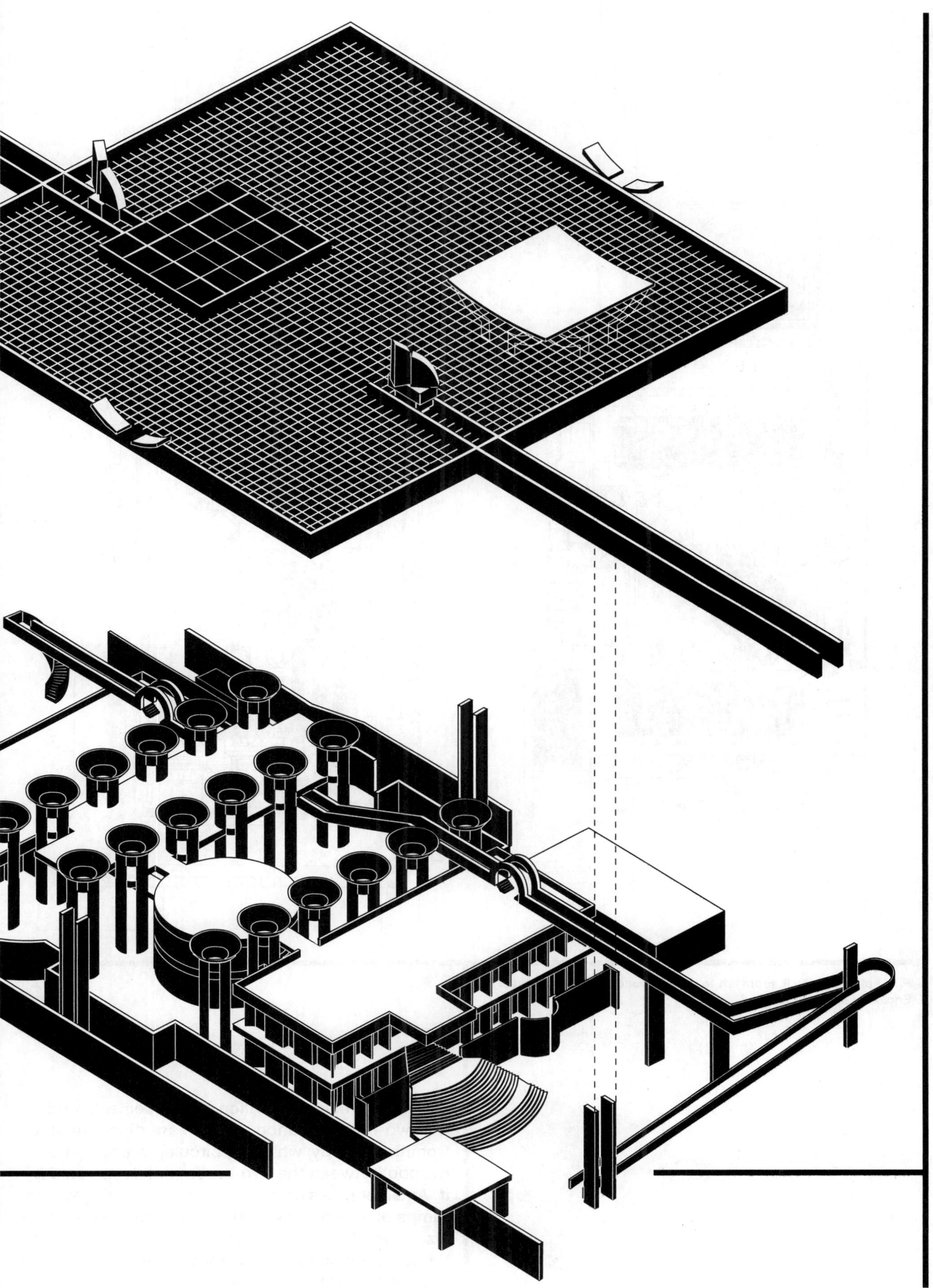

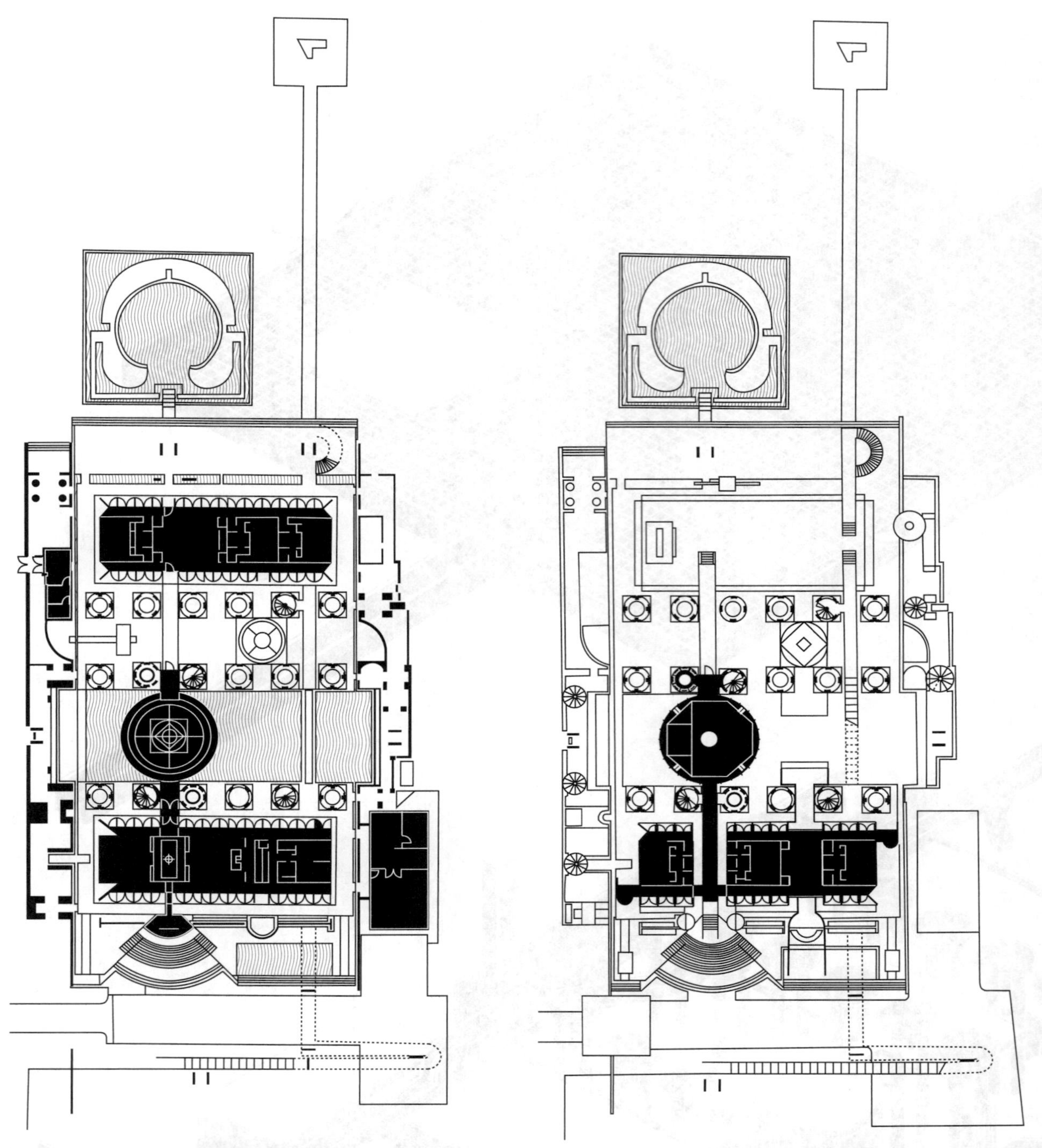

Plans of Entelechy II. From left to right: ground level, level 1, level 2. Enclosed space in black.

The one-level lanai pavilion on the sea side and the two-level entrance pavilion are disconnected from the canopy, while the circular dining-living gazebo between the two is completely covered by it. An elaborate series of roof terraces, bridges and ramps all seem to be suspended from this over-sized roof that connects these disparate elements. What is remarkable is how much of the house is outdoors, and to a degree, open to the elements.

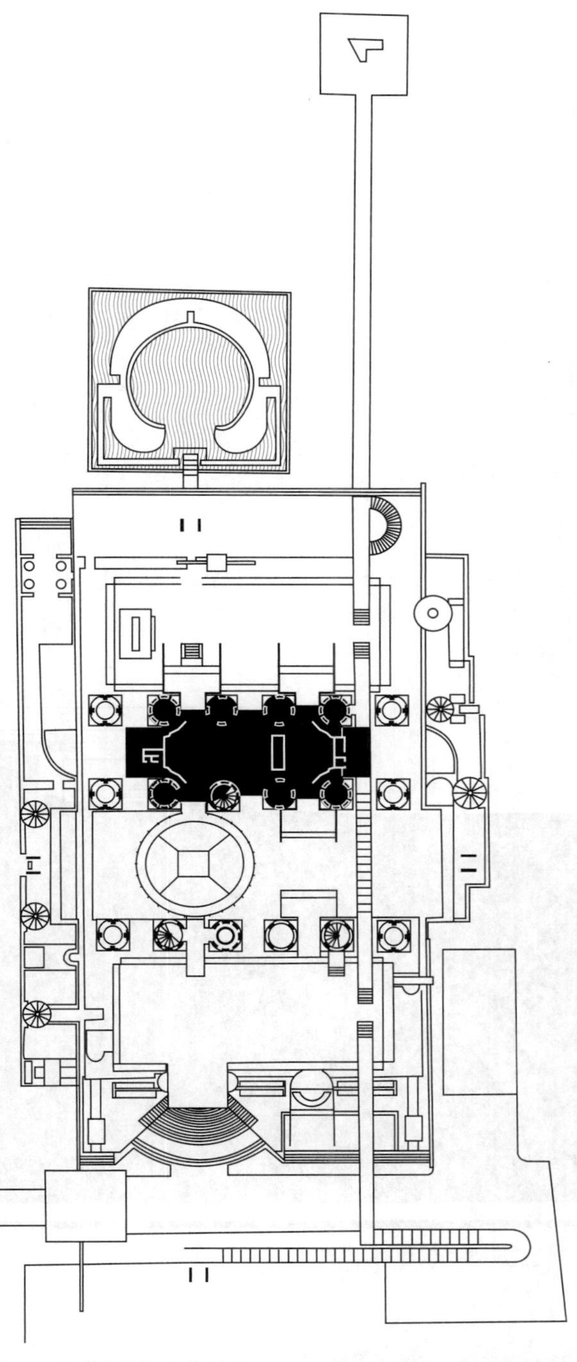

A forest of cylindrical columns, which partly double as small rooms, support the waffled canopy, but in contrast with the Entelechy house Portman built himself twenty-two years earlier, they never interfere with the volumes. Except for the second floor living room. It looks as if Portman cut a piece out of his first Entelechy house and glued it to the underside of the canopy, permitting a sea view. Here, the hollow columns act again as library, cabinet or staircase.[66]

Entelechy I, John Portman, Atlanta, 1964.

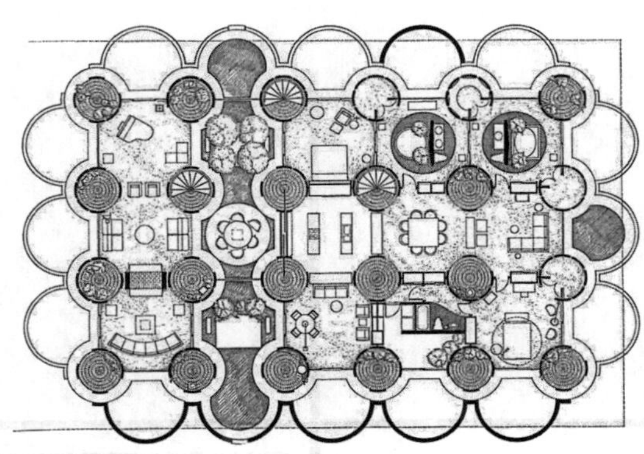

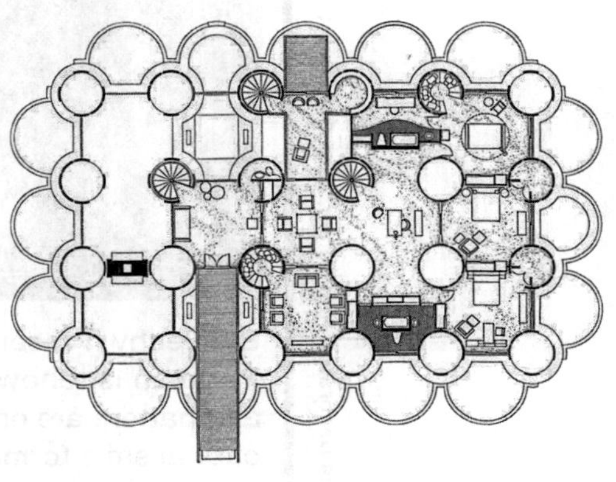

Plan of Entelechy I, with the same hollow columns.

Shadows broken by the gridded canopy and water reflected from below enliven a space already teeming with plants, figurative sculptures and abstract postmodern art (often made by Portman himself). There is even an artificial stream running through the house.

If it sounds complex, it's because it is. Almost every architectural element has something above it, below it, woven through it or surrounding it. This clutter conceals the scale of this 2000-square-metre living space. At no point can you really take it all in.

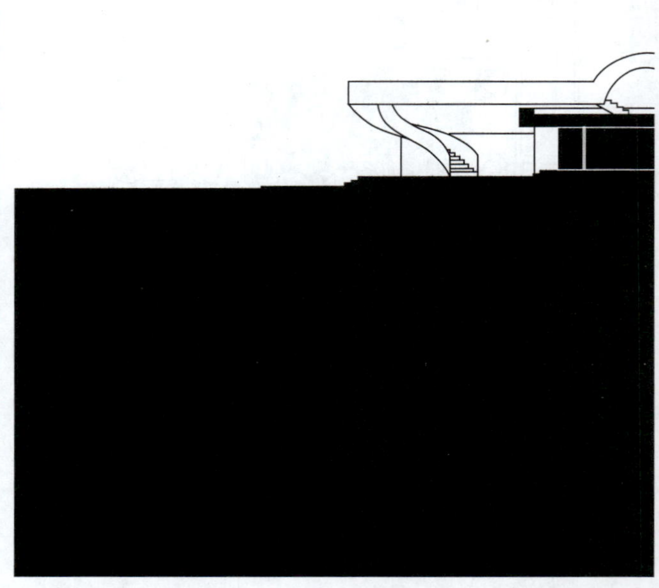

Atlanta Decorative Arts Center, John Portman, 1967.

Entelechy II resembles the internal atriums that Portman is renowned for, where repetition and pattern are employed to inspire awe, and for capitalism's formidable efficiency or for an imminent dystopian future, depending on your political persuasion.

The somewhat disappointing aspect is that despite the degree of porosity and integration of natural elements like light, air and water, the building is more of a museum cabinet for beautiful objects (nature included) than an experiment about how to live *with* nature. It is living proof that if you have the resources, you too can build your own private paradise in the form of a secluded over-sized house overgrown with plants.

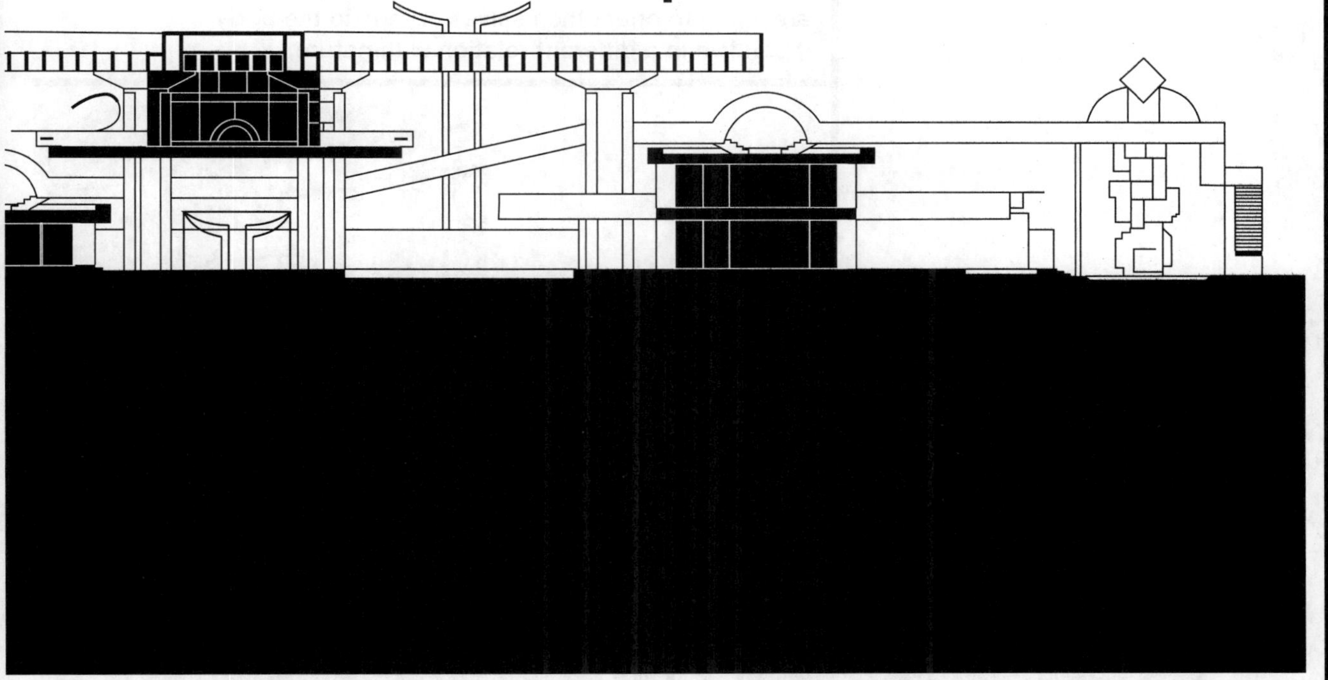

Section of Entelechy II.

Entelechy II is like an opulent postmodern Château de Versailles where postmodern beings can admire their achievements and influence.

Wooden House, Kumamoto, Japan, Sou Fujimoto, 2006.

But these experiments do exist. On the more modest scale, Giuseppe Perugini, Uga de Plaisant and Raynaldo Perugini did experiment with how to build an airy frame which nature and people could inhabit. Their brutalist tree house Casa Sperimentale floats above its wooded site in the seaside town of Fregene, near Rome, with a single drawbridge for access. It was referred to as the unfinishable or endless house. Why this was so remains a matter of conjecture, as Guiseppe died in 1995 and the house has since been repossessed by nature. Thirty years later, Sou Fujimoto's experimental house in Kumamura create a similar spatial experience in wood. Although they appear as more jungle-gym than dwelling, both have a comforting human scale. These frames are a little cavernous, a little open, lifted off the ground in places. Maybe they are trying to orient themselves or remind the body it can live in a different relation with nature.

Casa Sperimentale, Giuseppe Perugini, Fregene, Italy, 1968–1971.

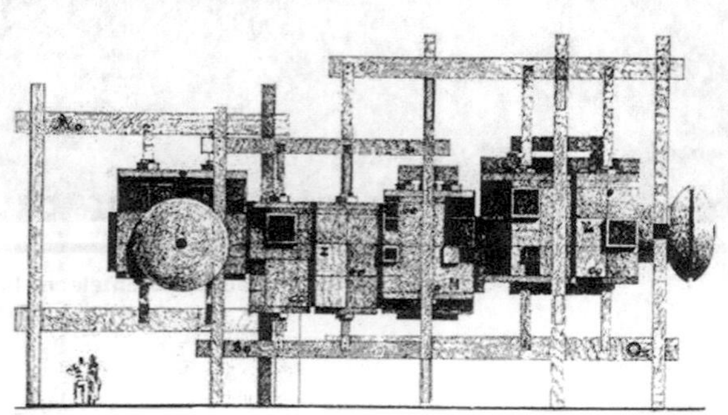

Sketch of Casa Sperimentale.

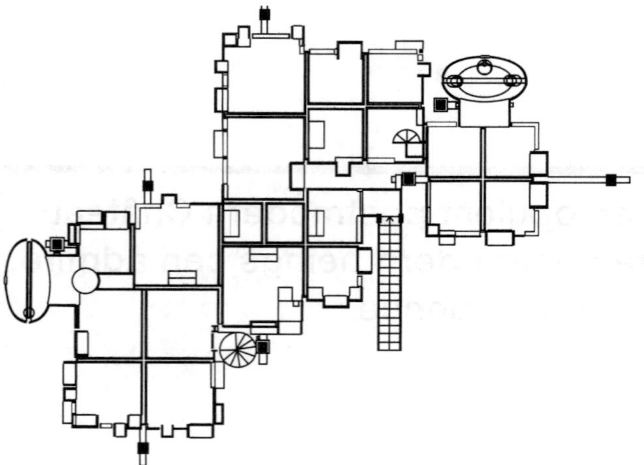

Plan of Casa Sperimentale.

John Portman
1986

Oculus and glass pavilion of dining room, Entelechy II.

For Portman, architecture came first, and nature was arranged around it. The dining room at Entelechy II says it all. Instead of painting an idealized landscape on the walls and ceiling, as Andrea Mantegna did in the Camera degli Sposi (bridal chamber) of the Ducal Palace of Mantua five centuries earlier, Portman draped plants over glazed walls and even built an oculus in the ceiling so his guests could see the sky. As Philip Johnson would say, "nature as very expensive wallpaper."[67]

Camera degli Sposi, Ducal Palace, Andrea Mantegna, 1465–1474.

Di sotto in sù ceiling panel of the Camera degli Sposi.

Espai Verd
Valencia, Spain
Antonio Cortés Ferrando (CSPT)
1986–1994

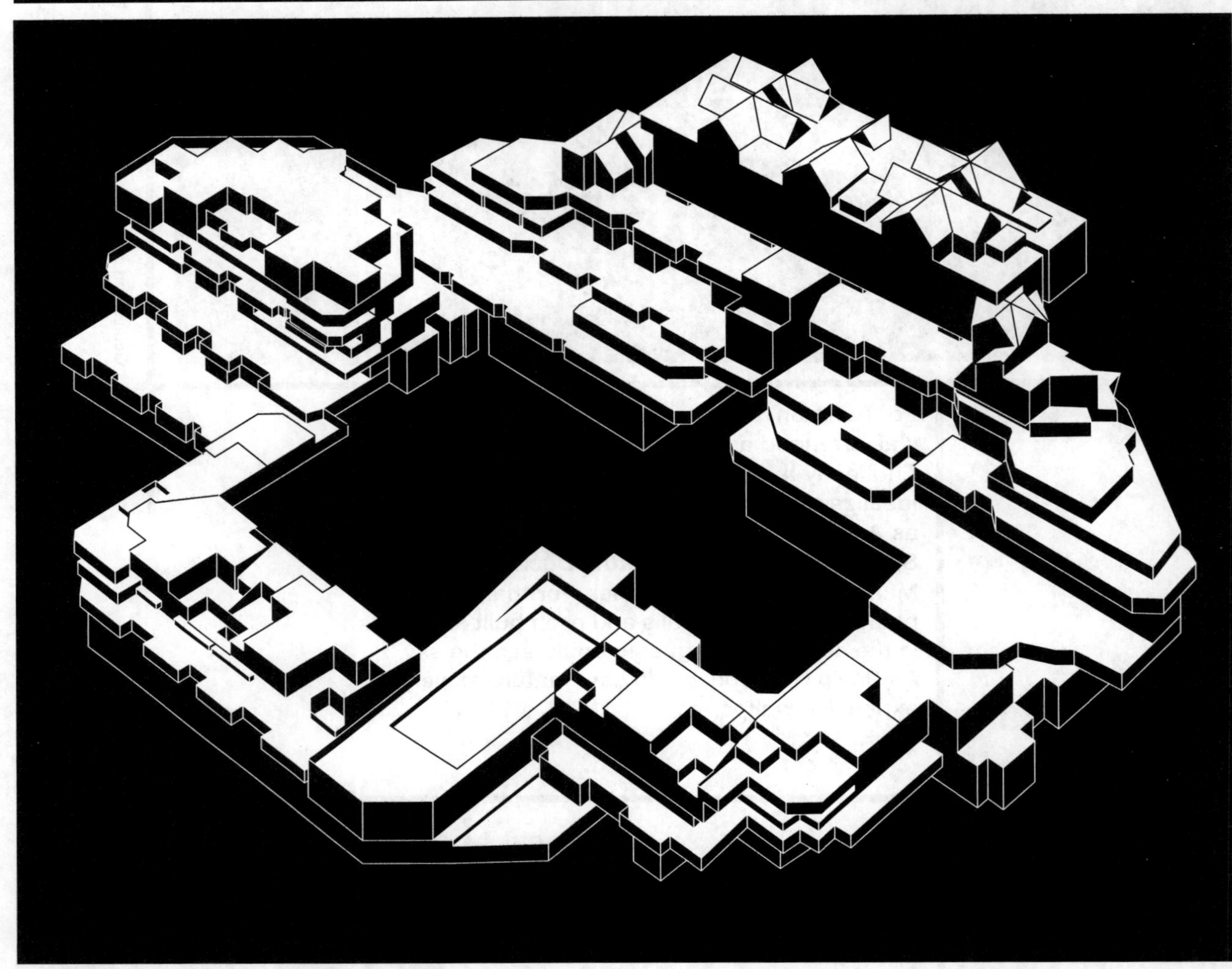

Axonometry of Espai Verd.

"In college, my professors taught me that in architecture there are three great spaces: the mathematical, which is the space assigned to objects; the experiential, which will be occupied by the inhabitant; and the sacred, where the inhabitant has the most complete experience: physical, social, intellectual and spiritual. This last space is the one that has always interested me the most."[68] —Antonio Cortés Ferrando

This urban cathedral was designed in the second half of the 1980s by architect and computer scientist Antonio Cortés Ferrando. What makes this *espai verd* (green space) fascinating is Ferrando's definition of 'green'. This building is not born out of a desire to preserve or protect a natural condition; it is conceived as a futuristic, technological and social novelty. More Bill Gates than bearded tree-hugger.

To satisfy the mathematical challenge of building a green space in the sky, Ferrando bought himself a mainframe computer (the size of a full room in his house at the cost of several houses) and started the pioneering company Espacio S.L. in 1983.[69] He developed software that allowed him to calculate the structure needed to carry fifteen levels of soil and plants, and by varying the thickness of concrete columns he was able to optimize the construction.[70]

At a time when almost no one knew what the internet was, or its potential to revolutionize how people work, Cortés Ferrando prepared apartments for a broadband network, and built a studio with independent access in each dwelling. He really thought decades ahead, pre-empting a technological utopia where inhabitants could work without leaving home. This futuristic mindset was paired with something even more important.

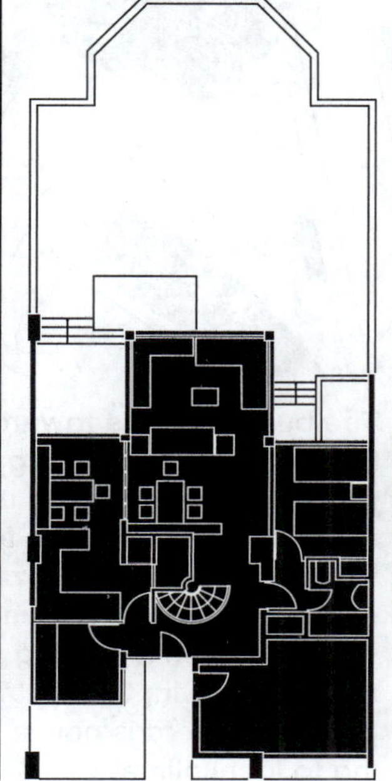

Duplex apartment plan.

Devised during a dinner with friends, Espai Verd was designed, funded and built by a cooperative, which continues to operate today. For Cortés Ferrando (himself a resident), this participatory model was a way of ensuring quality of life over profit.

Site plan of Espai Verd.

The building turns towards the sun and leans back to maximize solar gain. Situated on the urban periphery and stepping up from five to fifteen storeys, Espai Verd is a forceful silhouette. The volume is broken by zigzagging stairways, elevated streets, fountains, common gardens, a swimming pool and even a jogging track. Once criticized for aligning with the sun rather than the surrounding grid, Espai Verd is now a poster child for responding to local climate.

Sectional axonometry of Espai Verd.

Like Habitat 67, Espai Verd aspires to elevate the house-and-garden typology out of suburbia.[71] Each apartment has 95 square metres of outdoor space. Patios and balconies open out on both sides for cross ventilation, plants spill out over every level, and full trees grow within the interior. There is not a limp pot plant in sight.

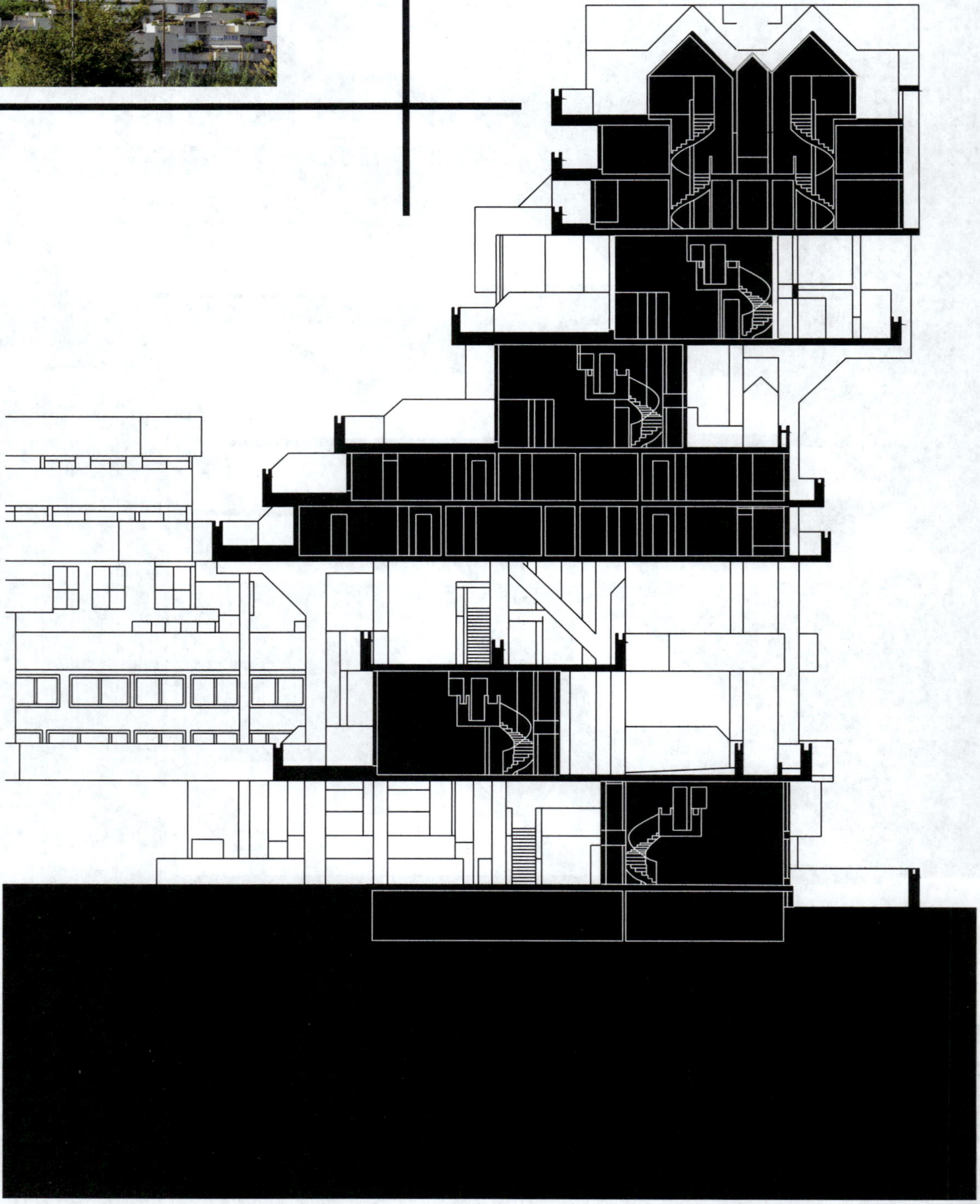

Section of Espai Verd.

As soon as you enter the building, a huge fountain provides a humid climate. From here you can see a pond and a four-storey mountain with a pool on top, created with the earth that was extracted in the construction of the car park. The ground floor and the fourth floor serve as horizontal connections throughout the building, which, in turn, is full of landscaped streets that are certainly labyrinthine.

Central fountain.

Espai Verd balances humanist, technological and ecological ideals.[72] It is one of the most fascinating and unknown urban utopias, offering a model for dense, urban living without disconnecting from nature. At times it is crudely brutalist, but it is also undeniably romantic. This romanticism is not pastiche, and Cortés Ferrando doesn't want to return to a once-natural state. Instead, nature is the future, and connections between made and born can be built. He has already shown us how.[73]

Árbol para Vivir
Lecherías, Venezuela
Fruto Vivas
1990

"I talk about 'trees for the living' as a possible dream. To coexist with nature without being more important than the flower of the mastranto or a butterfly."[74] –Fruto Vivas

There have been many attempts to construct a treelike architecture. As early as the 1920s there was El Lissitzky's Wolkenbügel, followed by Lazar Khidekel's Aero City and Yona Friedman's Ville Spatiale.[75] It took until 1974 before Gyorgy Chakhava could build his version, Space City in Tbilisi. But although Chakhava patented it, I doubt Fruto Vivas ever paid royalties for his steel version, Árbol para Vivir.

Ville Spatiale, Paris, Yona Friedman, 1959–1960.

Conceptual sketch by Fruto Vivas.

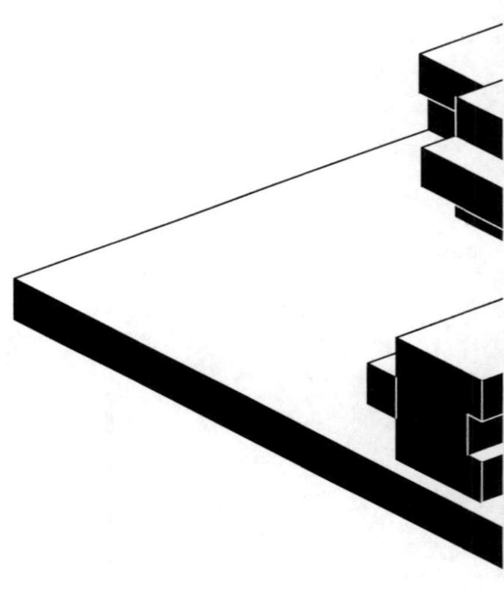

All these earlier models paved the road for this project. Árbol para Vivir was relatively free from the yoke of being a statement of avant-garde art and Vivas could focus on its compelling social and political motives. Perhaps that is precisely the reason why it was realized.

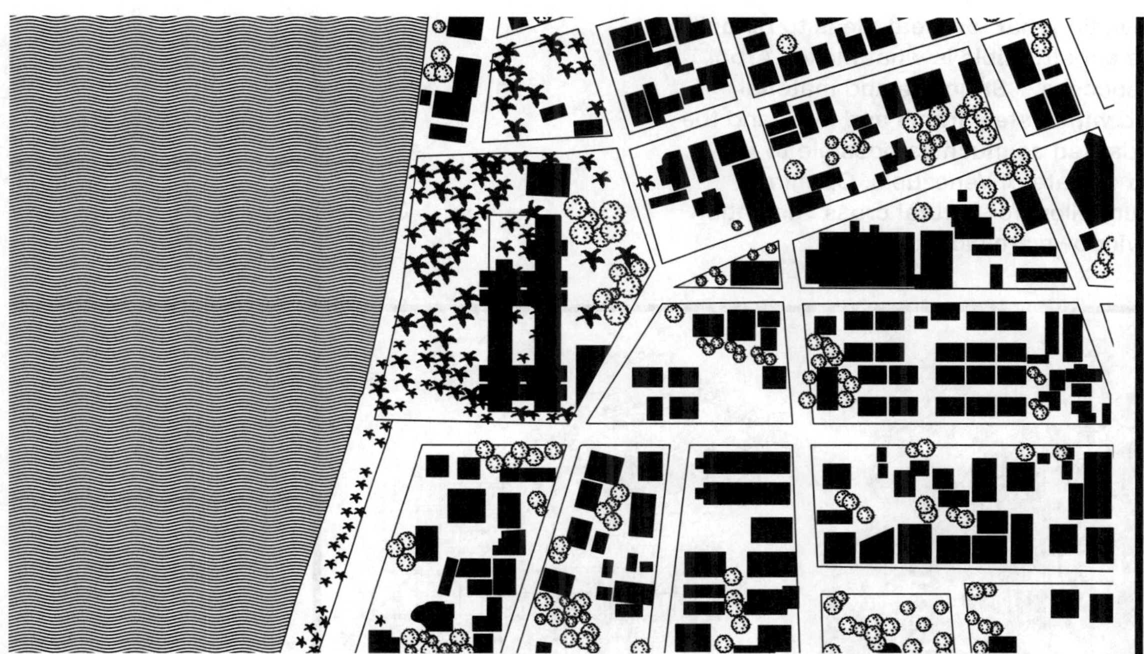

Site plan.

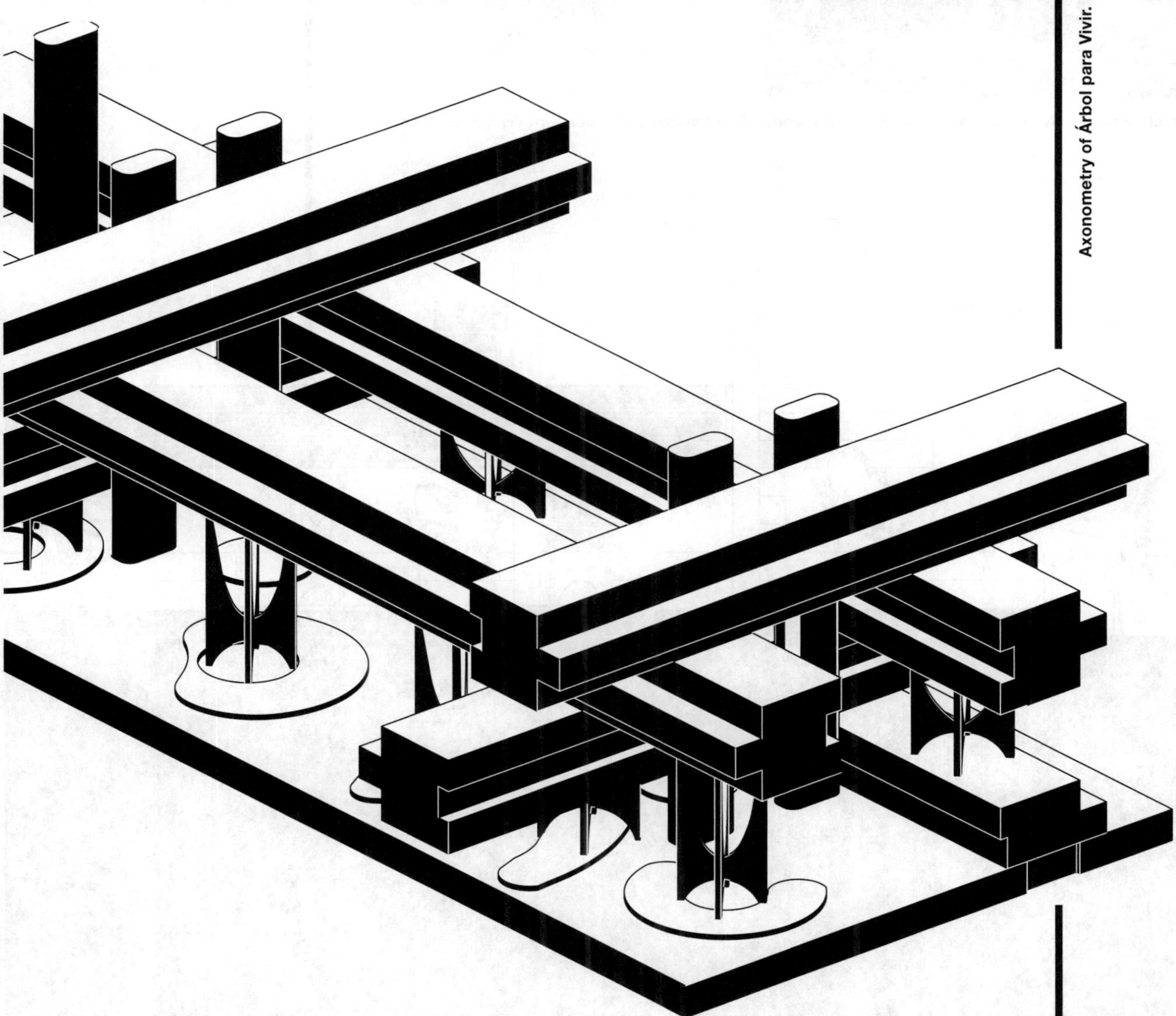

Axonometry of Árbol para Vivir.

The firm conviction that for great ideas to be built they must be constructible is what makes Árbol para Vivir a success.[76] Structure and material are optimized with a steel frame and infill, and the housing is adapted as much as possible to the warm, humid climate of Venezuela. Openings in the structure allow for natural cross ventilation even when windows are closed.

Steel framing of Árbol para Vivir under construction. 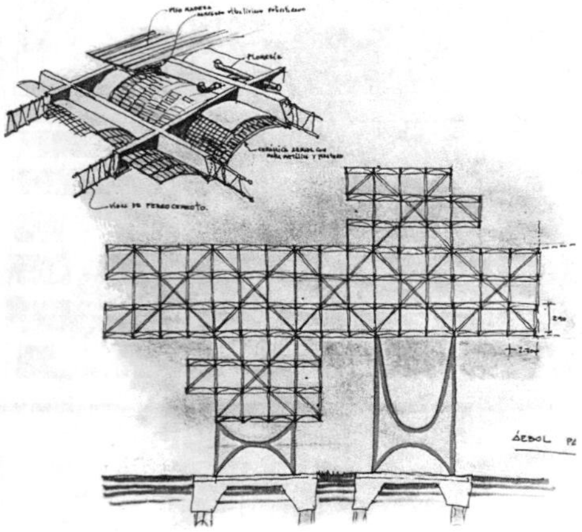 Short section of Árbol para Vivir, Fruto Vivas.

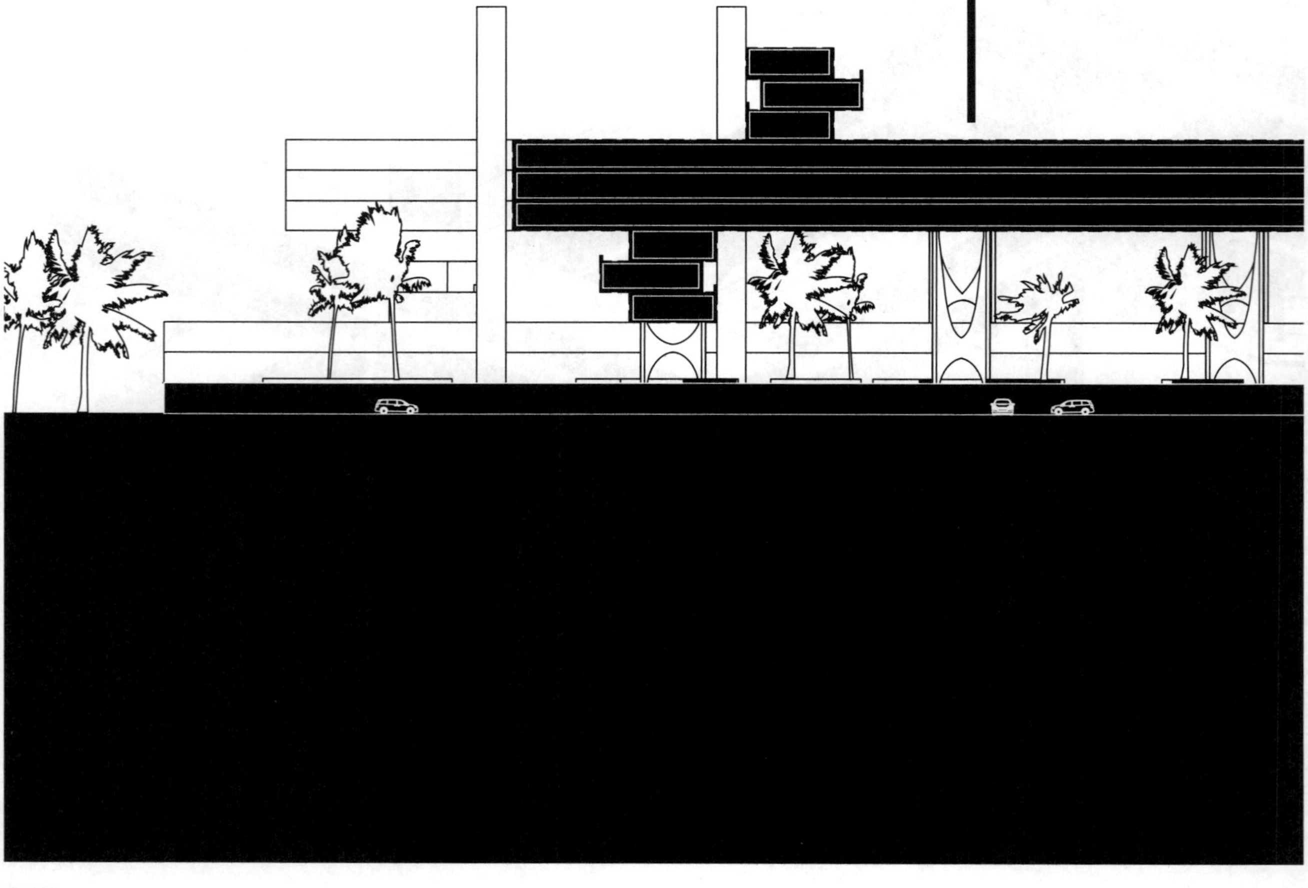

This pragmatism was driven by a deep understanding and appreciation of nature. Vivas believed that to achieve maximum efficiency and push the limits of structure, a building should learn to change as the forest does, to mutate in harmony with nature to support gregarious man.[77] For Vivas, the tree is the best manager of convective air currents. When the sun evaporates water held in the leaves, a drop of temperature produces an updraft, so the interior air of the trees is permanently refreshed. This was the quality he applied to Árbol para Vivir. Hence the name, Tree for Living.[78]

There is undeniably a common thread in getting the buildings in this chapter off the ground. Jean Renaudie had a communist municipality sympathetic to his vision for Jean Hachette; Antonio Cortés Ferrando started a cooperative of owners to protect the interests of Espai Verd; and Fruto Vivas realized Árbol para Vivir for the Cooperativa de Trabajadores de Pequiven, a worker's union. A humanist and ecological approach is needed to build an urban landscape that emphasizes quality of life over profit. Vivas and his accomplices planted the seeds of this idea over the past century. Now it's time for the trees to grow.

Section of Árbol para Vivir.

ACROS
Fukuoka, Japan
Emilio Ambasz
1995

Emilio Ambasz strongly believes in 'green over grey', envisioning a high-density city where you can "open your door and walk out directly to a garden, regardless of how high your apartment may be ... [and] reconcile our need for building shelters with our emotional requirement for green spaces..."[79]

Aerial view of ACROS and Tenjin Central Park.

View of ACROS from the park.

Site plan. ACROS gives its 13 000-square-metre footprint back to the park.

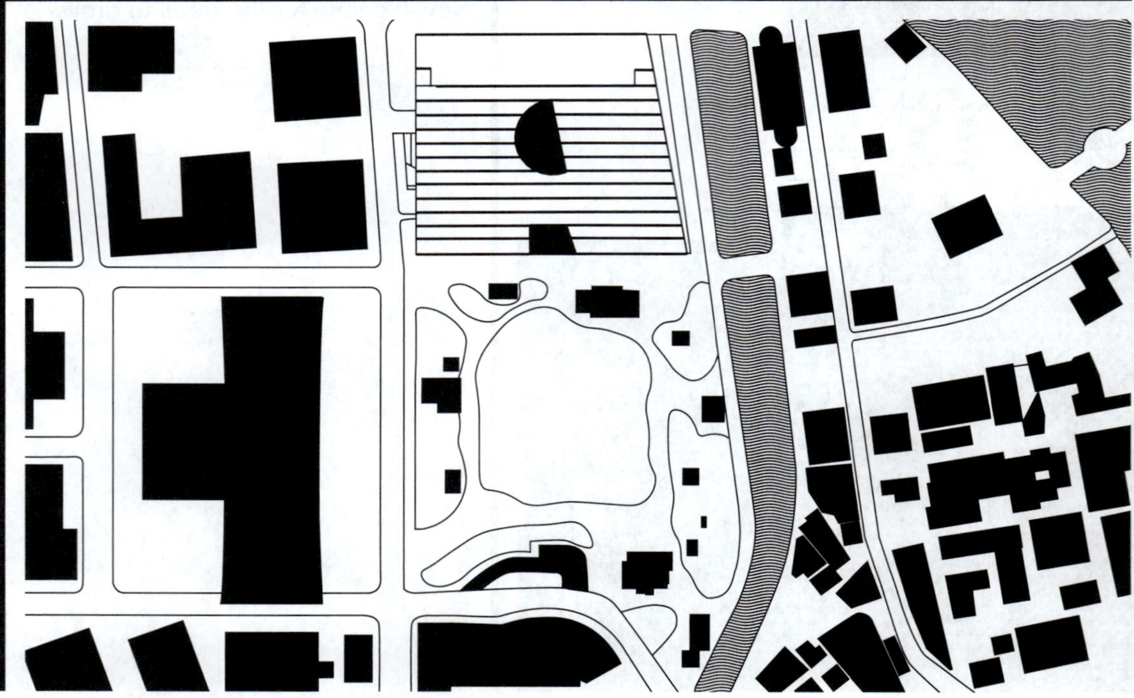

Fukuoka needed a new government building and the only available site was the last remaining green space in the city centre. Ambasz united these conflicting interests by lifting the park at two corners and draping it over a building. The various functions – congress, concert hall, offices and commercial spaces, car park – are contained within the distinctively stepped volume that extends the park over the building. Is this just another building neatly tucked under a green roof so as not to be a nuisance, or is it a brilliant move?

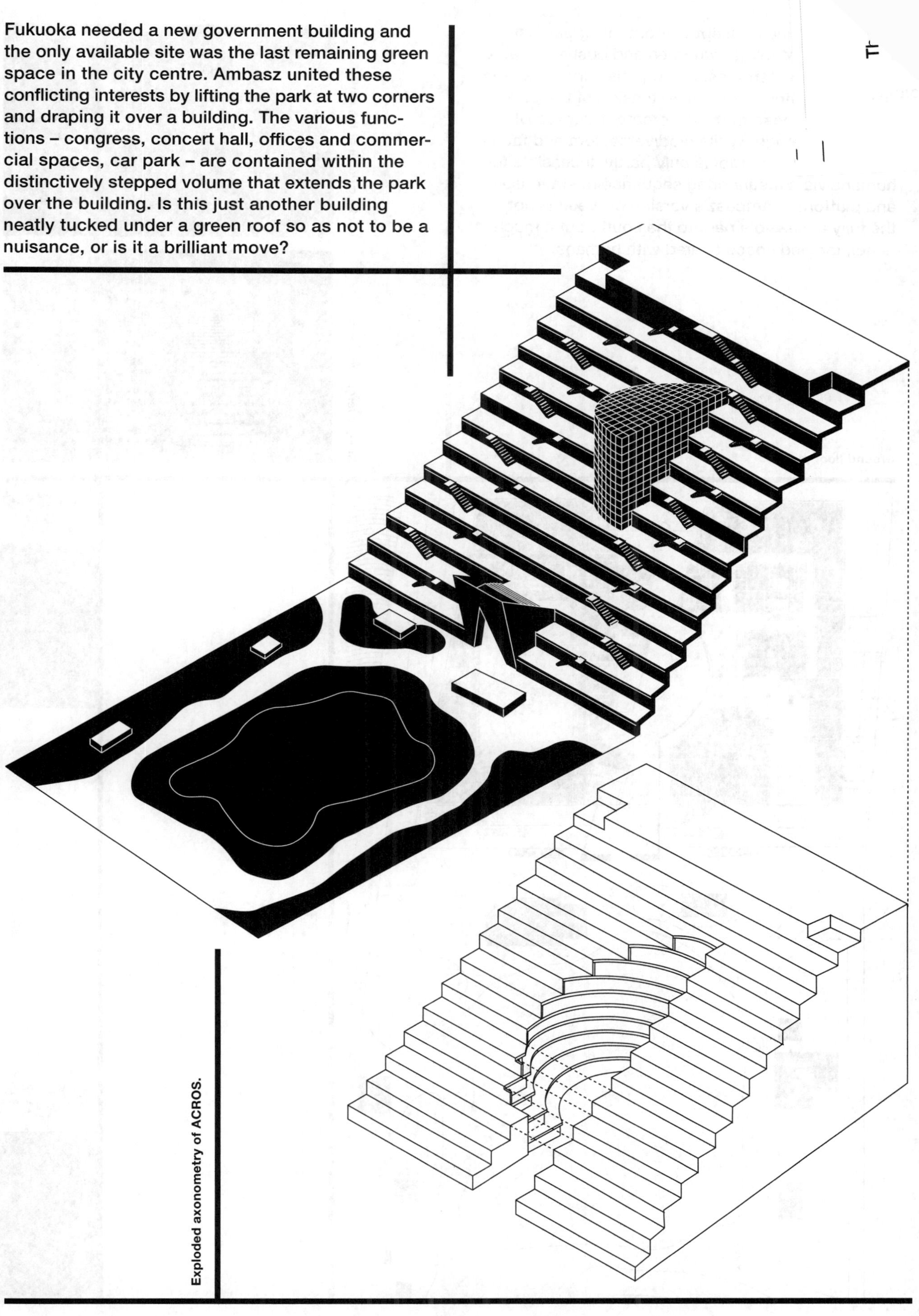

Exploded axonometry of ACROS.

ere is nothing antiseptic about this green carpet. Abundant full-grown trees and bushes inhabit these stepped terraces. In fact, this surface is more of a rocky outcrop than an extension of the park, with a steepness that may create a degree of unease or vertigo. While biodiverse flora and fauna have free rein, the roof is only partly accessible for humans via a meandering sequence of staircases and platforms. Ambasz's version of green is not the fully accessible park to the south, but a much richer, tangled space shared with humans.

Looking down at the park.

Steep overgrown steps.

Ground floor plan.

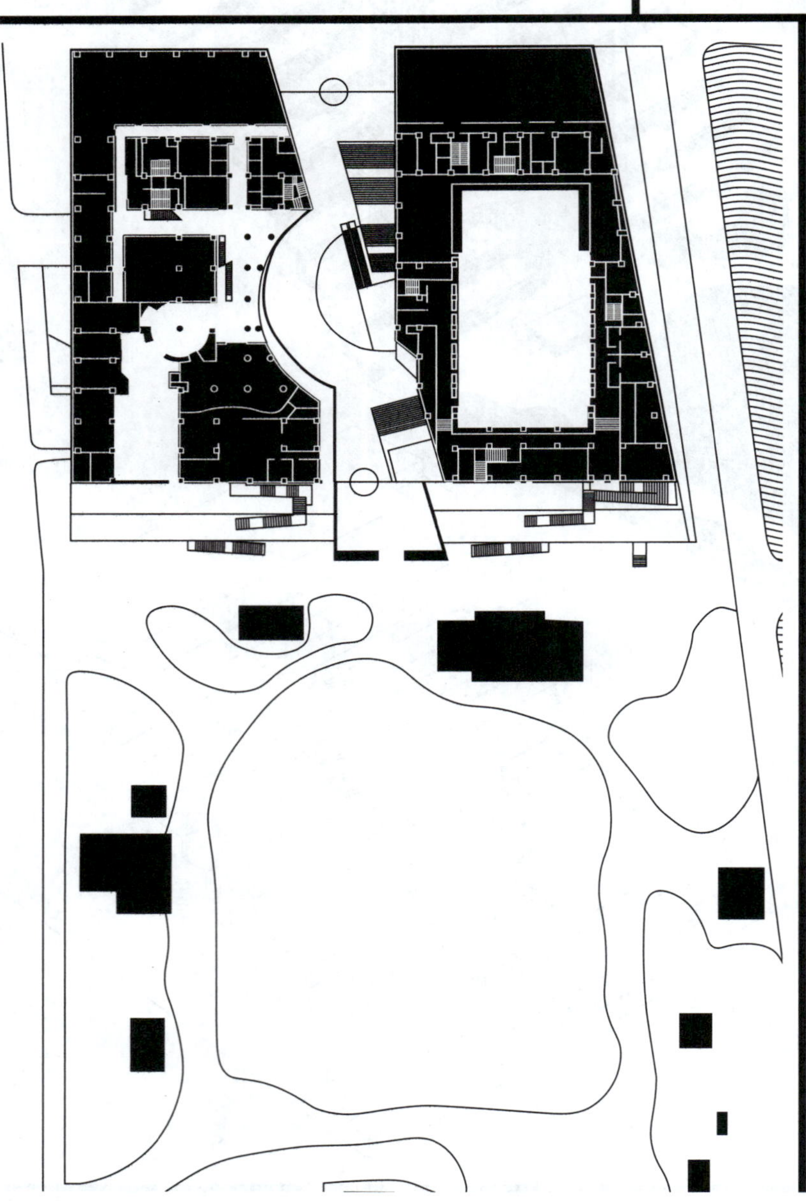

While greening rooftops has had varied rates of success elsewhere, Ambasz argues that it is not rocket science to use local plants found no further than twenty kilometres from the site, and use local gardeners for advice and maintenance.[80] ACROS proves it can be done, and done well, by balancing economic, humanistic and ecological interests. Rental space for the municipality, a place for the public, and a jungle for the park. "Having your cake and eating it too. Sometimes an architect can satisfy this paradox."[81]

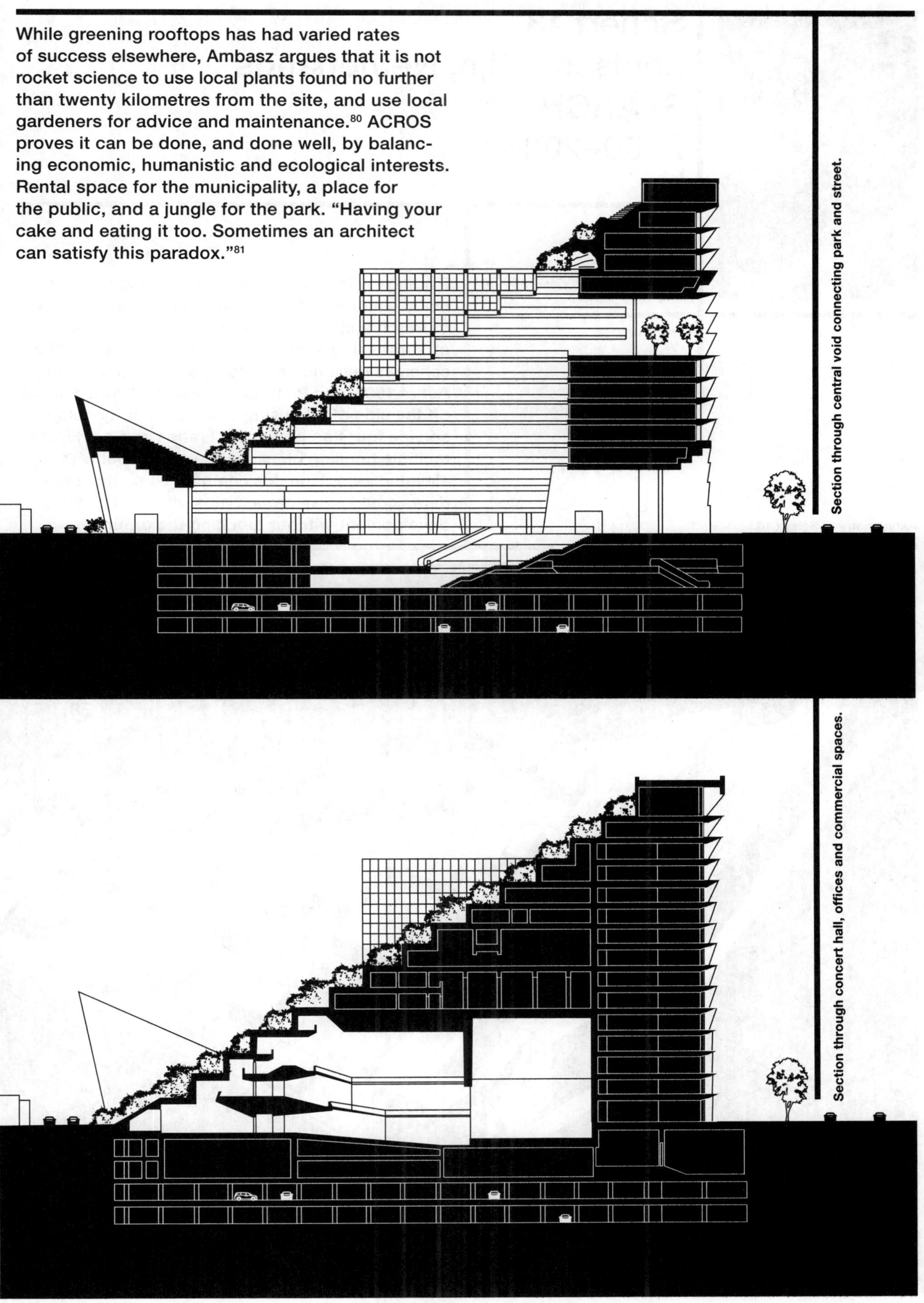

Section through central void connecting park and street.

Section through concert hall, offices and commercial spaces.

Scherf 13
Leidsche Rijn, Netherlands
SeARCH
2000–2006

Finding joy in efficiency and expressing the pragmatic elements of buildings cuts to the very core of Dutch architecture. There is a long tradition of addressing access that dates back to the first schemes designed according to the new Housing Act of 1905. Jan Piet Kloos hung an elevated street off the side of a housing block so that it could service four floors at once. Frans van Gool linked multiple housing blocks in Plan van Gool with elevated aeroplane docking bridges so that residents could move around most of the 1100-unit development without touching the ground.

Axonometry of Scherf 13.

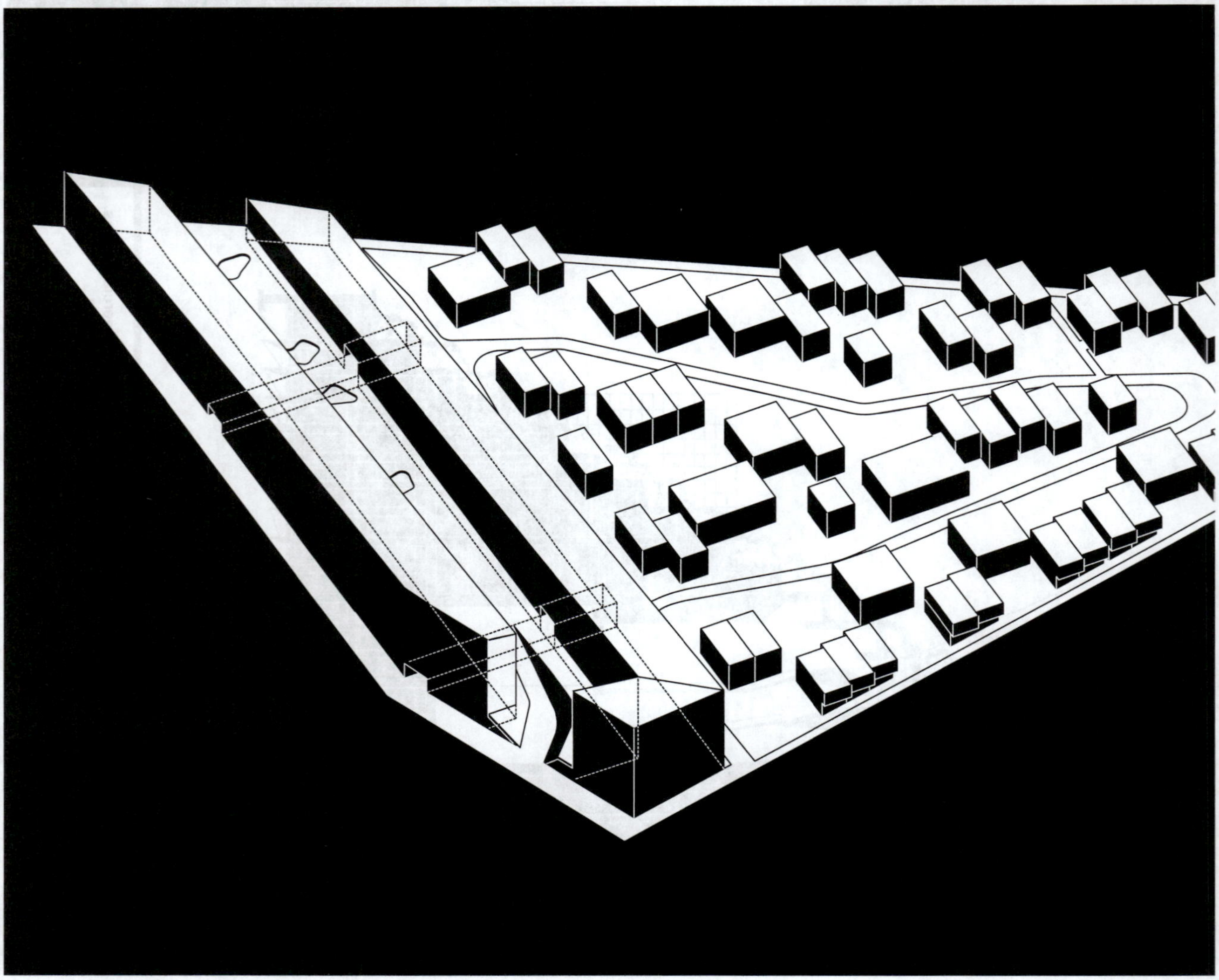

'Suspension bridge' duplex blocks, Amsterdam-Osdorp, Jan Piet Kloos, 1970.

The elevated streets of Plan van Gool, Amsterdam, Frans van Gool, 1962–1968.

Suspension bridge of Jan Piet Kloos connecting two duplexes.

Since the 1970s, attention has shifted to the pesky car. Especially in the Netherlands, where land is scarce, finding an efficient way to park has become a decisive element in a housing scheme's organization and success. At first, parking encircled developments, and later it pushed the building upwards, since parking at ground level is both cheap and desirable.

Gerard Noodtstraat, Nijmegen, SeARCH, 1993–1996. Rooftop parking, freeing the ground floor completely.

Oeverpad, Amsterdam, SeARCH, 1994–1998. Semi-underground parking topped by a garden.

Zuiveringspark, Amsterdam, SeARCH, 1994–2000. Ground-floor parking with new ground over former sewage facility.

De Meester Amsterdam, SeARCH, 2006–2009. Ground-floor parking enclosed within development, topped by an elevated deck.

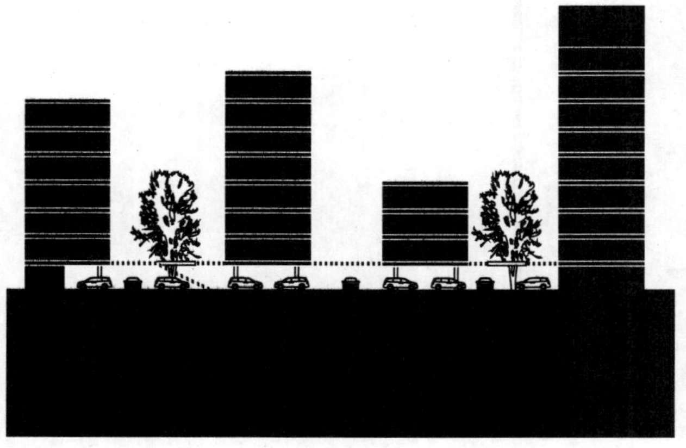

Section of Scherf 13, showing ground-floor parking and manipulated first-floor surface to mediate level change.

The paradox of suburbia is that people, often with kids, abandon the concrete jungle of the city centre in search of private green space, and end up in car-dependent neighbourhoods, complete with concrete kerbs, culverts, cul-de-sacs and driveways.

Pathway within car-free neighbourhood.

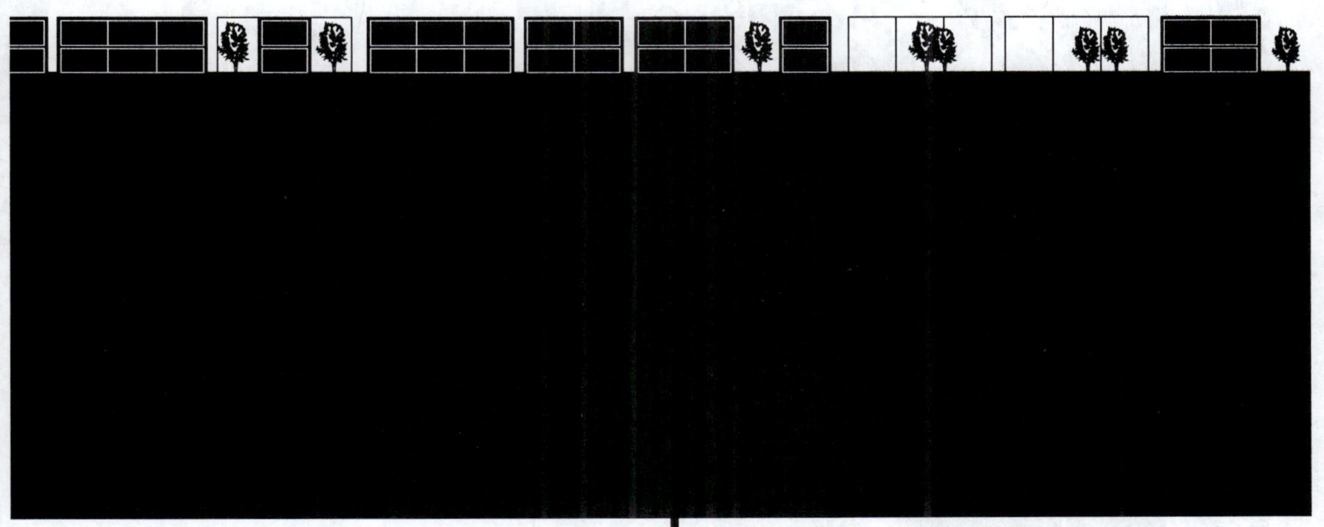

To resolve this dichotomy, pulling the car out of these residential spaces is key. At Scherf 13, all the necessary parking space is tucked under the main apartment building, so the gardens of the detached houses can be thirty per cent larger. It is not just about size but quality, creating a genuinely car-free neighbourhood that is lush and verdant.

Site plan of Scherf 13.

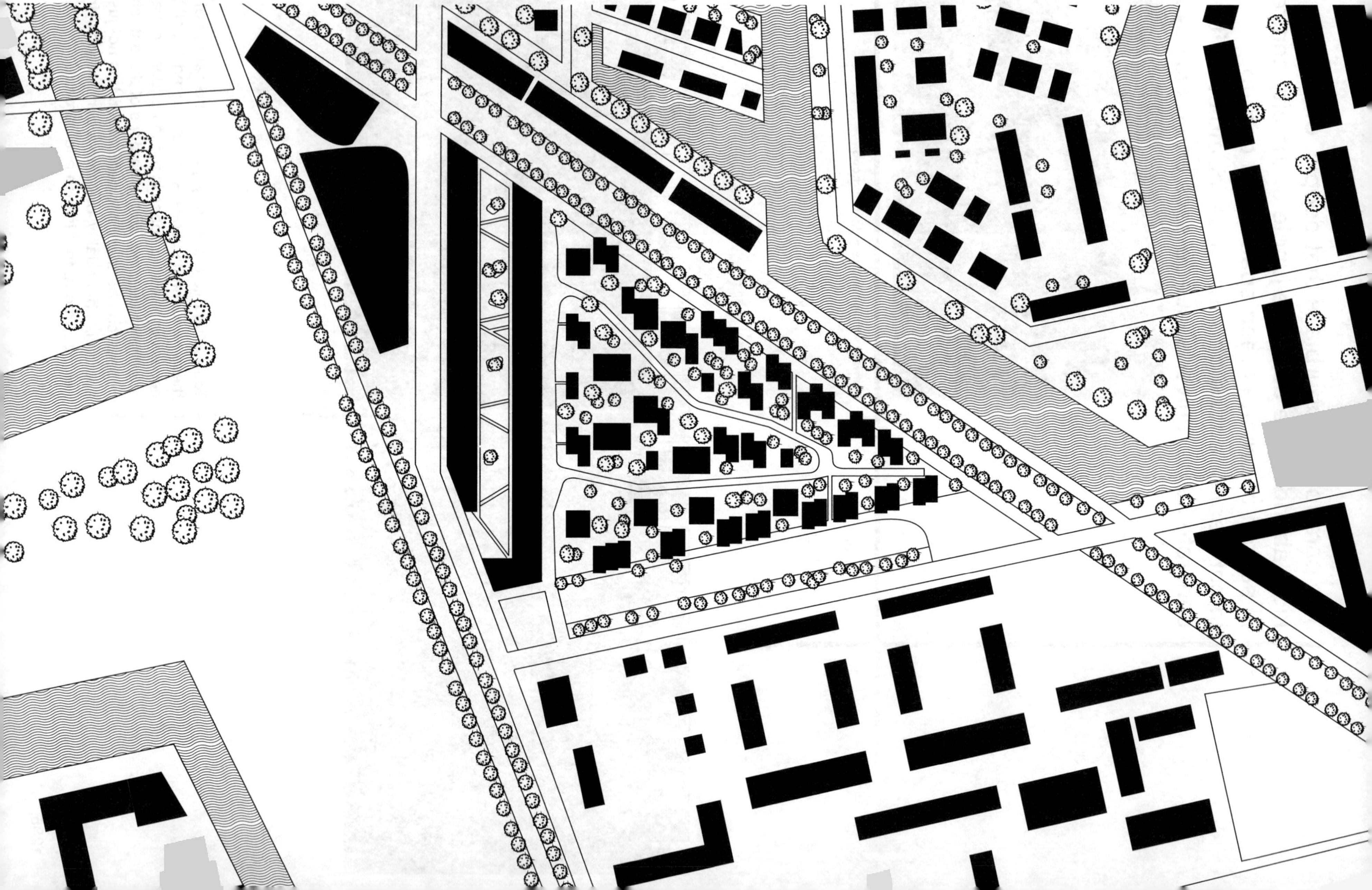

343
341

217
205
183
171
169

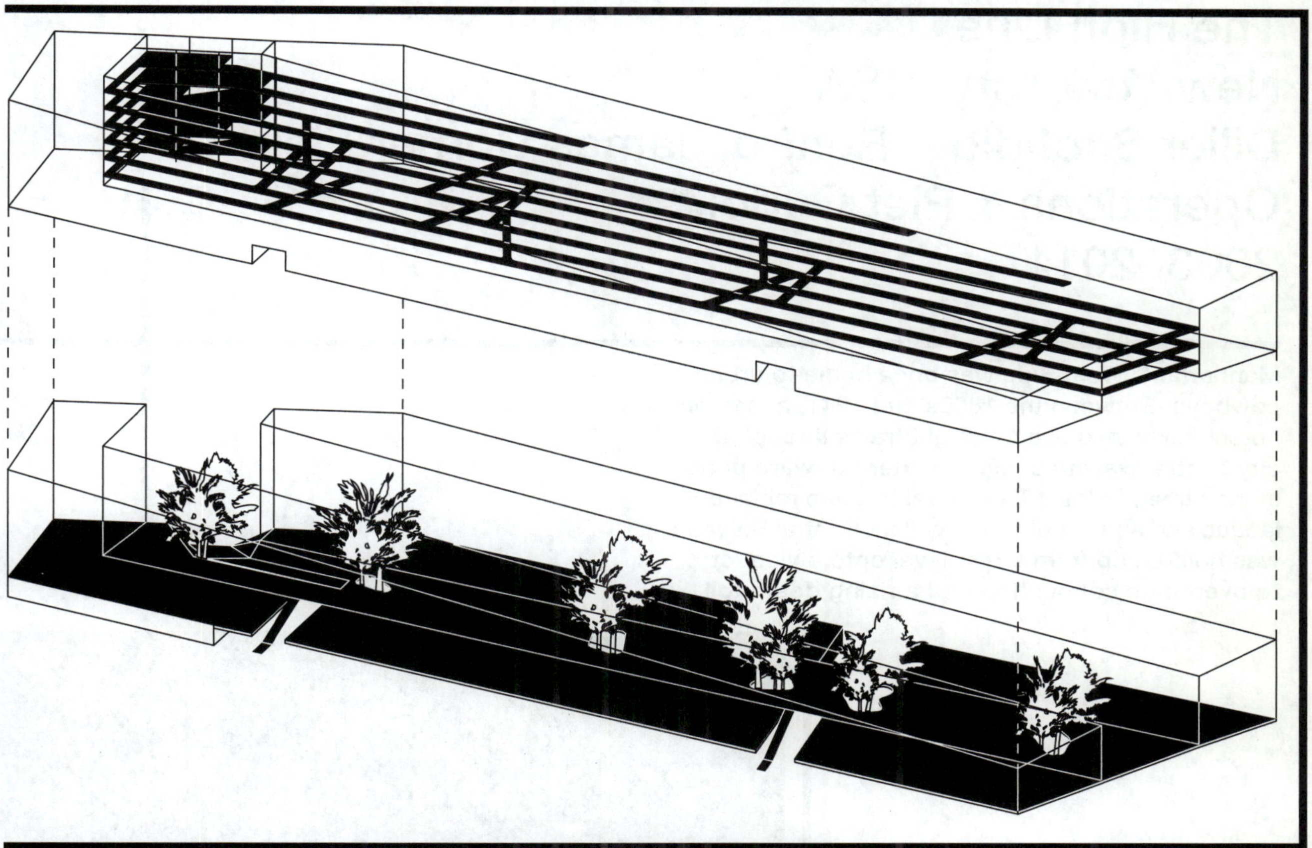

Exploded axonometry of apartment complex.

Within the apartment complex, an elevated deck slopes gently down towards the adjacent park, and large openings bring daylight into the garage while allowing mature maple trees to grow through. Above, bridges connect the two apartment blocks, limiting the number of lifts. Like its 1960s predecessors, the block shows that the careful consideration of a small element of efficiency can enhance the day-to-day experience of residents.

The High Line
New York City, USA
Diller Scofidio + Renfro, James Corner Field Operations & Piet Oudolf
2003–2014

Manhattan's West Side was once home to urban cowboys. Between the 1850s and 1941, a man on horseback would escort freight trains through the city centre, waving a flag or lantern to warn people in the street. In the 1930s, infrastructure replaced labour, and a piece of the New York Central Railroad was hoisted up from street level onto a viaduct to overcome congestion and a rising death toll.

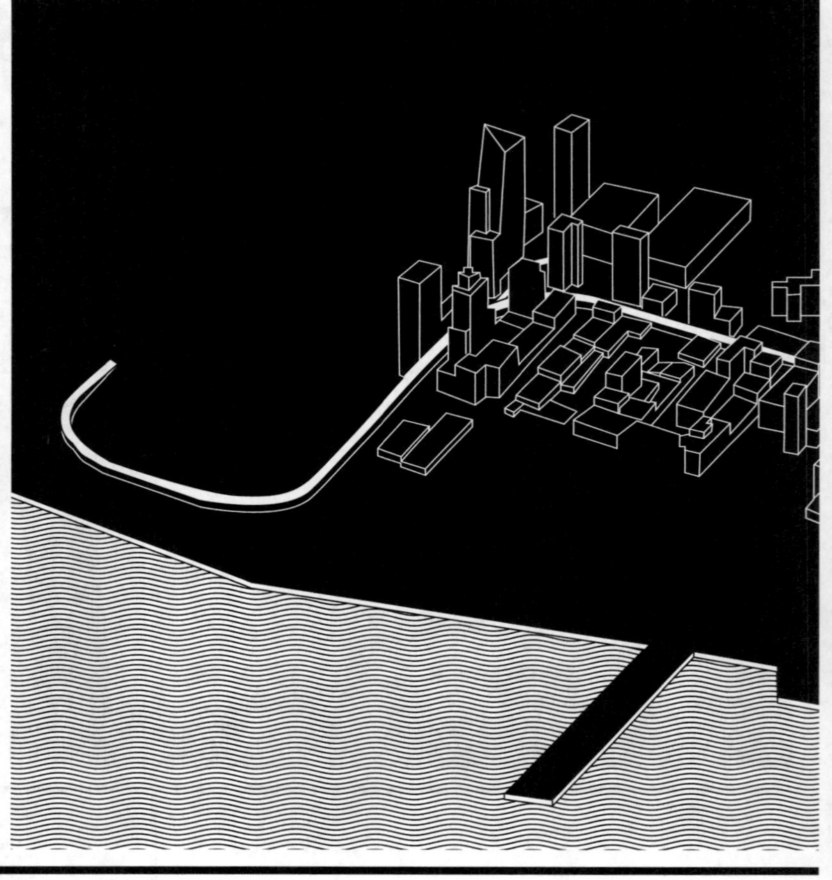

Axonometry of the High Line.

A West Side cowboy escorting a train.

Congestion on 11th Avenue, which became known as Death Avenue due to freight train accidents.

The High Line, New York City.

Promenade Plantée, Paris, Jacques Vergely & Philippe Mathieux, 1993.

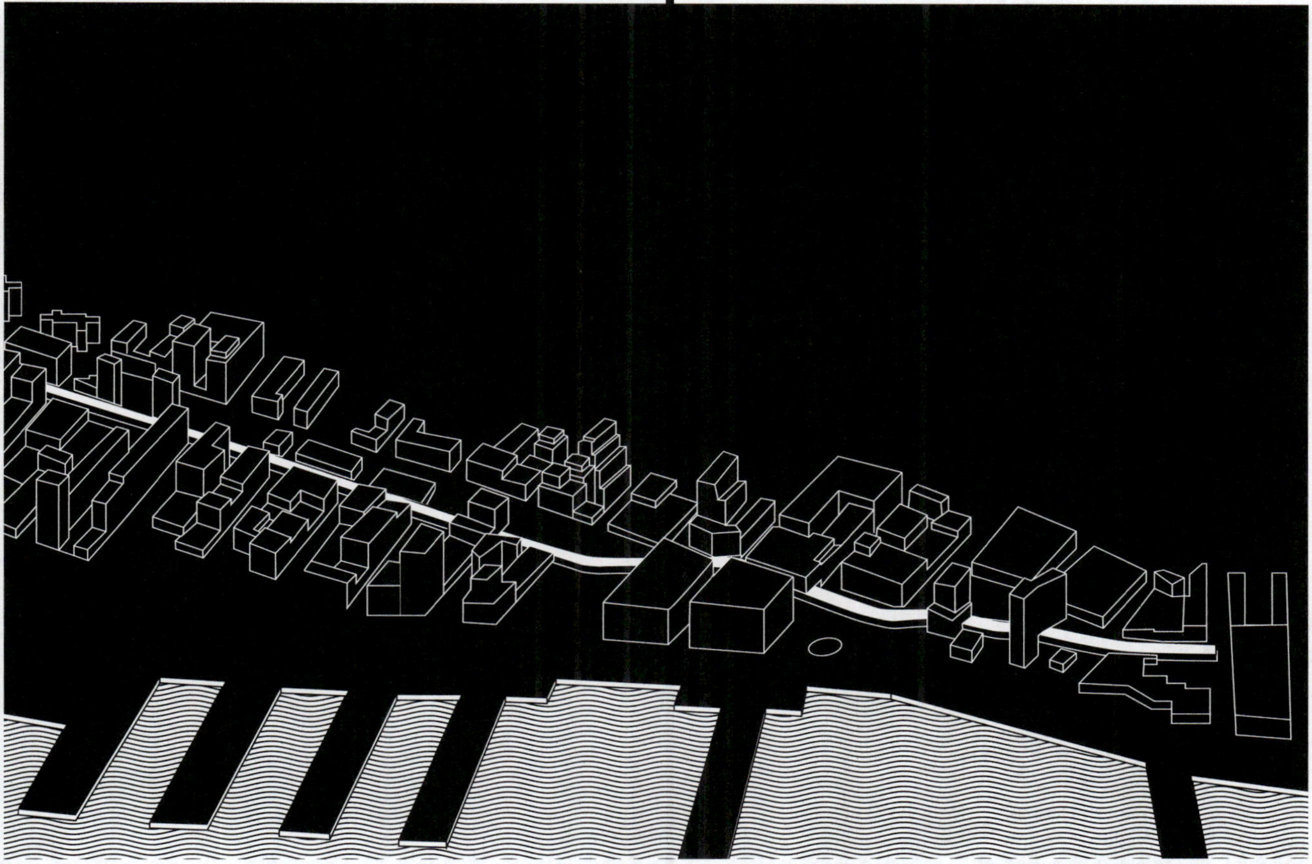

Today, this disused piece of infrastructure has been redeveloped as a public park. The High Line is championed globally, inspiring countless other elevated linear parks, including the Goods Line in Sydney, the Peckham Coal Line in London, 11th Street Bridge Park in Washington, DC, and the Skygarden in Seoul. One of the first and finest examples is the Promenade Plantée in Paris, built a decade before the High Line, which even boasts its own pool.

The establishment of a new park within the contemporary city is no easy feat. Ground has become such a coveted and profitable commodity that to not build is considered a wasted opportunity. Through reuse, the High Line and its many copycats take a different approach by revealing the incredible potential the city's redundant infrastructure represents.

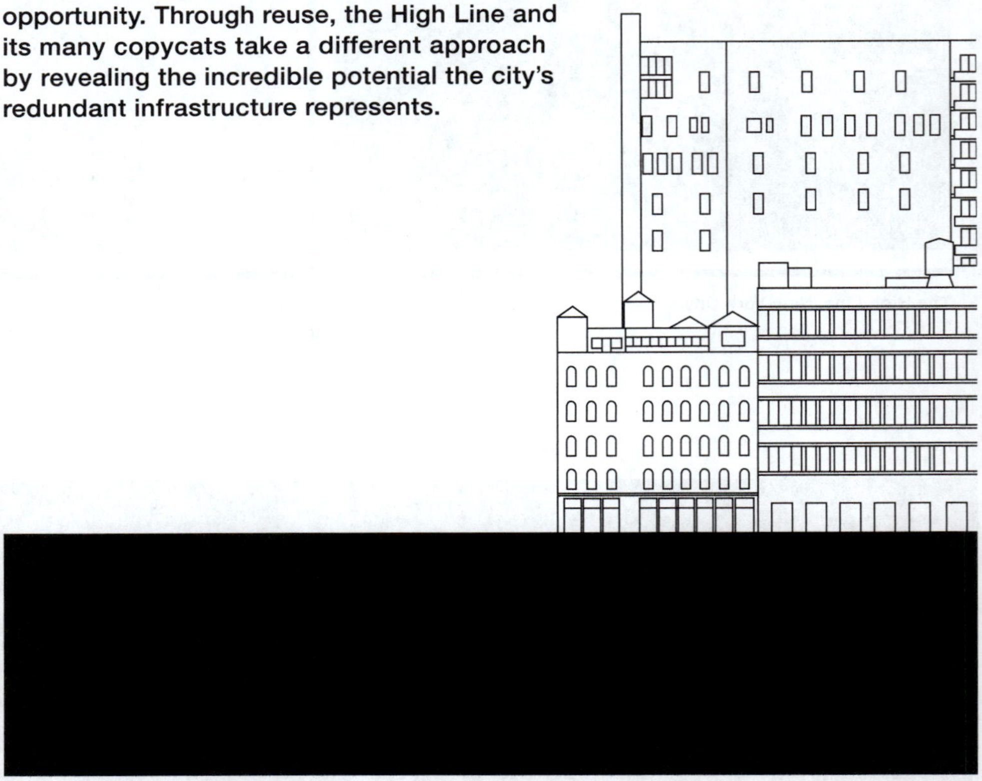

Section of the High Line running down 10th Avenue.

But, inevitably, economics eventually kick in. The High Line has gentrified its surroundings, raising the value of real estate around it many times over and spawning projects that are more folly than functional public space. At the end of the recently finished second section of the High Line, Hudson Yards, is a new billionaires' playground. Here the Vessel, a huge meshwork of stairs to nowhere, floats above the train tracks.

The giant shawarma, aka the Vessel by Heatherwick Studio.

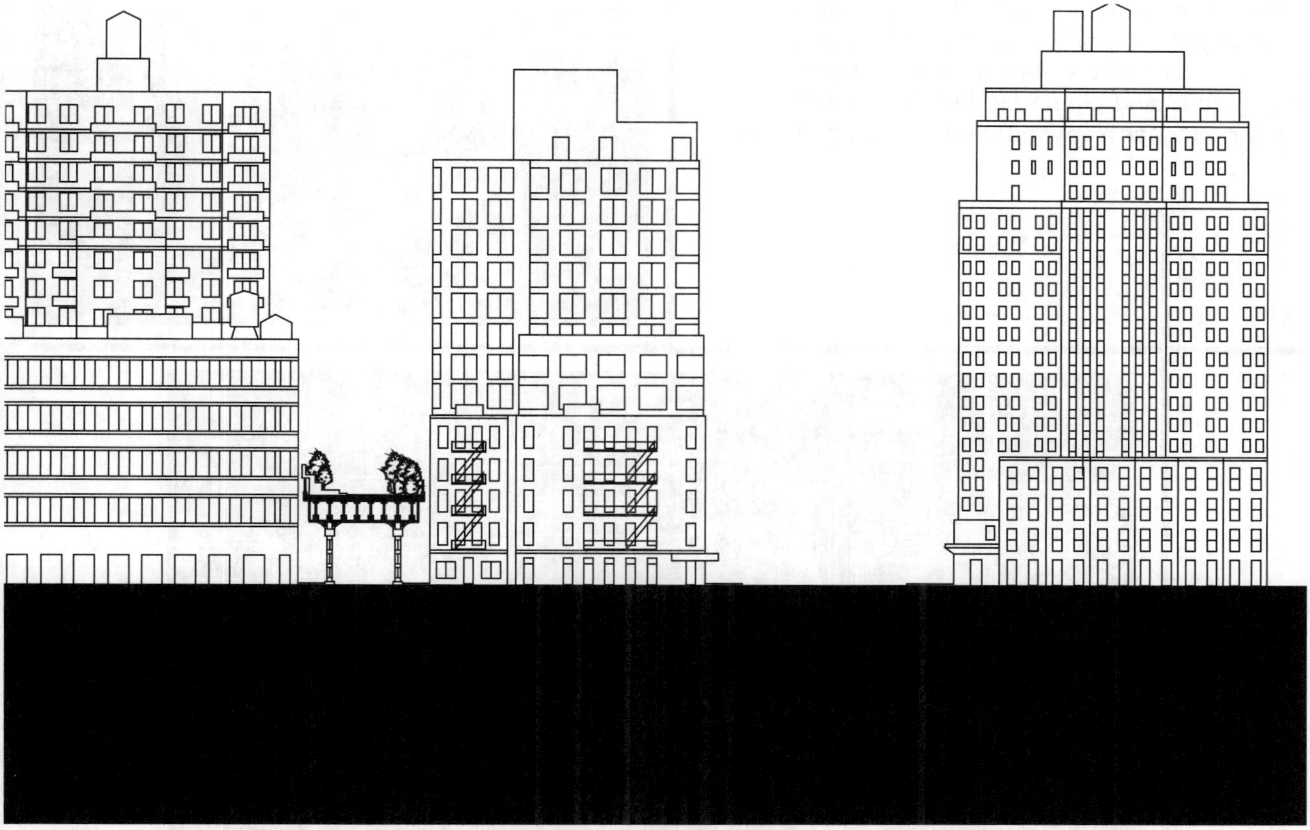

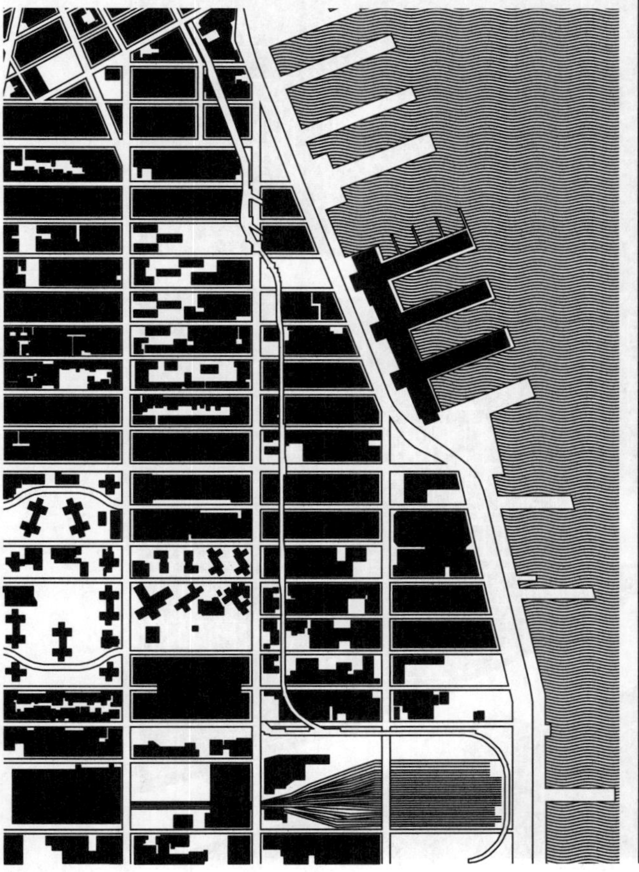

Site plan of the High Line.

In many ways the High Line breaks all the rules for a grounded building. It is an elevated promenade, with minimal physical and visual connections to street level. The public floats along, completely engrossed by this recreational surface, a little like those trapped on cruise liners, enjoying the view.

But curiously, a little isolation from the street functions very well; it heightens an awareness of the surrounding urban fabric. The surface, vegetation and character of the High Line differs from area to area, creating a varied meander over, along and even through the city, cutting through buildings and squeezing between blocks. It even drops down to a giant window over 10th Avenue, reconnecting those gliding above with the congestion below.

Landscape architect Diana Balmori believed these moments of connection between ground and viaduct are crucial and should have been pushed further. Her vision for the High Line would have gone beyond the adaptive reuse of a piece of infrastructure. She would have not just created new ground and planted it, but "thickened the crust of the earth" by merging above and below.

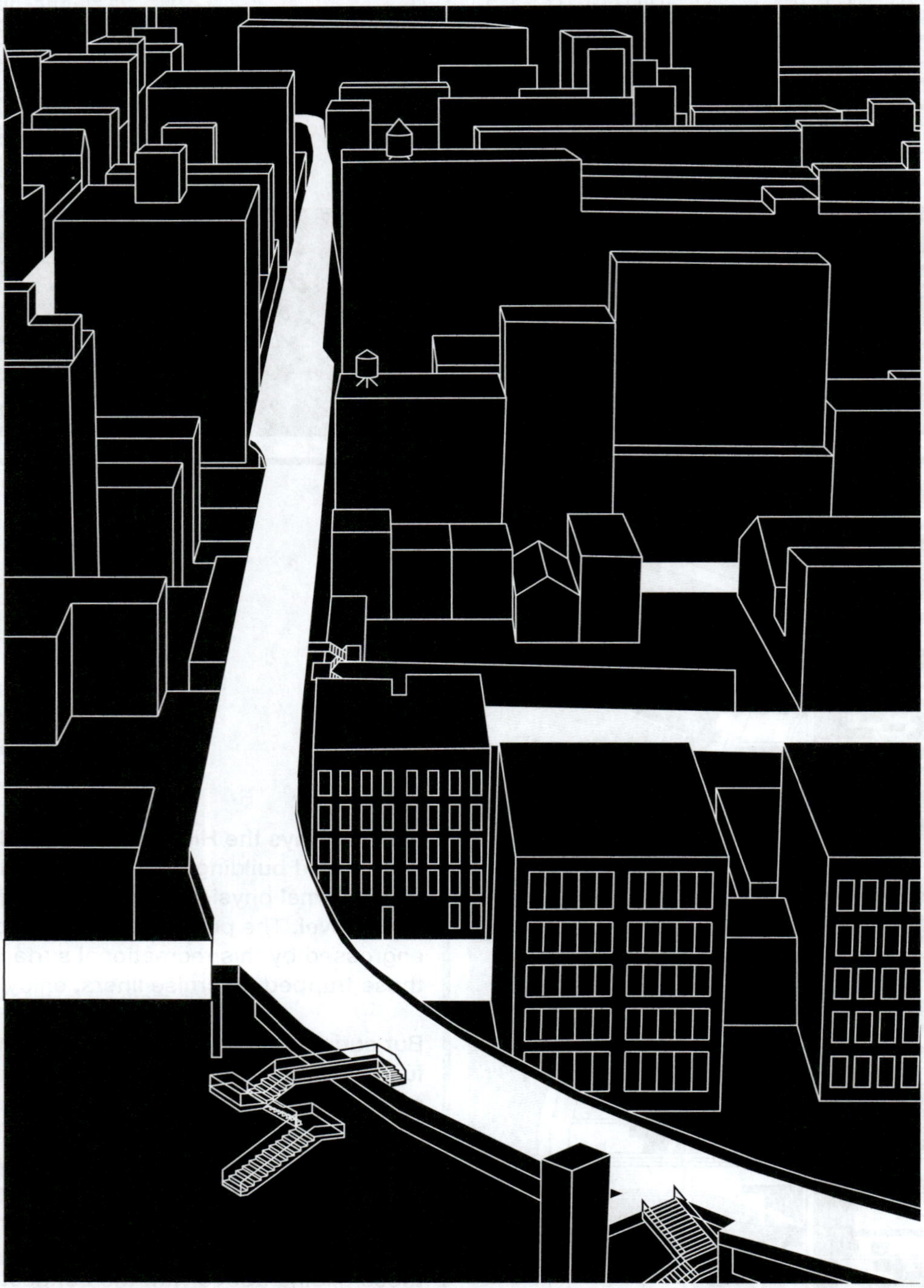

Perspective of the High Line.

Balmori argued that successful twenty-first-century parks are linear parks. They connect neighbourhoods and are more about movement than place. The fragments of our industrial past, the abandoned industrial riverbanks and harbour fronts, railyards and train tracks are ripe for conversion, adaption and reconstruction.[82]

Perhaps this vision will be answered in time. At the foot of the Williamsburg Bridge in Manhattan, an abandoned underground yard next to Delancey Street Station will be converted into a cavernous park with advanced optics and heliostat mirrors that beam daylight down to the vegetation. This Lowline, a kind of architectural antidote to its elevated buddy and its temporary lab, has already attracted over 110 000 people to the Lower East Side.[83]

Full-scale testing at the Lowline Lab, 2016.

Combined with the coastal resilience plans for Lower Manhattan and the future covering of expressways like FDR Drive, a substantial number of linear elevated parks are in the pipeline, thickening Manhattan's crust.

Rendering of East Side Coastal Resiliency Project, BIG, 2018.

In Conversation

In May 2014 Bjarne Mastenbroek sat down with landscape architect Diana Balmori and architectural historian and critic Hans Ibelings to discuss the reciprocal relationship between architecture and landscape. This discussion was inspired by Balmori's provocative book, *A Landscape Manifesto,* which argues that the city should be considered a part of larger natural systems and designed as such.

The conversation started with a remark about the beautiful view from the window of Diana Balmori's office on Broadway, overlooking Lower Manhattan. She had recently moved to this location, after the lease in Chelsea rose steeply because of the widely acclaimed High Line.

[Diana Balmori] Parks always gentrify and raise the value of land around them. No matter where we do a park, the value of the land around it rises.

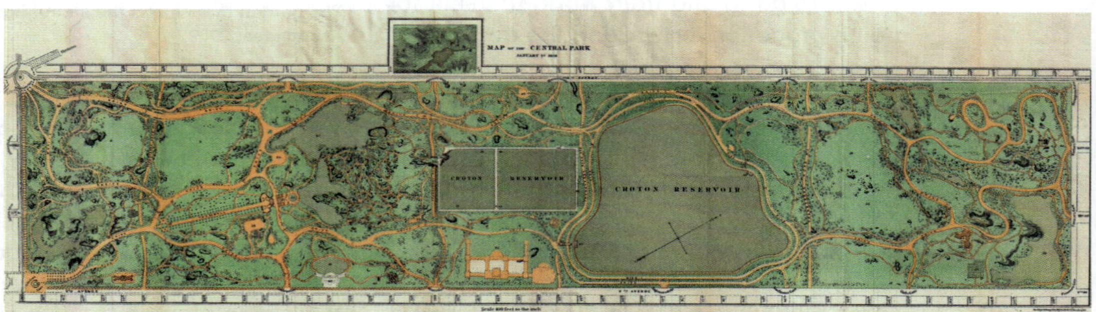

Map of New York City's Central Park, Calvert Vaux and Frederick Law Olmsted, 1870.

Olmsted-type parks, like Central Park here in New York, have been idolized in America, although the idea originated in Europe, especially England. In the last ten years there's been a move towards other formats. I think the first ones to represent another direction and a different intention in their use have been linear parks. They started to appear on abandoned railroad lines, under electric conduits and by the sides of rivers. They produced trails that became much more like parks. At first the linear park was considered to be suburban. As much as one admires Olmsted and his parks, it's quite obvious that you can't do Olmsted parks today. You can't do them because they were based on taking pieces of land that were not yet urbanized and turning them into parks as part of new city growth, and they were of a scale that's no longer possible in cities. To plunk a park in the city as a piece of nature set in opposition to the rest of the built environment is not in tune with our way of thinking today. Today you need to consider the whole city as part of a natural system, where you can work with nature at different scales. This human-made artefact called city is also part of natural systems. Our task now is to make them visible and put them to work on behalf of the city.

[Bjarne Mastenbroek] You say the linear park is often a conversion, like the reuse that increasingly happens in architecture. Does it relate to your idea of 'thick lines'?

[DB] That's a concept I felt was important in some of the work I was doing. The 'thick line', in my use of the term, means that you work not only at the ground level, but beyond that as well. It means connecting at different levels and across the division of inside-outside. Landscape architects here in the States start their work five feet outside the building envelope contractually. So that line is very precisely set and is thin, and the spaces on both sides of the line are radically different. But now there are efforts to bring the landscape in, and the architecture to morph as it goes out, and this creates a blurry thick line or zone, which represents a passage from one system to the other, from an architectural system to a landscape system. That passage can also be vertical, from below to above the earth. That passage has to mediate changes of scale which are quite marked between architecture and landscape. What seems large when you have a roof on top of it becomes menial under the open sky.

[BM] This morning I walked along the High Line. In my work I almost neurotically try to connect, and what really irritates me is that the High Line is not very well connected. It's simply stairs and an elevator. But since it is such a success, maybe the biggest connection is the mental connection it makes and how the line radiates beyond itself. Perhaps sometimes it's not even that important to physically connect.

[Hans Ibelings] The High Line is a linear world unto itself.

[DB] Right. Where it connects most effectively to what is below is not by stairs or elevators but in the sloping area with benches where you can see Tenth Avenue run below you.

[HI] And I think those trails are really interesting because they give a new programme to parks that are otherwise just places for a kind of innocent pleasure and nothing else.

[BM] It should be connected enough so people can use it as a trail on a day-to-day basis. To go to and from work, to use it for doing groceries, or walking the dog.

[DB] More connections would have made for a livelier floor below the High Line. What is underneath isn't used for anything; the streets alongside it have more stores on them now, usually on the basis of the new buildings going up, but the area just underneath it is not utilized, except in some places as a parking lot, and it would have been much more interesting to have a two-level thing. It could have been a 3D design. But that was a land ownership issue. Nearly all these linear parks that are trails have had difficulties in entering the city. The city wants to stop the trail because they see it as valuable real estate. Landscape architecture is a discipline that moves very slowly. It is much slower than the ideas generated in it. I think it's a twenty-year cycle. First there is the idea; it's rejected at the beginning; then there are very modest attempts, which usually fail, or are too modest to make the idea feasible; then more tries and a 'Well, maybe'; and then something happens and it begins to be believed. To me that's clearly shown in all the talk about climate change, with nobody accepting it was real, and certainly nobody doing anything about it. Nobody was taking it seriously. Then along comes Hurricane Sandy and everybody's convinced that climate change is here. But moving into action is proving very difficult.

[BM] And then you see a High Line being built, which is an enormous success, and other cities simply want to copy that success.

[HI] I think the High Line is the equivalent of the Guggenheim Bilbao, which cannot be replicated with the same effect.

The garden that climbs the stairs, Bilbao, Balmori Associates, 2009.

[DB] We are in the running for a competition for the Eleventh Street Bridge in Washington, DC, which they want to convert into a park. The first thing they said was that it should be something like the High Line. But it has nothing to do with the High Line. It is crossing a very wide river, so there's nothing on the two sides, and it's very urban at the ends.

[BM] So what are you proposing?

[DB] Well, we're not proposing anything yet because we have to be chosen in order to enter the competition.

[HI] But you've been thinking about it.

[DB] Yes, and I really think unless that bridge is able to do something for the people at both ends, it's not going to work. And I think that one of the big challenges may be to avoid gentrification, to find strategies so that this bridge is not simply going to kick out the people living in the modest neighbourhoods around it while attracting economic development to the area. And somehow I feel that the challenge for the designer is how to integrate that into form.

[BM] One of the reasons I wanted to talk to you is because of your manifesto in relation to our research into how architecture and landscape merge. We have done a quick scan of magazines from the 1960s, simply counting how many buildings really integrate with the landscape, and there were very few. And then we looked at recent magazines, where it turned out that over half of the published works show a clear integration of the two. At the same time, there is no analysis, no theory, no reflection on strategies of how to integrate architecture and landscape. Do you have some advice on how that could work in architecture?

[DB] The architecture field is in a very strange moment because it is only dealing with itself, and has cut itself off from other disciplines. There are many very intelligent and capable people like Peter Eisenman who feel that everything has to come from within architecture, that it is a self-generating field, and I think that is a mistaken idea. Architecture, particularly right now, needs an infusion of ideas from the arts and from landscape architecture. Landscape architecture has been dormant for a very long time because it separated itself from other disciplines. Then it was forced to deal with ecology, and after it began to absorb ideas from a series of other fields. It has benefited from this, philosophically, artistically, technically, scientifically.

[HI] What really struck me in your manifesto is the use of the word 'landscape artist'.

[DB] Landscape really needed another form of expression. I looked at the landscape architecture field and realized it was not communicating, or communicating the wrong things. What was interesting was the work of artists working in landscape or landscapers influenced by art. I've always had an enormous admiration for Robert Smithson because he dealt with change over time, a central issue in landscape. Landscape has communicated with the public poorly, with the result that the public doesn't understand what landscape is. They think it's shrubbery around buildings. In fact, landscape has a philosophy, it has an artistic vision, it's scientific. And most importantly, it shapes three-dimensional space. None of this ever enters the mind of the public on hearing the word 'landscape'. I thought that finding a different way of representation could be a way of attracting attention to landscape as a field with an artistic mission. So that's where we are, and again you know it's going to take twenty years to make the public see and understand what landscape is.

[HI] Do you feel your landscape manifesto hasn't landed yet?

[DB] It's quite surprising for me to see the interest in it growing, within and outside the profession. It's like throwing a stone into water and seeing the ripples spreading out. But how long the ripples will last, I don't know. I think it's having an effect in changing the field and in the way it thinks about itself.

[HI] I find it extremely interesting that you are experimenting with the representation of landscape architecture. How do you think that representation is influencing our perception of the landscape?

[DB] Landscape architecture is about the design of space rather than of objects in space, on which landscape has focused excessively. It has to do with an aesthetic intent. It is an art. So I really think that drawings are a way of expressing this.

[BM] Coming back to landscape versus building, I see two elements which are very different in architecture. First, the dominance of the building industry. It seems that in landscape it's not as much of a problem as in architecture, where suppliers and builders are extremely dominant. And second, every building is by definition commercial, so the client always has an extremely important say.

[DB] But landscapes face colossal commercial pressures as well.

[HI] In which way?

[DB] There is always a list of programmes that any landscape has to respond to, and they are very dated and rigid.

Speculative projects which thicken the earth's crust, SeARCH.

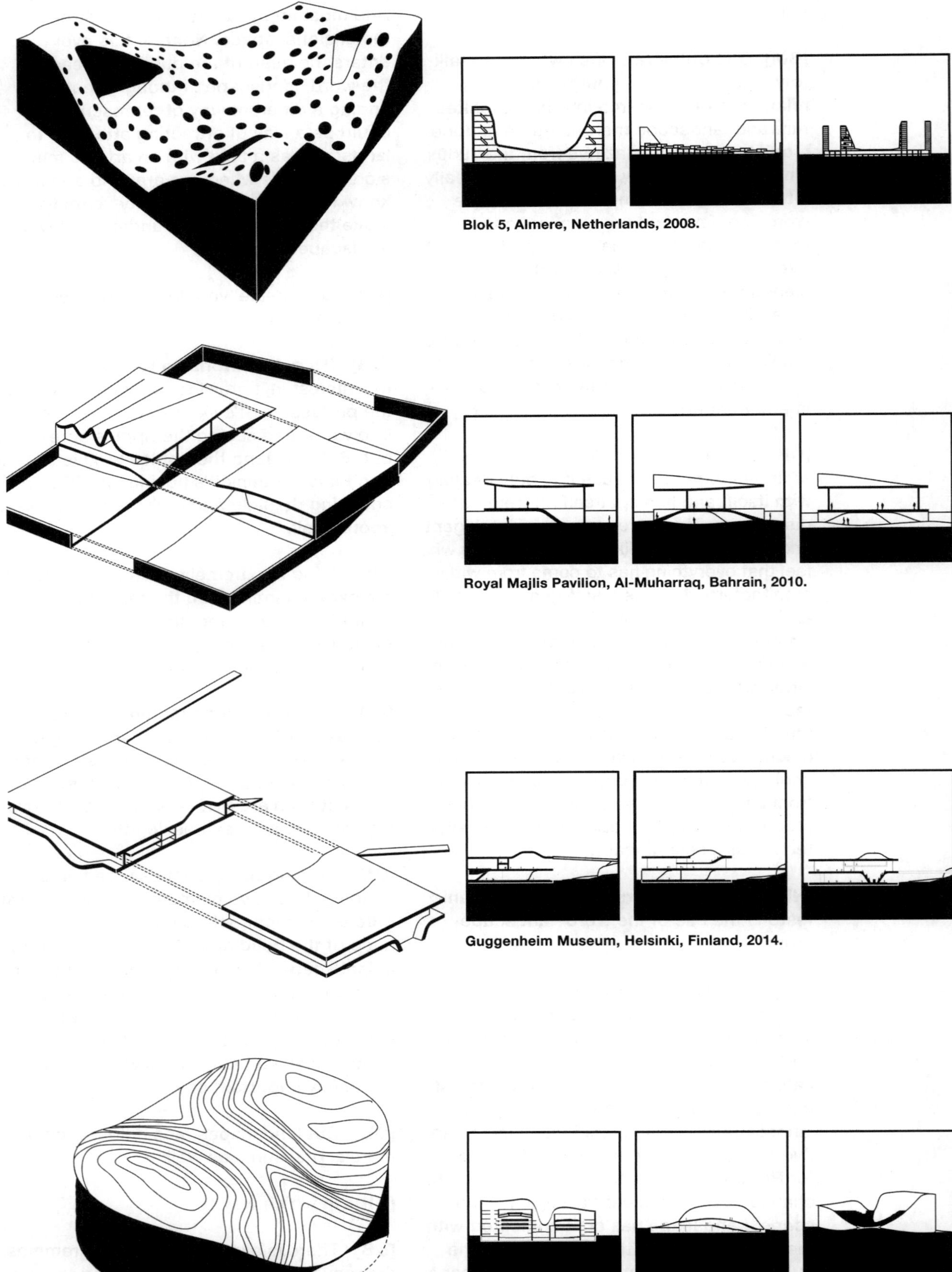

Blok 5, Almere, Netherlands, 2008.

Royal Majlis Pavilion, Al-Muharraq, Bahrain, 2010.

Guggenheim Museum, Helsinki, Finland, 2014.

Stavanger Concert Hall, Norway, 2003.

[BM] You mean, for example, that you have to make it possible for the park to be heavily used for large-scale commercial events?

[DB] For commercial events, but also that it has to have things for small children to play in, and they are quite defined as to how they have to play in it. And then there is always a highly regimented element of water, and there has to be a place where you sit on the grass, another place where you don't sit on the grass, and the benches have to be divided so that homeless people cannot sleep on them, and so on and so forth.

[HI] Is such a programme driven by social engineering or commerce?

[DB] Commerce. It's commerce in the sense that people are not willing to pay for a park unless it has the formulas in them. It also has to be cheap and easy to maintain and safe. You can't have a shrub that's any higher than four feet because it's considered unsafe; the list of to-dos and not-to-dos is very long. Otherwise you don't get the investment for the park. Parks usually start out with a budget from the city, but there's never a method to make them economically viable in themselves, so they always depend on commercial interest. Like how the High Line was built: the money put in by the city would never have been sufficient. They provided the money to preserve the line, but the money for building the park really came from private donations.

[HI] In your manifesto you say that you are in favour of porosity of buildings, does that suggest collaboration with architects?

[DB] That's a good point. I would say that the most important thing is that the architect and landscape architect start the job together, and I think that this would make for a much richer result than when we're brought in after everything has been designed.

[BM] If we do a project and the landscape designer comes in too late, we see problems arising immediately. Aside from that, most Dutch landscape architects tend to work with hard surfaces, like furniture, and they postpone the green. Sometimes I'm very happy that the municipality insists that buildings should be highly sustainable, because then at least you have tools to convince the client that a holistic approach is necessary. But even then, there is hardly ever a landscape architect involved.

[DB] To go back to the question of the relationship with the architect, it was long taken for granted that the architect led and that the landscape architect followed, given the task of shrubbing up leftover land. But then ecology began to affect the building. As a result, the relationship became a little bit unstable, and at that point architects felt that they had to take total command. But I really think that both fields could gain a lot from the architects talking about landscape and the landscapers talking about building.

[HI] Has there ever been a period when there was a kind of harmonious relation between architects and landscape architects?

[DB] I think that definitely in seventeenth-century France, and I think that Versailles was an experiment in putting them together harmoniously.

[HI] But that is the Guggenheim Bilbao of the seventeenth century. Incomparable to anything else. Isn't there a kind of natural friction between architecture and landscape?

[DB] I don't think so.

[BM] There shouldn't be.

[DB] There shouldn't be, but there is.

[BM] I think there's a natural friction between the artist and the gallery, the author and the publisher, the architect and the builder.

[HI] Aren't you too modest by saying that there should be a porous meeting point of architect and landscape? It means that you more or less stop at the edge of the building.

[DB] Well, I think that porosity belongs not so much to how landscape goes into the building but how much it affects the ideas of the building, that the idea may take a different form because of landscape.

[HI] There is a common idea that architecture frames the view and exposes the landscape.

[DB] But then it starts from within architecture, while you could also say we're looking from the landscape to the building. That is what happened in eighteenth-century England, when the landscape became informal while the buildings remained classical.

[BM] John Portman built houses where there is a completely porous nature literally entering to them. It's almost hilarious to see. Many architects look at it as completely ugly, but I think it has an interesting beauty to it.[84]

[DB] Portman was the first who made these wild commercial landscapes in the middle of the building, those courtyards his hotels became famous for.[85]

[BM] Jean Nouvel started cladding his building with vegetation, but he has also tried to let the landscape invade his buildings. I don't see that in many other architectural works, this extreme merging of landscape and architecture.

[HI] Talking about representation, the images of Nouvel's projects are usually better than the buildings themselves. But maybe it's not about representation but about performance?

[DB] What I mean by performance is that if I discover how a system in nature works, I may build it as an engineered form in such a way that it performs as that natural system. So it becomes a learning curve about how living systems work. That for me is a reason for optimism. Bio-computation is one of the tools by which you can achieve this. Some biological systems are very complex and require many parameters, particularly in hydrology. When you're working with water and you work with hydrologists, the data they bring and the interpretations they give get you working more intelligently and faster.

[HI] How does this scientific knowledge affect your design work?

[DB] It has enabled us to challenge hard engineering solutions, and use soft engineering solutions instead.

[HI] It sounds as if it was already your intuition that those soft solutions work.

[DB] Well, I was testing it on a project and seeing that it worked. So, yes, we did know something about it, but not enough. Now we can sustain it with data, we can really say we know it's going to work.

[HI] Would you say that in this respect current landscape design is better than it was maybe a few decades ago?

[DB] Oh definitely. In the past you knew a bit about soils and a bit about plants but not about systems and how they were interrelated. Learning this has transformed the field completely. We even had a major change in the thinking of the engineering body that regulates all river and marine waters in the US. When working on the HUD Rebuild by Design project after Hurricane Sandy, an engineer told us they were rewriting all the guidelines to incorporate soft engineering. I found this unbelievable, because previously they forced us to use hard engineering. I think it's the first major breakthrough, and it was Hurricane Sandy that brought this about.

[HI] There's always that issue with architects and landscape architects that they are do-gooders. It's kind of unavoidable. Yet, you can see that architecture can be potentially repressive or aggressive. Is it possible to have a slightly more subversive role for landscape architecture? Or does it always have to be nice and pleasant?

[DB] I'm actually very interested in that other dimension of landscape. The only time that there was some reference to that was in the concept of the sublime. The sublime included terrifying things and terrible things that fell apart, swept you away or killed you. I think that Smithson was playing with some of those ideas, mainly the idea of entropy – that everything in the world is slowly diminishing in energy. Bringing out such qualities in the landscape is sorely needed. Terrifying forests, caves, underground spaces, enormous waterfalls, precipices. And darkness. What becomes critical is the edge of that experience.

[BM] Where did your idea of the 'thick line' come from?

[DB] I developed the idea while visiting the summer palace in Kyoto. I simply began to observe how you went up to the teahouse at the top of the hill, which is the highest point in the whole garden. There are a series of changes in the paths as you walk up through the garden from the bottom of the hill. The paths keep changing in texture and quality until you finally reach the teahouse. Once you reach the teahouse itself you come across these stones on the ground. You can sit on the edge of one and take your shoes off. Then there is a first platform without a roof. It is followed by a second one with a roof. I thought this is really like a very thick line, where there are different gradations of textures and steps preparing you for the passage into the teahouse. I think that in modern terms one could compress these intricate changes into smaller spaces or time, which still give you the sensation of this thick line.

Gonai-Tei (top) & Oikeniwa Garden (bottom) in the Imperial Palace, Kyoto.

[HI] Do you think you should enhance the perception and experience?

[DB] You have to densify. It's like turning the volume up. You can do it with textures, smells, sounds, colour. These are a few ways of marking the transition from one to the other.

[HI] Would it be possible to design an unprogrammed landscape?

[DB] The park is itself a programme. It comes with a frame: 'park'. You would have to remove that frame. Then you can begin to think of landscape as unprogrammed. Landscape as a park is a very constraining idea. It's a nineteenth-century idea but an incredibly successful one. It's been good for cities, but it's not what we need today. So I think that if you remove the frame and the word 'park', then you take the programmes away and you can think of other things like how you traverse a space that is under constant change. I think we need the juxtaposition of being under a roof and not being under a roof. The moment I can have this infinite dimension of the sky above: that's what I consider landscape. So everything that does not have a roof is landscape; and the moment I have a roof above me, I'm passing into another realm and into another, totally different scale.

Sadly, Diana Balmori passed away in November 2016. We are very grateful for her contribution to this book; her unique perspective was a key source of inspiration.

Forest Tower
Putten, Netherlands
SeARCH
2004–2009

The Forest Tower is a meandering vertical pathway through the Schovenhorst Estate. Designed around a species of tree that flourishes in two pinetums, an arboretum and a forest, each part of the promenade looks out over the surroundings. The branches of the tower offer several views along the route, of the skies, the branches, the ground, or the surroundings.

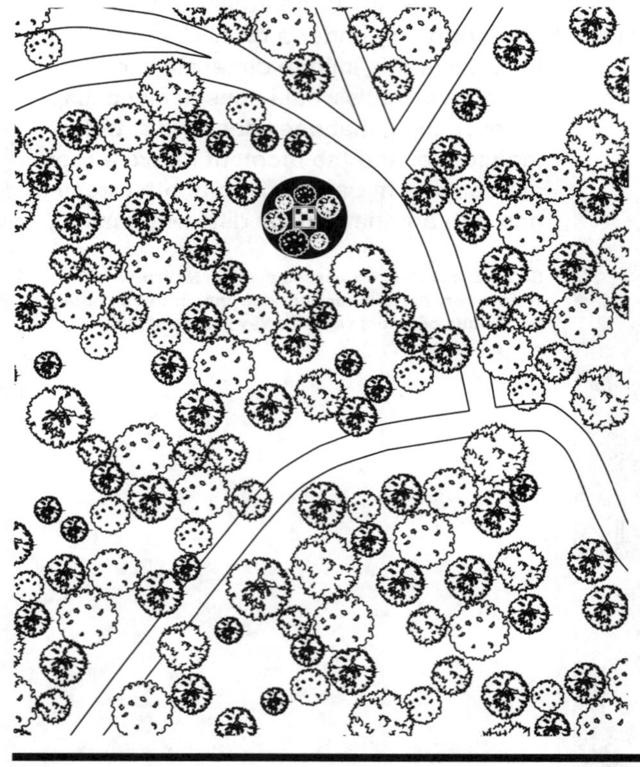

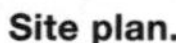

Site plan.

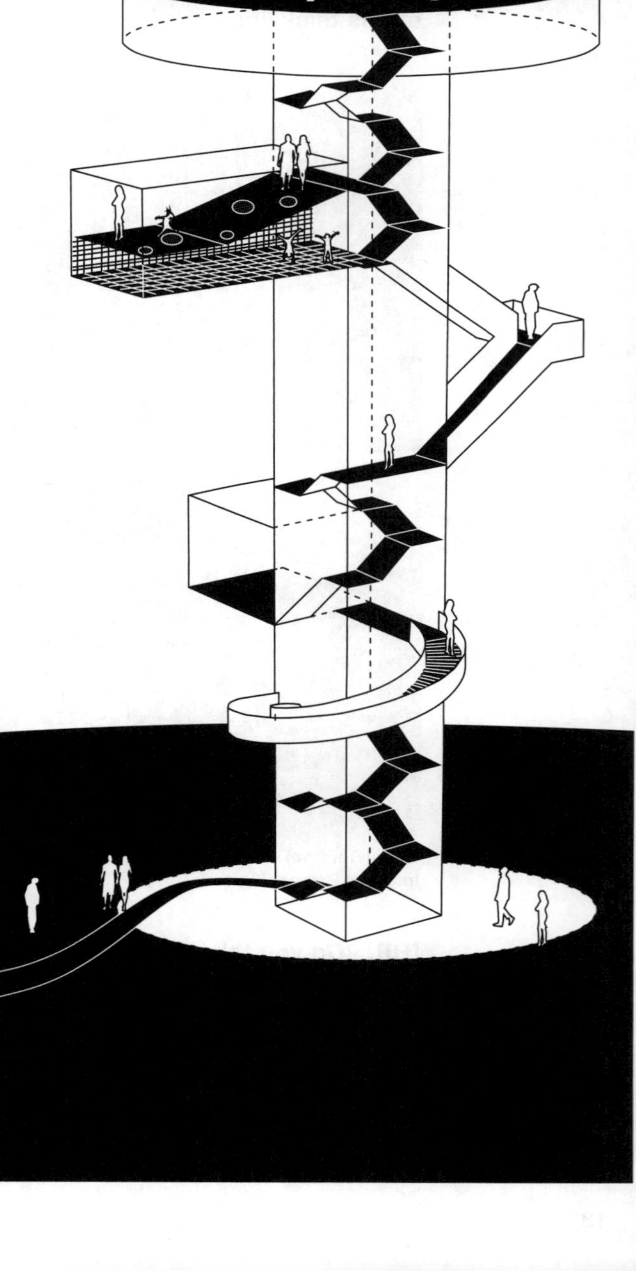

Schovenhorst Estate.

Aerial watchtower, Oudemirdum.

Research on forest towers showed that most have a tapered section, with stairs at the core and a platform on top. The idea is to reach the top in one go. We were looking for a more interesting walk, emphasizing the different layers of the forest (ground, trunks, lower branches, foliage, wide views), and stumbled on a series of post-war Dutch watchtowers.[86] Of the 138 that were built, 19 survive today. Spread around Holland, they are all unique, varying in location, height, structure and function. Constructed of concrete mesh owing to a shortage of steel, they are placid in appearance, as though they were not erected as watchtowers – they were quickly obsolete, with only a single Russian aircraft ever spotted – but to be admired, like a Sol LeWitt sculpture or a petrified tree.

Axonometry of Forest Tower.

Aerial watchtower 7T1, Winschoten.

At Schovenhorst, we designed the Forest Tower to embody this sculptural quality, rather than being simply a pathway up.

Section of Forest Tower.

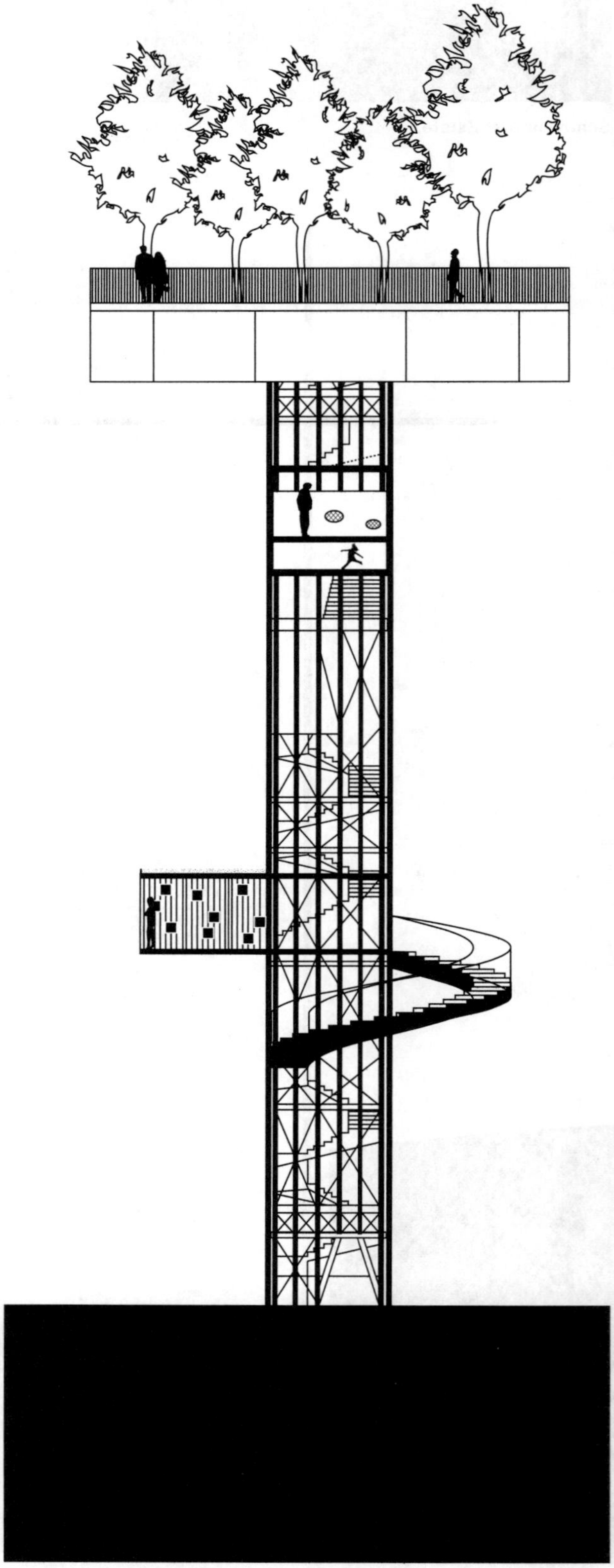

At a height of seven metres, a spiral stair leaves the tower core and leads to a cantilevered bird-house on the other side. The stairs rise further, passing the branches of trees and a net at a height of 30 metres before reaching a small theatre space.

Plan of Forest Tower.

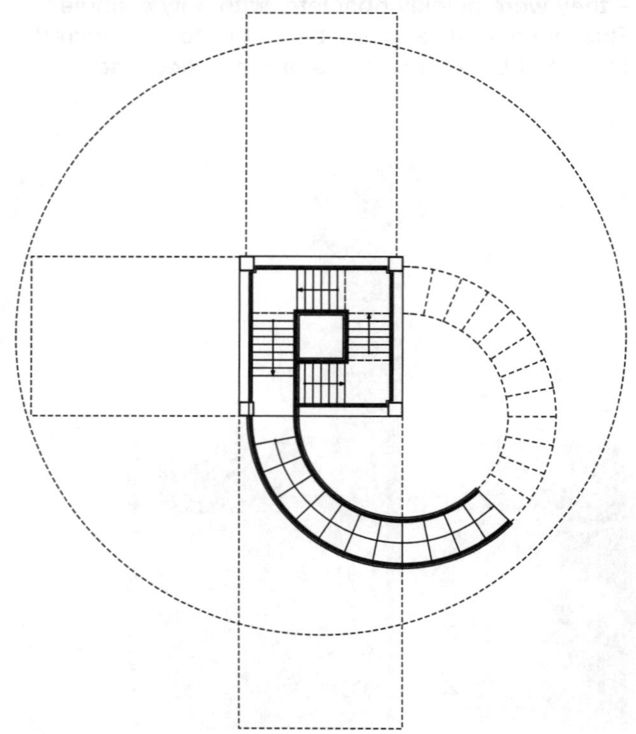

The tower's summit is not the customary lookout platform, but part of the forest itself. In fact, it is the forest that has been removed at ground level to make way for the tower. This elevated platform, with over a metre of soil in it and weighing five hundred tons, not only provides soil for experiments with conifers, but also offers visitors a powerful experience of ascending to a higher place.

Section of Forest Tower.

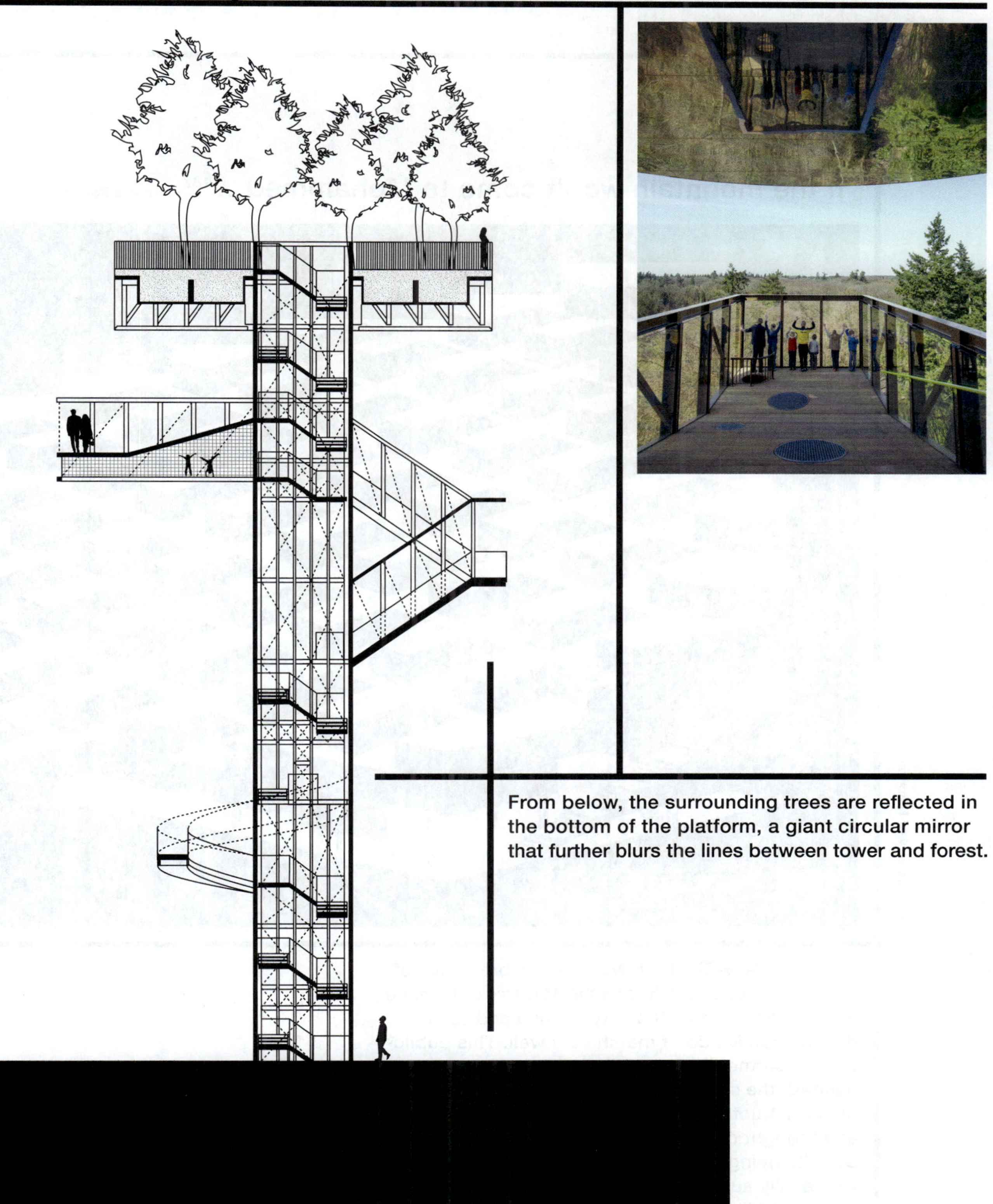

From below, the surrounding trees are reflected in the bottom of the platform, a giant circular mirror that further blurs the lines between tower and forest.

Mountain Dwellings
Copenhagen, Denmark
PLOT (JDS + BIG)
2008

"If the mountain won't come to Mohammed..."[87] —Francis Bacon

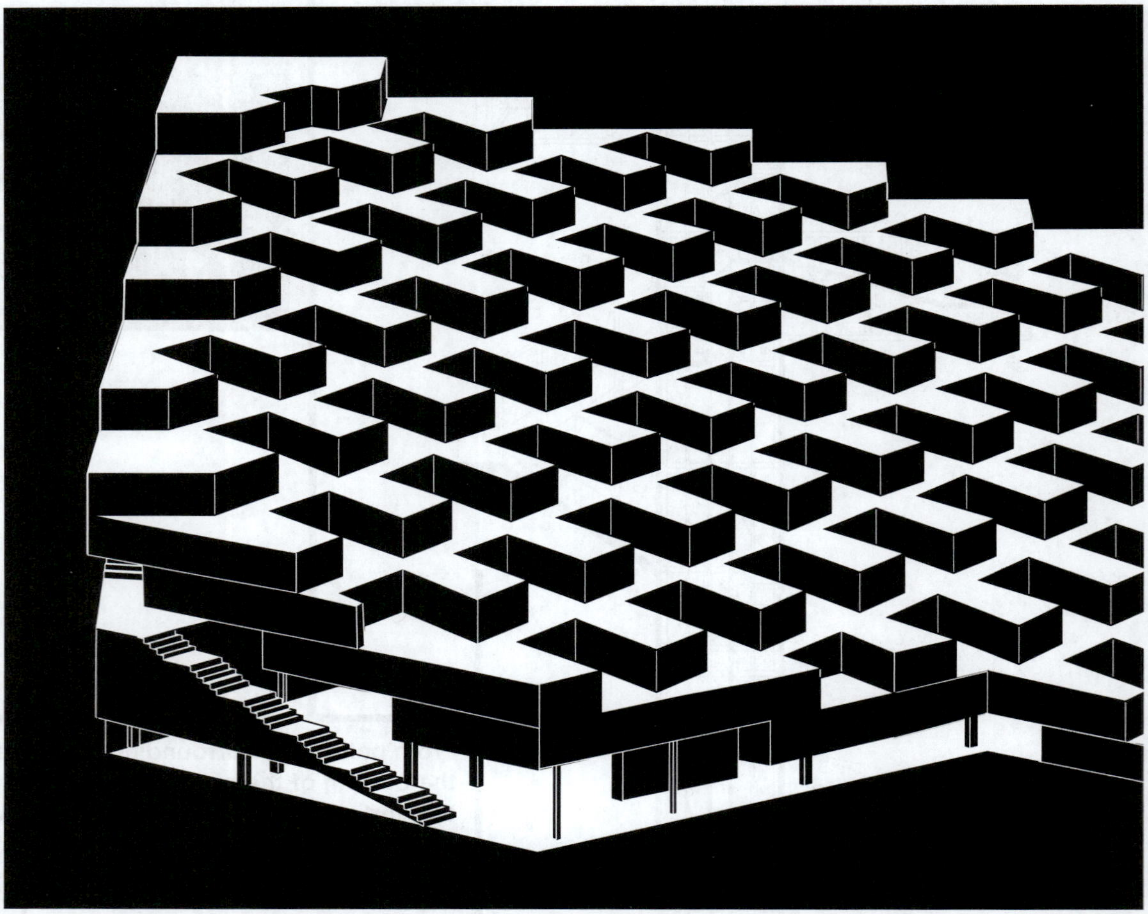

Axonometry of Mountain Dwellings.

The linear New Town of Ørestad, the brainchild of the city of Copenhagen and the Ministry of Finance in Denmark, is proof that city-making and calculative economics don't match very well. This public-private partnership was top down and heavy handed; the scale of the investment and the focus on infrastructure meant there was very little money and thought devoted to the final urban quality.[88] Despite being well located and well connected, with a fully automated metro line, it failed to attract even half of its expected 20 000 inhabitants.[89]

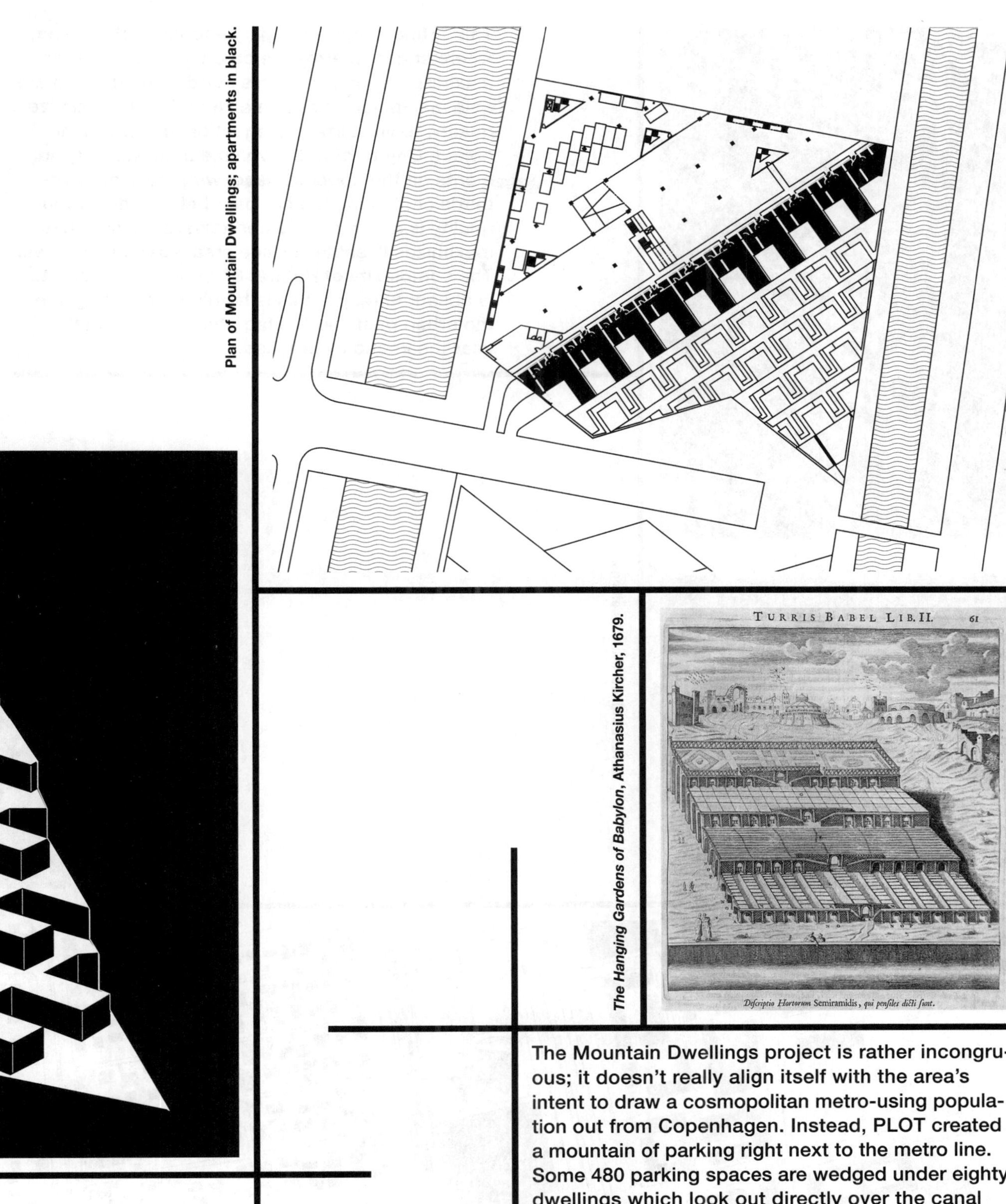

Plan of Mountain Dwellings; apartments in black.

The Hanging Gardens of Babylon, Athanasius Kircher, 1679.

The Mountain Dwellings project is rather incongruous; it doesn't really align itself with the area's intent to draw a cosmopolitan metro-using population out from Copenhagen. Instead, PLOT created a mountain of parking right next to the metro line. Some 480 parking spaces are wedged under eighty dwellings which look out directly over the canal to the suburban town of Sundby and the housing typology they mimic: a house with a garden.

Mountain Dwellings sell the suburban dream and do it extremely well. It is an incredibly simple idea. Stack individual homes up and step them backwards and up one storey so the roof of one becomes the garden of the next. These huge terraces, fenced with planters, are like a contemporary version of the Hanging Gardens of Babylon.

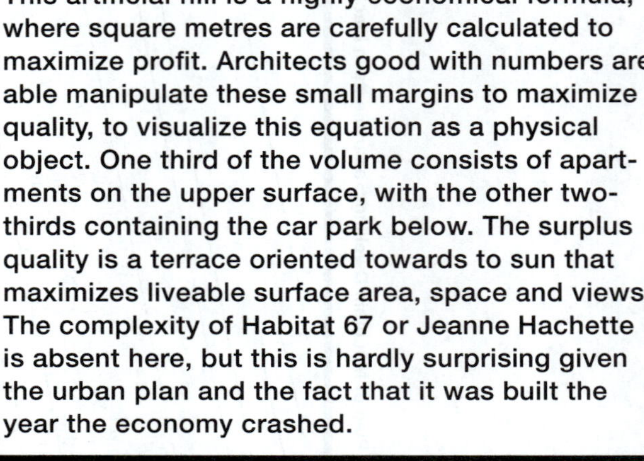

This artificial hill is a highly economical formula, where square metres are carefully calculated to maximize profit. Architects good with numbers are able manipulate these small margins to maximize quality, to visualize this equation as a physical object. One third of the volume consists of apartments on the upper surface, with the other two-thirds containing the car park below. The surplus quality is a terrace oriented towards to sun that maximizes liveable surface area, space and views. The complexity of Habitat 67 or Jeanne Hachette is absent here, but this is hardly surprising given the urban plan and the fact that it was built the year the economy crashed.

Terraces of Mountain Dwellings.

Site plan of Mountain Dwellings.

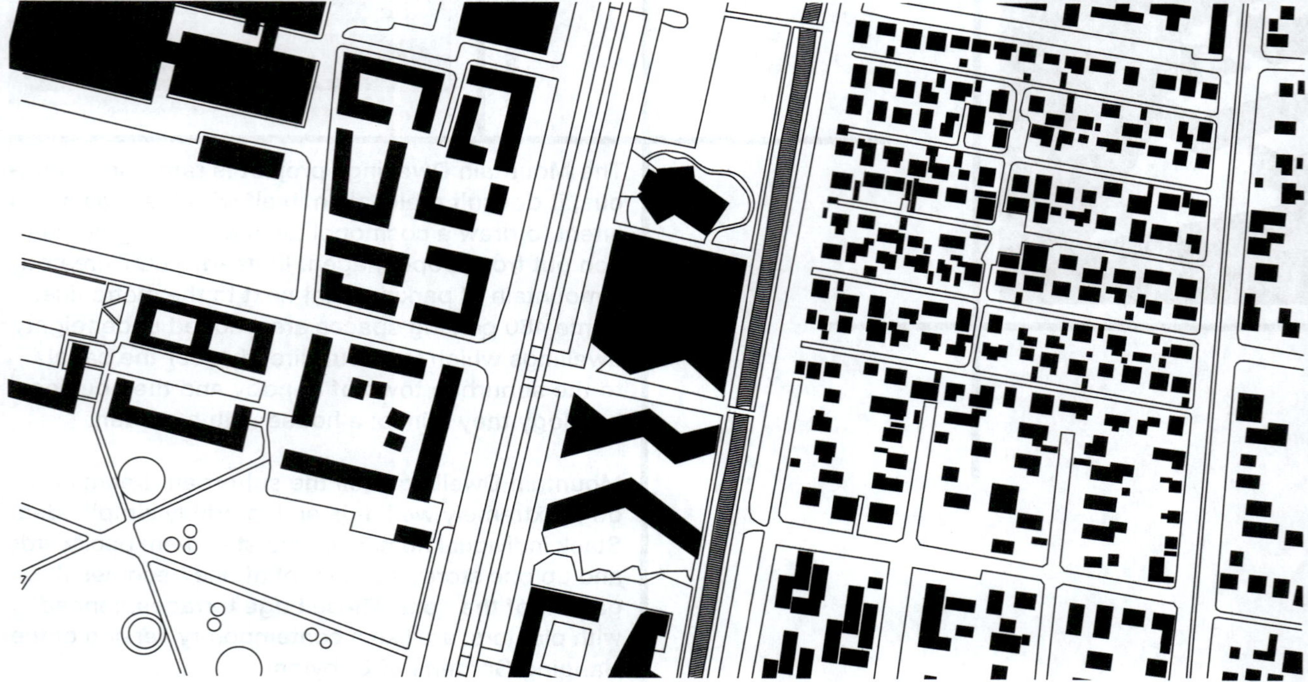

Section of Mountain Dwellings; apartments in black.

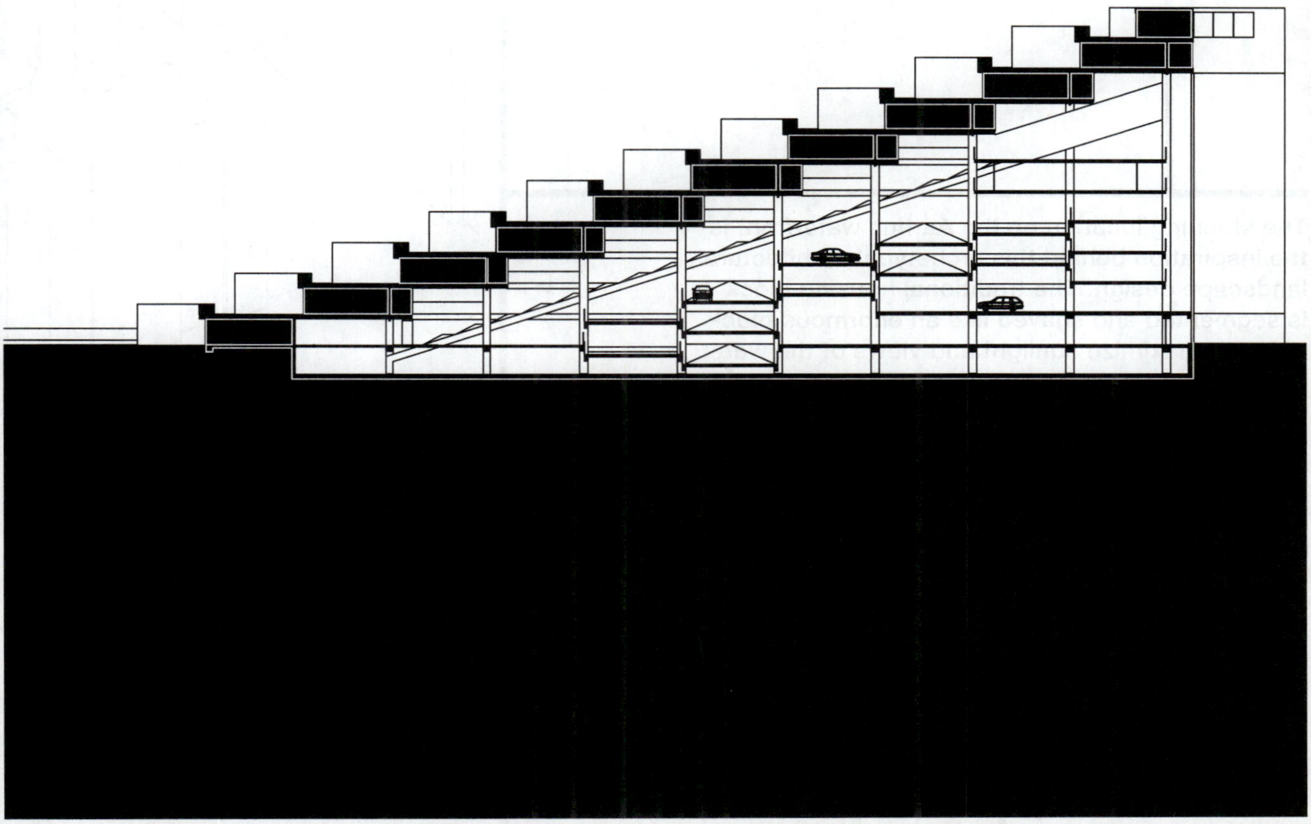

Perhaps it's hard to romanticize this child of the economy, but there are elements of lightness and playfulness. The interior of the car park is wrapped in rainbow colours and murals by the French street artist Victor Ash, depicting wildlife scenes such as moose standing atop mountains of wrecked cars. Perforations in the facade bring natural ventilation into the garage and form a large image of Mount Everest on the exterior. Although small, these acts are a sincere attempt to inject some humour and character into the building, and bit of a nod from the architects to acknowledge that they are well aware of the project's shortcomings.

The car park below the houses.

Isbjerget
Aarhus, Denmark
SeARCH + CEBRA + JDS
2008–2013

The stunning location on the Aarhus waterfront is the inspiration behind this archetypal architectural landscape design. The traditional housing block is segmented and shaved like an enormous block of ice to maximize sunlight and views of the water.

Aerial view of Isbjerget.

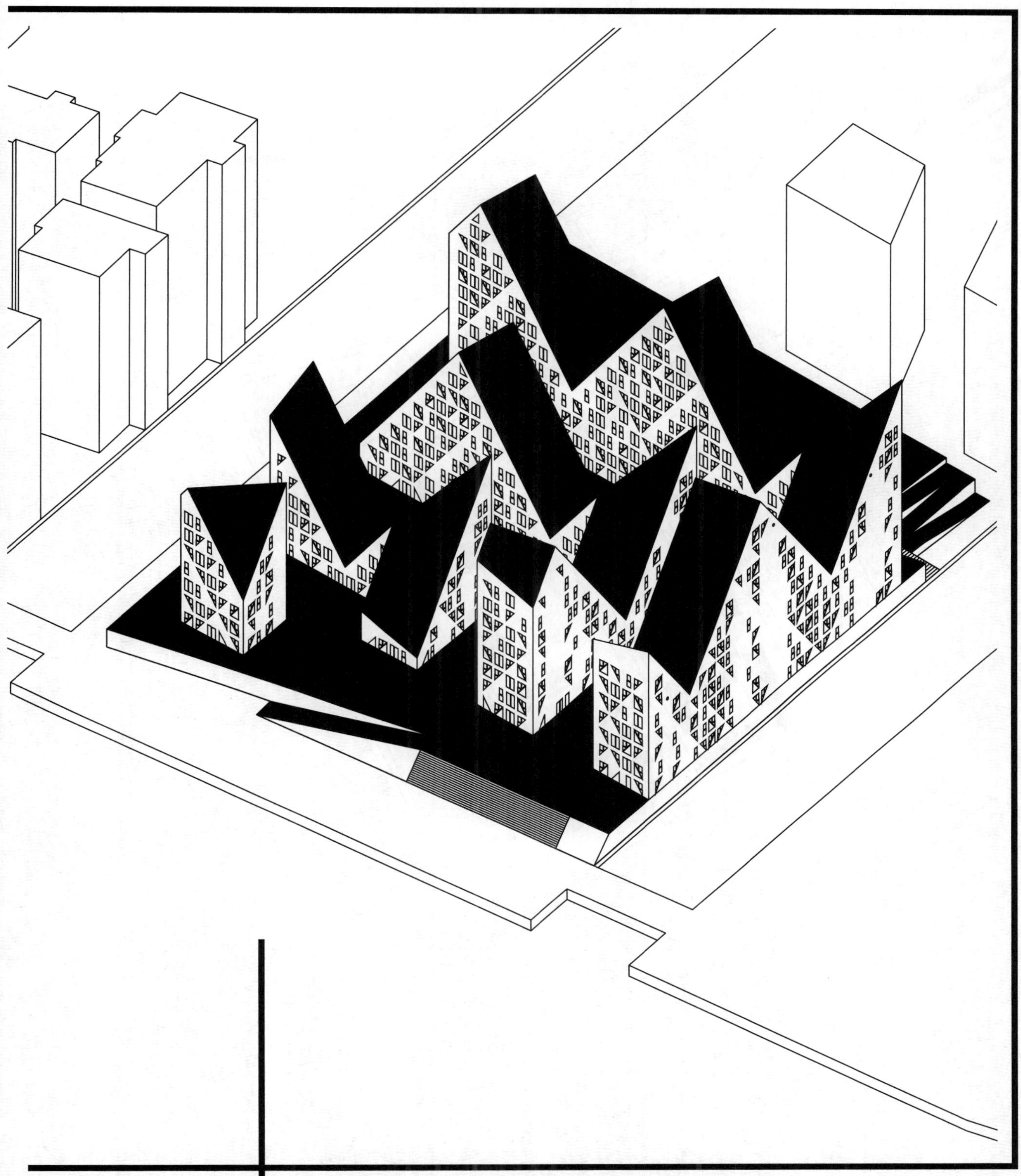

Axonometry of Isbjerget.

SeARCH, Cebra and JDS turned the typical Aarhus perimeter urban block with inner courtyard into L-shaped rows of housing that open up towards the water. The peaks and valleys of the volume maximize sunlight and views from almost every apartment. Mimicking the mesmerizing colour range you see when looking into the cavities of icebergs, balconies shift from bright blue at lower level to pale blue at the top.

Site plan of Isbjerget.

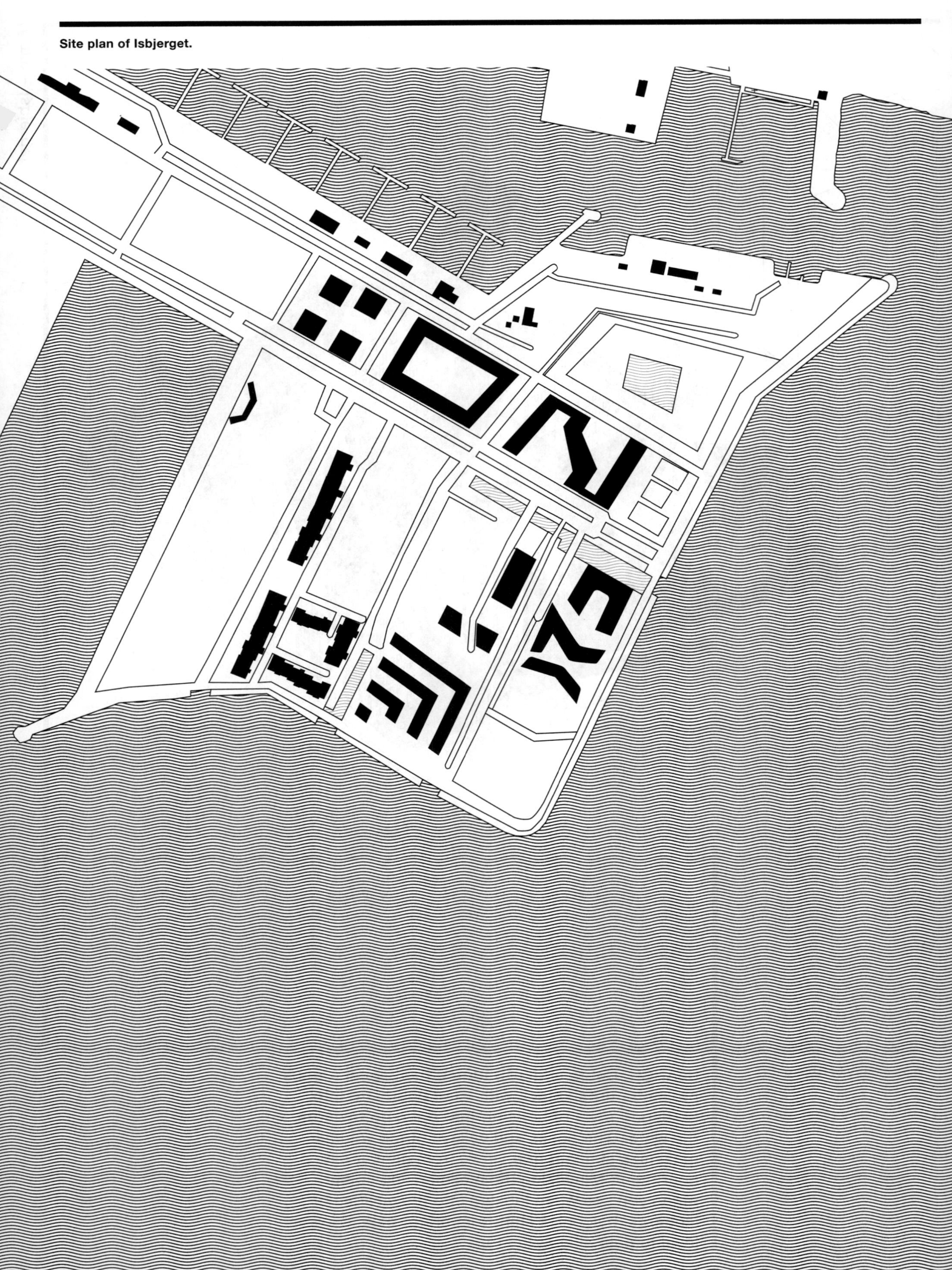

weber

Section of Isbjerget.

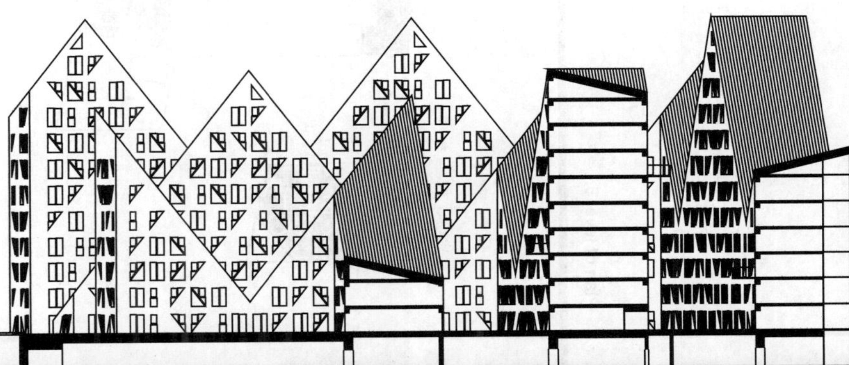

Colour gradient of balconies.

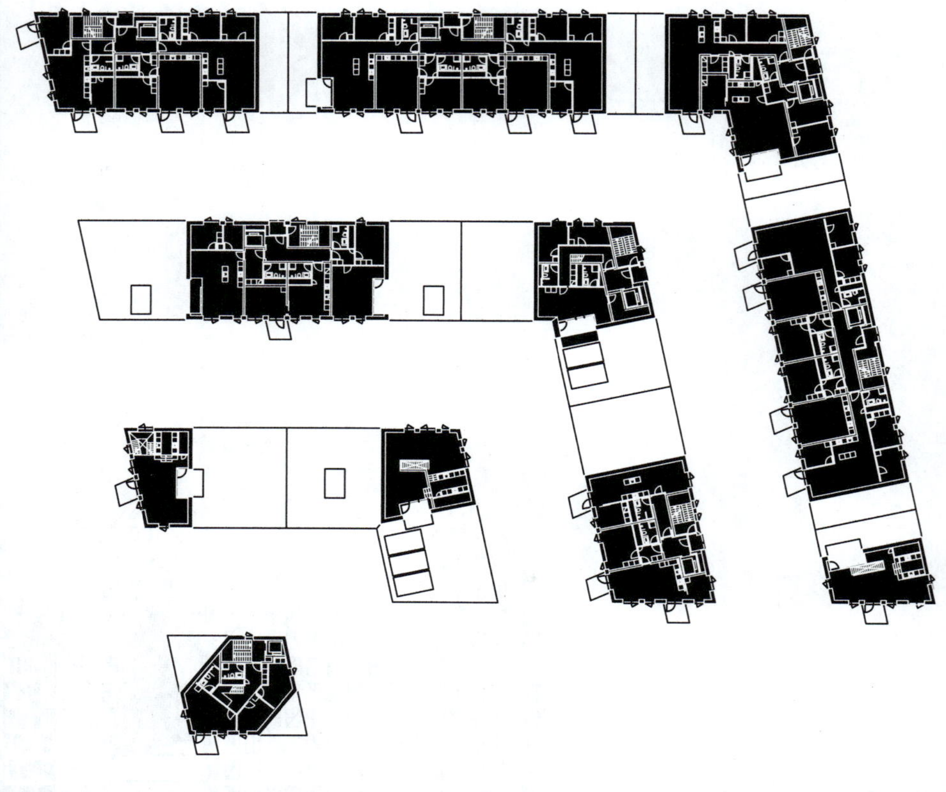
Plan of level 5.

These references to an iceberg make the building easily comprehensible. It has become a strong architectural landmark, its bold form completely at home alongside silos on the post-industrial harbour front, reconnecting the city with the sea.

Ground level plan of Isbjerget.

View from a balcony.

Summertime
Amsterdam, Netherlands
SeARCH
2014–2016

A Sunday on La Grande Jatte, Georges Seurat, 1884.

The not-so-new kid on the block, the pixel, was born around 1964. Over a century earlier, a similar picture element, the *Bildpunkt*, was patented by Paul Nipkow, and painters like Georges Seurat were experimenting with a pointillist style of painting.[90] Divisionists believed that by dissecting and juxtaposing colours, rather than physically mixing pigments, the painting would have a greater luminosity.[91] Shortly afterward, at the dawn of the twentieth century, the Lumière brothers developed the Autochrome photography technique, which produced natural colours through the superimposition of fine grains of potato starch. Cubism followed, with Piet Mondrian working as Vincent van Gogh once did, breaking colours apart and abstracting the image. A truly pixelated style is evident in his *Boogie Woogie* paintings.

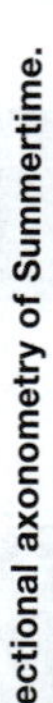

Sectional axonometry of Summertime.

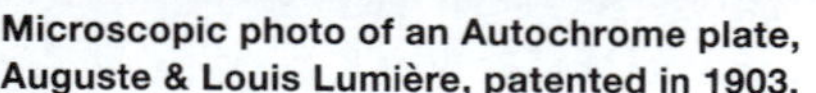

Microscopic photo of an Autochrome plate, Auguste & Louis Lumière, patented in 1903.

Victory Boogie-Woogie, Piet Mondrian, 1944.

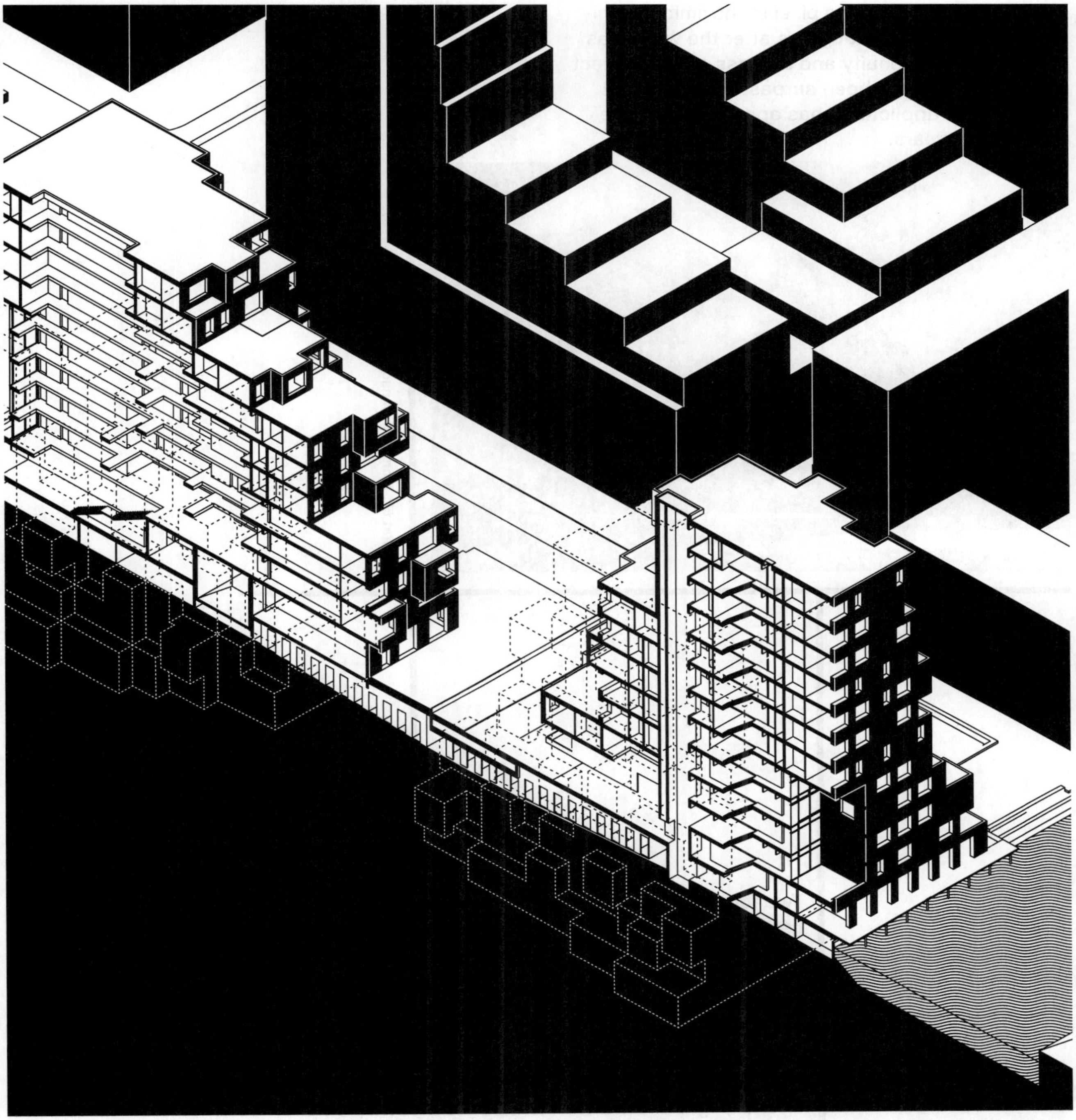

Abraham Lincoln, Béla Julesz, 1971.

All of these minimal point-and-colour-based techniques pivot around the idea that the eye is able to build a clear picture from very little input. Our ability to recognize Abraham Lincoln in Béla Julesz's image of only ten by ten pixels increases if we squint. The power and applicability of the pixel has turned out to be immense, and what molecules are for organic and inorganic life, the pixel has come to represent everything visually in the digital era.

Moshe Safdie pushed the pixel to the limit in architecture, just a couple of years after the word was coined.[92] The ingenuity and airiness of this project has seldom, if ever, been surpassed, and a real schism in its application has appeared over the past twenty years.

Habitat 67, Montreal, Canada, Moshe Safdie, 1967.

Two forms of architectural pixilation can be identified. The first aggregates smaller units to create a collective building. The size and position of these smaller parts respond and react to the surroundings and the inhabitants, as if receiving information and processing this into a larger form. This form of pixilation is about functionality, increasing the surface area of the building to offer air, light and views. Perhaps the most extreme version of this is found in informal development and vernacular building practices, where buildings are packed together tightly out of sheer need and mutual survival.

At the other end of this spectrum, the second form of pixilation attempts to disintegrate the overall volume of the building to create a visual statement. Everywhere from New York City to Bangkok, the sleek high-rise has begun to blur its silhouette. Here the pixel serves no functional purpose; it is purely formal, creating a 'larger image' rather than constituting a smaller grain. The only thing that links these two forms is the pixel itself. A pixel doesn't judge; it only registers.

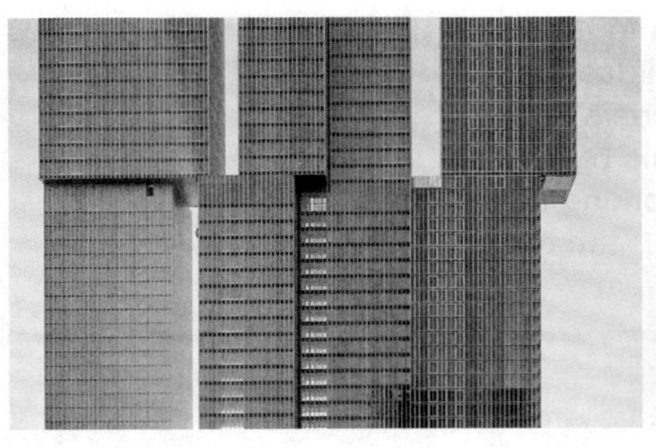

A.

B.

C.

D.

E.

F.

G.

H.

A. De Rotterdam, Rotterdam, Netherlands, OMA, 2013.
B. Hamburg Science Center, Hamburg, Germany, OMA, (unbuilt).
C. 56 Leonard Street, New York, USA, Herzog & de Meuron, 2017.
D. MahaNakhon Tower, Bangkok, Thailand, Buro Ole Scheeren, 2018.
E. 251 1st Street, New York, USA, ODA, 2017.
F. Pixel, Abu Dhabi, United Arab Emirates, MVRDV & BIG, (unbuilt).
G. LEGO House, Billund, Denmark, BIG, 2017.
H. Favela of Rocinha, Rio de Janeiro, Brazil, c.2010.

The Summertime towers stand out among the phallic office towers of Amsterdam's Zuidas, or south axis. As a result of the financial crisis of 2007, housing has been injected into this business district, but instead of rethinking or reworking the urban blocks, most projects simply keep the tower typology, perhaps terracing it slightly.

Site plan of Summertime.

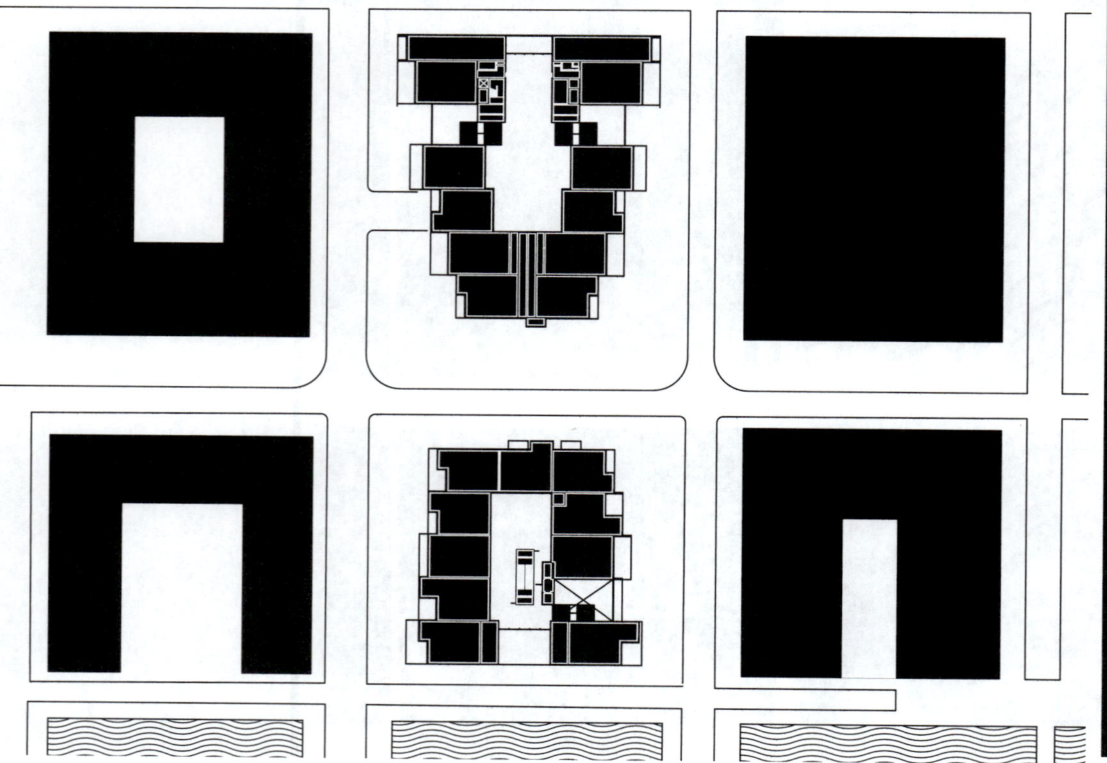

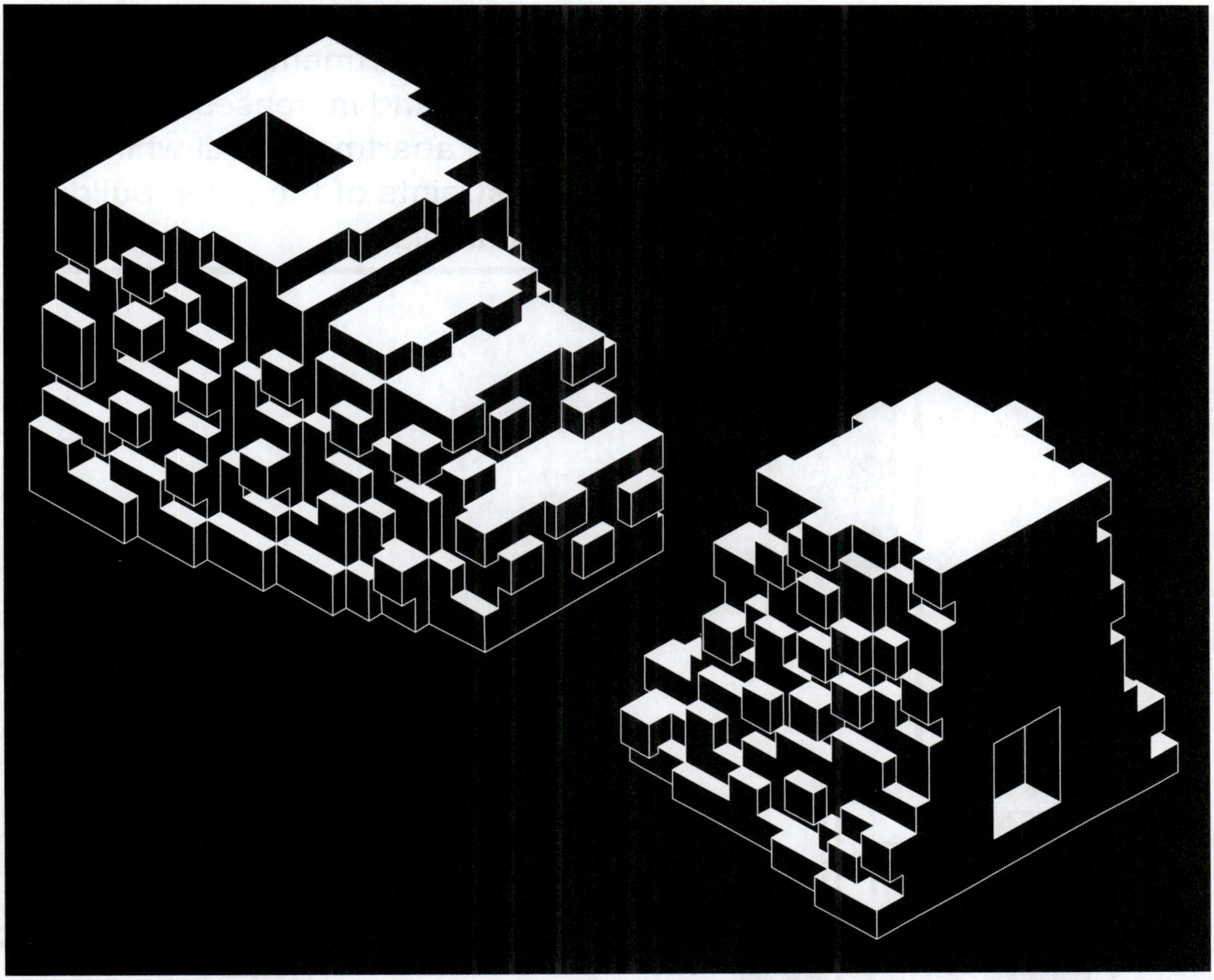

Axonometry of Summertime.

By stacking and shifting apartments like three-dimensional pixels, SeARCH was able to maximize views, sunlight and privacy within a high-density urban environment. Small shifts in and out give the towers a surprisingly random look, while the overall building is based on an economical and regular building grid.

This clever offsetting of spaces stretches the relative distance between apartments, offers a wide variety of outdoor spaces, and increases the individual legibility of the apartments. All while keeping within the constraints of the given building envelope and strict urban plan.

Section of Summertime. The tapered atrium is the result of three setbacks at levels three, six and eight.

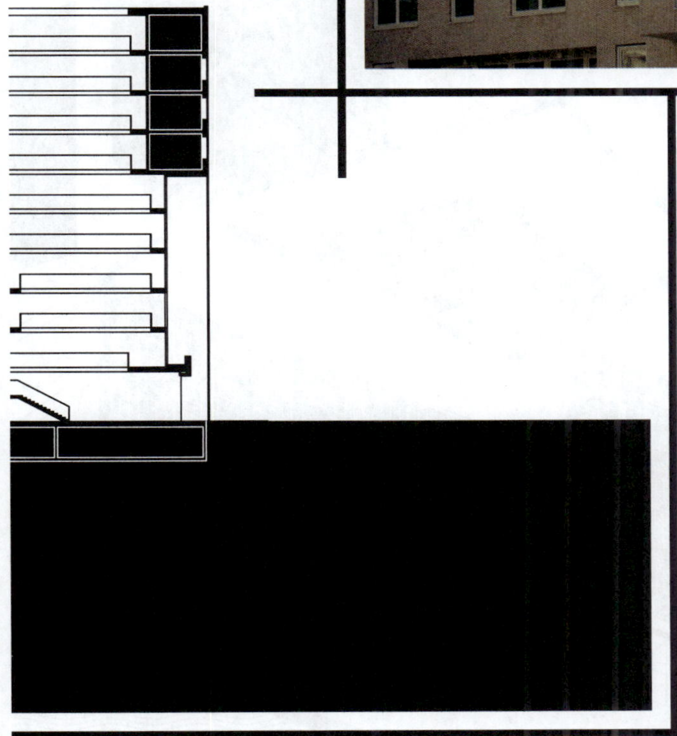

Another layer of pixilation is added to the facade and within the interior. As a tribute to the beautiful banknotes designed by Ootje Oxenaar, which disappeared with the appearance of the euro, images of the yellow fifty-guilder *Sunflower* and the purple 250-guilder *Lighthouse* are blown up and pixelated in both hallways. They also informed the coloured glass balustrades of the balconies that animate the facade.

Hotel Jakarta
Amsterdam, Netherlands
SeARCH
2014–2018

Hotel Jakarta juts out at the very tip of Java island, like a light flat-iron building about to set sail. To pay tribute to the significance of the site, where ships once sailed to Indonesia, a Dutch colony at the time, the idea arose to team up with both the 400-year-old Hortus Botanicus, Amsterdam's botanical garden, and the Tropenmuseum, the ethnographic museum, to realize an innovative and highly sustainable hotel.

Axonometry of Hotel Jakarta.

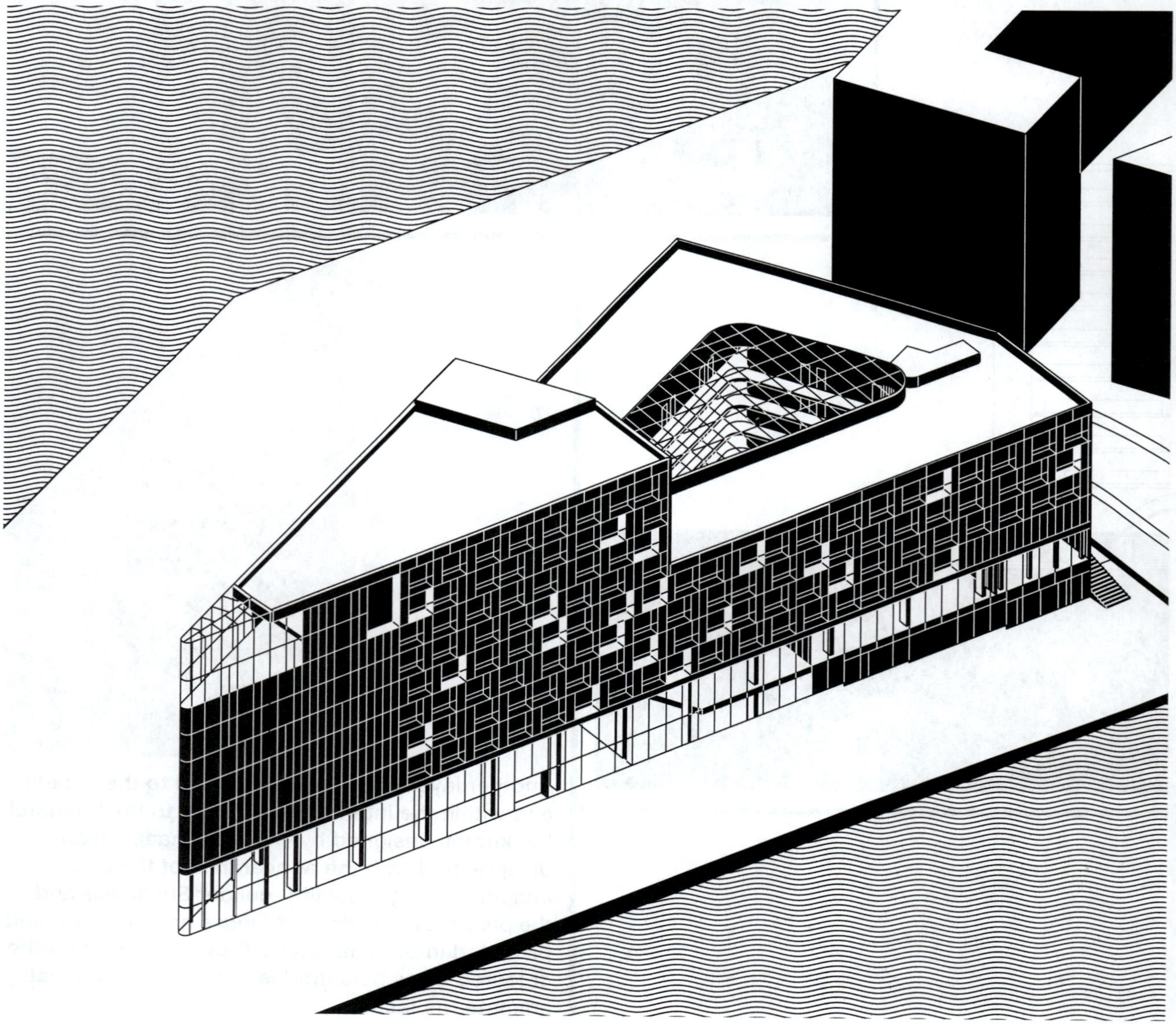

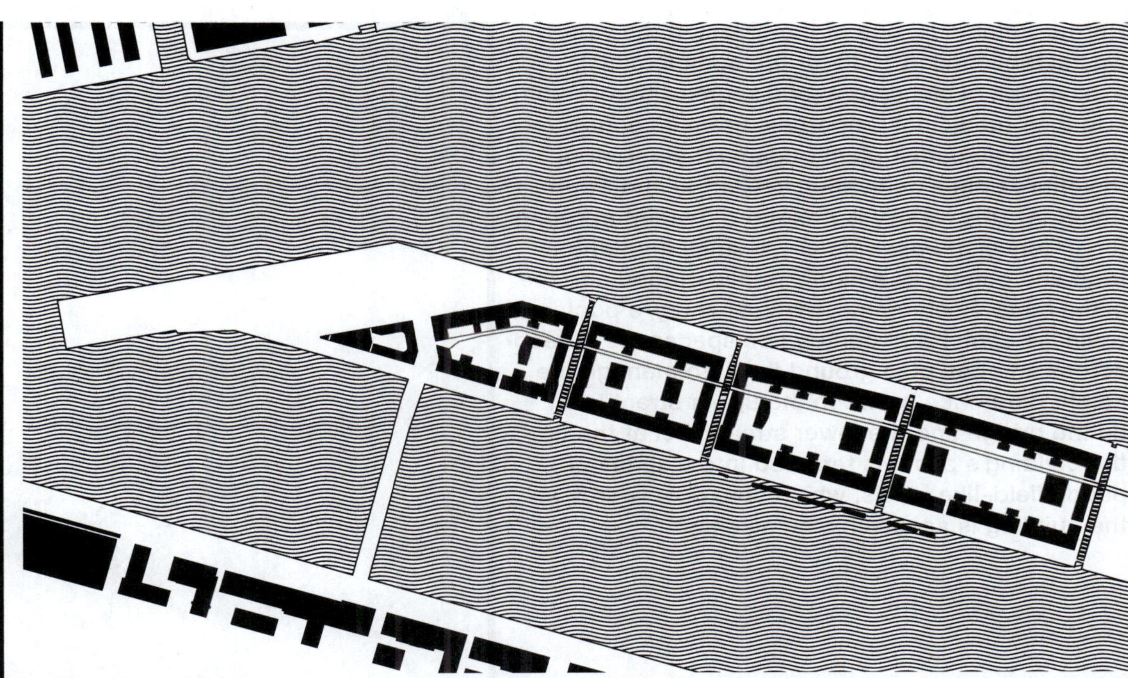

Site plan of Hotel Jakarta.

Hotel Jakarta is an energy neutral building, with a 30-metre-high load-bearing timber structure. Over two hundred rooms, of identical prefabricated timber modules, wrap around the full perimeter of the strict triangular urban envelope. Instead of filling the remaining internal space with programme, a subtropical garden extends the full height of the central void. This satellite of Hortus Botanicus is comprised exclusively of Indonesian flora.

For hotel guests and Indonesian jungle to cohabit, natural elements of air, light and water must be let in. Stored beneath the building for irrigation are 160 000 litres of water (collected from the roof and drawn from the IJ River beside it). The roof is a delicate balance of semi-transparent photovoltaics and glass to provide both shade and light, and both roof and facade can be opened so the building can breathe.

Hortus Botanicus, one of the oldest in the world, was established in 1638 for the commercial exploitation of plants as a food source and research into their medicinal properties. From its conservatory, a single coffee plant became the parent of the entire coffee cultivation in Central and South America. This history is honoured by reinterpreting the Indonesian *Pasar Malam*, a small market for food and coffee, as a highly public ground surface in the hotel. Restaurants, bars, a bakery, a pool, a wellness centre and conference spaces are spread across an open plan ground floor. To manage the height difference between the upper street level by the bridge and the lower street level at the tip, the building's plinth is terraced into a series of paddy field–like levels, which step downwards so the building is accessible on all sides.

Rendering of terraced ground floor.

Botanical illustration of *Coffee arabica*.

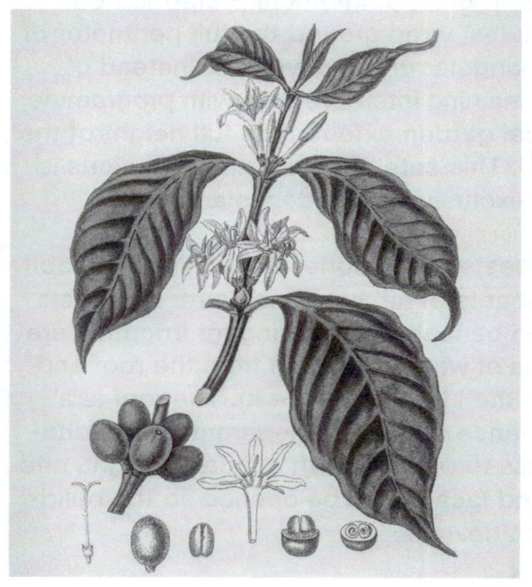

Hotel Jakarta dissolves the stuffy, dark European hotel into a light, airy frame that invites natural elements in and opens itself up to the neighbourhood around it.

Level 4 plan of Hotel Jakarta.

Section of Hotel Jakarta.

HOTEL JAKARTA
DWAW

MSC

HOTEL JAKARTA

7
6
5
4
3
2

67 [p. 1267] Alexandra Lange, "Philip Johnson's Not Glass Houses", *New York Times Style Magazine* (13 February 2015). Accessed June 2018.

68 [p. 1268] María Jesús Espinosa de los Monteros, "Espai Verd una catedral urbana", *Desfici Magazine* 9 (November 2017). Translated by Paula Ferro Delgado.

69 [p. 1268] The company name in full was Espacio S.L. Centro de Investigación de Arquitectura, Ingenieria, software e inteligencia artificial.

70 [p. 1269] Grupo Malavarrosa, "Ciclo de Visitas de Arquitectura. Espai Verd", *Viernes* (11 March 2016). Alvaro G. Devis, "¿Y si el Futuro se Estuviera Escribiendo en Valencia?", *Las Provincias* (7 May 2018).

71 [p. 1272] Parallels can be drawn with "Walden 7", Carve, 1042, and "Habitat 67", Mimic, 1188.

72 [p. 1273] Discussed by Professor Serra in María Jesús Espinosa de los Monteros, "Espai Verd una catedral urbana" (above, note 68).

73 [p. 1273] Ibid.

74 [p. 1274] Fruto Vivas quoted in Juan Pedro Posani, *Fruto Vivas, Una Hipótesis Explicativa* (Caracas: Ediciones MiNCI, 2018), 7. Translated by Paula Ferro Delgado.

75 [p. 1274] See speculative urban models, "Introduction", Mimic, 1160.

76 [p. 1276] Juan Pedro Posani, *Fruto Vivas, Una Hipótesis Explicativa*, 10. Translated by Paula Ferro Delgado.

77 [p. 1277] "We push the limits of the structure in order to reach the maximum efficiency, with the least matter. In doing so, we ask the building to evolve as life does. Let the city change as the forest does: without dying, in harmony with nature, in an intimate relation with a dialectical world (but on the gregarious scale of man) and where love becomes possible in urban structures." Posani, *Fruto Vivas, Una Hipótesis Explicativa*, 2 . Translated by Paula Ferro Delgado.

78 [p. 1277] "In nature we find the management of convective air currents. Trees are the best example. Heat from the sun causes water to evaporate in the leaves and this drop of temperature produces an updraft, so the interior air of the trees is permanently renewed. In developing this work, I applied this quality to the building, and baptized these buildings Trees for Living." Fruto Vivas quoted at the building's website. Accessed 4 December 2018. Translated by Paula Ferro Delgado.

79 [p. 1278] Vladimir Belogolovsky, "Emilio Ambasz: I Detest Writing Theories, I Prefer Writing Fables", *Arch Daily* (27 January 2017). Accessed 4 November 2019.

80 [p. 1281] Amy Kraft, "Why Manhattan's Green Roofs Don't Work and How to Fix Them", *Scientific American* (17 May 2013); and Jim Schneider, "Vegetated-Roof Failure Teaches Lessons", *Architect Magazine* (13 May 2009).

81 [p. 1281] Emilio Ambasz, quoted in Y-Jean Mun-Delsalle, "ACROS Fukuoka Prefectural International Hall Shows How Japan Is at the Forefront of Façade Greening", *Forbes Magazine* (19 February 2017). Accessed 2 February 2019.

82 [p. 1299] Diana Balmori, "In Conversation", Mimic, 1301–1307.

83 [p. 1300] Jake Nevins, "The Upside Down: Inside Manhattan's Lowline Subterranean Park", *Guardian* (6 April 2019). Accessed 16 April 2019.

84 [p. 1306] See "Entelechy II", Mimic, 1248–1267.

85 [p. 1306] See "Westin Bonaventure", Carve, 1054–1071.

86 [p. 1309] Prefabricated concrete aerial watchtowers, with a honeycomb-like structure, were built by the Schokbeton company in the 1950s, located in Bladel, Maashees, Oudemirdum, Winschoten and Schoonderbeek. Also see documentary "Onzichtbaar Nederland over veiligheid", *VPRO*, 6:40, Netherlands, 2016.

87 [p. 1320] Francis Bacon, *Essays* (1625); and John Owen's writings (1643).

88 [p. 1320] Lea Olsson and Jan Loerakker, "The Story Behind Failure: Copenhagen's Business District Ørestad", *Failed Architecture* (12 September 2013). Accessed 3 March 2019.

89 [p. 1320] Stan Majoor, "Urban Megaprojects in Crisis? Ørestad Copenhagen Revisited", *European Planning Studies* 23, no. 12 (5 March 2015).

90 [p. 1338] Paul Julius Gottlieb Nipkow invented a spiral-perforated disk which divides a picture into a linear sequence of points, patented on 15 January 1885. Neo-Impressionism was a term coined by French art critic Félix Fénéon in 1886 to describe the pointillist style of Georges Seurat.

91 [p. 1338] Additive luminosity is only applicable in the case of coloured light, not juxtaposed pigments; in reality, the luminosity of two pigments next to each other is just the average of their individual luminosities. Alan Lee, "Seurat and Science", *Art History* 10 (1987), 203–224.

92 [p. 1340] The word 'pixel' was coined in 1965 by Frederic C. Billingsley to describe the picture elements of video images from space probes to the Moon and Mars. Billingsley, "Processing Ranger and Mariner Photography", *Computerized Imaging Techniques, Proceedings of SPIE* 10 (1967), 1–19.

dig it!
Building Bound to the Ground
—
List of figures
Bibliography
About the authors
Credits
Acknowledgements

List of figures:

All photographs made by Iwan Baan and all drawings made by SeARCH unless otherwise stated.
In reproducing the images contained in this publication, SeARCH has made every effort to obtain the permission of the rights holders. In any instances where the rights holders could not be located, it requests any contact information concerning such rights be forwarded, so that they may be contacted for future editions.

p.80 Plan of ideal city by Vincenzo Scamozzi, 1615. JR James Archive.
p.80 Seventeenth-century map of the city of Palmanova, 1597. Georg Braun & Frantz Hogenberg. *Cities of the World*, Cologne, 1572–1680.
p.81 Depiction by Giovanni Battista Piranesi, Antichità Romane, 1756. Le antichità Romane, t. 1, tav. IV. Forma Urbis Romae, 1756.
p.81 Fragment of the Forma Urbis Romae, 200–300 CE. Stanford Digital Forma Urbis Romae Project.
p.82 A section of La Nuova Topografia di Roma, Giovanni Battista Nolli, 1748. Courtesy of Vincent J. Buonanno. Nuova pianta di Roma data in luce da Giambattista Nolli l'anno MDCCXLVIII, etching and engraving, 1748.
p.83 Hôtel de Beauvais by Antoine Le Pautre, 1652–1655. Derived from Michael Dennis, *Court and Garden*, 1986. Altered by SeARCH.
p.84 Hôtel de La Vrillière, François Mansart, 1635–1640. Derived from Michael Dennis, *Court and Garden*, 1986. Altered by SeARCH.
p.85 Ground floor (below) and first floor (above), Hotel Lambert by Louis Le Vau 1642–1644. Derived from Michael Dennis, *Court and Garden*, 1986. Altered by SeARCH.
p.86 Hôtel Guimard by Claude-Nicolas Ledoux, 1770–1772. Derived from Michael Dennis, *Court and Garden*, 1986. Altered by SeARCH.
p.87 Hôtel de Thelusson by Claude-Nicolas Ledoux, 1778–1783. Derived from Michael Dennis, *Court and Garden*, 1986. Altered by SeARCH.
p.87 Villa Almerico Capra, commonly known as La Rotonda, by Andrea Palladio, 1567–1592. Hans A. Rosbach.
p.88 A. Painted garden, Villa of Livia in Rome, 39 BCE. Miguel Hermoso Cuesta, 2014.
C. Painted wallcoverings of the Bartolotti House by Isaac de Moucheron, eighteenth century. Bjarne Mastenbroek.
D. The Crystal Palace, Joseph Paxton, 1851. Philip Henry Delamotte, 1854. Smithsonian Libraries.
F. *The Paintings (with Us in the Nature)*, Gilbert & George, 1972. Collection Kröller-Müller Museum, Otterlo, Netherlands. Purchased with support from the BankGiro Lottery, through the Kröller-Müller Fund, the National Acquisition Fund of the Ministry of Education, Culture and Science, the Mondriaan Foundation, the Rembrandt Association and its Titus Fund, the SNS REAAL Fund.
p.89 Painted garden, Villa of Livia in Rome, 39 BCE. Miguel Hermoso Cuesta, 2014.
p.91 Painted wallcoverings of the Bartolotti House by Isaac de Moucheron, eighteenth century. Bjarne Mastenbroek.
p.92 The Crystal Palace, Joseph Paxton, erected for The Great Exhibition of 1851. Philip Henry Delamotte, 1854. © Victoria and Albert Museum. Prints, Drawings & Paintings Collection.
p.94 *The Paintings (with Us in the Nature)*, Gilbert & George, 1972. Collection Kröller-Müller Museum, Otterlo, Netherlands. Purchased with support from the BankGiro Lottery, through the Kröller-Müller Fund, the National Acquisition Fund of the Ministry of Education, Culture and Science, the Mondriaan Foundation, the Rembrandt Association and its Titus Fund, the SNS REAAL Fund.
p.95 *The City as an Egg*, Cedric Price, 1982. Cedric Price fonds, Canadian Centre for Architecture, Montréal.
p.95 Urban sprawl of Greater London, Patrick Abercrombie, 1944. Courtesy of the JR James Archive.
p.96 The Thames in London was referred to as a 'monster soup', William Heath, 1828. Hand coloured etching, Trustees of the British Museum, 1828.
p.96 The three magnets of Ebenezer Howard, Garden Cities of Tomorrow, 1902. Ebenezer Howard. *Garden Cities of Tomorrow.* London : Swan Sonnenschein & Co., 1902.
p.97 Model for a ward and centre of a Garden City, Ebenezer Howard, 1902. Ebenezer Howard. *Garden Cities of Tomorrow.* London : Swan Sonnenschein & Co., 1902
p.98 Satellite towns around London, C. B. Purdom, "An Introductory Chapter", in *Town Theory and Practice*, London: Benn Brothers Limited, 1921, 32.
p.99 Aerial of Letchworth Garden City. Letchworth Garden City Heritage Foundation.
p.100 Modernist space was defined by air, light and freedom, Le Corbusier, 1935. © Fondation Le Corbusier/ADAGP, c/o Pictoright Amsterdam 2019.
p.101 Ville Contemporaine, 1922. © Fondation Le Corbusier/ADAGP, c/o Pictoright Amsterdam 2019.
p.101 Le Corbusier's Plan Voisin proposed the erasure of the traditional urban fabric of Paris in favour of a grid of twentieth-century towers, 1925. © Fondation Le Corbusier/ADAGP, c/o Pictoright Amsterdam 2019.
p.102 During the 1950s large areas of central New York City, like the site above which is now the Lincoln Center, were demolished. This slum clearance displaced thousands and forever altered the urban fabric. Committee on Slum Clearance. *Lincoln Square*. New York: Charles Francis Press. The New York Public Library Digital Collections, 1956.
p.103 Los Angeles's Four Level Interchange of 1953 was a connector within the modern decentralized metropolis. Courtesy of the California Historical Society Collection, USC Libraries.
p.104 Democracity designed by Henry Dreyfuss, 1939. Vogue Magazine, May 1, 1939.
p.104 New York World's Fair organized by Robert Moses, 1964. AP Photo/John Lindsay.
p.105 Nuclear weapon testing at Bikini Atoll, mid-1946, less than a year after the destruction of Nagasaki. The "Baker" explosion, July 1946. United States Department of Defense.
p.106 Aerial spraying of DDT to control the tussock moth, Latah County, Idaho, 1947. Philip C. Johnson, 1947. Western Forest Insect Work Conference archives, Bureau of Entomology and Plant Quarantine, Coeur d'Alene Forest Insect Laboratory, 1175. USDA Forest Service, Pacific Northwest Region.
p.106 Apollo 8's view of earth rising over the moon has proved to be the most enduring image we have of our fragile world. NASA, 1968.
p.107 Deep ploughing of virgin topsoil caused severe dust storms from 1934 to 1940 in Texas and Oklahoma. *Heavy black clouds of dust rising over the Texas Panhandle, Texas, March 1936.* Library of Congress, Prints and Photographs Division, 20540.
p.107 This affected 400,000 square kilometres of land, earning the area the name the Dust Bowl. *Buried machinery in barn lot, May 1936.* United States Department of Agriculture, 00di0971.
p.108 The Great Leap Forward was an effort to rapidly transform the People's Republic of China from an agrarian to an industrialist society, 1958 to 1962. Unknown photographer, 1958.
p.109 François, a local postman, becomes obsessed with keeping up with the speed and efficiency of the US postal service air delivery by retrofitting his bicycle. *Jour de Fête,* Jacques Tati, 1949. Jour de fête de Jacques Tati (1949) © Les Films de Mon Oncle – Specta Films C.E.P.E.C.
p.109 Frustrated with automated, ultra-modern surburbia, Monsieur Hulot pines for his muddled urban apartment. *Mon Oncle*, Jacques Tati, 1957. Mon Oncle de Jacques Tati (1958) © Les Films de Mon Oncle – Specta Films C.E.P.E.C.
p.109 The homogenous architecture of the modern city in *Playtime*, Jacques Tati, 1967. PlayTime de Jacques Tati (1967) © Les Films de Mon Oncle – Specta Films C.E.P.E.C.
p.110 The five Hötorget buildings (1952–1966) of Stockholm were designed by various architects but their similarity highlights a certain dogmatism. They would be completely at home in Tati's *Playtime*. John Willian Reps, John Reps Papers, #15-2-1101. Division of Rare and Manuscript Collections, Cornell University Library.
p.111 Social centre for a factory in Baden, Switzerland. *L'Architecture d'Aujourd'hui*, January 1957, 78-79.
p.112-113 The J Hancook Company, Kansas (left) and the Bank of Commerce Dusseldorf (right). *L'Architecture d'Aujourd'hui*, January 1964, 12-13.
p.114 Dreischeibebhaus, Düsseldorf, Germany, by Helmut Hentrich & Hubert Petschnigg, 1957–1960. Unknown photographer.
p.115 Golden Lane project, Alison & Peter Smithson, 1952. The Smithson Family Collection.
p.116 Housing for the elderly. De Drie Hoven, Amsterdam (Demolished). Herman Hertzberger. Internal street of De Drie Hoven, 1975. Herman Hertzberger. © Willem Diepraam.
p.118 Yona Friedman envisioned a *Spatial City* of adaptable habitats suspended over Paris, 1960. © Yona Friedman.
p.119 Cushicle, Michael Webb, 1964. Archigram / unknown photographer.
p.119 Buckminster Fuller's Geodesic dome, US pavilion, Expo 67, Montreal. Bill Engdahl, Montreal, Canada,

p.205 Section of Chaitya hall, 200–100 BCE. Plate XXXVI, Longitudinal section of Ajanta Cave XIX. Drawn by James Burgess in James Fergusson. *The Cave Temples of India*. London: Allen, 1880. Altered by SeARCH.
p.222 Recycling nails, Addis Ababa. Bjarne Mastenbroek.
p.222 Plastic strapping from cargo packaging. Bjarne Mastenbroek.
p.239 At Biete Ghiorgis, the entry is via a slit in the earth, pictured here on the lower right. Allen Jones.
p.241 Ethiopian headrest. Jean Doresse. Inventory number: 999-210. Museum of Natural History and Ethnography Colmar. 1999.
p.255 Samuel Aroutiounian.
p.256 Stone Age burial mound, Newgrange, Ireland 3200 BCE. Tjp Finn.
p.256 Clava Clairn burial mound, Scotland, 2500 BCE. Dave Conner.
p.256 Barclodiad y Gawres burial mound, Wales, 3000 BCE. © Crown copyright Cadw. 2019.
p.258 Jorge Láscar.
p.261 Jorge Láscar.
p.262 Wilderness Act of the United States, 1964. Mark Lisac, U.S. Fish and Wildlife Service.
p.262 Goat with a Bird by Jean Dubuffet, 1954. Ink transfer and ink on paper, 46.2 x 56.7 cm. The Joan and Lester Avnet Collection. Acc. no.:65.1978. New York, Museum of Modern Art (MoMA). © 2019. Digital image, The Museum of Modern Art, New York/Scala, Florence.
p.263 City, Michael Heizer, 1972–2020. © 2019 Google Maps.
p.264 Roden Crater, James Turrell, 1979–present. © 2019 Google Earth.
p.265 Ecokathedraal by Louis Guillaume le Roy, 1970. Esther Mecredy.
p.267 Montaña de Tindaya. Jose Mesa.
p.267 *Consejo al Escpacio* (Advice to space VIII), Eduardo Chillida, 2000. Bjarne Mastenbroek.
p.270 House to Watch the Night Skies, Aladab, Not VItal, 2006. Not Vital.
p.270 JOSUJO (Disappearing house), Sent, Not Vital, 2007. Not Vital.
p.272 Aitor Ortiz. Not Vital / Archiv Kerber Verlag.
p.272 NotOna, Patagonia by Not Vital. Aitor Ortiz / Not Vital.
p.274 Ensamble Studio.
p.275 Ronald Halbe.
p.279 Eight villas in Dali, China, by Junya Ishigami, 2017. © Giovanni Emilio Galanello.
p.280 Construction of House & Restaurant. © junya. ishigami+associates.
p.282 © Gordon Calder.
p.283 Pei Cobb Freed & Partners.
p.286 Unknown.
p.287 Tomas Peterson.
p.288 © John Gollings.
p.291 Richard Powers. Michael Wee.
p.293 Unknown photographer.
p.294 *Death of St. Rodegunda*, Federico García Lorca, 1929. Laura García-Lorca, Fundación Federico García Lorca.
p.294 *Two Figures over a Grave*, Federico García Lorca, ca 1929–1931. Laura García-Lorca. Fundación Federico García Lorca.
p.296 Petr Šmídek
p.296 *Kleine Welten XI*, Vasily Kandinsky, 1922. Lithograph from a portfolio of twelve prints, six lithographs (including two transferred from woodcuts), four drypoints, and two woodcuts, plate: 23.7x 19.7 cm; sheet: 30.3 x 26.8 cm. Publisher: Propylaeen-Verlag, Berlin. Printer: Reineck & Klein, Weimar. Edition: 230 (including deluxe edition of 30 on "japan" paper and regular edition of 200 on "Buetten" paper). Purchase. Acc.n.: 335.1940. © 2019. Digital image, The Museum of Modern Art, New York/Scala, Florence.
p.297 Dieter Janssen.
p.298 Houndstooth, or 'Pied-de-poule'. Kotivalo.
p.298 *Day and Night*, M.C. Esher, 1938. M.C. Escher's "Day and Night" © 2019 The M.C. Escher Company-The Netherlands. All rights reserved. www.mcescher.com.
p.302 *Jardin d'émail*, Jean Dubuffet, 1974. Dqfn13.
p.303 *The Endless House*, Frederick Kiesler, 1950–1960. Exterior view of the Endless House, model, 1958. New York, Museum of Modern Art (MoMA). Gelatin silver print, 25.4 x 20.3 cm. Architecture & Design Study Center, photograph by Geroge Barrows. Acc. n.: AD521.© 2019. Digital image, The Museum of Modern Art, New York/ Scala, Florence.
p.304 Laurian Ghinitoiu.
p.309 Leonardo Finotti.
p.309-310 Bjarne Mastenbroek.
p.315-322 Bjarne Mastenbroek.
p.323 Allegorical engraving of the Vitruvian primitive hut in the frontispiece of Marc-Antoine Laugier, *Essai sur l'architecture*, 2nd ed. 1755. Engraving by Charles-Dominique-Joseph Eisen. The Miriam and Ira D. Wallach Division of Art, Prints and Photographs: Art & Architecture Collection, The New York Public Library Digital Collections.
p.324 Gerard Noodtstraat, Nijmegen, Netherlands, SeARCH, 1993–1996. Rik Klein Gotink.
p.325 Section of the dome of Santa Maria del Fiore, 1613. Drawn by Lodovico Cardi. Department of Prints and Drawings. Uffizi, n.7980A.
p.327 I struzioni per l'uso di Salottobuono, Abitare, 499, 2010. Altered by SeARCH.
p.328 Typical Valser barns. Heinrich Malling, circa 1903–1908.
p.338 Kate Gowan.
p.340 Bjarne Mastenbroek.
p.342 Graubündner chalet. Bjarne Mastenbroek.
p.345 Cow identifier. Teunis Bunt.
p.361 Map of the New Dutch Waterline, 1815. *Zuider Waterlinie*, Studio Marco Vermeulen, 2016. Altered by SeARCH. *Jonah and the Whale*, Pieter Lastman, 1621. Düsseldorf, Museum Kunstpalast. © Museum Kunstpalast - Walter Klein - ARTOTHEK.
p.362 Fort Vechten, 1925. Netherlands Institute of Military History.
p.363 Ossip van Duivenbode.
p.363 Bjarne Mastenbroek.
p.367 Rienbouw.
p.368 Partly sunken car park. Bjarne Mastenbroek.
p.369 Maison à Bordeaux, OMA, 1998. © Hans Werlemann.
p.371 Bjarne Mastenbroek.
p.372 Cross section of an Iglulik Snowhouse (igloo), Franz Boas, 1888. Franz Boas, *The Central Eskimo*, 1888.
p.372 Villa Cassel, Switzerland. Fiesch.
p.376 Clochán (beehive hut), Ireland. Dirk Huth.
p.376 Igloo, Alaska. Frank E. Kleinschmidt, 1924. Library of Congress Prints and Photographs Division, LC-USZ62-135985.
p.376 Ocmulgee Earth lodge, USA. Ahoerstemeier.
p.377 Fred Ernst.
p.378 Ossip van Duivenbode.
p.380 Johannes Schwartz.

Embed:

p.393 Null Stern Hotel, Teufen, Switzerland, Atelier für Sonderaufgaben, 2009. Frank and Patrik Riklin, Concept Artists. Daniel Charbonnier, Hospitality Professional.
p.395 Lever House, New York, US, Gordon Bunshaft and Natalie de Blois, 1952. Unknown photographer.
p.396 Zonnestraal Sanatorium, Hilversum, Netherlands, Jan Duiker, 1931. Edward Tyler.
p.397 A. Olympic Archery Range, Barcelona, Spain, Enric Miralles & Carme Pinos, 1991. Bjarne Mastenbroek.
B. Siedlung Halen, Bern, Switzerland, Atelier 5, 1955–1961. Atelier 5.
C. Buddhist Academy, Larung Gar, Tibet, 1980. Valerian Guillot.
D. Settlement of Oia, Greece. Harvey Barrison.
E. Rockland Ranch, Moab, Utah, 1980–present. Keofilms.
F. Sar Agha Seyed, Chaharmahal-Va-Bakhtiari province, Iran. Mirjam Terpstra.
G. Athfield House & Studio, Wellington, New Zealand, Ian Athfield, 1965–present. Grant Sheehan.
H. Guadix, Spain. Luis Irisarri.
I. Il Magistero, Urbino, Italy, Giancarlo De Carlo, 1968–1976. Fulvio Palma.
J. Nawarla Gabarnmang, Australia. Dr. Bruno David.
K. Hanging Temple, Datong, China, 490 CE. Nicor.
L. Kumbum chorten, Tibet, 1427–1437. Jan Reurink.
M. The Great Wall of WA, Western Australia, Australia, Luigi Rosselli Architects, 2015. Edward Birch.
N. Alemdoune, Morocco. Jean-Marc Astesana.
O. Vardzia Monastery, Georgia, twelfth century. Ben van der Ploeg.
P. Positano, Italy. VV Nincic.
Q. Acusa Seca, Canary Islands. Sophie Merkens.
R. Mühlehalde Housing, Umiken, Hans Scherer, Strickler & Weber, Switzerland, 1962–1971. Edward C. Olencki. Art, Architecture & Engineering Library Online Image Collection.
S. Tolo House, Ribeira de Pena, Álvaro Siza,

Modulor. © Fondation Le Corbusier/ADAGP, c/o Pictoright Amsterdam 2019.
p.515 'Roq' seen in relation to the old towns, Le Corbusier, 1949. © Fondation Le Corbusier/ ADAGP, c/o Pictoright Amsterdam 2019.
p.515 Le Corbusier's Cabanon, 1952. Tangopaso.
p.517 Marvin Zilm.
p.520 Rotsteinpass, Switzerland (top) and Siedlung Halen (bottom). Manfred Morgner, 2001. © lovingswitzerland, 2013.
p.521 Yukio Futagawa. Unknown.
p.522 Athfield House growing down the hill, 1990. Athfield Architects.
p.522 Ian Athfield and family on the roof. Athfield Architects.
p.528 Early stages of the Athfield House, 1974. Athfield Architects.
p.528 Athfield's village. Photograph by Grant Sheehan.
p.528 Ian Athfield on his roof. Athfield Architects.
p.529-534 Bjarne Mastenbroek.
p.538 Circulation space around the circular void. Photograph by Giorgio Casali. John Mckean. *Il Magistero: De Carlo's Dialogue with Historical Forms* [Speaking of Places]. Places, 16(1). 2004.
p.539 Fulvio.palma.
p.541 Limoncellista.
p.545 Veuveclicquot.
p.546 Staatsgalerie Stuttgart. travelux blog.
p.548 Ximo Michvilla, Flickr. Chia-Hsien Liao, Flickr.
p.550 Bjarne Mastenbroek.
p.551 *The Glass Mountain Shattered* by David Hockney in *Six Fairy Tales from the Brothers Grimm,* 1969. David Hockney, *The Glass Mountain (Old Rinkrack)*, 1969 (published 1970). Etching and soft-ground etching on handmade paper. Minneapolis Institute of Art, The Ethel Morrison Van Derlip Fund, P.74.53. © David Hockney.
p.553 Bjarne Mastenbroek.
p.553 Castillo de Morella, zwinger and bent entrance, 1300–1400. Millars.
p.553 Aerial view of terraced agricultural land, town of Morella and castle. NASA U.S. Geological Survey. © Google Earth.
p.555 Bjarne Mastenbroek.
p.556 Detail of the floor plan of the Olympic Archery training facility. Fundació Enric Miralles.
p.557 Painting of a battle between archers dated to the late Mesolithic in dubbed the earliest surviving image of combat, in Cueva del Roure, Morella la Vella, Spain. Eduardo Hernández Pacheco. *Estudios de arte prehistórico, Prospección de las pinturas rupestres de Morella la Vella*. Madrid, 1924.
p.558 Giant boulders at 2750m altitude in Valsertal, near the Dachberg summit. Bjarne Mastenbroek.
p.559 Micha L. Rieser.
p.560 Early sketch of Therme Vals by Peter Zumthor.
p.560 Detail of landscape near Dachberg summit, showing boulders at the same scale as the project in sketch. Bjarne Mastenbroek.
p.560 Cracks in quartzite stone layers. Bjarne Mastenbroek.
p.560 Kazunori Fujimoto.
p.561 Summer forest at Peil, the valley directly south of the village of Vals. Bjarne Mastenbroek.
p.564 Therme Vals rooftop extends the slope outwards. Kazunori Fujimoto.
p.565 Slender recesses in the roof let light into centre of Therme Vals. Kazunori Fujimoto.
p.567 From left to right, Borneo, Sporenburg and KNSM island, 1980. Archief van de Dienst Ruimtelijke Ordening. Stadsarchief Amsterdam. Rietveld Schröder House, Utrecht, Gerrit Rietveld, 1923–1924. © Gerrit Thomas Rietveld, Rietveld Schröder house, 1923–1924 c/o Pictoright Amsterdam 2019.
p.568 Row of 28 units with an alternative typology at the end. Christian Richters. Conceptual photo with real Smart cars, 1997. Christian Richters.
p.570 Christian Richters.
p.573 View from the hillside. Forgemind ArchiMedia.
p.575 The Q'eswachaka Bridge has been rebuilt continuously since the time of the Incas. Mi Perú.
p.575 *The Drawbridge* by Giovanni Battista Piranesi, 1761. Etching, 55 x 41 cm, plate 7, *Carceri d'Invenzione* (Imaginary Prisons), The Arthur Ross Collection, Yale University Art Gallery.
p.575 Forgemind ArchiMedia.
p.577 Hisao Suzuki.
p.592 Plan of the Red Fort in Dehli by John Murray, 1901. *A Handbook for Travellers in India, Burma, and Ceylon*, digitized by Prof. Emerita Frances W. Pritchett, Columbia University Library, May 2006.
p.592 *Red Fort* by Ghulam Ali Khan, 1852–1854.
p.592 Archaeological site of Mahasthangarh, Paundravardhanapura, 300 BCE. Shafiqul Islam Shiplu.
p.594 Ossip van Duivenbode.
p.594 Hotel Zodiaque, a mega-chalet in Anzère. Unknown.
p.594 Multi-gabled chalet, Anzère. Unknown.
p.597 Grand Chalet Balthus, Rossinière, 1752–1756. Bjarne Mastenbroek.
p.598 Ossip van Duivenbode.
p.599 Ossip van Duivenbode.
p.600 Ossip van Duivenbode.
p.600 Farnsworth House, Mies van der Rohe, 1945–1951. Victor Grigas.
p.600 Glass House, Philip Johnson, 1948–1949. Staib.
p.601 With heavier rainfall and overdevelopment along the riverbank, the frequency and intensity of flooding at the Farnsworth House has increased. Vince Michael.
p.602 Johnson's Painting Gallery is tucked within the same estate as the Glass House, 1965. Original plan by Philip Johnson, altered by SeARCH. Staib.
p.603 Historical map of the tidal environment of the Zuiderzee region, Christiaan Sgroten, 1573. "Delineatio Sinus Meridionalis Maris, Vulgo De Zuyder Zee; Phrisia occidentalis, et Watterlandia", Westfries Archief.
p.603 Skewed Stolp within the polder. © 2018 Google Maps.
p.615 Existing stolp on the left and skewed extension to the right. Ossip van Duivenbode.

Absorb:

p.623 Ideal cross section of the earth's crust. Traugott Bromme, *Atlas zu Humboldt's Kosmos*, 1854. Traugott Bromme & Alexander von Humboldt. *Atlas zu Alex. v. Humboldt's Kosmos*. Stuttgart: Krais & Hoffmann, Plate 8, 1854.
p.623 The largest man-made hole in Europe is the Hambach surface mine, Germany. Johannes Fasolt. Inspired by Ulrike.
p.624 Monastery of Simonos Petra, Mount Athos, 1257. Photograph by Frank R. Horlbeck. Copyright Board of Regents of the University of Wisconsin System. 1983.
p.626 Deep foundation pit of IJdock, Amsterdam, 2009. Ton van Rijn, Stadsarchief Amsterdam.
p.627 A. Fallingwater, Mill Run, USA, Frank Lloyd Wright, 1938. National Park Service.
B. Raymond Loewy House, Palm Springs, USA, Albert Frey, 1947. Julius Shulman.
C. Casa Prieto-Lopez, Mexico City, Luis Barragán, 1950. Steve Aldana.
D. Federico Gómez House, Mexico City, Francisco Artigas, 1951. Roberto Luna.
E. Berggasthaus, Äscher, Switzerland, 1856. ilirjan rrumbullaku.
F. Polonatalawa Estate, Nikarawetiya, Sri Lanka, Geoffrey Bawa, 1964. Sebastian Posingis.
I. Elrod House, Palm Springs, USA, John Lautner, 1968. Nelson-Moe Properties.
J. Volcano House, Newberry Springs, USA, Harold J. Bissner Jr, 1968. Zillow Group.
K. Casa do Penedo, Moreira do Rei, Portugal, 1974. Leonardo Finotti.
L. Casa Gerber, Angra dos Reis, Brazil, Paulo Mendes da Rocha, 1975. Feliciano Guimarães.
M. Fundación de César Manrique, Tahíche, Canary Islands, Cesar Manrique, 1982. Julian Weyer.
N. Kandalama Hotel, Dambulla, Sri Lanka, Geoffrey Bawa, 1991. Geoffrey Bawa.
O. Posbank Pavillion, Rheden, Netherlands, SeARCH, 2002. Christian Richters.
P. Massaro House, USA, Frank Lloyd Wright & Thomas Heinz, 2008. realtor.
Q. The Pierre, San Juan Island, USA, Olson Kundig, 2010. Benjamin Benschneider, Dwight Eschliman.
R. Summer House, Storfjord, Norway, Jensen & Skodvin Architects, 2013. Jan Olav Jensen.
S. Knapphullet, Sandefjord, Norway, Lund Hagem, 2014. Ivar Kvaal.
U. Museum Susch, Engadin Valley, Switzerland, Chasper Schmidlin & Lukas Voellmy, 2019. Conradin Frei.
p.628 Military bunker, Switzerland. Kecko.
p.629 Costa Brava Clube, Ricardo & Renato Menescal. 1962–1965. Ricardo e Renato Menescal Arquitetos.
p.629 Villa Malaparte in *Le Mépris*, Jean-Luc Godard, 1963. Jean-Luc Godard, *Le Mépris*, Georges de Beauregard, Carlo Ponti. Italy, 1963.
p.630 Boulder Garden Resort, Sri Lanka, Lalyn Collure, 2008. Ji Min An.

p.772 Seattle Central Library, OMA, 1999–2004. Philippe Ruault.
p.773 Acacia parquet of the Posbank Pavilion. Rheden, SeARCH, 1998–2002. Christian Richters.
p.774 The spiral across scales: DNA, shell, plant, hurricane, galaxy. SeARCH.
p.774 To fasten: Screw patent, P.L. Robertson, 1909. Unknown.
p.775 To raise water: Archimedes' screw, 250 BCE, still in common use for hydro power and water turbines. Ianmacm. In: *Chambers's Encyclopedia*, Philadelphia: J. B. Lippincott Company, 1875.
p.775 To fly: Spiralling Ornithopter, Leonardo da Vinci, 1485. Museo nazionale scienza e tecnologia Leonardo Da Vinci.
p.775 To define theory of elasticity: Coil sprint experiments, Robert Hooke, 1678. De potentia restitutiva.
p.775 To propel: Screw propeller, Francis Pettit, 1836. Unknown.
p.776 To sleep: Bed spring Patent No. 16972A, 7 April 1857. Unknown.
p.776 To light: Bulb patent No. 223898 with a coil as glowing tip, Thomas Edison, 27 January 1880. U.S. Patent.
p.776 To write: Stylographic Pen patent, No. 232804, Alonzo T. Cross, October 1880 (the spring was not for releasing the tip but for forcing ink into the tip of the scriber. U.S. Patent.
p.776 To drive (electric): Elektro Magnetic Motor, Nikola Tesla, 1 May 1888. Nikola Tesla Universe.
p.780 Chogha Zanbil, Khuzestan, Iran, 1250 - 640 BCE. ©2019 CNES, Google Earth.
p.780 Chogha Zanbil drawn by J.H. Sixties, 1966. Drawing by J.-H. Sixtus. After Ghirshman, 60, fig. 40. 1966.
p.780 View from the base of Nanna Ziggurat. Samantha Ciaramitaro. Operation Iraqi Freedom. U.S. Army.
p.781 Eanna Ziggurat at Warka, Iraq, 2018. Essam Al-Sudani.
p.782 Axonometry of the Nanna Ziggurat. Based on drawing by F.G. Newton in Leonard Wooley, *Sumerians*, 199. 1965. Drawn by SeARCH.
p.783 Tell el-Muqayyar, Iraq. ©2002 Digital Globe, Google Earth.
p.783 Plan of Nanna Ziggurat within the palace structure. Unknown.
p.786 Plan of the Palace of Sargon II, Dur Sharrukin. Derived from John Henry Wright. *A History of All Nations from the Earliest Times*. New York: Lea Brothers & Company, V.2. 81. 1905. Drawn by SeARCH.
p.787 City of Dur-Sharrukin, with the citadel and palace to the north. Derived from John Henry Wright. *A History of All Nations from the Earliest Times*. New York: Lea Brothers & Company, V.2. 80. 1905. Drawn by SeARCH.
p.787 Reconstruction of the ramped Ziggurat of Dur-Sharrukin by John Henry Wright, 1905. *A History of All Nations from the Earliest Times*. New York: Lea Brothers & Company, V.2. 93. 1905.
p.789 Plan of Etemenanki Ziggurat within city of Babylon. Deutsche Orient-Gesellscaft.
p.790 Shape of Etemenanki carved on a black stone, The Tower of Babel. Stele, 604-562 BCE. The Schoyen Collection.
p.791 Reconstruction by Zénaïde A. Ragozin, 1889. Mary Evans Picture Library.
p.791 Reconstruction by Robert Koldewey, 1913. Deutsche Orient-Gesellscaft.
p.791 Reconstruction by Hans-Jörg Schmid, 1999. Deutsche Orient-Gesellscaft.
p.791 Reconstruction by J.L Montero Fenollós, 2013. Univeristy of A Coruña.
p.793 A. *The Tower of Babel*, Cornelis Anthonisz, 1547. Rijksmuseum, Amsterdam, Netherlands.
B. *The Tower of Babel*, Pieter Bruegel the Elder, 1563. Museum Boijmans Van Beuningen, Rotterdam, Netherlands.
C. *The Tower of Babel*, Lucas van Valckenborch, 1568. Landesmuseum, Zürich, Switzerland.
D. *The Tower of Babel*, Abel Grimmer, 1570–1619. Alain.R.Truong.
E. *The Tower of Babel*, Tobias Verhaecht, 1585–1600. Norwich Castle Museum and Art Gallery. England
F. *The Tower of Babel*, Lucas van Valckenborch 1594. Musée du Louvre, Paris.
G. *The Tower of Babel*, Marten van Valckenborch, 1595. Staatliche Kunstsammlungen Dresden. Germany.
H. *The Tower of Babel*, Abel Grimmer, 1604. The Hatton Gallery King's College.
I. *The Tower of Babel*, Jan Micker, 1650. ARTNET.
J. *The Tower of Babel*, Athanasius Kircher, 1679. Universitätsbibliothek Heidelberg. Germany.
p.795 Reconstruction of the Pharos of Alexandria lighthouse, 280 BCE–1320 CE by H. Thiersch 1909. Hermann Thiersch. *Pharos; Antike, Islam und Occident; ein Beitrag zur Architekturgeschichte*. Lepzig: Teuber, 1909.
p.795 The Minaret al-Malwiya part of the Great mosque of Samarra. Reuters.
p.797 Depiction of the Minaret al-Malwiya in *The Confusion of Tongues* by Gustave Doré, 1865. Private collection.
p.799 The city of Samarra in Iraq. © 2005 Digital Globe, Google Earth.
p.800 Banked slope of the Rundetårn spiral ramp. Peter Hartley.
p.802 Ole Ritter set the current record of 55.3 seconds in the Rundetårn bike race in 1971. Morten Langkilde.
p.802 Kids during the Uniracer Rally, held since 1982, with a record time in 1989 of 1.48 minutes. Rundetaarn.
p.804 A. Mule ramp, White Tower of Thessaloniki, Greece, reconstructed in 1430. Unknown.
B. Doppelwendeltreppe, The Burg, Graz, Austria, 1439. Unknown.
C. Tour des Minimes, Chateau d'Amboise, 1470–1498. Unknown.
D. Scala Contarini del Bovolo, Venice, Giovanni Candi, 1499. Un ospite di Venezia.
p.805 E. Spiral staircase of François I, Château de Blois, 1515–1524. University of Notre Dame. Architecture library. Paris, France.
F. The Grosse Wendelstein, Castle Hartenfels, Germany, 1533–1537. Unknown.
G. Double Helix Staircase, Chateau de Chambord, France 1520. Unknown.
H. Painted spiral stair, Melk Abbey, Austria, 1702–1736. Herbert Frank.
I. Spiral road, Hohenzollern Castle, Germany, 1846. Unknown.
J. Spiral horse ramp, Palau Güell, 1886–1888. Unknown.
p.806 The core of Tour des Minimes, Château d'Amboise. Laurent Massillon.
p.806 Château d'Amboise above Amboise, France. Zebree.
p.807 Plan of Château d'Amboise, Tour des Minimes above and Tour Heurtault below. Robert de Cotte, 1718.
p.807 Plan and section of Tour des Minimes. Drawn by Victor Ruprich-Robert. Plate 70 in Anatole de Baudot, Anatole Perrault-Dabot, Archives de la Commission des Monuments Historiques. Vol. 3. Paris: Laurens.
p.808 The spiralling approach to Hohenzollern Castle, Hechingen, Germany, 1846. Heinrich Grube. Staatsarchiv Sigmaringen FAS, 862. 1879.
p.808 Zairon. 7 November 2009.
p.808 Rainer Wiest. Altered by SeARCH.
p.809 Pena Palace, Sintra, Portugal, 1852. © Google Earth.
p.811 View from the bottom of the initiation well. Stijndon.
p.813 Subterranean fiction novel *Journey to the Centre of the Earth* by Jules Verne, 1864. Antipodean Books.
p.813 Plan the Impossible, Hendricus Theodorus Wijdeveld, 1944. Het Nieuwe Instituut.
p.814 Dgtmedia – Simone. Wikimedia Commons, July 7, 2008.
p.816 Vespa race on the roof, 2011. Chris Lesser.
p.816 Banked test track. Tijmen Stam, IIVQ.
p.817 Lily-pad-like radial concrete structure by engineer Vittorio Bonadè Bottino. Gabrielle Basilico, 1915.
p.818 Rib-vaulted ceiling of the Chapter House of Wells Cathedral, Somerset, England, 1286–1310. David Iliff.
p.818 Reinforced concrete slabs with isostatic ribs in the Palazzo del Lavoro (Palace of Labour), Turin, Pier Luigi Nervi, 1961. The Pier Luigi Nervi Project Association.
p.818 The corrugated vaulted roof of the Turin Exhibition Hall is made of a series of ferrocement components, Pier Luigi Nervi, 1947–1954. The Pier Luigi Nervi Project Association.
p.818 The fan-vaulted ceiling of Gloucester Cathedral cloisters dates back to 1351–1377. Michael D. Beckwith.
p.819 Vertical letter file of the Central Social Insurance Institution, Prague, 1936. ibkeepr. *Reddit*, 2018.
p.819 The director's office within a five-by-five-metre elevator, Bata Headquarters, Zlin, 1937. Bjarne Mastenbroek.
p.819 Rendering of the Tesla Gigafactory covers one million square metres (140 football fields). Courtesy of Tesla.
p.820 Mundaneum, Musée Mondial (World Museum), Geneva, Switzerland, Le Corbusier, 1929.

Carve:

Panini, 1734. Online Collection of National Gallery of Art, Washington D.C.
p.972 Basilica of Maxentius and Constantine, Rome, ca 312 CE. Auguste-Rosalie Bisson, 1861. Gifted by Joyce F. Menschel. Courtesy of the Metropolitan Museum of Art.
p.972 The nave of the Basilica of Maxentius and Constantine is twenty-five metres wide and eighty metres long. Georg Dehio, Gustav von Bezold. Kirchliche Baukunst des Abendlandes. Stuttgart: Verlag der Cotta'schen Buchhandlung, Plate No. 5, 1887–1901. Altered by SeARCH.
p.973 Section of Grotta di Seiano, a cave excavated into a 770-metre-long tunnel, Naples, 37 BCE. Planimetria della Grotta di Seiano a cura dell'Archivio Disegni SANC, Studio Falanga. Altered by SeARCH.
p.973 Depiction of Grotta di Seiano, Gustaf Söderberg, 1820. Thaw Collection, Jointly Owned by The Metropolitan Museum of Art and The Morgan Library & Museum, Gift of Eugene V. Thaw, 2009.
p.974 Son Doong Cave, Phong Nha-Kẻ Bàng National Park, Vietnam. Photograph by Ryan Deboodt. Courtesy of Oxalis Adventure Tours, Vietnam.
p.975 Grotta Azzurra (Blue Grotto), Anacapri, Italy, ca. 27 CE. Photograph by Roberto Rive, 1875.
p.975 Upper level of Saint Samaan the Tanner Hall, Mokattam. Hoba offendum.
p.976 Saint Mark's Church, below Saint Simon the Tanner Hall, Mokattam, 1993. Vagabonblogger.
p.977 Westminster Hall, London, 1097. The present-day roof was built in 1393. Drawn by Thomas Rowlandson and Augustus Pugin. R. Ackermann. *The Microcosm of London*, 1808–1811. Altered by SeARCH.
p.977 In 1923, Frank Baines of the Ministry of Works saved the roof of Westminster Hall by inserting steel trusses and largely relieving the medieval timber roof of its structural function. Public Records Office. Altered by SeARCH.
p.978 Comparative sections of Amiens Cathedral, 1220–1270 (left) and Beauvais cathedral, 1225–1284 (right). Edouard Corroyer, *Gothic Architecture*, New York: Macmillan & CO, 1893, 73 & 79. Altered by SeARCH.
p.978 Transept and north stained-glass window of Amiens Cathedral, France. Benh Lieu Song.
p.979 Plan of Amiens Cathedral. Drawn by R. Garland in Benjamin Winkles. *French Cathedrals*. London: Charles Tilt, 1837. Altered by SeARCH.
p.980 *Restauration de la Bibliothèque nationale*, Étienne-Louis Boullée, 1785. Gallica Digital Library. Bibliothèque nationale de France.
p.980 *Coupe du Cimetière de la Ville de Chaux*, Claude-Nicolas Ledoux, 1773–1806. C. N. Ledoux. *L'architecture considérée sous le rapport de l'art, des moeurs et de la législation*. National Library of France. Paris: H.L. Perroneau, Vol. 1. 99, 1804.
p.981 Interior of the transept of Crystal Palace, Joseph Paxton, 1851. Philip Henry Delamotte (photographer), Plate from portfolio ''Views of the Crystal Palace, London, England", Albumen silver print, Collection Centre Canadien d'Architecture/ Canadian Centre for Architecture, Montréal, PH1978:0074:010.
p.981 First sketch of Crystal Palace, Joseph Paxton, 11 June 1850. Vawebteam.
p.981 Paxton's patented 'Ridge-and-Furrow' system has become the standard covering for atria ever since. Peter Berlyn and Charles Fowler. *The Crystal Palace: Its Architectural History and Constructive Marvels*. Adamant Media Corporation, 36, 2015. Courtesy of Project Gutenberg.
p.982 The Great Stove, Chatsworth, Joseph Paxton, 1836–1841. Unknown photographer, before 1920.
p.982 The privately funded tropical gardens, Jardin d'Hiver, stood south of the largely empty Champs-Élysées, Paris, Meynadier & Rigolet, 1847–1952. Clerget, Hubert. Musée Carnavalet, Histoire de Paris.
p.983 Palais de l'industrie, Exposition Universelle, Paris, 1854. Max Berthelin, 1854. © RMN-Grand Palais (Musée d'Orsay) / Hervé Lewandowski.
p.983 Galerie des Machines, Ferdinand Dutert & Victor Contamin, 1889. Brown University Library. Unknown photographer, 1889.
p.984 Engraving of the Exposition Universelle, Paris, Paul Destez, 1889. Brown University Library.
p.985 The Eiffel Tower, Gustave Eiffel, 1887–89, measures 124.9 × 124.9 metres in surface area, is 324 metres high, and contains 7300 tons of iron. Unknown. Altered by SeARCH.
p.986 Österreichische Postsparkasse (Austrian Postal Savings Bank), Otto Wagner, 1906. Jorge Royan. Altered by SeARCH.
p.989 Mercado de Abasto, Buenos Aires, Viktor Sulčič with José Luis Delpini and Raúl Bes, 1931–1934. Unknown photographer. Archivo General de la Nación Argentina, ca.1945.
p.989 The gothic vaulted ceiling of Bath Abbey built by George Gilbert Scott in 1539 (left) and the glazed ceiling of the Mercado de Abasto, Viktor Sulčič, 1931–1934 (right). Adrian Pingstone. Unknown photographer.
p.990 The Great Workroom sits within an almost blind, brick box of the Johnson Wax Headquarters. Carol M. Highsmith Archive, Library of Congress, Prints and Photographs Division.
p.990 The Great Workroom of Johnson Wax Headquarters. Carol M. Highsmith Archive, Library of Congress, Prints and Photographs Division.
p.991 Section of Piscine des Amiraux, Paris, Henri Sauvage, 1922–1927. Fonds Henri Sauvage (1873–1932). SIAF/Cité de l'architecture et du patrimoine/Archives d'architecture du XXe siècle.
p.992 Five stages of the One Times Square building, later the Allied Chemical Corporation building (left to right): under construction in 1903, unveiling in 1905, recladding in 1964, unrealized proposal in 1985 by the artist Christo, and finally fully billboarded in 2003. A perfect showcase of the real forces in the development of cities. Unknown photographer. *The New York Times.*
p.993 The Whitney Museum, New York City, Marcel Breuer, 1964–1966. © Ezra Stoller / Esto.
p.997 Interior of the pool. Deide Von Schaewen & Canal.
p.998 Light well of Piscine des Amiraux. Fonds Henri Sauvage (1873–1932). SIAF/Cité de l'architecture et du patrimoine/Archives d'architecture du XXe siècle.
p.998 Street section illustrating setback. Alexannder Tzonis. *The Architectural Drawings of Henri Sauvage*. V.2. London: Taylor & Francis, 97, 1994.
p.988 Balconies of Piscine des Amiraux. Lucille Daunay.
p.1003 Giant Hotel, Paris, Henri Sauvage, 1927. Fonds Henri Sauvage (1873–1932). SIAF/Cité de l'architecture et du patrimoine/Archives d'architecture du XXe siècle.
p.1003 University of East Anglia, Halls of Residence, Sir Denys Lasdun 1964–68. Paul Hayes.
p.1005 MASP above the Trianon Terrace. Wilfredor.
p.1006 Within the public void of MASP. Harry Wood.
p.1006 Demonstration against evictions by the Brazilian Homeless Workers Movement, 2013. Marcelo Camargo/ Agência Brasil.
p.1009 Lina Bo Bardi's watercolour painting of the Trianon Terrace, 1965. Preliminary Study for sculptural stage props on Trianon Terrace, Museum of Art São Paolo, 1965. Instituto Lina Bo & E.P. Bardi.
p.1009 Within the levitated block. Leonardo Finotti.
p.1010 The curved canopy of Ibirapuera Park, Oscar Niemeyer, 1954. Daderot.
p.1010 Spider sculpture by Louise Bourgeois in the Museu de Arte Moderna de São Paulo (MAM). Corrector-Carvalho.
p.1013 Diffuse light in the atrium of Phillips Exeter Academy Library, New Hampshire, Louis Kahn, 1965–1975. Gunna Klack.
p.1013 Natural light in reading spaces along the perimeter of Phillips Exeter Academy Library. Kathia Shieh.
p.1013 Laurian Ghinitoiu.
p.1014 Laurian Ghinitoiu.
p.1014 Laurian Ghinitoiu.
p.1017 *Conical Intersect*. Gordon Matta-Clark, Paris, 1975. Photo Marc Petitjean.
p.1017 Plan of Atelier Bardill, Scharans, Valerio Olgiati, 2007. © Archive Olgiati. Altered by SeARCH.
p.1017 Exterior of Atelier Bardill. © Archive Olgiati.
p.1017 Within the void of Atelier Bardill. © Archive Olgiati.
p.1030 Kevin Roche holding a model of the Ford Foundation facade. Courtesy of Kevin Roche John Dinkeloo and Associates.
p.1032 © Ezra Stoller/Esto.
p.1034 The recessed facade and lowered entrance hall patio. © Erik Torkells.
p.1035 View from under one of two tree-like columns with twelve branches which hold up the whole r oof of St. John's University Alcuin Library, Marcel Breuer, 1966. Peter J. Sieger.
p.1036 *Portrait of Mlle Pogany,* Constantin Brâncuşi, 1912. Postcard from the Armory Show, New York, February 1913, Walt Kuhn family papers, and Armory Show records, Archives of American Art, Smithsonian Institution.
p.1036 Barbara Hepworth at Trewyn Studio, 1961. Photograph by Rosemary Mathews. Courtesy of Hepworth Estate.

P. Jaarbeurskwartier Utrecht, Netherlands, SeARCH, 2016. SeARCH.
Q. Green City Hall, Bac Ninh, Vietnam, Vo Trong Nghia Architects, 2016. Vo Trong Nghia Architects.
R. 1000 Trees, Shanghai, China, Heatherwick Studio, 2017. Heatherwick Studio.
S. Digbeth Hanging Gardens of Babylon, Birmingham, England, Architects of Invention, 2017. Architects of Invention.
T. Triango, Paris, France, Rau & SeARCH, 2017. Rau & SeARCH.
U. Zhangjiang Future Park, China, MVRDV, 2018. MVRDV.

p.1150 Lower gardens of Villa di Pratolino, Giusto Utens, 1599. Giusto Utens. Museo di Firenze com'era.

p.1150 Apennine Colossus, Villa di Pratolino, Giambologna, 1580. Antonio Scaramuzzino.

p.1151 The Mouth of Hell, Sacro Bosco, Bomarzo, Pier Francesco Orsini, 1552. Alessio Damato.

p.1151 View towards the Grand Canal, Château de Versailles. Christopher Macsurak.

p.1152 General plan of the gardens of Versailles, Nicolas de Fer, 1700. Engraved by Charles Inselin.

p.1153 Blenheim Palace grounds redesigned by Capability Brown around 1765. Drawn by Nicolas Vergnaud, 1835. Narcisse Vergnaud & Joseph Disponzio. L'Art de Créer les Jardins.The British Library: Petit Génie, Plate I, 2015.

p.1153 Blenheim Palace grounds, 1705. © Blenheim Palace, 2019.

p.1154 *Apollo and the Muses on Mount Helion* (Parnassus), Claude Lorrain, 1680. Museum of Fine Arts Boston.

p.1154 Marie Antoinette's Hameau de la Reine at Versailles, 1783. Daderot.

p.1155 *Der Stein zu Wörlitz*, Wilhelm Friedrich Schlotterbeck, 1797. © Kulturstiftung Dessau Wörlitz, Heinz Fräßdorf.

p.1155 Eruption of Wörlitz volcano in 2010 after the restoration. H.U. Küenle.

p.1156 *Interior of the Temple of Neptune,* Giovanni Battista Piranesi, 1778. Etching, 45 x 67 cm, Vue des restes de la celle du Temple de Neptune, The Arthur Ross Collection, Yale University Art Gallery.

p.1156 Cenotaph for Newton, Étienne-Louis Boullée, 1784. Bibliothèque nationale de France, FRBNF40299118.

p.1157 Inspector's House at the Source of the Loue, Claude-Nicolas Ledoux, 1773–1779. Arnaud 25, 2015. Claude-Nicolas Ledoux, L'architecture considérée sous le rapport de l'art, des moeurs et de la legislation, Vol. 1, 1804, 57.

p.1157 Reading room of the Bibliothèque Nationale Richelieu, Paris, Henri Labrouste, 1860. Unknown photographer.

p.1157 Stairway of Art Nouveau-style Tassel House, Brussels, Victor Horta, 1892–1894. Unknown photogrpher.

p.1158 Wolkenbügel, El Lissitzky, 1925. El Lissitzky, "Cloud Iron. Ground Plan. View from Strastnoy Boulevard", 1925. Black and white photography with annotations by the artist. Van Abbemuseum, Eindhoven.

p.1158 Sketch for a futuristic city (on poles), Lazar Khidekel, 1926–1928. Khidekel Family Collection, New York.

p.1160 A. Giant Hotel, Paris, France Henri Sauvage, 1927. © Fonds Sauvage. SIAF/Cité de l'architecture & du patrimoine/Archives d'architecture du XXe siècle.
B. Wohnberg, Walter Gropius, 1928. Robert Gorny.
C. Spatial City, Yona Friedman, 1958. Yona Friedman.
D. Ville Flottante, Paul Maymont, 1959. Unknown.
E. Shibuya Project: City in the Air, Isozaki Arata, 1962. Fede___G.
F. Marine City, Kiyonori Kikutake, 1963. Misfits' architecture.
G. Proposal for Tsukiji District, Tokyo, Kenzo Tange, 1963. Peter Gössel, Gabriele Leuthäuser.
H. Plug-in City, Peter Cook, Archigram, 1964.
I. Hexahedron, Paolo Soleri, 1964. Aerial Perspective. Gift of the Howard Gilman Foundation. Courtesy of the MoMA. Gili Merin. Gili Merin.
J. Triton, Buckminster Fuller, 1967. Escola de Arquitetura da UFMG-Departamento de Urbanismo.
K. Instant city, Stanley Tigerman, 1968. Archive of Affinities.
L. Intrapolis, Walter Jonas, D. F. 1968. dpr-barcelona.

p.1161 Offshore mobile oil drilling platform "Mr. Gus II," in the Gulf of Mexico, 1957. E.F. Patterson, United States Geological Survey.

p.1161 Sea fort in the Thames Estuary, 1939–1945. Created and released by the Imperial War Museum.

p.1161 Sea fort in the Thames Estuary, 1939–1945. Created and released by the Imperial War Museum.

p.1162 Former Ministry of Transportation, Tbilisi, Georgia, Gyorgy Chakhava and Zurab Jalaghania, 1974. Labdabudi, 2015.

p.1162 Unrealized Hotel, Yalta, Crimea, Gyorgy Chakhava, 1967. Gyorgy Chakhava.

p.1163 Biosphere 2, Oracle, Arizona, 1987–1991. Katja Schulz.

p.1164 Agriculture inside Biosphere 2. Abigail Ailling, one of the crew members.

p.1164 The crew inside. Dartmouth Alumni Magazine.

p.1165 Holon diagram, Ken Wilber, 1970. Permaculture Productions LLC.

p.1166 Giant's Causeway, Ireland. Detroit Publishing Co. Under license from Photoglob Zürich. Between 1890 and 1900.

p.1166 Hairpin bends of the lacets de Montvernier, Col du Chaussy. Frédéric Prayer.

p.1168 The Bodrum, Torba, Turkey. Priyanka Agarwal, "A sneak peek at Bodrum's newest resort; Turkey's favourite beach town is getting busier", Condé Nast Traveller, April 27 2017. Accessed January 29 2019.

p.1168 World's largest Cruiseliner The Harmony of the Seas. © 2019 Royal Caribbean International.

p.1168 Roof of the Unité d'Habitation, Marseille, Le Corbusier, 1945–1952. Vincent Desjardins.

p.1169 A. Orquideorama, Medellín, Colombia, Plan B & JPRCR, 2006. Plan B & JPRCR Architects.
C. Ewha Womans University, Seoul, South Korea, Dominique Perrault, 2008. Ewha Womans University.
H. Marcel Sembat High School Sotteville-lès-Rouen, France, archi5, 2011. Thomas Jorion.
I. Metropol Parasol, Seville, Spain, J. Mayer H Architects, 2011. David Franck.
J. Groupe scolaire Aimé Césaire, Nantes, France, Mader, Mabire & Reich, 2011. © Jean-Dominique Billaud/Samoa.
K. Primary school for Sciences and Biodiversity, Paris, France, Chartier Dalix Architect, 2014. © P. Guignard.
O. Hotel Jakarta, Amsterdam, Netherlands, SeARCH, 2018. Bjarne Mastenbroek.

p.1171 Sirius Building, Sydney, Tao Gofers, 1980. © Barton Taylor 2016.

p.1175 Boyd159.

p.1177 Aerial view of Monte Albán complex, Mexico. Addison Berry. Unknown photographer.

p.1178 Competition Plan of the Sydney Opera House plinth, 1956. Oxyman.

p.1185 Model of the roof shell concept as built. The meridian lines allowed the ribs to be identical, only to be shortened to the appropriate length, making the construction of the shells much more economical. *Architectural model, Sydney Opera House, roof geometry, designed by Jorn Utzon, 1961-1965*, Museum of Applied Arts & Sciences, 2003/34/1-1.

p.1187 Guy Debord and Asger Jorn, *The Naked City*, 1957. Illustration de l'hypothèse des plaques tournantes en psychogéographique, Guy Debord. Simon Ford, *The Situationist International: A User's Guide*, London: Black Dog, 2005.

p.1187 *Carte du pays de Tendre*, Francois Chauveau, 1654. Giuliana Bruno. *Atlas of Emotion: Journeys in Art, Architecture, and Film*. New York: Verso, 2002.

p.1188 Photograph by Timothy Hursley, courtesy of Safdie Architects.

p.1188 Illustration from Traffic in Towns, England, Colin Buchanan, 1963. © Department for Transport, 2014.

p.1188 The Vertical City, Ludwig Hilbersheimer, 1927. Hochhausstadt, Perspective View: North-South Street, Ludwig Karl Hilberseimer, 1924. Gift of George E. Danforth, The Art Institute Chicago, 1983.992.

p.1190 Upper street of the Justus van Effen complex, Rotterdam. Het Nieuwe Instituut.

p.1191 Plan of the Justus van Effen complex by Michiel Brinkman, 1922. Het Nieuwe Instituut.

p.1192 Barbican Centre, London, Chamberlin, Powell and Bon, 1982. Sam.

p.1192 Elevated walkway, Barbican Centre, London, Chamberlin, Powell and Bon, 1982. Andy Mabbett.

p.1193 Thamesmead Housing Estate, London, 1968. Jon Bennett.

p.1194 Photograph by Sam Tata, courtesy of Safdie Architects. Alexi Hobbs.

p.1195 Alexi Hobbs.

p.1199 Habitat 67 under construction. Safdie Architects.

p.1200 Model of Habitat Puerto Rico, Safdie Architects, 1968–1970. Safdie Architects.

p.1309 Schovenhorst Estate. Bjarne Mastenbroek.
p.1309 Aerial watchtower, Oudemirdum. Still from the documentary "Onzichtbaar Nederland over veiligheid" from VPRO, 6min 40, © vpro / onzichtbaar nederland.
p.1309 Aerial watchtower 7T1, Winschoten. Cultural Heritage Agency in the Netherlands.
p.1311-1318 Jeroen Musch.
p.1319 Jeroen Musch.
p.1321 The Hanging Gardens of Babylon, Athanasius Kircher, 1679. Athanasius Kircher. *Images from the Rare Book and Manuscript Collections. 'Rare Books'*, Division of Rare and Manuscript Collections, Cornell University Library, 61, 1679.
p.1324 Aerial view of Isbjerget. Soeren Kjaer.
p.1328-1331 Mikkel Frost.
p.1332-1334 Bjarne Mastenbroek.
p.1336 Colour gradient of balconies. Bjarne Mastenbroek.
p.1337 View from a balcony. Bjarne Mastenbroek.
p.1338 *A Sunday on La Grande Jatte*, Georges Seurat, 1884. Art Institute of Chicago.
p.1338 Microscopic photo of an Autochrome plate, Auguste & Louis Lumière, patented in 1903. Janke.
p.1338 *Victory Boogie-Woogie*, Piet Mondrian, 1944. Gemeentemuseum Den Haag.
p.1339 *Abraham Lincoln*, Béla Julesz, 1971. Béla Julesz, 1971.
p.1340 Habitat 67, Montreal, Canada, Moshe Safdie, 1967. Thomas Ledl.
p.1341 B. Hamburg Science Center, Hamburg, Germany, OMA, (unbuilt). Visualization by OMA.
D. MahaNakhon Tower, Bangkok, Thailand, Buro Ole Scheeren, 2018. Hufton + Crow Photography
E. 251 1st Street, New York, USA, ODA, 2017. Courtesy of ODA New York-Miguel de Guzman.
F. Pixel, Abu Dhabi, United Arab Emirates, MVRDV & BIG, (unbuilt). Visualization by MVRDV.
H. Favela of Rocinha, Rio de Janeiro, Brazil, circa 2010. Chensiyuan.p.1342 Bjarne Mastenbroek.
p.1343 Ossip van Duivenbode.
p.1344-1345 Bjarne Mastenbroek.
p.1348 John Stephenson & James Churchill, *Medical Botany*, London: King's College London, 1836.
p.1354 Bjarne Mastenbroek.
p.1359 Bjarne Mastenbroek.
p.1362 Bjarne Mastenbroek.

Bibliography:

Alberti, L. B., *De re aedificatoria*, Florence, 1485.

Allain, Y., Christiany, J., *L'Art des Jardins en Europe*, Paris: Citadelles & Mazenod, 2006.

Allen, S., *Points + Lines: Diagrams and Projects for the City*, New York: Princeton Architectural Press, 1999.

Allen, S., McQuade, M., *Landform Building: Architecture's New Terrain*, Zurich: Lars Müller Publishers, 2011.

Al-Murādī, A. I. K., *Kitāb al-asrār fī natā'ij al-afkār* (1000 CE) / *The Book of Secrets in the Results of Ideas*, trans. Soha Bayoumi and Ahmed Ragab, Milan: Leonardo 3, 2009.

AlSulaiti, F., "Minaret", *Ancient History Encyclopedia* website, 6 February 2013.

Amit Khanna Design Associates, "The Profanity of Solace by Amit Khanna", *WAN, World Architecure News,* 17 December 2012.

Amos, J., "Welcome to the Meghalayan Age: A New Phase in History", *BBC*, 18 July 2018.

Andrianova, G., "Architecture of Soviet Housing and Main Soviet Urban Planning Concepts", Xi'an Jiaotong-Liverpool University, Department of Architecture, Suzhou, China, May 2015.

Anthony, D. W., Chi, J. Y., *The Lost World of Old Europe: The Danube Valley, 5000–3500 BC*, New York: Institute for the Study of the Ancient World, 2010.

Arranz-Otaegui, A., Gonzalez Carretero, L., Ramsey, M., Fuller, D. Q., Richter, T., "Archaeobotanical Evidence Reveals the Origins of Bread 14,400 Years Ago in North-eastern Jordan", *Proceedings of the National Academy of Sciences*, 16 July 2018.

Auerbach, J., "Victorian Prism: Refractions of the Crystal Palace", *Victorian Studies* 50, no. 3, Spring 2008.

Aureli, P. V., "Life, Abstracted: Notes on the Floor Plan", *Het Nieuwe Instituut*, 19 October 2017.

Bacon, F., *Essays*, 1625.

Bakema, J. B., *Van Stoel tot Stad: Een verhaal over mensen en ruimte*, Zeist: W. de Haan, 1964.

Baldwin, S., Holroyd, E., Burrows, R., "Luxified Troglodytism? Mapping the Subterranean Geographies of Plutocratic London", *ResearchGate*, May 2018.

Balmori, D., *A Landscape Manifesto*, New Haven: Yale University Press, 2010.

Barzilay, M., Ferwerda, R., Blom, A., *Predicaat experimentele woningbouw 1968–1980*, Verkenning Post 65, Cultural Heritage Agency, Ministry of Education, Culture and Science, 2018.

Bechtel, D., "Stone and Water Temple Delights the Senses", *swissinfo.ch*, 2004.

Beck, H., *UIA International Architect*, London: International Architect, 1985.

Beck, R., *The Durable House: House Society Models in Archaeology*, Carbondale: Center for Archaeological Investigations, 2017.

Bêka, I., Lemoine L., *Koolhaas Houselife*, Rome: BêkaFilms, 2008.

Belogolovsky, V., "Emilio Ambasz: I Detest Writing Theories, I Prefer Writing Fables", *ArchDaily*, 27 January 2017.

Belogolovsky, V., "The New Generation Will Not Accept Standard Solutions. We Need an Entirely Different City", *Arch Daily*, 8 October 2015.

Bergdoll, B., "Marcel Breuer and the Invention of Heavy Lightness", *Places*, June 2018.

Bergdoll, B., Massey, J., *Marcel Breuer: Building Global Institutions*, Zürich: Lars Müller Publishers, 2018.

Berthier, S., "Timber in the Buildings of Jean Prouvé: An Industrial Material", *Construction History* 30, no. 2, 2015.

Billingsley, F., "Processing Ranger and Mariner Photography", *Computerized Imaging Techniques, Proceedings of SPIE* 10, 1967.

Blake, P., *Form Follows Fiasco: Why Modern Architecture Hasn't Worked*, Boston: Little Brown & Company, 1977.

Blake, P., "Slaughter on Sixth Avenue", *New York Magazine*, May 1969.

Bloom, J. M., "The Minaret: Symbol of Faith and Power", *Saudi Aramco World Magazine* 53, no. 2, March/April 2002.

Bofill, R., *Ricardo Bofill Taller de Arquitectura* website.

Bradley, K., "Why Museums Hide Masterpieces Away", *BBC*, 23 January 2015.

Brammanis, L., Dawson, K., Goodman, Z., Lenny, E., Neskovic, O., *The Siedlung Halen Rowhouses*, 2015.

Brand, S., *Whole Earth Catalog*, Fall 1968.

Bratishenko, L., "No Parks?", Nature Reorganized, *CCA*, May 2017.

Breuer, M., Papachristou, T., *Marcel Breuer: New Buildings and Projects*, New York: Praeger, 1970.

Brillembourg, A., Klumpner, H., "Metro Cable Caracas / Urban-Think Tank", *ArchDaily*, 23 September 2013.

Brown, P., "Buddhist Rock-cut Architecture: The Early or Hinayana Phase, 2nd Century B.C. to 2nd century A.D.", *Indian Architecture: Buddhist and Hindu Periods,* vol. 1, Bombay: Taraporevala Sons, 1940.

Brown, R. A., *Castles: A History and Guide*. Dorset: Blanford Press, 1980.

Brownlee, D. B., De Long, D. G., *Louis I. Kahn: In the Realm of Architecture*, Museum of Contemporary Art & Rizzoli, 1991.

Bruno, G., *Atlas of Emotion: Journeys in Art, Architecture, and Film*, New York: Verso, 2002.

Carandell, J. M., "The Peculiar Charm of Walden 7", *Archisearch*, 8 March 2016.

Carlin, G., "Jammin' in New York", *HBO*, April 1992.

Carson, R., *Silent Spring*, Boston: Houghton Mifflin, 1962.

Cescinsky, H., Gribble, E. R., "Westminster Hall and Its Roof", *Burlington Magazine for Connoisseurs* 40, no. 127, February 1922.

Chevez, A., Huppatz, D., "A Short History of the Office", *The Conversation,* 14 August 2017.

C-Lab, "Mechanization of the Office", *Volume* 37, 16 November 2013.

Colomina, B., "The Endless Museum: Le Corbusier and Mies Van Der Rohe", *Log* 15, 2009.

Colomina, B., Wigley, M., *Are We Human? Notes on an Archeology of Design*, Switzerland: Lars Müller Publishers, 2016.

Colquhoun, K., *The Busiest Man in England: A Life of Joseph Paxton, Gardener, Architect & Victorian Visionary*, Boston: David R. Godine, 2006.

Corner, J., *Recovering Landscape: Essays in Contemporary Landscape Architecture*, New York: Princeton Architectural Press, 1999.

Crozier, M., Huntington S. P., Watanuki J., *The Crisis of Democracy: On the Governability of Democracies to the Trilateral Commission*, New York: New York University Press, 1975.

Curry, A., "Gobekli Tepe: The World's First Temple?", *Smithsonian Magazine*, 2008.

Curry, A., "Here Are the Ancient Sites ISIS Has Damaged and Destroyed", *National Geographic*, 1 September 2015.

Curtis, W. J. R., *Denys Lasdun: Architecture, City, Landscape*, London: Phaidon Press, 1994.

Curtis, W. J. R., *Modern Architecture Since 1900*, New York: Prentice-Hall, 1983.

Danielsson, C. B., Chungkham, H. S., Westerlund, H., Wulff, C., "Office Design's Impact on Sick Leave Rates", *Ergonomics* 57, no. 2, 2014.

Debord, G., *Report on the Construction of Situations and on the International Situationist Tendency's Conditions of Organization and Action*, Italy, June 1957.

Denison, C., Rosenfeld, M. N., Wiles, S., *Exploring Rome: Piranesi and His Contemporaries*, Cambridge: MIT Press, 1994.

Dennis, M., *Court and Garden: From the French Hotel to the city of Modern Architecture*, Cambridge: MIT Press, 1986.

Desmoulins, C., "Bernard Zehrfuss – le Musée Gallo-Romain de Lyon (1969–1975)", *AMC* 23, December 2015.

Devis, A. G., "¿Y si el Futuro se Estuviera Escribiendo en Valencia?", *Las Provincias*, 7 May 2018.

Dine, A., *Identifying Atlanta: John Portman, Postmodernism, and Pop-Culture*, Bard Undergraduate Senior Projects, Spring 2017.

Dishman, L., "Hate Your Cubicle? Thank Medieval Monks", *Fast Company*, 21 September 2014.

Donis, F., "Evolution in the Age of Crisis", *Conditions* 1, 2009.

Duerden, P., "Great Detail: Duerden on Baines' Westminster Hall Roof Repair", *Architects' Journal*, 9 December 2016.

Duffy, F., "Office Buildings and Organizational Change", in *Buildings and Society: Essays on the Social Development of the Built Environment*, London: Taylor and Francis, 1984.

Easterling, K., "Subtraction", *Perspecta* 34, 2003.

Egelius, M., *Ralph Erskine, arkitekt*, Stockholm: Byggförlaget, 1988.

El-Khoury, R., Robbins, E., *Shaping the City: Studies in History, Theory, and Urban Design, about Atlanta*, London: Routledge, 2013.

Ellis, E., "Utzon Breaks His Silence", *Sunday Morning Herald*, 31 October 1992.

Ellis, E. C., Goldewijk, K. K., Siebert, S., Lightman, D., Ramankutty, N., "Anthropogenic Transformation of the Biomes, 1700 to 2000", *Global Ecology and Biogeography* 19, September 2010.

Espinosa de los Monteros, M. J.,"Espai Verd un Cathedral Urbana", *Desfici Magazine* 9, November 2017.

Fay, L., *Shostakovich: A Life*, Oxford: University Press, 1999.

Fenollós, J. L., "La ziggurat de Babylone: un monument à repenser", in *La Tour de Babylone*, Béatrice André-Salvini (ed.), *Documenta Asiana* 10, 2013.

Fernando, H., "Notas sobre una Isla", *Revista Arquitectura* 165, 1972.

Flam, J., *Robert Smithson: The Collected Writings*, Los Angeles: University of California, 1996.

Fletcher, R., *The Limits of Settlement Growth*, Cambridge: University of Sydney, 1995.

Foreign Office Architects, *Phylogenesis: FOA's Ark*, London: Actar Publisher, 2004.

Foster, H., *The Anti-Aesthetic: Essays on Postmodern Culture*, New York: New Press, 1998.

Frearson, A., "Thomas Heatherwick Reveals Zeitz MOCAA Art Galleries Carved Out of Cape Town Grain Silo", *Dezeen Magazine*, 15 September 2017.

Gargarin, M., Fantham, E., *The Oxford Encyclopedia of Ancient Greece and Rome*, vol. 1, Oxford: Oxford University Press, 2010.

Gatley, G., *Athfield architects*, Auckland: Auckland University Press, 2012.

Germán, J. G., *Canarias y Las Salinas; Fernando Higuares*, Madrid: CentroCentro, 2015.

Giedion, S., *Space Time and Architecture: The Growth of a New Tradition*, Cambridge: Harvard University Press, 1941.

Giovannini, J., "Claude Parent, Visionary Architect of the Oblique, Dies at 93", *New York Times*, 29 February 2016.

Goodyear, D., "A Monument to Outlast Humanity", *New Yorker*, 29 August 2016.

Graham-Harrison, E., "Downward Spiral: How Venezuela's Symbol of Progress Became Political Prisoners' Hell", *Guardian*, 15 September 2017.

Großmann, G. U., *Burgen in Europa*, Regensburg: Schnell & Steiner, 2005.

Guggenheim Museum, *Frank Lloyd Wright: From Within Outward*, New York: Solomon R. Guggenheim Foundation, 2009.

Hall, P., Ward, C., *Sociable Cities: The Legacy of Ebenezer Howard*, Chichester: Wiley, 1998.

Hancox, S., "Contemporary Walking Practices and the Situationist International: The Politics of Perambulating the Boundaries Between Art and Life", *Contemporary Theatre Review* 22, no. 2, 2012.

Harari, Y. N., *Sapiens: A Brief History of Humankind*, London: Vintage Books, 2015.

Harvey, D., *The Condition of Postmodernity: An Enquiry into the Origins of Cultural Change*, Oxford: Blackwell, 1989.

Hauben, M., "Participatory Democracy from the 1960s and SDS into the Future On-line", Columbia University, 1995.

Hejduk, J., "Adalberto Libera's Villa Malaparte", *Domus* 605, 1980.

Hernandez, M., Maurer, C., *Line of Light and Shadow: The Drawings of Federico García Lorca*, Durham: Duke University Press in association with Duke University Museum of Art, 1991.

Hertzberger, H., "Centraal Beheer Offices, Apeldoorn (1968–1972)", *AHH* website.

Hertzberger, H., *Space and the Architect: Lessons in Architecture 2*, Rotterdam: 010 Publishers, 2010.

Hodder, I., "This Old House", *Natural History Magazine*, June 2006.

Holborn, M., "Under the Volcano", *Independent*, 11 April 1993.

Howard, E., *Garden Cities of Tomorrow*, London: Swan Sonnenschein & Co, 1902.

Hulshof, M., Roggeveen D., "Facing East: Chinese Urbanism in Africa", *Storefront for Art and Architecture*, 2015.

Hustvedt, S., *The Summer Without Men*, London: Hodder & Stoughton, 2011.

Huxtable, A. L., "Anti-Street, Anti-People", *New York Times*, 10 June 1973.

Huxtable, A. L., "Ford Flies High", *New York Times*, 26 November 1967.

Huxtable, A. L., "How to Kill a City", *New York Times*, 5 May 1963.

Jacobs, J., *The Death and Life of Great American Cities*, New York: Random House, 1964.

Jensen, D., Keith, L., "Earth at Risk: Building a Resistance Movement to Save the Planet", *PM Press*, 2012.

Jorn, A., "Formsprakets Livsinnehåll", *Byggmåstaren* 26, no. 17, 1947.

Jorn, A., "What Is an Ornament?"(1948), in Ruth Baumeister (ed.), *Fraternité avant tout: Asger Jorn's Writings on Art and Architecture, 1938–1958*, Rotterdam: 010 Publishers, 2011

Judd, D., "Statement for the Chinati Foundation/ La Fundacion Chinati", *VAGA*, New York, 1987.

Juniper, T., *What Has Nature Ever Done for Us?: How Money Really Does Grow on Trees*, London: Profile Books, 2013.

Khidekel, R., *Lazar Khidekel & Suprematism*, London: Prestel, 2014.

Koeck, A., "Invisible Cities – The Last Remnant of Modernism", *Australian Design Review*, 24 October 2014.

Kohlmaier, G., von Sartory, B., *Houses of Glass: A Nineteenth-Century Building Type*, Cambridge: MIT Press, 1986.

Kraft, A., "Why Manhattan's Green Roofs Don't Work and How to Fix Them", *Scientific American*, 17 May 2013.

Kroyanker, D., *Architecture in Jerusalem: Modern Construction Outside the Walls*, Jerusalem: Keter Press, 1991.

Kuijt, I., Finlayson, B., "Evidence for Food Storage and Predomestication Granaries 11 000 Years Ago in the Jordan Valley", *Proceedings of the National Academy of Sciences* 106, no. 27, July 2009.

Kurapkat, D., "Bauwissen im Neolithikum Vorderasiens", in *Wissensgeschichte der Architektur. Band I: Vom Neolithikum bis zum Alten Orient*, Jürgen Renn, Wilhelm Osthues, Hermann Schlimme (eds.), Berlin: Open Access, 2014.

Lal, R., *Encyclopaedia of Soil Science*, New York: Taylor & Francis, 2002.

Langdon, D., "AD Classics: Montreal Biosphere / Buckminster Fuller", *ArchDaily* 25, November 2014.

Lange, A., "Philip Johnson's Not Glass Houses", *New York Times Style Magazine*, 13 February 2015.

Latour, B., *Facing Gaia: Eight Lectures on the New Climatic Regime*, New York: Wiley, 2017.

Laurence, P. L., *Becoming Jane Jacobs*, Philadelphia: University of Pennsylvania Press, 2016.

Le Corbusier, *The City of To-morrow and Its Planning*, London: Rodker, 1925.

Le Corbusier, *Le Corbusier, Oeuvre Complet 1946–1952*, Zurich: Editions Girsberger, 1955.

Le Corbusier, *Towards an Architecture*, Paris: Cres & Cie, 1923.

Lee, A., "Seurat and Science", *Art History* 10, 1987.

Leone, A., *Changing Townscapes in North Africa from Late Antiquity to the Arab Conquest*, Bari: Edipuglia, 2007.

Le Roy, L. G., Vollaard, P., Hendriks, R., "Leven en Werken in Ruimte en Tijd", *Stichting Tijd*, 2006.

Lewis, M., "Yesterday's City of Tomorrow", *The Lewis Mumford Reader*, New York: Pantheon Books, 1986.

Livingston, M., Beach, M., *Steps to Water: The Ancient Stepwells of India*, New York: Princeton University Press, 2002.

Maak, N., Klonk, C., Demand, T., "The White Cube and Beyond", *Tate* 21, Spring 2011.

Mabulla, A. Z. P., "Tanzania's Endangered Heritage: A Call for a Protection Program", *African Archaeological Review* 13, 1996.

Macdonald, H., "Estate of the Art", *Monocle* 7, no. 65, July/August 2013.

Madanipour, A., *Designing the City of Reason: Foundations and Frameworks*, London: Routledge, 2007.

Majoor, S., "Urban Megaprojects in Crisis? Ørestad Copenhagen Revisited", *European Planning Studies* 23, no. 12, 5 March 2015.

Mann, C. C., "The Birth of Religion", *National Geographic*, June 2011.

Marchese, K., "Millions of Lasers Project 3D Scan Allowing Ensamble Studio's Contemporary Intervention of Abandoned Quarry", *Designboom*, 29 May 2018.

McClean, J., "Il Magistero: De Carlo's Dialogue with Historical Forms", *Places* 16, no. 1, 2004.

McLeod, M., "Architecture and Politics in the Reagan Era: From Postmodernism to Deconstructivism", *Assemblage* 8, February 1989.

Mead, A., "Putting Down Roots", *Architects Journal*, 16 August 2001.

Mertins, D., "Cracking the Glass Ceiling: A Look Back at the Career of Trailblazing Architect Natalie de Blois", *SOM Journal* 4, 2006.

Miller, J., *Democracy Is in the Streets*, New York: Simon and Schuster, 1987.

Miralles, E., *Works and Projects 1975–1995*, New York: Monacelli Press, 1996.

Mohsen, M., *Portman's America & Other Speculations,* Zürich: Lars Müller Publishers, 2017.

Monbiot, G., "Putting a Price on the Rivers and Rain Diminishes Us All", *Guardian*, 6 August 2012.

Monotti Graziadei, R., "The Space City Method", *Journal of Biourbanism* 4, no. 1 and 2, 2015.

Montaner, J. M., Villac, M. I., *Mendes da Rocha*, Barcelona: Editorial Gustavo Gili, 1996.

Mostafavi, M., Doherty, G., *Ecological Urbanism*, Zürich: Lars Müller Publishers, 2010.

Mun-Delsalle, Y., "ACROS Fukuoka Prefectural International Hall Shows How Japan Is at the Forefront of Façade Greening", *Forbes Magazine*, 19 February 2017.

Murphy, D., "Notopia: The Fall of the Streets in the Sky", *Architectural Review*, 9 June 2016.

Muschamp, H., "Looking at the Lawn, and Below the Surface", *New York Times*, 5 July 1998.

Musser, G., "The Origin of Cubicles and the Open-Plan Office", *Scientific American*, 17 August 2009.

Myerson, J., *The Handbook of Interior Architecture and Design*, London: Berg Publishers, 2013.

Neuhart, J., Neuhart, M., *Eames Design: The Work of the Office of Charles and Ray Eames*, New York: Harry N. Abrams Publishers, 1989.

Nevins, J., "The Upside Down: Inside Manhattan's Lowline Subterranean Park", *Guardian*, 6 April 2019.

Newton, N. T., *Design on the Land: The Development of Landscape Architecture*, Cambridge, Mass: Belknap Press of Harvard University Press, 1971.

Nieuwenhuys, C., "Nieuw Urbanisme", *Provo* 9, 12 May 1966.

"Not Vital", *Du* 881, January/February 2018.

Nuwer, R., "Future Fossils: Plastic Stone", *New York Times*, 9 June 2014.

Obiol, A., "Miralles & Pinós: Igualada Cemetery & Archery Range", *Transfer*, 13 March 2017.

O'Day, K., "Tropical or Colonial?: A Reception History of Jean Prouve's Prefabricated Houses for Africa", master's thesis, Louisiana State University, 2009.

O'Haganot, A., "Inside the Many Houses of Not Vital, Maker of Dreamscapes for Adults", *New York Times Style Magazine*, 18 October 2013.

Olalquiaga, C., "Tropical Babel", *Failed Architecture*, 11 September 2014.

Olsson, L., Loerakker, J., "The Story Behind Failure: Copenhagen's Business District Ørestad", *Failed Architecture*, 12 September 2013.

Osborn, F. J., *New Towns After the War*, London: J. M. Dent and Sons Ltd, 1918.

Oudenampsen, M., "Re-tracing the Garden City", *MO*, 3 April 2013.

Parker, G., "Military Revolution 1560–1660 a Myth?", *The Journal of Modern History* 48, no. 2, June 1976.

Parker, G., *The Military Revolution: Military Innovations and the Rise of the West 1500–1800*, Cambridge: Ohio State University, 1996.

Patel, R., "One of the Largest Underground Caverns Ever Constructed", *Arup* website.

Patteeuw, V., "Delirious Architects and Globes",

The Ball, *MacGuffin: The Life of Things* 6, 2018.
Pausanias, *Pausanias's Description of Greece*, trans. J. G. Frazer, vol. 1, New York: Biblo and Tannen, 1965.
Piper, O., *Burgenkunde: Bauwesen und Geschichte der Burgen*, Würzburg, 1995.
Plato, "The Allegory of the Cave", *The Republic*, 380 BCE.
Posani, J. P., *Fruto Vivas, Una Hipótesis Explicativa*, Caracas: Ediciones MiNCI, 2018.
Prévot, P., *Histoire des Jardins*, Bordeaux: Editions Ulmer Sud-Ouest, 2002.
Renaudie, J., *La Ville est une Combinatoire*, Paris: Movitcity, 2014.
Renaudie, J., Goulet, P., Schuch, N., *La logique de la complexité,* Paris: Institut français d'architecture, 1992.
Rich, N., "Losing Earth: The Decade We Almost Stopped Climate Change", *New York Times Magazine*, 1 August 2018.
Risselada, M., "Conglomerate Ordering, Growing Houses", in *Alison and Peter Smithson: From the House of the Future to a House of Today*, Rotterdam: 010 Publishers, 2004.
Roberts, M., *The Military Revolution, 1560–1660: An Inaugural Lecture Delivered before the Queen's University of Belfast*, Belfast: Boyd, 1956.
Rowe, C., *Five Architects: Eisenman, Graves, Gwathmey, Hejduk, Meiser*, New York: Oxford University Press, 1975.
Rudofsky, B., *Architecture without Architects: A Short Introduction to Non-pedigreed Architecture*, London: Academy Edition, 1964.
Safdie, M., "Moshe Safdie Tells the Tale of Habitat 67 and Predicts Housing's Future", *Metropolis*, 16 June 2017.
Salhani, P., "Revisited: The Seidlers' Killara House", *Architecture AU*, 1 October 2011.
Salter, P., "The Romantic and Pragmatic History of the Fan Vault Has Lessons for Contemporary Structures", *Architectural Review*, 21 December 2010.
Sandaker, B., Eggen, A., Cruvellier, M., *The Structural Basis of Architecture*, London: Routledge, 2011.
Scalbert, I., *A Right to Difference: The Architecture of Jean Renaudie*, London: Architectural Association, 2004.
Schmitt, A. K., et al. "Identifying the Volcanic Eruption Depicted in a Neolithic Painting at Çatalhöyük, Central Anatolia, Turkey", *PLOS ONE*, 8 January 2014.
Schneider, J., "Vegetated-Roof Failure Teaches Lessons", *Architect Magazine*, 13 May 2009.
Seisenbacher, P., Schörghuber, A., "Sar Agha Seyed and the Bakhtiari People of Iran", *IN EXTENSO Photography* 12, October 2017.
Sennett, R., "Beyond Freedom and Dignity", *New York Times*, 24 October 1971.
Sennett, R., *The Fall of Public Man*, New York: Knopf, 1977.
Shaw, H. J., *The Consuming Geographies of Food: Diet, Food Deserts and Obesity*, London: Routledge, 2017.
Simon, M., "Lab Grown Meat Is Coming, Whether You Like It or Not", *Wired*, 16 February 2018.
Sire, H. J. A., *The Knights of Malta*, New Haven: Yale University Press, 1994.
Skinner, B. F., *Beyond Freedom & Dignity*, Indianapolis: Hackett Publishing Company, 1971.
Skinner, B. F., "Some Thoughts about the Future", *Journal of the Experimental Analysis of Behaviour* 2, 1986.
Skinner, B. F., *Walden Two*, Indianapolis: Hackett Publishing Company, 1948.
Staal, J., "Art. Democratism. Propaganda.", *E-flux Journal* no. 52, February 2014.
Steele, J., *Eames House: Charles And Ray Eames; Architecture In Detail*, London: Phaidon Press Limited, 1994.
Storrie, C., *The Delirious Museum: A Journey from the Louvre to Las Vegas*, London: I. B. Tauris, 2006.
Super-Kamiokande website.
Swilling, M., "The Curse of Urban Sprawl: How Cities Grow, and Why This Has to Change", *Guardian*, 12 July 2016.
Tarasen, N., "About Michael Heizer", *Double Negative* website.
Taub, L., "The Historical Function of the 'Forma Urbis Romae'", *Imago Mundi* 45, 1993.
Ten Velden, J., "Het domein van architect Le Corbusier", *NRC-Handelsblad*, 27 August 1990.
Tice, J., "The Nolli Map and Urban Theory", *Nolli Map* website.
Tremlett, G., "Spanish Island Allows Massive Cave to Be Bored into 'Magic' Mountain", *Guardian*, 20 January 2011.
Utzon, J., "Platforms and Plateaus", *Transfer Global Architecture Platform: Monograph* 1, 15 September 2016.
Van den Heuvel, D., "Total Space: Considering Dutch Structuralism Today", *Archis* 50, 2017.
Van Eyck, A., "Dogon: Mand-Huis-Dorp-Wereld", *Forum* 17, no. 4, 1963.
Van Hensbergen, G., *Gaudi: A Biography*, New York: HarperCollins, 2001.
Van Mensvoort, K., *Next Nature*, Amsterdam: Next Nature Network, 2015.
Vaughan, A., "Humans Have Destroyed a Tenth of Earth's Wilderness in 25 Years – Study", *Guardian*, 8 September 2016.
Vegas, F., Mileto, C., "La cultura de la montaña sagrada", *Publicat a Asimetrías*, Valencia: Universidad Politécnica de Valencia, 2006.
Venturi, R., *Complexity and Contradiction in Architecture*, New York: Museum of Modern Art, 1966.
Virseda, A., "Reversing the Promenade: Homage to Le Corbusier after UNESCO World Heritage Site Listings", *Bigmat International Architecture Agenda*, 8 September 2016.
Wachtel, E., "Moshe Safdie Architect", *Queen's Quarterly* 115, no. 2, 2008.
Wainwright, O., "I Want to Make the Sky", *Guardian*, 3 April 2018.
Wainwright, O., "One Never Builds Something Finished: The Brutal Brilliance of Architect Paulo Mendes da Rocha", *Guardian*, 4 February 2017.
Wainwright, O., "Walkways in the Sky: The Return of London's Forgotten 'Pedways'", *Guardian*, 2 October 2018.
Walker, R., "Portraits of Ath", *ARCHITECTURE-NOW*, January 2015.
Wang, F., Yu, F., Zhu, X., Pan, X., Sun, R., Cai, H., "Disappearing Gradually and Unconsciously in Rural China: Research on the Sunken Courtyard and the Reasons for Change in Shanxian County, Henan Province", *Journal of Rural Studies* 47, part B (October 2016).
Ward, S., "Jane Jacobs: Critic of the Modernist Approach to Urban Planning Who Believed That Cities Were Places for People", *Independent*, 3 June 2006.
Warsza, J., *Ministry of Highways: A Guide to the Performative Architecture of Tbilisi*, Berlin: Sternberg Press, 2013.
Watkin, D., *A History of Western Architecture*, London: Laurence King Publishing, 2005.
Wijdeveld, H., "15 Miles into the Earth" (design), NAI Collection and Collection Het Nieuwe Instituut, 1944.
Wilber, K., *The Holographic Paradigm and Other*

Paradoxes: Exploring the Leading Edge of Science, Boulder: Shambhala, 1982.
Wilde, O., "The Decay of Lying: An Observation", *The Complete Writings of Oscar Wilde*, vol. 7, New York: Nottingham Society, 1909.
Winterson, J., "The Hole of Life", *Tate Magazine* 5, 1 June 2003.
Wolf, G., "Steve Jobs: The Next Insanely Great Thing", *Wired*, 1 February 1996.
Woodburn, J., "Egalitarian Societies", *Man, New Series* 17, no. 3, September 1982.
Woolley, L., "Ur: Ancient City Iraq", *Encyclopædia Britannica* website, 29 August 2017.
Wright, F. L., *Frank Lloyd Wright: An Autobiography*, New York: Duell, Sloan and Pearce, 1943.
Wright, R. P., *The Ancient Indus: Urbanism, Economy, and Society*, Cambridge: Cambridge University Press, 2009.
Xie, J., "Meet John Portman, the Architect Behind the Dystopian Backdrops of 'The Walking Dead' and 'The Hunger Games'", *Curbed Magazine*, 2 April 2015.
Zein, R. V., *Brutalist Connections*, São Paulo: Altamara, 2014.
Zhu, X., Liu, J., Yang, L., Hu, R., "Energy Performance of a New Yaodong Dwelling, in the Loess Plateau of China", *Energy and Buildings* 70, February 2014.
Zimmer, C., "The Lost History of One of the World's Strangest Science Experiments", *New York Times*, 29 March 2019.
Zimmerman, C., Chang, D., Joslin J., *The Path of Kahn* (digital exhibition), Taubman College of Architecture & Urban Planning, 2014.
Zoetmulder, A., "Jean Renaudie (1925–1981)", *Local Heroes*, Winhov.nl, March 2018.

About the authors:

Architect Bjarne Mastenbroek and photographer Iwan Baan share a fascination with buildings and their powerful connection to the crust of the earth.

To their great surprise, many of these amazing projects lack clear documentation. Some projects were never drawn. Some projects, due to their remoteness, lack photographic documentation. And some are unknown or unfamiliar to the architecture discipline and therefore have never been written into it.

For over ten years, Bjarne Mastenbroek and his architectural practice SeARCH has been engaged in researching the intertwining of architecture and landscape, sifting through the last millennia and scouring the globe to highlight historically overlooked projects and fascinating examples.

Capitalizing on Iwan Baan's constant globetrotting, SeARCH has slowly compiled a rich and broad survey of a building culture bound to the ground. The richness of this architecture is captured through over 500 highly graphic analytical drawings and the almost anthropological photographs of Iwan Baan.

Bjarne Mastenbroek:

The work of Bjarne Mastenbroek is characterized by a continuous exploration into the intimate and reciprocal relationship between architecture and site. As a Dutch architect, Mastenbroek is well aware of the scarcity of land and believes strongly in using this resource more intelligently in order to give 'nature' more space to survive.

Mastenbroek has been practicing architecture in the Netherlands and abroad for over 20 years. He has seen first-hand how architecture is all too often pushed in the opposite direction for perceived economic gains, especially within dense urban conditions. Since founding the pratice SeARCH in 2002, Mastenbroek has witnessed and actively pushed for a more site-specific or connected approach to architecture to overtake a modernist approach to building.

Mastenbroek was chairman of the Royal Institute of Dutch Architects in 2010–2011. He has been a jury member in prestigious competitions and has lectured around the world. Mastenbroek was 'Dutch Architect of the Year' in 2009. He has taught at the Academy of Architecture in Amsterdam, TU Delft, the International University of Catalonia and the University of Auckland.

SeARCH:

SeARCH stands for Stedenbouw en ARCHitectuur (Urban Planning & Architecture) and as the name suggests the practice sees both the building and its environment as inseparable components of design. The projects of SeARCH are conceived as landscapes — the most essential and generous element. Without boundaries, landscapes are endless and open; they connect architecture with urban, interior with exterior.

SeARCH won the Aga Khan award for the Dutch Embassy in Addis Ababa and the Green Good Design award from the Chicago Athenaeum and the Wallpaper Design Award for Villa Vals — both clear examples of how SeARCH designs architecture to exist in nature without dominating it. Isbjerget in Aarhus won the MIPIM award 2013 (best residential buildings) and is an example of pioneering urbanism and architecture in an area in transition. The recently completed Hotel Jakarta on Java island in central Amsterdam has received considerable praise for its unique sustainable design concept, based on prefab timber hotel units stacked around a subtropical interior garden. Hotel Jakarta is the WAF 2018 winner in the hotel and leisure category and won the American Architecture Award, the public building of the year 2018 award, the Green Good Design award 2018 and the public prize in the Golden A.A.P. 2019.

Through careful consideration of the surrounding environment, SeARCH is able to introduce a high degree of sustainability and awareness into its projects. To achieve this, SeARCH believes in collaborating with clients, users and specialists. This sets the stage to create innovative, original and unexpected design solutions. Research into new building methods, products and materials is a natural extension of our work.

Iwan Baan:

Dutch photographer Iwan Baan is known primarily for images that narrate the life and interactions that occur within architecture. After his studies in photography at the Royal Academy of Arts in The Hague, Baan followed his interest in documentary photography, before narrowing his focus to record the various ways in which individuals, communities and societies create, and interact within their built environment.

With no formal training in architecture, his perspective mirrors the questions and perspectives of the everyday individuals who give meaning and context to the spaces that surround us. Baan challenges a long-standing tradition of depicting buildings as isolated and static by representing people in architecture and showing the building's environment. This artistic approach has given matters of architecture an approachable and accessible voice.

Today, architects such as Rem Koolhaas, Herzog & de Meuron, Zaha Hadid, Diller Scofidio & Renfro, Toyo Ito, SANAA and Morphosis turn to Baan to give their work a sense of place and narrative within their environments. Baan's work has been exhibited in the Museum of Modern art, the Architectural Association in London, the AIA New York Chapter and the Marta Herford Museum and appears frequently in publications such as *The Wall Street Journal, The New York Times, Architectural Record, Domus, Abitare and Architectural Digest.*

Credits:

Author:
Bjarne Mastenbroek
with Esther Mecredy

Editor: Julius Wiedemann

Photographer:
Iwan Baan
Assisted by Suzanne Tóth-Pál

Design:
Mevis & Van Deursen
with Virginie Gauthier
and Nerijus Rimkus
Assisted by Maria Mitcheva

Editorial coordination:
Meike Nießen
Billy Nolan

Production:
Thomas Grell

Proofreaders:
Thea Miklowski
Nick Axel

Researchers:
Andrea Verdecchia
Jurjen de Gans
Jeroen Mensink
Karlijn de Jong
Ayla Ryan

Each and every TASCHEN book plants a seed!
TASCHEN is a carbon neutral publisher. Each year, we offset our annual carbon emissions with carbon credits at the Instituto Terra, a reforestation program in Minas Gerais, Brazil, founded by Lélia and Sebastião Salgado. To find out more about this ecological partnership, please check: www.taschen.com/zerocarbon.
Inspiration: unlimited.
Carbon footprint: zero.

To stay informed about TASCHEN and our upcoming titles, please subscribe to our free magazine at www.taschen.com/magazine, follow us on Instagram and Facebook, or e-mail your questions to contact@taschen.com.

© 2021 TASCHEN GmbH
Hohenzollernring 53
D–50672 Köln
www.taschen.com

Printed in Italy
ISBN 978-3-8365-7817-2

Acknowledgements:

We would like to thank everyone who enriched and supported this research over the last eight years. Especially the Creative Industries Fund NL, without whom this book wouldn't have been possible.

Thank you to the staff at SeARCH (past & present) who contributed to the research, analytical drawing and realization of the book, and equally to those who kept the office running while they did so.

Kathrin Hanf
Kim François
Harry Kurzhals
Samantha Gazzolo
Lucille Daunay
Niels Limburg
Niels Boswinkel
Annamaria Pisani
Tudor Nedelcu
Aiva Dorbe
Chrysanthi Karakasi
Bram Dekker
Simone Cardullo
Teresa Avella
Koen Smulders
Ad Bogerman
Theo Tulp
Gabriel Boutsema
Tjerk Boom
Gabija Veronika Turek
Blanka Borbely
Mariagrazia Dalò
Juan Miguel Bienvenido Zambrana
José Sanmartín Gonzalez
Pietro Degli Esposti
Nicole Passarella
Roman Popadiuk
Leen Kooman
Jaap Baselmans
Tsvetomira Nekova
Uda Visser
Marijn Mees
Remco Wieringa
Anouk Bras
Ivo de Jeu
Katariina Minits
Richard Schwartzenberg
Javier Martinez Avila
Ramona Enache
Alina Vogel
Marielena Papandreou
Justina Stefanovic
Michal Hondo
Andrija Matotan
Martyna Maciaszek
Andrea Levorato
Sergio Balestrieri Spadon
Julia Kneiss
Julia Streletzki
Nuno da Graça Ribeiro
Paolo Erriquez
Paula Ferro Delgado
Suzanne Tóth-Pál
Tang Yuchen
Julia Katarzyna Woch

Contributors and interviewees:
Diana Balmori, Balmori Associates.
Hans Ibelings, architectural historian and critic.
Matthew Stadler, author.
Marco Casamonti, Archea Associati.
Hubert Klumpner & Alfredo Brillembourg, Urban Think Tank.
Max Risselada, Emeritus Professor of Architecture TU Delft.
Koert van Mensvoort, Next Nature Network.
Victoria Lautman, author.
Jurriaan van Stigt, Partners Pays-Dogon.
Christian Müller, CMA.

Financial contributions / sponsors:
Creative Industries Fund NL for both a grant for research and a grant for publication.

creative industries
fund NL

Niels Wouters for hosting us at Citroen Garage.

Advice:
Sander Knol, Xander Uitgevers
Ernst van der Hoeven, MacGuffin
Florian Kobler, Taschen

Photographic contributions:
Mirjam Terpstra
Samuel Aroutiounian
Laurian Ghinitoiu
Alexi Hobbs
Ossip van Duivenbode
Ronald Tilleman
Fernando Schapochnik
Zac Athfield
Leonardo Finotti
Laura García-Lorca
Piermario Ruggeri
Gordon Calder
John Gollings
Petr Šmídek
Dieter Janssen
Peter J. Sieger
Yann Arthus-Bertrand
Gabriel & Gwen Fagan
Eva Bloem
Richard Powers
Filip Dujardin
Hereward Longley
Christian Richters
Andy Tye
Brandt Graves
Nelson Kon
Michael Reisch
Moshe Safdie
Grant Sheehan
Zvi Hecker
Alexa Rhoads
Herman Hertzberger
Willem Diepraam
Harry & Penelope Seidler
Antón García-Abril and Débora Mesa
Not Vital
Aitor Ortiz
Jeroen Musch
Kate Gowan
Yona Friedman
Ian Kuijt
Sonia Mangiapane
Giovanni Emilio Galanello
Junya Ishigami and Yuki Sudo
Antonio Cruz Villalón
Antonio Ortiz
Mikkel Frost
Lucille Daunay
Max Dupain
Ken McCown
Laura Cioncì
Roy Winkelman
Cesar Rolando Moreno Ramire
Frutas Vivas
Valerio Olgiati
Frank R. Horlbeck
Steve Aldana
Takehiko Nagakura
Peter Hempfling
Patrick Berden
Celso Kuwajima
Harvey Barrison
Thomas Jorion
David Franck
Luigi Rosselli
Felipe & Federico Mesa
Alberto Campo Baeza
Marco Nervi
Barton Taylor
Ricardo Bofill
Sergio Grazia
Carl Theodor Sørensen
Jakob Tigges
Nigel Young
André Morin
Sergio Grazia
David Hartt
Andreas Angelidakis
Ray Charter
Richard Langendorf
Edward C. Olencki
Aldo & Hannie van Eyck
Roberto Ceccacci
Allen Jones
Fred Ernst
Johannes Schwartz
Edward Tyler
Jan Reurink
Micheal Panse
Duccio Malagamba
Micha L. Rieser
Darren Foltinek
Sebastian Posingis
Conradin Frei
Philippe Ruault
Allan T. Kohl
Deide Von Schaewen
Patrick Rubin
Michel Denancé
The Smithson Family Collection
Serge Renaudie

Thank you to all those who opened the doors to their homes and countries to be photographed by Iwan Baan and his partner Jessica Collins who travelled with him around the world during these years to research, plan and organize access to all these places.

This book has been a long time coming and we apologise wholeheartedly if we have missed anyone who has given their time and knowledge.